MOON HANDBOOKS

WISCONSIN

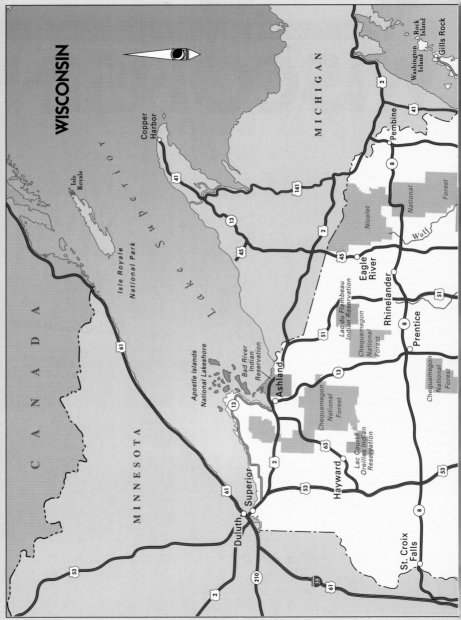

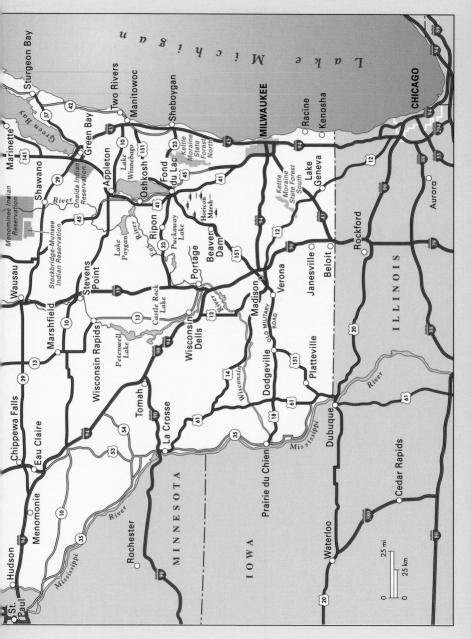

MOON HANDBOOKS
WISCONSIN

INCLUDING DOOR COUNTY
SECOND EDITION

THOMAS HUHTI

AVALON
TRAVEL
publishing

MOON HANDBOOKS: WISCONSIN
SECOND EDITION

Published by
   Avalon Travel Publishing, Inc.
   5855 Beaudry St.
   Emeryville, CA 94608, USA

All photos by Thomas Huhti unless otherwise noted.
All illustrations by Bob Race unless otherwise noted.

Some photos and illustrations are used by permission
and are the property of the original copyright owners.

ISBN: 1-56691-277-6
ISSN: 1531-555X

Editors: Helen Sillett, Ellen Cavalli, Valerie Sellers Blanton,
   Erin Van Rheenen
Index: Vera Gross
Graphics Coordinator: Erika Howsare
Production: Carey Wilson
Map Editor: Mike Ferguson, Naomi Dancis
Cartographer: Mike Morgenfeld, Chris Folks, Allen Leech

Front cover photo: Kayaking off Sand Island © Craig Blacklock/Larry Ulrich Stock

Distributed in the United States and Canada by Publishers Group West

Printed in the USA by R.R. Donnelley

Although every effort was made to ensure that the information was correct at the time of going to press, the author and publisher do not assume and hereby disclaim any liability to any party for any loss or damage caused by errors, omissions, or any potential travel disruption due to labor or financial difficulty, whether such errors or omissions result from negligence, accident, or any other cause.

Please send all comments, corrections, additions, amendments, and critiques to:

**MOON HANDBOOKS: WISCONSIN
AVALON TRAVEL PUBLISHING, INC.
5855 BEAUDRY ST.
EMERYVILLE, CA 94608, USA
e-mail: info@travelmatters.com
www.travelmatters.com**

Printing History
1st edition—1997
2nd edition—March 2001
   5 4 3 2 1

To Hyeon, for always being there,
even when so far away.

CONTENTS

SPECIAL TOPICS

SPECIAL TOPICS

ABBREVIATIONS

AYH—American Youth Hostel Association
CCC—Civilian Conservation Corps
CR—County Road
CVB—Convention and Visitors Bureau

d—double
DNR—Department of Natural Resources
DOT—Department of Transportation
FR—Forest Road
IAT—Ice Age Trail

NPS—National Park Service
s—single
USFS—United States Forest Service
USGS—United States Geological Survey

ACKNOWLEDGMENTS

Travel writing can be partly defined as professional mooching, availing oneself of whatever generosities strangers and especially friends offer. Some are inveterately predisposed to max out this credit line: crashing on couches, constant milking for information, and so on. *Moon Handbooks: Wisconsin* would never, ever have been possible without the latent Elvis in all of the following members of Chambers of Commerce and/or CVBs: Sharon Benda, St. Germain; Patty Schauf, Wisconsin Dells; Wendy Haase, Milwaukee; Alisa Goetsch, Eau Claire; Dorothy Bliskey; Denny Moyer, Sheboygan; Ginnie Davis, Cedarburg; the entire chamber office in Lake Geneva; and especially Kim Bednarczyk in Kenosha. Many thanks to the travel information center staffers statewide who are always in such good moods, helping us clueless travelers out in so many ways.

In civilian life, thanks as always to the WESLI family for being the place of sanctuary when off the road, especially Company Man Dan Perreth for being there to bounce things off of; Judy, Dawn, Laila, Jen, and Gregg, for being great friends, colleagues, and office-mates for all these years; and Amy Duit and Carlos Osorio, for letting me get away with it all, like usual.

Also a nod to my family, for absolutely everything. As always.

For help with the mojo during tedious crunch times, or along those millions of miles, I gratefully acknowledge Bob Uecker ("get up, get outta here, GONE!"), National Public Radio in any of its manifestations, Richard Buckner, Counting Crows, and Jimmy Lafave.

MAPS

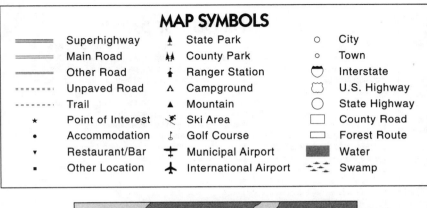

MAP SYMBOLS

═══	Superhighway	⚲	State Park	○	City
══	Main Road	⚲⚲	County Park	○	Town
──	Other Road	⚲	Ranger Station	⬡	Interstate
∷∷∷	Unpaved Road	∧	Campground	⬠	U.S. Highway
-----	Trail	▲	Mountain	○	State Highway
★	Point of Interest	⚡	Ski Area	☐	County Road
•	Accommodation	♌	Golf Course	▭	Forest Route
▾	Restaurant/Bar	✛	Municipal Airport	▓	Water
▪	Other Location	✈	International Airport	≈≈	Swamp

HANDBOOK DIVISIONS

MICHIGAN

Superior

NORTHWESTERN WISCONSIN

Eagle River

NORTHEASTERN WISCONSIN

Eau Claire

Sturgeon Bay

GREAT

Wausau

THE DOOR PENINSULA

RIVER

CENTRAL WISCONSIN SANDS

Green Bay

La Crosse

MINNESOTA

ROAD

EAST-CENTRAL WATERS

Dodgeville

Madison

MILWAUKEE

SOUTHWESTERN WISCONSIN

SOUTHEASTERN WISCONSIN

IOWA

ILLINOIS

IS THIS BOOK OUT OF DATE?

Although we make Herculean efforts to check our facts, the task is an enormous one and sometimes gets away from us. You can help us keep up.

If something we mention here no longer exists, if certain suggestions are misleading, if you've uncovered anything new, please write in. Letters from Wisky residents are especially appreciated. Although we try to make our maps as accurate as possible, we are always grateful when readers point out any omissions or inaccuracies. When writing, always be as specific and exact as possible. Notes made on the spot are better than later recollections. Write your comments in your copy of *Moon Handbooks: Wisconsin* as you go along, then send us a summary when you get home. This book speaks for you, the independent traveler, so please help us be relevant and accurate.

The author would also like to make this a reader-participation event. In particular, sub-sequent editions of *Moon Handbooks: Wisconsin* would benefit greatly from readers who scour their closets, attics, garages, and basements and send us *copies* of any historic photos, the older the better. Of course, all will be treated preciously and credited dutifully, though return can only be guaranteed by the enclosure of a S.A.S.E.

Likewise, photographers, poets, or other struggling artists may wish to contribute work with a Wisconsin theme. If you want it back, please enclose directions and funds to do so.

Address your letters to:

Moon Handbooks: Wisconsin
c/o Avalon Travel Publishing
5855 Beaudry St.
Emeryville, CA 94608, USA

email: info@travelmatters.com
www.travelmatters.com

INTRODUCTION

No region can be more appropriately designated the heart of North America . . . than that which lies within the embrace of the upper Mississippi, Lake Superior, and Lake Michigan . . . and of this territory Wisconsin embraces the greater part.
—HARPER'S MAGAZINE, 19TH CENTURY

Oh, that glorious Wisconsin wilderness!
—JOHN MUIR, 20TH CENTURY

Wisconsin is truly Midwestern. Incapable of braggadocio, it's generally content to remain in the middle on most things—except such important issues as livability quotients, at which it tends to excel. Superlatives about the place abound: it's one of the top five most livable states in the nation; it's the Midwest's overall most popular travel destination; it's one of the country's most ethnically rich regions; it boasts a north woods encompassing over three million acres of public verdance, the planet's most diverse glacial topography, nearly 16,000 primeval glacial lakes, and 800 miles of Great Lake and Mississippi River littoral stretches. Wisconsin puts the lie to all those clichés about the "bland and boring" Midwest.

THE LAND

Topographically, Wisconsin may lack the jaw-dropping majesty of other states' vaulting crags or shimmering desert palettes. But it possesses an equable slice of physicality, with fascinating geographical and geological highlights—many of them found nowhere in the country outside of Wisconsin. Plainspoken and modest, Wisconsin's geology may seem a bit wanting, but take a little while with it and you'll appreciate the understatement.

Where in the World . . . ?
Where *is* the state? Well, it depends on whom you ask. Sticklers describe it as lying in the "eastern north central United States." (In fact, Wisconsin lies in the northern section of the east north-central states between 86° 30' and 93° longitude and latitudes 42° 30' N at the Illinois border and 47° at the Apostle Islands.) In a guidebook (*another* guidebook), one outlander classified it simply as "north," which makes sense only if you

Continental

Ice

Sheet

of

Extent

Superior
Lobe

Chippewa
Lobe

Wisconsin
Valley
Lobe

Terminal

Moraine

Chippewa
Moraine

Glaciated

Green Bay
Lobe

Two Creeks
Forest

**WISCONSIN
GLACIATION**

Northern Kettle
Moraine
Campbellsport
Drumlins
Horicon
Marsh

Terminal

Area

Lake
Michigan
Lobe

0   40 mi

Moraine

0   40 km

© AVALON TRAVEL PUBLISHING, INC.

even prefer you call it a Great Lakes State.

The Basics
Extend your left hand, palm outward. There's your fairly decent approximation of Wisconsin (albeit with a large pinky knuckle and superfluous index finger).

One-third of the U.S. population lives within a day's drive of the state. Its surface area of 56,514 square miles ranks it 26th largest in the nation.

Wisconsin is by no means high, but misguided notions of epic flatness do not apply here. This is a state of rolling topography, chock-full of hills and glacial undulation. The highest point is Timm's Hill in north-central Wisconsin. Though, at 1,953 feet, paltry by Rocky Mountain standards, it's nothing to sneeze at for the Midwest.

Hydrophiles love it here. Even

look at a map. Wisconsinites themselves most often consider their state a part of the Midwest—more specifically, the Upper Midwest. And some excluding all the access to the Great Lakes, approximately four percent of the state's surface is water—including over 16,000 ancient glacial lakes

WISCONSIN'S TOP ATTRACTIONS

Apostle Islands National Lakeshore, Northwest Wisconsin

Cave of the Mounds, Blue Mounds

Circus World Museum, Baraboo

The Dells, Wisconsin Dells

Door County, Door Peninsula

EAA Air Adventure Museum and Fly In, Oshkosh

Green Bay Packers Hall of Fame, Green Bay

Holy Hill, Hubertus

House on the Rock, Spring Green

Johnson Wax Building, Racine

Manitowoc Maritime Museum, Manitowoc

Mid-Continent Railway Museum, North Freedom

Milwaukee breweries, Milwaukee

Milwaukee County Zoo, Milwaukee

Milwaukee Public Museum, Milwaukee

Mitchell Park Horticultural Conservatory (The Domes), Milwaukee

National Freshwater Fishing Hall of Fame, Hayward

National Railroad Museum, Green Bay

Old World Wisconsin, Eagle

Pendarvis, Mineral Point

Road America, Elkhart Lake

Summerfest, Milwaukee

Taliesin, Spring Green

University of Wisconsin, Madison

Villa Louis, Prairie du Chien

Wisconsin State Capitol, Madison

(40% of which have yet even to be named).

Most of Wisconsin's perimeter is natural, side-stepping surveyors' plotting. The grandest borders—Lakes Michigan and Superior—are unique to Wisconsin and only one other state (Michigan). Superior occupies the far-north cap of the state, ensconcing the Bayfield county promontory and its Apostle Islands. More subdued Lake Michigan runs for an enormous stretch down the state, interrupted only by the magnificent Door County Peninsula.

FORMATION AND PHYSIOGEOGRAPHIC REGIONS

Before Pre-Cambrian period heaving and shifting of continental plates positioned them where they are today, Wisconsin was Earth's equatorial belt buckle. The plate shifting created the Canadian Shield, which includes some two-thirds of eastern Canada along with Wisconsin, Minnesota, Michigan, and New York. During this period, Wisconsin also experienced sedimentation and constant erosion. In the late Cambrian period, up to half a billion years ago, a glacial lake flooded the Wisconsin range—the northern section of present-day Wisconsin. What had been mountains during this period were rounded off in the north and completely covered with sediment in the south. In the later stages of the Upper Cambrian, the northern part of the state rose (up to eight feet per mile) while the southern half was covered with sedimentary debris. The Paleozoic and Pleistocene periods brought intermittent stream erosion, which formed salient cuestas (slopes) in the south (resulting in today's erosionary lines) and more uplifts in the north (the reason for the region's current splendid cataracts).

Glaciation is responsible for Wisconsin's variegated, one-of-a-kind topography. During the two million years of the four glacial periods—geologically, a blink of an eye—over one-third of the earth's surface was covered. The final advance, occurring 70,000 to 10,000 years ago, was even named the Wisconsin period. Wisconsin endured five glacial "lobes" penetrating the state, each carving out rock and leaving detritus in its wake. The Wisconsin period in part reduced the state's previous ambitious heights to knobs and slate-flat lands and established riverways and streambeds. Only the southwestern lower third of the state escaped the glaciers' penetration, resulting in the world's largest area surrounded completely by glacial drift.

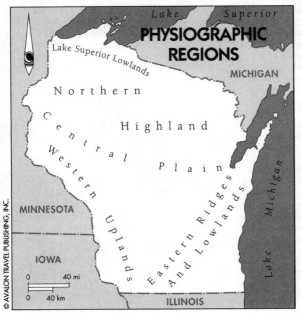

Northern Highland

Covering 15,000 square miles, the Canadian Shield is the most salient feature of northern Wisconsin and one of the larger physiogeographical subdivisions. It is underlain by crystalline rock on a peneplain, rolling or flat landscape once a mountain range. One of the higher points of this concave shield is east of Crandon.

A few elements of glacial lobe penetration can still be seen in the southern counties. The bedrock and glacial soils are particularly suited to growing timber. As a southern border

THE INLAND SEAS

In their interflowing aggregate, these grand fresh-water seas of ours,—Erie, Ontario, and Huron, and Superior, and Michigan,—possess an ocean-like expansiveness, with many of the ocean's noblest traits.

-HERMAN MELVILLE, *MOBY DICK*

Together, the Great Lakes account for 20% of the planet's fresh water. Fifty million people drink from its basins. Lake Michigan, the only Great Lake wholly within U.S. boundaries, is so large that it has its own tide (albeit a minute one). Lake Superior, however, is the second-largest lake in the world. Although Superior has twice its surface area (larger than South Carolina), Lake Baikal in Russia is more voluminous. Superior contains three billion gallons of water—one-eighth the world's water supply. It would take about 111 years to drain it.

Creating a State

At 820 miles, Wisconsin is second only to Michigan in possessing Great Lake frontage property, with shorelines along hydro-behemoths Michigan and Superior. The Great Lakes were largely responsible for perpetuating Wisconsin as a state, and in many ways they still do today. Early shipbuilding and commercial fishing industries have been joined by sportfishing, now a $67 million-a-year industry. Superior, Wisconsin, remains one of the largest and busiest ports in the world, and Wisconsin's 12 ports contribute about $115 million to the state's economy.

Geology

In geological terms, the Great Lakes are young—about 2,000-3,500 years old—but initial geological machinations started half a billion years ago, with successive volcanic action and earth shifting during the Pre-Cambrian period. The basic formations resulted from movements of the Canadian Shield and rising and falling geosyncline regions during the Paleozoic period. Ancient seas later flooded the entire region, and glaciers bulldozed the existing trenches. Most of what makes up today's Great Lakes was formed in the glacial epoch, streams and waterways gouging and forming channels. Wisconsin's Lake Superior Lowlands, surrounded by higher palisade-like ridges, is unique in Great Lakes geology. Both Lakes Michigan and Superior were once conjoined as part of vast, ancient Lake Nipissing, which also included Lake Huron.

Environmental Issues

Lake Michigan, at the edge of the Rust Belt, was particularly toxic following WW II's economic boom. Industrial effluents were the primary cause—factories dumping at will, along with ignorant citizens who saw nothing wrong with disposing of car batteries and refrigerators in the lakes. Development was (and is) another killer, ravaging littoral marshes that once filtered nutrients and pollutants and acted as buffers for runoff. Prior to the advent of the Clean Water Act of 1972, more than 20 billion pounds of toxins were dumped into the Great Lakes each year, and three-quarters of Great Lakes shorelines were unsafe for any use.

A dozen hydrocarbons, pesticides, paper-mill and other industrial waste, and agricultural runoff are the primary toxins still lurking in the Great Lakes. Because the groundwater in the Great Lakes basins is not renewable, very little of Lake Michigan or Lake Superior is active in a hydrologic cycle. Currently, air currents are bringing toxic materials from as far away as Russia. Among the toxins, Chlordane, Dieldrin, DDT, HCB, mercury, OC5, PCBs, and Toxaphene are the most pervasive. DDT and PCBs leach out of heat-resistant industrial fluids dumped into the lakes and are ingested by small fish, which are in turn consumed by larger fish, until, naturally, the "top" of the order—humans—eat the victors for dinner. The chemicals pile up in piscine fatty tissues with a horrifyingly efficient concentration. Effects on children are the most pernicious: short attention spans, lower IQs, and increased likelihoods of developing reading problems are some of the tamer outcomes.

Though dead zones still exist in the Great Lakes, all isn't really lost. The waters of Superior were, until very recently, so clean (due in part to the primeval iciness of the water, so cold it inhibited bacterial growth) that you could cup your hand and drink the water. It isn't this way anymore, but Lake Superior remains the only Great Lake whose native predatory fish—lake trout, for example—can still spawn. A 1986 council of Great Lakes Governors signed a ban on all discharges. Intertribal agencies, the EPA, and especially Canada have also begun cooperating to clean up the waters. Cynics roll their eyes, since the Clean Water Act was initially ignored by industry, but scientists claim to have detected progress—up to a 90% drop in DDT and PCBs detected in human milk (though mercury was up) since 1972.

Still, there are worries. Scientists are most concerned by a tremendously quick rise in average lake temperatures; this may be the canary-in-the-mine to global warming. If it's true, one lethal certainty is that the warmer waters would allow an absolute invasion of non-native species. Communities have also had to deal with average drops of five to six feet in water levels.

So are the Great Lakes safe? In most cases, the fish you're eating will be safe, since most Great Lakes fish—except Lake Superior lake trout—aren't commercially marketed. The feds say it's safe to eat, while alarmists claim that people risk a one-in-ten chance of developing cancer by having one meal of large lake trout per week. Most dangerous are large lake trout and salmon, both of which are fattier and grow old. As a general precaution, never eat a fish over 30 inches long from either lake. Remember that children and pregnant women are always more at risk. Skinning, filleting, and trimming *all* fatty tissue can reduce contaminants by up to 60%. Or just stick to tiny fish, or leaner species like perch and panfish.

of an Arctic Circle belt, the area has a high concentration of peat bogs and a predominance of spruce and tamarack trees. Besides its admittedly modest relief, its high concentration of lakes is what separates the region from the rest of the Midwest—and, in fact, distinguishes it in the world, since only the remotest parts of Quebec and Finland have more lakes per square mile.

Other highlights include the Gogebic Iron Range, which stretches from Iron County and the Chequamegon National Forest into Michigan's Upper Peninsula; Rib Mountain and Timm's Hill; and the underappreciated Blue Hills near Rib Lake.

Lake Superior Lowlands
Wisconsin's northern cap along Lake Superior displays a geological oddity, unique in the Great Lakes—a fallen trench of Lake Superior, flanked by palisades. Before the glaciers arrived, shifting lowered this 10- to 20-mile-wide belt (technically a graben); glaciers subsequently carved the trench. The area is now a half-mile lower than the surrounding land. This wedge-shaped red clay plain skirts Bayfield County and the Apostle Islands and runs along Douglas County across Ashland and Iron Counties; it consists mainly of copper-hued outcroppings and numerous streams and rivers. Most of the state's waterfalls cascade off a 400-foot escarpment abutting the southern ridge.

Eastern Ridges and Lowlands
Bordered by Lake Michigan on the east and north, this 14,000-square-mile physiogeographic region is the state's most populous. Glacial deposits were much richer in this region, and the fecund soils attracted the first immigrant farmers. The impeded waterways were ideal conduits for floating timber to mills.

Cut by the Fox River Valley, the region has a smooth, low relief but three prominent cuestas: the Niagara, which forms the eastern side of Lake Winnebago and stretches east all the way to Niagara Falls; another near Ripon in Fond du Lac County; and the last in Marinette County. The Kettle Moraine region southeast of Lake Winnebago is a physical textbook of glacial geology.

Central (Sand) Plain
Bisected by the mighty Wisconsin River (and including the Chippewa River Valley), the crescent-shaped Central Plains region spreads for 13,000 square miles south of the Northern Highlands. Once the bottom of enormous glacial Lake Wisconsin, the region is most noted for its oddball topography of sand dune-esque stretches mingled with peat bog, cranberry marsh, and jack pine and scrub oak—all made famous by Aldo Leopold's *A Sand County Almanac*. The central section of this region is relatively flat, but the lower third contains buttes and outliers (younger rock formations isolated in older rocks),

rock arch at Natural Bridge State Park

large sandstone hoodoo-shaped rises visible from many highways. Most impressive are the multi-hued post-glacial sandstone canyons of the Wisconsin Dells region—a must-see for any geology buff.

Western Uplands

The Western Uplands subsumes the radical Driftless Area. Geologically the roughest and wildest sector of Wisconsin, it contains rises up to 400 feet higher than the contiguous Central Plain. The unglaciated plateau experienced much stream erosion, and the result is an amazing chocolate-drop topography of rolling hillock and valley capped by hard rock and sluiced by the lower Wisconsin and Mississippi Rivers. It varies from plateau to severe drop-off (near the Mississippi) to wide valleys of huge rounded ridges resembling West Virginia uplands. Most areas feature exposed craggy dolomite.

CLIMATE

Contrary to what you may have heard, Wisconsin weather ain't all that bad. Sure, tempera-tures varying from 110° F to -50° F spice things up a bit and, come late February, most people are psychotically ready for the snow to go, but overall it isn't terrible. (And those halcyon days of spring, summer, and autumn more than make up for any winter day!)

Wisconsin is situated in the mid-latitude belt of the Upper Midwest, near the path of the jet stream, and it lacks any declivity large enough to impede precipitation or climatic patterns. Its northerly latitude produces seasonal shifts in the zenith angle, which result in drastic temperature fluctuations. It's not unusual for farmers near Lake Geneva to be plowing while ice fishers near the Apostle Islands are still drilling holes in the ice.

Commingled air masses from three seriously disparate sources affect the state's weather: dry polar air from the Rocky Mountains (the only buffer zone between weather and Wisconsin), warm tropical air from the Gulf of Mexico, and dry, bitterly cold polar air from the Arctic.

Temperatures and Precipitation

The state's mean temperature is 43° F, though this is not a terribly useful statistic. You'll find 100° in the shade come August, 40 or more below with wind chill in winter, and everything in between.

The annual mean temperature ranges from 41° F in the "Snow Belt," which stretches from Douglas County (Superior) in the west through northern Vilas County, to 48° F in southeastern Kenosha County. This breaks down to a high of 54° and low of 36° March-May, 81° and 57° June-Aug., 59° and 36° Sept.-Nov., and 32° and 12° Dec.-Feb.

The average precipitation amount is 38.6 inches annually. Northern counties experience more snowfall than southern ones, and anyplace near the Great Lakes can see some sort of precipitation when the rest of the state is dry. Snow cover ranges from 140 days per an-

AVERAGE TEMPERATURES

All temperatures are listed in degrees Fahrenheit.

LOCATION	JULY HIGH/LOW	JANUARY HIGH/LOW
Superior	78/52	20/0
Ashland	79/54	22/0
St. Croix Falls	82/58	20/-1
Eau Claire	81/58	20/0
Eagle River	78/52	19/1
Wausau	80/57	20/1
Stevens Point	81/58	23/4
Green Bay	80/58	23/6
Sturgeon Bay	76/56	26/11
La Crosse	83/62	23/5
Wisconsin Dells	82/59	25/6
Prairie du Chien	85/62	27/8
Madison	81/57	27/9
Milwaukee	81/59	28/12
Kenosha	81/60	29/13

num in the north to 85 days in the south. Snowfall ranges from 30 inches in the extreme south to 120 inches or more in Bayfield County and the Lake Superior cap.

Cooler Near the Lake
With an elevation of a mere 1,940 feet (and change), the state lacks the topography necessary to create its own elevated climates. It does, however, have two massive sea-sized bodies of water contiguous to it, and these give rise to their own littoral microclimates. Anywhere along the Great Lakes shoreline, you should get used to hearing "cooler near the lake" in summer and "warmer near the lake" in winter.

The Great Lakes act as moderating influences on shoreline climates; thus, eastern and northern coasts avoid the climatic extremes experienced in the interior. This moderating influence is particularly helpful for the orchards and gardens in Door County on Lake Michigan and Bayfield County on Lake Superior.

When to Visit
Wisconsin is a four-season stop, so the timing of your visit is really up to you. In some parts, winter vacationers may outnumber summertime campers and anglers. In general, late January is the coldest period, late July the warmest.

Winter weather creeps in in mid-November, though permafrost and a hoary landscape usually don't arrive in earnest until the first week of December. They last until early March, and then the real doldrums kick in—the blustery, brown, mucky spell of mid-March—until blossoms and grass finally recover near the end of April.

"Summer" really means mid-July to around the end of the third week of August. May and June are generally great, but precipitation levels are slightly higher than during the rest of summer.

Autumn—a time of moderate temperatures—reveals itself as early as late September and lasts through early or mid-November. Rainier autumn days most likely occur in late October.

Tornadoes
Generally, not much here in Wisconsin can kill you. There are few floodplains, no hurricanes, no snakes, few insects, no freeway snipers, no grizzlies. But the state does endure the eye-popping experience of tornadoes, generally aver-aging six serious twisters and many more near-misses or unsubstantiated touchdowns each year, though it's nothing like Mississippi or Tornado Alley in Texas and Oklahoma. But, unlike with a hurricane or an earthquake, there's always a bit of gamble involved—you might get hit while your neighbor remains unscathed.

Wisconsin lies along the northern edge of the region of maximum tornado frequency extending from northern Texas, Oklahoma, and Kansas into Iowa. They can hit anywhere in the state, but generally the extreme northern and eastern counties and possibly the Great Lakes experience fewer.

A tornado usually appears as a rotating funnel-shaped cloud that extends toward the ground from the base of a thundercloud. They vary in color from white at formation to light gray (from condensation of water vapor) to black (from ground debris), and they can be thin as snakes or a mile wide. Very often, large hail and lightning are continuous throughout. Tornadoes usually form within severe thunderstorms with cloud tops extending 40,000 feet or more into the stratosphere. Many drop down from hundred-plus-mile-long squall lines and move out ahead of eastward-advancing cold fronts. They often, but not always, move from the southwest.

Tornado development depends on a large supply of warm, moist air near the surface. If this air rises to great heights in the unstable atmosphere and gets high velocity inflow near the ground and outflow at the top, conditions are ripe. Upper-level winds provide suction above a thunderstorm, while updrafts of warm, humid air rise to the top, and more warm air rushes to replace it. Combined with the earth's rotation, the updrafts begin spinning and eventually extending, creating the funnel. Pressure inside the tube drops, creating an inward force, while the rotation creates an outward pull, sealing off the tube and causing air to be sucked in through the bottom; the updraft becomes stronger, the tube spins faster, and on and on.

Winds inside a twister are believed to hit up to 300 miles per hour, though no wind instrument has ever survived an attempt at measurement. This wind shear emits the ominous sound of a locomotive. Major property damage is caused more by the pressure than the winds, although both are destructive. Air inside buildings does not have time to escape through holes or cracks, so buildings explode, their roofs lifted and their walls falling out, while objects inside can remain untouched. (Opening windows is not a solution—you won't have time, and the winds are going to rip everything to hell no matter what you do.)

Tornado season begins in March and peaks during late May, June, and July. A secondary spike occurs during September and extends occasionally into mid-October. Many of the midsummer tornadoes are smaller and less intense than the ones in April to June or in September.

What to Do: The first thing to remember is not to panic. Don't be ignorant and sit out on the front porch with a beer waiting for a tornado to arrive, but don't run off screaming either. Lightning still causes more deaths per year than tornadoes and hurricanes combined.

A **tornado watch** means conditions are favorable for the development of a tornado. A **tornado warning** means one has been sighted in the vicinity. In either case, emergency sirens are active almost everywhere in Wisconsin. Tornadoes appear most often between 3 and 7 p.m. but can occur at any time.

Seek shelter in a basement and get in the southwest corner, under a table if possible. Avoid windows at all costs. If there is no basement, find an interior room, like a bathroom, with no windows. Avoid rooms with outside walls on the south or west side of a building. If you are driving, position yourself at right angles to the tornado's apparent path. If that's not possible, get out of your car, find a low depression in the ground and lie flat in it, covering your head with your hands.

Dane County historically has the most tornadoes in Wisconsin, though the southwestern sector—Waukesha County, Dodge County, and the area around Eau Claire—also sees quite a few.

Thunderstorms and Lightning
Lightning still kills some 200-300 people per year. Wisconsin averages two serious thunderstorms per year, with a midsummer average of two relatively modest ones each week. Don't let this lull you into complacency in autumn, however; once, on the penultimate day of October, as the original edition of this book was being feverishly scribbled, southern Wisconsin experienced the worst thunderstorm of the year,

replete with marble-sized hail, flash floods, and tornadic activity.

Thunderstorms are generally regarded as less dangerous than tornadoes, but they're often deadlier, particularly when driving or when isolated in open areas. Lightning is serious stuff. The cardinal rule when lightning is present: do the opposite of what gut instincts tell you. Avoid anything outside—especially trees. If you cannot get indoors, squat on the balls of your feet, hugging your knees in a balled position, reducing your contact with the ground and your apparent size. If indoors, stay away from anything that has a channel to the outside: telephones, TVs, radios, even plumbing.

Snowstorms
Technically, four inches of snow per 24-hour period qualifies as heavy snowfall, but it takes a lot more than that to faze anyone from Wisconsin. Six inches in eight to 12 hours will cause serious transportation and infrastructure disruptions and definitely close airports for a while. Snow generally begins to stick in mid- to late October in Northern Wisconsin, and early December in Southern Wisconsin, though snow has fallen as early as September and as late as May on rare occasions.

Odds are, if you're in Wisconsin in the winter you're going to be driving in the stuff. Still, even the hardiest winter drivers need to practice prudence. If you're a novice at winter driving, don't learn it on the road, especially on a crowded highway at dawn or dusk. Always drive safely—it's important to *slow down*. Be cautious on bridges, even when the rest of the pavement is okay; bridges are always slippery. In controlled skids on ice and snow, take your foot off the accelerator and steer *into* the direction of the skid. Follow all owner's manual advice if your car is equipped with an Anti-Lock Braking System (ABS); unlike other brakes, which you should pump steadily and carefully, ABS brakes require you to depress the pedal and hold it there, allowing the computer to do the work. Most cars come equipped with all-season radials, so snow tires aren't usually necessary. **Tire chains are illegal in Wisconsin.**

During nighttime snowstorms, keep your lights on low-beam. If you get stuck, check your owner's manual for the advisability of "rocking" the car between Drive and Reverse; be sure to keep the front wheels cleared *and pointed straight ahead.* Do not race the engine.

Winterize your vehicle. Most important, carry an emergency kit including booster cables, sand or gravel (in a pinch, try sandpaper strips, or kitty litter works marvelously), flares, candles, matches, a shovel and scraper, flashlight and extra batteries, blankets (space blankets are excellent), extra heavy clothing, high-calorie non-perishable food, and anything else you might need if you have to spend the night in a snowbank.

And please, if you see someone hung up in a snowbank, stop and help push him or her out.

The Department of Transportation's website (www.dot.state.wi.us) updates winter driving conditions from November to late-March four times daily. You can also call the state's toll-free winter driving conditions hotline at 800-ROAD-WIS.

Wind Chill and Frostbite
The most dangerous part of winter in Wisconsin is the wind-chill factor—the biting effect of wind, which makes cold colder and more lethal. For example, when the temperature is 30° F, with a wind of 40 mph the temperature is actually six below zero; if the temperature were zero, 40 mph winds would make it 54° below zero—the point at which it's no longer a joke how cold a Wisconsin winter is. The wind-chill factor is currently being debated; new analysis of data from Antarctica suggests a reworking of the calculations, using more modern methods of heat transfer theory, may be needed, but nobody disputes that wind-chill does exist and does cause major injury every winter to the unprepared.

When the wind chill takes temperatures low enough, exposed skin is in immediate danger. **Frostbite** is the result of skin's prolonged exposure to cold. Like burns, frostbite can range in severity: in minor cases it hurts to take off

WIND-CHILL FACTOR

Wind chill numbers indicate the approximate equivalent temperature when combined with wind speed.

DEGREES (F)	35	30	25	20	15	10	5	0	-5	-10	-15	-20
WIND SPEED (MPH)	RESULTING WIND-CHILL FACTOR											
0	35	30	25	20	15	10	5	0	-5	-10	-15	-20
5	33	27	21	16	12	7	1	-6	-11	-15	-20	-26
10	21	16	9	2	-2	-9	-15	-22	-27	-31	-38	-45
15	16	11	1	-6	-11	-18	-25	-33	-40	-45	-51	-60
20	12	3	-4	-9	-17	-24	-32	-40	-46	-52	-60	-68
30	5	-2	-11	-18	-26	-33	-41	-49	-56	-63	-70	-78
40	1	-4	-15	-22	-29	-36	-45	-54	-62	-69	-76	-87

your boots and mittens, and even lukewarm water is excruciating, but the pain will go away. Lots of Badgers still remember one serious case that they swear they can still feel today when the weather changes. The most serious cases of frostbite—you've seen photos of mountain climbers with black ears and digits—can require amputation.

Worse, without proper clothing, you're at risk for **hypothermia,** a lethal condition in which the body loses the ability to warm itself. Warning signs of hypothermia include unvanquishable chills, slurred speech, and disorientation, among other symptoms.

Dress appropriately for the weather at all times—that includes wearing a hat. Generally, the more fashionable an outfit, the less effective it is. The best way to stay warm is by layering. Against your skin, wear a thin insulative layer that can wick body moisture away. Most decent sporting good stores have lots of options; good materials include silk, polypropylene, and caliprene. Over that, fleece is a godsend for trapping warmth. On top, many find jackets with a Gore-Tex shell invaluable, since it keeps out wind and precipitation but also "breathes." However, these are very expensive. For the recreation-oriented, layering is the only way to go, as you can shed layers when exertion raises your core body temperature. Again, most body heat is lost through the head, so wear a hat. One relatively new item that really works is a head tube (popularized by pro football players). It's very thin, stretchable, and magnificently versatile; it acts as scarf, hat, ear warmer, and face mask, all in one. Plus, it folds up to the size of a handkerchief. Do not come to Wisconsin in winter without a good pair of gloves. Mittens are warmer than gloves, since the fingers are not insulated from each other as they generate heat. Inuit-worthy mittens are something you'll be ever so grateful for on a sleigh ride or while you await a tow truck. A good pair of boots is also a necessity; some people carry a heavy-duty pair in the car at all times, in case of an emergency.

yellow lady's slipper

FLORA AND FAUNA

Flora

The Eastern Transition and Great Lakes Forest Zones cover most of Wisconsin. Both are primarily mixed meadow and woodland, a far cry from pre-settlement periods when 85% of the state was covered by forest and the rest by tall grass. By settlement periods, in the mid-19th century, those numbers had dipped to 63% forest, 28% savannah, and nine percent grassland. Today, the state's forest cover is 37%, and precious little of that is original. Of the two million acres of prairie that once covered the state, only 2,000 scattered acres survive. In all, Wisconsin has over 2,100 species of plants, approximately a tenth of which are classified as rare, and some of them are threatened.

Four major vegetation types cover Wisconsin. **Boreal forest,** a subarctic coniferous spread across northern North America, is found near Lake Superior in the north. Stretching across the central lowlands of the U.S., **deciduous forest** makes up the second-largest swath of Wisconsin woodlands. **Mixed forest,** consisting of species of both, is found throughout the state. **Nonforest/grasslands** are located throughout the southern third of the state and up into west-central Wisconsin along the Mississippi River.

Pines of all kinds are the most common tree type in Wisconsin. Commercially valuable, they grow quickly (key to recouping harvested lands) and hold well in the sandy, humus-poor soil of Wisconsin's central regions. Virtually all of northern Wisconsin's verdance is pine trees intermingled with northern hardwoods like maple, birch, and aspen. In the extreme north, along Lake Superior, swamp conifers such as spruce and fir are common, along with tamarack and balsam. In the midsection of the state and to the south, you'll see oak, hickory, beech, and hemlock trees. To the east, lowland hardwoods like elm, ash, and some cottonwood still grow.

In settlement periods, Wisconsin had a huge expanse of wetlands, including over 10,000 acres along Green Bay alone. Today, that amount has dwindled by more than half but still constitutes the largest amount remaining on the Great Lakes—a pathetic indication of rapacious development and overuse.

Fauna

Wisconsin lies within three well-defined "life zones" conducive to species diversity: the Canadian, the transition, and the upper austral (or Carolinian). The Canadian, not surprisingly the coldest, features small mammals like the snowshoe hare but also the state's primary large mammals, the deer and the black bear. The warmest zone, the Carolinian, falls in the southern tier of the state and lacks big game mammals. In total, Wisconsin has 73 species of mammals, 339 native bird species, and over 200 species of amphibians, reptiles, frogs, bats, butterflies, and insects.

Of Wisconsin's two large mammals, the ubiquitous **white-tailed deer** is so great in number that in 1996 the state Department of Natural Resources instituted an unheard-of two-season deer hunt including a special hunt specifically designed to thin out the doe and fawn population. (See the special topic "Roadkill.") The other resident big mammal, the **black bear,** is still relatively common in the north woods and has also been seen in central counties; see the special topic "Smokey Bear and Friends."

Wisconsin lies smack in the middle of several migratory waterfowl flyways, so birding is a big activity in the state. **Tundra swans, sandhill cranes,** and **Canada geese** are three of the most conspicuous species. The latter is so predominant at the Horicon Marsh National Wildlife Refuge that ornithologists make pilgrimages there each spring and especially fall. (The state's fish population is detailed in the "Recreation" section of the On The Road chapter.)

Threatened, Endangered, Exterminated

Like many other states, Wisconsin is paying the price for a century of ravenous exploitation of its natural resources, untrammeled development, and simple ignorance. Wisconsin has 121 plant species listed as either endangered or threatened and 90 threatened or endangered mammals, birds, reptiles, amphibians, fishes, insects, snails, and mussels. The last plains buffalo was shot five years before the state became a territory; the next to become extinct withinthe state of Wisconsin were the Richardson's cari-bou, the American elk, the cougar, the Carolina paroquet, the passenger pigeon (the world's last was shot in Wisconsin), the peregrine falcon, the pine marten, the trumpeter swan, the whooping crane, the wild turkey, the moose, the fisher, and, in 1922, the common wolverine.

Of these, the fisher, falcon, pine marten, trumpeter swan, and wild turkey have been reintroduced to varying degrees of success. In 2000 the state received clearance to establish nesting sites for whooping cranes over 100,000 acres in central Wisconsin; eventually nests will be found at the Sandhill State Wildlife Area, Necedah National Wildlife Refuge, and two other sites. By 2020 hopes are to have 125 of the majestic birds in the state. Most amazing was the return of a nesting pair of **piping plovers** to the shores of the Apostle Islands National Lakeshore in 1999. In the entire Great Lakes only 30 nesting pairs exist, all in Michigan. As a result, the U.S. Fish and Wildlife Service has proposed setting aside nearly 200 miles of shoreline—20 in Wisconsin—for critical habitats, and possibly to establish a colony.

Though never extinct, the bald eagle, once perilously close to vanishing, may have had the most successful recovery of all. The state now harbors some 600 pairs of breeding eagles, and the birds are so prevalent along the Wisconsin and Mississippi Rivers that certain communities make much of their tourist income because of them. And in 1996, bald eagles were officially

removed from the threatened and endangered lists. In 2000 the state announced plans to gobble up riverine land near Prairie du Sac to continue the comeback.

Despite the grim extinction figures, Wisconsin is taking steps. It was the first state in the U.S. to designate Natural Areas throughout the state. These vigilantly protected areas harbor fragile geology, archaeology, or plant and animal life; some are even being nudged toward a return to their pre-settlement ecology.

In the 1990s, the state began serious efforts to bring back the **timber wolf,** which had been all but exterminated by the 1940s due to misinformation, fear, and rapacious bounty-hunting. State-instituted programs such as selling specialized license plates to pay for research and reintroduction made such an impact that plans are being formulated to reclassify the wolf from endangered to threatened. Currently up to 245 wolves in 28 breeding pairs roam throughout 13 counties; one wolf was even spotted just 30 miles north of Madison. This is great news for a species down to just 15 survivors in 1985. In

FRANKEN(HOL)STEIN

The latest dairy crisis in Wisconsin is the Franken-(Hol)stein. Or, as one news headline put it, "Robo-Cow." It's the result of profit-mongering through mega-technology. The nearly-cyborg superbovines are the result of rBGH, better known as Bovine Growth Hormone. More correctly termed "rBST" and marketed by Monsanto under the name Posilac (hereafter rBGH), it's a synthetic, genetically engineered growth hormone designed to increase the milk output of a cow. The dilemma: Will it lead dairying into the 21st century, or is it a health time-bomb working its way through the food chain, like some 21st-century PCB?

Indeed, the use of rBGH can increase a cow's milk production by at least 10%. In 1996, a Wisconsin holstein pushed out a record-breaking 63,444 pounds of milk, beating the old record by 1,740 pounds. This is staggering considering that the average dairy cow produces 16,000 pounds of milk per year.

The FDA approved rBGH in 1993, stating that it found no evidence of consumer peril. As a result, mandatory labeling—as called for by a network of agriculture- and health-industry advocates—was not enforced. In fact, dairy interests in certain states wielded enough clout to have bans put into effect *against* labeling; Wisconsin is one of the few states allowing voluntary rBGH-free labels. Canada and the EU have both banned rBGH in toto.

The Debate

Critics of rBGH say that claims praising its safety are typical PR glossings. Monsanto has grudgingly admitted to 20 side effects. Mastitis, a pus-producing infection of the udder, is the most salient and perni-

cious effect; it must be treated with antibiotics, which critics say appear subsequently in residual amounts in milk. The hormone also makes cows relatively voracious and increases their feed intake by a large percentage—the costs of which offset any profitability. There are also negative economic effects of using rBGH. For farmers, it means an increase in the management time required for a herd injected with the hormone. They eat more, and then they require more attention and a shift in methodology. It's not an easy, or manageable, change for a struggling family farm. Alarmists also predict it will screw up the milk supply system, driving prices into the ground. Worst of all to some are the potential medical consequences. Monsanto, of course, claims rBGH cannot and does not enter the cow's milk. And if it did, it would havde no effect on humans. But no test exists for tracing residual amounts in humans, and the FDA has not begun to develop one.

Leading the Charge

As a whole, Wisconsin is one of the states most stridently opposed to the hormone. In 1994, Wisconsin Congressman David Obey asked the General Accounting Office to investigate the FDA's handling of the matter, and Wisconsin Sen. Russ Feingold is a major opponent of its use. At the height of the debate, Wisconsin dairies and groceries—even chain stores—reported a surge in consumer demand for rBGH-free milk, one reason the state's labeling law was passed. Nationwide, the use of rBGH has dropped, some estimates say, by as much as 80%, and less than 10% of all farmers use it. But it's still big business—sales top $90 million per year.

fact, as this book was being updated, the state Department of Natural Resources (DNR) announced that if the wolf numbers reached 250, they would consider removing it from the endangered list. Environmentalists are furious, since delisting it would allow property owners to seek permission to shoot what they consider pest wolves. Worse, if the population hits 350, the state may sell $100 "lottery licenses," which would allow hunting, including using traps and dog packs. So much for a progressive regard for nature. Consider yourself eminently blessed if you see one.

In 1995, the state launched a project to reintroduce **elk,** importing 25 from Michigan into the Chequamegon National Forest. Hopes were high when the elk survived their first winter; if successful, Wisconsin will be one of approximately 20 states with free-ranging elk.

If there is one endangered fish all Badgers worry about, it's the **perch,** especially the yellow perch. In a state that treats fish fries as quasi-religious experiences (there is no better fish than perch for a fish fry), plummeting lake perch populations in the early 1990s absolutely freaked the fish-loving population out. But in 2000, for the first time in five years, sufficient numbers were being seen for the DNR to be "cautiously optimistic."

Still, the picture could be much better. In 1996, 23 more native species were added to the threatened and endangered lists. Up to three percent of native plants are now threatened or endangered.

Zebra Mussel

One culprit for the decline in Lake Michigan's yellow perch population could be this pesky little mollusk, the species best representing what can happen when a non-native species is introduced into an environment. Transplanted most likely from a visiting freighter from the Caspian Sea in the mid-1980s, the zebra mollusk is a ferocious, tough little Eurasian mollusk that found it loved the warmer waters and phytoplankton of the Great Lakes. Problem is, it loves to breed near warm areas—like at discharge pipes around power plants. They breed so rapidly they create unbelievably dense barnacle-like crusts that do serious damage. Worse, they're being blamed for the decline if not decimation of native species as they literally suck all the nutrients out of an area. Now the state is frantically fighting a war to keep them from spreading into inland lakes and streams.

ENVIRONMENTAL ISSUES

A state that produced both John Muir and Aldo Leopold must have a fairly good track record of being "green." If you discount the first century of statehood, during which the state—like most states at the time—pillaged the natural world fullbore, Wisconsin has in fact been ahead of its time environmentally. The state government initiated exceptionally far-sighted environmental laws beginning in the 1950s, when tourism loomed as a major industry. The state was the first to meet the 1972 Clean Water Act; it had put similar legislation on its own books a half-decade earlier. Former Wisconsin governor and U.S. Sen. Gaylord Nelson founded Earth Day in 1970. Nearly 200 environmental periodicals are published here.

Still, as always, things could be better. Wisconsin retains more than 40 EPA Superfund sites (areas so contaminated that the EPA allots large amounts of money to clean them up). The Wisconsin Department of Natural Resources has found that some 900 miles of rivers in the state flunked environmental standards in the mid-1990s, and another 50 or so lakes were "questionable" or worse. Twenty-two percent of rivers and streams fail, one way or another, to meet the state's clean-water goals. Fish consumption advisories are in effect in 2000 for 341 lakes and rivers. Though the figures may constitute less than five percent of riverways and an even lower percentage of lakes, it is indicative of a state resting on its laurels and portends worse things to come. And environmentalists in 2000 were chagrined at the state's killing of its mercury reduction program.

With 90.1 people per square mile, Wisconsin ranks in the middle of American states for population density. However, two-thirds of the people dwell in the dozen southeastern counties, creating a serious land-use and urban-sprawl issue. In southeastern Wisconsin, agricultural land is being converted to urban use at a rate of 10 square miles per year, and the rate of wetland destruction increased 200% between 1970 and 1985. Northern forests are being encroached upon as flight from burgeoning urban areas continues. This sprawl results in diminished air quality (from excess use of commuters' automobiles), loss of farmland and wildlife habitat, more toxic runoff, and continued erosion.

Air Quality

At one point in the 1970s, fully half of Wisconsin counties failed standards for ozone, total suspended particulates, and sulfur dioxide. All have gotten better, save for ground-level ozone—the main ingredient of smog—still found in 11 southeastern counties. The problem is so severe that southeast Wisconsin was forced by federal law to begin using expensive reformulated gas in the mid-1990s. (Wisconsinites naturally blamed Chicago for the pollution!)

Once a grave crisis for northern lakes and forests, acid deposition, known as acid rain when it falls from the sky, has been slowed, largely through strict national legislation enacted in the mid-'80s. It's still a problem however; 90% of the pollutants in Lake Superior come from the air.

Water Quality

Though the state passed the earliest and strictest groundwater standards in the country and is pointed to by the EPA as one of three exemplary states, not enough local water sources pass muster. Land use, particularly agriculture, forestry, and construction, often creates eroded soils and runoff polluted with fertilizers and toxins. But agriculture cannot hold all the blame; urban runoff potentially causes up to 50 times as much soil erosion. Non-point-source pollution (so called because it isn't traceable to a single source) is no higher than point-source pollution such as factory or industrial discharge. Non-point-source water picks up contaminants from whatever it comes in contact with—soil, pesticides, manure, oils, grass clippings, heavy metals—and winds up in surface water, sediment, or groundwater. Wisconsin's animal-waste runoff problem is among the nation's worst.

Contaminated sedimentation from decades of abuse remains a secondary problem. In 1970, pulp and paper mills discharged almost 300 million gallons of wastewater, most of it untreated, into surface water, leaving a toxic legacy. In 1999 the EPA asked to declare 39 miles of the Fox River—the heart of papermaking—a Superfund site because *40 tons* (of an original 125 tons) of toxic PCBs (polychlorinated biphenyl) remained from factory waste discharge.

As a result of other pollution, the Wisconsin DNR issues almost 200 "boil water" notices annually (one Wisconsin county found half of its 376 wells to be seriously contaminated by pollutants such as atrazine and nitrates). Over 90% of state lakes have been affected one way or another, including sedimentation, contamination, and (the most common and difficult to handle) eutrophication—when increased nutrients in the water lead to algae blooms and nuisance weeds, which eventually kill off aquatic life. The DNR is in the process of publishing consumption advisories for fish in certain state lakes and the Great Lakes.

In 2000 the state took aim at non-point-source pollution with a set of proposed guidelines that caused immediate debate when Wisconsinites got the bill: $2 billion. The act covers everything from manure spreading to pet droppings.

The Crandon Brouhaha

The most recent environmental flap concerns the Wolf River region. It arose after Exxon Corp. (who later sold the project to Rio Algoma, then they to Nicolet Minerals, but everybody still blames Exxon) announced plans to create the planet's largest zinc-sulfide mining operation near Crandon, precariously close to the headwaters of Wisconsin's officially designated Outstanding Water Resource (and National Wild and Scenic River), the whitewater-wild and primitive Wolf River.

Opposition was quick and effective. Environmentalists statewide, along with other citizens and Indian tribes throughout the state—including some of the same groups that squared off at boat landings just a few years earlier in spearfishing protests—launched fast and furious grassroots campaigns to halt Exxon before its bid for permits got too far (see the special topic "Trouble in Paradise" for more on the spearfishing issue).

Environmentalists recite a litany of harrowing statistics: the U.S. Bureau of Mines has identified acid drainage from sulfide mines as the most difficult problem it faces with similar mines out west; 2,000 gallons per minute of treated mine waste would flow into the Wolf River; lethal sulfuric acid would be an unavoidable consequence;

the 365-acre, 90-foot-deep waste pond would be the largest waste-disposal facility in state history; the company's own geologists admit that no protective system could work forever; and EPA mock-up tests showed that containment ponds holding residual tailings from the mine had a life of merely 30 years. Exxon's initial forays into this mine ended quickly in face of the opposition in 1986 and were only reopened recently, cynics asserted, when one of Exxon's ex-lobbyists became Wisconsin's Secretary of Administration.

Exxon and the state counter that the mines are absolutely, positively safe and will offer probably hundreds of jobs in the Crandon area alone. With a 70-million-ton lode under the ground, the mine could operate for some 30 years. They claim pollution won't happen, as no smelting will take place, only concentrating, and the water discharged into the Wolf will be as pristine as what is already there.

Environmentalists are fighting an uphill battle, no matter what the minor victories. Already over 350,000 acres of land—including national forest—has been leased for "exploratory" purposes by mining groups. Since not enough damage from similar operations can be documented, and the companies spend millions on public relations (buying libraries for cash-strapped northern villages, for example), it's merely a matter of time before permits are passed through and the earth-movers set about stripping. Indeed, environmentalists were chagrined to learn that the entire northern region of the state is being eyed by many mining consortiums.

As this book is being updated, endless studies have been read at endless court battles for a decade and a half and still the Crandon mine project sits in limbo. The company has set a target date of 2004, by which time opposition in court or in Department of Natural Resource Board meetings will be essentially exhausted. If the courts haven't stopped the project by then, there may be no more chance for discussion or opposition. Ironically, what may eventually stop mining cold in the north isn't citizens' advisory groups or angry sportsmen showing up at DNR public meetings but rather the very treaty rights of Native Americans that caused a previous uproar over spearfishing. The 11 tribes of Wisconsin may hold the trump card as to whether the north woods are carved up by multinationals. And, if nothing else, at least previous foes—average citizens, environmentalists, sportsmen, and the tribes—have found some common ground.

Visually Busy

On a personal note, there's another piece of the pollution puzzle—not lethal but certainly important—that needs scrutiny: Wisconsin's lovely countryside is absolutely scarred by the visual pollution of "litter on a stick," or billboard advertising. While states and communities across the nation have awakened to the fact that not only is it disgustingly ugly, it can also distract drivers. The state has nearly 15,000 ugly popsicles gracelessly attesting to our state's, well, if not greed then certainly bad taste; only three states have more billboard advertising than Wisconsin.

HISTORY

EARLY ARRIVALS

The Siberia-to-Alaska Beringia theory, which posits that the progenitors of North America's Native Americans arrived over a land bridge that rose and submerged in the Bering Strait beginning as many as 20,000 years ago, was dealt serious blows in the late 1990s. Provocative new anthropological discoveries in Latin America have forced a radical reconsideration of this theory (a Wisconsin archaeologist was one of the first to bring up the topic). According to the original postulation, the three possible periods of human migration into Wisconsin coincide with the retreat of the great glaciers of the Ice Age. The last of the glacial interludes of the Pleistocene era, the Two Rivers, probably saw the first movement into the state of early Paleo-Indians some 11,500 years ago. The time is based on examinations of fluted points as well as a rare mastodon kill site, the Boaz Mastodon, which established Paleo-Indian hunting techniques of the Plains Indians in Wisconsin.

Glacial retreat helps explain why the Paleo-Indian groups entered the state from the south and southwest rather than the more logical north. Nomadic clans followed the mastodon and other large mammals northward as the glaciers shrank. Thus divergent Indian cultures formed in northern and southern Wisconsin, each in a distinct biotic zone created by retreating glaciers, the incipient woodland and prairie, and even nascent littoral environments.

Later Stages

Solid archaeological evidence establishes definite stages in Wisconsin's earliest settlers. The **Archaic** period, approximately 8000 B.C. to 750 B.C., is generally determined according to slight typological shifts in the design of fluted points and stone tools, as well as an absence of pottery and of burial mounds. The region's deciduous forests and moderate climate required little lifestyle modification. The tribes were still transient, pursuing smaller game and the fish in the newly formed lakes. Around 2000 B.C., these Indians became the first in the new world to fashion copper, which was abundant in the region.

The later **Woodland** Indians, with semi-permanent abodes, are generally regarded as the first natives in Wisconsin to make use of ceramics, elaborate mound burials and, to a lesser extent, domesticated plants such as squash, corn, pumpkins, beans, and tobacco. Lasting from around 750 B.C. until European exploration, the Woodland Period was a minor golden age of dramatic change for the native cultures. Around 100 B.C., the Middle Woodland experienced cultural and technological proliferations, simultaneous with the period of Ohio's and Illinois' Hopewell societies, when villages formed and expanded greatly along waterways. The Late Woodland culture is best represented by the residual ground formations of the effigy mound cultures in the southern third of the state. Original state archaeologists devoted themselves solely to recording and studying the mounds, before the settlers' plows did their work. Still, then—as now—the effigies baffled scientists.

The people living during the tail end of the Woodland period have been classified into two additional groups: the **Mississippian** and the **Oneota.** The former's impressive sites can be found from New Orleans all the way north into Wisconsin and parts of Minnesota. Mississippian culture showed high levels of civic planning and complex social hierarchies, and it lasted at least until the Spanish arrived (Spanish records reported contact). Trade was enormous during this period but declined during the Oneota, as did the flowering of culture.

EUROPEAN CONTACT

The Spanish (and Portuguese) in the latter part of the 15th century—the watershed of Europe's first great westward expansion—blazed the trail west looking for the East. The main directive was to circumvent the Arabs, reach the courts of the Great Khan, and establish channels to appropriate the riches of new lands. Along the way, the natives, if any, were to be "pacified" under papal hegemony. After England came to naval power under the Tudor monarchies and began taking swipes at the French, the New World became the proving ground for the European powers.

New France: Black Robes and the Fur Trade

The French, relative latecomers to maritime and thus expansionist endeavors, were, thanks to the Reformation, conveniently freed of papal dicta for divvying up the new continent and its inherent wealth. Nevertheless, Spanish strength closed them out of much of the Caribbean and Gulf Coast. The up-and-coming English established a foothold in what would become the mid-Atlantic colonies. Hence, France was effectively forced to attempt to penetrate the new land via the northern frontier.

Jacques Cartier first opened the door to the Great Lakes region with his "discovery" of the Gulf of the St. Lawrence River, in 1534. His tales, however, lacking mention of lustrous gold and silver, failed to woo the insular French monarchy, who were obsessed with keeping up with the Spanish. As a result, the French, content to fish the shoals of Newfoundland, left the scattered outposts to simmer for another 40 years—except for several fur traders, who, it turns out, were on to something.

When, with an eye to establishing a permanent "New France," the French did establish sparse settlements in the early 16th century, they were dismayed by the lack of ready riches, the roughness of the land, and the bitter weather. However, the original traders possessed one superlative talent: forging relationships with the natives, who became enamored of French metal implements—firearms in particular. Eventually, the French found their coveted mother lode: beavers.

Paris hatmakers discovered that beaver pelts—especially those softened for a year around the waists of Indians—made a superior grade of felt for hats, and these soon became the rage in Paris and other parts of Europe. As beaver was readily available and easily transportable to France from the wilds, it became the lifeblood of the colonies, sustaining the region through the mismanagement and general vagaries of both British and French rule.

Facilitating both the fur trade and French control over the colonies were the missionaries of the Society of Jesus—the Jesuits. These "Black Robes" (so-called by the Huron and Ottawa because of their long dark frocks) first arrived during a time of atavistic religious fervor in France. The Franciscans had originally set down here but found the task of conversion too daunting for their small order. The Jesuits became the very foundation upon which New France operated, serving crucial secular needs as well as religious ones. The traders needed them to foster harmony with Native American traders. More important, the often complicated French systems of operation required that all day-to-day affairs be carried out at the local level. By 1632, all missionary work in French Canada was under the auspices of the Jesuits.

The Jesuits also accompanied *voyageurs* (explorers) as New France attempted to widen its sphere of influence westward. Eventually, the Black Robes themselves, along with renegade fur traders, were responsible for the initial exploration and settlement of present-day Wisconsin.

THE FRENCH IN WISCONSIN

Samuel de Champlain, who first arrived in Quebec in 1603, was the province's most famous French governor and, in many ways, its most effective, despite ignoring mundane management duties to obsess on the legendary route to the "People of the Seas" and the Great Khan.

After arriving and hearing of the "People of the Stinking Waters" (the Winnebago), which he surmised to mean an ocean-dwelling people, he dispatched the first Europeans from Acadia to explore the wild western frontier.

Though there is speculative evidence that Étienne Brûlé, Champlain's first explorer, may have poked around Wisconsin as early as 1620—the same year many assume the pilgrims founded the new colonies—most historians credit Jean Nicolet with being the first European to turn up in Green Bay, landing at Red Banks in 1634. Garbed in Chinese damask and using thunderstick histrionics to impress the natives (the Potawatomi he met immediately dubbed him Thunder Beaver), Nicolet efficiently and diplomatically forged immediate ties with the Indians, who guided him throughout the region to meet other tribes, many of whom had never seen a European.

As before, Nicolet couldn't rouse the wilted interest of the French royalty—all it wanted to see was bags of Chinese silk—and the country once again let the matter drop. Legitimate French fur traders were scooped by Pierre Esprit Radisson and Médard Chouart des Groseilliers, two pesky *coureurs-de-bois* (renegade trappers) who couldn't be bothered to get licensed by the crown. They delved farther into Wisconsin than any had before but had nowhere to trade their furs after being blacklisted by the ruling powers in New France. This led them to England, which gave them a charter to establish the Hudson's Bay Company north of New France—one reason for the later conflict between France and Britain. In 1666, these two were followed by Nicholas Perrot, who extended Nicolet's explorations and consequently opened the French fur trade with natives in Wisconsin. Perrot was later named Commandant of the West and still later discovered the vast lead fields in southwestern Wisconsin.

In 1661, the first Black Robe, Father René Ménard, arrived to help the displaced Huron in Chequamegon Bay. Lost in the wilderness, he was replaced by the more seasoned Father Claude Allouez, who founded the first mission at La Pointe in the Apostle Islands. After Perrot opened official commerce with the Indians, Allouez founded St. Francois Xavier, Wisconsin's first permanent European settlement, at De Pere, south of Green Bay. Much of the knowledge of Native American cultures at the time comes from the journals of these Jesuit settlers.

The most famous Jesuit explorer was Father Jacques Marquette who, along with Louis Jolliet, was sent by La Salle in 1673 to discern whether the Mississippi emptied into the Gulf of Mexico. The first Europeans to cross Wisconsin, they made it to the Mississippi on June 17, 1673, and went as far south as Arkansas, where they saw Indians with European goods, confirming both a route to the Gulf and the presence of the Spanish. The French hesitated in buttressing their western frontier—and it wound up costing them dearly.

Conflict with the British and British Rule

The fate of New France and, thus, Wisconsin was determined not in the New World but on the European continent, as Louis XIV, who had reigned during a zenith of French power, frittered away French influence bit by bit in frivolous, distracting battles.

The French never fully utilized the western edges of the Great Lakes. With few royal overseers and inept central planning, the exploration was left to a hodgepodge of fur traders and Jesuits; it proved arbitrary and minimal. James II's rise to the throne in England marked the end of France's never-exactly-halcyon days in the Great Lakes. James forced Louis into wild strategies to protect French interests in the New World—strategies that did lead to further exploration of the hinterlands but also drove France to overextend itself and, eventually, collapse as a power in the region.

At the behest of the Jesuits, who hoped to corral the recalcitrant Indian tribes (who hadn't yet displayed either loyalty to the crown or subservience to God), Louis closed trade completely in the Great Lakes interiors, thus cutting off possible ties between the Indians and the English or the Spanish. Louis correctly reckoned that whoever the Indians sided with would end up controlling the new lands. After realizing this plan was overly rash—and likely was draining royal coffers—he changed tactics and decided instead to keep the Indians, the English, and the Spanish in check by exploring as far inland as possible and trying to establishing a line of garrisons from Montreal all the way to New Orleans.

Louis succeeded in this second plan but in the process alienated the uneasy Indians who *had* sworn loyalty to France and, worse, aroused the ire of France's bitterest enemies—the Iroquois and the Fox Indians. Wars with the Fox, which raged from 1701 to 1738, sapped the determination of the French temporarily, but they had enough pluck and military might—to string forts along the Mississippi to look for inroads into territories already held by the British in the Ohio River Valley. By 1750, British colonists in the western Great Lakes outnumbered French twenty-to-one, and many Indians, discovering that the English made higher-quality goods more cheaply, switched to the British side.

Franco-Anglo hostilities ignited for real in 1689, when William of Orange came to power, and the two nations fought four wars over a span of 75 years. These wars had little practical effect on the Great Lakes region, but the last one—the French and Indian War (1755-63)—was a thorough thrashing of the French by the British and greatly determined European spheres of influence in North America. The first Treaty of Paris, signed in 1763 as a result of the war, dictated France's ouster from Canada and the Northwest Territory except for minute fisheries on Newfoundland. Spain got New Orleans and Louisiana west of the Mississippi, and Britain got the rest.

Under the British, little changed in daily life. The American colonists were only marginally interested in relocating so far west, and even the military exerted only nominal control. The English never even had an official presence in present-day Wisconsin. One Englishman of note, however, was Johnathan Carver, a roguish explorer who roamed the state from 1766 to 1768 and returned to England to publish fanciful, lively, and mostly untrue accounts of the new lands west of the inland seas.

The British crown's ruling philosophy was, for the most part, hands off, except in crucial areas of diplomacy. The French had been content simply to trade and had never made overtures for the land itself. But the British who did come—many barely able to conceal their scorn for the less-than-noble savages—began parceling up property and immediately incited unrest. Pontiac, an Ottawa chieftain, led a revolt against the British at Muscoda.

Additionally, the British monarchy's finances were in disarray from the lengthy conflicts with the French in North America and with other enemies in European theaters. The American colonists had paid very little for the military protection they enjoyed, but the monarchy now decreed that the colonies could foot their own bill for the new lands and instituted the Stamp Act.

THE AMERICAN REVOLUTION

British settlers in Wisconsin who remained after the area was made part of British Quebec Province under the Quebec Act of 1774 stood resolutely loyal to the British crown but never got a real chance to test their mettle. Settlers in Wisconsin remained out of the American Revolution other than scattered attempts by both sides to enlist the Indians.

The 1781 surrender of Cornwallis at Yorktown sealed the fate of the British in the New World. John Adams, Benjamin Franklin, and the other colonial peace negotiators at the second Treaty of Paris, in 1783, never dreamed the British would be so generous in the scope of lands surrendered. Though they ceded a great portion of their holdings, including the Northwest Territory, which included Wisconsin, practical British influence remained in the state until after the War of 1812.

British commercial interests had little desire to abandon the still-lucrative beaver trade, and the Indians had grown if not loyal to, then at least tolerant of, the British. When hostilities broke out in 1812, the British, aiming to create a buffer zone of Indian alliances in Indiana and Illinois, quickly befriended the Indians—an easy venture, as the natives were already inflamed over the first of many U.S. government snake-oil land treaties.

The Northwest, including Wisconsin, played a much larger role in this new bellicosity than it had in the Revolution; British loyalists and American frontiersman fought for control of the natives as well as of the water-route forts of the French and British. British forts, now occupied (and undermanned) by U.S. troops, were easily overwhelmed by English and Indian confederates. However, Commodore Perry's victory on Lake Erie in 1813 swung the momentum to the American side. Treaties signed upon reaching a stalemate in 1814 allowed the U.S. to regain preexisting national boundaries and, once and for all, sweep the British from the Great Lakes and

the Mississippi River. Almost immediately, John Jacob Astor's American Fur Company set up operations in Wisconsin, but by this time the golden age of beaver trade in the area was over.

Though not yet even a territory and despite both the intractability of the Indians and the large populations of British and French, Wisconsin was fully part of the United States by 1815. In 1822, the first wave of immigration began, with thousands of Cornish and other miners burrowing into the hillsides of southwestern Wisconsin to search for lead (the origin of the Badger State moniker). As miners poured into Wisconsin to scavenge lead, speculators multiplied, land offices sprang up, and the first banks opened; everyone was eager to make money off the new immigrants. Before the area achieved territorial status, in 1836, more than 10,000 settlers had inundated the southern portion of the state.

NATIVE AMERICAN RELATIONS

Unfortunately, none of the foreign settlers consulted the indigenous residents before carving up the land. The United States practiced a heavy-handed patriarchal policy toward the Native Americans, insisting that they be relocated west—away from white settlers on the eastern seaboard—for the betterment of both sides. Simultaneously, the new government instituted a loony system designed to reprogram the natives to become happy Christian farmers. American leaders assumed that weaning Native Americans from nomadic hunting tracts would minimize conflict with settlers. Land cessions, begun around the turn of the century, continued regularly until the first general concourse of most western Indian tribes took place, in 1825, at Prairie du Chien, Wisconsin, at which time the first of the more draconian treaties was drawn up. The first New York Indians—the Oneida, Stockbridge, Munsee, and Brothertown—were moved to Wisconsin beginning in 1823. The cocktail of misguided U.S. patronization and helplessly naive native negotiations turned lethal when many tribes came to realize what had been done to them. The U.S. began enforcing treaty eviction small print bit by bit, and the forlorn Native Americans, deserted earlier by both the French and the British, were encroached on more and more by a hostile new White Father. Inevitable retaliation followed.

The first skirmish, the so-called Winnebago War of 1827, was nothing more than a frustrated attempt at vengeance by a Winnebago chieftain, Red Bird, who killed two settlers before being convinced to surrender to avert war. The second was more serious—and more legendary.

The Black Hawk War

In 1804, William Henry Harrison, a ruthless long-time foe of Indians in the West, rammed through a treaty with Native Americans in St. Louis that effectively extinguished the tribes' title to most of their land. Part of this land was located in southwestern Wisconsin, newly dubbed the "lead region."

Mining operations—wildcatters, mostly—proliferated but ebbed when the miners began to fear the natives more and more. The ire and paranoia of the federal government, which had assumed carte blanche in the region, was piqued in 1832, when a militant band of Fox-Sauk Indians refused to recognize treaties, including the one that had forcibly moved them out of the southern portion of Wisconsin.

Their leader was Black Sparrow Hawk, better known as Black Hawk, a warrior not so much pro-British as fiercely anti-American. Black Hawk had allied with the English during the War of 1812 and defeated U.S. forces in several battles. He was angry at an Indian nemesis—Keokuk, who had befriended U.S. agents—and for being excluded from land negotiations. With blind faith in the British, obdurate pride, and urging from other Indian tribes (who would later double-cross him), Black Hawk initiated a quixotic stand against the United States, which culminated in tragic battles staged in Wisconsin.

Black Hawk and his group of some 1,000 recalcitrant natives, dubbed "the British Band," balked at U.S. demands that the tribe relocate across the Mississippi in accordance with an 1829 treaty. Insisting that they were exempt because Black Hawk had been blacklisted from the treaty negotiations and hadn't signed anything, in April 1832 the band began moving up the Rock River to what they deemed their rightful lands. Other tribes had promised support along the way, in both provisions and firepower. Instead, Black Hawk found his erstwhile exhorters—the Potawatomi, Sioux and Winnebago—turning on him. Worse, news of Black Hawk's actions was sweeping the region

Chief
Black Hawk

with grotesque frontier embellishment, and the U.S. military, private militias, and frontiersmen under their control were all itching for a fight. The U.S. quickly mustered several bands of overzealous—nay, bloodthirsty—militia brigades and banded them under Gen. Henry Atkinson, an old hand at fighting natives.

His people lacking provisions (one reason for the band's initial decampment was a lack of corn in the area after the settlers squeezed in) and soon tiring, Black Hawk wisely realized his folly and in May sent a truce contingent to Atkinson. Jumpy soldiers under Maj. Isaiah Stillman instead overreacted and attacked. Black Hawk naturally counterattacked and, although seriously outnumbered, his warriors chased the whites away—an event that became known as Stillman's Run. Nevertheless, the fuse was lit.

The band then crossed into Wisconsin near Lake Koshkonong and began a slow, difficult journey west, back toward the Mississippi River. Two commanders, under Atkinson but bearing no official directive, led their forces in pursuit of the hapless Indians, engaging in a war of attrition along the way. They cornered Black Hawk and fought the quick but furious Battle of Wisconsin Heights along the Wisconsin River. The tribe escaped in the darkness, with the soldiers pursuing hungrily. One large group of mostly women, children, and old men tried to float down the Wisconsin toward the Mississippi but were intercepted by soldiers and Indians; most were drowned or killed.

What followed is perhaps the most tragic chapter in Wisconsin history, the Battle of Bad Axe, an episode that garnered shocked national attention and made Black Hawk as well known as the President. On August 1, 1832, Black Hawk made it to the Mississippi River. Hastily throwing together rafts, the band tried to cross but was intercepted by a U.S. gunboat. The U.S. forces opened fire mercilessly for two hours, despite a white flag from the Indians. Black Hawk and a group of 50 escaped, assuming the other group—300 women, children and elderly—would be left alone. Instead, this group was butchered by Atkinson's men and their Sioux cohorts when they reached the opposite shore.

Black Hawk and the 50 warriors were pursued by legions of soldiers and Indian accomplices. Black Hawk was eventually brought in alive to St. Louis (guarded by Jefferson Davis) and later imprisoned on the East Coast, where he found himself in the media spotlight. He later wrote a compelling autobiography, one of the first documents offering a glimpse of the baffled, frustrated Native American point of view. Black Hawk was eventually sent back to Wisconsin.

In truth, Black Hawk was likely never half as belligerent as he's been characterized. By the 1830s he was well into his 60s and weary of protracted and unbalanced negotiations and battles with the whites. The Black Hawk War marked a watershed of native presence in Wisconsin: by 1833, the few cessions the U.S. had gained to Native lands below the Fox-Wisconsin Rivers had been extracted. However, in 1837 the northern Wisconsin tribes signed away for a pittance more than half of the land area north of the Fox River, giving free reign to the rapacious lumbermen. Perhaps due directly to Black Hawk's sad grasp for legitimacy, the U.S. government began playing hardball with the Native Americans.

THE WISCONSIN TERRITORY

The Northwest Ordinance of 1787 established many of the borders of present-day Wisconsin; Thomas Jefferson had initially envisioned dividing the region into 10 states. Later, prior to the War of 1812, Wisconsin became part of first the Indiana Territory and then the Illinois as the Northwest was chiseled down. In 1818, the Illinois Territory was further hacked to create the Michigan Territory. Finally, in 1836, the Wisconsin Territory was established, taking in all of modern Wisconsin, the Upper Peninsula of Michigan, Iowa, Minnesota, and parts of North and South Dakota.

Despite the loss, the Black Hawk fiasco had another effect contrary to the Sauk leader's intentions: the well-publicized battles put Wisconsin on the map. This, combined with the wild mining operations in the southwestern part of the state, burgeoning lumber operations along the Great Lake coast, and discovery of the fecund soils outside of Milwaukee, ensured Wisconsin's status as the Next Big Thing. The new Erie Canal provided immigrants a direct route to this new land. By 1835, 60,000 eager settlers were pushing through the Erie Canal each year, and most were aiming for what the following year became the Wisconsin Territory. Two years later, in 1838, when the chunk of Wisconsin Territory west of the Mississippi was lopped off, over half of the 225,000 settlers were in Wisconsin proper. With the enforcement of Indian land cessions following Black Hawk's defeat, up to three *billion* acres became available for government surveyors; the first land title sales started in 1834. Wisconsin had fully arrived—and it still wasn't even a state.

STATEHOOD: GROWING PAINS

Wisconsin's entrance into the Union as the flag's 30th star was a bit anticlimactic; there wasn't even a skirmish with Canada over it. In fact, the populace voted on the issue of statehood in 1841, and every year for nearly the entire decade, but distinctly disinterested voters rejected the idea until 1848, when stratospheric levels of immigration impelled the legislature to more animated attempts, and the first measures passed.

Incessant immigration continued after statehood. Most newcomers arrived from New England or Europe—Ireland, England, Germany, and Scandinavia. The influx of Poles was still decades away. Milwaukee, a diminutive village of 1,500 at the time of territorial status, burgeoned into a rollicking town of 46,000 by the start of the Civil War, by which time the population of the state as a whole was up to 706,000 people

During the period leading up to the Civil War, Wisconsin was dominated by political (and some social) wrangling over what, exactly, the state was to be. With the influence of Yankee emigrants and the Erie Canal access, much of Wisconsin's cultural, political, and social makeup finally resembled New England. In fact, New York legislation was the model for many early Wisconsin laws. The first university was incorporated almost immediately after statehood, and school codes for primary and secondary education soon followed—a bit ahead of the Union as a whole.

Abolition was a hot issue in Wisconsin's early years. It reached top-level status following the annexation of Texas and the Mexican-American War; as a result of this and many other contentious issues, Ripon, Wisconsin, became the founding spot of the Republican Party, which soon took hold of the legislature and held fast until the Civil War.

During the Civil War, despite being among the first states to near enlistment quotas, Wisconsin suffered some of the fiercest draft rioting in the nation. Many new immigrants had decamped from their European homelands for precisely the reasons for which the government was now pursuing them. Eventually, 96,000 Wisconsinites would serve.

Post-Civil War: Immigrants, Dairy, and Industry

Following the Civil War and through the turn of the century, Wisconsin began getting its economic bearings while politicians wrestled over issues as disparate as temperance, railroads, and immigrants' rights. The latter hot potato galvanized enormous enclaves of German-Americans into action; they mobilized against anti-immigration laws sweeping through the legislature. Despite the mandates (banning the German language in schools, for one), successive waves of immigrants poured into the state.

The first sawmills had gone up in Wisconsin at the turn of the 19th century. Yankee and British settlers put them up to use the timber they were felling in clearing farmland. Commercial timber exploitation hadn't begun in earnest until the 1830s, initially along the Lake Michigan coast and Fox/Wisconsin Riverway, then creeping northward as the perimeter of forest was hacked

away. By 1870, over one billion board feet of lumber was being churned out through the state's 1,000-plus mills each year, easily making Wisconsin the country's largest timber producer. In time, over 20 billion board feet were taken from the shores of Green Bay alone; one year, 425 million board feet were shipped through Superior. Wisconsin wood was used in other parts of the expanding country to make homes, wagons, fences, barns, and plank roads. As a result, by the turn of the 20th century, over 50 million acres of Wisconsin (and Minnesota) forest had been ravaged—most of it unrecoverable. By 1920, most of the state was a cut-over wasteland and the timber industry declined to more rational levels, although papermaking continued in overdrive, as it still does today.

A handful of years after the Civil War, the state kicked its wheat habit (by 1860, Wisconsin was producing more wheat than any other state in the U.S.) and began looking for economic diversity. Wheat was sapping the soil fertility in southern Wisconsin, forcing many early settlers to pick up stakes once again and shift to the enormous golden tracts of the western plains states. Later, when railroads and their seemingly arbitrary pricing systems began affecting potential income from wheat, farmers in Wisconsin began seriously reviewing their options. Farmers diversified into corn, cranberries, sorghum, and hops, among others. Sheep and some hogs constituted the spectrum of livestock, but within two decades, the milk cow would surpass everything else on four hooves.

Myriad factors influenced the early trend toward dairy. Most of the European immigrant farmers, many of them dairy farmers in the old country, found the topography and climate in Wisconsin similar to those of their homelands. Transplanted Yankees had seen it before in New York and Vermont and knew a dairy revolution was coming. Led by foresighted dairying advocate William Hoard and his germinal journal, *Hoard's Dairyman,* and by the new Wisconsin Dairymen's Association, farmers began adding dairy cattle to their other crops and livestock until, by 1899, 90% of Wisconsin's farmers were keeping cows predominantly.

Butter production initially led the new industry, since it was easier to keep than milk. But technology and industrialization, thanks in large part to the University of Wisconsin Scientific Agriculture Institute, propelled Wisconsin into milk, cheese, and other dairy-product prominence. The institute was responsible for extending the dairy season, introducing several highly productive new methods, and the groundbreaking 1890 Babcock butterfat test, a simple test of chemically separating and centrifuging milk samples to determine its quality, thereby ensuring farmers were paid based on the quality and not just the weight of the milk.

By 1880, despite less-fecund land and a shorter growing season than other agricultural states, Wisconsin ranked fourth in dairy production, thanks to university efficiency, progressive quality control, Herculean effort in the fields, and the later organization of powerful trade exchanges. The southern half of the state, with its minerals in the southwest and rich loamy soils in the southeast, attracted European agrarian and dairy farming immigrants and speculators. "America's Dairyland" made it onto state license plates in the 1930s.

Wisconsin's grand network of northern and central forests and connected waterways, which had supplied humans the means of existence for 10 millennia, were not overshadowed by the southern dairy boom. Ever since the mid-1830s, immigrant tie-hacks had moved north along the Lake Michigan coast in search of lumber. The timber industry surpassed dairy until well into the 20th century.

Boom-bust logging ravaged Wisconsin's virgin tracts. One area of the Chippewa River possessed one-sixth of all the pine west of the Adirondacks—and Wisconsin pine was larger and harder than that in surrounding states. Easily floated down streams and rivers, pine became an enormous commodity on the expanding plains. In Wisconsin, even the roads were fashioned from pine and hardwood planks. Though declining in sheer volume after a zenith in the 1870s, lumber led all manufacturing 1890-1910; in 1893, the timber industry provided one-fourth of all wages in the state.

The inevitable downside was the effects of raping the environment. Land eroded, tracts of forest disappeared and weren't replaced, and riparian areas were destroyed in order to dam for "float flooding." Worst, the average pine tree size was shrinking rapidly, and the lumber barons expressed little interest in preparing for the ultimate eradication of the forests. The small settlement of Peshtigo and over 1,000 of its people perished in a furious conflagration made worse by logging cut-over in 1871, and in the 1890s vast fires swept other central and northern counties.

THE PROGRESSIVE ERA

Wisconsinites have a rather fickle political history. Democrats held sway in the territorial days; then, in 1854, the newly formed Republican Party took the reins. The two monoliths—challenged only occasionally by upstarts such as the Grangers, the Socialists (Milwaukee consistently voted for Socialist representatives), Populists, and the Temperance movement—jockeyed for power until the end of the century.

The Progressive Party movement, formed of equal parts reformed Democrats and Republicans, was the original third-party ticket, molted from the frustrated moderates of the Wisconsin Republican Party keen on challenging the status quo. As progressivism gained steam and was led on by native sons, the citizenry of Wisconsin—tireless and shrewd salt-of-the-earth workers—eventually embraced the movement with open arms, even if the rest of the country didn't always. The Progressive movement was the first serious challenge to the United States' political machine.

Fightin' Bob: Legacy of Progressivism

If there is one piece to the Wisconsin political mosaic that warrants kudos, it's the inveterate inability to follow categorization. Whether politically prescient or simply lacking patience, the state has always ridden the cutting edge. These qualities are best represented physically by the original Progressive: Robert La Follette, a.k.a. "Menace to the Machine." One political writer at the turn of the century said of La Follette: "The story of Wisconsin is the story of Gov. La Follette. He's the head of the state. Not many Governors are that." The seminal force in Wisconsin, La Follette eschewed the pork-barrel status quo to form the Progressive Party. In Wisconsin, the La Follette family dominated the state scene for two generations, fighting for social rights most people had never heard of.

Robert M. La Follette was born on a Dane County farm in 1855, where the typically hard-scrabble life prepared him for the rigors of the University of Wisconsin, which he entered in 1875. He discovered a passion and talent for oratory but, too short for theater, gravitated to politics—a subject befitting the ambitious young man. He was elected Dane County district attorney in 1880. Well-liked by the hoi polloi, he gave them resonance with his hand-pumping and his off-the-cuff speeches on hard work and personal responsibility in government. An entrenched Republican, he was more or less ignored by the party brass, so in 1884 he brashly ran for U.S. Congress on his own—and won. He was the youngest state representative in U.S. history.

Initially, La Follette toed the party line fairly well, though he did use his position to crow elegantly against the well-oiled political infrastructure. After the Republicans were voted out en masse in 1890, La Follette returned to Wisconsin and formed the Progressive Party. He ran for governor and, after two tries, landed the nomination. A tireless circuit and chautauqua lecturer, he relied on a salt-of-the-earth theme and left audiences mesmerized. This marked the birth of the "Fightin' Bob" image, which persists to this day. He was elected governor three times, returned to the Senate for a tempestuous career, and made serious runs at the presidency.

La Follette's critics found him as self-righteous and passionately tactless as he was brilliant, forthcoming, gregarious, and every other superlative by which he remains known today. This driven man of the people was no more enigmatically contradictory than many other public figures, but historians have noted that even his most vehement opponents respected his ethics. Under him, Wisconsin instituted the nation's first direct primary and watershed civil-service systems, passed anti-corruption legislation and railroad monopoly reforms, and, most importantly, formed the Wisconsin Idea.

Progressivism and the Wisconsin Idea

Progressivism represented a careful balance of honest-to-goodness idealism and what may today be termed Libertarian tenets. La Follette saw it as an attempt to overcome, on a grassroots level, the dehumanizing aspect of corporate greed and political corruption. *The Progressive,* the Madison-based periodical he founded, remains the country's leading medium for social justice.

THE OTHER LA FOLLETTE

While Robert La Follette, Sr., dominated Wisconsin politics for most of three decades and left a political footprint still discernible today, he by no means did it alone. He and his wife, Belle, were an inseparable team, both passionate crusaders for social justice—and both well ahead of their time.

Belle La Follette was behind Bob in every way and in many cases, it could be said, *was* Bob. She was born into a New England family; her grandmother inculcated in her a fierce determination to obtain the education she herself had been denied. Belle's parents sent her to the University of Wisconsin, where she excelled. It was there that this very independent woman caught the eye of her soulmate, Bob La Follette. The two rewrote many of society's constricting traditions. They were the first couple in Wisconsin to delete "obey" from their marriage vows. Belle later became the first woman to graduate from the University of Wisconsin law school—this after having their first child.

Her post-collegiate life was an amazing blend of supporting Bob and maintaining her own crusading career as a journalist, editor, and suffrage leader. She marched in the state's first major suffrage parade and became a leading researcher and writer on practices of segregation, welfare, and other social issues. In addition to all that, she lectured, acted as her husband's attorney, and raised the La Follette brood.

Her education and activities were deliberately designed for both herself and Bob. She knew he would need an enlightened insider, so she chose to study law. She immersed herself in the issues and became his most trusted advisor; he rarely made a move without her. When Bob La Follette died, she refused public life; instead, she devoted herself to the *Progressive* magazine, which Bob had founded. Her own activism may be best remembered in her moving, eloquent 1913 speech to a transfixed U.S. Senate Committee on Woman's Suffrage, during which she quoted Abraham Lincoln in asking, "Are women not people?"

Fightin' Bob's most radical creation was the Wisconsin Idea. Officially a system whereby the state used careful research and empirical evidence in governing, in reality it meant that La Follette kept a close-knit core of advisors as de facto aides. His was the first government—state or federal—to maintain expert panels and commissions, a controversial plan around the turn of the century. Some criticized it as elitist, but he argued that it was necessary to combat well-funded industry cronyism.

EARLY 20TH CENTURY

Robert La Follette's most (in)famous personal crusade was his strident opposition to U.S. participation in World War I. It was engendered in no small part in Wisconsin's heavy German population, but also in La Follette's vehement pacifism. He suffered tremendous regional and national scorn and was booted to the lower echelons of politics. Interestingly, when the United States officially entered the war, Wisconsin was the first state to meet enlistment requirements. Eventually, La Follette enjoyed something of a vindication with a triumphant return to the Senate in 1924, followed by a final real presidential run.

Also a political activist, Bob's wife, Belle La Follette, mounted a longstanding crusade for women's suffrage that helped the 19th Amendment get ratified; Wisconsin was the first state to ratify it. In other political trends starting around the turn of the century, Milwaukee began electing Socialist administrations. Buoyed by nascent labor organizations in the huge factory towns along Lake Michigan, the movement was infused with an immigrant European populace not averse to social radicalism. Milwaukee was the country's most heavily unionized city, and it voted Socialist—at least in part—right through the 1960s. The Progressive banner was picked up by La Follette's sons, Phil and Robert, Jr., and the Wisconsin Progressive Party was formed in 1934. Robert, Jr. took over for his father in the U.S. Senate, and Phil dominated Wisconsin politics during the '30s. Despite these efforts, the movement waned. Anemic and ineffective from internal splits and WW II, it melded with the Republican Party in 1946.

Dairying became Wisconsin's economic leader by 1920 and gained national prominence as well. The industry brought in nearly $210 million to the state, wholly eclipsing timber and lumber. This turned out to be a savior for the state's fortunes during the Depression; dairy products were less threatened by economic collapse than either forest appropriation or manufacturing, though farmers' management and methodology costs skyrocketed. Papermaking, in which Wisconsin is still a world leader, ameliorated the blow in the jobless cut-over north- and east-central parts of the state. Concentrated fully in southeastern Wisconsin, heavy industry—leather, meat packing, foundries, fabrication, and machine shops—suffered more acutely during the Depression. Sales receipts plummeted by two-thirds and the number of jobs fell by nearly half in five years. Brewing was as yet nonexistent, save for root beer and some backroom swill.

POST-WW II TO THE PRESENT

Wisconsin's heavy manufacturing cities drew waves of economic migrants to its factories after WW II, and agribusiness rose in income despite a steady reduction in the number of farms. The state's economic fortunes were generally positive right through the mid-1980s, when the state endured its greatest recession since the catastrophic days of the Depression. Wisconsin companies lost control to or were bought out by competitors in other states. In the early '90s, agribusiness, still one of the top three Wisconsin industries, became

schooner at Kewaunee Harbor circa late 1800s

vulnerable for the first time when California challenged the state in production of whole milk.

The one industry that blossomed like no other after the war was tourism. Forethinking Wisconsin politicians enacted the first sweeping environmental legislation, and north woods resort owners instituted effective public relations campaigns. By the late 1950s, Wisconsin had become a full-fledged, four-season vacation destination, and by the early 1990s tourism had become a $6 billion industry in Wisconsin, which established a cabinet-level Department of Tourism and opened regional travel centers in other states.

Politically, Wisconsin went through periods of readjustment following World War II. The GOP briefly took control, but then Wisconsin put its foot squarely with the Democrats, where it's been pretty much since 1960. Wisconsin has always been a hot spot for Democratic candidates, even during periods of Republican landslide.

GOVERNMENT

Wisconsin entered the Union as the 30th state by Congressional vote in 1846, following two contentious Constitutional Conventions. The final signing, by President James K. Polk, came on May 29, 1848.

Wisconsin has a bicameral legislative system, with a 99-member Assembly elected every two years and a 33-member Senate elected every four years. Both share lawmaking duties with a governor, who is elected every four years. The governor wields veto power and also has a line-item veto. Wisconsin has been fighting proposals to shift districts at the national level, which would reduce the state's representation in the House of Representatives by one member.

Wisconsin has always relished its penchant for progressive, and occasionally even radical, politics. In 1854, Wisconsin made a grand entrance into the national spotlight when dissenters within the Whig Party formed the Republican Party. Wisconsin's real political zenith came with the birth of the Progressive movement, led by Fightin' Bob La Follette. Still, the Republicans retained power whenever the Progressives couldn't cobble together enough votes to sweep them out. By the late 1950s, Wisconsin was showing its Democratic colors. The Democrats constituted the majority in both houses of the state legislature through 1993. Democratic governors have outnumbered Republicans historically, though in recent years a GOP member has been residing in the governor's mansion. Conservative Republican Gov. Tommy Thompson was first elected in 1986 and has been exceedingly popular, serving for four terms, despite Wisconsin's liberal history. The success of his radical welfare reform program had him mentioned as a potential vice presidential nominee in 1996 and 2000. Thompson does not plan to seek re-election in 2002.

ECONOMY

Wisconsin may be "America's Dairyland" but it isn't *only* America's Dairyland. The economic triumvirate of the state is agriculture, manufacturing, and tourism. Wisconsin is an international exporter, tallying $6 billion in receipts in 15 to 20 foreign markets. Leading exports include computers, industrial machinery, and transportation equipment (crops come fifth).

Since 1990, the state has had one of the country's fastest-growing per capita income levels, topping $18,000. Since the mid-'80s, it's been one the top ten nationally for fastest-growing economies. This is tempered somewhat by the state's high income tax. As of the late-'90s and into the 21st century, Wisconsin has paralleled national economic trends by maintaining a strong growth rate (around 3 percent per annum). It has also defied logic by maintaining an unemployment rate of near *zero* in some communities, though multinational mergers and reorganization of paper companies in the Fox and Wisconsin River Valleys are causing layoffs in the hundreds now, perhaps thousands in the next decade.

THE BUTTER BATTLE

You doubt Wisconsin's a dairy state? Consider the Butter Battle, or Oleo Wars. Oleomargarine was developed in 1895. It would take until 1967—that's right—that selling or purchasing the creamy concoction wasn't a *crime.*

Farmers initially feared that the golden-colored spread would ruin them and demanded the ban; later they would march and protest for a ban on anything resembling butter or anything used like butter. Of course, margarine smuggling started up (kinda lacks the romanticism of moonshine running, doesn't it?) and those consumers watching their diets would cross the Illinois line to the "margarine villages" that sprouted up alongside border service stations. Butter's most partisan supporter was Gordon Roseleip, a Republican Senator from Darlington, whose rantings against oleo could occasionally overshadow Joseph McCarthy's anti-Communist spewings. But the good senator doomed the butter industry in 1965 when he agreed to take a blind taste test between butter and oleo. And lost. His family later admitted that he had been unknowingly consuming oleo for years; he weighed 275 pounds and his family had switched, hoping to control his weight.

Manufacturing accounts for up to 30% of Wisconsin's income—$37.1 billion. Wisconsin leads the nation in the fabrication of small engines, metals, paper products, printing, food processing, mineral extraction equipment, electrical machinery, and transportation equipment. The paper product industry is particularly strong, number one in the nation since 1953. Its 35 facilities account for 4.7 million tons of paper, or more than 12% of the national total, to the tune of $12.4 billion. One of every 11 jobs in the state is tied to paper.

The new kid on the block, economically speaking, is tourism, which really got its start after World War II. The state now rakes in more than $6 billion annually.

Agriculture is still the linchpin. Forty-one percent of the state remains devoted to agricultural products. It's another more-than-$6 billion industry, with 60 percent of that from dairying. Wisconsin ranks number one in the U.S. for production of milk, cheese, condensed milk, corn and silage, sweet corn, and snap beans; it ranks second or third in butter, oats, maple syrup, cranberries, carrots, beets, green peas, cucumbers, and cabbage.

THE PEOPLE

Wisconsin in 1999 reached the six million mark; it averaged 6.7% growth in the 1990s. With 90.1 people per square mile, the state ranks 24th nationally in population density. (It rarely feels that crowded.) General population growth in the state is 3.9 percent annually, unusual because the Upper Great Lakes as a whole shows steadily declining numbers, though this decline is slowing. Wisconsin traces most of its ethnicity (single or multiple ancestries) to Europe, specifically Germany. At the turn of the 20th century, it was the most ethnically diverse state in the Union.

Distribution

Though born of its northeastern waterways, Wisconsinites established themselves in the south among the ports and factories of Lake Michigan. Likewise, the Fox River Valley region—from Oshkosh north to Green Bay along Lake Winnebago—is now heavily populated after

decades as a center of paper and pulp production. The remainder of the state is a bit sparser. A handful of cities with populations of around 20,000 line major riverways and the Great Lakes, but beyond that it's wide-open spaces peppered with one-horse towns. Flight from the big cities continues: Milwaukee County lost three percent of its population in a half-decade, while every other county in the state experienced an influx. Madison grew 11% 1990-97. Northwestern and northeastern counties, former population wastelands, are exploding at 10% annual growth.

Native Americans

Wisconsin has one of the most diverse Native American populations of any state, taking into account the number of cultures, settlement history, linguistic stock, and affiliations. The state is home to six sovereign Native American nations on 11 reservations, not all of which are demarcated

WISCONSIN LINGUISTIC PRIMER

A 19th-century American travel writer once aptly noted, "There is no limit to the eccentricity of American nomenclature." As with any state, great fun—and occasional consternation—can be had with the anti-English rhythms of Wisconsin place names. The source of the majority of Wisconsin's names is illiterate (and occasionally innumerate) trappers and traders struggling to filter non-Indo European words and speech through Romance and Germanic language sensibilities. Toponymy generally falls into several categories—bastardized Native American lexical items (the peskiest to suss out), practical monikers pertaining to local landforms or natural wonders, and memorials to European-American "founding" fathers.

Even "Wisconsin" is etymologically slippery; a historical linguist has called Wisconsin's name the most cryptic of all 27 states with Native American names. As early as 1673, Father Marquette named the river from which some say the state's name derived Meskousing ("red stones"), perhaps because of a red tinge of the banks. "Ouisconsin" appeared on a Jesuit map in 1688. But most widely accepted is the Ojibwa word for the state, "Wees-kon-san"— "gathering place of waters."

Wisconsinisms

Perhaps the most famous example of a Wisconsinism is "bubbler," for drinking fountain, as in the cheesehead who travels to another state and asks, "Excuse me, I'm thirsty. Where's the bubbler?" The Dictionary of American Regional English (out of UW-Madison) says that the other truly Wisconsin word is "golden birthday," the birthday year that matches the date of the month (for example, if you were born on January 13th, your 13th birthday is your golden birthday).

More cultural linguistic gems like "fish fry," "supper club," and "brat[wurst]," and others are defined in the Introduction. One important one to know is "yooper," for a denizen of Michigan's Upper Peninsula.

Milwaukee colloquialisms—though some vociferously deny it—include "bumbershoot," for umbrella, and "ainah hey?" for "isn't that so?" You'll also hear "down by"—everything is "down by" something. Or, even "Grease yourself a piece of bread and I'll put you on a hamburger"—a Milwaukeeism if ever there was one. Wisconsinites also seem somewhat averse to liquid sounds; it's "M'waukee" as often as not.

Howzat Again?

The phonology of Wisconsin English contains only one dramatic sound: the "ah," seriously emphasized and strongly run though the nasal cavity, as in Wis-KHAN-sin. (And please, never, ever, is it WES-khan-sin.)

Algoma—al-GO-muh
Chequamegon National Forest—shuh-WAHM-uh-gun
Fond du Lac—FAHN-duh-lack
Green Bay—green-BAY, not GREEN-bay
Kenosha—kuh-NO-shuh
Lac Court Oreilles—la COO-der-ray
Manitowoc—MAN-ih/uh-tuh-wock
Menominee/Menomonie—muh-NAH-muh-nee
Minocqua—min-AHK-wah
Muscoda—MUSS-kuh-day
New Berlin/Berlin—new BER-lin
Nicolet National Forest—nick-oh-LAY (but don't be too surprised to hear "Nickle-Ett")
Oconomowoc—good luck!
Oshkosh—AHSH-kahsh
Prairie du Chien—prairie du SHEEN
Racine—ruh-SEEN
Ripon—RIP-pin
Shawano—SHAW-no (though SHAH-no is possible)
Sheboygan-shuh-BOY-gun
Trempealeau-TREM-puh-low
Waupun-wau-PAHN

by boundaries. In addition to the six nations, Wisconsin historically has been the home of the Illinois, Fox, Sauk, Miami, Kickapoo, Satee, Ottaway, and Mascouten Indians. The total Native American population is around 40,000. Native Americans lived in relative harmony with European explorers and trappers and early settlers until federal expansionist efforts began in earnest. Intertribal warfare also intensified, simultaneous with European contact. Full-scale military conflict and the Black Hawk War of 1832 wore down Native American resistance. Major land cessions followed. In the 1836 Treaty of Cedars, the Menominee gave up four million acres for $700,000. By 1842, all Native American lands were in U.S. control.

The largest native group is the **Ojibwa**. (Formerly rendered by the white man as "Chippewa," the Euro-transliteration of what trappers thought they heard, it has returned to the more appropriate approximations of Ojibway, Ojibwe, and Ojibwa. Ethnologists, historians, linguists, and even tribal members disagree on the spelling. *Ojib* means "to pucker up" and *ubway* "to roast," and the words together denote the tribe's unique moccasin stitching. In any event, all are really Anish'nabe anyway.) Wisconsin has five Ojibwa tribes. The Ojibwa inhabited the northern woodlands of the upper Great Lakes, especially along Lakes Huron and Superior. They were allied with the Ottawa and Potawatomi but branched off in the 16th century and moved to Michigan's Mackinac Island. The Ojibwa said that their migration westward was to fulfill the prophecy to find "food that grows on water"— wild rice. The **Bad River** group today resides on a 123,000-acre reservation along Lake Superior in Ashland County. It's the largest reservation in the state and is famed for its wild rice beds on the Kakogan Sloughs. The **Red Cliff** band, the nucleus of the Ojibwa nation, has been organized along the Bayfield Peninsula's shore since 1854. The **St. Croix** band—"homeless" tribes scattered over four counties with no boundaries—resides in northwest Wisconsin. The **Lac du Flambeau** band is the most visited and recognizable, due to their proximity to Minocqua and state and federal forests and for exercising their tribal spearfishing rights. **Lac Courte Oreilles** is originally of the *Betonukeengainubejib* Ojibwa division. **Sokaogan** (Mole Lake) band of Lake Superior Ojibwa is known as the "Lost Tribe" since their original legal treaty title was lost in an 1854 shipwreck. Originally from Canada, they moved along to Madeline Island before defeating the Sioux near Mole Lake in 1806.

The Algonquian **Menominee** have been in Wisconsin longer than any other tribe. The Menominee once held sway south to Illinois, north into Michigan, and west to the Mississippi River, with a total of some 10 million acres. Known as the "Wild Rice People"—the early French explorers called them "Lords of Trade"—Menominee were divided into sky and earth groups, then subdivided into clans. Though the hegemony of the Menominee lasted up to 10,000 years in Wisconsin, they were almost exterminated by eastern Canadian Indians fleeing Iroquois persecution and by pestilence imported by the Europeans. Today the population has rebounded to around 3,500, and the Menominee reservation constitutes an entire Wisconsin county. The Menominee have been recognized for their forestry conservation methodology.

The Forest County **Potawatomi**, also Algonquian, are the legacy of the tribe that made the most successful move into Wisconsin, beginning in the 1640s. Originally inhabitants of the shores of Lake Huron, the Potawatomi later moved to Michigan, Indiana, and places along the St. Joseph's River. The name means "People of the Fire" or, better, "Keeper of the Fire," after their confederacy with the Ojibwa and Ottawa. The Potawatomi stretched from Chicago to Wisconsin's Door County and was one of the tribes to greet Jean Nicolet when he arrived in 1634. Wisconsin's band of Potawatomi was one of the few to withstand relocation to Oklahoma in 1838.

Wisconsin's only Mohicans, the **Stockbridge-Munsee**, live on a reservation bordering the Menominee. The Stockbridge (also called Mahican—"Wolf") originally occupied the Hudson River and Massachusetts all the way to Lake Champlain. The Munsee are a branch of the Delaware and resided near the headwaters of the Delaware River in New York, New Jersey, and Pennsylvania.

The **Oneida** belonged to the Iroquois Five Nations Confederacy consisting of the Mohawk, Oneida, Onondaga, Cayuga, and Seneca. The Oneida, originally from New York, supported the colonists in the American Revolution but were forced out by Mohawks and land-grabbing settlers along the Erie Canal following the war. Beginning in the 1820s, the Iroquois-speaking Oneida merged with the Mahican, Mohegan, Pequot, Narragansett, Montauk, and other tribes in Wisconsin.

The erstwhile **Winnebago Nation** has reverted to its original name, **Ho Chunk**, or, more appropriately, **Ho Cak** ("Big Voice" or "Mother Voice"), an attempt to restore the rightful cultural and linguistic heritage to the nation. Also known as Otchangara, the group is related to the Chiwere-Siouxan Iowa, Oto, and Missouri Indians, though their precise origin is unknown. Extremely powerful militarily, they were nonetheless relatively peaceful with the Menominee and Potawatomi, with whom they witnessed Jean Nicolet's 1634 arrival. French scourges and encroaching tribes fleeing Iroquois hostilities in New York devastated Ho Chunk numbers; later, forced relocation nearly killed off the rest. The tribe pulled up stakes in Oklahoma and walked back to Wisconsin, following its chief, Yellow Thunder, who bought the tribe a tract of land, deftly circumventing relocation and leaving the federal government no way to force them out of Wisconsin.

European-Americans

At statehood, only 10 nationalities were represented in Wisconsin. The state organized an emigration council in New York City and on Ellis Island to tout Wisconsin's myriad opportunities to arriving immigrants. By 1900, 25 nationalities populated the state; by 1950, over 50 could be counted. The vast majority of these were European, and Wisconsin is still 92.3% Caucasian.

A decidedly **German** state, Wisconsin boasts more residents claiming Teutonic roots (54%) than anywhere else in the country. So thick is the German milieu of Milwaukee (34%) that German chancellors visit the city when they're in the U.S. for presidential summits. The 1990 census showed that Wisconsin has 60,000 native speakers of German—quite remarkable for a century-old ethnic group. Germans came in three waves. The first arrived 1820-35 from both Pennsylvania and southwestern Germany. German farmers were lured by the chance to purchase their own lands—at the time for $1.75 an acre. The second wave, 1840-1860, came mostly from northwest Germany and included the legendary "48ers"—enlightened intellectuals fleeing political persecution. A fairly large number of Catholics and Hussites also came at this time. During this wave, as many as 215,000 Germans moved to

Wisconsin each year; by 1855, fully one-third of Wisconsin's Germans had arrived. The third wave occurred after 1880 and drew immigrants mainly from Germany's northeastern region to southeastern Wisconsin, where they worked in the burgeoning factories. Today, the southeast and south-central regions' toponymy reflects its heavily German heritage.

The state's **French** roots can be traced back to the *voyageurs*, trappers, and Jesuit priests. They started the first settlements, along the Fox and Wisconsin River Valleys. Though Wisconsin shows no strong French presence in anything other than place names, the Two Rivers area still manifests an Acadian influence.

As the **British** and the French haggled and warred over all of the Wisconsin territory, many crown-friendly British Yankees did relocate here, populating virtually every community. The **Irish** began arriving in the late 19th century in numbers second only to the Germans. Irish influence is found in every community, especially Milwaukee's Bay View, Erin in Washington County, Ozaukee County, Adell and Parnell in Sheboygan County, and Manitowoc County.

Pockets of **Welsh** and **Cornish** are found throughout the state, the latter especially in the southwestern lead-mining region of the state. A distinct **Belgian** influence exists in Kewaunee County, where Walloon can still be heard in local taverns.

Poles represent the primary Eastern European ethnic group. The largest contingent is in Milwaukee, where kielbasa is as common a dietary mainstay as bratwurst. Most Poles arrived 1870-1910. At that time, Poland was not recognized as a country, so Ellis Island officials erroneously categorized many of the immigrants as Prussian, Austrian, or Russian. While 90% of Wisconsin's Polish immigrants moved into the cities, some three-tenths of those who arrived farmed, mostly in Portage and Trempealeau Counties; the latter is the oldest Polish settlement in the United States. By 1920, 90,000 Poles inhabited Milwaukee. **Czechs,** another large Eastern European group, live mostly in north and east-central Wisconsin, especially Kewaunee and Manitowoc Counties.

Many **Norwegians** also emigrated to the Upper Midwest, primarily Minnesota and Wisconsin. Most were economic immigrants trying to escape Norway's chronic overpopulation (85% of its people were forced onto three percent of the arable land). Most Norwegians in Wisconsin wound up in Dane and Rock Counties between 1835 and 1850. **Finnish** immigrants to the U.S. totaled 300,000 between 1864 and 1920, and many of these settled in the Upper Peninsula of Michigan and northern Wisconsin. **Swedes** made up the smallest Scandinavian contingent, the original settlement made up of a dozen families near Waukesha.

By the turn of the century, Wisconsin was home to almost 10% of all the **Danes** in the U.S.—the second-largest national contingent. Most originally settled in the northeast (the city of Denmark lies just southeast of Green Bay), but later emigrants wound up farther south. To this day, Racine is nicknamed "Kringleville," for its flaky Danish pastry.

The **Dutch** settled primarily in Milwaukee and Florence Counties beginning in the 1840s, when potato crops failed and protests flared over the Reformed Church. These southeastern counties today sport towns like Oostburg, New Amsterdam, and Holland.

In 1846, a large contingent of **Swiss** from the Glarus canton sent emissaries to the New World to search out a suitable immigration site. Eventually, the two scouts stumbled upon the gorgeous, lush valleys of southwestern Wisconsin. After much travail, hundreds of Swiss forded their way across the country and endured a tough winter to establish themselves here. A great deal of Swiss heritage remains in Green County.

Italians began arriving in the 1830s—many Genoese migrated north from Illinois lead camps to fish and scavenge lead along the Mississippi River—but didn't arrive in substantial numbers until the early 1900s. Most settled in the southeast, specifically Milwaukee, Racine, and especially Kenosha.

Perhaps most unique to Wisconsin is the large population of **Icelandic** immigrants, who settled on far-flung Washington Island, northeast of Door Peninsula. It was the largest single Icelandic settlement in the United States when they arrived in 1870 to work as fishers.

African Americans

Some theories hold African Americans first arrived in Wisconsin in 1835, in the entourage of Solomon Juneau, the founder of Milwaukee. But records from the early part of the 18th century detail black trappers, guides, and explorers. In 1791 and 1792, in fact, black fur traders established an encampment estimated to be near present-day Marinette. Though the Michigan Territory, which would become the Wisconsin Territory, was ostensibly free, slavery was not uncommon. Henry Dodge, Wisconsin's first territorial governor, had slaves but freed them two years after leaving office. Other slave owners were transplanted southerners living in the new lead-mining district of the southwest. Other early African Americans were demi-French-African immigrants, who settled near Prairie du Chien in the early 19th century. Wisconsin's first African-American settlement was Pleasant Spring, outside Lancaster in southwest Wisconsin; the State Historical Society's Old World Wisconsin in Eagle has a brand-new exhibit on it.

After passage of the Fugitive Slave Act, which allowed slave catchers to cross state lines in pursuit, many freed and escaped slaves flocked to the outer fringes of the country. Wisconsin's opposition to the act was strident. One celebrated case involved Joshua Glover, an escaped slave who had been living free and working in Racine for years. He was caught and imprisoned by his erstwhile master but later broken out by mobs from Ripon, Milwaukee, and southeastern Wisconsin. The state Supreme Court ruled the act unconstitutional.

Following the Civil War, the African-American population increased, and most chose to live in rural, agricultural settings. Large-scale African-American migration to Milwaukee, Racine, and Kenosha took place after WW II, as northern factories revved up for the Korean War and, later, the Cold War. Today, the vast majority of Wisconsin's 245,000 African Americans—81%—reside in these urbanized southeastern counties.

Hispanics

Wisconsin's Hispanic population stands at around 100,000 and is growing fast. **Puerto Ricans** began arriving in Milwaukee following WW II as blue-collar laborers. In the 1950s, estimates put the Puerto Rican population at perhaps 500; today, the number is near 20,000. **Mexicans** represent one of the more recent immigration waves, many of them having arrived in the mid-1960s, though Mexican immigrants have been in the state since as far back as 1850. Mexicans today reside mostly in southeastern Wisconsin—Milwaukee, Madison, but especially Racine.

Asians

Wisconsin has upwards of 60,000 residents of Asian descent. One of the fastest-growing elements, **Laotian Hmong,** began arriving during the Vietnam War and settled mostly in Appleton, Green Bay, the Fox River Valley, Manitowoc, Eau Claire, La Crosse, and pockets in southeastern Wisconsin. The state also has substantial **Chinese** and **Korean** populations.

LITERARY HISTORY

Wisconsin has contributed to the canon of American literature more than to any other art form, but surprisingly few Wisconsinites realize it. In the late 1980s and early 1990s, Wisconsin experienced a minor artistic renaissance. Prominent authors such as Lorrie Moore *(Anagrams),* Kelly Cherry *(My Life and Dr. Joyce Brothers),* Jacqueline Mitchard *(The Deep End of the Ocean),* and others took up residence in Madison, while Jane Hamilton, who sells fruit with her family at Madison's Saturday farmers' market, received national acclaim for *The Book of Ruth* and *A Map.* The state itself figured prominently in Mona Simpson's wondrous first novel, *Anywhere But Here.*

Native American

Wisconsin's amazingly diverse Native American cultures shared their form of literature—the oral tradition—with early explorers and settlers. The Anish'nabe (Ojibwa) told stories of the Great Protector of all Algonquian peoples and explanatory narratives of their westward migration in search of *manomin* (wild rice). The Menominee spoke of the Great Water Panther, and the Hocak (formerly Winnebago) had an interwoven collection of trickster tales that represent one of the most elaborate literary cycles in Indian North America.

Black Hawk, the Fox-Sauk chief who defied U.S. government forces and saw his tribe massacred in the 1832 Black Hawk War, penned from his prison cell one of the most evocative autobiographies ever and became for a time the most famous man in America.

Early European

Initial European explorers in the state—the few who were literate—returned to Europe and lied through their teeth in tales about the wild Northwest Territory in order to earn money for return trips. These accounts sold like gangbusters. (Consult Louis Hennepin and especially Jonathan Carver for tales exemplary of the genre.)

John Muir was the first European Badger author to become well known. Born in Scotland, he immigrated with his family to the U.S. while a very young boy. Settling in Wisconsin's Juneau County, he spent his formative years entranced by the surrounding wilderness. He worked and attended the University of Wisconsin before dropping out and setting off into the "university of the wilderness." His classic *Story of my Boyhood and Youth* spans his early years (1849-60) in the state along with his first two years at the university.

Settler Life and the 20th Century

In the mid- and late 19th century, Wisconsin entered its settlement and land-clearing period, laying the foundation for the literary ethos of the Midwest, as agrarian met industrial and literary all in the same heady epoch. Hamlin Garland was born near La Crosse, in West Salem, and is best known for his bittersweet account of life as a farmsteader, *Son of the Middle Border.* A fervent practitioner of natural and social realism, he was painfully blunt in his evocations. He won the Pulitzer Prize for Literature in 1922.

Another Pulitzer Prize winner, two years after Garland, was Edna Ferber, whose novels and books detail life all around Wisconsin. Likely her most popular Wisconsin book, *Come and Get It* recounts the raucous, hellaciously ribald years of Hayward and Hurley during the state's lumber days.

A contemporary, Zona Gale, was born in Portage. Early on a respected newspaper writer, she left for New York, hated it, and returned to stay forever, where she and a hodgepodge of Wisconsin writers formed their own version of the Algonquin roundtable. She was aggressively devoted to Wisconsin's progressive politics of the time.

Glenway Wescott grew up near Kewaskum and, like Garland, evoked rural community life. His early, quasi-autobiographical writings are generally considered his best. Unlike Garland, who had mixed emotions, Wescott harbored pure resentment toward the bucolic prairies. He eventually became one of the famous Lost Generation of Paris expatriates in the 1920s.

Two-time Pulitzer winner Thornton Wilder was born and raised in Madison, where his parents were prominent in academics and society. He won his first Pulitzer for *The Bridge of San Luis Rey* in 1927 and his second for the eternally popular *Our Town* a decade later.

Even Carl Sandburg gave Wisconsin credit for his works, having spent five of the most important years of his life in the state. He would later say of Milwaukee, "Ah, Milwaukee. I got my bearings there. The rest of my life has been the unrolling of a scene that started in Wisconsin."

There are great writers as obscure inside the state as out. Edna Meudt wrote fiction and later poetry. Despite a late start due to her family, she eventually became a brief star of Wisconsin literature. Arguably Wisconsin's best poet, Lorine Niedecker is also totally obscure—except to the British, who loved her (for more, see the special topic "Her Life by Water"). Another nonnative, Aldo Leopold, produced graceful, engaging prose, which to many represents the acme of Wisconsin writing (see the special topic "Sand County Sage").

Wisconsin's Door County has inspired artists and writers for generations with its rustic isolation. Among the most famous regionally is **Norbert Blei,** who produced a cycle of three "Door" books written out of a converted chicken coop. The books are full of observations on life and nature and contain his own watercolor work.

Derleth: The Full Picture

If one writer attempted to capture the gestalt of Wisconsin, it was August Derleth. He's omitted from most American literature anthologies. Even most Wisconsinites have never read him. And

August Derleth

yet, at one time this laudable Badger was in no uncertain terms heralded as one of America's best young writers by the Guggenheim Foundation, which awarded him a grant in 1938. Sinclair Lewis admired him so much that he called him Wisconsin's Homer. Declaring him Wisconsin's de facto poet laureate would almost be a slight—he was so much more—a sweaty, unvanquishable workaholic wordsmith who churned out up to one million words a year. His 150-tome output runs the Dewey Decimal gamut of novels, short stories, poetry, children's books, journals, mysteries, romances, fantasy, and more—all of it the work of a kindred spirit to the soul of the land and its people.

Derleth was born in Sauk Prairie, the dual villages of Sauk City and Prairie du Sac in south-central Wisconsin along the lower Wisconsin River. He sold his first piece of juvenilia to *Weird Tales* at age 16. He later founded a publishing house for the sole purpose of preserving the works of his hero, H.P. Lovecraft. A graduate of UW in English and history, he spent some time in Minneapolis as editor of *Mystic Magazine* before returning to his beloved hometowns.

None save Twain, some claim, have written more about more. Profoundly moved by the Wisconsin River, he devoted his life to writing about his fictionalized Sauk Prairie in what has been dubbed the Sac Prairie Saga, a journey into the persona of the lower Wisconsin River country. In the saga, successive generations of Sac Prairie residents are examined in novels, poetry, journal scribblings, short stories, and whatever else he could cook up—all combining history, ethnography, a seminal eco-awareness, and his own infectious spirit.

Derleth's detractors decried his propensity for overwriting, and it's true that the motive in the madness can be hard to suss out. But Derleth's real magic is his amazing facility for over-the-top emotionalism and intricate detail. This is also one reason most people can't wade completely or even halfway through his collected works. A good primer is the Prairie Oak Press edition of his selected works, a respected and well-executed sampling of Derleth at his most inspired; it also features a concise, bulls-eye introduction about the man himself.

Derleth's home—the "Place of Hawks"—is still in Sauk Prairie, now privately owned and not open to the public. His grave sits in the local Catholic cemetery. The August Derleth Memorial Bridge spans the Wisconsin River. The lower level of the local library is devoted to his life and works. A local restaurant features "Augie's Room." And in Sauk City's Derleth Park a hiking trail takes in a splendid vista of the river Derleth spent so many evenings pondering.

ON THE ROAD

ROAD TRIPS

Travel media have consistently voted Wisconsin one of the greatest road-touring states in the country; *RV* magazine readers are particularly devoted to the state. The Door Peninsula has routes for road trippers like nowhere else on earth. NBC's *Today* TV show travel correspondent once called Wisconsin the U.S.'s undiscovered gem, marveling at how its roadways offered up the very antithesis to "flyover land."

Heritage Tourism
Part of a federally initiated project on regional tourism—and by far the most successful nationally—the **Wisconsin Ethnic Settlement Trail (W.E.S.T.)** stretches along the entire Lake Michigan coast and is marked by distinctive yellow and brown signs. Wisconsin boasts the nation's largest concentration of 19th-century old world settlements. Travelers can follow the migration of generations of immigrants along 18 routes originally used by Native Americans.

Other heritage highlights include the **Fox-Wisconsin Riverways Heritage Corridor;** the **Frank Lloyd Wright Heritage Tour; Pineries to the Present** and **Timber Trails in the Chippewa Valley,** both of which provide an overview of the state's early timber industry; **Iron County**

Rooted in Resources Trails; Lake Superior Heritage Highways; Southwest Wisconsin Point of Beginnings; and the **Lac du Flambeau Band of Lake Superior Chippewa Indians.** The state is also developing a rural tourism initiative to focus on what the state is all about. Other tours for Native and African American heritage have been mapped out, and good travel materials are available.

For more information on all of the above, contact the **Wisconsin Department of Tourism,** tel. (800) 432-TRIP, for a free 100-page *Wisconsin Heritage Traveler* outlining 125 historic sites around the state that are included in the above tours.

Great River Road
Wisconsin shares with Minnesota and Iowa a grand, approximately 200-mile stretch of mighty Mississippi riverway, chock-full of somnolent old river towns and some of the most gorgeous scenery the state has to offer. Best of all: no crowds. *Great* fun!

Rustic Roads
The state Department of Transportation has highlighted the state's best back-roads trips—on

some of the Midwest's oldest roads—in an effort to preserve the lightly traveled avenues into the real Wisconsin. Brown and yellow signs mark the short (usually less than 10 miles long) historic highways, farm-to-market roads, forest roads, and others. It's a phenomenal way to view the countryside and the culture up close and personal. The book *Rustic Roads: A Positive Step Backward* outlines the routes and is available free from tourist centers or by writing the **Wisconsin Department of Transportation,** Rustic Roads, P.O. Box 7913, Madison, WI 53707.

RECREATION

"Work hard, play hard" is the ethic in Wisconsin. There's always a trail, a lake, or an activity within shouting distance. The free *Wisconsin Recreation Guide* is an 80-page compendium of state and national parks and forests and sites for hiking, biking, boating, fishing, and any other kind of recreation you could imagine. Light as a map, it's nonetheless the best and most comprehensive all-in-one guide to state recreation. It's available free by calling the state's toll-free information line at (800) 432-8747. Furthermore, the friendly staffers answering the phone can point you to other, more specific, and also free information for travelers, including good maps.

PARKS, FORESTS, AND TRAILS

Wisconsin contains a fairly remarkable 65 state parks and forests, ranging in size from Green Bay's 50-acre living museum **Heritage Hill** to the 225,000-acre **Northern Highlands-American Legion State Forest** near Woodruff and Minocqua. A state park lies within an hour of every Wisconsin resident, a deliberate feature of the state park system. The parks offer an admirable mix of history, archaeology, anthropology, recreation, and state preservation; they've been dubbed the most diverse in the Midwest. A few of them—**Devil's Lake State Park, Peninsula State Park,** and the **Kettle Moraine State Forest,** for example—rival other major state parks in the nation. Each of the first two receives more visitors annually than Yellowstone National Park.

The state also boasts two mammoth national forests: the **Chequamegon** and **Nicolet,** totaling a million and a half acres. (Technically, they merged into one entity in 2000, but the change is just administrative.) And the final jewel is a rare national lakeshore—**Apostle Islands National Lakeshore.**

National forests now charge a $3 daily user fee for things like picnic areas and beaches, and camping runs $7-12. State parks and forests require a park sticker, which can be purchased hourly ($3 resident and nonresident), daily ($5 resident, $7 nonresident) or annually ($18 and $25). Camping fees in state parks are also $7-12, depending on location and campsite (some primitive camping is free). See "Camping" for reservation information.

Wisconsin's mammoth multi-use trail system is also under the Department of Natural Resources, and a trail pass ($3 daily, $10 annually) is needed; note that some trails are not *state* trails but county trails and you'll need a different pass—them's the rules! Also note that hikers do *not* need to pay; only those using bikes, horses, skis, or ATVs do.

BIKING

Bicycling magazine rates Wisconsin one of the top three states for cyclists. Madison is second only to Seattle in the list of the nation's most bike-friendly cities; the Elroy-Sparta State Trail was the country's first rail-to-trail system and is regarded as the granddaddy of all multipurpose state recreational trails; and the Chequamegon Area Mountain Bike Trail (CAMBA) system is among the most respected outside Colorado and Utah. All this, combined with the immense concatenate labyrinth of rural farm-to-market roads, makes it obvious why Wisconsinites leave bike racks on their cars year-round. In total, the state maintains over 10,000 miles of established, mapped, and recommended bike routes. A sweeping way to take in Wisconsin is

biking along the Sugar River State Trail

July's GRABAAWR-the GReat Annual Bicycle Adventure Along the Wisconsin River, which departs from the headwaters of the Wisconsin River near Eagle River and moves along the Wisconsin River all the way to Prairie du Chien.

Rails-to-Trails and State Trails

Since the completion of the Elroy-Sparta State Trail, the state has added 34 other rail beds, logging roads, and state park trails to its State Trail System for a total of nearly 1,000 miles. It's impossible to keep up with how many more miles are added annually since cities and counties are establishing their own networks to link up with state trails. Most are mixed-purpose—hiking, skiing, and cycling (some also allow horses and ATVs)—and surfaced with screened crushed limestone. All have facilities of some sort at nodes along the route.

Maps and Information

The state of Wisconsin dispenses excellent free cycling route maps. A recent addition is the (also free) *Wisconsin Biking Guide,* a glossy book with 14 on-road, 14 off-road, and 15 traffic-free touring routes, with plenty of maps and detail.

Trail passes are required for cyclists, skiers, equestrians, and ATV operators (hikers are exempt). Daily passes cost $3, and an annual pass is $10. They can be purchased at state parks, some local businesses, and usually, but not always, at the trail.

HIKING

With over two million acres of state and federal land open for public consumption, along with 33 state recreation trails, hiking opportunities are endless. Two trails of interest to serious backpackers are the **Ice Age National Scenic Trail** and the **North Country National Scenic Trail.** The former (although still being completed) is Wisconsin's pride—a 1,200-mile (when finished) serpentine route across residual moraine through nine federal scientific reserves. Wisconsin's state government has okayed a plan to look into establishing a statewide network of bike-hike trails, allowing one to bike or hike from Milwaukee to the Mississippi River. The ultimate goal is to link Wisconsin's 35 rails-to-trails trails via city-county-state plans. This would double the state's trail mileage. The plan is viewable at www.dnr.state.wi.us/org/land/parks/reports/trails. The North Country National Scenic Trail is one of three interconnected loops that will eventually stretch across the northern U.S. from the East Coast and link with the Pacific Crest Trail. Wisconsin's 40-mile segment served as the inspiration for building the entire trail and gave it its name.

Hiking seasons are fairly consistent statewide, though climatically speaking the far north will always be up to a month behind the extreme south. The snows recede across the state in March and April, and it isn't until late April that

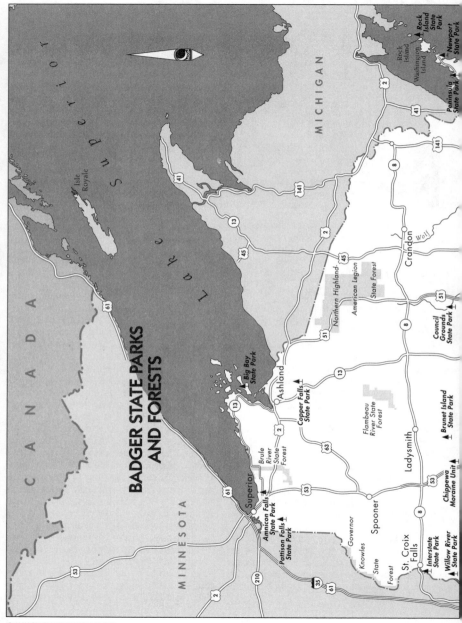

BADGER STATE PARKS AND FORESTS

Map of Wisconsin showing recreation areas and state parks.

Lake Michigan

Green Bay

Whitefish Dunes State Park
Sturgeon Bay
Potawatomi State Park
Marinette

Copper Culture State Park
Shawano
Green Bay
Appleton
High Cliff State Park
Oshkosh
Fond du Lac

Manitowoc
Sheboygan
Kohler-Andrae State Park
Harrington Beach State Park
MILWAUKEE
Racine
Kenosha

CHICAGO

Bong State Recreation Area

Kettle Moraine State Forest North

Pike Lake State Park
Aztalan State Park
Kettle Moraine State Forest South
Janesville
Big Foot Beach State Park

Horicon Marsh Wildlife Area
Beaver Dam

Wausau

Rib Mountain State Park

Stevens Point
Hartman Creek State Park
Roche-A-Cri State Park

Puckaway Lake

Lake Poygan

Wisconsin Dells
Devil's Lake State Park

Madison
Lake Kegonsa State Park
New Glarus Woods State Park
Monroe

ILLINOIS

Lake Wissota State Park

Eau Claire

Wisconsin Rapids
Buckhorn State Park
Rocky Arbor State Park

Castle Rock Lake

Petenwell Lake

Mirror Lake State Park
Natural Bridge State Park
Tower Hill State Park

Blue Mound State Park
Governor Dodge State Park
Dodgeville
Mineral Point
Yellowstone Lake State Park

Browntown-Cadiz Springs Recreational Area

Black River State Forest

Mill Bluff State Park
Wildcat Mountain State Park

La Crosse

First Capitol State Park

Hoffman Hills State Park

Merrick State Park
Perrot State Park

Prairie du Chien
Wyalusing State Park
Nelson Dewey State Park

Hudson
Kinnickinnic State Park

MINNESOTA

IOWA

Mississippi River

25 mi
25 km

everything is dry enough for point-to-point hiking. If you don't mind getting mucked up, most trails are open earlier in the spring and late in the fall as well. Many trails permit winter hiking, though they're not always maintained.

FISHING

Given that Wisconsin has more than 16,000 lakes, 27,000 miles of fishable river and stream, and over 1,000 miles of Lake Superior, Lake Michigan, and Mississippi River coastline, and that most of the state's 135 native species of fish are fair game, it's no surprise that the number-one activity is angling. Wisconsin ranks in the top five states nationwide for number of fishing licenses dispensed and is first in number of nonresident licenses sold annually. Most of the north woods resorts cater to muskie anglers and tagalong families. Boulder Junction and Hayward both claim to be the Muskie Capital of the World. Though the **muskellunge** is revered as king of the waters (see the special topic "Wisconsin's White Whale"),

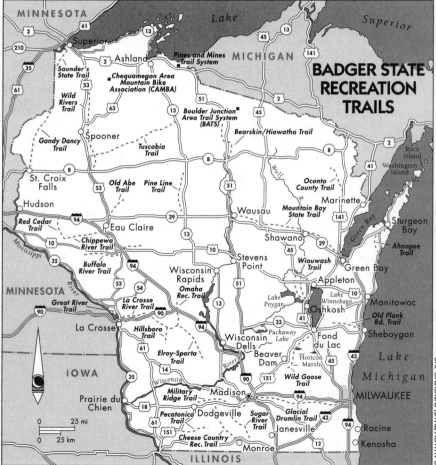

BADGER STATE RECREATION TRAILS

© AVALON TRAVEL PUBLISHING, INC.

in sheer numbers the most popular sportfish is the **walleye** *(Stizostedion vitreum vitreum)*. This aptly named marble-eyed fish is the largest member of the perch family and justly famed as the favorite Friday fish fry entrée. This doesn't mean it's easy to reel in—you'll spend eight hours on the water for each walleye you catch. Annually, Wisconsin anglers take over five million walleye.

Wisconsin's only native stream trout is the **brook trout** *(Salvelinus fontinalis),* closely related to the lake trout.

Other popular hook-and-line species include **smallmouth** and **largemouth bass, rock bass, white bass, northern pike, pickerel, sauger** (closely related to the walleye), and **catfish.** Common panfish include the pervasive whiskered **bullhead** species, **bluegill, pumpkinseed** (sunfish), **yellow perch,** and **crappie.**

Regulations, Maps, and Information
Enumerating all the regulations for fishing Wisconsin waters would require more room than is possible here. In short, species open all year for fishing are rock, yellow, and white bass; all panfish (sunfish, bluegill, crappie, and yellow perch); bullhead; catfish; cisco and whitefish; rough fish; and shovelnose sturgeon. All other species—the ones most anglers want—have specific seasons, bag limits, and size requirements.

A license is required for all anglers 16 years and over. Licenses are sold at most Wisconsin Department of Natural Resources offices, all county clerk offices, and most bait shops, sporting goods stores, and marinas. Valid April 1 through March 31, a four-day license costs $15 for a nonresident (additional surcharges are tacked on for trout and salmon stamps).

Though it doesn't routinely print or stock lake maps for public distribution, the DNR, Box 7921, Madison, WI 53707, does have a few lake maps at the Madison and district offices. More complete maps are available from the **Clarkson Map Company,** 1225 Delanglade St., Box 218, Kaukauna, WI 54130, tel. (920) 766-3000. Each extremely detailed map ($1) shows depth, area, scale, and even grids through ice. Clarkson is also the source for Lake Michigan charts and county maps ($11.75), good for locating trout streams.

Another good source of information, available in just about any state bookstore and many outdoor supplies shops, is the *Fishing Hot Spots* series of books, detailing lakes and rivers by geographic area. The same stores also sell large lake contour maps marked with fishing spots for individual lakes or chains of lakes. For catalogs, maps, or detailed lake reports, contact **Fishing Hot Spots,** P.O. Box 1167, Rhinelander, WI 54501, tel. (800) 338-5957.

State Publications, 222 N. Midvale Blvd, Suite 26, Madison, WI 53705, tel. (800) 236-4710 or (608) 233-4710, sells reprints of the indispensable *Wisconsin Trout Streams* (also known as "the blue book"), an out-of-print DNR reference, for $7.

Great Lakes Fishing
Great Lakes fishing has grown to become an enormous industry, with entire fleets devoted to working the well-stocked waters. Not all the fish in the Great Lakes are native species, but nobody seems to mind. Much of the restocking took place in response to early-century overfishing and the decline of fish stocks due to exotic species. In terms of fish taken per angler hour, Kenosha, Racine, and the Kewaunee/Algoma stretch rate extremely high. The entire Door Peninsula is also hugely popular. In all, the state Department of Natural Resources stocks over 2.1 million coho and chinook salmon, a million lake trout, and two million brook, brown, and steelhead trout.

The **lake trout** *(Salvelinus namayucush),* is a Lake Michigan native, a slow-growing fish common to cold, deep lakes. The **brown trout** is a European transplant. The **rainbow trout, coho salmon,** and **chinook salmon** are all West Coast transplants that have adapted well to the Great Lakes. Chinook are particularly popular, since some reach 40 pounds (perhaps the reason for its "king salmon" nickname).

The state of Wisconsin's *Recreation Guide* features an exhaustive listing of charter fishing operators on both Lake Michigan and Lake Superior.

lake sturgeon

Ice Fishing

Driving the truck out on a frozen lake to a village of shanties erected over drilled holes, sitting on an overturned five-gallon pail, stamping your feet quite a bit, and drinking a lot of schnapps is a time-honored tradition in the Great White North. Ice fishing is serious business in Wisconsin: up to two million angler-days are spent on the ice each year, and ice fishing accounts for up to one-fifth of the state's annual catch.

In general, panfish can be caught year-round. On inland waters, walleye and northern pike can be fished for through March 1, but the season then closes until the first Saturday in May. Muskie are always out of season in winter, and so are trout except in Columbia, Grant, Iowa, Lafayette, Richland, and Sauk Counties and certain limited areas in other counties, which allow trout fishing January 1 through September 30.

On Lakes Superior and Michigan, trout, salmon, northern pike, walleye, and perch can be fished year-round except Superior lake trout, which are off-limits October 1 through November 30. (You can spear northern pike through the ice on Lake Superior.)

Lots of minor regulations exist—and regulations vary on boundary waters with Minnesota, Iowa, and Michigan—so be sure to get the rundown from a local bait shop before drilling your hole.

HUNTING

Personal misgivings aside, hunting, like fishing, is a well-established business in Wisconsin, though far less so on a tourist level. The nine-day gun deer season alone generates $250 million for the state. Fortunately, hunters are often more conservation-oriented than their civilian brethren. Many animal species owe their continued existence to hunting and conservation groups.

Deer hunting is essentially a rite of passage in Wisconsin's north woods even today. Entire school districts in the area shut down for the November white-tail deer season. Other popular hunts include **goose, duck, pheasant,** and especially **ruffed grouse.**

Direct all hunting queries to the Wisconsin Department of Natural Resources, Box 7921, Madison, WI 53707. The DNR issues separate pamphlets on trapping, big-game, pheasant, and waterfowl hunting. An annual nonresident license for fur-bearers costs $175; small game is $75; archery $135; deer $135. Migratory-bird hunting requires additional federal *and* state stamps, adding another $22 to the total, and a pheasant stamp runs an extra $7.25.

SKIING

Wisconsin mountains will never be mistaken for the Rockies or the Grand Tetons, but the state's heights, compared with the rest of the Midwestern flatlands, gives it a fairly decent concentration of downhill ski facilities. Cross-country ski buffs can indulge themselves in an orgy of skiing statewide. It's such a big deal in Wisconsin that the nation's largest cross-country ski race, the Birkebeiner, is held here every year in February, in Hayward.

Including private recreation centers as well as county, state, and federal lands, Wisconsin has 34 downhill facilities and 350 established cross-country ski areas. The tourism department's free book, *Wisconsin Winter Recreation,* details all the sites.

SNOWMOBILING

Snowmobiling is a big deal here. Back in 1924, a Wisconsinite strapped a single-stroke engine to a pair of skis and *voila!*—the first snowmobile was born. Since then, things haven't been the same in this state, a place where local high schools provide snowmobile parking lots in winter and get more 'biles than cars. In 1996, Antigo passed ordinances giving snowmobiles rights similar to those of cars on city streets. Restaurants and nightspots often list their addresses according to the snowmobile route you'll find them on.

In some communities, snowmobiling accounts for more business than even fishing. In fact, with over 175,000 registered riders spending $40 million, it accounts for more money in some parts of the state than angling, hunting, and skiing combined. In *Snowgoer* magazine, reader polls have ranked northeastern Wisconsin and Minocqua best overall, eclipsing better-known, better-financed Rocky Mountain operators.

In total, the state maintains 25,000 miles of interconnected trails, so well linked that you can travel on them continuously from Kenosha in southeastern Wisconsin all the way to Lake Superior in the northwest. Fifteen of the 33 state recreation trails permit snowmobiling; so do 15 state parks and forests; and the national forests are wide open. The highlight of snowmobile season is Eagle River's crazy World Championships, when 30,000 boisterous 'bile fans pile into the tiny north woods town.

The state tourist office has addresses of county contacts and local snowmobile clubs; it also maintains lists of regional businesses offering rentals. It also offers an invaluable 50-page free guide to the state's snowmobiling options; you can get it from any information center or by calling the state's toll-free number. Myriad regulations cover the use of snowmobiles; contact local chambers of commerce, the local DNR office, or even rental shops for specifics. Snowmobile rentals do not come cheap—only a bit less than renting a car. Personal health insurance should be a prerequisite for anyone who rides one.

CANOEING AND KAYAKING

Imagine 15,000 lakes, 27,000 miles of stream and river, almost 1,000 miles of Great Lake and Mississippi River shoreline, and 144 established canoe trails. Wisconsin features unbeatable canoeing and kayaking. Nationally regarded or federally designated Wild Rivers include the **Wolf River,** a federal Outstanding Water Resource coursing through the Menominee Indian Reservation; the **Flambeau River** system, one of the wildest in the Midwest; the **Bois Brule River,** famed for its trout; the **Montreal River,** home of the Junior World Kayak Championships; the unknown but exquisite **Turtle River,** leading into Wisconsin's Turtle-Flambeau Flowage in the most unspoiled section of the state; the **Pine** and **Popple Rivers** in the Nicolet National Forest; the wild **Peshtigo River;** the lazy, classic **Lower Wisconsin State Riverway;** the **La Crosse River;** the **Kickapoo River** (the "crookedest in the world"); the **Yahara River,** one reason *Canoeist* magazine calls Madison a canoeing mecca; and perhaps the most popular, the **Manitowish River,** in the Northern Highlands/American Legion State Forest in one of the planet's densest concentrations of lakes.

The **Namekagon-St. Croix National Scenic Riverway** stretches west from northeast of Cable, joins the St. Croix River and its smashing geology, and eventually flows to the confluence with the Mississippi River.

Kayakers enjoy the superb **Apostle Islands National Lakeshore** along Lake Superior—an experience impossible to overstate—and, to a lesser extent, the magnificence of Door County on the Lake Michigan side. Rentals are plentiful at all locations; kayaks are always much more expensive to rent than canoes but offer a wider range of use, since they can handle rougher waters.

Serious aficionados of water-borne activities should not overlook the funky fun of mucking around in Mississippi River sloughs or wetland and marsh—the best way to experience the landscape and wildlife.

GOLF

Believe it or not, forlorn, wintry Wisconsin has one of the nation's highest concentrations of golf courses per capita. Go figure. Nearly 430 courses are listed in the state's *Wisconsin Golf Guide.* Among the courses most often pursued are **Blackwolf Run** in Kohler, **Lawsonia** in Green Lake, **Sentryworld** in Stevens Point, **University Ridge** in Madison, and **Brown Deer Golf Course** near Milwaukee.

ARTS AND ENTERTAINMENT

THE POLKA

Wisconsinites possess a genetic predisposition to polka, which was established by a 1994 statute as the state's official dance. Given the state's heady 19th-century influx of Eastern and Central European immigrants—the highest concentration in America at the time—it's only natural that the peasant dance would take root here. Some cultural historians claim Wisconsin harbors more species of polka than anyplace else in the world. Polka music emanates from dozens of stations on the AM dial across the state. At weddings, one polka per hour is virtually an unwritten house minimum. Polka at Brewers games, polka in the Capitol building, and plans in Milwaukee for a Polka Hall of Fame, in a seven-story accordion-shaped edifice. In Wisconsin, polka is king.

Origins

The polka is an ethnic dance in 2/4 time (the polka-mazurka is a variation in 3/4 time) derived by peasants from Bohemian folk dancing in Eastern Europe in the 1830s. Both Poland and the former Yugoslavia claim to be its birthplace, though its first manifestations as a social dance appeared in Prague.

The world "polka" means "half step," but the "step" could really be "hop," since that's the dance's trademark move—the bounce before the twirl. Simple and easily improvised, the polka is essentially a pastiche of hops, dips, swings, and slides. It caught on in Central and Eastern Europe and by the 1840s began a rage across Europe. Picked up in part by dance experts, it was showcased in Paris and later London. It then wafted across the Atlantic to the U.S., where, unlike in Europe (the snobbish elite there considered it a madness of the lowest base order), it caught on like wildfire.

Modern Polka

Each culture in Europe stylized the polka with its own distinctions. The Swiss did the polka step on the first beat of a bar, while the Austrians did it on the last half beat, made it more prominent, and included some zig-zags. The Dutch used a backward swing and omitted the hop, replacing it with only a slight rise or roll of the body to mark the last whole or half beat of a bar. The Poles' polka stepped in measures of four, with the polka lead foot every second step. Czechs did it without a hop. Finns used a 4/4 rhythm and an abrupt heel step and added bits from their own baleful tango. Generally, polka couples turn right continuously without reversing and always move to the right.

Polka has had an unmistakable influence on the Americas. Eastern and Central Europeans also gravitated to the south, where predomi-

Everybody polka party!

nantly African-American steps were incorporated. A large population of Europeans took their music to Texas and melded border flavors into the music called *conjunto*. Today, some country-western two-steps are being traded back and forth between country and polka camps.

And in Wisconsin, all forms have melded into one eclectic, happy dance. Wisconsin polka is mainly the Polish mazurka and the Dutch, Swiss, and Czech polkas. The best way to experience it is at one of the state's many polka festivals. For information, contact the **Wisconsin Polka Booster, Inc.,** W2813 Neda Rd., Iron Ridge, WI 53035. The group sponsors the annual **Wisconsin Polkafest** in mid-May in diminutive Concord.

HANDICRAFTS

There are dozens of types of handicrafts in Wisconsin, as is true of the Midwest in general. Every community has artisans specializing in various ethnic styles: Norwegian rosemaling, for example, is a flowery, colorful, painted trim artwork. Unique are the creations of the Amish and the Hmong. A large contingent of Amish families, famed for their quilting, crafts, bent-hickory furniture, and outstanding bakery, live in the southwestern and west-central sections of Wisconsin.

Hmong crafts include storycloths, which recount narratives visually, and exquisite decorative *paj ntaub,* a 2,000-year-old hybrid of needlework and applique, usually featuring geometric designs and, often, animals. These quilts and wall hangings require more than 100 hours of work. Some Amish and Hmong young women are synthesizing their quilt styles into wonderful bicultural mélanges. Hmong artisans are often found at craft fairs and/or farmers' markets. Amish wares are found both in home shops throughout southwestern Wisconsin and in a few stores.

EVENTS

The following listing of events in Wisconsin is by no means complete—dozens and dozens of opportunities exist to attend festivals and events somewhere in the state. A comprehensive biannual magazine-size events guide is available by calling the state Department of Tourism hotline, tel. (800) 432-8747.

Holidays
During the following national holidays, government offices and many businesses, including banks, close: **New Year's Day,** January 1; **Martin Luther King, Jr.'s Birthday (observed),** third Monday of January; **President's Day,** third Monday in February; **Memorial Day,** last Monday of May; **Independence Day,** July 4; **Labor Day,** first Monday of September; **Veteran's Day,** November 11; **Thanksgiving,** fourth Thursday of November; and **Christmas,** December 25.

MONTH BY MONTH

January
In mid- to late January, the wild **World Championship Snowmobiling Derby** is held in Eagle River. The world's best snowmobile drivers compete on a half-mile, iced oval track. Thirteen classes feature stock to super-modified. During special pre-race tours, you can ride with the champs.

February
In Hudson, the **Hot Air Affair** features up to 50 hot air balloons in racing and precision-flying events, with mass ascensions daily. In the evenings, great photo ops abound of the tethered balloons illuminated from within.

The largest cross-country ski race in North America, the **American Birkebeiner,** is held in Hayward and Cable in northwestern Wisconsin. Six thousand competitors from around the world race on the grueling 55-km course. The four-day event features tons of smaller races, elite sprints, champion skier challenges, a telemark downhill race, and a great feast the night before the big race.

Following January's screaming 'biles with barking are the sled dogs running the **Klondike Days and World Championship Oval Sled Dog Sprints** in Eagle River. Sled dog teams compete in freight races and weight pulls on a half-mile iced oval track. Simultaneously, the event features a frontier winter rendezvous, lumberjack demonstrations, chainsaw carving, sled dog rides, and an authentic Native American powwow.

March

During the doldrums of spring, Wisconsin gears up for the high tourist season at the **Journal-Sentinel Sports Show** in Milwaukee. While the show is geared primarily toward consumerism, it's also a great place to pick up information on travel, tours, and resorts in the state.

May

Mid-May heralds the beginning of the festival season, which runs through autumn. Tiny Muscoda celebrates the obscure, tasty morel mushroom at its **Morel Mushroom Festival,** while across the state at the same time Burlington throws a hoedown with its **Chocolate Days.** Later in the month, Burlington also hosts **National Hydroplane Races,** when more than 300 hydroplane racers gather for competition.

Norwegian rosemaling, Stoughton's Syttende Mai *Festival*

The state's Norwegians—and many others—kick up their heels mid-May for independence day during the **Syttende Mai Folk Festival** in Stoughton, outside Madison. Folk dancing and arts displays are the big draws; a personal favorite is the Ugly Troll contest.

June

Some of the top sprint-car racers in the nation gather in Elkhart Lake for the **June Sprints,** with 22 classes and 450 drivers on a top U.S. road course.

The largest bike ride in the country takes place in early June when 13,000 cyclists undertake the **Miller Lite Ride for the Arts** in Milwaukee. The ride consists of 2-, 15-, 30-, and 50-mile routes; all proceeds benefit the Milwaukee United Performing Arts Fund.

Fond du Lac's **Walleye Weekend** is part of the National Walleye Tournament. Along with the fishing tournament, the crowds enjoy musical entertainment and 40 other events.

Milwaukee's **Polish Fest** is one of the larger ethnic festivals in the country, but the city really gets into high gear the last week of June when it hosts the mammoth **Summerfest,** billed as the largest music festival in the United States. In the 11-day extravaganza, more than 2,500 national acts perform everything from big band to heavy metal. A great place to sample Wisconsin food.

Wausau hosts the **National Kayak Racing Competition** to coincide with its **Logjam Festival** late in the month. The kayak races pass right through the heart of downtown. The Logjam Festival re-creates the state's bygone settlement era.

Another huge event is the **Timberfest and Lumberjack Tournament of Champions** in Woodruff. North America's best lumberjacks converge on the town and compete in chopping, log rolling, pole climbing, and lumberjack entertainment—it's the real thing, even televised by ESPN.

July

The **Oneida Pow Wow and Festival of Performing Arts** takes place west of Green Bay on the Oneida Indian Reservation and is a full competition powwow open to the public.

The largest automotive festival in the Midwest—third-largest in the world—the **Iola Old Car Show and Swap Meet** takes place in the southeastern town of Iola. Over 2,500 show cars are exhibited, and vendors walk around wearing T-shirts stenciled with lists of parts for sale or parts they want to buy.

Top-name country music stars perform in a natural outdoor ampitheater at Rhinelander's **Hodag Country Festival** the first week of the month.

A favorite of many is Milwaukee's **Great Circus Parade.** Re-creating the circus street shows of a century ago, over 700 horses and close to 100 authentic circus wagons, along with circus performers and wild animals, make the trip through Wisconsin along the "Great Circus Train" from its Baraboo headquarters to Milwaukee. Get there early; people line the streets up to two days in advance. Yet another classic ethnic festival is Milwaukee's **Festa Italiana** following the Great Circus Parade. Milwaukee's third major ethnic festival of July is **German Fest.** Second only to Summerfest in size, it's the third-largest ethnic festival in the country.

Wisconsin's Lac Courte Oreilles Indians honor the Earth with a powwow and homecoming celebration of ceremonial dancing, drumming, food, games, workshops, and speakers.

The most prestigious event outside of Summerfest is likely Oshkosh's **EAA International Fly-In Convention,** the world's most significant aviation event. Fifteen thousand experimental and historic aircraft—including NASA-designed craft—descend on the city and surrounding area for a week. Also present are some 500 exhibitors, from international aviation notables to the FAA. Daily flight shows are wildly popular.

August
During the first week of the month, Milwaukee's African-American community celebrates **African World Festival** with ceremonies, dance, food, and art. At about the same time, Milwaukee hosts the **Wisconsin State Fair,** the state's largest annual event, with more than a million visitors over 11 days. In late August, Milwaukee features **Irish Fest,** the world's largest Irish cultural event.

In early August, Seymour celebrates its status as the **Home of the Hamburger.** There's a Giant Hamburger Parade, Hamburger Olympics, Bun Run, and occasionally the world's largest hamburger (or, actually, cheeseburger).

An up-and-coming event is La Crosse's **Great River Festival of Jazz.** It features continuous jazz over an entire weekend, with jam sessions, jazz liturgies, and even a Mardi Gras-style parade.

Fond du Lac welcomes the world's greatest aerobatic pilots at its **International Aerobatic Championships** in mid-August. Individual and team combinations are sidelighted by stunt pilots and air shows.

September
New Glarus shows itself as North America's most Swiss village during its **Wilhelm Tell Pageant** in early September. The famous Tell drama is presented in both English and Swiss-German. And, of course, there's plenty of yodeling, log throwing, and the like.

Also in Green County is the Swiss village of Monroe, which every two years throws the wild **Cheese Days Celebration** featuring the world's largest wheels of Swiss cheese, plenty of parades, and more.

Wisconsin's largest Native American cultural celebration is Milwaukee's **Indian Summer,** in mid-September. Featured are a full competition powwow as well as Native American entertainment and artwork.

The nation's premier off-road bike race is the **Chequamegon Fat Tire Festival** in Hayward and Cable in mid-September—three days of off-road racing, orienteering, 16- and 40-mile events, and criterium lap racing.

Believe it or not, up to 80,000 people crowd west-central Wisconsin, near Warrens, for late September's **Cranberry Festival,** which celebrates the tart little fruit.

Nature's autumn majesty is a big deal in Wisconsin, drawing thousands of tourists annually. Local news reports even feature nightly leaf color watches. The trees begin to turn in extreme northern Wisconsin in late, late September and peak sometime in the first weeks of October. The leaf-color peak moves gradually southward; during the last week of October and sometimes into the first few days of November, the southern half of the state experiences the full palette of colors. A 24-hour **leaf color hotline,** (800) 432-8747, tells you where and when to go on leaf-color road trips.

October
One of October's major festivals is **Oktoberfest** in La Crosse, fashioned after Munich's Oktoberfest celebrations. There's a Maple Leaf Parade, music, rides, and a lot of beer.

Being America's Dairyland, it seems appropriate for Wisconsin to hold the world's largest dairying trade show, the **World Dairy Expo.** More than 50 countries participate in the event, held yearly in Madison.

Bayfield closes out the season of warm-weather festivals with its early October **Apple Fest,** featuring food booths, parades, arts and crafts, carnivals, and music. It's worth going just to see the Apostle Islands.

November
In mid-November, over 50 ethnic groups participate in the Milwaukee **Holiday Folk Fair.** The largest annual multiethnic festival in the country, it's a great place to shop for folk art, and the ethnic dancing is quite popular.

ACCOMMODATIONS

Prices
Since Wisconsin remains primarily a summer destination, prices in certain hotels—particularly those in areas saturated by *auslander*—jump significantly between Memorial Day and Labor Day. And prices generally, though definitely not always, drop in winter. Places near ski areas or winter recreation spots—Hayward during the Birkebeiner cross-country ski race, for example, or anyplace popular with snowmobilers—do have higher winter rates; others will be dirt cheap or boarded up tight.

For consistent off-season rates around the state, spring (pre-Memorial Day) is a good time to come. However, the best opportunity to maximize the dollar is without question autumn. After Labor Day (usually into the first week of October), prices dwindle, the heat retreats, wood smoke fills the air, and the leaves begin turning. There are some good deals to be found if you scout around.

All rates quoted in this book are top-end prices, although *significant* off-season deals are noted. Otherwise, figure a 10-20% drop in the off-season. Be aware that local municipalities have the option to tack on room taxes beyond the state's five percent sales tax.

HOTELS AND MOTELS

Wisconsin's hotel and motel offerings run the gamut from sleazy dives to cozy mom-and-pop operations to opulent, five-star gems. Generally, as in most U.S. states, the farther out in the sticks you are, the more of a bargain you'll find. However, keep in mind that at times the sticks *are* the tourist draw, and so you may arrive in a one-horse town and find yourself shelling out big bucks for meager accommodations.

All quotes in this book are based on single occupancy, since in many places singles and doubles cost the same. Both single and double prices are listed if available. Motel rooms for under $20 do still exist in Wisconsin, though you'd have to spend a lot of time in state before coming across one of them. In general, expect to pay $30-40 for the lowest-end motels of decent comfort; if you find one for below $30 (and quite a few do exist), consider yourself lucky. In larger cities, you'll more likely pay $40 for the same amenities. Most luxury hotel rooms cost around $200 at the most, though a couple in this book start at $250.

Little distinction is made in this book between most national chains—Motel 6, Super 8, Ramada Inn, and the like—since the differences tend to be minuscule. The rooms are always about the same size, the walls are creamy white or pastel hued, forgettable artwork adorns the walls, and there are usually two or three faux brass lamps and a perfectly adequate bed. Light blue pile carpeting versus wall-to-wall deep shag matters little, but if one of the chain hotels offers above-average amenities (and this author is a liberal judge), it's mentioned.

RESORTS

Here's the hardest to define of all Wisconsin accommodations options. Popular tourist destinations, like Door County, show a growing number of sprawling, condo-style developments, essentially self-contained city-states with hedonistic amenities.

But the true Wisconsin resort is a much different animal. Most north woods establishments—and many others in the state—use the term "resort" pretty freely.

One may be a ramshackle shotgun shack built as a hunting camp hut in the 1930s, with busted glass or flapping screens, bunk beds lining the walls, and an oil heater thrown in; the proprietor will often be an engaging old cuss who'll probably clean your fish for you. You can get these for as cheap as $200 per week.

Then there are the classic mom-and-pop "resorts." Generally, these consist of different-sized cabins grouped together, each a modest homelike cottage with sitting room, linoleum-floored kitchen area, and bedrooms. The better ones have screened sitting porches. All have ersatz wood paneling and at least one wildlife print on the wall. The furnishings consist of 1950s-era chairs and couches. Kitchens are equipped with cooking utensils, even old-style percolator coffeepots. Some proprietors have knuckled under to modernity and now include TVs with cable. Lake breezes mixed with the scent of sun-baked forest pervade. All resorts, by definition, lie on a lake or riverfront, so most come with rowboat and, if you're lucky, beaches. Almost all are housekeeping cabins, meaning you bring and change your own linens and towels. Rates vary, but around $300 per week is average.

With so many definitions of resort, travelers need do their homework well in advance. Contact the local chamber of commerce or the resort ahead of time and request brochures. Knowing what you're getting into ensures a pleasurable experience. Remember: the owners may be hovering around, and one person's dump is another's treasured find.

And do it fast. Some cultural preservationists have called the traditional Wisconsin resort one of the most doomed of the state's cultural highlights. Even natives are shocked to discover that the dream of owning a rustic cabin on a lake is well-nigh impossible in some touristed areas up north. Everybody wants his or her own retreat, and so pretty soon everybody *is* up north. That means development, that means sprawl, that means lakefront property that once sold for $150 per square foot now can command $2,000 due to development. It's virtually impossible for a mom-and-pop operation *not* to sell out.

BED AND BREAKFASTS

As in other regions of the country, Wisconsin bed and breakfasts have a loyal following. A bed and breakfast is essentially a private home that rents rooms. All include breakfast, but these vary from light continental fare to full bacon-and-eggs feasts. Many also offer extras such as afternoon tea and homemade cookies.

These establishments often have rules you won't be subjected to at a motel, such as mandatory late-afternoon check-in and lots of quiet-hour stipulations. Some B&Bs offer rooms with private baths, but often facilities are shared.

Visitors will also encounter B&B-style accommodations in places called "historic inns." What's the difference between a historic inn and a bed and breakfast? Cynics answer, "About $50." But in fact, most places billed as historic inns have been recognized by state or federal authorities as structures worthy of preservation and study. As a consequence, prices are ratcheted up. Historic inns can function as quasi-hotels, with regular check-in times, pools, and restaurants. Others are simply B&Bs with more rooms than average and more authentic period decor.

Wisconsin's B&Bs are mostly, but not always, late 18th-century gingerbread Victorians, originally owned by local lumber, paper, or brewing executives and now restored to their previous opulence by private owners. However, wonderful variations exist—1830s homestead cabins cobbled together, old barns, settlement-era farmhouses, old general stores, stone silos, and more.

The **Wisconsin Bed & Breakfast Association** maintains tough standards for membership—reportedly the most stringent in the nation. Thus, its free book, *Wisconsin Bed & Breakfasts,* is an invaluable source for choosing a B&B.

HOUSEBOATS

A funky way to see the state is aboard a houseboat, particularly along the southern terminus of the St. Croix National Scenic Riverway or anywhere on the Mississippi River. La Crosse is a hot spot for houseboat rentals. Count on paying about $750 for a four-day rental, although most go by the week only and start at $1,000. Everything is included in a houseboat rental except navigational skill (though you don't have to be a riverboat captain to rent one). The state's **Recreation Guide** has a lengthy list of houseboat operators.

FARM VACATIONS

An increasingly popular form of seeing Wisconsin is getting your hands dirty on a working farm. These generally are basic B&Bs that allow visitors to get up close and personal views of rural life. Most people adore the experience. The Wisconsin *Recreation Guide* also has extensive lists of these operations. Lodging rates for farm vacations are generally reasonable, usually similar to those of mid-range B&Bs.

HOSTELS

Wisconsin has only a handful of hostels, but more are being planned. You'll find one in Milwaukee, one in Madison, one 25 miles southwest of Madison, one in the Nicolet National Forest, one in Cable near the Chequamegon National Forest, and several others.

Hostels are a good place to mingle with other travelers. Conditions vary, but most are clean and quiet. Some have strict curfews, while others are more relaxed. Some offer a few private rooms, but most have gender-segregated dorms. If you haven't brought your own, sleeping sheets (two sheets sewn together to make a bag) can be rented at any hostel. Hostel rates in Wisconsin run $11-18 per person per night. Membership in AYH guarantees the lowest rate but is rarely required; nonmembers pay approximately $3 extra.

CAMPING

In regional media polls, Wisconsin's state park system is generally singled out as the best. One reason: a profusion of campgrounds. With over 50 state parks, forests, and recreation areas featuring campgrounds, chances are good you'll have a place to pitch your tent. The state parks and forests all have some reservable sites. For the most popular state parks (like Devil's Lake, Peninsula, and anything in Door County or along Lake Michigan), make your reservations as early as possible—February might be too late. You can reserve sites from 11 months up to 48 hours in advance. Contact (888) WI-PARKS or the DNR Website (www.wiparks.net) to reserve; there is an additional $9.50 fee to reserve sites. Camping fees in state parks and forests are $7-9 for Wisconsin residents, $9-12 nonresidents; sites with electricity are $3 more. Note that unlike

canoe camping in the Northern Highlands American Legion State Forest

RACHEL FRIEDMAN

bordering states, Wisconsin's parks are often full. The most popular parks are even booked during the week. Many people will come a week early on a Monday, get a site, then drive back and forth between the park and work all week just to maintain the site for the upcoming weekend. (This is due to the fact that the number of campers has increased dramatically, but Wisconsin hasn't created a new state park with a campground since the 1960s.) Make plans as early as possible or head for federal land.

Additionally, Wisconsin's two enormous national forests sprawl over 1.5 million acres, with dozens and dozens of established campgrounds that fill up only on Memorial Day and Labor Day. Also, camping is legal *anywhere* on federal land, within certain guidelines. So even if the campgrounds are chockablock, you can still tramp into the forest and set up a tent.

Some county parks accept campers and are usually less cluttered than state parks. The state Department of Transportation highway map marks all county parks with red squares.

Campsites in all national and county parks and forests range in price from $7 to $14. A few primitive backpack and/or canoe sites in the national forests are free. Reservations for national forest campgrounds are available by calling (877) 444-6777 daily 7 a.m.-11 p.m. Central Standard Time, or by logging onto the reservation service's website (www.reserveusa.com). Reservation fees are $9 in addition to the campsite fee. You can reserve up to 240 days in advance, or not fewer than five days ahead of time.

The Department of Tourism publishes a free guide to Wisconsin private campgrounds; it's available by calling (800) 372-2737.

FOOD

Midwestern Cuisine

An oxymoron? Hardly. Banish those visions of tuna casserole dancing in your head. Midwestern cuisine—real, original fare handed down generationally—is more eclectic and more representative of "American" heritage than better-known, better-marketed cooking styles.

If you search out the latent Americana in Wisconsin cooking, you'll be amazed. Wisconsin's best cooking is a thoughtful mélange of ethnicities, stemming from the diverse populace and prairie-cooking fare that reflects a heritage of living off the land. Midwest Regional cuisine is a blend of originally wild food such as cranberries, wild rice, pumpkins, blueberries, whitefish livers, catfish cheeks, and morel mushrooms incorporated into standard old country recipes. Added to the mix are game animals, like deer, pheasant, and goose. Many Midwesterners simply shoot their own, rather than raising them or buying them from a grocery wholesaler. It's a home-based culinary style, perfected from house to house over generations of adaptation.

And while the state features a panorama of European fare, the rest of the culinary spectrum is also represented. Milwaukee's got real-deal soul food and a fantastic array of Puerto Rican and Mexican restaurants, and in Madison you'll find a plethora of Asian eateries. In short, despite the preponderance of hot beef and meatloaf, it's quite possible to find good imaginative food in Wisconsin.

Prices

In general, food is not outrageously expensive here. Greasy spoons are low-scale cafes where you can get two eggs, toast, and bacon with coffee for three bucks or less. Such establishments may call themselves cafes, but true cafes are generally a bit more upscale. Supper clubs vary widely in entrée prices, generally between $8 and $25 for a dinner entrée, $6-12 for lunch. Fish fries are all-you-can-eat and almost always cost $7-10 (a few are lower priced). At fine dining places, expect to pay at least $15 for an entrée, and don't dress too casually, unless you plan on being the center of attention.

SUPPER CLUBS

What, exactly, is a supper club? What the *zócalo* is to Latin Americans, the sidewalk cafe to Parisians, the *biergarten* to Bavarians, so is the supper club to Wisconsinites. It sometimes seems as if state charter requires every Badger-

FISH FRIES

Cuisine experience number one in Wisconsin is a Friday-night fish fry. Its exact origins are unknown, but it's certainly no coincidence that in a state contiguous to two Great Lakes, featuring 15,000 glacial pools, and undergoing three successive waves of German Catholics, followed by Italian, Irish, and Polish Catholics (Catholics don't eat meat on Fridays during Lent), people would specialize in a Friday-night fish-eating outing.

Fish fries are myriad. Corner taverns, family restaurants, diminutive cafes and greasy spoons, supper clubs, and even local churches and VFW posts all have their own take on the tradition. Milwaukee does it bigger and better than anywhere else—it's so popular there that the local fast-food restaurants even have them; the American Serbian Hall serves 2,500 people at a drive-through; Chinese, Mexican, and other ethnic restaurants get in on the act; and even Milwaukee County Stadium has fish fries at Friday Brewers games.

Everybody has an opinion on who has the best fish fry but, truthfully, how many ways can you deep-fry a perch (or one of the other species variants—haddock, walleyed pike, and cod)? Those with an aversion to deep-fried food can usually find one broiled option.

Generally set up as smorgasbords (sometimes including platefuls of chicken, too), the gluttonous feasts are served with slatherings of homemade tartar sauce and a relish tray or salad bar. The truly classic fish fry joints are packed to the rafters by 5:30 p.m.—and some even have century-old planks and hall-style seating (the kind of place where you gaze at the tartar sauce on the table and wonder really how long it's been sitting out, unrefrigerated).

Consider yourself truly blessed if you get to experience a smelt fry. This longtime tavern tradition has pretty much disappeared; in the old days, smelt, milk-dipped, battered, and even *pickled* were *the* thing.

state community to have one. It's the social and culinary underpinning of Wisconsin. Indeed, though supper clubs exist in many Midwestern states, Wisconsin's density is difficult to fathom.

Equal parts homey, casual meat-and-potatoes restaurant and local kaffeeklatsch (better make that "brandyklatsch"), supper clubs traditionally have a triumvirate of obligatory specialties: prime rib, always on Saturday, although some serve it every day; homestyle chicken; and invariably a Friday-night fish fry. No fish fry, no business. Most menus feature steaks in one column, seafood in the other. Regional variations buttress these basics with anything from Teutonic carnivore fare to Turkish food. This being Wisconsin, venison occasionally makes an appearance. One side dish will always be a choice of potato. If it's a true supper club, a relish tray comes out with the dinner rolls. On it, you'll find everything from sliced vegetable sticks to pickles to cole slaw—and sometimes an indescribably weird "salad" concoction like green Jell-O with shaved carrots inside.

No two supper clubs look alike (the only prerequisites are an attached bar and faux wood paneling), but all can be partially covered by clichés such as "rustic," "cozy," and "like someone's dining room." Nicer supper clubs will have crackling fireplaces; low-end joints feel more like run-down family restaurants, in both decor and menu. The coolest ones have animal heads dangling above the diners, the tackiest ones feature overdone nautical decor. Dress is completely up to you. Wear a suit and you'll be conspicuous. Jeans are perfectly acceptable. In many places—especially Madison—Badger red is de rigeur on football Saturdays. Beware impostors: in recent years, the words "supper club" have been adopted by fancy restaurants on both coasts, but a co-opted supper club is not the real thing. If you ever see a dress code posted, you're not at a real supper club.

CHEESE

Wisconsin produces over a third of the nation's cheese (leading in cheddar, colby, brick, muenster, limburger, and many Italian varieties). Over 200 varieties of cheese come out of Wisconsin, all influenced by German, Swiss, Scandinavian, Dutch, French, and Italian styles. And, yes, we really do eat a great deal of it as well. The loyal dairy consumption shouldn't come as a surprise—laws prohibiting the use of margarine remained on the books until 1967.

The most common cheese in Wisconsin is the ever versatile **cheddar.** It ranges in color from nearly white to orange, and its flavor can be almost bland to bitingly sharp (aged versions). For something different, eat it with fruit (apples are best) or melt it on hot apple pie.

Colby cheese was invented in the northern Wisconsin town of the same name. The cheese has a very mild, mellow flavor and a firm, open texture. It's most often eaten breaded and deep-fried, but try cubing it in fruit or vegetable salads. Firmer, with a smooth body, **Colby Jack** cheese is marbled white and yellow—a mixture of the mellow Colby cheese along with the distinctive broad taste of **Monterey Jack,** a semisoft, creamy white cheese used mostly in Mexican restaurants as a substitute for cheese from the Mexican state of Chihuahua.

Wisconsin effectively brought **Swiss** cheese to prominence in the United States over a century ago. Firm and smooth with large shiny eyes (holes), Swiss has an unmistakable nutty flavor. Swiss cheese fans should head immediately for the town of Monroe in southwestern Wisconsin; there you'll find the greatest Swiss you've ever tasted, as well as a milder **baby Swiss.** While there, slip into a tavern or sandwich shop and really experience Wisconsin culture by sampling a **limburger** sandwich—the pungent, oft-misunderstood Swiss on pumpernickel, with onions and radishes. Wisconsin may be the last place on earth where it's couth to munch limburger in polite company; it *is* the last place in the world making the cheese.

Another Wisconsin original is **brick cheese,** a semisoft cheese with a waxy, open texture. Creamy white, young brick has a mild flavor; when aged, it becomes sharp. It's perfect for grilled cheese sandwiches or with mustard on pumpernickel bread.

Two transplants the state produces to near perfection are **Gouda** and **Edam** cheeses, imported by Western Europeans. They're semisoft to firm and creamy in texture, with small holes and mild, slightly nutty flavor.

Finally, for the most authentic cheese-eating cultural experience, go to a bar and order **cheese curds,** commonly breaded and deep fried. When purchased at a dairy or a farmers' market, cheese curds leave a distinctive squeaky feeling on the teeth and are a perfect snack food. Another unique cheese dish, especially in Green Bay, is beer cheese soup.

The *Recreation* guide, an indispensable, free tourist publication available at any Wisconsin tourist center, details cheese factory tours around the state.

DRINK

Yes, Badgers drink a lot. We rank fourth nationally in per capita consumption; 69% of drinking-age population report participation in legal imbibing. Madison, and Dane County around it, have one of the highest percentages of binge drinkers in the United States. Alcohol is the social lubricant of the state, and many out-of-staters are a bit wide-eyed when they move here. At last count, the state had more than 13,000 taverns, by far the most per capita in the country.

Beer

To disabuse: Wisconsinites do not drink more beer (per capita, anyway) than residents of any other state in the country. Alas, the days of quaffing a brew with breakfast and finding a *biergarten* on every street corner are long gone.

Wisconsin beer drinking began with the hordes of European immigrants. The earliest brewery has been traced back to an 1835 operation in Mineral Point, but there may have been one a few years before that. Though what most early southwestern Wisconsin brewers were making was actually top-fermented malt liquor (which to some aficionados is akin to cutting a porter with antifreeze). Surprisingly, Germans did not initiate Milwaukee's legendary beermaking industry; it was instead a couple of upstarts from the British Isles. But massive German settlement did set the state's beer standard, which no other state could hope to match. By 1850, Milwaukee alone had almost 200 breweries, elevating beermaking to the city's number-one industry. Throughout the state, every town, once it had been platted and while waiting for incorporation, would build three things—a church, a town hall, and a brewery, not necessarily in that order.

The exact number of breweries in the state in the 19th century isn't known, but it is easily in the thousands; up to 50 years ago, local brew was still common. At that time, beermaking went through a decline; industry giants effectively killed off the regional breweries. But by the 1970s, a backlash against the swill water the big brewers passed off as beer sent profits plummeting. In stepped microbreweries and brewpubs. Currently, the nation is going through a renaissance of beer crafting, and Wisconsin is no different; Madison and Milwaukee have numerous brewpubs and a few microbreweries. In other parts of the state, anachronistic old breweries are coming back to the fore, usually with the addition of a restaurant and lots of young professional patrons. Time will tell if this trend marks a permanent national shift toward traditional brews (made according to four-century-old purity laws), or if it's simply a fad.

Some local standards still exist. **Leinenkugel's** (or Leinie's) is the preferred choice of north woods denizens, closely rivaled by Point, which is brewed in Stevens Point. In the southern part of the state, Monroe's Joseph Huber Brewing Company puts out the college-student-standard (cheap but tasty) **Huber**—the Bock is worth the wait. In Middleton, west of Madison, the **Capital Brewery** has been restored to its early-century standards.

Brandy

What really makes a Badger a Badger, drinkwise? Brandy, of any kind. Wisconsin not only leads the nation in brandy consumption, but it's up there with other brandy nations of the world. It is the default drink for bartenders at supper clubs. (The author's father still gets stares from *auslander* wait staff with the very Wisconsin drink request of "brandy old-fashioned with mushrooms, not fruit"—they're surprised by the brandy, not the mushrooms, and they usually get it wrong.) Only in Wisconsin is it as perfectly acceptable to drink brandy from a plastic cup while ice-fishing as at a wedding.

BRANDY OLD-FASHIONED

Here's how to make Wisconsin's fave drink: Put ice cubes in a glass. Add two oz. brandy (any kind you wish), one lump sugar, and one dash cocktail bitters. Fill remaining glass with water or white soda. Top off with fruit or mushrooms.

When the Wisconsin Badgers play a football game on the road, the 30,000-plus cheeseheads who follow generally get newspaper articles written about their bratwurst, post-game polka dancing, and prodigious brandy drinking. In 1993, when the rowdy Badger faithful descended on the Rose Bowl in a friendly invasion, Los Angeles hotels essentially ran dry of brandy; by the time the Badgers returned in 1999 (and again in 2000), local hoteliers had figured it out!

Wisconsinites are decidedly *not* connoisseurs of brandy; you'll never hear discussions of "smoky" versus "plump" varieties, or vintages. Try to chat somebody up about cognac versus brandy in a bar and you'll probably just be met with an empty stare. Nope, stop by a liquor store and most folks will be trudging out with a perfectly average, low-end priced bottle of brandy. And a good number will be walking out with a fruit brandy, a decidedly sweet variation. (For the record, cognac is a spirit distilled from the white wine grapes of Cognac in France; brandy is a more general term for a spirit distilled from wine.)

Wine

Few people would think of snowy Wisconsin as a wine-producing region, but thanks to the temperate climate afforded by the two Great Lakes and a somewhat less severe winter in southern counties, southern wineries can cultivate grapevines, which has resulted in a few decent wines. On Door Peninsula, you'll find the best known of Wisconsin's wineries, **Von Stiehl** in Algoma and the **Door Peninsula Winery** in Sturgeon Bay. Both are well known for their seasonal fruit wines (Door County is one of the nation's top cherry-producing areas). Most other wineries are in southwest Wisconsin.

JACOB LEINENKUGEL BREWING COMPANY

SHOPPING

Pick a direction and point. More than likely you'll be pointing to a cheese store or a cheese and sausage outlet. Thousands of places will ship genuine Wisconsin cheese across the country. And most will also stock foam-rubber cheeseheads—tacky souvenir gift numero uno—as well as innumerable holstein-style black-and-white spotted clothing.

The state's free *Recreation Guide* features page after page of small, family-run dairies and cheese factories, some in antiquated turn-of-the-century buildings. These are the places to buy cheese. Still better places to shop are the fair days—now called farmers' markets—on Saturday (and sometimes one weekday as well) in small towns. Local farmers come into town and sell their vegetables off card tables. It's a regular Saturday institution in Madison and a great experience out in the sticks, where you'll find an unrivaled mix of food and flea market. They're good opportunities to rub elbows with the locals. The state Department of Agriculture, P.O. Box 8911, Madison, WI 53708, maintains a complete listing of state farmers' markets.

Road warriors are generally also interested in antiques and/or artisans' crafts. It's always a tough call to recommend specific galleries (which this author doesn't do) since everything is subjective. However, there are definitely areas that have large populations of artists and/or collectors. Door County in its entirety is an artists' haven and draws millions from around the Midwest annually, most of whom return home with something. For an outstanding and enormous assortment of galleries of all sorts, it's hard to beat Mineral Point in southwestern Wisconsin. It's been recognized by virtually every major medium for its extraordinary diversity in galleries.

If you're in southwestern Wisconsin, head for Amish country. First, savor the wonderful home cooking, especially the pies. Then take a look at the crafted furniture and, especially, quilts. You won't find better anywhere.

For unique shopping, cruise the Great River Road and find your perfect freshwater pearl for a ring, earrings, or necklace; it's a gorgeous, precious thing, and it's perfectly representative of the culture on the river side of Wisconsin.

TRANSPORTATION

BY ROAD

In *Midwest Living* magazine reader surveys, Wisconsin's roadways rank the best in most categories—best roads overall, best maintained, and others. Despite a few problem areas, the state's 110,290 miles of roads are all in pretty good shape. The stretch of I-94 running through Milwaukee is one of the nation's 10 most congested highways, and the resultant transit problems remain unaddressed. The next-worst roads you'll experience are Madison's Beltline Highway and I-90 interchange, both of which, along with Milwaukee's interstates, are inhospitable during rush hours (7-10 a.m. and 4-6:30 p.m.). There are also a few congested spots on US 51 and US 53 in northern Wisconsin. The state

Department of Transportation is now operating under a 20-year plan to improve existing multilane highways and expand certain two-lane highways, including roads linking key tourist centers. These two-lane roads are crucial, as they constitute only four percent of the state's highways but carry 42% of the traffic.

The designation "CR" stands for "County Road" and is always followed by letters. You can determine in advance the general condition of the road by the letters designating it. The road deteriorates in direct proportion to the number of letters. Thus, CR RR will be narrower than CR R—and possibly decaying. County roads are generally paved, but don't be surprised if they're not. State highway numbers are preceded by the abbreviation "WI," federal highways by "US," and interstates with "I."

Regulations and Etiquette

Wisconsin permits radar detectors in cars. There is a mandatory motorcycle helmet law for persons under 18 years old. All vehicle passengers are required by law to wear seatbelts. Child restraints are mandatory for children under four.

The speed limit on Wisconsin interstates is 65 mph, reduced to 55 mph in metropolitan areas. Milwaukee's fringes are well monitored, so be forewarned. You can travel 65 mph on some four-lane highways in the northern part of the state, to the relief of many travelers.

Drivers in the state are very courteous. In fact, many acquaintances of this author have grumbled about the, er, *methodical* pace of Wisconsin traffic. The interstate arteries surrounding larger cities, especially Milwaukee, are the only places conducive to speeding.

Road Conditions

The state Department of Transportation maintains a **road condition hotline,** (800) ROAD-WIS, detailing the conditions of all major roads across the state; it also has construction delays listed. The department updates its website (www.dot.state.wi.us/dsp/road-cond.html) four times a day.

It's important to winterize your vehicle while driving in Wisconsin. Always keep your antifreeze level prepared for temperatures of 35 below (half water, half fluid usually suffices). Most important: keep a full tank of gas.

BY AIR

The major U.S. airlines have few direct domestic flights into Wisconsin; you almost always have to stop first in Chicago, Minneapolis, St. Louis, or another major hub. Ticket prices vary wildly depending on when you travel and, more important, when you purchase the ticket. Every so often, the major carriers have so-called fare wars, which drive prices way down. However, you usually have to fly within a spec-

ified period and purchase tickets in advance. Prices are predictably higher around the major holidays (4th of July, Thanksgiving, Christmas) and to southern destinations in winter, while other times you can fly for around $400 from the West Coast, slightly less from the East Coast; sometimes you can get tickets for half that! The best way to find out about deals is through a travel agent or, yes, mucking about on the Internet.

Milwaukee's Mitchell International Airport is the only international airport in the state and the only airport offering direct flights across the country. The very wonderful Midwest Express is the key carrier to the city and state. Other airlines serving the airport include **Delta,** tel. (414) 223-4770 or (800) 221-1212; **Northwest,** tel. (800) 225-2525; **America West** and **America West Express,** tel. (800) 235-9292; **American** and **American Eagle,** tel. (800) 433-7300; **American Trans Air,** tel. (800) 225-2995; **Comair,** tel. (800) 354-9822; **Continental** and **Continental Express,** tel. (414) 342-3099 or (800) 523-3273; **KLM,** tel. (800) 374-7747; **Lufthansa,** tel. (800) 645-3880; **Northwest,** tel. (800) 225-2525; **Skyway,** tel. (414) 747-4646 or (800) 452-2022;

WISCONSIN DRIVING DISTANCES

© AVALON TRAVEL PUBLISHING, INC.

TWA and **TWA Express,** tel. (414) 933-8292 or (800) 221-2000; **United** and **United Express,** tel. (800) 241-6522; **USAirways** and **USAirways Express,** tel. (800) 428-4322; and **Virgin Atlantic,** tel. (800) 862-8261.

Madison, Green Bay, Stevens Point/Wausau, La Crosse, Oshkosh, Eau Claire, Marinette, Rhinelander, Appleton, and a few other minor locations are served by intrastate airlines, often branches of the major carriers. Memorial Day to Labor Day in Eagle River and Minocqua/Woodruff, **Trans-North Aviation,** 3418 Park Dr., Sturgeon Bay, WI 54235-9011, tel. (920) 743-6952, operates a once-daily shuttle Thurs.-Fri. and Sun.-Mon. to and from Chicago's Palwaukee Airport (along Milwaukee Ave. in Wheeling, west of Tri-State Toll Road 294). The fare is $100.

Midwest Express is a Milwaukee-based service with direct flights and undoubtedly the best service in the country. Imagine two-person-wide leather seats throughout the cabin, exquisite meals (cookies baked on board!), and genuinely solicitous service. If you call at least 36 hours in advance, you can choose from an amazing gourmet menu. The prices are competitive, too, on nonstop flights to Atlanta, Boston, Columbus, Cleveland, Dallas/Fort Worth, Denver, Kansas City, Grand Rapids, Las Vegas, Los Angeles, Newark, La Guardia (NYC), Philadelphia, San Diego, San Francisco, Washington D.C., and seasonal flights to Tampa, Fort Lauderdale, Fort Meyers, and Phoenix. The airline offers excellent package deals including tickets, rental car, and accommodations from a dozen major U.S. cities. For information on Midwest Express, call (414) 747-4646 or (800) 452-2022.

BY BUS

Greyhound, tel. (800) 231-2222, operates in all major Wisconsin cities, if somewhat irregularly. In the northern counties, a few regional carriers serve Michigan's Upper Peninsula. The communities of Janesville, Beloit, Racine, Kenosha, Milwaukee, and Bayfield Peninsula have bus systems linking nearby communities. Madison and Milwaukee are linked by the oft-running **Badger Bus,** tel. (608) 255-6771. **Van Galder,** tel. (800) 747-0994, operates between Chicago and Madison, making stops at Wisconsin communities along the way. Chicago and Milwaukee are linked via Kenosha and Racine by **United Limo,** tel. (800) 833-5555, and **Wisconsin Coach Lines,** tel. (800) 236-2015.

BY TRAIN

Amtrak, tel. (800) 872-7245, operates about 20 trains through Wisconsin. The long-distance **Empire Builder** originates in Chicago and runs through Milwaukee, Columbus, Portage, Wisconsin Dells, Sturtevant, Tomah, and La Crosse on its way to Seattle/Portland.

The very controversial, interminably debated **Hiawatha** is an on-again, off-again train that travels between Milwaukee and downtown Chicago; at present, it runs four times daily. In 2000 Amtrak somewhat inexplicably initiated service from Chicago to Janesville, WI and from Milwaukee to Fond du Lac (the latter route was still a through-bus as this was being prepared). Many Midwestern states are beginning discussions about creating a Midwest rail network, with Chicago as the hub and Milwaukee as one of many branches. Express light rail between Madison and Milwaukee will probably be debated until the end of time.

Several old steam engines traverse portions of the state, including great trips from New Freedom through the Baraboo Valley and through the Nicolet National Forest.

BY WATER

The **SS *Badger,*** the only active passenger/car steamship left on the Great Lakes, is a fantastic way to experience Lake Michigan. It runs on a daily basis in season between Manitowoc, Wisconsin, and Ludington, Michigan.

On a much smaller scale, one of the few remaining interstate ferries left in America, the **Cassville Car Ferry,** operates seasonally in southwestern Wisconsin. It shuttles passengers across the Mississippi River between Wisconsin and Iowa.

With 1,000 miles of Mississippi River and Great Lakes shoreline, Wisconsin is entered easily in your own craft. Racine has the Great Lakes' largest marina, and every community along both Lake Michigan and Lake Superior offers slips and rentals.

MONEY, MEASUREMENTS, AND COMMUNICATION

MONEY

Wisconsinites are taxed to high heaven, but in general travelers don't have to share the burden; the state doesn't even have toll roads. Prices in general are lower in Wisconsin than in the rest of the country, and gasoline here is usually cheaper than anywhere else in the Midwest except maybe Iowa. Once you get out into the rural areas, prices for goods and services are absolutely dirt cheap. Wisconsin's sales tax is five percent. Some counties or cities can tack on an additional half percent. There may also be additional room taxes.

Traveler's checks are accepted in most hotels and motels; those that don't take them are few and far between, usually the low-end places. Some restaurants will accept them, others won't—inquire ahead of time. Credit cards are widely accepted in cities, but the number of places guaranteed to take them slips in direct proportion to how far out into the rural areas you go.

Automatic Teller Machines (ATMs) are found adjacent to most every bank in cities and towns; actually, they're absolutely everywhere these days. Remember that you're probably going to get $1 or $1.50 tacked on to *each* transaction; Madison seems to be the only place where you can still find fee-free terminals.

Exchanging foreign currency can be a bit more problematic; Wisconsin will never be confused with an international banking center. If you arrive with foreign currency, it may be difficult to exchange it for U.S. dollars. Banks in Madison and Milwaukee will often have just one branch that deals with moneychanging. (For example, the M&I Bank branch handling currency exchange in Madison is the one in the Hilldale Shopping Mall, 1 W Main St., Madison, tel. 608-242-5885.) In smaller cities, such as Green Bay, La Crosse, and Appleton, it isn't advisable to arrive with foreign currency.

MEASUREMENTS

Voltage
Electrical outlets in the U.S. run on a 110V or 120V AC. Most plugs are either two flat prongs or two flat and one round. Transformers and adapters for 220V appliances are available in hardware or electronics stores.

The Metric System
Let's just say it doesn't come up a whole lot in Wisconsin. Foreign visitors can reference the U.S.-Metric Conversion Table in the back of this book for help with distance and temperature conversions.

COMMUNICATIONS

Time Zones
All of Wisconsin falls on Central Standard Time, which is six hours earlier than Greenwich Mean Time. However, if you plan a trip north of the border into Michigan's Upper Peninsula, you'll enter the Eastern Standard zone, which is one hour ahead of CST.

Postal Service
Generally, post offices are open 8 a.m.- 6 p.m. weekdays. Some branches may open or close an hour earlier or later, and a few main offices have Saturday-morning hours. Post offices are *rarely* open past 6 p.m.

If you need mail sent to you while traveling in Wisconsin, have it addressed to you c/o General Delivery in the specified city, with the corresponding zip code (ask the post office if you're unsure of the zip code). Poste restante mail is held for 10 days. You'll need a 33-cent stamp to mail a letter weighing one ounce or less within the U.S.; postcards require only 20 cents postage. Letter-weight postage overseas starts at 60 cents (less for Canada).

Privately owned shipping services—**Mail Boxes, Etc.** is one international chain—ship packages via U.S. mail or private shippers such as United Parcel Service and Federal Express. These stores are often open later than post offices and offer fax and photocopying services, as well.

Telephone

Wisconsin has five area codes. Currently, Milwaukee and most of southeastern Wisconsin are in the 414 area; areas immediately outside of Milwaukee are 262 area code; Madison and the southwestern and south-central regions fall in the 608 area code; and the rest—most of the northwest—lies in the 715 area code. All else is area code 920.

Public pay phones are widely available on street corners and outside convenience stores and gas stations. Maintained by a variety of private companies, pay phones cost 30 or 35 cents for local calls. You can use any combination of silver coins, but if you put in two quarters, you won't get change. Dialing directions are usually provided on the face of the phone. If you're stumped, simply dial "0" for an operator who will direct your call, but expect to pay an additional $1-2 charge. When using a universal calling card, follow the instructions on the back of the card, or dial "0" for operator assistance.

SERVICES AND INFORMATION

For information on anything and everything in the state, contact the **Wisconsin Department of Tourism,** tel. (608) 266-2161, 123 W. Washington Ave., P.O. Box 7976, Madison, WI 53707. You can also call the office at (800) 372-2737 Mon.-Fri. 8 a.m.-4:30 p.m. or (800) 432-8747 every day, around the clock.

Wisconsin's tourism department website (www.travelwisconsin.com) has garnered accolades for its design and practical information, including information on events, attractions, and recreational facilities. It also features links to nonprofit tourism organizations' websites.

The state operates eight information centers along major highways entering Wisconsin from neighboring Iowa, Minnesota, Illinois, and Michigan. In addition, there's a Wisconsin information office in downtown Chicago at 342 N. Michigan Avenue.

Freebies

The Department of Tourism hands out reams of worthwhile free publications. Request the *Wisconsin Recreation Guide,* an 80-page rundown of every conceivable recreation highlight in the state, including cheese factory tours, NFL summer camps, sleigh rides, and houseboat vacations. The fairly new *Wisconsin Biking Guide* is better than most current books on the subject. If you're into the bed and breakfast experience, the state's catalog-size *B&B Guide* features plenty of information. There are also seasonal events catalogs, golf course directories, private campground lists, fishing locations lists, good heritage and ethnic travel information, private lodging directories, and state park information.

MAPS

You can get a decent Department of Transportation state road map free by calling the state Department of Tourism hotline. County and state highway maps (scale: half inch equals one mile) are available for 50 cents (county) or $1.50 (state) from Wisconsin Department of Transportation Map Sales, 3617 Pierstorff St., P.O. Box 7713, Madison, WI 53707. The best maps for snooping around the state are those contained in the *Wisconsin Atlas and Gazetteer,* available from any outdoors store or direct from the **DeLorme Mapping Co.,** P.O. Box 298, Freeport, ME 04032, tel. (207) 865-4171. On a somewhat smaller scale than topo maps, the maps in this 100-page, large-format book are absolutely indispensable for exploring the back roads.

Topographic, planimetric, and 7.5-minute quadrangle maps can be obtained from the **Wisconsin Geological and Natural History Survey,** 3817 Mineral Point Rd., Madison, WI 53705, tel. (608) 263-7389. Seven-and-a-half- or 15-minute maps cost $3.50 each. County topographical maps (1:1,000,000 scale) are available for $4 each.

Obtain upper Mississippi River navigation charts from the **U.S. Army Engineer District,** P.O. Box 2004, Rock Island, IL, 61204. They cost $7 plus $5.50 for first-class shipping. Lake Winnebago, Fox River, and Great Lakes maps are also available from the **Distribution Division, National Ocean Service,** Riverdale, MD 20737.

MEDIA

The only publication that covers Wisconsin on a macro scale is the monthly magazine *Wisconsin Trails,* P.O. Box 5650, Madison, WI 53691. It's a slick periodical with a nice balance of road warrior personality and nostalgia. It dispenses with the political and social and just focuses on where and when to go, providing lots of good cultural bits and stunning photography. *Midwest Living* magazine, another monthly, features Wisconsin regularly. More for the conservation-minded, *Wisconsin Natural Resources,* 101 S. Webster St., Madison WI 53702, is published by the state DNR. The well-put-together periodical features detailed natural history and is so well-written and -photographed that it might let you truly understand and appreciate science for the first time.

Newspapers

In 1995, the *Milwaukee Journal* and *Milwaukee Sentinel* melded into the high-quality *Journal Sentinel,* the largest and best of Wisconsin's newspapers. This leaves Madison as the only major Wisconsin city with two papers—the morning *Wisconsin State Journal* and the afternoon *Capital Times*—but there's no telling how long the afternoon daily will last. In general, folks consider the former more conservative, the latter more liberal.

Internet

If you need to log on, you generally have two choices: the public library or a local business services and copy shop like Kinko's. Internet cafes are essentially nonexistent in Wisconsin thus far, even in Madison and Milwaukee, at least in areas where tourists can expect to be.

The library is a good option, but there are some drawbacks. First, local libraries are usually among the first to suffer budget cuts and therefore have restricted hours, and often no hours on weekends. Second, you may have to go through the annoying process of signing up for a library card before you can log on. Thus, it's often best to head for a local Kinko's and pay for the Internet time, especially because those places are open 24-7.

WEATHER AND ROAD INFORMATION

Many communities broadcast weather information in a variety of locations. You can also call (800) ROAD-WIS (within Wisconsin and from contiguous states only) for a report on detours, road closures, accidents, and, perhaps most important, winter road conditions. The state has 50 phone lines, so even during the brunt of a blizzard, you should be able to get through. For similar information in Madison, call (608) 246-7580; in Milwaukee, call (414) 785-7140.

Weather information is also updated frequently on the Department of Transportation website (www.dot.state.wi.us/dsp/roadcond.html).

SOUTHEASTERN WISCONSIN

Ironically, the gateway to the state—Wisconsin's southeastern quadrant—wasn't the first entry point for paleolithic hunters or white explorers. The area didn't beget the state, it simply perpetuated it. Steamships laden with European immigrants landed at Milwaukee and the southern ports, making southeastern Wisconsin the site of the state's major population centers, where some 90% of Wisconsinites live today. Major manufacturing industries, reliant on cheap labor and water transportation, also established themselves here, giving the state its only real Rust Belt presence.

In Wisconsin's southeastern tier, the trees have long since been felled, replaced by agricultural tracts on the fecund glacial till. Since within a short bike trip one can find towering skyscrapers, ethnic neighborhoods, and classic pastoral dairyland, southeastern Wisconsin may best represent the state itself.

KENOSHA

Kenosha generally evokes images of steel-gray skies punctuated by factory smokestacks and blaring work whistles. Though its primary employer for decades was an automobile plant, Kenosha belies that blue-collar stereotype. In fact, in 1998, *Reader's Digest* declared it the second-best "Family Friendly City" in the U.S. (Sheboygan, WI, was first). The southernmost Lake Michigan port in Wisconsin, it offers endless stretches of inspiring littoral parkland (the city owns eight out of 10 lakefront plots), lots of blue sky, and an appealing array of early-century buildings mixed with careful gentrification. In 2000, as this book was being updated, the city was in fact gutting a 69-acre theretofore blighted zone downtown to put in greenspace, a promenade, a farmers' market, trolley lines, and new residential area. It already looked splendid.

History
New Englanders first inhabited this region in 1835, naming their town for Pike Creek, which flows through the northern section; the name was later changed to Kenosha. Though farming was the primary draw, a harbor and docks made it a permanent lake port. The town would never rival Milwaukee or Racine since its harbor—even after extensive and costly improvements—still proved less amenable to large ships.

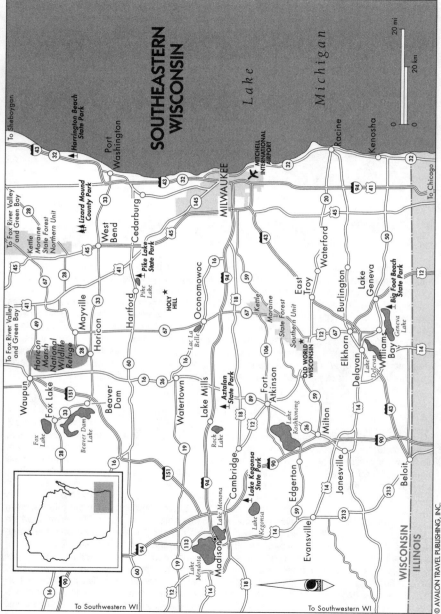

SOUTHEASTERN WISCONSIN

Lake Michigan

To Sheboygan

Harrington Beach State Park

Port Washington

MITCHELL INTERNATIONAL AIRPORT

MILWAUKEE

Racine

Kenosha

To Chicago

Lizard Mound County Park

To Fox River Valley and Green Bay

Kettle Moraine State Forest Northern Unit

West Bend

Cedarburg

Mayville

Hartford

Pike Lake State Park

Pike Lake

HOLY HILL

Oconomowoc

Horicon

Lac La Belle

To Fox River Valley and Green Bay

Horicon Marsh National Wildlife Refuge

Waupun

Fox Lake

Beaver Dam

Fox Lake

Beaver Dam Lake

Watertown

Lake Mills

Kettle Moraine State Forest Southern Unit

East Troy

Waterford

Burlington

Lake Geneva

Big Foot Beach State Park

Elkhorn

Delavan

Lake Delavan

Williams Bay

Geneva Lake

OLD WORLD WISCONSIN

Fort Atkinson

Aztalan State Park

Rock Lake

Lake Koshkonong

Milton

Beloit

Cambridge

Lake Kegonsa State Park

Edgerton

Janesville

Lake Monona

Madison

Lake Mendota

Lake Kegonsa

Evansville

WISCONSIN
ILLINOIS

To Southwestern WI

To Southwestern WI

20 mi

20 km

© AVALON TRAVEL PUBLISHING, INC.

Major growth did not occur until after the Civil War, when a tannery and a wagon factory became the first large-scale manufacturing plants in the city. By the turn of the century, over 100 modest to large factories employed a quarter of the city's population (then around 21,000). Kenosha remains an industrial linchpin for Wisconsin today; manufacturing falls a close third to retail and service industries in the economy. The hardy city of 84,000 is also gaining a reputation as a center for fishing and shopping.

SIGHTS

Orientation
The grid system within Kenosha offers no special difficulties. Streets run east-west, avenues north-south. Numbers for the avenues start at the lake-front and rise as you go west. Numbers for streets begin at the Racine/Kenosha County line to the north and rise to the south. The major arteries into town are: WI 50 (75th Street), WI 158 (52nd Street), and WI 142S.

Bristol Renaissance Faire
Brigands, knights, mimes, and maidens wander the 30-acre grounds done up in 16th-century medieval style south of Kenosha for the Bristol Renaissance Faire, and more than 15 stages and 200 artisan and demonstration areas feature garbed drama. The Faire is open late June to late August 10 a.m.-7 p.m., rain or shine. For information, call (847) 395-7773. Admission is $15, $14 for students and those over age 54, $7 ages 5-12. To reach the Faire, take I-94 south of Kenosha to Exit 347 (Russell Road). Signs lead the way from there; the address is 12420 128th St.—right on the Wisconsin-Illinois border.

Carthage College
Picturesque Carthage College is a school of liberal arts and sciences affiliated with the Evangelical Lutheran Church. It was established in 1847. The **Palumbo Civil War Museum,** in the college's art gallery, displays worthy antebellum and war memorabilia. Free to the public, it's open Sept.-May by appointment. The college is at 2001 Alford Dr. north of town along WI 32 on the lake, tel. (262) 551-8500.

Farmers' Markets
Every day of the week from June through November, the farmers' market occupies a different spot. On **Monday,** head to Roosevelt Park, 68th St. and 34th Ave.; **Tuesday,** Union Park, 7th Ave. and 45th St.; **Wednesday,** Columbus Park, 22nd Ave. and 54th St.; **Thursday,** Lincoln Park, 18th Ave. off 70th St.; **Friday,** Baker Park, 66th St. and Sheridan Rd. On **Saturday,** it returns to Columbus Park. The markets offer mostly food and some craft items. Participation increases dramatically in the summer months. For more information call (262) 605-6700.

Harmony Hall
This Tudor-style mansion at 6315 3rd Ave., tel. (262) 653-8440, sits in a lovely setting by the lake. It's home to the **Heritage Hall Museum of**

SOUTHEASTERN WISCONSIN HIGHLIGHTS

Aztalan State Park, Lake Mills

Clown Hall of Fame, Delavan

Danish *Kringle,* Racine

Golden Rondelle Theater, Racine

Harley-Davidson Plant, Milwaukee

Hoard Museum and Dairy Shrine, Fort Atkinson

Horicon Marsh National Wildlife Refuge and Wildlife Area

Kemper Center, Kenosha

Kettle Moraine State Forest

Lake Geneva

Logan Museum of Anthropology, Beloit

Memorial Union Terrace, Madison

Miller Beer, Milwaukee

Milwaukee County Zoo, Milwaukee

Milwaukee Public Museum, Milwaukee

Pabst Mansion, Milwaukee

Picnic Point, Madison

Rotary Gardens, Janesville

The Domes, Milwaukee

Tiffany Bridge, Tiffany

University of Wisconsin Arboretum, Madison

Wild West Museum, Elkhorn

Wisconsin State Capitol, Madison

Barbershop Harmony, a small video theater, and the headquarters of the Society for the Preservation and Encouragement of Barber Shop Quartet Singing in America. Free tours are available year-round weekdays 9 a.m.-4 p.m.

Historic Districts

Kenosha has three major historic districts. The visitors bureau has extensive information on each. The **Library Park District,** between 59th and 62nd Streets and 6th Avenue and Sheridan Road, was once the site of homes on the

Underground Railroad, now marked by a plaque. It was patterned after New England communities with village commons (and was originally even called the Commons). In addition to the mishmash of architectural styles, visitors can view the birthplace of Orson Welles at 6116 7th Ave.

East of the Library Park District and fronting the lake between 61st and 66th Streets, the **Third Avenue District** is the most popular historic stroll. It features Kemper Hall, the Anderson Arts Center, Harmony Hall, and most of the ornate mansions of the wealthy early-century citizens.

Northwest of the Library Park District, roughly between 55th and 58th Streets and 8th and 11th Avenues, the **Civic Center District** was the first district to undergo massive experimental civic rejuvenation, during the late 19th century. As part of a "City Beautiful" campaign, this district has been credited with effecting political reform. Numerous buildings are exquisite examples of period architecture; even the post office is a neoclassical revival gem. Highlights now include the Kenosha Public Museum, the county courthouse, a miniature Statue of Liberty in Civic Center Park, and the Kenosha Area Convention and Visitors Bureau.

Kemper Center

One of seven gorgeous county parks—most of them right on the lake—this is among the largest, at 18 acres, and the only one in the nation listed in its entirety on the National Register of Historic Places. The Gothic Revival and Italianate antebellum hall was originally a school for girls but now serves as a multipurpose center for the city. Its grounds include an arboretum with over 100 species of flora (including more than 100 types of roses and a flower and herb garden designed for those without sight), numerous tennis courts, and a handicapped-accessible fishing pier. Also in the park is the impressive **Anderson Arts Center,** 121 66th St., open Tues. and Thurs.-Sun 1-5 p.m., grounds open dawn 'til dusk.

Kenosha County History Center

Located in the Third Avenue Historic District, just north of the Kemper Center grounds, this organization, in operation since the 1870s, is housed in a Colonial Revival mansion. The permanent collections include decorative and folk arts, toys, and artifacts of the previous century, and there's a Victorian ensemble and exhibits on ethnocultural highlights of the past three centuries. An interesting exhibit highlights Kenosha's impact on America's early transportation industry (it was a major automobile manufacturing center). The center, 6300 Third Ave., tel. (262) 654-5770, is open Tues.-Fri. 10 a.m.-4:30 p.m., weekends 2-4:30 p.m.

Outlet Malls

Shopping in Kenosha is a sight in itself—a big reason many trek here. At the junction of I-94 and WI 50, the **Factory Outlet Center** is an amalgamation of 110 factory shops dispensing clothing, shoes, clothing, electronics, clothing, outerwear, clothing, and other miscellaneous items dirt cheap. **Prime Outlets,** near the junction of I-94 and WI 164, has a mere 76 stores featuring mostly—you may have guessed—clothing.

Kenosha Public Museum

The Kenosha Public Museum, 56th St. at 1st Ave., tel. (414) 656-8026, is the rectangular edifice downtown with the Doric columns in front; note however that by the time you read this the whole shebang should have moved eastward near the lake. Exhibits include details on Wisconsin's natural history, especially the geology, flora, and fauna. Its most exciting exhibit is on the Schaeffer Mammoth, the oldest butchered mammoth found in the Western Hemisphere; the bones date to 12,000 years ago, and it helped prove human existence during that era. Other sections feature priceless ivory and carved Oriental artworks, African masks, and Native American artifacts. A popular recent addition is a life-size *Deinonychus* dinosaur, a rival for the resident black bear. By the time you read this, the museum will also have numerous interactive exhibits. The museum is open Mon.-Fri. 9 a.m.-5 p.m., Saturday 9 a.m.-4 p.m. in summer (closes earlier on Saturdays after November 1) and Sunday 1-4 p.m. Free admission.

Parks

Over a half dozen gorgeous parks line the Lake Michigan lakefront in Kenosha. **Lincoln Park,** along 22nd Ave. to the south of 75th St., is one of the most picturesque, but you really can't go wrong at any of them. The city owns over three-quarters of the lakefront acreage and has converted most of it into greenspace. **Southport Marina,** 58th St. at 3rd Ave., features Wolfenbuttel Park, with tot playgrounds, picnic areas, a public beach, a beautiful garden, lakefront promenade, and a unique children's water fountain.

University of Wisconsin-Parkside

A University of Wisconsin extension, UW-Parkside has greenhouse-style walkways. The campus also offers cross-country skiing and nature trails for visitors. Central campus buildings are along Wood Road in the 900 block. Located next to the campus is **Petrifying Springs Park,** the oldest county park, with picnic areas and over seven miles of trails for walking, biking, or cross-country skiing.

ACCOMMODATIONS

Under $50

Most of Kenosha's hotels and motels are found along I-94 west of town, along WI 50 (75th Street), and on 122nd and 118th Avenues. Cheaper options are north along WI 32 between Kenosha and Racine.

The least expensive lodging in Kenosha is probably the **Beach-Aire Motel,** 1147 Sheridan Rd., tel. (262) 552-8131. It offers swimming along the lake, free coffee, and rates from around $30.

$50 to $75

The **Knight's Inn,** 7221 122nd Ave., tel. (262) 857-2622, has more than 100 guest rooms, a dozen or so with kitchenettes. Rooms go for around $45 s or d. The **Days Inn,** 12121 75th St., tel. (262) 857-2311, has an indoor/outdoor pool, jacuzzi, a dining room open all night, and rates from $50.

$75 to $100

You'll get great views at the **Holiday Inn Harborside,** 5125 6th Ave., tel. (262) 658-3281, right on the lake. It has 110 rooms, an indoor pool, jacuzzi, whirlpool, wading pool, and restaurant with lounge and nightclub. Rates are $89 s or d.

A few of the 115 units at the **Best Western Executive Inn,** 7220 122nd Ave., tel. (262) 857-7699, are multi-room patio suites. Amenities include an indoor pool, jacuzzi, sauna, a lounge, in-room coffee, and free continental breakfast. Rates are $80.

Camping

The closest decent public campground is at the mammoth, 4,500-acre **Bong State Recreation Area,** tel. (262) 652-0377, along WI 142, a mile west of WI 75 in Brighton, about 25 minutes northwest of Kenosha. One of the oddest state parks in Wisconsin, it's named after a famed WW II ace and was slated to be an Air Force base. Therefore, it's not surprising that you'll see hang gliders, parasailors, and remote-controlled planes buzzing around. A visitor center features exhibits and maps detailing recreation opportunities. Dozens of ponds and lakes dot the recreation area, and 15 miles of trail wind through diverse terrain. There are three family campgrounds, 217 sites total, some with electricity.

About 10 miles west of Kenosha, in Bristol, is the private **Happy Acres,** tel. (414) 857-7373. It has over 150 campsites and a separate tent area. Sites cost $21 and up. To get there, head north on US 45 from its junction with WI 50, then west on CR NN.

FOOD

Taste of Wisconsin

Don't bypass this original family restaurant, so popular it provides catering service to several local hostelries and shopping centers. The post-and-beam construction, fieldstone fireplace, and antique barn trimmings smack of rich north woods history, and all the refurbished, relocated furnishings come from Wisconsin farms. But the menu outdoes the surroundings—a pan-ethnic foray into Wisconsin's immigration history. Everything down to the syrup is from Wisconsin: New Glarus beer, Door County cherries, Bayfield apples, and Jackson County cranberry pie. An attached shop dispenses Wisconsin cheese, sausage, and assorted foodstuffs. At 7515 125th Ave., tel. (262) 857-9110, Taste of Wisconsin is open daily for breakfast, lunch, and dinner. Selections from $5.

Fish Fry

Lots of pubs and family-style restaurants have fish fries; figure $7 for all-you-can-eat. Decent are the ones at **Boathouse Pub and Eatery,** 4917 7th Ave., tel. (262) 654-9922, and **Hobnob,** 277 S. Sheridan Rd., tel. (262) 552-8008, which some say is actually in Racine since it lies directly between the two towns.

Try the **Italian American Club,** 2217 52nd St., tel. (262) 658-3177, for an old-fashioned Friday-night fry. The place also serves Italian dishes, including wicked Sicilian-style pork chops.

Quick Bites and Greasy Spoons

The greatest diner in America? Never seen a better one than **Frank's Diner,** 508 58th St., right downtown—purportedly the oldest one in the United States. It's a cubbyhole caboose chock-full of authors poring over manuscripts, businessfolk chatting, and a gum-cracking staff busy chiding the chowderheads. Refill your own coffee—but you have to refill everybody else's cup too! Dishes from, say, a buck.

Here's a joint to get a quick bratwurst, that key to Wisconsin culture. **The Brat Stop,** I-94 and WI 50, has great brats and a full menu; it's also got three separate bar areas, lots of imports, and live entertainment weekends. Menu items from $2.50.

Steakhouses and Supper Clubs

Since the early '30s, **Ray Radigans,** 11712 S. Sheridan Rd., tel. (262) 694-0455, has been a supper club and lounge. It offers freshly prepared steaks and seafood, which has a particularly devoted following. Entrée highlights include crushed black peppercorn pork chops, roast Wisconsin duckling, and daily specials (always including a vegetarian choice). Open for lunch and dinner daily except Monday. From $6.

Bohemian

There's not much left of this wonderful cooking style, a pastiche of German, Polish, and Serbian cuisine. But Kenosha has **Little Europe at Timber Ridge,** 6613 120th Ave., tel. (262) 857-2925, along a frontage road near I-94. The many styles of pork are the specialty, but you can get hearty stews, dumplings, and a wonderful Bohemian meatloaf. From $7.

German

The **House of Gerhard,** 3927 75th St., tel. (262) 694-5212, specializes in German fare but occasionally offers an "American" specialty. The interior is strictly Old World. It's open Mon.-Fri. for lunch and dinner and Saturday for dinner only. From $6.

Similar prices at the **Candlelight Club,** 3927 75th St., tel. (262) 658-3738, a supper club with Teutonic delights like *rouladen, kessler ripchen,* and the like. Open for dinner daily except Tuesday.

Italian

While Racine is Danish to the core, Kenosha is distinctly Italian. Travelers would be remiss not to visit **Mangia,** 5517 Sheridan Rd., tel. (262) 652-4285, while in town. Open daily for dinner, it's regularly praised by culinary scribes but hasn't rested on its laurels. One of the finest simple restaurants in the state, this basic trattoria pushes out unbeatable wood-fired pizzas and exquisitely done pastas, meats, and roasted entrées from $9. It's a regular stop for gourmands from both Milwaukee and the equidistant Windy City.

Some say the most authentic Italian comes from longtime fave **Tenuta's Deli,** 3203 52nd St., tel. (262) 657-9001, open Mon.-Sat. 9 a.m.-9 p.m., Sunday until 6 p.m. A good place to stop if you're in a hurry, it's got a smattering of pastas, salads, and ready-made entrées. It's also an outstanding Italian grocery store. Dishes from $4.

Asian

Whey Chai, 510 57th St., tel. (262) 654-6300, is primarily a Chinese eatery but also offers some Thai fare. The lunch combos are cheap and worth the money. **Panda,** 8021 22nd Ave., tel. (262) 652-0010, has Sichuan-style Chinese with good specials and low-fat and vegetarian options. Both from $5.

On the Waterfront

Operated by a family that lives to fish, the **Boathouse Pub and Eatery,** 4917 7th Ave, tel. (262) 654-9922, sports a harborside dining room and an outdoor veranda for alfresco dining. A full menu, including lots of fresh seafood and 25 different sandwiches, and lots of entertainment are all found here. Lots of Long Island Iced Teas are on the bar menu; a smokehouse puts out good smoked fish. Choices from $5.

Overlooking the harborfront, **Villa D'Carlo,** 5140 6th Ave., tel (262) 654-3932, features Italian and American dishes with a hefty number of steaks and pizzas. Anglers often have their catch grilled here. Menu items from $5.

Overlooking Lake Michigan between Kenosha and Racine is **Hob Nob,** WI 32, tel (262) 552-8008. Hob Nob is a steaks and prime rib place with live jazz Friday nights and a Saturday night piano bar. Dishes from $8.

Brewpubs

Kenosha's only brewpub, **Brewmaster's,** 4017 80th St., tel. (262) 694-9050, has good food and a regular array of live music. It's housed in a renovated masonry barn with plenty of rough cedar and polished brass everywhere. Selections from $6.

ENTERTAINMENT AND EVENTS

Events

Two of the largest annual events revolve around shopping (no surprise in this city of factory outlets); over Memorial Day weekend, Fourth of July, and Labor Day weekend, the **Prime Outlets** and other outlet malls have enormous tent sales. In June, **Cohorama** draws thousands for a coho fishing derby and festival. Several art fairs and festivals come to town in July. In early August, at the five-day **Kenosha County Fair**, locals and visitors enjoy displays, rides, and carnival games. Later that month, the **Polkafest** celebrates the state's official dance.

Spectator Sports

Kenosha has the oldest operating velodrome in the United States. Every Tuesday in summer, the **Kenosha Velodrome**, at WI 142 and 18th Ave., has bike races at 7 p.m.

Sound and Stage

October through May, the **Kenosha Symphony Orchestra**, tel. (262) 654-9080, performs a season of classical music and boasts a quarterly slate of nationally renowned guest musicians. Performances are held at Reuther Central High School Auditorium.

The **Lakeside Players Theater**, 514 56th St., tel. (262) 657-7529, puts on a full season of plays in an old opera house fronting Lake Michigan.

Mid-June through August the **Kenosha Pops** and other entertainers put on free shows at the Sesquicentennial Bandshell, 35th St. and 7th Ave.

RECREATION

Charter Fishing

As of 1994, Kenosha sportfishing rated number one in terms of fish caught per hour. As for trout and salmon, it may be even better.

Before setting out, it's worth the time to investigate captains and charter operations, since you'll be the one spending an entire afternoon on the water with a captain and crew. One person's dream crew is another's ship from hell.

The most consistent periods for fishing are the last two weeks of May and the first two weeks of June. These present the greatest opportunity to catch all species of coho salmon, rainbow trout, king salmon, brown trout, and lake trout. From late July to mid-September, you can catch all of these except coho.

Rates vary but average around $275 for a weekend five-hour charter with four or fewer people. Charters generally run 6 a.m.-1 p.m. or 1-6 p.m. Lots of package deals are available; a weekend overnight with six people runs up to $145 per person.

Kenosha is well represented with a fleet of over 20 charter captains. Contact them at (800) 522-6699.

Trails

The **Pike Trail** runs 14 miles south along Lake Michigan to the Illinois border and through **Chiwaukee Prairie** (near Carol Beach), the only unbroken stretch of mixed-grass prairie in Wisconsin. The prairie is home to more than 400 native plant species, including the endangered pink milkwort. The area is now protected as both a National Natural Landmark and a State Natural Area. The trail also goes north to Racine. Eventually one will be able to bike from the Illinois border north through Milwaukee to Cedarburg, Grafton, and who knows how much farther north? The trails at UW-Parkside run through an arboretum and nature center. Travelers can also enjoy hiking Bong State Recreation Area trails (see "Camping," above).

SERVICES AND INFORMATION

You'll encounter solicitous and chatty folks at the **Kenosha Area Convention and Visitors Bureau**, 812 56th St., tel. (262) 654-7307 or (800) 654-7309, www.kenoshacvb.com. It's open Mon.-Fri. 8 a.m.-4:30 p.m. and maintains a 24-hour information line at (414) 658-4FUN.

A **Wisconsin Travel Information Center**, tel. (262) 857-7164, is near Kenosha on I-94 north of the Illinois state line.

The *Kenosha Daily News* is a respectable daily for a city Kenosha's size. It costs 50 cents a copy. The Friday edition features a "Get Out" section with rundowns on entertainment and current happenings.

The **post office** is just off the corner of 56th St. and 8th Ave. in the Civic Center District.

Kenosha's **Simmons Library** is at 711 59th Place, tel. (262) 942-3700. **Southport Bank,** 7027 Green Bay Rd., tel. (262) 942-1111, is the only locally owned bank in Kenosha—and they give you fresh-baked cookies! If you've got **laundry** to do, Midwest Laundries, 1730 22nd Ave., tel. (414) 551-0299, has lots of different-sized machines, along with air-conditioning and televisions.

The **United Hospital System,** tel. (262) 656-2011, is a local hospital network with a central location at 6308 8th Avenue. Dial 911 in the event of a medical emergency.

GETTING THERE AND AWAY

Intercity Bus
Kenosha is connected to Milwaukee by **Wisconsin Coach Lines,** tel. (800) 236-2015, which runs eight buses every weekday 5:30 a.m.-7 p.m. and four buses on the weekend 8 a.m.-7 p.m. The bus stops in Kenosha at the Metra Station. En route to the Beer City, you can get off at Racine, Oak Creek, or Mitchell International Airport, and there are numerous stops in downtown Milwaukee. One-way fare to Milwaukee is around $5. This is more convenient than **Greyhound,** which is far out at 2105 Roosevelt Road.

You can also hop aboard **United Limo,** tel. (800) 833-5555, which goes north to Milwaukee via Racine and south to Chicago. All buses stop at the Brat Stop at the junction of I-94 and Hwy 50. Southbound buses leave the site nine times daily 5:30 a.m.-9:30 p.m., and northbound buses nine times daily 8:40 a.m.-12:25 a.m. One-way to Milwaukee is $5, to Chicago's O'Hare airport is $14.

Train
Metra, tel. (312) 322-6777, offers train service between Kenosha and Chicago's Madison Street Station. Trains depart the Kenosha Transit Center, 5410 13th Ave., tel. (262) 653-0141, eight times a day 5:50 a.m.-6 p.m. (an additional one departs at 11:30 p.m.) on weekdays; five times on Saturday 5:50 a.m.-10:20 p.m.; and 6:45 a.m., 8:45 a.m., and 6:45 p.m. Sunday. A one-way ticket to Chicago is $7, and the trip takes a little over an hour.

GETTING AROUND

Kenosha Transit
The Kenosha City Transit System, tel. (262) 653-4BUS, has eight bus routes, but none that take you close to the Kenosha Transit Center. Route 7, the yellow one, runs from downtown to the factory outlet mall and also gets you within shouting distance of the Burger King at the junction of I-94 and WI 50, where United Limo stops (though double-check with the driver before boarding). Kenosha's museum is served by routes 1 and 5. Route 1 also goes to Carthage College.

Fares are $1 per ride, 60 cents for students with ID, and 50 cents for senior citizens. Route maps can be found at the Convention and Visitors Bureau.

Lakeshore Trolley/Electric Streetcar
May through September Kenosha's old trolley rolls through downtown giving narrated tours. The ride begins at 7th Avenue just north of 58th Street at the top of each hour and *usually* follows this route: 6th Avenue downtown to Library Park to the Historical Society and Kemper Center to Southport Marina and Tot Park to the Holiday Inn to Simmons Island to Harborside on 7th Avenue. Fares are $2, free for children three and under.

Kenosha's new—and wildly popular—electric streetcar rumbles through the downtown area to the Metra Train station and back. A bus pass works for the streetcar. For information call (262) 653-4000.

RACINE

Racine is a heavily industrialized city; more than 320 industries still operate in the county, significantly buttressing the area's economy. The city leads the nation in the manufacture of farm machinery; metal casting and finishing; injection molding; production of electrical motors and parts, lawn mowers, prestressed concrete, rubber, and glass; lithography; and printing.

Like its de facto sister city to the south, Kenosha, Racine suffers somewhat from its association with manufacturing. A few sections do show their age and their blue-collar roots. But the stereotypical drab image of gritty soot clinging to building facades simply doesn't hold up. The mid-sized (pop. 77,000) city perches on a promontory swooping into Lake Michigan from a point just below the Milwaukee County line. The city lakefront, once a true-to-form, ugly-as-hell mill town with a horizon of gas tanks and brown sloughs, was mostly razed in the early 1990s and spruced up to the point of meticulousness. Now, it's full of landscaped parks and plenty of public boat launches, and the city sports the largest marina on Lake Michigan— over 100 acres.

Ethnically, Racine is home to the same Northern and Eastern European mosaic as the rest of Wisconsin's southern regions. While in the early 20th century the city boasted the nation's most appreciable Bohemian influence, it is now known for its Danish contingent—it's got the largest Danish population outside of Denmark—and West Racine is even referred to as "Kringleville," for the pastry produced in huge numbers by local bakeries.

History
The Root River, named by early Native Americans for its gnarled, knife-resistant roots, was first explored by French *voyageurs* around the 1670s. Thoroughly unimpressed by the river, which they deemed essentially unnavigable, they decamped. Potawatomi, Winnebago, Menominee, and Sauk Indians were the only inhabitants for another century or so, until white settlers arrived in 1820 to set up trading outposts in present-day Caledonia, as well as at lakeside.

Jacques Vieau, a seminal figure in Milwaukee history, also established a post near Racine.

In 1834, once the federal government had rammed through its final treaties stripping the Potawatomi and Menominee of their lands in southeastern Wisconsin, an opportunistic former naval officer named Gilbert Knapp scooped up riverside property and sold sites to settlers. This initial assemblage of dwellings was called Port Gilbert in his honor.

Within a half decade, the population climbed to 300, and in 1841 the town incorporated under the name Racine, which means "root" in French. Like Kenosha, Racine was plagued by the maddeningly shifty river mouth and resultant sandbars. Citizens got the jump on federal Lake Michigan improvement projects by digging out the sandbars and constructing the first piers in 1843-44. Initially, lake traffic was the lifeblood of the city. Later, agricultural implement manufacturing was among the first economic supplements to shipping, and by the mid-1850s small factories were producing over 20 wares. By the 1880s, manufacturing had eclipsed both transportation and agriculture. By the turn of the century, Racine was a leading national figure in farm implement and wagon production and had become a primary Midwestern manufacturing city, a position it retains today.

SIGHTS

Charles A. Wustum Museum of Fine Arts
Housed in a historic 1856 Italianate farmhouse on a 13-acre spread of park and formal garden, this museum exhibits art in various media and is home to an interpretation, education, and collection program. The 2,000 holdings include 20th-century American watercolors, photographs, and graphics and one of the largest collections in the Midwest of Works Project Administration Federal Arts Program works. Fourteen major exhibitions are scheduled throughout the year, including some local artists. The Racine Theater Guild is also on site. The museum, 2519 Northwestern Ave., tel. (262) 636-9177, is open Mon.-Sat. 11 a.m.-5 p.m.,

with extended hours Monday and Thursday, and Sunday 1-5 p.m. Admission is free.

Other Museums

The **Racine County Historical Museum,** 7th and Main Streets, tel. (262) 636-3926, in a Carnegie building on the National Register of Historic Places, contains the dusty detritus of a century and a half. Admission is free; it's open Tues.-Fri. 9 a.m.-5 p.m. and weekends 1-4 p.m.

A former fire station full of antique equipment constitutes the **Firehouse 3 Museum,** 700 Sixth St., tel. (262) 637-7395. It's open only Sunday 1-4 p.m.

The **Dillinger Exhibit** isn't a museum but a fun look at the bad old days of cops and robbers. On November 20, 1933, four brazen robbers held up a downtown Racine bank, stole $27,700, and relieved a security guard of his machine gun. When Dillinger was finally taken down in Arizona, the gun was recovered—complete with Dillinger's signature on the stock. It's now on display in the Racine Police Department lobby, 730 Center Street.

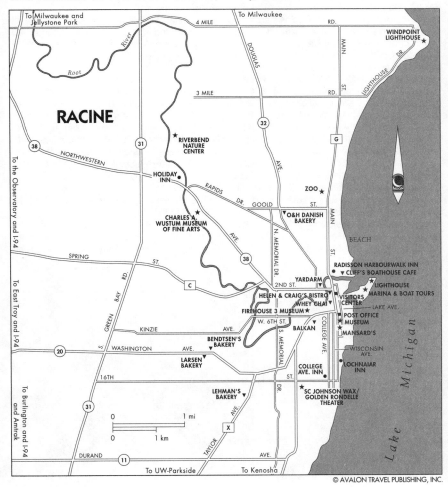

© AVALON TRAVEL PUBLISHING, INC.

Just north of the terminal of Racine's Batten Airport, 3333 N. Green Bay Rd., is the **Southeast Wisconsin Aviation Museum,** where you can see exhibits on an SC Johnson Wax Taperwing WACO, the restoration of a Fairchild 24, barnstorming, and early air shows.

SC Johnson Wax and Golden Rondelle Theater

It's hard to miss the SC Johnson Wax Co. on the city's south side, especially with the globular-shaped Golden Rondelle Theater, 1525 Howe St., tel. (262) 631-2154, on the corner. The theater is the most distinctive of Racine's architectural landmarks. It was unveiled at the New York World's Fair in 1964-65. It was even more dramatic then, with 90-foot columns arching over the top. At the fair, the short documentary about the theater, *To Be Alive,* riveted the crowds and garnered an Oscar for best documentary short. Following the fair, Taliesin Associate Architects, founded by Frank Lloyd Wright, was commissioned to bring the theater to Racine and incorporate it into the grounds of SC Johnson Wax near the administration building, which was designed by Wright. Now the offices of the Johnson Wax Co. guest relations staff and a sometimes conference center, the theater screens free films for public viewing Tues.-Fri. (coinciding with company tours). The films include the original short film from the World's Fair along with Living Planet, and *On The Wing,* a sensational leap into flight. Free tours of the SC Johnson Wax administration building depart the theater Tues.-Fri. at various times; reservations are necessary. The Great Workroom in the administration building is worth the entire tour.

Modine-Benstead Observatory

Located in Union Grove west of Racine, the Modine-Benstead Observatory, CR A and 63rd Dr., tel. (262) 878-2774, offers free stargazing from dusk until 11 p.m. every clear Thursday June through August.

Mound Cemetery

The remnants of 14 conical burial mounds of the Woodland Mound Builders, dating to AD 900, can be found in this cemetery along West Boulevard and Washington Avenue.

Parks and Nature Centers

Racine's got its share of good parks and white sand strands. The spring-fed waters at **Quarry Lake Park,** 3800 Northwestern Ave., make the lake a great swimming hole. Along the shore, **Racine County Harbor Park** draws most people. Artificially created, it comprises the massive 100-acre Reefpoint Marina and an observation tower directly across from the landmark red light beacon.

The **Riverbend Nature Center,** 3600 N. Green Bay Rd., tel. (262) 639-0930, is an 80-acre preserve of woodland, pond, prairie, and wetland, through which flows the Root River. Numerous serpentine multipurpose trails wind

the Golden Rondelle Theater, designed by Frank Lloyd Wright

through the preserve. The nature center building has wildlife and natural history exhibits. It's open daily weekdays 9 a.m.-4:30 p.m. and weekends 12:30-4:30 p.m., and admission is free.

Racine Zoo

The free **Racine Zoological Gardens,** 2131 Main St., tel. (262) 636-9189, features over 200 animals from around the world, including a rare white tiger (one of half a dozen endangered species). There is an Australian exhibit, an ibis and flamingo area, a popular "wolf woods," and an interactive prairie dog section. You can even meet Bender, a three-ton white rhinoceros. One ambitious elephant paints with her trunk. A popular petting zoo is located on site and a beach is near the exhibits. Free Wednesday night jazz concerts during the summer are popular. The zoo stays open year-round except major holidays. High-season hours are daily 9 a.m.-8 p.m.; off season, it closes at 4:30 p.m.

Toward the end of the year, the local Kiwanis club transforms the zoo grounds with millions of lights strung to portray shooting stars, doves, Christmas messages, and more.

Windpoint Lighthouse

Many visitors associate Racine with the eye-catching red beacon atop the breakwaters across from Reefpoint Marina. Racinians would likely rather be associated with Windpoint Lighthouse, north of town between Three Mile and Four Mile Roads. Believed to be the oldest (built in 1880) and tallest (112 feet) lighthouse on the Great Lakes, it is still in use today. You can't go inside, but you can stroll the grounds at most hours of the day.

Scenic Drives

The city of Racine boasts a historic chunk of roadway. Three Mile Road, beginning at 108th Street and running east to 80th Street, was laid out in the early part of the 19th century and has remained virtually untouched (and unwidened). It still has old oaks and rail fences at its verges and makes a beautiful tour.

There's also lots of worthy snooping around to be done in the vicinity of Racine. State Rustic Roads are everywhere you look. One heads north of town along Honey Lake Road, Maple Lane, and Pleasant View Road to CR D and WI 83, passing along the way a woodland preserve,

dairy farms, and marshes with muskrat houses. Backtrack to CR DD and it picks up with another Rustic Road adjacent to the **Honey Creek Wildlife Area.** This route also passes the **Franklyn Hazelo Home,** which is on the National Register of Historic Places. Southeast of Burlington off WI 142 via Brever Road or Wheatland Road, a Rustic Road passes under an expanse of oak and black walnut trees. Highlights include old barns, an old farmhouse, marshes, and lots of great fishing along the Fox River, accessed from Hoosier Creek Road.

Northeast of Waterford via WI 164 and WI 36 is Loomis Rustic Road, originally an 1840 territorial road that's little changed. Along the way, you'll pass Colonel Heg Memorial Park, commemorating Wisconsin's highest-ranking Civil War officer. A park museum describes the region's settlement by Norwegians, and an 1830s cabin sits nearby.

Burlington

The town of Burlington sits some 25 miles west of Racine. For a town of only 8,900 people, it's sure got a bunch of damn liars. The home of the world famous Burlington Liar's Club, it hosts an annual yarn- and fib-spinning festival and also distributes a brochure about the town's **Tall Tales Trail.** Also called Chocolate Town USA (a Nestlé plant is located here), Burlington has many streets named after candy bars.

The **Spinning Top Exploratory,** 533 Milwaukee Ave., tel. (262) 763-3946, has more than 1,500 examples of yo-yos, tops, and anything else that revolves. Some pieces are quite rare. Visitors can play with the three dozen hands-on display tops. With advance reservations, you get a tour featuring videos, demonstrations, and game-playing, as well as a look at prototype tops used in a feature film on the subject. Open by reservation, the Exploratory charges admission of $5 per person (discounts for large groups).

The **Burlington Area Arts Council,** 112 E. Chestnut St., offers revolving exhibits detailing local arts. The usual fare awaits at the **Burlington Area Historical Museum,** Jefferson St. and Perkins Blvd., tel. (262) 767-2884, open Sunday 1-4 p.m. At 503 Browns Lake Rd., the ethereally subdued **St. Francis Retreat Center** features gardens and a grotto open to the public.

Try the Bohemian food at **Johnnie Reynolds' Dinner,** 6291 Hospital Rd., tel. (262) 763-9908. Great prime rib, too. Right downtown, **B.J. Wentker's,** tel. (262) 767-1514, is a pub with incredibly creative and well-prepared entrées (well worth the drive); the restoration of this place's interiors is amazing (also worth the drive). Selections from $6.

North of Burlington along WI 36 is Waterford, site of the **Hoppe Homestead Family Dairy Farm,** at 33701 Hill Valley Dr., tel. (262) 534-6480. This century-old dairy farm invites visitors to do any of the many chores—milking included—or just enjoy hay and wagon rides. The hearty family-style breakfast spreads, served Sunday 9 a.m.-1 p.m., are semi-legendary. Farm tours are available May-Oct.; tours are daily 10 a.m.-2 p.m. and cost $5. There are also sleigh rides.

Another large-scale farm open to the public out this way is **Green Meadows Farm,** three miles west via WI 20, tel. (262) 534-2891. Green Meadows has over 200 farm animals you can help tend, more milking, pony rides, tractor hayrides, and picnics. It's open daily May 1 through October 31, 9:30 a.m.-2:30 p.m. Admission is $8. Also in Waterford, **Rausch's Bear Den,** 6831 Big Bend Rd. (WI 164), is a family-owned petting zoo that does hayrides. Admission is charged.

ACCOMMODATIONS

Hotels and Motels

The lowest-priced lodgings in Racine are at the **Knight's Inn,** 1149 Oakes Rd., tel. (262) 886-6667 or (800) 722-7220. Some rooms have microwaves or refrigerators. Rates start at $50.

East of I-94 along WI 20, the **Fairfield Inn by Marriott,** 6421 Washington Ave., tel. (262) 886-5000 or (800) 228-2800, has an indoor pool, whirlpool, and good rooms from $50.

The Racine **Holiday Inn,** 3700 Northwestern Ave., tel. (262) 637-9311 or (800) 465-4329, has 110 rooms (from $60, slightly less off season), a restaurant, lounge, outdoor pool, recreation room, and a decent riverside site.

The **Racine Marriott,** 7111 Washington Ave.,

tel. (262) 886-6100 or (800) 228-9290, is the largest hotel in town with 225 rooms (from $150), a restaurant, lounge, indoor pool, whirlpool, and sauna. Airport transportation is offered. Some rooms have refrigerators.

Then there's the only over-the-water hotel on southern Lake Michigan. The **Radisson Harbourwalk Inn,** 223 Gaslight Circle, tel. (262) 632-7777 or (800) 333-3333, has 80 guest rooms (from $115), all affording gorgeous lake views, and 25 suites with whirlpools on balconies. Boaters can dock at slips lining the perimeter of the hotel. The Chancery Restaurant on site is well regarded. There is also a small indoor pool. Extras include 24-hour room service, in-room coffeemakers, and airport transportation.

Historic Inns and B&Bs

Racine has a host of historic inns and bed and breakfasts. A European-style guest inn, the grand **Lochnaiar Inn,** 1121 Lake Ave., tel. (262) 633-3300, has been named as one of the 10 best in the Midwest by many travel media. It was built in 1915 by a Scottish immigrant industrialist, and the name, which translates as "on the water," fits—it's perched on the crown of a bluff overlooking Lake Michigan. The inn supplies modern conveniences like fax machine and meeting room, and all rooms have telephones and TVs. Some rooms have private whirlpool baths and/or fireplace. Rates are $80-175.

Mansard's on the Lake, 827 Lake Ave., tel. (262) 632-1135, is a Second Empire post-Civil War mansion on a bluff overlooking Pershing Park and Lake Michigan. It was built by the inventor of J.I. Case threshers and pulls. Early 20th century suffrage meetings were held here. Residential suites have private baths with Empress tubs, parlors with TVs, bedrooms, and full kitchens. Rates are $55-65.

Camping

Sanders County Park, tel. (262) 886-8457, is at 4809 Woods Rd. and has 50 campsites, along with a playground and hiking trails. About 10 miles or so northwest of Racine, near Caledonia, **Cliffside County Park,** 7320 Michna Rd., tel. (262) 886-8457, has nearly 100 sites. Both cost around $11.

FOOD

Kringle

Racine is still lovingly called Kringleville, and almost all travelers leave town with white wax-paper bags stuffed with *kringles*. *Kringle* is a flaky, ovoid kind of coffeecake filled with a variety of fruits and almond paste or pecans. Family bakeries vie annually for top honors of best *kringle*, and they still make it the Old World way—some taking three days to prepare the dough alone. Aficionados who have written in with advice say: 1) pecan kringles are best; and 2) always go for the thinnest slice on the plate, since it always has the most filling.

O&H Danish Bakery, 1841 Douglas Ave., tel. (262) 637-8895, does the most advertising and probably ships the most *kringles,* but those in the know claim **Larsen Bakery,** 3311 Washington Ave., tel. (262) 633-4298, or **Bendtsen's,** 3200 Washington Ave., tel. (262) 633-0365, have the best.

Another Danish highlight is *aeblewskiver,* a lovely spherical waffle.

Fish Fries

The Summit, 6825 Washington Ave., tel. (262) 886-9866, is a cloth-napkin kind of place but puts on a great Friday-night fish fry. Equally upscale is the **Hob Nob,** 277 Sheridan Rd., tel. (262) 552-8008, which Kenosha also claims as its own. **Cliff's Boathouse Cafe** is a popular joint, too (see "Greasy Spoons and Cafes" below). Not here on a Friday? No problem, the **Yardarm** bar and grill, 920 Erie St., tel. (262) 633-8270, has fish fries nightly; its burgers are much talked about, as well. **Madden's on Main,** 1659 N. Main, sports an 1800s Brunswick bar, a fish fry, and Kankakee bowling. Fish fries generally cost around $7 for all-you-can-eat.

Supper Clubs and Steakhouses

The **Corner House,** 1251 Washington Ave., tel. (262) 637-1295, serves enormous tender roasts and exquisite prime rib. Around since WW II, this is the institution of institutions. Corner House is open daily from 5 p.m. Meals from $7.

West of Racine in diminutive Kansasville, **Auctioneer's Inn,** 4614 Sheard Rd., tel. (262) 878-4100, is a hip New York City jazz club in an Old West saloon. The combination works better than you might imagine (some, however, have reported mediocre food considering the prices—from $18.) Famed for its three-pound Australian lobster and escargot, it's also got an array of great steaks. Open daily for dinner; reservations are good idea. To get there, head west on WI 11, then south on CR B. Also in Kansasville is **Giovanni's on Eagle Lake,** 3101 Eagle Rd., tel. (262) 878-4500, operated by the owners of a popular downtown Milwaukee eatery. The Sicilian food here is good, and the views are great. Dinner is served Tues.-Sun., from $12.

Greasy Spoons and Cafes

Not a greasy spoon per se, **Kewpee,** 520 Wisconsin Ave., tel. (262) 634-9601, rates a nod as the best burger joint in perhaps all of southern Wisconsin. Devotees regularly come from as far away as the Windy City. Decades old (it started in 1927), this erstwhile teen hangout doesn't have much in the way of ambience now. It's as fast as fast grub gets, but you can't beat the burgers or malts. It's standing-room-only at lunchtime. Selections from $1.

Get outstanding potato pancakes, made from an age-old recipe, at **Cliff's Boathouse Cafe,** 301 Hamilton St., a block north of the Main Street Bridge, tel. (262) 633-1767. A popular breakfast joint, it's closed Monday but open from 8 a.m. Sunday and 6 a.m. all other days; it closes at 2 p.m. Choices from $2.

Balkan

Sample food from the Balkan Peninsula, from *sarma* to *chevapcici* to gyros, at the **Balkan Restaurant,** 605 6th St., tel. (262) 632-8292. It has daily specials and a Friday fish fry. Open every day except Sunday for breakfast, lunch, and dinner. From $5.

Bistro

Rated as one of the best modestly elegant eateries in the state, **Helen and Craig's Bistro,** 340 Main St., tel. (262) 637-4340, features European-influenced fare including wood-fired brick-oven pizzas, wood-roasted chicken, salmon, swordfish, and succulent desserts. The building itself might be even better—a 19th-century structure that used to be a drugstore and still sports the original dark walnut cabinetry and wall trims. Casually upscale. Open daily for lunch and dinner and Sunday for brunch; it's also got a Friday fish fry. From $6.

Finer Dining
The Summit, 6825 Washington Ave., tel. (262) 886-9866, is a wonderful place. This restaurant has marvelous lunches and dinners from $5 in an upscale atmosphere, but you might want to check out its incredible Sunday brunch, if only for the extraordinary array of *kringle* available.

Asian
Two Chinese restaurants stand out in Racine. Downtown at 400 Main St., **Whey Chai,** tel. (262) 633-8000, is a pan-Cathay spot oft voted tops in the local newspaper's annual survey. Open daily for lunch and dinner, from $5. Also popular is **Great Wall,** 6025 Washington Ave., tel. (262) 886-9700, offering Cantonese, Mandarin, and Sichuan selections from $5.

Enjoy Vietnamese food at **Saigon Dining,** 6034 22nd Ave., tel. (262) 658-4433.

Italian
Totero's, 2343 Mead St., has been dishing up homemade pasta for more than 50 years in a delightful family tavern atmosphere. It's also got out-of-this-world lasagna and banana cream pie. Choices from $5.

Get excellent pizza at **Wells Brothers,** 2148 Mead St., tel. (262) 632-4408. It's highly rated by national pizza associations and is generally voted best Italian by locals. Open daily for lunch and dinner.

ENTERTAINMENT AND EVENTS

Events
Dismiss the blahs at February's **Winter Carnival.** Held the first week of February, it's three days of sports, games, and entertainment. The first weekend of May brings the **Lakefront Artists Fair,** which includes the biggest breakfast—a pancake feast—in the state. The following week, little Burlington whoops it up during **Chocolate Days.**

Racine's Fourth of July celebration is the largest in the state, replete with mock-ups and replicas of 18th-century clippers prowling the harbor and the longest parade in Wiscsonsin.

The granddaddy of all events is mid-July's **Salmon-A-Rama,** during which over 4,000 fishers from 25 states land about 18 tons of fish and another 200,000 people crowd the lakefront for a huge blowout of a festival. It's the largest freshwater fishing festival in the world.

Spectator Sports
The **Racine Raiders** are a scrappy affiliate of the Minor Football League Alliance and have been national champs so many times that the league declared them Franchise of the Decades. They play weekends July-Nov. at Horlick Field, 1648 N. Memorial Dr., tel. (262) 634-8842. Tickets are $7.

Drag racing takes place Tues.-Sun. from April to November at the **Great Lakes Dragway,** CR KR, four miles west of I-94, tel. (262) 878-3783.

Entertainment
The **Racine Symphony Orchestra,** tel. (262) 636-9285, is the oldest continuous symphony orchestra in Wisconsin, founded in 1932. It performs a seven-concert classical series, a three-concert chamber series, and a summertime array of pops.

The **Racine Theater Guild,** 2519 Northwestern Ave., tel. (262) 633-4218, produces eight plays annually. An award-winner at competitions in the U.S. and abroad, it also occasionally hosts international festivals.

RECREATION

Charter Fishing
Along with Kenosha, Racine has one of the most productive charter operations on Lake Michigan. Racine also has the largest marina on the Great Lakes—over 100 acres. Six different species of salmon and trout cohabit near three reefs lying outside the harbor. April and early June are the best times to come for coho salmon, the middle of summer for steelhead, mid-July for Chinook, March 1 through October 31 for lake trout (the state-record lake trout was caught off Racine). The finicky brown trout can be taken all year.

For more information, contact the **Fishing Charters of Racine,** P.O. Box 1393, tel. (262) 633-6113 or (800) 475-6113.

Bicycling

The county has a 117-mile on-road bicycle trail marked; portions are on a multi-use trail. Six county scenic multi-use trails exist; the North Shore Trail links to Kenosha; this trail links up with the Racine/Sturtevant Trail. Other trails in Waterford and Burlington are downright lovely.

Canoeing

The Root and Fox Rivers and Honey Creek west of Racine are good for canoeing. **Riverbend Nature Center,** 3600 N. Green Bay Rd., tel. (262) 639-0930, rents canoes.

SERVICES AND INFORMATION

The **Racine County Convention and Visitors Bureau,** 345 Main St., tel. (262) 634-3293 or (800) C-RACINE, www.racine.org, is open regular business hours (with weekend hours in summer) and operates a 24-hour **events line,** tel. (262) 634-4654.

The **post office** is downtown in the 600 block of Main Street. Kinko's, 2500 W. Green Bay Rd., tel. (414) 554-5000, has 24-hour **internet access** for $12/hour or 20 cents per minute. The **Racine Public Library** is at 75 7th St., tel. (414) 636-9241.

GETTING THERE AND AWAY

Racine has a private airport, but no commercial service is available. There's also no Amtrak service directly to Racine, but trains do stop at 2904 Wisconsin St., tel. (800) 872-7245 in Sturtevant to the west. Racine city buses travel to Sturtevant.

Bus

United Limo, tel. (800) 833-5555, makes stops in Racine on its routes to and from Chicago and Milwaukee. The Racine stop is at the Highlands Mobil Travel Plaza at WI 20 and I-94. In Chicago, catch the bus to Racine at O'Hare Field; in Milwaukee, catch it at the airport, the United Limo stop on S. 13th St., the Amtrak station, and the Marquette University Library. Buses run nine times daily to Chicago ($18 one-way) 4:35 a.m.-8:20 p.m. and nine times daily to Milwaukee ($2 one-way) 8:25 a.m.-1:20 a.m.

Wisconsin Coach Lines, tel. (262) 634-4156, also stops in Racine on its run between Milwaukee and Kenosha. The local agency is Eastside Emporium, 300 Sixth Street. Weekdays, there are eight trips north and south 5:50 a.m.-7:30 p.m.; weekends, there are four trips 8:30 a.m.-7:30 p.m. Racine stops are at WI 32 and Durand Ave., 14th & Racine Streets, Monument Square, Douglas and Goold, Douglas and Three Mile Rd., and Douglas and Six Mile Rd. One-way fare to Milwaukee is $3.50, to Kenosha $1.50.

GETTING AROUND

City Bus

The **Belle Urban System,** 730 Washington Ave., tel. (262) 637-9000, has 10 bus routes served 5:30 a.m.-7:30 p.m. weekdays, shorter hours Saturday. Fares are $1 adults and children 6-17, 50 cents seniors and passengers with disabilities. The routes run as far west as the Amtrak station in Sturtevant, north to Six Mile Road, east to the lake, and south to UW-Parkside.

Trolley

The favorite way to move around is aboard one of the two trolleys that spin along the lakefront shopping and business districts. One buck gets you as far north as Reefpoint Marina and as far south as 7th Street. The trolleys run daily Memorial Day-Labor Day 10 a.m.-5 p.m.; on Friday and Saturday, the "pub and grub" run stops at 17 restaurants and bars downtown from 5 p.m. to midnight. For more information, call (262) 636-8025.

Sailing Charters

Great Lakes Charters, 1427 Park Ave., tel. (262) 633-0550, has $50 per hour charters for a minimum of two hours; deluxe trips include beverages, snacks, and photos. Dinner cruises can be arranged. The company also offers sailing instructions aboard a 34-foot Grampian sloop.

MILWAUKEE

Travelers and provincial Wisconsinites have been comparing and contrasting Madison and Milwaukee—Wisconsin's two population principals—for as long as they've existed. And Milwaukee has gotten somewhat of a bum rap, even from fellow Wisconsinites. The stereotypes have it that Madison is a loopy mishmash of students, time-warp radicals, and button-down Capitol yuppies, whereas Milwaukee is blue-collar to the core, replete with belching smokestacks and a gritty veneer.

A friendly rivalry exists between the two cities. While Madison denizens picture Milwaukeeans as beer-and-bowling knuckleheads, Milwaukeeans see Madisonians as people convinced that they live at the center of the universe. Milwaukee *is* decidedly more lunch-box than bento box, engendering not a few of those stereotypes—but that's only one piece of the mosaic.

The state's most populous and significant city both historically and economically, Milwaukee is equal parts sprawling metropolis, upwardly mobile financial center, hard-working industrial linchpin, and amalgamation of funky Old World neighborhoods. With a population of 1.5 million, it's the 19th-largest metropolitan area in the United States. It rates in the top five percent in the nation in arts, attractions, and recreation.

For all that, however, it has an awfully low-key, rootsy feel to it. The *lingua franca* in the city's older neighborhoods is often a mother tongue peppered with accented English. You'll often hear people speak of *gemütlichkeit* (warmth, hospitality) in Milwaukee, and it's by no means hyperbole.

All things considered, Milwaukee is essentially a big Midwestern city—and an underrated Great Lakes coastal city. Hang out here long enough and you'll appreciate it.

Climate

Milwaukee can be downright lovely, generally in direct proportion to your proximity to Lake Michigan or one of the three rivers that wend through the city to the crown of a modest bluff and a debouchment into the lake. In every weather report, you'll hear the tagline "cooler near the lake."

The Great Lakes establish their own microclimates and influence inland areas for miles. Temperatures along littoral stretches don't show the extreme fluctuations you find in inland communities, and on days when flurries are forecast for Madison, Milwaukee can get five inches of slick glop. The lake is best appreciated during the dog days of summer, when its breezes take some of the swelter out of the weather. On the beaches even during August, sweaters are not unheard of in late afternoon. Seasonal average temperatures are 52° in spring (March-May), 77° in summer (June-Aug.), 58° in autumn (Sept.-Nov.); and 29° in winter (Dec.-Feb.).

A popular local forecasting method is to espy the tear-shaped light atop the Wisconsin Gas Co. building downtown: yellow means cold; red means warm; blue means no change; and any color flashing means precipitation is predicted.

The local number to call for weather reports is (414) 936-1212.

HISTORY

The Mascoutin and Fox Indians were the first to reside in the tamarack swamps along the Milwaukee, Menomonee, and Kinnickinnic Rivers near their discharge into Lake Michigan. They were succeeded at various times by Menominee, Winnebago, Ojibwa, and Sauk Indians. Prior to the 17th century, the Potawatomi domain stretched northward along the Lake Michigan coast, which means that it was most likely they who welcomed the initial French *voyageurs,* Jesuit Black Robes, and renegade beaver-pelt traders paddling south. The earliest of these arrived around 1675, four decades after Jean Nicolet's splashy arrival in Red Banks. The city's name purportedly originates in an Algonquian language: *Mahn-a-waukee, Millioki,* and any number of other conjectures have all been translated as, roughly, "gathering place by the waters," a fitting appellation.

Fur traders, hoping to cop some of the untapped wealth of the Northwest Territory for New France, built the first cabins in the malarial muck-lands of the river valleys prior to the 19th century, while the Jesuits languished in their efforts at conversion. Northwest Fur Company trader Jacques Vieau is generally credited with erecting the first shack, along the Menomonee River in 1795. Yankee speculators arrived not long after, and all parties cooled their heels while the nascent U.S. government figured out a way to stick it to the natives. The U.S. duped the Potawatomi and Menominee into ceding all lands east and north of the Milwaukee River in 1831; a couple of years later, all Native American lands in southeastern Wisconsin were gone.

The Bridge War

The first of Milwaukee's famous native sons, Solomon Juneau—the city's first permanent European—arrived around 1820 to scoop up the former Native American landholdings. Juneau, George H. Walker, and Byron Kilbourn built rival communities in and around the rivers near Lake Michigan. Landed opportunists being what they are, none of the three could deflate his ego enough to cooperate on creating one city. The situation got so bad that the men refused to follow construction guidelines that would complement the others' roads and, especially, bridges. For years, bad blood lingered until finally the internecine squabbles escalated into claim-jumping and city sabotage in what became known as the Bridge War. Irate east-siders considered actually going to war with the west side and at one point even buried a cannon pointed across the waters at Kilbourntown. (Attentive visitors can still discern traces of the Bridge War on a walk of the downtown streets and bridges.)

Immigrants

While the power triumvirate worked out their civic engineering problems, a steady tide of settlers streamed into the area. The first of three massive waves of German immigrants occurred in 1836. By the 1880s, 35% of Milwaukee would be German-born, making up 70% of Milwaukee's total immigrant population and contributing to its status as the most ethnically rich area in the country. (It was even dubbed the German Athens.) The population jumped from over 9,500 in 1846 to nearly 50,000 in 1851. Germans make up the vast majority of the city's ethnic heritage, followed by Poles, Serbs, Italians, Irish, African-Americans, Dutch, Scandinavians, Bohemians, and Hispanics; in the 1990 census, over four dozen ethnic groups were represented. Milwaukee had the country's first Polish-language newspaper, and the German publishing industry there rivaled any contemporary press group.

American Made

The Civil War provided Milwaukee's biggest economic boon. Manufacturing moved to the Great Lakes during the war, and Milwaukee's deep-water harbor provided both an outlet for goods and an inlet for immigrant labor. Over 3,300 tanneries, meat-packing plants, and machine and ironworks were the industrial stalwarts that bolstered brewing and drove the city's economy for the ensuing century. Wheat cultivation gradually declined in Wisconsin as the Great Plains opened, but through the 1870s Milwaukee remained the wheat milling and transport capital of the world, with five dozen mills and grain elevators. Nowadays, though Milwaukee has shed a bit of its rough exterior and the downtown can seem downright glossy, since 22% of the population is still employed in manufacturing the city has retained the moniker "machine shop of America" (and possibly the world).

Socialist Central

Immigrant labor gave Milwaukee its trademark socialistic overtones. As the factories sprang up, workers—many of them enlightened free-thinkers from Germany fleeing oppression—organized the first trade and labor unions and played a direct role in the establishment of the country's first unemployment compensation act. In 1888, Milwaukee elected the first socialist ever elected in a major city. Socialist Mayor Dan Hoan once said, after refusing to invite the King of Belgium to the city, "I stand for the common man; to hell with kings." Socialists were later elected to a few county posts, and Milwaukee eventually sent the first socialist to the House of Representatives. Milwaukee labor unions and their strikes are legendary in the Midwest. They were among the initial and definitely most vociferous proponents of workplace reform; by the mid 1880s, up to 15,000 workers at a time would stage demonstrations, and in 1886 militia groups fired on crowds in the eastern European enclave of Bay View, killing five immigrant laborers.

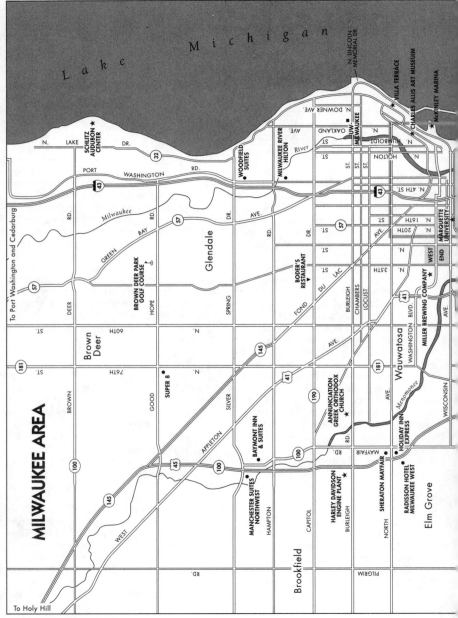

MILWAUKEE AREA

Lake Michigan

SCHLITZ AUDUBON CENTER ★

VILLA TERRACE
CHARLES ALLIS ART MUSEUM ★
McKINLEY MARINA

N. LINCOLN MEMORIAL DR.

N. DOWNER AVE.

WOODFIELD SUITES

MILWAUKEE RIVER HILTON

UW-MILWAUKEE ■

N. OAKLAND AVE.
N. HUMBOLDT
N. HOLTON ST.
N. 4TH ST.
N. 16TH ST.
N. 20TH

MARQUETTE UNIVERSITY

WEST END

BROWN DEER PARK GOLF COURSE

Glendale

BODER'S RESTAURANT

MILLER BREWING COMPANY ★

Wauwatosa

To Port Washington and Cedarburg

To Port Washington and Cedarburg

Brown Deer

SUPER 8

ANNUNCIATION GREEK ORTHODOX CHURCH ★

BAYMONT INN & SUITES

HOLIDAY INN EXPRESS

MANCHESTER SUITES NORTHWEST

HARLEY DAVIDSON ENGINE PLANT ★

SHERATON MAYFAIR

RADISSON HOTEL MILWAUKEE WEST

Elm Grove

Brookfield

To Holy Hill

© AVALON TRAVEL PUBLISHING, INC.

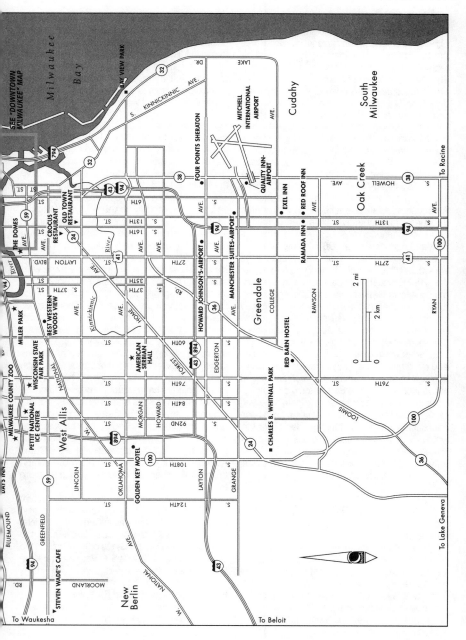

20th Century

World War I was not a particularly good time for Milwaukee or its German citizens, but worse was the Prohibition that followed—the city was already the brewing capital of the United States. The brewers switched to root beer, the socialists organized quasi-WPA relief agencies that predated the Depression, and everybody held on tight. (However, at 12:01 a.m. on the day Prohibition was officially repealed, Milwaukee somehow managed to ship 15 million bottles of beer, and the city erupted into a paroxysm of celebration.)

Following World War II, Milwaukee remained steadfastly blue-collar, though not quite so socialist. As African-Americans migrated to factory jobs along the Great Lakes, Milwaukee's African-American population reached 17% within three decades. Unfortunately, Milwaukee remained one of the nation's most segregated cities, as riots and marches of the 1960s pointed out.

Slowly but surely, the lucrative factory days waned, and the central city declined throughout the '70s. Exhaustive machinations to overhaul the downtown began in the mid-'80s, and a careful gentrification of the downtown has avoided giving it the sickening ersatz sheen manifest in so many other cities going for the tourist shakedown. There's real history here. Still, that's not to say Milwaukee doesn't want a new image: much time and effort have gone into a zillion-dollar convention center, an entertainment district facelift, and Milwaukee's version of San Antonio's riverwalk, complete with gondolas ferrying camera-toting tourists. These efforts to boost tourism have been necessitated in part by the slow decline of Milwaukee's major breweries—at present only Miller remains—and the manufacturing industry. In all, tourism in Milwaukee generates over $2 billion, accounting for over 22% of the state economy.

SIGHTS

Orientation

There's a lot to see in Milwaukee, and that's not just guidebook gush. There's also a lot of Milwaukee to see, as the city comprises 96 square miles in a big rectangle backing off the lake. The city is fairly well laid out and not too hard to maneuver. A few roads bend off at an angle after crossing either the Menomonee or Milwaukee River, but overall the scheme isn't a nightmare to follow.

Beware: Jaywalking is illegal and strictly enforced in Milwaukee, especially during lunchtime hours. You *will* be ticketed ($40); don't even try it. On the other hand, the police dole out equal numbers of tickets to drivers who don't give way to pedestrians, so it works out.

From the west, I-94 is the primary thoroughfare; I-894 skirts the southern and western fringes north to south, and I-43 meets I-94 at the Marquette interchange downtown, then heads north toward Green Bay or south to Beloit.

Off the freeways, most of the sights—save the Historic Third Ward or outlying sights—are concentrated in a rough square bounded by WI 145 to the north, I-43 to the west, I-794 to the south, and the big old lake to the east (although the lakefront highlights seem closer to the downtown highlights than they really are). The Milwaukee River splits the square down the middle and separates the city into its east and west sections. The river is also the line of demarcation for street numbering, so if you bear in mind where the river is, you should be fine. There are no major one-ways to worry about, and Wisconsin Avenue is the main east-west drag downtown.

There's plenty of **parking** everywhere. East of the river, the city has 25 structures or surface lots. To the west of the river, nearly 50 lots, mostly surface, provide parking. The only time you're going to have trouble is during Summerfest or other festivals and when the Bucks are playing at the Bradley Center, when parking prices shoot up precipitously. On the west side are the huge parking areas north of the public museum and to the south and west of the Grand Avenue via N. 4th Street. Parking rates vary; in general, expect $2-4 per hour, and no more than $10 for the whole day.

Skywalk: A comprehensive skywalk system connects the Hyatt Regency Hotel with the new Midwest Express Convention Center, the Federal Plaza, and the Grand Avenue. One stretch, the Riverspan, when built was the only skywalk in the U.S. built over a navigable riverway, here the Milwaukee River.

Historic Third Ward and Riverwalk

Up until the mid-1980s, downtown Milwaukee roughly south of I-794 and the Milwaukee River

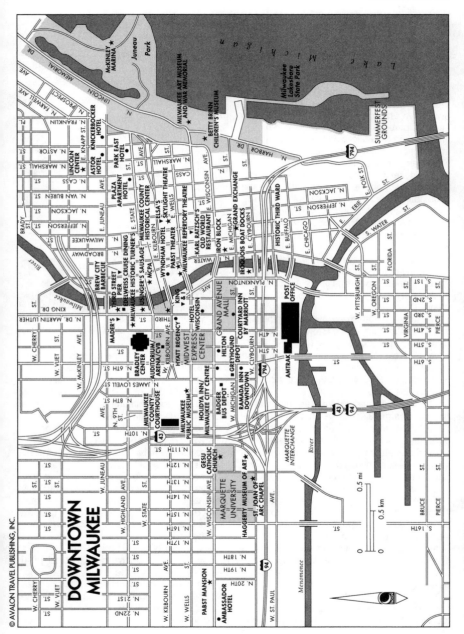

DOWNTOWN MILWAUKEE

© AVALON TRAVEL PUBLISHING, INC.

cupping it to the west was, in no uncertain terms, a deteriorating zone threatening to fall in on itself. This was nothing new for the area. The one-time bustling ethnic warehouse district suffered a catastrophic conflagration in 1892 in which over 500 buildings burned (only one was left standing), displacing thousands of immigrants. Though rebuilt, the district never regained its prior verve. Halfway through the 1980s, however, the city renovated much of the downtown, including requisite bricks on the streets and old-style lampposts lining the walkways. Antique stores and art galleries are the norm now, in among dozens of cafes, upscale shops, and a few longtime holdovers. It's also the fruit and vegetable district, quite a sight in the morning as the trucks roll through. Among the antique shops is the huge **Milwaukee Antique Center,** 341 N. Milwaukee St., tel. (414) 276-0605, with 75 dealers crammed into three stories. North Broadway and the ever-popular N. Water Street have most of the remaining arts and antiques shops. Handfuls of art galleries are sprinkled throughout the neighborhood. The Italian Community Center is also here.

The unofficial "off-Broadway" area of the city, the Third Ward has a new **Broadway Theatre Center,** 158 N. Broadway, tel. (414) 291-7800, which smacks of an 18th-century European opera house; juxtaposed with that is a smaller experimental theater. Many local theater companies call this home.

The well-regarded **Milwaukee Institute of Art and Design,** 273 E. Erie St., tel. (414) 276-7889, is housed in an old terminal, rebuilt in the days after the ward fire. An on-site gallery exhibits student and faculty work, some quite off-the-wall. It's open during school sessions Tues.-Sat. 10 a.m.-5 p.m. and until 7 p.m. Thursday; admission is free.

There are more and more places to eat in the Third Ward district; tops is the **Third Ward Caffe,** creatively eclectic and housed in the only building to survive the 1892 conflagration.

As this book was being updated, a $6 million river walk was being developed in the Third Ward; it will stretch from Clybourn to Young Street and will include a marketplace with vendors.

North of I-794 is another modestly gentrified zone along both sides of the Milwaukee River. To the east is Water Street, the happening mélange

boats along the Milwaukee River

of microbreweries, sports pubs, restaurants, and cultural attractions. To the west is the Old World Third Street, with more classic Milwaukee edifices, original old hotels and factories, the Bradley Center, and more restaurants. Milwaukee's new $13 million Riverwalk stretches from Clybourn Street north to E. Pleasant on the west side and to Highland Avenue on the east bank. The Riverwalk includes **Pere Marquette Park,** with a gazebo, pavilion, and boat dock for tours, along with permanent decks and slips over the water. You can also rent boats here for $25; **Laacke & Joys,** tel. (414) 271-7878, right on the river, has kayak rentals for $16 per day. A water taxi service has been proposed and would likely depart from the park.

Also along N. Old World Third Street is **Usinger's,** 1030 N. Old World Third St., tel. (414) 276-9100, known as the Tiffany of sausagemakers. In a city raised on *fleisch,* Usinger's has been the carnivore's heaven since 1880 and partially explains the occasional odd olfactory sensation downtown—the sweet scent of wood smoke mingling with the smell of brewers' yeast. Usinger's old-style store, right in front of the factory, dispenses over 75 varieties of sausage; not surprisingly, the bratwurst tops the list. In 2000 *Food & Wine* dubbed Usinger's bratwurst the best sausage in America. Usinger's also ships Old World ham and gift boxes. Open Mon.-Sat. 8:30 a.m.-5 p.m.

Lakefront

Milwaukee sits on the deepest harbor on the western edge of Lake Michigan. For miles, the city rolls like a sideways wave along the lake. You can drive the entire lakefront on WI 32 or bike most of it on separate county park bike paths. You pass nine beaches along the way; the most popular include **South Shore Beach** along South Shore Drive, **McKinley** and **Bradford** Beaches, both along N. Lincoln Memorial Drive; and **Grant Beach,** in South Milwaukee.

Lincoln Memorial Drive is what most visitors see; it stretches some three miles from north of the Summerfest grounds along greenspace to Lake Park at the tip of a modest promontory. Three miles of park, park, and more park. Lake Park was designed by Frederick Law Olmsted, planner of New York City's Central Park and San Francisco's Golden Gate Park. Adjoining the nucleus (prehistoric Native American burial mounds) at Lake Park is the **North Point Lighthouse,** originally a guiding light downtown built in 1837 and still in use today. At the top of North Avenue is the **Northpoint Watertower,** a Victorian gothic structure dating from the 1870s and one of the few extant water towers like it in the United States. Along Lincoln Memorial Drive, you can't help but experience the War Memorial and the Art Museum or pass by large Juneau and McKinley Parks, the latter of which has a huge marina and Government Pier—great for coastwatching. To start at Lake Park and walk south is a good way to while away a day. Take the 30 Jackson-Downer bus eastbound along Wisconsin Avenue and get off at North Avenue and Lake Drive.

Near where Harbor Drive connects with N. Lincoln Memorial Drive is the newer **Milwaukee Maritime Center,** 500 N. Harbor Drive. A Coast Guard education and sailing center-cum-repository of maritime history, it's housed in an old ferry building. The interiors include a quasi-museum of Great Lakes heritage; the center is in the process of building an enormous replica schooner; see "River and Lake Tours" for information. The center is open Sat.-Sun. noon to 5 p.m.

High Roller Bike and Skate Rentals, tel. (414) 273-1343, has locations at both Veterans Park on the lakefront and Greenfield Park, 2028 S. 124th St. They rent and sell bikes, tandem bikes (child accoutrements available), inline skates, and volleyball sets. Both stores are open daily April through early September 10 a.m.-8 p.m. Some other city parks have private rental vendors. At 140 N. Lincoln Memorial Dr., a **sailing center,** tel. (414) 225-9393, rents sailboards and jet skis. **Welker Water Sport Rentals,** McKinley Pebble Beach, tel. (414) 630-5387, has jet ski, kayak, and canoe rentals. You can paddle the Juneau Park lagoon just off the lakefront in a paddleboat rented from the contiguous Veterans Park.

South of the Milwaukee Art Museum and the Municipal Pier is Wisconsin's newest state park—not yet named when this book was being updated—a 20-acre parcel of land adjacent to the Summerfest grounds. It will consist of a small-craft landing, fishing pier, and trails linking it to the Glacial Drumlin Trail, Military Ridge Trail, and others.

To reach the lakefront by bus, any eastbound Route 10 bus will get to the War Memorial Center and Art Museum; the 30 Prospect-Maryland bus also goes to the complex.

Neighborhoods, Historic Districts, and Walking Tours

Early travelogues touted the city's lines and lines of palatial residences. "Indeed, it is not easy to recall any busy city which combines more comfort, evidences of wealth and taste and refinement, and a certain domestic character, than this town on the bluffs," one impressed easterner observed.

The unusually high concentration of magnesium and calcium in Milwaukee clay created the yellowish tint that gives much of the city's original architecture a distinctive flair. Factories produced top-quality bricks of such eye-catching light hues that the city became known as Cream City.

Virtually all of the **Northpoint District** is on the National Register of Historic Places. This longtime exclusive community lies west of N. Lincoln

Memorial Drive and south of E. Park Place to E. Woodstock Place, tracing the northern stretch of Milwaukee's coastal bight. The Northpoint Watertower occupies the central radial point, and the northern section is bookended by Lake Park. Strolling through the Northpoint District, you'll see gracefully aging residences built for Milwaukee's wealthier financiers and industrialists in the 1890s to the 1930s.

For all of Northpoint's well-to-do elegance, **Yankee Hill** makes that neighborhood appear raffish. This, the premier Milwaukee neighborhood, arose north of E. Mason Street to E. Ogden Avenue, and west off the lakefront to N. Jackson Street. Originally owned by Milwaukee's first resident, Solomon Juneau, this became the city's center of government, finance, and business. Populated by East Coast transplants, it was known also as Yankeeburg. Churches are everywhere, along with lovely old rowhouses and townhouses as well as examples of Victorian gothic, Italianate, and every other 19th-century architectural predilection. Milwaukee's original luxury hotels went up along these stretches.

Juneautown constituted the east side of the 19th-century internecine Milwaukee wars. Originally encompassing 160 acres extending from the river to Lake Michigan, this high-and-dry real estate enjoyed a prime location. As such, it developed into the effective heart of the original city. It was populated by early Yankee opportunists who erected much of the city's commercial and governmental addresses, primarily along Water Street, then along Wisconsin Avenue; toward the lake, residential districts expanded in tight grids. Eventually, commercial activity hopped the river to Kilbourntown, but Juneautown continued to dominate finance, insurance, and local government. Today, both Water Street and Wisconsin Avenue atavistically claim the title of most-happening area in the city. Original architectural gems like the Milwaukee City Hall, Pabst Theater, Iron Block, and funky old Milwaukee Street are still chockablock with baroque Victorian buildings.

Kilbourntown went up as a direct rival to Juneautown—and at about the same time. Speculator Byron Kilbourn also platted his 300 acres snugly; Kilbourn, however, refused to align his bridges with Juneautown's, the consequence of which is apparent today. Low-lying and marshy, there wasn't much going for the land, other than

location—spreading west from today's Old World Third Street, the community was an important transit point to Madison. Yankees populated the enclave initially but were soon overrun by the waves of Germans who put their stamp on the town beginning in the 1830s. Not much of that 19th-century flavor remains. Other than N. Old World Third Street, much of the architecture was razed for mega-projects such as the Bradley Center, the Midwest Express Convention Center, and the early 20th-century retail and commercial enterprises that rejuvenated the town. Highlights in Kilbourntown include the Mediterranean Revival Riverside Theater along W. Wisconsin Avenue; the Germania Building on W. Wells Street, once the site of a German-language publishing empire and notable for its carved lions and copper-clad domes (endearingly dubbed "Kaiser's Helmets"); the odd-shaped Milwaukee County Historical Center; the legendary Turner Hall; the Milwaukee Public Museum; Milwaukee Public Library; and the enormous Grand Avenue Mall.

A case can be made that the **West End** rivals Yankee Hill's opulence. A couple miles west of the commercial districts, West End became the city's first residential suburb, between N. 27th St., N. 35th St., W. Wisconsin Ave., and W. Vliet Street. Yankee bluebloods and prominent German-American families competed in building the most opulent mansions, rivaling the decadence of the lakeshore mansion rows. Highland Boulevard was at one time referred to as "Sauerkraut Boulevard." Though most of the well-to-do left for wider pastures just decades after the mansions went up, district by district preservation efforts have restored lots of the original grandeur. Three historic districts are now located within the West End. Highlights of the area include the Tripoli Shrine Temple on W. Wisconsin Avenue, Harley Davidson Co., Miller Brewing Co., and entire blocks of refurbished Victorian primness.

Brady Street spans a land bridge connecting the Milwaukee River and Lake Michigan. Another major overhaul of the local architecture has restored this area, originally Milwaukee's version of Little Italy. Today the residual effects of a century of Italian immigration pervade, but there's also an appreciable quotient of hipsters and misunderstood geniuses lining coffeehouse windows. The refurbishing has nice touches, such as the etching of Brady Street history into the sidewalk cement.

In 2000 the city announced plans to renovate **Bronzeville,** an erstwhile African-American cultural and entertainment center that has faded, doing a Brady Street gentrification to make it hip and happening. The district will run from N. 4th Street to N 7th Street, using America's Black Holocaust Museum (see below) as the premier attraction.

Immediately north of the Allen-Bradley clock, between 1st and 2nd Streets on W. National Avenue, is a stretch of Milwaukee that looks sadly akin to a Depression-era photo during the day but by night becomes one of the city's most underappreciated tip-the-elbow neighborhoods. Bit by bit, **Walker's Point** is being rejuvenated by renovation—good and slow, without glossy gentrification. This small peninsula, once completely occupied by marshy lowlands, was settled by George Walker, who built his little cabin at the confluence of the Milwaukee and Menomonee Rivers. While most scoffed at him, Walker knew that when the swamplands were drained, he would have an overland route between the east and west sides of the city. Palatial residential streets went up around Walker's Point and industry filled in the marshes. Many of the city's primary manufacturing employers got started on the Point. Walker's Point is also one of the most ethnically mixed neighborhoods in Milwaukee. German, Scandinavian, British, Welsh, Irish, Serb, Croatian, and Polish settlers came in originally, and Hispanics and Southeast Asian immigrants have arrived more recently.

Activated in 1962, the **Allen-Bradley clock,** the second largest in the world—but the largest four-faced clock in the world, according to the *Guiness Book of World Records*—has octagonal clock faces twice the size of the clocks of Big Ben in London. The hour hands are 15 feet 9 inches long and weigh 490 pounds; the minute hands are 20 feet long and weigh 530 pounds. It's still crucial as a lake navigation marker. Stop by **Tivoli Gardens,** home of the Milwaukee Ballet Company, to see another good example of gentrification. An original al fresco produce market was renovated into a biergarten by the Schlitz Brewing Co. and in the past decade was redone yet again, but without undoing the better aspects of its design.

The CVB offers detailed brochures covering all Milwaukee neighborhoods; they also have lists of tour companies, including **Historic Milwaukee, Inc.,** tel. (414) 277-7795, which offers 90-minute walking tours of the early settlement areas, eastside mansions, and other things. See below for easier trolley tours.

Annunciation Greek Orthodox Church

"My little jewel—a miniature Santa Sophia," is how Frank Lloyd Wright described the final major work of his life—the Annunciation Greek Orthodox Church, 9400 W. Congress St., tel. (414) 461-9400. Its imposing rondure is a landmark to Milwaukee architecture—a dramatic inverted bowl into which Wright incorporated symbolic golds and blues and the Greek cross. The blue-tiled dome rises 45 feet above the floor and spans 104 feet. During the most recent update the congregation was involved in a heated dispute as to whether the original murals should be changed to more, er, "religious" themes. Individual tours are not possible, but groups can reserve tours. From N. 4th St. at Wisconsin Ave., take the 57 Walnut-Lisbon bus westbound and disembark at 92nd and Grantsosa.

Other Churches

St. Mary's Church, 836 N. Broadway, is precisely the same age as Milwaukee. Made of Cream City brick in 1846, it is the oldest Catholic church in the city. The Annunciation painting above the altar was a gift from King Ludwig I of Bavaria.

The only thing remaining of a Teutonic settlement in New Coeln (founded in 1840), **St. Stephen's Church,** 5880 S. Howell Ave., now resides here in Milwaukee and houses a collection of famed woodcarvings.

The first Polish basilica in North America was built in Milwaukee, **St. Josaphat's Basilica,** on Lincoln Ave. at S. 6th Street. Parishioners built the structure out of salvaged rubble from the Chicago Federal Building. The capacious dome is modeled after St. Peter's in Rome; inside is a rather astonishing mélange of Polish iconography and hagiography, relics, stained glass, and woodcarvings. Take any southbound Route 80 bus from N. 6th St. at Wisconsin Ave. and get off at 6th and Lincoln.

The progressive **Central United Methodist Church,** 639 N. 25th St., tel. (414) 344-1600, is partially enclosed by earth and incorporates radical energy-saving and solar-energy measures (the tower holds solar panels). Tours can be arranged on weekdays.

It's not a church per se, but the **Tripoli Shrine Temple,** 3000 W. Wisconsin Ave., is worth a look, if only for the oddly appealing Taj Mahal nature of the place. It was built during a period of "fantasy architecture" and was indeed based on the Taj Mahal of India. The main dome is 30 feet in diameter and is flanked by two smaller domes. Camels, lanterns, and floral designs are some of the artwork decorating the interiors. Self-guided tours are available weekdays 9 a.m.-4 p.m.

Architectural Odds and Ends

A block from the Public Museum, the distinctive **Milwaukee Public Library** is an impressive 1895 edifice. You can find it by looking for the dome. Inside, a spacious rotunda displays well-preserved original detail work. Any westbound bus on Wisconsin Ave. will get you there; get off between 8th and 9th Streets.

In the 200 block of E. Wells St., **Milwaukee City Hall** is a navigational aid for first-timers, with its can't-miss-it Flemish Renaissance design (and also because many remember it from the television sitcom *Laverne & Shirley*). Antechambers there have extant woodcarving, century-old hand-designed ceilings, leaded stained-glass windows, and a lovely eight-story atrium. The 10-ton bell in the tower now rings only for special occasions, and it rocks the entire downtown when it does.

On the southeast corner of Water Street and Wisconsin Avenue, the antebellum **Iron Block** is the only example of cast-iron architecture left in Milwaukee, and one of three in the Midwest.

Wisconsin's one-time status as leading world grain producer explains the lavish interiors of the **Grain Exchange,** 225 E. Michigan Street. Located in the Mackie Building, the three-story exchange was built in 1879 (the first centralized trading center in the U.S.); recent touch-ups resulted in atavistic Victorian opulence—gold motifs and enormous paneled murals adorn the 10,000-square-foot room.

The Brewery that Made Milwaukee Famous . . . and Others

Milwaukee was once home to dozens of breweries churning out the secret sauce of *gemütlich-*

keit. Though breweries are no longer the economic champions of the city, the pungent malt scent can still pervade, and beer does remain a cultural linchpin.

Once the sixth-largest (and the oldest) brewery in the U.S., **Pabst** was perhaps the most representative of old-time Milwaukee and its predilection for lagers. The Victorian buildings with their German gothic shadows, the copper kettles, and the stained-glass windows served as eye-catching remnants of a bygone era. Sadly, the turn of the millennium brought an end to the reign of the old king. Though the name lives on—the Pabst brand is among the most popular beers in parts of *China,* of all places—operations have ceased in Milwaukee.

King of the hill in Milwaukee is mega-brewer **Miller,** 4251 W. State St., tel. (414) 931-BEER. This slick, modern operation is the very antithesis of a neighborhood brewer. Frederic Miller apprenticed and served as a brewmaster at Hohenzollern Castle in Sigmaringen, Germany, before striking out for the U.S. in 1855 at age 28 and starting a small brewery there. His original Plank Road Brewery, bought from the son of the Pabst progenitor and not to be confused with Miller's shrewdly named contemporary brewing operation, put out 300 barrels per year—no mean feat, but nothing stellar. Today, Miller—now owned by Phillip Morris—is the second-largest brewery in the nation, with six satellite operations and a total production of *45 million* barrels a year (the warehouse is the size of five football fields). Brewery visits start with a mammoth-screen multimedia history and devotional to Frederic Miller. Hour-long tours then depart, taking in the ultra-high-tech packaging center, the hangar-size shipping center, and, finally, the brewhouse. Tours end at the Caves Museum, a restored portion of Miller's original brewery in which kegs of beer were cooled prior to the advent of refrigeration. Historic brewing equipment and memorabilia are on display. The ineluctable Bavarian hut dispenses free samples and features an antique stein collection and ornate woodwork. Tours are free and run Tues.-Sat. 10 a.m.-5:30 p.m. Miller is considering a **brewing museum** at its west-side corporate headquarters.

Any northbound Route 71 bus will get to the brewery; get on at N. Water St. and Wisconsin and disembark at 42nd and State.

THE BEER CITY

It's hit the skids to a certain extent, but in a state that conjures up images of beer halls and morning quaffs, Milwaukee was the place that gave rise to the stereotype. King Gambrinus, the mythical Flemish king and purported inventor and patron of beer, would no doubt have called the city home.

The Beginnings and the Rise

The first brewery in Milwaukee wasn't started by a German. In 1840, Richard Owens and two other Welshmen founded a lakefront brewery and began producing mostly ales. Germans got into the act not much later with Herman Reuthlisberger's brewery in Milwaukee—and the city's character was never the same. In 1844, Jacob Best started the neighborhood Empire Brewery, which later became the first of the mega-breweries, Pabst. The same year saw Milwaukee's first beer garden—that all-inclusive picnic/party zone with lovely flower gardens and promenades so essential to German culture—open, and this was two years before the city's charter was approved! The next half decade saw the establishment of the progenitors of Milwaukee's hops heritage—in order, Blatz, Schlitz, and the modern leviathan, Miller.

Milwaukee's stranglehold on the brewing industry can be traced to a number of factors. Without question, the primary spur was the massive immigration of people accustomed to satisfying their thirst with a brew. Of these, most influential were the waves of German immigrants, which earned Milwaukee the nickname "German Athens" by the 1880s. Other ethnic groups were also involved, but breweries and state beer consumption rose and fell in direct proportion to the level of Teutonic immigration. Further, when the government levied a whiskey tax of $1 per barrel, tavern patrons immediately began asking for beer instead. Later, tastes for light German-style lagers rose outside the state.

Another factor in Milwaukee's brewery success was location; Wisconsin was a world agricultural player in grains, hops among them. In addition, Milwaukee's plethora of natural ice gave it an edge over other U.S. brewers. The Great Chicago Fire of 1871 also helped, by devastating virtually all of Milwaukee's competition.

As a result, Milwaukee breweries proliferated and enjoyed a meteoric rise. Breweries sponsored their own salons throughout the city. The city became famous for production and consumption—by the Civil War, there was one tippler's joint for every 90 residents—and *during* the war, the breweries doubled their production yet again. At one time, there were nearly 600 breweries in the state. This led Temperance crusader Carrie Nation to declare in 1902, "If there is any place that is hell on earth, it is Milwaukee. You say that beer made Milwaukee famous, but I say that it made it infamous."

The brewers' vast wealth allowed them to affect every major aspect of Milwaukee society and culture; ubiquitous still are the brewing family names affixed to philanthropic organizations, cultural institutions, and many buildings. So popular was Pabst beer that it could afford to place real blue ribbons on bottles by hand; so pervasive were the beers that Adm. Robert Peary found an empty Pabst bottle as he was nearing the North Pole.

The Decline

At its zenith, untold numbers of large breweries were in operation in Milwaukee. With perhaps 60 at the peak, that number dwindled to only a dozen or so after Prohibition, and today there is just one, Miller.

The whole system started going haywire when the first of the original large breweries, Blatz, ceased operations in 1959. In 1982, Stroh's of Detroit purchased the Jos. Schlitz Brewing Company. Pabst, long under absentee ownership, closed here in 1999. In the years before Blatz's demise, Milwaukee could still claim to produce nearly 30% of the nation's beer; as of 1996, the number was less than five percent.

Microbreweries and brewpubs (not the same thing) have inevitably cut into the mega-brewery markets: the fickle tastes of aging yuppies and the protean nature of trendy youth don't bode well for tradition. Today, the nation boasts over 2,500 different beers. And yet microbrews are a throwback of sorts. The first beer brewed in Milwaukee came from neighborhood brewers, most of which put out only a barrel a week, just enough for the local boys. As the major breweries gained wealth, they gobbled up large chunks of downtown land to create open-atrium *biergartens* and smoky *bierhalls,* in effect shutting out the smaller guys. Milwaukee has three ambitious microbreweries, and brewpubs are on the rise.

Most telling of all may be the deconstruction of yet another Wisconsin stereotype: Cheeseheads, despite being born clutching personalized steins, do not drink more beer per capita than any other state—that honor goes to Nevada.

Brewing on an epic scale established Milwaukee's early fame, but now that that era is dissipating, microbreweries and brewpubs are picking up the slack.

The **Lakefront Brewery,** 1872 N. Commerce St., tel (414) 372-8800, started as a kitchen experiment for some Milwaukee brothers and now puts out 2,000 barrels annually. Tours Friday at 5:30 p.m. and Saturday afternoons at 1:30, 2:30, and 3:30 p.m. take in Larry, Moe, and Curly on the tanks; the tour's free, but a $3 donation (which goes to charity) is urged. Lakefront brews include specialty beers like pumpkin and cherry-flavored varieties. This microbrewery is the most unique and the best place for tastings. All its beer is dispensed in Milwaukee, especially in Riverwest taverns. The brewery also has a boat dock and riverwalk.

Larger in scale is **Sprecher,** 701 W. Glendale Ave., tel. (414) 964-2739, in Glendale, one of the original Milwaukee microbrews, which has expanded its 10 labels throughout the state. The Special Amber can be found just about anywhere in southern Wisconsin and is a personal favorite. The brewery also makes a killer root beer and cream soda and has one of the city's best microbrewery tours.

Other brewpubs are found downtown, most along N. Water Street. The **Water Street Brewery,** 1101 N. Water St., tel. (414) 272-1195, is the original, and though there are no established tours, they pretty much always talk up beer if you want to visit. A few blocks south is the **Stout Bros. Public House,** 777 N. Water St., tel. (414) 273-1080, which had just opened as this book was being researched. The **Milwaukee Ale House,** 233 N. Water St., tel. (414) 226-2337, is just up the street and also offers impromptu tours. One outpost of a national chain, the **Rock Bottom Restaurant and Brewery,** 740 N. Plankinton Ave., tel. (414) 276-3030, is a huge place and possibly the most popular, especially for food.

If you visit during summer, check and see if water-based weekend brewery tours are offered aboard the *Brew City Queen.* The three-hour tours start at Lakefront Brewery, then head to Rock Bottom Restaurant and Brewery, followed by the Milwaukee Ale House. Tour times vary and cost $12 plus $3 if you're going to drink (it's bottomless). Reservations are required; call (414) 283-9999.

Beer Corner
The only-in-Milwaukee award goes to **Forest Home Cemetery,** 2405 W. Forest Home Ave., and its designated sector of eye-catching monuments to the early Milwaukee brewing giants: Blatz, Pabst, Best, and Schlitz rest in peace beneath the handcrafted stones. Kooky or spooky, heritage is heritage. You can usually enter the cemetery weekdays until around 4 p.m. and on Saturday mornings.

Harley-Davidson
Hogs and Ultra-Glides are not actually assembled in the Beer City anymore. In fact, the only part of the motorcycle-manufacturing process visitors can witness in Milwaukee is at the **Harley-Davidson engine plant** (which also assembles transmissions), 11700 W. Capitol Dr., tel. (414) 535-3666. The plant produces Sportster and Buell engines. Even if you know zilch about motorcycles, it's kind of a thrill to walk down a Harley assembly line. Free hour-long tours vary week to week according to seasonal demands, so call ahead. Children must be 12 years old, and no cameras are allowed.

The best way to experience Harley otherwise is to be around for annual Harley riders' conventions, when literally 100,000 Harleys descend on the city to fete the metallic beasts. It's an indescribable experience to see the parade of Harleys roaring down I-94 toward Miller Park on their way to a Brewers game. As this book was being updated, the city was breaking ground for the **Harley-Davidson Experience Center** to be built in Schlitz Park, the gorgeous old brewhouse of defunct Schlitz Brewing Co. This $30 million project will feature an interactive museum and exhibits on the history, culture, and lifestyle engendered by the company and its slavishly devoted riders. There will also be lots of vintage vehicles and a restaurant.

See "Organized Tours" for a way to get aboard a growling Harley.

Pabst Mansion
First stop for any historic architecture buff is the grandest of the grand—the Pabst Mansion. Built in 1890-93 of those legendary cream-colored bricks, it was the decadent digs of Capt. Frederick Pabst, an erstwhile steamship pilot turned heir to the Pabst fortune. The Flemish Renaissance man-

HOG HEAVEN

Beer may have made Milwaukee famous, but a certain classic Americana keynote also roared out of the city nearly a century ago—the Harley-Davidson Motorcycle Co. To some, Harley-Davidson—the bikes, the slavishly devoted riders, and the company—truly represents the ethos of Milwaukee: blue-collar tough, proud, and loyal. Anyone who witnessed Harley's 90th Anniversary Reunion in Milwaukee knows what it's all about. Nearly a quarter of a million Harley riders invaded the city in a thunderous cacophony, effectively shutting down the interstates, then taking over the lakefront festival grounds and Milwaukee County Stadium for a Brewers game. All in celebration of the only American motorcycle maker and its return to the stuff of legend.

The Company

William S. Harley and Arthur Davidson were boyhood friends in Milwaukee, the former an apprentice draftsman, the latter a fabricator. Fascinated by the bicycle craze around the turn of the century and by German Daimler motorcycles made as early as the 1880s, the two took it one step further. In 1903, they rigged a single-cylinder engine (the carburetor was a tin can) and leather-strap drive chain onto a thin bicycle frame—with no brakes. Thus began the first putterings of the company known for roaring.

They only sold a couple the first year, but within three years they were getting a dozen orders a month; the company eventually incorporated in 1907, bringing in additional family members, and within a decade became the largest motorcycle maker in the world. Harleys' reputation for endurance made them popular with the U.S. Postal Service and especially police departments. But it was during WW I that Harley gained the U.S. government's devotion—Harleys with sidecars equipped with machine guns pursued pesky Pancho Villa into Mexico in 1917. Europeans found a great enthusiasm for the machines, too, following the Great War; within five years, 20% of the company's business was exported.

Harley-Davidson's mammoth success was due to many things, primarily sound engineering (Harley's first real motorcycle—without a bicycle frame—lasted 100,000 miles). In the first Federation on American Motorcyclists endurance test, the co-founder's brother Walter Davidson and his hog scored above a perfect 1,000 points, leading to a Harley dominance in motorcycle racing for decades. Constant innovations, like the first clutch, also fueled success. Finally, Harleys were tough enough for the U.S. military to designate the company its sole supplier.

Further, no motorcycle maker could claim the innovation or the zeal with which Harley-Davidson catered to its riders. Original dealers were instructed to employ the consumers in as much of the process as possible. Harley-Davidson open houses were legendary. *The Enthusiast,* the company's newsletter, is the longest-running continuously published motorcycle organ anywhere. (All this effort beat Saturn cars by half a century.)

The Bikes

The original Harleys were derisively dubbed "Hardly Ablesons" because of their tendency to break down and the maddeningly high requirement of patience and maintenance—or so said owners of arch rival Indian Motorcycles. Harley-Davidsons, despite the tinkering required early on, reinvented the way the country thought about motorcycles and design.

The prototype that rolled out of the backyard shop in 1903 was followed by the first real motorcycle, the 1916 Model J. The company hit eternal fame with the goofy-looking, radically designed Knucklehead in 1936, when a public initially dismayed by the bulging overhead valves (hence the name) soon realized its synthesis of art and engineering—it has been called the most perfect motorcycle ever made. The Sportster, introduced in 1957, also gets the nod from aficionados—it's called the Superbike. In the 1970s, the Super Glide—the *Easy Rider* low-rider's progenitor—singlehandedly rescued the company. The modern Softail and Tour Glides are considered by Harley-Davidson to be the best ever engineered.

Good Times, Bad Times

By the 1940s, two-thirds of all U.S. bikes were Harley-Davidsons. By the 1950s, swelled by demand, Harley managed to push out its main competitor, Indian Motorcycle. But somewhere along the line, something happened, and the

(continued on next page)

HOG HEAVEN

(continued)

company took it on the chin. When AMF (American Machine and Foundry) took control of the company in 1969, sales were plummeting. Some blame incompetent corporate oversight, others blame a toxic image problem brought on by Hollywood. (Marlon Brando and *The Wild One* had established the archetype of the motorcycle renegade, and by the 1960s, most people's clearest images of Harleys were as the ride of choice among Hell's Angels and the final scenes of *Easy Rider*.) Whatever the cause, sales hit the wall, morale of the company's workforce hit an all-time low, and things got so bad that manufacturing was doled out to separate factories around the country.

In 1981, a group of about 30 Harley employees (most of them long-time vets of the original company but some from AMF) bought the company back and virtually reinvented it. With top-of-the-line products, brilliant marketing, and a furious effort at regaining the trust of the consumer, Harley-Davidson moved steadily back into the market. By the late-1980s, the company was again profitable against Japanese bikes. The effects are manifest: there's a

veritable renaissance of the Harley craze, an extensive waiting list for bikes (all 75,000 produced in a year are spoken for up to a year in advance), and Harley groups tooling even the streets of Hong Kong. The bikes are now priced beyond the reach of most of the "beards, booze, and broads" crowd. Over half of Harley owners are senior citizens, married, college-educated, and have high incomes. In the last few years, some of Harley-Davidson's highest-profile proponents have included the late Malcolm Forbes and Jann Wenner, founder and publisher of Rolling Stone.

The contemporary Harley-Davidson headquarters sits very near the site of that shed/workshop that cobbled together the first bike. The bikes aren't assembled here anymore—just transmissions and engines—but the company remains firmly committed to its downtown location. It has programs encouraging employees to live in the neighborhood and is one of the most in-touch corporations in town. An enormous Harley-Davidson museum-cum-place of worship is under construction in Milwaukee in a lovely old beer factory building.

sion, unique in a city that didn't have much like it, is staggering even by the baroque standards of the time: 37 rooms, 12 baths, 14 fireplaces, 20,000-plus feet of floor space, carved panels relocated from Bavarian castles, priceless ironwork by Milwaukeean Cyril Colnik, and some of the finest woodwork you'll likely ever see. It enjoyed Milwaukee's first electricity and central heating. An adjacent pavilion, now the gift shop, was the Pabst showcase at the World's Columbian Exposition in Chicago in 1893 but was later renovated to resemble St. Peter's basilica.

The mansion, 2000 W. Wisconsin Ave., tel. (414) 931-0808, is open Tues.-Sat. 10 a.m.-3:30 p.m., Sunday noon-3:30 p.m. Admission is $7 adults, $6 seniors, $3 ages 6-17, and free for children under 6. To get there on the bus, take any westbound Route 10, 30, or 31 bus on Wisconsin Ave. and get off at 20th Street.

Milwaukee County Zoo

Though its innovative designs have been mimicked nationally and internationally for the past

three decades, none have quite duplicated the charm or ingenuity of the Milwaukee County Zoo. The animals' environments, grouped in specific continental areas with a system of moats, creates apparent juxtaposing of predator and prey. Almost 5,000 specimens live in the zoo, many of them also residents of the endangered species list. Perennially popular are the polar bears and other aquatic leviathans viewable through subsurface windows, and the children's petting zoo. In a century-old barn is a dairy complex—an educational look at milk production. New for this edition is a renovated timber wolf area. Zoomobiles ($2.50) roll about the expansive grounds, and mini trains ($1.50) also chug around. On occasion, you can even hop aboard an elephant or a spitting camel. Animal shows take place throughout the day. The grounds are large enough to provide cross-country ski trails in winter; rentals are available.

At 10001 W. Bluemound Rd., tel. (414) 771-3040, it's open daily 9 a.m.-4:30 p.m.; from late May to October 1, it's open Mon.-Sat. 9 a.m.-5 p.m. and Sunday and holidays 9 a.m.-6 p.m. The Children's Zoo, rides, and animal shows have varied schedules. Admission is $8, $7 ages 60 and over, $6 children 3-12; parking is $5. All rides and activities within are extra. Milwaukee County residents get in for half price every Wednesday. To bus it, take any westbound Route 10 Wells-Wisconsin bus to 103rd and Bluemound Rd.; from Highway 100, take Route 28 to Bluemound Road.

Milwaukee Public Museum

Of the nearly two dozen museums in the city and nearby, among the most respected nationally and number-one nationwide in exhibits (it holds 6.2 million specimens), is the Milwaukee Public Museum, 800 W. Wells St., tel. (414) 278-2700. It initiated the concept of walkthrough exhibits in 1882 and total habitat dioramas (with a muskrat mock-up) in 1890; today, its "Old Milwaukee" street life construct is quite possibly Milwaukee's most visited tourist spot. New for this edition is an African American 1850s home added to the street, only the second permanent addition to the "Streets" exhibit in 20 years. The museum's multi-level walkthrough Rain Forest of Costa Rica—featuring its own 20-foot cascade—wins kudos and awards on an annual basis. Among the catacombs of displays on archaeology, anthropology, geology, botany, ethnography, and more are its jewels of paleontology: the world's largest dinosaur skull and a 15-million-year-old shovel-tusk elephant skeleton obtained from the Beijing Natural History Museum.

The museum is constantly expanding to allow some of the six million-plus pieces in storage to see the light of day. One heartwarming new display will be the skeleton of beloved Samson, the 600-pound gorilla and long-time resident of the zoo, who died in 1981. Opened in 2000, the Live Butterfly Garden has already become the most popular exhibit. Its 15,000 total square feet features flowering plants, a waterfall, and a 2000-square-foot vivarium.

Take walking shoes, as the three floors—and you'll want to see every one—will wear you down. The museum has completed a huge, dome-shaped, $17-million IMAX theater and the adjacent **Discovery World Museum.** Relocated here from the cramped public library, Discovery World houses hundreds of hands-on exhibits on science and technology.

The museum is open daily 9 a.m.-5 p.m. Admission is $5.50, $4.50 seniors, $3.50 children 4-17 or students with ID. Discovery World costs $5, $4 seniors, $3 children 4-17. Any bus on Wisconsin Ave. will get you to the museum; get off at 8th and Wisconsin and walk north a block to Wells.

Milwaukee Arts Museum

Among the tops in the Midwest for visual arts museums is the Milwaukee Arts Museum, 750 N. Lincoln Memorial Dr., tel. (414) 224-3200, a landmark designed by Eero Saarinen. The museum houses over 20,000 paintings, sculptures, prints, and decorative art. The most noteworthy exhibits include a panorama of Haitian art, collections of German Expressionism and the School of Eight, and the repository of Frank Lloyd Wright's Prairie School of Architecture. Pieces date back as far as the 15th century, and the permanent displays are impressively diverse—Old Masters to Warhol through the Ash Can School. The Bradley Wing houses a world-renowned collection of Modern Masters.

The museum is open Tuesday, Wednesday, Friday, and Saturday 10 a.m.-5 p.m., Thursday noon-9 p.m., and Sunday noon-5 p.m. Admission is $5, $3 seniors and students, children under 12 free. Milwaukee County residents get in free Wednesday and Saturday 10 a.m.-noon. On the transit system, take any Route 10 bus eastbound along Wisconsin Ave., or take the 30 Prospect-Maryland, and disembark at Prospect and Mason.

The MAM is actually one piece of the vast **Milwaukee County War Memorial Center,** a complex comprising several parts of the immediate lakefront and assorted buildings throughout the city. The front of the memorial features an enormous mosaic memorial to WW II and the Korean War. By the time you read this the city will have finished a massive, $50-million architectural enhancement to the museum by international designer Santiago Calatrava. The addition—gull-like wings, which can be raised or lowered to let sunlight in, soaring above the complex—features a breathtaking suspended pedestrian bridge. Even in mid-construction it is a truly stunning spectacle and something that could put Milwaukee on the map. The center's completion will give the museum over 200,000 square feet, an auditorium, an al fresco dining room, an education center, and an additional gallery.

Across from the arts museum in O'Donnell Park, the **Betty Brinn Children's Museum,** 929 E. Wisconsin Ave., tel. (414) 291-0888, is housed in a park pavilion. The museum has dozens of hands- and feet-on experiences for kids; one exhibit is marine oriented. *Parents* magazine rated it in the top 10 for best museums for families. It's open Tues.-Sat. 9 a.m.-5 p.m., and Sunday noon-5 p.m. Admission is $4.

Other Museums

The campuses of the University of Wisconsin-Milwaukee and Marquette University have additional museums. **Mitchell International Airport** has an aviation museum housing a number of aircraft, including a zeppelin. More appealing is the retrospective of the iconoclastic and innovative military aviation pioneer Billy Mitchell, a Beer City native. The museum, on the airport's upper level, is open daily 8 a.m.-10 p.m.; admission is free.

Northeast of downtown, the **Charles Allis Art Museum,** 1801 N. Prospect Ave., tel. (414) 278-8295, is in a Tudor mansion built by the first president of Allis-Chalmers, a major city employer. It has a superb collection of world art, fine furniture, and nearly 1,000 objets d'art dating back as far as 500 B.C. and covering the entire world. The museum's posh interiors feature Tiffany windows, silk wall coverings, and loads of marble. The museum is open Wed.-Sun. 1-5 p.m. and Wednesday nights 7-9 p.m. On Sunday 2-4 p.m. garbed docents lead tours. Admission is $3, children 12 and under free.

Also on the east side and within walking distance of the Charles Allis Museum, the lavish Mediterranean Italian Renaissance **Villa Terrace,** 2220 N. Terrace Ave., tel. (414) 271-3656, was built in 1923 as a private home on another of Milwaukee's palisades along the shoreline. Today it houses an eclectic collection of decorative arts, including art and handcrafted furniture from the 16th through the 20th centuries. Wrought-iron work is also on display. New for this edition is the Garden Renaissance program, which includes the restoration of a variety of botanical collections; it will be one of the country's only existing examples of Italian Renaissance

garden art and design. The museum is open Wed.-Sun. 1 p.m.-5 p.m., and admission is $2, children under 12 free. To get there by bus, get on an eastbound 30 Jackson-Downer bus along Wisconsin Ave. and get off at North Ave. and Lake Drive.

Constructed during a Greek Revival craze in the 1840s, the **Kilbourntown House,** 4400 N. Estabrook Park Dr., tel. (414) 273-8288, is no longer in Kilbourntown, one of the city's original enclaves. Precariously close to demolition in 1938, it was instead moved and restored by the WPA. Inside, the collection of mid-19th-century furniture and decorative art, while not as extensive as the one at Villa Terrace, may be more impressive. Open Tuesday, Thursday, and Saturday 10 a.m.-5 p.m. and Sunday 1-5 p.m. Admission is free.

Adjacent to Pere Marquette Park on the west side of the Milwaukee River, the triangular **Milwaukee County Historical Center,** 910 N. Old World Third St., tel. (414) 273-8288, features the historical detritus of a large, multi-ethnic city along with fascinating explicative displays on the city's legendary Bridge Wars and roiling Socialism, including some large mock-ups of various turn-of-the-century offices and shops. A painting alcove displays works of the Panorama painters—an obscure Milwaukee specialty. The center is open Mon.-Fri. 9:30 a.m.-5 p.m., Saturday 10 a.m.-5 p.m., and Sunday 1-5 p.m. Admission is free. Take any northbound Route 19 N. 3rd St.-S. 13th St. bus from N. Plankinton Ave. at Wisconsin Ave. and get off at N. 3rd St. and W. Kilbourn Avenue.

Located in the lower level of the Grand Avenue Mall, the **Clown Hall of Fame** features clothes, exhibits, demonstrations, videos, and regular summertime slapstick performances. Open Mon.-Sat. 10 a.m.-4 p.m., also occasional Sundays 11 a.m.-4 p.m. in summer. Admission is $2, another $3.50 for the clown show.

A fairly new museum in town, **America's Black Holocaust Museum,** 2233 N. 4th St., tel. (414) 264-2500, is an exposé of nearly three centuries of de facto ethnic cleansing. (The museum's Milwaukee location is ironic, given Milwaukee's history of segregation.) The museum's founder witnessed friends' lynchings in the 1930s; he survived one, the only known survivor of a lynching in America. It's open Mon.-Sat. 9

a.m.-6 p.m. Admission is $5 adults, $2.50 children; as often as not, you'll get the museum's founder and director as a guide.

Milwaukee's newest museum, the **Eisner Museum of Advertising and Design,** 208 E. Water St., tel. (414) 203-0371, is only the second facility related to this subject in the country (the other is the American Advertising Museum in Portland, Oregon), and the only one owned by an art school. Extensive exhibits include Burma Shave signs, the automobile in advertising, beer in ads (natch), and "The Shopping Bag: Portable Art." It's open Tues.-Sat. 11 a.m.-5 p.m.; admission is $4.50 adults, $2.50 seniors and students 13 and up.

University of Wisconsin-Milwaukee

UWM is second in enrollment only to the main campus in Madison; it's well known for its civil engineering program. The *Golda Meir Library,* 2311 E. Hartford Ave., tel. (414) 229-6282, houses the **American Geographical Society Collection,** a priceless collection of over half a million maps, atlases, logbooks, journals, globes, charts, and navigational aids, including what is reportedly the world's oldest known map, dating from the late 15th century. The library is open weekdays 8 a.m.-5 p.m., and admission is free.

Three art galleries are also on the campus. The **UWM Art Museum,** in Vogel Hall, 3253 N. Downer Ave., is the most substantive (and permanent); the **Fine Arts Gallery,** at 2400 E. Kenwood Blvd., has student and faculty displays; and the **Art History Gallery,** Mitchell Hall, 3203 N. Downer Ave., rotates exhibits in the largest exhibition hall. Galleries are generally open Tues.-Sat. or Mon.-Fri. noon-5 p.m. Call (414) 229-5070 for information. Free admission.

Marquette University

Though the university's namesake was not particularly enamored of the Great Lake coastline, this Jesuit university was founded in 1881 and christened for the intrepid explorer. (The university purportedly even has bone fragments from the Black Robe.) The primary attraction here is the **St. Joan of Arc Chapel,** an inspiring, five-century-old relic from the Rhone River Valley of France. Transported stone by stone, along with another medieval chateau, it was reassembled on Long Island in 1927 by a raiload magnate (the French government put the kibosh on cultural relocation following this). The chapel passed through several hands before it was donated to Marquette in 1964. It was lovingly redone by some of the nation's premier historic architects and renovators. It's the only medieval structure in the Western Hemisphere where Mass is said regularly. Stories regarding St. Joan and the chapel may or may not be apocryphal; she is said to have kissed one of the stones while worshiping in the chapel during the war between France and England, and that stone has been colder than the surrounding ones ever since. The chapel is generally open daily 10 a.m.-4 p.m.

Another genuine treasure of architecture on campus is the **Gesu Church,** dating from 1894. This splendid Brobdingnagian gothic structure was named after a church in Rome. The vertiginous heights of the spires are enough, but the gorgeous rose stained glass, divided into 14 petals, is equally memorable.

Also on the campus is the **Haggerty Museum of Art,** 530 N. 13th St., tel. (414) 288-1669, easily one of the city's most challenging galleries and worth it for anyone jaded by excessive exposure to the old masters. It's multicultural and multimedia with a modernist bent. The priciest piece is the Bible series of over 100 hand-colored etchings by Marc Chagall. The gallery is open Mon.-Sat. 10 a.m.-4:30 p.m., Sunday noon-5 p.m., and some Thursday evening hours. Admission is free.

One fascinating item at the **Marquette University Memorial Library,** 1415 W. Wisconsin Ave., is the world-renowned J.R.R. Tolkien Collection, over 10,000 pages for "Lord of the Rings" alone, but also thousands of other documents. There are plenty of display cases on Tolkien's works.

Any westbound bus on Wisconsin Ave. from downtown (except Routes 1 and 12) will get you to Marquette; get off at 14th and Wisconsin and walk a block south.

The Domes

Though it's officially the **Mitchell Park Conservatory,** 524 S. Layton Blvd., tel. (414) 649-9800, everybody knows this complex as "the Domes." You'll know why once you take a gander at the conical seven-story, 148-foot-tall glass-encased buildings. The capacious interiors, totaling some 15,000 square feet, are isolated into arid desert, traditional floral, and tropical rainforest bio-spheres. Two have permanent flora, while the third is re-landscaped up to half a dozen times annually. The Domes puts on extremely popular special shows every year. Outside, the conservatory, ringed with more sunken gardens, is the only structure of its type in the world.

The Domes are open daily 9 a.m.-5 p.m. Admission is $4 adults, $2.50 for children under 18 and senior citizens, free to Milwaukee County residents Sunday 9-11:30 a.m. From N. 2nd St. at Wisconsin Ave., take any southbound Route 18 bus and get off at 27th and National, then walk a block north.

Greenspaces

On the far north side of the city, in Bayside, the **Schlitz Audubon Center,** 1111 E. Brown Deer Rd., tel. (414) 352-2880, abuts the edge of Lake Michigan on the grounds of an erstwhile Schlitz brewery horse pasture. A six-mile network of trails winds along the beach (no swimming) and through diverse prairie, woodland, and wetland. An observation tower with parapet offers lake views. Primarily an education center, the reserve has an ongoing slate of retreats, seminars, and lectures. An interpretive center features lots of displays. It's open daily except Monday 9 a.m.-5 p.m. A $4 fee is collected for trail use.

Along CR Y in Newburg, the **Riveredge Nature Center,** 4458 W. Hawthorne Dr., tel. (414) 375-2715, is a 350-acre preserve along the Milwaukee River with 10 miles of trails through diverse topography. Visit weekdays 8 a.m.-5 p.m., weekends noon-4 p.m. Admission is $1.50 adults, $1 children.

One place you don't hear much about is the **Timber Wolf Farm,** 6669 S. 76th St., tel. (414) 425-8264, home to a dozen captive wolves and an education center on the demise of the wolf.

Charles B. Whitnall Park is a mammoth, 600-acre park, the cornerstone of Milwaukee County's enormous park system. It's even got its own 18-hole golf course. To enjoy more formal gardens, visit **Boerner Botanical Gardens,** 5879 S. 92nd St., tel. (414) 425-1130, located in Whitnall Park in Hales Corners. Forty acres of roses, perennials, wildflowers, and more thrive here; the 1,000 acres of arboretum surrounding the gardens includes the largest flowering crabapple orchard in the United States. The

roses, totaling over 3,000 bushes, are a particularly large draw. Tour the gardens daily mid-April through October, 8 a.m.-sunset. Entry is free, though parking costs $3.50.

Also in Whitnall Park is the **Todd Wehr Nature Center,** designed as a living laboratory of eco-awareness, with nature trails and an ongoing mixed-grass prairie restoration. The center houses wildlife exhibits. Also free, it's open daily 8 a.m.-4:30 p.m.; parking costs $2.50.

River and Lake Tours

Increasingly popular are Milwaukee River cabin cruiser tours, some offering dining cruises as well. Check itineraries—some do only a simple traipse up and back, while others do a good deal of snooping around on century-old canals and river branches. Best for river dining is **Edelweiss,** at the Riverfront Plaza, 1110 N. Old World Third St., tel. (414) 272-3625, which has sleek, single-level Rhine River-style cruisers that chug along the river and into the harbors. The lunch, brunch, and dinner cruises are catered by a prominent local restaurant. The cruises run April-Oct., with fares from $20 to $60. Reservations far in advance are usually necessary.

The venerable **Iroquois Boat Tour,** 3225 N. Shepard, tel. (414) 384-8606, departs from the Clybourn St. Bridge on the west bank of the Milwaukee River daily June-August at 1 and 3 p.m. Fares are $9.50 adults, $6.50 ages 12-17, and $4.50 children under 12.

As this book was being updated, construction of Wisconsin's first tall ship in over a century was ongoing. The *Denis Sullivan* is Wisconsin through and through, with all lumber culled from northern Wisconsin forests; it is over 130 feet long with three 95-foot native white pine masts. Tours were to be available, likely from the Milwaukee Maritime Center.

Brand new to Milwaukee is something folks in the Wisconsin Dells have known about for a generation: Duck rides. The old WW II-issue land-sea craft now prowl land and river. Weekdays the ducks roam the lakefront, weekends they plunge into the Milwaukee River. Call (414) 831-0000 for information.

Freebies

The Riverwalk stroll along the Milwaukee River is the best free activity in town, especially if you're pressed for time. Along the lake at **Pere Marquette Park,** the city screens "river flicks"—free movies alongside the river every Thursday in August. Cathedral Park Square at Jefferson and Wells features free **live jazz** Thursday evenings. At noontime along N. Water St. in the summer, more live music is staged as part of Milwaukee's annual Rainbow Summer. In fact, keep your eyes peeled throughout the week during summer—you're virtually guaranteed a free show daily or nightly at a park somewhere in town.

ACCOMMODATIONS

Hotels and Motels
Downtown Milwaukee is full of gracefully aging anachronisms, some wearier than others. The central area has also seen a boom in new hotels, due to the construction of the Midwest Express Convention Center. Newest is the **Courtyard by Marriott,** which is a good option if you're attending a convention or plan on shopping at the Grand Avenue mall, since it's connected to both by a skywalk.

The **Hotel Wisconsin** 720 N. Old World Third St., tel. (414) 271-4900, fax (414) 271-9998, used to be the best budget choice in town; no frills and ticking radiators for ambience, but it was undergoing extensive remodeling at the time of writing. Still, prices weren't set to rise too dramatically, and if you get the right room (one of the ones on the corners), they're absolutely enormous accommodations for the price. The lobby sports a gallery-worthy assortment of historic photos and newspaper clippings detailing the Old World Third Street area. Similar is the **Astor,** 924 E. Juneau St., tel. (414) 271-4220 or (800) 558-0200, with character (and characters strolling about) through and through, down to the original fixtures. A bit away from central downtown, the **Ambassador** is the cheapest budget hotel.

The hotel causing most buzz is **Hotel Metro,** 411 E. Mason St., tel. (414) 272-1937 or (877) 638-7620, fax (414) 223-1158, with a posh but creative design. The Art Deco stylings include environmentally friendly practices like bamboo-wood floorings and wood from sustainable forests. It's got one of the best cafes in Milwaukee as well.

The **Hilton Milwaukee City Center,** 509 W. Wisconsin Ave., tel. (414) 271-7250 or (800) 445-8667, fax (414) 271-8841, is perhaps the best example of restored charm downtown. This incarnation features limestone ashlar, pink granite, and buff terra-cotta; it's Milwaukee's sole Roaring '20s art deco-style hotel, right down to the geometric marble motifs in the lobby. In late 2000 it opened an interesting recreation center, an island-themed water recreation area with water slides and a real sand beach!

The granddaddy of Milwaukee hotels—called the "Grand Hotel" in fact—is the **Pfister,** 424 E. Wisconsin Ave., tel. (414) 273-8222 or (800) 558-8222, fax (414) 273-8082, built in 1893. This posh city-state-size behemoth oozes Victorian grandeur. The somewhat overwhelming lobby is done with such ornate intricacy that the hotel organizes regular tours of its displays of 19th-century art. It was planning an extensive reconstruction of its 23rd floor to house a state-of-the-art recreation facility.

B&Bs and Historic Inns
Milwaukee surprisingly doesn't have that many B&Bs to choose from. Among the options is the 1897 Queen Anne **Acanthus Inn,** 3009 W. Highland Blvd., tel. (414) 342-9788, fax (414) 342-3460, a 10-room B&B that has retained most of its original design. Period lighting and artwork add a nice touch. Rates are $85-120.

B&B aficionados would do well to scout out communities surrounding Milwaukee—in particular Cedarburg to the northwest. Along the same highway, Mequon also has a few classic old 19th-century Victorian gingerbread and antebellum dwellings. **American Country,** 12112 N. Wauwatosa Rd., Mequon, tel. (414) 242-0194, is an 1844 stone cottage with a patio, wood-burning fireplace, kitchen, private bath, and rates from $80. Port Washington is another good bet.

Hostels
The well-run **Red Barn Hostel,** 6750 W. Loomis Rd. (WI 36), tel. (414) 529-3299, is in southwestern Milwaukee, in the suburb of Greendale, near Scout Lake and Whitnall Parks. The hosts are efficient and you can't beat the digs—a genuine old red barn. It's located on the Milwaukee '76 bike trail, at Root River Parkway and Loomis Road MSA; hiking trails aren't far away. The

MILWAUKEE ACCOMMODATIONS

Note: Milwaukee has a 9% room tax

DOWNTOWN

Ambassador Hotel, 2308 W. Wisconsin Ave., tel. (414) 342-8400, fax (414) 931-0279; $59-99; newly remodeled art deco rooms, good budget choice, some suites and kitchenettes, fitness room, lounge

Astor Hotel, 924 E. Juneau St., tel. (414) 271-4220 or (800) 558-0200, fax (414) 271-6370; $89-119; near lake, gracefully aged historic, some kitchen suites, many original fixtures, health club privileges, newspaper, shuttle, weekend rates, restaurant

Courtyard Inn by Marriott, tel. (414) 291-4122 or (800) 321-2211, fax (414) 291-4188; $89+; linked to downtown attractions via skywalk, pool, fitness room, restaurant/lounge, spacious rooms, ergonomic furnishings, data ports

Holiday Inn-Milwaukee City Centre, 611 W. Wisconsin Ave., tel. (414) 273-2950 or (800) HOLIDAY, fax (414) 273-7662; $75-155; valet parking, pool, restaurant, lounge, higher rates during special events

Hotel Metro, 411 E. Mason St., tel. (414) 272-1937 or (877) 638-7620, fax (414) 223-1158; $145-175; sleek newly refurbished historic boutique hotel with environmentally friendly materials, many suites, reputable restaurant

Hotel Wisconsin, 720 N. Third St., tel. (414) 271-4900, fax (414) 271-9998; $79-95; historic and newly renovated, some special rates for Bradley Center events, hip lounge, good restaurant

Hyatt Regency, 333 W. Kilbourn Ave., tel. (414) 276-1234 or (800) 233-1234, fax (414) 276-6338; $155-175; second-largest in city, landmark 18-story atrium, room service, enclosed walkways to downtown, numerous restaurants including Wisconsin's only rooftop revolving restaurant, exercise equipment

Knickerbocker on the Lake, 1028 E. Juneau Ave., tel. (414) 276-8500, fax (414) 276-3668; $96-110; hotel rooms and apartments, dining room, weekly and monthly rates

Hilton Milwaukee City Center, 509 W. Wisconsin Ave., tel. (414) 271-7250 or (800) 445-8667, fax (414) 271-8841; $179-199; largest in city, 1920s Art Deco style, totally renovated in 1996, ornate marble interiors, indoor pool, sauna, barber, beauty shop, enormous indoor water recreation facility, many more amenities

Park East Hotel, 916 E. State St., tel. (414) 276-8800 or (800) 328-7275, fax (414) 765-1919; $85-120; lounge, dining room, health club, whirlpool, modem hookups, downtown shuttle

Pfister Hotel, 424 E. Wisconsin Ave., tel. (414) 273-8222 or (800) 558-8222, fax (414) 273-8082; $129-189; four stars, sumptuous atmosphere, numerous restaurants, lounges, pool, 24-hour room service, art displays and tours, exercise rooms, multi-bedroom suites

Plaza Apartment Hotel, 1007 N. Cass St., tel. (414) 276-2102, fax (414) 276-0404; $60-80; furnished apartments with full kitchens, restaurant

Ramada Inn-Downtown, 633 W. Michigan St., tel. (414) 272-8410 or (800) 228-2828, fax (414) 272-4651; $75-120; three blocks from Bradley Center and public museum, restaurant, lounge, outdoor pool, 24-hour room service

Wyndham Milwaukee Center, 139 E. Kilbourn Ave., tel. (414) 276-8686 or (800) WYNDHAM, fax (414) 276-8007; $130-520; four stars, in theater district, highly respected restaurant, some minimum multi-night stays, exercise rooms, whirlpool, sauna, steam room

AIRPORT AND SOUTH

Exel Inn of Milwaukee-South, 1201 W. College Ave., tel. (414) 764-1776 or (800) 356-8013, fax (414) 762-8009; $40 and up; good budget choice, transportation, continental breakfast

Four Points Sheraton Hotel Milwaukee Airport, 4747 S. Howell Ave., tel. (414) 481-8000 or (800) 558-3862, fax (414) 481-8065; $79-185; restaurants, health club, tennis and racquetball courts, indoor and outdoor pools, nightclub, hair salon, free transportation, exercise room, some refrigerators

Howard Johnson-Airport, 1716 W. Layton Ave., tel. (414) 282-7000 or (800) 446-4656, fax (414) 282-7000; $50-90; dining room, lounge, outdoor heated pool, airport shuttle, laundry

Manchester Suites-Airport, 200 W. Grange Ave., tel. (414) 744-3600 or (800) 723-8280, fax (414) 744-4188; $80 and up; across from airport, courtesy shuttle, tasteful living-room-like setting with refrigerators and microwaves, made-to-order complimentary breakfasts

Ramada Inn Convention Center, 6401 S. 13th St., tel. (414) 764-5300 or (800) 228-2828, fax (414) 764-4405; $65-115; rooms and some suites, restaurant, coffee shop, lounge, enormous ballroom, free airport shuttle, indoor pool, sauna, whirlpool, indoor and outdoor recreation areas

Red Roof Inn, 6360 S. 13th St. (in Oak Creek), tel. (414) 764-3500 or (800) THEROOF; $50 and up; free morning paper and coffee

SOUTHWEST

Best Western Woods View Inn, 5501 W. National Ave., tel. (414) 671-6400 or (800) 528-1234, fax (414) 671-1029; $64-89; in-room coffee, some kitchenettes, restaurant and lounge, indoor pool, good for zoo

Golden Key Motel, 3600 S. 108th St., tel. (414) 543-5300; $35-60; outdoor pool, refrigerators

WEST

Note: Many of the hotels to the west are strung along or in Milwaukee's first suburb, Wauwatosa; most are in proximity to the state fairgrounds, the zoo, and County Stadium.

Holiday Inn Express, 11111 W. North Ave., tel. (414) 778-0333 or (800) HOLIDAY, fax (414) 778-

0331; $84-109, more on weekends; complimentary continental breakfast, close to Mayfair Mall

Days Inn, 11811 W. Bluemound Rd., tel. (414) 771-4500, fax (414) 771-4501; $40 and up; newly refurbished rooms, restaurant and lounge, continental breakfast

Radisson Hotel Milwaukee West, tel. (414) 257-3400, fax (414) 257-0900; $119 and up; pool, fitness center, across from upscale mall

NORTHWEST

Baymont Inn & Suites, tel. (414) 535-1300 or (800) 301-0200, fax (414) 535-1724; $69; coffee makers, microwaves, refrigerators, some newly renovated rooms

Manchester Suites, 11777 W. Silver Spring Dr., tel. (414) 462-3500 or (800) 723-8280, fax (414) 462-8166; $79 and up; complimentary made-to-order breakfast, voice mail system

NORTHEAST

Milwaukee River Hilton Inn, 4700 N. Port Washington Rd. (Glendale), tel. (414) 962-6040 or (800) 445-8667; $100-125; dining room, lounge, indoor pool

Port Zedler Motel, 10036 N. Port Washington Rd., tel. (262) 241-5850, fax (262) 241-5858; $40 and up; good budget choice

Woodfield Suites, 5423 N. Port Washington Rd., tel. (414) 962-6767 fax (414) 962-8811; $115-135; indoor pool, whirlpool, exercise room, voice mail to rooms, secretarial services, complimentary evening beverages

hostel also rents canoes. To get there, take US 41/S. 27th St. south to Loomis Rd., and then south to the intersection of Root River Parkway. The #35 southbound bus takes you there on a long, long meander to the end of the line. From Wisconsin Ave. downtown, take the westbound #10 bus to 35th St. and request a transfer. The hostel takes guests from April to October only; the office is open 7:30-9:30 a.m. and 5-10 p.m. General facilities are available; rates are $10, day-use $2. Other Hostelling International (HI) hostels are located in Kettle Moraine State Forest—one in Eagle, tel. (262) 594-2765; one in Monches, tel. (262) 628-8259; and Newburg, tel. (262) 675-6755. Milwaukee is the site of the Wisconsin Council offices of **HI-AYH,** 5900 N.

Port Washington Rd., Suite 146, Milwaukee, WI 53217, tel. (414) 961-2525.

Camping

The best public camping is a half hour to the west in the **Kettle Moraine State Forest**; it's very popular and is often booked, so arrive early. The nearest private campground is southwest of Milwaukee along I-43 in Mukwonago at the **Country View Campground,** S110 W26400 Craig Ave., tel. (414) 662-3654. Country View is open mid-April to mid-October and offers a pool, playground, hot showers, and supplies. Campsites are $19-24. RVs can camp at the Wisconsin State Fairgrounds, west along I-94 in West Allis, but it's crowded and cacophonic with freeway traffic.

FOOD

Milwaukee boasts a large array of cuisine—a pan-ethnic food heaven spanning the gamut from fish fries in cozy 120-year-old neighborhood taprooms to four-star *prix fixe* repasts in state-of-the-art gourmet restaurants. If you're seriously into Old World ethnic food, a unique guide exists to the markets, grocers, and bakeries in Milwaukee's enclaves of original cuisine. It's Cari Taylor-Carlson's *The Food Lover's Guide to Milwaukee—An Insider's Guide to Ethnic Bakeries, Grocery Stores, Meat Markets, Specialty Food Shops, and Cafes,* available from Serendipity Ink, P.O. Box 17163, Milwaukee, WI 53217. She eschews large restaurants but includes smaller neighborhood cafes.

Landmark

The oldest civic and cultural organization in Milwaukee (founded in 1833), **Turner Hall,** 1034 N. 4th St., tel. (414) 273-5590, presents a defining Milwaukee dining experience. Before an extensive 1996 renovation, the interiors were dingy, and a foreboding sense of the place caving in at any minute was almost unavoidable. The renovation was overseen by the owners of popular Trattoria Della Via, and the newly christened **Milwaukee Historic Turner's** is refreshingly warm and wondrously bright, allowing a look at the classic Old World interiors: stained glass, photographs, murals, and century-old memorabilia. And yes, it's still got the legendary fish fry, although it's a menu item now and not quite the socializing buffet of before. Along with the fish fry is an eclectic array of appetizers, sandwiches, creative salads and pastas, and a few traditional German dishes. Open daily for lunch and dinner. Selections from $5.

Also there is the **Heritage Tourism Center,** with rotating exhibits and information on ethnic areas and multicultural events along the Lake Michigan Settlement Trail and in Milwaukee. It's open Mon.-Sat. 10 a.m.-10 p.m.

Fish Fries

In Milwaukee, you'll find a fish fry everywhere—even at the chain fast-food drive-through and Milwaukee County Stadium during Friday night Brewers games. Dozens of neighborhood taverns and bars still line up the plank seating and picnic tables with plastic coverings on Friday nights. The tables are arrayed with tartar sauce and maybe pickles (you better like cole slaw, because that's what you get as a side dish). Most fish fries come in under $7 for as much as you can stuff in.

No longer an actual neighborhood taproom but still a glimpse of old Milwaukee is the **Brown Bottle Pub,** 221 W. Galena. It was originally a Schlitz brewery beer parlor and is now a pub. A personal favorite is the classic Wisconsin-style fish fry held at any VFW post—an unbeatable experience. A good bet is **Tanner Paull Post-American Legion,** 6922 W. Orchard St., tel. (414) 476-0434. Or, head for a Catholic church; Milwaukee's got 275 parishes, so you'll find a good one. For 30 years **St. Veronica Congregation,** 4001 S. Whitnall Ave., has served up to 700 people on the last Friday of the month. It's a steal at $5.75 for adults, $2.75 for kids.

For the most one-of-a-kind fry in town, head for the **American Serbian Hall,** 53rd and Oklahoma, tel. (414) 545-6030, recognized as the largest in the nation. On Friday night, this hall serves over a *ton* of Icelandic-style or Serbian baked fish to over 2,500 people. The operation got so big that a drive-through has been added, which serves an additional 1,200 patrons.

Greasy Spoons and Family Restaurants

The greasy spoon of choice is any of the **George Webb** diners in town, the quintessential open-all-night, gum-cracking place to get road food. Downtown, there's one on N. Old World Third, up from the Hotel Wisconsin. Food from $2.

The seven locations of **Heineman's,** the local favorite family-style restaurant, have been around forever. Germanic influences can be detected, and the food's unsurprising but decent. Choices from $3.

Perhaps owing to that "Soup Nazi" episode on *Seinfeld,* Milwaukee has its own new soup restaurant, and it's great. **Soup Bros.,** 209 W. Florida St., tel. (414) 860-SOUP, is in Walker's Point. Outstanding soups from a New York City-trained chef. Open 8 a.m.-4 p.m. Menu items from $2.

Late Night Eats

Great honest-to-goodness Mexican at **El Chico,** 1814 N. Ave., tel. (414) 276-1277, open daily until 3 a.m. A place to see and be seen is another jewel of chic-dom, **Elsa's,** on N. Jefferson St. The former from $2, the latter $4.

Coffee and Tea

The **Fuel Cafe**—great name—at 818 E. Center St., is exceedingly young, hip, and alternative; you'll find cribbage players and riot grrls. The decor is mismatched rummage-sale furniture with an arty flair, and the service gets rapped as lousy. It isn't—and there's a great menu of coffee drinks, bakery items, salads, sandwiches, even Pop Tarts! Try the "Kevorkian Krush," three shots of espresso and mocha. From a buck.

Also try **Brewed Awakenings,** in the 1200 block of E. Brady St., and the great **Jitterzz,** an underground Old World-looking cafe at 7532 W. State Street. Possibly the other most popular hangout is **Rochambo,** 1317 E. Brady Street.

Watts Tea Shop, 761 N. Jefferson St., tel. (414) 291-5120, heads the list for afternoon tea and homemade everything, from scones to chicken salad. The shop is ensconced in the ritzy Watts store, purveyor of prohibitively fragile china, silver, and crystal. Choices from $3.

Custard Stands and Drive-ins

Frozen custard is an absolute must of a Milwaukee cultural experience; the dozens of Milwaukee family custard stands were the inspiration for Big Al's Drive-In on the 1970s TV show *Happy Days.* In an informal poll, 20 questions determined a dozen different recommendations for where to experience frozen custard. The three most often mentioned follow (but you really can't go wrong anywhere). **Kopp's,** 5373 N. Port Washington Rd., tel. (414) 961-2006, does custard so seriously that it has a flavor-of-the-day hotline. An institution since the early '40s is **Leon's,** 3131 S. 27th St., tel. (414) 383-1784; it's got the best neon. **Charlie's A&W,** at 5572 S. 27th St., has Friday and Saturday classic car shows. It's open daily March-October. At 830 E. Layton Ave., the **Nite Owl Drive In** has been dishing up ice cream and doling out burgers by the same family for a half century; even Elvis loved to eat here. All have ice cream from a buck or so.

Supper Clubs and Steakhouses

Coerper's Five O'Clock Club, 2416 W. State St., tel. (414) 342-3553, has been around for-

ever and is so popular for steaks you absolutely need a reservation. It has the largest portions in town, from $10.

Jake's, 21445 W. Capitol Dr., Brookfield, tel. (414) 781-7995, and 6030 W. North Ave., tel. (414) 771-0550, offers casual fine dining in a supper club atmosphere. It's famous for flown-in fish, pepper steak in a crock, and onion rings. Items from $17.

Butch's Old Casino Steakhouse, 1634 N. Water St., tel. (414) 271-8111, is casual and chockablock with steak lovers. Plenty of chops, seafood, and chicken are on the menu as well. Classic Midwestern—you get a relish tray to start. Choices from $15.

The best steak might not even be in Milwaukee itself—the perennially popular **Eddie Martini's,** 8612 Watertown Plank Rd., tel. (414) 771-6680, is west of the city, in Wauwatosa. Also in Wauwatosa is the spanking new **Mr. B's, a Bartolotta Steak House,** 17700 W. Capitol Dr., tel. (262) 790-7005, run by one of Milwaukee's most successful restaurateurs (he also owns an eponymous Italian restaurant in Wauwatosa—see "Italian"). The steaks are grilled over hardwoods, an excellent method to cook them; Italian entrées are also available. Items from $17.

Fine Dining

Grenadier's, 747 N. Broadway Ave., tel. (414) 276-0747, is a four-star *prix fixe* continental restaurant. Specialties include lamb, veal, and beef, with magnificent sweetbreads and an award-winning wine cellar. You choose from multi-course sets (from $20); à la carte menus are also available. New ownership has affected the menu: there's lots of fresh seafood now, and a vegetarian menu is available. Grenadier's is open weekdays for lunch, Saturday for dinner only, Sunday seasonally. Jackets required.

Nouvelle cuisine is done magnificently at **Sanford,** 1547 N. Jackson St., tel. (414) 276-9608, one of the state's most original and respected innovators of cuisine. This is without a doubt the place to cook up an excuse for a splurge. Diners choose from a tasting menu, selecting a three-, four-, five-, or seven-course meal ($42-69) instead of separate entrées and appetizers. The same owners also recently opened the more casual but still creative and outstanding **Coquette Cafe,** 316 N. Milwaukee St., tel. (414)

291-2655, which has items from $7 and they're all worth it.

A couple options exist outside of downtown. Consistently one of Milwaukee's best restaurants, **Steven Wade's Cafe,** 17001 W. Greenfield Ave., New Berlin, tel. (262) 784-0774, always features challenging, rewarding nouvelle cuisine from $12. A newer restaurant that is also excellent is **The Riversite,** 11120 N. Mequon Rd., Mequon, tel. (262) 242-6050, which features seasonal cuisines—excellent steak and lamb from $19.

Boder's on the River, 11919 N. River Rd., tel. (414) 242-0335, has been a mainstay of the community since 1929, still operated by the same family. Four dining rooms spread out along fireplaces and through formal gardens in this 1840s homestead. Open for lunch and dinner Tues.-Sun., with a Sunday brunch. Menu items from $15.

In the Cudahy Towers at 925 E. Wells St., the **Boulevard Inn,** tel. (414) 765-1166, rates a nod for its varied cuisines—German to seafood to vegetarian, from $7.50.

Most downtown Milwaukee hotels have popular dining rooms, including the superb outdoor dining patio of the seafood-heavy **Anchorage Restaurant** in the Milwaukee River Hilton, the **Pfister** dining rooms, the outstanding, creative **Cafe Metro** in the Hotel Metro, and the chicest of the chic **Cafe Knickerbocker** in the Knickerbocker Hotel. The **Polaris Restaurant** atop the Hyatt Regency is Wisconsin's only revolving restaurant.

Water Views
Pieces of Eight, 550 N. Harbor Dr., tel. (414) 271-0597, is Victorian with a mariner complex and incessantly popular. It boasts a busy bar, a wide array of food, and genuinely grand lake vistas. In summer, the deck is crammed; firepits lick flames at the water. The menu runs the gamut of soups, salads, sandwiches, seafood, and other substantial entrées from $7. The 100-item Sunday brunch is also wildly popular. Open daily for lunch and dinner. This is no longer the only restaurant with a lake view. **Nola's,** 931 E. Wisconsin Ave., tel. (414) 298-0000, used to be a spotty South Asian place. It's now a great restaurant featuring creative New Orleans cuisine; try the $10 brunch.

An exquisitely restored 19th-century park structure is now **Bartolotta's Lake Park Bistro,** 3133 E. Newberry Blvd., tel. (414) 962-6300. Housed in an exquisitely restored century-old park pavilion, this newer bistro is becoming very popular. Opened by a prominent local restaurateur, its French cuisine is superb and, if nothing else, the view from the drive along the lake is worth the time. It's a popular Sunday brunch spot. Open weekdays for lunch and dinner, Saturday for dinner only, Sunday brunch and dinner. From $7 lunch, $12 dinner.

Set along but slightly off the Milwaukee River, the riparian **Third Street Pier,** 1110 N. Old World Third St., tel. (414) 272-0330, is one you can hardly help passing downtown. It has the feel of a businessperson's lunch joint; it's got a slew of seafood entrées daily and a whole mess of seafood all day on Friday. Definitely worth a try for the huge and cheap buffet—superb choices under $7. It also has piano music.

Also popular along the river is the casual **Wells St. Station,** 117 E. Wells St., tel. (414) 276-7575, featuring a deck over the river and a mix of pizzas, sandwiches, burgers, chicken, and fish from $5.

Harp Irish Pub, 113 E. Juneau, is hugely popular and has a boat deck along the river, as does **John Hawke's Pub,** 100 E. Wisconsin Avenue.

Seafood
The **Anchorage Restaurant** in the Milwaukee River Hilton serves up great seafood. No frills but worth the trip is the unpretentious **Red Rock Cafe,** 4022 N. Oakland Ave., tel. (414) 962-4545; the chef is an American Culinary Institute grad. You never know what's being flown in that day, so the scrawled special is a definite fresh treat. Choices from $7.

Also outstanding is the chic **Eagen's on Water,** 1030 N. Water St., tel. (414) 277-6900, with decent sushi. The regular airmail cod-cheek delivery is a bit gimmicky, but the seafood is very good at **River Lane Inn,** 313 W. River Lane, Brown Deer. Both from $7.

Vegetarian and Health Food
A healthy option for a low-key cafe-style meal is **Beans and Barley,** 1901 E. North Ave., tel. (414) 278-7878. Very much a hip (though low-priced) eatery, it's housed in what smacks of an

old grocery store warehouse encased in glass walls from an attached grocery and small bar. Brightly lit, it's got simple tables, tile floors, and large paintings. Everything from straight-up diner food to creative vegetarian is on the menu, with Indian and Southwestern options. Juices and smoothies, too. Items from $2.

For take-away health food, a number of co-ops and natural-foods stores are in the downtown area. The largest is **Outpost Natural Foods,** 100 E. Capitol Dr., tel. (414) 961-2597, easily mistaken for any other mega-grocery store save for the organically grown veggies, dietary-restriction sections, and juice bar—there's also a good bakery and deli.

German

Rollicking, boisterous, and full of lederhosen, **Mader's,** 1037 N. Old World Third St., tel. (414) 271-3377, has held its position as *the* German restaurant for the hoi polloi since 1902. Purists sometimes cringe at the over-the-top atmosphere (it's packed to the rafters with German knickknacks), but the cheeriness is unvanquishable and the prices are the best in town for genuine German fare (from $10). Try the *knudel,* which doesn't taste like it came out of a box, *Rheinischer* sauerbraten, oxtail soup, or Bavarian-style pork shank. Mader's also serves a Viennese brunch on Sunday.

Karl Ratzsch's Old World Restaurant, 320 E. Mason St., tel. (414) 276-2720, is superbly realized. This decidedly more upscale multiple award winner is split into two levels. The lower level features a bar with an extensive stein collection, impressive dark interior woodwork, handpainted murals, and antiques; the upper level gives a great bird's-eye view of the dining and bar areas. The menu is copious and decidedly carnivorous—sauerbraten, braised pork shank, *rouladen, käse spätzle,* special strudels, and even some vegetarian offerings. Early dining is available here, and Bavarian music is featured nightly. Open daily for lunch and dinner and Sunday for great breakfasts. From $13.

Another reputable and upscale casual German restaurant is **John Ernst,** on Ogden at Jackson, tel. (414) 273-1878, slavishly worshiped by more than one travel journal. It's open for lunch and dinner daily and features live music daily. Selections from $9.

Italian

Consistently garnering raves for top-shelf Italian cuisine is **Giovanni's,** 1683 N. Van Buren St., tel. (414) 291-5600. Complimentary limousine service is offered to and from downtown hotels and offices. The city's best purveyor of *alta cucina,* **Osteria del Mondo,** 1028 E. Juneau Ave., tel. (414) 291-3770, is in the Knickerbocker Hotel and features a one-page rundown of real-deal antipasti, fresh salads, pastas, fish, and a handful of meat dishes, all from $13. The restaurant also has an atmospheric Italian wine bar.

A diminutive trattoria with solid regional Italian is **Louise's,** 801 N. Jefferson, a trendy place popular with theatergoers. Items from $10.

You'll find bocce courts and the whole works at the **Italian Community Center-Trattoria 631,** 631 E. Chicago St., tel. (414) 223-2180, which appears to have stepped out of a prior era. But possibly the most popular Italian eatery is **Ristorante Bartolotta,** 7616 W. State St., tel. (414) 771-9710, a warm and gregarious trattoria in Wauwatosa—definitely worth the trip. Bartolotta may well be the best-realized Italian experience in the state. Choices from $12.

Mimma's Cafe, 1307 E. Brady St., tel. (414) 271-7337, constantly gets national write-ups for its cuisine; over 50 varieties of pasta and weekly regional Italian specialties are highlights. Selections from $13.

If you're cash-poor, a great option is always **Buca di Beppo,** 1233 N. Van Buren St., tel. (414) 224-8672, since the excellent family-style Italian dinners are absolutely *enormous* (don't get the large!). You'll likely wind up with enough food for two meals. From $8.

Mexican

You'll find the most substantial Mexican menu at **3 Hermanos,** 1100 W. National Ave., tel. (414) 384-8850, and at 1332 W. Lincoln Ave., tel. (414) 384-8885, specializing in seafood in virtually every form—particularly a soup that'll knock your socks off. Quite a bit of grilled seafood, too. From $7.50.

Cempazuchi, 1205 E. Brady St., tel. (414) 291-5233, is a newer restaurant that has a very nice variety of Mexican food represented (items from $10). Ditto the menu at **Rey Sol,** 2338 W. Forest Home Rd., tel. (414) 389-1760, which has items from $7. On a straw poll most Milwaukeeans offered **La Fuente,** 625 S. Fifth St., tel.

(414) 271-8595, as their favorite, and it does have an extraordinary shrimp soup. Items from $5.

Milwaukee's southeast side is a haven for unpretentious authentic Mexican eateries; some Mexican grocers have lunch counters in the back or sell delectable tamales ready for take-out. **Conejito's,** 4th and Virginia Streets, is a neighborhood bar-restaurant with authentic atmosphere and real-deal Mexican food from $4. The same is true at **Jalisco's,** which has numerous locations (one at 2207 E. North Ave.) but whose original is at 9405 S. 27th St., tel. (414) 672-7070. The original perished in a fire, but with a complete rebuild the place has a new look to go with the great food. Jalisco's restaurants are open 24 hours Fri.-Sat. and serve creative burritos as big as your head. Items from $5.

Enjoy Mexican as well as some Puerto Rican choices at **Cafe El Sol,** 1028 S. Ninth St., tel. (414) 384-3100, in the lower level of the United Community Center. Selections from $4.

Cajun
Scotty's Crab House, 1533 E. Belleview Place (two blocks west of Oakland), tel. (414) 964-5400, serves seafood with a special nudge toward Cajun. It's open Tues.-Sat. for dinners, from $15. If you really crave Cajun food, head to Wauwatosa and **Jolly's on Harwood,** 7754 Harwood Ave., tel. (414) 476-7393, a great place with entrées from $12.

African
Very central is the **African Hut,** 1107 N. Old World Third St., tel. (414) 765-1110, whose special is *lumumba,* peppered wings. Items from $7. Open Mon.-Sat. for lunch and dinner.

Barbecue
Serafino's, 1228 N. Astor St., tel. (414) 273-1430, has been synonymous with Milwaukee barbecue for generations, beginning with the present restaurateur's father. Chops, chicken, and racks are slathered and encrusted with the special homemade sauce. Serafino's is open Mon.-Sat. for dinner, from $6.

An interesting take on barbecue can be found at **Brew City Barbecue,** 1114 N. Water St., tel. (414) 278-7033. In addition to the usual racks, they serve a heavenly smoked prime rib. Items from $10. Outstanding, too, is **Speed Queen BBQ,** 1130 W. Walnut St.

Soul Food
Mr. Perkins, 2001 W. Atkinson Ave., tel. (414) 447-6660, is the place to go for soul food, with tons of downhome specialties—collard greens, catfish, chitterlings, fried apples, turkey legs, and the like, as well as homemade sweet potato pie and peach cobbler like you'll find nowhere else. Items from $4.

Grant's Soul Food, 411 W. North Ave., tel. (414) 263-2929, has mostly seafood and chicken, with a lunch special daily.

The **Bungalow,** on Milwaukee's north side, 3466 N. 14th St., tel. (414) 265-9117, is so good that the Green Bay Packers pay it to cater their meals. The menu is a homesick Southerner's dream: short ribs of beef, black-eyed peas, fried corn, peach cobbler, smothered chops, and excellent barbecue. Basic orange Formica decor, but there is some Packer regalia. Open Tues.-Sun. 11 a.m.-1 a.m.

Serbian
Enjoy top-notch Serbian food in a delightful Old World atmosphere at **Three Brothers,** 2414 S. St. Clair St., tel. (414) 481-7530, in Bay View. The 1897 turreted brick cornerhouse, an original Schlitz brewery beer parlor, was turned into a restaurant by the present owner's father, a Serbian wine merchant. Not much has changed—the high paneled ceilings, original wood, dusty bottles on the bar, mirrors, and mismatched tables and chairs. All of it is charming. The food is heavy on pork and chicken, lots of *paprikash* and stuffed cabbage. The signature entrée is *burek,* a filled phyllo dough concoction the size of a radial tire; you wait a half hour for this one. Items from $11. The restaurant is difficult to find—this neighborhood is the real Milwaukee—you'll likely wind up asking for directions from a horseshoe club outside a local tavern. You can take Superior to Bay View, then take a left on Russell; that should get you to St. Clair. The views from Bay View's side streets are absolutely splendid.

One of Three Brothers' three brothers also owns the **Old Town Restaurant,** 522 W. Lincoln Ave., tel. (414) 672-0206, featuring ethnic entertainment and food from $15.

In South Milwaukee, the **Balkanian New Star Maric,** 901 Milwaukee Ave., tel. (414) 762-6397, is a restaurant, deli, and bakery. From under $5.

One little-known place for Serbian in Milwaukee is **Fritz's Pub** at 20th and Oklahoma, with a decent selection of Serbian-style sandwiches. From under $5.

Polish
Polonez, 2316 S. Sixth St., tel. (414) 384-8766; **Cracovia,** 1531 W. Lincoln Ave., tel. (414) 383-8688; and **Crocus,** 1801 S. Muskego Ave., tel. (414) 643-6383, all serve authentic Polish fare. Very good *czarnina* (a raisin soup with noodles) at Polonez, which makes seven soups daily as well as pork dishes, stuffed cabbage, a Sunday roast duck special, and a Friday fish fry with potato pancakes. Meals from $10.

Greek
Ask a Milwaukeean where to find the best Greek food and odds are you'll be pointed to **Mykonos,** 1014 N. Van Buren St., tel. (414) 224-6400. Don't go wearing a tie; this unassuming gyro joint isn't even a sit-down restaurant. But the fare is copious and well prepared and, best of all, served until 2:30 a.m. weekdays and 3:30 a.m. weekends. Selections from $4.

Middle Eastern
The great new incarnation of Zam Zam, **Yafa,** 2410 N. Farwell Ave., tel. (414) 276-2765, is run by a local Middle Eastern bakery owner. Try the *sayadyah,* fish in tahini sauce. It's open Mon.-Sat. for lunch and dinner. Another local fave is the diminutive **Abu's Jerusalem,** 1978 N. Farwell Ave., tel. (414) 277-0485, where the rosewater lemonade enraptures. Both from $5. **Sahar,** 307 E. Wisconsin Ave., tel. (414) 270-0970, has top-notch Persian cuisine from $5.

Indian
Milwaukee's got a couple of good Indian restaurants. **Dancing Ganesha,** 1692-1694 N. Van Buren St., tel. (414) 220-0202, offers an extensive list of less-than-usual items on its menu, from $7. If you're an aficionado of southern Indian food, you're generally out of luck. But Milwaukee recently saw the opening of **Tandoor,** 1117 S. 108th St., West Allis, tel. (414) 777-1600, and it's a godsend. Everything's divine here. The lunch buffet is fabulous too. Items from $8.

Chinese
China Gourmet, 330 E. Kilbourn Ave., tel. (414) 272-1688, gets rave reviews. Never a bad dish, but go especially for the salmon steamed in black bean sauce. Choices from $7. The Sunday brunch here is popular. In a straw poll, most Cathay-minded eaters recommend **Yen Ching,** 7630 W. Good Hope Rd., tel. (414) 353-6677, with items from $7. Enjoy Chinese noodles with Korean overtones at one of Milwaukee's first realistic noodle shops—**San Dong Express,** 220 W. Layton Ave. The noodles are all homemade and the many soup or plate-style noodle concoctions keep noodleheads satisfied. The *cha jang myun* (noodles in a dark, soy-flavored sauce with shredded pork and assorted minced greens) is excellent, and this is the only place in town to get authentic Korean-style seafood soups. Menu items from $4.

Japanese
A longtime standard for Japanese in town, especially when you have a sushi craving, has

FAMOUS SAUSAGE
MADE IN MILWAUKEE SINCE 1880

been **Izumi's,** 2178 N. Prospect Ave., tel. (414) 271-5278. It's open for lunch and dinner weekdays, dinner only on weekends. Choices from $5. Most folks don't know about the excellent Japanese food at **Restaurant Hama,** 333 W. Brown Deer Rd., Bayside (in Audobon Court), tel. (414) 352-5051, which has excellent Japanese and Pacific Rim food from $5.

Vietnamese
The name belies the fare somewhat, but **West Bank Cafe,** 732 E. Burleigh St., tel. (414) 562-5555, has some of the most solid Vietnamese cuisine in the state, from $5.

Thai
No doubt the best-known Thai place in Beer City is **King and I.** This diminutive but richly decorated restaurant (with the most comfortable dining chairs in town) has worthy Thai right down to the mango custard desserts. Specialties of the house are *panang nau* and *pla lad prig.* From $7.

Located in Prospect Mall downtown is the **Bangkok Orchid,** 2239 N. Prospect Ave., an unknown Thai place that deserves more recognition. From $7.

NIGHTLIFE

Milwaukee is no Austin, Texas, but there's a lot more music here than people realize. Then again, it's also the city where sheepshead (a native card game) tournaments might get equal billing with live music in the same bar. Milwaukee has over 5,000 bars, in keeping with tradition, so there's something out there for everyone. Unless otherwise noted, most of the clubs listed here charge a cover. It's best to verify everything before making the trip.

The free weekly, *Shepherd Express* gives a rundown of most of the clubs. Another free weekly is *The Paper.* Less thorough is the "Let's Go" section of Friday's *Milwaukee Journal-Sentinel.*

Weekly Regulars
Hear Irish and Celtic music at **Nash's Irish Castle,** 1328 W. Lincoln Ave., tel. (414) 643-9654. **Nomad,** 1401 E. Brady, tel. (414) 224-8111, a coffee/beer/wine house, features free early shows. A popular neighborhood bar with good

pub grub and a lengthy list of Milwaukee microbrews offering a regular mix of music on Monday is the Farwell-North-triangle institution **Hooligan's,** 2017 E. North Avenue, tel. (414) 278-7878. Join in the open reggae jams at the **Tasting Room,** 1100 E. Kane Pl., tel. (414) 277-9118, on Wednesday.

Rock
Shank Hall, 1434 N. Farwell Ave., tel. (414) 276-7288, offers a constant barrage of prominent local, regional, and national acts. It was once a stable, so the interior isn't exactly a delight when the lights come up. Acts that have achieved something of a name will make an appearance at the narrow (but high) **Globe East,** 2028 E. North Ave., tel. (414) 276-2233, also a good spot for local rock groups. More good spots for local rock or regional alternative acts and mostly college crowds include **Points East Pub,** 1501 N. Jackson St., tel. (414) 272-0122; and the acoustically atrocious **Rave,** 2401 W. Wisconsin Ave., tel. (414) 342-RAVE.

Latin
Best place for anything Latin, along with a varied menu of other musical styles, is **Matisse,** 1806 E. North Avenue. Salsa and merengue dancing is found on weekends at **El Babalu Caribbean Club and Restaurant,** 611 W. National Avenue.

Blues and R&B
It's all blues all the time at the **Up and Under Pub,** 1216 E. Brady St., tel. (414) 276-2677. There's free parking in lot a half block east at the corner of Brady and Arlington. On the south side, **Bunker's Mainstreet,** 8031 W. Greenfield Ave., tel. (414) 257-1012, is mostly blues, but reggae, Caribbean, and other musical styles (including great Cajun nights) are sometimes featured.

The Riverwest neighborhood is a prime spot for soulful music. A small neighborhood tavern unconcerned with decor, **Linneman's River West Inn,** 1001 E. Locust St., tel. (414) 263-9844, has blues and some folk. The **Uptowner,** 1032 E. Center St., tel. (414) 372-3882, has rock, blues, and a smattering of gospel and R&B.

Jazz
A place most people don't know about, **The Estate,** 2423 N. Murray Ave., is so small you can't

stretch your arms. The **Main Event,** 3418 N. Martin Luther King Blvd., tel. (414) 263-9481, offers jazz on a more consistent basis. Serious jazzers should head for the **Jazz Oasis,** 2379 N. Holton Ave., tel. (414) 562-2040.

Folk
As always, start with the coffeehouses for folk. **The Coffee House,** 631 N. 19th St., tel. (414) 744-FOLK, features lots of folk music and occasional poetry readings. **Zur Krone,** 839 S. Second St. in Walker's Point, tel. (414) 647-1910, has mostly acoustic music.

Eclectic
Blues, jazz, and hip-hop stream out of the **Blues Oasis,** 2433 N. Holton Ave., tel. (414) 562-4111, reminiscent of a Sinatra-esque martini bar. You name it, they feature it at **Harpo's,** 1339 E. Brady St., tel. (414) 278-0188, which admirably sees no problem in mixing Jazz Butcher with a Chicago blues band or a faux Black Sabbath.

A broad palette of acts is represented at yet another Riverwest nightspot, the **Stork Club,** 2778 N. Wiel St., tel. (414) 265-2300. You never know what you're going to get at **Truman's,** 7924 W. Appleton Ave., tel. (414) 461-0777—a local rock band or a keyboard and a crooner—but there's no cover charge and it's bound to be interesting.

Dancing
Clubs come and go so this list will likely be different by the time you read it. Currently the most varied music is at **Mad Planet,** 533 E. Center Street. Techno to modern rock to retro is at **Metropolis,** 788 N. Jackson St. The **Empire Room,** 5401 N. Lovers Lane Rd., near Hwy 100 and Silver Spring Dr., has a multi-level assortment of bars and music. Swing tunes are mixed with contemporary music at **Victor's Cocktail Lounge,** 1230 N. Van Buren Street. **La Cage** is a gay bar, but straights feel at home too. It's huge, with six bars, two DJs, and lots of light shows.

Concertina
Experience an absolutely tickling time at **Art Altenburg's Concertina Bar,** 1920 S. 37th St., tel. (414) 384-2570, a Thurs.-Sat. institution for old Milwaukeeans. Squeezebox aficionados crowd in and launch into impromptu waltzes,

ballads, and the ineluctable polkas and chicken dances; patrons are welcome to bring their own accordion or borrow one from behind the bar (tambourines are available for the musically inept). Closed on Sunday.

Walker's Point
More and more shops, boutiques, and restaurants are moving into this neighborhood. Walker's Point nightspots range from a pub with a sand volleyball court outside to a Teutonic watering hole, dark sippers' pubs, and a whole lot more. **Zur Krone,** 839 S. 2nd St., tel. (414) 647-1910, would make any northern European proud with its beer selection (more than 225). Join the **Meister Beer Schmeckers Verein** and work your way up from apprentice to journeyman to meister; low-key acoustic music is also featured semi-regularly. **Shaker's,** near Zur Krone, is a slightly yuppified restaurant in a funky atmosphere. It holds gastronomic events, cigar nights, wine tastings, and more. **Tony's,** also nearby, is a dark place with good whiskeys and low-key atmosphere.

The Walker's Point Tavern Association also generally throws a late-summer/Labor Day block party blowout.

Jefferson Street
Elsa's on Park, Louise's, and the new **Taylor's** bar, all in the same area, have given North Jefferson Street and environs the feel of a subdued scene—all in the ritzy section of town full of boutiques, galleries, and the like. These are the clubs for you if you want to avoid the fun but occasionally wild contingent on Water Street.

Water Street
Stretching along the Milwaukee River, aptly named Water Street draws a preponderance of Marquette students and lots of downtown business types. Nightlife ranges from a microbrewery to sports bars and dance clubs. A block away is one of the many sports bars downtown, **Luke's Sports Spectacular,** 1225 N. Water Street.

The **Water St. Brewery,** 1101 N. Water St., tel. (414) 272-1195, is one of the popular newer microbreweries in town but similar to others with gleaming copper kettles on display. It has appetizers, sandwiches, and a host of rotating entrées. Very trendy.

Get the best bar food around at **Rosie's Water Works,** 1111 N. Water St., tel. (414) 274-7213, and good barbecue at **Brew City Barbecue** across the way.

Taps, Taverns, and More Nightspots
The **Safe House,** 779 N. Front St. (look for the "International Exports" sign), tel. (414) 271-2007, is a bar-restaurant done to the hilt in espionage decor. The drinks have spy names, you may be asked for a password, on Monte Carlo theme nights you can learn roulette, etc. ad nauseum. It's a ritual watering hole for Milwaukee first-timers, others think it's the biggest joke in town.

Along bopping N. Farwell Avenue, **Von Trier,** 2235 N. Farwell Ave., tel. (414) 272-1775, could pass for a German *bierhall* with its long heavy wooden bench seating and a summertime *biergarten;* it's got 20 imports on draft and another 75 or so bottled. In true Bavarian and Wisconsin style, there's a buck's head affixed to the wall. A block away on North Avenue, **Vitucci's** is a quieter place and a personal favorite watering hole.

Another Schlitz taproom is **Benjamin Briggs Pub,** 2501 W. Greenfield Ave., tel. (414) 383-2337, where they still serve beer in stainless steel pails. It also has good pub grub and occasional live music.

At **Landmark Lanes,** 2220 N. Farwell Ave., tel. (414) 278-8770, in the bowels of the Oriental Landmark Theater, there's bowling—this is Milwaukee, after all—but mostly it's a happening young nightclub with three separate bars, pool tables, and dart boards.

The British-style waterside place, **John Hawk's Pub,** in the basement at 100 E. Wisconsin Ave., offers an oak bar and cozy fireplaces as well as live music—usually blues. **Nash's Irish Castle,** 1328 W. Lincoln Ave., is owned by Irish transplants and has draft Guinness, Gaelic newspapers, and a good deal on its Friday fish fry.

If you're looking for a more upscale place, try the **Hi-Hat Lounge,** Brady and Arlington Streets. With cool jazz wafting in the background it's got a classy but not showy feel and an older, sophisticated crowd.

Nomad World Pub is a tiny, tiny place— part coffee shop, part unpredictable drink-pouring bar where you can get betel nuts while listening to world beat music, sometimes live.

Too many neighborhood taverns to count exist in Milwaukee, and everybody's got a different recommendation. The since-1908 **Wolski's,** 1836 N. Pulaski St., tel. (414) 276-8130, is a corner tavern that defines a Milwaukee tippler's joint.

OTHER ENTERTAINMENT

In Rand McNally's *Places Rated,* Milwaukee hit the top five percent of big cities for cultural attractions and the arts. In the past decade, over $100 million has been poured into downtown arts districts. Per capita, Milwaukeeans donate more to the arts than any U.S. city besides Los Angeles. Four dozen cultural organizations call the city home.

Both **Marquette University,** tel. (414) 288-7504, and **UW-Milwaukee,** tel. (414) 963-4308, offer full schedules of artistic and cultural performances throughout the year.

Rundowns for all cultural activities can be found in the Friday and Sunday editions of the *Milwaukee Journal-Sentinel. Milwaukee Magazine* also has a comprehensive monthly compendium of music, theater, art, dance, and more; you can find it around town or at the convention and visitors bureau.

Theater
The city has over a dozen theater companies, performing in many locations. The **Pabst Theater,** 144 E. Wells St., tel. (414) 286-3663, an 1895 Victorian piece of opulence which still today seems as ornate as ever, is a majestic draw in its own right, but it also continues to attract national acts of all kinds. The **Marcus Center for Performing Arts** (MCAP), 929 N. Water St., tel. (414) 273-7206, has a regular season of theater, symphony, ballet, opera, children's theater, and touring specials. It is the home of the Milwaukee Symphony Orchestra, the Milwaukee Ballet Company, the Florentine Opera Company, and First Stage Milwaukee.

One respected local company is **Theater X,** 158 N. Broadway, tel. (414) 278-0555, creating original works that have garnered an Obie Award and a Pulitzer Prize nomination. The nation's only African-American professional theater group is the **Hansberry-Sands Theatre Co.,** tel (414) 272-PLAY.

Both the **Skylight Opera Theatre,** tel. (414) 291-7800, and **Milwaukee Chamber Theatre,** tel. (414) 276-8842, are residents of the lovely new Broadway Theatre Centre downtown. The latter's language-centered contemporary plays are always a challenge. The **Milwaukee Repertory Theater,** 108 E. Wells St., tel. (414) 224-9490, is part of an international network of co-operating organizations and offers classical, contemporary, cabaret, and special performances Sept.-May.

Music
The **Milwaukee Symphony Orchestra,** 330 E. Kilbourn Ave., tel. (414) 291-6010, one of the nation's top orchestras, performs Sept.-July. The oldest arts group in Milwaukee (five decades old), the **Bel Canto Chorus,** tel. (414) 272-7950, offers a repertoire of classics.

A low-cost alternative is the performances of faculty, students, or guest artists at the **Wisconsin Conservatory of Music,** 1584 N. Prospect Ave., tel. (414) 276-5760.

Dance
Milwaukee has a thriving modern dance culture; New York City companies make regular visits to do performances, often at Alverno College and UWM. The classics aren't ignored. Ranked among the top ballet companies in the country is the **Milwaukee Ballet Company,** 504 W. National Ave., tel. (414) 643-7677, whose December production of *The Nutcracker* always packs the house. Enjoy a diverse array of performances from the **Milwaukee Dance Theatre,** tel. (414) 273-1999.

Nationally renowned is Milwaukee's modern **Ko-Thi Dance Company,** 2001 W. Capitol Dr., tel. (414) 442-6844.

EVENTS

Another term of endearment for Milwaukee is the City of Festivals. Almost every week of the year brings yet another celebratory blowout feting some cultural, ethnic, or seasonal aspect of the city—and sometimes for no reason at all. There are many ethnic festivals in the city throughout the year; the city's festival rundown is one large database. Show up any weekend from late May to early November and you're guaranteed something to do at a festival grounds in town.

The Short List: German Fest, the largest multi-day festival in the country (July); Bavarian Folk Fest (June); Oktoberfest; Polish Fest (June); Lakefront Festival of Arts (July); Festa Italiana (July); Bastille Days (July); Greek Festival (July); Mexican Spring Festival-Cinco de Mayo (May); Mexican Fiesta (August); Irish Fest (August); African World Festival (August); Serbian Days (August); Indian Summer (September); Asian Moon Festival (September); and Holiday Folk Fair (November).

The largest party of all is early August's **Wisconsin State Fair,** at the fairgrounds west along

the Great Circus Train
arriving in Milwaukee

I-94. This fair of all fairs features carnivals, 500 exhibits, livestock shows, entertainment on 20 stages, and the world's greatest cream puffs.

A uniquely Milwaukee event is July's **Great Circus Parade,** when the big top makers from Baraboo, Wisconsin's Great Circus Museum, load up the ornate boxcars and head for the Cream City for a massively popular cavort through downtown.

All summer long Cathedral Square downtown is home to a large **farmers' market.**

Summerfest

This is the granddaddy of all Midwestern festivals and the largest music festival in the world (so says the *Guiness Book of World Records*). For 11 days in late June, top national musical acts perform on innumerable stages along the lakefront, drawing millions of music lovers and partiers. Agoraphobics need not even consider it. Tickets cost $8 in advance and $9 at the gate, but shop around for discount coupons at grocery stores and assorted businesses, or consider a multi-day pass, available at businesses all around town.

SPORTS AND RECREATION

Milwaukee has been rated in the top 10% of like-sized U.S. cities for recreational opportunities in and around the city. Consider the 137 parks and parkways and 15,000 acres of total passive and active greenland.

The Brew Crew

Is Milwaukee truly a major-league town? Sports fans in the area have endured this debate ever since the Braves decamped for greener pastures in 1965. The answer is yes and no. Milwaukee remains something of an anomaly—the smallest of the small markets. And most markets of comparable size support just one major league franchise, not two, as Milwaukee does— baseball's National League **Milwaukee Brewers** and basketball's **Milwaukee Bucks.**

Debate over a proposed $200 million (now $400 million) retractable dome stadium for the Brewers raged before the bill to pay for it was finally passed—some say rammed through—in an epic all-night session of the Wisconsin Legislature that cost at least one legislator his job in

a recall election. Whatever your take on it, the stadium is absolutely magnificent. It has been described as the most perfect synthesis of retro and techno in the world—do check it out.

But personally, that's not the best reason to go to a game. The Brewers have the coolest stunt in pro sports: the Sausage Race. Halfway through the game while the field is being tailored, four ground crew members stick themselves into big, clunky sausage outfits and lumber around the field to a thrilling finish at home plate. It's so popular that opposing players beg for the opportunity to be a Milwaukee sausage for the day; other teams ask the Brewers to bring the costumes along when they go to other cities.

Baseball season runs early April through late September, and obtaining tickets, rarely an issue while the Brewers played in creaky old County Stadium, may now be a more difficult when popular teams come to town. Tickets are always hot when the arch enemy Chicago White Sox or Chicago Cubs come to town. There are even plenty of bargains for tickets, depending on the season and the opponent. For ticket information, call (414) 933-9000.

Even if you're not a baseball or even a sports fan, a Brewers game is something of a cultural necessity. Nobody but nobody parties before a ballgame like Wisconsinites, and Milwaukeeans (and Green Bay Packers fans) have perfected the pre-game tailgate party. The requisite pregame attraction is the meal of beer, grilled brats, and potato salad, eaten while playing catch in the parking lot. (The *Guinness Book of Records* recognized Milwaukee County Stadium as the site of the world's largest tailgate party.) And the food inside Milwaukee County Stadium was superb: NBC Sports commentator emeritus Bob Costas deemed the stadium's bratwurst tops in the major leagues. Concessions at the new Miller Park are said to be even better, if such a thing is possible.

Milwaukee Bucks

The Milwaukee Bucks are on more solid ground. Their fiscal shakeouts occurred a decade ago, when local philanthropists donated the new digs at the Bradley Center and ownership was taken over by grocery magnate and U.S. Senator Herb Kohl. This allowed an injection of capital sufficient to pursue stratospherically priced free agents. Bucks tickets are generally available on game days. The Bucks offer great deals on their Bonus Nights, when certain seats (and not all of them at nosebleed elevation) are dirt cheap—by NBA standards, anyway. For ticket information, call (414) 227-0500.

Other Pros

Also in the major leagues, though a bit out of the mainstream, are the professional indoor soccer **Milwaukee Wave,** tel. (414) 962-WAVE, and the arena football **Milwaukee Mustangs;** both also play in the Bradley Center. The Mustangs are one of the best teams in the newer, completely wild forum of arena football. The **Milwaukee Rampage** play professional outdoor soccer at Uihlein Field on Good Hope Road April-August.

Other Spectator Sports

Also playing in the Bradley Center are the **Milwaukee Admirals,** of the International Hockey League. The IHL is a bruising minor-league quasi-farm system of the National Hockey League (NHL), and if you follow hockey now and again you'll see retread veterans or up-and-coming college players on the rosters.

The local hometown Division 1A Golden Eagles of **Marquette University,** the perennially popular basketball team, also play at the Bradley Center.

The **University of Wisconsin-Milwaukee Panthers** are known for excellence in Division 1A sports, including basketball and especially soccer.

Milwaukee Mile

Located at Wisconsin State Fair Park, the Milwaukee Mile is a legendary stop on the Indy car and CART circuit in the summer.

Trails

The **Milwaukee '76 Trail** wends along the lakefront for 13 miles, from O'Donnell Park on E. Wisconsin Ave. to Kilbourn Town Historic House. The Oak Leaf Trail is a 90-miler and is popular. Other popular multi-use trails run along the Menomonee River between Good Hope and Bluemound Roads, along the Milwaukee River from Good Hope Road to the lakefront near McKinley Marina, along the Root River from Greenfield Avenue to Loomis Road, and along

the south lakefront through Cudahy and South Milwaukee. Find great ski trails at a number of parks, including Schlitz Audubon Center, Whitnall Park, and, believe it or not, the zoo.

Charter Fishing

With the deep waters right off the harbor, it's no wonder that Milwaukee leads the state in charter operations and salmonoids taken annually. On a scintillating summer day, the marina and harbor areas of Milwaukee appear to be discharging a benevolent, whitewashed D-Day flotilla. Though toxic no-man's-lands in southern Lake Michigan have dissipated somewhat since the death-zone days of the '50s and '60s, PCB contamination in fatty tissues of fish remains a concern. Contact the DNR for specific fish requirements.

Charter operators include **A Seagull Charters,** tel. (414) 224-7707, a state record holder for steelhead, located at McKinley Marina, 1750 N. Lincoln Memorial Drive.

The CVB can provide more detailed information. Investigating charter operators prior to sailing can save quite a lot of personality friction; the boats are not that big, and you are the one who'll have to sit out on the big lake with the skipper all day.

Bowling

A joke: Wisconsin's the only state where you can factor your bowling average into your SAT score. Of the city's *81* regulation bowling centers, **Red Carpet Bowling Centers** are the big-name lanes. Locations include Red Carpet Celebrity, 5727 S. 27th St., tel. (414) 282-0100; and Red Carpet Lanes Regency, 6014 N. 76th St., tel. (414) 464-8800.

A couple of neighborhood joints have old-style duckpin bowling; the **Holler House,** 2042 W. Lincoln Ave., has the two oldest sanctioned bowling lanes (lanes 1 and 2) in the United States. A true Milwaukee treasure is longstanding **Koz's Mini Bowl,** 2078 S. Seventh St., with four 16-foot lanes and orange-sized balls; the pin setters still make 50 cents a game plus tips. These two places truly represent a once-important aspect of Milwaukee social life.

Pettit National Ice Center

A longtime national center for speed skating, the Milwaukee area finally cornered the market as top spot when a local philanthropist donated this enormous, quarter-million-square-foot training facility for the U.S. Olympic teams. It's the only one of its kind in the country and one of only five of its scope in the world. National and international competitions are held here regularly. The public can enjoy the 400-meter ovals and two Olympic-size hockey rinks throughout the day; skating costs $5 adults, $4 seniors and children under 13, with an additional $2 for skate rentals. Tours cost $3. The center is located at 500 S. 84th St., off I-94, tel. (414) 266-0100.

Golf
Milwaukee is often mentioned for its nearly 20 golf courses within a short drive. Most prominent in the near vicinity is **Brown Deer Park** 7835 N. Green Bay Rd., tel. (414) 352-8080, site of the Greater Milwaukee Open; for a public course, it's amazing. Whitnall and Oakwood Parks also have excellent courses. Farther afield **The Bog** near Cedarburg is newer and very highly rated by golf media.

SHOPPING

There's more to shopping in Milwaukee than the requisite cheddar cheese foam wedge hat and cheese and bratwurst gift packs. The **Grand Avenue** isn't a bad mall—a synthesis of old and new. Originally built in 1915 as the Plankinton Arcade, much of the architecture was retained when the four-block area was gentrified into a lower level of shops and an upper level of sidewalk cafes and peoplewatching heights.

North Old World Third Street has a few longstanding shops, and the Jefferson Street area around the Pfister Hotel is chockablock with expensive antique shops, galleries, and boutiques.

The world's largest selection of model railroad cars is at **Wm. K. Walthers, Inc.,** 60th St. and Florist, tel. (414) 527-0770, a factory and warehouse that also offers tours.

SERVICES AND INFORMATION

The **Greater Milwaukee Convention and Visitors Bureau,** 510 W. Kilbourn Ave., tel. (414) 273-3950, or (800) 554-1448, www.milwaukee.

org, is across the street from the Midwest Express Center. It's open weekdays 8 a.m.-5 p.m. and Saturday 9 a.m.-3 p.m. Memorial Day-Labor Day. Rumors were circulating that this office would move to a vacant Marshall Field's Department Store building in the Grand Avenue, so don't be surprised if it happens. Additional offices are located at Mitchell International Airport, tel. (414) 747-4808, open weekdays 7:30 a.m.-9:30 p.m., Saturday 9 a.m.-6 p.m., and Sunday 1-9:30 p.m.; and at the Midwest Express Center, tel. (414) 908-6205, open weekdays 8 a.m.-5 p.m.

The city also maintains visitor information offices in Chicago, 101 W. Grand Ave., Suite 200, tel. (312) 595-1589; and Washington D.C., 1101 17th St., N.W., Suite 1005, tel. (202) 293-6969.

The local sales tax totals out at 5.6%. There is a 9% tax on hotel rooms in addition to the sales tax, and a.025% tax on food and beverage purchases.

Media
Once one of Wisconsin's oldest newspapers, the *Milwaukee Sentinel* in 1995 merged with its afternoon rival, the *Milwaukee Journal,* to form the *Milwaukee Journal-Sentinel,* another of those morning dailies resulting from two competing papers owned by the same conglomerate. The Friday paper has a complete listing of weekend cultural events, music, clubs, and movies. Fans of alternative views pick up weekly copies of the free *Shepherd Express,* which is also a good source of local arts and nightlife info. The local monthly repository of everything Milwaukee is *Milwaukee Magazine.*

Listen to the eclectic, student-run **WMSE** at 91.7 FM—it might surprise you.

Bookstores
The bookstores-per-capita quotient is pretty high here. Two blocks north of Grand Avenue Mall, **Renaissance Book Shop,** 834 N. Plankinton Ave., tel. (414) 271-6850, has an amazing six stories of books.

Post Office
Post offices are located at 345 W. St. Paul Ave., tel. (414) 291-3544; and 606 E. Juneau Ave., tel. (414) 289-8336; an additional outlet at the airport, tel. (414) 291-2348, is open 24 hours a day 365 days a year.

GETTING THERE AND AWAY

By Air

General Mitchell International Airport, 5300 S. Howell Ave., tel. (414) 747-5300, is southeast of downtown, near Cudahy. It's best accessed by traveling I-94 south and following the signs. From downtown, you can head south on 6th St. N.; it should get you to WI 38 (Howell Ave.). Named for a native-son Army Air Corps general who was run out of the armed forces for his outspokenness, it's not bad as airports go. Over 90 cities are reached direct from Milwaukee; 220 flights per day depart.

A genuine treat for Milwaukee-bound travelers is the chance to experience what is doubtless the nation's best domestic carrier, Milwaukee-based **Midwest Express.** Travelers who try Midwest Express vow they'll never step aboard another cattle carrier again. How can you compete with double-wide leather seats throughout the whole cabin, exquisite meals, and genuinely solicitous service. If you call at least 36 hours in advance, you would not believe the amazing menu choices you're offered. The prices are competitive, too. Nonstop flights are available to Atlanta, Boston, Columbus, Cleveland, Dallas/Fort Worth, Denver, Kansas City, Grand Rapids, Las Vegas, Los Angeles, Newark, La Guardia (NYC), Philadelphia, San Diego, San Francisco, and Washington, D.C., with seasonal flights to Tampa, Ft. Lauderdale, Fort Meyers, and Phoenix. The airline offers excellent package deals including airfare, car rental, and accommodations from a dozen major U.S. cities. For information on Midwest Express, call (414) 747-4646 or (800) 452-2022.

The 15 other airlines serving the airport include **Delta,** tel. (414) 223-4770 or (800) 221-1212, 250 E. Wisconsin Ave.; **Northwest,** tel. (800) 225-2525; **America West** and **America West Express,** tel. (800) 235-9292; **American** and **American Eagle,** tel. (800) 433-7300; **American Trans Air,** tel. (800) 225-2995; **Comair,** tel. (414) 354-9822; **Continental** and **Continental Express,** tel. (414) 342-3099 or (800) 523-3273; **Skyway,** tel. (414) 747-4646 or (800) 452-2022; **TWA** and **TWA Express,** tel. (414) 933-8292 or (800) 221-2000; **United** and **United Express,** tel. (800) 241-6522; **USAirways** and

USAirways Express, tel. (800) 428-4322; and Sun Country Airlines, tel. (800) 359-6786 (800-FLY-N-SUN). The last one is a good cheap way to get to and from Minneapolis.

Milwaukee County Transit System **bus** #80 goes to the airport 6 a.m.-12 a.m.; almost any bus can get you there if you ask the driver for transfer help. The fare is $1.35. A taxi from downtown costs $15-20 and takes 20 minutes. Airport limousines cost half that. **United Limo,** tel. (800) 833-5555, runs between Marquette University, Mitchell International, and Chicago's O'Hare airport nine times daily 4 a.m.-7:15 p.m. with rates of $20 one-way, $32 roundtrip.

Airport parking is $1.50 per hour with a $10 maximum.

For all ground transportation questions, call the airport's hotline, tel. (414) 747-5308.

By Bus

The **Greyhound** station, tel. (414) 272-2259, is in the 600 block of N. James Lovell St., between W. Wisconsin and W. Michigan Avenues. Buses leave 10 times daily for Chicago ($13 one-way); buses also go to Minneapolis ($51 one-way); Madison ($12 one-way); Eau Claire; three to Fond du Lac; three to Green Bay; three to La Crosse; and twice each to Stevens Point and Wausau. Verify all schedules and fares. The depot closes at 11:45 p.m.

The Greyhound station is also the northern terminus of the **Wisconsin Coach Lines** buses, tel. (262) 542-7434 or (262) 542-8861, which run south to Racine and Kenosha and west to Waukesha County; they also make stops at the airport, Marquette University, UWM, and other downtown locations. Heading south, buses make up to eight trips daily and stop along Michigan Ave. in the downtown area before heading to the airport. Starting from Kenosha, buses return 5:30 a.m.-7:05 p.m.

The express also makes some two dozen trips daily from the Greyhound station to Marquette University, then at the I-94 ramp stops through Brookfield and New Berlin before arriving in Waukesha. Buses also make a sporadic schedule of afternoon trips to Oconomowoc and Mukwonago. Check for the scheduling.

Up the street from the Greyhound station is the **Badger Coaches** hangout, 635 N. Seventh St., tel. (414) 276-7490. Buses leave this location for Madison up to eight times daily 7 a.m.-8 p.m. (the last trip varies); the fare to Madison is $12 one-way.

United Limo, tel. (800) 833-5555, doesn't stop at the Greyhound depot, but departs from the Marquette University Library, 1415 Wisconsin Ave., nine times daily, then stops at the Amtrak station, 5th and Paul Streets, and at the United Limo Depot, 4960 S. 13th St., before swinging out to Mitchell airport and heading on to Chicago's O'Hare Airport via Racine and Kenosha. To O'Hare is $20 one-way.

By Train
Is **Amtrak** alive or dead? This is the question dogging train service between Milwaukee and Chicago. One year it seems near death, then it's revived by government monies, then it's dead, etc.

Presently, four trains operate daily, with hefty fares of $20 one-way on off-peak weekdays, $30 on the weekend. Service to Minneapolis is less imperiled; one train still leaves daily. The Amtrak station, 433 W. St. Paul Ave., tel. (414) 933-3081, is scheduled for a facelift. Many Midwestern states are now attempting to coordinate an independent rail network through Chicago, of which Milwaukee would likely be a node.

In 2000, daily service to Fond du Lac was instituted by Amtrak. Experimental commuter rides west to Wauwatosa, Elm Grove, Oconomowoc, and Watertown were also undertaken; it remains to be seen if they'll remain in service.

By Boat
Plans for a high-speed ferry from Milwaukee to Muskeon, MI, were being debated as this book was going to press. The proposed 244-foot catamaran boat would carry up to 300 passengers and 80 vehicles daily May-October, and the journey would take just under two hours, a remarkable feat if they can pull it off.

GETTING AROUND

Taxi
Taxis are all metered and have a usual drop fare of around $2 for the first mile and about $1.50 for each additional. **Veterans Taxicab**

Cooperative, tel. (414) 291-8095, is the state's largest operator and has computer-assisted dispatching.

Bus
The **Milwaukee County Transit System,** tel. (414) 344-6711, operates from 6 a.m. to well past midnight on certain routes with loads of buses. Fares are $1.35 adults, 65 cents children 6-11, senior citizens, and riders with disabilities.

Rental Cars
Every major rental car agency is represented at Mitchell International Airport, including **Avis,** tel. (800) 831-2847; **Budget,** tel. (414) 541-8750; **Enterprise,** tel. (414) 486-3600; **Hertz,** tel. (414) 747-5200; and **National,** tel. (414) 483-9800. National has outlets at the Embassy Suites and Milwaukee Hilton, and most others have a half dozen or so representatives throughout the city. There is a three percent tax on car rentals.

Organized Tours
Nine companies prowl the land on organized tours, and another handful ply the waters of the Milwaukee River. The CVB can provide a detailed listing. Each specializes in something slightly different.

You can do it yourself by hopping aboard an old fashioned **trolley** from Milwaukee County Transit System, tel. (414) 344-6711. There's a River Route and a Lake Route that run year-round; an extension of the River Route covers the Brady St. area Memorial Day-Labor Day and Saturday only Labor Day-New Year's Eve. A Walker's Point extension of the River route runs year-round. The Lake Route runs from the Art Museum along the lake west along Wisconsin Ave. to 10th St., then north to Wells St. before looping back along Wisconsin Avenue.

BRIAN BARDWELL

The River Route runs along Water St. south through the Historic Third Ward. Trolleys run every six to nine minutes 9 a.m.-10 p.m. Mon.-Thurs., until 1 a.m. Friday, 10 a.m.-1 a.m. Saturday, and 11 a.m.-10 p.m. Sunday. The fare is all of 50 cents. A Downtown Trolley ($1) operates May-Oct. and stops in the Third Ward, at the Grand Avenue, Brady Street, Old World Third Street, and other locations. The transit system has also offered popular guided tours in summers.

Perhaps the most Milwaukee way to tour the city would be aboard a rumbling Harley-Davidson. **Milwaukee Iron Motorcycle Tours,** tel. (262) 628-9421 or (800) 964-1257, provides a fully chauffeured Hog tour of Milwaukee and surrounding areas.

VICINITY OF MILWAUKEE

Cedarburg

What candy-facade original-13-colony spots such as Williamsburg are to the East Coast, Cedarburg is to Old World Wisconsin. It's been seemingly preserved in a time vacuum, thanks to local residents who successfully fought off wholesale architectural devastation from an invasion of Milwaukeeans looking for an easy commute. Cedarburg, about a half-hour north of downtown Milwaukee, was originally populated by German (and a few British) immigrants, who hacked a community out of a forest and built numerous mills along Cedar Creek, which bisects the tiny community, including the only worsted wool mill and factory in what was then considered the West. Those mills, and over 100 other original Cream City-brick buildings have been painstakingly restored into the state's most concentrated stretch of antiques dealers, shops, galleries, bed and breakfasts, and proper little restaurants. For curio browsers, it's heaven. For jaded roadsters who suspect a stratospheric kitsch quotient, don't worry—it isn't all that bad. Plus, as this book was being updated, Cedarburg was in the midst of a further prettying up along its main drag. Stop at the visitor center for an excellent booklet on historic structure walking tours.

The heart and soul of the town is **Cedar Creek Settlement,** an antebellum foundation mill once the village's center of activity but now a several-blocks-long hodgepodge of shops, restaurants, and galleries. The **Cedar Creek Winery** is also on the premises; tours take in the aging cellars. Hours are Mon.-Sat. 10 a.m.-5 p.m., Sunday 11 a.m.-5 p.m. West of the main drag (Washington Road), Portland Road features one of the original structures in Cedarburg, the enormous, five-story **Cedarburg Mill,** now home to yet another antique shop. Along Riveredge Drive is the **Brewery Works,** tel. (262) 377-8230, a restored 1840s brewery housing the Ozaukee County Art Center. You can sometimes see artists at work. Open Wed.-Sun 1-4 p.m.

North of town three miles is the last extant **covered bridge** in the state, dating from 1876; to get there, head to the WI 143/60 junction on Washington Avenue. This is an excellent bike tour! Northeast of Cedarburg in Grafton is the **Family Farm,** a newly opened turn-of-the-20th-century rural museum with a petting zoo, horse-drawn wagon rides, nature walks, antique farm implements, gardens, and a handful of buildings. Open May-Oct., Tues.-Sat. 9 a.m.-4 p.m., Sunday 11 a.m.-5 p.m. in peak seasons. Admission is $6, $5 seniors, $3.50 children 3-12. Southeast of Cedarburg via Hamilton Rd. is the original settlement of **Hamilton,** with another picturesque creekside mill.

A proposed 11-mile bike trail to Belgium via Port Washington would allow Lake Michigan access as well as linking to a trail all the way to Milwaukee.

The town has a great **Performing Arts Center,** tel. (262) 376-6161, with a full slate of visiting artists and performances. The **Cedarburg Cultural Center,** tel. (262) 375-3676, has regular jazz and folk performances ($12) along with art exhibits. The local **visitor center,** tel. (262) 377-9620 or (800) 237-2874, www.cedarburg.org, is here; very friendly and useful staffers will point you in the right direction. A small **general store museum** is also in the complex.

Gorgeous lodging options exist; nobody comes here to stay in a *motel.* The **Stagecoach Inn and Weber Haus Annex,** tel. (262) 375-0208 or (888) 375-0208, is a historic inn and pub on the old Milwaukee-to-Green Bay stagecoach line. Nine lovely rooms are in the main inn; three are in a restored 1847 frame building across the street where you can stroll in a private garden. Six suites have whirlpools; two have gas fireplaces. Rumors say a benign, black-garbed apparition wafts through the inn! Rates are $80-140. Cedarburg's first inn was the **Washington House Inn,** tel. (262) 375-3550 or (800) 554-4717, and it's now another sybaritic B&B, with rates from $75.

For food, you can get classic Wisconsin German tavern food, or the casually upscale fare found at most gentrified enclaves such as this. Best known (for five decades) is **Barth's at the Bridge,** along WI 57, tel. (262) 377-0660, with solid German and American cuisine, including a luscious sauerbraten, what may be the state's best meatloaf, a Friday seafood buffet, and Sunday brunch. Choices from $7. Open Tues-Sat. for lunch and dinner, Sunday for brunch and dinner. It's a chichi name and menu at **Cream and Crepe Cafe,** but the crepes are delectable, as is the creekside dining area. Choices from $4. **Settlers Inn,** W63-N657 Washington Ave., tel. (262) 377-4466, has a casual restaurant with family fare; the pies are award-winning and there are good vegetarian items. Items from $4. A newer steak joint, known now for its smashed garlic Black Angus steak, is the **Farmstead,** W62-N238 Washington Ave., tel. (262) 375-2655, which also has crab, ribs, seafood, and a wine list. Options from $8. **New Fortune,** W62-N547 Washington Ave., tel. (262) 376-0908, has good Chinese with a few Cambodian items, from $5.

Landmark Tours, P.O. Box 771, Cedarburg, WI 53012, tel. (262) 375-1426, leads group tours through Cedarburg and Ozaukee County.

Port Washington

A half hour north of Milwaukee is Port Washington, a littoral Lake Michigan community that links up with east-central Wisconsin. Port Washington put itself into the history books with its quixotic anti-Civil War draft riots, when mobs took over the courthouse and trained a cannon on the lakefront until the Army showed up and quelled the disturbance. Part Great Lake fishing town and part preserved antebellum anachronism, Port Washington, a declination backing off the lake, is known for its enormous downtown **marina** and fishing charters. You can stroll along the breakers, snapping shots of the art deco **lighthouse,** now a historical museum. Another renovated lighthouse houses the **Port Washington Historical Society Museum,** 311

Johnson St., open Sunday 1-4 p.m. in the summer. The **Eghart House** on Grand Avenue at the library is done up in turn-of-the-century style and open Sunday 1-4 p.m. Also along Grand Ave., what's known as the **Pebble House,** site of a tourist center, was painstakingly arranged of stones scavenged from the beaches along the lake. All of Franklin Street, dominated by the thrusting spire of St. Mary's Church and various castellated building tops, rates as one of the most small-town-like of any of the Lake Michigan coastal towns. Upper City Park, on a bluff overlooking the water, affords wondrous views of the lake and horizon.

Port Washington claims to hold the **world's largest fish fry** annually on the third Saturday of July, though they've got a couple of in-state rivals for that title.

For a basic place to stay, the **Best Western Harborside Inn,** 135 E. Grand Ave., tel. (262) 284-9461, has good rooms from $60. The city offers lots of B&Bs, including the huge Victoran **Grand Inn,** 832 W. Grand Ave., tel. (262) 284-6719, with two rooms and a nice sitting parlor with a wood-burning stove. Rates start at $100.

Plenty of good food is available in Port Washington—every place will have a decent fish selection, if not a particular specialty—including the venerable **Port Hotel,** 101 E. Main St., tel. (262) 284-6195, with the best prime rib for miles (not to mention frog legs); and **George Wilson's House,** 200 N. Franklin Place, tel. (262) 284-6669, with a good pub. A block north of George Wilson's, the **Fish Shanty,** tel. (262) 284-5592, specializes in seafood and serves a killer lemon pie. The best fish selection may be at unpretentious **Newport Shores,** 407 E. Jackson St., tel. (262) 284-6838, a block east of downtown and sitting right on the lake. **Buchel's Colonial House** south of town features northern European, Teutonic-oriented fare, done by a family that has catered to European royalty for over a century. **Bernie's Fine Meats Market** on N. Franklin is a good place to scout out Wisconsin-style smoked meats—especially sausage varieties.

Farther north is **Harrington Beach State Park,** unknown to most outside of the Milwaukee area, which is too bad. It's got great lake and limestone bluff views, an abandoned limestone quarry and quarry lake, and hiking trails, some a bit treacherous. No camping.

BETWEEN MADISON AND MILWAUKEE: NORTH OF I-94

Linked by the I-94 artery, dipolar Madison and Milwaukee appear as the ends of a barbell. Skirting to the north, though, there are pockets of classic Wisconsin dairyland, famed national wildlife refuges, a national shrine, and more.

HOLY HILL

Even recovering Catholics might appreciate a side trip to Holy Hill, with the neo-Romanesque church dominating the skyline, simply for its splendid location. In 1855, a handicapped mendicant hermit experienced a "cure" atop the 1,340-foot bluff and established Holy Hill as a pilgrimage site. One of the church spires, 180 steps up, affords commanding views of variegated kettle moraine terrain and, on clear days, the downtown Milwaukee skyline. Around the church are 400 heavily wooded acres crossed by the National Ice Age Scenic Trail; the grounds also contain a half-mile trail and a grotto. The monastery has guest rooms and retreat facilities; reservations are required. There is also a cafeteria open weekends year-round and daily June 1 through October 31; the Sunday brunch is another nice reason to visit. To get there, head 30 miles north of Milwaukee via US 41/45, then west on WI 167. For more information, call (262) 628-1838.

Kettle Moraine Railway

Near Holy Hill in the little town of North Lake is the Kettle Moraine Railway, tel. (262) 782-8074, a steam train offering eight-mile trips through the Southern Unit of the Kettle Moraine State Forest. Schedules and rates vary, but trips run on Sunday only June-Sept., on Labor Day, and on Saturdays in October.

Hubertus

Sneeze and you'll miss Hubertus—one of those places you can find on maps but doesn't really seem to be *on* the map. One of southern Wisconsin's landmark restaurants, **Fox and Hounds,** 1298 Friess Lake Rd., tel. (262) 251-

4100, is here, in a log structure at least part of which predates territorial status. Owned by the proprietors of Milwaukee's legendary Karl Ratsch's, it serves steaks and seafood as well as forgotten Midwestern items like goose and has one of the best wine lists around. Open for dinner Tues.-Sun. with a Sunday brunch as well. Menu items from $15.

HARTFORD

Little Hartford is a few miles north of Holy Hill via WI 83. It's worthy of a stop just to see the art deco interiors and smashing pieces of auto history at the **Hartford Heritage Auto Museum,** 147 N. Rural St., tel. (262) 673-7999. The museum displays over 80 antique automobiles, motorcycles, farm equipment and other engine-driven machines in pristine condition, including Wisconsin-produced Nash automobiles and high-caliber Kissels, which were built in Hartford 1906-1931. Open May-Sept. Mon.-Sat. 10 a.m.-5 p.m., Sunday noon-5 p.m., shorter hours the rest of year. Admission is $5 adults, $4 for seniors over 65, $2 children 8-15.

East of town is **Pike Lake State Park,** a large and relatively underappreciated greenspace of glacial terrain. The large park is dominated by 1,350-foot-high Powder Mountain. Actually a kame, the conical mountain was formed by glacial backwash pouring through ice crevasses. The park has close to a dozen miles of trails on six primary loops. The second-longest is the Blue Trail, from the beach to the campground; it's moderately challenging. The toughest is the Orange Trail, about 2.4 miles from the main parking lot as it runs through the heart of the park on hilly stretches. The four-mile Brown Trail leaves from the beach and wends through a variety of ecosystems. A stretch of the National Ice Age Scenic Trail cuts through the park on CR CC one-quarter mile south of WI 60 and leaves near Glassgo Road. The park's popular campground has 32 sites ($8); a car sticker must be purchased upon entry. Memorial Day through Labor Day, rates increase on Friday and Saturday nights.

WEST BEND

West Bend lies 15 minutes northeast of Hartford along US 45. You may know this busy manufacturing center as the point of origin of dozens of small kitchen appliances. There's a lot of parkland, too, in the city limits. The **West Bend Art Museum,** 300 S. 6th Ave., tel. (262) 334-9638, boasts a large holding of early 19th-century Wisconsin art. In addition to the works of Milwaukee-born German Carl von Marr, an antique dollhouse spans an entire room. It's open Wed.-Sat. 10 a.m.-4:30 p.m., and Sunday 1-4:30 p.m. Free admission.

The **Washington County Historical Society Museum,** 320 S. 5th Ave., tel. (262) 335-4678, is in a funky old 1880s county jail and courthouse. It covers county history with exhibits and walk-throughs of the main floor and the cellblock of the old jailhouse. Open the second Sunday of every month 1-4 p.m. and, April-Dec., Tuesday and Thursday 1-4 p.m. as well. Free admission.

North of town on WI 144 and CR A is the awe-inspiring **Lizard Mound County Park,** along with Aztalan State Park, one of the state's most important archaeological sites. The Mississippian Indians here predated Aztalan's by perhaps 500 years and built amazingly detailed earthworks in geometric and animal forms. Well worth a trip.

The place to stay right in town is the **West Bend Inn,** 2520 W. Washington St., tel. (262) 338-0636, with its somewhat bizarre but thoroughly intriguing FantaSuites, which are done up in ways you wouldn't believe—one's a space capsule, for example. Rates start at $65 but go way down to around $46 in low periods.

East of West Bend, in Newburg, is one of Wisconsin's most unique experiments in accessible living. **Welcome H.O.M.E,** 4260 CR Y, tel. (262) 675-2525, is a nonprofit organization dedicated to people with disabilities. It features 18 acres of semi-wooded meadow and prairie; fully accessible trails are free and open year-round (but are not maintained in winter), including a four-season self-guided trail for visitors without sight. A center with fully accessible accommo-dations is also on site. The group has recently opened a 3,600-square-foot living laboratory so that people with disabilities can experiment with independent living. Two suites are available with advance reservations; rates are $50. Northeast of Newburg is the **Riveredge Nature Preserve and Center,** with trails and activities.

Farther north, in Waubeka, you'll find the **Ozaukee County Historical Pioneer Village,** CR I, tel. (262) 377-8432, an assemblage of numerous pioneer homes and structures now populated by artisans who practice and demonstrate period crafts. Open every Wednesday and weekends noon-5 p.m. Memorial Day through Labor Day, then weekends only through October.

Food

West Bend has a couple of great places to eat. The **Old Courthouse Inn,** 518 Poplar St., tel. (262) 335-6302, is in a cozy, bilevel, 125-year-old brick building and has a full slate of creative entrées alongside classic Teutonic-inspired fare. It's open for lunch weekdays and dinner Fri.-Saturday. Choices from $5. **Tastings Food and Spirits,** 315 N. Main St., tel. (262) 335-0340, has equally creative continental fare from $5. Closed Sunday and Monday.

Timmer's, 5151 Timmer Bay Rd., tel. (262) 338-8666, is a classic country-style supper club out of town on Big Cedar Lake. Built in 1864, this antebellum eatery is on the National Register of Historic Places and has a big-time fish fry and a great Sunday brunch. It's open daily except Tuesday. Also on Big Cedar Lake is **Schultz's Whitetail Inn,** WI 144 and Anring Dr., known for its Jack Daniels prime rib.

HORICON MARSH

One of nine nodes of the National Ice Age Reserve, the Horicon Marsh is divided into two parts: the National Wildlife Refuge in the north and the Horicon Marsh Wildlife Area in the southern tier of the greenery. Spreading over 32,000 acres, the marsh was formed by the Green Bay lobe of the Wisconsin Glacier beginning around 70,000 years ago. The result was a shallow glacial lakebed filled with silt—the largest freshwater marsh in North America, often called the "Little Everglades of the North."

The marsh was populated originally by nomadic Paleo Indians, who hunted animals right along the edge of the receding ice floes. In turn, Hopewellian tribes, mound builders, Potawatomi, and Winnebago all resided in or around the marsh. Europeans showed up and began felling the region's deciduous forests, and, once the dry land was cleared, the farmers moved in farther. A dam was later built to facilitate floating timber logs on the Rock River and to create power for a gristmill and a sawmill, both built in 1846. The water levels rose nine feet, resulting in the world's largest man-made lake. Around the time of the Civil War, far-thinking conservationists succeeded in having the dam removed and reconverting the marsh to wetland. It became a legendary sport-hunting paradise; private clubs removed whole wagonloads of birds after hunts.

Around the turn of the century, agricultural interests once again lobbied to drain the marsh and reestablish farming. What couldn't be drained off was going to be used for profit-rich muck farming or moist-soil agriculture. The efforts failed, though the dikes the companies built still exist in a gridlike pattern today. Citizens' groups finally organized in the 1920s to call for legal designation of the marsh as a refuge. In 1927, the state legislature passed the bill, which officially protects the lower one-third; the federal government still maintains the upper two-thirds.

The marsh has a few Indian mounds along the east side, accessed by a driving route, as well as a four-mile-long island, an educational barn, and plenty of fishing.

But birds are the big draw. Annually, over 1,000,000 migrating Canada geese, ducks, and other waterfowl take over the marsh in a friendly—if histrionic and cacophonic—invasion. The geese alone account for three-quarters of the total.

The marsh has an established 30-mile-long **Wild Goose Parkway,** a drivable loop that takes in the whole of the marsh and offers some spectacular vistas. There are innumerable pulloffs with educational displays. The gates open 8 a.m.-3 p.m. weekdays and some Saturdays mid-April through mid-September.

Wildlife

Wetlands, upland grassy fields, and deciduous woodlands harbor a panorama of flora and

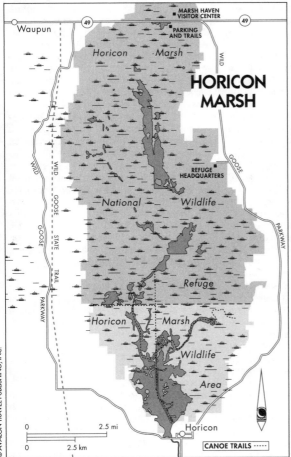

© AVALON TRAVEL PUBLISHING, INC.

fauna. The deep marshes are flooded every year except during severe droughts; water levels can rise four feet—crucial for nesting waterfowl, especially diving ducks, grebes, and fish-eating fowl. Wet meadows may flood annually, but never very much. Rich with insects, the meadows are key for shore birds and migratory waterfowl. The shallow marshes are usually six inches to one foot deep. The denser vegetation brings security in nesting, breeding, and rearing young. Well, at least all that was true until 1999 when the carp population reached such epic proportions that they literally started choking the ecosystem to death. Carp are a scavenging non-native pest species that breed like, well, rabbits. Thus, the Wisconsin Department of Natural Resources instituted a somewhat-controversial carp-kill to allow native species to return and the ecosystem to achieve a natural equilibrium again. The problem was that the winter ice melted faster than normal and, instead of being forced to the bottom to act as bottom fertilizer, the carp wound up floating down tributaries into Lake Sinnissippi, creating an epic stench and a nightmare for the DNR. However, by 2000 water quality had improved 100%, twice as fast as expected. Even wild rice grows again in the great marsh.

Mammals in the marsh include white-tailed deer, foxes, squirrels, raccoons, minks, skunks, opossums, muskrats, and coyotes. Some of the over 260 species of birds include mallards, blue-winged teals, coots, ruddy ducks, cormorants, herons, and terns. The marsh is the largest nesting area east of the Mississippi River for redhead ducks, almost 3,000 of which show up each year. Birds are most often spotted during spring and fall migrations. Rookeries—particularly one on Cotton Island—attract egrets, herons, and cormorants. In 1998, for the first time in over 100 years, trumpeter swans returned to the marsh. No state has spent more time or money to bring trumpeter swans back to native areas, and after years of preparation, a dozen swans were released. The goal is to have 20 nesting pairs eventually.

What of those honking geese? They come from the watery tundra near Hudson Bay in northern Canada. Some begin arriving by mid-September, with a gradual increase through October and sometimes into November. Upon arrival, they establish a feeding pattern in surrounding fields, eating waste corn and grass. Picture-perfect mass takeoffs occur right around sundown. The geese remain until dwindling temperatures freeze their water supply.

Recreation and Tours
The Horicon Marsh Wildlife Area, in the southern half of the marsh, has several established **canoe trails** through the wetlands, Mieske Bay, and along the east branch of the Rock River.

Six miles of **hiking trails** are accessible on the south side of WI 49, nearly three miles from the western boundary of the marsh. The trails spin deep into the marsh, occasionally on boardwalks, sometimes shrouded by cattails. A two-mile hiking trail starts near the foot of Conservation Hill at the north end of Palmatory Street in Horicon—a great spot for watching the waterfowl. Although not officially maintained as a trail, One Mile Island is also accessible for wildlife watching; to get there, follow WI 33 through town to the boat landing at the end of Nebraska St., where a hiking trail leads a half mile out to the island and Main Ditch.

Canoes can be rented at the **Blue Heron Landing,** WI 33 at the bridge in Horicon. All-day rental is $16, a shuttle is an extra $10. This is also the place to get aboard a **pontoon boat tour** of the marsh with **Blue Heron Tours,** tel. (920) 485-4663. Tours run daily at 2 p.m. May-Sept., weekends only in the off-season. A one-hour tour is $8 adults, $5.50 children 12-15, $3.50 children under 12. A special two-hour tour, taking in the largest heron and egret rookery in Wisconsin, is twice the price.

Marsh Haven Visitor Center
Three miles east of Waupun along WI 49 is the marsh's **visitor center,** tel. (920) 342-5818. It has a theater, art displays, and exhibits on the natural history of the marsh—including a live display of birds—and trail access from the parking lot. Admission is $1; hours are Mon.-Fri. 10 a.m.-4 p.m., Sat.-Sun. 9 a.m.-5 p.m.

Marsh Headquarters
The DNR Headquarters of the Horicon Marsh Wildlife Area is along WI 28 outside of Horicon, tel. (920) 387-7860. It's open weekdays 8 a.m.-4:30 p.m. The National Wildlife Refuge Headquarters is at W4279 Headquarters Rd., in the

Marsh, tel. (920) 387-2658, open weekdays 7:30 a.m.-4 p.m.

Plans are underway to create a unique public-private partnership to establish a $5 million addition to the headquarters building for a new education center, hiking trails, and wildlife viewing area. Plans looked gorgeous.

Horicon

The small town of Horicon has camping ($7.50), its own hiking trails, and Indian caves under the bluffline at **Ledge Park,** east of town via WI 28 and Raasch's Hill Road. Truly a spectacular place to hang out, it's the western edge of the Niagara Escarpment, which stretches all the way up to Niagara Falls. There's also the **John Deere Horicon Works,** 203 E. Lake St., tel. (920) 485-4411, producing the distinctive green and yellow lawn-care tractors along with snow throwers and other essentials. Plant tours are offered during the week before 10 a.m. by appointment. History buffs will like the **Horicon Historical Museum/Satterlee Clark House,** 322 Winter St., tel. (920) 485-2830, an old Civil War-era mansion full of period pieces and historical artifacts. It's open May-Oct. on the second and fourth Sunday of the month 1-4 p.m.

Horicon also has an access trail to the **Wild Goose State Trail,** a 30-mile multipurpose trail skirting the western edge of the marsh all the way north to Fond du Lac. Brief sections of the trail allow horses, ATVs, and snowmobiles. Trail passes ($3 daily) are required.

Waupun

Even with a maximum-security prison casting a shadow over the town, Waupun somehow manages to maintain an attractive, if somewhat subdued, downtown. (It was described by the old WPA Wisconsin guidebook as "almost oppressively pleasant.") Noteworthy are its five life-size bronze statues scattered throughout town, presented to Waupun by a late industrialist/sculptor, some of whose own sculptures are also seen in the town and vicinity. One of the life-size statues, on Madison Street, is the first casting of James Earl Fraser's *End of the Trail,* part of a series commemorating the genocidal expansionism of the frontier. The **Waupun Heritage Museum,** 22 S. Madison St., tel. (920) 324-3625, is housed in an old library and open the first and third Sunday of every month 1-4 p.m.

Geese are everywhere in Waupun, both as decoration and physically during migration. The city fetes all those geese the first week of October during **Wild Goose Days,** with a dance, car show, and craft festival. Great ethnic festivals in Waupun include the **Klompen Fest,** a Dutch fair in June in which townsfolk literally "klomp" through town and scrub the streets in one particularly memorable parade; and **Volksfest,** a German blowout the first week of September.

Waupun has an access trail leading east to the Wild Goose State Trail; **TJ's** is right along the trail on WI 49 and has bike rentals; better, it opens early, at 8 a.m. Memorial Day-end of season.

Mayville

East of the marsh in the town of Mayville is the **White Limestone School,** on N. Main St., tel. (920) 387-3474, known mostly for its collection of rural Wisconsin photographs taken by Edgar Mueller. There are also arrowhead and wild game exhibits. Admission is charged. The local historical society operates the **Hollenstein Wagon and Carriage Factory,** 11 N. German St., tel. (920) 387-5530, an old factory that once produced wagons. Several wagons are on display, and within the structure is a museum-esque display on the town's early iron industry, an old church, and a fire station. The factory is open May-Oct. every second and fourth Sunday 1:30-4:30 p.m. Free admission.

BEAVER DAM

It's not hard to guess the toponymic history behind this hardworking city of 14,200 once you espy Beaver Dam Lake, one of the 11 largest lakes in the state and one of a group heavily used in the area. The town got its start in 1840, when two intrepid homesteaders erected cabins alongside a narrow gurgling spring up from the confluence of a narrow stream that flowed to the Beaver Dam River. Hard work has always been the credo in Beaver Dam—even the local preacher owned the first gristmill and flourmill.

Sights

About the only sight is the monstrous **Beaver Dam Historical Society Museum,** 105 Park Ave., dominating the end of the main drag just to the right of the chamber of commerce. This 1890 Romanesque structure was built as the library and today contains a host of historical artifacts. It's open Tuesday 11 a.m.-1 p.m. and Wed.-Sat. 2-4 p.m. Down the street, the **chamber of commerce,** tel. (920) 887-8879, www.beaverdam-chamber.com, sits in an old train depot; unvanquishably chatty, the staff has more tourist info on paper than most cities its size. Open weekdays 9 a.m.-noon and 1-4:30 p.m.

Also in town is **Swan City Park,** with quaint Spring House, the bottling center for a mineral spring resort in operation from the 1880s through the 1940s. **Crystal Lake Park** features a spring that dumps 60,000 gallons of clear water per hour into the lake.

The city hosts the **Dodge County Fair** in mid-August, as well as **Beaverfest** in May, which isn't to be confused with July's **Beaver Dam Lake Days.**

Lakes

Ages ago, at **Beaver Dam Lake,** lunker fish were caught with regularity, but a takeover by rough fish reduced lunker numbers, and it's been a tough comeback, though restocking and carp traps have helped. One excellent thing about Beaver Dam Lake—not many resorts and no amenities crowd its shores. On its 14 miles of shoreline, you can always find a nook somewhere to be alone. If you're fishing, northerns and walleye currently predominate here. **D&D Bay Marina,** tel. (920) 885-4038, west of town on CR G, has rentals and sales. Jet skis go for around $20 per half hour, a pontoon boat $15 an hour, a sailboat $4 an hour, and canoes $4 an hour.

More heavily used is **Fox Lake,** just to the north. Over 175,000 fish it annually—mostly for walleye, though it's got muskie as well.

Practicalities

The cheapest rooms you'll find in Beaver Dam are on the southern edge along WI 33—the **Grand View Motel,** 1510 N. Center St., tel. (920) 885-9208, has rooms from $31. The **Campus Inn Motor Lodge,** 815 Park Ave., tel. (920) 887-7171 or (800) 572-4891, is a Best Western with a couple of pools, some suites with whirlpools, and a putting green. Rates run from $68.

For camping, the county operates **Derge Park,** six miles west of town with sites from $8.

The Pyramid, five miles east of Beaver Dam on WI 33, tel. (920) 885-6611, is a pyramid-shaped restaurant and definitely Egyptian on the inside. It's got a supper club menu and live entertainment on weekends; the Sunday brunch is also quite popular. Another distinctive supper club, in an old mansion, is the **Schaumburg Dinner Club,** corner of CR AW and CR A, tel. (920) 928-3348, north and west of Beaver Dam approximately 10 miles, near Randolph. The menu features the quintessential Midwestern Americana fare—broasted chicken specials Tues.-Thurs., a Friday fish fry, and prime rib on Saturday and Sunday nights. Both from $7.

Much less elaborate fare is available right in town. **Edith's Cakes and Catering,** 103 Front St., has a tasty cafe menu. Personal favorite **Chili John's,** 223 Front St., tel. (920) 885-4414, has not only good chili but also great unusual entrées such as stuffed Hungarian peppers. Both from $4.

At 831 WI 33, **Benvenuto's** is a very good bet for solid Italian. The wood-fired pizzas are great, and you can get bruschetta, calamari, a half dozen other excellent entrées, and lots of sides. Menu items from $5.

WATERTOWN

Watertown justifies its name: it lies at the bifurcation of the Rock River as it wends through an oxbow bend in the valley. Yankee settlers appeared as early as 1836 and harnessed the channel's water power—it drops 20 feet on its course through town—for grist- and flourmills, some of which still stand.

Historically, besides water power, Watertown was known for geese and Germans. Watertown goose livers were the top of the pâté de foie gras line. The city exported up to 25 tons of the rich organ to eastern markets annually. (Watertown perfected the art of "noodling"—force-feeding the geese with noodles to fatten them up.) The local high school's team nickname is the Goslings—not exactly ferocious, but at least historically relevant.

Until quite recently, the town's name was rendered Wasserstadt on a few business signs, a remnant of the heavy immigration of enlightened freethinkers fleeing political and social persecution in 1848 Germany. (This would be the reason that the city currently is being considered for a national Bratwurst Hall of Flame—yes, that's spelled right.) Most notable was Carl Schurz, a political reformer who arrived in Watertown in 1855 and eventually left his mark on U.S. politics. His wife put the town on the map, though, in contemporary terms; hers was the first kindergarten in the United States, which continues to be one of the city's primary tourist draws. At a critical transportation point in southern Wisconsin, Watertown was rumored at one time to be on the short list for state capital relocation.

Watertown is bisected by US 26 north to south, the south end being populated by much of the inevitable urban sprawl zones. East to west runs WI 19, or Main Street. Standing at the junction of Church and Main Streets, aside from one of the tallest steeples in Southeastern Wisconsin, the desiccated boulevard smacks of a previous-century daguerreotype. It's thoroughly small townish.

Watertown's gone through a sprucing-up in recent years. The Main/Water/First Street area now sports a riverside boardwalk and belching fountain. Across the way, a local entrepreneur has converted an old Water Street lumberyard two blocks south of Main Street into a tasteful mélange of artisan and Old World handicraft shops.

Sights

Watertown's **Octagon House,** 919 Charles St., tel. (920) 261-2796, may be the most impressive in the state. It is certainly the largest pre-Civil War fami-

ly residence in the Midwest, with over 8,000 square feet of floorspace and 57 rooms (although only one fireplace). Built over the course of 13 years by John Richards—who owned three mills on the river below the vertiginous hill upon which the house sits—the house is made of Milwaukee and Watertown bricks and sports one of the nation's only cantilevered spiral staircases, a basswood and cherry marvel that pirouettes 40 feet to the upper levels. This baby was so well built that reportedly not one of the stairs on the staircases creaks! Many of the house's furnishings are original Richards family pieces. The third floor today holds displays that provide an overview of Watertown's predominantly Germanic immigration and early history. Behind the house on the large grounds is the nation's first kindergarten, and nearby is a restored late 19th-century barn housing an array of agricultural implements. And a by-the-way: one of the owners of the house invented the golf ball washer. The octagon house hosts a variety of activities throughout the year and sits on the best sledding hill in the county. The house is open May-Oct., with docent-led tours 10 a.m.-4 p.m.; prior to Memorial Day and after Labor Day, hours are 11 a.m.-3 p.m. Admission is $3.50 adults, $3 seniors, and $1.25 children.

Accommodations

In the center of town along WI 19 is the **Heritage Inn,** 700 E. Main St., tel. (920) 261-9010, with a popular restaurant and sports pub in the lower level.

the largest antebellum octagon house in the Midwest

North of town along US 26 is the **Nite Cap Motel,** 760 N. Church St., tel. (920) 261-2452, with rooms from around $35; farther north, the **Flags Inn,** tel (920) 261-9400, has rooms at similar rates.

South of town along US 26 is the local **Super 8,** tel. (920) 261-1188, with an indoor pool and rooms from $55. Eight miles south, a grouping of chain motels lies at the junction of I-94.

Food

Classic artery-hardening greasy-spoon fare is on offer at **Zwieg's Grill,** 904 E. Main St., on the east end of downtown, across from the Piggly Wiggly grocery store. Going strong at 50-plus years, it's open at 5:30 a.m. Lunch is served within 10 minutes. Menu items from a buck.

The newest restaurant in town is also making a name for itself in southeastern Wisconsin. The **Upper Crust** is located in The Market, an old lumberyard just south of Main Street along Water Street gentrified into a chi-chi mix of antique and craft shops. It's a creative soup and sandwich place (from $4) but it's absolutely famed for its killer pies. You can't get near this place at lunch; it's so popular that traveling businesspeople will phone a day ahead to reserve pies, then take away a dozen at a time!

The building housing **Elias Inn,** a block north of Main St. at 200 N. Second St., tel. (920) 261-6262, has come a long way from the days when it was a German-style *bierstube.* Farmers coming into town to do their banking on Friday would stop off to quaff a brackish tap in a cloudy glass while suit-and-tie types from the bank munched head cheese or homemade venison sausage. Its present incarnation is a delicious amalgam of straight-up supper club with hints of Midwestern regional cuisine—all in a real-deal rustic interior. It's one of the best places to eat outside of Madison or Milwaukee. Open for lunch and dinner; on weekends, call ahead for a table for dinner. Closed Sunday and Monday.

For a lunch, quick bite, or, best of all, dessert, **Mullen's,** 212 W. Main St., tel. (920) 261-4278, is a southeastern Wisconsin landmark. Well into its sixth decade, it's got the best homemade ice cream you'll ever taste and a red and white checked interior reminiscent of bygone times. Lunchtimes are great for a chili dog or light sandwich; for dessert, there are dozens of ice cream concoctions, including the Bigger 'n Bill, named

after the proprietor—when you see it, you'll know it's for hardcore ice cream aficionados only.

OCONOMOWOC

That's "Oh-KAHN-uh-muh-wahk" (sometimes that first syllable sounds an awful lot like "uh"), but you'll hear it called simply "Cooney." It's the only city in America with a name spelled with five o's, one in every odd-numbered position in the word. Oconomowoc is another trim, spread-out Victorian city, this one wound around Lac La Belle and Fowler Lake, with other lakes in chip-shot range.

Oconomowoc is currently the center of attention for a radical new "living community" proposed and planned by August Pabst, grandson of the Pabst brewing magnate and owner of the nearby farm that once grew the hops and barley used by the brewery. The Pabst Farms European Country Village would create 800 new homes, 400 townhouses and apartments, condos, office parks, light industry, retail outlets, a golf course, stables, and a community center. The planners promise that over 600 acres of greenspace would be preserved and that Indian mounds and historic barns and structures would be spared. Cynics are appalled at the plan.

Sights

Oconomowoc is primarily a strolling town, and the local chamber of commerce along E. Washington Avenue has brochures for a **historical walking tour** around Fowler Lake. If you don't have any time to actually take the tour, go to the lobby of the First Bank of Oconomowoc, 155 W. Wisconsin Ave., where you'll find paintings of many of the homes in town. The lake edge and downtown are also done up in anachronistic red brick and boardwalk. The **Oconomowoc and Lake Country Museum,** 103 W. Jefferson St., tel. (262) 569-0740, has exhibits detailing the region, including 19th century architecture; there's also a theater with a video on area history. It's open weekends May-Dec.; free.

A dozen miles north of the city along WI 67, the **Honey Acres Museum,** tel. (920) 474-4411, has a one-of-a-kind showcase of the history and industry of beekeeping. There's a 20-minute multimedia presentation, a live bee tree (an apiarian version of an ant farm), displays, and a pleasant nature walk. And, of course, there are mouths-on activities as well. The museum is open weekdays 9 a.m.-3:30 p.m.; May 15 through Oct. 30, it's also open weekends noon-4 p.m. Free admission.

Every Wednesday night at the Lac La Belle bandshell downtown, the American Legion Band performs free concerts.

Accommodations

One of the larger all-season resorts in the southern part of the state, the 220-acre **Olympia Village Resort,** 1350 Royale Mile Rd., tel. (262) 567-0311 or (800) 558-3318, has rooms and villas, along with a ski hill, spa and fitness center, 18-hole golf course, seven indoor-outdoor tennis courts, a glamorous outdoor pool, and excellent dining. Rooms start at $90.

Find less pricey digs in town at the **Lake Country Inn,** 1367 W. Wisconsin Ave., tel. (262) 569-9600, a very nice place with rooms from $48 s, $57 d; a few suites have whirlpools.

Quaint **Inn at Pine Terrace,** 351 E. Lisbon Rd., tel. (262) 567-7463, has 13 guest rooms, most with high, flared ceilings, intricate woodwork, and antiques. Modern creature comforts include double whirlpool baths, TVs, phones, and a swimming pool. Rooms start at $65.

Food

A branch of Wisconsin's 24-hour diner institution, **George Webb,** is at 645 E. Wisconsin Ave., known for chili and soups. Right downtown at 159 E. Wisconsin Ave. is the casual **Simply Seafoods,** tel. (262) 560-1115, obviously a seafood place (good food; try the seafood chili!) but with steaks and other options from $8. If you're not wild about seafood, the **Main Street Depot,** 115 East Collins St., tel. (262) 569-7765, is a casual place with lots and lots of creative takes on soups, sandwiches, steaks, and more. Try the old-world meatloaf. Dishes from $6.

One of the most fabulous family restaurants you'll experience is **Spinnaker's,** 128 W. Wisconsin Ave., tel. (262) 567-9691, right on Lac La Belle. The menu runs the gamut from burgers to seafood and prime rib. Live entertainment is offered Wed.-Sat. nights. The service is outstanding, and it's one of the best places to take the whole family for a step above average family-style restaurants.

East of town on WI 16 is the **Golden Mast Inn,** 1270 Lacy Lane, tel. (262) 567-7047, with a hefty dose of German fare to buttress its steaks and seafood. An outdoor *biergarten* is lovely. There's also a Sunday brunch. Choices from $15.

Purportedly the oldest dining establishment in Wisconsin is the **Red Circle Inn,** tel. (262) 367-4883, established in 1848. Enjoy gourmet American and some French country cuisine. You'll find it along WI 16 east of Oconomowoc Lake at the junction with CR C. Selections from $18.

BETWEEN MADISON AND MILWAUKEE: SOUTH OF I-94

Interstate 94 links Madison and Milwaukee by some 80 highly forgettable miles. Real road-hogs know better than to suffocate on the gray swells of other mad travelers. Taking a souther-ly detour leads to the largest state forest in south-ern Wisconsin, funky Old World Wisconsin, an obscure Native American burial site, and the shrine to Wisconsin dairying.

KETTLE MORAINE STATE FOREST~ SOUTHERN UNIT

The Kettle Moraine State Forest-Southern Unit is sibling to the northern tier discussed later in this book. Debate continues—gets a bit bristly at times—over plans to acquire sufficient private lands to link the two, creating a green buffer against Lake Michigan suburban expansion. If expansion isn't curbed, development will de-stroy the region's residual glacial topography. A worst case scenario would have the Ice Age National Scenic Trail not even being able to link the two if development continues unchecked. The Wisconsin DNR hopes to add over 16,000 acres by 2010 or it may be too late.

Like the northern unit, the finger-thin southern section is representative of the state's oddball glacial heritage—landscape punctuated by resid-ual kames, eskers, and the eponymous kettles and moraines. Also within the forest are weather-beaten homestead log cabins, now one-eyed and decaying in the tall grass, and a handful of bluffline panoramas taking in all the glacial geology.

The southern unit, given its proximity to Mil-waukee and Madison, is unquestionably the more heavily used of the two. At 21,000 acres much smaller than its northern counterpart, the forest is packed, especially on weekends. But it does have an equal number of—if not more—trails than the north.

Recreation
You'll hear cyclists muttering about the parking lots being chockablock with autos, but those same whiners seem to forget innocent hikers, who can barely take a step without checking for gonzo mountain bikers careening along the paths. Yes, Kettle Moraine is popular. Show up on a Saturday in summer or fall and you'll likely be elbow-to-elbow with enthusiasts of all bents, so be prepared.

The forest offers 80 miles of trails, some hik-ing, some biking, some both; 30 of these are groomed for cross-country skiing in winter. The National Ice Age Scenic Trail cuts through the park from the Pine Woods Campground to Rice Lake—some 30 miles. Mountain biking is al-lowed on the **Emma Carlin** and **John Muir** Trails; the former has three loops and is found along CR Z, the latter is near La Grange along CR H. The Emma Carlin loops include the red loop (1.6 miles), which wends through hardwood forests with a steep razorback ridge and a good view of a glacial sand plain; the orange (2.2 miles), which continues along the same route on an old logging road; and the longest, the green (5.6 miles), a blend of open and wooded areas, winding through apple and walnut groves and affording vistas of Lower Spring Lake and, on a good day, Holy Hill. The John Muir trails are the most popular. They include a red loop (2 miles) through open fields and mostly pine forest, with one tough downhill; the orange loop (4.8 miles), which has a steep trail along leather leaf bogs (and a shelter for camping by permit); the green loop (7.4 miles), which has some of the rougher sections in the forest but which also boasts incredible blooms of pasque flowers in spring; the white loop (4 miles), which switch-backs through open areas and mature hard-wood and pine; and the blue loop (10 miles), the forest's longest, which has some of the best biking trails—diverse, challenging, and designed specifically for mountain bikes. Look at the twists and turns of the blue loop's southernmost point, stretching into a mature hardwood forest, and you'll see the outline of a squirrel.

The **Scuppernong** Trail, between CR ZZ to the south and CR G/GG on the east, is for skiing

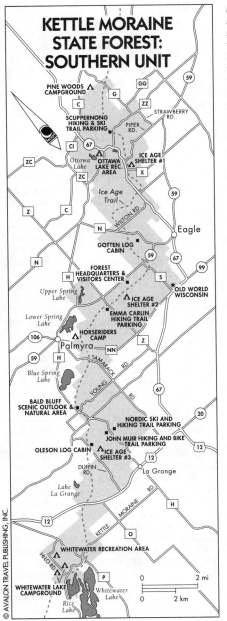

KETTLE MORAINE STATE FOREST: SOUTHERN UNIT

and hiking. This trail has three loops. The short and narrow red loop (2.3 miles) has quite a few steep parts through pine plantations and a good vista. The orange loop (4.2 miles) goes deep into the hardwoods of the forest; rare pileated woodpeckers and uncommon coopers hawks have been spotted here. The longest, the green loop (5 miles), skirts the Pine Woods Campground and goes through undulating terrain.

Adjacent to the John Muir trails along CR H, the **Nordic Ski and Hiking Trail** has five loops. The red loop (2.5 miles) goes over old farming pastures between four steep hills. The orange loop (3 miles) has one of the best views of the glacial topography, including a view of a wet kettle. The white loop (3.2 miles), keeping to mostly open areas, is the easiest in the forest. The green loop (4.3 miles) is similar to the white but a bit tougher. The blue loop (9.2 miles) is the toughest trail—for expert skiers only—with a fine cross-section of biotic zones.

The 30-mile **Ice Age Trail** is usually cut into four segments. From Pine Woods Campground to shelter #1 is 4.8 miles and runs through hardwoods; it has few open areas but two vistas. Shelter #1 is at the top of a spur trail and affords a commanding view of an outwash plain formed by retreating glaciers. To shelter #2 is another 8.3 miles over the dolomite limestone Niagara Escarpment. Lowlands and dry higher terrain are interspersed. To shelter #3 is another 10 miles and tangentially nips the Emma Carlin trails—it, too, offers vistas of Holy Hill and Lower Spring Lake. A switchback then traverses the top of a moraine, a prairie restoration, and a legendary stone elephant. The final leg is eight miles through hardwood forests and past Lake La Grange, with some spectacular views along the way. The Ice Age Trail can also be skied from the Mackie Area to Pine Woods; hiking is off-limits during winter.

As always in Wisconsin, there are plenty of lakes for beaches and boating. Two of the campgrounds are located along larger lakes.

Camping

Primitive camping is allowed at three Adirondack backpacking shelters along the Ice Age Trail; it's free, but you have to register at park headquarters. The forest also has 328 family campsites in four campgrounds; 50 of the sites have electricity. Not all campgrounds have showers. There is also a fully accessible camping cabin. Ottawa Lake is the most modern—with showers—but it's crowded and noisy. For tranquility, head directly to Pine Woods Campground; not only does it have the most isolated, shaded campsites, but it also has 32 sites where radios are banned! (A godsend—respite from the Yahoos.) You can also get to boat-in campsites ($10); check at the ranger station. Camping fees are $7-10, depending on the type of site, the season, and the day of the week (it's always $2 more on weekends). Vehicles must have admission stickers.

Food

Some of the charming little communities surrounding the forest have your usual bar grub; a couple other places have surprisingly good food. The **Kettle Moraine Inn** at the corner of WI 59 and WI 67 in Eagle is in an old hotel and has oodles of beers, including a Wisky resident's fave—cold Schlitz for $1 a bottle. You can also get steaks, fish, sandwiches, some Greek items, and homemade pizza. Its Friday fish fry might include New Orleans blackened varieties. Choices from $5.

Just south of Palmyra is the amazing **Nature's Trail Cafe**, N1242 WI 59, with all healthful entrées made from many locally grown organic ingredients. You can also get items like buffalo burgers, organic chicken from Oconomowoc farms, and other meats from local producers. Great breakfasts! Closed Tuesday. Items from $2. Equally impressive is **Camille's**, tel. (262) 594-6300, in diminutive Eagle. This place has superb French and Italian cuisine and an award-winning wine list. Selections from $8.

Rentals

The **La Grange General Store**, tel. (262) 495-8600, is conveniently located at the junction of US 12 and CR H. This welcome little gem inexplicably in the middle of nowhere dispenses a luscious array of deli, cafe, and natural food items—espresso, cappuccino, soups, salads, wines and beers, sandwiches, and cheeses. It also rents mountain bikes and cross-country skis and sells trail passes, as well as doing bicycle repairs and selling bike parts. Call ahead for the lowdown on trail conditions. Open Memorial Day through Labor Day 9 a.m.-8 p.m. weekdays, from 8 a.m. weekends; call for off-season hours.

Information

The **KMSF Headquarters** is at S91W39091 WI 59, tel. (262) 594-6200. Obtain free detailed maps here of the park's extensive trail system and recreation opportunities. It's open 8 a.m.-4:30 p.m.

OLD WORLD WISCONSIN

Along the eastern edge of the Kettle Moraine State Forest's Southern Unit is the blink-and-you'll-miss-it hamlet of Eagle, known solely as the home of the city-size Old World Wisconsin. Spread over 575 acres, Old World Wisconsin is an outdoor museum run by the state historical society. It comprises more than 50 immigrant structures relocated from around the state and organized here into Polish, Danish, Norwegian, Yankee, Finnish, and not one but two German homesteads, each populated by costumed docents leading discussions and exhibitions on pioneer life. Its collection of original log and wood buildings is the largest in the U.S. and considered the best. New for this edition are reconstructed buildings and a cemetery from Pleasant Ridge in Grant County in southwestern Wisconsin (five miles south of Lancaster); this was among Wisconsin's first African American communities. The complex is so big that trams ($2) make a circuit continuously.

Trails run throughout the complex. Walking the whole route is about two and a half miles, but there are shortcut nature trails through the woods or across meadows. A new Aldo Leopold Environmental Trail System includes nine ecological zones; another cultural history trail wends past more extant architectural gems. These same trails double as cross-country ski tracks on winter weekends. (Rentals available on site.) Sleigh rides are also offered. The visitor center presents slide shows.

Very popular is the **Clausing Barn Restaurant**, an octagonal 1897 barn designed by a Mequon immigrant. It offers casual cafeteria-style dining with an emphasis on heritage cuisine; open until 4 or 4:30 p.m. except on Fridays, when it stays open until 9 p.m. for its fish fry.

The complex is open May-June and Sept.-Oct. weekdays 10 a.m.-4 p.m. and weekends until 5 p.m. July and August, it's open 10 a.m.-5 p.m. daily. Admission is $7 adults, $6.50 ages over 65, $3 children 5-12. Admission stops one hour prior to closing; a ticket purchased after 3 p.m. can be used the following day.

FORT ATKINSON

Bisected by the Rock River, which flows sluggishly south and west of town into Lake Koshkonong, Fort Atkinson is a trim slice of Americana. It's been called by *Money* magazine one of the "hottest" small towns in the country in which to live.

The city was born when Gen. Henry Atkinson and his men hastily assembled a rough stockade and crude cabins at the confluence of the Rock and Bark Rivers while pursuing the Sauk Indians in the 1832 Black Hawk War. Dairying truly put the town on the map. William Dempster Hoard, the sort of patron saint of Wisconsin's dairy industry, began *Hoard's Dairyman,* a newsletter-cum-magazine, here in 1873. Today, Fort Atkinson enjoys a solidly diverse light-industry economic base. And it is an eye-catching classic small town.

Hoard Museum and Dairy Shrine

A primary draw here is the **Hoard Historical Museum,** 407 Merchants Ave., tel. (920) 563-7769, the repository for local history, housed in W.D. Hoard's family home, a gothic revival mansion later enlarged by Hoard in a mission oak style. The museum displays a restoration of the Dwight Foster House—the area's first frame house, built in 1841—along with two rooms of traveling exhibits, dolls, quilts, clothing, 400 specimens of a bird collection, and an extensive, 15,000-piece Native American artifact collection—so extensive the Smithsonian once eyed it. The museum's research archives include a wealth of information on the Black Hawk War. In progress is touch-up work on a new wing devoted to local Civil War memorabilia, which focuses on Abe Lincoln, who traveled through the county in 1832 with the militia chasing Black Hawk.

The museum is also the site of the **Dairy Shrine,** an assemblage of audiovisual displays, dioramas, and artifacts tracing the history of Wisconsin dairying.

Both are open Tues.-Sat. 9:30 a.m.-3:30 p.m. and, June-Aug., until 4:30 p.m. weekdays as well as the first Sunday of each month 1-5 p.m. Admission is free.

The Fireside

Since 1964 the ever-so-popular Fireside dinner theater has packed audiences in for Broadway-style musicals and international revues as well as a copious dinner in a 650-seat in-the-round theater. The restaurant itself seats about 1,100. The gift "shoppes" are as large as some grocery stores. A total of nine performances, including some matinees, generally run Wed.-Sunday. The Fireside is south of Fort Atkinson on US 26. Call (920) 563-9505 for information.

Lake Koshkonong

The second-largest lake in Wisconsin, Lake Koshkonong is fed by the Rock River. Primary communities on the lake include Newville—the gateway village to the lake—and Busseyville. The lake's entire circumference is lined with restaurants, inns, resorts, and marinas. For a small village town, Newville's got a lot of action, especially in the way of restaurants and pubs.

Tours of the lake and Rock River on the replica paddlewheel *Chief Black Hawk* are available from **Fort Boat Tours,** tel. (920) 563-2345. The paddlewheeler is a 48-person re-creation of turn-of-the-century Rock River vessels. Lunch cruises, afternoon sightseeing, and sunset excursions are offered. Rates are $7 adults, $6 seniors 62 and over and children 3-12. Tours run May-Oct. and depart from Loman Bicentennial Park, west of Main and WI 12/26 along Water Street.

Practicalities

The area's largest motel is the **Best Western Courtyard Inn,** two miles south on WI 26, tel. (920) 563-6444, with rooms from $60, an indoor pool, and a whirlpool.

The Fireside Dinner Theater garners most of the culinary attention locally. Also worthy is the **Cafe Carpe,** 18 S. Water St., one of the best eateries in the state. The food is a carefree, delicious blend of Midwestern diner and downscale cafe with Southwestern overtones; it's so popular that expansions are underway. But the Carp

HER LIFE BY WATER

Absolutely unknown to Wisconsinites—except those in her hometown of Fort Atkinson—Lorine Niedecker's simplistic, haiku-like poetry is arguably the most evocative interpretation of the ethos of a place in the canon of Wisconsin literature. In her own way, she pursued the underlying elements of life and place along the same lines as Wisconsin's other champion of the common—August Derleth. Overlooked as most poets are, she has been included by no less than the *Norton Anthology* as one of the 20th century's most significant U.S. poets.

Lorine Niedecker was born on May 12, 1903, on her beloved Blackhawk Island, a peninsular marshy swale through which the Rock River rolls into Lake Koshkonong, a rustic collection of shotgun-shack cottages, minor resorts, and fishing families. Blackhawk Island's isolation and ecology imbued Niedecker's works. Life was hard—the river flooded viciously, her father seined carp in scows for a modest living, and her mother developed deafness after Lorine's birth—all of which contributed to her leaving Beloit College to return home for good in 1922.

Reading Louis Zukofsky's "Objectivist" issue of *Poetry* magazine in 1931 changed her outlook and artistic life. She found resonance in the objectivist doctrine of viewing a poem as a pure form through which the things of the world are seen without the ambiguity of feeling. Like other prominent Wisconsin writers—among them Zona Gale, John Muir, Aldo Leopold—Niedecker's works were ecological in every sense; the earth and one's inextricable link to it was a permanent fixture around which the poetry revolved. Her spare but graceful poems literally flit across the page, designed to anticipate eye movement responding to rhythm. Her attention to the "condensory" (her word) called for using only words that contributed to a visual and aural presentation. Resolutely hermitic, Niedecker cloistered herself in her small hand-built cottage, which was stuck up on blocks to avoid the menacing spring floodwaters. This sense of isolation is fundamental to appreciating her passionately understated writing.

Niedecker never sold many books but was not interested in teaching, and so supported herself by scrubbing floors at Fort Atkinson General Hospital. Before this, she had worked as an assistant at the library, as a scriptwriter for WHA radio in Madison, and as a proofreader for *Hoard's Dairyman*. Her greatest work may have been as field editor for the classic Wisconsin guidebook—the 1942 WPA guide to the Badger State.

An unhappy first marriage ended in 1930. She remarried happily in 1961 and traveled widely throughout the Midwest for the first time. It was this travel that raised her poetry to another level; for the first time she wrote extended poems. Her output was prolific as she lived quietly on the island until 1971 when, after lingering in a coma following a cerebral hemorrhage, she passed away on January 3.

The Canon

Niedecker published her first book, *New Goose,* in 1946. A second, *My Friend Tree,* wasn't published until 15 years later by an obscure Scottish press. What many consider her greatest poem, "Lake Superior," was included in the great *North Central,* published in 1968 in London. Her *T&G: The Collected Poems 1936-66* was released in 1969, followed a year later by the classic *My Life By Water: Collected Poems 1936-68*. Most stores have to special-order any of these titles.

Some libraries may have a few thin critical biographies; the excellent *Granite Pail* (San Francisco: North Point Press, 1985; Cid Corman, ed.) is the most recent selection of her poems. *The Norton Anthology of American Literature* does include some poems.

is even more famous as Wisconsin's best venue for folk music. Low-key and friendly, this is one place you'll revisit.

Information

The **Fort Atkinson Chamber of Commerce,** 89 Main St., tel. (920) 563-3210 or (888) 733-3678, www.fortchamber.com, maintains a 24-hour information line at (920) 563-1870.

AZTALAN STATE PARK AND LAKE MILLS

Aztalan State Park, just off the interstate, is completely overlooked by 99% of passing travelers. Surrounded by agrarian stretches, the park feels eerily historic; the Rock River rolls by silently and the only sound audible is the wind shuffling through the leaves of the corn. One of the largest and most carefully researched archaeological sites in Wisconsin, Aztalan covers almost 175 acres and features remnant stockades and hiking trails snaking in and around the large burial mounds. Scientists theorize that this spot was a strategic northern endpoint of a Middle Mississippian culture, whose influence stretched south to New Orleans and into Mexico. The inhabitants—approximately 500 of them—lived here from A.D. 1000 to 1300. No camping is allowed today, but it's definitely worth a stop. Next to the park sits the **Aztalan Museum** in an old building on the site of the original Lake Mills community church. It's full of dusty old artifacts; a cabin and school supplement the old church. It doesn't keep regular hours—whenever a local volunteer has time to staff it, it's open.

Lake Mills is an engaging classic small Victorian town. Encircling a central park, it has wide tree-lined avenues, mansions, and droopy willow trees. Visitors can enjoy Lake Mills' free Bartles Beach, or, for a fee, Sandy Beach, on the other side of Rock Lake. (An aside: there are those who believe—this is no joke, universities have sent research teams—that there are pyramids beneath the black surface of Rock Lake. Apparently, these structures were produced by copper-mining expeditions from Asia and Europe several thousand years ago. Why they would halt mining and create pyramids hasn't been explained.) The less leisure-minded should head to the junction of WI 89 and CR A, a node for the **Glacial Drumlin Trail,** a 47-mile multipurpose recreation trail spanning from Waukesha to Cottage Grove east of Madison. The Lake Mills segment may be the most picturesque along the entire trail, with an old depot and trestle at the trailhead not far from Rock Lake. Other parking areas or rest stops are in Wales, Dousman, Sullivan, Jefferson, Deerfield, and Cottage Grove. Trail passes are required—$3 per day, $10 per season. There's also a good wildlife area south of Lake Mills.

Cuisine-wise, Lake Mills is classic supper club country; **The Pine Knoll,** N7755 WI 89, tel. (920) 648-2303, is one of the most popular. For road

silence of history at Aztalan State Park

grub, **Cafe on the Park,** 131 N. Main St., tel. (920) 648-2915, has famous breakfast skillets that weigh a ton and a Friday fish fry. The community arguably has the best burgers in the state as well—butter-filled little heart-attack patties called sliders served all summer by the VFW. An upscale eatery recently opened in town, too.

CAMBRIDGE

A perfect day-trip from Madison, Cambridge lies along US 12/18 to the east. Actually a mosaic of communities around the minor resort-area nucleus of Lake Ripley, Cambridge is now mostly associated with the village of Cambridge and its myriad pottery shops and quaint architecture, eateries, and antique shops. Yet the architecture is not at all cloyingly artificial—it's worth a gander. Best known of the local artisan workshops is the huge **Rowe Pottery Works,** 217 W. Main St., tel. (608) 423-3935, specializing in 19th-century salt-glaze stoneware. The **Cambridge Antique**

Mall packs 25 dealers into a century-old church complex. Out of town, you'll find the **Gallery in the Woods,** 245 Hoopen Rd., tel. (608) 423-4502, set back into gorgeous groves of oak. The gallery itself features pottery and weaving. To get there, take CR B past Rockdale and go to Hillside Rd., then south to Hoopen Road. Downtown the community has just opened the **Cambridge Museum,** housed in a 1906 building that was the original community schoolhouse.

Non-browsers can head to the innumerable parks, including Ripley Park on the west end of Lake Ripley. Better is the **Cam-Rock Park System,** consisting of three parks with tons of trails around small ponds and lakes. The Glacial Drumlin Trail also passes north and west in Deerfield.

Great eats around here. Downtown the **Country Inn** is a pub and restaurant with hearty Midwestern fare like roast meat, along with pastas and homemade soups, all from $5. East of town along US 18 is **Cardinal Ridge Supper Club,** tel. (608) 423-3956, with excellent carnivorous fare from $9.

MADISON

A Wisconsin governor's aide once quipped, "Madison is 60 square miles surrounded by reality." His precision inarguable, it has become a proud bumper-sticker slogan in the city. Madison may be reminiscent of other leftist hotspots such as Berkeley and Ann Arbor, but the salad days of revolution are long gone. There are conspicuously more financial institutions than cubbyhole political storefronts, and corpulent lobbyists seem to outnumber radicals. The student population rarely raises a fuss anymore, unless to celebrate Badger Rose Bowls or Final Fours or torch a neighborhood during the (in)famous (and now officially defunct) Mifflin Street Block Party.

Still, it is a wacky place. Octogenarian Progressives mingle with aging hippies and legions of university professors, and corporate and Capitol yuppies don't seem out of place. The student body omnipresence is a given—everyone in Madison is considered a de facto student anyway. It is still the "Madtown"—one agreeable, engaging, oddball mix.

Sanctuary
No guidebook hype—Madison is a lovely town. Ensconced erratically on an isthmus between two of the city's four lakes, it's got endless patches of green, a low-key downtown, a laid-back way of life, and a populace appreciably content if not downright enjoying themselves. Civic pride runneth over. It's no surprise, then, that after years of being a bridesmaid, Madison was finally named by *Money* magazine in 1996 the best place to live in America; it would repeat the honor two years later. It's also no coincidence that Madison is populated by droves of people who came for college and never left.

HISTORY

Perhaps appropriately for such an enclave of iconoclasm, Madison did not even exist when it was picked as the capital site. Judge James Duane Doty plied legislators away from the original capital—tiny Belmont—with offers of free land in what were no doubt termed lush river valleys to the northeast. Territorial legislators, probably dismayed by the isolation of Belmont, fell over themselves to pass the vote. Not one white person lived in the Madison area at the time.

Four Lakes

Originally dubbed "Taychopera" (Four Lakes), these marshy lowlands were originally home to encampments of Winnebago Indians. The first whites trekking through the area—most heading for lead mines in the southwest—remarked upon it in journals as a preternaturally beautiful, if wild, location. One early solider wrote that "the country . . . is not fit for any civilized nation of people to inhabit. It appears that the Almighty intended it for the children of the forest."

It remained that way until 1837, when a solitary family set up a rough log inn. Its occupants were workers who arrived to start construction on the Capitol. As Wisconsin lurched toward statehood, the city of Madison added civic particulars: a school, a church, a general store. (And, of course, bars, which also doubled as the first churches.) Still, a half decade after it became the capital, only 150 or so people called this semi-wilderness home.

After Statehood

In 1848, the territory became a state, just as finishing touches were being added to the Capitol. The population had mushroomed to over 700, yet there was still not even a semblance of established roads. At this point a munificent Milwaukee millionaire, Leonard Farwell, showed up and, most likely aghast at the beastly conditions,

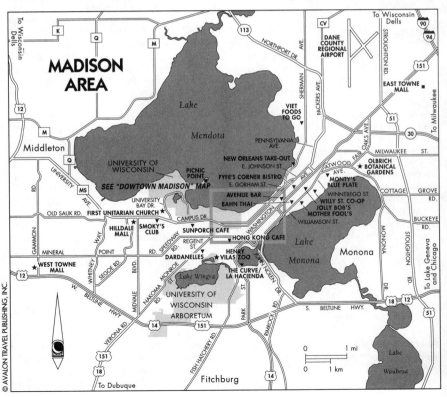

© AVALON TRAVEL PUBLISHING, INC.

scooped up land and began major changes. Streets were established, marshlands drained, and the initial mills built.

Through the 1850s, Madison exploded into a full-scale community, with commercial districts, foundries, and the new University of Wisconsin—only five years old in 1853. When the railroad arrived, in 1854, the city had a rollicking population of just under 7,000.

Civil War spending allowed the city's finances to expand rapidly; a decade after the end of the hostilities, Madison had nearly 500 factories of all sorts. By the turn of the century, more than 19,000 inhabitants resided in Madison. Still, despite the numbers, wild animals gamboled through the remaining thickets, and one contemporary Eastern visitor remarked that Madison resembled nothing much more than an exaggerated village, down to a village's mannerisms and conduct.

20th-Century Madison

Madison in the first half of the 20th century is noteworthy for a dearth of juicy history. One historian said of most of Madison's past, "The historian finds little of stirring interest; and that little almost always the reflex of the legislature." Political machinations have always played a central role in the image of Madison. From the boozy, brawling first legislators, Madison has always had a sideshow accompaniment to its vast cultural arenas. This was perhaps never more manifest than in the 1960s, during implosions over the Vietnam War, when Madison truly became the Mad City—one of the nation's foremost leftist concentrations.

Overtones of radicalism still exist, but the city really is too busy to get all worked up over issues, having transformed itself into a financial and commercial center. Its remarkable new Frank Lloyd Wright-designed Monona Terrace seems contrived deliberately to draw a national spotlight.

SIGHTS

Orientation

You're never more than eight blocks from a lake in Madison. The city spreads along a narrow isthmus between two large lakes, and to the

west it gradually unravels around their edges, which doesn't bode well for traffic grids.

Traffic can be maddeningly circuitous in downtown Madison. If you always keep an eye on the Capitol, you should do all right. Also keep in mind that east and west in street names are approximations—it's actually closer to northeast and southwest. *All east-west streets use the Capitol as the dividing point.*

The main thoroughfare down the throat of the isthmus is E. Washington Avenue (US 151); it leads directly to, and then around, the massive state Capitol, which is connected to the university by State Street.

North of E. Washington are one-way Johnson and Gorham Streets, the former running east, the latter heading west. Gorham crosses State, then bears hard right, becomes University Avenue, and takes you into Universityville. Washington Avenue continues west to Park Street, which leads to the main artery between east and west Madison: the white-knuckled swells of the Beltline—US 12/14 and 151/18 (or any combination thereof). It's unlikely you'll be able to avoid the Beltline altogether; just avoid rush-hour peaks. Both East Washington Avenue and the Beltline link up with the interstate east of Madison.

There's generally plenty of parking downtown in parking structures; the closer you get to the university, the more frustrating it is to try to park. Parking starts at 35 cents an hour in the structures. Municipal parking areas have great deals on Saturday. Be exceedingly aware of parking regulations in Madison; they're enforced stringently winter and summer. As a matter of fact, parking sentinels are thought to be omniscient, so do use prudence. Finally, travelers will note that some downtown traffic signs have been color-coded to facilitate traffic flow (unfortunately, it's unlikely locals will know what "color" you're talking about if you ask them).

State Capitol

Standing atop the most prominent aerie in Madison, the stately white bethel granite Wisconsin State Capitol is one of the largest in the country and definitely one of the most magnificent, inside and out. Designed by George Pesi, who also designed the New York Stock Exchange, it stands 300 feet above the morainic rise—a bea-

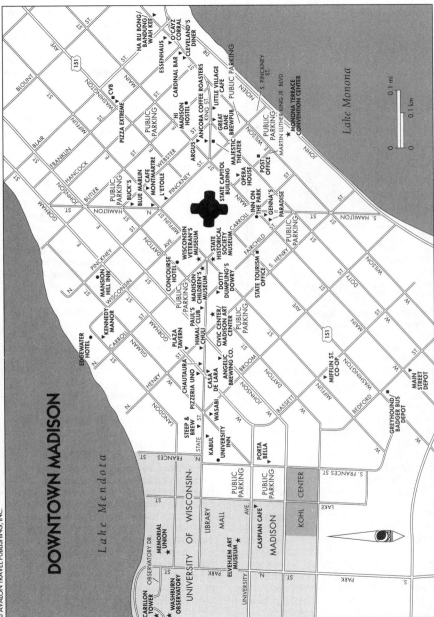

© AVALON TRAVEL PUBLISHING, INC.

DOWNTOWN MADISON

Lake Mendota

Lake Monona

CARILLON TOWER ★
WASHBURN OBSERVATORY ★
OBSERVATORY DR.
MEMORIAL UNION ★
UNIVERSITY OF WISCONSIN-
ELVEHJEM ART MUSEUM ★
LIBRARY MALL
CASPIAN CAFE ▼
MADISON
KOHL CENTER

EDGEWATER HOTEL ●

STEEP & BREW ▼
KABUL ▼
UNIVERSITY INN ●
PORTA BELLA ▼

CHAUTAURA ▼
PIZZERIA UNO ▼
CASA DE LARA ▼
WASABI ▼
ANGELIC BREWING CO. ▼

KENNEDY MANOR ●
MANSION HILL INN ●
PLAZA TAVERN ▼
BUCK'S ▼
BLUE MARLIN ▼
CAFE MONTMARTRE ▼
L'ETOILE ▼
PINCKNEY
HIMAL CHULI ▼
PAUL'S CLUB ▼
CIVIC CENTER/ MADISON ART CENTER ★

PIZZA EXTREME ▼
CVB ●
HA RU BONG/ BANDUNG/ WAH KEE ▼
O'CAYZ CORRAL ▼
CLEVELAND'S DINER ▼
ESSENHAUS ▼
CARDINAL BAR ▼
HI MADISON HOSTEL ●
ANCORA COFFEE ROASTERS ▼
LITTLE VILLAGE CAFE ▼
ARGUS ▼
GREAT DANE BREWPUB ▼
KING ST.
MAJESTIC THEATER

STATE CAPITOL BUILDING

CONCOURSE HOTEL ●
WISCONSIN VETERAN'S MUSEUM ★
MADISON CHILDREN'S MUSEUM ★
STATE HISTORICAL SOCIETY MUSEUM ★
DOTTY DUMPLING'S DOWRY ▼
OPERA HOUSE
INN ON THE PARK ●
GENNA'S ▼
PARADISE ▼
POST OFFICE
MONONA TERRACE CONVENTION CENTER
MARTIN LUTHER KING JR. BLVD.

STATE TOURISM OFFICE ■

MIFFLIN ST. CO-OP ■

MAIN STREET DEPOT ■
GREYHOUND/ BADGER BUS DEPOT ■

S. PINCKNEY ST.

0   0.1 mi
0   0.1 km

Streets (partial): BLOUNT ST, BLAIR ST, FRANKLIN ST, HANCOCK ST, BUTLER ST, HAMILTON, PINCKNEY ST, WEBSTER ST, KING ST, NOLEN DR, WILSON, JOHN, JOHNSON ST, GORHAM ST, DAYTON, MIFFLIN ST, N. CARROLL, FAIRCHILD, S. HENRY, BROOM, BASSETT, BEDFORD, DOTY ST, WASHINGTON, S. HAMILTON, WILSON, MAIN ST, FRANCES ST, S. FRANCES ST, LANGDON ST, HENRY ST, N. FRANCES, STATE ST, GILMAN ST, WISCONSIN, PINCKNEY, CARROLL, PARK ST, LAKE, UNIVERSITY AVE, N. PARK ST, S. PARK ST, 151

It's not as big as the one in Washington, DC, but this one could hold more beer!

con for lost out-of-towners. Crowning it is the three-ton gilded bronze statue *Wisconsin,* a golden lady with a badger on her head—she was being burnished back to glossy splendor as this edition was being updated!. The current building (the first two burned) was constructed over 11 years and cost $7.25 million dollars—25 cents per state resident per year of construction. It resembles the nation's Capitol from afar: the powers that be in D.C. took this as a sign of homage, but that quickly passed when they realized plans were to build Wisconsin's Capitol taller than the nation's Capitol. Though the Badgers were forced to reduce the height of their Capitol to three feet below that of the federal one, Wisconsin's volume is greater. The interior features 43 different types of stone from eight states and six foreign countries, including semiprecious marble nonexistent today. The mosaics, imported and domestic hand-carved furniture, massive murals, and hand-stenciling make the building priceless. Interesting Capitol tidbits: one stone on the south side near a window was left

unsealed with a notch cut in it—some believe this has something to do with ghosts; also, the Capitol always wins local surveys for cleanest public bathrooms.

The building is open 6 a.m.-8 p.m. Free tours leave daily every hour Mon.-Sat. 9-11 a.m. and 1-3 p.m. For information call (608) 266-0382.

State Street and Museum Mile

Bookended by the Capitol on one end and the university on the other, State Street is a quasi-pedestrian mall (buses and taxis are allowed, and you need to be fully aware of bicycles and in-line skaters when walking). It's full of shops, boutiques, coffeehouses, restaurants, bookstores, museums, cultural centers, and much of the downtown's character. People-watching along these seven blocks is a long-standing tradition.

Note that as this book was being updated, Madison was preparing to break ground—well, concrete actually—on a grand new **Madison Arts District** that would take up the 100 block of State Street along with a few blocks on either side of it. Not all the wrinkles have been worked out, but plans tentatively would create galleries, art spaces, museums, and performance venues. It was brought about by the amazingly generous donation of $50 million—later increased—by a local Madtown philanthropist. Though benign on the surface, the project has not come without some controversy. Many felt that the city simply kowtowed to the whims of yet another rich white guy; did Madison really need another arts venue for wine-sipping yuppies? Some thought the money would have been better spent on genuine arts space, support for local artists, or arts education for youth. (In fact, the only teen center in Madison was forced out by the project, and the city ridiculously put the new center almost a kilometer away, on noisy, polluted East Washington Avenue. Teens don't frequent the new place and instead loiter on State Street.) A couple local businesses refused to sell, insulted by what they termed patronizing treatment by the project's leaders; they were in the midst of what seemed a Phyrric battle as this book was being prepared. Dissenters at least got a few crumbs. The original plans had, quite unbelievably, planned on gutting the grand Oscar Mayer Theater inside the Civic Center. It now won't be gutted but simply divided up—a moral victory but a victory nonetheless for those opposed to the project.

Six museums and a couple other highlights are currently located along State Street. On the State Street corner of the Capitol Square, the **State Historical Museum,** 30 N. Carroll St., tel. (608) 264-6555, and the **Wisconsin Veterans Museum,** 30 W. Mifflin St., tel. (608) 264-6086, sit across the street from one another. The former has permanent multimedia exhibits that detail the state's geological and Native American history. Visitors can walk through a talking mud hut or punch up online geological dioramas. The lower level is a gallery area featuring revolving exhibits; two more floors were recently opened to hold permanent exhibits. The museum is to be commended for its varied, challenging exhibits. Free public programs occur every Saturday at 10:30 a.m. This museum has unquestionably the best bookstore for Wisconsin titles. Free, it's open Tues.-Sat. 10 a.m.-5 p.m. and Sunday noon-5 p.m.

The Veterans Museum has two impressive main galleries of exhibits, dioramas, and extensive holdings tracing Wisconsin's involvement in wars from the Civil War to the Persian Gulf Conflict; the Battle of Antietam is well represented. Even Mexican border campaigns are detailed. Main attractions are the mock-ups of the Battle of Antietam, the Battle of the Bulge, and jungle fighting in Papua New Guinea, as well as the aircraft hovering overhead—a Sopwith Camel, a P-51 Mustang, and a military helicopter. Children will love the submarine periscope sticking out of the gallery's roof, which allows for a true panoramic view of downtown Madison. The museum is open Mon.-Sat. 9 a.m.-4:30 p.m. and, April-Sept., Sunday noon-4 p.m.; admission is free. Call (608) 267-1799 for information.

Note that the next two items will definitely be affected by the new arts district. Kids also love the next museum along the route: the **Madison Children's Museum,** 100 State St., tel. (608) 256-6445, is housed in this old triangular corner edifice. Visitors can romp through and get their hands on a variety of traditional and computer-oriented activities. Significant is the display regarding Madison's lake environment. It's open Tues.-Sun. 10 a.m.-5 p.m. and Thursday 5-8 p.m. Admission is $4, children

under 1 free, and free to all the first Sunday of every month.

One block nearer the university from the Children's Museum is the distinctive Madison Civic Center and, within it, the **Madison Art Center,** 211 State St., tel. (608) 257-0158. The prominent gallery window is always attracting the attention of passersby, most staring quizzically at the art or, occasionally, the performance artist trapped inside. The small galleries are interspersed through three floors of the civic center complex and feature contemporary art—mostly paintings and some photography. A good gift shop is located here. Free, it's open Tues.-Thurs. 11 a.m.-5 p.m., Friday 11 a.m.-9 p.m., Saturday 10 a.m.-9 p.m., and Sunday 1-5 p.m. The Civic Center also houses the 2,200-seat Oscar Mayer Theatre, which hosts modern and classical music, touring shows, and Broadway plays. The Isthmus Playhouse inside is a thrust-stage venue home to the Madison Repertory Theatre.

The remaining museums operate under the auspices of the University of Wisconsin. As State Street runs its final block and melds with the Library Mall, walk past the bookstore and a church, then bear left down a cul-de-sac. The **Elvehjem Museum of Art,** 800 University Ave., tel. (608) 263-2246, contains almost 15,000 holdings, the oldest dating from 2300 B.C. The open, airy design features three levels of permanent collections including Egyptian and Greek porcelain, a Roman cask, Japanese prints, Indian figurines, Russian icons, early European and American art, and a somewhat moody roomful of Renaissance church art. The top floor showcases modern American artists. The museum is open Tues.-Fri. 9 a.m.-5 p.m. and weekends 11 a.m.-5 p.m., and admission is free.

Farther along the campus proper, the **UW Geology Museum,** 1215 W. Dayton St., tel. (608) 262-2399, is rather small but has large exhibits, including a scaled version of a limestone cave, a 30-some-foot-long dinosaur and a mastodon skeleton. Of course, you'll also view the detritus of millions of years of the machinery of fossilization, meteorites, and minerals. It's open weekdays 8:30 a.m.-4:30 p.m. and Saturday 9 a.m.-1 p.m. The **Entomology Museum,** 1630 Linden Dr., tel. (608) 262-0056, has staff happy to lead tours, showing folks lots of the nearly two million specimens. You can even see really, really big and really ornery hissing cockroaches from Madagascar. One retreat from throngs of folks that most people don't know about isn't really a museum. But **Birge Hall,** in front of Bascom Hall atop Bascom Hill, is the nucleus of the botany department and its greenhouses are wonderful. Tours are available whenever the hall is open—generally weekdays 8 a.m.-3:45 p.m.

University of Wisconsin-Madison

Bascom Hill on the other end of State Street affords a view similar to the one from the state Capitol rise. Crowning this is belvedere Bascom Hall, one of the original university buildings, established in 1848. North Hall, down the hill toward the lake, was the campus's original building and served until 1850 as a one-room university. A statue of a relaxed Abraham Lincoln sits in a tiled courtyard between Bascom and North Halls; the tiered hill is a favorite sack-out spot for students between (or skipping) classes. From a handful of students and wild animals in 1848, the university has grown to 1,000 acres and over 50,000 students and faculty. A world-renowned institution, the University of Wisconsin is consistently ranked in the upper echelons in engineering, mathematics, numerous languages, and many other disciplines.

Since its inception, UW has imbued the fabric of the community to a larger extent than even the state government has. The campus sprawls gorgeously for nearly two miles along the southern cusp of capacious Lake Mendota. The nucleus of campus is **Memorial Union,** 800 Langdon St., tel. (608) 262-1331. Perched beside Lake Mendota, it's a must-stop for any visitor. Visitor information, tel. (608) 263-2400 or (608) 265-9500, is available in the "Old Red Gym" next to the Union; it's open weekdays 7:30 a.m.-12:30 p.m. Guided tours depart weekdays at 3 p.m. and weekends at noon.

Not far from Bascom Hall is a **carillon tower** with 56 bells and sporadic Sunday afternoon performances. Up the hill from the tower is **Washburn Observatory,** 1401 Observatory Dr., tel. (608) 262-WASH, one of the first observatories to use radio astronomy. April-Oct., it's open the first and third Wednesday of each month at 9 p.m. (every Wednesday mid-June-late July); the rest of the year, it opens at 7:30

p.m. Generally there's somebody around. If for nothing else, hike up to the observatory to drink in the views of Lake Mendota. A hundred yards away from the Union along Observatory Drive, at the corner of Babcock Drive, is a conglomeration of 22 gardens on a two-and-a-half-acre Victorian estate that once belonged to the university deans. Another gem is just below Birge Hall on Bascom Hill; **Botany Garden** has nearly 1,000 plants arranged in evolutionary sequence.

Lots of UW's departments offer tours; it's best to call ahead and verify it is possible. Most popular might be the **Babcock Hall Dairy Plant,** 1605 Linden Dr., tel. (608) 262-3045, where you can get up close and personal looks at the creation of UW's famed ice cream; the department also makes cheese. Babcock hours are weekdays 9:30 a.m.-5 p.m., Saturday until noon. Biotechnology is a new addition to the **agricultural campus.** On the guided "Biotrek," beginning in the Dairy Barn, 1915 Linden Dr., you take in the Dairy Research Building, the milking parlor, Babcock Hall, Horse Barn, and the School of Veterinary Medicine. The barn itself is of note: designed in 1898 by a UW professor, its cylindrical style became a world standard. Call (608) 265-2420 to schedule a tour.

Where State Street ends and the university begins stands the **Memorial Library.** Ranking in the top five nationwide for its collection (it holds over five million volumes), it also has a few areas with rare books. A plan to add floors to the library raised a hullabaloo, since it would block the view of the Capitol.

Bus lines serve just about everything. For general campus information, call (608) 262-2400.

Picnic Point: A lakeshore path runs from the popular terrace of the Memorial Union, bypasses dormitories, boathouses, beaches, and playing fields, and winds up at one of the university's two gorgeous natural areas—Picnic Point. This narrow promontory jutting into Lake Mendota is split by a screened gravel path and is popular with hikers, joggers, and bikers. You can walk to the tip in under 20 minutes; along the way there are offshoot roads and trails as well as firepit picnic sites. The views of the city are great. If you can't hoof it, bus lines wind along nearby University Bay Drive from the Memorial Union; get off when you see signs for Eagle Heights, a university housing area.

Henry Vilas Zoo

One of the few nationally accredited zoos in the U.S. that remain delightfully free to the public, the vastly popular Henry Vilas Zoo, 702 S. Randall, tel. (608) 266-4732, sits adjacent to a park and the popular beach on Lake Wingra. For a city of Madison's size, the array of 800 wild animals, representing almost 200 species, is quite impressive. Though most zoos are inherently disquieting, this does an admirable job. It underwent a massive "rezoovenation" in the late 1990s to expand facilities, especially for big cats and primates. A second aviary is also in the works. A new Herpetarium and Discovery Center offers hands-on entertainment for kids; they can also get free camel rides Sunday mornings in summer. The zoo is open daily June through Labor Day 9:30 a.m.-8 p.m. and Sept.-May until 5 p.m.

University of Wisconsin Arboretum

Covering a rough triangle between US 151, the Beltline, and Monroe St./Nakoma Rd. on the south side of Madison, the Arboretum is one of the most expansive and heavily researched of its kind in the nation. Its 1,260 acres comprise stretches of natural communities from wetland to mixed-grass prairie; the restoration work on some is unique—designed to resemble Wisconsin and the Upper Midwest prior to settlement. More than 300 species of native plants flower on the prairies, some of which are the world's oldest restored tallgrass prairie and the site of the first experiments (in the 1940s) on the use of fire in forest management. The deciduous forests include one virgin stand dating to the time of European settlement in the lower half of the state. In the deciduous forests along Lake Wingra, Native American burial mounds dating as far back as A.D. 1000 can be found. Best of all are the more than 20 miles of trails and firelanes. Note that no bicycles are allowed.

The McKay Center is a solar-heated visitor center plunked in the midst of the Arboretum, surrounded by fifty acres of ornamental gardens and shrubs. It was also being expanded as this edition was being researched. The center offers exhibits, slides, a library, and guidebooks; it often has free tours on Saturday and Sunday (8:30 a.m. summers, 1 p.m. rest of the year). It's open weekdays 9:30 a.m.-4 p.m., weekends 12:30-4 p.m. (11 a.m.-3 p.m. June-Aug.). The trails and landscaped areas are open 7 a.m.-10 p.m.

Olbrich Botanical Gardens

Along Madison's east side, these mammoth gardens feature a tropical forest conservatory with waterfall inside a 50-foot glass pyramid, along with a botanical education center and seemingly endless gardens covering almost 15 acres. The rose and herb gardens are particularly impressive; the rose displays include approximately 600 bushes. New expansions were underway for this edition. Concerts (free every Tuesday in summer), plant sales, and educational events are held throughout the year. The conservatory is open daily 10 a.m.-4 p.m., the gardens earlier. Admission to the conservatory is $1, free to children under age five, free to all Wednesday and Saturday 10 a.m.-noon. Admission to the gardens is always free.

Monona Terrace Community and Convention Center

Garish white whale or architectural cornerstone? You be the judge of the new Monona Terrace. Madisonians may never come to terms with their decades-old love-hate relationship with it. Supporters hoped that the structure, which some call Frank Lloyd Wright's masterpiece, partially atop Lake Monona on pylons, would draw attention (and moneyed conventioneers) to Madison; critics moaned that it was yet another civic white elephant—and a monument to what they considered an egotistical SOB. After innumerable false starts, a referendum in the early '90s barely passed, setting off another round of cacophonic protest, including enlisting the EPA to declare it a Superfund site (Lake Monona was built over early 1900s ash and waste piles). Perhaps most clamorous were the powerful cycling contingents in town, irate that the only bicycling artery along the lake was to be closed. The groups shut down traffic sporadically along the route until the planners factored in bike lanes.

In any case, the thing's finally built. Those who come (or don't come) will eventually be the judge of the complex's success or failure. Wright's hoped-for design included much, much more than was finally constructed, and only three years after it opened its structures already required repairs; they also wonder why it's called a "community" center since everything people do here seems to cost money. But even opponents admit that nothing like it exists in a city of comparative size.

The building is open daily 9 a.m.-5 p.m. The rooftop garden area is open Sun.-Thurs. 8 a.m.-10 p.m., until midnight Friday and Saturday. The cafe on Level 4 is open weekdays 7 a.m.-1 p.m., from 8 a.m. Saturday. Guided tours are available daily at 11 a.m. and 1 p.m.; they cost $3 but are free Monday and Tuesday. Free concerts are offered Wednesday (and some Fridays). For information, call (608) 261-4000.

First Unitarian Church
Frank Lloyd Wright has left his mark on Madison in more ways than the Monona Terrace center. Several residences in town show his handiwork, and one structure he designed that attracts many viewers is the First Unitarian Church, 900 University Bay Dr., distinctive for its acclivitous triangles.

Farmers' Market
Madison's farmers' market—the largest of its kind in the U.S.—has become a draw in and of itself. Bright and early every Saturday April-October, more than 200 farmers line Capitol Square and dispense everything you could possibly imagine. The only-in-Madison juxtapositions include an organic herb farmer, a free-range-chicken vendor, a Hmong family selling vegetables, jugglers, local politicos pressing the flesh, and radical political or social organizations of many bents. Add to this zillions of gapers circling counterclockwise. Agoraphobics won't take to it at all.

Capital Brewery
The Capital Brewery, 7734 Terrace Ave., tel. (608) 836-7100, is actually in Middleton, west of Madison. A long-time brewer that shut its doors ages ago, it's undergoing a rejuvenation of sorts and is now a popular purveyor of local beers. Tours of the traditional-style brewery take in the brewhouse, fermenting and aging cellars, and kegging area; they're offered in summer Wed.-Thurs. at 1 p.m., Friday at 1 and 3:30 p.m., and Saturday at 1 and 2:30 p.m.; in the off-season, they're Saturday at 1 and 2:30 p.m. More popular than the brewery is the rollicking biergarten on the premises, with live music weekends.

ACCOMMODATIONS

Madison has some 6,600 hotel beds, and more are on the way following completion of the Monona Terrace Convention Center downtown. Most accommodations are strung along the Beltline (US 12, 14, 18, 151), the artery linking east and west Madison. Another concentration of motels is found at the junction of US 151 and US 51 and east along US 151 (E. Washington Ave.) to East Towne Mall—the major commercial portion of the east side. The cheapest room you'll find is around $35 in the low season. Always check ahead—football Saturdays and many UW events max out rooms in town.

B&Bs and Historic Inns
Highly recommended is the **Mansion Hill Inn,** 424 N. Pinckney St., tel. (608) 255-3999, an opulent 1858 Romanesque Revival on the National Register of Historic Places. Set snugly along a quiet residential street close to downtown, this ornate piece of Victoriana features a distinctive gabled roof and wrought-iron railings encircling the etched sandstone facade. Inside, the opulence is breathtaking, with thrusting round-arched windows, ornate cornices, and hand-carved marble. The four-story spiral staircase leads to the rooms and a wraparound belvedere. Victorian gardens surround the inn. The eight rooms vary from Empire style to a Turkish nook, Chinese silk, an Oriental suite, a room done up as a study, and more. Great extras include 24-hour valet parking, silver-service breakfast delivered to rooms, and shoeshine service. Rates are $100-250 weekends, with good midweek rates.

Given Madison's progressive environmentalism, it's little surprise that the **Arbor House B&B,** 3402 Monroe St., tel. (608) 238-2981, was renovated using all recycled materials, from the frames to the beams to the tiling; it calls itself an "environmental inn". Highly respectable and perfect for accessing the UW Arboretum. Rates from $85.

In a historic district near UW's west side, the **University Heights B&B,** 1812 Van Hise Ave., tel. (608) 233-3340, is a 1923 craftsman-style home. Much of the oak trim is original; the commons area is capacious and warm. One of the rooms is a two-room suite with a whirlpool. Rooms run $65-125.

MADISON ACCOMMODATIONS

DOWNTOWN

Best Western InnTowner, 2424 University Ave., tel. (608) 233-8778 or (800) 258-8321; $82-140; near University and VA Hospitals on near west side, pool, whirlpool, fitness center, airport/campus/hospital shuttle

Edgewater, 666 Wisconsin Ave., tel. (608) 256-9071 or (800) 922-5512; $99-375; on excellent Lake Mendota property, very close to campus, lakefront rooms, patio and deck, popular dining rooms, entertainment, large rooms

Howard Johnson Plaza, 525 W. Johnson St., tel. (608) 251-5511 or (800) 654-2000; $80-135; indoor pool, whirlpool, airport shuttle, in-room coffee

Best Western Inn on the Park Hotel, 22 S. Carroll St., tel. (608) 257-8811 or (800) 279-8811; $70-169; across from Capitol with superb nighttime views, top-floor dining room, whirlpool, fitness center, airport shuttle

Ivy Inn Hotel and Restaurant, 2355 University Ave., tel. (608) 233-9717; $65-75; excellent dining room with popular vegetarian Sunday brunch, shuttle service

Madison Concourse Hotel, 1 W. Dayton St., tel. (608) 257-6000 or (800) 356-8293; $99-250; outstanding renovation, some rooms with beautiful views, popular bistro and lounge, sauna, fitness center, indoor pool, outdoor hot tub

Madison Inn, 601 Langdon St.; tel. (608) 257-4391; $70-800; some suites, dining room

University Inn, 441 N. Francis St.; tel. (608) 257-4881 or (800) 279-4881; from $65; centrally located, just off State Street pedestrian mall, closed mid-December to mid-January

EAST

Budget Host-Aloha Inn, 3177 E. Washington Ave., tel. (608) 249-7667 or (800) 825-6420; $45-70; heated indoor pool, whirlpool, sauna, good rooms for the price

Comfort Inn, 4822 E. Washington Ave., tel. (608) 244-6265 or (800) 228-5150; $69-199; brand new room decor, complimentary breakfast, indoor pool, whirlpool, fitness center, executive suites

Crowne Plaza, 4402 E. Washington Ave., tel. (608) 244-4703 or (800) 465-4329; $89-110; dining room, indoor pool, sauna, in-room whirlpool, fitness center, shuttle

Holiday Inn Madison East, 3841 E. Washington Ave., tel. (608) 244-2481 or (800) 272-6232; $79-124; indoor pool, sauna, shuttle, in-room whirlpools, continental breakfast, dining room

East Towne Suites, 4801 Annamark Dr., tel. (608) 244-2020 or (800) 950-1919; $70-105; large rooms, dining room, indoor pool, fitness center, shuttle

Exel Inn, 4202 E. Towne Blvd., tel. (608) 241-3861 or (800) 356-8013; $44-80; in-room whirlpools

Fairfield Inn, 4765 Hayes Rd., tel. (608) 249-5300 or (800) 228-2800; $55-70; bright rooms, complimentary breakfast, microwaves, refrigerators, outdoor pool

Hampton Inn East, 4820 Hayes Rd., tel. (608) 244-9400 or (800) 426-7866; $79-100; indoor pool, sauna, fitness center, continental breakfast, rooms with irons and ironing boards

Red Roof Inn, 4830 Hayes Rd., tel. (608) 241-1787 or (800) 843-7663; $40-61; lowest prices on far east side

Residence Inn by Marriott, 4862 Hayes Rd., tel. (608) 244-5047 or (800) 331-3131; $80-140; continental breakfast, outdoor pool, sauna, fitness center, full kitchens, some fireplaces

Select Inn, 4845 Hayes Rd., tel. (608) 249-1815 or (800) 641-1000; $43-48; continental breakfast, sauna

Spence Motel, 3575 E. Washington Ave., tel. (608) 244-8877; $35 and up; in congested area but decent rates

WEST

Best Western West Towne Suites, 650 Grand Canyon Dr., tel. (608) 833-5614 or (800) 847-7919; $55-200; large rooms, business center, continental breakfast, dining room

Baymont Inn and Suites, 8102 Excelsior Dr., tel. (608) 831-7711 or (800) 428-3438; $60-95; continental breakfast, indoor pool, sauna, fitness center, shuttle service, dining room, microwaves, refrigerators, free local calls

(continued on next page)

MADISON ACCOMMODATIONS
(continued)

Colonial Motel, 3001 W. Beltline Hwy., tel. (608) 836-1131 or (800) 821-5994; $30-45; outdoor pool, sauna, lowest prices on west side

Comfort Suites, 1253 John Q. Hammons Dr., tel. (608) 836-3033 or (800) 221-2222; $85-200; continental breakfast, indoor pool, sauna, fitness center, shuttle, some efficiencies

Hampton Inn Madison West, 516 Grand Canyon Dr., tel. (608) 833-3511 or (800) 426-7866; $70-90; outdoor pool, sauna, fitness center

Marriott Madison West, 1313 John Q. Hammons Dr., tel. (608) 831-2000; $79-159; dining room, indoor pool, sauna, fitness center, in-room whirlpools, shuttle, some suites, microwaves, refrigerators, nightclub

Merrill Springs Inn, 5101 University Ave.; tel. (608) 233-5357; $50 and up; continental breakfast

Residence Inn West, 501 D'Onofrio Dr., tel. (608) 833-8333 or (800) 225-5466; $90-120; dining room, continental breakfast, outdoor pool, sauna, fitness center, shuttle, courts, fireplaces in some rooms

Radisson Inn, 517 Grand Canyon Dr., tel. (608) 833-0100 or (800) 333-3333; $92-120; well maintained, tasteful decor, excellent dining room, indoor pool, sauna, fitness center, shuttle

SOUTH

Days Inn-Madison, 4402 E. Broadway Service Rd., tel. (608) 223-1800 or (800) 329-7466; $60-80; continental breakfast, indoor pool, sauna, fitness center, in-room whirlpools, some efficiencies, microwaves, refrigerators

Edgewood Motel, 101 W. Broadway, tel. (608) 222-8601 or (800) 732-8492; $44-60; coffeemakers, refrigerators

Expo Inn, 910 Ann St., tel. (608) 251-6555; $40; continental breakfast

Holiday Inn Express, 722 John Nolen Dr., tel. (608) 252-7400 or (800) 574-3935; $70-85; newest in Madison, close to Coliseum and Expo Center, large continental breakfast, 24-hour indoor pool and whirlpool, fitness center, game room, some whirlpool rooms, free local calls

Sheraton Madison Hotel, 706 John Nolen Dr., tel. (608) 251-2300 or (800) 325-3535; $85-150; across from Coliseum and Expo Center, dining room, indoor pool, sauna, fitness center, shuttle

Trails End Motel, 99 W. Beltline Hwy., tel. (608) 271-7100; $40-50; decent budget option

---

A much cheaper B&B option is the **Stadium House B&B,** 810 Oakland Ave., tel. (262) 251-0674, with rooms from $35.

Hostel
Madison's **HI Madison Hostel,** 141 S. Butler St., tel. (608) 441-0144, costs $15 members and $18 nonmembers and should be a year-round facility by the time you read this. It's central, progressive and has lots of activities throughout the year. Two six-bed dorms, two rooms for four, and two doubles total out to two dozen guests. It does book out in summer so try and make reservations.

Camping
The nearest public campground is **Lake Kegonsa State Park,** approximately 15 miles southeast off I-90 on CR N. Not a particularly breathtaking park, but it's large and the lake is nice.

There is an 80-site campground with the usual rates: $8 per site, plus entrance sticker. No mention-worthy private campgrounds lie within or even decently close to Madison.

FOOD

Given the cosmopolitan-minded citizenry—not to mention the presence of a world-renowned university—the cuisine in town covers a wide range. Madison since the late 1990s has seen an absolute explosion of new eateries; it's nearly impossible to keep up with a population that apparently doesn't like to stay home and cook. As an example, King Street, leading away from the State Capitol, from 1998 to 2000 saw every single business save two in its first block change into a restaurant. You'll find something you like.

Alfresco

A Madison dining tradition is to buy a box from a food cart and sprawl on the Mall at the university end of State Street or at the Capitol. You'll find half a dozen carts at either end; usually for around $3 or $4 you can fill up. At the Capitol, Chinese and Vietnamese cuisine are the best represented.

At the university end, currently you'll find Thai (two carts), Chinese, Cuban, Jamaican, barbecue ribs, vegetarian, and a whole lot more.

Barbecue

Find the city's largest ribs, chicken, and beef smoked so delicately the meat slides from the bone at **Big Mama & Uncle Fats'**, 6824 Odana Rd., tel. (608) 829-2683, now doling out tons of smoked catfish, too. Dirty rice, cobbler, and all the other accompaniments to a ribfest are available. Live blues every Friday and Saturday night. Open for lunch and dinner Tues.-Fri., dinner only on weekends. Choices from $5.

Also delicious are the handful of slow-smoked meats—chicken, beef, pork shoulder, brisket, turkey, and fish—at **Smoky Jon's**, 2310 Packers Ave., tel. (608) 249-7427, in funky little digs near the airport. Barbecue aficionados also swear by **Fat Jack's**, 6207 Monona Dr., tel. (608) 221-4220.; from $7.

Burgers

Dotty Dumpling's Dowry, 116 N. Fairchild St., tel. (608) 255-3175, always wins local surveys for burgers, which really **are** sublime creations (if a bit pricey), and are whisked onto a smoldering pit right before your eyes. The cavernous interior is adorned with a visual cacophony of junkshop and antique-store merchandise. From $5. Note that this place was scheduled for demolition to make way for the new arts district, so it may have relocated down State Street.

For a less expensive burger option, head up State Street to the corner of Johnson and cut over to the **Plaza Grill**, a popular nighttime hangout that serves the legendarily tangy Plazaburgers—a slider of a sandwich if ever there was one. Menu items from $3.

If you're on the west side, head for the indescribably cool **Blue Moon Bar and Grill**, 2535 University Ave., where the burgers are great and the retro chic interiors are cool. Items from $3.

Cafes

A longtime favorite lunchtime (and dinnertime) eatery is **Little Village Cafe**, 211 King St., tel. (608) 255-6622, with an eclectic menu of Southwestern-inspired burritos, pastas, salads, and a killer Zuni stew from $4. A block west is the **Clay Market Cafe**, a popular Cambridge eatery that relocated here in 2000. It too has wonderful creative concoctions; the fish is always great. Selections from $4.

Best place to take guests when they show up unannounced on a Saturday morning for the farmers' market is the deliciously art deco cool blue interiors of **Monty's Blue Plate**, 2089 Atwood Ave., tel. (608) 244-8505, an upscale diner on the near east side. Here, you'll find the best synthesis of American meat-and-potatoes with trendy off-the-beaten-menu items. The chefs are equally adept with meatloaf and tofu and scrambled egg Mediterranean surprise. From $4.

More elegant and more expensive, **Deb & Lola's**, 227 State St., tel. (608) 255-0820, a downtown favorite, features an eclectic array of thoughtful entrées, with lots of Southwestern overtones to its creative American fare. Some food scribes have called it one of the best spots in the state. It's open Mon.-Sat. for dinner only.

For years, the funky old building about 10 blocks east of the Capitol stood empty. Finally, **Fyfe's Corner Bistro**, 1344 E. Washington Ave., tel. (608) 255-4674, appeared. The menu includes well-prepared California-style pastas and seafood as well as Angus steaks and other carnivore-friendly dishes from $8. The lounge has a semi-regular array of live jazz.

Tucked away in a mod setting, the **Wilson St. Grill**, tel. (608) 251-3500, is actually at 217 S. Hamilton and offers well-prepared creative entrées. Lunchtimes will be crowded by suits; reservations are recommended for dinner. Choices from $9.

On the near east side, **Coyote Capers**, 1201 Williamson St., tel. (608) 251-1313, has established itself as a rock-solid purveyor of creative, ethnically inspired cuisine. Most noteworthy, the cafe regularly hosts dinners focusing on one ethnic cuisine. Weekend brunches are excellent as well. Menu items from $10.

Not really a cafe per se but unclassifiable otherwise is the **Grand Lobby Cafe and Lounge** in the lobby of the Orpheum Theater, 216 State

Street. It's a totally cool take on breakfast, lunch, or dinner, in the stately interiors of a grande dame of Madison. Some items are quite creative; the Sunday brunch is great. Selections from $6.

Coffeehouses

State Street is crawling with the places. One venerable institution is **Steep & Brew,** 544 State St., tel. (608) 256-2902. An initiator of the coffee generation in Madison, it's got a cubbyhole lower level and a cozy—if a tad noisy—upper level, with muted lighting and artwork adorning the walls. Live music is offered here, too.

Mother Fool's Coffeehouse, tel. (608) 259-1301, on the near east side at 1101 Williamson St., has an eclectic array of acoustic world folk, mostly on weekends.

A very new entry—and an excellent one—is **Ancora Coffee Roasters,** 112 King St., tel. (608) 255-2900, which has the best interior of any coffee shop downtown. Warm and naturally lit, this is a place to relax with a latté; the coffee roaster dominates the room's interior.

Deli

The wildly popular **Ella's Deli,** 2902 E. Washington Ave., is a kosher deli and ice-cream parlor. The east side location is very family-friendly—a wild descent into circus kitsch, complete with a carousel outside. At the State Street location, you'll find mostly young students nursing coffee refills and plates of french fries. The menu at both, however, is a tome of outstanding cuisine. Ella's generally opens around 8 a.m. and remains open until anywhere from 8 to 10 p.m. Choices from $3.

Fine Dining

If you're only in town for one night, the place to choose is definitely **L'Etoile,** 25 N. Pinckney St., tel. (608) 251-0500, on Capitol Square directly opposite the Capitol. The creative regional fare has garnered nationwide raves and placed the owners in the national cuisine spotlight (they even serve as consultants to the White House kitchen). The restaurant is a supporter of local produce merchants and uses organic ingredients; it also truly strives to reach that esoteric netherworld of the harmony of cuisine, art, and culture. How many restaurants sit the entire staff down for a communal meal before opening and invite local farmers making deliveries to join in? Simply put, the menus, which change weekly, are incredible gastronomic representations of the geography and ethos of this place. Highly recommended. Dishes from $20.

The Opera House, 117 Martin Luther King, Jr. Dr., tel. (608) 284-8466, is in a smashing location looking out onto the walkway across from the Capitol through a large glass facade. The menu is diverse, ambitious, and very well executed by a respected local chef; it's also known for its wines (noted by *Wine Spectator* magazine) and a full array of scotches. From $5 at lunch, $17 at dinner. Open weekdays for lunch and dinner, Saturday for dinner only.

Another place with highly regarded cuisine is **Quivey's Grove,** 6261 Nesbitt Rd., tel. (608) 273-4900, an amalgam of restaurant and tap rooms on a four-acre 19th-century estate two miles south of Madison's Beltline Highway. The restaurant's numerous dining rooms are scattered throughout an enormous fieldstone mansion (so many doors and exits you'll get lost), while a 60-foot tunnel leads to the Stable, a taproom and grill with original hand-hewn beams, wagon-wheel tables, and a buffalo head trophy. Another structure, the Paddock, has a bar, barbecue pit, and picnic tables. The food is a tasteful blend of Midwestern regional fare. For non-Midwesterners, this is a wonderful crash course. Selections from $12. Call for reservations and exact hours.

The downtown hotels all have reputable restaurants. The Concourse Hotel's bistro is particularly nice, and Inn on the Park's top-floor restaurant has arguably the city's most coveted view of the Capitol dome. Another great vista can be had from **Admiralty,** the highly regarded continental dining room in the Edgewater Hotel. Many have said the Ivy Inn's dining room has the most diverse food—even vegetarian.

Fish Fries

Madison doesn't necessarily live and die for the fish fry, but there are some good ones here. Generally voted the best fish fry in Madison is the institution along E. Washington Ave., **The Avenue Bar,** 1128 E. Washington Ave., tel. (608) 257-6877, with a number of tables along its huge bar and a newer hall decorated in a pastiche of

Badger memorabilia and farm implements. It has classic family-restaurant tables and chairs and a supper club atmosphere. Prime rib is served Tuesday and Saturday, and the Avenue is equally famous for its pound steaks. From $6. Reservations recommended.

From the west side of town, it may be better to swing toward Middleton, where **The Stamm House at Pheasant Branch,** 6625 Century Ave., tel. (608) 831-5835, is a popular supper club housed in a century-old farmhouse. The place is absolutely jam-packed and very festive; given the crowds, service can be spotty, but the atmosphere is unbeatable. From $6.

Quivey's Grove (see Fine Dining) has a Wednesday night fish fry.

Greasy Spoons and Diners
Here's a guaranteed moneymaking opportunity—open a genuine greasy spoon in the Capitol vicinity. Come 7 a.m., I've been stopped more than a few times in the vicinity by weary out-of-towners looking for a place with chipped mugs. Sure, **Cleveland's Diner,** 410 E. Wilson St., is only a handful of blocks east, but its freshly scrubbed new interiors just don't have that divey feel. The potato pancakes are good, though. Choices from $2.

Aficionados of road food have some other outstanding choices. **The Curve,** with two locations (the original at 653 S. Park St.), is legendary for its copious breakfast plates. The line goes out the door Saturday mornings for a chance to sit at the counter. **Curve II,** 44 S. Fair Oaks Ave., is similar. Both from $2.

Still, the most classic downscale Madison breakfast place has to be **Mickie's Dairy Bar,** 1511 Monroe St., doling out awesome breakfasts (luscious pancakes) and malts since the '40s. The atmosphere is super here and the decor real-deal, down to the aging napkin dispensers and anachronistic knickknacks everywhere (the cafe's name harks back to the establishment's days as one of the largest milk and bread retailers in the city). Open for lunch and dinner daily except Monday. Try the Scrambler or the Frisbee-size flapjacks. From $3.

Harmony Bar
It doesn't feature the usual artery-clogging bar food; hell, it isn't even pub grub. The Harmony Bar, 2201 Atwood Ave., tel. (608) 249-4333, is the most perfect approximation of a neighborhood bar and eatery. An early-century east-side tavern and fish-fry server extraordinaire, the current incarnation is a comfortable tavern with one of the best jukeboxes in town and a menu of homemade pizzas, tuna steak with mango chutney, walnut burgers, and sesame-oil hot noodles—even the hot pretzels come with gourmet mustard, but the character is downhome and engaging. . Choices from $4. The back room features mostly blues and roots rock on Friday and Saturday.

Ice Cream and Desserts
Madison has caught the custard bug, up to a point. Personal favorites include **Michael's Frozen Custard,** with lots of locations, and **Culver's,** found throughout southwestern Wisconsin. But for the obligatory Wisconsin experience, head directly for the UW campus and **Babcock Hall,** where the university cooks up delectable batches of its own proprietary ice cream, which is also served at the Memorial Union.

Organic Foods
Natural-food stores and co-ops abound in Madison. The campus-area co-op of choice is the mural-decorated **Mifflin St. Co-op,** at the corner of W. Mifflin St. and Bassett St., while on the east side, the **Willy St. Co-op,** 1202 Williamson St., tel. (608) 251-6776, is even larger and has a good deli. The west side has one of the largest natural-food stores in the country, **Whole Foods,** on University Avenue.

Pizza
This is a university town, of course, so the varieties of pizzas are endless. Without question, Madisonians peg **Pizzeria Uno,** 222 W. Gorham St., tel. (608) 255-7722, as the place for unbelievable Chicago-style pies—and the place does deliver. From $5. An East Coast colleague insists **Sal's,** 313 State St., is the closest any Madisonian is going to get to "real" New York pizza.

Forget all the other slabs of crust with greasy cheese supported by legions of soused students—for the best low-priced delivery pies, **Pizza Extreme,** 605 E. Washington Ave., tel. (608) 259-1500, is the place; it also serves a huge number of sandwiches, pastas, chicken wings, and more.

Seafood

Way up the price scale is the crisp **Blue Marlin,** 101 N. Hamilton St., tel. (608) 255-2255, a white-linen place with fresh grilled swordfish, salmon, tuna, crab, and more—even a San Francisco fish stew. The classic, century-old aesthetics are hard to beat. For seafood, this is the place. From $12.

Much cheaper and still excellent are the imaginative Moroccan seafood dishes at **Oceans Brasserie,** 527 State St., tel. (608) 257-3107; it's got other dishes too, including some of the most unbelievable soups you've ever had. Choices from $3.

Supper Clubs and Steakhouses

Check any airline in-flight magazine and chances are you're going to find **Smoky's Club,** 3005 University Ave., tel. (608) 233-2120. One of a dying breed, it's a real charcoal-killer place. The classic supper club-cum-steakhouse, Smoky's is the type of place where the waitresses have been bustling for four decades and the bartender will remember your drink on your second visit. Big Ten sporting teams make pilgrimages here when they're in town. The decor is simple but homey, and the atmosphere most definitely frenetic. Reservations are essential. Dishes from $10.

Best bet for a prime rib (you can damn near cut it with a fork)—according to a UW Meat Sciences staffer—is **Fitzgerald's,** 3112 W. Beltline Hwy., tel. (608) 831-7107, also good for steaks and seafood. It's open weekdays for lunch, daily for dinner with a Saturday brunch. Choices from $8.

Vegetarian

Madison has a very large vegetarian population, so virtually everyplace offers a vegetarian option. One local cafe gets lots of recognition for a menu nicely balanced between meat and meatless dishes: **Sunporch Cafe,** 2701 University Ave., open for breakfast, lunch, and dinner daily with live music occasionally. The **Ivy Inn,** 2355 University Ave., is well respected for its attention to vegetarian options; it offers a superb full-vegan Sunday brunch every first and third Sunday.

Afghan

With overtones of Mediterranean and Middle Eastern cuisine, **Kabul,** 541 State St., tel. (608) 256-6322, is unique in Wisconsin—most likely the only Afghan restaurant. It's well worth it, and you can dine outside in summer. Open daily for lunch and dinner. Menu items from $6.

Cajun

A longtime favorite is the takeout only **New Orleans Take-out,** 1920 Fordem Ave., tel. (608) 241-6655, with the hottest dirty rice you'll find in Madison and some delectable sweet potato pie. Dishes from $5.

A new place on the near-west side is **Luther's French Quarter Cafe,** 1401 University Ave., tel. (608) 257-1164, which has Cajun and Creole dishes but is even more well known for its all-blues music line-up. From $5.

Still farther west, excellent food—American and creative Cajun—and great entertainment are to be had at **Louisianne's, Etc.,** 7464 Hubbard Ave., tel. (608) 831-1929, in Middleton. From $8. There's also almost always blues on Friday and Saturday nights and jazz some weeknights, all in a historic structure with great ambience. Reservations are wise on the weekends.

Chinese

At last count, Madison had a couple dozen Chinese restaurants, so you'll no doubt find something you like. Madison residents cried when famed **Temple Garden** left for Lake Geneva, but its smaller offshoot noodle place just off State St. at 411 W. Gilman St. serves up real-deal noodle bowls that are great. And cheap—from $4.

Hong Kong Cafe, 2 S. Mills St., tel. (608) 259-1668, has consistently good Cantonese fare. The large menu is a plus-even dim sum weekends. Delivery is available, too. Choices from $5.

At 600 Williamson St. in the Gateway Mall, the underappreciated **Wah Kee,** tel. (608) 255-5580, has a diverse pan-Cathay menu, emphasizing Cantonese and Hong Kong but also with some Shanghai items and oddities such as *yangchou*-style fried rice. The specials are well priced, and you can get live lobster and other seafood. They also have a vegetarian night (the curried eggplant is great). From $5.

Continental
An old transient hotel done up in original 1930s decor, down to the brass elevator, **Kennedy Manor Dining Room,** 1 Langdon St., tel. (608) 256-5556, is a subdued, casually elegant European-style restaurant across from the Edgewater. The creative concoctions range from homemade pastas to delicate fish. The decor is dim black-and-white and straight out of a '30s picture show. At times the food has been inconsistent, but recently it's greatly improved. Parking is tricky, so ask for advice when making reservations. Dishes from $9. It's open for lunch and dinner Tues.-Fri., dinner only Saturday.

German
Cuisine seems almost a secondary consideration at the **Essenhaus,** 514 E. Wilson St., tel. (608) 255-4674. With all the oompah, boots of beer, and raucous Teutonic songs, who has time for food? Even so, the place, open for dinner Tues.-Sun., does have a dense, copious menu for the sauerbraten-deprived, from $13.

Indian
Madison's had a run of hard luck with Indian cuisine. The latest entry is **Maharaja,** 6713 Odana Rd., tel. (608) 833-1824. Not far away is the **India Garden Restaurant,** 6119 Odana Rd., tel. (608) 277-8070. Both are good with choices from $5. The former gets a nod for its huge number of vegetarian options (nearly 20); it's also got a great lunch buffet ($6).

Indonesian
Wisconsin's only Indonesian restaurant is **Bandung,** 600 Williamson St., tel. (608) 255-6910. The Indonesian food is solid, but it also has Thai choices. From $5.

Iranian
Do not miss **Caspian Cafe,** 17 University Square, tel. (608) 259-9009, in University Square Mall at the corner of University Avenue and Lake Street. It's one of those amazing finds you can tell won't last long in this neglected warren of a site once enough people experience its inex-

pensive creative Persian cuisine. Open for lunch only Mon.-Thurs. and Saturday, for lunch and dinner on Friday. From $4.

Italian
Heavy on the Italian fare is newer **Cafe Continental,** 108 King St., tel. (608) 251-4880, with good pastas, gourmet pizzas, and other continental fare, with reasonable prices. There's even a good brunch. From $5.

Downtown, **Porta Bella,** 425 N. Frances St., tel. (608) 256-3186, has been dishing out Italian, along with steaks and seafood, since 1968. It's got a quiet ambience and the downstairs wine cellar has a good selection of wines and microbrews. From $5.

Jamaican
Get top-notch jerk at **Jolly Bob's,** 1210 Williamson St. The service is occasionally spotty, and it's sometimes hard to get a table, but the food is more than worth it. The bar has a huge array of rums. Menu items from $7. A block east is **Jamerica,** which also has great Jamaican food in a much more relaxed setting; it has vegetarian options.

Japanese
Downtown Madison has **Wasabi,** 449 State St., tel. (608) 255-5020, featuring four dozen types of sushi and a relatively inexpensive menu, from $8. A great noodle shop is **Kitakuni,** 437 W. Gorham St., tel. (608) 251-3377. Japanese friends say the food is "like home." Closed on Sunday. From $4.

Korean
Two recommended Korean restaurants in town are **Ha Ru Bong,** 600 Williamson St., tel. (608) 255-1988, downtown; and **New Seoul Kitchen,** 2503 University Ave., tel. (608) 238-3331. Both from $5.

Laotian
The original Laotian restaurant in Madison is **Vientiane Inn,** 1124 S. Park St., tel. (608) 255-5538 (a newer location with the old name, Vientiane Palace, sits a block off State east on Gorham St.), essentially a Thai restaurant with some Laotian dishes. It's open for lunch and dinner Mon.-Sat., dinner only Sunday. From $6.

The food is a bit better at **Lao Laan-Xang,** 1146 Williamson St., tel. (608) 280-0104, which has good specials—and delivers! It also serves a traditional Laotian brunch that is a godsend if you're sick of eggs and bacon. From $6.

Mediterranean

Hints of Spanish, Italian, French, and Turkish can be found at **Dardanelles,** 1851 Monroe St., tel. (608) 256-8804, a newer entry on trendy Monroe Street. After struggling initially, this place really has found its niche among the downtown eateries. From $7.

Mexican

The title of top Mexican eatery now belongs to **La Hacienda,** 515 S. Park Street. Owned by the same Milwaukee family that has given southeast Wisconsin the outstanding Jalisco restaurants, La Hacienda has spartan decor as stereotypically Mexican-restaurant as any you'll find, but the service is always friendly. The menu is an encyclopedic traipse through home-style Mexican, down to a great daily *comida corrida,* menudo, huge burritos, sweetly tart mole sauce, and a killer *chile de arbol* sauce. The lunch specials are good deals and, best of all, it doesn't close until 3 a.m. daily (it opens at 8 a.m.). From $3.

You might pop in to **Las Palmas Deli,** 2105 Sherman Ave., tel. (608) 245-1810, an intriguing little deli-restaurant that synthesizes Mexican cuisine with, believe it or not, Italian and American. It's got amazingly good *barbacoa* and great daily specials. From $3.

Middle Eastern

For years and years, **Lulu's,** 2524 University Ave., tel. (608) 233-2172, was Madtown's only Middle Eastern restaurant. Though it's got competition now, it still holds its own, with succulent meat dishes and outstanding *babaganoush* and *moussaka.* From $6.

Nepali

The Madison institution for Nepali cuisine has always been **Himal Chuli,** 318 State St., tel. (608) 251-9225, a great little place with a menu that will never let you down. Lovers of Himalayan food were orgasmic when the owners opened the equally delightful **Chautaura,** 334 State St., tel.

(608) 255-3585, which serves Nepali with heavy overtones of Indian and even Tibetan. Both of these places are highly recommended. Both are open Mon.-Sat.for lunch and dinner. From $7.

Pakistani

Shalamar Garden, 5518 University Ave., is brand new and does good curries—go for the chicken. It even offers a "Pakistani fish fry" on Friday. From $7.

South American

Restaurant Magnus, 120 E. Wilson St., tel. (608) 258-8787, is a newer eatery and wildly popular for its creative cuisine, often a fusion of Brazilian, Argentinian, Chilean, and other Latin American cuisines. Its bar is also a local favorite. The service has been very spotty for the prices, but the food is good. From $14.

Spanish

A wonderful Spanish eatery, **La Paella,** is at 2784 S. Fish Hatchery Rd., tel. (608) 273-2666. The three dozen tapas include an exquisite *embuchado*—a cold roast pork loin with pine nuts, spinach, and herbs, which gives a hint of the succulence to come. Beyond the tapas bar, the menu features a wide range of well-prepared seafood. From $3. La Paella is open for dinner Mon.-Sat.; the tapas bar is open Mon.-Sat. from 3:30 p.m.

Thai

The first Thai restaurant in Madison was **Bahn Thai,** 944 Williamson St., tel. (608) 256-0202. Its additional location, at 2809 University Ave., tel. (608) 233-3900, underscores its reigning title as king of the city's Thai restaurants. The food at both locations is generally solid; the biggest plus is that they deliver. From $5.

While Bahn Thai garners the most attention, little **Sa Bai Thong,** 2840 University Ave., tel. (608) 238-3100, is arguably the best Thai restaurant in the state. Ensconced drearily in another of those endless strip-mall hells on the near west side, its menu really isn't extensive but the food is generally done to perfection. It's so popular they've recently expanded into the suite next door. Sa Bai Thong is open Mon.-Sat. for lunch and dinner, Sunday for dinner only. From $5.

Vietnamese

A personal favorite is the takeout only **Viet Foods to Go,** 1018 N. Sherman Ave., tel. (608) 249-5399, in a little cubbyhole. The *pho* is great, as you'd expect, but you can't miss with just about anything.

NIGHTLIFE

You'll find the city's best nightlife downtown and on the east side. The west side is mostly a zone where Hooters is a draw among the predominant chain bars, mega-mall sprawl, a couple of good restaurants, an okay brewpub, and a tiresome array of sports bars.

Check Thursday's *Wisconsin State Journal* and especially the *Isthmus* for club happenings. Lots of places have blues or rock on any given night of the week. An outstanding resource for those who like to make pub runs is the free *Madison Bar and Tavern Guide* available at many liquor stores; it's an incredible resource, detailing (really detailing) every bar, tavern, dance club, bowling alley, etc in the region. The maps are splendid.

Memorial Union

It's free, open to all ages, and a local tradition: an alfresco music mélange Thurs.-Sat. on the Memorial Union's outdoor terrace. The whole place really gets bopping Friday and Saturday—the music cranks up and the beer starts flowing. During inclement weather, the whole she-bang moves indoors to the cavernous Rathskeller (an acoustic death zone). You must have a UW ID *and* valid driver's license to buy beer; heavy-handed staff cards for underage drinkers often here, unlike in the old days.

Pubs

A lot of Madison's nightlife is predictably situated in the vicinity of the campus; the closer you are to the university, the greater the population of students in the raucous pubs and bars. Most of the bars on State Street are usually full of students. Another string of bars chock-full of students is found along Regent Street down from Camp Randall stadium. It's mostly students at the well-lit and capacious **Plaza,** just off State Street at the corner of Johnson St.; known for its tangy burgers, it's also got a killer jukebox. Two floors of twentysomethings—the upper level looks for all the world like a house party—at **Genna's,** across from the Capitol along W. Main Street. A half block away is the dimly lit **Paradise Lounge,** once home only to serious rumrats but now a hangout for the black-and-flannel crowd. Lots of Capitol suits enjoy good pub grub at the **Argus,** 123 E. Main St., an antebellum building with pressed-tin coffered ceilings; at night, legions of the netherworld mingle with the lategoing yuppies. Pheromones rage at **Buck's,** 113 N. Hamilton St., but the drinks are strong for the price.

You'll find jazz groups, local art and photography on the wall, and a light sandwich menu at **Cafe Montmartre,** 127 E. Mifflin St.; this brick-walled subterranean wine bar has an atmosphere most amenable to sipping wine.

Another place on the student path (but equally popular with nonstudents) is the film noir **Paul's Club,** in the 200 block of State St., known mostly for the personalized steins on the wall and the tree growing up through the center of the floor.

In the Regent Street neighborhood, the hordes of students generally don't stray as far as the subdued **Greenbush Bar,** 914 Regent St., an excellent Italian neighborhood eatery and *the* place in the area for a glass of wine or a scotch.

If you find yourself waiting for a Greyhound bus, wander over to the **Main Street Depot,** 627 W. Main St., housed in the town's original phone company building. No frills, but an Old World feel to the interiors and it's never overcrowded. This is the best spot for nursing a drink in an unobtrusive tavern.

A bit far from downtown but a Madison legend is the **Laurel Tavern,** 2505 Monroe St., a tippler's joint since 1939. Huge burgers are here.

The west side of Madison may be a dreary slice of strip-mall hell, but there is one unique option. **Le Tigre Lounge,** 1389 S. Midvale Blvd., is next to a hardware store in an antiseptic strip mall, but step inside and you'll see why it's named such. As for the atmosphere, it's a time trip back to the Rat Pack. West-side friends, defending the honor of their geography, have insisted I include **J.T. Whitney's,** 674 S. Whitney Way, a brewpub, so I will. And I will add that the beer is certainly creative.

Oompah

Get your personalized mug filled with one of over 250 beers and join in a boisterous bout of singalong or polka with lederhosen- and dirndl-clad help at the **Essenhaus,** 514 E. Wilson St., tel. (608) 255-4674. A local tradition is to imbibe a boot of beer—a prodigious amount. If that gets too much, the **Come Back Inn,** a huge adjoining beerhall, is a great place to quaff a tap.

Near East Side

The near east side begins four or five blocks east of the Capitol, downhill along E. Wilson Street to the hairy junction of some six or seven roads at the cusp of Lake Monona. At this junction, legendary Williamson Street ("Willy St.") begins. Willy St. and its neighborhoods are a pleasant hodgepodge of students—grad or otherwise—and families, with an up-and-coming array of restaurants, clubs, bars, and shops. The cornerstone is the **Crystal Corner Bar,** at the corner of S. Baldwin and Willy Streets; this neon-lit bar is the hot blues (especially blues), roots rock, Cajun, and R&B spot in town.

Up the road to the west is funky **Mother Fool's Coffeehouse,** with eclectic music Friday and Saturday. Continuing east you'll find one of the greatest neighborhood bars in Madison: **Mickey's,** 1524 Williamson. It's famous for rock-bottom beer prices, coasters made from well-worn carpeting, and large crowds.

Brewpubs

The Great Dane, 123 E. Doty St., is a brewpub occupying what was Madison's landmark Fess Hotel. The interior upstairs is fairly spacious, but it's best known for its great courtyard. The catacomb-like downstairs is a great place for moody swilling. The Great Dane has been ranked in the top 10 brewpubs in the nation in terms of beer consumption; no surprise in a university town in Wisconsin. The food is exceptional pub grub, and the place has got a new billiards hall and cigars for aficionados.

Angelic Brewing Co., 322 W. Johnson St., is another spot with fine brews and a decent menu—and live music three or four nights per week.

Live Music

Regular eclectic big-name music acts—roots rock, alternative, hip-hop, folk, international—appear at the neighborhoody **Barrymore Theatre,** 2090 Atwood Ave., tel. (608) 241-2345, recognizable for its distinctive-hued dome. This old vaudeville hall (which also hosts film festivals) has an endless schedule, so something is bound to be in town.

The venerable **O'Cayz Corral,** 504 E. Wilson St., tel. (608) 256-1348, used to be the scuzziest-looking club in Madison, but it's still the place to see local heroes thrash or newcomers try to belt one to the crowd across the bar from the window overlooking the street. It's a terrible stage situation and impossible bathroom set-up, but true rock-and-roll atmosphere. The slate almost always features local or regional bands, with an occasional big name popping in. It's been spruced up a bit, but the decor still leans heavily on Christmas lights and assorted cowpoke memorabilia. And cheap beer. A blues jam goes down every Tuesday.

If you're on the far west side, consider the **Club,** 1915 Branch St. in Middleton. Every Thursday it's got blues, and every Tuesday there's jazz. Otherwise, it features rock and alternative acts.

Folk Music

Located inside the Wil-Mar Center, the **Wild Hog in the Woods,** 953 Jenifer St., tel. (608) 283-3464, regularly welcomes folk artists and holds barn dances and the like. See "Near East Side" above for folk at Mother Fool's Coffeehouse.

If you're a big folk-music fan, decamp for Fort Atkinson's **Cafe Carpe,** about a half hour east along US 12. Nationally known performers appear here.

Dancing

Without question, the hottest dance club is **The Cardinal,** 418 E. Wilson St., tel. (608) 251-0080, with a wide musical selection. Friday is hip-hop (disco before 11 p.m.), with salsa and merengue on Saturday. Sunday brings jazz, martinis, and cigars. You'll even find a fetish night.

Bullwinkle's, 624 University Ave., a downtown meat market with dancing Tues.-Sat., has music that spans the spectrum from industrial to Top 40.

ENTERTAINMENT

A cornerstone of local culture is the **Madison Civic Center,** 211 State St., tel. (608) 266-9055, home to the 2,200-seat Oscar Mayer Theatre and a 300-seat thrust-stage theater. Isthmus Playhouse welcomes touring shows of all kinds at the Oscar Mayer Theater, while the smaller one houses the Madison Repertory Theatre and Children's Theater of Madison.

Theater

The University of Wisconsin's Vilas Hall has two theaters presenting university dramatic and musical productions throughout the year. Call (608) 262-1500 for information. The **Madison Theatre Guild,** tel. (608) 238-9322, performs in the renovated Esquire Theater, corner of Pinckney and Mifflin Streets. The **Madison Repertory Theatre,** tel. (608) 256-0029, performs both modern and classic stage works. Also in the Civic Center, **Children's Theater of Madison** offers family entertainment.

The long-standing **Broom Street Theatre,** 1119 Williamson St., tel. (608) 244-8338, always has the most experimental offerings in town. Shorter one-acts and obscure, challenging vignettes are presented by the **Mercury Players Theater Company,** tel. (608) 251-1886.

Classical Music

The popular **Madison Symphony Orchestra,** tel. (608) 257-3734, performs in the Madison Civic Center a dozen or more times during the year. On campus, the **UW-Madison School of Music,** tel. (608) 263-1900, has a year-round slate of performances by faculty, students, and visiting musicians; the Elvehjem Art Museum has a popular Sunday Afternoon Live series in autumn and winter.

Cinema

In operation since its 1906 vaudeville days, **The Majestic,** a block from the Capitol on King St., is a great venue for offbeat and independent movies, even if they never, but never, start on time. It was recently renovated and looks smashing inside.

Freebies

Grab a picnic basket and head for the Capitol Square Wednesday evenings for free concerts put on by the **Wisconsin Chamber Orchestra.** Though the weather is incessantly bad for these concerts, they are wildly popular. The **Memorial Union** at the UW is the most popular place to be Thurs.-Sat. for its free concerts.

Every Saturday April-Oct., the Madison Civic Center features free entertainment for kids.

EVENTS

In January, the city participates in the **Badger State Winter Games,** a sort of Olympics for everyman. In June there is **Cows on the Concourse,** a fun way of highlighting Wisconsin's dairy industry; you can get up close and personal with dairy cows, as they're scattered all over the Capitol area. July's biggie is the now-annual **Rhythm and Booms** choreographed fireworks display on the Fourth. Later that month, the **Art Fair on the Square** is a huge draw—one of the largest events in the Midwest and one of the largest juried art fairs in the country; the **Dane County Fair** also brings many visitors. In mid-August, the **Drum Corps International World Championships** is held at the UW's Camp Randall stadium. It's a weeklong blowout of serious marching bands in a highly competitive campaign. It's really a serious deal, and if you're in town during the week you can see and hear marching bands from across North America practicing at the playing fields of virtually every elementary school in the city. Late August brings the **Madison Blues Festival,** a two-day event that draws national and international blues and R&B acts along the Lake Monona shoreline. October brings the world's largest dairy show, the **World Dairy Expo,** a very important event, with agriculturalists and scientists from all over the globe coming to check up on any new dairy industry progress; regular folks can get a lifetime of knowledge about dairy just by wandering around and looking at exhibits.

SPORTS AND RECREATION

You may notice that Madisonians spend all their time jogging, biking, 'blading, skiing, or participating in some other cardiovascular exercise. In fact, this may be why *Outside* magazine has declared Madison a dream spot to live.

Cycling

No doubt about it, cycling is king in Madison. *Bicycling* magazine called Madison the fourth-best biking city in North America. Second only to Seattle in number of bikes per capita, Madison pedals virtually everywhere it goes. There are—quite seriously—bike traffic jams on certain routes in peak hours since 10% of the citizenry commute by bicycle. There are 25 miles of established pathway on innumerable trails. Most popular paths include the Lake Monona loop, easily accessed along John Nolen Drive (especially at Olin-Turville Park); it's about 12 miles long and cruises through residential neighborhoods. For a jaunt off that loop, many head over to the UW Arboretum for a lovely ride (note that the Arboretum's trails are for feet only; you'll have to lock your bike in the racks provided). Nearing completion just as this book was being updated was Madison's wonderful new Capital City State Trail. (You can access it from the Lake Monona loop where the lakeshore path bisects the Beltline Highway at Waunona Way; there are signs pointing you underneath the overpass 300 yards to the official trailhead.) The trail should, by the time you read this, stretch west from Lake Monona all the way to Verona, where it would link with the existing Military Ridge State Trail, a grand journey. Eventually, the trail should lead down along Madison's isthmus before heading east to Cottage Grove to link up with the Glacial Drumlin State Trail, allowing one to bicycle all the way to Milwaukee. The Madison segment is part of a visionary project dubbed E-Way, a corridor encompassing over 3,200 acres for ecological, educational, and recreational use. It isn't just a trail—it's an established "necklace" of linked islands of educational or environmental importance. Madison environmentalists lobbied and fought hard for 25 years to see it established.

Or, from Memorial Union, a path leads along Lake Mendota to Picnic Point.

Budget Bicycle Center, 1230 Regent St., tel. (608) 251-8413, and **Williamson St. Bike Shop,** 601 Williamson St., tel. (608) 255-5292, both rent bikes of all kind, with rates of $7-10 per day, $18-38 for a weekend, and $21-55 for a week. They also stock maps of city bicycle routes, as does the visitor center along E. Washington Avenue. The former is closer to the Arboretum, the latter is right on the Lake Monona Bike Path. The latter also has inline skates and ski rentals.

Hiking

Any cycling trail in the city is also open to hikers. The UW Arboretum has the most bucolic trails, some of them quite superb for an urban area.

Cross-Country Skiing

Madison has around 20 miles of groomed trails for cross-country skiing. Parks include Warne Park, 1511 Northport Dr.; Monona Golf Course, 111 Dean Ave.; Olin-Turville, 1155 E. Lakeside St.; Elver Park, 1301 Gammon Rd.; and Odana Golf Course, 4635 Odana Road. An excellent county park west of town via US 12 and WI 19 is **Indian Lake County Park.** Currently, there's a $2 day-use fee to ski at county parks.

Fontana Sports, 251 State St., tel. (608) 257-5043, rents skis.

Golf

Madison has four public courses, of which **Yahara Hills,** 6701 E. Broadway, tel. (608) 838-3126, is the least crowded. Don't even bother trying to get a time at **Odana Hills,** so crowded at times it's like Disneyworld.

An outstanding course is the University of Wisconsin golf center, **University Ridge Golf Course,** 7120 CR PD, tel. (608) 845-7700, a championship par-72 course with the tightest slingshot fairways you'll find in town.

Canoeing and Water Sports

Canoeing magazines also rave about the city. This comes as little surprise since the city boasts four lakes, the larger two of which—Mendota and Monona—are connected by the Yahara River, a superb ribbony urban stream passing through locks and a series of smaller lakes. The Yahara connects to the Rock River, which itself flows through southern Wisconsin. **Carl's Paddlin',** 110 N. Thornton Ave., tel. (608) 284-0300, rents canoes and kayaks by the day.

Hoofer's, attached to Memorial Union, rents windsurfing equipment, boats, canoes, and sailboats, and also gives lessons. On the west side, **REI,** tel. (608) 833-6680, also has rentals of all sorts of outdoor gear.

Spectator Sports

UW is what draws the sports nuts to Madison. The university is NCAA Division 1A in all sports, and the citizenry is gaga over the Badgers. Camp Randall Stadium on a football Saturday is an experience you'll not soon forget. If the opponent is a Big Ten foe, forget about a ticket, but for early-season games an occasional ticket may be available. Ditto with the perennial Western Collegiate Hockey Association champion (and five-time national champion) Badgers, who play at Dane County Coliseum; the fans here may be more rabid than the football legions. (The blasting of "Sieve!" at opposing goaltenders after scores is truly cacophonous.) The men's and women's basketball teams have both had a renaissance in the 1990s; no longer doormats, both regularly get to their respective tournaments, and the men's team shocked the nation in 1999 by making it to the "Final Four," the semifinals of the national championship tournament. For information on ticket availability, call the ticket office at (608) 262-1440. For general information on men's sports, call (608) 262-1811, for women, (608) 263-5502.

Lesser-known UW sports are well worth the money, particularly track, cross-country, and men's and women's soccer, consistently ranked in the nation's top 20. The men's soccer team won the NCAA championship in 1995.

SERVICES AND INFORMATION

Post Offices

The main post office, tel. (608) 246-1249, is at 3902 Milwaukee St., not very accessible to downtown. Additional satellite branches are one block from the Capitol along Martin Luther King, Jr. Blvd. in the City Building and in the University Mall at the corner of University Ave. and Lake St. near campus. The University Mall location has brief Saturday hours. Postage for average letters (one ounce) within the U.S. is 33 cents, 20 cents for postcards.

Visitor Information

The **Greater Madison Convention and Visitors Center,** tel. (608) 255-2537 or (800) 373-6376, www.visitmadison.com, is at 615 E. Washington Ave. and is open Mon.-Fri. 8 a.m.-4:30 p.m. A satellite office operates at the airport from 11 a.m. to 8 p.m. daily.

The main **Wisconsin Division of Tourism,** tel. (608) 266-2161 or (800) 432-TRIP, operates a visitor center with gregarious hosts a block west of the Capitol on W. Washington Avenue. It's open Mon.-Fri. 8 a.m.-4:30 p.m.

Bookstores

Madison is an amazing place for a bookworm, with over 50 bookshops. The country's largest **Barnes and Noble** mega-store (outside of New York City's original) has opened on the west side, at 7433 Mineral Point Rd., with over 150,000 titles in stock. **Borders,** 3416 University Ave., is another huge chain store.

You'll find many bookstores by strolling along State Street. A worthy, musty used bookseller is **Shakespeare's Books,** 18 N. Carroll, across from the Capitol. Not far around the corner is **Bookworks,** for serious bibliophiles. Four blocks or so down State St., a right on Gilman St. takes you to the great selection at **Avol's.** The granddaddy, though, has always been **Paul's,** at the far end of State St., just off the Lake St. corner; it's been around since the '50s.

Newspapers

Though both *The Capital Times* and the *Wisconsin State Journal* are puppets of the same master, Madison is one of the few remaining two-paper towns in the country. *The Cap Times* is the more liberal, the *WSJ* a bit denser in news coverage. Consult the Friday *Cap Times* and Thursday *WSJ* for rundowns of weekend cultural events.

Neither of these really compares to the free weekly *Isthmus,* distributed en masse throughout the downtown on Thursday, when Madisonians dutifully trek to java shops for a scone and a folded *Isthmus* with their lattés. A civic watchdog, it's got the most energetic writing and especially kicks in entertainment scribblings. This is the best resource on entertainment, movies, clubbing, and other nightlife.

Other Media

A delightful mélange of progressivism, half-assed professionalism, at times near-anarchy, and great music, **WORT** (89.9 FM) is a local community-sponsored Pacifica station. It's the only place to hear jazz, blues, genuine alternative rock, Latin, and experimental music, along with hefty doses of community issues. Little else like it in town, as you'll soon discover.

GETTING THERE AND AWAY

By Air
The **Dane County Regional Airport,** tel. (608) 233-4680, is served by **Midwest Express** and **Skyway,** tel. (800) 452-2022; **Northwest,** tel. (800) 225-2525; **United** and **United Express,** tel. (800) 241-6522; **American Eagle,** tel. (800) 433-7300; **COMAIR,** tel. (800) 221-1212; **Chicago Express/ATA,** tel. (608) (800) 435-9282; and **Trans World Express,** tel. (800) 221-2000. You'll have to suffer shuttles to major hubs via all these airlines.

City buses run to the airport. The closest bus stop is a couple hundred meters after you walk left out the doors of the airport along International Lane.

A taxi ride from the airport to downtown costs $10 minimum.

By Bus
The local intercity **bus station** is at 2 S. Bedford St., or about six blocks west of the State Capitol on W. Washington Ave. The station also houses Greyhound, tel. (800) 231-222, offering numerous daily departures to all points; the schedule changes regularly.

The depot is also home to **Badger Bus,** tel. (608) 255-6771, which has up to eight daily departures to Milwaukee 7 a.m.-8 p.m., some via Mitchell International Airport. An additional run is added Friday and Sunday. Two buses make stops in Lake Mills and outside Milwaukee at Goerke's Corners. For a quick and cheap ($12 one-way) trip to downtown Milwaukee, this is hard to beat.

Those heading to downtown Chicago via O'Hare Field can either go in a Greyhound or, better, head for Memorial Union on campus, where the **Van Galder** bus, tel. (608) 257-5593 or (800) 747-0994, leaves nine times daily 2 a.m.-6 p.m. for O'Hare—four of these continue to downtown Chicago's Union Station and the Best Western Hotel. The Van Galder makes a stop at the park-n-ride wayside at US 151 and the Beltline. A one-way ticket downtown is $19, $18 to O'Hare. The Van Galder makes stops in Janesville and Beloit as well.

GETTING AROUND

Bus
Madison buses generally run from 6 a.m. to 10 or 11 p.m., though this varies by line. If in doubt, always head to Capitol Square, around which spins just about every bus in town. Route information can be had by calling (608) 266-4904 or (608) 266-4466 6:15 a.m.-6 p.m. weekdays, shorter hours weekends. Fares are $1.50 adults, $1.25 cents youth 17 and under, 90 cents seniors. The city has in the past had free fare zones within downtown but these are slowly being phased out.

Rental Cars
National, tel. (608) 249-1614, is at the airport (as are all other major car rental agencies); it also has a satellite in the Concourse Hotel, tel. (608) 257-6611. Find **Thrifty,** tel. (608) 251-1717, downtown at 332 W. Johnson Street. On the west side, **Enterprise,** tel. (608) 276-6444, has an office at 1601 W. Beltline.

Taxi
Three taxi services operate in Madison. The most common choice is **Badger Cab,** tel. (608) 256-5566, since it operates a shared-ride (read: cheaper) service. If that's not an option, **Madison Taxi,** tel. (608) 258-7458, and **Union Cab,** tel. (608) 242-2000, are both fine.

Women's Transit Authority
The WTA, tel. (608) 256-SAFE or (608) 256-3710 during the day, is an independently run rape-prevention ride service for women, operating Sun.-Wed. 9 p.m.-1 a.m. and Thurs.-Sat. 8 p.m.-2 a.m.

Bicycle
If you see a clunky old Schwinn or other cruiser painted red right down to the rims, hop on for a free ride. These have been donated, fixed up by local bike shops, and distributed for the public's use.

Note that the bikes are not to be locked up or considered personal property. Just ride to where you're going and leave it for someone else to use.

Organized Tours

Madison has proposed a new trolley, which would circulate between the university, downtown, and the Dane County Expo Center, running along Lake Monona; if it gets off the ground it would be a cheap do-it-yourself tour.

A couple of places offer water tours of Madison lakes, including **Spirit of Madison Cruises,** tel. (608) 280-9170, which has dining and sightseeing cruises on Lake Monona.

JANESVILLE

Often overlooked in Madison's glare to the north, this bustling community of 52,100 is a hardworking town known mostly for its General Motors truck assembly lines. It was founded in 1836 by Henry Janes, who carved his initials in a tree on the bank of the Rock River. Janes, who had heard tales of the river's lush valleys from soldiers returning from the Black Hawk War, built the village's first ferry and, of course, tavern and became the town's first postmaster.

Development spread rapidly as riverways allowed Mississippi riverboats to travel all the way up to the city. The river powered mills, and the fecund agricultural expanses sustained farmers. Light manufacturing turned into heavy manufacturing when GM bought out a local factory in 1919 and began Janesville's first assembly line. Within a decade, over half of the city owed its economic fortunes to GM. Another prominent local manufacturer is Parker Pen, whose writing instruments are used in the White House at official signing ceremonies.

Janesville received worldwide attention in 1994 with the birth of Miracle, the white buffalo. Native Americans pilgrimaged from across North America to witness this incredible (and, to many, sacred) rarity. The farm where it happened is at 2739 South River Rd., exit 1777 off I-90; call (608) 752-2224 for information.

SIGHTS

Rotary Gardens

These gardens spread over a dozen acres and encompass several landscaping techniques—Japanese rock, English Cottage, French, Italian, sunken, and perennial. Each displays flora of a different geographic region, though all are united by a theme of Dialogue: World Peace Through Freedom. Rotary Park itself is an enjoyable stroll—a good place dedicated to international peace. Lions Beach is right next door. Across the street you'll find a segment of the Ice Age Trail. Rotary Gardens hosts a farmers' market Saturday mornings May-October. The gardens are open year-round during daylight hours; the visitor center is open weekdays 8:30 a.m.-4:30 p.m., weekends and holidays 10 a.m.-6 p.m. May-Oct., lesser hours weekends and holidays rest of year.

Not far from Rotary Gardens is **Palmer Park,** a large greenspace with a wading pool, tennis courts, and the CAMDEN Playground, the largest fully accessible playground in the United States. It's got a moat, towers, games area, and a performance stage.

General Motors

The GM plant spreads over 137 acres, making it the largest automobile facility in the country. Total output is about 192,000 units per year; it takes an average of 21 hours to build a Suburban on this, the shortest truck assembly line in the world. The factory burns 22,000 tons of coal per year. One-hour tours of the General Motors Truck Assembly Line are available April-Dec. Mon.-Thurs. at 9:30 a.m. and 1 p.m., though they may be down during midsummer line changes. Children must be accompanied by an adult, and no cameras are allowed.

To get there, go south on US 51 and east on Delavan St. to Industrial Avenue. For information, call (608) 756-7954.

Gray Brewing Company

An old-fashioned root beer or ale can be sampled after a tour at the **Gray Brewing Company,** 2424 Court St., tel. (608) 752-3552, a brewery dating from 1850. Tours are given at 1:30 p.m.

the first and third Saturday of each month and cost $2.

Historic Tours

Approximately one-fifth of all of Wisconsin's buildings on the National Register of Historic Places can be found in Janesville. Historic districts are in Look West, Courthouse Hill, Old Fourth Ward, and Main and Milwaukee. **Forward Janesville,** 20 S. Main St., can help with tour information, or stop by the historical society museum.

Lincoln-Tallman House

The Lincoln-Tallman House, 440 N. Jackson St., tel. (608) 752-4519, is the only private residence in Wisconsin in which Abe Lincoln hung his hat. This domestic 26-room Italianate mansion was constructed in 1855 by a prominent local abolitionist. Architecture mavens have called it the one of the finest of its kind in America. Also on site are the original horse barn and a Greek Revival stone house used by servants.

The grand mansion was built with Milwaukee cream brick; it boasted the first indoor plumbing and gas lighting in Janesville, among other amenities. A million-plus dollar renovation added heating and air conditioning to preserve the original decorations and interiors, including the bed in which Honest Abe slept. The house is open weekends Feb.-May and October, Tues.-Sun.

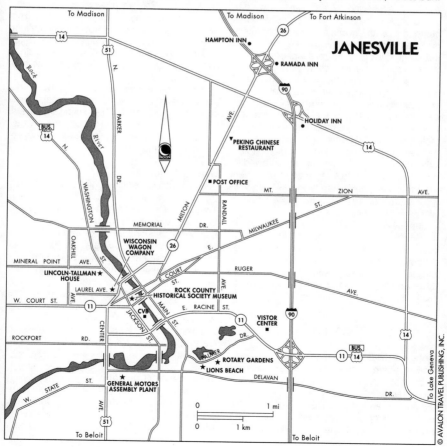

© AVALON TRAVEL PUBLISHING, INC.

9 a.m.-4 p.m. June-Sept., and for lots of special holiday tours. Admission is $8 adults, $7.50 seniors, $4 children 5-17.

Rock County Historical Society Museum

The detritus of Rock County is on display at this museum, 10 S. High St., tel. (608) 756-4509, along with occasional traveling exhibitions. The museum is open weekdays 10 a.m.-4:30 p.m. Admission is $2, less for seniors and students.

Wisconsin Wagon Co.

This Janesville company, at 507 Laurel Ave., tel. (608) 754-0026, makes replicas of wooden American Classic coaster wagons—an outstanding bit of Americana brought to life, since the original factory went out of production in 1934 and the Sears-Roebuck catalog was never the same. Tours are available Mon.-Tues. by appointment and cost $2.

ACCOMMODATIONS

Under $50

Cheapest dependable digs are without question at the local **Motel 6,** 3907 Milton Ave., tel. (608) 756-1742, where rooms go for $35 or under. East of town along WI 11 is the **Baymont Inn,** 616 Midland Rd., tel. (608) 758-4545 or (800) 428-3438, with that classic room-delivered continental breakfast, in-room coffee, a tiny indoor pool, and a whirlpool. Clean and comfy for $45 s, $50 d.

$50 to $100

The **Hampton Inn,** 2400 Fulton St., tel. (608) 754-4900, offers complimentary continental breakfast, free local calls, an indoor pool, and whirlpool. Rooms—some mini suites and a hospitality suite—can also feature refrigerators, microwaves, or whirlpools. All have an attractive, chic feel. Well worth the $57 s, $65 d.

The **Holiday Inn Express and Conference Center,** 3100 Wellington Pl., tel. (608) 756-3100, is a nicely designed large facility with all the amenities (no restaurant, however). Rates from $93.

Camping

No private camping exists in Janesville. The nearest you'll find is five miles northeast in tiny Milton, which, oddly enough, has a plethora of private grounds. The largest—almost 600 sites!—is **Lakeland,** 3407 E. Blackhawk Dr., tel. (608) 868-4700, with rates from $20.

FOOD

Pub Grub

The **Looking Glass,** 18 N. Main, tel. (608) 755-9828, has great big burgers, good soups, and a slew of lunch specials. The interior is a rustic blend of original high, pressed-tin ceilings and polished brass and dark wood bar. Menu choices from $3.

Supper Clubs and Steakhouses

Roherty's, 2121 WI 26, tel. (608) 752-2393, has been a local staple for over 90 years. It serves a host of prime rib and steak choices, along with some sandwiches, chicken, Italian dishes, and salads. From $5. Open daily for lunch and dinner.

Cafes

Creative is the **Alfresco Cafe,** 3900 WI 26, tel. (608) 757-4444, offering salads, seafood, a fish fry, pasta, California pizza, and some excellent meat-centered entrées. From $6.

Chinese

Peking Chinese Restaurant, 2632 WI 26, tel. (608) 754-0251, has very good Sichuan dishes along with more general Cathay fare in a cozy atmosphere. From $4.

ENTERTAINMENT AND EVENTS

Nightlife

TAASBAG, 1717 Milton Ave., tel. (608) 754-5667, has live music and no cover charge; it's the place to start for local live music.

Cultural Events

The **Beloit-Janesville Symphony Orchestra,** tel. (608) 362-2554, maintains an Oct.-March schedule of pops and classical music performed at the Marshall Middle School, 408 S. Main Street.

The **University of Wisconsin Center-Rock County** has an art gallery of student and faculty works, along with a Fine Arts Series featuring

AMERICA'S DAIRYLAND

In the Beginning

Surprise, surprise: dairying was not the first gear in the state's agricultural machine—wheat was. Wisconsin was a leading world wheat producer and exporter through the 1870s. Chronic pest plagues, tiring soils, poorly timed financial panics, lunatic overproduction and consequent lower prices, and the settlement of the Great Plains doomed the state's wheat industry before the century turned.

Wisconsin cheese had an inauspicious beginning, to say the least. The state's initial forays into home butter- and cheesemaking were derisively called Western Grease. Wisconsin cattle were initially miscegenational hybrids of hardier species bred essentially for an ability to withstand the elements. Milk production was an extra but hardly a necessity; wheat provided the bulk of the state's coffers.

The Birth of a Stereotype

The rise of dairy was initiated by transplanted New Yorkers. Beginning in the 1850s, New York farmers organized the first commercial cheesemaking factory systems, supplied by outlying farmers. In addition, the first experiments in modern herd management and marketing were undertaken. One New Yorker, Chester Hazen, opened a cheese factory in Ladoga and in 1864, its first year, produced 200,000 pounds. Within a half decade, the state had nearly 50 factories, and in some spots the demand for milk outstripped the supply.

What Yankees had started, the immigrants finished. Mostly Germans and Swiss populated the southern regions of the state, finding the topography reminiscent of home and the glacial till profoundly fecund (one spot of Dane County has been termed the world's richest agrarian soil). Not as quick to incorporate the new Eastern concepts, the conservative immigrants were nonetheless insistent upon top-quality dairy products.

Old World pride mixed with Yankee ingenuity created an explosion of Wisconsin dairying. The first dairy organizations were founded following the Civil War; a dairy board of trade was set up in Watertown in 1872, opening access to Eastern and European markets. The state's dairies shrewdly diversified the cheesemaking and took the western markets by storm. By the turn of the century, a stereotype was born: Jefferson County, Wisconsin, was home to 40,000 cows and 34,000 people.

W.D. Hoard

A seminal figure in Wisconsin's rise to dairy prominence was William D. Hoard, an otherwise unknown dabbler in lumber, hops, and publishing. In 1870, Hoard published the first issue of *The Jefferson County Union,* which became the mouthpiece for southeastern Wisconsin farmers. The only central source for disseminating information, the paper's dairy columns transmogrified into *Hoard's Dairyman.* It was the most influential act in Wisconsin's dairy industry.

Hoard had never farmed, but he pushed tirelessly for previously unheard of progressive farm techniques. Through Hoard, farmers learned to be not so conservative, to keep records, and to compare trends. Most significantly, Hoard almost singlehandedly invented the specialized, milk-only cow. He became such a legend in the industry he was elected governor in 1889.

The University of Wisconsin followed Hoard's lead and established its College of Agriculture's experimental stations in 1883. The renowned department would invent the butterfat test, dairy courses, cold-curing processes, and winter feeding.

How You Gonna Keep 'Em down on the Farm?

Dairying in Wisconsin is a $17 billion industry, accounting for just under a tenth of the state's total economic output. One-quarter of all the butter and a third of the cheese in the U.S. are produced in Wisconsin. It produces 2.1 billion pounds of milk per year on average; that's fourth highest of any nation in the world. It also produces nearly 30% of the nation's butter. And as for quality, at a recent U.S. Championship Cheese Competition, Wisconsin cheeses took 13 of 20 first-place awards; California took two. Two.

In the area of cheese, Wisconsin a leg up on California in several respects. Wisconsin had 33% of the cheese market in the U.S. in 1919. It has 27.1% today, while California has 17.4%. Wisconsin produces 2.15 billion pounds of cheese, California 1.4 billion pounds per year. Wisconsin is desperately trying to keep its lead in specialty cheeses, which is Wisconsin's main cheese industry today. It currently leads in every cheese type except mozzarella. Wisconsin has 350 varietals, California 130. Economists say that California's cheese industry is dangerously tied to the stock market, since many of its consumers are Double Income No Kids types— every time the stock markets hiccup, California's markets quake, but not Wisconsin's. (Wisconsin's have been around for over a century). California cheeesemakers, also, are mostly huge factory operations, as opposed to small family operations in Wisconsin. Seventy-five percent of Wisconsin cheesemakers grew up in an operation in which a grandparent had worked in the industry. Only 20% of California's cheesemakers can say that. Wisconsin cheesemakers have won 33% of World Cheese Championship first prizes; California, two percent.

And yet, the horizon appears dark.

In 1993, the unspeakable occurred: California edged ahead of Wisconsin in whole-milk output. Wisconsinites stayed in a fog of denial until 1994. California's dairy output is now hovering around 10% more per annum than Wisconsin. Further, Wisconsin has seen its family dairy farm numbers dwindle from post-WW II figures approximating 150,000 to under 28,000 in the mid-1990s to 23,000 in 2000; annually since 1989, the state has lost an average of 1,000 dairy farms. Farm acreage drops roughly 4 million acres every five years. And at present, dairy farms garner only one-quarter of their income from actual dairy practices. Apparently, "America's Dairyland" is a title under siege.

Badger State politicians on Capitol Hill blame the dairy problems on outdated federal milk-pricing guidelines, which pay other states higher rates than Upper Midwest farmers. Eau Claire is the nucleus; the farther you get from that point, the higher the price—up to $3 more per 100 pounds (milk paying a farmer $1.04 per 100 pounds in Wisconsin fetches a South Florida farmer $4.18!). The Wisconsin delegation was outraged in 1996 when Congress passed—and President Bill Clinton signed—a divisive regional compact giving northeastern markets free reign to rewrite milk guidelines as they see fit. Doomsayers foretold the end of Wisconsin dairy; even proponents were unsure of the long-term effects on Wisconsin. Things didn't improve in 2000 when Cheesehead representatives once again couldn't stop the madness on Capitol Hill, though this time they actually got a hearing.

Not to be completely apocalyptic, Wisconsin, though in a decline, is in little danger of completely losing its cultural underpinnings of rural Americana. Supplying one-third of the cheese in the U.S. still equals a huge market. And Badger farmers are finding ways to stem the wave of disappearing farms. One innovative program involves rural villages banding together, pooling resources, and purchasing family farms to keep them operational. It may not be able to compete in whole numbers, but on a per capita basis, Wisconsin is still America's Dairyland.

---

guest speakers, plays, musical and comedy performances, and more. For information, call (608) 758-6530.

Janesville supports several community theatrical groups, including **Stage One,** which performs three productions annually at the UW Center campus. The **U-Rock Players,** tel. (608) 758-6538, present annual theater of all types.

Freebies
The **Lower Courthouse Ampitheater** has free concerts June-July at noon and 6 p.m. The **Rock Aqua Jays** waterski team performs at Traxler Park, US 51 south on Wednesday and Sunday evenings at 7 p.m.

SERVICES AND INFORMATION

The **Janesville Area Visitors and Convention Center,** 51 S. Jackson St., tel. (608) 757-3171 or (800) 487-2757, www.janesvillecvb.com, is right along the south side of the river.

The *Janesville Gazette* is a local daily paper with information on local events and nightlife.

A **post office** is along WI 26 a little north of Black Ridge Rd., next to a huge mall. Another branch is downtown in the Old Town Mall at 20 S. Main Street. The Janesville Public **Library** is at 316 S. Main St., tel. (608) 758-6588. The Janesville **Urgent Care Center,** tel. (608) 757-1217, is at 1409 Creston Park Drive.

TRANSPORTATION

Amtrak established service between Janesville and Chicago in 2000. Currently the Lake Country Limited runs to Chicago at 6 a.m. and costs $22. The train returns to Janesville at 8:15 p.m.

Van Galder buses, tel. (608) 752-5407, stop in Janesville en route to Madison and Chicago 10 times a day, from 3:20 a.m. to 7 p.m. south-bound and 5:45 a.m.-1 a.m. northbound. The bus stops at the terminal at 3120 N. Pontiac. To Madison it costs a couple of bucks, less to Beloit. Chicago is $18 one-way.

Greyhound is at the corner of Main and Racine. Janesville has five **Beloit-Janesville Express** buses weekdays 7:15 a.m.-5 p.m. leaving from its downtown terminal along W. Court St., with a stop at State and Center. Fares are $2 one-way.

You can call **Janesville Taxi** at (608) 757-1006.

VICINITY OF JANESVILLE

Milton

Five miles northeast of Janesville along WI 26 is flyspeck Milton. At the junction of this highway and WI 59 is the **Milton House Museum**, tel. (608) 868-7772, a 20-room hexagonal erstwhile stagecoach inn once used as part of the Underground Railroad—the stone and earth tunnels still lie beneath it. It was also purportedly the first building made from poured grout "concrete" in the United States. Also on the grounds is an 1837 log cabin (the terminus of the subterranean tunnel) and plenty of 19th-century artifacts. The museum is open daily June-Sept. 10 a.m.-5 p.m., weekends only in May and from Labor Day to October. Admission is $5 adults, $4 seniors, and $3 children 5-17.

Milton at one time had Milton College, whose founding predated statehood by a half decade. It shut its doors in 1982 and today the whole campus—essentially the 500 block of College Street—supports an antique haven, specialty shops, and the **Main Hall Museum,** detailing the college's and to some extent the community's history. The museum is open weekend afternoons in summer.

Edgerton

Whiz through the fields surrounding Edgerton and you'd swear you were in North Carolina or eastern Virginia by the odor of tobacco on the air. Edgerton is Wisconsin's "Tobacco City," the tobacco-growing and distribution center. Thus it makes sense that the **Tobacco Museum,** 210 E. Fulton St., tel. (608) 884-4319, resides here. Any memorabilia pertaining to the trade is found here, as well as at many downtown shops. The city celebrates tobacco in late July at its **Tobacco Heritage Days** festival with many festivities (due to politically correct swells, the tobacco spitting contest has been discontinued).

Brodhead

On the Rock County line west of Janesville along WI 11, Brodhead is the terminus of the Sugar River State Trail, leading to New Glarus. It's also got the **Brodhead Historical Museum,** 1100 1st Center Ave., tel. (608) 897-8048, an old railroad depot housing local history exhibits.

BELOIT

The city of Beloit (pop. 35,600) lies along a wide expanse of the Rock River at its confluence at Turtle Creek. After the Winnebago, in the 1820s, trappers came here and scooped up Native lands for Yankee speculators. It is a lovely spot, explaining in part the migration of virtually the entire village of Colebrook, New Hampshire, to this town in 1837. Called Turtle initially, then Blodgett's Settlement, and finally New Albany, it settled on Beloit in 1857.

The city's founders erected a college (respected Beloit College, patterned after Eastern religious seminaries) and a church before much of anything else and landscaped the town around designs of a New England village with a square. It must have had a positive effect. In the rough-and-tumble 1840s, a traveler wrote of it as "an unusual community, amid shifting pioneer conditions already evincing character and solidity."

Today, the college still leaves its imprint on the community, though light industry is the economic linchpin; food processing (the world's largest chili can sits in front of the Hormel factory) and automotive and diesel engine manufacturing are the chief contributors. Anthropologist Margaret Mead once called busy and vibrant Beloit "a microcosm of America." The city recently finished a massive facelift, complete with a riverfront revitalization stretching from Grand Avenue on the south to Pageant Park on the north—transforming coal and rail eyesores into a river tourist hotspot.

SIGHTS

Orientation

Keep in mind what side of the river you're on and you'll do okay. The main pedestrian area downtown is Grand Avenue. The Riverwalk makes the entire expanse easy to maneuver on foot. It's a four-mile-long multi-use path connecting downtown with Riverside Park. Old railroad bridges have been converted into fishing

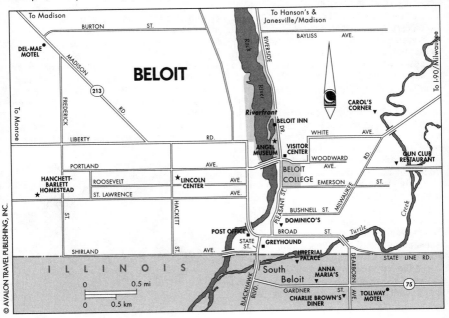

platforms. Illuminated fountains spray on the riverfront.

Angel Museum

The world's largest privately held collection of angel artifacts is on display at Beloit's **Angel Museum,** 656 Pleasant St., tel. (608) 362-9099, housed in a restored church located right on the Rock River. Angels of all sorts are on display—over 12,000 and counting—but the highlight is no doubt the nearly 600 African-American angels donated by Oprah Winfrey. Hours are Mon.-Sat. 10 a.m.-5 p.m., Sunday 1-4 p.m. May-Oct., Tues.-Sat. 10 a.m.-4 p.m. rest of the year. Admission is $5, $4 seniors and children 13-17, $3 children 12 and under.

Beloit College

Founded on the Rock River's east bank as Beloit Seminary, Beloit College is a nationally respected liberal-arts school, the oldest college in Wisconsin. Its founding philosophy was to preserve Eastern mores and culture in the heathen "West"—though they could only pay their two professors $600 a year "if they can raise it." The eye-catching buildings represent a mélange of architectural styles, most notably Georgian colonial. The Middle College building, dating from 1847, is the oldest college building north of Chicago. Well respected for its anthropology and archaeology departments, Beloit's Victorian gothic **Logan Museum of Anthropology,** at College and Bushnell Streets, tel. (608) 363-2677, was just a collection of Civil War memorabilia upon inception in 1893, but is now one of the best museums in the state, with almost a quarter of a million artifacts from around the globe, including the most extensive Stone Age and paleolithic collections outside of Europe. It's also got a respected Native American collection. Pieces have been collected from six continents on school expeditions, ongoing since the turn of the century. For a private college of 1,000 students, this is an amazing museum. Extensive renovations took place in 1996 to make room for more displays to be added. The museum is open weekdays 10 a.m.-5 p.m., weekends 8 a.m.-6 p.m. (until 4 p.m. Sunday). Free admission.

The **Wright Museum of Art,** Bushnell St. and Campus Dr., tel. (608) 363-2677, displays faculty and student art and hosts art events. Its permanent holdings include American and European paintings and sculpture, Asian decorative arts, and graphics.

The **Thompson Observatory** is at the corner of Emerson and Pleasant Streets and offers tours in mid-fall and mid-spring. Over two dozen Indian burial mounds also dot the campus.

Historic Tours

Though most cities claim to be worthy of a walking tour, Beloit is not guilty of hyperbole. The two most historically significant districts are the **Near East Side,** with over two dozen structures east of Beloit College, and the **Bluff Street** area. Houses in the Near East Side include the unique cobblestone Rasey House, Beloit College's original president's home, and a mélange of mid- to late 19th-century styles. The Bluff Street area was settled across the river a few blocks from the college and includes homes built for the wealthier industrialists and businessmen beginning in the 1840s. A couple also feature delightful cobblestone construction. Maps are available at the visitor center, the Chamber of Commerce, the Historical Society (845 Hackett St.), or the third floor of City Hall Building (100 State St.).

Hanchett-Bartlett Homestead

This limestone Greek revival and Italianate mansion, built from locally quarried stone, sits on 15 acres and has been restored to period detail, with special attention to the original color schemes. A great limestone barn filled with farm implements sits on the property, along with a smokehouse nearby. A rural school has been relocated here, and the grey shed-planked Beckman-Howe mill, on the National Register of Historic Places and dating to the post-Civil War pe-

Beckman-Howe mill

riod, is being restored not far away on CR H. The mill has been selected as one of the 10 most endangered historic sites in Wisconsin. At 2149 St. Lawrence Ave., tel. (608) 365-7835, it's open Wed.-Sun. 1-4 p.m. June-Sept., and admission is $2.50.

Lincoln Center
The home of the **Beloit Historical Society,** 845 Hackett St., tel. (608) 365-7835, the Lincoln Center houses a permanent exhibit on Beloit sports history and a Hall of Fame, along with a memorial gallery to Beloit's wartime dead and a few local antiques. It's open weekdays 10 a.m.-4 p.m. and 1-4 p.m. first and third Saturday of each month. Free admission.

Recreation
The area isn't known as a recreational paradise, but there are some trails about, including some along Turtle Creek. Access is available at three spots: I-43 at Milwaukee Road; Cranston Road; and Canterbury Road near the I-43/I-90 interchange. No trails span more than a couple of miles.

Side Trips
Tough-to-find little **Tiffany** lies northeast of Beloit on CR S, but it's worth a search; it's got one of the most unique **bridges** anywhere, a remnant five-arch iron-truss span based on Roman architecture. Built by the Chicago and Northwestern Railroad in 1869, the structure was modeled after a bridge in Compiegne, France. Each arch spans 50 feet with a 26-foot radius. To reach Tiffany, head east on CR S from Shopiere and then turn left onto Smith Road. You can really view the bridge only from the Smith Road iron truss bridge, built in 1890. Tiffany is a personal favorite, an anachronistic relic in the dewy midst of nowhere. The **Tiffany Country Store** is a wonderful place for breakfast, and even better is the **Tiffany Inn** for dinner—the fish fry is amazing, and they polka down Friday and Saturday.

Back in Shopiere, check out the village's antique weight-driven timepiece adorned with four lion heads.

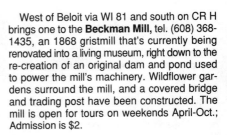

bridge in Tiffany

West of Beloit via WI 81 and south on CR H brings one to the **Beckman Mill,** tel. (608) 368-1435, an 1868 gristmill that's currently being renovated into a living museum, right down to the re-creation of an original dam and pond used to power the mill's machinery. Wildflower gardens surround the mill, and a covered bridge and trading post have been constructed. The mill is open for tours on weekends April-Oct.; Admission is $2.

ACCOMMODATIONS

Under $50
Cheapest is likely the **Driftwood Motel,** 1826 Riverside Dr., tel. (608) 364-4081, with rooms from the mid-$30 range. Similar rates prevail at **Finnegan's Del-Mae Motel,** 1850 Madison Rd., tel. (608) 362-8888, which has some rooms with kitchenettes.

$50 to $75
The **Comfort Inn,** 2786 Milwaukee Rd., tel. (608) 362-2666 or (800) 221-2222, has some rooms with kitchenettes, an indoor pool, and a whirlpool. Rates are $50-80.

Nearby is the **Holiday Inn Express,** 2790 Milwaukee Rd., tel. (608) 365-6000, which is one of two in town; the other is in South Beloit at the US 51 and IL 75 junction. The Van Galder bus stops here on the way to Chicago. The Express has some rooms with whirlpools and coffeemakers. Rates start at $70.

Finishing touches were being put on the **Beloit Inn,** 500 Pleasant St., tel. (608) 362-5500, right downtown. This attractive place has studio and one-bedroom suites with lots of extras. Rates hadn't been established but won't be on the cheap end.

Camping
The **Turtle Creek Campground** is two miles northwest of town just off of I-90. It's open May-Oct. with campsites from $14; the **Pearl Lake Campground** is two miles south on US 251 and has similar rates.

FOOD

Greasy Spoons
Best place to meet the locals is at **Carol's Corner**, 1655 Copeland Ave. Carol's has about three booths and that's it. Only open for morning feeds, it's got a classic combination called The Mess (a ton of eggs)—with or without "scrap metal." You can get a Half Mess if you're not that hungry. Menu items from $2.

The truck stop of choice—complete with country music—is **Charlie Brown's Diner**, 1334 Gardner St., in South Beloit off I-90 across from the Holiday Inn. From $2.

Burgers and Fish Fries
Enjoy *huge* burgers at **Hanson's**, at 615 E. Cranston on the river along US 51. This is the place for a fish fry as well. It's also the place to experience local flavor, hands down. Choices from $2.

The **Circus Drive-In**, 3525 Riverside Dr., tel. (608) 362-9375, is a classic, complete with trays hooked on half-open windows. There's also a children's play area with rides. From $2.

Brewpub
McClintock Brewery and Grill, 132 W. Grand Ave., tel. (608) 363-7683, is right downtown and brews up to 10 different beers on-site. Its menu consists of lots of appetizers, salads, sandwiches, and a limited entrée menu. From $3.

Chinese
Local favorite and winner of the largest menu award goes to **Imperial Palace**, 302 S. Park St. in South Beloit, with a pan-Cathay array of food including steaks and seafood. It's also got a popular Sunday brunch. It's open daily for lunch and dinner. From $5.

Pizza and Italian
Dominico's, 547 E. Grand Ave., tel. (608) 365-9489, is the pizza joint of choice, with a good veggie pie. Also featured are Italian goodies like chicken primavera, veal *a'dominico*, and lots of shrimp and seafood. Dominico's is open daily for lunch and dinner. Selections from $6.

Anna Maria's, 823 Gardner St., tel. (608) 389-2645, has pizza and Italian food, along with steaks, chicken, and seafood. It's open daily for dinner. From $5.

Supper Clubs and Fine Dining
The institution in these parts is the **Gun Club**, Colley Rd., tel. (608) 362-9900, serving prime rib nightly, along with steaks, seafood, exquisite duck, ribs, and homemade seasonal desserts. Antiques dominate the interior. Open Tues.-Sun. for dinner, the Gun Club presents live entertainment Friday and Saturday. From $9.

Equally traditional, casually ritzy, and open for about six decades is **The Butterfly Club**, CR K east of town, tel. (608) 362-8577. Enjoy supper club dining on a patio and likely the best fish fry around (available Wednesday nights as well as Friday). Live entertainment is featured on Friday. It's open Tues.-Sun. for dinner, and the outside is covered with beautiful tulips in season. From $9.

A Victorian charmer is **The Manor**, intersection of I-43 and I-90, tel. (608) 365-1608, with six dining rooms and a lounge serving standard supper club fare. The Manor is open daily for dinner, with a Sunday brunch. From $8.

ENTERTAINMENT AND EVENTS

Nightlife
Young visitors will want to head straight for the **C House** on the Beloit College campus. A dark hall, it feels like the inside of somebody's home, with a loft apartment upstairs. The long bar has all bottled beer (kegs are banned on campus), and there are pool tables and dartboards upstairs. Best of all, there are bands at times, from grunge to jazz-fusion.

You'll find live music and DJs at **TAASBAG Too**, 2683 Prairie Ave., tel. (608) 365-0999 (and get a buck if you can guess what the acronym stands for).

Events
The summer brings July's **Riverfest**, a four-day musicfest that's one of the largest of its kind in the country, with over 50 national acts performing. It ranks second in Wisconsin; only Milwaukee's Summerfest is larger.

In September, the city hosts **Heritage Days**, recounting Beloit's 19th-century founding; the highlight is a dramatic reenactment of Abraham Lincoln's 1859 campaign appearance.

Cultural Events

The **Neese Performing Arts Center** has a full schedule of academic year cultural events; call (608) 363-2000 for campus information. The **Beloit-Janesville Symphony Orchestra** has scheduled performances in Beloit Oct.-March.

Spectator Sports

The **Beloit Snappers** used to be the Beloit Brewers and are indeed a farm team (single-A) of the Milwaukee Brewers. The shift in names was to spur marketing sales, and it's been quite successful—the Snappers logo-adorned paraphernalia are among the country's most sought-after souvenirs. The Snappers play at Pohlman Field and are perennial playoff contenders.

SERVICES AND INFORMATION

The **Beloit Visitor Center,** 1003 Pleasant St., tel. (608) 365-4838 or (800) 4-BELOIT, www.visit-beloit.com, is housed in the city's refurbished pump house, built in 1880. You can still wander around and see the workings.

A big hello to the Land of Lincoln is at the Wisconsin Travel Information Center south of Beloit at Rest Area 22 on I-90, tel. (608) 364-4823. It's staffed daily 8 a.m.-6 p.m. (till 4 p.m. Sunday) May-Oct., only Tues.-Sat. the rest of year.

The **post office** is at 300 Mill St., tel. (608) 365-7755. The local public **library,** tel. (608) 364-2905, is on the southeast corner of Public Avenue and Pleasant Street. The **Beloit Memorial Hospital,** tel. (608)364-5151, is at 1969 West Hart Road.

TRANSPORTATION

Bus

Van Galder buses, tel. (608) 752-5407, stop in Beloit on their forays to and from Madison and Chicago (O'Hare airport and downtown). The 10 daily buses (each way) stop at the Holiday Inn Express in South Beloit, junction of IL 75 and US 51. To Madison costs $6; to O'Hare is $17.

The local **Greyhound,** 454 St. Paul Ave., tel. (608) 365-7808, has three daily departures to Madison and three to Chicago. The fare to Madison is $6.

Beloit Transit System

The Beloit Transit System, tel. (608) 365-7433, has routes covering the city as well as an express bus to Janesville five times on weekdays 7 a.m.-5 p.m.; the fare to Janesville is $2 one-way. The Express starts from a transit system transfer point along Henry Ave. and stops at the Beloit Mall and Beloit Shopko. The E-Line runs to the Holiday Inn, where the Van Galder stops. The B-line runs near Lincoln Center. Fare is $1.

LAKE GENEVA AND ENVIRONS

Interstates 90 and 94, along with the Illinois State Line, form a tight quadrilateral in southeastern Wisconsin. Bisecting this neatly is I-43, and just south of the region's midpoint is Wisconsin's southernmost lakes playground, the gateway resort city of Lake Geneva.

Relatively overlooked by most Wisconsinites, it's primarily visited by Windy City summertime refugees who'd prefer not to tackle the five-hour drive all the way to the northern woods. Some 60% of annual visitors in fact call Chicago home; another quarter come from Milwaukee. In the town and around the entire perimeter of the lake are eye-catching anachronistic residences, cau-

tious development (a modicum of tacky ersatz New England does exist), a state park, and sites of historical interest.

History

Spring-fed Geneva Lake, carved out by the Michigan glacier during the ultimate glacial epoch, was originally settled by Potawatomi Indians on its western cusp. Big Foot State Park is named for a Potawatomi chief—bleakly ironic since the Potawatomi were forcibly relocated to Kansas. They originally lived side by side with white settlers, who in the early 1830s set up a dusty stagecoach stop on the route between

Kenosha on Lake Michigan and inland Beloit. The first dwellings wrapped around the east side, where the lake forms an outlet at the White River. Water power and mills were the first industries in the community. Those humble, somnolent days lasted until the Iron Rooster steamed into town on freshly laid tracks, carrying Chicago's elite. The Windy City wealthy began raising palatial summer homes and estates on the east end of the lake. The Great Fire of 1871 cemented the city's status as a getaway when it became a retreat for Chicago's refugees. So many magnificent estates lined the shores it was dubbed "Newport of the West," a moniker still applicable today.

SIGHTS

Orientation

Lake Geneva is but one piece of the Geneva Lake area mosaic. Actually composed of four lakes—Delavan, Comus, Como, and Geneva—the area forms a rough triangle with the city of Lake Geneva to the east, Delavan 10 miles to the west, and little Fontana to the south on the western cusp of Lake Geneva. Williams Bay is also included, along the northern perimeter of Lake Geneva. Lakeless little Elkhorn lies to the north, outside the immediate area.

Geneva Lake

With a surface area of 5,262 acres (7.6 miles long by 2.1 miles wide) and a depth of 135 feet, Geneva Lake is one of the larger lakes in southern Wisconsin. The most popular way to experience it is on a tour in either a replica Mississippi paddlewheeler, lake steamer, or even7 an official U.S. Mail boat (!) from **Geneva Lake Cruise Lines,** Riviera Docks, tel. (262) 248-6206 or (800) 558-5911. Tours leave the docks for an hour spin six times daily 10 a.m.-4:15 p.m. mid-June through

early September, twice a day in spring and fall. Full tours range from one hour up to just under three hours and cost $12-50 adults, $11-43 seniors, $8-36 students, and $6-30 children; the higher cost tours are daily luncheon cruises, Thurs.-Fri. dinner cruises, or the Sunday brunch cruise. In peak summer season boats seem to depart constantly. Other boats in the cruise line include genuine lake steamers, including one still using a 75-year-old steam engine, the only large steamboat left in Wisconsin.

Lake Geneva residents still get their mail delivered by boat, just as in the '30s. Visitors can also hop on the mail boat, the *Walworth II,* in operation for over 100 years, seven days a week in summer.

Downtown Lake Geneva has a small **historical museum.** For a great freebie, head for the **library,** which has comfy chairs and a four-star view of the lake. You can also peruse detailed county guidebooks on historical structures and local history.

Most fun is a 26-mile-long **footpath** which circles the lake via linked ancient Native American footpaths. You can access it at any park

LAKE GENEVA

along the lakefront. Along the way, the path passes those same gargantuan summer homes (palatial manors), a state park, and the **Yerkes Observatory,** tel. (414) 245-5555, which has the world's largest refractor telescope and can be toured Saturdays 10 a.m.-noon; free.

ACCOMMODATIONS

Dozens of motels, hotels, inns, bed and breakfasts, and resorts line Geneva Lake and fill downtown Lake Geneva town as well as the small communities surrounding the lake, including Fontana and Williams Bay. If things are booked solid in Lake Geneva town, try little Lake Como a few minutes to the west on CR H, or head up to Delavan Lake via WI 50.

Hotels and Motels
Wells Street has most of Lake Geneva's motels and hotels. Expect to pay a minimum of $50 for a single in the high season (summer). Some good ones to try are the **Ambassador Motel,** 625 Wells St., tel. (262) 248-3542, on a 10-acre plot with a pool and recreation area, and the **Plaza,** 304 Wells St., tel. (262) 248-3049. Both have rates from $70; the latter drops significantly Sun.-Thursday.

The **Budget Host Diplomat Motel,** 1060 Wells St., tel. (262) 248-1809 or (800) BUD-HOST, is an award-winning property with an outdoor pool. The decor is pleasant, and some rooms have waterbeds and/or refrigerators. Rates are from $50 s or d in summer, much less Sept.-April.

The **Best Western Harbor Shores,** 300 Wrigley Dr., tel. (262) 248-9181 or (888) 746-7371, is right on the lakefront and has an indoor pool, whirlpool, sauna, restaurant, private dock, and tennis and golf privileges. Rates begin at $90.

Resorts
The **Abbey,** in Fontana on the west side of the lake, tel. (262) 275-6811 or (800) 558-2405, is an enormous spread of 13 parlors and 140 villas, some fireplace suites, and standard rooms. Amenities include indoor and outdoor pools, a health club, water skiing, tennis, bicycling, and golf. It has four restaurants, four lounges, and a full spa. Rates are $85-200.

Relax in a lodge and cozy villas at the **Interlaken Resort,** W 4240 WI 50, tel. (262) 248-9121 or (800) 225-5558. It features three pools, children's activities, restaurants with entertainment and dancing, valet and concierge service, a barber, beauty shop, and tennis courts. Lodge rooms are $60 and up; villas start at $140 and can hold up to six persons.

The **Grand Geneva,** east of town at the junction of US 12 and WI 50, tel. (262) 248-8811 or (800) 558-3417, is a three-story lodge with over 300 rooms. Amenities include indoor tennis, a 36-hole golf course, driving range, boat and ski rentals on-site (a downhill ski mountain is adjacent), bicycles, skeet shooting, a recreation room, indoor exercise facilities, massage therapists, weights, whirlpools, sauna, and steam room. Its private land holdings include almost 1,500 acres of diverse meadow and forest, along with its own lake. Rates are from $100.

The **Geneva Inn,** N2009 WI 120, tel. (262) 248-5680 or (800) 441-5881, is a hodgepodge of spacious rooms in a variety of floorplans. All have panoramas of the lake. The inn has a private pier, boat slips, an excellent lakeside dining room decorated as an English inn, an atrium, and more. Rates are from $150.

Historic Inns and Bed and Breakfasts
Central to Lake Geneva, a block off Broad Street, is the **T.C. Smith Inn B&B,** tel. (262) 248-1097 or (800) 423-0233. It may not be very quiet, but it's got the most authentic historical feel—an eclectic mélange of architectural styles in an 1845 mansion set amidst a formal courtyard, gardens, and a waterfall. The posh interiors feature oriental carpets, antiques, artwork, original gasoliers, and an original *trompe l'oeil* (a still-life painting designed to give the illusion of reality), as well as fireplaces everywhere. Rates run from $125.

Bugs Moran used to hang out at the **Waters Edge of Lake Geneva,** W4232 West End Rd., tel. (262) 245-9845, in the '20s and '30s. Four guest rooms full of antiques—each with its own private deck—are available. Waters Edge rates start at $75.

The sybaritic rooms at the **French Country Inn,** WI 50 West, tel. (262) 245-5220, are some of the nicest in the area. Partially constructed in Denmark and shipped stateside a century ago to serve as the Danish pavilion in the 1893

World's Fair, the house later did time as a Chicago rumrunner's joint during Prohibition. All rooms have TV and air-conditioning; some have fireplaces. There's a swimming pool and a modest French country-style dining room serving excellent steaks, fresh fish, and from-scratch cooking. Rates are $110 and up.

Camping
Just outside of Lake Geneva to the south along WI 120, **Big Foot Beach State Park** features great swimming and picnicking. The short trails make for easy strolls and great cross-country skiing. The campsites ($7 and up) are less than impressive; there are too many of them for a 270-acre park.

FOOD

Greasy Spoons, Family Restaurants, and Cafes
It's red vinyl and tubular steel straight out of the '30s at the **Harborside Cafe,** Wrigely Dr. adjacent to Popeye's. Straight-up diner fare here, along a classic breakfast counter. Menu items from $2.

Fran's Coyote Cafe, 522 Broad St., has a typical eggs-and-omelettes menu also featuring cube steak, a Coyote melt, the basics, and some limited Italian choices; it's also open for lunch. From $2.

On the corner of Dodge and Broad Streets, salt-of-the-earth **Hanny's Restaurant,** obvious for its huge neon sign, is a spacious family-style restaurant. In business since around WW II, it's got the cozy charm of a classic. The food tastes old-fashioned homestyle—they still use the original buttermilk pancake recipe. Hanny's is open daily for lunch and dinner. Best of all, it stays open 24 hours Friday and Saturday. From $2.

Waterfront
Legions keep coming back to **Popeye's,** corner of Broad St. and Wrigley Dr., tel. (414) 248-4381, for fare from the roaster, which smokes up chicken, pork, and lamb (each on a different day). The menu also features Yankee pot roast, Middle Eastern salad, liver and onions, pot pies, and veggie burgers. From $5. Adjacent is **Scuttlebutt's,** another American joint with sandwiches, burgers, and, interestingly, some Swedish specialties. From $6.

Supper Clubs and Steakhouses
In a reconverted Victorian farmhouse once serving as a capacious antiques dealer, the **Red Geranium,** US 50 E., tel. (262) 248-3637, is an outstanding supper club that grills its own steaks and seafood in standard-to-creative style. The intimate dining rooms are open for lunch and dinner daily, and the Sunday brunch is a smash hit. Choices from $7.

An institution on the lake is the tavern downstairs at **Chuck's** on Lake Avenue in Fontana; upstairs is a casual dining spot for lunch and dinner (and breakfast on weekends). The "seven-mile view" is legendary. From $5.

Most of the resorts have their own restaurants. Of note is **The Abbey** in Fontana, which has three. **La Tour de Bois** is a continental fine dining room under the resort's legendary A-frame; **The Monaco** features Wisconsin specialties and a great Sunday brunch. Both from $7.

Worth a side trip just for the ambience is **Fitzgerald's Genoa Junction Restaurant,** 772 CR B, tel. (262) 279-5200, in Genoa City approximately 10 minutes southeast of Lake Geneva. Housed in a historic octagon house, the supper club features grilled chicken, ribs, and shrimp but is known for its outdoor fish boils Wed.-Sat. 5-9 p.m. and Sunday 3-7 p.m. From $7.

Continental
Kirsch's, US 50 W, tel. (262) 245-5756, on the shores of Lake Como at the French Country Inn, has tremendous panoramic views, outdoor patios, and award-winning French/American cuisine with Pacific Rim overtones. From $17. A second location is also in Williams Bay.

A mosaic of European food—heavy on Hungarian and German, with a bit of French—is at **Chef's Corner Bistro,** Geneva Street in Williams Bay, tel. (262) 245-6334, open Wed.-Sun. from 5 p.m. From $8.

Chinese
Arguably the most important Chinese restaurant (this China expert thinks it is) in Wisconsin, **Temple Garden,** 724 W. Main St., tel. (262) 249-9188, relocated to Lake Geneva in 1998 from Madison; Madisonians were beside them-

selves. The Tibetan-Taiwanese owners are masters of Chinese cuisine and nothing is overlooked. Let the experts guide you here; you won't be sorry. Options from $6.

Mexican/Southwestern
Once a local hot spot for steaks, the **Cactus Club,** 430 Broad St., tel. (262) 248-1999, now has Mexican and U.S. steakhouse fare and Southwestern adobe decor. You'll find tacos, enchiladas, fajitas, burgers, ribs, and steaks on the menu, though it makes a claim of synthesizing Native American, Spanish, Mexican, and U.S. cuisine (try the sopaipillas). It's open daily for lunch and dinner and has live music Saturday nights. From $6.

Lighter Fare
Along Broad Street, the **Bottles Restaurant,** 259 Broad St., tel. (262) 248-2020, has homemade soups and sandwiches, along with creative salads such as a shrimp, artichoke, and snap pea combination. Bottles is open daily for lunch and dinner. From $4.

Best option for dessert is **Annie's Ice Cream Parlor and Restaurant,** 712 Main St., tel. (262) 248-1933. The interior is done up in turn-of-the-century style, and the light menu offers fresh sodas, lots of waffles, salads, quiches, and big sandwiches. From $3.

Delavan
It's worth the trip to **Millie's,** N2484 CR O, tel. (414) 728-2434, for the delectable Pennsylvania Old World-style, from-scratch cooking—not to mention the expansive, farm-like setting. It's open daily July-Aug. for breakfast, lunch, and dinner; closed Monday the rest of the year; open weekends only Jan.-Feb. From $5.

The restored 1900 Victorian is charming, but reviews have been mixed for the cuisine at the **Latimer House,** 523 E. Walworth Ave., tel. (262) 728-7674, with a wide range of steaks, pastas, and other creative entrées. From $7.

Believe it or not, Delavan is becoming known for Mexican food. It now has not one, not two, but three very good Mexican restaurants. Guadalajaran dishes wonderfully done are found at both **Buena Vista,** 239 E. Walworth St., tel. (262) 728-2180, and **Guadalajara,** 308 WI 50, tel. (262) 740-1810. Both have dishes from $3. **Her-** **nandez El Sarape,** 212 S 7th St., tel. (262) 728-6443, has excellent versions of food from San Luis Potosi state. From $2.

ENTERTAINMENT AND EVENTS

The third weekend of August, the community has **Venetian Nights,** when the town and lake turn into an ersatz Venice with torch-lit boat rides, festivities, and lots of fireworks. In late September, there's a **classic car show.**

Most **nightlife** is confined to the resorts or restaurants themselves. **Hogs 'N Kisses,** downtown on Broad St., features nightly dancing and live music on Sunday.

For six decades, the **Belfry Theatre** in Williams Bay, tel. (414) 245-0123, has been the home of entertainment for the lakes region. Currently it houses the "Eddie Cash: America's Musical Storyteller" show, a Branson-style hoedown.

RECREATION

Boating
Lake Geneva has a marina with boat rentals at **Marina Bay Boat Rentals,** 300 Wrigley Drive, tel. (262) 248-4477. Marina Bay offers fishing, skiing, and some cruises.

Gordy's, tel. (262) 275-2163 (Fontana) and **Jerry's,** tel. (262) 275-5222 (Fontana), both have four locations—Fontana, Lake Lawn Lodge, Abbey Resort, and Interlaken Resort. Gordy's has ski boats, ski schools, sailboats, and cruises; Jerry's offers waverunners, parasailing, pontoon boats, and cruises.

Golf
There are plenty of golf courses in the county. Noteworthy is **Geneva National,** tel. (262) 245-7010, four miles west of Lake Geneva town on WI 50. Rated in the state's top 10 by *Golf Digest,* it's got championship courses designed by Arnold Palmer and Lee Trevino. Fees on weekends, including cart, range balls, valet parking, on-course food and beverage, and more, are $90; lesser fees are charged weekdays, and Tuesday brings a two-for-one special. Contact the Lake Geneva Chamber of Commerce for other courses.

Horseback Riding

Lake Lawn Lodge, tel. (262) 728-7950, and **Fantasy Hills Ranch, Ltd.,** tel. (262) 728-1773, provide horses for rides throughout the lake edge areas. The latter also has children's pony rides, buggy rides, hayrides, and a petting zoo.

SERVICES AND INFORMATION

The **Lake Geneva Chamber of Commerce,** tel. (262) 248-4416 or (800) 345-1020, www.lakegenevawi.com, is at 201 Wrigley Drive.

The Lake Geneva **post office** is a block off Broad Street, at the corner of Main and Center Streets.

There is a 24-hour Urgent Care medical facility, **Mercy Walworth Medical Center,** in Lake Geneva at Hwys 50 and 67, tel. (414) 245-0535 or (800) 637-2901.

Amtrak is currently debating whether to bring train service to/from Chicago on its Lake Country line from Chicago to Janesville.

VICINITY OF LAKE GENEVA

Elkhorn

This trim village up US 12 northwest of Lake Geneva lies splayed around a somnolent tree-shaded square. Settled by speculators in the 1830s, it was named by a U.S. Army colonel who espied a set of elk antlers in a tree. It is a picturesque place; in fact, it's sometimes called "Christmas Card Town"—and you'll know why if you show up anytime around Christmas. It's the kind of place where local businesses list their home phone numbers as well as their business phones. The oldest municipal band in the state, established in the 1840s, still toots it out summer Friday evenings at Sunset Park. This seems singularly appropriate because five primary industries of the town are related to the manufacture of musical instruments.

One rumor running rampant around Elkhorn concerns the existence of a large-eared, werewolf-type beast said to prowl the surrounding forests. Over the last century, many sightings have been reported; the local humane officer once even had a file labeled "werewolf."

While in Elkhorn don't miss **Watson's Wild West Museum,** east off US 12/67 (look for the sign), tel. (414) 723-7505. This is the lifelong labor of love of the proprietor, who's got a serious Western obsession. Over 35 years, his collection has grown to museum-worthy proportions. Branding irons seem to be a specialty, but there are also animal heads, ropes, clothing, photos, a saloon bar, a real covered wagon, "Wanted" posters, and thousands of assorted knickknacks. The interiors are done up to resemble an 1880s general store and dance-hall saloon. The owner may even show up, dressed like Wyatt Earp. The museum is open May through October Mon.-Sat. 10 a.m.-5 p.m., Sunday 11 a.m.-5 p.m. Admission is $3.75 adults, $2.50 children.

The **Webster House Museum,** 9 E. Rockwell St., tel. (262) 723-4248, once served as the territorial land office and later the home of composer Joseph P. Webster, who penned over 1,000 songs, including "The Sweet By and By." The collection includes a music room, a bird collection, and Civil War-era books and documents. It's open Thurs.-Sun. 1-5 p.m. Admission is $2 adults, $1 children 6-12.

Delavan

Delavan's two lakes are great reasons to visit—excellent fishing on Delavan Lake—but for non-hydrophiles, Delavan is also home to a bit of clown history. For some 50 years in the 19th century, Delavan was the headquarters for most of the country's traveling circuses, including the prototype of P.T. Barnum's. It was also home to the Clown Hall of Fame and Research Center until 1997, when the center moved to Milwaukee. Local cemeteries at the end of Seventh Street are full of circus performers and workers dating from this time; Tower Park is chock-full of colorful circus memorials and statuary.

Delavan is also home to the **Dam Road Bears,** 4310 Dam Rd., a teddy-bear factory. Open to the public, it's got variable hours. Visitors can wander about trails at the **arboretum** north of town along the shores of Lake Comus. Delavan Lake was once one of the most polluted in Wisconsin, heavily soiled by phosphorous runoff; however, an aggressive rehabilitation campaign has turned it into one of the southeast's cleaner lakes.

See above under "Food" in Lake Geneva for Delavan restaurants.

East Troy

Head 20 minutes up I-43 to East Troy to view the **East Troy Electric Railroad,** 2002 N. Church St., tel. (262) 542-5573, dedicated to the preservation of electric rail history. Also excellent is the 11-mile spin on a refurbished trolley. Some grand dinner tours are offered in an old-style art deco lounge car; this car also hosts traditional tea rides. Open Memorial Day through October on weekends and holidays noon-4 p.m. and mid-June through August Wed.-Fri. 11 a.m.-1 p.m. There may be additional trips available. Admission is $8 adults, $4 children.

East Troy is also known for the **Alpine Valley Resort,** south and east along CR D, tel. (262) 642-7374 or (800) 227-9395, with 12 ski runs, 90 acres of skiable terrain, and a vertical drop of 400 feet (longest run is 3,000 feet). There are a half dozen triple chairlifts, five doubles, and five rope tows. Inside, the lodge offers two dining rooms, two cafeterias, a pizza shop, equipment rentals, a game room, and more. Full lift ticket and run privileges run around $35 on weekends; rentals are an additional $19. Rooms start at $100 weekends; some package deals are available.

While in the area, travel five miles northeast off the interstate, near Mukwonago in the town of Vernon. There, **Heaven City Restaurant,** S91-W27850 National Ave., tel. (262) 363-5191, is one of the best Wisconsin regional cuisine restaurants in the state. The flapper-era decor seems a bit out of place, but the food is unbeatable.

Lady of the Lake

EAST-CENTRAL WATERS

Stretching south of the Wisconsin-Michigan border, winding around Green Bay and down almost as far as Milwaukee and west halfway to the Wisconsin River, the east-central region is easily overlooked by travelers winging north to the north woods or the Door Peninsula. Yet this area owns bragging rights to much of the state's heritage. It is the most historically significant region, having served as the initial and one of the most important doorways to the state and, later, site of the first permanent settlements and of the state's commercial center when Wisconsin's economy depended on the region's rivers, concatenate lakes, and tracts of forest.

Part of east-central Wisconsin—the vast stretch from the cusp of Green Bay to Oshkosh and beyond—constitutes the oft-mentioned Fox River Valley. It includes all communities along the Fox River/Lake Winnebago corridor—Green Bay to the north, Oshkosh to the south, and the Fox Cities. And Wisconsin's understated old man riverway, the Fox, flows through it all.

The Fox is one of the few rivers in North America to flow north, from its source at Portage in central Wisconsin to the mouth at Green Bay. For well over a century the Fox River Valley has been a big player in the nation's paper and pulp manufacturing, so much so that it's sometimes referred to as "Paper Valley."

Dominated cartographically by Lake Winnebago, the region also includes the Fox River Valley towns of Appleton and Neenah/Menasha, Oshkosh, Fond du Lac, and the progenitor of all towns in Wisconsin, Green Bay. Fanning out west from the lake are tiny north woods-type towns.

The Heritage Corridor
In the waning years of the 19th century, when the Portage Canal linking the Upper Fox and Lower Wisconsin Rivers was completed, two of the most crucial waterways in the Great Lakes system were finally joined, allowing transport from the Atlantic Ocean all the way to the Gulf of Mexico. The Fox River engineering was no mean feat for the time—it required 26 locks and dams to corral the rapids and negotiate a 200-foot drop. Within a century, though, the decrepit condition of the Fox River locks in Kaukauna earned them the distinction of being one of the 10 most endangered historic sites, according to an official state commission.

So, in 1990, the state of Wisconsin established the Fox-Wisconsin Riverways Heritage Corridor to preserve what was left, one of four pilot projects in the state. (The Kaukauna locks were finally placed on the National Register of Historic Sites.) The entire length of the Fox River is being eyed by the National Park Service as a

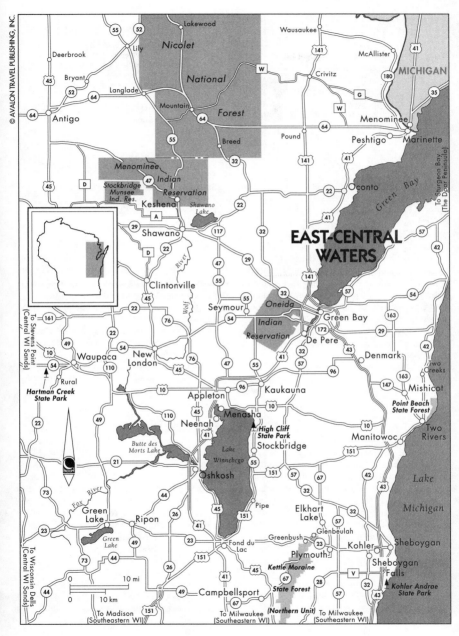

National Heritage Corridor, which would ensure preservation of historic structures and prevent wholesale pillaging for development. The Lower Wisconsin is protected by its official State Riverway status. In addition to the locks, some of the only extant French-style agricultural developments can still be seen—they're recognizable by their long, narrow drawbacks from the river, as opposed to the usual patchwork parallelograms of the other European immigrants.

HISTORY

Early nomadic Paleo-Indians arrived on the nascent littoral shores of Lake Michigan between 6,000 and 10,000 years ago as the glaciers retreated and the prehistoric lake waters subsided. By the time Jean Nicolet came calling in 1634, the region was well populated by Native Americans. The Jesuits first settled somewhere on the shore of Green Bay as early as 1669 and for the next century attempted, along with itinerant trappers, to establish the westernmost fringe community of New France. Their main missions were to harvest beaver hides and civilize the Indians. After a century of skirmishes between French, British, and Native Americans for control of the region, immigrants began pouring in. One big draw was the ready-made timber treasures, perfect for satisfying the rapacious needs of a burgeoning nation. The Fox River

---

EAST-CENTRAL WATERS HIGHLIGHTS

Birthplace of the Republican Party, Ripon
EAA Convention, Oshkosh
Fox River Heritage Corridor, Green Bay-Oshkosh
Houdini Historical Center, Appleton
Kettle Moraine State Forest-Northern Unit Campbellsport
Lake Winnebago, High Cliff State Park
Point Beach State Forest, Two Rivers
Sheboygan Bratwurst Festival, Sheboygan
SS *Badger,* Manitowoc
SS *Cobia* and **Marine Museum,** Manitowoc
The Pack, Green Bay
Wolf River, Shawano/Keshena

Valley, once the route of inquisitive *voyageurs,* became famed for floating immense wealths of lumber. For a while, with the hinterlands timber industry and the prodigious fishing harvests and shipping receipts from the long, long Green Bay shoreline and Lake Michigan coast, this was the richest section of the state.

Though the timber has slowed to a less heady trickle and the shipbuilding and fishing fleets are mostly gone, the region remains an intriguing highlight of the state's past, juxtaposing some great recreation with the zenith of Wisconsin's early economic triumvirate.

SHEBOYGAN

Sheboygan has come a long way, touristically speaking. Two decades ago, this phlegmatic, gritty industrial town was so aesthetically weary travelers wouldn't even think of stopping here.

Fast-forward to the city's remarkable recovery. Herculean efforts and millions of dollars have made possible the renovation of marinas, promenades, lighted walkways, bike trails, building facades, and harbor breakwaters—truly gentrifying the city. It's almost nearing postcard cliché realms.

Through it all, Sheboyganites kept a stiff upper lip. Eventually, somebody noticed the underlying luster. In 1998 *Reader's Digest* named Sheboy-

gan the number one "Family Friendly" city in the United States.

Sheboygan has never lacked fame for one other thing: bratwurst. The self-proclaimed Bratwurst Capital of the World might get some debate from regions of Bavaria—or even a certain Wisconsin city to the south—but for rentention of and rabid devotion to a culinary heritage, nobody touches Sheboyganites and their brats. Innumerable neighborhood butchers still turn out family-secret-recipe bratwurst (everyone is slobberingly devoted to his or her own butcher), and Bratwurst Days in the summer is one of Wisconsin's largest food festivals.

HISTORY

What is today Sheboygan actually grew out of an initial settlement three miles upriver from the mouth of the Sheboygan River, at what is now Sheboygan Falls. These falls inspired the Ojibwa name *Shaw-bwah-way-gun,* "the sound like the wind of the rushing waters." Sawmills and clapboard shacks sprang up in 1835, and though many settlers decamped by 1840, enough remained for the territorial legislature to initiate road-building and establish new villages. One of these was "The Mouth" (Sheboygan), finally permanently settled by 1844. Initial expansion was helped by Sheboygan's location along the Lake Michigan shipping lane, equidistant from Milwaukee and Manitowoc. The village erected one of the first decent piers along Lake Michigan, allowing lake schooners and ferries to bring tens of thousands of German, Dutch, and English immigrants to town. With the arrival of the immigrants, dairying and agriculture buttressed the lake trade. The new labor force—and federal road-building—also initiated manufacturing.

Sheboygan's real boom occurred during the final wave of German immigration, between 1880 and 1890, when 20,000 northern Germans flooded the community. Some townships in the county were (and are) 95% German; diminutive St. Nazianz, northwest of Sheboygan, was founded and populated in the 1850s solely by Baden German Catholics, and at first glance today it appears that not much has changed. Most of

© AVALON TRAVEL PUBLISHING, INC.

the immigrants were woodworkers, so several furniture and wood-product factories opened. Thus, Sheboygan also became known as the city of cheese and chairs.

SIGHTS

The Boardwalk
One of the major features of the new city center is this winding walkway alongside the Sheboygan River and Riverfront Drive, trailing gentrification as it goes. The old fishing shanties have been transformed into antique shops, art galleries, restaurants, and other retail outlets. A few old weatherbeaten shacks remain, and a very few are still actually used.

Lakefront Promenade
This paved trail is great for jogging, inline skating, or just strolling. It circumvents the trendy clutter of the Boardwalk. Stretching from the boat launching area to North Point, it's a great way to get right atop the roaring lake, passing plenty of sandy beaches along the way.

Lottie Cooper
Lake Michigan has sunk 62 vessels off Sheboygan. The *Lottie Cooper,* a three-masted lumber schooner, went down in a gale off Sheboygan on April 9, 1894. The white oak ship went down in 15 feet of water. One crewmember lost his life. During preliminary preparations for the Harbor Centre project in 1992, routine cultural excavations revealed the wreck. The subsequent salvaging operation brought up a treasure—much of the ship, still intact, including one of the longest salvaged keels of a Great Lakes wreck. Originally displayed in the Harbor Centre, the vessel now rests in Deland Park, near the North Pier.

Sheboygan Indian Mound Park
One of the city's most eerily impressive parks is this archaic relic along the Black River region in south Sheboygan. The approximately 18 Native American effigy mounds, in myriad geometric and animal shapes, date from A.D. 500. A beautiful nature trail runs along a creek, and an exhibit of materials is displayed inside the mounds. Admission is free.

John Michael Kohler Arts Center
This superlative arts center, 608 New York Ave., tel. (920) 458-6144, is one of Sheboygan's cultural landmarks. The wondrously progressive, eclectic grouping of galleries is devoted to contemporary art in all media—sculpture, painting, photography, and dance—along with workshops, artist show-and-tells, and more. Of note are its galleries devoted to self-taught artists. Housed in an 1882 Italianate villa, which recently added 70,000 square feet of gallery space, the center has been nationally recognized for its unusually broad scope and its efforts to incorporate the community in its undertakings; its newest conglomeration of pieces called "The Matrix" focuses on linking all the ethnic groups of the county. It's open Mon.-Fri. 10 a.m.-5 p.m., Tuesday and Thursday evenings until 8 p.m., and weekends 10 a.m.-4 p.m. Free admission.

Sheboygan County Historical Museum
On the city's west side, in one of the oldest brick buildings in the community (early 1850s), this complex features individually themed rooms in a main house, while outside stands the Weinhold Homestead—among the only remaining log cabins in east-central Wisconsin. An old barn contains creaky antique agricultural implements, and the newest draw is an 1867 cheese factory. The museum is open April-Oct., Tues.-Sat. 10 a.m.-5 p.m. and Sunday 1-5 p.m. Admission is $3 adults, $1 children 12 and under.

Kohler-Andrae State Park
A personal favorite, the underappreciated Kohler-Andrae State Park may well be the best stretch of beach along Wisconsin's Lake Michigan shoreline. Consisting of a park and a natural area, it includes two miles of windswept beach and a plank trail that meanders through the fragile Kohler Dunes Natural Area, one of the state's rarest habitats (an interdunal wetland), and winds up and over the gorgeous, chocolate-drop-shaped dunes through stark sandblow—when lakefront sand gets blown back and intermingles with grassy areas—and huge ridges tufted with grassy outcroppings. Don't be surprised if you stumble across white-tailed deer among the dunes. The chilly waters off the park are home to some 50 shipwrecks (a diver's paradise). Many of the re-

covered wrecks are on display at the Sanderling Center at the end of the boardwalk. Located at 1520 Old Park Rd., tel. (920) 451-4080, the park is open year-round. Admission is $5 for residents, $7 for nonresidents.

RECREATION

Charter Fishing
Sheboygan's massive urban renewal project included the 300-slip **Harbor Centre Marina,** 821 Broughton Dr., tel. (920) 458-6665. With it came a radical rejuvenation of the harbor and coastal region around Sheboygan. Today, some 35 licensed skippers operate out of Sheboygan. Trips range from mini to half-day to full-day outings. Prices vary, but it's generally $220-260 (not including tip and a Wisconsin fishing license) for one to four people for a half-day charter; some outfits offer mini charters. Full-day, 10-hour charters are also available, but that means *lots* of wind, water, and sun.

A complete listing of all charter operators can be obtained from the visitors bureau.

Old Plank Road Trail
In 1843, the territorial legislature, hoping to effect permanent settlement in today's Sheboygan County region, began building the first plank road, to reach all the way to Fond du Lac. It was completed in 1852. Today, the Old Plank Road Trail is a paved 17-mile-long multipurpose recreation trail running from western Sheboygan to Greenbush and the Kettle Moraine State Forest's Northern Unit, via Kohler and Plymouth, a lovely ride in spots.

Pigeon River Environmental Park
This picturesque area, at 3615 Mueller Rd., actually includes three separate parks along Sheboygan's northern city limits. Totaling almost 300 acres, the parks are bisected by the Pigeon River (all are connected by bridges) and contain three nature trails, hiking trails, and swimming, along with an Eco Center and wildlife enclosures. Natural springs percolate down the hillsides into the river. The Eco Center is open Tues.-Fri. 9 a.m.-4 p.m. and is free. The park is open 6 a.m.-10 p.m. To reach the park, take Calumet Dr. (bus 42) west.

ACCOMMODATIONS

Under $50
Sheboygan doesn't have that many motels. All the budget places have rates within five dollars of each other. Price reductions may occur in winter or off-season, though, so shop around.

The best budget lodging, the **Parkway,** CR V and CR OK, tel. (920) 458-8338 or (800) 341-8000, is right up the road from Kohler-Andrae State Park a handful of miles south of town. The rooms are all pleasant, some have individual themes, with rates from $40—much less in the off-season.

$50 to $75
Best bet downtown would be the **Harbor Winds,** 905 S. 8th St., tel. (920) 452-9000, the only place on the water in Sheboygan. An observation deck affords a great view, and residents get a free morning newspaper and breakfast (though those are the only perks). Rooms from $60.

In town northwest of the city center is the **Baymont Inn,** 2932 Kohler Memorial Dr., tel. (920) 457-2321 or (800) 428-3438, a clean, attractive and newly renovated place with rooms from $59 year-round.

North of town along I-43 is a **Comfort Inn,** 4332 N. 40th St., tel. (920) 457-7724, with attractive rooms, a small heated indoor pool, and a whirlpool. Also included is a free continental breakfast and newspaper. Rates begin at $55.

B&Bs
Overlooking Lake Michigan is the **Lake View Mansion,** 303 St. Clair St., tel. (920) 457-5253, a gorgeous historic structure. The four rooms all have private baths and a view of the lake. Rates from $95.

FOOD

Brats
Not so long ago in Sheboygan, most taverns and a whole bunch of diners and cafes served up charcoal-fried bratwurst. Not all do today, though some places still serve Sheboygan's finest.

The **Charcoal Inn,** 1313 S. 8th St., tel. (920) 458-6988, and 1637 Greele Ave., tel. (920) 458-

BRATWURST: THE WISCONSIN DISH

Bratwurst, a Germanic legacy of Wisconsin, is the unofficial state dish. The brat (pronounced to rhyme with "plot," not "splat") is pervasive here—every picnic, get-together, barbecue, and especially tailgate party centers around this carnivore's delight. At major sporting events, forget about eating anything else (the farthest you'll get is a Milwaukee specialty, the Polish kielbasa, or maybe an Italian sausage). Supermarkets devote entire lengths of freezers to accommodate sausage-makers. Many towns still have old butcher shops that string up homemade flavors. Watertown, WI, is being considered for a national Bratwurst Hall of Flame (that's right, Flame). Sportscaster Bob Costas, a baseball purist if ever there was one, decreed the old Milwaukee County Stadium bratwurst the top of the major league line.

The Immigrant Epicure

Wisconsin sausage is a myriad thing: there's summer sausage, venison sausage, Italian sausage, pols-

Wisconsin's state dish

ka kielbasa, liverwurst, braunschweiger, blood sausage, *mettwurst, landjaeger, lachschinken,* and so on. But the bratwurst is the king of 'em all, in any form. Strictly speaking, the bratwurst is but one of hundreds of varieties of sausage, according to official (and draconian) German food law. Many people presume the bratwurst and other sausage varieties came to Wisconsin with the large-scale German immigration to the state. But sausage-making was here with the Native Americans, who had long stuffed deer intestines and hides with wild rice, grains, meats, offal, and herbs to produce pemmican, which is, technically, a sausage.

From the earliest settlement of the state, immigrants did make their own sausage. Wisconsin's bratwurst, unlike some varieties, is almost strictly made from pork. All immigrant groups traditionally used intestines for bratwurst casings. The internal mixtures would consist of meat, fat, and seasonings, along with occasional starches like rice and bread. Concoctions were and are highly secret—similar to the recipe for Coca-Cola.

Infinite Varieties

The main categories of Wisconsin sausage are outlined below. In addition, the Czech method includes a rice sausage and head cheese; the Norwegians make *sylte,* which is spiced and salted in brine.

German: There are a zillion kinds of German sausage. The four basic preparation methods are smoking, boiling, parboiling, and "raw." Boiled sausages include liverwurst and occasionally the frightening *blutwurst* or "black pudding." Parboiled sausages are by far the most common; they include *fleischwurst* (bratwurst), *bockwurst* (the incredible sausages made with bock beer), *knackwurst* (similar to bratwurst), and hot dogs. Bratwurst are most often seasoned with marjoram, pepper, salt, caraway, and nutmeg, though there are no hard and fast rules. You might also see *weisswurst*—a white veal Munich specialty sausage that most Wisconsin forebears made—and *bauernwurst,* a smoked pork sausage often made by farmers (many farms had their own smokehouses out back with the sheds).

Italian: Italian sausage, found mostly in southeastern Wisconsin or along the Wisconsin-Upper Peninsula border, is sweeter and hotter. Coarse pepper and fennel, a key ingredient, give it its trademark flavor.

Polish: In Polish, the word "kielbasa" means "sausage," but the name has been generally corrupted into one specific type—a garlic-heavy ring of two-inch-thick, dark pink bologna-esque sausage traditionally steam-fried for dinner (then cut into sandwiches for leftovers and lunchboxes). Polish recipes often call for red cabbage and mustard sauces.

Brats in Sheboygan

Germans might blench when they hear this, but Sheboygan bills itself the Bratwurst Capital of the World. Scores of local butchers still put out individual versions of the big B. The place to go is **Miesfeld's Triangle Market,** 4811 Venture Dr. (two blocks north of the intersection of I-43 and WI 42), tel. (414) 565-MEAT, where Chuck and the boys have been putting out national-award-winning sausages (15 varieties of bratwurst have thus far garnered 68 national awards) for as long as anybody can remember. The town has a celebratory fit of indulgent mayhem come August with its Bratwurst Days, when over 100,000 visitors come to town to inhale brats.

Some brat-related Sheboygan-only linguistic tips: "double"—you simply cannot eat just one brat "fry out"—used as both a noun and a verb (the rest of the state prefers the pedestrian "grill out") "fryer"—whatever thing you cook the brat on (again, most non-Sheboyganite Cheeseheads say "grill")

"hard roll"-it looks like a hamburger bun but it's bigger and harder (sometimes called sennel rolls) and absolutely essential.

Preparation

Microwave a brat and you'll incur the wrath of any Wisconsinite. Frying one is okay, but traditionally a brat must be grilled. Brats work best if you parboil them in beer and onions for 10 to 15 minutes before putting them on the grill, though many people just rip them out of the package and put them straight on the fryer—which is an excellent way to get a blackened casing and a dangerously undercooked midsection. Sheboyganites absolutely cringe at parboiling, so don't tell them I told you. Another no-no is any sort of roughage crammed in the bun—lettuce, tomatoes, etc.; even sauerkraut, loved by Milwaukeeans, is barely tolerated by Sheboyganites.

Another Option: Parboil brats briefly. Sear in butter in a frying pan. Set aside. Pour 2 cups dark beer into fry pan and scrape residue. Combine a finely chopped onion, some beef stock, juice from one lemon, and maybe one chopped green pepper. Put brats back in and boil 12-15 minutes. Remove brats and place on hot grill. Sauce can be thickened with flour or cornstarch and poured over the top. A Cheesehead will stick the sauce in a bun alongside the brat with mustard.

1147, still fires up a fryer every morning to supplement its unpretentious Midwest fare. From $4.

But if it's German you crave, head for the local institution, **Hoffbrau,** 1132 N. 8th St., tel. (920) 458-4153, a boisterous barn of *gemütlichkeit.* The place has, hands down, the best steaks in Sheboygan, and the hickory-wood fires also sear native-made brats. This supper club is also the place for German classics (schnitzels, rouladen, and possibly sauerbraten) and over 100 beers. It's one of the few supper clubs with a salad bar left in the state. Hoffbrau opens for lunch and dinner Mon.-Sat., closes Sunday. From $8.

Greasy Spoons and Drive-Ins

Jumes, 504 N. 8th St., tel. (920) 452-4914, is the place to go to rub shoulders with the locals, read the compendious menu, and enjoy the dirt-cheap heart-stopping breakfast. My Sheboyganite friends swear by this one. From $2.

Cruisers, a retro drive-in, and a Harley-Davidson showroom all in one at **Route 43 Harley**

Davidson, 3736 S. Taylor Dr., tel. (920) 458-0777. There are huge burgers, malts, and Harley memorabilia.

American

Enjoy good American food at **Rupp's Lodge,** 925 N. 8th St., tel. (920) 459-8155, in downtown Sheboygan for six decades. Aged, hand-cut steaks are the specialty here, along with standard supper club fare from $5. Through a glass partition, you even get to watch the food being prepared in the kitchen. On Friday and Saturday nights, patrons join in singalongs at a piano. Rupp's is open Mon.-Thurs 11 a.m.-10 p.m., Fri.-Sat. 11 a.m.-11 p.m., and Sunday 10:30 a.m.-10 p.m.

You'll find deli-style sandwiches and the best chicken salad in town at **Ella's Dela,** along with huge sub sandwiches and homemade soups and salads. The brownies melt in your mouth. Located at 1113 N. 8th St., tel. (920) 457-3034, Ella's is open Mon.-Fri 8 a.m.-7 p.m., Saturday 9 a.m.-5p.m. From $3.

One of Sheboygan's most creative menus is at **City Streets Riverside,** 712 Riverfront Dr., tel. (920) 457-9050, in a historic building overlooking the Fish Shanty Village along the Boardwalk. The most menu space goes to seafood—quite an impressive spread—but you'll also find steaks and prime rib, and more delicious homemade soups. From $6. It's open weekdays for lunch and dinner weekdays, Saturday for dinner only.

Fish Fries

A good bet for a Friday fish fry is a bar, though any supper club or family restaurant wanting to remain in business more than a week will also offer one. The **Scenic Bar,** 1635 Indiana Ave., tel. (920) 452-2881, has standard supper-club-in-a-tavern fare, with a fish fry Friday at noon and night (half-orders available). Otherwise, it's chicken, chops, seafood, steaks, and some decent homemade soups. From $4. The Scenic is open seven days a week from 10 a.m.

It's takeout only at **Schwarz's Retail Fish Market,** 828 Riverfront Dr., tel. (920) 452-0576, the best place in town for fresh fish.

Italian

Dishing up the best Italian is the ever-friendly **Trattoria Stefano,** 522 S. 8th St., tel. (920) 452-8455, a casually upscale place with a bright pastel environment and excellent service. The brick here is handmade, and the pastas are great. This place has just installed a wood-fired pizza oven. Menu items from $6. The Trattoria is open for lunch Tues.-Fri. 11:30 a.m.-1:30 p.m. and for dinner Mon.-Thurs. 5 p.m.-9 p.m. and Fri-Sat. 5 p.m.-10 p.m. Reservations are accepted.

Coffeehouses

New York on 8th, 632 N. 8th St., tel. (920) 457-6565, isn't just a coffee and espresso bar. Yes, it is the place to go for that latté fix, but it also serves up light lunches, continental breakfasts, and excellent homemade breads and is the best option in Sheboygan for a vegetarian meal or a quick, eclectic daily special. The floor-to-ceiling windows and vaulted ceilings create the best people-watching atmosphere, too. It's open weekdays 7:30 a.m.-8 p.m., Saturday until 3 p.m. From $3.

Health Foods

Nature's Best, on the Boardwalk at 809 Riverfront Dr., tel. (920) 452-6176, offers health and diet foods, along with fresh-roasted coffee, espresso, and some specialty drinks.

ENTERTAINMENT AND EVENTS

Live Music

None-too-common rock is relegated to a number of forgettable tavern environments. Otherwise, the best bet for live music would be the John Michael Kohler Arts Center, which brings in national touring acts.

Bars and Nightlife

Happy Days, 2538 N. 15th St., tel. (920) 452-2270, features pub games and live entertainment—and also serves decent food, from broasted chicken to steak sandwiches and a fish fry.

A great local tavern is **Meyer's Lakeview Pub,** 550 Wilson Ave., tel. (920) 457-9610, a working-class corner tap with a killer view, billiards, a decent jukebox, and one enormous moosehead.

The best beer selection is found at either the American Club's **Horse and Plow** or **TD Beach Club,** 2401 Calumet Dr., tel. (920) 457-6457. The beer selection is all these two have in common; the former is dark-stained wood and brass upscale, while the latter is decidedly more hoi polloi.

The local dance club is the **Dreamers Club,** 821 N. 8th St., tel. (920) 452-0020, a two-level thumping joint in what was once an old saloon. It's loud, loud, loud and has one of those great security systems of large men walking around with walkie-talkies and earpieces.

Spectator Sports

The **Sheboygan A's** baseball team plays May-Aug. at Wildwood Baseball Park. Affiliated with the Wisconsin State Baseball League, it's the usual zany minor-league-esque family fun with oodles of giveaways—all for the princely sum of $2 adults, $1 students. For information, call (920) 458-4377.

SERVICES AND INFORMATION

The **Sheboygan County Convention and Visitors Bureau** is located along the Boardwalk at 712 Riverfront Dr., Suite 101, tel. (920) 457-9497 or (800) 457-9497, www.sheboygan.org.

You'll find the **post office** at 522 N. 9th St., tel.

(920) 458-3741. The **Mead Public Library,** tel. (920) 459-3422, is at 710 N 8th Street. An urgent care walk-in clinic is at the **Sheboygan Clinic,** 2414 Kohler Memorial Dr., tel. (920) 457-4461.

TRANSPORTATION

Getting There
There is no Greyhound or public inter-city bus service in Sheboygan; the only consolation is that it's on an interstate. The nearest commercial air service is in Milwaukee.

Getting Around
Sheboygan's quaint, battery-propelled replica trolley buzzes about the downtown area during summer. The route runs from the Transit Center to Fountain Park, the visitor center and along the Lakeshore Promenade. Fares are quite reasonable—$1 for adults, 50 cents for seniors.

Otherwise, **Sheboygan Transit System** buses run from 5:15 a.m. and cost $1.25. Buses do go to Kohler and Sheboygan Falls. No Sunday service.

The local taxi service is **Citi Taxi,** 1217 Superior Ave., tel. (920) 457-3030.

VICINITY OF SHEBOYGAN

KOHLER

For many travelers, Kohler is the reason for a trip to Sheboygan. A planned workers' community surrounding the operations of the Kohler Company, it's trim and attractive—thoroughly inspiring for a sense of community. Kohler also houses the state's most incredible resort/restaurant and puts on unforgettable factory tours.

Sights
The **Kohler Design Center,** 101 Upper Rd., tel. (920) 457-3699, is a must-see. The international manufacturer of bathroom fixtures here showcases the company's early factory and factory-town history along with its wares in an incredible "Great Wall of China." Also featured are a theater, ceramic art gallery, and more. The free two-and-a-half-hour factory tour is up-close-and-personal and better than you can imagine. The center is free and open Mon.-Fri. 9 a.m.-5 p.m., weekends and holidays 10 a.m.-4 p.m.; tours leave at 8:30 a.m. and require advance registration.

The younger daughter of company founder John M. Kohler commissioned Austrian architect Kaspar Albrecht to design and build a dwelling based on homes from the mountainous Austrian Bregenzerwald region. The result, **Waelderhaus** (House in the Woods), 1100 W. Riverside Dr., tel. (920) 452-4079, contains antique furnishings and highlights such as candle-reflected water-globe lighting. Tours are free and offered daily 2-4 p.m.

In the Shops at Woodlake in Kohler is a fine museum and art gallery, **Artspace: A Gallery of the John Michael Kohler Arts Center,** tel. (920) 452-8602. A full range of contemporary art in all media is featured; the sales gallery features art and crafts from some 200 American artists.

Hands down the best golf in Wisconsin—and some say the Midwest—is found in Kohler at The American Club resort, detailed below. **Blackwolf Run** offers two PGA championship courses—one of them was the highest-rated gold medal course in the U.S. according to *Golf* magazine. Newer are the preternaturally lovely courses of **Whistling Straits,** designed to favor the old seaside links courses of Britain; they've even got sheep wandering about! There is the Straits course and a challenging Dunes Course, both PGA championship courses. In 2000 Whistling Straits unveiled its new Irish Course, a companion course to the first Straits course; among other things it features some of the tallest sand dunes in the United States. All these course are on the PGA and LPGA tour for major events. Phone (920) 457-4446 for details; neither cheap nor easy is it to golf these courses.

Accommodations and Food
Easily Wisconsin's most breathtaking resort, **The American Club,** Highland Dr., tel. (920) 457-8000, is a member of Historic Hotels of America and the Midwest's only AAA five-diamond resort. The 1918 red brick facade of an erstwhile workers' hostel and dormitory has been retained, along with the original carriage house,

though both have been poshly retrofitted. A full slate of recreation is offered, of note two championship Pete Dye golf courses (one of them considered one of the most perfect examples in the world of a shot-master's course). There's also a private 500-acre wildlife preserve to explore. If that's not enough, the seven dining rooms and restaurants include the state's best—the Immigrant Room, winner of the prestigious DiRoNa Award. Here, various rooms offer the ethnic cuisine and heritage of France, Holland, Germany, Scandinavia, and England. The food is created with regional Wisconsin ingredients. Jackets are required. The nearly 250 guest rooms run from $160 in high season, $125 in low—the best splurge in the state; they top out at a very princely $690 for the presidential suite, not such a bargain.

A step down is the **Inn on Woodlake,** 705 Woodlake Road, tel. (920) 452-7800 or (800) 919-3600, a minor resort compared to the American Club, but of excellent value, with a small beach on the lake, a health club, golfing, and more. Rooms start at $130 in the high season, $80 at low periods.

Another solid restaurant is **Cucina,** 725 E. Woodlake Rd. in the Shops at Woodlake, tel. (920) 452-3888, with excellent Italian food. The huge round room takes in a gorgeous lakeside setting. Cucina is open daily for lunch and dinner. Selections from $7.

SHEBOYGAN FALLS

Sheboygan actually got its start near these somewhat thundering falls of the Sheboygan River. The town (pop. 5,456) has a great riverwalk with views of the falls and two very historic districts. The visitors bureau offers great guided ethnic heritage tours of German, Dutch, Irish, and Yankee buildings; tours include crafts, shopping, and a representative meal. For information, contact the chamber of commerce at (920) 467-6206.

Accommodations
The grandest bed and breakfast in town is **The Rochester Inn,** 504 Water St., tel. (920) 467-3123 or (800) 421-4667, a massive 1848 general store. The rooms all have parlors with wingback

lounges, and there are four split-level luxury suites and a grand internal spiral staircase. Rooms start at $100.

Food
A wonderful restored firehouse is the perfect setting for the **Falls Firehouse Pizza,** 109 Maple St., tel. (920) 467-8333. Specialty pizzas have names such as Appetite Extinguisher; sandwiches, homemade soups, and desserts are also offered. It's closed Tuesday but open for lunch and dinner the rest of the week. Menu items from $4.

Enjoy copious and hearty Midwest ethnic family fare at **The Villager,** 124 Pine St., tel. (920) 467-4011. The pies and soups here have won awards. From $4.

Richard's, 501 Monroe St., tel. (920) 467-6401, in an 1840s stagecoach inn, features excellent finer dining. Specialties of the house range from exquisite meats to oysters Rockefeller. From $6. Richard's is open daily for lunch and dinner, closed Sunday. More fine dining is found at **Broadway Bistro,** 334 Broadway St., tel. (920) 467-9082, an eatery that really lives up to the word "bistro" with a flair for the creative. Lots of ingredients come from local producers; the decor is attractive and cozy. From $6.

PLYMOUTH

Plymouth (pop. 7,655) lies just west of Sheboygan and would definitely be on a National Register of Quaint Places—the aesthetics of its early Yankee settlements remain amazingly intact. Initially a solitary tavern-cum-stage stop along the Mullet River, it grew into an agricultural and transportation center, as all rail traffic passed through the little burg. It eventually became the center of the cheese industry in eastern Wisconsin (the first Cheese Exchange was located here).

Sights
Plymouth is a small town, easily explored on foot. It's worth a stretch to view the historical buildings and picturesque ponds. The local chamber of commerce has an impressively mapped and detailed historical and architectural walking tour highlighting some 50 buildings. The visitor center is itself located in an architec-

tural highlight, the **Plymouth Center** on East Mill St., tel. (920) 893-0079, a restored 1920s edifice that also houses a historical museum and art galleries. It's open year-round weekdays 9 a.m.-4 p.m., Saturday noon-4 p.m., from 1 p.m. Sunday.

The town is most often remembered, however, for **Antoinette,** a 20-foot-long, half-ton replica Holstein standing at the west end of downtown.

Accommodations

Historic bed and breakfasts are everywhere you turn here. The longest standing is **Yankee Hill,** 405 Collins St., tel. (920) 892-2222, the oldest B&B in the county. The 12 rooms spread throughout two residences of cozy antiquity. The owners have won awards for the place. Rooms run from $75.

The countryside **Spring Farm Cottage,** N4502 CR S, tel. (920) 892-2101, is a classically quaint private English-style cottage right in the Kettle Moraine Forest. Artwork adorns the walls, and a spiral staircase leads to the loft bedroom. Nightly rates start at $95.

Food

Listed on the National Register of Historic Places and definitely a structure woodworkers will want to see is the **52 Stafford Irish Guest House,** 52 Stafford St., tel. (920) 893-0552. The 19 guest rooms are well worth the price, but the main attraction here is the food. The limited but ambitious menu changes a lot; the signature meal is an Irish beef brisket basted in Guinness—it'll wow you. The rich woods, ornate stained glass, and original fixtures give the place a special atmosphere.

ELKHART LAKE

Northwest of Sheboygan is one of the region's first resort areas. Around the turn of the century, well-to-do Chicagoans sought out the quiet getaway, and, later, so did high-profile mobsters like John Dillinger. (The town's name is deliberate—the Potawatomi thought the lake resembled an elk's heart.) The bustling trade has ebbed somewhat, but it's still a popular and picturesque spot. Another major draw is the international

speedway **Road America,** which hosts Indy cars, AMA and U.S. Grand Prix motorcycles, sprint cars, and vintage vehicles on North America's longest natural road-racing course.

Sights

Besides Road America, Elkhart Lake has the **Depot Museum,** corner of Thine and Lake Streets, tel. (920) 876-2922, with exhibits on the century-old structure and the community's history. Open summers, but keeps very irregular hours.

Another tiny museum is **Henschel's Museum of Indian History,** Holstein Rd., tel. (920) 876-3193, a private collection and archaeological dig of Indian pottery, copper wares, and other Native American implements. It's open summers; admission is charged.

Practicalities

Plenty of family resorts (budget to expensive), bed and breakfasts, guesthouses, and campgrounds surround the lake. One of the oldest and most established (family-run since 1916) is **Siebkens,** 284 S. Lake St., tel. (920) 876-2600, a turn-of-the-century resort with two white-trimmed main buildings (open only in summer) and a year-round lake cottage. The main buildings are the remains of the Belleview Hotel, built in 1882. The classic tavern and dining room serve up regional fare on an old porch. The dining room is open seven nights a week and Fri.-Sun. for lunch. Rooms start at $75 in the high season.

On the other hand, the state's newest upscale condominium resort is **The Osthoff,** 101 Osthoff Ave., tel. (920) 876-3366. It's a full-service, absolutely everything place, with high season rates running $169-359.

For all lodging requests, contact the **Tourist Housing Program** of the chamber of commerce, 104 S. East Street, tel. (920) 876-2922 or (877) ELKHART.

KETTLE MORAINE STATE FOREST~NORTHERN UNIT

A crash course in geology helps preface a trip through the 29,000 acres of the Northern Unit of the Kettle Moraine State Forest, spanning three eastern Wisconsin counties. During the initial planning stages of the state's 1,000-mile-long

Ice Age National Scenic Trail, the northern unit was chosen as the site of the Henry Reuss Ice Age Interpretive Center because of its variegated topography of kettles (deep depressions shaped like kettles and formed by large glacial ice blocks), terminal moraines (large deposits of glacial wash tracing the edge of the glacier's farthest penetration), kames (cone-shaped hills resulting from debris as water cascaded through vertical crevasses in the ice), and eskers (sandy residual lines tracing glacial sub-streams), as well as for the forest's large Jersey outwash plain—sand and gravel detritus pushed forward by the glacier and its meltwater.

This northern swath of forest is the complement to its sibling southwest of Milwaukee in Waukesha and Walworth Counties. Early creators envisioned the two sections of forest as the nascent stages of a superforest, concatenate segments of lands acting as an urban buffer zone. Certain politicians and environmental groups are still leading the fight to link the two to create a 120-mile ecocorridor. The fight has just begun.

The forest runs north to south, with a slight eastward lean, for some 25 miles. Glenbeulah is the northernmost town and Kewaskum the last village at the southern end. The largest of the Ice Age Trail's nine units, it's got everything an outdoors person could want—country forest road tours to primitive backpacking. Unlike the southern unit's predominance of pines and spruce, this forest supports hardwoods like maples and sumac. Surrounded by suburban expansion, it somehow manages to hold 12 State Natural Areas inside its borders.

Park headquarters are open weekdays 7:45 a.m.-4:30 p.m. For information, contact HQ, Kettle Moraine State Forest-Northern Unit, Campbellsport, WI 53010, tel. (414) 626-2116.

Henry Reuss Ice Age Interpretive Center
Along WI 67 near the CR G junction a mile south of Dundee is the Henry Reuss Ice Age Interpretive Center. The back deck has outstanding vistas of the whole topographical shebang. Inside is a theater with rotating film programs, educational exhibits on the region's geological formations, and good relief maps. You can take a self-guided 40-mile auto geology tour from the center (get maps there). A short nature trail winds from the building outside.

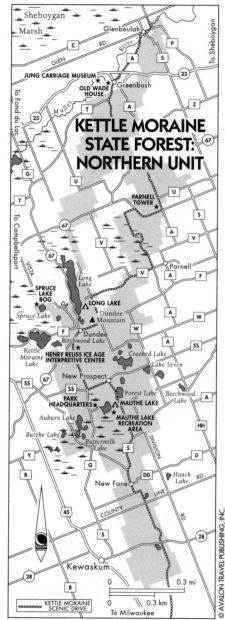

KETTLE MORAINE STATE FOREST: NORTHERN UNIT

© AVALON TRAVEL PUBLISHING, INC.

The center is open weekdays 8:30 a.m.-4 p.m. and weekends 9:30 a.m.-5 p.m., tel. (920) 533-8322. Admission is free.

Wade House and Jung Carriage Museum

Just outside of the forest's northwestern perimeter along WI 23 in Greenbush is the **Old Wade House**, one of eight official sites preserved by the Wisconsin State Historical Society. The Wade Inn went up in the 1850s along the oak plank road that stretched from Sheboygan to Fond du Lac. It was established to serve bone-weary stage travelers. Also on-site is the painstakingly restored Greek revival home of the Wades' in-laws. Across a wooden footbridge spanning the Mullet River is a blacksmith forge.

Perhaps the biggest draw is the impressive **Wisconsin Jung Carriage Museum,** a repository of the state's largest collection of hand- and horse-drawn vehicles; for $1, you can view the museum on a carriage ride. Throughout the summer, period-garbed interpretive guides demonstrate soapmaking, cooking, baking, gardening, and other skills of the 18th century. Located at the junction of Kettle Moraine Scenic Dr. and CR T, tel. (920) 526-3271, it's open May-Oct., daily 9 a.m.-5 p.m. Admission is $7.25 adults, $3.25 for children 12 and under.

Scenic Drives

The most convenient departure point for the Kettle Moraine Scenic Drive is to the north in Greenbush at the Old Wade House. But if you start even farther north, along partially paved CR S in Glenbeulah (an official Rustic Road), you'll trace the oldest geology in Wisconsin, 10,000-year-old outwash of the last glacial period. (You'll have to bop back onto the Scenic Drive via WI 23.)

The scenic drive is linked in the south with other great back roads all the way to the Southern Unit, some 40 miles away. It's hard to get lost; just follow the acorn-shaped road signs. From Sheboygan Marsh in the north to Whitewater Lake in the Southern Unit, the road totals about 120 miles and passes through six counties.

Visit an ancient bog environment at the **Spruce Lake Bog National Natural Landmark,** highlighted by moccasin-flower, west of Dundee along CR F.

Recreation

Over 140 miles of trails snake through the forest's narrow northern unit. The forest's sublime segment of the **Ice Age National Scenic Trail** is the 31-mile ecological and geological highlight of the entire system. It runs the length of the park and hooks up with five other forest trails for plenty of options. Five shelters are located along the way. Backpackers must have permits (generally easy to obtain, but plan ahead for high season). This trail tangentially touches many of the other trail systems in the forest. More shelters are found along the **Zillmer Trail.**

The **Dundee Trail,** off the Scenic Drive south of Long Lake, winds (easily) through the forest to Dundee Mountain—actually a conical kame—with a superb view from the top.

The oldest and best-established trail is the multipurpose **Greenbush Trail,** with a maximum distance of five miles, mostly along old logging roads, trailing a lot of meadow, some hardwood, and even marsh to the north. One spur offers a great look at Bear Lake. The trail is accessed via the Scenic Drive.

The best-known trail is the 11-mile **Zillmer Trail,** accessed via CR SS, a mostly meadow meander through bits of evergreen, pine plantation, swamp, and upland brush along one tough ridge with a great vista.

Some say the best view is the one from **Parnell Tower,** two miles north of WI 67 via CR A, then an easy four-mile jaunt around the observation deck through swamp and forest plantation. You're over 1,300 feet above sea level and 450 feet above the surrounding forest here, at the highest point in the region.

The **New Fane Trails** are for hiking, cycling, and skiing and are accessed in the north via CR S, CR DD, and County Line Road. Follow the Scenic Drive to get there.

The **Parkview General Store,** tel. (414) 626-8287, north of the Mauthe Lake Recreation Area entrance, has paddleboat, canoe, and rowboat rentals starting at $3 per hour, $10 for four hours. A 12-foot rowboat or 15-foot canoe can be rented for five days for $50.

Camping

Long and **Mauthe Lakes** have the largest established campgrounds with showers, pit toilets, and fire pits. Two enormous group camp areas—one indoors—are also available. In all, 400 campsites are available. Only Mauthe Lake has electrical hookups. If you're at Mauthe Lake, request the "A" area—it offers the most shade and a lake view. Section G is more isolated and is touched by the Ice Age Trail but has no lake view. Primitive shelter camping is possible along the Glacial Trail. Mauthe Lake also has a tepee for rent.

MANITOWOC AND TWO RIVERS

Another in the vein of "twin cities," these two Lake Michigan shoreline communities were originally home to tribes of Ojibwa, Potawatomi, and Ottawa Indians. The tranquil harbors attracted fur traders as early as the 1670s, and by 1795, the Northwest Fur Company had built its post here. Under Europeans, the area prospered during the heady early decades of whitefish plunder and shipbuilding. Both industries have slowed considerably today, but the shipbuilding and commerce are still around in some fashion. Neither town is unattractive, and both give outstanding glimpses into the coastal heritage of Lake Michigan.

Charter Fishing

As with other places along the Great Lakes coast, charter fishing is big business. Coho and king salmon, along with lake and brown trout (and some rainbow), are most popular for skippers in these waters. Salmon and rainbow and brown trout fishing generally starts in April (and runs through October), while lake trout season runs the first week of May through September.

Charter fishing operations are prolific. One central location for information is **Two Rivers-Manitowoc Sport Fishing Charters**, P.O. Box 82, Two Rivers, WI 54241, tel. (800) 533-3382 or (920) 793-3474, all of whose captains are licensed by the Coast Guard. They offer plenty of special bus tours and some packages.

MANITOWOC

This small bight was a port of call for wary Great Lakes travelers—the earliest ones in birchbark canoes—heading for Chicago. Equally wary Native American fishers were there to greet them when they disembarked.

Lumbermen competed with the quizzical English, German, Polish, and Bohemian farmers trying to scratch out a living from the difficult land.

Drive out into the countryside and you can still see smokehouses and bake ovens on early farmsteads, log threshing barns large enough to drive machinery through, split-rail fencing, and unique cantilever house designs.

An enormous fishing industry came and, thanks to an 1850 cholera epidemic and intense overfishing through injudicious use of drift nets and seines, went. However, the so-called Clipper City shifted to producing ships of all sorts and did well that way for more than a century. Clipper sailing ships were first produced in the 1800s; production here crested during WW II, when Manitowoc's shipyard became one of the most important naval production facilities in the country. (The industry fell with the advent of ore supercarriers—these were too big to be built in Manitowoc's narrow channel.) Today, a once-again bustling commercial fishing industry has picked up some of the slack, taking over as the town's major industry. General industrial manufacturing companies have also entered the market.

Wisconsin Maritime Museum

At peak WW II production, Manitowoc eclipsed even major east coast shipbuilding centers. This grand history is housed in Manitowoc's major attraction, the Wisconsin Maritime Museum, 75 Maritime Dr., tel. (920) 684-0218. Housed in a new $2-million riverfront building protected by the USS *Cobia* submarine (a National Historic Landmark), the museum is an amazing conglomeration of Great Lakes maritime history. Two stories re-create old port towns and harborfronts, with permanent displays of early shipping developments on the Great Lakes, early Manitowoc commerce, steamships (including a replica, the *Christopher Columbus*), old harbor equipment, drydocks, navigational aids, extensive examinations of WW II industries, a detailed model-ship gallery, and thousands of maps, documents, and pieces of nautical hardware. Regularly scheduled events take place throughout the year. The museum is open seven days a week 9 a.m.-6 p.m. Memorial Day weekend-Labor Day weekend, until 5 p.m. in April and Sept.-Oct., and 11 a.m.-5 p.m. the rest of the year. Admission (including a tour of the *Cobia*) is $6 adults, $4 ages 6-12; it costs $2 less for the museum only. The submarine can only be toured in combination with museum admission.

Other Sights

The **Pinecrest Historical Village,** tel. (920) 684-5110 or (920) 684-4445, is located west of town. Travel three miles on CR JJ, then turn left on Pine Crest Lane. Pinecrest is an ensemble of over 20 extant buildings brought here and painstakingly restored over 60 acres. Structures date from as far back as the 1840s. You'll also find gardens and a nature trail. It's open May 1-Labor Day, 9 a.m.-4:30 p.m.; weekends only thereafter 10 a.m.-4 p.m.; and the last weekend in November and first weekend in December 11 a.m.-4 p.m. Admission is $5 adults, $3 children, $13 family, higher during festivals.

The **Rahr-West Art Museum,** 610 N. 8th St. at Park St., tel. (920) 683-4501, is an 1891 Victorian with intricate woodworking and grand beamed ceilings. It houses one of the finer collections of art—some exhibits change regularly—in the Midwest. It's open Mon., Tue., Thurs., and Fri. 10 a.m.-4 p.m., weekends 1-4 p.m., and admission is free.

More for the gearhead set is **Zunker's Antique Auto Car Museum,** 3722 MacArthur Dr., tel. (920) 684-4005, with over 40 fully restored vehicles, along with an antique gas station, old motorcycles, and a doll and lunch box collection. Zunker's is open by appointment May-Sept., 10 a.m.-5 p.m. Admission is $2.

The name of **Natural Ovens Bakery,** 4300 CR CR, tel. (920) 758-2500, is a bit of a misnomer. This progressive operation has grown from a small organic bakery to a state-of-the-art operation spread over 55 acres, supplying over 1,150 grocery stores nationwide. The bread is still fantastically healthy, as are the rolls, cereals, muffins, and bagels. Free tours are given

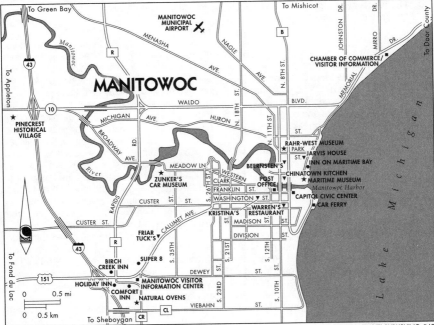

The S.S. Cobia *stands guard outside Manitowoc's Maritime Museum.*

Monday and Wed.-Fri. hourly 9-11 a.m. A newly opened museum displays vintage farm equipment collections in an old 1837 log dwelling; everything is hands-on, including the animals.

Architecturally speaking, the neoclassic **Manitowoc County Courthouse,** 8th and Washington Streets, is eye-catching, with a lovely copper dome and open lantern.

Recreation

Sixteen miles west of town on CR JJ, the **Collins Marsh Wildlife Refuge** is open May-October. In town, the **West of the Lake Gardens,** tel. (920) 683-4501, a five-and-a-half-acre estate built in the 1930s, features sweeping expanses of annual and perennial plants and flowers. Free, it's open Memorial Day through September 30 and is great for a relaxing stroll.

Baseball nuts can see the **Manitowoc Skunks,** a member of the Northwoods League (marginal college talent but always great fun), play at Municipal Field, S. 23rd and Grand Ave., tel. (920) 682-8810.

Accommodations

Most motels and hotels, including several chain operations, are clustered around the I-43/US 151 interchange. If you want dirt-cheap, head for Two Rivers. The **Birch Creek Inn,** 4626 Calumet Ave., tel. (920) 684-3374 or (800) 424-6126, recently sank over $1 million in renovations to turn itself into a quaint little spot. Rooms are still only from $50.

The luxury accommodation in town is the **Inn on Maritime Bay,** 101 Maritime Dr., tel. (920) 682-7000 or (800) 654-5353, the only place right on the lake and adjacent to the Maritime Museum. A host of amenities (including pool) complement the excellent Breakwater restaurant. Rooms range from $95.

Food

Enjoy basic good grub and a pleasant atmosphere (old red vinyl swivel seats) at **Warren's Restaurant,** on Washington St. between 9th and 10th, open Mon.-Fri. 7 a.m.-6 p.m., Saturday until 8 p.m., and Sunday until 1 p.m.

Farther up Washington Street, **Kristina's,** 1306 Washington St., tel. (920) 683-1787, offers healthful salads and sandwiches, along with a luscious fresh veggie sauté; dishes from $4. Sandwiches such as the Turk (jalapeño bread with turkey) and the Inferno (a Cajun-style concoction) give you an idea of what to expect from the lively, rustic **Fat Seagull,** 807 Quay St., tel. (920) 684-9123. From $4. A large number of sandwiches can also be found at an eastern Wisconsin favorite, **Friar Tuck's,** 3702 Calumet Ave.; from $4.

Serving Sichuan, Cantonese, and some surprisingly diverse Hunan dishes is **Chinatown Kitchen,** 807 Buffalo St., tel. (920) 683-9330. The house specials, *chow har kew* and *ta-chien* chicken, are excellent. It's open daily for lunch and dinner. From $5.

For more upscale dining, head to the **Coach Lite Inn,** 4709 Menasha Ave., tel. (920) 682-

4262, featuring traditional beef, pork, and chicken, along with some seafood. House specialties include chicken Oscar and homemade pizzas. From $6. It's closed on Monday. Chocolate fanatics and the dessert-minded should not miss **Beernsten's,** 108 N. 8th St., tel. (920) 684-9616, a renowned local chocolatier for some 50 years. Beernsten's now serves light lunches and sundaes in a warm atmosphere of rich old walnut and is open daily 10 a.m.-10 p.m.

Cultural Events

Right at the bridge downtown the **Capitol Civic Center,** 913 South Eighth St., tel. (920) 683-2184, hosts a full slate of plays, musical performances, and kid-dedicated shows.

Services and Information

The **Manitowoc Information Center,** tel. (920) 683-4388 or (800) 627-4896, www.manitowoc-cvb.com, is prominently housed on the western edge of town by the Holiday Inn motel enclave and is open Mon.-Fri. 8:30 a.m.-4 p.m. and Saturday 9:30 a.m.-4 p.m. The 24-hour foyer features a kiosk with direct phone links to area hotels and a display of local brochures. The Manitowoc Chamber of Commerce has another office north of town along WI 42 with the same brochures.

The locally produced weekly *Lakeshore Chronicle* has a dearth of news but is good for local interest.

The **post office** is located on Franklin Street, a few blocks west of the lake.

Transportation

Greyhound was planning to put Manitowoc on its routes from Chicago and Milwaukee at the time this book was being updated but hadn't even found a depot yet.

SS *Badger:* Of all the tourist draws, likely the biggest is the SS *Badger* ferry, running between Manitowoc and Ludington, Michigan. Originally one of seven railroad and passenger ferries plying the route, this 4,244-ton, 414-foot-long behemoth (able to hold 620 passengers and 130 autos) is a wonderful anachronism. Though technically a steamship—and the last of its kind on Lake Michigan—you can hardly tell due to modern pollution controls. Bypassing the horrible urban sprawl around southern Lake Michigan,

it's a great way to reach Michigan, and it's just a lot of fun. Crossings take four hours and depart seven days a week mid-May to mid-June and Sept.-Oct. at 2 p.m., mid-June to September at 1 p.m. and 12:30 a.m.(20% fare discount for this night trip). Fares are $39 one-way, $63 roundtrip adults, $36 and $58 seniors 65 and over, $18 and $31 ages 5-15, free for children under 5. You can also get a stateroom to overnight in Ludington for $55 but only in spring and fall (and there's no shower). Vehicles are additional: autos, vans, and pickups cost $47, motorcycles $27, bikes $5, and all trailers and motorhomes $3-5 per foot. It is possible to stay overnight (one night only) in Michigan and return on the ferry the next day on a roundtrip ticket, but only if you have no vehicle. There are plenty of extras aboard the *Badger,* including a cafe and snack bar, an arcade, a gift shop, storytime for children, movies, and even a bingo game. For more information, call (920) 684-0888 or (800) 841-4243.

TWO RIVERS

The Native American name Neshotah was translated into "Two Rivers" not long after whites first arrived. It was named for the East and West Twin Rivers, which trisect the city as they flow into Lake Michigan. Along with Germans, Poles, and Czechs, many French-Canadians came to Two Rivers.

Though the shipping industry here, too, has waned, Two Rivers is still the fishing capital of Lake Michigan. But residents are even prouder of another claim to fame: the ice cream sundae was invented here in 1881 at a 15th Street soda fountain. The mammoth historic **Washington House Museum and Visitor Center,** downtown at 17th and Jefferson Streets, tel. (888) 857-3529, is open every day of the year and dispenses information as well as great ice cream. Featuring a mock-up of the original fountain that made the town famous, it was once an immigrant hotel complete with saloon and dance hall, now serves as the visitor center, but still has the original murals and stencils in the ceilings—great for browsing. The chatty, solicitous volunteers often give impromptu tours. And a three-day rummage sale held in 1991 to raise funds has never stopped, so it's a good place find bargains.

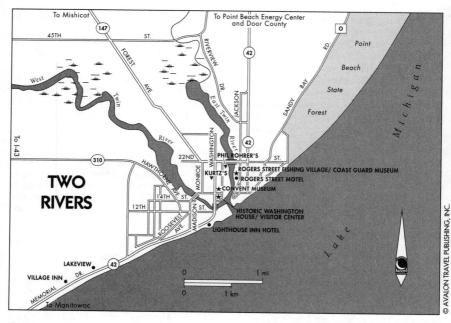

Sights

Two impressive museums downtown are the contiguous **Great Lakes Coast Guard Museum,** 2022 Jackson St., tel. (920) 793-5905, and the **Rogers Street Fishing Village,** 2102 Jackson St., tel. (920) 793-5905. The former contains roomfuls of artifacts related to the USCG, especially its lighthouse operations. There is a lot of shipwreck memorabilia—they say it's Wisconsin's largest shipwreck exhibit—and plenty of retired vessels (including one fascinating old cutter, the *Escanaba*) and equipment. The latter has an outstanding 1886 lighthouse on the riverbank, the old fishing tug *Buddy-O,* an art gallery, and museum. Both are open daily mid-May to mid-September 10 a.m.-4 p.m. Admission is $2 to both museums.

The recently opened **Convent Museum,** 1810 Jefferson St., tel. (920) 793-1103, is down the street from the Washington House information center. The museum includes a chapel, religious artifacts, an art deco room, and a room detailing French, German, Bohemian, Polish, and Lithuanian immigration to the area. It's open daily 9 a.m.-5 p.m. and admission is free.

Just north of town is a gorgeous tract of state forest—**Point Beach State Forest,** off CR O six miles east of town, tel. (920) 794-7480. You can't miss it: the majestic white lighthouse towers above the sandy pines. The wind-whipped 2,700 acres spread along latté-colored sandy beaches; the wicked shoals offshore have pulled plenty of ships to their graves. The lighthouse is functional but public access is currently unavailable. The preserved ridges along the shoreline are residual effects of a glacial lake last seen retreating some 5,500 years ago. The entire forest is a State Scientific Area. There's plenty of camping and, in winter, superlative cross-country skiing. Park admission is $4. One of Wisconsin's official **Rustic Roads** stretches along the park— CR O, a.k.a. Sandy Bay Road. This is one of the most densely wooded roads along the lake, a tunnel of conifers offering occasional views of windblown dunes.

Up the road farther is the **Point Beach Energy Center,** 6600 Nuclear Rd., tel. (920) 755-6400. The Point Beach nuclear plant has caused some controversy in Wisconsin due to plans to store waste aboveground in concrete casks.

Nonetheless, the energy center, an offshoot of the plant, was recently constructed and is impressive; it features worthwhile hands-on exhibits on energy, as well as a great nature trail and observation tower. The views are impressive. The center is open daily 9 a.m.-4:30 p.m. April-Oct., 10 a.m.-4:30 p.m. the rest of the year. Admission is free. General tours of the nuclear power plant are given the second and fourth Wednesday of each month, and reservations are necessary.

One of nine Ice Age National Scientific Reserves in Wisconsin is the **Two Creeks** area, 12 miles north of Two Rivers. Two Creeks contains the remnants of a 12,000-year-old buried glacial forest.

Excellent are the **Woodland Dunes,** off Memorial Drive at Woodland Drive and Goodland Road. The eponymous spiny mounds were the littoral edges of a glacial lake. Northern and southern areas of plants and animals surround a nature center. It is an official wildflower sanctuary and wildlife research station, with a bird-banding operation. It's open Mon.-Sat., and trails are accessible 24 hours. No camping.

Accommodations

Almost all of Two Rivers' lodging options, save for a few B&Bs, lie on WI 42. Farthest south from town toward Manitowoc, the **Village Inn,** 3310 Memorial Dr. (WI 42), tel. (920) 794-8818 or (800) 551-4795, is a decent, family-run operation, a two-level motel of 28 clean rooms—some are theme rooms—with a coffee shop and mini-golf course on the premises. Rooms run from $55 high season. Village Inn also operates a charter-fishing service. Near this motel are other dirt-cheap options.

Smack in the center of town is the **Rogers Street Motel and Marina,** 2010 Rogers St., tel. (920) 793-5678 or (800) 533-3382. Situated right on the river, the place offers extra-long beds, dockside pickup for pontoon river cruises, and boat and bicycle rentals. Rooms start at $36.

Top of the line is the **Lighthouse Inn on the Lake,** 1515 Memorial Dr., tel. (920) 793-4524 or (800) 228-6416. The standard rooms aren't exactly capacious, but they do have magnificent vistas of Lake Michigan—and some higher-priced rooms *are* quite large. The Water's Edge, the hotel restaurant, has the best views in the city, and the food is excellent. Other amenities include indoor pool, jacuzzi, sauna, and exercise room. Lakeside rooms are $75-89.

Camping: Point Beach State Forest, tel. (920) 794-7480, one of the most beautiful segments of Lake Michigan shoreline in the state, offers campgrounds under towering pines. Sites for residents start at $8, nonresidents $10, slightly higher in summer months. Vehicle admission fees for residents are $5, nonresidents $7; annual passes are available.

Food

Hole-in-the-wall **Phil Rohrer's,** 1303 22nd St., tel. (920) 794-8500, serves up classic diner fare. One of my personal favorites, it has a handful of swivel seats, fewer booths, and since 1962 has had some of the state's greatest "ho-made" soups to go with the slider burgers (which cost all of 60 cents) and daily specials such as meatloaf, pork steak, liver 'n' onions, and fish on Friday. From 60 cents! It's open late for lunch and dinner.

M&M Lunch, 1210 Washington St., tel. (920) 794-7616, has downhome casual dining along with Friday fish specials and serves up a traditional fish boil Wednesday through Sunday in season. It also serves bison burgers and has a 20-item salad bar. From $3.

Not well known but worth a trip for the pizza is **Port Sandy Bay,** 6421 Sandy Bay Road, tel. (920) 793-2345. Founded in the 1940s by a Wisconsin senator, it has recently undergone a change in management, which goes the extra mile by making fresh sauces and dough and grinding and stuffing its own sausage; in addition, the cheeses are specially ground to have a lower fat content.

One of the best-known restaurants in this region is **Kurtz's,** 1410 Washington, tel. (920) 793-1222. Established in 1904 to serve the rollicking sailors hopping off Great Lakes steamers and clippers, today it's an upscale pub. A wide spread of deli sandwiches are the foundation here, along with a handful of salads, a large array of beers, and killer desserts (many using Door County fruits).

For supper club fare, try **River Falls,** 6460 CR B, tel. (920) 682-3400, perched above the falls of the West Twin River. Open Tues.-Sun. for dinner, with a Sunday brunch, it offers some Italian entrées as well.

It doesn't get any quainter than **Berner's Ice Cream Parlor,** 1622 Jefferson St., tel. (920)

793-2490, housed in the Washington House. The first ice cream sundae was concocted here, and you can reminisce with the real thing while wandering the dusty interiors of the old building. The ice cream shop is open daily 9 a.m.-9 p.m.

Services and Information

The **Two Rivers Visitor Information Center,** tel. (920) 793-2490 or (888) 857-3529, is located in the Washington House mentioned above. It's open daily May-Oct. 9 a.m.-9 p.m., until 5 p.m. the rest of the year.

The post office, tel. (920) 794-7014, is at 1516 8th Street. The Lyster Public Library is at 1001 Adams St., tel. (920) 793-8888. For urgent care, try the **Two Rivers Clinic,** 2219 Garfield St., tel. (920) 793-2281.

MISHICOT

On the way to Green Bay, take a trip to small Mishicot. The **Old Rock Mill,** tel. (920) 863-2812, on CR R, dates from 1848 and has a functioning water wheel. The waterfalls are gorgeous. Tours and slide shows are given hourly Tues.-Sat. 10 a.m.-4 p.m. and Sunday 1-4 p.m. in summer.

In town, **The Old School,** 315 Elizabeth St., tel. (920) 755-2291, features a collection of shops in a 1905 schoolhouse. Of note is the Rockwell Center, perhaps the largest private (non-museum) collection of Norman Rockwell works. **River Edge,** 432 Main St., tel. (920) 755-4777, is an excellent two-story art gallery and antique store in a building once used for meat processing. It's open daily May-Oct., weekends only off-season.

It wouldn't be a small town without a local historical museum. The **Mishicot Historical Museum,** corner of Rockway and Randolph Streets, tel. (920) 755-2076, is another restored schoolhouse (this one was later used as a town hall). It's got the usual historical collections and is open weekends 1-4 p.m. during summer.

Mishicot's **Fox Hills Resort and Country Club,** 250 W. Church St., tel. (920) 755-2376 or (800) 955-7615, is a full-service resort with an enormous golf resort (45 holes) and hundreds of hotel rooms, condo suites, and multi-bedroom villas. Some decent package deals with car ferry service are available. Rates begin at $60.

West of town eight miles along WI 147 is the **Cedar Ridge,** tel. (920) 863-8691, an exceedingly friendly family-style eatery serving three squares a day, with good specials including grand buffets. German delights such as pork hocks, spareribs, and dumplings with sauerkraut are also offered. From $2. Featured are the trout boils held the first and third Friday of each month May-October. This unique place even has a mini-farm and groomed hiking trails.

DENMARK

Also a hop off the interstate on the way to Green Bay is the Danish enclave of Denmark, known heretofore as Copenhagen. There's lots of old Danish architecture downtown, and more cheese shops per capita than anywhere else. Get Danish fare at **Lorrie's Home Town Cafe** and Danish everything at the **Dansk Hus B&B,** 223 Elm St., tel. (920) 863-3138.

GREEN BAY

The vast stretch of Wisconsin from the cusp of Lake Michigan's Green Bay to Oshkosh and along the Fox River beyond represents the state's original *raison d'etre*—exploration, settlement, and economics.

La Baye

Early French *voyageurs* and itinerant trappers christened the sanctuary of the Green Bay's waters La Baye (only later did it become La Baye Verte). It served as a haven from the volatility of Lake Michigan and was a natural doorway to the wilds of the northwestern region. Yet it took until 1669 for New France to establish an official settlement at the mouth of the bay (near the present-day suburb of De Pere). Under the auspices of Jesuit Father Claude Allouez, it was the first permanent settlement in what would be Wisconsin, though trappers had been hanging around at an unofficial trading post here since 1655.

The bay region quickly proved its worth as a gateway to the entire Fox River Valley, which led explorers and trappers to immense numbers of beaver and, more important, to new networks of inland waterways. Not to mention trees. By 1684, the legendary Nicolas Perrot was made commandant of the region; under his command the wilderness produced more than any other region in New France.

After a century of changing hands, the bay was the transportation conduit—for both commerce and immigration—to the rest of Wisconsin and, via the Mississippi, the country.

The City

Forts erected by the French, mostly during periods of Native American unrest, gave permanence to east-central Wisconsin's most populous community, Green Bay (pop. 96,500). Settlers, including Augustin de Langlade (considered by many the father of Green Bay, and indisputably one of the early monopolizers of Native business), began inhabiting the Fox River mouth around the turn of the 18th century. Maintaining peace with the Native Americans, the French prospered in the region until they were forced to surrender La Baye to the British following the French and Indian Wars. The British promptly renamed it Fort Howard. It was Yankee settlers who finally anglicized the original French name to Green Bay.

The fur trade made up the bedrock of the city's fortunes early on, but Green Bay began growing in earnest upon completion of the Erie Canal in 1825, when the state's first European immigrants, buoyed by news of cheap fertile lands in the Northwest Territory, descended en masse into Wisconsin, most via Green Bay. Many put down roots immediately, working in Green Bay's burgeoning agricultural, logging, and iron smelting industries. Before the city was even a thought, the paper industry had solidified its future. The city's lumber industry quickly surpassed the beaver trade. Until the turn of the century, growth continued as the transportation, lumber, paper, and manufacturing sectors drew boatload after boatload of eager European workers.

Despite recent subtle gentrification, the city will never forget its blue-collar roots. The downtown area is well kept and the tourist spots are spruced up, but enormous amounts of ship and railroad transportation still muscle through, and tight working-class bungalows still line street after street.

But remember: history and economics notwithstanding, Green Bay translates culturally as "football." If there is one dominant cultural ethos underpinning the city, it is the beloved Green Bay Packers. The *The Sporting News*—among many, many other national media—has rated the entire city the number-one sports fans in the National Football League, literally in a league of their own. Need more proof? The waiting list for season tickets is longer than a phone book in a midsize city; at present if you apply now, you'll get tickets in about 200 years. This is a city where 60,000 people pay to watch a *practice.*

Orientation

Cupping the lower tip of Green Bay and bisected by the Fox River, the city and its streets can sometimes be a confusing jumble. In addition, the town lies at the junction of several major highways, which run every which way in and around the city. Worst of all, every map published by the city is good but no bullseye. Two tips: (1) always keep in mind which side of the river you're on, and (2) when in doubt, head for Lake Michigan and start over.

SIGHTS

The Pack

One of the oldest professional football teams in the United States—and the only community-owned team in professional sports—the Green Bay Packers are *it* in this town; check out the glazed-eyed, slobbering Packer fans from around the globe jumping in glee in Lambeau Field's parking lot.

Tourists and locals often crowd the free, twice-a-day practices (usually 8:15 a.m. and 2:30 p.m.-ish) during the Packers' late-summer **training camp,** held at the practice facility along Oneida Street across from Lambeau Field. Sometimes practices are held indoors in the team's state-of-the-art Hutson Practice Facility (named for early Packer great, wide receiver Don Hutson). Practices begin in mid-July and run until preseason games begin in late August. There are usually morning practices and less strenuous post-lunch

© AVALON TRAVEL PUBLISHING, INC.

workouts. Call (888) TO-SEE-GB for up-to-the-minute practice schedules. Times vary.

A totally cool day would be to watch some of the practice sessions (those standing along the fence line to watch are known as "railbirds," and it's a tradition for Packer players to ride local kids' bikes to and from the playing field), then take a tour of Lambeau Field and check out the Hall of Fame. Then head next door to the Packer Experience, a two-football-field-sized opportunity to relive your glory days. You can toss footballs, run the 40-yard dash, snap, kick, even wear Brett Favre's shoes. Outside you can shag punts and run the obstacle course like a real pro. You'll be sore the next day, guaranteed, but enjoy! The Experience only runs concurrent with training camp. If you're really lucky, you can also catch a glimpse of initial mini-camps, which open as early as April. For information, call (920) 496-5700.

While there, you *can't* miss the **Lambeau Field** tour, 855 Lombardi Ave., tel. (920) 499-4281 or (920) 442-7225. Visitors explore virtually every corner of this local landmark (except—sadly—the Packers' locker room), including the pressbox, the visitors' locker room, the skyboxes, and even the field itself. Hour-and-a-half tours aboard funky green-and-gold John Deere tractor-trains and are given daily June through Labor Day 10:30 a.m.-4:30 p.m. and start from the Packer Hall of Fame, across the street. Cost is $7.50 adults, $5 children.

The number-one Packer destination is the **Green Bay Packer Hall of Fame,** 855 Lombardi Ave., tel. (920) 499-4281, across from Lambeau Field. The Green Bay Packers are the only professional team to have its own hall of fame; 700,000 people visit the Pro Football Hall of Fame every year, but 760,000 visit the Pack. The museum has displays from the early days of pro football and the numerous world championships won by Green Bay. Besides the Lombardi Trophy display—named, of course, for legendary Packers coach Vince Lombardi—play-by-play highlights run on video screens everywhere, with Packer backers sit-

Vincent T. Lombardi

ting rapt in absolute ecstasy watching Bart Starr's one-yard plunge in the 1967 Ice Bowl again and again and again. The Hall of Fame also features fantastic (very extensive) memorabilia collections and a downstairs multi-screen video history of the team. Children particularly love the passing and field-goal kicking room, if they can push the hyperactive adults out of the way, of course. The museum is open year-round, 10 a.m.-5 p.m. Sept.-May, 9 a.m.-6 p.m. June-August. Admission is $7.50 adults, $6 children. The gift shop overflows with wares.

See "Organized Tours" below for more Packer options.

Museums

One of the most impressive local museums is the staggering **National Railroad Museum,** 2285 S. Broadway Ave., tel. (920) 437-7623. With over 80 railroad cars and locomotives, this respected collection is one of the originals of its kind in the nation. Stored on the grounds and available for close-up inspection are Big Boy (the world's largest steam locomotive), the Bayonet train Dwight Eisenhower rode throughout the European campaign of WW II, the experimental 1950s Rock Island "Aerotrain," and dozens of others, including steam locomotives and narrow-gauge railroads. There's also a multimedia presentation, shown five times a day, which provides an overview of railroading in the U.S.; a diorama collection in a reception center; and a great room devoted to the local HO model railroaders club. Of course, train rides are also available, five times daily in summer. Included in the admission is a mile-long jaunt on a narrow-gauge railroad. Guided tours depart at 10:30 a.m. and 1:30 p.m. in summer. Open daily 9 a.m.-5 p.m., Mon.-Sat. only Oct.-April. Admission is $6 adults, $4 youth, $18 family, and rates drop by half in winter.

Equally popular is the most unique state park in Wisconsin—**Heritage Hill Living History Museum** 2640 S. Webster Ave., tel. (920) 448-5150 or (800) 721-5150. More than 25 historic buildings from around Wisconsin have been reconstructed at this 50-acre site. Separated into four distinct thematic areas—Pioneers, Military Life, Small Towns, and Agricultural—the buildings include mock-ups of flimsy original sapling-and-bark dwellings of the Jesuits and some of the oldest extant buildings in Wisconsin. All areas are accessible via wagons. Period-dressed guides, located in most of the buildings, give educational spiels while spinning wool, carving, cobbling, etc. A recent addition is a relocated cheese factory dating from the 19th century. Lots of special events take place. The museum is open daily Memorial Day weekend to Labor Day 10 a.m.-4:30 p.m., from noon on Sunday; through the end of September it's open weekends only. Admission is $6 adults, $4 children.

The spacious **Neville Public Museum,** 210 Museum Place, tel. (920) 448-4460, contains art, history, and science exhibits. Traveling art exhibits are on the ground floor. The second floor is a respectable grouping of five galleries covering local history, natural sciences, paleontology, technology, local art, and the outstanding main hall exhibit "On the Edge of the Inland Sea," a 7,500-square-foot diorama of a retreating glacier. The view of the city skyline is impressive from here. It's open year-round Tuesday and Thurs.-Sat. 9 a.m.-4 p.m., Wednesday 9 a.m.-9 p.m., and Sunday noon-4 p.m. Suggested donation for admission is $3 adults, $2 children.

The **Children's Museum of Green Bay,** in the Port Plaza Mall, 320 N. Adams St., tel. (920) 432-4397, features hands-on displays on Green Bay's cultural and economic history, cross-cultural exhibits, and new environmental displays. Kids love the 911 fire interactive exhibit; there's even an exhibit for toddlers and infants. The museum is open Saturday 10 a.m.-5 p.m. and Sunday 11 a.m.-5 p.m.

Hazelwood Historic Home

Located in the historic Astor district, at 1008 S. Monroe Ave., tel. (920) 437-0360, one of northern Wisconsin's oldest buildings is quite a piece of work. This resplendent 1837 Greek revival structure was the original home of the president of Wisconsin's second Constitutional Congress, Morgan L. Martin, who got his start in the area as an Indian agent. It contains original Duncan Phyfe and Sheraton furnishings, along with the table where the state constitution was composed. Tours depart Monday and Wed.-Fri. 10 a.m.-2 p.m., Sat.-Sun. 1-4 p.m. June-Aug., weekends only in May; admission is $3 adults, $2 children.

Bay Beach Amusement Park

One of my favorites in Green Bay is the anachronistic gathering of 12 rides—a couple for adults—along the bay shoreline at the Bay Beach Amusement Park, 1313 Bay Beach Rd., tel. (920) 391-3671. There are concession stands, a fast-food restaurant, and picnic areas. The best part: rides cost as little as *10 cents.* The park is open daily Memorial Day through late August 10 a.m.-9 p.m., then until 6 p.m. through the first week of September, and 10 a.m.-6 p.m. weekends most of the rest of September and from mid-April to late May. Park admission is free.

Green Bay Botanical Garden

Just north of the Northeast Wisconsin Technical College is this 60-acre site of undulating hills and gurgling streams. You'll find four-season gardens, a nice rose garden, an American perennial garden, and an imaginative children's garden. A visitor center has more exhibits. Hours are May-Oct. Tues.-Sun. 10 a.m.-6 p.m.; free admission. It's located at 2600 Larsen Rd., tel. (920) 490-9457.

Wildlife Sanctuary

Up the road from the amusement park is the excellent Wildlife Sanctuary, 1660 E. Shore Dr., tel. (920) 391-3671, a 700-acre spread with exhibits on Wisconsin fauna, including the new and very popular timber wolf house, about 1,000 geese, and a nature center. There are seven miles of nature trails doubling as cross-country ski trails, and tours are available. It's free, and open September 15 through April 14, 8 a.m.-5 p.m., then April 15 through September 14, 8 a.m.-8 p.m.

NEW Zoo

The well-regarded **NEW Zoo,** 4378 Reforestation Rd. (Hwy. IR), tel. (920) 448-4466, eight miles north of Green Bay, is one of the better ones. Constant expansion has allowed the animals greater freedom to roam. Animal compounds include Prairie Grassland, Wisconsin native, and International—you're as likely to see a Galápagos tortoise as you are a Wisconsin red fox. The zoo has tripled in size in recent years and added many new exhibits, including a black-footed penguin zone. A children's area allows interactive experiences. The zoo is open 9 a.m.-6 p.m. April 1 through October 31 and 9 a.m.-4 p.m. November 1 through March 31. Admission is free.

L.H. Barkhausen Waterfowl Preserve
Green Bay has yet another sanctuary for animals: the Barkhausen Waterfowl Preserve, 2024 Lakeview Dr., Suamico, tel. (920) 448-4466. These 925 acres along the western edge of the bay contain nature trails, interactive displays on local endangered fauna, and nine miles of hiking and skiing trails. The trails are open daily 8 a.m.-sunset, the interpretive center Mon.-Fri. 9 a.m.-4 p.m. and Sat.-Sun. noon-4 p.m. Admission is free.

Side Trip
West of Ashwaubenon is zany **Seymour,** which bills itself as the "Home of the Hamburger," purportedly invented here. The townsfolk fete their title with the annual **Hamburger Festival,** the first Saturday in August. You can head straight for the **Hamburger Hall of Fame,** 126 N. Main St., tel. (920) 833-9522, for an astonishing variety of burger-focused displays. The Hall of Fame is open summers daily 10 a.m.-4 p.m., and is, believe it or not, one of the top tour-bus destinations in the country.

ACCOMMODATIONS

A caveat: Don't even think of showing up in Green Bay on a weekend when the Packers are playing at home with any hope of getting budget lodging. (In fact, many places raise rates over Packer weekends.)

Downtown
Cheapest accommodations downtown are at the **Village Inn,** 119 N. Monroe, tel. (920) 437-0525. Rates run $34 s, $43 d.

The **Best Western Washington St. Inn** 321 S. Washington St., tel. (920) 437-8771, has a full list of amenities including pool, sauna, whirlpool, recreation, putting green and restaurants, for reasonable prices: $55 s, $60 d Friday and Saturday.

The **Days Inn Downtown,** 406 N. Washington St., tel. (920) 435-4484, overlooks the Fox River and offers rooms from $60 s, $65 d. There is a heated indoor pool and a restaurant and bar.

Upscale downtown digs are at the **Regency Suites,** 333 Main St., tel. (920) 432-4555. It's more or less a self-contained city, so everything you need is here, including a free breakfast in the morning. Rooms cost $110 and up.

South (Allouez)
Between De Pere and Green Bay proper is the suburb of Allouez, a good place to stay when visiting Heritage Hill State Park. The **Mariner Motel,** 2222 Riverside Dr., tel. (920) 437-7107, has rooms from $40 s, $44 d, health club privileges, and its own jogging path; the supper club here is recommended. The **Marriott Residence Inn,** 335 W. St. Joseph St., tel. (920) 435-2222, features a full line of offerings but significantly higher rates ($99) than the Mariner. Both offer free continental breakfasts.

Southwest: Airport and Stadium
The southwest section of Green Bay includes Oneida and Ashwaubenon and provides the easiest access to Lambeau Field and the airport.

The best hotel closest to the airport is the **Radisson Inn,** 2040 Airport Drive, tel. (920) 494-7300, with rooms from around $109 and a full range of services. Decidedly less expensive is the **Airport Settle Inn** 2620 S. Packerland Dr., tel. (920) 499-1900, not far from the Radisson. Rooms are in the $65 range, and the hotel has a pool, whirlpool, and continental breakfast. (Settle Inns tout themselves as the nation's first luxury budget motel, and the rooms certainly are worth the money, though I've seen some tacky decorating jobs in whirlpool suites.)

Otherwise, at the interchange of US 41 and WI 172, you'll find eight chain motels with similar prices and amenities. Farthest away from the airport but the busiest is the **Holiday Inn Airport Holidome,** 2580 S. Ashland Ave., tel. (920) 499-5121, east of the interchange along WI 172. Rates here are from $65, with the usual line of Holiday Inn services but no sauna.

Ramada Way off of US 41 south of the interchange contains a large motel ghetto. The **Ramada Inn,** tel. (920) 499-0631, offers the full line of services for high-season rates of $75 s, $85 d. All rooms feature free movies and cable TV; some have coffeemakers, microwaves, or refrigerators.

The area near Lambeau Field is another cluster of accommodations, though not as tightly grouped. North of the Airport Holidome is the **Sky-Lit Motel,** 2120 S. Ashland, tel. (920) 494-5641, which has rooms for $35 s, $50 d, and free cable. West of Lambeau Field along Lombardi Avenue are others. The cheapest—at $35 and up—is the **Arena Motel,** 871 Lombardi Ave., tel. (920) 494-5636.

Where Lombardi Avenue swings around to hook up with Military Avenue is the **Bay Motel,** 1301 S. Military Ave., tel. (920) 494-3441. Rooms run $36 s, $52 d, and all have free cable and movies; some have mini-refrigerators. The in-house cafe here is popular; the food is made from scratch and the place has its own bakery.

Northwest

The northwest of Green Bay includes the suburb of Howard. Right off US 41 is **Comfort Suites,** 1951 Bond St., tel. (920) 499-7449. Rooms go from $79, though I've gotten late-night mark-downs, and amenities include a restaurant, pool, whirlpool, sauna, gym, and free breakfast. South of Dousman Street, the **Valley Motel,** 116 N. Military Ave., tel. (920) 494-3455, offers inexpensive rooms in the $35 range, some with refrigerators or kitchenettes.

De Pere

De Pere has a couple of interesting lodging choices. The historic **Union Hotel,** 200 N. Broadway, tel. (920) 336-6131, has rooms from $40 and a cool ambience. A new boutique hotel overlooking the Fox River, the **James St. Inn,** 201 James St., tel. (920) 337-0111, is in a historic mill. Great views are afforded from a deck. There are also whirlpools. Rooms from $70.

Bed and Breakfasts

The **Astor House,** 637 South Monroe Ave., tel. (920) 432-3585, was Green Bay's original B&B. Built in the 1880s, the mansion has five rooms stocked to the hilt with amenities. Rates run from $79 to $129 with some specials available.

Camping

The camping nearest to Green Bay is toward Door County north on WI 57, 15 miles out of town. Here, the **Bay Shore County Park,** tel. (920) 448-4466, is open May 1-November 1. Tent sites run $11.

FOOD

Greasy Spoons and Diners

If you really want to rub elbows with the locals, check out the mostly Greek **Viand's,** in a strip mall along Military Ave., tel. (920) 497-9646. There are good early-bird specials; it's open Mon.-Sat. 5:30 a.m.-9 p.m. and Sunday 6 a.m.-8 p.m. Menu items from $3.

At Military Ave. and Ninth St. is the **Bay Family Restaurant,** tel. (920) 494-3441, one of the most popular eating establishments in Green Bay. The Bay uses ingredients direct from family farms and serves homemade pies and piles of hash browns the size of encyclopedias. From $3. It's open daily for breakfast, lunch, and dinner. There are two other locations: 1245 E. Mason St. and 1100 Radisson.

The **Walnut St. Cafe,** at the corner of Walnut and Monroe Streets, tel. (920) 432-8878, features an interesting "walnut scramble" and basic but dependable fare. Open daily for breakfast and lunch. From $2.

For great chili, around $3, the best place is **Chili John's,** 519 S. Military Ave., tel. (920) 494-4624; it might mean a bit of a wait, but it's worth it. From $3.

Kroll's, the best family restaurant in town, has two locations; the more convenient one is downtown at 1658 Main Street, tel. (920) 468-4422. It's open 10:30 a.m.-11 p.m. (until midnight weekends). The other is on S. Ridge Road, closer to Lambeau Field, tel. (920) 497-1111. This is the older of the two and appears to have come straight out of the movie *Diner.* Great walleye and perch supplement the usual selection of burgers and sandwiches. This Kroll's also features wall buzzers that customers can use to summon the wait staff.

The best pizza in town is at **Jake's,** 1149 Main St., tel. (920) 432-8012. You'll have to wait up to half an hour, but it, too, is well worth the time. From $4.

Supper Clubs

For exquisite rib-eye steak, **Ziggey's Inn,** 741 Hoffman Rd., tel. (920) 339-7820, can't be beat—and the rest of the menu is outstanding as well. Choices from $7.

River's Bend Supper Club, 792 Riverview

Dr., off US 41 at the Velp exit, tel. (920) 434-1384, has some of the best steaks in town. The restaurant also displays local artwork. If for no other reason, go for the gorgeous view of Duck Creek. Open daily for lunch and dinner. From $5.

A cheerful, popular place with an expansive menu is the **Rock Garden Supper Club,** 1951 Bond St., tel. (920) 497-4701. In addition to the copious steak entrées are pasta, veal, barbecue ribs, chicken, and duck dishes. Rock Garden is open daily for supper, weekdays for lunch and dinner, and Sunday for brunch. From $5.

Fish Fries

Any of the supper clubs above will have a popular fish fry; Kroll's, mentioned above, has great fish. A popular one is at **The Stein,** 126 S. Adams, tel. (920) 435-6071, which also has German food. Fish fries usually start at $6. If you're attending a cultural event at the Weidner Center at UWGB, consider **Willie Wood's Shorewood Inn,** 2607 Nicolet Dr., tel. (920) 468-1086, owned by an ex-Packer great.

Brewpubs

Green Bay's got a couple of lively brewpubs. Right downtown at the west end of the Fox River Bridge along WI 29 is **Titletown Brewing Co.,** 200 Dousman St., tel. (920) 437-2337, with an above-average menu of quite creative fare. From $8.

Ethnic

Italian restaurants are the dominant ethnic specialty in Green Bay. One of the best is **Victoria's,** 2610 Bay Settlement Rd., tel. (920) 468-8070. The food is scrumptious and the portions outrageously huge. From $5.

The **Dragonwyck,** 1992 Gross Ave., tel. (920) 498-9801, is just a block behind the CVB and has a full range of Chinese (across the regional spectrum) and is open daily for lunch and dinner. From $5. **Khan's Mongolian Barbeque,** 2245 University Ave., tel. (920) 468-9500, has the best Mongolian barbecue in town.

Cafe Expresso, 119 S. Washington St., tel. (920) 432-9733, is multi-ethnic, mostly Greek but also lots of Mexican and Italian. This is the hip place to hang out; trendsetters, would-be poets, and misunderstood geniuses can be seen quaffing excellent coffee and downing the copious gyros. From $3. Open daily (until midnight!) for

dinner and weekdays for lunch as well.

Fine Dining

The Wellington, 1060 Hansen Road, tel. (920) 499-2000, is a Green Bay institution of sorts. An exclusive lunch and dinner spot done up as an English drawing room, it specializes in beef Wellington (no surprise) and excellent duck, steer tenderloin, and seafood dishes. The Wellington is open weekdays for lunch and dinner, Saturday for dinner only, closed Sunday. From $6 at lunch, $16 at dinner.

Eve's Supper Club, 2020 Riverside Dr., tel. (920) 435-1571, has the grandest view of any dining establishment, perched atop the 2020 Riverside office building overlooking the Fox River, almost directly across from the railroad museum. It specializes (for some 30 years now) in superb steaks and seafood, though you most certainly pay for your view. Open weekdays for lunch and dinner, weekends for dinner. From $6.

East of downtown is the new, well-regarded **Bistro John Paul,** 1244 Main St., tel. (920) 432-2897, known for its country French cuisine. Open for dinner. From $16.

De Pere

The Union Hotel, 200 N. Broadway, tel. (920) 336-6131, has been run by the same family for 75 years, and though rooms are used by boarders now, it remains *the* fine-dining place in the area, with sumptuous food served in a turn-of-the-20th-century atmosphere.

Giving it a serious run for its money is the luscious creative fare at the new **Black and Tan Grille,** 101 Howard Ave., tel. (920) 336-4430, with outstanding creations from a well-known local chef. From $13.

Cafe Olé, 365 Main Ave., tel. (920) 336-3087, features excellent gourmet Mexican; try the seafood. It's open weekdays for lunch and daily for dinner. Right next door, **The Alamo** has hedonistic portions of barbecue ribs and good steaks.

ENTERTAINMENT

For local entertainment listings, check the schedules in either the free weekly *Bay Beat,* stocked in several places around town, or the Thursday *Green Bay Press-Gazette,* which has a rundown in its "More" section. Unfortunately, neither is particularly detailed.

Another freebie floating about the Fox River Valley, the monthly *The Valley Scene,* includes Green Bay but offers more coverage of the Fox Cities area of Appleton and Oshkosh.

The Arts
On the University of Wisconsin-Green Bay campus, the smashingly modern **Weidner Center for the Performing Arts,** tel. (920) 465-2217, showcases national and regional musicians, plays, musicals, dance performances, and the annual Green Bay jazz fest. The **City Center Theater,** 217 E. Walnut St., also brings in national acts. The city boasts its own symphony orchestra and two community theater groups. In De Pere, **St. Norbert College,** tel. (920) 337-3181, also offers concerts and theater throughout the year.

Sports Bars
Without question, thanks in no small part to the Packers' presence, Green Bay's specialty is the sports bar-cum-restaurant. One of the most popular is **Gipper's,** 1860 University Ave. (east of Henry St.), tel. (920) 435-1515, with an impressive display of sports memorabilia.

Coaches Corner, 501 N. Adams St., tel. (920) 435-9599, across from the Holiday Inn City Centre, is an enormous place with the usual multitudinous TVs throughout. Don't leave without trying the legendary beer-cheese soup, served in a homemade bread bowl.

The area surrounding Lambeau Field, not surprisingly, is home to a handful of boisterous sports bars. The most popular is **Stadium View,** 1963 Gross St., tel. (920) 498-1989, right down the street from the visitor's office and the Packer Hall of Fame.

Glory Years Pub, 321 S. Washington St., is in the Best Western Washington St. Inn. This sports pub, rife with Packer fans, was once the Packers' corporate office and ticket office. Check out the memorabilia worshiping Vincent T. Lombardi.

Live Music
A great dive for music is **Heroes,** 401 S. Washington, tel. (920) 435-5587, which has lots of roots rock, rock, and especially blues bands on weekends. It's cramped and smoky, and there are odd, larger-than-life murals of comic-book heroes on the walls, but the music is usually good and there's often no cover charge. Otherwise, the most varied music scheduling comes from **Gallagher's on Broadway,** 163 Pearl St., tel. (920) 435-4992, and **The Bar,** 2001 Holmgren Way, tel. (920) 499-9989.

Jazz can be heard most consistently at **Purcell's,** in the Radisson Inn. It consistently gets great entertainment—good jazz to the odd rockabilly band or two. In De Pere, **A's Dockside,** 112 N. Broadway, tel. (920) 336-2277, offers a slew of folk, reggae, and jazz throughout the week, as well as open-mic nights.

EVENTS

May/June
Green Bay's hootenanny, **Bayfest,** takes place at the UW-Green Bay campus at the beginning of June. The festival includes five musical stages (jazz, rock, blues, country, and reggae bands play nonstop), some 25 international cuisine tents,

powwow at Oneida Indian Reservation

HYEON LEE

*the Pilgrimage:
arrival at Mecca,
a.k.a. Lambeau Field*

games, a carnival, and a huge fireworks display.

At the end of June, the **Rail Fest,** at the National Railroad Museum, features exhibit tours of the capacious grounds, a railway post office demonstration, and assorted uniqueness such as a hobo encampment.

July

Immediately prior to the Fourth of July, Lambeau Field hosts the **Shopko Fireworks.** Another large fireworks display takes place over the Independence Day holiday at the **Celebrate Americafest** in downtown Green Bay.

The **Oneida Pow Wow and Festival of Performing Arts,** held at the Norbert Hill Center in Oneida just west of Green Bay, includes a traditional powwow and dancing competition, along with Native American foods, athletic events, and contests.

August/September

Since Green Bay is synonymous with football, the highly anticipated NFL season is kicked off each year at the **Great Green Bay Kickoff,** held at the Brown County Expo Center usually in late August or early September. Featured are lots of food, Packer appearances, and general delirious revelry.

SPORTS AND RECREATION

Football

It's virtually impossible to get tickets to regular-

season Packers games, especially if the Pack's success continues; preseason games are another matter. Call (920) 496-5700 for ticket information. (See "The Pack" under "Sights," above, for more information on tours and team activities.)

Hockey

The minor-league Green Bay Gamblers, a newer addition to the city, are becoming wildly popular and have already won two USHL crowns, 1901 S. Oneida St., tel. (920) 494-3401. There are 20 home games stretching from late October or early November into mid-March; all games start at 7:30 p.m.

University of Wisconsin-Green Bay

The Phoenix are relative newcomers to big-time college athletics. Not long ago moved up to Division I, the teams do well in national competition. The men's basketball team is a perennial giant-killer; its games may sell out, depending on the opponent. For ticket information for all teams, call the area's events line at (920) 437-3955, then dial 2931. Or contact the local ticket distributor **TicketStar** at (920) 494-3401.

SERVICES AND INFORMATION

The main **post office** downtown is at 118 N. Monroe Ave., tel. (920) 498-3912, and is open regular business hours and somtimes for limited

TITLETOWN

It is ever the same: Sunday morning, 11:59 a.m. The network feed fades to black. Then, as always, a still shot of Him. And, slowly, with the melodrama of sports announcers, the voice-over: "The Man. Vincent T. Lombardi." Or, even more powerfully, "Titletown . . . " It incites goosebumps, followed by the shakes of unvanquishable dumbbell belief.

The Religion

If there are any awards for professional sports fandom, the Pack and its beloved legions sweep—hands down. One grizzled sportswriter wrote, "The Dallas Cowboys were only another football team; the Packers were a practicing religion." If he only knew the ambivalence, the bittersweet . . . well, *curse* of being born a Packerbacker. (This author was unlucky enough to be born on the demise of the last Packer empire, following Super Bowl II, back in 1968, and don't think his family hasn't reminded him of the lethal coincidence.)

Every sport has its knucklehead legions. But nobody—*nobody*—equals the Packers for their absolutely astonishing, mystical grip on their faithful. The Green Bay Packers are the only passively proselytizing franchise in all of professional sports. Hardcore travelers and football aficionados will find Packer bars and Packer fan clubs in every state in the union—as far away as jolly old England. I've even found scads of Packer faithful bellowing for Sunday satellite-dish equity as far away as Taiwan and Thailand. A Packer publicist from the Lombardi years, getting away from football in the off-season (he thought), on fishing islands off the coast of Italy, was approached in a diminutive, foggy village by a grizzled old fisherman who had noticed the small "G" on the publicist's golf shirt. The fisherman stopped him and asked in great animation, "How's Bart Starr's arm?"

Early Years

The Packers were founded in 1919 as one of the handful of teams that would eventually make up the National Football League. The team was born in the back room of the *Green Bay Press-Gazette,* where the cigar-chomping sports editor, George Calhoun, and legendary ex-Notre Damer Curly Lambeau agreed to found a local team. They convinced a local industry bigwig to supply a practice field and uniforms, thus obligating the team to call itself the Indian Packing Co. Footballers. This was later shortened to you-know-what. Almost immediately, the team was a hit. Going 10-1 its first season, the dynasty had begun.

After literally passing the hat in the crowd for the first season, the Packers, in need of financial stability, hit upon one of the most unique money angles in sports. The community issued $5 non-dividend public shares in the team; almost beyond logic, the citizens scooped up the stocks.

The *only* nonprofit, community-owned team in professional sports, the Green Bay Packers have become a true anomaly: a small-market team with few fiscal constraints on finding and wooing talent. And they can never desert the town—if they try to move, the organization is dissolved and all money goes for a Veterans of Foreign Wars memorial.

Titletown

After The Packers whomped their opponents in the first season, they became the first NFL team to win three consecutive NFL titles, and they did it twice—1929-31 and 1965-67. In all, they won 11 championships through 1968 and the Lombardi years. In fact, though the Lombardi-led teams get all the glory, the teams of the early years were even more dominant, amassing a 34-5-2 record.

Then the well went dry. Before major front-office changes in the early 1990s brought in more forceful management, the Packers suffered through their longest drought ever between NFC Central Division Championships: 24 years. Twenty-four long, unbearable, embarrassing years. Still, the fans dutifully packed the stadium every Sunday. They always believed.

And now the Pack is back. January 26, 1997, is now a de facto state holiday in Wisconsin—the day the Pack beat the New England Patriots 35-21 for their third Super Bowl title and their 12th NFL championship. Words cannot do justice to the state of Wisconsin on that day. Half the state whooped in apoplectic glee, the other half succumbed to a mixture of crying and sedate disbelief.

hours Saturday, but call ahead.

The **Green Bay Area Convention and Visitors Bureau,** P.O. Box 10596, Green Bay, WI, 54307, tel. (920) 494-9507 or (888) TO-SEE-GB, www.greenbay.org, is at 1901 S. Oneida St., across the street from Lambeau Field in the Brown County Expo Center. It's open Mon.-Fri. 10 a.m.-5 p.m. You can also tune your radio to 530 AM for local events information.

The *Green Bay Press-Gazette* is Wisconsin's oldest newspaper, started in 1833 as the *Green Bay Intelligencer.* It is a bit denser than the *Green Bay News Chronicle,* though both offer adequate local information.

The main public **library** branch, tel. (920) 448-4400, is located at 515 Pine Street. The local **Kinko's,** 2279 S. Oneida St., tel. (920) 496-2679, has Internet access for $12/hour or 20 cents per minute.

Green Bay has two InstaCare clinics for **urgent care.** Centrally located is the branch at 211 N. Broadway Ave., tel. (920) 497-5711, but it's only open weekdays. Open daily at 7 a.m. is the branch to the west at 1727 Shawano Ave. (same telephone).

GETTING THERE AND AWAY

By Air
Austin Straubel International Airport, tel. (920) 498-4800, located in southwest Green Bay off WI 172, is served by **American Eagle,** tel. (920) 498-4803; **Comair,** tel (800) 354-9822, **Northwest,** tel. (920) 498-5011; **Skyway/Midwest Express,** tel. (920) 498-5024; and **United Express,** tel. (920) 498-4840.

By Bus
The **bus depot,** 800 Cedar St., just east of the corner of Main and Webster Ave., tel. (920) 432-4883, is served by Greyhound to most points in southern Wisconsin; there are two other regional lines, which are fairly reliable for travel throughout northern Wisconsin and Michigan's Upper Peninsula.

GETTING AROUND

Taxi
For taxi service, try **Ace-Yellow Cab,** tel. (920) 468-1585; **Bay City Cab,** tel. (920) 432-3546; or **Green Bay Taxi Service,** tel. (920) 469-9774.

Organized Tours
The *Foxy Lady,* tel. (920)432-3699, docked behind the Holiday Inn City Centre, offers sightseeing, lunch, cocktail, sunset, dinner, and moonlight cruises Wed.-Sun. mid-April through mid-October. Rates start at $11 for a narrated cruise and go up to $28 for a sunset dinner. Reservations are required for all but the sightseeing cruise.

A do-it-yourself tour is to hop aboard the *Titletown Trolley* that departs from the Packer Hall of Fame daily during training camp (usually 10 and 11:30 a.m. and 1 p.m.) and rolls past several attractions, with narrated highlights the whole way. This "Legends of Lombardi Ave." one-hour tour costs a mere $7.50, free to children 5 and under.

ONEIDA NATION

West of Green Bay are the 12 square miles making up the **Oneida Indian Reservation.** Known as the "People of the Standing Stone," the Oneida were members of the League of the Iroquois and once a protectorate of the Stockbridge-Munsee bands on the east coast. They moved westward en masse (save for a small band still in New York) not long after the turn of the 18th century.

One of the only repositories of the history of the Oneida is the **Oneida Nation Museum,** W892 EE Rd., tel. (920) 869-2768. Exhibits in the main hall focus on Oneida history and culture; outside is a longhouse and stockade as well as a nice nature trail. The museum is open Tues.-Fri. 9 a.m.-5 p.m. and Sat.-Sun. 10 a.m.-5 p.m., but closed every second and fourth Sunday. Admission is $2 adults, $1 children. The Oneida **powwow** takes place on or near the Fourth of July.

APPLETON

Known as the Queen of the Fox Cities and the Princess of Paper Valley, Appleton (pop. 65,695) dominates the Fox Cities region. Bisected by the Fox River, this spread-out city is still supported predominantly by paper processing. Yet it hardly seems industrial when you're traipsing about the gentrified downtown area of shopping, dining, and entertainment. A major goal of the ambitious downtown development project is to turn Appleton into a city that never sleeps. Time will tell.

The central city is influenced by the presence of well-respected Lawrence University, a small liberal-arts college founded by the Episcopal Church and the state's first co-ed institution of higher education. Seventy years ago, Lawrence initiated the first post-graduate papermaking institute; today, many of its departments are nationally recognized, especially the music department and conservatory.

Appleton's most famous sons are magician Harry Houdini and Senator Joseph McCarthy—whom many Appleton residents will tell you was-

n't from here, just came here. Houdini (who, as it happens, came from Hungary) is immortalized with a plaza and a bust, while McCarthy has been relegated to a minor statue by the courthouse.

Like other communities of east and central Wisconsin, Appleton grew up around a mill. But unlike other Fox Valley communities, paper did not dominate initially. Agricultural interests in the region found wheat production more profitable than floating log rafts from the north. Not until after the Civil War did local industrialists turn their attention to Wisconsin's ready-made paper wealth. The Fox-Wisconsin River corridor facilitated the mammoth timber traffic and brought the Fox River Valley to national prominence in papermaking. It is still so—the region is known alternatively as Paper Valley.

Hydroelectricity

The Fox River drops 200 surly, not always cooperative feet along the length of the valley; within Appleton's city limits, the old Fox drops al-

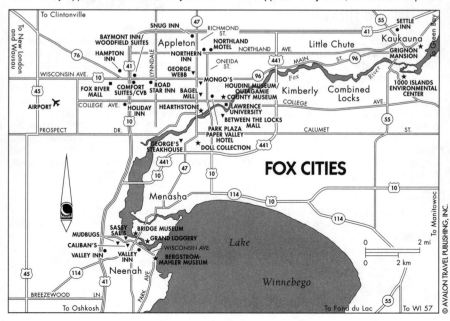

most 40 feet, much of it in angry rapids. In 1886, enterprising businessmen established one of the first streetcar lines in the U.S., certainly the first powered mostly by hydroelectricity. The Hearthstone, the city's major architectural draw, was the first home to be lit by a self-contained hydroelectric plant.

The Fox Cities and Fox Valley

Between Neenah and Kaukauna along Lake Winnebago's northwestern cap lie a dozen concatenate communities making up the Fox Cities region—a region part of but distinct from the Fox River Valley, which itself stretches along the Fox River/Lake Winnebago corridor and takes in all communities between Green Bay and Oshkosh. Appleton is the region's economic anchor; the smallest town is Combined Locks. All take their inspiration from the Old Man Riverway of Wisconsin, the Fox River—one of the few rivers in North America to flow north. Together, the Fox Cities constitute the third-largest metropolitan area in the state (pop. 180,000), a statistic even most Wisconsinites find surprising.

Harry Houdini

SIGHTS

Appleton is the proposed new home for a new **Papermaking Industry Hall of Fame** which is currently in the Octagon House in Neenah.

Orientation

College and Wisconsin Avenues are the main east-west arteries; Oneida Street splits them into east-west.

Houdini Historical Center/ Outagamie County Historical Museum

Born Ehrich Weiss in Hungary in 1874, the enigmatic Houdini spent most of his life in Appleton until running away from home for the big city. The Houdini Historical Center, 330 E. College Ave., tel. (920) 735-8445, is maintained as part of the Outagamie County Historical Society. The center's pride and joy is the Sidney H. Radner Collection of Houdini Memorabilia, the foremost such collection in the world. (Prior to Radner, Houdini's own brother maintained it for 40 years.) Amazingly comprehensive, the exhibits range from rare and private photos to publicity flyers to the original leg irons and locks Houdini used in his show. Rarest are the Guiteau handcuffs which bound President Garfield's assassin and from which the magician later escaped. The center has its own multimedia showcase on Houdini's life, as well as a detailed walking tour of the city (marked with brass plaques) taking in the sites of his childhood. There are also lots of magic shows and plenty of Houdini merchandise.

The Outagamie County Museum, 330 E. College Ave., tel. (920) 735-9370, on the same corner of the block, contains an excellent and award-winning exhibit ("Tools of Change") on the workers and economic history of the Lower Fox region, composed of minirooms-a turn-of-the-century wire-weaving loom and a Roaring '20s newsroom. The museum is open Tues.-Sat. 10 a.m.-5 p.m., Sunday noon-5 p.m. Admission is $4, $2 ages 5-17, and includes the Houdini Historical Center.

Hearthstone

This massive 1882 Victorian looks like another imposing Paper Valley *grande dame* mansion from the outside, but it's the insides that count. In 1882, this Queen Anne-style dwelling became the world's first home to be powered by a central hydroelectric plant. The rich original appointments have been preserved, from the Minton-Hollins hearth tiles (the owners were rabid fans of the Aesthetic Movement, of which Sherman Minton was a pioneer) to period electroliers and light switches designed by Thomas Edison. New hands-on displays—namely the Hydro Adventure Center—teach visitors about electricity and allow you to operate the controls of a power plant. Along with the education center came the inevitable gift shop. The house is at 625 W. Prospect Ave., tel. (920) 730-8204. It's open Tuesday, Thursday, Fri-

TAIL GUNNER JOE

I have in my hands a list of 205 names that were made known to the Secretary of State as being members of the Communist Party and who nevertheless are still working and shaping policy in the State Department.

The words remain a mystery. The effects, however, remain palpable. Uttered by Sen. Joseph McCarthy in Wheeling, West Virginia, these words—in what became known as the 205 Speech—thrust him into the national political spotlight for a torturous half decade. Before he shot himself in the foot politically, he dominated U.S. politics, electrified the nation, aided Tricky Dick, and inspired a new word. Wisconsinites still wonder how they feel about one of their most (in)famous native sons.

Tail Gunner Joe

McCarthy was born in 1908 near Appleton in the Fox River Valley. Little is known of his early childhood, other than it was typically hardscrabble. Shy and awkward, he never fit in and eventually left school. Either latent skill or over-compensatory zeal kicked in later in life; while managing a grocery store full time, he completed high-school coursework in less than one year. It was a pattern he followed the rest of his life—dogged sweat transcended acumen or detail. No longer shy, he now favored in-your-face braggadocio.

He graduated from Marquette Law School in 1935 and set up a law practice in Shawano (later Waupaca), and astonished everyone by winning a judgeship in 1938 through sheer grassroots toil—living on the road and pressing the flesh throughout the voting district.

He was not a widely respected judge and came under fire for controversial bench rewrites. He further infuriated opponents by stumping for higher office from the South Pacific, while in World War II. Upon arriving home, he licked his chops and dug in. The press was already his; he had the limelight. Somewhat overstating his military career, Tail Gunner Joe was born.

The Junior Senator

Upon return from WW II, McCarthy went head to head with a La Follette—Robert, Jr.—and stunned the state by defeating the waning Progressive Party family-name candidate in the Republican primary. He then unleashed a blitzkrieg whistle-stop tour. He was swept up in the GOP wave of 1946 and made it to Washington. Typical of his style, he immediately called a press conference to air opinions about national strike leaders. The press gallery later voted him Worst Senator.

Politically, McCarthy started as a Democrat—and history reveals him as being all over the board. He incessantly angered the Senate with his intractable attitude, personal attacks, and rules violations. Seeming ever ill prepared, he nonetheless plowed on and managed to steal the show with his histrionic demagoguery. By 1949, the congressional leadership loathed him, and most assumed he was simply a lame-duck embarrassment.

What no one counted on was his shrewd prescience about the national paranoia over Communism. In a mysterious, legendary meeting with advisors in a Washington, D.C. restaurant, McCarthy concocted the Red Scare and focused the general national uneasiness into a real fear of Communists in the federal government. By the time the resulting spark became an inferno, Americans identified Joe McCarthy singularly with the topic, and the embarrassed GOP had no choice but to silently watch him take off. He was once again re-elected. His path culminated in his antics in the Special House Committee on Un-American Activities. McCarthyism was born.

By 1953, he had reached the pinnacle of his powers, attacking his peers and fending off constant attacks from his many Senate enemies, who regularly attempted to bring charges or censure against him. One charge finally stuck—a kickback scheme in which he had pocketed $10,000. This was hardly a major blow to McCarthy, but a closed committee began investigating him and on December 2, 1954, he was officially censured, diminishing the blindly firing junior senator from Wisconsin.

Wisconsin and McCarthy

Was he a nutcase obscenity? A prescient, passionate Red fighter? Or a simple populist expediently grabbing an issue? Strident opposition to McCarthy was ever-present throughout his reign. Drives to have him recalled were ongoing, and the large press in Madison and Milwaukee lobbed as many editorial shells as they could to bring him down. Sauk City was a leading anti-McCarthy crusader. Its 2,000 residents organized a "Joe Must Go" campaign, which collected almost half a million signatures statewide.

Ask Wisconsinites today about McCarthy and they'll likely dodge the question or roll their eyes and shudder. There *are* still those who support him.

Perhaps most tellingly, Appleton, his adopted hometown and the place he lies buried, pays its respects to him with a minor bust in the county courthouse, while favorite resident Harry Houdini (Ehrich Weiss) is celebrated throughout downtown. Central Square is now Houdini Plaza, with a huge memorial sculpture in his honor.

day, and Sunday 1-4 p.m., closed Fridays after summer. Admission is $4, $2 ages under 18.

Gordon Bubolz Nature Preserve

North of Appelton, these 762 acres of greenspace protect a lowland white cedar forest and its diverse ecosystem. Eight miles of trails wind through the preserve. Two rental cabins are on-site, one for overnighting, though advance registration is required. A nature center (sheltered by earth) features natural history exhibits and a nature store. The preserve hosts plenty of fun outings, from maple syruping to ski clinics and craft workshops. Trails are open daylight hours, the nature center Tues.-Fri. 8 a.m.-4:30 p.m., Sat. 11 a.m.-4:30 p.m., Sun. 12:30-4:30 p.m. Admission is free.

Art Galleries

Lawrence University's **Wriston Art Center,** along E. College Ave., tel. (920) 832-6621, features rotating and permanent exhibits of student and guest artists in traditional and mixed media. If for no other reason, go to see the building's otherworldly design.

The **Appleton Art Center,** 130 N. Morrison St., tel. (920) 733-4089, has three galleries, with an emphasis on regional artists, and hosts the largest summer art fair in the state and a Sunday High Tea series of chamber music. The Fine Art Exhibition showcases Fox River Valley artists. The center is closed Sunday and Monday. Admission is free, but a $2 donation is requested.

Bubolz Doll Collection

In the main building of the Secura Insurance Co., over 1,000 dolls from a private collection are displayed; some are incredibly rare, dating from the 1830s. Secura Insurance is at 2401 S. Memorial Dr., tel. (920) 739-3161. It's open Mon.-Fri. 7:30 a.m.-4 p.m. Admission is free.

Side Trips

In nearby New London, along the Wolf River, the **Mosquito Hill Nature Center,** N3880 Rogers Rd., tel. (920) 779-6433, offers some good hiking trails and the very intriguing Wisconsin Butterfly House, showcasing Wisconsin's native butterfly species. The American water spaniel, bred by a local resident, also originated in New London.

Among the oldest paved trails in Wisconsin is hard-to-find number 53 on Wisconsin's Rustic Road system. Beginning in 1857, work was done on what today are Garrity, McCabe, Greiner, and Bodde Roads, northwest of Appleton along US 41 at CR JJ. (Keep your eyes peeled—it's somewhat confusing.) Along the way, you'll pass scenic double-arch bridges, a stone silo, and a wildlife conservation area.

ACCOMMODATIONS

In Appleton itself, the vast majority of lodgings are clustered around the interchanges of US 41/10 between Wisconsin Avenue and Spencer Street—the general area of the Outagamie County Airport. Three low-end options are found on the north side of town along Northland Avenue (CR OO) and Richmond Street. Downtown, the only option is a good one, the Park Plaza Paper Valley Hotel.

North

The least expensive lodging is along Northland Ave. (follow Oneida St. north). The **Northland Motel,** 138 E. Northland Ave., tel. (920) 739-8847, is no-frills but decent; rates are about $30 d. Another cheapie is to the west.

The **Snug Inn,** 3437 N. Richmond, tel. (920) 739-7316 or (800) 236-4444, located at the US 41-WI 47 interchange, will run $36 d.

West

For the budget-conscious, the **Road Star Inn,** 3623 W. College Ave., tel. (920) 731-5271, has 102 basic rooms and a continental breakfast for $40 s, $46 d; a few blocks west is the **Baymont Inn,** 3920 W. College Ave., tel. (920) 734-6070, with an outdoor pool, continental breakfast, and rooms from $50. Also nearby, at 3730 W. College Ave., is the trim **Woodfield Suites,** tel. (920) 734-9231, with two pools, sauna, whirlpool, a dining room, and continental breakfast. Rates run from $85 s, $95 d.

The Appleton **Hampton Inn,** 350 Fox River Dr., tel. (920) 954-9211, has been rated one of the top 10 Hampton Inns nationwide. Visitors enjoy free local calls, large rooms, a pool, whirlpool, and continental breakfast in a well-maintained facility. Rooms run from $69 s, $79 d.

One of the largest recreation centers in the U.S. is at the Appleton **Comfort Suites Comfort Dome,** 3909 W. Wisconsin Ave., tel. (920) 730-3800. Some rooms have kitchens and microwaves; rates run from $65 s, $75 d. The **Holiday Inn,** 150 Nicolet Dr., tel. (920) 735-9955, has every extra desirable for its guests at $84 s, $94 d.

Downtown

One of Wisconsin's best, the **Park Plaza Paper Valley Hotel,** 333 W. College Ave., tel. (920) 733-8000, features over 400 rooms of all types and pays meticulous attention to detail and service. There's a full array of recreation, including a putting green. Christie's restaurant is one of the top eateries in the region. A bargain at rates of $99 and up.

Bed and Breakfast

The downtown area of Appleton features a couple of large historic dwellings offering B&B accommodations. A few blocks north of the Avenue Mall is the 1897 Victorian **Franklin Street Inn,** 318 E. Franklin St., tel. (920) 739-3702. Original pocket doors, oak and maple hardwoods, and original chandeliers give the place a nice feel. The three rooms run from $67.

FOOD

Coffee

In addition to bookselling, **Conkey's,** 226 E. College Ave., tel. (920) 735-6223, now offers basic coffees and some specialty drinks in a cafe area in the back. The original architecture of this city landmark makes it a great venue aesthetically for sipping java. Publisher copies of books are available for preview. From $2.

Greasy Spoons and Diners

The southern Wisconsin institution **George Webb** dishes out its famous dense breakfasts and other diner fare 24 hours a day at 1939 N. Richmond. It's got that great clinking china and harried waitress atmosphere. From $2.

Quick Bites and Burgers

Get jen-yoo-wine Upper Peninsula pasties at **Stella's Pasty Shop,** 3130 W. Wisconsin Ave., good if you're staying in motels on the west side, and at the **Pasty Koop,** 135 E. Wisconsin Ave., tel. (920) 830-0896. The latter has real-deal pasty—they even use rutabaga, a unique regional ingredient. Choices include ground chuck, turkey, vegetarian, and even breakfast pasties that are to die for. From $2. It's open 6 a.m.-6 p.m. daily.

Enjoy full one-third-pound burgers at the **Badger Station Charcoal House,** 1025 N. Badger Ave., tel. (920) 739-4062, Appleton's best. Good fish, too. **Friar Tuck's,** 2120 W. College Ave., tel. (920) 730-1004, features a zillion bigger-than-a-breadbox sandwiches, and all bread is baked fresh daily. From $3.

Popular with Appleton residents is **Mr. Cinders,** 1309 E. Wisconsin Ave., tel. (920) 738-0100. You can't go wrong with the burgers or the delicious grilled steak sandwich. Best of all, there's a fish fry all day Friday from 10 a.m. From $4.

Healthy

Healthy is **Ecotopia,** 101 E Wisconsin Ave., tel. (920) 993-1212. The fare is made from natural ingredients and ranges from wild rice salads to gourmet pasta, with an eclectic international bent. From $4.

Pizza

Frank's has been making every ingredient of its pizzas from scratch for over 40 years—including the sausage—and it's still going strong. Located at 815 W. College Ave., tel. (920) 734-9131, Frank's is open daily for dinner and Wed.-Sun. until 3 a.m. for late-night dining. From $4.

Fish Fry

For classic Wisconsin-style dining, visit **Forester Banquet Hall,** 4001 W. Spencer, tel. (920) 734-1821, open Wednesday, Friday, and Sunday for piscatory feeds and tenderloin tips and chicken in a capacious hall that seats 300. From $6.

Trim B's Restaurant and Catering, 201 S. Walnut St., tel. (920) 734-9660, features a huge seafood selection nightly along with steaks and pasta. Trim B's breads its own perch and is open for lunch and dinner weekdays, dinner only on weekends. From $6.

Supper Clubs

Though not a supper club per se, **Greenville Station,** tel. (920) 757-6999, does have possibly the best prime rib in the region. Also offered are pasta, veal, and lots of seafood. Housed in a historic 19th-century hotel, Greenville Station is located along WI 76, five minutes from the Fox River Mall. Lunch and dinner are served weekdays, dinner only weekends. From $4.

Open for 50 years and still going strong is **George's Steak House,** 2208 S. Memorial Dr., tel. (920) 733-4939. It's strictly steaks and seafood here, with piano music nightly. It's open for lunch and dinner Mon.-Saturday. From $5.

Eclectic

Enjoy California-style and general eclectic cuisine at **Cali,** 201 N. Appleton St., tel. (920) 830-0700, with good seafood (specialty of the house is oysters). Cali is open Tues.-Fri. for lunch and dinner Saturday for dinner only. From $6.

The menu at **Gibson's Grill,** 211 W. College Ave., tel. (920) 954-1001, features American, Cajun, and Italian cuisines. Trendy art deco black lacquer decor gives the place a sheen, and an antique auto in the window is a nice touch. Gibson's was built right into an old two-story auto repair shop that used to have a ramp from the lower level to transport the cars up. Diners hear classical music while indulging in traditional sandwiches, pastas, steaks, and seafood. From $6. Gibson's is open daily for lunch and dinner, Sunday for dinner only.

The Willow, 3301 Prospect Ave., tel. (920) 993-9515, is a fantastic restaurant, one of the state's best since 1997. It's housed in a building that had one of Wisconsin's previous faves, Le Bon Appetit. It is basically a chic American bistro with creative fare from $8. Highly recommended.

Asian

Bustling **Chef Chu's** 719 W. College Ave., tel. (920) 749-0330, is the place to go for Mandarin-based Chinese food. It's always busy and is considered the takeout leader in town. From $5. Open daily for lunch and dinner.

The Mongolian barbecue—with great, smoky, hammered-steel inverted woks that the long-sticked wizards use to stir-fry your choice of meats and vegetables—is at **Mongo's** 231 W. Franklin St., tel. (920) 730-8304. It's open for dinner daily, lunch Friday, closed Sunday. Live entertainment is offered Wednesday and Fri.-Sat. From $5.

Right downtown is the new **Nakashima Sushi Bar and Yakitori,** 124 N. Appleton, behind city hall, tel. (920) 830-0444, an offshoot of long-standing Nakashima at 4100 W. Pine Street. The new place has noodle sets, *don buri,* a huge selection of sushi, central Wisconsin's only *yakitori* (fish or beef grilled on a skewer), and some reasonably priced bento boxes for lunch. The original Nakashima is the place for hibachi-grilled chicken. It's open for lunch and dinner daily except Sunday. From $7.

Taste of Thai, 321 E. College Ave., tel. (920) 830-2030, has good Thai food, with Indian overtones. It's open daily for lunch and dinner, dinner only weekends. The lunch buffet is a steal. From $6.

German

Mark's East Side, 1405 E. Wisconsin Ave., tel. (920) 733-3600, features a significant number of German entrées, along with seafood, steaks, chicken, roast duck, and barbecued ribs. Mark's is open for lunch and dinner weekdays, dinner only weekends. From $6.

Another supper club highlighting German cuisine is **The Crown Supper Club,** 2318 S. Oneida St., tel. (920) 730-9190, with a Wednesday-night German buffet. Good *rouladen.* It's open daily for dinner, Sunday until 8 p.m. only.

Fine Dining

Christie's, downtown, is without a doubt the most popular restaurant in the area. Semiformal, it has often been praised for its service and atmosphere. The white linen, crystal, attentive staff, English library décor—it's all superlative, as is the best Sunday brunch in town. Located in the Park Plaza Paper Valley Hotel, 333 W. College Ave., tel. (920) 733-8000, Christie's is open weekdays for lunch and dinner, Saturday for dinner only. From $12.

NIGHTLIFE

Keep your eyes peeled for a copy of the free monthly *The Valley Scene,* which has a good listing of entertainment happenings and occasionally some useful information on restaurants.

Park Central

At 318 W. College Ave. is this mini-mall comprised of seven different bars, comedy clubs, and sports bars. There's even line dancing. Something is always going on here. Call (920) 738-5603 to see what.

Watering Holes

Closer to Lawrence University, naturally, there's a higher quotient of pubs and bars, usually filled with students. One place to check out is **Houdini's Lounge,** 117 S. Appleton St., tel. (920) 832-8615, a pub with Houdini as a central theme (no surprise) and over 60 beers available.

Packed to the rafters by 8 p.m. is **Cleo's Brown Beam,** 205 W. College Ave., which bills itself the "Cheers of Appleton" and has an amazing display of Christmas lights all year.

It's hard to beat the beer selection (almost 100 varieties) at **Caliban's,** 134 W. Wisconsin Ave., in Neenah, along with specialty pizzas, sandwiches, and vegetarian fare. Caliban's has a great tin ceiling and old hardwood floors, as well as offshoot rooms for privacy. **Bazil's,** 109 W. College Ave., tel. (920) 954-1770, features an amazing 135 microbrews.

The Between the Locks Mall, 1004 Olde Oneida St., tel. (920) 735-0507, is an 1858 brewery reconverted in 1989 into the **Appleton Brewing Company.** It makes the trademark Adler-Brau beer, served in the mall's Dos Bandidos Mexican restaurant and Johnny O's brewpub. Tours of the brewery, which only has a seven-barrel-capacity brew kettle, are available to restaurant patrons (sometimes at all hours). There's also a beer garden in summer. Open Mon.-Sat. for lunch and dinner, Sunday for dinner only.

USA Today called **The Wooden Nickel,** 217 E. College Ave., tel. (920) 735-0661, the best sports bar in Wisconsin, and it's hard to argue with that—this place is channels, channels everywhere.

Live Music

Gibson's Grill 211 W. College Ave., tel. (920) 954-1001, maintains a regular weekend jazz schedule and charges no cover.

Blues aficionados head to **Emmett's,** 139 N. Richmond St., tel. (920) 733-7649, for great weekend blues gigs.

ENTERTAINMENT

Lawrence University has almost always got something happening, from a remarkable speaker series to regular performing arts productions (130 musical performances a year at the conservatory alone) at the Memorial Chapel and Stansbury Theatre, in the Music-Drama Center. For information, contact the Office of Public Events, tel. (920) 832-6585.

Appleton also has 18 music or theater groups—from boys' choirs to barbershop quartets—with performances throughout the year, including the 75-member **Fox Valley Symphony,** tel. (920) 729-5000, a cultural fixture for three decades.

The **Grand Opera House,** tel. (920) 424-2355, is an outstanding place to experience any of more than 200 performances per year. The dramatic 1883 Victorian underwent restoration and touch-up work in 1974, and the result is elegant and impressive.

The **Arts Alliance,** a consortium of arts groups, publishes an excellent and comprehensive listing of all performances and venues in the quarterly *Focus,* often available at the Appleton visitors center.

SPORTS AND RECREATION

Wisconsin Timber Rattlers
Goodland Field is the home of the **Wisconsin Timber Rattlers,** a single-A minor league franchise of the Seattle Mariners. The season runs April through September. You can't beat the price (the most expensive seat is $6), and there are always zany promotions and between-innings fun—all in all, it's great family entertainment. The field is located at 2400 N. Casaloma Drive. Call (920) 733-4152 for ticket information.

SHOPPING

Malls
Appleton is mall country, with so much mall space that bus tours make regular pilgrimages here. The **Valley Fair Mall,** one of many in Appleton, was the nation's first indoor mall. The unity of the **Fox River Mall,** the state's largest indoor mall, is admirable. There's a full-time consultant/scout/guide who maintains up-to-the-minute information on sales, bargains, and anything else you need to know about the almost 200 outlets, boutiques, and restaurants here. Call (800) 876-MALL for information.

Cheese
One of the only original farm-cheese factories left in the state, **Mossholder Farm Cheese Factory,** 4017 N. Richmond St., tel. (920) 734-7575, is one of a vanishing breed. Tours aren't available, but it still sells its white brick cheese out of a tiny retail shop in the basement. It's open regular business hours and Saturday 9 a.m.-noon.

SERVICES AND INFORMATION

The **Fox Cities Convention and Visitors Bureau,** tel. (920) 734-3358 or (800) 2DO-MORE, www.foxcities.org, is at 3433 W. College Avenue.
The only morning paper is Oshkosh's *Northwestern,* but the afternoon *Appleton Post-Crescent* is fairly dense and has local information.
The downtown **post office** is at 410 W. Franklin St., tel. (920) 734-7141. The public **library,** tel. (920) 832-6173, is at 225 N. Oneida Street. **Kinko's,** 3303 W. College Ave., tel. 920-

832-9300, has Internet access for $12 per hour or 20 cents per minute.
A walk-in urgent care center, **Appleton Medical Center,** 1818 North Meade St., tel. (414) 738-6343, can answer general health questions or refer you to area clinics 24 hours a day. There is also a direct line to speak to a nurse, tel. (414) 738-2230.

GETTING THERE AND AWAY

By Bus
Greyhound, 100 E. Washington St., tel. (920) 733-2318, departs nine times daily between 7 a.m. and 8 p.m. **Lamers** bus line also has one departure daily to Milwaukee's Amtrak station and one to Wausau (departures times vary; check with the terminal). All buses leave from the same terminal.

By Air
The **Outagamie County Airport** is the fourth busiest in Wisconsin and is served by the following commuter airlines: **United Express,** tel. (800) 241-6522, with six departures weekdays and five on Saturday; **Skyway (Midwest Express),** tel. (800) 452-2022, with multiple daily flights; **Northwest Airlink,** tel. (800) 225-2525, with seven departures weekdays and five or six on weekends; and **Comair,** tel. (800) 354-9822, with four departures weekdays and three on Sunday.

GETTING AROUND

The **Appleton-Neenah-Menasha Taxi** service is located at 705 W. Wisconsin Ave., tel. (920) 733-4444.
Valley Transit Authority operates between Appleton, Grand Chute, Kaukauna, Kimberly, Little Chute, Menasha, and Neenah. For information, call (920) 832-5800. There is a great downtowner circuit with free riding Mon.-Fri. 6:30 a.m.-6:30 p.m.; it makes a short loop of the downtown every 15 minutes. Fare is $1.
At the airport, you can rent a car from **Avis,** tel. (920) 730-7575, or **Budget,** tel. (920) 731-2291. Closer to the downtown area are **Enterprise,** 2700 W. College Ave., tel. (920) 832-2555, and **Best Value,** 1401 W. Wisconsin Ave., tel. (920) 739-9416.

VICINITY OF APPLETON

NEENAH-MENASHA

The twin cities of Neenah-Menasha are casually regarded as one entity, though their governments are separate. They share Doty Island, where Little Lake Butte des Mortes of the Fox River empties into Lake Winnebago.

Two Fox River channels flowing past the island and two minor promontories made available ready-made water power and gave rise to the birth of both villages by the 1840s. Depressed industries spurred papermaking, and within three decades Neenah-Menasha ruled the powerful Wisconsin papermaking region.

Bergstrom-Mahler Museum
This massive dwelling was once home to early area industrialist John Bergstrom. The highlight of the museum is a world-renowned collection of paperweights, many dating from the French classic era of 1845-60. The glass menagerie, as the museum calls it, is made up of 2,100 exquisite pieces. Other features include exhibitions of contemporary glass, photography, painting, textiles, and sculpture. Located at 165 N. Park Ave., tel. (920) 751-4658, the museum is open Tues.-Fri. 10 a.m.-4:30 p.m. (until 8 p.m. Thursday), weekends 1-4:30 p.m. Admission is free.

Downtown Neenah and Menasha Riverfront
The scenic, landscaped Fox River north channel walkways in Menasha feature a marina and over 30 picturesque historic buildings, many straight neoclassical in design. The best view is from the still-hand-operated lock on the canal. There's also a new museum along Tayco Street, the **Bridge Tower Museum,** in an 80-year-old bridgetender's tower. The building itself is worth a gander, and inside are plenty of historical artifacts. It's open daily May-Sept. 10 a.m.-7 p.m.

Downtown Neenah is equally resplendent, and the homes are decidedly more palatial. East Wisconsin Avenue, near Riverside Park, gives the best glimpse into 19th-century opulence and great river vistas. The mansions along this stretch were the partial setting for Wisconsin native Edna Ferber's novel *Come and Get It.* At 336 Main Street is an **octagon house**; it currently houses materials for the Papermaking Industry Hall of Fame, which may be moved to Appleton. Hours are Tuesday, Thursday, and Friday 9 a.m.-noon and 1-4 p.m., Sunday 1-4 p.m.

Neenah's Doty Park contains a reconstruction of **Grand Loggery,** the home of James Doty, the state's second territorial governor. With scant artifacts of family and area history, Grand Loggery is open June-Sept. Mon.-Thurs. 1-5 p.m. and Fri.-Sun. 11 a.m.-3 p.m. Donations are encouraged.

Menasha's **Smith Park** has a few Native American burial mounds. **Kimberly Point Park,** at the confluence of Lake Winnebago and the Fox River, has a great lighthouse and some good views of the river. The big draw is the world-class **Barlow Planetarium,** 1478 Midway Rd., tel. (920) 832-2848, on the campus of UW-Fox Valley. It has virtual reality exhibits and new public shows every week; no reservations required. Admission is charged.

Cloverleaf Factory
The Cloverleaf Factory, 2006 Irish Rd., tel. (920) 722-9201, is another of the old breed of cheese factory, rarely seen these days. The first cheese was produced here in 1884, and some of the original infrastructure is still visible. Experience up-close-and-personal views of the cheddar-making process. It's open Mon.-Fri. 7 a.m.-3 p.m.

Practicalities
The best place to stay in the twin towns is **The Valley Inn,** 123 E. Wisconsin Ave., tel. (920) 725-8441, whose excellent facilities include a pool, exercise room, and very clean guest rooms for $88 s or d. Rates are half that at **Twin City Motel,** 375 S. Green Bay Rd., tel. (920) 725-3941, which offers a large yard and a putting green in addition to adequate rooms.

The best coffee is at **Blue Moon Coffee,** 303 N. Commercial St. in Neenah, tel. (920) 729-4426. Open from 6 a.m. daily, there's live jazz and blues weekends, poetry readings Tuesday, books and board games, and some fresh-baked goodies.

The best place to eat is **Caliban's,** 134 W. Wisconsin Ave., tel. (920) 725-0573, with a large menu of specialty sandwiches and preservative-free pizzas, along with the largest beer selection around. From $4. Across the street is **Sassy Sal's,** sometimes called "The Pink Palace" and legendary for abusive waitresses. At 208 W. Wisconsin Ave. is **Mudbugs,** tel. (920) 720-9338, with great Cajun fare and some vegetarian options; there's great live zydeco music constantly, too. From $5.

A great bistro in town is **Milagro's Eclectic Bistro,** 230 Main St., tel. (920) 729-6041. It's the place to go for diverse sandwiches, salads, and quiches with a definite Middle Eastern flair. It's the best place in the valley for vegetarian, too. Milagro's is open 11 a.m.-4 p.m. From $5.

If there's an institution here, it's **Julie's Breakfast Club,** 1304 Midway Rd., a popular place with pancakes as big as a pizza. It burned down a few years ago, and locals breathed a sigh of relief when it reopened here. The restaurant now serves dinner as well. From $3.

KAUKAUNA

The word *gran ka-ka-lin* is a French-Ojibwa pidgin hybrid describing the long portage once necessary to trek around the city's 50-foot cascades, which ultimately required five locks to tame. Most know Kaukauna through a more humorous anecdote: in 1793, the area's land was purchased—the first recognized deed in the state—by Frenchman Dominique Ducharme for the princely sum of two barrels of rum.

Sights

Not far from the pesky rapids of old stands the **Grignon Mansion,** along Augustine St., tel. (920) 766-3122. Built in 1838 by Augustin Grignon, grandson of northeastern Wisconsin's legendary Charles Langlade, to replace the log shack lived in by rum-dealing city founder Dominique Ducharme, the house became known as the mansion in the woods. It has been thoroughly renovated, down to the hand-carved newel posts and imposing brick fireplaces. (Though from the outside it doesn't look much

like a "mansion.") Garbed docents conduct tours, and plenty of fur trading-era encampments, rendezvous, and even a Christmas candlelight pageant are held. Or you can simply wander through the gardens and an apple orchard. Several of Kaukauna's legendary locks can be reached via the grounds. Open June-Aug. Mon.-Sat. 10 a.m.-5 p.m., Sunday noon-5 p.m., shorter hours April-May and in October. Admission is $4, half price under 18.

Across the river at a bight is the aptly named **1000 Islands Environmental Center,** 700 Dodge St., tel. (920) 766-4733, a vital stop on the Mississippi Flyway for waterfowl and predatory birds. A huge number of mounted animals are displayed, and live versions include plenty of native Wisconsin fauna, such as great blue heron, coot, and bitterns. The acreage also supports a stand of chinquapin oak, rare in the state. Plenty of great trails run along the Fox River here. The center is open weekdays 8 a.m.-4 p.m., weekends 10:30 a.m.-3 p.m., and admission is free.

Practicalities

The best lodging in Kaukauna is the **Settle Inn,** 1201 Maloney Dr., tel. (920) 766-0088, with an indoor pool and outstanding budget rooms from $45.

A valley staple for 130 years is the venerable **Van Abel's Supper Club,** 8108 CR D, tel. (920) 766-2291, with varieties of chicken, chops, and seafood. It's open daily except Monday for dinner and offers a Sunday brunch. From $6.

Another excellent eatery is the **Out-O-Town Club,** 2127-718 Town Club Rd., tel. (920) 766-0414, a supper club with a Friday fish fry and nightly specials. Tenderloin Oscar is served Thursday, and the roast duck is a specialty. It's open Tues.-Thurs. for lunch and dinner, Fri.-Sat. for dinner only, and closed Sunday after Labor Day. From $6.

HIGH CLIFF STATE PARK

The drama of this sheer escarpment draws over half a million travelers annually to High Cliff State Park, located southeast of Appleton on the northeast side of Lake Winnebago. The cliff is actually the western edge of the Niagara Escarpment, a jutting, bluff-like dolomite rise formed during the time the Silurian Sea covered the region. It stretches almost a thousand miles to the east, through Door County and beyond to Niagara Falls. It is the prime spot to view big ol' Lake Winnebago. From the top, almost 250 feet above the waters, you can see all of the Fox River Valley—Appleton, Oshkosh, Neenah, Menasha, and Kaukauna.

High Cliff, the only state-owned recreation area on the lake, was founded on an old limestone quarrying and kiln operation. Extant materiel and former Western Lime and Cement Co. structures still stand. Effigy mounds found along trails originated from an unknown prehistoric Native American tribe; the mounds range from 28 to 285 feet in length. Sometime after those original occupants, the Ojibwa moved in. A statue of Red Bird, their Chief, graces the bluff. Red Bird loved to come sit and listen to the lake. An observation tower along the trails offers unbelievable panoramas.

Park flora includes battle-scarred sugar maples (scarred by sugarbushers' spikes and quarrying), cottonwood, shagbark hickory, and hophornbeam (ironwood). Critters aren't common, but you might spot a 13-striped ground squirrel or red fox.

Camping

The park's 1,200 acres have 112 fairly isolated campsites, most occupied early in the high season. Sites cost $8 residents, $10 nonresidents most of the year, slightly more in the summer high season. A vehicle admission fee is levied. You can make reservations May-October. Contact the park at N7475 High Cliff Rd., Menasha, WI 54952, tel. (920) 989-1106.

Recreation

The park maintains both a swimming beach and an 85-slip marina for anglers and boaters. Sand and walleye pike, large-mouth bass, and panfish are taken most often in the park's pond; sand pike, white bass, and walleye are caught in Lake Winnebago. Hikers have seven miles of somewhat steep trails to choose from, and cross-country skiers can access four of those come winter. The **Lime-Kiln Trail** is just over two miles and runs from the lime kiln ruins to the lake, then up the east side of the escarpment. The longest is the **Red Bird Trail,** mostly gentle and passing by the family campground. In addition, five miles of snowmobile trails and eight miles of bike and horse trails run through the park.

STINKING WATER

Geographically, Lake Winnebago dominates east-central Wisconsin; in fact, most Wisconsinites take it for granted. At 10 miles across and 30 miles north to south, this shallow lake—once a glacial marsh—is among the largest freshwater lakes fully locked within one state. It totals 88 miles of shoreline comprising 138,000 acres. Formed over 25,000 years ago by a lobe of the Wisconsin glacier, the lake is actually the western rim of the dolomite rock layer known as the Niagara Escarpment, which stretches almost 1,000 miles to Niagara Falls.

The lake was always crucial to Native Americans as a portion of the water transport system along the Fox and Wolf Rivers. The name purportedly comes from a linguistic mix-up—or deliberate pejorative snub—from the French, who dubbed the Native American tribe they discovered here the "stinkers" (an updated transliteration); "Stinking Water" was a natural follow-up.

Lake Winnebago today crosses the heavily populated Fox River Valley region and, come summertime, is heavily populated with fishers and pleasure-crafters. It is always thronged with anglers, whatever the season; in winter, up to 10,000 cars park on the frozen lake at any one time. Top catches include walleye, perch, and great white bass runs; if you're around in February, do not miss the annual throwback to Pleistocene days—the sturgeon spearing season.

The best places to check out the lake are Fond du Lac's littoral park, spreading around a great white lighthouse. Or wind east out of Fond du Lac via US 151 to skirt the eastern shoreline along what locals call "the Ledge," the high breathtaking rise above Deadwood Point. The small town of Pipe along this route is home to Columbia Park and its awesome 80-foot tower. Farther north is Calumet County Park, also with inspiring vistas and some superb trails, along with six rare panther effigy mounds. (At the entrance to the park, stop at **The Fish Tale Inn** to see the largest male sturgeon ever caught on the lake.) An even better place to experience the lake is one of Wisconsin's most outstanding state parks—High Cliff State Park, along the northeastern edge.

OSHKOSH

In 1987, former President Jimmy Carter said in a speech at the University of Wisconsin-Oshkosh campus, "I have never seen a more beautiful, clean, and attractive place." He was referring to this Fox River Valley city of 55,000—the one with the weird name. Situated on the western bight of Lake Winnebago, Oshkosh truly is a trim and tidy city. Bisected by the Fox River, it is still an important manufacturing center but lacks the ugly mill-town patina that often goes along with that.

The city is often associated, by both Wisconsinites and outsiders, with two disparate images—bib overalls and bizarre airplanes. Since 1895, Oshkosh B'Gosh has turned out functional, fashionable bib overalls and children's clothing and launched the city's tongue-twisting name onto the international scene. (And, yes, they *have* heard people say things such as "Is this Oshkosh, b'gosh?") As for bizarre airplanes, the annual Experimental Aircraft Association's Fly-In is the largest of its kind, a not-to-be-missed highlight of itinerant edge-dwelling avionics.

HISTORY

Strategically located on Lake Winnebago at the mouth of the Fox River, Oshkosh had always been a historic gathering spot along the Fox River and its tributaries—for Native Americans, then French and English *voyageurs,* missionaries, and opportunists. The primary Jesuit Black Robe himself, Father Jean Claude Allouez, even came in 1670 to preach to the Fox and Menominee Indians. While relations were generally harmonious, the Fox Indians blockaded the route in 1733, inciting the only major skirmish. The Winnebago teamed with the French to defeat the Fox; the carnage was memorialized in the renaming of the nearby lake and hill Lake Butte des Mortes—Hill of the Dead.

The first permanent white settlement was a lonely trading post established in 1818, relatively late considering the importance of the area, the midpoint between Forts Howard and Winnebago. Shrewd land grabbers established a new village on the north side of the Fox River, stretching to the mouth at Lake Winnebago. Called Athens, it grew opposite friendly rival Algoma, which later became Brooklyn—the little trading outpost that grew into a city. Athens was renamed Oshkosh in honor of the local Menominee chief; speculative stories are all that explain why the village honored him in this way. Certainly it was expedient for gaining access to timber, much of which the Menominee controlled. And the name should really be Oskosh; the first "h" was added later since everybody got it wrong anyway.

Sawdust City

A century and a half ago, the north woods of Wisconsin extended much farther south than they do today. Initial operations began at the same time as the establishment of new settlements; in 1848, the first large-scale sawmills appeared. By the close of the Civil War, some 35 factories were processing lumber in the city. The result was constant light showers of wood dust—at times an inch thick on the back streets. Hence, Oshkosh earned the moniker "Sawdust City." Excavations along Oshkosh riverbanks still reveal marbled layers of compacted sawdust.

This sawdust condemned the city to a painful series of conflagrations; four major fires between 1859 and 1875 virtually leveled the downtown, which was constructed entirely of the inexpensive timber. The 1875 fire was so bad that the city finally learned its lesson and rebuilt with stone; ironically, some of this stone came from Chicago—itself recently devastated by fire and rebuilt mostly with wood from Oshkosh sawmills.

SIGHTS

Orientation

Oshkosh streets can be confusing at first, since they parallel the Fox River. Some streets change names when they cross the Fox and some when they bisect North Main Street. North Main is the east/west dividing line for major streets. US Highway 45 becomes Jackson Street in the north, Oregon Street to the south.

EAA Air Adventure Museum

The state has officially decreed this museum a state treasure, a consequence no doubt of the 800,000 or so visitors who converge on Oshkosh for the annual fly-in sponsored by the Experimental Aircraft Association (EAA). Almost 100 airplanes of every possible type are displayed—aerobatics, home-built, racers, and more. The popular Eagle Hangar spotlights WW II planes and flying aces. Five theaters, numerous display galleries, and tons of multimedia exhibits make this well worth the admission. If you're re-ally lucky, you'll be there on one of the weekends when flights are offered in a historic 1929 Ford TriMotor Airliner, complete with the leather hat, goggles, and wind-blown hair. The flights take off from the museum's Pioneer Airport, tel. (920) 426-4800. Located off US 41 at the WI 44 exit, next to Wittman Regional Airport, along Poberezny Dr., the museum is open Mon.-Sat. 8:30 a.m.-5 p.m. and Sunday 11 a.m.-5 p.m. Admission is $7.50 adults, less for students (with ID) and seniors. Children under 8 get in free. Family rate is $20.

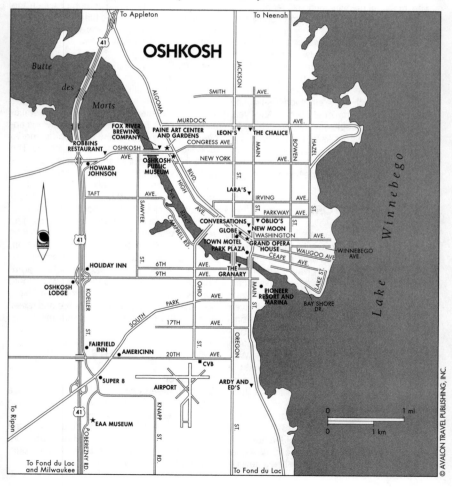

© AVALON TRAVEL PUBLISHING, INC.

Paine Art Center and Gardens

Across the street from the Oshkosh Public Museum is this superlative piece of eye candy, a lumber baron's Tudor revival house dating from the 1920s. The meticulously appointed rooms showcase period furnishings and antiques, along with 19th-century French Barbizon and U.S. art. Particularly impressive are the oriental rugs and solid oak panel balustrade staircase hand-carved by a Bavarian master. Outside lie acres and acres of equally well-cared-for greenspace including six gardens; one, modeled after the Dutch Pond Garden at Hampton Court in England, features over 100 varieties of rose. Legend has it the place is haunted, but the caretakers disavow any knowledge. Located at 1410 Algoma Blvd., tel. (920) 235-6903, it's open Tues.-Sun. 11 a.m.-4 p.m., Friday until 7 p.m. Admission is $5 adults, less for seniors and students, free for ages under 12.

Oshkosh Public Museum

In 1994, the Fox River Valley community held its breath as the grand 1907 English-style home of the Oshkosh Public Museum—replete with iridescent Tiffany stained glass—caught fire, threatening three floors of holdings. Much *was* lost, but much was also saved, and the rebuilding efforts have been nothing short of inspirational. A new addition adjoins the original mansion, once belonging to lumber baron Edgar Sawyer. This is one of the best public museums you'll see in a town of Oshkosh's size. Permanent holdings range in subject from local and natural history, china, and pressed glass to Native American ethnology and archaeology. One highlight is an eight-foot-tall Apostles Clock designed and built in the late 1800s by a German immigrant; it's considered one of Wisconsin's most treasured pieces of folk art. The museum is at 1331 Algoma Blvd., tel. (920) 424-4731, open Tues.-Sat. 9 a.m.-5 p.m., Sunday 1-5 p.m., and admission is free.

Grand Opera House

While in Oshkosh, try to attend a cultural performance at this architectural gem, at 100 High Ave., tel. (920) 424-2355, an 1883 edifice designed after majestic halls in Italy. After some neglect, it was brought back to life in 1986. A variety of local cultural organizations share the magnificent structure, and international touring acts perform regularly. Public tours ($2) are possible by appointment.

Oshkosh B'Gosh

This clothier, established in 1895, put Oshkosh on the map, fashion- and function-wise. Tours of the factory, where the dandy pinstriped bib overalls come together, are sadly no longer offered. Instead, head for the **Oshkosh B'Gosh stores.** The factory store, at 3001 S. Washburn, tel. (920) 426-5817, features outlet prices. And the showcase store, 206 State St., tel. (920) 231-4458, has the latest offerings in the company's line of children's clothing.

Menominee Park and Zoo

Menominee Park, at Hazel and Merritt Streets, tel. (920) 236-5080, along Lake Winnebago, is a city park featuring the closest swimming beach. Also in the park is the **Menominee Zoo,** a menagerie of native Wisconsin and some exotic species. The zoo also features paddleboats, bumperboats, canoe rentals, and a mini-train for children. The zoo is open May-Sept. daily 8 a.m.-7:30 p.m., and admission is free.

Scenic Drives and Tours

The Oshkosh Convention and Visitors Bureau has maps of a concise and visually well-plotted scenic drive and bike tour—a quick, efficient, and gorgeous way to take in the city, its sights, and more.

The Pioneer Inn, 1000 Pioneer Dr., tel. (920) 233-1980 or (800) 683-1980, offers the summertime **Pioneer Princess Excursion Yacht Cruise.** The 63-foot-long luxury yacht plies the waters of Lake Winnebago and the Fox River. Some dinner cruises are also available. Rates run from $11 for adults on the basic "Cookies and Cruise" to $30 for a moonlight dinner cruise. You'll find a whole bunch of different cruises, even a Jimmy Buffet-themed shindig.

ACCOMMODATIONS

Downtown

The least expensive option in downtown Oshkosh is the **Town Motel,** 215 Division St., tel. (920) 233-0610. Fresh brewed coffee is the only extra, but rates are under $40.

A step up is the **Pioneer Inn and Marina,** 1000 Pioneer Dr., tel. (920) 233-1980 or (800) 683-1980. Perched on small Kini Island at the mouth of the Fox River, the resort offers 200 plush rooms. Amenities include indoor and outdoor pools, whirlpools, marina and moorings, cross-country and water skiing, and more. Rooms go for around $90, with some package discounts.

A few blocks away is the Oshkosh **Park Plaza,** 1 N. Main St., tel. (920) 231-5000 or (800) 445-8667, which has superlative views of the Fox River and Lake Winnebago. The hotel offers two pools, a whirlpool, and a workout room. Basic rooms in this sleek-looking building begin at around $65, while the luxury-level ones start at around $110.

West
Most Oshkosh accommodations are spread along the highway interchanges of US 41 west of town. Cheapest of these is the always-economical **Oshkosh Lodge,** 1015 S. Washburn St., tel. (920) 233-4300, at the 9th St. exit. Rooms are spartan but clean for a mere $33 s or d.

The **Marriott Fairfield Inn,** 1800 S. Koeller Rd., tel. (920) 233-8504 or (800) 228-2800, is also off the 9th St. exit and offers a pool, whirlpool, and game room for $56 s or d.

Upscale lodging on the west side is the **Holiday Inn-Oshkosh,** 500 S. Koeller Rd., tel. (920) 233-1511 or (800) HOLIDAY, featuring a slew of amenities for $80 s or d.

Camping
There are unfortunately no state or county park camping options very close. Two private options—and the crowded misery often attendant— are **Circle R Campground,** 1185 Old Knapp Road (exit WI 26 from US 41 to CR N, east 1 mile), tel. (920) 235-8909, and, slightly farther away, **Kalbus' Country Harbor,** 5309 Lake Road, tel. (920) 426-0062, seven miles south of town. Both have sites in the $15 range.

FOOD

Quick Bites and Family Fare
Exceedingly low-key but consistently good is **The Chalice,** 1741 N. Main St., tel. (920) 233-4400, a dark and intimate restaurant with a fireplace. Enormous sandwiches and outstanding homemade soups. From $3.

Not far from Oshkosh, in little Omro, is the **Main Street Restaurant,** tel. (920) 685-5980, housed in an 1881 grocery, shoe, and millinery store. Wednesday features 40-pound turkeys and outstanding dressing to supplement the hearty family fare. You can also pick up a fishing lure at Al's Lure Shop, in the corner of the restaurant. It's open Mon.-Sat. 5 a.m.-9 p.m. and Sunday 6 a.m.-8 p.m. From $4.

Drive-Ins
Believe it or not, Oshkosh has two good drive-ins. **Leon's,** 121 W. Murdock Ave., tel. (920) 231-7755, is a classic neon kind of place with Michael's Quality Custards and a mouth-watering homemade sloppy joe-style concoction. The turtle sundaes are marvelous. The other, **Ardy & Ed's,** 2413 S. Main St., tel. (920) 231-5455, has been around since 1948 and does not appear much changed. It still plays '50s tunes and the wait staff still gets around aboard roller skates.

Coffee Shops
Spacious and aesthetically underdeveloped is **New Moon,** corner of N. Main and Algoma Blvd., tel. (920) 232-0976, is the place for coffee or a light meal. The java list is extensive, the short menu runs from sandwiches to creative soups (an African peanut chicken soup, for instance). Housed in a historic 1875 building, it also offers live blues, jazz, and reggae regularly and poetry readings on Tuesday. Blue Moon is open 7 a.m.-11 p.m. most nights, until midnight Fri.-Sat., and until 9 p.m. Sunday.

Cafe
The Globe, 107 Algoma Blvd., tel. (920) 235-1111, is housed in an old Odd Fellows Lodge built around the turn of the 20th century. The interiors, recently refurbished, are spectacular, and the small but rewarding menu features creative entrée salads, sandwiches, pastas, and more, with lots of veggie options. Behind the Grand Opera House, the Globe is open Tues.-Sat. for lunch and dinner; an attached bakery opens around 7 a.m. It also has live jazz regularly. From $4.

Natural Foods and Vegetarian
Kitchen Korner Natural Foods, 507 N. Main St., tel. (920) 426-1280, sells Manitowoc, Wisconsin's Natural Ovens products, along with health magazines and assorted products. It's

open daily except Sunday. A block away at 457 N. Main St. is **Conversations,** a teahouse with a light vegetarian menu. From $4.

Fish Fries

Jansen's, 344 Bowen St., tel. (920) 231-0690, is in an impressive turreted building and is at least as much restaurant as bar. Steaks and seafood are the rule here, with Thursday prime rib specials and great lake perch on Friday. Jansen's is open for lunch and dinner Mon.-Sat., closed Sunday. From $5.

The same owners run **Jeff's,** 1005 Rugby St., tel. (920) 231-7450. With more emphasis on the seafood, here Alaskan whitefish replaces the perch at the Friday fish fry. Also on the menu are walleye pike, lobster, shrimp, and scallops, along with steaks, chicken, and a large selection of sandwiches. Prime rib is available Wednesday and Saturday. From $4.

A lesser-known good bet for fish fry is **Parnell's,** 2932 Fond Du Lac Rd., tel. (920) 235-9770, which specializes in broasted chicken in addition to its fish fry. From $4.

Brewpub

Fratello's Cafe is part of the complex of the **Fox River Brewing Company,** 1501 Arboretum Dr., tel. (920) 232-BEER. The attractive cafe interiors overlook the river; you can even boat up to the outdoor deck. A biplane strung above diners adds a nice touch. The fare is solid steak, pizza, pasta, sandwiches, and seafood. From $5. It's open for lunch, dinner, and late-night eats. Brewery tours are available Saturday 1-4 p.m. or by appointment.

Mexican

Head for **Lara's Tortilla Flats,** 715 N. Main St., tel. (920) 233-4440. Oshkosh's first Mexican restaurant is a real-deal family affair turning out excellent *norteño* food—the recipes came up with grandma from her Salinas boardinghouse a century ago. The mole is outstanding, as is the *pozole,* a traditional northern Mexican corn and pork soup. Everything's made from scratch, including an exquisite creamed corn, white cheese, and chili pepper cornbread. The decor features images of the clan's role in the Mexican Revolution as well as great-grandpa's role in capturing legendary *bandito* Gregorio Cortez. The bar fea-

tures 14 different tequilas. Lara's is open Mon.-Sat. 11 a.m.-10 p.m., Sunday 4-9 p.m. From $4.

Supper Clubs and Fine Dining

The proprietors may dispute categorization as a supper club, but **Robbins,** 1810 Omro Rd., tel. (920) 235-2840, closely fits the bill. You can go casual or formal, although the food is decidedly not casual, featuring a host of excellent steaks and fresh fish. Best of all, this is the place to experience the Wisconsin tradition of in-house sausage-making and meat smoking. From $5.

Justman's Gasthaus Inn, at the corner of 6th and Knapp, tel. (920) 235-8167, features over 60 German entrées, but it's classic supper-club steaks and seafood. Justman's is open Tues.-Sun from 4:30 p.m. From $6.

Another top spot in Oshkosh is **The Granary,** 50 W. Sixth Ave., tel. (920) 233-3929, south of the Fox River. Herculean renovations have transformed an 1883 stone flour granary into Oshkosh's most character-rich eatery. Diners can gaze upward into the massive barley chutes; the original enormous wood sifters now separate the foyer and lower dining room; and the two-level, ladder-back bar is graced by horse-team rigging. The menu is basic. For lunch, there's a variety of light fare— veggie salads, seafood, deli and butcher-block sandwiches—as well as lasagna and swordfish. Dinner is prime rib, miller's cut, and a variety of other steaks, along with seafood. House specialties include tenderloin Oscar, seafood Alfredo, a variety of veal dishes, and shellfish Provençale. Hours for lunch are Mon.-Fri. 11 a.m.-2 p.m., dinner Mon.-Thurs. 5-10 p.m., Fri.-Sat. 5-10:30 p.m., and Sunday 5-9 p.m. From $6.

For the spectacular view of Lake Poygan, it's worth a short trip northwest of Oshkosh in Larsen to the **Lake Poygan's Duck Inn,** 7502 Richter Lane, tel. (920) 836-2321. The signature dishes are duck but also some outstanding fish and meats. Open for lunch and dinner; closed Monday. From $5.

NIGHTLIFE

The local newspaper is decent and generally includes a thorough listing of entertainment in the area. The same goes for the free monthly *The Valley Scene,* which also lists Appleton and

Green Bay happenings; check the coffee shops for this one.

Bars and Music

Mentioned above, the **New Moon** coffee shop offers folk music. **Peabody's Ale House,** 544 N. Main St., has live music—blues to rock.

For jazz, **The Granary,** 50 W. 6th Ave., tel. (920) 233-3929, has something most nights; on Thursdays the **Algoma Club** above the Globe restaurant has jazz. For a basic watering hole without the cacophony of college students downing shots, try **Oblio's.** It's got a pressed-tin ceiling, an antique wood bar, and photos of old Oshkosh.

Cultural Events

In addition to the Grand Opera House (see "Sights"), stage and theater shows are found on the campus of UW-Oshkosh at the **Frederic March Theatre,** 926 Woodland Ave., tel. (920) 424-4417.

EVENTS

EAA International Fly-In Convention

Oshkosh aviation pioneer Steve Wittman—erstwhile manager of the airport renamed for him—designed and built racing planes; one of them is on display at the Smithsonian. He was so impressive he drew the attention of Orville Wright and other airplane aficionados. After the Exper-

imental Aircraft Association was formed, it moved to Wittman's hometown, Oshkosh. Soon after, a tradition began: the gathering known as the Fly-In, now a legendary, jawdropping display of airplanes that draws hundreds of thousands of people from around the world. Rivaled only by Milwaukee's Summerfest, this event draws as much or more national exposure.

And it's certainly a spectacle. The skies in the last week of July and into August are filled with planes and pilots who'll never shake their appetite for aviation the way it used to be done—strictly by the seat of your pants. Handmade and antique aircraft are the highlights, but lots of contemporary military aircraft are also on show. (A personal favorite is the seaplanes at the seaplane base.) Thrilling air shows go on nonstop. In all, almost 12,000 aircraft and more than 750,000 people are on hand for this one. Free shuttles run all over the grounds and to the EAA Air Adventure museum, but remember to wear good shoes, a hat, and sunscreen. You may also want to carry water; it's an enormous place.

The Fly-In is held the last week of July and first week of August and runs 8 a.m.-8 p.m. daily; air shows start at 3 p.m. It doesn't come cheap; for nonmembers, prices are $29 a day, $16 ages 7-13. For members, prices are lower; memberships can be purchased on-site for $40, which brings the ticket cost down to $16 a day, $87 for the week for adults, $12 and $40 kids. (Tickets also get you into the museum the day of purchase.) Tack on $5 for parking ($7 RVs) and it adds up.

Oshkosh's
Experimental Aircraft
Association's Fly-In

Other Events

Over the Fourth of July holiday, Oshkosh celebrates its timber heritage with **Sawdust Days,** a multi-day party featuring carnivals and an extensive fireworks display. The **Winnebago County Fair** is held in August. Thanksgiving weekend brings brightly decorated trees, downtown wreaths, and lots of gingerbread for the **Festival of Trees.**

SPORTS AND RECREATION

Fishing

Walleye and perch are the predominant prey. Winnebago-region specialties are the white bass run (generally mid- to late May) and sheepshead. The Wolf and Fox Rivers generally have the best walleye fishing in April. For a one-of-a-kind, only-in-Wisconsin experience, be here in February for the sturgeon spearing season. **Boat rentals** are available from the Fox River Marina, 1100 Pioneer Dr., tel. (920) 236-4230. Hot spots include Rainbow Park, Riverside Park, and the river mouth at Bowen Street.

Parks and Beaches

Asylum Point Park has no swimming but does have some nice views—its trails run from marshland to prairie to lakefront. It's an established wildlife restoration area. Even more stunning nature trails run through the **Waukau Creek Nature Preserve** north of Waukau on Delhi Road, off CR K; steep ravines follow the only flowing creek in the county.

For swimming, try the enormous **Winnebago County Community Park** in the far northern reaches of town, bordered by County Roads A and Y and WI 45. Or, jump in Lake Winnebago itself at the **Menominee Park** swimming beach along Millers Bay at Hazel and Merritt Streets.

Trail Systems

There are some 75 miles of multipurpose trail in Winnebago County, much of it an abandoned railroad corridor. The main route is the **WIOUWASH Trail,** a crushed limestone surface meandering through woods, marshes, farm fields, and tallgrass prairie from Oshkosh to the Winnebago County line. The access point is along Westwind Road. The Convention and Visitors Bureau has a map of a scenic bike tour through the area.

SERVICES AND INFORMATION

The **Oshkosh Convention and Visitors Bureau** is at 525 W. 20th Ave., not far from the airport, tel. (920) 303-9200 or (877) 303-9200. It's open Mon.-Fri. 8 a.m.-4:30 p.m. The website is www.oshkoshcvb.org.

The *Oshkosh Northwestern* is a daily (except Sunday), and for a city of Oshkosh's size it isn't bad.

The Oshkosh **post office** is at 1025 W. 20th Ave., tel. (920) 236-0200. The public **library,** tel. (920) 236-5200, is at 106 Washington Avenue, between Jefferson and Mt. Vernon Streets. **Kinko's,** 1971 Koeller Ave., tel. (920) 426-5580, has Internet access for $12 per hour or 20 cents per minute.

The **Aurora Medical Group,** 855 N. Westhaven Dr., tel. (920) 303-8700, has urgent care facilities.

TRANSPORTATION

Air

Wittman Regional Airport, 525 W. 20th Ave., tel. (920) 424-0092, has a few flights daily from **United Express,** tel. (920) 426-2854.

Bus

The local **Greyhound** stop is at Wittman Regional Airport, tel. (920) 231-6490, adjacent to the Convention and Visitors Bureau. Not too many buses serve Oshkosh.

Oshkosh Transit System local buses operate Mon.-Sat. 6:15 a.m.-6:15 p.m.; exact change only.

Taxi

City Cab Co., 124 N. Main St., tel. (920) 235-7000, offers 24-hour service.

Rental Cars

Budget rents cars out of a small office at the Wittman Field Regional Airport, tel. (920) 235-5900. Downtown, **Enterprise Rent-A-Car** is at 1245 S. Washburn St., tel. (920) 236-6777.

FOND DU LAC

Fond du Lac often refers to itself as "First on the Lake"—sort of a loose take on the French, which translates literally as "bottom [or far end] of the lake." It wasn't the first body of water French *voyageurs* saw in the late 17th century, but for travelers winging north from southern Wisconsin's population centers, it afforded the first glimpse of big Winnebago. A winding, sprawling city on the lake, it is modestly prosperous and home to a diverse array of recreation and industry, including the world headquarters of Mercury Marine. Out-of-staters likely know Fond du Lac as the home of the Miracle Mile, a stretch of Main Street downtown that has produced an inordinate number of lottery winners and $185 million in winnings. If you're ever going to indulge in this form of gambling, this is the place to do it.

History

Three separate Winnebago villages were on this site at various times. Before Europeans arrived for good, in 1785, the primary community was Winnecomeyah (the city's original name). Despite its strategic location—at the base of a big lake and equidistant to the Fox-Wisconsin riverway—the town grew painfully slowly. Everywhere-to-be-seen town father, and later Wisconsin's first territorial governor, James Doty had the town platted in 1835.

Boomtown status effectively eluded the place—so much so that the local constabulary, the story goes, couldn't afford a pair of handcuffs. Doty's anticipated timber traffic never materialized because the town was too far from the fast-receding lumber lines to the north. However, a plank road, laboriously laid down from Sheboygan, be-came a vital channel of transportation from the Lake Michigan coast. By the late 1860s, the arrival of the railroad transformed the city into a transportation hub (though the first train was de-railed by an ox on the tracks) before manufacturing moved in.

SIGHTS

Galloway House and Village

The stately mid-Victorian Italianate villa Galloway House, 336 Old Pioneer Rd., tel. (920) 922-6390, is the cornerstone of Fond du Lac's

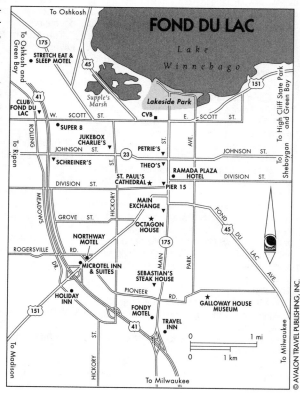

sightseeing. This beast, originally finished in 1847, features 30 rooms, four fireplaces, and much Victorian opulence. Spread out along E. Pioneer Road behind the house is a turn-of-the-20th-century village containing 23 restored regional dwellings and structures. Village highlights are the original carriage house, a flat-log cabin, a Main Street mock-up, gristmill, old depot, general store, and more. The grounds also include the Blakely Museum, an assortment of pioneer and early-20th-century Fond du Lac stuff, including an extensive local private Native American collection (with an original cigar-store wooden Indian), a doll collection, miscellany from U.S. martial involvement, machines, and even a mounted passenger pigeon.

The whole compound is open 10 a.m.-5 p.m. Memorial Day through Labor Day and weekends in September. Admission is $5.50 adults, $3 students 17 and under, preschoolers free.

Octagon House

Yet another proud historic structure in Fond du Lac, this 12-room private home was originally raised as a stockade against Native American attack. After the Civil War, it became a node on the Underground Railroad (you can add almost a dozen secret places to the number of rooms, including secret passages, tunnels, and one hidden room). And it wouldn't be complete without the requisite ghost reportedly wafting about. Inside are plenty of period antiques and a number of displays and collections ranging from Native American artifacts to model ships and dolls. Located at 276 Linden St., tel. (920) 922-1608, Octagon House is open Monday, Wednesday, and Friday afternoons Memorial Day through Labor Day. Admission is $8, $5 children.

St. Paul's Cathedral

This Episcopalian English gothic stone cathedral, 51 W. Division St., tel. (920) 921-3363, houses the Oberammergau unified collection, a priceless assemblage of woodcarvings. Rare vestments are also on display. The tiny garden is tranquil. Open by appointment 8 a.m.-4 p.m. Admission is $2.

Lakeside Park

One of the better municipal parks anywhere on Lake Winnebago is this 400-acre tract, separated into two parts. The western section is made up of Supple's Marsh, a wetlands with launch ramps and picnic areas. The eastern part is what attracts most folks. The park's eye-frying-white sentinel lighthouse is probably Fond du Lac's most recognizable symbol. This section of the park also includes landscaped islands, a deer park, a mini-train, a harbor, and a marina, among other things. You can rent bumperboats, windsurfing boards, canoes, and aquabikes at the marina. A carousel dating from the 1920s here is one of the few extant wooden merry-go-rounds left in the state; it still runs on a simple two-gear clutch. All the horses are pegged—constructed wholly without nails. This is a great place to spend an afternoon in Fond du Lac.

white lighthouse at Lakeside Park

Talking Houses and Historic Places Tour

Fond du Lac does the usual historic tours one better with its Talking Houses tour. The city-wide driving tour of 24 homes features AM radio transmissions at 14 of the highlights (AM 1020, 1100, 1210). And it's not just houses. Also featured are a Spanish-American War soldier statue, a Soo Line locomotive, Lakeside Park's carousel, a Victorian bandstand, and Lookout Lighthouse. The local visitor's bureau, 19 W. Scott St., tel. (920) 923-3010 or (800) 937-9123, provides an excellent companion brochure.

Eldorado Marsh

Just a few miles west of Fond du Lac along WI 23 and CR C is an unknown canoeists' paradise, the 6,000-acre Eldorado Marsh, which subsumes the 1,500-acre shallow flowage marsh. Locals refer to it as the "Everglades of the North." I'm not sure about that, but it is a tranquil, solitary spot. Fauna typically include deer and small game, along with tons of ducks and geese.

ACCOMMODATIONS

Downtown
There's only one option near the central area, the full service **Ramada Plaza Hotel**, 1 N. Main St., tel. (920) 923-3000 or (800) 2-RAMADA. It has an indoor pool, whirlpool, lounge, restaurant, health club, covered parking, and some suites. Rates begin at $69, though they jump steeply late July through late August.

West
Cheapest on the west side is the spartan but comfy **Stretch Eat and Sleep**, on Pioneer Rd. at CR OO and US 41, tel. (920) 923-3131, featuring a/c, a restaurant, and rooms from $26.

The city's newest lodging is the **Microtel Inn and Suites**, 649 W. Johnson St. (WI 23), tel. (920) 929-4000 or (888) 771-7171, with a health club, whirlpool, and continental breakfast. Rooms from $44.

Southwest
The **Northway Motel**, 301 S. Pioneer Rd., tel. (920) 921-7975, offers decent, inexpensive rooms. Amenities include a continental breakfast, a restaurant, and some rooms with refrigerators. It's along one of those unpleasant frontage roads, but it's set back far enough. Rooms start at $30.

On the other end of the spectrum, the sybaritic **Holiday Inn Holidome**, 625 Rolling Meadows Dr., tel. (920) 923-1440 or (800) HOLIDAY, offers its usual amenities and rooms from $80 in winter, $100 in summer.

South
The bottom-budget **Fondy Motel**, 108 S. Main, tel. (920) 921-5820, has rates from $29 but not much else to recommend it. **Travel Inn**, 1325 S. Main St., tel. (920) 923-0223, a large complex of motel and busy restaurant, is slightly more expensive. Rooms are decent and there's an indoor pool and whirlpool, lounge, restaurant, and a few other perks. Rates from $33.

Camping
Try first the Kettle Moraine State Forest, tel. (262) 626-4305, approximately 15 miles southeast of town. There, camping fees are $7. If the state forest is full, there's also the **KOA**, five miles south of Fond du Lac on US 41, tel. (920) 477-2300. Rates here are $18. The Fond du Lac County Fairgrounds offers 18 sites, though it's geared for RVers.

FOOD

Burgers
Faro's Custard and Jumbo Burgers, 609 W. Johnson St., tel. (920) 922-8050, also serves burgers noteworthy for their, well, enormity. Huge and delicious. From $3.

The teenybopping **Jukebox Charlie's**, 248 N. Hickory St., tel. (920) 923-8185, features poodle-skirted waitresses, '50s music on the jukebox, and a dance club. Burgers, malts, and the like are available as well. Outside, under a 35-foot jukebox sign, carhops move on wheels.

Fish Fries
Pier 15, 15 W. Division St., tel. (920) 921-2200, has excellent fish every night, a good fish fry, and other seafood and steaks; you can grill your own here. From $6.

Another excellent fish fry is at **Wendt's on the Lake**, which has as classic a Wisconsin supper club atmosphere as you'll find anywhere. Famous for perch, it also has great prime rib. From $6. It's located seven miles north of town along WI 45, tel. (920) 688-5231.

Supper Clubs
On a local straw poll, most chose **Sunset Shores Supper Club**, N7364 Winnebago Dr., tel. (920) 922-4540, as the place to sit, gaze at the big lake, and go at a steak. From $6.

If it's steak you want, another place to go for sure is **Sebastian's Steakhouse**, 770 S. Main St., tel. (920) 922-3333, which is certainly good for the number of choices it gives you and for the excellent value. Open for dinner daily except Monday; from $4.

Jim and Linda's Lakeview serves four-course dinners Tues.-Sun., seven days a week in high season. If nothing else, come for the view of the lake—the place is 30 feet from the eastern shoreline. It's located in little Pipe; take US 151 east to CR W, then west, tel. (920) 795-4116.

The **Idlewile Inn** garners local kudos for its food and its old 1920s hotel decor. Not really a supper club, it has an eclectic menu with more than just steaks and seafood; the house specialty is barbecue ribs, and this is the place near town for Sunday brunch. The fish fry is great. Go 12 miles east on WI 23, north on CR G, tel. (920) 999-4404. It's open for dinner every day except Tuesday. From $6.

The only place featuring anything remotely decent for vegetarians is **Club Fond du Lac,** 977 W. Scott St., tel. (920) 923-8190, which does also serve flame-seared steaks and seafood. From $5.

Check out the diversity at **Theo's,** 24 N. Main St., tel. (920) 922-8899. Pastas are wonderful—the fennel sausage with red pepper in particular. Also featured are gumbos, grilled chicken marinated in rosemary and lemon olive oil, beef tenderloin stir-fry, some excellent salads, and fantastic Angus steaks. From $5.

Family Dining

Arguably *the* Lake Winnebago culinary institution is **Schreiner's,** 168 N. Pioneer Rd., tel. (920) 922-0590, a hearty American-style family restaurant serving meals since 1938. The menu is broad, the servings copious, and the specials Midwestern. But the real highlight is the bread, made fresh on-site in the bakery. The New England clam chowder is also superb. Schreiner's is open daily 6:30 a.m.-9 p.m. and longer in summer. From $3.

Since the '30s, **Petrie's,** 84 N. Main St., tel. (920) 921-9150, has served three square meals daily. Enormously popular, its buffet draws so many people that it's had to maintain a buffet hotline, (920) 921-8087, recounting the day's offerings. It's famous for fried chicken and ham (and it's also known as the Bavarian Inn). From $4.

NIGHTLIFE

Bars

The largest drink selection is, ironically, at a restaurant—**Main Exchange,** 161 S. Main, tel. (920) 923-8180, a Mexican, steaks, and sandwiches eatery with great old tin work and oak bars. **Dillingers,** Main and Division Streets, tel. (920) 923-6776, is another eatery-cum-bar,

with a live DJ Wed.-Sat. and some decent drink specials.

Of course, many of the big hotels feature their own pubs, lounges, and/or nightclubs. The **Country Woods Pub,** inside the Holiday Inn, features live entertainment Wednesday, Friday, and Saturday.

EVENTS

Though it might get some argument from Port Washington to the southeast, Fond du Lac purports to hold the world's largest fish fry in June—over 5,400 fish dinners and sandwiches are consumed in one gluttonous three-day **Walleye Weekend** in 1994.

Fond du Lac's Marian College hosts a two-day **jazz festival** in mid-April. During the summer, the **Buttermilk Performance Center,** corner of S. Park Avenue and Old Pioneer Road, features open-air concerts by the Fond du Lac Symphonic Band. Performances are free and given Monday and Wednesday.

SPORTS AND RECREATION

Bicycling

Directly on Lake Winnebago. A 400-acre waterfront park. The Kettle Moraine State Forest just a hop away. Fond du Lac sounds pretty promising for biking, and it is. The city has a balanced system of rural trails including the great **Ledge Lookout Ride,** 45 miles on the eastern shore of Lake Winnebago along the Niagara Escarpment. Better yet is the **Wild Goose State Trail,** of which Fond du Lac is the northern terminus. The screened limestone trail stretches 34 miles south to the Horicon National Marsh, the city of Horicon, and beyond. A trail pass ($10 annually) is necessary. The trail is open year-round. Hook up with the trail at Rolling Meadows Drive, across from the Holiday Inn Holidome.

Trails

See "Eldorado Marsh," above, for canoeing trails. Short nature trails are available a few miles south of Fond du Lac via Hickory Street Road at the **Hobbs Woods Natural Area,** 60 small acres of picturesque greenspace along a creek.

STURGEON SPEARING

Anyone with any piscatory ambitions should experience the Wisconsin pastime of ice fishing. Every winter, seasonal villages of clapboard shacks or tent-like awnings sprout up on the frozen surfaces of just about every one of the state's 15,000 lakes. And while Wisconsin's great white whale may be the musky come summertime, for lore and legend nothing rivals the prehistoric leviathan prowling the waters of east-central Wisconsin—the lake sturgeon.

Of Brobdingnagian proportions, sturgeon and its variegated 23 species are found only in the northern hemisphere. Sturgeon are some of the world's largest predominantly freshwater fish; a western-U.S. relative of the lake sturgeon, the white sturgeon, can grow to 500 pounds. The largest and most prized come from Russia—the beluga sturgeon can approach an incredible 3,500 pounds. The most prehistoric of fish, these shovel-nosed behemoths have scudded through murky waters for 300 million years and counting.

Its physiology is monstrous: an overlapping armor of scutes—dense, mottled cartilage—four small barbed tentacles (barbels) off the bottom of the snout; opaque, myopic eyes; an ovoid mouth devoid of teeth and with enormous lips; a torpedo-shaped body with a heterocercal fin, which gives it its sinister, sharklike appearance. Some say it resembles a cross between a crocodile and a platypus.

Living as a sort of custodian in a lake's shallower depths, the sturgeon scours the bottom, feeling with its barbels. It sucks up virtually everything and spits out only the most unwholesome of bottom muck and detritus, ingesting clams, snails, larvae, and other invertebrates (along with the odd beer can).

Who Would Want This Fish?

Everyone. We want it mainly for the roe—caviar to most, but, strictly speaking, it's roe in the lake sturgeon. Only Russian belugas—the granddaddies of 'em all—can be said to produce caviar as it is known in this country. Up to one-fifth the body weight of the average female is roe. The meat of the fish is also rich and healthful.

European epicureans long treasured the sturgeon's offerings. One of England's King Henrys reportedly banned sturgeon consumption by any but royalty to preserve its availability for himself. In the U.S., Longfellow revered it as "the monster, Mishenama . . . the King of Fishes" in *Hiawatha*. Sturgeon is no longer considered a trash fish in the U.S.; chic restaurants today are in on the action. Trendy bistros in Los Angeles, New York, and the Bay Area serve variations as diverse as sturgeon salad and grilled sturgeon with lentil-and-arugula salad.

Wisconsin's Sturgeon

Wisconsin has two species of two genera. Most common is *Acipenser fulvescens*, or lake sturgeon—also called rockfish, dogface sturgeon, and other pejoratives. Most live in east-central regions, but they are found all the way to the Wisconsin-Iowa border and up the Mississippi to the St. Croix River region.

Native Americans long treasured the valuable fish, but by the turn of the 20th century Wisconsin settlers, like most of the country, considered the sturgeon a vile, meddlesome water-borne varmint. With their large numbers, they choked canals and disrupted river traffic. As a result, sturgeon were slaughtered at every opportunity and left to rot on shorelines or chopped up for animal fodder. Parts were even ground up to clarify beer.

Eventually, however, by the 1870s, the caviar craze caught on here and Wisconsin became the nucleus of U.S. caviar production. Wholesale slaughter combined with greedy harvesting seriously reduced the sturgeon population. Add a century's worth of dam and hydro-plant building (sturgeon swim upstream to spawn like salmon) and you can see why there is now a serious problem with the survival of the species. By 1920, they were virtually extinct.

New management efforts have curtailed the decline. Most crucial were laws prohibiting the capture of mature females, which only spawn sporadically (25 years to mature, and then they spawn only two to three times per decade) and are the source of the valuable roe. The results were salutary enough to make Lake Winnebago's sturgeon population the highest in the world and give Wisconsin one of the country's few sturgeon spearing seasons. Most species are still listed nationwide as threatened (or extinct). It is illegal to sell the meat or roe of sturgeon in Wisconsin but, as in other places, the state still has a serious poaching problem.

Spearing

Some limited hook-and-line fishing for sturgeon is permitted, but old-timers know the only way to do it is to get down and dirty with—gulp—a spear. The first thing you need is patience—lots and lots of it. Then, you need a hole the size of a refrigerator cut into the ice. Multicolored coaxers—bright beach balls, homemade fish-shaped decoys, sometimes even beer cans—are dropped into shallow water near the bottom to attract the fish. A multi-pronged pike, the trident, is affixed with a rope, and the wait begins. When a sturgeon appears, you plunge the spikes into the gelatinous cartilage around the head and hold on for dear life; a sturgeon's fight can rival that of an angry marlin.

Annually in Wisconsin, up to 10,000 grizzled Lake Winnie vets trudge out for a two- to three-week sturgeon-spearing season in February, when up to 31,000 fish are taken. The days of 300-pounders are long gone, but 100 pounds is not uncommon. Most spearers have their own rigs, but neophytes can rent complete outfits right from shore.

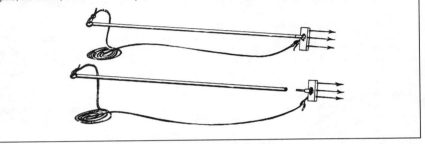

Fishing

Fond du Lac is the southernmost access point for fishing on Lake Winnebago, the most popular fishing lake in the state. Primarily, walleye, perch, sand pike, white bass, saugers, and those old beasty sturgeon are taken on the lake. A list of fishing guides is available from the visitor center. Lakeside Park downtown offers easy access, with full-service marina facilities and launch ramps.

SERVICES AND INFORMATION

The **Fond du Lac Area Convention and Visitors Bureau** is at the Main St. entrance to Lakeside Park, 19 W. Scott St., tel. (920) 923-3010 or (800) 937-9123.

The local **post office** is at 99 W. 2nd St., tel. (920) 921-9300. The public **library,** tel. (920) 929-7080, is at 32 Sheboygan Street. **Urgent care** is available at Aurora Health Center, 20 Wisconsin American Dr., tel. (920) 907-7000.

TRANSPORTATION

At the time of this edition's writing, Amtrak was initiating train service to and from Milwaukee, but it wasn't up yet (it was using Greyhound Thruway service for the time being). The local **Greyhound** stop is at the Hardee's restaurant along S. Main Street.

The **Fond du Lac Transit** system operates daily within the city; for schedules and fares, call (920) 929-2935.

THE REPUBLIC OF WINNECONNE

In 1967 the state of Wisconsin issued its annual highway map. Puzzled taverngoers in Winneconne—let's get this out of the way now; it's west of Oshkosh—tried to no avail to find their village. Gone, absent, forgotten, ignored.

With tongues nudged a bit into cheek, the village board voted to secede from the state; then it declared war. The new Republic of Winneconne's banner boasted: "We like it—where?" To which the Governor, in Madison, said smiling, "By the way, where *is* Winneconne?" The brouhaha continued as the little village that wouldn't be ignored went through machinations of re-creating itself as a sovereign nation; all of this as the nation chuckled along with the resulting media barrage. The state Department of Transportation has never overlooked the town again.

WEST OF WINNEBAGO

RIPON

Winding Ripon (pop. 7,241) has an oddball heritage. Originally founded in 1844 by an organization called the Wisconsin Phalanx as an experiment in communal living, it was named Ceresco, after the Roman goddess of agriculture, and attempted to implement in pure form the democratic principles of French social progressive François Charles Marie Fourier. Ironically, a decade later, it came to fame as the birthplace of the Republican Party (a claim hotly disputed by a few other communities in the U.S.). From a contemporary perspective, however, the two events are not quite so inherently contradictory.

Later, Ripon became the birthplace of another political pioneer—Carrie Chapman Catt, one of the founders and first presidents of both the American Women's Suffrage Association and the League of Women Voters; it was under her lead that the 19th Amendment to the Constitution was finally passed.

Ripon today is a well-worn, tidy little town with some outstanding early architecture still preserved, including an octagon house. Ripon College, a highly regarded liberal arts college, is also located here.

Sights

Along the 300 block of Blackburn Street (WI 44) stands the birthplace of the Republican Party, the **Little White Schoolhouse,** tel. (920) 748-4730. This official national monument doesn't hold much more than a few mementos, but it's still fun to poke around in. It's open May-Oct. Mon.-Sat. 10 a.m.- 4 p.m., shorter hours on Sunday. Free.

Ripon College, tel. (920) 748-8364, overlooks the town from a hill and houses the C.J. Rodman Center for the Arts, containing two paintings by Sir Anthony Van Dyck. The college's Caestecker Fine Arts Series is a constant source of cultural events during the year.

Five miles or so south of town on WI 44/49, then east along Reed's Corner Road, is **Larson's Famous Clydesdales,** tel. (920) 748-5466. Over a dozen of the equine giants made famous by sentimental Budweiser beer commercials are bred and raised here, including a national champion six-horse hitch. Demonstrations are given, and visitors can pet the horses. Reservations are required. It's open Mon.-Sat. May-October. Tours are usually $8, half that for children.

Along the western edge of town stands one of Fourier's followers' communal log structures—the **Log House.** It's on private property near

the Little White
Schoolhouse, birthplace
of the Republican Party

BIRTH OF THE REPUBLICAN PARTY

By the early 1850s, the issue of slavery was as divisive as any issue in American history. The powers within the contemporary political parties were either impotent, willfully ignorant, or, like all entrenched political organizations, hamstrung by both sides. Anti-slavery activists within the Whig Party in Ripon ultimately grew tired enough to call for action. In 1852, Alvan Earle Bovay visited Horace Greeley in New York City to discuss matters. It was clear that the end was near for the Whig party, but what to do about it wasn't as clear.

Then, Senator Stephen Douglass of Illinois provided an opportunity for a minor revolution with his Kansas-Nebraska Bill, introduced in June of 1854; the proposal was to extend slavery beyond the perimeters of the earlier Missouri Compromise. An entertaining chaos of a debate followed and roiled for three months before the bill was passed through the Senate.

Bovay immediately and quietly summoned 53 other voters back to Ripon to devise a battle plan for opposing the slavery proponents. Ripon had long been a nerve center of the abolitionist movement. So strong was its opposition, in fact, that the city was the site of what's known as "Booth's War," a guerrilla skirmish between Milwaukee abolitionist Sherman Booth, who helped escaped slaves along the Underground Railroad, and the federal authorities; local citizens helped Booth and frustrated the authorities over a five-year period.

Bovay hoped to organize the abolitionists into a cohesive force to be called Republicans ("a good name . . . with charm and prestige," he said). His oratory was effective, and the Republican Party was born on March 20, 1854, in the Little White Schoolhouse in Ripon. Official declaration of its platform came two years later in Pittsburgh; standing near the podium was Abraham Lincoln, who, four years later, would become the party's first successful presidential candidate. Note that Ripon is but one of a few places to claim the title of birthplace of the party; the potshots fly back and forth over who legitimately owns the title.

Ceresco Park and isn't exactly obvious, so ask at the Little White Schoolhouse or stop by the chamber of commerce for specifics.

The **Northwestern Trail** is a three-mile-long trail extending from downtown west to CR PP along an old railroad bed.

Accommodations
Ripon offers a handful of places to stay, including the inexpensive **Best Western Welcome Inn**, 240 E. Fond du Lac St., tel. (920) 748-2821, only a block from downtown with rooms from $56.

Food
Many a traveler whipping through Ripon has mistaken the **Republican House**, 303 Blackburn St., tel. (920) 748-2150, for *the* Republican House, where the Republican Party started. Until they see the ideographs, that is. Long a Ripon culinary tradition, this proud, imposing 1857 structure, an erstwhile American eatery, has now become a highly regarded Chinese restaurant. The menu is enormous, and all the copious entrées are well prepared. (An aside: when the new owners took over, they discovered an antique histor-

ical mural painted a century ago). Weekends feature a lunch buffet; an evening buffet is offered Tuesday nights; there's even the inescapable Friday fish fry, here a smorgasbord.

An excellent place to eat is the reconverted bank turned eatery **The Treasury,** 114 Watson St., tel. (920) 745-2000. This impressive place has a main dining room, private dining rooms in old offices, and a cognac bar. Live music tinkles. Luscious continental and American fare turns up on the menu, all well turned out. From $7 lunch, $9 dinner. Open for lunch and dinner weekdays, dinner only Saturday.

Services and Information
The **Ripon Area Chamber of Commerce,** 214 Jefferson Street, tel. (920) 748-6764 or (800) 662-6927, www.ripon-wi.com, is along the edge of the main square.

GREEN LAKE

Green Lake (pop. 1,060) is approximately one-sixth the size of Ripon, but this flyspeck town pulls in tons of visitors, all coming for the eponymous lake—the deepest in the state. The area was first settled in 1840. In 1867, the first resort west of Niagara Falls was built here (thus its self-given moniker, "historic resort community"). When Chicagoans heard about it, the rush was on. Within three decades, posh resorts dotted the circumference of the 7,320-acre lake. Despite its granddaddy status as a resort, the tourists are neither condescending bluebloods nor so numerous that the small-town charm is obliterated.

The lake dominates the psyche here—water or waterfowl references appear in just about every name. If you don't like water, Green Lake may not be for you. The lake trout fishing here is some of the best in the state.

Sights

Heidel House Resort operates the popular **Escapade Tours,** 643 Illinois Avenue, tel. (920) 294-3344. Brunch, cocktail, dinner, and sight-seeing excursions are offered aboard a 57-foot yacht; a basic sightseeing tour is $10. On-the-lake recreation comes from **Zephyr Kayak Tours,** tel. (920) 294-3949, and no paddling experience is necessary.

There's not too much to see "downtown," save for an old railroad depot housing historic artifacts and memorabilia.

You can make some fine day-drives from the Green Lake area, particularly through the diminutive villages of Berlin and Princeton. Princeton has an impressive historical collection in two old buildings downtown and one of the largest—and most varied—flea markets in the state every Saturday May-October. Princeton is also site of the long-running **Cattle Fair.**

You could also make an extensive spin for eco-worship. A number of miles west, to the little town of Montello, then south on CR F, takes you to **Muir Park and Fountain Lake Farm.** Fountain Lake—now called Ennis—was the boyhood home of John Muir and is a National Historic Landmark, as well as a birder's paradise. Many sandhill cranes can be seen here—the Fox River Unit of the Horicon National Wildlife Refuge is across the road. The sandhill crane is mentioned often in Muir's writings; it's estimated that Marquette County alone holds one of North America's highest concentrations, some 1,100 of them winging their way to and from Florida along the Mississippi Flyway.

Scenic Drive

Rustic Road 22, also known as White River Road, ends at CR D, north of Princeton, but affords the experience of two original plank bridges and views of mostly DNR-protected wetlands. From Green Lake, head west along WI 23 to Princeton, then north on CR D.

Accommodations

Rates are *really* high around here during the summer; these are high season rates, but you'll find steep drop-offs in lower periods.

The well-worn sign doesn't accurately represent the **Lakeside Motel,** 488 South Street, tel. (920) 294-3318, a good budget option at around $70.

A motel with a resort complex sums up **Bay View,** 439 Lake Street, tel. (920) 294-6504, another good deal for the money. Anglers love this place—there's plenty of fishing and boat rentals. Rates run around $80 in summer and drop precipitously in the off-season. Some kitchenettes and suites are available.

One of Wisconsin's best and best-known resorts is the **Heidel House Resort,** 643 Illinois Ave., tel. (920) 294-6128 or (800) 444-2812, fax (920) 294-6128, a 20-acre, self-contained sybaritic universe fully deserving its reputation. Over 200 guest rooms, including some estate buildings, run the gamut of elegance and luxurious antiquity. Four-season activities include water sports and on-site trails. The dining is superb. Rates run $85-350.

Part English country home and part traditional New American restaurant (only open for scrumptious dinners), **Carver's on the Lake,** N5529 CR A, tel. (920) 294-6931, is classic Green Lake coziness, a 1920s mansion filled with antiques. The dining room is also well regarded. High-season rates run $65-165.

Built in 1866, the historic **Oakwood Lodge** bed and breakfast, 365 Lake St., tel. (920) 294-6580, features 11 large guest rooms with no telephones. There are fantastic balcony views, and breakfast is served on a screened porch alongside the lake. Rates run $85 s or d.

If you really want to rough it, 13 miles west along WI 23 (near Princeton) is **Mecan River Outfitters,** tel. (920) 295-3439. The primitive secluded lodge with five rooms and three cabins has no electricity and no phones but wood heat and gaslights, the way the northlands used to be. This outfit also organizes canoe and hunting trips and has 10 miles of trails for skiing.

Food

You'll have no problem finding great food of any kind. A good casual dining spot is the **Nordic Hill Restaurant,** W1917 WI 23, tel. (920) 294-0230, perched above Dartford Bay. A deli complements the balanced menu; Friday nights feature an excellent selection of seafood, from stuffed sole to a Jamaican brown fish stew. Nordic Hill is open Tues.-Sun. for breakfast, lunch, and dinner. From $4.

Enjoy fast food the way it used (and ought) to be at **Hinky Dink's,** 304 S. Lawson Dr., tel. (920) 294-3150, where the fries are still hand cut and fried in peanut oil. It's mostly standard burgers and Chicago red-hots, but they do serve mean potato pancakes and make their own bread. A few veggie options. It's open daily mid-April through early September until around 10 p.m. From $2.

Though basically a sports bar, there's a decent view and an even better menu at the **Goose Blind, Etc.** 512 Gold Street, tel. (920) 294-6363. A lengthy, eclectic menu offers creative sandwiches (cucumber, sprout, and mushroom), burgers, seafood (shrimp to snow cod or pike), Mexican entrées, pastas, and California-style takes on standard entrées (chicken strips with artichoke hearts and Parmesan). Best of all, the pricing is reasonable, considering the variety. From $3.

The local supper club of repute (for 25 years and going strong) is **Alfred's Supper Club,** 506 Hill St., tel. (920) 294-3631, with one of the area's most extensive menus in a pleasant ersatz-Victorian atmosphere. Italian pasta dishes supplement the house specialty—aged and hand-cut steaks and exquisite seafood. Another excellent choice is **Norton's,** S. Lawson Dr., tel. (920) 294-6577, the only supper club on the lake accessible by water. Both from $9; Norton's is open for lunch as well and has grand alfresco dining on a lakeside deck.

If a dress-code kind of place is what you're after, **Carver's on the Lake,** N5529 CR A, tel. (920) 294-6931, has elegant dinner dining in a historic English-style cottage. The menu concentrates on seafood and Midwestern cuisine; the restaurant does its own baking. The great room bar is a great place for a drink before dinner. The patio has a spectacular lake view. Reservations are a good idea. From $16.

Ready to splurge? Rated one of the best restaurants in Wisconsin is the **Grey Rock Mansion Restaurant,** 643 Illinois Avenue, tel. (920) 294-3344, in the Heidel House Resort and Conference Center. Housed in an 1890s building, the charming rich woods interiors and fireplaces support the food. The walleye here will knock your socks off. From $11.

Sports and Recreation

There's an awful lot to do in Green Lake, but fishing tops the list. **Walker's Guide Service,** tel. (920) 748-3661, runs trips for lake trout, walleye, bass, northern, or pan fish; trips are fully outfitted aboard pontoon or Starcraft boats. Contact the service by mailing to: Rt. 2, Box 91, Ripon, WI 54971.

For your own recreation, the **Green Lake Marina,** 485 Park Dr., tel. (920) 294-6221, rents ski boats, pontoon boats, fishing boats, and slips. Numerous motels and cottages in the area rent boats and supplies, including the **Green Lake Conference Center,** WI 23 West, tel. (920) 294-3323, and the **Bayview Motel and Resort,** 439 Lake St., tel. (920) 294-6504.

For land-based recreation, there may be more golf courses per capita in the Green Lake vicinity than anywhere in Wisconsin. The **Golf Courses of Lawsonia,** WI 23 West, tel. (920) 294-3320, have been rated as among America's top public courses, according to *Golf Digest* magazine, which gave the elevated tees and merciless bunkers four stars. (It was designed to resemble Scottish links-style courses.) They also noted the affordability, given the quality. Tee times are recommended here. **Tuscumbia Country Club,** tel. (920) 294-3240, is Wisconsin's oldest course; it's known as one of the best manicured courses in the Midwest. The local chamber of commerce has information on some of the great golf/lodging packages available.

Services and Information

The **Green Lake Area Chamber of Commerce,** tel. (920) 294-3231 or (800) 253-7354, www. greenlakecc.com, maintains information booths at both ends of the town in summer. Address written requests to P.O. Box 337, Green Lake, WI 54941.

WAUPACA AND THE CHAIN O' LAKES

The Waupaca area lies at the western edge of the east-central waters region, approaching the central Wisconsin River Valley and Sand Country. But it still qualifies as hydrophilic: 22 spring-fed lakes southwest of Waupaca form one of the longest recreational stretches in the lower half of Wisconsin—240 lakes in the county alone. Settlement began in the region around 1848; the first flourmill went up a year after the state's birth. The city was named for an altruistic Potawatomi chief, Sam Waupaca, who collapsed and died after convincing local Natives not to kill the white settlers.

Sights

The most popular activity in the Chain O' Lakes area is to take a breezy ride aboard an authentic sternwheeler, the former flagship of a brewery, the *Chief* (or on the more sedate motor yacht *Lady of the Lakes*). The one-and-a-half hour tours take in eight to eleven lakes of the chain, including Indian Crossing Bridge to Long Lake and the mouth of the Crystal River. Sunday champagne brunch tours ($13.50) are available. Tours begin running Memorial Day weekend and depart three times daily 11:30 a.m.-4 p.m. for the eight-lake tour aboard the *Chief;* rates run $6.75 adults, $3.50 children under 12. There are fewer departures during the weeks prior to Memorial Day and after Labor Day. The 11-lake tour on the *Lady of the Lakes* costs the same and lasts two hours; it departs at 4 p.m.

Unique to Waupaca is the **Wisconsin Veteran's Home,** a self-contained community for war veterans and their spouses founded in 1887. The city of Waupaca purchased the Greenwood Park resort hotel and 80 acres to donate to the Grand Army of the Republic, the veteran's group that initiated the project. The Marden Center inside the grounds contains a small museum of war memorabilia and artifacts; there's also a gift shop and coffee shop. Located in King, via CR QQ, tel. (715) 258-5586, the center is open daily 8 a.m.-4 p.m. Free admission.

Just southwest of Waupaca along WI 22 lies tiny **Rural,** honest to goodness a town that time forgot. It's a Yankee town stuck in the middle 1800s. Virtually the entire city, along the switch-backing banks of the Crystal River, is on the National Register of Historic Places. The architectural renaissance is impressive; it's gotten so popular that WI 22 was rerouted *around* the town to avoid spoiling it. It's also a good spot to pick up antiques. Check out the unbelievable selection at **Walker's Barn,** a converted chicken farm that now seems to have about half the antiques in Waupaca County.

Another short jaunt out of the city via CR K takes you to **Red Mill.** The biggest water wheel in the state, it's been converted into a hodge-podge of shops offering handicrafts, antiques, and lots and lots of scented candles in an original interior. One of the few extant covered bridges in Wisconsin is also there (400 hand-crafted oak pegs were used in its construction), along with the Chapel in the Woods. Red Mill lies along a beautiful stretch of the Crystal River with a picturesque park.

Scenic Drives

Two of those farm-to-market narrow country lanes in the area are **Rural Road** and **Emmons Creek Road,** both jutting westward out of Rural toward Hartman Creek State Park. The former serpentines across the Crystal River several times; the latter takes in a tributary trout stream of the Crystal and lots of woodland.

South of Waupaca along CR E (itself fairly narrow) is Saxeville and, still farther south, **26th Road,** along CR W out of town. 26th Road stretches to CR H along the Pine River Valley, a Class II trout stream. This drive passes several dwellings—one a log cabin—predating the Civil War.

Accommodations

This is another resort/cottage area, and the local chamber of commerce maintains a complete listing. The cheapest motel in town and the only one on the east side is the **Park Motel and Library Lounge,** E3621 WI 10/49, tel. (715) 258-2691, with basic rooms for around $35.

Upscale lodging is at the **Baymont Inn and Suites,** 110 Grand Seasons Dr., junction of WI 10 and 54, tel. (715) 258-9212 or (877) 880-1054, which has a pool, health club, sauna, and enormous game room. Doubles start at $66.

Bed and Breakfasts: Close to town is **The Thomas Pipe Inn,** 11032 Pipe Rd., tel. (715)

824-3161, an 1855 farmhouse that was once a stagecoach inn. Four rooms start at $70. In anachronistic Rural is the **Crystal River Inn,** E1369 Rural Rd., tel. (715) 258-5333 or (800) 236-5789, an older (by two years) farmstead. The six original farmhouse guest rooms are done up with antiques and brass beds. All the rooms have views of either the river, a wildwood garden, or the backyard garden; three of them have fireplaces. Rooms run $65-90.

Camping: Hartman Creek State Park is the best bet, with over 100 good sites available. An entrance fee and site fee ($8) are required. Otherwise, in or near the city are six private campgrounds, including two right in town: **Waupaca Camping Park,** E2411 Holmes Rd., tel. (715) 258-8010, with rates from $18.25; and **Rustic Woods,** E2585 Southwood Dr., tel. (715) 258-2442 (open all year), with rates from $20. Both cater more to RVs but do offer tent sites, especially at the former, which has a separate tenting area.

Food and Entertainment

Many restaurants in the Chain O' Lakes area cater to the footloose summertime crowd, so dinner may include live entertainment—DJs, loud music, or live bands.

The Clear Water Harbor, N2757 CR QQ, tel. (715) 258-2866, (known locally as the "Har Bar") is the departure point for the *Chief* and *Lady of the Lakes* tour boats. It serves a menu varying from pub grub sandwiches (try its famous 'shroomburger) to salads and a Friday fish fry. From $3. It's also popular for summer entertainment, with a huge deck on the lakeside. It's open seasonally. (From here, you can do the Wally Walk up the road into King to the very local **Wally's Bar,** where you can get a Lunch Box shot: beer with amaretto and orange juice. It's tasty if you can down it quickly.)

Another popular lakeside eatery, **The Wheelhouse,** along CR Q off CR QQ, tel. (715) 258-8289, features simple sandwiches, some of the best pizza around, and lasagna. It also has a lakeside deck, this one complete with a deck-locked boat with its own mast. Some live entertainment is offered, particularly the Wednesday open jams. The tavern preserves the tradition of sticking dollars to the ceiling with pins. From $4.

The most recognized Waupaca restaurant is **Weasel's,** in Waupaca's City Square, tel. (715) 258-5900. The "pretty-good chili" is better than its name, and they serve up the best stone oven-baked pizza around. Swedish pea soup is available daily. There's even a Waupaca specialty—the Waupaca slider, a dinner roll with different combinations of fish, meat, and a pickle. Try the variation of a calzone called the "Weasel-oni." Weasel's is open for lunch and dinner. From $4.

Some traditional fish boils have been offered Friday in summer at **King's Table,** CR QQ in King, tel. (715) 258-9150, which also has great skillet breakfasts in the morning, fresh-baked bread daily, and some decent Mexican choices. From $4.

A respectable eatery (a place you'd take your grandma) is **Simpson's,** a subdued supper club also known as the Indian Room, 222 S. Main Street. Simpson's has been serving lunch and dinner since the 1930s, specializing in chicken with mushrooms and wine sauce. From $4.

Best place for dessert is the **Danes Home Lodge,** 301 N. Main St., established in 1877 for the social and literary pursuits of Danish settlers in the region. Membership grew so much it had its own Danish library and offered its own insurance, but it disbanded in the 1930s. This one now doubles as an ice cream shop, open daily 10 a.m.-6 p.m., Friday until 8 p.m., and weekends until 4 p.m. Tours of the 1894 building are available. Get good ice cream also at the old-fashioned general store **Main Street Marketplace,** 103 N. Main St., tel. (715) 258-9160, with fresh fudge and lots, lots more. Open seven days a week. Both from $3.

Find live comedy on Sunday at the **Beach Club,** CR QQ in King; the club also has DJs spinning blues, jazz, reggae, and '50s and '60s music. Come summertime, the best entertainment is the free **band concerts** Friday nights in the historic 1898 bandstand at the downtown square.

J.R.'s Bar and Grill, near the junction of WI 10 and WI 54 northwest of town on WI 54 (near the overpass), is one of the weirdest bars you're likely ever to encounter. In addition to the fireplace, pool tables, and general tavern atmosphere, there is a game farm and petting zoo with over 100 exotic animals. (And many more mounted on the walls.) Tigers, bears, giraffes, cougars, and an inordinate number of ducks are just a few. The zoo is open May-Sept. 10 a.m.-7 p.m.

Events
Waupaca County holds one of Wisconsin's few PRCA-sanctioned rodeo events the first week of July in nearby Manawa. Events include bareback and saddle bronc riding, calf roping, steer wrestling, bull riding, team roping, and girls' barrel racing. Tickets cost $8 for reserved seats.

Sports and Recreation
A segment of the National Scenic Ice Age Trail is located in **Hartman Creek State Park;** the county section totals 20 miles and links up on both ends with Portage County's segment. The park has a hike-in primitive cabin offered on a first-come, first-served basis. The state park also maintains off-road bike trails. Maps are available at the chamber of commerce, 221 S. Main St., tel. (715) 258-7343 or (800) 236-2222. The park is also popular with canoeists and boaters, since most of the upper Chain O' Lakes are either in or adjacent to state park lands.

The lolling, tranquil Crystal River is perfect for canoeing. Organized excursions leave from **Ding's Dock** along CR Q, tel. (715) 258-2612 (it also rents decent cottages); or on the Little Wolf River from the **Wolf River Trips and Campground,** in New London, tel. (715) 982-2458.

This is prime touring area for bikers; trails run along waterways and through some Amish farmstead areas; northwest of the city, the topography shifts to rolls of kettles and moraines. Check **Harbor Bike and Ski,** tel. (715) 258-5404, for maps.

Shopping
Besides the myriad opportunities for antiquing in the area, **Woodcrafters,** 114 N. Main St., tel. (715) 258-3210, offers Amish crafts, including wonderful bent-hickory furniture, quilts, and more. It's open daily from 9 a.m. but closes Sundays after Labor Day.

Services and Information
The **Waupaca Area Chamber of Commerce** is at 221 S. Main St., tel. (715) 258-7343 or (800) 236-2222.

THE WOLF RIVER REGION

MENOMINEE INDIAN RESERVATION

The Menominee nation represents the oldest established inhabitants of the territory of Wisconsin, going back as far as five millennia, though precise dating is impossible. Unlike the diasporic nature of many U.S. tribes, the Menominee are strictly Wisconsin residents. The reservation lies a chip-shot north of Shawano and abuts the southern perimeter of the Nicolet National Forest and the northern edge of the much smaller Stockbridge Indian Reservation. While many Wisconsinites never seem to notice the reservation—spearfishing controversies don't predominate here as they do farther north—they do pay attention to its crown jewel, the Wolf River, one of the region's top draws.

History

Anthropologists have surmised that the Menominee, an Algonquian-speaking tribe, may have been in the Wisconsin territory as far back as 10,000 years ago. They probably originated around the mouth of the Milwaukee River. The tribe and its many bands once controlled regions of the Upper Great Lakes from as far south as Milwaukee to the Escanaba River in Michigan's Upper Peninsula and the entire breadth of Wisconsin. They were called *O-Maeq-No-Min-Ni-Wuk*, or "Wild Rice People"; much of the regional toponymy arises from their language and often has roots in the word *manomin* (wild rice). French trappers got it wrong when they saw the Menominee's main grain and dubbed them the Folle Avoine Nation—Followers of the Oats.

Beginning in 1817, a series of breached federal treaties gradually eroded Menominee sovereignty until, by 1854, they were only allowed 12 townships on the present-day reservation; some of the ceded land was turned over to the Oneida and Stockbridge Indians for their own reservations. Almost 10 million acres dwindled to 200,000.

Along with other Native American nations, the Menominee, who had been given reservation status by a treaty signed near the Wolf River's Keshena Falls, asked for their status as natives to be terminated in 1961 in an attempt at federal assimilation. It was a dismal failure, and reservation status was reinstated in 1973. The tribe today numbers approximately 6,500, more than half of whom reside on the reservation.

In 1995, the Menominee received statewide attention when they filed a federal district lawsuit attempting to reestablish fishing and hunting rights over the 10 million acres the tribe once controlled, insisting that the federal government had given them access to the lands in 19th-century treaties. The tribe lost the case in 1996. It would have been an astonishing coup if they had won, since the lands in question represent most of eastern Wisconsin and Lake Michigan, along with the Wolf, Fox, and Wisconsin Rivers.

Menominee Indian Reservation Forest

The 223,500 acres of forest surrounding the reservation include some of the most pristine stands of hardwoods, hemlock, and pine in the Great Lakes region; it's regarded as an invaluable ecosystem. The tribe has had a lumber operation since 1908, one of the first and largest Native-owned in the U.S.; they had been trading lumber with the Winnebago long before European contact. Their high-tech present-day plant is the largest and most modern in the region. Over two billion board feet have been removed from the forest—more than twice the entire yield. Yet the Menominee have been lauded by international environmentalists—including Robert F. Kennedy, Jr., who toured the forest in 1995—for instituting a radical sustainable ecosystem model, presently being examined by Indian bands from the Atlantic Coast to the Nuu-chah-nulth group of tribes from Vancouver Island. Forestry experts from as far away as Cambodia and Indonesia have come to the tribe's new forestry institute.

Wolf River

Meandering through the reservation from its headwaters in Lily to the north is the nascent Wolf River, a part of the Fox River system, which includes the Fox and Wolf Rivers headwaters, the lower Fox River, and Lake Winnebago. This stretch of the state-designated Outstanding Water

the Wolf River Dells near the Menominee Indian

Resource and federally designated wild river is perhaps the most spectacular. It drops almost 1,000 feet as it crosses the reservation, from the multi-hued juttings and whitewater of Smokey Falls to the eerie canyons of the Wolf River Dells. Water conditions range from placid—below Post Lake—to hair-raising—in sections near Smokey Falls. One of Wisconsin's designated fly-fishing-only stretches of blue-ribbon waterway is located below Hollister. For more river-running information, see tour operators listed under "Recreation" in "Shawano," below.

Sights

Don't miss the **Menominee Logging Camp Museum,** tel. (715) 799-3757, the largest and most comprehensive exhibit of timber heritage in the United States. Seven hand-hewn log buildings and over 20,000 artifacts re-create an early 1900s logging camp. The mock-ups are well presented, and the rustic feel adds to the experience. Of note are the 12-to-a-bunk bunkhouse and the 1,000 pairs of oxen shoes, not to mention a 400-year-old pine log. Located at Grignon Rapids along the Wolf River, north of the Wolf at CR VV

along WI 47. The museum is open May 1 through October 15, Tues.-Sat. 9 a.m.-4 p.m., Sunday 11 a.m.-4 p.m. Admission is $3 adults, $2 seniors, 75 cents children 10-15, or $6 family.

Any of the bends in the Wolf River off the road are worth investigating on foot. **Wolf River Dells** has a short nature trail leading to rough multi-colored granite cliffs overlooking the Wolf for hundreds of yards along both the upper and lower dells. The outcroppings set you right on top of the aggressive waters. In summer, a small snack stand operates. The Dells are located four miles from a well-marked turnoff from WI 55 along a road that alternates from hardpack gravel to nerve-wracking sand and dirt that gets good and goopy in the spring—so take care. A footbridge crosses the 40-foot gurgling Smokey Falls to a small mid-river island; a 50-cent "toll" is advertised. Purportedly, the mist from the waters is actually smoke from the pipe of a spirit living within the falls. **Spirit Rock,** located a couple of miles above Keshena Falls, is also significant. According to legend it's really a petrified Menominee Warrior who angered the Earth. This warrior, *Ko-Ko-Mas-Say-Sa-Now,* allegedly asked for immortality and was thrust into the earth forever. The legend also says that when the stone erodes, the Menominee tribe follow. Some believe kind spirits come to offer rings of tobacco, and their willowy vapors can be observed flitting among the trees in the dusky night.

Powwows

Two powwows are held annually here. Over Memorial Day weekend, the **Veteran Powwow** honors the reservation's military veterans. Larger is the **Annual Menominee Nation Contest Powwow,** held the first weekend in August. The biggest highlight is the dancing contest and all its finery. This is one of the largest cultural events in the Upper Midwest. Both are held in the natural amphitheater Woodland Bowl. Admission is $8 for the weekend, $4 for a daily pass. Children five and under and seniors 60 and over get in free.

STOCKBRIDGE-MUNSEE INDIAN RESERVATION

The Stockbridge-Munsee are an Algonquian-speaking band of the Mohican Indians. The three tribes composing the band (along with a fourth, which eventually opted for assimilation) stretch throughout the Connecticut and Hudson River Valleys. This band is one of the best traveled of any in the state, though that's hardly of their own doing; the word "Mohican" means, aptly enough, "people of never-still waters." They first appeared in Wisconsin in the early 1820s, living in the Fox River Valley (hence, the town of Stockbridge on the eastern shore of Lake Winnebago; the Stockbridge cemetery there is a National Historic Site) along with the Munsee, a Delaware tribe also forced west by European expansion. Some Stockbridge Indians decamped to Indiana Territory in Kansas, others moved to Red Springs, Wisconsin, to live on land ceded to them in 1856 by the Menominee (who got $20,000 for 2.5 million acres). The reservation has been occupied since 1937 and consists of 40,000 acres; the tribe numbers some 1,500.

Sights

The **Stockbridge Munsee Historical Library Museum** has one of the best archives of Native American material in Wisconsin, including maps dating from the 1600s (not on public display). Available for viewing are exhibits and collections arranged chronologically. Most exhibits are on the day-to-day life of the Stockbridge and the later fur trade. Of note is the section on the missionaries—those stoic Jesuits—including a catechism written in Mohican and a 1745 Bible presented to the Stockbridge by an emissary of the Prince of Wales. The library and museum are located four miles east of Bowler and are open Mon.-Fri. 8 a.m.-4:30 p.m.

In nearby Gresham, the **Gresham Railroad Museum**, CR A, tel. (715) 526-3536, a tiny exhibit of railroad memorabilia, is open on Saturday afternoon in summer. The tribe also operates a nine-hole golf course and holds an annual powwow.

SHAWANO

Shawano (pop. 7,598) lies along the proud Wolf River at one of its widest points and serves as the recreational heart of the Wolf. The lake bearing the name Shawano sits to the east, full of fish.

The name (pronounced "SHAW-no") is another mellifluous result of the Menominee term for the large lake, *Sha-Wah-Nah-Pay-Sa*—"Lake to the South").

Settlers first came to work in lumber mills built in the 1840s, then to serve traffic on an old military road (Main Street was part of it). The city now has one of the country's largest milk-products plants and a leading artificial breeding cooperative; it's also third in butter production.

But it's recreation that draws most visitors—fishing on Shawano Lake and whitewater rafting on the icy Wolf River. The area is noticeably less garish than the Wisconsin Dells strip and less nouveau-riche than Door County. This is true-blue, mom-and-pop, basic family-style resort country.

Sights

In Shawano proper, visit the **Heritage Park Museum,** tel. (715) 526-3536, with a restored old schoolhouse, a stone building with artifacts from a hardware store, a log house, and (in Gresham) an old depot, adjoining the Wolf River and Sunset Island downtown on a somewhat dusty compound. The museum features cheesemaking exhibits and a collection of early street lamps. Follow the signs downtown to get there. It's open June-Sept. Wednesday and weekends 1:30-4:30 p.m. Admission is $3 adults, 50 cents children.

Seven miles south of town, the almost unknown **Navarino Wildlife Area** is a restored 1,400-acre glacial lakebed, once a swamp and wetland that was drained and farmed for a century. Conservation efforts were begun in the 1950s. Oak and pine stands predominate, under a shelterwood replacement system. Fifteen dikes have re-created the wetlands—sedge meadow to cattail marsh. Prairie and oak savanna restoration work is underway. The marshes support a resident family of sandhill cranes; the best wildlife viewing is along the Wolf River drainages on the western fringes, near McDonald Road. A nature center, tel. (715) 526-4226, is located at the site. Access the wildlife area via WI 156 and McDonald Road.

The **Mielke Theater,** a mile north on WI 29, then follow signs along CR HHH, stands in an isolated, bucolic setting with a country garden and offers year-round cultural events ranging from an arts and crafts fair (a good time to scout for Midwestern handicrafts) to children's theater and plenty of concerts.

In Clintonville to the southwest, you can visit the **Four-Wheel Museum,** along 11th St., tel. (715) 823-2141, an assortment of antique vehicles manufactured in town by the FWD Corporation.

Scenic Drives

West of Shawano approximately 25 miles is tiny Wittenburg, the endpoint of one of Wisconsin's Rustic Roads, this one CR M, which ends in Tigerton. There are lovely scenes on this route—historic round barns and stone buildings (including a gas station), and closet-size historical museums in both Wittenburg and Tigerton.

Tigerton is also the home of Wisconsin's first anti-government militia, the Posse Comitatus, who made some waves in the early 1980s before retreating into obscurity after several of its leaders were jailed. They've been pretty quiet since, though there are definitely still members out there. An important thing to remember in these days of militias under every rock is that these folks have always been around.

Cheese

Shawano County is one of the top agricultural areas of the state. Cheesemaking was among the original agricultural pursuits to solidify the regional economy. Since 1913, the **Grass Lake Cheese Factory** has been producing cheddar, Monterey Jack, Colby, and, more recently, a slew of specialty cheeses. Located five miles southwest of Shawano along Grass Lake Rd., tel. (715) 526-5558, the factory (fresh curds on Friday) is open Mon.-Sat. 8 a.m.-4 p.m.

Accommodations

Rock-bottom lodging done right is available along the main drag at the surprisingly nice **Wisconsin House Inn,** 216 E. Green Bay St., tel. (715) 524-4488 or (800) 245-0692. The site has offered lodging of some sort since 1887. Today, travelers enjoy a very cozy lobby in Early American decor, spartan but clean rooms, a large restaurant, and a lounge with local artwork displayed. A couple of whirlpool suites are available, and there is a sauna. All this for as low as $20 off-season, $30 in summer.

An equally good budget option is the strictly motel **Pine Acre,** 1346 E. Green Bay St., tel.

(715) 524-6665 or (800) 788-6665, with few amenities but excellently appointed rooms (and one cottage) and low prices—around $30. It's on a nicely wooded lot.

Find very nice rooms and tasteful decor at the cozy **Country Inn,** 104 Airport Rd., tel. (715) 526-2044 or (800) 456-4000, with an indoor pool and continental breakfasts for $60 s or d.

Most of Shawano is classic Wisconsin rustic lodging country—cabins and cottages that are clean but very, very simple. Rates vary: you can find a cabin for six folks for as low as $400 a week—not a bad deal. A good example is **Bamboo Shores,** tel. (715) 524-4992 or (800) 408-4992, which has cottages that can sleep 6-10. The chamber of commerce has a comprehensive listing of cabins and cottages, many with pictures.

Closest public **camping** is on the north shore of Shawano Lake, via CR H, with 90 campsites in a decent wooded area with a great big beach. Sites run $9. For private campgrounds, check the family resorts, which at times have separate camping areas. Otherwise, the closest is **Brady's Pine Grove,** 12 miles west on WI 29, then north on Campground Rd., tel. (715) 787-4555. Sites begin at $14.

Food

The specials range from country ribs to dumplings and sauerkraut to Reubens at **Pop-p's,** 132 S. Main, tel. (715) 524-6240, open Mon.-Sat. 6 a.m.-6 p.m., Sunday 7 a.m.-6 p.m. From $5. More Germanic inspired cuisine at **Black Forest Pub,** 114 S. Main St., tel. (715) 524-4592, which also has lots of sandwiches and Upper Peninsula (MI) pasties; from $4.

Anello's Torchlight, 1276 E. Green Bay, tel. (715) 526-5680, is a favorite supper club, with reasonable daily specials. From $4. Another popular supper club is **The Ribs,** W6026 Lake Dr., tel. (715) 526-5435, with jambalaya and specials varying daily—Italian Tuesday, stuffed pork chops Wednesday, applewood-smoked ribs Thursday, and the usual Friday fish and Saturday prime rib. It's open for dinner daily except Monday. From $6.

Enjoy German food until your tummy creaks at **Happy Corners,** just west of town along WI 29, tel. (715) 787-4114. House specialties include sauerbraten, *rouladen,* and even *Jager Schnitzel,* along with rarities like rabbit. The old-style architecture is noteworthy; this used to be a cheese factory. From $5.

You can get some very good Chinese at **Hunan's,** 145 S. Main St., tel. (715) 526-5820. There's a surprisingly good lo mein selection and outstanding Hunan specialties, particularly the two-flavor shrimp and Happy Nest. Good prices on weekday lunch specials. From $4.

Events

Every August, Shawano hosts three days of fiddlin' and pickin' during the **Old Time Music Festival** at Mielke Theater and Park. Featured in prior years have been national acts like Sally Rogers and Peter Ostroushko, along with such diverse activities as Japanese *koto* and tea ceremonies.

In October, the area's German heritage is celebrated at the Shawano version of **Oktoberfest,** with the usual dining, drinking, and dancing, along with great potato pancake feeds. (It's also a good time to catch the fall colors.)

Sports and Recreation

The Shawano stretch of the Wolf River is a prime area for whitewater rafting and also offers more leisurely stretches for canoeing. The river itself begins quietly in Lily, then picks up speed as it crosses Langlade; by the time it reaches the Menominee Reservation, it's built up quite a head of steam. The colorful toponymy describes it well: Little Slough Gundy, Sherry Rapids, Horse Race Rapids, Twenty Day Rips, and more. The stretch of river between Gilmore's Mistake and Smokey Falls—the lower terminus for most rafters—can be rife with mid-range rapids, some up to eight feet. During high-water periods, operators shut down trips—proof it can be serious business. Outfitters in these parts generally don't supply guides or captains, so you're on your own.

There's a handful of tour operators in the area; many just rent boats, others run full six-hour trips. **River Forest Rafts,** tel. (715)882-3351, has rentals, is also a campground, and has trails for mountain bikes.

Shotgun Eddy, north of Shawano via WI 55, tel. (715) 882-4461, offers four trips—two tough ones requiring skill and strength, two easier ones. All operate between Shotgun Eddy and Smokey Falls. Rustic campsites are available.

Operating out of Keshena on the Menominee Indian Reservation is **Big Smokey Falls Rafting,** tel. (715) 799-3359 or (715) 799-4945, with three runs between the W.W. Bridge paralleling WI 55 through three falls areas, the lush, moss-covered Wolf River Dells, and the bumpy Teakettle Rapids. Smokey Falls, the end of the trip, is the wildest section. Trips cost $11-18 per person.

The **Mountain Bay Trail** is a 65-mile multi-use trail connecting Green Bay, Shawano, and Wausau. It's a grand trail and leads to numerous other trails.

Services and Information

The well-stocked visitors center of the Chamber of Commerce is at 1404 E. Green Bay Rd., tel. (715) 524-2139 or (800) 235-8528, www.shawano. com. Open weekdays 8:30 a.m.-5 p.m. and Saturday 9 a.m.-1 p.m., the chamber has a comprehensive listing of over 45 motels, motor hotels, spartan cabins, family resorts, and even the occasional B&B.

DOOR COUNTY

Hold your left hand up for a moment, palm out. The thumb is, as the Depression-era WPA Wisconsin guidebook put it, "the spout, as it were, of the Wisconsin teakettle." That's the Door Peninsula. Early French inhabitants called the watery cul-de-sac formed by the peninsula *La Baye* (later, *La Baye Verde,* and finally, Green Bay).

"Cape Cod of the Midwest" and other silly likenings (I've even heard "California of the North," and that *really* gets me going) are the rule here. Incessant comparisons to Yankee seaside villages don't wholly miss the mark, though in spots the area smacks just as much of chilled, stony Norwegian fjords. Bays in all the colors of an artist's palette are surrounded by variegated shoreline—alternately rocky beach, craggy bluff, blossom-choked orchard, bucolic heath, and meadow. Generation upon generation of shipbuilders, fishers, and farmers benefited from the magical microclimate here, and there's a predisposition within the populace not to get worked up about much.

Door County is the place most people come to visit. The county boasts 250 miles of gorgeous coastline (more than any county in the U.S.) and agricultural expanse. Fantastic isolated state parks, including outlying islands, offer an abundance of one-of-a-kind Midwest camping and hiking options. (Door County's established park-

land acreage—county, state, and municipal—is staggering, considering its size.) There are endless pages to be written about the hybrid of culture and activities on the peninsula—the cherries, the cheese, the fish boils, the dunes, the theater and art, the parks and recreation, and on and on.

Ups and Downs

Summer tourists first discovered the Door Peninsula around the start of the Civil War; the first hotel went up near Sturgeon Bay in 1866. Around the turn of the century, handfuls of other tourist homes and modest resorts sprang up in communities up and down the coast. But the Door somehow always deftly avoided swells of tourists.

Until now, that is. The peninsula (Door County especially) has in 25 years eclipsed the state's north woods regions and Wisconsin Dells to position itself as Wisconsin's number-one overall tourist destination. One of every six travelers to Wisconsin—that's approaching two million folks—head to the Door. It's no longer a one-season kind of place—always a summer retreat, it is in fact even more popular now during autumn. Roughly half of the tourism infrastructure on the peninsula was created in the past two decades.

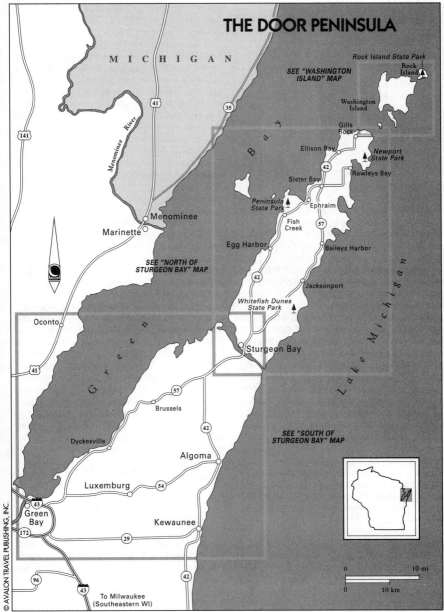

THE DOOR PENINSULA

MICHIGAN

Menominee River

Menominee

Marinette

Oconto

Green Bay

Luxemburg

Kewaunee

Dyckesville

Algoma

Brussels

SEE "NORTH OF STURGEON BAY" MAP

SEE "SOUTH OF STURGEON BAY" MAP

Green Bay

Sturgeon Bay

Whitefish Dunes State Park

Jacksonport

Egg Harbor

Fish Creek

Peninsula State Park

Ephraim

Sister Bay

Ellison Bay

Gills Rock

Baileys Harbor

Rowleys Bay

Newport State Park

Washington Island

SEE "WASHINGTON ISLAND" MAP

Rock Island State Park

Rock Island

Lake Michigan

Bay

To Milwaukee (Southeastern WI)

0   10 mi

0   10 km

© AVALON TRAVEL PUBLISHING, INC.

DOOR COUNTY HIGHLIGHTS

Blossom Festival
Cana Island and Range Lights Lighthouses, Baileys Harbor
Charter Fishing, Algoma
The Clearing, Ellison Bay
Door County Maritime Museum, Sturgeon Bay
Peninsula Players, Fish Creek
Peninsula, Whitefish Dunes, and Newport State Parks
Washington and Rock Islands

With that resurgence comes the inevitable debate about whether it all is a good thing. As weekenders throw up multimillion-dollar resorts and condos around them, year-round residents eventually find themselves priced out of their own family homes due to stratospheric property taxes. The fragile water table takes a severe hit annually, and no amount of technology can provide water that simply isn't there. Most telling: at times, both state highways serving the peninsula are absolutely gridlocked.

Chambers of commerce and other anti-alarmists reason that very little new development has actually been done in Door County (true) and, if caution is exerted, more can be done without damaging ecosystems, agricultural economics, or culture (seriously debatable). Why then, alarmists ask, did Door County civic groups in 1996 get together and formulate an unheard-of agreement essentially banning development in order to preserve the quality of life?

The bottom line: old hands in Door County constantly bemoan the degradation and awful gentrification of what was once among the wildest retreats on the Great Lakes; locals worry about the future; benevolent hordes of tourists pile in. It's still a place unlike any other. In other words, the Door Peninsula is the same as it ever was.

Climate
Jacksonport, Door County, is on the 45th parallel, exactly halfway between the equator and the North Pole, but don't let that fool you—the peninsula's climate is far more temperate than in other northerly Wisconsin areas. The fero-cious waters of Lake Michigan, legendary for their unpredictability and furor, can also ameliorate the weather, keeping things cool in the dog days and taking the bite out of winter's Alberta Clippers. (Early weather accounts from Door County point out that the northern tip is generally a few degrees warmer than the southern end, though the bayside vs. lakeside difference is more important climatically.) This in part explains the rather one-sided habitation of the Door; most of the residents live on the western, or bay, side. With Lake Michigan in a huff, blowing fog, spray, and mist, Green Bay, in the lee of fifteen miles of limestone windblock, remains sedate (if a bit cloudy).

Lakeside vs. Bayside
South of Sturgeon Bay, WI 42 traces Lake Michigan, and WI 57 follows Green Bay. Six miles outside of Sturgeon Bay, they link up and do the clogged-four-lane thing all the way to the ship channel. North of the city the road regains rationality, and thus two lanes, for three miles. The two split again (and crisscross) and you've got a decision to make: travel along Green Bay (now WI 42) or Lake Michigan (WI 57) for nearly 30 miles to Sister Bay. In a nutshell, the Lake Michigan route takes in a state park with mocha-colored beaches and communities far less built up than those on the Green Bay side. There are few structures in Jacksonport or Baileys Harbor, both sometimes sadly featuring a pretentious film of charm. The Green Bay shoreline is rife with aesthetic eye candy—real or improvised. Sybaritic resorts and posh B&Bs outnumber rustic cottages, restaurants hit the wallet hard, and shoppers will find a plethora of opportunities. Conversely, south of Sturgeon Bay, the lakeside (WI 42) has the large communities, and the bayside (WI 57) very little at all.

HISTORY, NATURAL AND OTHERWISE

The area's most salient feature is the limestone bedrock rising 220 feet out of Lake Michigan. It's part of the same Niagara Escarpment that stretches south to Lake Winnebago (and east all the way to Niagara Falls). The heights don't eclipse those of the lower Fox River Valley, but their beauty is transcendent. Eons of waves have carved rough sea caves into the multi-hued red and smoky black cliffs. (The shores on the western side of Green Bay are dramatic in contrast—mostly low-slung topography crawling toward the shore through marsh or beach.)

Porte des Mortes

At the tip of the peninsula is the only major gap in the escarpment, Porte des Mortes, the fabled "Door of Death"—so named by petrified early French explorers. The ferocious local climate has devoured hundreds of ships here. Accounts vary wildly (travelers will believe anything—and pass it along at the next inn) regarding which tragedy gave rise to the name Door of Death, but all are remarkably harrowing. Most accounts point to a band of 300 to 500 Potawatomi—some say Winnebago—who were dashed against rocks. Gales swirl up so quickly that it's still a dangerous crossing, modern technology notwithstanding. Before the advent of modern navigation and large, diesel-driven screws, most ships could not overcome the shifting currents or conflicting wind shears. The waters, ruinous outer depths and shallows alike, are littered with hundreds and hundreds of wrecks.

Human History

Human habitation at what today is Whitefish Dunes State Park dates back to 100 B.C., to judge by traces of the North Bay People, who spread from the mouth of the bay all the way to Rock Island. Woodland Indians arrived in the mid-1600s, when hostile, large-scale Iroquois expansion in Acadia forced the Hurons to flee. They likely arrived on Rock Island, which had been populated by Potawatomi, who would later return to open the doors to the Europeans. With the aid of Winnebago and Ottawa Indians, one of the largest ramparts in the New World was constructed on Rock Island to repel Iroquois invaders. (The U.S. government would later forcibly evict the Potawatomi from Rock Island so lumbermen could enter.)

Most evidence of initial European settlement points to Frenchman Jean Nicolet's 1634 landing at a low-banked rise of ruddy clay and rock cliffs—Red Banks. On Washington Island two decades after Nicolet's arrival, the Potawatomi would initiate commercial operations with Pierre Esprit Radisson, who considered the island one of his favorite sites in all New France. The Native Americans and the French spent a good five decades in trade before permanent settlement began in the 1830s.

Fishermen were the first to occupy most points along the Lake Michigan coast, including Rock and Washington Islands. Fishing camps later spread south along the water's edge to Kewaunee and north to wrap around the tip of the peninsula clear to Fish Creek. Some of the largest fish ever caught on Lake Michigan were landed off Rock Island. Those communities, which also began commercial shipping and shipbuilding, cemented the regional economy in the 1830s. In shipbuilding, Sturgeon Bay always played second fiddle to Manitowoc farther south, but it still managed to parlay its ship factories into one of the major facilities on Lake Michigan.

Cherries

The Door's microclimate fostered the county's remarkable fruit-growing industry—one of the tops in the U.S. for a solitary county.

Immediately prior to the Civil War, a Swiss immigrant disembarked from his Great Lakes steamer and found a remarkably equable climate. The land was already rife with wheat farmers, so this farmer planted an orchard. Yields were so astonishing that the University of Wisconsin came to investigate—and went away impressed. By the turn of the 20th century, the first commercial apple, plum, and cherry orchards were established, and cherries eventually became a large-scale industry. The UW kept up its involvement, in 1922 establishing a research station near the original cherry orchard. By the 1930s, the peninsula had over 10,000 acres of orchards, including what at the time was the world's largest cherry orchard. Crop picking being so labor intensive, German prisoners of war were used to harvest the fruit during WW II, along with migrant labor from south Texas, which is still utilized today. Door County maintains over 100 orchards totaling 2,100 acres, which ranks it the third most productive county in the United States. The total take tops out at 4,250 tons per year. Some are worried, however, that corporate farms are bleeding the county of much of its charm; only five large farms produce the bulk of the county's cherries. In addition, with a proposal to widen WI 57 between Green Bay and Sturgeon Bay, farmers could be forced to sell their smaller properties to developers. For now cherry and apple orchards are equal with dairy farming as economic mainstays in the county; during the summer, cherry stands sprout up along the roads, dispensing fresh fruit, jams, jellies, wines, and more. Restaurants across the state use Door County cherries in their pies, cookies, and ice cream concoctions; brewers from Sturgeon Bay all the way to New Glarus brew seasonal cherry beers. And around here you don't dare think of attending a fish boil without finishing it off with cherry pie or cobbler.

SIGHTS AND ACTIVITIES

Blossoms
Show up in mid-May and you're likely to be plowed under by camera-toting tourists here for the popular blooming season. Cherry trees taking advantage of the lake's moderating influ-

Bailey's Harbor Range Lights

ence are lovely enough, but much of the county's cutover land and agricultural pasture has been left to regrow wild, and the county contains five state parks and the Ridges National Natural Landmark, a wildflower preserve with 13 species of endangered plants. The county is now also making a concerted effort to become one of the daffodil capitals of the world, planting over 100,000 bulbs annually. Look for the white-and-peach colored daffodil—I mean, doorfodil (seriously), developed locally.

Northern winter vagaries creep in here as everywhere else, but generally by the second or third week of May, blooms are peeking out. The bay side will bloom first, the lake side following a week to 10 days later. As soon as the blossoms are out, it's time for the **Festival of Blossoms,** a month-long shindig of blossom field trips, midway rides, pageants, fish boils, shipyard tours (your only chance to see the operations up close, $5 and worth it), lighthouse tours ($7 and also worth it), parades, and special cherry-centered celebrations.

If you miss the festival, wildflower hikes are held at Newport State Park every weekend in spring and summer.

Lighthouses
Door County has more lighthouses (they like to quiz you on this around here) than any other county in the United States. Starting in 1836 with Rock Island and in 1858 on Pilot Island (which can be toured only from the water), 10 lighthouses were constructed along the coasts and canals to hold Lake Michigan's stormy temperament somewhat in check. Almost all are still in some recognizable condition, and tours of some are offered regularly. See the individual cities below for more detail.

Charter Fishing
Idiotic overuse of gill nets and parasitic alewives penetrating the Great Lakes essentially killed off the commercial fishing industry in the first half of the 20th century. But an almost accidental renaissance of fishing—this time sportfishing—occurred when Michigan introduced nonnative salmon. Sportfishing has grown to serious economic mainstay proportions.

Sturgeon Bay's sportfishing charter fleet ranks sixth in the state in total salmon takes on a seasonal basis, but that's in numbers only. Factoring in relative populations, the Door Peninsula's communities are way ahead of the pack. Around here, lunkers prevail—in 1994, a record 44.92-pound chinook salmon was landed by a 16-year-old off Sturgeon Bay; however, Algoma won't let you forget that it was from an Algoma charter boat. Ten- to 20-pound rainbow and brown trout and 20- to 30-pound lake trout are not uncommon. A newer species of rainbow, skamania, is noted for its muskie- or bass-like surface gymnastics. Most people don't know that the smallmouth bass fishing here is some of the best in Wisconsin, especially for flyfishing in late spring. As always, obtain a local list and do some advance work. Learn the ins and outs of charter offerings—not to mention the personality traits of captains and mates. It's worth the time. Do-it-yourself rentals are also available from innumerable marinas throughout the peninsula. Door County operates a **24-hour fishing hotline**, tel. (920) 743-7046.

PRACTICALITIES

Accommodations
There is a coma-inducing array of accommodations throughout Door County—motels, hotels, inns and B&Bs (often but not always the same thing), swank resorts, homes, luxurious condos, and the ubiquitous Wisconsin "cottage" (anything from a step above a deer-hunting shack to an exquisite A-frame). Remember also that this is Wisconsin's number-one tourist destination during certain times of the year: rates jump and room availability shrinks to zilch—and if you can manage to track down a room or a condo at all, you might be required to stay more than one night.

Rates could be $35 a night or $250; you might get a two-story minor mansion or a half-bath "cozy cottage." In the summer and autumn, you'll be more than lucky to find something under $55 for a single. Off-season, there are still rooms under $30. Though local variations apply, May 1 through Labor Day and late September through early November are considered peak seasons, reflected in room availability and prices.

With such a disparity, it's a good idea to request a copy of the glossy Door County vacation planner from the chamber of commerce; it contains detailed descriptions of cottages, homes,

and condos (the listings in *this* book are by no means comprehensive). As always, the more homework you do, the happier you're going to be with the room you get.

Camping
For campers, the Door Peninsula offers five state parks (including the state's largest, visited by more people per annum than Yellowstone), a handful of county parks (though there's not much camping in them), and 12 private operations. Rock Island has the most isolated campgrounds, but Newport State Park has rustic, pack-in sites as well.

On weekends or holidays in summer, don't even think about showing up to a state park without advance reservations. If you do, get there early—and if you get a site, congratulations; you're one of the lucky ones. Door County's state parks take reservations and often fill up months ahead of time; Peninsula State Park's best sites are often gone minutes after the January reservation period begins.

Shopping
Unless something earth-shaking warrants it, the following pages don't cover shopping. Simply put, the peninsula has the state's most astonishing concentration of artists, crafters, antiques, vendors, galleries, chi-chi boutiques, and plenty of other ways to pry greenbacks from your wallet. Good news, though: the ratio of quality to tacky is decidedly in the former's favor.

Services and Information
Snag a copy of the free *Door County Go Guide*. This comprehensive listing of dining, arts, entertainment, and the usual tourist amusements is heavy on shopping opportunities but also has some good village maps. Other media include the *Door Reminder* and small-townish *Resorter Reporter* from the *Door County Advocate,* a twice-weekly paper (good if you need TV listings).

The **Door County Chamber of Commerce,** tel. (920) 743-4456, doorcountyvacations.com, is located just south of Sturgeon Bay on WI 42/57. It has the usual array of brochures. Even better are the Innline touch-screen information centers spread around the county at various information centers; they provide up-to-the-second information on lodging vacancies, along with shops, restaurants, recreation, services, and the arts.

Transportation

Door County well represents the American antipathy toward public transportation. Hoi polloi disembarking from a Greyhound evidently doesn't fit well in a Cape Cod sunset postcard scene. There are no buses, no trains, and no ferries from towns south along the interstate. (Sounds isolated and great, but just wait until you see the auto traffic!)

Very small and very limited air shuttles from Chicago to Sturgeon Bay have occasionally popped up, but these generally last a season or two and close up shop. Your one air choice is to fly into Green Bay and take the **Door County-Green Bay Shuttle,** tel. (920) 746-0500 to any destination on the peninsula. To Sturgeon Bay is $55, and all the way to Northport costs $80. Reservations are required.

Auto Rental: Once in Sturgeon Bay, **Avis** has rental offices at 29 N. Second Ave., tel. (920) 743-7976, and at the Quarter Deck Marina, 910 WI 42-57, tel. (920) 743-4991. Avis also has rentals available in Sister Bay, tel. (920) 854-4820, and Baileys Harbor, tel. (920) 839-2973

SOUTH OF STURGEON BAY: BAYSIDE

Sturgeon Bay sits approximately at the midpoint of Door County. For many folks, the county begins only when they have buzzed the bridge spanning Sturgeon Bay's Lake Michigan ship canal; others claim that you're not in the county until WI 42 and WI 57 bifurcate into bayside and lakeside routes northeast of town. Still, Door County proper includes a chunk of 15 or more miles south of the ship channel; and the *peninsula* comprises underappreciated Kewaunee County as well. Many travelers forsake this southern section altogether, while others prefer its relative solitude.

Note that WI 57 is going to undergo dramatic changes in the life of this edition of Wisconsin Handbook. Between Green Bay and Sturgeon Bay the road will bend away from the lake and split into a hyperdrive four-lane divided highway. At least that's the plan; somehow transportation engineers have to figure out a way to plat the road and not damage archaeological sites, wetlands, and threatened species, all of which have slowed the project. For now, almost immediately upon leaving Green Bay and beginning the bayside northeasterly spin along WI 57, you'll find an easy-to-overlook little county wayside. At **Red Banks** wayside, a statue to Jean Nicolet stands a few hundred yards from the red clay bluffs overlooking the serene bay. Those in the know agree that it was here that Jean Nicolet first came sloshing ashore, cracking his harquebuses to impress the Winnebago village that stood at this site in 1634. But scenery-wise, WI 57 leaves much to the imagination. More adventuresome travelers might attempt to locate

CR A out of Green Bay; it spins along the same route, but right atop the lake. Bypassing Point Sable—once a boundary between Native American tribal lands—the road offers views of a state wildlife area across the waters. Farther up, you can see Vincent Point and, immediately after that, Red Banks itself. This byway continues on through Benderville before linking up with WI 57 again, and there's camping in a county park up the road. Before crossing the Kewaunee-Door County line into Belgian territory, about the only thing to mention is **Joe Rahr's,** off WI 57 on CR A in little Duvall, just beyond Dyckesville— a classic Wisconsin salt-of-the-earth tavern with bowling ball-size burgers.

Beyond that, Brussels and surrounding towns like Champion, Euren, Maplewood, Rosiere, and Forestville constitute the country's largest Belgian-American settlement. The architecture of the region is so well preserved that over 100 buildings make up Wisconsin's first *rural* National Historical Landmark. Right along WI 57, the homes and Catholic chapels show distinctive Belgian influences along with a lot of reddish-orange brick and split cedar fencing. On alternating weekends through the summer, the villages still celebrate *Kermiss,* church mass during harvest season.

Brussels is the area's capital of sorts, with **Belgian Days** the first week of July—plenty of Belgian chicken, *booyah* (thick vegetable stock), *jute* (boiled cabbage), and tripe sausage. A handful of restaurants serve Belgian fare in Brussels, including **Marchants Food, Inc.,** 9674 WI 57, open daily for 50 years. **Joe and Nancy's** is in

Rosiere and open Tues.-Sun. for lunch and dinner. The proprietor can even spin a yarn in Walloon for you. The burgers are awesome, the folks are chatty, and you can expect a long wait to sit. It's near the junction of CR C and CR X. A quick side trip takes in lots of Belgian architecture. In Robinsville, a mile and a half east of Champion along CR K, sits the **shrine grotto**, a home and school for disabled children founded by a Belgian to whom the Virgin Mary is said to have appeared in 1858. North of Brussels along CR C, the **St. Francis Xavier Church and Grotto Cemetery** is representative of Belgian rural construction; farmers contributed aesthetically pleasing stones from their fields to raise a grotto and crypt for the local reverend.

Three miles northeast of Brussels via CR C is **Quietwoods Campground,** tel. (920) 825-7065, with sites ($20 and up) adjacent to the **Gardner Swamp State Wildlife Area** and along Keyes Creek.

SOUTH OF STURGEON BAY: LAKESIDE

KEWAUNEE

Perched on a hillside overlooking a lovely historic harbor, Kewaunee was another in the long line of trading posts established by the Northwest Fur Company. At one point in its history the town seemed bent on rivaling Chicago as maritime center of the Great Lakes and could likely have given the Windy City a run for its money when an influx of immigrants descended after hearing rumors of a gold strike in the area. But Chicago had the rail, while Kewaunee, despite its harbor, was isolated and became a minor port and lumber town. The area—including Sleepy Hollow, Stangelville, Pilsen, and other rustic villages—still shows a strong Czech heritage; you'll even hear Czech spoken.

Sights

Kewaunee is worthy of a short stroll and the chamber of commerce has brochures of a nifty **walking tour,** taking in some three dozen historical structures. Among the most photographed sights in the state, the **Kewaunee pierhead lighthouse** was built in 1909. After nearly a century of tinkering, the structure consists today of a steel frame base and steel tower with a cast-iron octagonal lantern some 50 feet high. At the harbor you can take a tour ($3) aboard a retired **tugboat**. The central **Kewaunee County Courthouse,** at the corner of Vliet and Dodge, tel. (920) 388-4410, has a historical museum open daily 10:30 a.m.-4:30 p.m. in summer. The usual assortment of historical displays are housed in an old sheriff's home, part of which doubled as the jail, including gruesome dungeon cells. Statues of Father Marquette and solemn, pious Potawatomi are likely what you'll be shown first. Head, too, for the replica of the USS *Pueblo*. The ill-fated Navy ship, involved in an incident with North Korea in the 1950s, was built in Kewaunee during WW II. The most impressive exhibit is the wood carving of Custer's Last Stand, done over a span of six years by two local craftsmen. Hours are daily 10:30 a.m.-4:30 p.m., Memorial Day-Labor Day. Admission is $2.

Three miles west of town, the Wisconsin Department of Natural Resources operates a state-of-the-art **Anadromous Fish Facility,** N3884 Ransom Moore Lane, tel. (920) 388-1025. Detailed are the spawning practices of anadromous fish, viewed through underwater panels. It's open daily usually 10 a.m.-5 p.m. Southwest of town in Montpelier township is a **Rustic Road** scenic drive involving parts of Hrabik, Cherneysville, Sleepy Hollow, and Pine Grove Roads. Close to here, south of Krok, is the only known Wisconsin rooftop windmill; it's listed on the National Register of Historic Places.

At **Svoboda Industries,** tel. (920) 388-2691, along WI 42 North, you'll see what is purportedly the world's largest grandfather clock—39 feet tall. Open daily 10 a.m.-5 p.m.

If a leg-stretch is all you're up for, a quarter-mile north of town you'll find a picturesque overlook along the Kewaunee River at the marsh where it empties into the lake. Near here is the local **visitor information center,** tel. (920) 388-4822 or (800) 666-8214, www.kewaunee.org, right on WI 42.

Accommodations

A couple of fine B&Bs are in town, but one interesting one is found southwest of Kewaunee. Precious is the **Historic Norman General Store,** E 3296 CR G, tel. (920) 388-4580, as its name says the original (1876) general store now done up as a B&B. Rooms from $65.

Also commendable in town right along WI 42, near the bridge, the **Harbor Lights Lodge,** tel. (920) 388-3700 or (800) 736-3700, offers comfy rooms, an indoor pool, sauna, whirlpool, sun deck with great lake views, and rates from $45. Rock-bottom prices are found in diminutive Alaska, between Kewaunee and Algoma. At this dry and eternally sunblinded village, rooms as cheap as $31 for four people can be found.

For those prices, right on the harbor in Kewaunee is the **Harrison Harbour House,** tel. (920) 388-0606, built for a former governor and best described by the proprietors as a "hunting cabin for fishermen," with bunk beds, stone walls, rough-hewn board ceilings, and a definite feel of lake life. It isn't for everyone, but some folks just groove on it. Rooms are $32.

If Door County camping is too far for the day, 15 bucks gets you a basic site at **Kewaunee Village,** north of town along WI 42. An okay lake view, a 15-acre nature area with trails, and complete facilities are located on the grounds.

Food

The local specialty is Czechoslovakian and Bohemian food, including *kolace* (yeast buns with fruit filling) and *buhuite* (pronounced "bu-ta"—thin dough filled with seeds or fruit), sauerkraut rye bread, and *rohlik.* These delectable baked goods are available at **Tom's Pastry Shoppe,** 409 WI 42, tel. (920) 388-2533, which is also a deli. **Les's Steak Joint** is right on WI 42 and has good steaks and fresh fish; the relish tray to start the meal is a treat. From $8. Near the bridge in town are a couple of places for great **smoked fish.**

Five miles north, in Alaska along WI 42 is the well-known **Alaskan Supper Club,** tel. (920) 388-2483, best known for Tuesday-night carnivorous German buffets. Otherwise, it offers straight supper club fare with rib-eye specials on Wednesday. From $8.

ALGOMA

The whole drive along WI 42 from Manitowoc to Algoma is spectacular—a resplendent, beach-hugging route only occasionally straying from scintillating lake views. Nowhere is the view as blinding as the few miles swooping into Algoma from the south, where seemingly endless miles of wide, empty beach begin, both road and beach unencumbered by travelers. This freshly scrubbed little community of friendly folks might be said to be a wonderful poor man's Door County (were one to approve of such distinctions).

Originally called Wolf River by English and Irish settlers in the mid-1800s, the town grew quickly with influxes of Bohemian, Belgian, and northern Europeans. The small town is known today mostly for its killer sportfishing, and its

SOUTH OF
STURGEON BAY

marinas account for the state's most substantial sportfishing industry. The latest record broken locally was a 35-pound, 11-ounce brown trout landed in 1996; prior to that, a 44.94-pound chinook salmon was landed here in 1994.

Sights

The top draw in Algoma, the **Von Stiehl Winery,** 115 Navarino St., tel. (920) 487-5208 or (800) 955-5208, is the oldest licensed winery in Wisconsin and listed on the National Register of Historic Places. The award-winning winery is housed in what was once the Ahnapee Brewery (named after the local river), built in the 1850s. Its three-foot-thick limestone walls are a ready-made underground catacomb system for aging wines. The house specialty is cherry wine, but you'll find grape, apple, blueberry, cranberry, and other Wisconsin fruit wines, all guarded by a patented system to prevent premature aging and light damage. Guided winery tours are offered daily during regular business hours May-October. Free wine tastings are also given daily.

Algoma is also the southern terminus of the **Ahnapee State Trail,** a section of the Ice Age National Scenic Trail stretching 18 miles to the southern fringe of Sturgeon Bay along an abandoned railroad grade. Packed for the most part with limestone screening, the route's highlights are the miles along the grand Ahnapee River. (Note that during spring flooding, this trail can get spongy if not waterlogged altogether.) It's a fine place to get an up-close view of native wildlife. Communities with pit-stop practicalities are at either end and at two midpoints. A state pass is required to hike the trail. Another trail runs from Algoma to Casco.

The **Netto Palazzo,** is a renovated hotel and net factory. The highlight is an Italian motorcycle museum displaying over 30 classic Italian roadsters, including the Cagiva Elephant. Also on-site you'll find myriad shops including an espresso shop. The Netto is found at Navarino and 4th Streets and is open daily.

Algoma once had a legendary "fishing mayor," Art Dettman. His name lives on in a restored fish shanty on the National Register of Historic Places. It's currently being renovated into a museum to early commercial and sportfishing.

Algoma's is without a doubt the cutest movie theater in Wisconsin—my living room is larger.

North of town via CR S, **Zillmer's Antique Farm,** tel. (920) 487-5785, is a sixth-generation family farm, and it appears they've kept all the equipment. You can view hundreds of old pieces of equipment; Zillmer's also holds the world's largest antique haying show in July. Kids love the petting zoo. Open Memorial Day-Labor Day weekend Tues.-Sat 10 a.m.-4 p.m.; admission is charged.

Charter Fishing

Algoma's charter boats barely rank second to Port Washington in numbers of salmon taken—meaning that this is a prime place to smear on the zinc oxide and do the Ahab thang. Early-season lake trout are generally hot in May, but June is Algoma's biggest month; rainbow trout and chinook salmon are everywhere. Steelhead and especially king salmon are added to the mix come July, and brown trout get big in August. September fishing is great for the fish—adult salmon reach maximum weight then—but the weather gets a bit unsettled, and iron sea legs become a necessity.

Fishing is such a big deal in Algoma that the city maintains a 24-hour hotline for up-to-date fishing dope, tel. (920) 487-3090 or (800) 626-3090.

The most logical thing for hopeful anglers to do is contact the chamber for a complete listing of guides and then do some shopping around. After all, you're the one who has to sit on the water all day with these folks. Call (920) 487-3722 or (888) 343-3722 to be linked to the Algoma Wisconsin Charter Association.

Among Algoma's vast fleet you'll find **R.V. Charters,** tel. (920) 487-5158 or (800) 487-0022, with its own dockside condos and three ultra-modern Bertram and Chris Craft vessels of over 30 feet each. Rates, of course, are myriad, but an absolute rock-bottom, midweek price might be $160 per person for six people. The price includes eight hours on the water, one night's stay, all licenses, a continental breakfast, and all onboard conveniences. Deluxe packages can go as high as $489 per person for a four-day charter.

Accommodations

At the lowest end (and I make no claims to quality), you'll find the **Barbie Ann Motel and Inn,** right downtown at 533 Fourth St., tel. (920) 487-5561, which has rooms for $25 or less. More expensive, but with a killer view for a basic motel, the **Algoma Beach Motel,** 1500 Lake St., tel. (920) 487-2828, offers a whirlpool and some kitchenette units starting at $70.

Along Michigan Street on the north end of town and right along the water you'll find the **Harbor Inn Motel,** tel. (920) 487-5241. Clean and well run, it has a decent view and rates from $60 Some rooms have three beds and most have refrigerators.

You can find basic camping at **Ahnapee River Trails Campground,** E6053 W. Wilson Rd., tel. (920) 487-5777, offering a huge assortment of amenities including a solar-heated swimming pool. It's right on the Ahnapee Trail. From the junction of WI 42 and WI 54, go two miles north on WI 42, then a mile west on Washington Rd., then a mile south on CR M to Wilson Road. Rates are $15.

Food

The basic, downscale **Captain's Table,** off the corner of WI 42 and 2nd St., is perhaps the busiest and most classic roadfood eatery in Algoma. The place is cozy and packed, with won-
derful service. It offers better-than-average breakfasts, lunches, and dinners, and all-you-can-eat trout boils daily, Holland perch smorgasbords Friday nights, and a popular Sunday brunch. The **Hudson Restaurant,** 205 Navarino, tel. (920) 487-5493, overlooks the harbor and offers steak-and-seafood lunches and dinners. Open daily. The staple at **Penguin City Restaurant,** 604 WI 42 (4th St.), tel. (920) 487-9917, is pizza, but it also serves Belgian *booyah* and Belgian pie.

Bearcat's, at the corner of WI 42 and Navarino Streets, has great smoked fish.

Services and Information

You can get cheerful and solicitous help at the squat little **tourist information center,** tel. (920) 487-2041 or (800) 498-4888, www.algoma.org, on the south edge of Algoma. Open Mon.-Fri. 8 a.m.-4 p.m., the information center is also the departure point for **historical walking tours** of downtown. Tours depart at 10 a.m. mid-May through mid-September and cost $2; personal tours departing at 4:30 p.m. can also be arranged.

STURGEON BAY

The anadromous leviathans for which Door County's gateway community is named once crowded the harbor waters in such plenitude that ships would literally run aground atop heaps of them. They were speared, shot, netted, and left to rot, their pungence choking the air.

Whether or not Sturgeon Bay is properly the heart and soul of the county, it lies at a most strategic location. Halfway up the peninsula,

safely within the crook of the bay, it was used for eons by Native Americans, and, later, early Europeans, as the launching point for a transpeninsular portage, obviating a trip through the Door of Death. When the 6,600-foot-long canal was blasted, chiseled, hacked, and dug through to link the bay with Lake Michigan, the town of Sturgeon Bay was set to become the largest community in the county. A plentiful wood supply

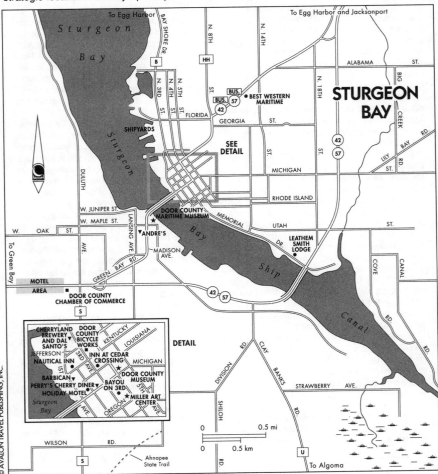

made way for a shipbuilding industry in the 1850s; by the 1880s, the industry here was rivaled only by that of Manitowoc to the south. The heyday is over now, but Sturgeon Bay still has specialized shipbuilding and repair facilities—behemoths up to 1,200 feet long continue to ply the waters.

Sturgeon Bay today is a vibrant village of 9,200, not at all rural despite its bucolic setting. Lying mostly on the island (northern) side of the peninsula, a small section lies across the bridge on the peninsula (southern) side. Both parts of town are off the main highway along an easy declivity. Most of the county's cherries are processed here. The genuine graciousness of the folks is palpable. Sturgeon Bay was voted Wisconsin's Friendliest Small Town by those who really know—the readers of *Wisconsin Trails* magazine. Some jaded

SHIPBUILDING

Given its welcome promontory jutting into the waters, it was natural that the Door Peninsula and environs became important links in the water chain. The peninsula offers much: 425 miles of shoreline, the safe haven of Green Bay, innumerable bights in the craggy limestone coast offering linked harbors, and, most important, a channel toward the Fox and Wisconsin Rivers and eventually the Mississippi. Those factors created an area ripe for shipbuilding. One major advantage Door Peninsula shipbuilders had was a plethora of native oak, relatively untouched by loggers and transportable with little effort to the shore communities.

As early as the 1830s, Manitowoc began to turn out oak sailing ships sturdy enough for the travails of the Great Lakes on the way to the St. Lawrence seaway. The city later unveiled its crowning achievement: the Great Lakes schooner, a wooden ship with tight ends front and back that met below the water, a shallow draft, and a raisable centerboard, designed specifically to tackle Lake Michigan. By the early 1900s, though, the schooner's days were numbered and thus Manitowoc and lower Lake Michigan builders had to completely redeploy workforces.

Door County to the north, meanwhile, was just being settled, and its newer shipyards didn't have to go through the refitting pangs the more southerly builders had—namely, converting facilities to turn out steamships instead of clippers.

Sturgeon Bay churned out ships in amazing numbers. The first one left Sturgeon Bay shipyards in the mid-1850s, but it wasn't until the prime of the schooner days, in the mid-1860s, that the town really hit the big time. In the decade following the Civil War, perhaps two dozen ships in all were manufactured in the new shipyards; the superb quality of Sturgeon Bay ships was immediately recognized.

The first major shipbuilder in Sturgeon Bay was Leathem and Smith, predominantly a ship-repair facility that opened in the 1880s, but which also put out sculls, barges, and a few schooners of its own. By World War I, it had expanded its operation into a prosperous boatworks and, during the Great War, produced more tugboats than any other outfit. Now called Bay Shipbuilding, it is still in operation in Sturgeon Bay. In fact, it's the number-one operation, comprising a number of Sturgeon Bay builders in one grand merger, and can handle boats up to 1,100 feet long.

Many shipbuilders relocated here for the environment and abundant resources. In 1896, Riebolt and Wolter moved an entire drydock from Sheboygan. Over the past half-century, various corporate mergers have resulted in most of the Michigan Street Bridge area of Sturgeon Bay being an arm of one or more subsidiaries of the same company. Whatever the ownership, and despite the decline in shipping brought about by the advent of railroad and later autos, some 40 ships were still constructed during the decade and a half leading to 1986.

Peterson Builders, Inc., started just after the turn of the century and constructed yachts, fishing tugs, and rowboats. Business boomed during the 1930s and the war years—24-hour operations cranked out sub chasers and minesweepers. After the war, hydrojets and research craft entered the company's catalog. Today, the output includes wooden naval minesweepers, gunboats, torpedo retrievers, steel tugs, and landing craft. During the 1980s, Peterson was the primary employer in the industry.

The final jewel in Sturgeon Bay's shipping crown is Palmer-Johnson, still going strong after its incorporation following World War II. Devoted to racing craft and custom yachts, it puts out million-dollar private vessels and acts as a repair facility. So renowned for yachts is Palmer-Johnson that offices and facilities have opened in four countries as well as Florida and Georgia.

and wearied city dwellers are made uneasy by these folks, who've been known to pump gas for travelers without being asked.

SIGHTS

One great freebie is to wander north of downtown to the shipyards, where **Bay Shipbuilding** is located. This huge operation is a great place to espy behemoth vessels as they're being launched or brought in for fixing. You can't get in the grounds but you can still get some good views.

Canal Station Light House
One of the oldest of its kind, dating from 1899, this lighthouse originally used an experimental design in which only latticework guy wires supported the tower and lantern. The station was redone after the turn of the century, constructing the skeletal steel framework around the hundred-foot-tall light. It's not open for regular tours, but you can snoop around outside the perimeter and along the jetty without the Coast Guard shooing you away. To get there, head north of town on WI 42/57, turn east just past the Bay View Bridge onto Utah St., then right onto Cove Rd., then left on Canal Road.

Door County Maritime Museum
One of two marine museums in the county, the **Door County Maritime Museum,** tel. (920) 743-5958, is hard to miss, right at the western base of the bridge joining the two sides of the city, in a sparkling new complex finished just as this book was being updated. The 20,000-square-foot museum has four galleries and a balcony level with splendid views of the bay. There's a room-by-room walk-through of the shipbuilding industry. The newest addition is a periscope from a nuclear submarine that offers 360-degree views of the city; it's part of an ambitious exhibit on the crucial role Manitowoc played in building subs in WW II. A bridge room with working global positioning system (GPS) units is a hit with kids. Numerous other exhibits include an engine room, a small craft workshop, a steamship office, and the story of raising an ore carrier from the bottom of Lake Michigan. Open daily 9 a.m.-6 p.m. Memorial Day-Labor Day weekend, 10 a.m.-5 p.m. rest of the year. Admission is $5, $2.50 children 5-17, family rate $12.50.

Door County Museum
At 4th Ave. and Michigan St. you'll find a small museum originally built by the WPA during the Great Depression and now operated by the county historical society. The *Chicago Tribune* called it the "Best Small Museum in the Midwest." The most popular sight is the old-time firehouse, complete with refurbished pumper vehicles including a horse-drawn model predating the end of the Civil War. Lots of taxidermy, Door County prehistory, and settlement history, and artwork is also here. The museum is child-friendly; climb-aboard, hands-on vehicles are on display. Open daily 10 a.m.-4:30 p.m. May-October. Free admission.

Miller Art Center
This fine art center, 107 S. 4th Ave., tel. (920) 746-0707, is located in the Sturgeon Bay library. The top floor houses the permanent collection, with an emphasis on 20th-century Wisconsin artists. Downstairs, the main gallery features revolving exhibits in various media. One room houses Gerhard Miller's works. Open year-round Mon.-Sat. 10 a.m.-5 p.m., and also 7-9 p.m. Mon.-Thursday. Free.

William S. Fairfield Public Gallery and Museum
To be opened by the time this edition is out is this gallery, 242 Michigan St., tel. (920) 746-0001, which features the works of Henry Moore and other contemporary artists. It hosts traveling exhibits and lots of other events.

The Farm
The Farm, four miles north of Sturgeon Bay along WI 57, tel. (920) 743-6666, bills itself as a living museum of rural America, and it lives up to that. On 40 acres of an original homestead, various old-style dwellings and structures dot the compound and pioneer implements line the walls. But the primary draw is the menagerie of farm animals, many of which can be petted, milked, or bottle-fed. You'll also find nature trails, gardens, and many informative displays about the diverse peninsular ecology. It's exceedingly family friendly. Open Memorial Day through

Labor Day daily 9 a.m.-5 p.m. Admission is $7, $3.25 ages 13 and under.

Potawatomi State Park
Three miles south of Sturgeon Bay along WI 42/57 on Park Dr., unfolding along the western edge of Sturgeon Bay and flanked by Sherwood and Cabot Points, Potawatomi State Park is known for rolling birch-lined trails atop the limestone ridges scraped off the Niagara Escarpment. Residual geology—tide lines—of a prehistoric lake can be seen along several trails. The geology of the park is significant enough that Potawatomi marks the beginning of the Ice Age National Scenic Trail.

Almost 11 miles of trails wind through the park. A four-mile **off-road bicycle trail** also meanders through grassy meadows. The easiest walk is the two-and-a-half-mile **Hemlock Trail,** along the limestone scree of the bay's shoreline. At the northern end of this trail, the **Tower Trail** quickly ascends the ridges through thicker vegetation, leading to a 75-foot-tall **observation tower.** This is a belvedere vantage point with spectacular views all the way to Michigan's Upper Peninsula on a good day, and a killer spot for viewing the sunset. Islets rimmed in hues of blue and gray pepper the outlying reaches off the park (bring a polarizing camera lens on a sunny day). The rest of the Tower Trail is a somewhat challenging mélange of rises and falls up the bluffs. Some stretches are fairly steep and present sharp drop-offs. Fishing in the naturally protected bay is some of the best in the lower Door.

Door County's only downhill ski area is found in Potawatomi park, but it's not exactly fright-inducing. More popular are the 14 miles of cross-country skiing trails and winter camping areas. Two rings of camping areas with a total of 125 sites are available, and half are reservable. Reservations are accepted starting the first working day following New Year's Day, and it is recommended that you not wait too long to make your reservations for a weekend. The usual state park rates of $5 resident, $7 nonresident apply, and a park sticker is required.

South of the park entrance, at the airport, **plane rides** are available for $30-129. Directly across the road you'll find a golf course. For a quick road trip, head back toward WI 42/57 but turn right onto CR C, then right onto CR M, which

takes you all the way around Sherwood Point to the **Sherwood Point Lighthouse** (it's a bit tough to spot). Constructed in 1883 and automated in 1960, the 38-foot-high house guarding the bayside entrance into Sturgeon Bay was constructed with a 10-sided cast-iron light. Closed to the public, it and the old keeper's house are used today as a retreat for the Coast Guard. (It is open during the Festival of Blossoms tour.)

Collector's Showcase
The **Chal-A,** 39010 WI 42/57 north of town, is a great diversion (and also offers the cheapest lodging in Door County)—a hodgepodge of assorted antique autos, thousands of dolls (1,000 Barbies alone) and toys, and several hundred old Marshall Fields window mechanicals. Despite the collections, the place is not at all tacky. Open mid-May through mid-October daily 9 a.m.-5 p.m. Admission is $2.50, $1 ages 12 and under.

Tours
You can still get out in the harbor and on the lake without having to hook a chinook. A few resorts or lodges offer boat tours at their marinas, including the **Leathem Smith Lodge,** tel. (920) 743-5555, which has waterfront and sunset tours for $40; they depart at 9:30 a.m. and 1 and 5 p.m. **Snug Harbor Inn,** tel. (920) 743-2337, has boat rentals.

North of town, the **University of Wisconsin agricultural research station** is open for public perusal. Groups have to register, but individuals can obtain a map for a self-guided tour of the 120-acre fruit and potato research center.

Nothing else to do? Head down to the city dock to take in the U.S. **Coast Guard Cutter Mobile Bay,** open weekdays 1-4 p.m., weekends 11 a.m.-4 p.m.

Beers and Wines
Sturgeon Bay Brewing, 6613 WI 42/57, tel. (920) 746-7611, is a newer brewer and Texas barbecue joint; tours are available.

Eight miles north of Sturgeon Bay, in Carlsville, **Door Peninsula Winery,** 5806 WI 42, tel. (920) 743-7431, is housed in an old schoolhouse. Tours are given sporadically throughout the day and take in the cellars and winemaking rooms where 29 Door County California-style fruit wines are produced. Open year-round daily from 9 a.m.

ACCOMMODATIONS

There seems to be an aversion to the word "hotel" in Sturgeon Bay—everyplace has to be a "resort" or an "inn and conference center," and on the peninsula as a whole, no similar towns have quite the number of B&Bs or historic inns. Expect multiple-night minimums during peak season (and year-round if your stay includes a Saturday night). Unless specified otherwise, all listed accommodations are open year-round.

Motels

Most motels offer high-season rates in the $55-60 range for a single in summer but dip much lower (as low as $28) in non-peak times. Among the best budget choices is the **Holiday Motel,** 29 N. 2nd Ave., tel. (920) 743-5571, tucked away off a corner of the bridge spanning the canal. This is no-frills accommodation, but the rooms have a fresh feeling, the owners are gracious and helpful, and they don't skimp on the free continental breakfast spread. All rooms have refrigerators. Rates start at around $45 s in summer, lots less off-season. The **Nightengale,** 1547 Egg Harbor Rd., tel. (920) 743-7633, claims rates as low as $30 all year but that seems hard to believe.

Long known for its economical rates (and bizarre collection of antiques and toys), the **Chal-A,** 3910 WI 42/57 north of town, tel. (920) 743-6788, is still a solid deal. Located in a quiet setting (right on ski and snowmobile trails), the motel has very nice rooms and rates around $45 year-round.

Cherryland Motel, south on WI 42/57, tel. (920) 743-3289, features a legendary indoor tropical whirlpool, a swimming pool, game room, regular rooms, and a few cottages. Rates are from around $50 for some rooms high season but most are around $65.

Between the bridges in Sturgeon Bay, **Snug Harbor,** 1627 Memorial Dr., tel. (920) 743-2337 or (800) 231-5767, is under new ownership and it shows. Basic motel rooms, cottages, and brand-new luxury suites are available. The suites are multi-level gems with fireplaces, skylights, full cooking facilities, and refrigerators. The spacious grounds have barbecue facilities and picnic areas. Boat rentals are also available at the small marina on site. Basic motel rates of $79 and luxury-suite rates of $140 are the rule in high season but you may scare up a $55 room.

Resorts and Lodges

The **Bay Shore Inn,** 4205 Bay Shore Dr., tel. (920) 743-4551, was voted by a couple of national magazines as one of the most family-friendly resorts in the United States. Three dozen luxurious kitchenette suites overlook the bay, and the facility has two pools (one indoor), a whirlpool, a private beach, and some rooms with balconies. Rates start at $174 s, $260 d, with some multi-night stays required mid-June through August.

On what was once an expansive cherry orchard now sits Door County's most luxurious digs—the **Cherry Hills Lodge and Golf Course,** 5905 Dunn Rd., tel. (920) 743-4222 or (800) 545-2307. Though the thoroughly modern rooms and suites are well appointed and meticulously maintained and feature an expansive balcony overlooking the links, the golf is what draws people. The championship course is carved into pure Door County craggy forests and heaths. The restaurant is also excellent. Rates start at $99 s and $137 d during high season, much less at other times.

Built in 1937, as Door County reached its first summertime tourism zenith, the **Glidden Lodge,** 4676 Glidden Drive, tel. (920) 746-3900 or (888) 281-1127, was the epitome of hedonistic delight at the time—a massive, fieldstone main building offering stunning lake views. Located a handful of miles out of Sturgeon Bay, near Whitefish Dunes State Park (right off of WI 57 onto CR T), in the area known as the "quiet side of the peninsula," it's got prime peninsular location. The one- to three-bedroom condo units all offer breathtaking lake views and eastern exposure to allow the sunrise to manifest itself fully. The Glidden offers a full list of recreational and diversionary amenities. Rates in high season run $175-275.

The most solid, all-around Door County resort experience, with rates that don't induce apoplexy, the **Leathem Smith Lodge,** 1640 Memorial Dr., tel. (920) 743-5555, has been recognized even by the county's chamber of commerce for its superlative efforts in maintenance and operations. In the mid-1990s the entire resort underwent a careful overhaul, and it shows nicely—spacious, well-appointed rooms with tasteful decor and wood beams and deck ceilings in most. The suites are magnificent. The well-regarded dining room, besides serving a popular fish boil, is a pleasure—a hangar-like chamber with basic furnishings but super food. The hardwood dance floor in the lounge overlooks the water and is a great place to dance under a full moon in summer. All this for respectably modest rates of $89-192.

The most unique lodging in Sturgeon Bay is **Cliff Top Lodge,** tel. (920) 743-1626, cresting a bluff above Green Bay in High Cliff Park, five miles south of Sturgeon Bay. Built in 1919 by Norwegian craftsmen as the main lodge of a local estate, the entire structure was carefully taken down, moved from Newport State Park, and reassembled here. With one large master bedroom and two huge dorm-style rooms, the lodge can comfortably hold 12—and 14 is not unheard of. The gorgeous living area features a fieldstone fireplace, a wrought-log staircase, and dead fauna adorning the walls. The bathroom, exceeding some apartments in size, features a sauna. Three people can stay for $400 a week; each additional person is $50.

Inns and B&Bs

A century-old commercial building (and erstwhile soda fountain), the **Inn at Cedar Crossing,** corner of 3rd and Louisiana Streets, tel. (920) 743-4200, has set the standard for Sturgeon Bay lodging since its inception as a Victorian inn in 1986. Victorian country would be a more precise description; the owner's flair and passion for folk art decoration is expressed in the rooms (room 6 is particularly warm and spacious). Each of the nine rooms is loaded with antiques, and most come with a fireplace, a

the White Lace Inn

whirlpool, or both. Rates run $95-135, and a few packages are available.

So picturesque that it regularly adorns postcards and magazine covers, the **White Lace Inn,** 16 N. 5th Ave., tel. (920) 743-1105, is actually three late 19th- and early 20th-century homes ensconced in a well-realized version of a charming Victorian neighborhood. Ringed with floral gardens and white picket fences, all that's missing are spinning parasols. Folk art decoration and antique furnishing aficionados will have a field day here. Rooms run $109-229.

Another reputable multi-building inn, the **Barbican,** 132 N. 2nd Ave., tel. (920) 743-4854, features two restored late 19th-century estates of a local lumber baron. Suites are each two rooms, and some take up *three levels.* Numerous fireplaces are not uncommon, and all rooms have whirlpools. Rates run $110-150.

Outside the picturesque historic Sturgeon Bay neighborhoods, the restored farmhouse **Chanticleer,** north to CR BB, then north on CR HH, tel. (920) 746-0334, sits on a 30-acre orchard. Rooms and suites are available, and some are quite stupendous—multi-level suites with 15-foot vaulted ceilings and private terraces, lofted suites with bisque pine ceilings and rafters, and a head-shaking array of amenities in each. Notable extras include a solarium, sauna, hiking trails, and a heated pool. Rates run $120-190.

North of Sturgeon Bay five miles, then right on the road to Whitefish Dunes State Park, you'll find the rustic and very popular **Whitefish Bay Farm B&B,** 3831 Clark Lake Rd., tel. (920) 743-1560. This 1908 American farmhouse has four sunny rooms. Transplanted Milwaukeeans own the working farm and instead of quotidian day jobs, they now raise Corriedale sheep. The farm covers 75 acres of meadow and orchard and is very close to Whitefish Dunes State Park and Cave Point County Park. With all that wool, the owners are accomplished weavers and give spinning and weaving demonstrations in their barn-cum-art gallery. Rooms start at $70.

Cottages

Cottages are the quintessential Wisconsin experience and may also be the most economical way to take in Door County. Sturgeon Bay has a huge assortment of them. Some are just uninhabited B&Bs for a zillion dollars; but hey, they are cottages.

On the economical end, **Lake Lane Breezes,** 5647 Lake Lane, tel. (920) 743-3463, sleeps two to four people. A very family-friendly operation, it's even got a treehouse outside for the kids, and pets are welcome. Rates are $60 by the day, $300 weekly, but verify these by phone before making plans.

Much more expensive would be a private home, but the positive is that you can often bring a group and split the cost. **Mary's Beach House,** 3746 Glidden Dr., tel. (847) 891-4716, has three bedrooms, two baths, and lots of private beach. It's a cool $150 per night or $1000 and up weekly.

Camping

Try not to imagine camping anywhere other than the state parks, but if you have to, Sturgeon Bay has **Quietwoods North,** a mile and a half southwest at 3668 Grondin Rd., tel. (920) 743-7115 or (800) 472-3677, with 260 sites from $20.

FOOD

Fish Boils

There are a couple of fish boil standards in Sturgeon Bay. (Reservations are always advisable in high season.) The **Mill Supper Club,** 4128 WI 42/57 North (right where the highways separate north of town), tel. (920) 743-5044, is a basic Wisconsin supper club serving beef, chicken, and seafood, with fish boils every Tuesday and Thursday, usually at 6:30 p.m. The **Leathem Smith Lodge,** 1640 Memorial Dr., tel. (920) 743-1783, has boils Wednesday and Sunday at 6:30 p.m. June-October. Fish boils are usually $15-20.

Greasy Spoons and Diners

Cover your eyes from the glaring white interior and throwback '50s-style decor at **Perry's Cherry Diner,** 230 Michigan St., tel. (920) 743-9910. Perry's has a large menu for such a small place, offering basic comfort food—burgers, hot beef sandwiches, and "hot plates" (chicken platter, grilled ham, lake perch)—along with a few Jamaican and Greek items like pinatas (small Greek pizzas). From $4. It's also got a new espresso bar. Best of all, it's smoke-free. Open Mon.-Sat. 6 a.m.-9 p.m., Sunday 8 a.m.-3 p.m.

Much more typical is the Americana **My Sister's Cafe,** right along N. Third. Slinging egg-heavy hash, this is the type of place where you might meet the local town council having a breakfast klatsch. From around $3. Open Mon.-Thurs. 5 a.m.-2 p.m., Friday until 8 p.m., weekends 7 a.m.-2 p.m.

Supper Clubs

Besides the aforementioned Mill Supper Club, Sturgeon Bay's historic west side has **Andre's,** at 23 W. Oak St., tel. (920) 743-4179. You'll find good daily lunch and dinner specials here, including standards like chicken and pan-fried perch, walleye, and whitefish, and a Saturday night choice of roast duck, prime rib, or tenderloin with crab legs. From $6. Every night but Friday, the house specialty is Cajun-style steak. Big band music is played Sunday nights, when diners line up for the smorgasbord of baked chicken and meatballs.

Go by road or by boat to the utilitarian (family-kitchen-style chairs, plywood paneling, and thick brown coffee mugs) **Shore Line,** 9254 Lime Kiln Rd., tel. (920) 824-5760. The house specialty—one-pound lobster tails and 18-ounce T-bones—is served nightly. It also has a popular Sunday brunch and family-style chicken and ribs dinners in the evening. Open April-Oct. Mon.-Sat. 4 p.m. until whenever and Sunday from 10 a.m., shorter hours the rest of year.

Italian

Dal Santo's, 341 N. Third Ave., tel. (920) 743-6100, in a historic depot, offers one of the most impressive meals downtown for the money. The specialties are spinach fettucine Alfredo, gnocchi alla Romona, and some very creative pizzas. From $5. The ambience is warm and casually elegant, with tall booths and scattered plants. Open from 11 a.m. daily.

Cajun

Bayou on 3rd, 50 S. 3rd Ave., is another new addition for this book; it's garnered lots of rave reviews for its Cajun food, from $9.

Fine Dining

Arguably the most incredible culinary experience in Door County—and among the top restaurants in Wisconsin—is the dining room of

DOOR COUNTY FISH BOIL

Just when travelers think they've come to understand Wisconsin's predilection for fish fries, Door County throws them a curveball on the fish fetish—the fish boil, which is not at all the same thing as a fry.

Though Scandinavian immigrants came with their own recipes for fish soups and stews, the fish boil likely came from pure practicality. Door County had few cows and fewer pigs, but was rich with whitefish; potatoes and onions, hardy vegetables, were also abundant. Dumping them together was quick, fast, and cheap.

The modern version is a different story. As some tell it, the proprietor of Ellison Bay's Viking Restaurant concocted the first modern fish boil back in the 1960s, ostensibly searching for something unique to serve at the restaurant. It was an immediate hit that snowballed into the de rigueur culinary experience of Door County. Whatever the historical genesis of the boil, it has become a cultural linchpin for the peninsula community, almost a county ordinance.

The Works
Essentially, a Door County fish boil requires only a couple of things: a huge witch-quality iron cauldron, kindling and firewood sufficient to blaze a light for Great Lakes ship traffic, and the innards—fish steaks, small potatoes, onions, and a heck of a lot of salt. Whitefish is for purists, but don't let that stop you from trying other varieties such as trout.

Add salt to the water and bring to a boil (the salt raises the boiling temperature of the water and helps keep the fish from flaking apart in the water). Add potatoes and boil for 15 minutes. Add onions and boil another 4-5 minutes. Add fish, which is often wrapped in cheesecloth to prevent it from falling apart, and boil for another 10 minutes. Now, here's the fun part: right before the fish is done, use kerosene to jack up the flame to space-shuttle-launch proportions. The kerosene induces a boil-over, which forces the oily top layers of water out of the cauldron to be burned off in the fire. Drain the rest and slather it with butter. The requisite side dishes are coleslaw, dark breads, and, this being Door County, cherry pie or cobbler for dessert.

the **Inn at Cedar Crossing,** corner of 3rd and Louisiana Streets, tel. (920) 743-4200, an epicurean delight well documented by professional travel scribes and gourmands. Though quite modern and posh, the inn features original decor down to pressed-tin ceilings and ornate glasswork, and a fireplace roars in each dining room. The menu, heavy on fresh fish and seafood, emphasizes regional ingredients—as many foods as possible come from Wisconsin. The trademark entrées include harvest pheasant linguine, capered whitefish, and tenderloin stuffed with lobster. The owner is proud of the to-die-for desserts (and patrons swoon over them with somewhat alarming passion). Lunch from $5, dinner from $9. The inn also features live classical and flamenco guitar on weekends. Open daily for breakfast, lunch, and dinner year-round.

However, the Cedar is being given a run for its money by new **Restaurant Sage,** 136 N. 3rd Ave., tel. (920) 746-1100, with an impressive menu of creative cuisine; examples include Thai shrimp, New Zealand lamb, and a macadamia nut-encrusted salmon. A wine bar with live jazz and piano adds to the atmosphere. Menu items from $20.

NIGHTLIFE AND RECREATION

Sturgeon Bay is not a happening place when the sun goes down, to be sure. For live entertainment, check out a few of the restaurants listed above. One consistent place for catching live music is **Roadhouse,** 5790 WI 42, tel. (920) 743-4966, which is actually in Carlsville, nine miles north of Sturgeon Bay. You can get steaks, chicken, chops, burgers, and outstanding deep-fried lobster there, but best of all, they offer live blues performances Saturday nights July-October. Closed Monday.

Pick a direction and you'll find grand bike touring. The **Ahnapee State Trail,** best suited for mountain bikes, starts just south of town (see "Algoma," above). Even better, splash out onto the coastline in a sea kayak. **Latitude 45,** 20 N. Third Ave., tel. (920) 743-4434, rents bikes and has half-day sea kayak tours for novices.

SERVICES AND INFORMATION

The **Sturgeon Bay Visitors Center,** tel. (920) 743-3924, www.sturgeonbay.net, and the **Door County Chamber of Commerce,** tel. (920) 743-4456 or (800) 52-RELAX, doorcountyvacations.com, are located contiguously and intelligently, just south of town. The latter is generally full of all the information you're likely to need. It's got a 24-hour touch-screen information service, most often used to find lodgings. Open summers Mon.-Fri 8:30 a.m.-5 p.m. and weekends 10:30 a.m.-4 p.m., winters weekdays only 8:30 a.m.-4 p.m.

The **post office** is at the corner of Louisiana and 4th Streets.

NORTH OF STURGEON BAY: LAKESIDE

Otherwise known as the "quiet side," this area shows less commercial development than the rest of the peninsula. North of Sturgeon Bay, the lakeshore side of the Door is a wonderland of pristine heath, healed cutover forest, rocky sea caves, some of Lake Michigan's finest beaches, biome preserves, picture-postcard lighthouses, and two of Wisconsin's best state parks.

The quick way into the area is WI 57, branching off WI 42 north of Sturgeon Bay. Farther off the beaten path, get right above the water along the coast starting southeast of Sturgeon Bay at the Sturgeon Bay canal North Pierhead Lighthouse. From there, an established State Rustic Road hugs the coastline all the way to Whitefish Dunes State Park, bypassing Portage and Whitefish Points and the Lilly Bay curve. Don't worry about getting lost once you find CR T; there are no other roads as you buzz through the splendid wetlands scenery.

WHITEFISH DUNES STATE PARK

Some say Whitefish Dunes is the most pleasant park in the state system. The beach is indisputably so—miles and miles of mocha-colored dunes sculpted into ridges by the prevailing winds.

Archaeologists surmise that the littoral site's proximity to inland lakes and creeks (nearby Clark Lake is over 800 fish-rich acres) was likely the primary reason for settlement. Thus far, eight temporary encampments or semi-permanent small villages have been identified, dating as far back as 100 B.C. and spreading over three acres now comprised by the park. The North Bay natives were the earliest, occupying the shores from Green Bay north to Rock Island seasonally until A.D. 300. The water levels of Lake Michigan rose and flooded the site. The Heins Creek and Late Woodland inhabitants occupied the area from A.D. 500-900, and by that time, the itinerant camps had grown into a sizable semi-permanent village. The Oneota Indians, descended from the Late Woodland tribe, held sway on the peninsula at two different periods beginning in A.D. 900. This site was occupied in A.D. 1200 and A.D. 1400—on either side of another flood. European settlers arrived in 1840, when a commercial fishing operation on Whitefish Bay was begun by the Clark brothers (who lent their name to the nearby lake), working side by side with the Winnebago.

Today, everybody comes for the big dunes—among the highest on Lake Michigan, east or west. They were formed by numerous advances and retreats of ancient lakes and, later, Lake Michigan, and zillions of storms. Sand banks first closed off Clark Lake in what is now the mainland, and as vegetation took hold three millennia ago, wind deposits began piling up atop the sandbar. The result is a microcosm that couldn't possibly occur on the bay side of the peninsula—a wide beach rising to forested dunes. The tallest, Old Baldy, stands 93 feet high.

The one rule to follow dutifully is *stay off the dunes.* Many of the grasses holding together the mounds are peculiar to this park, and once

Cave Point County Park hollow formations

they're gone, the dunes are done for (just take a look at the lifeless gashes created by motorcyclists before the park was established). The most popular walk is the **Red Trail,** a three-miler with an optional shorter loop that skirts the shoreline. Plank-and-rope boardwalks allow beach access. Bicycles are allowed on this trail, and at the midpoint it branches away from the water to link with longer trails through mixed hardwood, red pine, or oddball wooded dune areas—13 miles total, most of it maintained for skiing in winter. Continuing on the Red Trail to its southern end, hikers can access the only climbable dune—Old Baldy, which offers panoramas of Lake Michigan and Clark Lake inland. From there, it's possible to link with the longer trails in the mixed sand and hardwoods, including a spur trail to Whitefish Creek, which drains Clark Lake. Farthest to the north a short access trail to the White Trail leads to **Cave Point County Park,** likely the most photographed parkland in Door County.

From south to north in Whitefish Bay, the geology shifts from dunes to mixed sand and stone, and finally, at Cave Point, to exposed limestone ledges thrusting up to 50 feet above the water of the Niagara Escarpment—the bedrock of the peninsula. Eons of crashing waves have hewn caves and cenotes that show up as blowholes of sorts as the surf pounds and crashes, echoing like rolling thunder. The whole effect is not unlike the crumbled parapets of a time-worn castle. Sea kayakers have a field day snooping around this small promontory. Straight-faced old-

timers tell of a schooner that slammed into the rocks at Cave Point in 1881 (true). Laden with corn, the ship cracked like a nut and spilled its cargo (true), and within a few days, corn had mysteriously appeared in Green Bay on the other side of the peninsula (hmm).

A caveat: do not take swimming lightly here. The concave bend of Whitefish Bay focuses all the current, forming tough riptides. Predicting where these form is never possible, but most occur in a well-marked 200-yard zone near the first ramp to the beach. Obviously, swimming within this zone is foolhardy. When waves are large enough to really notice, move as far down the beach as possible and do not go in farther than waist depth. The waves create long shore currents, which serve only to funnel you into the rips. If you are ensnared, do the usual: swim parallel to the shore until you're out of its clutches (generally riptides are no more than 30 yards wide). *Lifeguards are never on duty.*

This park is day-use only; no camping. Great picnicking, though, is found right atop the limestone ledges overlooking the lake. Do check out the nature center for its exhibits on the geology and anthropology of the area; it's one of the most comprehensive you'll see in a state park.

JACKSONPORT

You can always tell those who have explored the bay side of the peninsula first, then backtracked through Sturgeon Bay to come back up this side. Generally, these are the ones who race right through Jacksonport as if they didn't know it was there, then turn around to try and find what they missed.

At one time, Jacksonport rivaled Fish Creek as epicenter of economic booms on the Door. Once the local lumber was depleted, Jacksonport's docks were relegated to fishing boats. The last community to be settled in the county, Jacksonport caught one of the Germanic immigrant waves, and its annual **Maifest** is among the larger shindigs held throughout the summer.

Somnolent Jacksonport today sports a few antique shops and gift cottages selling wares and crafts from dozens of Door County artists. A lazy strand of sand acts as a beach, and top-notch fun comes in the form of the sweets at the **Town Hall Bakery,** 6225 WI 57.

Just north of town (and halfway between the equator and the north pole), the village presents **Meridian County Park** right on the 45th Parallel (we'll have to take their word for it). Adjacent to this is a vast **wildlife sanctuary.**

Right downtown is the pinnacle of Jacksonport's developmental ambition: the **Square Rigger Lodge and Cottages,** 6332 WI 57, tel. (920) 823-2404. Over a dozen basic but comfortable modern motel units overlook the water (a couple do not), and most have private balconies or patios. One- to three-bedroom cottages also line the waterfront. Rates run $92-128.

For food, get the basics at **Mike's Port Pub and Grill,** 6269 WI 57, tel. (920) 823-2081; it has tons of Packer paraphernalia. The most substantial eats are found at the aforementioned **Square Rigger Galley,** which also serves fish boils in summer. The supper club of choice is **Mr. G's,** 5890 WI 57, tel. (920) 823-2112, with a ballroom and live entertainment during the summer. From $9. **Bright Eye Farm Market,** south of Jacksonport, sells organic produce.

BAILEYS HARBOR

Lake Michigan sportfishing really shows itself as you enter Baileys Harbor. Every inch of roadway, alleyway, and parking lot is crammed with trucks and empty boat trailers—perhaps fitting, as it was boats that got the town founded in the

first place. In 1844, a Captain Bailey and crew were foundering in a sudden squall when they espied this cove and took shelter. They were amazed to find a deep, well-isolated harbor and gorgeous cedar stands backing off the beach. So enthralled was the captain that he and the shipping company owner persuaded the U.S. government to construct a lighthouse at the entrance some years later. It was the first settlement in Door County. With just the right amount of development, it's still an important spot for ships, as its harbor is the only designated Harbor of Refuge on the lake side of the peninsula.

Sights

Baileys Harbor is sandwiched between the strategic safe harbor on Lake Michigan and Kangaroo Lake, the peninsula's largest inland lake. Travelers are so preoccupied with these two sights that it's easy to miss the two large promontories jutting off the peninsula just north of town, forming Moonlight Bay. These two capes may be the state's most awesome natural landmarks and definitely have the best lighthouses. North of Baileys Harbor along CR Q a critical biotic reserve, the **Ridges Sanctuary,** 1,000 acres of boreal bog, swamp, dune, and a complete assortment of wildflowers in their natural habitat. The eponymous series of ancient spiney sand ridges mark the advance of ancient and modern Lake Michigan. All 23 native Wisconsin orchids are found within the sanctuary's confines, as are 13 endangered species of flora. The preserve was established in the 1930s by hardcore early ecologists (like Jens Jensen) in one of the state's first environmental brouhahas, incited by a spat over plans for a trailer park. The Department of the Interior recognizes the site as one of the most ecologically precious in the region; it was the first National Natural Landmark in Wisconsin.

Also accessible via the short, meticulously laid out trails and boardwalks across the dunes are the famed **Baileys Harbor Range Lights,** a pair of small but powerful lighthouses—a shorter, wooden octagonal one across the road on the beach, the other 900 feet inland—raised in 1869 by the Coast Guard. The inland house, also home to the lightkeeper, was built up by 15 feet to allow ships to align the two lights for guidance into the harbor. Three easy trails, ranging from just under two miles to five miles, snake throughout the tamarack and hardwood stands—20 miles in all and well worth the effort. Wintertime cross-country skiing through the Ridges trails in the contiguous county park is amazing. Donations are requested for upkeep; tours are $2 adults, $1 children. Also on the grounds you'll find a nature center, open Mon.-Sat. 9 a.m.-4 p.m., Sunday 1-4 p.m.

Continue on Ridges Road out of Baileys Harbor to additional sites deemed National Natural Landmarks by the Department of the Interior and dedicated by the Nature Conservancy. **Toft's Point** (or Old Lighthouse Point) is along a great old dirt road that winds through barren sands with innumerable pulloffs. There are no established recreational sites and no camping, but a few trails for hiking and skiing are found throughout the 600-plus acres that take up the whole of the promontory and include almost three miles of rock beach shoreline. To the north of the Ridges, also off CR Q, the **Mud Lake Wildlife Area** is over 1,000 acres protecting the shallow lake and surrounding wetlands. A prime waterfowl sanctuary, Mud Lake and its environs may be even more primeval and wild than the Ridges. Again, there are no established facilities, but you can hike and ski. Canoeing is also very popular, as Reibolts Creek connects the lake with Moonlight Bay.

And the bays don't end yet. North of Moonlight Bay is isolated North Bay, site of a handful of cottages and resorts. On the southern promontory you'll find undoubtedly the most popular lighthouse on the peninsula, **Cana Island,** accessible via CR Q to Cana Island Dr. to a narrow spit of gravel that may be under water, depending on when you get there. Impressively tall and magnificently white, the lighthouse is framed naturally by white birch. One of the most crucial lighthouses in the county, it stands far off the coast on a wind-whipped landform. Built in 1870, it was obviously considered a hardship station during storm season. It's not open to the public for tours, but you can wander the grounds daily 10 a.m.-5 p.m. North Bay is also the site of **Marshall's Point,** an isolated stretch of wild land completely surrounded by private development once touted as a possible state park for its remarkable microclimate (no plans have yet advanced beyond speculation).

South of Baileys Harbor and along a splendid stretch of beach is a decidedly different kind of vacation, an educational seminar at **Bjorklunden,** tel. (920) 839-2216, more a relaxed, soul-searching means of personal growth than a for-credit school experience. Participants live in a recently reconstructed Norwegian-style lodge built of local fieldstone and undertake courses in humanities and natural sciences. Fees for lodging, meals (the food is outstanding), and seminars are $600 s, $850 d, far less for those with lodging off-site. Just to stay at the lodge, which looks like a Viking ship, is around $400 a week, meals included. Visitors can tour Monday and Wednesday 1-4 p.m. and check out the Norwegian *stavkirke* (church).

Accommodations

Baileys Harbor has a couple of basic, modestly priced motels, including **Journey's End,** 2528 CR EE/F, tel. (920) 839-2887, with 10 rooms, all with two beds, from $60 in peak season. You'll find some of the nicest motel rooms in Door County, and a lovely setting to boot, at the **Garden Inn,** a block west of WI 57 on Guy St., tel. (920) 839-2617. Rates from $63 and up.

The **Blacksmith Inn B&B,** 8152 WI 57, tel. (920) 839-9222, is a renovated 1912 half-timber and stovewood home offering seven rooms, and, yes, it was a real blacksmith shop in bygone days. Many of the antiques filling the house were made in the shop. Set on two beachfront acres, it's even got a gurgling spring and footbridge. Rates run $80-135.

An 1860s-era log home was painstakingly dismantled near Pulaski, WI, and relocated to the village, where it has become the showpoint lodging option of **Scofield House North,** tel. (877) 376-4667. The gorgeous two-story log home has two bedrooms with skylights, two fireplaces, a washer/dryer, cathedral ceilings, and a lovely sunroom. A cottage and huge main house are also available. Rates for the log house are a cool $250 per night, or $1400 per week, with a three-night minimum. The cottage is a mere $125 per night with a three-night minimum.

The ever-expanding **Ridges Resort,** 8252 WI 57, tel. (920) 839-2127, adjacent to the Ridges Sanctuary (a big plus, with all that hiking), features a main lodge with comfy motel-style rooms as well as one- and two-bedroom cottages. More options will likely exist by the time you read this. The lodge rooms have vaulted ceilings and fireplaces, and the cottages offer super views of the sanctuary from private balconies. A newer guesthouse features four luxurious suites. Rates run from $110 weekends in peak season, much much less other times.

The gorgeous, well-designed and -appointed accommodations at **Baileys Harbor Yacht Club Resort,** 8150 Ridges Rd., tel. (920) 839-2336 or (800) 927-2492 feature living-room-style lodge rooms and various cottages. High-season rates of $75-150 might be the steal of Baileys Harbor.

What may be the most enviably sited lodging in all of Door County is the **Gordon Lodge,** 1420 Pine Dr., tel. (920) 839-2331. Spread across the tip of a promontory jutting into Kangaroo Lake's north bay, the long-established Gordon Lodge sprouted up in the 1920s as an offshoot of a popular Sturgeon Bay doctor's summer home. The main lodge has a lake view, while villas with fireplaces creep out right atop the water. Some original cottages are set back and nestled under the pines. Fitness trails and other recreational activities are offered. The dining room is casually elegant and the Top Deck lounge, originally a boathouse, is unsurpassed for after-dinner dancing. Rates start at $110.

For camping, Newport and Peninsula State Parks are fantastic—and usually full. A mile west on CR EE you'll find **Bailey's Bluff,** tel. (920) 839-2109. Open seasonally, it has lots of wooded areas and, best of all, no minimum stays; rates from $18.

Food
There are a number of food options for such a small place, and all are impossible to miss—they're right downtown. The local nucleus of the food industry is the **Sandpiper,** tel. (920) 839-2528, a most informal family-style place with sandwiches, meat platters, and some from-scratch items (from $3). The popular fish boil ($12) is held Mon.-Sat. throughout summer and autumn. Open April through mid-October for breakfast, lunch, and dinner.

The supper club of choice is the **Florian II,** tel. (414) 839-2361, serving steaks, fowl, and seafood, along with a western-style barbecue buffet ($11) Sunday nights in July and August

and a breakfast buffet ($7) on weekends. The **Common House,** on WI 57, tel. (920) 839-2078, is a bit more creative in its entrées (from $10) and features a wood stove in the dining room. For a special Door County evening, the dining room at the **Gordon Lodge,** 1420 Pine Dr., tel. (920) 839-2331, cannot be surpassed.

Recreation
Chinook salmon and rainbow and brown trout are the quarry for local fishing captains and charter boats, and the fishing in Baileys Harbor is some of the best in the county—Lilliputian Baileys Harbor (pop. 780) boasts a salmon harvest one-half the size of *Milwaukee's*. The **Baileys Harbor Charter Fishing Association,** P.O. Box 72, Baileys Harbor, WI 54202, tel. (920) 839-9111, acts as a clearinghouse for information and as a contact point for the half dozen boats operating out of the harbor. Charter outfits include the **Fish Doctor,** 10309 Old Stage Rd., Sister Bay, tel. (920) 854-5109, operated by Capt. Lynn Frederick, a Ph.D. in fisheries and a fishing charter captain since 1975; she also teaches occasional fishing and ecology seminars. Another outfit, **Salmon Depot,** tel. (920) 839-2272, offers charter fishing along with wreck scuba diving and scenic shoreline cruises.

Services and Information
The Town Hall (can't miss it) has the local **visitor information center,** tel. (920) 839-2366, open daily in summer and fall.

ROWLEYS BAY

Out of Baileys Harbor, WI 57 swoops back toward Sister Bay to WI 42. The next lakeside community, Rowleys Bay, is mostly a massive and well-established resort and campground. To get there, take CR Q northwest out of Baileys Harbor to Woodcrest Rd., then go north to CR ZZ all the way to CR Z, which will lead you right to **Wagon Trail Resort, Restaurant, and Conference Center,** 1041 CR ZZ, tel. (920) 854-2385 or (800) 99-WAGON. Originally a bare-bones fishing encampment and later a rustic lodge, Wagon Trail has transmogrified into what is certainly the most comprehensive operation on the upper Door Peninsula; from campground to posh suites, somehow the place does it all and does it well. Two- and three-bedroom rustically upscale vacation villas are set on wooded or waterfront sites. Rates run from $109 in peak season for the main lodge, though there are innumerable seasonal packages (and multi-day minimums).

The resort's campground, spread throughout 200 acres along the bay, is really quite fastidious and professionally run—campsites are isolated by tall, thick pines. The options here include basic tent sites ($20), secluded RV sites with electricity and water ($31), and "tent suites" ($40), plus a laundry list of extras. The campground is very popular, and reservations are recommended.

Several miles of trails wend through the resort's acreage; one leads to Sand Bay Beach Park on Rowleys Bay, another to the Mink River Estuary. On the bay, the resort's marina offers bicycles, canoes, kayaks, paddleboats, charter fishing boats, and scenic excursions.

The reason most folks show up here, though, isn't for the cozy rooms but rather for **Grandma's Restaurant and Bakery,** a magnet for sweet tooths from around the country hungry for Gran's 10 kinds of homemade bread, cardamom coffee cake, cherry pie, Old World-style bread pudding, and scads of muffins, cookies, and pastries. The specialty is Swedish sweets—*limpa* and *skorpa* (thinly sliced pecan rolls sprinkled with cinnamon sugar and dried in the oven). The place also sells 47 kinds of flour. This is the place for breakfast or lunch—Swedish buffet-style or straight à la carte. A Swedish all-you-can-eat dinner buffet is also served twice a week, and fish boils are held in summer. From $5. Expect a wait in the summer; use the time to peruse the historical book written on this institution—chock-full of recipes.

Mink River Estuary

Stretching southeast from Ellison Bay to the edge of Newport State Park, the Mink River Estuary acts, by grace of the Nature Conservancy, to protect the river system as it empties into the bay through marsh and estuary. Primarily a crucial ornithological migratory site, the waters also act as a conduit for spawning fish. The topography of the 1,500 acres is astonishingly diverse and untouched; two threatened plant species—the dune thistle and dwarf lake iris—are found within the boundaries, and over 200 species of birds pass through.

To get there, most take WI 42 out of Ellison Bay to Newport Drive; go south and keep your eyes peeled. Mink River Road also leads directly from Ellison Bay. Hike in from Newport Drive, or canoe in across the bay from CR Z at the Wagon Trail Resort.

NEWPORT STATE PARK

The best place to capture the wild side of the Door Peninsula, this rough, isolated backwoods park constitutes half of the tip of the county—it stretches for almost 12 miles along the Lake Michigan coast through an established scientific reserve. A remarkable diversity of hardwood and conifers, isolated wetland, bog, and even a few hidden coves along the lakeshore make the hiking appealing. Once an up-and-coming lumber village in the 1880s, the town decayed gradually as the stands of forests became depleted. By the 1920s, the village and its dwellings had disappeared. (Ghostly outlines of foundations are still scattered about in the underbrush.) With the appropriation in the mid-1960s of the Europe Lake region, what some have called a perfect park was established.

The park's environment has made a remarkable recovery; from wasted white pine cutover, the inner confines of the park are now dense tracts of bog forest. The southern section of the park is an established scientific reserve on 140 acres of mixed hardwoods. The park's magnificent ecosystem draws one of the planet's highest concentrations of monarch butterflies, which make a mind-boggling trip from Mexico's Yucatán Peninsula to San Juan Capistrano and then all the way here. Unfortunately, biologists have noted a dramatic drop-off in monarch numbers, mostly due to pollution and logging.

Trails

The park maintains 28 miles of trails, along which you'll find wilderness campsites. By far the most popular area of the park is the northern tier and the two trails along Europe Lake—one of the largest of the county's inland lakes—a pristine, sandy gem uncluttered by development. From a parking area, **Europe Bay Trail** leads more than three miles to the lake. Along the way, the topography is similar to that of Whitefish Dunes—a sandy forest with dune-like mounds that isolate Europe Lake from Lake Michigan. Almost immediately, **Fern** and **Lynd Point Trails** bifurcate and wind around Lynd Point into Newport Bay. Along here and to the north are a rocky beach and some great views of Porte des Mortes and the surrounding islands. Gravel Island, viewable from Lynd Point, is a national ornithological refuge. The **Holtz loop** branches off Europe Bay Trail later and skirts the edge of the lake through stands of hardwood. Crane your neck along this route and all you'll see is water.

North of the park office is a short **Upland Trail** and new for this edition, a two-mile-long **Sugar Bush Trail.**

In the southern section of the park, the **Newport Trail** pokes through hardwood and significant stands of conifer. This and **Rowley Bay** and **Ridge Trails** alternately pass through meadows, wooded areas, and along limestone headlands on the coast, mostly along old logging roads. Spider Island, viewable from the Newport Trail, is another wildlife refuge for nesting gulls. A few other tiny trails, including a well-marked nature trail leaving from the welcome center, line the park.

Fifteen of the park's 28 miles of trail allow mountain bikes, and bike camping is possible, though the park warns of porcupine damage to bikes overnight! Note that the trails are for the most part hardpacked dirt but are regularly pocked with bikers' land mines—potholes of quicksand, python-size tree roots hidden under leaves, and more than a few spots of gravel. Essentially, anywhere that hikers go a bike can get to, just not always on the same trail. Keep those eyes peeled, because things can get confusing on the network. The most conspicuous off-limits areas are the shoreline routes—it's too tempting for bikers to whip down onto the fragile sands. Note that Rowley Bay Trail is definitely an advanced trail.

In winter, 23 miles of trail are maintained for cross-country skiing—grand, isolated, wooded skiing. The Fern and Lynd Point Trails from Newport to Europe Bay are open to hikers and, especially, snowshoers, but these are the only trails exclusively for nonskiers. Ski trails are ungroomed.

Camping
Here's the reason outdoor aficionados pilgrimage here regularly—there's no vehicular access to campsites. Sites are strictly walk-in (a modestly strenuous hike to some, a serious pack to most, but it sure beats the traffic death of Potawatomi and Peninsula; the shortest hike in is one-half mile, the longest nearly four miles). Thirteen of the 16 sites are reservable. Two sites on Europe Lake are waterside, so canoes can land and camp; the Lake Michigan side has plenty of lakeside sites. Winter camping is outstanding here.

NORTH OF STURGEON BAY: BAYSIDE

Wisconsin Highway 42 has perhaps the most intriguing history of any country road. Not your average farm-to-market remnant, it was hewn from a tundra-like wilderness in 1857 by starving millers and fishers desperate when winter arrived earlier than expected and froze supply boats out of the harbor.

On the way to Egg Harbor out of Sturgeon Bay, a great on-the-water side trip is along CR B. It starts out as N. Third Avenue in downtown Sturgeon Bay, then changes to Bay Shore Drive before the names peter out and it simply becomes CR B. Eventually, it merges with CR G around Horseshoe Bay and leads directly to Egg Harbor.

EGG HARBOR

There's something of a contrived (officially, "revitalized") feel to Egg Harbor, back on WI 42. A couple of structures smack of the early days, now redone with fresh facades. But there's more than a little new development, including an ersatz-Victorian strip mall that could have been plunked down in any city suburb or fringe sprawl in America.

This isn't to denigrate the lovely village at all, built on a rise overlooking one of the most accessible and well-protected harbors along either coast. The harbor had long been in use by the Winnebago before military materiel and trade ships necessarily anchored here—the only safe spot between Fish Creek and Little Sturgeon Bay. The first permanent European presence was established in the late 1850s, when Jacob and Levi Thorp, two brothers of the founder of Fish Creek, collaborated to build a pier to allow transport of local cordwood. By the 1890s, despite the tough precipice and local swampland, Egg Harbor had become the southernmost resort village in the county, and a rivalry with Fish Creek was born. Over time, the population has ebbed to a stable 200 permanent residents.

Oh, and that name. It doesn't stem from any ovoid land configuration but from a legendary 1825 battle between vacationing rich folk. While rowing to shore in longboats, boredom apparently got the best of the well-to-do, who started winging picnic-packed eggs back and forth. When the shells settled, a name was born.

Sights and Activities

Winding off WI 42 and down the hillside, your first sight is probably the most picturesque village park in the county, this one with a small strand of smooth-stoned beach. Farther south a couple of miles you'll find an even better view of Horseshoe Bay and another beach at Frank E. Murphy County Park.

Just out of town on an old dairy farm is the **Birch Creek Music Center,** three miles east on CR E, tel. (920) 868-3763. Evening concerts by budding students and national names in the big barn are regularly scheduled (generally mid-July through Labor Day) and something of an institution in the area—the big band series is particularly popular. Percussion performances are the specialty.

Sight of sights and a landmark for denizens of the Door is the gothic revival **Cupola House,** a massive building constructed in 1871 by Levi Thorp as local cordwood made him among the wealthiest men in the county. During the summer, resident artists at the Birch Creek Center give performances at the house; the mansion has been restored and now houses an assortment of shops and boutiques.

Kurtz Corral, CR I, tel. (920) 743-6742, offers a large variety of rides throughout the area. They also have winter rides complete with fireside cider breaks. Open daily 9 a.m.-3 p.m. May-Sept., by appointment thereafter.

The local library has a small **visitor information center,** tel. (920) 868-3717, www.eggharbor-wi.com, open Tues.-Sat. seasonally.

Accommodations

The cheapest accommodations to be found in Egg Harbor will run you $50-55, including those at the most notable resort in town, the rambling, seemingly endless **Alpine Inn and Cottages,** tel. (920) 868-3000, stretching some three-quarters of a mile southwest of town along the bay. A heated pool, private sand beach, pier, 27 holes

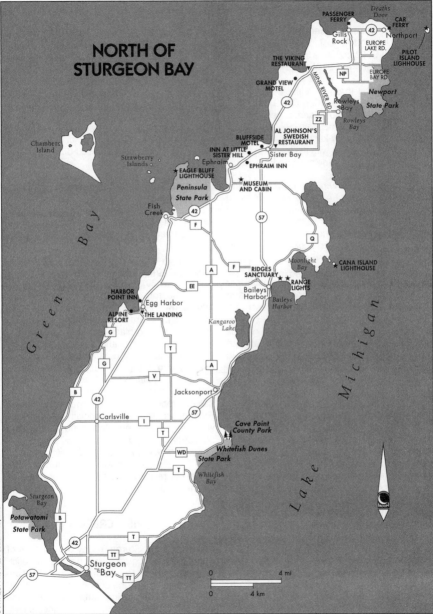

NORTH OF STURGEON BAY

PASSENGER FERRY

Deaths Door

CAR FERRY

Gills Rock

Northport

EUROPE LAKE RD.

42

PILOT ISLAND LIGHTHOUSE

THE VIKING RESTAURANT

MINK RIVER RD.

NP

EUROPE BAY RD.

GRAND VIEW MOTEL

42

Rowleys Bay

Newport State Park

ZZ

Rowleys Bay

Chambers Island

Strawberry Islands

BLUFFSIDE MOTEL

AL JOHNSON'S SWEDISH RESTAURANT

INN AT LITTLE SISTER HILL

Sister Bay

Ephraim

EAGLE BLUFF LIGHTHOUSE

EPHRAIM INN

MUSEUM AND CABIN

Peninsula State Park

Fish Creek

42

57

F

Q

Green Bay

F

Moonlight Bay

CANA ISLAND LIGHTHOUSE

A

RIDGES SANCTUARY

EE

Baileys Harbor

RANGE LIGHTS

HARBOR POINT INN

Egg Harbor

Baileys Harbor

ALPINE RESORT

THE LANDING

Kangaroo Lake

G

T

Lake Michigan

G

A

B

V

42

Jacksonport

Carlsville

57

I

Cave Point County Park

T

WD

Whitefish Dunes State Park

T

Whitefish Bay

Moon

Sturgeon Bay

Potawatomi State Park

B

42

T

TT

Sturgeon Bay

TT

57

0   4 mi

0   4 km

of golf, and free tennis, boats, and bikes are just the tip of the iceberg. The Hof Restaurant gets good reviews and offers live entertainment nightly in July and August. Open Memorial Day through mid-October. Rates from $60 s, $72 d in the inn; cottages run $105 a day or $640 for the week.

A good motel that looks like a resort, the **Mariner,** two miles south on CR G, tel. (920) 868-3131, has beautifully landscaped grounds along the shore (they maintain their own nature trails) with 26 clean, well-kept rooms and rates as low as $60 for a double with the least appealing view. There are also some multi-bedroom family cottages.

You'll find award-winning rooms at **Ashbrooke Suites,** 7942 Egg Harbor Rd., tel. (920) 868-3113, with one- and two-bedroom suites done up in a French country atmosphere. The facility includes an indoor pool, whirlpool, sauna, fitness room, and private whirlpools in some suites. Rates are $107 in peak periods, less thereafter.

One of the largest and most impressive resort complexes in the entire county, in fact Door County's largest resort, **Landmark Resort and Conference Center,** is a mile south of town off of CR G down an access road, tel. (920) 868-3205 or (800) 273-7877, and has almost 300 condos with various numbers of bedrooms—all with spectacular views. You'll need both hands to count the swimming pools, another two for the tennis courts. There's also an excellent restaurant. Rates start at $150 for a one-bedroom unit.

For a non-resort option in town, try **Woldt's Intown Farmette,** north of town on WI 42, then north on Church St., tel. (608) 873-8884. This two-story cottage is adjacent to a reconstructed Dutch colonial barn and windmill. Daily rates start at $75, weekly at $450. **The Cottage Retreat,** 4355 CR T, tel. (920) 743-4420, has also been reconstructed, from collected fieldstone. The sun-soaked two-bedroom cottage can sleep six and offers a combined kitchen/dining room/living area; full-length windows overlooking a deck; and a boardwalk to a sauna. Rates are $79 daily, $450 weekly.

Cornerstone Suites, 6960 WI 42, tel. (920) 868-3005 or (888) 495-3005, has cozy rooms in a spectacular refurbished 19th-century barn; one suite has sublime views of the countryside. Rates run from $114. The owners of the **Honey**

Dew Lodge, 6543 Division Rd., tel. (920) 743-2456, have gotten tremendous write-ups, for their cheeriness and for the lovely hand-hewn log home (it should be in great shape; they built it for their eventual retirement!). Cathedral ceilings, wood-burning stoves, kitchen, the whole works is here. Rates are $125 per night and up.

There are four private campgrounds nearby, three of which allow individual tenters. For the best wooded sites and a clean facility, **Door County Camping Resort,** 4906 Court Rd., is south on WI 42 to Sunny Point Rd., then east, tel. (920) 868-3151. Rates run $20-60.

Food

The **Olde Stage,** 7778 Egg Harbor Rd., is another tavern-cum-restaurant. It has a breakfast buffet and serves Italian-American food, with weekly smorgasbords—including a fish fry—and the largest beer selection you'll find. From $5.

The early meal (and lunch) of choice is at the longstanding **Village Cafe,** at the north end of town, tel. (920) 868-3342, a breakfast/lunch place. The from-scratch bakery, soups, salads, and sandwiches, and early-bird breakfast specials (7-8 a.m.) are worth the effort. This is Egg Harbor's favorite place for evening fish boils, too, served up Friday and Saturday. From $4.

The restaurant for gourmands in town, however, is **Trio,** tel. (920) 868-2092, an eclectic and ambitious Italian and Country French eatery serving fantastic antipasti and entrées such as Italian lamb shank and an orgasmic whitefish Provençale. The house specialty is *cassoulet,* white beans baked with lamb, duck, and sausage. Serving dinner from 5:30 p.m.

Shipwreck'd, 7791 Egg Harbor Rd., tel. (920) 868-2767, is a brewpub and restaurant (from $6) in the resort of the same name; it serves lunches and dinners daily.

FISH CREEK

Some consider Sturgeon Bay the nucleus of Door County. Geographically it may be, but strictly speaking this graceful community is what generally offers visitors the anticipated coffee-table pictorial and rustic fishing camps. Not to mention oodles of lodgings worthy of magazine covers, shops, restaurants, and lengthy harborside strolls. It may be the soul, as it were, of the county, and yet, it's also another Door County village—with a population right at 200.

Arguably the most picturesque view in the county is along WI 42 as it winds into the village from a casual bluff. The official village history describes the town's situation succinctly—"with its back to a rock and its face to the sea." A treasured stretch of road with a few hairpin perils, a roller-coaster gut-lifter, and suddenly you're in a trim and tidy Victorian hamlet that could have come out of a Currier & Ives print. Fish Creek boasts the most thoroughly maintained pre-20th-century architecture on the entire peninsula, some 40 historic structures.

In 1844, trader Increase Claflin, the first non-native permanent settler in Door County, left Sturgeon Bay after a few less-than-propitious incidents with the Potawatomi and wound up here. About this time, an Eastern cooper afflicted with terminal wanderlust, Asa Thorp, made his way to Door County via southeastern Wisconsin, searching for his fortune. With his two brothers, Thorp constructed a loading pier and began a cordwood cutting business to supply steamships plying the coast. Later, Fish Creek transformed itself into the hub of commercial fishing on the Door Peninsula. Tourism was fortuitously there to take up the slack when the shipping supply industry petered out. By the late 1890s, locals were already putting out "Tourist Home" signs. Within a decade, even the home of Asa Thorp had been transformed into the Thorp Hotel.

Sights and Activities

Most visitors to Fish Creek prefer to simply stroll about, getting a look-see at the original architecture in an old county. The harbor area also has remnants of the earliest cabins. Even the remains of an 1855 cabin built by the founding Thorp brothers stands on the grounds of the newfangled Founders Square mélange of shops and restaurants in the village center. Razed by a conflagration, they were rebuilt as closely as possible to the original designs. As this book was being updated, Fish Creek was busily putting final touches on its famous "haunted house," the 1875 Greek Revival Noble House, to recapture its original lavish looks. Tours are available; check at the visitor information center.

The Gibraltar Historical Association, tel. (920) 868-2091, has historic walking tours of Fish Creek Tuesday at 2 p.m. and Friday at 9 a.m. Free but donations would be a good idea.

Billed as the country's oldest summer theater, the Peninsula Players, north of Fish Creek off WI 42 on Peninsula Players Rd. inside the state park, tel. (920) 868-3287, perform a spate of Broadway plays and musicals in a gorgeous garden setting with bayside trails late, June through mid-October, a tradition in its seventh decade. Reservations are recommended. Performances are Tues.-Sun. evenings under an all-weather pavilion.

Less than half as old, but with boatloads of attitude, the tongue-in-cheek American Folklore Theatre, tel. (920) 839-2329, is an acclaimed theater-and-song troupe as likely to perform the rollicking original "Belgians in Heaven" (with the catchphrase "cheese curds, booyah, and beer") as a ghost story series or the works of the Bard. Performances are held May through mid-October, also in the state park, and now include an autumn Town Hall Series performed around the county. Mixed with the zaniness, as the name suggests, is an admirable amount of state and national heritage.

During August, professional musicians from across the country assemble in Fish Creek for the annual Peninsula Music Fesival, tel. (920) 854-4060, offering Renaissance, Reformation, baroque, and chamber ensembles, along with an array of thematic material. Nationally known folk musicians make an appearance at Gibraltar School Auditorium, 3924 WI 42, tel. (920) 868-2728; theater and dance performances are also held regularly. Peninsula Dance, run through the University of Wisconsin, has regularly scheduled dance events (and classes) at the Fish Creek Town Hall. The Peninsula Art School, tel. (920) 868-3455, offers 60 classes and has a regular Sunday-night series of demonstrations and lectures by staff members, free of charge.

At the north end of town, the Skyway Drive In is a throwback movie experience, and you'll have boisterous fun at the nearby Thumb Fun Park and Waterworld, with tons of water activities and rides, a haunted mansion, narrow-gauge railroad, and mini golf. Open daily Memorial Day through mid-October 10 a.m.-9 p.m., until 5 p.m. thereafter. Admission is $11.

Without chartering a boat or flying your own plane, the easiest way to take in Chambers Island across the Strawberry Channel is via the *Stiletto,* at the Fish Creek Harbor Boat House, tel. (920) 868-3745. The sailboat cruises depart five times daily and take an hour (a sunset sail is an hour and a half). Reservations are recommended; the trip costs $25 per person. Slightly less expensive sailboat rides (not to the island) also depart the Boat House, and canoes, kayaks, boats, and motors are available for rent.

Accommodations

The Fish Creek Chamber of Commerce, in the library complex, maintains a photo album of places to stay if you show up unannounced. It also has a phone and a touch-screen service to monitor last-minute cancellations. You might get lucky ringing up a place you've got your heart set on. In prime season, expect nothing under $60.

Travel media scour every inch of the peninsula annually, looking to scoop others on an undiscovered gem, though they generally rehash the same old thing—always the stately grace and charm of the **White Gull Inn,** three blocks west of WI 42 at 4255 Main St., tel. (920) 868-3517. A proud old guesthouse since 1897, it's truly the *grande dame* of Door County. A number of rooms—a couple with private porches—run $108 and up; a few cottages ($155 and up) and rooms in a cliff house ($125 and up) are also available. The dining room serves a spectacular array of continental, creative regional, and seafood in a country inn atmosphere that's not at all stuffy. And then there's that legendary fish boil, so popular that people swear they've made the return trip just to experience the boisterous one here, where it's made extra special by the boilmasters, who often preside over impromptu singing. Fish boils ($15.50) are served Wednesday and Fri.-Sun. in summer and Wednesday and Saturday other seasons; reservations are needed. Candlelight dinners are Mon.-Tues. and Thursday in summer and fall, Sun.-Tues. and Thurs.-Fri. in winter.

The cheapest rooms in prime season are likely at the **Fish Creek Motel and Cottages,** at the end of Cottage Row a block and a half past the stop sign off WI 42, tel. (920) 868-3448. This amazing motel was actually built in Ephraim and boated around the point in 1981. Basic rooms start at around $68, cottages at $95.

Cheap comfy cottages are also available at **Edgewater Cottages,** in the 4000 block of WI 42, tel. (920) 868-3551. Rates start at $60.

A main rival to the White Gull Inn is the **Whistling Swan,** along WI 42 in the village center, tel. (920) 868-3442. Constructed a decade prior to the White Gull Inn, this one has the better story—it was originally constructed across Green Bay in Marinette and scudded across the winter ice in 1907 to its present site. Five period rooms and two suites are available; the arched windows, fireplace, and high ceilings of the lobby are a draw for casual browsers in the shops on the main level. Rates run $99-150.

You'll find the most history of all at the **Thorp House Inn and Cottages,** 4135 Bluff Rd., tel. (920) 868-2444, on lands originally belonging to Freeman Thorp, nephew to Fish Creek's founding father. The inn is backed up along the bluff overlooking the harbor. When Thorp perished in a 1903 shipwreck, his widow was forced to convert their new Victorian into a guest home. In addition to the four lodge guest rooms, six country-style cottages are available, each sleeping up to five. Rooms run $75-120, cottages $75-140 (cottages rent for a week minimum in peak season).

The most unique place you'll likely find in Door County is the four-floored **Silo Guest House,** 3089 Evergreen Rd., tel. (920) 854-2363, near the state park. It's got two bedrooms and is fully furnished. The top floor is the living room offering a grand view of the surrounding areas. It rents by the week only July-Aug. ($525), for $85 a night thereafter.

Peninsula State Park has almost 500 campsites and is the place to camp; weekends it's almost always full and reservations max out about 10 minutes after the computers go online in January. Otherwise, there is the **Path of Pines,** 3709 CR F, tel. (920) 868-3332, with 91 sites though no separate tent area. Rates from $22.

Food

Just a decade ago, Fish Creek had the usual slew of standard surf-and-turf supper clubs and soup-and-sandwich nooks. No longer. The White Gull's main fish boil rival is **Pelletier's,** 4199 Main St., tel. (920) 868-3313, a nautically themed restaurant heavy on breakfasts (get the French crêpes) and soups and chowders from scratch (from $4). Fish boils ($11.50) nightly; reservations recommended.

The coziest and brightest cafe along the coast, and many visitors' favorite breakfast spot, is **The Cookery,** in the village center on WI 42, tel. (920) 868-3634, a sunny cafe with great, healthy takes on standards. Breakfast packs the place—the menu of pancakes reads like an apartment lease—and healthy options abound; even vegetarians aren't forgotten. Classic farmer's breakfasts—hash browns with peppers, mushrooms, and slathered in cheese—are listed side-by-side with trendy items such as pesto garlic burgers. From $4. Do try the house specialty whitefish chowder. The Cookery also produces its own semifamous line of jams, jellies, mustards, pie fillings, and assorted seasonal condiments, all using Door County ingredients. Open daily April-Oct., weekends thereafter. More vegetarian options are found at **Julie's Cafe and Motel** adjacent to Peninsula State Park.

The food at the historic **Summertime Restaurant,** 1 N. Spruce St., tel. (920) 868-3738, runs a similar vein. Breakfast, lunch, and dinner are served in a large hall, a loft dining room, or on an outside patio. Built in 1910 as one of the original village cafes, it's definitely still got that old-fashioned feel. Fare runs from fish to steaks, with a bit of Italian thrown in. The specialty of the house is South African back ribs. Open 7 a.m.-11 p.m. seasonally. From $4.

C&C's Supper Club, where WI 42 bends right in the village center, tel. (920) 868-3412, used to be about the only game in town. C&C's serves straight steaks and seafood, with an assortment of house specialties. From $9. Open daily for dinner late April through November and weekends thereafter. Live entertainment is offered nightly June through Labor Day.

Kortes' English Inn, between Fish Creek and Ephraim on WI 42, tel. (920) 868-3076, serves a wide variety of specialty entrées nightly. Don't be surprised to see a tableside flambé here. From $10. The Friday-night seafood buffet is quite popular. Open daily from 5:30 p.m.

Digger's, across from the entrance to Peninsula State Park, tel. (920) 868-3095, also has a large number of burgers and sandwiches. Open May-Oct. 11 a.m.-midnight. This is the place for late-night eats. The **Bayside Tavern,** on WI 42 downtown, also serves food until midnight. Both from $4.

South of Fish Creek, in tiny Juddville, **Theo's American Bistro,** W4240 Juddville Rd. in an old farmhouse, tel. (920) 868-1550, has dining tables on a screened-in porch. Another of Door County's up-and-coming bistros, this one serves hearty creative American regional that is worth the trip. Closes from late October until late spring. From $8.

North of town one mile is the **Rock of Gibraltar,** tel. (920) 868-3054, with Mediterranean and American cuisine; from $5.

Recreation

Boat and bike rentals are available in town at **Nor Door Sport and Cyclery,** 4007 WI 42, tel. (920) 868-2275, which is the place to get a hybrid bike ($5 an hour, $15 a day), mountain bike ($7 an hour, $25 a day), or a single-speed cruiser ($3 an hour). Plenty of other equipment is also for rent. In winter, you can rent cross-country skis ($9 a day) and even snowshoes and ice skates. At the entrance to Peninsula State Park is **Edge of Park, Inc.,** tel. (920) 868-3344, which also rents bikes and mopeds; moped rentals include a park sticker. You can rent boats from **Bayou Boat Rentals,** tel. (920) 619-6356.

Services and Information

The **Fish Creek Information Center,** tel. (920) 868-2316 or (800) 577-1880, www.doorcounty-wi.com/fishcreek, is in the library complex. Fully equipped to deal with your travel snafus or last-minute needs, it also has a phone on which you can ring accommodations and a touch-screen info kiosk to track available lodging. It's open Thurs.-Sun. varied hours mid-May through mid-June, daily 9 a.m.-5 p.m. through Labor Day, daily except Sunday through mid-Oct., then varied hours Fri.-Sun. mid-October through mid-May.

PENINSULA STATE PARK

Consider: 3,400 acres stretching from the northern fringe of Fish Creek, past Strawberry Channel, past Eagle Bluff, past Nicolet Bay, and finally to Eagle Harbor and Ephraim—that's the scope of this peninsular park. Deeded to the state for a state park in 1909, Peninsula is the second-oldest park in the state system, and with no statistical manipulation the park is numero uno in usage in Wisconsin—with good reason.

The peninsula, rising 180 feet above the lake at Eagle Bluff, is a manifestation of the western edge of the Niagara Escarpment, here a steep and variegated series of headlands and reentrants. The ecosystem here is unparalleled. Near Weborg Point in the southwest, the Peninsula White Cedar Forest Natural Area is a 53-acre stand of spruce, cedar, balsam, and hemlock, and the boggy residual tract of an ancient lake. South of Eagle Tower is the larger, 80-acre Peninsula Beech Forest Natural Area. Not only is this a primitive example of northern mixed hardwood, but it is a relatively uncommon stand of American beech. Within both confines are a handful of threatened species, including the vivid dwarf lake iris. Other rarities include gaywings, Indian paintbrush, blue-eyed grass, and downy gentian.

Human History

As usual, the first European, Increase Claflin, was a squatter; he parked his cabin high above the Strawberry Islands in 1844. But these parts had long been inhabited by several tribes of Native Americans. Plano Indian encampments have been examined and dated to 7000-4000 B.C., and since that time a host of other tribes has been in continuous residence. Following the arrival of the Europeans, the Menominee, Fox,

Winnebago, Iroquois, and Potawatomi Indians all occupied littoral sites. The Native American presence—and for once, overtly harmonious relations—is symbolized by the **Memorial Pole.** This 40-foot totem pole commemorates Potawatomi Chief Simon Khaquados, laid to rest here in 1930 before thousands of admirers. Unfortunately, the settlers didn't love him enough to preclude building a golf course around his grave; the pole today sits between the number 1 and number 9 fairways.

Sights and Activities

Obligatory is the **Eagle Bluff Lighthouse.** Built during the Civil War by U.S. lighthouse crewmen as the second of the peninsula's lighthouses, a square tower some 45 feet tall attached to the keeper's house. It stands atop the bluff and can be seen for 15 miles. The prized assignment for lighthouse keepers in the peninsula, it had a commanding view and the best salary, the princely sum (for 1880) of $50 per month. Public interest prompted local historical societies to peel off 80 layers of paint and set to work refurbishing it in the late 1950s. Today, tours are given weekdays in early summer and autumn every half hour 10 a.m.-4:30 p.m., lesser times rest of year. Admission is $3 adults, $1 children 6-17.

Two 75-foot towers were erected at the park's inception and used as fire spotting towers (one was later removed due to dry rot). **Eagle Tower** was placed where it is simply because so many

Eagle Bluff lighthouse, Peninsula State Park

people wanted to spot a pair of long-term nesting eagles—the two for whom the bluff, the harbor, and the peninsula itself were eventually named. The easiest way to Eagle Tower is through Ephraim's entrance; drive through the golf course along Shore Road. More ambitious visitors can take Minnehaha or Sentinel Trail.

Before hiking, most visitors head to the **White Cedar Nature Center** to walk a nature trail and view a host of exhibits covering the park's natural history. Regularly scheduled nature programs including hikes take place mid-June through Labor Day.

Golf

Deemed by the golf press one of the gems of Midwestern courses, this 18-holer is plunked right in the eastern swath of the park. Built by a group of Ephraim businessmen in the early 1900s and originally a nine-hole course with sand greens, it was later altered to a verdant 18 holes. Administered by the DNR, the par-71 course has a pro-length of 6,224 yards. Tee time reservations are obviously necessary—as early as you can make them. Call (920) 854-5791 for information.

Other Recreation

Over 20 miles of hiking trails network through the park and along the shores of the bays. Fifteen miles of on- and off-road bike trails exist, and a state trail pass ($3 daily, $10 annual) is required on certain marked routes. What may be the most heavily traversed recreational trail—**Sunset Trail**—roughly parallels Shore Road for five miles through marsh and hardwood and conifer stands. At dusk it is definitely not misnamed. This hardpack, multi-use trail links with innumerable side trails. An extra few miles take in the littoral perimeter of Nicolet Bay and lead back to Fish Creek via back roads.

In the 1930s, the park was a winter sports hotbed, but while trails are still maintained for cross-country skiing and the golf course has one sledding hill, that's about it these days. The toughest trail, but also the most rewarding, the **Eagle Trail,** covers two miles skirting the harbor and a couple of natural springs and affords challenging scrambles over 200-foot bluffs. The easiest hike is either the three-quarter-mile **Minnehaha Trail,** linking Nicolet Bay Campground

and Eagle Trail, or the **White Cedar Nature Trail,** which loops near a nature center between Bluff and Skyline Roads.

Peninsula State Park has its own bike and boat rentals, at Nicolet Beach, tel. (920) 854-9220. Bikes start at $6 an hour for a basic model (no mountain bikes). Kayaks ($5 an hour), canoes ($8), sailboards ($12.50) and paddleboats ($6) are the cheaper ways to get on the bay; a 14-foot sailboat, the most basic wind-driven craft, starts at $15 an hour. See "Fish Creek" for additional concessionaires.

Camping

Originally, camping was generally allowed in any direction the ranger waved his hand and cost from free to 50 cents per week. Today, the DNR receives up to 5,000 applications for summer reservations in January. At last count there were, let's see, tons of campsites—469 to be exact, separated into four sectors. Only one sector is open year-round.

EPHRAIM

As the map tells it, five miles separate Fish Creek and Ephraim, but you'd hardly know it. On the way north, passing the north entrance of Peninsula State Park, a modest jumble of development appears, then vanishes, and shortly the fringes of beautiful Ephraim appear. Another of those endlessly long Door County villages along a vivid harbor, Ephraim isn't the oldest community in the county, nor are its structures the most historically distinguished. But aesthetically it may have them all beat and in many other respects, the community is the most perfectly preserved slice of Door County. The quaintness isn't accidental—for a while the village dictated via social pressure that all structures were to be whitewashed in proper fashion. And it's stuck. The town is set along gorgeous Eagle Harbor. An enclave of pious fortitude, it was settled by Norwegian Moravians and christened Ephraim, which means "doubly fruitful" in Hebrew.

Sights and Activities

The oldest church in the county, the **Moravian Church,** built out of necessity when the village founder's living room no longer sufficed, is, appropriately enough, along Moravia Street. It was built in 1857 out of cedar from the Upper Peninsula (local logs were too rough for such a sacred house). Also on Moravia Street, the **Pioneer Schoolhouse Museum,** tel. (920) 854-9688, doubles as a repository of local history, with artifacts and effects from early settlers. There's also a nice local art display, with various media represented from juried shows and chosen by locals arts associations. Open Mon.-Sat. 10:30 a.m.-4 p.m. in summer, Fri.-Sat. thereafter through October. The final historic structure along the street is the **Thomas Goodleston Cabin,** an original and one of the peninsula's first cabins. Dating from 1857, the cabin has been authentically restored and furnished with period pieces.

Down off the bluff are the **Anderson Barn and Store.** The ruddy barn was built in 1870 and restored in 1990 to be used by the Ephraim Foundation as a historical archive. During the summer, it's open for browsing; the salient square silo is a rarity. The ever-popular store has also been restored, but it was always a country general store. Built in 1858 by Aslag Anderson, one of the original Scandinavian settlers, it is now on the National Register of Historic Places. Old-time store items are on display along with museum-like pieces. Open Mon.-Sat. 10:30 a.m.-4 p.m. in summer, Fri.-Sat. thereafter through October. Free.

Summertime **walking tours** of all the historic structures depart Monday, Wednesday, and Friday (usually, but call to verify) at 10:30 a.m. from the Anderson Barn. Admission is $2, $5 for a family.

South Shore Pier, in the heart of the village, has a large number of water-based recreation and tour opportunities. Two-hour tours ($25) daily to Horseshoe Island, Eagle Bluff Caves, and along the bay's coastline are offered by **Bella Sailing Cruises,** tel. (920) 854-2628; departure times are 10:30 a.m., 1 and 3:30 p.m., and sunset. Hour-plus catamaran cruises ($19), including a sunset cruise ($25), depart seven times daily aboard the *Stiletto,* tel. (920) 854-7542. Or, rent your own pontoon boat, kayak, Waverunner, paddleboat, or fishing boat from the **South Shore Pier, Inc. Boat Rental,** tel. (920) 854-4324. Canoes are $10 an hour, and prices go all the way to $60 for two hours on a

pontoon boat. You can go charter fishing through **Eagle Harbor Charters,** tel. (920) 854-4667, with individual rates of $38 and up for a 6 p.m.-sunset cruise, higher rates earlier in the day. Newer operations have started offering windsurfing lessons and parasail rides; **Mayberry's,** tel. (920) 868-3479, has sleigh rides ($6) and carriage rides. You can call the same day to make arrangements for a ride.

The highlight of the entire year in Ephraim is the Scandinavian summer solstice celebration **Fyr Ball Festival.** Bonfires dot the shoreline and fish-boil cauldrons gurgle to commemorate the arrival of summer. A "Viking chieftain" is crowned and then blesses the ships and harbor. The accompanying art fairs are less Norse in nature.

Ephraim's **information center,** tel. (920) 854-4989, is right along WI 42 and open 9 a.m.-4 p.m. daily June through early September, Friday and Saturday May, daily except Sunday early September through mid-October. A 24-hour kiosk is there in season for last-minute motel scroungers.

Accommodations

Unlike other spots in Door County, there's a dearth of city-state-size resort complexes; a "resort" here is basically an overgrown motel.

If you're really looking for the cheapest place to stay in Door County, it might be **Billerbeck's Cottage and Rooms,** 9864 Hidden Spring Rd., tel. (920) 854-2528. One log cabin with an upstairs sleeping loft ($70 daily, $320 weekly) and three rooms with shared baths upstairs in the family house ($25 and up) are available.

You'll find slick lodge-style rooms and a couple of cottages at the **Edgewater Resort,** 10040 WI 42, tel. (920) 854-2734, which also has a heated pool, sun deck, sand beach, and private pier. This interesting resort is actually two late-19th-century resorts conjoined. It's also got a fish boil. Rates start at $125.

Trollhaugen, north on WI 42, tel. (920) 854-2713, is part motel, part lodge and log cabin, with rates of $80, much less off-season. It's in a quiet wooded setting with updated lodge decor.

There are those who say that the **Eagle Harbor Inn,** 9914 WI 42, tel. (920) 854-2121, is the best inn in Door County, if not the Midwest, and that's saying a mouthful. The elegant nine-room inn is antique-strewn and offers a sumptuous country breakfast in the garden. The one- to three-bedroom cottages on nicely wooded grounds are also very appealing. High-season rates for the inn are $89 for basic rooms, $150 for suites.

There really is not a bad location in the entire community, but the most inspiring of all belongs to the **High Point Inn,** north on WI 42, tel. (920) 854-9773, atop the bluffs. Guests have a choice of one- to three-bedroom suites with kitchens, living areas with fireplaces, and whirlpool baths. Also on-site are indoor and outdoor pools, an exercise room, and indoor whirlpool. Rates August through mid-October are $145-205; in winter, they can drop by half.

Pioneer Acres, 2965 CR Q, tel. (920) 854-2425, has one- to three-bedroom cottages; some are rustic log lodges. All have fireplaces, kitchens, and cable TV and are in a quiet wooded setting just three blocks from the village center. Daily rates run $90-180, weekly $600-1100.

Food
There are precious few restaurants here; the lodges and resorts take the lion's share of the food business. **Leroy's Water St. Coffee Shop** is tucked behind the Shorewood Village Shops. The coolly named **The Singing Bowl Cafe, Deli, and Market,** WI 42 and Townline Rd., tel. (920) 854-7376, has gourmet and healthy foods, including vegetarian salads, soups, and prepared foods. From $3.

The most popular restaurant in town is undoubtedly the **Old Post Office,** 10040 WI 42, tel. (920) 854-4034, known mostly for one of the biggie fish boils in the county, but also for Belgian waffles. Another widely touted lodging dining room is **The Second Story** at the Ephraim Shores Motel, offering family-style soups, sandwiches, and quiches, seafood, a salad bar, and a smattering of Mexican dishes. Open for breakfast, lunch, and dinner. The latter two have items from $5.

If you're around between April and October, it's nearly a Door County law that you stop at **Wilson's** old-fashioned ice cream parlor, right in the heart of the village. Opened in 1906 and serving pretty much ever since, it's got ice cream cones as big as bullhorns, as well as burgers and homemade soups and salads. You'll feel like you're in a Norman Rockwell painting hanging out on the white-framed porch.

SISTER BAY

Sister Bay can sure get congested on a typical summer Saturday—symbolic of its status as the largest community north of Sturgeon Bay (though the population is a mere 695). It's also the only spot north on the peninsula where a minor mall or village-size grocery chain of any sort reveals itself from the roadway. Named for twin islands offshore, the bay—not offering quite the windbreak of Eagle Harbor—never got much notice from southbound steamers until Scandinavian settlers discovered the dense forest land in the surrounding hills. The first settlers erected cabins in 1857, and a spurt of growth took place in the 1860s.

Activities
Sister Bay's quaint village park, with one of the prettiest stretches of beach around, hosts the huge Fall Festival and is the linchpin of a fine community network of parks, which offer regular doses of free big band, jazz, country, and folk concerts. The **Door County Storytelling Festival** takes place May-October with over 75 performances. If it's not solitude you're looking for, an amusement park and game center, **Pirate's Cove Adventure Golf,** is just south of town in one of the county's very few sickeningly overdeveloped stretches. Also on the south edge of town is the **Old Anderson House Museum,** a restored house dating from 1895; this baby was built in Marinette, WI, and dragged across the ice to get it here. It's open weekends and holidays mid-May through mid-October for tours; free.

Bayshore Outdoors, tel. (920) 854-7598, has daily guided kayak tours ($45) three times daily, along with rentals of cross-country skis ($6-18), snow shoes ($7), and bikes. **Sunset Concert Cruises,** tel. (920) 854-2986, offers concert and dinner tours ($42).

South of town along WI 57, **Carole's Corral,** tel. (920) 854-2525, is a huge farm, zoo, and stable that allows hands-on petting or goat walking for the little ones and trail rides and midweek cookouts for the adults. (If you stay at the Patio Motel, you get a deep discount.)

Accommodations
One of the cheapest motels on the Door is the delightfully rustic **Century Farm Motel,** 10068 WI

57, between Sister Bay and Ephraim. A real country farm, it's got four individual units with TVs and refrigerators, and you might get one for under $50, especially in the off-season. Also for the budget cruncher is the rustic, century-old **Liberty Park Lodge,** north on WI 42, tel. (920) 854-2025. The main lodge has four rooms with washbowl and shared bath from $45 in high season, $35 in low. Also available are Cape Cod-style woodland ($75) and shore ($98) cottages.

A definite hop up, **The Inn at Little Sister Hill,** 2715 Little Sister Hill Rd., tel. (920) 854-2328, sits in a wooded setting south of Sister Bay—not on the water but close enough. These very comfortable surroundings also cater to families. One- and two-bedroom condo suites come fully equipped, each with fireplace and private patio, and the complex boasts a heated pool. Rates in prime season start at $109, lots less in winter.

Similarly priced and a 75-year tradition in Sister Bay, the **Hotel Du Nord,** a mile north of town on WI 42, tel. (920) 854-4221 or (800) 582-6667, offers rooms of all types—an adjacent lodge, a cozy inn, woodside suites, multi-bedroom cottages, even a beach villa. The restaurant gets raves. The lowest-priced rooms are in the lodge ($85), edging upward to $165 for a two-bedroom suite.

Forty-five large (up to 600-square-foot) and attractive rooms are available at the **Country House Resort,** 715 N. Highland Rd., tel. (920) 854-4551 or (800) 424-0041. All feature refrigerators and private waterside balconies, and some have whirlpools and other miscellaneous amenities. The grounds cover 16 heavily wooded acres with private nature trails and a 1,000-foot shoreline. Recreational facilities are free for guests. Rates start at $90 in peak season.

The top-ranked condo resort in the state, **Sister Bay Resort and Yacht Club,** 504 Mill Rd., tel. (920) 854-2993, has one- and two-bedroom suites right over the marina. All feature fireplaces, full facilities, and a winner of a view. Tennis and trails through the spacious grounds are free to guests. There is a two-night minimum in summer, and a week's stay knocks your per-night price way down. Peak-season nightly rates run a minimum of $190 for a two-person suite.

Food

For the "only in Wisconsin" file: the **Sister Bay Bowl and Supper Club,** 504 Bay Shore Dr.,

tel. (920) 854-2841, does have bowling. But, believe it or not, it offers one of the better fish *fries* around. Just because fish boils are the rage in these parts is no reason to eschew the tried-and-true fry (the day *is* called Friday, after all). Open daily April through January 1, weekends only Jan.-March. From $3.

The **Mission Grille,** at the junction of the two big highways, tel. (920) 854-9070, is a turn-of-the-century church-turned-cozy restaurant. Steaks, prime rib, and seafood—all good—support the menu. Vegetarians aren't ignored. From $5. The summertime dining on a tri-level patio and veranda is not to be missed.

The name **Sister Bay Cafe,** 611 N. Bay Shore Dr., tel. (920) 854-2429, is misleading. It's got your basics, but much more, like some creative dinners, usually seafood-oriented—tuna steak with dill sauce, for example—and then a whole slew of authentic Scandinavian fare, including *apskaus,* a Norwegian farmer's stew; *rødgrød med fløde,* red fruit pudding with cream; and *frickadillar,* beef and pork patties styled after a Danish dish. From $4.

The most famous ethnic eatery in the county, if not the state, is **Al Johnson's Swedish Restaurant,** 702 Bay Shore Dr., tel. (920) 854-2626, where cars regularly screech to a halt when drivers see the legendary live goats munching the sod roof. The menu offers tremendous Swedish and American food. Pound after pound of Swedish meatballs are served nightly, and other favorites are the Swedish beefsteak sautéed in onions and lingonberry pancakes for breakfast. Open 6 a.m.-8 p.m. It's often standing room only, and the restaurant doesn't take reservations. From $3.

You'll find creative regional cuisine, and a meal worthy of splurging on, at the **Inn at Kristofer's,** 734 N. Bay Shore Dr., tel. (920) 854-9419. Tiny in size but eminently dependable in its fare, the inn is a highlight of any true culinary experience in Door County. A sample item from the menu: focaccia sandwich with grilled eggplant and Havarti sauce, grouper, and wild rice ravioli. The Inn also gives gourmet cooking lessons. Open for lunch and dinner daily May 1 through October 31 daily, Thurs.-Sun. late November through late April. From $10.

The desserts at the **Door County Ice Cream Factory and Sandwich Shoppe,** WI 42 at

Beach Rd., tel. (920) 854-9693, are worth a drive. The ice cream is made right before your very eyes, and the sandwich bread is baked in back. The trademark sandwich is the Door County Shell—check it out.

Information
Sister Bay has a quaint **tourist information center,** 416 Gateway Dr., tel. (920) 854-2812, in a refurbished log schoolhouse on a hillock overlooking the junction of WI 42 and WI 57. Open May-October.

ELLISON BAY

Plunked along the decline of a steep hill and hollow tunneling toward a yawning bay, Ellison Bay gets little respect in the tourism industry. The village facade isn't as spectacular as Ephraim's, the architecture isn't as quaint as Fish Creek's, and it's a fifth the size of Sister Bay. Nonetheless, there is something engaging about the place. It begins with what may be the best view from the highway in the whole county. Atop the 200-foot bluff on the south side of town, you can see clear to Gills Rock, farther up the peninsula. Founded in the early 1860s, the village originally served as a hub for lumber, courtesy of the operations in nearby Newport State Park. As recently as the 1930s, the town's commercial fishery take led Wisconsin in tonnage—

perhaps the reason a local restaurant is credited with the first fish boil.

Sights
The name is often misinterpreted as an approximation of the 130 lovely acres overlooking the northern fringe of Ellison Bay, but in fact, **the Clearing** refers to something a tad more metaphysical—closer to "clarity of thought." A contemplative retreat for the study of art, natural science, and the humanities—philosophy is ever-popular—the school was the result of a lifetime's effort by famed landscape architect Jens Jensen. Much like contemporary Frank Lloyd Wright, Jensen's maverick style and obdurate convictions grated with the entrenched elitism of landscape architecture in the early 20th century. His belief in the inseparability of land and humanity was considered foolish, if not outright heretical, in those early days. A Danish immigrant, Jensen arrived in the U.S. in 1884 and became more and more enamored of the wild Midwestern landscape while simultaneously cultivating his radical notions of debt to the earth and the need to connect with it despite living in a rat race. While in Chicago creating the parks that made his name, he began purchasing land around Ellison Bay. By the 1930s, everything had gelled into a cohesive plan, and he spent the next 15 years establishing his retreat according to folk educational traditions in northern Europe.

*view from
Ellison Bay bluff*

The grounds contain a lodge, a library, a communal dining area, and cottages and dormitories for attendees. Summer classes are held May-Oct. and last one week. Meals are included. Lots of group work, outdoor exploration, campfires, and other traditional folk systems are the rule. Fees, including room and board (except Thursday supper, when attendees are encouraged to explore the town for a fish boil), are $480 a week in the dormitory, $520 a week in a double room. Non-participants can visit on weekends 1-4 p.m. mid-May through mid-October. The estate has two large chalets for rental. Rates are $775 per week down to $485 for a three-day weekend; this is not bad considering there are three bedrooms and two baths.

Ellison Bay has a grand county park three miles southwest along WI 42 then off toward the lake. Nearly 100 wild acres atop 100-foot bluffs overlook the lake. There is no camping, but some rough trails (none to the water) wind through the area.

Accommodations

Hands down, the best view per dollar spent is from the aptly named **Grand View Motel,** WI 42, tel. (920) 854-5150 or (800) 258-8208, on the south edge of town on the brow of Ellison Bluff. Located on 16 acres of land homesteaded by the family over 125 years ago, the motel offers 30 rooms with private decks and panoramic views. There is also a central sun deck and a main lobby with a fireplace. Bicycles are rented on the premises. High-season rates start at $80.

A Cape Cod-esque 1910 mansion and summer home since the 1920s, complete with open gazebo on the five-acre front lawn, **The Griffin Inn,** 11976 Mink River Rd., tel. (920) 854-4306, has the advantage of being on the way to Rowleys Bay and Newport State Park. Ten rooms in the house and four cottages are available all year. Rates are $79 s, $89 d, $99 triple in the main rooms and $84 for a cottage.

A 1902 hotel turned B&B, the **Hotel Disgarden,** 12013 WI 42, tel. (920) 854-9888, still has a distinctive turn-of-the-century feel in its seven rooms and suites. Room-service breakfast is offered. Rooms start at $75.

Food

The eatery of choice in town has for a long spell been **The Viking,** 12029 WI 42, tel. (920) 854-

2988. Credited with filling that first iron cauldron with whitefish, potatoes, and onions, and brewing up a culinary tradition, the Viking still builds a roaring kettle fire daily. Open 6 a.m.-7 p.m. Mon.-Sat., Sunday until 2 p.m. Fish boils are served daily 4:30-8 p.m. May-October. From $3.

Besides that, the **Voigt Supper Club,** right along Hwy 42, tel. (920) 854-2250, has a lengthy standard supper club menu, with a variety of seafood and excellent roast duck and ribs. Even better is the substantial fresh fruit bar. Open daily for dinner, with a Sunday brunch. From $9.

Services and Information

The smallest visitor center on the peninsula is either Ephraim's ticket-booth-sized closet or the **information kiosk** in Ellison Bay, tel. (920) 854-5448, across from the Viking Restaurant. Open May-October.

A wowser of a Wisconsin bookseller, **William Caxton,** 12037 WI 42, tel. (920) 854-2955, has an unbelievable number of hard-to-find titles in stock—this is also the place in Door County to shop for titles on Wisconsin.

GILLS ROCK/NEWPORT

Out of Ellison Bay, WI 42 cuts east, then changes its mind and bends 90 degrees north again into the tightly packed fishing village of Gills Rock (pop. maybe 75) and the first of the ends of the road. Parked high atop 150-foot Table Bluff overlooking Hedgehog Harbor across from Deathdoor Bluff, pleasant Gills Rock is as far as the tourist road goes on the Door—that is, until you hop islands. Sleepy and quaint and known as the tip or top of the thumb, Gills Rock has the feel of an old tourist camp from the 1930s. Up WI 42 a couple of miles is truly the end of the line, Northport.

Sights and Activities

Door County's "other" maritime museum is parked on a little dusty side road in Gills Rock—the **Door County Maritime Museum,** tel. (920) 854-2860. Whereas the Sturgeon Bay collection centers mostly on shipbuilding, this one features gill nets and more gill nets—or rather, the commercial fishing industry. The highlight is an old fishing tug, and there is plenty of other old equipment. Open June-Sept. Mon.-Sat. 10 a.m.-4 p.m. and Sunday 1-4 p.m., Memorial Day to June Fri.-Sun. 1-4 p.m. only. Admission is free.

Capt. Paul's, tel. (920) 854-4614, ubiquitous in Gills Rock, is a motel, cottages, and a popular marina and fishing charter, all in one. Chinook salmon and German brown trout are the specialties, and the rate of $58 per person for a four-hour trip isn't bad at all. Trips depart May through mid-October 9 a.m.-1 p.m., 1-5 p.m., and 2:30-6 p.m. for the evening trip. With this set-up, solo travelers and novices can take advantage of Great Lake sportfishing, a service difficult to find on other charters.

You'll find the best views of the bay and solitude at the largest park in the county, **Door Bluff Headlands,** almost 200 acres of wild trails and woodland. From WI 42, take Cottage Road to Garrett Bay Road.

Washington Island Ferries and Cruises

The most luxurious way to Washington Island is a narrated cruise aboard the *Island Clipper,* tel. (920) 854-2972, a 65-foot cruiser specifically designed by a Sturgeon Bay boatbuilder for the Death's Door crossing. A basic tour ($8 adults, $3.50 children) is available, as is a ferry plus "Viking Train" island tour ($13 and $7). The grand tour includes lunch ($19 and $12). Tours operate late May through early October, with up to 10 departures daily 10 a.m.-5 p.m. in peak summer season. Island Clipper also leads a one-of-a-kind tour that most don't know about. Departing Gills Rock, passing Porte des Mortes, you'll cross Green Bay to Michigan's Upper Peninsula and Fayette State Park, a reconstructed Civil War iron smelting community. Call for details. There are also sunset cruises with assorted live music and buffet suppers.

Also from Gills Rock, the **C.G. Richter Cruise Line,** tel. (920) 847-2039, offers narrated cruises of the Death's Door and can link you up with the Cherry Train on Washington Island. The tour operates mid-May through late October. Five departures 11 a.m.-5:45 p.m. head for the island (9:15 a.m.-5 p.m. from the island). A combo ferry, train, and lunch tour runs $19 adults, $9 children 6-11.

Northport exists solely to accommodate the second of the ferry lines to Washington Island. This pier was established as an escape from fierce prevailing winds on the Gills Rock side. Northport, in fact, has eclipsed Gills Rock as a departure point to Washington Island, as it is virtually always free of ice and saves precious crossing time. Those who wish to drive their cars over to Washington Island will have to come here for the **Washington Island Ferry,** tel. (920) 847-2546 or (800) 223-2094, which takes autos and passengers. It also hooks up with the Cherry Train tour of the island if you take the 9:45 a.m. or earlier crossing from Northport, 11 a.m. from Gills Rock. The schedule for the ferry is staggering; check the wall map. In high season, July 1 through late August, 23 roundtrips depart to and from the island beginning at 6:30 a.m. from the island, 7:15 a.m. from Northport (no early trip on Sundays!). The farther you are from this zenith chronologically, the fewer trips depart. By Dec.-Jan., there are only three trips per day, and Jan.-March there is only one per day, and vehicle reservations are mandatory. Call anyway for verification in the off season. A car costs $8.50, each adult is $3.75, a child 6-11 is $2, bicycles are $1.50, and motorcycles are $5—all prices are one-way.

Accommodations

Prominent in Gills Rock, the **Shoreline Resort,** 12747 WI 42, tel. (920) 854-2606, offers waterfront rooms with patios and a popular rooftop sun deck; the views are grand! Charter fishing tours and assorted sightseeing cruises (the sunset cruise, with live entertainment, is perennially popular) also leave the on-site marina. There is a shipwreck dive charter operator with dive supplies here; the company has recently added snorkeling trips (no dive experience necessary). It also rents bikes. Rates for rooms run from $100.

Much cheaper is the **Harbor House Inn,** tel. (920) 854-5196, a 1904 Victorian with a grand lighthouse suite, more basic rooms, and a cottage; rates start at a reasonable $60. There are bike rentals and a private beach.

Unheard-of **On The Rocks,** 849 Wisconsin Bay Rd., tel. (920) 854-4907, is possibly the most private Door County experience. This jewel is a massive 3,500-square-foot A-frame lodge with fieldstone fireplace atop a 60-foot cliff. Each of the five bedrooms runs $200 a night and has a large array of extras. Open April-November.

Food

The best food you're going to get in Gills Rock is some of that grand smoked Lake Michigan fish.

You'll find the best maple-smoked chub and whitefish in the world at **Charlie's** on the dock, just about your only choice. The **Shoreline Resort** is the other dining option, with good whitefish and basic hearty fare for breakfast, lunch, and dinner May-October.

WASHINGTON ISLAND AND ROCK ISLAND

Rustic, time-locked Washington Island, an easy (and safe) ferry ride from the mainland across Death's Door, very nearly wasn't included as part of the Door, but in 1925, the Supreme Court ruled in Wisconsin's favor in a border dispute with Michigan. At issue were a number of the dozen or so islands in the Grand Traverse Chain, of which Washington and the surrounding islands are a part.

The island isn't what most expect. Many envision a candy-facade Mackinac Island, full of historically garbed docents or fudge sellers every two steps. Not at all. Populated by 650 permanent residents, development is unobtrusive. The place has a pleasant weatherbeaten seaside look to it, rather than the sheen of a slick resort. Best of all, Washington Island has the feel of a small Midwestern town, right down to the well-used community ballparks.

HISTORY

Natural History

Beyond Washington Island is one of the Niagara Escarpment's longest gaps as it stretches under the waters to Michigan and on to Ontario. Of the islands stretching across the lake to Michigan's Upper Peninsula, Washington is the granddaddy, geologically and historically. With 36 square miles, the island's circumference is just over 25 miles. The escarpment is on a consistent, gradual declivity (two to five degrees) a mere 160 feet above the lake's surface, surrounding Washington Island's rough, wave-battered exterior. Nowhere on the Door Peninsula does nature manifest itself with more force—wind-whipped stretches of open meadow or scattered hardwoods equally wind-bent—than on this tough island.

Human History

The Door, a macabre caveat of death for those foolhardy enough to attempt the savage waters here, fits Washington Island, truly the door to Wisconsin. Washington and Rock Islands were populated long before the rest of northeastern Wisconsin. Before vandals and thickets of ambitious brush got ahold of the sites, the island was one of the richest Native American archaeological time capsules in the Midwest. The original island dwellers were likely the Potawatomi and later the Huron (the island's original name was Huron Island), among others, who arrived in flight from the bellicose Iroquois in modern Quebec.

Island-hopping *voyageurs* plying the expanses of New France found a ready-made chain of havens and temporary fishing grounds stretching from Michigan to the Door Peninsula, and thus to the Fox and Wisconsin Riverways. Purportedly, Jean Nicolet himself was the first European to set up camp on Washington Island. Pierre Esprit Radisson, who wintered here with the Huron, dubbed it the most pleasant place he had experienced in the Great Lakes. The most famous European presence still lends itself to the murky legends swirling in the cruel straits. In 1679, Robert La Salle sailed the *Griffin* into Detroit Harbor, where he met and bartered fur and iron wares with the Potawatomi, then left, destined for Mackinac Island. The ship vanished, and mariners have regaled the gullible with stories of a shrouded ship matching its description haunting the shoals around the Door ever since.

A large-scale European presence appeared in the early 1830s, when immigrants into Green Bay heard of trout the size of calves being taken from the waters around the island. The first fishers were Irish, but the true habitation mark on Washington Island is pure Icelandic—richest in the United States. Several thousand of the nation's first Icelandic settlers arrived, took readily to the isolation, and set down permanent roots. Their heritage is clearly manifest in the *stavkirke*—the wooded stave church—being built gradually by island residents, one massive white pine log at a time.

SIGHTS

There is a lighthouse on Washington Island, the **Bowyer Bluff light** on the northwest side. Un-

fortunately, you can't see it, but you may wish you could—at 210 feet, it's the tallest on the Great Lakes.

Art and Nature Center

A mix of natural and cultural island history is displayed here, at the corner of Main and Jackson Harbor Road in an unassuming building resembling an old schoolhouse. Permanent artwork displays are housed within, and nature trails branch from the rear. Art classes are offered, and regular musical events are held during a

© AVALON TRAVEL PUBLISHING, INC.

weeklong midsummer festival. Open weekdays 10:30 a.m.-4:30 p.m., Sundays 11:30 a.m.-4:30 p.m. mid-June through mid-September, lesser hours after Labor Day. Admission is $1 adults, free ages under 18.

Museums

The top stop for museum hoppers is the **Jackson Harbor Maritime Museum,** at the east end of Jackson Harbor Rd., opposite the ferry landing. The museum retains a significant presence—what little remains of the island's commercial fishing industry operates out of secluded Jackson Harbor. You'll find a reconstructed fish shed, a couple of ice houses, an old fisherman's house, some outdoor displays (a Kahlenberg engine, an old Coast Guard boat, and remnants of a wreck), and the site itself, housed inside two fishing shacks. Open weekends 10:30 a.m.-4:30 p.m. Memorial Day to July 1, daily thereafter until Labor Day, weekends again until Columbus Day. Admission is $1.

The **Jacobsen Museum** is housed in a vertical log building owned by early settler Jens Jacobsen, on the south shore of Little Lake. The packrat progenitor collected a huge number of natural history artifacts, mostly Native American arrowheads and beads. Also inside you'll find Danish scrollwork, maps, models of shipwrecks, fossils, and tools. There's also a whole bunch of weird stuff lying out front, like an ancient leviathan rudder from the steamer *Louisiana,* which ran aground in 1913, ice cutters, and huge capstans for raising anchors. Open daily 10 a.m.-4 p.m. Memorial Day through mid-October. Admission is $1.

The smallest of all is the **Farm Museum,** a spread of pioneer structures off Airport Road along Jackson Harbor Road. A pioneer log home, a double log barn and shed with a collection of hand tools, 15 pieces of horse-drawn machinery, a forge and blacksmith shop, a reconstructed stone building, and a popular petting zoo are on the grounds. A nominal 25 cents is requested. Open June 17 through mid-October with regularly scheduled kids' activities starting on Wednesdays after July 5 and running through mid-August.

Sievers

In its second decade, the **Sievers School of Fiber Arts,** Jackson Harbor Rd., tel. (920) 847-2264, is the most intriguing of island highlights. It's less a school than a retreat into weaving, papermaking, spinning, basketweaving, batik, tapestry, drafting, Scandinavian woodcarving, and any other number of classes in vanishing folk arts. On any given day, the solitude is accentuated by the thwack of looms or the whirring of spinning wheels. Classes are offered May-Oct., and weekend or one-week classes are available. Fees range $125-225, plus up to $100 for dorm fees for a weeklong class. A downtown consignment shop displays and sells the works created, as well as cherrywood looms.

Dunes

No visit to the Jackson Harbor Maritime Museum is complete without a stroll on the nature trail through the ecosystem of the **Jackson Harbor Ridges,** a 90-acre State of Wisconsin Scientific Reserve. The fragile mix of shore meadow, dune, and boreal forest is not found anywhere else in the peninsula. Northern plant species such as the rare dwarf lake orchid and arctic primrose, along with white cedar, fir, and spruce, are found here. A part of the ridges was established with a Nature Conservancy tract. There is an isolated and generally underpopulated beach adjacent to the reserve.

More great Lawrence of Arabia dunescapes are found across the island southeast of Detroit Harbor along South Shore Drive at **Sand Dunes Public Beach.**

Parks

The generally gravelly shoreline is rimmed with parks and beaches: **Schoolhouse Beach** in Washington Harbor, with tough and chilly swimming in a secluded setting; the Ridges in Jackson Harbor; and **Percy Johnson Park** on the eastern side at the tip of Lakeview Rd., offering vistas of Hog Island and a nesting sanctuary. None allow camping.

Inland is where you'll find the two interesting parks. A small picnic area and park is adjacent to the airport, of all places, and people head out with a lunchtime sandwich to watch the odd plane arrival. To get there, take Main Rd. north, then Town Line Rd. east to Airport Road. The most commanding views of all are at the 200-foot heights of **Mountain Park Lookout,** just about the geometric center of the island.

ACCOMMODATIONS

Washington Island features a patchwork of lodging options, stemming from its isolation. You'll find basic motels, intriguing and microscopic kiosk-cottages, spacious but threadbare cabins that look like deer-hunting shacks heated with oil furnaces, even the odd resident's spare bedroom.

Ferry Landing

You probably won't want to stay here—it's congested and loud. But there is a motel here if you need a quick morning getaway.

Detroit Harbor

North up the road from the ferry landing at the mouth of the harbor is another smattering of accommodations, restaurants, and services. The best-known lodging here is **Findlay's Holiday Inn** (not affiliated with the chain), with a bundle of newer units at **Holiday Too,** both tel. (920) 847-2526. The former has eight suites in a Norwegian-style home; rooms have private baths, and the dining room overlooks the harbor. Rates run $80 s, $96 d, with a maximum of $105 for four people. Holiday Too offers eight additional rooms with a common living room. Rates are $65 s, $79 d, maximum of $90 for four persons.

At Main Rd. along Detroit Harbor are the apartment-like digs of **Viking Village,** tel. (920) 847-2551. Standard units run $55 s, $65 d, $75 triple; also available are studio and one-and two-bedroom suites with fireplaces. Rates for the bedroom suites start at $80 s, $95 d.

West Harbor

A handful of modest cottages and a couple of similar resorts lie along a stretch of Old West Harbor Road. The most rustic of all are the cabins, apartment-style rooms, and small bedrooms in the main residence of **Cedar Lodge,** tel. (920) 847-2124. The small rooms are probably among the cheapest and certainly most no-frills on the entire island. The cabins are heated by fireplace, and one features a funky old oil heater. There is a boat ramp and dock here, and the proprietor is a local trout and "lawyer" fishing guide.

The most popular along the harbor road, **Sunset Resort,** tel. (920) 847-2531, has 12 lodge units overlooking the water. There is also a pri-

vate sand beach and tennis court, and the restaurant is fairly popular for breakfast. Rates from $75. Open May through mid-October.

Inland

The **Inn at Froghollow Farm B&B,** tel. (920) 847-2835, has rooms from $65 on a real farm, available seasonally.

Cross-Island: Jackson Harbor

You'll find gracious hosts and fishing charters at the wonderful **Jackson Harbor Inn,** tel. (920) 847-2454, within walking distance of the Rock Island Ferry. The inn has rooms ($30 s, $40 d), suites ($60), and a snug cottage ($50 d). The greatest rooms are the loft suites in the old barn ($60). Some rooms share a bath.

Camping

The isolated beach camping and hiking in Rock Island State Park shouldn't be missed. If you do miss the Karfi ferry or arrive at an off-season time and still want to pitch a tent, there is the **Island Camping and Recreation Area,** tel. (920) 847-2622, on East Side Rd., with 100 somewhat secluded sites, a game room, laundry room, mini golf, tennis courts, and more. Rates are in the $18 range.

FOOD AND DRINK

Food for the obvious reasons, drink because you'll hear quite a bit about the potent "bitters"—an antifreeze-proof Scandinavian tradition still served in local pubs. If you can stomach a shot, you're in the club.

Quick Bites

A summertime drive-in—**The Albatross,** Lobdell Rd. and Main Rd., tel. (920) 847-2203, specializes in, that's right, the Alby Burger, a half-pound of Swiss cheese slathered on ground beef with bacon and assorted condiments. Open daily in summer 11 a.m.-10 p.m. From $3.

Breakfast

To-die-for Icelandic pancakes are the house specialty at breakfast at **Sunset Resort,** Old West Harbor Rd., tel. (920) 847-2531. This local hot spot serves morning grub, including homemade breads, daily 8-11 a.m. July-Aug., weekends only June and September. From $2.

Main Course

Landmark **Bitter's Pub and Restaurant,** Main Rd., tel. (920) 847-2496, is located in Nelson's Hall, a century-old structure in the center of the island. Famed for its Bitter's Club, initiated in 1899, it draws some 10,000 visitors annually. Bitter's is the best elbow-rubbing option on the island; the restaurant is classic Americana—steaks, seafood, and chicken. A $5 breakfast buffet, lunch, and dinner are served daily.

The **KK Fiske Restaurant,** tel. (920) 847-2121, is also on Main Rd. downtown and specializes in Lake Michigan fish, in particular "lawyer" (that's burbot, not counselors) and whitefish. It also has fish boils Wednesday, Friday, and Saturday nights. Some home-baked goods are available. From $5.

The dining room at **Findlay's Holiday Inn,** up the road from the ferry landing, tel. (920) 847-2526, gets good notice. At this warm Norwegian country home with bay windows overlooking Detroit Harbor, every Friday night is a perch fry, and Saturdays always have something different—maybe prime rib, maybe a theme night. Three meals a day; from $3.

ENTERTAINMENT

The **Red Barn,** south of Gislason Beach along South Shore Dr., features a regular assortment of local talent—musicians or whoever else can be drummed up. The **Art and Nature Center** offers a weeklong mid-summertime music festival during which concerts and programs are offered.

As this book was going to press, the island was preparing for the groundbreaking of a philanthropic gift to the arts, the **Trueblood Theater of the Arts,** offering upon completion a full slate of cultural events and lectures.

RECREATION

With 75 miles of paved roadway, Washington Island was made for biking. A weekend here is just about enough time to spin around the main perimeter and nose off on a few side roads. Much of the eastern littoral roadway is gravel, as is the main artery, Michigan Road, in the center of the island. Bikes can be rented at a couple of places at the ferry dock ($3 per hour, $12 per day), and trails are marked by green signs.

Field Wood Farms, one-half mile west of Main Rd. on West Harbor Rd., tel. (920) 847-2490, offers trail rides on descendants of original Icelandic stock horses—a rarity anywhere. Pony rides, riding instruction, and horse-drawn wagon rides are also available by appointment.

Daily and vacation passes are available to the public at the surprisingly modern **Washington Island Recreation Center,** tel. (920) 847-2226, with a 30- by 60-foot indoor pool, whirlpool, weight room, and two outdoor tennis courts.

On Main Rd. there is a nine-hole **golf course,** tel. (920) 847-2017, with a nice run through heavily wooded fairways; 18 mini-golf holes with electric-powered challenges await the less ambitious.

Fishing

Thirty-pound salmon are not unheard of in the sheltered waters around the island's bays; other big takes include perch, smallmouth black bass, rock bass, and especially northern pike, right in Detroit Harbor. The local variety of note is the "lawyer"—another name for the burbot, a mud-dwelling gadid fish with barbels on the chin. A number of charter operations run about, including salmon and bass charters and gracious service from **Captain Mike Lane's,** tel. (920) 847-2454. Five-hour salmon trips are $275 per trip for up to six persons; bass charters are $40 an hour for two people.

SERVICES AND INFORMATION

The **Washington Island Chamber of Commerce,** tel. (920) 847-2179, can be reached at P.O. Box 222, Washington Island, WI 54246. Another worthy spot for information is the community archives of the library (both are located in the community center), a wellspring of historical information.

The Door County newspaper is called the *Door County Advocate,* a pretty thin twice-weekly. You can buy the Green Bay papers on the island as well. Other local media are shopping/ad rags called the *Resorter Reporter* and *Key to the Door,* published by the same company. These contain coupons and some travel info.

The public **library,** tel. (920) 847-2323, is located at the junction of Main and Lakeview Roads. The **Washington Clinic,** tel. (920) 847-2424, and **post office,** tel. (920) 743-2681, are also along Main Road.

TRANSPORTATION

Ferry lines to and from Washington Island via the "top of the thumb" are outined in "Gills Rock," above. Ferries have made the seven-mile crossing somewhat quotidian, but it wasn't always so. Winter crossings used to be made by horse-drawn sleigh or—unimaginably—car, but weather conditions could change the ice or eliminate it altogether within a relatively short period. Today the ice freezes the crossing nearly solid for just over 100 days each year, usually Jan.-March, but modern ferries can take much of the ice thrown at them. When ice floes pile up during extreme cold, the ferries either "back up" and try to make an end run, or "back down" and run right at the ice. At those times, ferry service is preciously light and reservations are necessary to cross with an automobile.

You could theoretically paddle a sea kayak from Northport all the way to Washington Island—and it has been done. The lunatic fringe aspect of that notwithstanding, it would be the most breathtaking way to meet the Porte des Mortes head on. Obviously, you'd better be a damn good—and experienced—paddler.

On Island
If you've come over sans car but with a rucksack, **Vi's Taxi,** tel. (920) 847-2283 or 1-493-2388 (toll-free cell phone), has rides to the center of the village for $1.25 per person for four or more persons. Guided tours of the island run $6 per person for four or more. The hour-and-a-half tour takes in Jackson Harbor's Fishing Village, Washington Harbor, Little Lake, the Maritime Museum, the Art Center, Sievers School, and other sights. Right at the dock are also a couple of **mopeds** for rent.

Two "train" tours (essentially a Chevy Suburban pulling carriages) depart from the ferry dock regularly, linking with the ferries from Northport and Gills Rock. Times and prices are outlined in "Gills Rock," above. The Cherry Train meets the Washington Island Ferry out of Northport Memorial Day into early fall, offering four tours daily between 9:45 a.m. and 3 p.m. mid-June through mid-August. The 9:45 a.m. tour is Tues.-Thurs. only.

ROCK ISLAND STATE PARK

Less than a mile from Washington Island's Jackson Harbor as the crow flies is one man's feudal estate-turned-overgrown state park. Getting to Rock Island, the most isolated state park in Wis-

runic inscriptions, Rock Island

consin's system, necessitates not one but two ferry rides. In 1910, Milwaukee inventor Chester H. Thordarson plunked down $5,725 for the 775-acre island, formed of Silurian dolomite over 450 million years ago. Over the next 55 years, Thordarson gradually tamed the wilds and carefully transformed at least part of the island into his own private retreat.

Native Americans lived in sporadic encampments along the island's south shore from 600 B.C. until the start of the 17th century. In approximately 1640, Potawatomi Indians migrated here from Michigan; allied Ottaway, Petun, and Hurons fleeing extermination at the hands of the Iroquois nations followed in the 1650s. The Potawatomi were visited in 1679 by Rene Robert Covelier, Sieur de la Salle, whose men built two houses, the remains of which are still visible amidst the weed-choked brambles off the beach. Eventually, the French and the Potawatomi returned, establishing a trading post that lasted until 1730. Until the turn of the 20th century, the island was alternately a base camp for fishers and the site of a solitary sawmill. Rock Island is thus arguably the true "door" to Wisconsin, and a ready-made one at that—the first rock on the way across the temperamental lake from Mackinac Island.

Thordarson initially restored a few squat settler's cabins and lived there while he pondered his masterpieces—a boathouse hewn meticulously from island limestone, and, later, his grand mansion (it was never built), as well as gardens and other experiments in horticulture.

Remarkable is that this was no simple exercise in rich man's indulgence. As prescient as he was entrepreneurial (he made his fortune inventing more than 100 patentable devices, including the world's first million-volt transformer), Thordarson developed only 30 acres of the island, with the full intent of leaving the remaining 745 as an experiment in ecological preservation. With a profound knowledge of the natural world, much of it the result of self-educated sweat, he spent the rest of his days analyzing the biological minutiae of his island. Because of this, in 1929 the University of Wisconsin gave him an honorary Master of Arts degree. The school also purchased his entire island library, containing one of the world's greatest collections of Scandinavian literature.

Flora and Fauna

Here's why the isolated island is so great—no ticks, no pesky raccoons, no skunks, and no bears. In short, no perils for backpackers. The worst thing out there are the rather pernicious fields of **poison ivy** (though these are usually well marked). There are white-tailed deer, lemmings, foxes, and a few other small mammals and amphibians. Plenty of non-poisonous snakes can also be seen.

The northern hardwood forest is dominated by sugar maple and American beech. The eastern hemlock is gone. The perimeters have arbor vitae (white cedar) and small varieties of red maple and red and white pine.

Sights

Two off the most historically significant buildings in Wisconsin, as deemed by the Department of the Interior, are Thordarson's massive limestone **Viking Hall** and **boathouse.** Patterned after historic Icelandic manors, the structures were cut, slab by slab, from Rock Island limestone by Icelandic artisans and workmen ferried over from Washington Island. Only the roof tiling isn't made from island material. That's a lot of rock, considering that the hall could hold over 120 people. The hand-carved furniture, mullioned windows, and rosemaling-like detail, including runic inscriptions outlining Norse mythology, are magnificent.

The original name of Rock Island was Potawatomi Island, a name that lives on in one of the original lighthouses in Wisconsin, Potawatomi Light, built in 1836. The original structure was swept from the cliffs by the surly lake soon after being built but was replaced. Unfortunately, it's not open to the public except for occasional ranger-led tours. The house is accessible via a two-hour trail.

On the east side of the island are the remnants of a former fishing village and a historic water tower—don't laugh—it, too, is on the National Register of Historic Places. The village dwelling foundations lay in the midst of thickets and are tough to spot; there are also a few cemeteries not far from the campsites. These are the resting spots of the children and families of lighthouse keepers and even Chief Chip-Pa-Ny, a Menominee leader.

*Thorardson
Boathouse,
Rock Island*

Otherwise, the best thing to do is just skirt the shoreline and discover lake views from atop the bluffs, alternating at points with up to half a mile of sandy beach or sand dunes. Near campsite #15, you'll pass some carvings etched into the bluff, done by Thordarson's bored workers.

Recreation

At one time a sawmill buzzed the logs taken from the island; the wheel-rutted paths to the mill turned into rough roads. Thordarson let them grow over during his tenure on the island, but today they form the basis for a few miles of the park's nine and a half total hiking miles. The island is only 900-plus acres, so you've got plenty of time to cover everything, assuming you're not just spending an afternoon. If that's the case, you can hump double-time and cover the perimeter in just under three hours. You'll see all the major sights and an additional magnificent view on the northeast side—on a clear day you can see all the way to Michigan's Upper Peninsula. For those less aerobically inclined, just head for the **Algonquin Nature Trail Loop,** an hour-long (maximum) traipse.

No wheeled vehicles are allowed in the park. The dock does allow private mooring for a fee of 40 cents per foot.

Camping

The camping at Rock Island is absolutely splendid (next to the Apostle Islands, the best in the state), with sites strung along a beachfront of sand and, closer to the pier, large stones. Many of the sites farthest from the main compound are fully isolated, almost scooped into dunes and, thus, fully protected from wind but with smashing views (#13 is a favorite). Forty primitive campsites with water and pit toilets are located on the island—35 to the southwest of the ferry landing, another five spread along the shore farther southeast—these are isolated backpacker sites. Two additional group campsites are also available. Calling ahead for reservations is a good idea in summer and fall (and is essential on weekends during those times). Fees are $8 weekdays, $10 weekends for residents.

Note: the park is a pack in, pack out facility, so plan wisely.

Access

If you're not sea-kayaking over, the *Karfi* ferry, tel. (920) 847-2252, has regular service. Boats depart Jackson Harbor on Washington Island daily May 25 through June 30 and September 5 through October 9 at 10:30 a.m. and 1 and 3 p.m., with additional departures on weekends and holidays. July 1 through September 4, boats leave hourly 10 a.m.-4 p.m. and return after 15 minutes of waiting on the island. Roundtrip tickets cost $6.50 adults, $4.50 children under 10, and $7.50 campers with gear. In the off-season, you can arrange a boat, but it's prohibitively expensive.

Private boats are permitted to dock at the pier, but a mooring fee is charged.

OTHER ISLANDS

Plum and Pilot Islands

Prior to the establishment of the lighthouse on Plum Island, over 100 ships were pounded into the shoals of the Door. In one year alone, Plum Island became the cemetery for 30 ships. Though safer than any U.S. highway today, it will never be sweat-free; as recently as 1989 a ship was thrown aground by the currents. The U.S. Lighthouse Service established the Pilot Island Lighthouse in 1858. It stands atop what an early guidebook described as "little more than a rock in the heavy-pounding seas." Two brick structures stand on Pilot Island and are about the only things still visible. Once-dense vegetation has been nearly killed off, turned into a rocky field by the ubiquitous and odoriferous droppings of federally protected cormorants, which long ago found the island and stuck around.

Plum Island had to wait until 1897 to get its imposing 65-foot skeletal steel light, after which the mortality rate within the Door dropped significantly. Plum Island—so-called for its plumb-center position in the straits—is home to an abandoned Coast Guard building on the northeast side, an old foghorn building on the southwest tip, and yet another decaying Cape Cod-style lightkeeper's residence near the range lights.

Neither island is accessible—unless your sea kayak runs into trouble—except for boat tours given during the festival of blossoms ($6.50), usually offered three times daily 11 a.m.-3 p.m. from Gills Rock.

Detroit Island

Steaming into Detroit Harbor on Washington Island, look to the starboard side. The island with the crab-claw bay is Detroit Island, one of the largest satellite islands surrounding Washington Island. Settlers built the first permanent structures on the island in the early 1830s and gradually forced the displacement of the resident Ottawa and Huron Indians, who had been there for generations. Once an archaeological gem, thieves have laid waste to it. Today it is privately owned and not accessible.

CENTRAL WISCONSIN SANDS

Going north, US 51, the four-lane artery clogging the region's midsection, as soulless as any interstate, generally engenders a lash-the-wheel-and-doze traveling philosphy.

However, hop a mere mile off the major roads and you'll experience some of the state's most variegated and challenging topography—multicolored striations in mammoth sandstone cliffs, wetlands, residual prairie and woodland, superb major riverways, and that famous gritty soil. And contrary to general belief, there's plenty to do in central Wisconsin: the Wisconsin Dells, the highest points of Wisconsin topography, Devil's Lake State Park, the Wisconsin River, and more.

The Land

Gazing at a map, it's hard not to notice the Wisconsin River, the Sand Country's most salient feature, slicing through the heart of the region. This "Hardest Working River in the Nation" and its valley have given central-region residents sustenance and have sculpted an amazing topographical diversity. The region cuts across both the Northern Highlands and Central Plain geological subsections, and broaches the Western Uplands. The result is Wisconsin's third-highest point (in the north), flat lands (in the center), and a touch of chocolate-drop undulation (in the southwestern corner). Through it all, the terminal moraine line of glacial advancement meanders north to south from Sauk County to Marathon County near Wausau, then loops back to the south before cutting west out of Wood County.

Eons of primeval lakes and oceans washing in and out of the central region have produced a mishmash of predominantly bog and marshland interspersed with spinneys of forest, bits of grassland, and plenty of agricultural spreads. It also gave the central region its aesthetic highlight—

CENTRAL WISCONSIN SANDS HIGHLIGHTS

Aldo Leopold Reserve, Portage
Central Necedah National Wildlife Refuge, Necedah
Circus World Museum, Baraboo
Devil's Lake State Park, Baraboo
Eagle-watching, Sauk Prairie
International Crane Foundation, Baraboo
Kayak Championships, Wausau
Leigh-Yawkey Woodson Museum, Wausau
Merrimac Ferry, Merrimac
Natural Bridge State Park, Sauk Prairie
Portage Canal, Portage
Rib Mountain, Wausau
World-class kitsch, Wisconsin Dells

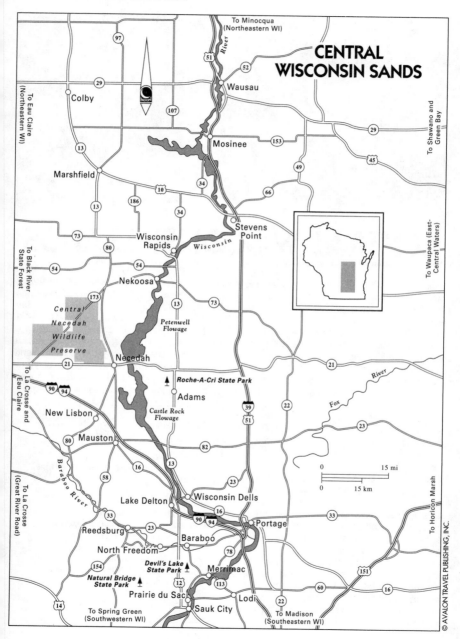

CENTRAL WISCONSIN SANDS

To Minocqua
(Northeastern WI)

To Eau Claire
(Northeastern WI)

Colby

Wausau

Mosinee

Marshfield

Stevens Point

Wisconsin Rapids

Wisconsin

Nekoosa

To Black River
State Forest

Central
Necedah
Wildlife
Preserve

Petenwell
Flowage

Necedah

Roche-A-Cri State Park

To La Crosse and
Eau Claire

Adams

Castle Rock
Flowage

New Lisbon

Mauston

Baraboo River

To La Crosse
(Great River Road)

Fox River

Lake Delton

Wisconsin Dells

Reedsburg

Portage

North Freedom

Baraboo

Natural Bridge
State Park

Devil's Lake
State Park

Merrimac

Prairie du Sac

Lodi

Sauk City

To Spring Green
(Southwestern WI)

To Madison
(Southeastern WI)

To Shawano and
Green Bay

To Waupaca (East-
Central Waters)

To Horicon Marsh

0   15 mi
0   15 km

© AVALON TRAVEL PUBLISHING, INC.

pockets of sandblow, soil-poor but geologically profound. A mile off the otherwise uninspiring interstate, you can find yourself amongst dunes—real sand dunes, in the landlocked Midwest. If it weren't for the hardy evergreens in lieu of cacti, you'd swear you were in the Sonoran desert.

History

According to stratigraphic dating, a spot in the southwestern tip of this region (Natural Bridge State Park) is one of the oldest inhabited sites in the Upper Midwest. Early settlement of this point was logical, since the glacial lobes had stopped dead at just about this point. As the glaciers retreated, the Paleo-Indians forged north with them.

European expansion into south-central Wisconsin followed only to that in the Fox River Valley. From the famed portage between the Fox and Wisconsin Rivers arose the town of the same name, and from there, intrepid fur traders plying the Wisconsin were followed by hardy settlers, who found the sandy or marshy soils often unsuited for agriculture. Timber opportunists found the northern stretches of dense woodland more hospitable, and by the 1820s, a permanent white presence had been hacked out of the forests. The residual lumber boomtowns stretched along the Wisconsin River from Sauk Prairie in the south all the way to Wausau in the north.

WISCONSIN DELLS

Once nothing more than a sleepy backwater bend in the river—albeit one that happened to have the most spectacular stretches of riverside geology in the state—the Wisconsin Dells is now the state's number-one tourist attraction, with a capital "T." Door County (not to mention Milwaukee) might squawk a bit at that statistic, but thanks in part to a public-relations campaign rivaling a presidential election, the Dells has become for some the free-associative symbol of Wisconsin. Three *million* people visit the Dells each year. And the winter season is beginning to gain popularity. They come for the inspiring 15-mile stretch of the upper and lower dells of the Wisconsin River, a serpentine, tranquil journey through breathtakingly beautiful 150-foot sandstone bluffs.

This popularity has not come without controversy. Spirit-killing crass commercialism has exploded in all directions. (One national tour operator association tagged it with the dubious honor of the "tackiest place in America.") Public relations means development. One golf course fairway was covered to make way for . . . a new resort and golf course. To some, the Dells is still unrivaled for its preternatural scenery; to others, it can never to be enjoyed again because of the miles-long frenetic commercial business strip devoted exclusively to summertime tourism dollars.

Serpents and Glaciers

The media kit on the Wisconsin Dells does a great PR two-step on the region's history by juxtaposing images and text from a Ho Chunk Nation tribal member and a University of Wisconsin geology professor. The Ho Chunk attributes the geology to an age-old serpent that slithered southward along the Wisconsin River fleeing the frigid beginnings of the ice ages. Upon reaching a large rock wall, it plowed through, scattering smaller snakes ahead of it. Voila!—a riverway and smaller canyons. The professor dryly explains that the Dells came about from the ineluctable advance of billions of tons of ice, primeval seas, and more—long before the ice ages. Take your pick. Somehow, the lower region of the Wisconsin River managed to carve magnificent dells through intensely colored sandstone escarpments.

What glaciers, particularly the Cambrian glacier, did and did not do best explains the exquisite geology of the region. The Cambrian penetrated as far south as the present-day Dells. Along with other northern states, most of Wisconsin was ravaged by the glacial movement. The Dells was partially hit, the river valley escaped onslaught, and the surrounding areas were carved flat. The city of Wisconsin Dells sits along the moraine, the perimeter of advance, of Pleistocene glaciers that stretched from west of Milwaukee as far north as Stevens Point.

All of this, however, was preceded by an enormous glacial sea that covered central Wisconsin in previous eons. The Sauk Sea carried metamorphic rock to the Wisconsin River Valley from

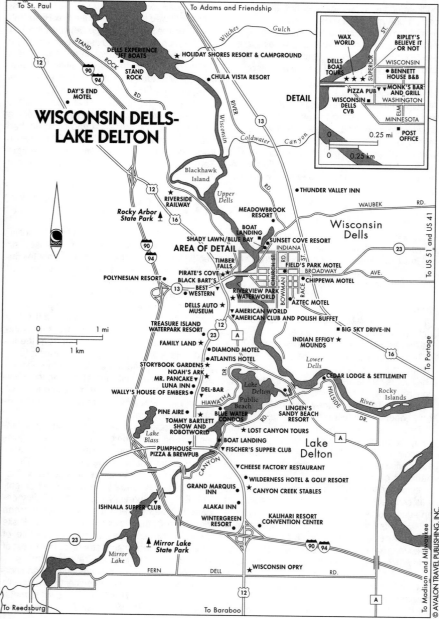

To St. Paul

To Adams and Friendship

Witches   Gulch

DELLS EXPERIENCE JET BOATS
★ HOLIDAY SHORES RESORT & CAMPGROUND

STAND ROCK

● CHULA VISTA RESORT

STAND ROCK

DAY'S END MOTEL

WISCONSIN DELLS-LAKE DELTON

Coldwater   Canyon

Blackhawk Island

Upper Dells

RIVERSIDE RAILWAY ★

Rocky Arbor State Park ▲

● THUNDER VALLEY INN

WAUBEK   RD.

Wisconsin Dells

MEADOWBROOK RESORT ●

BOAT LANDING
SHADY LAWN/BLUE BAY ●
● SUNSET COVE RESORT

AREA OF DETAIL

INDIANA
TIMBER FALLS ★
● FIELD'S PARK MOTEL
BROADWAY   AVE.
CHIPPEWA MOTEL ●

PIRATE'S COVE ★★
BLACK BART'S ▼
POLYNESIAN RESORT ●
BEST WESTERN ▼

RIVERVIEW PARK WATERWORLD ★

AZTEC MOTEL ●

DELLS AUTO MUSEUM ★

● AMERICAN WORLD
▼ AMERICAN CLUB AND POLISH BUFFET

● BIG SKY DRIVE-IN

TREASURE ISLAND WATERPARK RESORT ●

INDIAN EFFIGY MOUNDS ★

FAMILY LAND ★

● DIAMOND MOTEL
● ATLANTIS HOTEL

Lower Dells

STORYBOOK GARDENS ★
NOAH'S ARK ★
MR. PANCAKE ▼
LUNA INN ●
WALLY'S HOUSE OF EMBERS ▼
● DEL-BAR

● CEDAR LODGE & SETTLEMENT

Lake Delton

Rocky Islands

Public Beach

PINE AIRE ●

BLUE WATER CONDOS ●

LINGEN'S SANDY BEACH RESORT ●

Lake Blass

TOMMY BARTLETT SHOW AND ROBOTWORLD ●

★ LOST CANYON TOURS

PUMPHOUSE PIZZA & BREWPUB ●
● BOAT LANDING
● FISCHER'S SUPPER CLUB

Lake Delton

▼ CHEESE FACTORY RESTAURANT

● WILDERNESS HOTEL & GOLF RESORT

GRAND MARQUIS INN ●
★ CANYON CREEK STABLES

ISHNALA SUPPER CLUB ●

ALAKAI INN ●

WINTERGREEN RESORT ●

KALIHARI RESORT CONVENTION CENTER ●

▲ Mirror Lake State Park

Mirror Lake

● WISCONSIN OPRY

FERN   DELL   RD.

To Reedsburg

To Baraboo

DETAIL

WAX WORLD ■
RIPLEY'S BELIEVE IT OR NOT ●
WISCONSIN
DELLS BOAT TOURS ★★★
BENNETT HOUSE B&B ●
PIZZA PUB ■
MONK'S BAR AND GRILL ▼
WISCONSIN DELLS CVB ■
WASHINGTON
MINNESOTA
● POST OFFICE

0   0.25 mi
0   0.25 km

To Madison and Milwaukee

© AVALON TRAVEL PUBLISHING, INC.

0   1 mi
0   1 km

To US 51 and US 41

To Portage

as far away as Canada; weather processes pulverized the rock incessantly. Intermittent layers of the resulting mixed sand and quartz detritus was colored by pressed organic matter or iron oxide. Several state natural areas have been established in the canyons. The sandstone facings are home to unique plant species, including the state's only native rhododendron (endangered) and cliff cudweed, an aster found only in Wisconsin.

Human History

Indians of the Ho Chunk (formerly Winnebago) Nation were the first inhabitants in the region. Before the turn of the 18th century, fur trappers and traders showed up, taking advantage of the Wisconsin River waterway. And though lumber had always been transported on the river, precious little settlement took place until Newport sprouted up five miles south of present-day Wisconsin Dells, at a site where Indian trails and wagon-train routes had always naturally come together. A rival community, Kilbourn, expediently named itself after a railroad magnate and got the trains to stop there, and Newport shriveled up and effectively blew away, almost overnight.

Stopover rail passengers soon discovered the multi-hued striations of the sandstone, and by the 1850s, individual rowboats were carrying well-to-do passengers up and down the river in between train stops. In the 1870s, when George Crandall relocated to Kilbourn and saw opportunity, the first riverboats and steamships began plying the waters.

Opportunistic or not, Crandall is credited with applying the first preservationary eye on this stretch of magical beauty. By the 1880s, encroaching development threatened the shoreline. Crandall used the tourism money he'd amassed and began making wholesale riverfront purchases, letting the land revert to its natural state and planting trees where settlers had clearcut. He also established a conservation trust to see that others didn't muck it up later.

Crandall more than likely saved the day, although he was aided by the fact that newspapers nationwide were publishing photos of the area by Henry Hamilton Bennett, the inventor of the stop-action shutter. The pictures included the legendary first freeze-frame photograph—of Bennett's son jumping the crevasse at Stand Rock. By 1931, tourism was firmly entrenched as

the region's number-one economic base. Kilbourn had long passed on, so the town fathers, in another expedient move, renamed the town Wisconsin Dells, hoping the new name would draw even more tourists.

It did. But early tourist officials never dreamed what would become of the sleepy retreat town with local boys tugging tourists along in rowboats. In the 1960s, the Dells was still just another tourist town capitalizing on a local wealth of beauty. But the 1980s saw an explosion in growth and popularity. It hasn't ceased. Hotels and motels knock out endwalls every September to expand yet again. Every week another ride, attraction, feature, or museum is added. Still, for all its garish kitschiness and frustrating inanity, the town has managed to protect the beauty of the dells themselves. In fact, the Department of Natural Resources obtained riparian stretches to expand a long, narrow strip along the Upper Dells into a protected State Natural Area, enlarging one already established in 1994; in 1997 they expanded it yet again, doubling its size to over 2,130 acres and instituting strict rules on groundwater in the region. Plans are to build a two-mile hiking trail at Chapel Gorge and other recreational facilities. Once you're on the river, just a few miles from the strip, you get the feeling old George Crandall isn't spinning in his grave after all.

Orientation

Wisconsin Dells is effectively a sister city to Lake Delton; you can hardly tell the two strips of highway apart. The most common way to enter the Dells is off I-90/94 via WI 23/US 12; it's also the most effective, as it takes in both Lake Delton and Wisconsin Dells along a five-mile stretch.

SIGHTS

A caveat: the Dells don't come cheap. Be prepared to shell out top dollar. It's not really Big Apple pricing; it's more that there's such a wide range of irresistible stuff. Diverse discount packages are available from cooperating businesses. If you're going to stick around for a few days, check into these options, such as the Passport to Pleasure coupon book, which provides discounts based on the number of attraction tickets a visitor wishes to purchase.

Tommy Bartlett's Thrill Show

Tommy Bartlett's show is without doubt one of the most recognizable highlights in Wisconsin tourism; just count the "Tommy Bartlett" bumper stickers on Wisconsin roads. For over 45 years, this man defined the Dells, and the water-skiing show he founded has defined entertainment around these parts. The show itself is spectacular—so good it's been around the world dozens of times. It runs three times daily, rain or shine, through Labor Day. It's a two-hour grand mélange of vaudeville, three-ring circus, laser light show, and sheer daredevil gonzo on the stunt boats. Recent introductions have included contortionists and frenetic juggling acts. One of the best acts is the Sky Flyers Aerial Helicopter Trapeze. Tickets to the ski show, 560 Wisconsin Dells Parkway, tel. (608) 254-2525, are $12, $18 reserved seating, free for children five and under if they sit on a paying adult's lap.

Adjacent to the ski show is **Tommy Bartlett's Robot World and Exploratory,** a surreal mix of high-tech and kitsch set aboard an intergalactic cruiser and house of the future. Hundreds of hands- and feet-on activities explore gravity, energy, light, and motion. Robots actually guide the tours. They've recently introduced virtual reality (try the "Eat-a-Bug" sequence), wacky gyrotron rides, and touch-screen games. The original MIR space station is here too! (This is the only place in the world outside of Russia or outer space to have a MIR.) The exploratory is open daily in high season 8 a.m.-10 p.m., other months 10 a.m.-4 p.m. Admission is $8.75, $7 seniors, free for kids five and under.

Broadway: Museums, Freaks, and Kitsch

The Dells' main drag is Broadway, starting from the bridge and moving east. This is the netherworld of Americana, commercialism, and bad T-shirts.

At 115 Broadway is a branch of **Ripley's Believe it or Not,** tel. (608) 253-7556, with eight galleries of the unbelievable and an extra theater. The usual mélange of multi-spined vertebrates and King Tut curses. Get in for $19 as a family, or $7.95 adults 13 and up, $4.95 ages 6-12, five and under free. Open 8 a.m.-midnight July and August, more rational hours May-June and Sept.-October.

Next door to Ripley's is the **Wax World of the Stars,** tel. (608) 254-2184, perhaps the only place where Cher shares a stage with the Three Stooges. A hundred stars in all, heavy on comedians. Elvis is *in* the building. It's open 8 a.m.-11 p.m. Memorial Day through Labor Day, 10 a.m.-6 p.m. mid-April to Memorial Day and Labor Day through mid-October. Admission is $6 adults, $4 children 6-12, $22 family.

Across the road is **Count Wolff Von Baldasar's Haunted Mansion,** tel. (608) 254-7513, with nine theme dungeons. Admission is $5 ages 13 and over, $4 children. Top it all off with **Bill Nehring's Dungeon of Horrors,** tel. (608) 254-2980, open from 10 a.m., replete with tacky interiors and predictable scripted blood-curdling

a typical vista of Wisconsin Dells

narration. Admission is $5.50 adults, $3.50 children 12 and under.

The newest attraction slated to open downtown is the **American UFO and Sci-Fi Museum,** 740 Eddy St., tel (608) 253-5055, which features tributes to sci-fi movies, alien autopsies, Roswell and its legacy, and an exhibit on alien abductions. Admission will be around $6 for adults.

H.H. Bennett Studio and History Center

One attraction, at 215 Broadway, tel. (608) 253-2261, is the historic former studio of renowned photographer H.H. Bennett, the man who literally put the Dells on the map a century ago with his 18- by 22-inch glass negative prints of the sandstone escarpments (developed in the oldest darkroom and photographic studio in the U.S.). As this book was being updated, the state of Wisconsin was putting finishing touches on a $3 million renovation to turn it into the state's ninth State Historic Site. The center is organized into six interactive exhibits, with the overall theme of the evolution of the Dells region from prehistory to the 21st century. Obviously, lots of photography is featured: vintage prints adorn the walls; also check out the century-old furnishings and the eight-foot diamond-dust mirror. The Ho Chunk Nation isn't overlooked; there's also a replica of a traditional camp with rare Ho Chunk artifacts. Hours and admission hadn't been established at the time of writing.

Steam Train

A real 15-inch narrow-gauge railway (albeit on a one-quarter scale) journey begins at Hyde Park Station, a mile north of the Dells on Stand Rock Road. The **Riverside and Great Northern Railway,** tel. (608) 254-6367, takes you three miles through the countryside and takes in all the great Dells sights. Trains depart throughout the day from 10 a.m. to 5:30 p.m.; fares are $6 adults, $4 youths 4-15, $5 seniors, $18 family.

Storybook Gardens

It's straight family entertainment at the ever-popular Storybook Gardens, 1500 Wisconsin Dells Parkway, tel. (608) 253-2391, a theme park of fairy tale and nursery rhyme characters. A petting zoo is also on the grounds, and a mini-train loops about the whole park. Some live stage entertainment is offered. Admission is $9 adults/chil-

dren, $8 seniors. It's open summers daily 10 a.m.-5 p.m.

Dells Auto Museum

Antique convertibles are the hallmark of this impressive collection of vehicles spanning 1901-1984. The museum contains Indy pace cars as well as antique dolls, toys, license plates, and clothes. Located at 591 Wisconsin Dells Parkway, tel. (608) 254-2008, it's open mid-May through October 1 daily 9 a.m.-9 p.m., shorter hours in the off-season. Admission is $4.25 adults, $3.25 kids 6-12 and seniors, free for kids under six.

Park Lane Museum

A couple of miles west of the interstate toward Reedsburg on WI 23 is the **Park Lane Model Railroad Museum,** on Herwig Rd., tel. (608) 254-8050, displaying hundreds of meticulously detailed railroad cars and oodles of layouts. The museum is open mid-May through mid-September daily 10 a.m.-5 p.m., Sunday until 3 p.m. Admission is $4 adults, $2 for children 12 and under.

Petting Zoo

The **Wisconsin Deer Park,** south on US 12, tel. (608) 253-2041, features not only the state's official wild animal, the white-tailed deer, but also many other deer species, along with bison and game birds spread over almost 30 acres. It's open May 1 through mid-October, 9 a.m.-8 p.m. in high summer season, shorter times rest of season. Admission is $5.75, $3.50 children 4-11.

RECREATION ON THE WATER

The Dells

So what exactly is all the fuss about? What incited all of the clamor to get here in the first place were freaks of nature with oddball names like Devil's Elbow, Fat Man's Misery, Witches Gulch, Cold Water Canyon, and others. The scenic stretch of waterway that made the Dells famous is 15 miles long, with the upper and lower dells separated by a dam. The scenery truly is breathtaking—craggy palisades and soft-hued sandstone jutting right out of the water. Along the route are plenty of public beaches and boat landings, sandbars, wilderness trails, and superb, isolated spots to sit atop a towering bluff in the sun and watch the meandering river. The trademark of the Wisconsin Dells is **Stand Rock,** a mushroom-shaped sandstone protuberance made famous in 19th-century, first-of-its-kind, stop-action photography. Stand Rock is accessed via CR A and Stand Rock Road to the north of town.

If you're into exploring scenery on your own, there are plenty of marinas and rental options; a public boat launch is right off the strip. The **Lake Delton Water Sports Marina,** at the US 12 bridge, tel. (608) 254-8702, has paddleboats, canoes, Waverunners, pontoon boats, ski boats, and even parasail rides ($40). It opens the first week of May.

Wisconsin's Original Ducks

There are those who swear by the Ducks, to them the only way to experience the Dells. The Ducks are 14,000-pound amphibious landing craft that saw duty on foreign beaches in WW II. Brought out of retirement by some brilliant tour operator years ago, some 80 green and white awkwardly mobile behemoths plow along the main drag of the Dells, picking up passengers for a one-hour, eight-mile-plus trip taking in Fern Dell, Hop-Along Hill, Red Bird Gorge, Dell Creek, and Lake Delton. Also included are jaunts through restored prairie lands and access to wilderness trails, as well as a plow up and over a few sandbars for drama. Kiosks advertising the

Ducks are everywhere. Tours depart whenever enough passengers show up 8 a.m.-7 p.m. April-Oct., shorter hours the rest of the year. Tickets are $14.50 adults, $11.50 seniors, $8.75 kids 6-12. Call (608) 254-8751 for more information.

Dells Ducks

Not to be confused with the Ducks described above, this operation also tours the Lower Dells Islands and Sugar Bowl, Lone Rock, Grotto Island, and Twin Ink Well in Ducks. Tours depart the main dock along US 12 every 15-20 minutes 9 a.m.-6 p.m. May-Oct. and cost $15 adults, $9 kids 6-11. The company also runs the **Mark Twain Yacht Tour,** taking in 15 sites along the river. Tickets for this tour cost $12.

Dells Boat Tours

Another alternative for touring the Dells is on modern cabin cruisers. This tour offers separate Upper Dells tours (two hours), with a landing at the wild fern-draped canyons around Stand Rock and Witches Gulch. (This is the only boat tour that offers a stop at Stand Rock, another Dells trademark.) The Lower Dells tour takes half as long and goes nonstop through the Rocky Islands. Tours operate daily mid-April through October about every 20-30 minutes 8:30 a.m.-6 p.m. in high season, less frequently in lower spring and fall seasons. Upper Dells tours cost $15.75, $8 for children 6-12; the Lower Dells trip is $11.50, $6 ages 6-12. A combination ticket for both tours costs $20 adults, $11 children 6-12. A

taking in Wisconsin Dells on a boat tour

newer tour set to open is a dinner/dancing cruise with wine and cheese, a light buffet dinner, and a moonlight stroll through the tiki-torch-lit Witches Gulch . . . they claim it's 'romantic'. Boats depart from either the upper docks right along the riverside on Broadway or the lower docks, south on US 12 from the WI 13/16/23 junction. Call (608) 254-8555 for more information.

Other Boats

Two other water-borne options include **Captain CR Soma's Dells Cruises,** tel (608) 254-2628, with 90-minute tours aboard a double-decked 100-passenger cabin cruiser; there are also evening cruises.

For those looking for something a bit more gonzo, **Dells Experience Jet Boats,** tel (608) 254-8246, has jet boat rides five times daily 10 a.m.-6 p.m. for $16 adults, $11 children 11-15, $6 under 11.

RECREATION ON LAND

Water Parks

The Dells definitely has more big-draw water parks than any other tourist trap in the United States. It's become such a necessity that virtually every hotel or resort is caving in and operating a minor water-centered area of its own, from overblown pools to astonishingly complex slide systems.

The granddaddy is the wondrously large **Noah's Ark,** south on US 12/WI 23, tel. (608) 254-6351, the largest water park in the nation. Consider the superlatives: 70 acres with over 50 separate activities, 5,000 inner tubes, 600 picnic chairs, 550 employees, 12 restaurants, six separate swimwear shops, *ad nauseum.* The nuts and bolts: on-site are over 33 water slides, two wave pools, a kiddie pool, mini-golf, bumper boats, kids' world, go-carts, a surf pool, a whitewater raft adventure, and a new AquaXplorer submarine with working periscope, communicative helmets, and self-controlled water features. It's also recently unveiled a new Octopus Slide to rival its own legendary Big Kahuna, one of the largest wave pools in the country—big enough to offer surfing. All told, four million gallons of water gush through the place. Noah's Ark is open Memorial Day weekend through Labor Day daily 9 a.m.-8 p.m.; admission is $25 adults, $20 seniors, for an all-day pass to everything. Children two and under are admitted free.

Two lesser parks—though still massive by most standards—are **Family Land/Bay of Dreams,** south on US 12, tel. (608) 254-7766, and **Riverview Park and Waterworld,** also south on US 12, tel. (608) 254-2608. The former lives up to its name and has a price of $23 (two and under free) for a Spash/Slide/Ride pass. Limited access passes are available starting at $14. Family Land also has the one of the steepest and fastest water slides you'll likely ever experience—85 feet of precipitous drop. Riverview is another big one, totaling 75 attractions and specializing in kids (four children's activities pools alone) with 30 hydro-centered attractions in all along The Beach. And the best go-carts—mini Grand Prix driving! Individual rides cost up to $4 here, and water-only privileges run $11 ($1 off for night passes), while amusement ride only unlimited tickets cost $12. You're better off splurging for the all-inclusive ticket at $17, $9 ages three and under. Buy the ticket after 5 p.m. and it's only $9.

Mini-Golf

Duffer-delight holes abound in the Dells. Even if you don't like golf, the architectural ambition of some of the courses is mind-boggling. Top of the line is the lushly astroturfed **Pirate's Cove,** at the intersection of US 12 and WI 13/16/23 (look for the Country Kitchen), tel. (608) 254-8336, overlooking the sandstone sentinel rises. It has over 90 holes, with creative obstacles everywhere, from the traditional to the sublime. Pirate's Cove also has the longest average holes in the Dells. It's open April-October. During the high summer months, hours are 10 a.m.-midnight daily; it closes earlier the rest of the season. Eighteen holes cost around $7.

Timber Falls, at Wisconsin River Bridge and Stand Rock Road, tel. (608) 254-8414, also has five 18-hole courses (one an active volcano), along with its famous Timber Mountain Log Flume Ride ($4), a soaking-wet quarter-mile ride, partly through total darkness and then up and around a 40-foot mountain before the plummet. Enjoy—this baby cost over $2 million and is one of only five in the country. A $15 pass lets you play 90 holes of golf and ride the log flume.

Via Horse and Elk

One tradition in the Dells is taking a jaunt through the narrow back canyons via horse-drawn carriage from **Lost Canyon,** tel. (608) 254-8757. The simple half-hour trips wander through a spectacular mile of canyon; wagons accommodate up to 15 people and leave every 15 minutes from the south shore of Lake Delton. Basic rate is $6, $3.25 children 4-12. The operation also has a separate stable for individual horseback riding, **Canyon Creek,** tel. (608) 253-6942, located south on US 12; basic rates start at $16 per hour with a coupon. They have a popular daguerreotype photo operation, too. You can have your picture taken in Stetson atop a spotted horse; children also get a pony ring.

In 1996 a local couple opened an elk ranch, and within a few years so many curious tourists were poking around that they hardly had time for ranching. And thus was born a new attraction: **Nanchas Elk Ranch Tours,** tel. (608) 524-4355, located nine miles west of the Wisconsin Dells downtown on CR H on 160 acres of lovely undulating hills. Visitors take wagon tours throughout the grounds to get up-close ganders at the 50-odd calves and 25 (or more) bulls in full antler. Admission is $8 adults, $6 children 6-12.

Skiing

Christmas Mountain, S944 Christmas Mountain Rd., tel. (608) 254-3971 or (800) 289-1066, is a ski area outside of town with seven runs and a vertical drop of 250 feet; the longest run is 2,400 feet. Snowboarding is okay. It's a full-service ski resort, offering cross-country skiing, rentals, instruction, chalet, lodging, and restaurant. Open weekends 9 a.m.-10 p.m., lesser times weekdays.

Go-Carts

Not surprisingly, the Dells also has the nation's largest go-cart track, **Big Chief Go-Kart World.** There are actually 13 separate tracks, a multi-racer Grand Prix track, and the chilling wooden Cyclops roller coaster, rated in the country's top 10. The Big Chief has the only four-level track anywhere, and it's worth the price of admission. Big Chief has two locations—on the US 12 parkway and off US 12 along CR A.

Bungee Jumping

This fad is for neither the faint of heart nor the faint of wallet—$25 a pop for these bragging rights. Two jumps cost $40. **Air Boingo,** along the Strip in Lake Delton, tel. (608) 253-5867, also does bungee trampoline and an ejection seat ($30) to do an inversion on the gravity gonzo sport. **Dick Clark's Ultimate Rush,** tel. (608) 254-6911, has a kid's trampoline ($10) and the terrifying vertical accelerator ($25).

ACCOMMODATIONS

It's hard to believe that with room numbers totaling nearly *7,000* and long-time Dells families giving in and opening up yet another historic B&B, it would be iffy to expect to find a place to stay in peak season without a reservation. Still, odds aren't too bad that there's going to be something out there—excluding July 4 and Labor Day weekend. And what a bizarre and entertaining range of accommodations there is—posh resorts, water park hotels, spartan rustic cabins, historic bed and breakfasts, and plain-and-simple main-drag motels.

Note: Dells hotels, motels, and resorts are constantly adding pools, slides, wading pools, etc. Even the posh resorts will break down and put up water slides. At last count, some 40 properties had water-centered activities above and beyond the basic pool. Unless otherwise stated, all lodgings listed below include either an indoor or outdoor pool. All are also open year-round; plenty of others are seasonal. Single-night stays on weekends in summer are not allowed at many places. If you really want to combine lodging with water fun, see Water Parks below.

Rates: During the high summer months, you'll pay no less than $50 a night for one person, and as much as $200 in a swankier place. Myriad options exist in between. If you can stay that long, weekly rentals cost less, and securing a multi-person cabin and splitting the cost is a great way to save funds. Off-season, rates can dip as low as $30 for a single. All prices listed below are high-season rates. Remember, the Dells caters to the traveler, and with enough investigation ahead of time, you can save a lot with the tremendous discounts, coupons, packages, and other deals available.

One-of-a-Kind

Located inside tranquil Mirror Lake State Park in Lake Delton is the **Seth Peterson Cottage,** a

Frank Lloyd Wright-designed cottage available for overnighting. It's been described as having "more architecture per square foot than any other building Wright designed." The one-room cottage with a splendid view has recently undergone a thorough renovation and is fully furnished with a complete kitchen, enormous stone fireplace, flagstone terrace, floor-to-ceiling French doors and windows, and complete seclusion. Reservations are necessary; contact Sand County Service Co., 116 W. Munroe St., P.O. Box 409, Lake Delton, WI 53940, tel. (608) 254-6551. Per-night rate is a steep $205. Tours ($2) are also available the second Sunday of every month 1-4 p.m.

Water Parks and Water Activity Areas
The **Polynesian,** 857 N. Frontage Rd., tel. (608) 254-2883 or (800) 272-5642, has a fantastic three-story, 30,000-square-foot indoor water park separated into two sections including the Water Factory (a child-controlled geyser and fountain maker), tons of wiggling rides, 20-person hot tub, and more. All rooms include mini refrigerators, microwaves, coffeemakers, hairdryers, in-room movies, and the Disney channel. Many also include whirlpools, separate living areas, and poolview patios or balconies. Rooms are $95-320.

This pales in comparison to the area's water resorts, which comprise the most comprehensive indoor water facilities in the nation. Each is amazing in its own right but you'll find a general overarching theme to each, a mind-boggling array of rides, pools, slides, tubs, and lots of interactive exhibits. The **Kalihari Resort Convention Center,** 1305 Kalihari Dr., tel. (608) 254-5466, is over 105,000 square feet of fun, highlighted by numerous two- to four-person raft/tube rides and a tunnel body flume ride. Rooms have satellite TV, hairdryers, fridge, microwaves, hot tub, and fireplace. They run $139-499. Slightly cheaper rooms on average are found at both the **Treasure Island Waterpark Resort,** 1701 Wisconsin Dells Parkway, tel (608) 254-8560, and **Wilderness Hotel and Golf Resort,** 511 Adams St., tel (608) 253-9729, both of which have so many water attractions that they're broken into separate *wings.* Treasure Island has rooms with microwave, refrigerator, and coffeemaker; some have a whirlpool. A pub and grill overlooks the water park. Rooms run $89-350. The Wilder-

ness, akin to a city-state, comprises the largest indoor water facility in the United States. There's also an 18-hole championship golf course here. Rooms have satellite TV, hairdryer, whirlpool, fireplace, coffeemaker, fridge, and microwave. Rates are $95-500.

The Strip
The Strip is composed of Wisconsin Dells Parkway, stretching north to the bridge out of Lake Delton toward Wisconsin Dells proper, east of the lake and river; it also includes the bit of access west of the bridge toward the interstate, where a handful of lodgings are located. Not really part of the strip but a cheap option north of the strip along Hwy 12/16 is the **Day's End Motel,** tel. (608) 254-8171, which has very cheap and decent rooms from $54 even in high season.

Less expensive is the **Pine Aire,** 511 Wisconsin Dells Parkway, tel. (608) 254-2131 or (800) 635-8267, a stained brown structure with whirlpools, sauna, suntan beds, a game room, and some in-room jacuzzis and multi-room family suites. All units have their own balconies. Rates are $80. Some good off-season packages, especially involving the Ho Chunk Casino, are available.

Another local operation in the same price range is the new and very decent **Diamond Motel,** 1630 Wis. Dells Pkwy., tel. (608) 253-6500 or (800) 23-DIAMOND, between Noah's Ark and Familyland—thus, well located for families. It offers sauna, tanning, whirlpool, and game room, and some suites, with or without jacuzzi. Rates run $80 and up.

The non-chain **American World Inn and Resort,** 400 CR A and US 12, tel. (608) 253-4451, offers lots of pools (a rare diving board), whirlpools, saunas, and a more low-key, family-centered recreation area with volleyball and basketball courts. There's a huge Polish-American buffet here, too. Rates run from $89.

Big Best Western rooms at the **Best Western Ambassador Inn,** 610 Frontage Rd. S., tel. (608) 254-4477 or (800) 828-6888, with an incredible range of room types, some with kitchens or poolside locations. Private sun decks, laundry, waterfalls, and water slides are a few of the amenities. Lots of activity for room rates $108-218 on weekends, $20 less mid-week.

Clean and practical rooms at the **Skyline Motel,** 1970 Wis. Dells Pkwy., tel. (608) 253-

4841 or (800) 759-8475, along with six pools and jacuzzis, saunas, and some new package deal options. Rates are $89 and up.

Find always good though not always spacious rooms at the **New Concord Inn,** 411 Wis. Dells Pkwy., tel. (608) 254-4338 or (800) 348-2019, with the usual pools and whirlpool, and even a nice picnic area with grills provided. Rooms run $105-155 July and early August, much less the rest of the year.

Lake Delton

The relaxed-looking, low-slung **Alakai Hotel and Suites,** 1030 Wis. Dells Pkwy. S., tel. (608) 253-3803, has solid rooms, some with saunas and jacuzzis. Rates run $110-205.

Enjoy excellent rooms at the **Grand Marquis Inn,** 840 Wis. Dells Pkwy. S., tel. (608) 254-4843. Rates start at a princely $118 high season; some executive suites are offered, along with jacuzzis, sauna, and whirlpools.

A newer establishment located near the dog racing track—and conveniently eye-catching in a Kentucky Downs aesthetic—is the **Wintergreen Resort,** US 12, tel. (608) 254-2285 or (800) 648-4765, a full-service resort and conference center with the look and feel of a country inn, albeit an oversize country inn. New options include a couple of water-park areas. Some rooms have balconies. Rooms run $130-220 during the week, more on weekends; there's a two-night minimum on weekends.

A mile west of Lake Delton is the **Tamarack,** tel. (608) 254-6551, a villa complex of rough-hewn design. Interiors are grand: cathedral ceilings, skylights, satellite TV, courtyards, patios, and a great athletic complex on-site. Plenty of multi-sized units are available, starting from $115 per night.

Downtown Dells

The most inexpensive lodging in the area is along Broadway east of the river and north along River Road. Try the **Finch Motel,** 811 Oak St., tel. (608) 253-4352, with basic rooms. It's only open during the summer, with rooms from $45. All-season rooms and similar rates at the **Aztec,** 425 S. Vine St., tel. (608) 254-7404, featuring clean rooms with microwaves, refrigerators, and some connecting rooms. Picnic tables and grills are also available.

Chippewa Motel, 1114 Broadway, tel. (608) 253-3982, offers spacious rooms (some with jacuzzis), pool, sauna, whirlpool, and game room at rates of $78-170.

Another possibility includes **Field's Park,** 715 Broadway, tel. (608) 254-6100, which has a wide range of rooms from $40 and up.

River Road

To escape the cacophony of the central area, head north, to the area on and around River Road. The cheapest is **Shady Lawn,** 1038 River Rd., tel. (608) 254-7291, which has rooms as low as $42, along with a 24-hour pool, grills, and lots of equipment rentals. Rooms can sleep up to eight.

The **Blue Bay,** 1026 River Rd., tel. (608) 254-7303, is attached to the Shady Lawn and good for families, with a wide range of options—small cottages to kitchen suites. One cottage sleeps eight. The pool is open until midnight. Rates from $38.

Another outstanding secluded option for families is the cottage colony on 12 acres, **Meadowbrook,** 1533 River Rd., tel. (608) 253-3201, featuring a log motel, log lodge, and rustic-looking (though thoroughly contemporary) cabins. All have full facilities. Amenities include a huge pool, playground, large expanse of grounds, barbecue grills, and picnic tables. July and August rates run $88-299, but come in early summer and enjoy drastic discounts.

Best-known along River Road is undoubtedly **Chula Vista,** 4031 N. River Rd., tel. (608) 254-8366, a full-service resort on seriously attractive grounds. The resort recently redecorated in a Southern California "desert oasis" theme. It isn't tacky, as it may sound. A centerpiece is the 20,000-square-foot indoor pool, not to mention grounds large enough for nature trails and hiking trails. Myriad rooms and suites are available; the themed fantasy suites are popular. Rates are $135-275 in high season.

On the Waterfront

Most people naturally seek out lodging somewhere along the beauteous riverfront stretching from Mirror Lake to the south, through Lake Delton, and along the Wisconsin River. Most riverfront lodging is concentrated in the Lake Delton area and is expensive.

Good for groups is **Lighthouse Cove Condominium Resort,** off Hwy 12/23 at 530 E. Hiawatha Dr., tel. (608) 253-7616 or (800) 790-2683. In a magnificent lakefront setting, the units include modern kitchens; there's also a boat dock, pools, sauna, beach, tennis courts, and more. For four people, rates start at $135 per night, $850 per week; for six it's up to $240 and $1,300 respectively.

Cozy ponderosa-style interiors and a family atmosphere without the lunacy of the water-park resorts is offered at **Cedar Lodge and Settlement,** E11232 Hillside Dr., tel. (608) 254-8456. All rooms have decks, and most overlook the Wisconsin River; some have kitchenettes. Guests enjoy a large sandy beach, heated pool, and boating equipment. Two-night minimums are sometimes the rule in high season. Rates are $145-295. This operation is building fresh new villas.

The only resort along the Upper Dells is **Sunset Cove,** operated by Sand County Service, 116 W. Munroe St., P.O. Box 409, Lake Delton, WI 53940, tel. (608) 254-6551. There's a gorgeous view of Crandall Bay from here, all units are spacious and have patios, and it's just a hop to downtown. Plenty of extras, including a private marina. Rates run from $145 a day, $740 a week for a unit sleeping four.

Another Sand County Service property with a nice location is **Blue Water Condominiums,** tel. (608) 254-6551, along Lake Delton, on a hillside heavily wooded with evergreen, ash, and oak trees. The spacious one- and two-bedroom units all have fully equipped kitchens, are fully furnished, and have private patios. A four-person unit is a good deal at $108-287 a day, $550 a week.

Rivers Edge Resort and Motel, S1196 CR A, tel. (608) 254-7007, is a cozy log apartment-type complex above the Wisconsin River with one-, two-, and three-bedroom units, a log cabin, and basic motel units, all with fieldstone fireplaces. The resort has its own private boat launch and sandy beach. Rates vary—$70-170 for a basic room, $685 a week for an eight-person cabin.

Bed and Breakfasts

The **Bennett House,** 825 Oak St., tel. (608) 254-2500, is the former residence of the famed photographer H.H. Bennett, inventor of the stop-action shutter. This house, on the National Register of Historic Places, features a suite, English-style rooms, and garden rooms. Even the bedding was specifically designed for the home; the dining room has a grand fireplace. Rates are $75-95.

One of the best B&Bs in the Midwest is the isolated Scandinavian style 130-year-old *farmhus,* the **Thunder Valley Inn,** W15344 Waubeek Rd., tel. (608) 254-4145, also one of the best places to eat in the Dells. Original farm rooms have Franklin stoves; some feature balconies overlooking the woods. Entertainment includes fiddling hoedowns and some weekend chautauquas (outdoor cultural education assemblies) and threshing suppers. An old-fashioned schoolhouse contains artifacts from local Scandinavian homesteads and the Ho Chunk Nation. The lodging is available year-round, the restaurant only seasonally. Rates are $45-95.

Camping

State parks are far better than private campgrounds. Devils' Lake is the most appealing regional state park, but it's a ways from the Dells. The other options are **Mirror Lake** and **Rocky Arbor State Parks.** Mirror Lake is just south of Lake Delton along US 12 and is the better known—and, thus, more populated—of the two. It's known for its tranquil, placid waters, so canoeing is popular, especially to the dam that created the lake. For a large-capacity campground (145 sites), privacy is fairly decent. Rocky Arbor is closer to the Dells and not as well known; it's also fairly small, at just over 200 acres, but the geology here is half a billion years old and an excellent representation of the region. It offers a 90-site campground. Both state parks require a sticker for admission ($5 residents, $7 nonresidents), and the fee for sites is $8-12.

Eighteen private campgrounds are in and around the Dells. Come summertime, they will be chock-full and boisterous—not an isolated, bucolic experience. One of the smaller operations—and thus, theoretically, quieter—is **Blue Lake Campground,** 3531 CR G, tel. (608) 586-4376, with 45 total sites for RVs and a separate tenting area. There is a swimming beach here. Rates are $13-20. Also along this stretch of CR G is **K&L Campground,** 3503 CR G, tel. (608) 586-

4720, with 60 RV sites and an isolated tent site. Unlike Blue Lake, this one is open in winter, by appointment. Rates here are also $13-20.

A much larger popular operation is the **Holiday Shores Campground,** 3900 River Rd., tel. (608) 254-2717, a resort operation along the Wisconsin River with camping available. Hundreds of sites, separate tenting area, and a whole catalogue of extras for recreation are available, including bike and boat rentals. Rates run $26-31.

FOOD

Many, but by no means all, of these restaurants are open seasonally. These usually bolt shut for the winter sometime between late October and December, reopening in May.

Diners, Greasy Spoons, and Family-Style Dining

Paul Bunyan's Lumberjack Meals, near I 90/94 along WI 13, tel. (608) 254-8717, is every kid's favorite place to eat. All-you-can-cram-in meals are served here (figure $9 for adults), specializing in breakfast and chicken-and-rib feeds. Open daily for breakfast, lunch, and dinner; open seasonally.

Out on the strip, at 1405 Wis. Dells Pkwy., is a 30-year local tradition, **Mr. Pancake,** tel. (608) 253-3663, with almost three dozen versions of pancakes and breakfast combinations, all in admirably tacky riverboat decor (from $5). House specialty is a hot fudge banana split waffle. The photos on the walls are original H.H. Bennett shots of the Dells' early days. Mr. Pancake is open daily 7 a.m.-2 p.m. in season.

Buffets

Enjoy true Wisconsin-style food at **American World Polish-American Smorgasbord** (whew), 400 CR A (at US 12), tel. (608) 253-4451, with plenty of offerings including *pierogi, golabki,* and a host of American entrées (from $6). It's open daily 7 a.m.-noon and 3:30-8:30 p.m., Sundays and holidays 1-8 p.m.

Another huge buffet is found at **Black Bart's,** next to Lower Dells Tours tickets, exit 87 off the interstate, tel. (608) 253-2278, with breakfast, lunch, and dinner spreads (around $9) including a 50-item salad bar and a 50-foot dessert table.

Kids will love the "hold-ups," campfire singalongs, horse races, and the like.

Burgers and Pub Grub

One of the oldest bar-and-grills (sandwiches from $5) in the Dells is the venerable **Monk's,** 220 Broadway, tel. (608) 254-2955, the local burger joint and watering hole since WW II. The half-pound brats are nothing to sneeze at, either. The atmosphere is one of the best, the rich original interiors of the 1940s. Monk's is open daily at 11 a.m.

A family-friendly pub is **River's Edge,** S1196 CR A, tel. (608) 253-6600, with steaks, seafood, burgers, and chicken offerings (from $4). There's a century-old oak tree behind the bar, and a game room for the kids. Open year-round 11 a.m.-11 p.m.

The Dells' only true brewpub is the **Pumphouse Pizza and Brewpub,** tel. (608) 253 4687, right along WI 23 with lots of pizzas (from $6) and its own brews; they'll even deliver (pizzas, not the brew!) right to your campsite.

Pizza

You can get pizza—but also an even better, 80-item soup and salad bar and fresh pasta and Italian specialties (from $5)—at the **Pizza Pub,** 1455 Wis. Dells Pkwy., tel. (608) 254-7877. Loud and bustling with '50s and '60s music in the background. It's open daily 11 a.m.-late; seasonal.

Supper Clubs

Without question, the place to head is **Del-Bar,** a five-decade-old institution in the Dells. Bistrocum-supper club, it has the most exquisite custom dry-aged Angus steaks and prime rib as well as some creative pastas and excellent seafood, especially the Killer Shrimp. Menu choices for $13-30. Even better is the ambience—the building was designed by a protégé of Frank Lloyd Wright, and the dining rooms feature fireplaces. Located at 800 Wis. Dells Pkwy. S., tel. (608) 253-1861, it's open for dinner daily.

The rustic atmosphere at **Fischer's Supper Club,** 441 Wis. Dells Pkwy. in Lake Delton, a 50-year-old, family-owned place, has been made a bit fancy. But the ambience is still there. It's a good choice for a fish fry come Friday night. Dishes start from $6. Open daily year-round 4-11 p.m.

Savor luscious, hickory-smoked ribs from the proprietary smokehouse at **Wally's House of Embers,** along US 12, north of Tommy Bartlett's in Lake Delton, tel. (608) 253-6411, a newer supper club-style eatery. Also served are pastas, excellent seafood, and "flame-kist" steaks; dinner choices start at $10. The Sunday brunch is popular. Wally's is open year-round, 4:30-10 p.m.

Ishnala, Ishnala Rd., tel. (608) 253-1171, offers superlative vistas on a 100-acre spread of meadow overlooking Mirror Lake, as well as 40 years of steaks, prime rib, seafood, ribs, and a house special roast duck and baby back pork ribs. Dinner choices start at $11. Before-dinner cruises are available. Check out the Norway pines growing right through the roof. To reach Ishnala, take Gasser Rd., pass the dog track, then turn left onto Ishnala Road.

Something Else

Two restaurants stand out as unique to the Dells. The **Cheese Factory,** 521 Wis. Dells Pkwy., tel. (608) 253-6065, features—believe it or not—excellent international vegetarian cuisine, right here in the middle of prime rib country. And it's definitely international, from Thai sauté to mushroom-potato stroganoff and a very Greek spanikopita (items from $6). The interior of the multi-level '40s-theme eatery retains the original knotty pine and oak. Live entertainment is offered on weekends. A new espresso and specialty coffee bar is now open, and there's a great ice cream soda fountain. It's open daily 9 a.m.-9 p.m. except Tuesday, also for Sunday brunch. The restaurant opened a second branch in the White Rose B&B Inn and has similar cuisine with a Mediterranean cafe atmosphere.

The other place is a step back in time. Just north of town stands a pocket of old country dwellings, the **Thunder Valley Inn,** W15344 Waubeek Rd., tel. (608) 254-4145. The Thunder Valley, long an excellent lodging choice, is earning kudos for its food and environment. It's a working farm with goats and chickens dashing about; chores are optional. The food is in the grand Old World style, from German potato salad to roast chicken; and it does a superb

fish fry. Many ingredients are grown on-site; the restaurant even grinds its own wheat and rye berries. This is *the* spot for breakfast; the family-style breakfast is worth much more than the price, considering the work that goes into it, and each bite is a bit of Wisconsin culinary heritage. (Unbeatable Norwegian pancakes with lingonberries.) To top it all off, there are weekend chautauquas and sometimes bonfires, when the handmade fiddles come out and the hoedowns begin. Breakfast is served daily 7 a.m.-noon; there's a Friday fish fry, and dinner is served on Saturday. You'll need a reservation for the Saturday dinner and chautauqua. The restaurant is open seasonally, the inn year-round.

ENTERTAINMENT

Big Sky Twin Drive-In

Catch it while you can, this nearly dead American tradition. Two huge screens show four shows nightly—all first-run Hollywood stuff. The snack bar is huge. Big Sky is located one mile south via US 16E, tel. (608) 254-8025. Tickets are $6 adults, $3 children 5-11.

Rick Wilcox Theater

The eponymous illusionist has a theater along Wisconsin Dells Parkway, tel. (608) 254-5511, which has two Grand Illusion shows per day at 4 and 8 p.m. Tickets cost $17 adults, $12 children 5-12, $16 seniors.

Wisconsin Opry

Though Nashville's Grand Ole Opry stars do make appearances here, usually it's regional or local acts performing. It's the state's only real country music performance venue. Shows are at 8 p.m. Mon.-Sat. late May through late September. Sporadic Sunday matinees are also offered. A country-style dinner package with show is available. A weekend flea market is ongoing on the grounds, and hayrides will have been initiated by the time this book hits the press. The Opry is on US 12 at I 90/94, tel. (608) 254-7951 or (800) 453-2593. Tickets are $15 show, $27 show and dinner for adults, $7 and $10 children.

DOIN' THE DELLS

The first road signs—huge and color-splashed and screamingly designed—crop up somewhere around Madison if you're coming in from the south. With each mile clicked, the traveler becomes more fully informed as to the delights that the distant oasis offers. It's a numbing—nay, insulting—onslaught of countryside visual pollution.

Phantasmagoria of Kitsch

There are those (this author included) who believe—stridently—that the Wisconsin "experience" necessitates, without dissent, a descent into the kitschy, cacophonic purgatory of the Strip in the Dells and Lake Delton, that multi-mile Middle America meander clogged (by 10 a.m.) with belching RVs and minivans disgorging sunburned consumers like Marines wading ashore in Normandy. A giant corny shakedown.

Obscenity or pure Americana? Well, both. It's got the classic symptoms of a Niagara Falls: magnificent aesthetics and geological history mashed with the dizzying clatter of a tourist trap run amok. Miles and seemingly endless miles of water parks and water parks and water parks and braying, tape-looped haunted houses, embarrassingly stupid knickknacks and curio shops, freak museums, wax museums, miniature golf courses, greyhound racing, The Skreeeeeeeeeeeeeeeeemer, drive-in theaters, an "Opry," go-carts, bungee jumping, helicopter rides, an odd casino or two, otherwise rational people with arrows sticking out of their heads, the Cyclops, a ticket tout on every corner. And lately, the Dells has gotten real serious about roller coasters, so within a year a whole bunch of killers have sprouted up. The entire design of this Wisconsin city is aimed at the sheer, unadulterated, hedonistic delight of the child, real and inner. Mom and Pop have to choke on the exhaust, pray for parking, and get in line to start shelling out the cash.

It's as full of garishness as Niagara Falls. And it's wonderful—every damn frightening, wearying second of it. Sure, the jaded, the agoraphobic, the old, and anyone who opposes sprawling economic explosion should hunker down and barrel on through this area without stopping. But for those who appreciate an absolutely indescribable, surreal slice of Americana at its most over-the-top, it's a trip

Live Music

A newcomer to the Dells is the **Crystal Grand Music Theater,** WI 23, tel. (608) 254-4545 or (800) 696-7999, done up to resemble a stately mansion. The theater inside features a constant schedule of regional and national acts—no superstars yet but a popular slate of country-legend impersonators. Plenty of comedy and a modern vaudevillian atmosphere. Elvis hosts the show. Times and ticket prices vary.

Dancing

Just past Noah's Ark on the Parkway strip is **Brothers-in-Law,** 1481 Wis. Dells Pkwy., tel. (608) 254-2222, a full-service nightclub with high-tech sound system, dancing (reggae to classic '60s), sand volleyball, and lots and lots of noise; some live music, too. A DJ spins discs seven nights a week.

Bars and Pubs

The Dells caters almost solely to families, so expect a dearth of thumping nightclubs. What few exist are mostly along Broadway. One famous place, though, is **Nig's,** a very general bar whence come the T-shirts proclaiming "I Had a Swig at Nig's." Down the street is **O'-Connor's Irish Spirits and Saloon,** a typical pub open since the 1940s. Besides great burgers, **Monk's** is a good place to tip a few, one of the oldest—and thus most character-filled—watering holes in the Dells.

EVENTS

The biggest festival of the year in the Dells is January's **Flake Out Festival,** with a host of winter activities, including snowmobile radar running, music, and the state's only sanctioned snow sculpting competition.

In April there's a large **polka festival;** but it's outdone by the huge **Dells Polish Fest** the first weekend after Labor Day.

The newest festival, May's **Automotion,** is a showcase of over 750 cars—antiques, street machines, and classics—and includes swap meets, a car corral, cruises, and motorcycle classes.

There's also the popular **Autumn Harvest Fest** in mid-October, with lots of scarecrow stuffing, pumpkin carving, food, and very scenic boat/train/'Duck' tours.

SERVICES AND INFORMATION

The **Wisconsin Dells Visitors and Convention Bureau** is at 701 Superior St., tel. (608) 254-4636 or (800) 22-DELLS. This new facility has loads of brochures, good advice and, yes, public bathrooms. It was the first in Wisconsin to go cyber, as well: visit on the Web at www.wisdells.com.

The **post office,** tel. (608) 254-6411, is at 310 Minnesota Avenue. The **Kilbourn Public Library,** tel. (608) 254-2146 is at 620 Elm Street. The closest hospital is **Reedsburg Area Medical Center,** 2000 N. Dewey Ave., tel. (608) 524-6487, in Reedsburg.

TRANSPORTATION

Bus

Wisconsin Dells has no central bus station. **Greyhound** buses arrive and depart from the Mobil station at 802 Broadway, tel. (608) 253-2091; the schedule is ever-changing.

Train

There's also no **Amtrak** station, but the train does pick up and drop off behind the Wisconsin Dells Convention and Visitors Bureau, at the foot of Lacrosse Street; tickets can be purchased from any travel agent. At press time, the daily Empire Builder stopped around 5:45 p.m. for westbound travel, noon eastbound.

Rental Cars

Country Corner Cars, corner of WI 33 and US 12, tel. (608) 356-2181, has all types of vehicles for a flat $35 per day, including 100 free miles.

VICINITY OF THE DELLS

BARABOO

If you had to draw up quaint little communities for tourist brochures, this could be the model. Way back when in Baraboo, town founders were smart enough to lay the main highways away from the heart of the city, preserving the small-town charm. It's not exactly that small (pop. 9,203), but it sure feels like Tinytown, U.S.A.—life still revolves around the courthouse square. Baraboo consistently earns top-10 finishes in its category in media rankings of livability quotients of U.S. cities.

It's plunked down in an enviable locale, ensconced at the virtual midpoint of the canoe-shaped Baraboo Valley (and Range) of puce-colored quartzite escarpments and the grandeur and tackiness of the Wisconsin Dells, with a sampling of verdant Wisconsin countryside thrown in for good measure.

And then there's the circus. Though Baraboo was and is an important regional cog in dairy distribution, recent improvements to the local circus museum and highlights should make the town better known nationally for the Ringling Brothers. In 1882, a family of enterprising local German farmboys named Ringling, much enamored of a traveling troupe's performance in Iowa, organized the Ringling Brothers' Classic and Comic Concert Company and gave a performance in Mazomanie, to the south. Later renamed, the barnstorming caravan toured and grew slowly. The Ringlings eventually bought Barnum and Bailey out lock, stock, and barrel, securing the title to the Greatest Show on Earth. Wisconsin would become the "Mother of Circuses"—over 100 circuses have had their origins and based their operations here. Baraboo was home to the Greatest Show on Earth until 1918, and the Ringlings' legacy remains its biggest draw.

Sights

How about that **Circus World Museum,** 426 Water St., tel. (608) 356-0800, anyhow? It was the original headquarters of the Ringling Brothers circus, in an attractive setting along the Baraboo River. Cold weather eventually forced a decampment to warmer climes in Florida. Summertime (May-Sept.) is the best time to visit, when the capacious 51-acre grounds are open and the three-ring circus and sideshows reappear. Under the big top is Circus in America, a dazzling, frenetic, fun-as-heck mélange of jugglers, aerialists, clowns, bands, magic, circus nuts-and-bolts, steam-driven calliope concerts, and animal shows. Special fun is gearing up for the big train ride to Milwaukee and the Great Circus Parade. The Irvin Feld Exhibit Hall has memorabilia and displays from the past century of all circuses: rare circus miscellany from long-gone U.S. circuses, an exhaustive historical rundown of the Ringlings, and, in the video theater, ongoing films, including a tribute to legendary animal trainer Gunther Gebel-Williams. Also in the hall is the world's most complete collection of circus vehicles (214 and counting) and circus posters (8,000 and counting). Get lucky and maybe ride a pachyderm or a pony if you prefer. Newer attractions are the exhibit on Gargantua, the gorilla purported to be the largest ever ("The World's Most Terrifying Living Creature!!"), and the 1905 Gavioli band organ, which replicates an 80-piece

orchestra's sound. New for this edition are a kids' clown show, where ecstatic urchins can slap on the face paint and go wild; and a circus music demonstration, which features hands-on access to rare circus musical instruments. A new $2.5-million expansion has added a state-of-the-art facility for restoring circus wagons. The museum deserves recognition, too, for producing one of the most highly educational and richly detailed periodicals (and promos), *Circus Tails,* a newsletter packed with fascinating history, trivia, and games. It's open daily 9 a.m.-9 p.m. July-August, 9 a.m.-6 p.m. May-July and mid-August through mid-September, 11 a.m.-5 p.m. the rest of the year. Admission May-Nov. is steep but absolutely worth it—$12 adults, $6 kids 12 and under—but it's lower in the off-season.

The most inspiring attraction is the respected ornithological preservation ongoing at the **International Crane Foundation,** E11376 Shady Lane Rd., tel. (608) 356-9462. This world-renowned institution is dedicated to saving the world's largest flying birds, some 15 species of

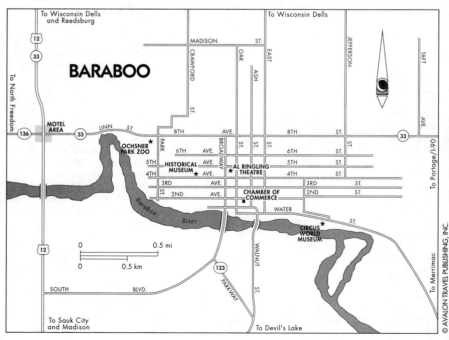

cranes, all of which are endangered or threatened; this is the only place in the world that houses all species. The whooping crane population, from a nadir of 15 birds in 1940, has amazingly rebounded to over 200 birds. This facility was the first to hatch Hooded and Siberian cranes. This place is so respected that its research facility welcomed the Crown Princess of Japan, who conducted research on-site in 1995. After a visit here, Indira Gandhi returned to India and founded the Keoladeo Ghana National Park to protect the Siberian crane. The center initiated an annual Crane Festival in May 1999; it's already wildly popular. Guided tours are given daily at 10 a.m. and 1 and 3 p.m.; self-guided tours to view adult birds, restored Wisconsin prairie, and marshland are available May-October. The center also has museum displays and slide shows and videos. The grounds have been restored to their pre-settlement ecological form. The center is open daily May-Nov. 9 a.m.-5 p.m.; admission is $7 adults, $6 seniors, $3.50 children 5-11. Incidentally, the center also sponsors an annual spring sandhill crane volunteer count, the largest such endeavor in the country. Wisconsin, a hot spot for cranes along the Mississippi Flyway, holds almost 13,000 sandhill cranes, with over 1,000 in Marquette County alone. It's quite a change from six decades ago, when sport and commercial hunters and predatory agricultural expansion had pared sandhill numbers to two digits.

Before Ringling Bros. abandoned ship for muggier climes in Florida, brother Al Ringling had a grand opera house built, modeled on European opera houses, in particular the Great Opera Hall at the Palace of Versailles. Tours are given in summer at the **Al. Ringling Theatre,** 136 4th Ave., tel. (608) 356-8844, or just show up for one of the movies or live music events held regularly. As this edition was being updated, the theater was in the midst of a multi-million dollar renovation to restore it to its original resplendence.

Most folks never even get to the **Sauk County Historical Museum,** 531 4th Ave., tel. (608) 356-1001, so caught up do they get in all the circus revelry or hiking at Devil's Lake. But it offers decent exhibits of regional history, including Civil War memorabilia, Native American artifacts, and more, all in a turn-of-the-century mansion. It's open May-Sept. Tues.-Sun. 2-5 p.m. Admission is $2 adults, $1 children 12-17. For a quick freebie, drop by **Ochsner Park,** corner of WI 33 and Park St., for a look at one of the best small-town zoos you'll ever see, featuring native Wisconsin and some exotic animals.

Not exactly in Baraboo, but in nearby North Freedom, is another astounding favorite—the chugging iron roosters at **Mid-Continent Railway and Museum,** west of Baraboo on WI 136 and CR PF, tel. (608) 522-4261. The last operating steam engine of the Chicago and North Western Railroad is the granddaddy here. All of these trains are refurbished originals; many serviced the area's quartzite mines. The grounds are loaded with railroad coaches, cabooses, snow fighters, and freight haulers; buildings include an original late-19th-century depot and a wood plank water tower. Most visitors come, however, for the nine-mile train ride through the Baraboo River Valley. Special seasonal trips also depart, including the most popular Autumn Color (first two weekends of October) and Snow Train (third weekend in February) trips, as well as Memorial Day's Railfest and the Santa Claus Express on Thanksgiving weekend. The Snow Train's evening dinner departure is a wonderful photo op. The museum is free and open mid-May through Labor Day and weekends through October 9:30 a.m.-5 p.m. Trains depart daily at 10:30 a.m. and 12:30, 2, and 3 p.m. Tickets are $9 adults, $5.50 children 15 and under, $8 seniors. Family rate is $25.

Totally cool is a one-of-a-kind sculpture collection just south of town via US 12. Dr. Evermor, better known as Tom Every, has placed a what-exactly-is-it? assemblage of sculptures created from what could best be described as the detritus of the Cold War and its belching factories; it is in fact located directly opposite the hulking remains of the dormant Badget Munitions Depot, which plied numerous Allied war efforts. This menagerie of machines has the **Forevertron** as its nucleus; it is a 400-ton monstrosity—the largest in the world, apparently (so says the *Guiness Book of World Records*)—and has been called a "space travel machine" by one critic. This author was amazed that it contained the decontamination chamber from the Apollo 11 moon landing. The creator would like to use the erstwhile armaments factory as a sculpture garden dedicated to the munitions industry of the U.S. throughout history; we'll see.

Scenic Drives

A great side trip out of Baraboo is a spin through Devil's Lake State Park and then a trip across the Wisconsin River via the *Colsac II,* one of the last free ferries in the country, operated by the state Department of Transportation. This site has had one form of ferry or another since 1844. Every year beginning in mid-April (until sometime in late fall), the only way to get from the town of Merrimac to Okee is on this 10-car chugger, recently re-outfitted with a new engine and transmission. It goes half a mile in 10 minutes or so, all-day, all-night. If you see flashing lights on the highway approaches, however, drive on; it means the ferry's down.

Enjoy it while you can—this one is loaded with controversy. Plenty of folks in the area would love to ditch the ferry in favor of building a highway bridge nearby. Incessant state and community meetings try to hash out one of five options; three involve keeping the ferry, two involve a bridge only. For now it's a superb memento of bygone days. On summer weekends, you might wait up to an hour or two to cross.

From there, you can head in to the scenic Lake Wisconsin resort area, which stretches 53 miles from Farmer's Bay, south of Portage, to Prairie du Sac. Every species of fish native to Wisconsin is found in the lake, so, needless to say, anglers flock here. Blue highways stretch the length of the river, offering splendid river vistas and access to trim Wisconsin towns. Little **Lodi** is the sleeper of southern Wisconsin, a picturesque off-river town of winding streets, cheery old buildings, and not much tourist traffic. Check out the Downtown Cafe here for classic Americana cuisine. From there, head northwest out of town to **Gibraltar Rock Park** (via, get this, CR J, then CR JV, then CR V, then, somehow, CR VA) and get a bird's-eye view of the Wisconsin River Valley. It's slightly less inspiring than Devil's Lake but has about a tenth of the crowd, if any. Lodi also contains an over-three-mile segment of the **Ice Age National Scenic Trail,** which passes through bluff-view topography (you can see Devil's Lake), a grand overlook, and oak savannahs. Many visitors head south to **Spurgeon Winery,** tel. (608) 929-7692, a.k.a. Bountiful Harvest Champagne Cellars. This is the second location of the winery; the original vineyards are in Highland in southwestern Wis-

consin. The Lodi winery specializes in mead and the labor-intensive *methode champenoise,* which requires each bottle to be disgorged separately. Tours are available; there's a small fee, but wine is at the end. Open daily 9 a.m.-5 p.m. April-Oct., 11 a.m.-5 p.m. the rest of the year.

Another side trip you don't hear about often is a hop east to a countryside park holding what is believed to be the only **man mound** in the world. From Baraboo, take WI 33 to T and Man Mound Road. The park's humanoid effigy mound is 215 feet long and 48 feet wide at the shoulders. Unfortunately, road engineers shaved off parts of the lower extremities around the turn of the century. You can combine this with a trip to the *Colsac II* Merrimac ferry; leaving the park, take Rocky Point Road south for some inspiring scenery in the bluffs of the Baraboo Range. East on WI 33 brings you to Bluff Road, another scenic trip through the South Range of the Baraboo Range leading directly to Merrimac.

Accommodations

Frantique's Showplace, 704 Ash St., tel. (608) 356-5273, is a 25-room Victorian filled to the gills with antiques and assorted nostalgic knick-knacks. Two sleeping rooms are offered, with feather-quilted brass beds; one has a full kitchen. Don't be surprised if you see an old Model T in the front yard. Rates are from $75.

Another interesting B&B is **Pinehaven,** E13083 WI 33, tel. (608) 356-3489, an enormous dwelling out of town atop a rise and near a spring-fed lake. There's also a private guest cottage. Four rooms are available, with rates $79-135.

More everyday lodgings are stretched out along Baraboo's 8th Street (Ringling Avenue), including the **Spinning Wheel Motel,** 809 8th St., tel. (608) 356-3933. The rooms are well kept and fresh, but better is the motel's location—set back off the road a bit. Rates run $55 s, $60 d in high season, much less other times.

More motel lodgings cluster about the highway interchanges to the west of town. The best in town is the **Quality Inn,** US 12W, tel. (608) 356-6422 or (800) 356-6422, with splendid commanding views of the Baraboo Range. A great sun deck supplements the indoor pool, sauna, whirlpool, restaurant, and good location. Rates of $75 s, $80 d are worth it.

Resorts: The family-style **Silverdale Resort,** E11878 CR DL, tel. (608) 356-4004, features five acres of housekeeping cabins and plenty of activities. This is in a good location for accessing Devil's Lake. The lounge/bar of the Silverdale has the best beer selection in the area—almost 100 choices. Rates run $67-90 a night, $300-485 a week. Nearby is **Nordic Pines,** tel. (608) 356-5810, another resort, this one cheaper, which also offers camping. Top of the line is **Devil's Head,** S6330 Bluff Rd., tel. (608) 493-2251 or (800) DEVILSX, in Merrimac, known primarily as one of the larger ski operations in southern Wisconsin. It offers 22 runs, three quad lifts, one triple, and six doubles, in addition to five rope tows. This resort's runs, especially the serious double-diamond run, are the most ego-building. The others are tame but varied enough to make it interesting. The longest run is a two-miler, but the vertical drop is about 600 feet at best. Snowboarders are tolerated. The golfing is excellent. Devil's Head also has all the self-indulgent resort amenities: chalet, condos, upscale motel, hot tubs, lounges, ski center, whirlpool, exercise room, and more. For skiing, it's open weekdays 9:30 a.m.-10 p.m., weekends from 8:30 a.m.; lift tickets are $33 adults, $28 children weekends, less weekdays; add $5 for nighttime skiing. Rentals are $18. Rooms start at $114 in peak periods, down to $70 otherwise.

Food

Baraboo is a city of cafes and diners. Every corner seems to have a classic, small-town eatery reminiscent of the pages of *Roadfood.* The Queen Mother is the **Alpine Cafe,** 117 4th St., tel. (608) 356-4040, in business since 1930. It still has rich woods, hammered-tin ceilings, and carnivorous heartland fare. Open weekdays 6 a.m.-3 p.m., weekends 7 a.m.-1 p.m. Not far away is **Teri's,** 111 4th St. tel. (608) 356-5647, which has the best pancakes anywhere and is known for from-scratch pies. Both have specials from around $3.50. Not far from downtown at 1215 8th St. (in East Baraboo), tel. (608) 356-8254, **Log Cabin** has solid family food at reasonable prices (from $4) daily from 6 a.m. to 10 p.m., including special omelettes and homemade breads.

Folks from the Madison area have always known about the hip Southwestern flavors of the **Little Village Cafe,** 146 Fourth Ave., tel.

(608) 356-2800, long a capital-area staple. Burritos are superb, along with the salads, chickens, assorted chilis, and heavenly stew. Dinner menus are also good, from jerk chicken to superb seafood. Vegetarians are generally able to find something great here. Items from $5. It's open for lunch Tues.-Sat. 11 a.m.-3 p.m. and dinner Thurs.-Sat. 5-9 p.m.

The closest thing to classic Midwestern fare is found at the **Hiway House,** US 12 and WI 33, tel. (608) 356-4147, with prime rib daily, a buffet 4-9 p.m., and a Sunday morning brunch. Items from $6.

South of town along WI 23 is **The Barn,** S5566 WI 123, tel. (608) 356-8320, in a handhewn century-old barn with fieldstone walls. Food ranges from continental to heartland here, and there's a Sunday champagne brunch. Open daily except Monday.

Definitely more upscale is the regional/international creative food at the **Sand County Cafe,** 138 First St., tel. (608) 356-5880, with entrées from $9. The chefs come from other well-known Wisky eateries and the food is excellent. Open Tues.-Sat for lunch and dinner.

Indulge in exquisite upscale dining at the **Sandhill Inn,** 170 E. Main St., Merrimac, tel. (608) 493-2203, a leisurely drive to the south. Madison gourmands flock to this place, a threestory 19th-century Victorian inn (it is also a B&B, but is better known for its food) rich with original beaded oak woodwork and spiral staircase. The menu includes salmon en croute, beef tournedos, and stuffed quail. The cuisine is renowned, but better is the casual feel to the place, a perfect balance of elegance and cheeriness. It's also worth supporting, since the restaurant uses as many locally produced ingredients as possible. It's open Tues.-Sat from 5:30 p.m., Sunday for brunch from 9:30 a.m. From $9.

Shopping

There's genuine Amish furniture at **Simply Amish,** 512 Oak Street, tel. (608) 356-7858, in downtown Baraboo. It also sells quilts, dolls, rag rugs, and basketry. Open Tues.-Sat. 10 a.m.-5 p.m. and, May-Sept., Sunday noon-4 p.m.

Information

The **Baraboo Chamber of Commerce,** tel. (608) 356-8333 or (800) BARABOO, is in a spanking new facility along 2nd St; check its website at www.baraboo.com/chamber.

DEVIL'S LAKE STATE PARK

The diamond-hard, billion-and-a-half-year-old quartzite bluffs of the Baraboo Range tower above a primevally icy lake of abysmal depth. The lake reflects the earthy rainbow colors of the rises—puce to steel to blood red—and mixes them with its own obsidian for dramatic results, to say the least. It's Wisconsin's number-one state park, in constant battle with Door County's Peninsula State Park. Devil's Lake is larger, at over 8,000 acres, and it draws more visitors annually than Yellowstone National Park.

Devil's Lake State Park lies at the junction of three imposing ranges of impenetrable geology constituting the Baraboo Range, formed of compressed silty glacial detritus. The rock-making started some 1.5 billion years ago as rivers fed the glacial lakes; the river deposits and lake wash accumulated millions of tons of sand throughout

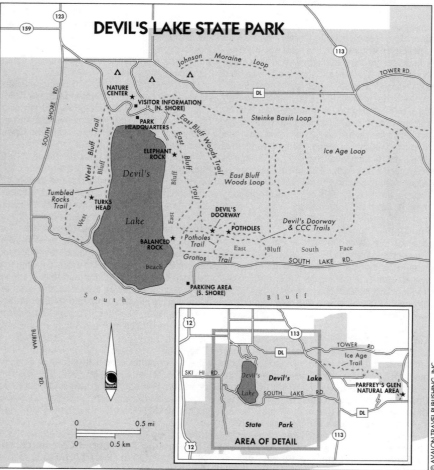

© AVALON TRAVEL PUBLISHING, INC.

the region. The seas retreated, revealing porous sandstone and lower levels of hard quartzite. Eons of hemming and pressure eventually rifted the quartzite into mountain ranges that now make up the park's majestic boundaries. Meanwhile, the interior naturally eroded, creating the Baraboo Valley. Additional flooding and retreating added residual sands and oxidizing coloring elements to stain softer layers.

Once again, glaciers starred in the final act, gouging out the eastern half of the range of hills but stopping just short of the western edge, where a terminal moraine lies today. The Wisconsin Glacier rerouted glacial rivers and gapped the endpoints of the north and south ranges, forming a lakebed, now fed by subterranean springs. The result is one of the most topographically diverse areas of Wisconsin—challenging bluffs adjacent to pastoral dairyland, both next to a tranquil river valley. The natural areas of Devil's Lake are among the most scrutinized by scientists in the state.

Or maybe, as the Winnebago story of the area's formation has it, giant thunderbirds warred with the spirits in the depths of the lake, hurling thunderbolts and dodging the water gods' boulders and water spouts. The battle raged for eons, until the thunderbirds flew away victorious, leaving the rocks and bluffs scarred from battle and the spirits in the depths licking their wounds and waiting.

Human History
The Winnebago Indians were the first known inhabitants of the area, fishing the lake and hunting nearby lowlands; several burial and effigy mounds are still within the park. Steam trains opened up the Devil's Lake region, but development was slow since the recalcitrant Baraboo Range made access difficult. After hacking and blasting through, a minor golden age of hotel building began following the Civil War. While not as extensive as in the Lake Geneva resort area of southeastern Wisconsin, neither was it less posh. Four grand hotels were raised but, due to inefficient train service and unmanageable vagaries of early summer weather, by 1910 resort owners gave up, leaving the lodging business to the more mundane mom-and-pop cottages and minor resorts. In 1911, the land was taken over and made into a state park.

Climate
One revealing aspect of Devil's Lake is how the ranges affect the temperature. It's over 500 feet from the top of the bluff to the lake; the quartzite traps the air and inverts it—warmer air up and cooler air down. Even the flora is affected—more climatically hardened plantlife flourishes at the base of the rises, while easygoing oak and hickory are scattered across the top reaches.

Hiking
The hiking cannot be beat here. Sixteen total miles encompass both the east and west bluffs. The west has only two trails and is a bit easier in grade. **Tumbled Rocks Trail** is a one-miler, easy and partially paved, running along the west shore in and around gigantic quartzite boulders.

On the east bluff, the best trails are the **Grottos Trail,** an easy one-mile skirt of the bottom of the south end of the bluffs; from here, you can connect to the heart-stopping, knee-bending, straight-uphill **Potholes Trail,** one-third of it torture (not for the faint of heart). At the top, you can continue on to favorites like **Balanced Rock** (spectacular views) and **Devil's Doorway,** an easier half-miler across the top of the east bluff. The top of the bluff is skirted by two other trails. Two more trails follow the woodland topography off the bluff (you can combine these). Another good idea is to connect them, then take a leg of the **Ice Age Trail** loop, which you come across; this in turn runs into the **Parfrey's Glen Ice Age Trail.** It may sound like a lot, but if you're in reasonably good shape and push it a bit you could do it in one day. Take water.

Many of these trails are used in winter for cross-country skiing. The **Naturalist Program** leads lots of hikes to the rock highlights as well as Elephant Rock and Cave. Check the schedule in the nature center, north of the park headquarters; the nature center also has displays of the regional geology, Devil's Lake being a prime node on the Ice Age Trail.

Rock-Climbing
The hard quartzite bluffs of the park are ready-made for excellent rock-climbing; it is, in fact, the only designated rock-climbing park in Wisconsin. Offering basic to advanced courses is **Adventures Unlimited,** tel. (800) 247-0176, which also teaches rope rescue classes.

Diving

The name Devil's Lake was applied since no one ever really knew just how deep the foreboding icy lake was. And no one really wanted to find out. If you're interested in plumbing those depths, **3 Little Devils**, S5780 WI 123, tel. (608) 356-5866, is a full-service scuba operation with equipment, training, repair, rental, and air fills. This outfit is also the departure point for three-hour ($23 adults) geologist-led van tours of the surrounding area; they're fascinating, if pricey. Call (608) 833-9446 for details.

Other Tours

Glacier Valley Wilderness Adventures, tel. (608) 493-2075, operates a canoe/kayak tour service in the area; it also conducts Saturday trips to the Wisconsin River ($55), dawn tours (5 a.m.! for $55) of the Upper Wisconsin Dells, and six-day tours to Lake Superior ($600). Basic Devil's Lake tours start at $35 and run Wednesdays 9 a.m.-4 p.m. The company also rents mountain bikes for $15 half-day, $25 full day.

Ice Age Reserve

Devil's Lake is one of nine official reserve segments of the **Ice Age National Scenic Trail.** The nature center has exhibits on the geology of the surrounding area and the trail itself, a moderately difficult four-miler, wooded and grassy, between Parfrey's Glen and the park's 16 miles of trails.

Parfrey's Glen Natural Area

It's astonishing how many people come through Devil's Lake and completely miss this place, not far from the Devil's Lake campgrounds. Thick, moss-covered ridge walls; hushed, damp silence; a creaking boardwalk; gurgling waters—it's all in the state's oldest natural area, four short miles from the perimeter of the park. A quarter-mile trek through a minor canyon, cool and dripping, is all that's required. The site once held a gristmill, built in 1846. Its inheritor, Robert Parfrey, turned the whole thing into a natural area; remains of the mill are still evident by the stream crossings. The area is meticulously studied by research scientists for its dramatic microclimates and oddball geology. Hundred-foot canyon walls are studded with enormous quartzite boulders (which shouldn't be here, having ridden four

miles on glacial wash); the flora consists of hardy northern-clime plants and ferns not found elsewhere in the state.

Camping

For its status as Wisconsin's granddaddy state park, the camping is sadly unimpressive. The three campgrounds have about 425 sites total, but they're little more than open-air sites spread over large expanses of grass, featuring little seclusion and a lot of popularity. Seventy sites stay open in winter. Campsites run $8-12.

REEDSBURG

Slightly off the beaten track 15 or so miles southwest of the Dells stands Reedsburg (pop. 5,834). It is notable for its very attractive downtown of rejuvenated and proud old structures and for being one of the planet's leading buttermakers.

Sights

The **Museum of Norman Rockwell Art,** 227 S. Park St., tel. (608) 524-2123, is a large, complete ensemble of Rockwell's life and work—groaningly sappy or a perfect rendition of small-town life, depending on your perspective. The museum is admirably willing at least to let the myths be disabused—Rockwell had other sides to his commercial art; it's not all rosy and wonderful. The museum is open daily year-round Mon.-Sat. 9 a.m.-6 p.m. and Sunday from 10 a.m. in high season, shorter hours the rest of the year. Admission is $5 adults, $4 seniors, $2.50 12-17, under 12 free.

The Reedsburg Historical Society operates a worthwhile **Log Village Museum,** tel. (608) 524-2807, a few miles east of downtown along WI 33. Eleven buildings dating from the mid 1800s are on-site, including the Oetzman log house, a log cabin, a church, a blacksmith shop, a country store, an apothecary, a one-room schoolhouse, and plenty of memorabilia. Take a stroll around the farm and surrounding wooded land. It's open weekends 1-4 p.m. in summer. Admission is by donation.

View the process of churning out millions and millions of pounds of butter per annum (a million pounds a week) at one of the planet's biggie dairies, **Wisconsin Dairies,** 501 S. Pine St., tel.

(608) 524-2351. It's got a viewing window and is open regular business hours, but it's a good idea to call ahead.

Reedsburg is the southern terminus of the grand 22-mile **400 State Trail,** a multipurpose resurfaced railroad-bed trail spanning from here along the Baraboo River to Elroy, where you can hook up with the Elroy-Sparta Trail for over 100 miles of superlative Wisconsin countryside.

For a great side trip, northwest of town via WI 33 and Woolever Road in tiny Valton is **The Painted Forest,** a venerable old 1890s camp hall. The name comes from the lovely folk art murals painted from 1897 to 1899 by an itinerant landscape painter, Ernst Hupeden. Viewing hours are generally 1-3:30 p.m. each Saturday in summer; call (608) 983-2352 for information.

Practicalities

The town's most complete lodgings are at the **Voyageur Inn and Conference Center,** 200 Viking Dr., tel. (608) 524-6431 or (800) 362-5483, a large facility done up in Scandinavian style. Features include a pool, sauna, whirlpool, and the Garden, one of the better dining rooms around, serving standard supper club fare. Rooms are $57 s, $67 d.

For just eats, try **Endehouse Brewery and Restaurant,** 1023 E. Main St., tel. (608) 524-8600, along the main drag, part of a huge old Victorian-style home. You'll find pub grub to even more creative options for lunch and dinner (from $6).

Services and Information

The **Reedsburg Chamber of Commerce,** tel. (608) 524-2850 or (800) 844-3507, dispenses information at 240 Railroad Street.

PORTAGE

The name says it all. In June of 1673, intrepid Jesuit Father Jacques Marquette, along with Louis Joliet, happened upon the half-mile gap between the Fox River and the Wisconsin River, which empties into the Mississippi in southwestern Wisconsin. The Winnebago had been well aware of the site for centuries, calling it *Wa-U-Na,* "Carry-on-Shoulder."

When trappers and traders began filtering through the new territory, *le portage* became a crucial point in the land-and-water trade routes. By 1828, European settlers decided that the

LINK-UP: THE PORTAGE CANAL

In the early 1800s, travel by water from Green Bay to the Mississippi River was still impossible; goods were hauled by ox-team along a rickety plank road built in the 1790s. A canal was proposed at *le portage,* the half-mile gap between the Fox and Wisconsin Rivers, to open these two crucial waterways in the West to quicker trade and river traffic. Or at least that was the plan.

Machinations on the Portage Canal were underway as early as 1829. And, like other opportunistic ventures of the period, canal-waiters suffered through now-you-see-them canal companies, joint-venture land grants, and general frontier avarice and ineptitude. Finally, in 1848, the state legislature got involved and, with federal monies and land grants, rammed through enough of the project's particulars to get a makeshift canal dug.

Yet at this point, the project was nearly out of money—perfect timing for a financial scandal. The state, mired in debt and fearful of not completing the canal, handed the project to a private investor, whose mysterious golden touch with federal regulators and legislators aroused suspicions. Somehow, by 1851, the canal was nearly finished, though most river traffic still couldn't get through until major—and costly—riverside adjustments were made.

During Wisconsin's financial panic of 1857 the project once again ran out of money. A canal was there, but still no river traffic. Another consortium of interests wrested control of the project but couldn't finish the Herculean task on the Wisconsin River side. Enter—again—the federal government, whose engineers this time frittered away three years and all of the project capital while not one commercial boat passed through the canal.

This comedy persisted until the late 1870s, when enough rough work was done on the Wisconsin side to allow for large transport barges and ferries. Unfortunately, by this time, the railroad had arrived, and the canal's necessity declined. Large pleasure boats mostly used the canal for 75 years, until the locks were filled in to create an earthen dam.

strategic waterways of the Fox River Valley and lower Wisconsin River warranted protection and began stringing forts along the route. Fort Winnebago was raised in 1828, a crucial midpoint between Fort Howard in Green Bay and Fort Howard at the Mississippi River confluence. Jefferson Davis, fresh from West Point, was posted there for a spell.

Sights

A quarter-mile or so east of town and a tight turn off WI 33 onto what must be the state's shortest Rustic Road (less than a mile) stands the **Old Indian Agency House,** tel. (608) 742-6362, opposite the site of Fort Winnebago. The house was built in 1832 for John Kinzie, the federal government's Indian agent with the Winnebago tribe. An enigmatic man, Kinzie spoke virtually every Indian dialect used in the Indiana Territory. The Kinzies must not have been enamored of the house, though extraordinarily plush by frontier standards; they decamped a little over a year after it was built. Juliette Kinzie later wrote a book of modest fame entitled *Wau-Bun,* recounting their tenure in the state. The house is carefully restored and filled with period antiques from the 1830s and earlier. It's open May-Oct. daily 10 a.m.-4 p.m. Admission is $3.50 adults, $1.50 children.

Two miles farther east along WI 33 is the **Surgeon's Quarters,** tel. (608) 742-2949, built during the 1820s and the only extant building from

Fort Winnebago. It once housed the medical officers of the garrison. Noteworthy among the rooms of artifacts and antiques are the original plans for the fort and some papers of Jefferson Davis. A historic school is also at the site. It's open May-Oct., daily 10 a.m.-4 p.m. Admission is $3.50 adults, $1.50 for children.

Downtown at 506 W. Edgewater is **Zona Gale's home,** built by Gale for her parents after her first novel was a success in 1906; she did most of her writing here until she won the Pulitzer Prize, in 1928. There are a few antiques and pieces of Gale memorabilia. It's open by appointment only, tel. (608) 742-7744, and charges a nominal fee.

Recreation

Get detailed instructions from the local chamber of commerce for the **Marquette Trail,** a marked hiking trail following the Fox River between the historic endpoints of *le portage.*

There's decent skiing three miles west at **Cascade Mountain,** W10441 Cascade Mountain Rd., tel. (608) 742-5588 or (800) 992-2SKI. More ambitious attempts at moguls, spread out on some of the 21 runs, are made here than in the lesser half of the state. You'll find more beginner-friendly hills, as well. The longest run is just over a mile, and the vertical drop is 460 feet. Three quads, three triples, and two double chairlifts are available. Snowboarders aren't allowed, at least for now. It's open for skiing weekends 9

old Indian Agency House

a.m.-10 p.m., from 10 a.m. weekdays; lift tickets cost $31 adults, $22 children. Night lift tickets are much less.

Accommodations

The cheapest accommodations (around $30) are found at either the **Lamp-Lite Motel**, tel. (608) 742-6365, fax (608) 742-3781, three miles south of town on US 51, or north of town along US 51 at the **Porterhouse Motel**, tel. (608) 742-2186.

A very well-kept place and the best non-chain option is the **Ridge Motor Inn**, tel./fax (608) 742-5306, two miles north on US 51 (turn onto New Pinery Rd.). The inn features a pool, exercise rooms, sauna, restaurant, and bar with entertainment. Rates from $55 s, $65 d.

Food

Portage has its share of great cafes and diners. **Gramma's Cafe**, corner of E. Cook and Dewitt, has excellent buttermilk pancakes and a classic, rustic interior with glass shelving and original counters. It's open daily 6 a.m.-2 p.m., Friday until 7 p.m.

Another good choice is the classic **Portage Cafe**, 111 W. Cook St., tel. (608) 742-4005, chock-full of memorabilia from its five decades in business. Best spot in town for liver and onions, it's open daily 5 a.m.-5 p.m., Friday until 7 p.m., and Sunday until noon. **The Saloon**, 123 E. Cook St., tel. (608) 742-2277, serves up a blend of gyros, steaks, and lots of sandwiches—croissants to French dips—in addition to Mexican. The place serves breakfast, lunch, and dinner, and a bar is attached.

In one form or another, **Rich's Landmark** 1016 Cass St., tel. (608) 742-2031, has been dishing up food since 1859; it's come a long way since its days as a stagecoach stop. A 16-ounce porterhouse is the king of the menu today, along with a good tenderloin poivrade. Try the Friday fish fry—cod, tilapia, and haddock are featured. It's open Tues.-Sat. from 4 p.m.

The local institution for hearty fare is **Blankenhaus**, 1223 E. Wisconsin St. (right along US 51), tel. (608) 742-7555, the town's unofficial supper club since way back. Heretofore known as The Roost, it's been operated by the same family for the past two decades. There's steak, chicken, and fish on the menu, and lively organ music

some nights. House specials include a sirloin steak topped with sautéed mushrooms, onions, and green peppers, and the German Melt—potato, onion, Bavarian sauerkraut, and German sausage under a glob of melted Swiss and cheddar cheese. Blankenhaus is open for brunch and dinner Sunday, lunch and dinner Tues.-Fri. (with a copious buffet on Wednesday), and dinner only Saturday. Closed Monday.

Services and Information

Portage's **Chamber of Commerce** operates out of a kiosk-size building along the main drag, 301 W. Wisconsin, tel. (608) 742-6242 or (800) 474-2525.

Transportation

The **Amtrak**, tel. (800) 872-7245, Empire Builder train, on its Chicago-Seattle run, makes a stop in Portage on its way to the Dells and from there to St. Paul. Trains leave at 5:30 p.m. from West Oneida Street. East toward Chicago the train stops at 12:25 p.m. It's always good to check ahead for schedule changes.

Mackenzie Environmental Center

Located in Poynette, 12 miles southeast of Portage, is this environmental education center and state of Wisconsin game farm (specializing in pheasant reintroduction). Begun in 1934, the operation is a slick multifaceted conservation institution as available to tourists as it is to specialists conducting research on-site. At the time of updating this edition, plans were underway to open by 2001 a museum dedicated to the oft-overlooked world of conservation game wardens. Yeah, you probably never give these folks a second thought, but they are on the front line of ecological conservation—the under-fire deputies of the environment. The collection, currently held in an extant 19th century barn, is huge and fascinating. A number of hiking trails through disparate ecosystems afford looks at the two dozen species of native state fauna and over 200 species of flora; highlights are the bison, wolves, and eagles. An observation tower provides the best viewing. Located along CR CS/Q, tel. (608) 635-4498, it's open May through mid-October daily 8 a.m.-6 p.m., weekdays only the rest of year. Admission is free.

SAND COUNTY SAGE

There are some who can live without wild things, and some who cannot. . . . Like winds and sunsets, wild things were taken for granted until progress began to do away with them.

—ALDO LEOPOLD, from the foreword to *A SAND COUNTY ALMANAC AND SKETCHES HERE AND THERE*

A quarter-century ago, leading experts on environmentalism were asked to name the most influential work in raising ecological consciousness. The winner was Aldo Leopold's *A Sand County Almanac*, a book that should be required reading for anyone planning a blitzkrieg vacation to Wisconsin's north woods, or for anyone even remotely sympathetic to the natural world. It'll also help you appreciate what might otherwise be dismissed erroneously as central Wisconsin nothing-country.

Aldo Leopold was a seminal naturalist, a pioneering figure in ecology and especially conservation. He introduced the idea of setting aside protected forest land and later devised the concept of wildlife management. Not a native Badger, Leopold nonetheless lived the better part of his life not far from where John Muir grew up—spending years of reflection and following scientific pursuits in south-central Wisconsin. His works, though five decades old, are still among the leading pan-discipline texts. Above all, he was a polished writer, with a lucid, engaging, eloquent style celebrating life and its connection to the land.

Young Aldo

Leopold was born in Burlington, Iowa, in 1887. He was always an avid outdoorsman and displayed a bent for ornithology while still in prep school. His decision to attend Yale was crucial, as its graduate forestry program was ultra-progressive, controversial, and the first of its kind. Also, the United States Forest Service (USFS) was instituted before a skeptical public while he was in school. Upon obtaining his master's degree in forestry in 1909, he went to work for the USFS, educating people on the need to coexist with forests instead of obliterating them in the name of progress.

He was still, though, a man of his times, one who viewed forests as usable and who believed "varmints"—like the wolf—existed solely for eradication. Leopold spent the early part of his career in the American Southwest—the USFS officially established the national forest wilderness system as a result of Leopold's work to establish the Gila River Wilderness. While there, upon looking into the eyes of a wolf he had shot, he realized that everything was interconnected. He would never be the same. He accepted a fortuitous transfer to a new USFS lab in Madison in 1924 and within a few years had revolutionized how we view the natural world. His newfound belief in a cause-and-effect relationship with the land led him to a two-year survey of game in North America and his founding of game management theory.

By 1933, he was named the chair of UW's new game management department. Part of his job was to examine and basically repair central Wisconsin, which had been laid waste during previous generations of misinformed agricultural exploitation.

Sand Country

Wisconsin Sand Country is not a misnomer. It is an area of geological mishmash, a bizarre juxtaposing of native Wisconsin deciduous and coniferous forest and bog with Gobi-esque outwash and genuine dunes, stretching from Portage's confluence of the Fox and Wisconsin Rivers north to the Wausau area, and west to the Mississippi. The region is a variegated dividing line of diverse ecosystems. His tenure oversaw reforestation, wetland restoration, establishment of innumerable state and county forests, game preserves, refuges, parks, and more; he saw life where none had been before.

Sand County Almanac

While covering the region for his work, Leopold finally found the perfect hunting retreat—a horribly dilapidated cowshed—which he dubbed his shack. With his family, he spent most of the rest of his life in examination of the land. Weekend scribblings turned into a determination to nail down the gist of it all. The result is his evenhanded and scientifically pragmatic masterpiece and legacy.

The organization of *A Sand County Almanac* is remarkable in its simplicity and originality. It has three sections: the first a touching month-by-month compendium of land husbandry, generally a reader favorite; the second he calls his scattered musings on natural history topics crisscrossing North America; and the third, aptly titled "the Upshot," outlines what, exactly, we and the land are all about. He sets us up and knocks us down, and we don't know it's coming until it happens. It is for this third section that he is justly famous, setting down what is now referred to as land ethic, the origin of modern-day land-use management—part moral witness-bearing and part reasoned science.

A Sand County Almanac was in essence a florid, cheerful way of describing the symbiotic nature of humans and the land. What we today couch in multisyllabic jargon (biodiversity or ecoawareness), Leopold recognized intuitively. This is not to say Leopold was a grave, somber pessimist, awaiting Mother Nature's vengeance. Part of the appeal of his writing is its simplicity and grace, not to mention a detectable sentimentality sorely lacking in most environmental texts.

Leopold died on April 21, 1948, of injuries suffered while fighting a marsh fire with neighbors. His beloved shack is now on the National Register of Historic Places. His original 80 acres, near Portage, along with 180 more donated over the years, is part of a Leopold Memorial Reserve (surrounding private donated lands raises the total to 1,400 acres), all dedicated to the research and advancement of ecological awareness. He was elected very soon after his death to the National Wildlife Federation's Conservation Hall of Fame.

One fantastic way to get a glimpse of the lands he so adored is to travel **Rustic Road 49,** Levee Road—10 miles stretching along the Wisconsin River between WI 33 and CR T and passing through the Aldo Leopold Reserve.

WISCONSIN RAPIDS

The nucleus of the nation's top cranberry-producing region, Wisconsin Rapids is also a leading reason for Wisconsin's status as the nation's number-one paper producing state. It's a few miles off four-lane US 51, but, tranquil and trim, it's worthy of a side trip, if for no other reason than to enjoy the roadway paralleling the wide Wisconsin River coming in from the south. Show up in autumn for glorious color photo opportunities in the surrounding cranberry bogs.

History
The first sawmills went up more than half a century before the town appeared, as early as 1831. Two communities arose upstream, near the chugging brown cascades—Centralia on the west bank, Grand Rapids on the east. During June 1880, forest fires raged through the area. No sooner had the beleaguered citizenry gone to bed after extinguishing one threatening fire than the Wisconsin River's charming rapids turned ugly, rising 100 feet after midnight and sweeping away much of the downtown area. The hardened residents rebuilt, incorporated as Grand Rapids, and later changed the name to avoid confusion with towns in both Michigan and Minnesota.

Wisconsin Rapids papermaking has always been a linchpin to Central Wisconsin's job force. That confident industry was shaken a bit in 2000, when the town's largest papermaking company was bought out by a Finnish paper consortium, and, though buoyed somewhat by encouraging statements from the corporate head office, the city was eyeing the future somewhat warily.

SIGHTS

The Convention and Visitors Bureau has an excellent fold-out map highlighting three local historical walking tours.

Paper
The major industrial force in Wisconsin Rapids, and still a fundamental reason why the state leads the nation in paper production, is **Consolidated Papers, Inc.,** which has three divisions in the area: the main 4th Avenue plant, a N. Biron Drive division, and, off WI 54, north of Biron, a nice forest. All are open for tours. The main plant, with its overbearing, hulking machinery, offers tours Wed., Thurs., and Sat. at 10

a.m. year-round; minimum age without an adult is 12 years. The Biron division tour is at 2 p.m. Friday year-round. The self-guided forest tour is available all year. For information, call (414) 422-3789.

Georgia-Pacific, 100 Wisconsin River Dr., tel. (920) 887-5076, also operates a plant near here, in Port Edwards, for manufacturing business communication papers. Tours of the mill are offered summers Mon.-Fri. at 1:15 p.m. No unaccompanied children under 12 and none at all under seven are permitted. Call to make sure times haven't changed.

Cranberries

You can tour the post-harvest processing at **Ocean Spray Receiving,** tel. (414) 421-5949, mid-September to early October. Call for more information. Wisconsin Rapids' Convention and Visitors Bureau has a map with its "Cranberry Highways" highlighted; September and October basically comprise a nonstop cranberry festival, with something going down every weekend.

Alexander House

South of Wisconsin Rapids a few miles along WI 54/73, the Alexander House, 1131 Wisconsin

River Dr., tel. (715) 887-3442, is the former residence of a Nekoosa Edwards Paper Co. executive. Now refurbished with original furnishings, it houses a ground-floor exhibit area displaying work of local, regional, and national artists. For a good in-depth view of area history, the second level has the extensive company archives. The holdings are intelligently organized into four theme rooms—lumber, founders, papermaking, and community. Plenty of photographs, too. The house is open Sunday, Tuesday, and Thursday 1-4 p.m. year-round. Free admission.

South Wood County Historical Society Museum

This stately 1907 mansion, at 540 3rd St. S., tel. (715) 423-1580, contains general historical flotsam. But there's some decent area snippets, from cranberry agriculture to a river pilot's raft, children's toy room, a surveyor's display, and the usual schoolroom, general store, and Native American artifacts. The museum is open Thurs.-Sun. 1-4 p.m. from the first Sunday after Memorial Day through Labor Day. Free admission.

Zoo

A small but engaging zoo, the **Rapids Municipal Zoo and Petting Zoo,** 1911 Gaynor Ave., tel. (715) 421-8240, features animals native to the state. The petting zoo is popular with little ones. It's open May 1 through October 15 daily 10 a.m.-8:30 p.m. Free admission.

Side Trips

Eight miles north of Wisconsin Rapids along WI 34 is a religious display nearing overzealousness, the **Rudolph Grotto Gardens and Wonder Cave,** tel. (715) 435-3120, on the grounds of St. Philip's parish. Inspired profoundly by the grotto at Lourdes, the Rudolph Grotto's founder, Father Philip Wagner, vowed to construct one if he recovered from an illness. Evidently, Our Lady responded; Father Wagner began construction in 1928 and worked diligently for 40 years—until his death—to create his dream. The gardens are a hodgepodge of flora and assorted rocks, including a boulder the size of a barn that the priest moved here somehow; the Wonder Cave is a representational collection of kitschy shrines and statues, and is devoted to Our Lady of Lourdes,

that goes on forever. The outdoor religious display and attractive gardens are free and open to the public; the Wonder Cave is open daily in summers 10 a.m.-5 p.m. and costs $2.50 adults, $1.25 teens, and 25 cents for children.

Eight miles south of Wisconsin Rapids is **Nekoosa,** the site of the original settlement along the rapids, dating from 1831. The town has attractive flower gardens, some nature trails, and a summertime Pioneer Festival. Historic Point Basse, located on the east bank of the Wisconsin River just south of Nekoosa, is an old cabin and is thought to date from 1837, probably the oldest building in the county. Many come here to visit **Rainbow Casino and Bingo,** 949 CR G, tel. (715) 886-4560, a 37,000-square-foot facility with 600 slot machines, blackjack, and a decent restaurant.

ACCOMMODATIONS

The local Convention and Visitors Bureau office has a vestibule from which you can make free calls to local places to stay.

Hotels and Motels

Cheapest lodgings are found at the basic but comfortable **Camelot Motel,** 9210 WI 13 S., tel. (715) 325-5111, with refrigerators in some rooms, and a pool. Rates are $35-49. It might be a good idea to spend a few more dollars and head for the large, very clean rooms at the **Chalet Motel,** 3300 8th St. S., tel. (715) 423-7000. Amenities include free continental breakfast and morning paper, a restaurant on the premises, and an adjacent mini-golf course. Rates run $40-45.

Undoubtedly the tops in town is **The Mead Inn,** 451 Grand Ave., tel. (715) 423-1500 or (800) THE-MEAD, in the heart of downtown along the river. Full-service amenities include a health club, lounge, indoor pool, sauna, whirlpool, and the best restaurants in Rapids. Excellent spacious units. Rooms cost $83-98.

Bed and Breakfasts

Sigrid's B&B, 340 Lincoln St., tel. (715) 423-3846, is a 19th-century Colonial Revival done up in a Norwegian theme and has rooms for $65.

Camping

There are no public campgrounds in Rapids. Three are located eight miles south, in Nekoosa, including **Deer Trail,** 665 CR Z, tel. (715) 886-3871, featuring tons of campsites, a private lake, and a heated swimming pool. Sites are $19.

Public camping is also available on the south side of the lake at **South Wood County Park,** five miles southeast along CR W ($11-13); another county park is five miles south of Pittsville on WI 80.

FOOD

Family Dining

Four Star, 2911 8th St. S., tel. (715) 424-4554, a step above the normal family fare (items from $4), specializes in breakfasts but also offers an impressive lists of entrées including excellent steaks. Open daily 6:30 a.m.-10 p.m. **Herschleb's,** 640 16th St. N., is a dairy store featuring homemade ice cream; it's been around since the 1930s.

Supper Clubs and Fine Dining

The Consolidated Papers-owned **Mead Inn,** 451 Grand Ave., tel. (715) 423-1500, and its restaurants are very popular—in part because of an excellent downtown location along the river. Good steaks, seafood, prime rib, and diverse daily specials (items from $5). There's one dining room with excellent Italian cuisine. There's live music Tues.-Sat, and a Sunday brunch.

SERVICES AND INFORMATION

The **Wisconsin Rapids Chamber of Commerce,** 1120 Lincoln St., tel. (715) 423-1830 or (800) 554-4484, www.wisconsinrapidsarea.com, has tourist information. Open daily 9 a.m.-5 p.m.

The *Daily Tribune* is a daily afternoon paper; the same publisher puts out the Central Wisconsin Sunday. Both have news and a smattering of information for travelers.

The **library** is just off the corner of Lincoln Street and Grand Avenue. The **Riverview Hospital** Association, tel. (715) 423-6060, has its main center at 410 Dewey Street.

TRANSPORTATION

No Greyhound service exists in Wisconsin Rapids, but a **shuttle** runs to nearby Stevens Point or Marshfield, departing from in front of the Wood County Courthouse. The shuttle costs $7 and generally leaves around 1:30, but it's a good idea to check first. Call (715) 421-1051.

VICINITY OF WISCONSIN RAPIDS

Castle Rock-Petenwell Flowages

The Castle Rock and Petenwell Dams are consummate examples of why the upper Wisconsin River has been called the "Hardest Working River in the Nation." These two dams—east and southeast of Necedah—created the fourth- and second-largest bodies of water in the state, respectively 23,300 and 32,300 acres. They were the first dams to be built on the sands of the central Wisconsin region. Of the floating-type construction, the dams have cutoff walls that are imbedded deep into the sands, far beyond normal standards, for stability.

Surrounding the two lakes are numerous county parks. Juneau County Wilderness Park on the west side of Petenwell Lake has a wonderful rustic campground with some 140 sites; Castle Rock Park, across the river from Buckhorn State Park, has 300 sites. Camping is also available at the nearby Roche-A-Cri State Park, west 10 miles on WI 21. You can't miss this park; it's dominated by a towering, 300-foot-tall crag jutting from a hill at the base, resulting in a height of over 1,200 feet above sea level. Technically a minor-league butte, it likely has the sheerest grade of any outcropping in Wisconsin. Only 41 campsites are here, so it's fairly quiet. A trail leads to the top of the spire, where outstanding views of the surrounding countryside unfold.

Portions of the Castle Rock dike system are being used as a trout fishery, and the local power company has constructed osprey nesting stands. Petenwell Dam sloughs are a great place to spot bald eagles. East of the Petenwell Dam is the **Van Kuren Trail,** a short multipurpose trail with excellent vistas; to the southwest is the **Petenwell Wildlife Area Hiking Trail,** skirting the shallow southern rim of Petenwell Lake through Strongs Prairie. These and other county parks are accessed along WI 21 and CR Z.

Also check out **Petenwell Rock** on the west bank of the river, the largest rock formation in the region. Apocryphal tales tell of a man who showed up and fell in love with an already betrothed maiden. They both leaped to their deaths rather than lose each other, and the maiden, Clinging Vine, had her spirit returned to this rock, which was named after her lover.

Central Necedah Wildlife Preserve

Sprawling north and west of Necedah and bordered by WI 80 and WI 21 is the stark, moving Central Necedah Wildlife Preserve, almost 44,000 acres of tight, winding dirt path roads that allow up-close glimpses at isolated wildlife and awesome scenery. Once in the confines, you'll understand soon why Native Americans dubbed the area Necedah, "Land of Yellow Waters."

The preserve is essentially what remains of an enormous peat bog—residual glacial Lake Wisconsin—eons ago called the Great Central Wisconsin Swamp. It's now one-quarter wetlands, home to 20,000 ducks and Canada and snow geese, all introduced beginning in the 1950s. The topography is dominated by a few 200-foot sandstone bluffs scattered across a four-county region, with plots of jackpine and scrub oak in the highlands and aspen and scrub willow in the lowlands. A few spiney sandstone ridges run throughout the refuge.

A total of 35 miles of hiking and skiing trails wind throughout the Necedah refuge; two observation towers also double as photo ramps. The 11-mile auto tours outlined in maps obtained from the nature center at the south end of the refuge are good. There's even great berry picking. Be careful while hiking, though; the state reintroduced the eastern massasauga rattlesnake in 2000. The nature center office is open 7:30 a.m.-4 p.m.

Contiguous to the refuge are three national wildlife areas: to the west is Meadow Valley Wildlife Area, bisected by WI 173; north is the Wood County Wildlife Area; and farther north along CR X and bordered to its north by WI 54, is the Sandhill Wildlife Demonstration Area, which houses a fenced-in bison herd, tons of eagles, a 12-mile loop trail, and a 20-mile hiking trail. At-

tempts are being made to reintroduce a native prairie oak savannah. The Sandhill WDA has an outdoor skills center devoted to instruction in game-tracking skills using firearms, bow, or camera. Both the Sandhill and Necedah confines are home to over 700 majestic sandhill and trumpeter swans, the latter transplanted from Alaskan nesting pairs.

Free, very primitive **camping** is allowed two miles west of Sandhill Headquarters in the Wood County Wildlife Area, September 1 through December 31. It is also allowed at the Wood County and Meadow Valley Wildlife Areas during the same times. Summer camping is not permitted. Campers can self-register; you'll need to stop at the nature center first to get specific maps and directions to these way-off-the-beaten-path campsites.

Buckhorn State Park

A perfect example of central Wisconsin Sand Country is this diverse 2,500-acre park located southeast of Necedah on a promontory that juts into the Castle Rock-Petenwell Flowages between the Yellow and Wisconsin Rivers. From the main entrance road, a stunning pulloff and short boardwalk trail lead to what could be the dunes and sandblow of the Sonoran Desert—if it weren't for the evergreens present. A wide array of ecosystems native to the state is protected here, from oak forests to restored grasslands. The park also has prime fauna watching—it's another segment of a crane flyway stretching south to Marquette County. Rare species of turtle can be found along a wonderful interpretive canoe trail in the backwaters; the canoeing overall is superlative here, very isolated and a good gaze into what land looked like a hundred years ago in these parts.

The **camping** is even better because there isn't much. Thus far, the state has resisted organizing a large-scale typical family campground. Primitive and backpack sites—only 20 of them—are the offerings now. Good bets for solitude.

New Lisbon

Due south of the Central Necedah Wildlife Refuge is this pleasant town of 1,491 folks. There's fascinating Native American heritage here: one of the Upper Midwest's largest groups of **effigy mounds** is located south of town off WI

12/16. Even rarer are the **Twin Bluff petroglyphs,** done by early Woodland tribes, west along CR A; hardy hikers can make it up Twin Bluff and to the caverns to check out the Thunderbird etchings. West of town five miles you can pick up the Omaha multi-use recreational trail as it passes through Hustler. Much of the area's history is on display at both the **New Lisbon Library** and **Raabe's Drug Store,** together representing the state's largest private prehistoric Native American artifact collection.

For lodging, your best bet is the **Rafters,** at the junction of I-90/94 and WI 80, tel. (608) 562-5141, a comfortable motor inn with a solid restaurant (gorgeous sandstone walls in the lounge). Rooms run from $40. The city also maintains **Riverside Park,** a clean park with hot showers with campsites with electricity for $9, $6 without. Three miles north of town, **Kennedy County Park** has free overnighting on a first-come, first-served basis.

For food, the venerable **Corner Cafe,** in the 100 block of Bridge St., has been around forever. Two other greasy spoon possibilities are **Grandma's** and **Northwoods Truck Stop,** both on the freeway.

The **Greyhound bus** stops in town at the drug store.

STEVENS POINT

At approximately the halfway point north-to-south in Wisconsin, Stevens Point (pop. 23,000) is a picturesque city spread out along the Wisconsin and Plover Rivers, smack within the fecund "Golden Sands" region, with an inordinate amount of greenspace and parkland.

Gateway to the Pineries

City settlement happened almost accidentally. Starting in 1830, enterprising lumber speculators had been pushing northward from the forts of the lower Fox and Wisconsin Rivers. Lumberman George Stevens temporarily deposited supplies at this spot, later called "the Point," and unwittingly founded the town.

The city wasn't close enough to the timber tracts to experience overnight or sustained boomtown status. By 1850, three years after the first platting of the town, there were only 200 citizens.

Later, sawmills became paper mills, and, blessed with prime agricultural fields surrounding,

the local economy drew more settlers—mainly Polish immigrants.

SIGHTS

Farmers' Market
The oldest continuously operated farmers' fair in Wisconsin is held spring through fall in the public square downtown. The market is open daily from early morning to early afternoon.

Point Brewery
One of the smaller and older (from 1857) breweries in Wisconsin, Point Brewery concocts the beers of choice for many a north woods resident and college student—rivaled only by Leinenkugel's. Brews include the ever-popular Point Special Lager, Bock, Light, Classic Amber, and even Spud Premier (after the region's agricultural heritage). The brews always nail down accolades at the Great American Beer Festival, and a Chicago newspaper called Point the best beer in America. Point is under new ownership and is making overtures to other parts of the country. The tour is still popular. You get a comprehensive peek at Old World brewing in the brewhouse and packing room, and finish up with a soft pretzel and free tasting. Located at 2617 Water St., tel. (715) 344-9310, Point gives tours June-Aug. Mon.-Sat. hourly 11 a.m.-2 p.m.; off-season, Mon.-Fri. at 11 a.m. and Saturday at 11:30 a.m. and 1:30 p.m. The cost is $2.

University of Wisconsin-Stevens Point
The UWSP's Museum of Natural History, adjacent to the Natural Resources building, contains a nationally recognized collection of ornithology. The planetarium, Fourth Ave. and Reserve St., holds regular free (and thus popular) programs every Sunday at 2 p.m. Oct.-May. The Edna Carlsten Gallery in the Fine Arts Center features student and faculty works in addition to rotating visiting exhibits. The Fine Arts Center

also holds regular performances throughout the year and houses a 1,500-piece glass goblet collection. For general information, call (715) 346-4242. When strolling around campus, check out the side of the Natural Resources building, which showcases the world's largest (25 tons of tile) computer-designed mosaic.

Wisconsin Forestry Hall of Fame/Aviary
One of Wisconsin's best environmental resources programs is housed at the UWSP—fitting, since these are the lands immortalized by naturalist Aldo Leopold. Leopold himself is immortalized in a corner of the hall of fame. In addition to the shrine to Leopold, there are exhibits on mammals, fish, turtles, and more. It's in the east lobby of the first floor of the Natural Resources building, tel. (715) 346-4617.

Schmeekle Reserve
Located on the northern edge of the university campus, this diminutive 200-acre tract could be the crown jewel of Stevens Point's already numerous natural sights. Supported by the university as an educational resource, it is an amalgam of pristine ecology with a quarter-mile interpretive trail (and observation tower), fitness trail, and other walking trails through the interspersed wetland, prairie, and woodland topography (the latter features an imposing stand of tall pines). There's even great fishing. The visitor center houses the Wisconsin Conservation Hall of Fame—UWSP initiated the country's first natural resources degree program. Bikes ($10 per day), canoes, boats, snowshoes, skis, and other recreation equipment can be rented at the UWSP's Recreational Services, 401 Reserve St. in the Upper Allen Center, tel. (715) 346-3848. The visitor center is open daily dawn-dusk; the visitor center is open weekdays 9 a.m.-4 p.m. and weekends noon-4 p.m. Free. For information, call (715) 346-4992.

George W. Meade Wildlife Area
Fourteen miles west of town via WI 10, in Milladore, is this prime wildlife viewing area, with

COURTESY OF THE STEVENS POINT BREWERY, STEVEN'S POINT, WI

28,000 acres of wildlife, marsh, and farmland. There are nesting eagles in parts of the preserve, a plethora of mammals, and a few prairie chickens. Over 70 miles of very rough and not-so-rough trails are planned. Free.

Historic and Scenic Tours

The downtown **Main Street Historic District** contains over 60 buildings in the Mathias Mitchell Public Square. A printed guide is available at many locations throughout town for a small fee.

Plenty of natural wildlife tours are available. Five auto or bike tours are detailed in a brochure available from the visitors bureau, 340 Division St. N., tel. (715) 344-2556 or (800) 236-INFO. The area has an abundance of osprey nesting sites, along with bald eagles, waterfowl, and even a few pesky river otters. See Schmeekle Reserve above for bike or canoe rentals.

ACCOMMODATIONS

Stevens Point's motels and hotels are mainly clustered around three areas: the north side of town along Business US 51, near North Point Drive; along WI 10 near the US 51 interchange; and finally, downtown on the long stretch along Church and Water Streets.

Under $50

Cheapest lodging downtown is at the basic but well-kept **Traveler Motel,** 3350 Church St., tel. (715) 344-6455, with large rooms from $35 s. Up the road is the **Point Motel,** 209 Division St., tel. (715) 344-8312 or (800) 344-3093, with clean rooms and a continental breakfast; rooms start at $37 s, $44 d.

To the east, at the junction of WI 10 and US 51 is the **Budgetel Inn,** 4917 Main St., tel. (715) 344-1900, offering good rooms and complimentary breakfast from $37 s, $47 d. Close by is the **Best Western Royale Inn,** 5110 Main St., tel. (715) 341-5110 or (800) 528-1234, with rates from $49.

$50 to $75

A step up in amenities and price is the **Comfort Suites,** 300 Division St. N., tel. (715) 341-6000 or (800) 228-5150, with exceptional decor, rooms varying in size, an indoor pool, exercise room, and more from $65 s or d.

$75 to $100

Still higher in price is the nearby **Holiday Inn,** 1501 N. Point Dr., tel. (715) 341-1340, a Holidome facility with a full range of facilities from $99 s, $109 d.

Bed and Breakfasts

The **Victorian Swan on Water,** 1716 Water St., tel. (715) 345-0595 or (800) 454-9886, is an 1889 pastel beauty full of wood floors, crown moldings, and black walnut. Rooms start at $55.

A slight step up in offerings (not to mention price) is the elegant **Dreams of Yesteryear,** 1100 Brawley St., tel. (715) 341-4525, with a half dozen rooms to choose from. Rates run $58-142.

Camping

The nearest public parks are **Lake DuBay,** tel. (715) 346-1433, northwest off WI 10 onto CR E, and **Jordan Park,** tel. (715) 345-0520, six miles northeast on WI 66. Both have sites for $9-11.

For private campgrounds, **Rivers Edge Campground,** tel. (715) 344-8058, is close to town at 3368 Campsite Drive. Sites begin at $16, but it's open only mid-April through mid-October. To get there, from US 51 N., exit on CR X, then go left on Sunset Dr., and left again on Maple Drive.

FOOD

Breakfast

Very cozy and aesthetically pleasing is the **Wooden Chair** 1059 Main St., tel. (715) 341-1133, a warm and spacious breakfast and lunch eatery downtown. It features open hardwood-floored areas, bookshelves, brick walls, fireplaces, and wide tables with elbow room. The two-buck breakfasts are a great deal. The specials change monthly, and the eggs selection is as diverse as it gets—eggs asparagus to the Banker's Omelette—a green onion-and-potato oddity. Good healthy options, too. It's open 7 a.m.-2 p.m.

Greasy Spoons and Quick Bites

The decor may be atrocious (Chicago Bears memorabilia everywhere, and way too much light blue), but **Al's Diner,** 3324 Jefferson St., tel. (715) 345-2300, is the best diner in town, with terrific French toast and pancakes and specials from $3.

Coffeehouses

The Mission Coffee House, 1319 Strongs, tel. (715) 342-1002, has coffees, beer, soup and salads, pastries, along with poetry readings, open-mic nights monthly, and live entertainment Friday and Saturday. Items from $3.

Brewpub

Point's first and only brewing company and restaurant is **Isadore Street,** 200 Isadore St., tel. (715) 341-1199, with decent pub grub and a small but respectable vegetarian selection. From $5. Open for lunch and dinner daily.

Fish Fries

A great fish fry is off US 51 at the **Hilltop Pub,** 4901 WI 10 E. (Main St.), tel. (715) 341-3037, with outdoor seating and great burgers to boot. This old pub is chock-full of Point memorabilia, including photos and an antique bottle collection. Diners eat on a comfy screened porch. It's open daily for lunch and dinner.

Supper Clubs and American Food

Carnivores will like **Anthony's,** 1511 2nd St. N., tel. (715) 344-5624, home of charcoal steaks and prime rib (Thurs.-Sat.); the house specialty, believe it or not, is a whopping 50-ounce sirloin steak. Items from $6.

An excellent creative eatery with a wide range of regional dishes is the local institution **Silver Coach,** 38 Park Ridge Dr., tel. (715) 341-6588, serving from a turn-of-the-century rail car since WW II. The ribs are killer here, as are the blackened steaks and the seafood. Wisconsin-themed artwork is displayed on the wall. Menu items from $6.

Northwest of town overlooking Lake DuBay is **Antler's Supper Club and Sandbar,** 1126 W. CR DB, tel. (715) 341-7080, featuring steaks, prime rib on Saturday, and a few pasta specials. Friday fish fry, too. From $6. The Sandbar is the lower-level lounge.

Best supper club of all might be the **Red Mill,** 1222 WI 10 W., tel. (715) 341-7714, once just another Point tavern with good food, now trans-

mogrified into the most country-style supper club imaginable (meaning *many* knickknacks and much eye-clutter). It sits in nicely landscaped grounds. The fare runs from excellent walleye to ribs and occasional creative takes on meats or fish. It's open daily except Monday for dinner. From $6.

The local Holidome of Stevens Point has the **Mesquite Room,** Bus. 51 and N. Point Dr., which serves tons and tons of mesquite-broiled baby-back ribs and also offers a dozen different northern Italian pastas. From $5. The Sunday brunch was voted tops in the state by *Wisconsin Trails* magazine readers. Open daily.

Pizza

Mickey's, on 2nd, tel. (715) 344-4843, has Italian, better pizza, and very good steaks, even though it doesn't look like much from the outside.

Asian

A longtime personal favorite is **Tempura House,** offering Japanese and Chinese cuisine in a thoroughly understated atmosphere. It relocated south of Point to Plover, 2529 Post Rd., Bus. US 51 and WI 64, tel. (414) 341-4944. The orange beef is mouth-watering, and there is a lunch buffet. From $5. Closed Monday.

Otherwise, **Hunan's,** 200 Division St., tel. (715) 344-7688, is another Japanese and mostly Chinese restaurant, three blocks south of the Holiday Inn.

German

Bernard's, 701 2nd St. N., tel. (715) 344-3365, the restaurant illuminated by small white lights, has fare ranging from American supper club (steaks and fish) to southern German dishes like veal schnitzel (five schnitzels in all) to a few French specialties. You can even get a "German" pizza with smoked sausage and sauerkraut. Bison is on the menu. Items from $9.

Continental

A historic 1861 dwelling in Plover, **The Cottage** specializes in beef Wellington and walleye pike in a bag, among its continental specialties. In summer, diners can eat on a nice balcony. Located at 2900 Post Rd., Bus. 51 at CR B, tel. (715) 341-1600, it's open for lunch weekdays, dinner nightly. From $7.

Fine Dining

The place to go in Point is **The Restaurant,** 1800 N. Point Dr., tel. (715) 346-6010, the eatery in the labyrinth of the SentryWorld Insurance complex. It is consistently rated as one of the top restaurants in Wisconsin. The Restaurant is actually a dinner-only partner to **Pagliacci Taverna,** featuring an Italian menu. If the food doesn't wow you—eclectic pastas and exquisite meats, including veal that melts in your mouth—the ambience will. It's got incredibly beautiful views, with expansive windows overlooking the oh-so-wide terraced concentric courtyards and a garden; you may even get a gander at wildlife through the windows. Both from $6. Open for dinner only, closed Sunday.

Ice Cream

No food is served here, but classic good times and the real thing are at **Belts' Soft Serve,** 2140 Division, tel. (715) 344-0449.

ENTERTAINMENT AND EVENTS

Bars and Nightlife

A consistent venue for live music—blues and more blues—is **Witz End,** 1274 N. 2nd Dr., tel. (715) 344-9045. Reggae to psychedelic blue-grass to funky folk to delta sweat.

The bars on the square downtown are student-centered; **Buffy's Lampoon** is one of the typical boisterous ones, open weekends only recently. The crowd is young but not necessarily student-aged at the nice **Partner's Pub,** 2600 Stanley on WI 66, the only place guaranteed to have Irish whiskey.

For dancing, **Brickhouse Tavern and Glass Haus Dance Club,** Clark and 2nd, tel. (715) 344-9186, is an all-ages thumping club housed in a 1900s building. There's always something happening at the **Holiday Inn** along N. Point Dr.; Wed.-Sun., "Vegas-style" entertainment is featured, though that can mean a few different things.

Culture

The best place for cultural events is the UWSP, tel. (715) 346-0123, or the **Sentry Theater,** which draws some national and international acts. For schedules and ticket information at the Sentry, call the university box office at (715) 346-4100.

The **Rising Star Mill,** tel. (715) 344-6383, is an 1860s mill in Nelsonville along WI 161 operated by the Portage County Historical Society with occasional poetry readings, concerts, and an art show.

Events

Stevens Point's big event is the annual **Badger State Winter Games,** an amateur Olympic-style games. Point hosts the figure skating competition at the Willett Ice Arena.

On a decidedly weirder note is UWSP's **Trivia Weekend,** held each April. The largest of its kind in the world, this event is a 54-hour, excruciating brain-tease hosted by the university radio station (WWSP 90 FM) and broadcast throughout central Wisconsin. Great fun—and hard as hell.

RECREATION

SentryWorld

The **SentryWorld Sports Center,** 601 N. Michigan Ave., tel. (715) 345-1600, is a highly rated golf and tennis/racquetball center. The golf course at Sentryworld is rated by a variety of sources as one of the best in the country and *the* best in Wisconsin; the trademark hole is the 16th, the "flower hole," adorned with over 90,000 individual plants.

Green Trail

The Green Trail is a fantastic 24-mile multipurpose loop trail that skirts the Wisconsin and Plover Rivers. It takes in many of Stevens Point's natural areas, with superlative vistas of the diverse forest, wetland, marsh, and prairie topography, including the Schmeekle Reserve and Joanis Lake. See Schmeekle Reserve for bike/canoe rentals. There's lots of wildlife and birdwatching. Ten parking areas are interspersed along the trail's length, easiest to access downtown along Main and First Streets.

SHOPPING

The 1100 block of Main Street is one building with nine shops—an antique-lover's heaven. The **Downtown Antique Shops** are open

Mon.-Sat. 10 a.m.-6 p.m. and Sunday noon-4 p.m. A great co-op is the **Stevens Point Area Co-op,** 633 Second Street, tel. (715) 341-1555, with fresh produce and about 500 other things.

Galleries

The **Koerten Gallery,** 2501 Church St., tel. (715) 341-7773, has grown from a small-scale custom framing operation to one of the Midwest's largest galleries, with constant shows featuring regional, national, and international artists. The enormous showcase room contains hundreds of prints along with collectibles too numerous to mention. Open Tues.-Thurs. 9:30 a.m.-8 p.m., Friday until 9 p.m., Saturday until 5 p.m., Sunday noon-5 p.m.

SERVICES AND INFORMATION

The **Stevens Point Area Convention and Visitors Bureau,** tel. (715) 344-2556 or (800) 236-INFO, is at 340 Division St. N., next to the Holiday Inn. The office maintains a 24-hour visitor information line, tel. (715) 341-6566, listing events and activities in Point. Also check the website at www.spacvb.com.

The **post office** is at 1320 Main St., along Smith St., tel. (715) 344-8432.

GETTING THERE AND AWAY

By Air

The **Central Wisconsin Airport** is located in nearby Mosinee, tel. (715) 693-2147, and is served by **Midwest Express,** tel. (800) 452-2022 or (715) 693-2147; **Northwest Airlink,** tel. (800) 225-2525; and **United Express,** tel. (800) 241-6522.

By Bus

The **Greyhound** station is at 1101 1st St., tel. (715) 341-4740. Schedules vary widely, but every major destination within Wisconsin (and most small ones, too) have a daily departure. Several approximate fares (all one-way): La Crosse ($27), Green Bay ($25), Wausau ($10), and Eau Claire ($33).

GETTING AROUND

PointTransit, tel. (715) 341-4490, operates some routes from as early as 6:45 a.m. Line 2 runs to UWSP, lines 3 and 4 pass downtown. The Greyhound station is served by line 5. Fares are $1 adults, 65 cents for children, 50 cents for seniors.

Checker Yellow Cab, tel. (715) 344-2765, is at 233 W. Clark.

MARSHFIELD

The Depression-era WPA guide summed up Marshfield with the line, "The city is sprinkled out on a flat green prairie . . . patterned rigidly as a chessboard, and industries are as diverse as pawns, knights, bishops, queens, and kings." West of US 51, it's also perhaps Wisconsin's most overlooked city. As far as overnight stops go, one could do far worse than this attractive burg (pop. 19,291). State residents associate the city mainly with its cutting-edge Marshfield Clinic, a major medical group practice of some national repute. But there's a whole lot more. Marshfield's livability quotient is always tops in the state and among the top five in the Midwest.

History

It's an All-American town today, cheery and gregarious, almost indescribably wholesome. But it started as a solitary tavern serving the construction workers hacking out trails and tracks through the wilderness. The town also served as the region's top railroad hub. Over 50 trains would stop at the depot.

Then it burned in a great conflagration, the sawmill and lumber piles torched by a fire fanned by a summer wind. Marshfield rose from the ashes and rebuilt with brick and fieldstone. The city is now one of the state's leading dairy research areas and hosts a dairy festival and the Central Wisconsin State Fair, over Labor Day weekend.

SIGHTS

Marshfield Clinic and New Visions Gallery

Not a tour spot per se, this clinic does sport some impressive credentials. One of the leading private group practice medical facilities in the

U.S., with 21 regional Wisconsin satellites, the Marshfield clinic began in 1916 as a dedicated group of six physicians trying to give the rural communities a higher standard of medical care. It now comprises three massive facilities—Marshfield Clinic, Saint Joseph's Hospital (19,000 patients per year), and the Marshfield Medical Research Foundation, a consortium of over 100 research projects. It employs more than 5,000 people.

Adjacent to the clinic, in a space it donated, **New Visions Gallery,** 1000 N. Oak Ave., tel. (715) 387-5562, is an educational gallery; permanent holdings include Marc Chagall prints, West African sculpture and masks, Australian aboriginal arts, Haitian painting, and world folk arts. All media are represented, with temporary exhibits changing every six to eight weeks. Art lectures, artists' receptions, museum tours, and sporadic workshops are also presented. It's open weekdays 9 a.m.-5:30 p.m., Saturday 11 a.m.-3 p.m. Free admission. St. Joseph's Hospital also has a corridor of Wisconsin artists—some 50 are displayed.

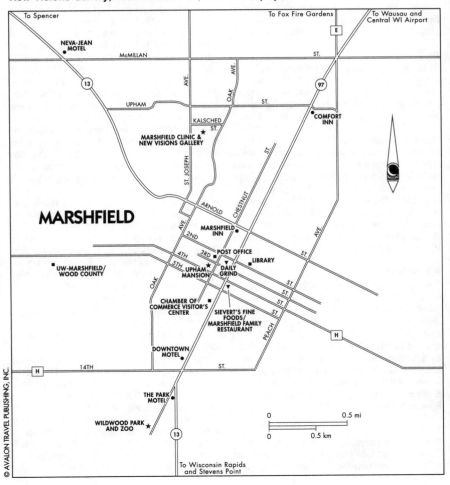

Wildwood Park and Zoo

For a city of Marshfield's size, this zoo is an astonishing feat—60 acres housing 200 species of mammal and bird, in total the fourth-largest zoo in Wisconsin. And expanding! Japanese snow monkeys are the featured attraction, though the grizzlies and bison garner about as much attention. Personal favorites are the rare auodad sheep and timber wolves. The surrounding park also has a swimming pool, walking and ski trails, Frisbee golf, and tennis courts. Located south of the Marshfield business district off 17th St. from Central Ave. S., it's open May 15 through September 15 8 a.m.-8 p.m., closed weekends thereafter. Free admission.

Foxfire Gardens

Japanese Zen design is juxtaposed with English formal garden at Foxfire Gardens, north of town, just west of CR E. Tranquil paths loop the private gardens, which are open May-September weekdays and Sundays noon-6 p.m.

Upham Mansion

This 1880 house belonged to early Marshfield industrialist William A. Upham, who made his capital in local factories before becoming the 18th governor of Wisconsin. The North Wood County Historical Society displays its holdings here. It's done up in period detail; better might be the lovely rose gardens around it. At 212 W. Third St., tel. (715) 387-3322, it's open Sunday and Wednesday only, 1:30-4 p.m. Free admission.

Stierle Bird Exhibit

The subdued Stierle Exhibit, 211 E. Second St., tel. (715) 387-8495, in the Marshfield Public Library, is one of the country's most complete and diverse collections of bird eggs (110 species and 1,900 or so eggs). It also features 140 species of birds (380 birds total), all collected by a local taxidermist and photographer. The library is open Labor Day through Memorial Day, weekdays 9 a.m.-9 p.m., Saturday 9 a.m.-5 p.m., Sunday 1-5 p.m., lesser hours during summer. Free admission.

Side Trips

Eerie silence pervades the **Highground,** Wisconsin's Veteran's Memorial Park located on 100 acres surrounded by one of the largest glacial moraines in the state. A most somber memorial, dominating a central rise, is the Vietnam Veterans' Memorial statue, while a nearby grove of trees forms a five-star pattern, dedicated to sacrifices of families in wartime. Statues to doughboys, wartime nurses, and others are scattered throughout. Most compelling is the Effigy Mound, an enormous dove-shaped earthen mound for POWs and MIAs and all those "prisoners of their own experience." (A similar mound is gradually being constructed in Vietnam by Vietnamese veterans, with the cooperation of Wisconsin vets.) An admirable mixture of flora and sculpture, the park is designed for the sound of wind chimes (many constructed from military hardware) to pervade the entire expanse. Lighted at night, the park is open 24 hours a day, seven days a week. The work is ongoing—future memorials will honor Native Americans and vets of the Persian Gulf War and the Korean War. Some picnic tables are available, and walking trails are constantly being developed. The whole experience is quite moving, particularly at night. Various festivals, including emotional powwows, take place throughout the year. It's located 37 miles south and west of Marshfield, via US 10; follow WI 13 south out of town to reach US 10.

Near Highground is charming little **Neillsville,** which is famed for a huge statue of Annabelle the cow on the east side of town. In town itself is an 1897 reconstructed jail listed on the National Register of Historic Places. Tours ($3) take place Memorial Day-Labor Day Sunday 1-4 p.m. **Wilderness Pursuit,** tel. (715) 743-4484, offers two-hour trail rides ($15) through Clark County Forest land, day-long rides with a steak dinner ($60), and multi-day trips (from $120) with all equipment included.

East of Marshfield is the 31,000-acre **George Meade Wildlife Area,** an excellent place for rustic trail hiking and wildlife watching; it's covered in detail under Stevens Point. Adjacent to Marshfield in the north/northwest is the McMillan Marsh Wildlife Area, with trails for bikes, hikes, and canoes. South of town via WI 13, then north on CR X leads to the 9,500-acre **Sandhill Wildlife Area,** a marshland dedicated to the restoration of sandhill cranes; there are also even a few bison herds. Automobile trails and observation towers make for great wildlife espying.

ACCOMMODATIONS

Under $50
Marshfield's most centrally located lodging is the **Downtown Motel,** 750 S. Central Ave., tel. (715) 387-1111, not far from the CVB office. There's a modest number of rooms, including multi-bedroom family units, kitchen efficiencies, and the basics. Rates run $35-60.

The **Park Motel,** 1806 Roddis Ave., tel. (715) 387-1741, is adjacent to Wildwood Park and the zoo. It offers basic but clean rooms $35-45.

Northwest on WI 13 is the **Neva-Jean Motel,** tel. (715) 387-3731. Here you'll find spartan but adequate rooms from $25; this is definitely the budget choice. Some kitchenettes available.

$50 to $75
North along WI 97, the best option is probably the **Comfort Inn,** 114 E. Upham St., tel. (715) 387-8691 or (800) 228-5150, with a fitness center, indoor pool, sauna, whirlpool, and continental breakfast. Rates run $35-50. Some suites are available for a higher price.

Camping
South on WI 13 is **Praschak Wayside** for basic camping. Thirteen miles south on CR A is **North Wood County Park.** Call City of Marshfield Parks and Recreation, tel. (715) 384-4642, or Wood County Parks, tel. (715) 421-8422 or (800) 422-4541 for rate and permit information.

FOOD

This is another city of cafes. Downtown's **Uncle Bud's Cafe,** 404 N. Central Ave., is a personal fave of the three along Central Avenue, open seven days a week 5:30 a.m.-7:30 p.m. with good homestyle food and even a drive-through. A few blocks away is the **Marshfield Family Restaurant,**. with similar stick-to-your-ribs fare; adjacent is **Sievert's Fine Foods,** with more substantial cuisine. The first two from $3.

Otherwise, get good java (about a million kinds) in a fancy little building at **The Daily Grind,** 230 S. Central Ave. The Grind has a spartan lunch menu to supplement its enormous coffee list and is chock-full of antiques. From $2.

The local supper club is the **Belvedere,** tel. (715) 387-4161, along WI 97 north of town. **Pandy's,** 1414 W. McMillan St., tel. (715) 387-3842, can't figure out if it wants to be a bar or a bistro (it is billed as a sports bar and casually elegant eatery). Whatever the case, some seafood is available here, along with pastas, steaks, veal, and chef's concoctions; it occupies an old cheese factory, so the decor is worthwhile. The lunch buffet is popular. The bar side has pizza, barbecue, and Italian pub grub. Open daily for lunch and dinner, Sunday for brunch. From $4.

ENTERTAINMENT AND EVENTS

The dairy industry is feted the first week of June at **Dairyfest;** mid-July welcomes the annual **Polka Fest;** and over Labor Day the city hosts the **Central Wisconsin State Fair.**

The **Helen Connor Laird Theater,** at the University of Wisconsin-Marshfield/Wood County, 2000 W. 5th St., holds various concerts, chorale performances, films, lectures, and plays throughout the year. Call (715) 389-6500 for information. Marshfield is also the base of the Wood County Symphony Orchestra and Chamber Chorale.

About the only place for live music is **The 9th Hole,** 104 W. 9th St., tel. (608) 384-4087, featuring blues or rock.

Every Saturday mid-April to mid-September, the **Marshfield Super Speedway,** west on CR H, has super stock and street stock car races in the Wissota circuit; there's also modified and some factory stock races.

SHOPPING

One of the country's leading mail-order companies, and likely the top place to sample typical Wisconsin wares, is **Figi's,** 1302 N. Central Ave., tel. (715) 384-1128, doling out cheese and sausage since before WW II.

SERVICES AND INFORMATION

The **Marshfield Chamber of Commerce and Industry,** tel. (715) 384-3454 or (800) 422-4541, www.marshfieldchamber.com, is at 700 S. Central Ave., and open weekdays 8 a.m.-5 p.m.

Check the thin daily *Marshfield News-Herald* for specific community happenings.

The **post office** is at 202 S. Chestnut Ave., tel. (715) 384-2198.

TRANSPORTATION

Marshfield is served by **Greyhound,** 103 W. McMillan St., tel. (715) 387-4030, but there aren't many departures. It's best to call for schedules and times. If you're heading for Wisconsin Rapids or Stevens Point, it'll be courtesy a taxi shuttle ($7 to Rapids or Point). In Stevens Point you can hook up with a proper bus.

Marshfield is also served by four satellite-of-a-major airline link services through the **Central Wisconsin Airport,** in Mosinee (see "Stevens Point," above, for more information).

WAUSAU

Immortalized by Wausau Insurance's television commercials poking fun at its name, the city of Wausau (pop. 37,060) is basically the gateway to the far north woods and Wisconsin's northeastern lakes triangle. It's the last city of any real size all the way to Superior in the northwest. Underrated and unseen by many, it features the mighty Wisconsin waterway and hourglass-shaped Lake Wausau; lots of river and lake walkways are in and around the gentrified downtown. Just south of town, Rib Mountain—for centuries erroneously assumed to be Wisconsin's pinnacle—dominates the topography. The heart of Marathon County, Wausau has become legendary over the past decade for something decidedly unexpected from north-central Wisconsin: ginseng. The county is now the nation's number-one producer of high-quality ginseng, second worldwide only to Korea in exports. Dairying hasn't completely been replaced, however; Marathon County is still number-one in milk and cheese output (colby cheese got its name from a town in this county). Wausau also acts as northern Wisconsin's primary industrial and manufacturing center, with over 160 plants in operation. You'll hardly notice it, though, other than in the occasional sweet smell of paper.

History

There's already a Wisconsin Rapids to the south, but the name might be more appropriate for Wausau—four communities stretched along a segment of roaring Wisconsin River cascades so incessantly punishing they were dubbed by early *voyageurs* Gros Taureau—"Big Bull Falls."

Around 1836, the first well-heeled Anglo speculators began showing up in Wausau, including George Stevens, the same trading tycoon who eventually established Stevens Point to the south. Plank roads were laid almost immediately, connecting the isolated area with regional transportation lines and allowing for the exploitation of the area's staggering wood supply. Within a decade, there was one sawmill for every 100 residents of the city, which was soon refitted with the Native American name Wausau—"Far Away Place."

Rib Mountain

Dominating the terrain—if not the local psyche—is Rib Mountain, for most of the state's history presumed by most to be the highest point in the state. Technically not a mountain, Rib is a 70-billion-year-old quartzite monadnock rising 1,940 feet above sea level and 800 feet above the surrounding peneplain, which, consisting of less-resistant quartz and igneous rocks, eroded around the rise and is now a "rib" of red granite. Though not exactly imposing in height, it's slopes are steep—there's a 1,200-foot rise per mile.

The Depot

The railroad depot now associated with the city of Wausau courtesy of national TV exposure isn't exactly mythical, but some marketing sleight of hand was involved. The ad takes a depot and superimposes it over the Wausau skyline as seen from a different depot. Through nonstop tourist badgering and civic pride, Wausau Insurance—one of the largest insurers in the nation—bought the depot in the commercial in 1977, constructed a replica at corporate headquarters, then donated the building to charity. It still stands at 720 Grant Street. The other, with the skyline, is along Washington Street and houses a travel agency.

SIGHTS

Leigh Yawkey Woodson Art Museum
About the time the international ginseng buyers descend on Wausau, another type of maven—ornithological—is showing up for the internationally regarded early autumn **Birds in Art** exhibition at the Leigh Yawkey Woodson

museum, when the museum rolls out its exquisite and astonishing menagerie of birds in all media. The little museum is in a grand Cotswold-style mansion; the modest holdings use nature and/or wildlife as a predominant theme. The eight to 12 exhibitions each year, plus a steadily growing permanent collection, include rare Royal Worcester porcelain, Victorian glass baskets, and complete multimedia artist collections with birds as the focus. There are also semi-rare porcelain and glass, paintings, and sculptures. The outdoor garden is a sculp-

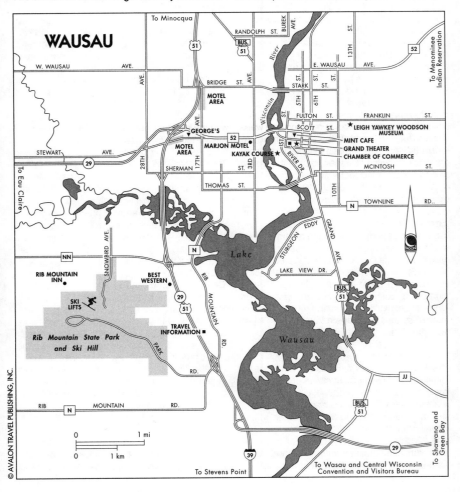

© AVALON TRAVEL PUBLISHING, INC.

ture in permanent progress, with a winding brick pathway cutting through. Located at 700 N. 12th St., tel. (715) 845-7010, it's open daily except Monday 9 a.m.-4 p.m., weekends noon-5 p.m. Free admission.

Marathon County Historical Museum
The progenitor of the Leigh Yawkey Woodson museum once owned the home now serving as the county historical society headquarters. This turn-of-the-century neoclassical mansion remains unaltered for the most part from the outside, and much of the inside is exactly as the Yawkeys left it; only the upper floors change—with revolving exhibits. The lovely formal garden is worthy of a stroll. At 403 McIndoe St., tel. (715) 848-6143, the museum is open Tues.-Thurs. 9 a.m.-4:30 p.m., weekends 1-4:30 p.m. Free admission.

Center for the Visual Arts
Local and regional artwork is displayed in another historic landmark, this one home to the Center for the Visual Arts, 427 Fourth St., tel. (715) 842-4545, a community-oriented arts organization offering courses and exhibits throughout the year. Good for viewing Wisconsin arts. Open daily except Monday 10 a.m.-3 p.m., Sunday 1-4 p.m. Free admission.

Grand Theater
See national performing arts in a painstakingly restored Greek revival opera house and vaudeville venue, the Grand Theater, 415 Fourth St., tel. (715) 842-0988, known for its intricate colonnades and Bedford limestone facade. There's something compelling about seeing irreverent guitarist Leo Kottke performing next to priceless marble statues in an opera house. Call for performances and prices.

Historic District
The lumber wealth of the area went to some superlative use. Over 60 structures of many architectural styles are showcased in a well-planned **walking tour** through part of downtown. The maps are available at the information center or local chamber of commerce, 300 Third St., tel. (715) 845-6231 or (800) 236-WSAU. Prairie school architecture is a dominant theme; also well represented are Greek revival and neoclassical.

The Center
Take WI 29 west to Poniatowski (follow the signs) and at some point you might start feeling some odd twinges inside. It could be you're approaching 45 degrees longitude and 90 degrees latitude—the exact center of the northwestern hemisphere and the midpoint of Greenwich, England, the international date line, the north pole, and the equator. It's well marked with a little park. Then head for local Gesicki Tavern and sign the logbook.

Something Else
Decidedly offbeat is the Salem Lutheran Church's **pipe organ,** designed after a 17th-century Bach favorite. The pipes are German, the intricate oak woodwork from the United States. Contact the church ahead of time and someone will arrange for demonstrations. It makes a lovely sound. The church is at 2822 Sixth St., tel. (715) 845-2822.

Ginseng
This trim, solidly Wisconsin city turns into an ersatz Asian nation come autumn, when buyers from Hong Kong, Taiwan, Korea, China, and all the American Chinese communities converge en masse to begin the cryptic ritual of sorting through the ginseng harvest.

If you're serious about ginseng, contact the **Ginseng Board of Wisconsin,** 1611 Menard Plaza, tel. (715) 845-7000, for details on regional growers and crops. Some offer tours (sometimes for a fee) of operations.

Dells of the Eau Claire Park
A gem by any standard is this Marathon County Park. Officially a state Scientific Area, it's a freak of geology, with striated rock outcroppings and, as the name hints, recessed water valleys with bluffs up to 70 feet high. In parts, the surrealistic rocky surfaces look like hardened cottage cheese. The park has superlative scenery and a segment of the Ice Age Trail to supplement the grand hiking. To get there, head out to CR Y, 15 miles east off WI 29.

Side Trip
Head out of town west along WI 29 some 30 miles and you'll come to little **Colby,** the birthplace of the eponymous cheese. Also of interest

GINSENG: WISCONSIN'S GOLDEN ROOT

Wisconsin may be America's Dairyland, but in the Wausau area, the revered root ginseng is an—if not *the*—economic mainstay. Between 90% and 95% of the United States' ginseng crop comes directly from the somewhat secretive farmers of Marathon County, now the world's fourth-largest ginseng producer at 1.6 million pounds of dried and powdered ginseng annually. Small potatoes? Hardly. Ginseng production can account for up to $90 million a year in Wisconsin coffers. It's now the number-one agricultural cash crop export for the state, most going to Hong Kong.

The Image of Man

Jin chen, ren shen . . . whatever transliteration method you use, "ginseng" means the "root in the image of man" or "man-root." And yes, Asians, primarily from East and Northeast Asia, prize the root. Ginseng's the cure-all for any ailment. The endless list of its functions includes panacea, aphrodisiac, stimulant, memory enhancer.

Ginseng's mysterious qualities work their magic by harmonizing the body's *chi,* that enigmatic life-force or life-spirit. In essence, ginseng preserves the crucial balance of yin (cool, dark, feminine) and yang (warm, light, masculine), as part of a balanced lifestyle. In Asia, you don't simply slam a glass of ginseng daily. It's part of a whole package of life. (And certain personality types—especially "hot" ones—shouldn't drink it at all.)

Ginseng is most highly revered in China and Korea. Legends tell of "mountain ginseng" as being a gift from the gods, caught in a mountain stream through lightning. Koreans say that if a fortunate event occurs in your dreams, you'll find wild ginseng . . . and maybe save someone's life. The Chinese will pay a month's wages for prime ginseng.

Russian scientists have purportedly substantiated Asian claims of ginseng's beneficial effects, but Western scientists remain divided. This mostly stems from lack of research—despite the boom in the popularity of supplements like ginseng, testing lags behind in this country. A stimulant-like effect has been observed on the central nervous and endocrine systems, and it has been shown to affect hormones and decrease blood sugar as well.

The Plant

All ginseng is not the same. All are members of the Aralinceae family, relatives of celery and carrots. Plants are up to two feet high and have five lanceolate leaves—some say it resembles wild strawberry. Ginseng has always grown wild across the eastern half of the U.S. from as far south as Mississippi. Daniel Boone traded it, and John Jacob Astor got his legendary fur company started by dealing it to the Chinese. Native cousins include sarsaparilla and English Ivy.

It's tremendously difficult to cultivate. Cash- and labor-intensive, the root is extraordinarily sensitive to temperatures and susceptible to rot and basically every known pest and blight. One acre can yield a good 2,000 pounds. Unfortunately, however, it takes four seasons to reach maturity—and, once an acre has grown ginseng, it's "dead" for at least another century.

Wisconsin Shang

Ginseng grows best in moderate northern latitudes such as Wisconsin. Known locally as "shang" or "sang," Wisconsin's ginseng *(panax quinquefolim)* is among the most valuable—economically and pharmacologically—in the world. First cultivated by German farmers, it was first commercially raised by a pair of Marathon County brothers around the turn of the century. A select breed of farmer has always been involved—a cliquey bunch, they nonetheless are for the most part cordial in their dealings with the enormously profitable root.

The future of Wisconsin ginseng is somewhat precarious, however. More and more neophytes are plowing under corn to raise the golden root, and this overproduction—along with new competition from British Columbia—has caused prices to plummet from highs of $70 a pound to a recent $15 a pound. Worse, Wisconsin has had to fight piracy of its name by unscrupulous buyers who mix and match inferior Chinese ginseng and label it all as Wisconsin-grown. The state has organized a Ginseng Board to coordinate efforts and smooth out problems.

here is the **Rural Arts Museum,** a weekends-in-summer kind of country museum with an old box factory, a depot, cabins, and more.

ACCOMMODATIONS

Under $50
The closest motel to downtown is the **Marjon Motel,** 512 S. 3rd Ave., tel. (715) 845-3125 or (800) 286-7503, on the west side of the river not too far from the central area. Twenty-six basic rooms, some with kitchenettes, are offered for rates of $33 and up.

The junction of Stewart and 17th Avenues on the west side of town, essentially the interchange of US 51/WI 29 and County 52, has the largest grouping of accommodations. Here you'll find the large **Baymont Inn,** 1910 W. Stewart Ave., tel. (715) 842-0421 or (800) 428-3438, with an indoor pool, whirlpool, and free continental breakfast. Rates are $48 and up.

To the north along 17th Avenue, the **Exel Inn,** 116 S. 17th Ave., tel. (715) 842-0641 or (800) 367-3935, offers 123 rooms (some suites), some with kitchenettes, and a free continental breakfast for basic rates of $38-60.

$50 to $100
The most full-service hotel in Wausau is the **Ramada Inn and Convention Center,** 201 N. 17th Ave., tel. (715) 845-4341 or (800) 754-9728, a sprawling complex of 250 rooms of all types and a restaurant (though no lounge). Also included are a slew of amenities—pools, whirlpool, sauna, recreation room, free breakfast, and more. Rates run $59-189.

Bed and Breakfasts
The **Rosenberry Inn,** 511 Franklin St., tel. (715) 842-5733, is a 1908 prairie school home with elegant stained glass and ornate oak woodworking. There are nine bedrooms total (yes, a big one), a few suites with fireplaces and whirlpools. Rates run $50-155.

Camping
At 1,940 feet, the campground at **Rib Mountain State Park** is unquestionably the highest camping opportunity in Wisconsin. The grounds have a mere 30 sites and, truth be told, privacy

here isn't the greatest. But the view you get after hiking up the seven miles of trails past eons-old quartzite geology sure is killer. A park sticker is required, as is a site fee of $7-11. Get here early to garner a site, since no reservations are taken for this park.

It's worth a drive to **Council Grounds State Park,** 15 miles to the north. There are 55 isolated sites in a heavily wooded park along the Wisconsin River. Not much else is here, but at least the camping's private, in some fairly impressive stands of proud pines.

Otherwise, Wausau has **Marathon Park,** along Stewart Avenue, a seasonal operation (May-Oct.) with 45 sites ($9-11), showers, water, a small museum, and some hiking trails. But this one pales in comparison to **Dells of the Eau Claire Park,** along CR Y, 15 miles east of town, with 25 sites ($6-8), a swimming beach, hiking trails, and some of the most isolated county park grandeur in the state. Definitely worth it.

Rib Mountain
The Rib Mountain area, south and west of Wausau, has the last grouping of lodgings. A topnotch facility is the **Park Inn and Conference Center,** 2001 N. Mountain Rd., tel. (715) 842-0711 or (800) 928-7281, with 120 well-appointed rooms offering myriad options. In addition to an indoor pool, whirlpool, and sauna, you get a putting green! Not to mention a restaurant with a lounge and live entertainment. Rates run $55-109.

A logical choice for skiers (at the base of the mountain) is the **Rib Mountain Inn,** 2900 N. Rib Mountain Way, tel. (715) 848-2802. There are two villas and 25 rooms here, many with balcony views of the mountain; fireplace studios to two- and three-bedroom townhomes are available. Naturally, some ski packages are possible, and golfing isn't far away, either. There's a sauna and picnic facilities. Some rooms have fireplaces, patios, and refrigerators. Rates run $52-145 (expect to see the higher end in winter).

FOOD

Family-Style and Quick Bites
A standing-room-only family eatery, **George's,** 1706 Stewart Ave., next to a service station, tel. (715) 845-7067, has your basic thick dark wood

tables with paper placemats and faded white china coffee cups, as well as a copious menu of dense heartland food (from $4). This is the best (and largest) breakfast in town, with mouth-watering pancakes. An irrepressibly helpful staff. Closed Saturday and Sunday, however.

"Upscale family-style" best describes **2510,** farther west on Stewart Avenue. The huge array of menu items runs the gamut from fresh-cut steaks, prime rib, and chicken to Mexican and Italian (from $5). The place also has its own bakery and deli. Open daily for lunch and dinner; the deli serves up breakfasts. It's at 2510 Stewart Ave., tel. (715) 845-2510.

The excellent **Mint Cafe,** 422 3rd St., tel. (715) 845-5879, on the pedestrian mall downtown, is not as ritzy as its ads imply, but it is clean and cozy. Featured are sandwiches—house special is a rib-eye sandwich—salads, meat-laden entrées, and some lighter fare, along with offbeat specials like lemon-pepper cod (from $4). The real sensations here are the homemade pies. Sit in the garish green booths by the counter; you'll hear the phone ring about a dozen times and the waitress shuffle over and answer by reciting the litany of the day's pie specials. Beer is served here. Open for lunch and dinner.

Just east of the mall at 606 N. 3rd St., the **Back When Cafe,** tel. (715) 848-5668, has healthful sandwiches on homemade breads along with gourmet meals in the evenings (from $4). This is the best local option for vegetarians. Jazz is here Fridays.

The best burgers in town are at the **Scott St. Pub,** 124 Scott St., tel. (715) 842-2424; they even have a great $1 burger special.

Fish Fry
Wausau denizens have more than once voted the fish fry at the **Hiawatha,** 713 Grant St., tel. (715) 848-5166, the best in town. It's also got sandwiches, steaks, salads, and pastas, from $6, and nice outdoor dining.

Supper Clubs and Fine Dining
One of the best-known supper clubs in northern Wisconsin is **Wagon Wheel,** 3901 N. 6th St., tel. (715) 675-2263, a five-decade-old local rustic eatery famed for dry aged steaks, barbecue ribs, and a dripping butterball tenderloin (over three inches thick) from $8; there are also

bison and New Zealand venison from $12. For dessert, the house specialty is flaming Irish coffee. *Wine Spectator* has favorably acknowledged its wine cellar, as well. Homemade everything. Open 5-10 p.m. Closed Sunday.

The most ambitious menu is found at **Gulliver's Landing,** 2204 Rib Mountain Dr., tel. (715) 842-9098, a marine-themed supper club (steaks and seafood) with some excellent Cajun-style entrées from $8. Open daily for lunch and dinner; lunches in summer can be eaten outside on a patio.

Another can't-miss steak and seafood place—with some very nice concoctions thereof—right nearby is the popular **Michael's,** 2901 Rib Mountain Dr., tel. (715) 842-9856, a very subdued, charming place. You'll also find veal and creative pasta concoctions here (from $10).

Italian
By Rib Mountain, **Carmelo's,** 3605 N. Rib Mountain Rd., tel. (715) 845-5570, has a fairly extensive Italian menu, but you can also get a very popular Italian fish fry on Friday. The homemade pasta is good. From $7. Open for dinner daily.

Italian with a great view on a screened porch overlooking the Wisconsin River is found at **Water's Edge,** 150 E. Stewart Ave., tel. (715) 849-9022. From $6.

ENTERTAINMENT AND EVENTS

Live Music
The upper-scale hotels in town have lounges with regular offerings of live music, normally on the easy-listening side. Hands-down the local favorite for live music is the **Scott St. Pub,** 124 Scott St., tel. (715) 842-2424, with folk to blues to reggae. The **Highland Grill,** 2002 Poplar Lane, tel. (715) 848-2900, is a casual cafe with steaks, pastas, a Friday fish fry and Saturday prime rib—along with creative dishes like tequila-sautéed shrimp—but it's also got live music Fridays and Saturdays. The **Back When Cafe** has regular jazz music.

Folk to blues to aggressive rock at **Players,** 4411 Stewart Ave., tel. (715) 842-0306. If you've got time, **The Cellar, Amherst Coffee Company,** 102 S. Main St., tel. (715) 824-2400, in Amherst has well-known alternative, acoustic, and jazz performers in an intimate setting.

Cultural Events

The **University of Wisconsin-Marathon County,** tel. (715) 261-6296, has performances from the drama and music departments, sometimes free. But the local big palace for cultural events is the **Grand Theater,** tel. (715) 842-0988, with Broadway touring shows and other big draws.

Spectator Sports

Minor-league style hardball without the minor leaguers, the **Wausau Woodchucks** are in the Northwoods League, a summertime mélange of college talent. Up to 30 games are played June-Aug. at Athletic Park; tickets are cheap at $5 adults, $3 children and seniors. For information, call (715) 845-5055.

Badger State Winter Games

The amateur-amateur Olympic-style Badger State Games take place at several sites across the region, but the headquarters of the winter games is Wausau. Events over the last week of January and early February include opening ceremonies in Marathon Park, downhill and cross-country skiing, ice hockey, curling, ski jumping, snowboarding, snowshoeing, and speed and figure skating.

Other Events

Wausau's Marathon Park hosts February's **Central Speedskating Championships.** Also of interest is a five-year-old and growing blues festival, the **Big Bull Falls Blues Fest,** in the middle of August.

RECREATION

Skiing

Long thought the highest point in Wisconsin, Rib Mountain was dethroned by Timm's Hill to the east. But that doesn't detract from the skiing—the highest ski hill in the state, it has the second-longest vertical in the Midwest at 624 feet. The longest run is a respectable mile. There are four bunny hills, three intermediate runs, and four challenging black-diamond runs. The hill has two double lifts, one triple, and a tow rope. Snowboarding is

allowed on all slopes. The half-century-old, split-stone chalet is a great place for a rest, with three huge fireplaces and plenty of great city views. The mountain also maintains a well-run ski school and hosts annual USSA freestyle competitions as well as the Badger State Games. Rates for skiing run around $30 for adults and $20 children during peak times (weekends and holidays), up to $10 less off-peak. Hours of operation are Mon.-Fri. noon-10 p.m., Saturday 9 a.m.-10 p.m., and Sunday until 5 p.m. Night skiing is available every night except Sunday. For snow conditions, call (800) 236-WSAU (recording). Note: the hill was recently sold and was going to be renamed, probably to Granite Peak; an $8 million renovation was also planned, so expect higher prices.

Much more basic is the **Sylvan Hill,** in town, with three tiny runs (longest is 1,800 feet) and four rope tows. Some like this hill since it combines cross-country skiing with downhill. On site are both a small chalet and rentals. For details, call (715) 847-5235.

Cross-Country: A personal favorite is the hidden, classical-style **Ringle Trail,** a three-plus mile trail for beginners in isolated hardwood stands east along WI 29, then north on CR Q, and east on Poplar Lane. Another remote trail is **Big Eau Pleine Park Trail;** several loops branch off this seven-miler along the backcountry peninsula jutting into the Eau Pleine Reservoir. Big Eau Pleine Park is fantastic even without the skiing, a densely wooded 1,450-acre promontory full of great trails and lots of isolation. From US 51 south, head west on WI 153 to Eau Pleine Park Road.

A couple of golf courses in town maintain trails; the easiest to get to is the **American Legion Golf Course,** right in town—follow N. 6th St. and then go east.

Kayaking

Lumber boomtowns in the Fox and Wisconsin Riverways notwithstanding, Wausau lays claim to the most persistent set of rapids. No longer powering the mills, the water now attracts thousands of whitewater aficionados and pro kayakers to make use of its downtown, dam-controlled whitewater course in national and international competitions. Not many other cities can brag about a course right through the city, complete with bankside seating. The city's program garnered kudos from the U.S. Canoe and Kayak Team, which has made Wausau its top training site. The Wisconsin River and Lake Wausau are part of a popular water trail; portaging is required. For the very active, a 10-hour trip from Merrill south to Wausau is possible. Contact the visitor information offices for maps and rental locations.

Bicycling

Wausau opened its segment of a new **Mountain-Bay Trail** in 1996. This 83-miler was constructed along the former Chicago and Northwestern Railroad railbed and stretches from Weston to Green Bay. The trailhead begins by the Weston Community Center, 5500 Schofield Avenue. A daily pass ($4) is required and can be obtained at the trailhead.

Outside of Wausau a few miles to the southwest, the county maintains 43 kilometers of off-road trails at **Nine Mile Recreation Area;** the paths double as cross-country trails in winter.

The city Convention and Visitors Bureau produces a fairly complete guide titled *Cycling,* also available at local bike shops including **Free Wheelin' Cyclery and Ski,** 1314 N. 3rd St., tel. (715) 845-2605, which also has rentals.

Snowshoeing

Rib Mountain State Park is one of the few in Wisconsin to offer trails specifically designed for snowshoeing—five miles total. The sport is so popular in the Wausau area you shouldn't have any trouble finding rentals at downtown sporting goods stores.

SHOPPING

Ginseng is widely available in Wausau. There are antiquing highlights here, too—**Rib Mountain Antique Mall,** 3300 Eagle Ave., tel. (715) 848-5564, is the biggie, one of the largest in the state, with some 70 dealers represented. Five miles west along CR U is the **Country Store,** tel. (715) 675-6574, with excellent Shaker furniture.

After visiting the downtown chamber of commerce, most people wander around the Washington Square area, a gentrified red brick zone with piped-in classical music. This is a nice enough way to pass the time, and there are plenty of shops and malls.

SERVICES AND INFORMATION

The local daily is the decent *Wausau Daily Herald;* check the Thursday edition's "Weekend Focus" section for goings-on around town. *City Pages* is a thin but intelligently written free weekly and another good font of information on what's going on around town.

One block west of the downtown chamber of commerce is **Rockwater Cybercafe,** with Internet access.

The **post office** has two locations: 1212 N. 1st, tel. (715) 848-5883, and 300 N. 3rd St., tel. (715) 845-4700.

The local **chamber of commerce,** 300 Third St., tel. (715) 845-6231 or (800) 236-WSAU, is downtown along Washington St., adjacent to the Wausau Center Mall and up on the second floor. Also try the **Rib Mountain Travel Center,** south along US 51 by the Rib Mountain Rd. exit (#188). In 2000 a spanking new **Wausau/Central Wisconsin Convention and Visitors Bureau,** tel. (888) WI-VISIT, www.wausaucvb.org, opened; it's a huge place at exit 185 of I-39/US 51 and is filled with information.

TRANSPORTATION

Air

The Wausau area is served by the **Central Wisconsin Airport** in nearby Mosinee, described in the "Stevens Point" section, above.

Bus

The **Wausau Bus Depot,** 2415 Trailwood Lane, tel. (715) 241-7799, is actually in Rothschild and serves Greyhound and Trailways. Some standard college discounts are offered, with valid ID. Schedules vary widely month to month, so call first.

Around town, the **Wausau Area Transit Authority,** WATS, services Wausau, Schofield, and Rothschild communities. For fare and schedule information, call (715) 842-9287.

Taxi

Taxi service is provided by **Wausau Yellow Cabs, Inc.,** tel. (715) 845-7346.

NORTHEASTERN WISCONSIN

Northeastern Wisconsin shows its true colors cartographically. Often dubbed "The Great North Woods," this region encompasses the majority of the county, state, and federal forest land. Peppered with one of the planet's highest concentrations of glacial lakes, it's of little wonder this area is so heavily frequented by tourists. The northeastern lakes region also has one of the world's highest ratios of lakes to land; 37% of the total surface area is water.

Whether you're on the lakes or in the forest, the region best approximates the "great woods escape" so craved by crazed city-dwellers from the south. Somewhere among the few highways crisscrossing the region is a north-south division oft discussed by Wisconsinites—an ethereal line akin to the Mason-Dixon Line, albeit more benign. It's thought of more as a Thoreau-

esque zone of tranquility. Some have suggested an east-west line through Eagle River. Fine enough, but as a popular Bayfield radio host once said, "Well, we basically consider everything south of US 2 to be Confederate." That's pretty far north.

Wherever you draw the line, the country is all wild escape. Bounded by the equally rustic Upper Peninsula of Michigan, northeastern Wisconsin is full only of people looking for solitude; it has by far the lowest population concentration of any region in Wisconsin. Local populations run in inverse proportion to the saturating numbers of tourists. Two counties, Iron and Florence, are among the least-populated in the entire state; Florence County has precisely zero incorporated towns. Thus, there's a whole lot of there there, to turn a Gertrude Stein-ism on itself.

GREEN BAY TO MARINETTE

Leaving Green Bay, US 41/141 heads due north for 18 forgettable miles before reaching tiny Abrams, where US 41 turns its four-lanes toward Lake Michigan and the Wisconsin-Michigan border at Marinette. Along the way you'll pass a few historical sites and photo ops, but for the most part, the great old lake isn't visible at all. (If you want a lakeside tour, County Highways J, S,

and Y, in that order, really track the lake and still get you almost all the way to Peshtigo.)

OCONTO

Along the way to Marinette, you'll pass through this little (pop. 4,500) community, home to the

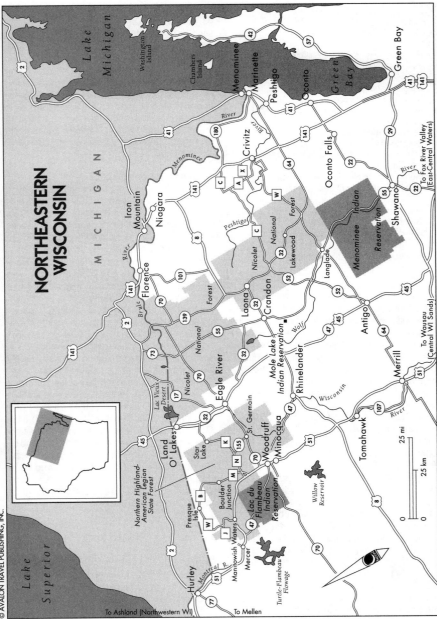

NORTHEASTERN WISCONSIN

NORTHEASTERN WISCONSIN HIGHLIGHTS

Hodags, Rhinelander
Iron County Courthouse, Hurley
John Dillinger's Hideout, Manitowish Waters
Muskie fishing, Boulder Junction
Nicolet National Forest
Northern Highland American Legion State Forest
Parkway Road, Crivitz
Peshtigo Fire Museum, Peshtigo
Piers Gorge and Long Slide Falls, Marinette County
Plummer Mine Headframe, Montreal
Snowmobile Hall of Fame and Museum, St. Germain
Superior and Potato River Falls, Iron County
Turtle-Flambeau Flowage
World Championship Snowmobile Derby, Eagle River
Waswagoning, Lac du Flambeau

Archaic Period's Copper Culture Native Americans five millenia ago, their burial site now a state park. Great Lakes historians debate whether Oconto—not De Pere—actually became the initial settlement site of the St. Francis Xavier Mission in 1669. With the West Main Street Historic District's rich, lumber-era architecture kept spruced up, it's a not-unattractive little town.

Sights

At the corner of Chicago and Main Streets is the first church ever built by the Christian Science religion. Located in the midst of the eye-catching downtown, the **Beyer Home Museum,** 917 Park Ave., tel. (920) 834-2260, is one of many Victorian-style mansions (this one dating from 1868) in northeastern Wisconsin. In addition to the usual artifacts relevant to county history, the annex contains a carriage house bulging with antique (and electric!) vehicles and a spiffy recreation of an 1890s Main Street. The museum is open June 1 through Labor Day (May 1 through October 1 for group tours) Mon.-Sat. 10 a.m.-4 p.m. and Sunday noon-4 p.m. Admission is $3 for adults.

The other draw in town, **Copper Culture State Park,** lies on the north bank of the Ocon-

to River, not far west from the intersection of US 41 and WI 22. Discovered in the 1950s, the site has yielded 45 ceremonial burial sites from 4,500 years ago, during the Old Copper Period. The cultures that developed during this period are of particular archaeological interest, being the first to develop commercial wares (some have been found as far away as New Mexico) and to fashion copper into tools. The park is quite understated (show up in winter and you'll probably be alone) and contains a minuscule museum, staffed on weekends in summer 9 a.m. to 4 p.m.

Accommodations and Food

There are a couple of decent places to stay in Oconto. Right downtown on US 41 by the river is an antiseptically clean **Ramada Inn,** tel. (920) 834-5559, which has singles from $60. Amenities include a jacuzzi, pool, continental breakfast, and morning newspapers by your door.

For campers, the community operates **Holtwood Park,** tel. (920) 834-7732, in the city, with 130 sites, electricity, showers, boat rental, and a sand beach. **Oconto County Parks,** 300 Washington St., tel. (920) 834-6820, issues $10 camping permits for the campgrounds maintained in the county. The North Bay Shore Unit is closest, a handful of miles north of town on CR Y right on Lake Michigan. Along the way, there's great birdwatching at the Oconto Marsh.

There's not much in the way of food in Oconto. If you're up to the drive, 12 miles west in downtown Oconto Falls you'll find the **Falls Restaurant,** 158 N. Main St., tel. (920) 846-8799. This quaint little place has irrepressibly cheery, spitfire-quick waitresses and solid and diverse cafe fare, including real potato pancakes. A good side trip for a drink, **Hunters and Fisherman's Bar,** in Lena, is chock-full of unbelievable taxidermy. While in Lena, stop by the great **Kugel Cheese Store,** too.

PESHTIGO

Sights

The one highlight in town, and it's a good one, is the old church turned into the **Peshtigo Fire Museum,** tel. (715) 582-3244, right on Oconto Ave., a block off the highway. The museum is

THE GREAT PESHTIGO FIRE

October 8, 1871, was quite literally a day from hell. Most of the country woke the following morning horrified at the news of the Great Chicago Fire and the incipient fame of Mrs. O'Leary's cow. But on the very same day, diminutive Peshtigo suffered an even more devastating fire, one most Americans have still never heard of.

By 1871, once-epic tracts of virgin pine forest in northern Wisconsin had been cut over and left to erode. Incessant dry weather gradually sparked repeated minor fires for hundreds of miles around Peshtigo. That October night, several fires merged, and, fanned by unusually hot winds unbroken by standing trees, swept across the new plains.

As the main body of flames joined with smaller fires, a virtual tornado of fire was produced, racing fast enough to destroy outlying villages before anyone realized what was coming. The wall of flame descended on Peshtigo—vulnerable, *wooden* Peshti-

go—and engulfed it seemingly within minutes. Sound asleep in the middle of the night, many of the 2,000 residents never knew what hit them. The fire eventually raged up the Green Bay coast, into Menominee, Michigan, and grazing Marinette, scorching 400 square miles in all.

Every building in the community save one (and a cross in the cemetery) was destroyed. Despite the steaming waters, helpless victims leapt into the Peshtigo River and thereby saved their lives. In Peshtigo alone, 800 (or more) people perished. The total regional death toll has been estimated at 1,200, though no official tally will ever make certain. Whatever the sum, Peshtigo was one of the worst conflagrations in United States history.

Despite the infernal calamity, Peshtigo persevered. Today, it's a sleepy little small town (pop. 3,200) of tight bungalows plunked down beside a meandering river.

---

rather spartan—scant objects survived the furnace heat—but as such is quite a powerful encapsulation of the grim 1871 Peshtigo fire. A few pictures in particular offer a powerful look at the tragedy. There's a somber cemetery adjacent, in which several hundred of the victims are interred. The museum is open daily June through October 8 (the anniversary of the fire) 9 a.m.-5 p.m. and is free.

The **Badger Paper Mills,** 200 W. Front St., tel. (715) 582-4551, offers free 45-minute tours of its facility weekdays June-August.

The **Peshtigo Wildlife Area** is located about six miles southeast on CR BB, on Peshtigo Point.

Accommodations and Food

The little **Drees Motel,** Highway 42 South, tel. (715) 582-2989 or (800) 245-0402, is the only motel in town, offering rooms from $30 d. To camp, **Badger Park,** tel. (715) 582-4321 or 582-3041, is at the north end of Emery Avenue on the banks of the Peshtigo River, west off of US 41. It's open mid-May until the first week of October and costs $6 per site.

Right on US 41, the no-frills **Anderson's Family Restaurant,** is open 24 hours. From $2.

What many consider the best in the county, **Schussler's Supper Club,** a mile west of downtown on CR B, tel. (715) 582-4962, has copious German (real schnitzel) and standard Midwestern fare. Closed Monday, it's open Tues.-Sun. at 5 p.m. From $4.

A very recent addition—and a joy to anyone looking for a break from stick-to-your-ribs heartland cooking—**Nom's Bangkok Supper Club,** 800 French St., tel. (715) 582-0522, is a real-deal Thai restaurant, along the highway on the southern edge of town. Get past the cheesy drink names—Pattaya Sunset—and you'll find admirable atmosphere and food. There is a huge menu offering good prices. The bar is large and a good place for a drink. From $6. Open for lunch weekdays, dinner daily.

Transportation

Believe it or not, there is bus service to this small town. The Green Bay-Calumet (Michigan) White Pine line stops at the Peshtigo pharmacy.

MARINETTE AND VICINITY

MARINETTE

The sister cities of Marinette, Wisconsin, and Menominee, Michigan, flank the Menominee River as it merges into Lake Michigan. The Wisconsin sibling was named for Queen Marinette, the daughter of a Menominee chieftain and the Chippewa-French wife of a local fur trader in the late-18th century. It provides all the incentive the locals need to affix *Queen* to everything, including the city's name.

For a period of six decades beginning in the 1840s, the city served as Wisconsin's lumber hub (producing more white pine than anywhere else in the world). A staggering 10.6 *billion* board feet of timber floated to town down the Menominee River—even more astonishing given the region's pervasive waterfalls.

The lumber boom has long since dwindled (though the industry stubbornly persists), and

the community's base has diversified into retail, services, and tourism, the latter the result of the immense county's recreation opportunities including 250-plus lakes. For sheer number of waterfalls, Marinette County can't be beat.

Sights

For its size and history, there's surprisingly little to actually *do* in the city proper. The **Marinette County Logging Museum,** tel. (715) 732-0831, by the river on US 41 in Stephenson Island Park, contains replicas of two logging camps, a stable, and a blacksmith shop (all done by one dedicated man). One can't help being impressed by the old sled-load of some 50 pine logs out front being consigned and hauled to the mills. The museum is open Memorial Day through Labor Day Mon.-Sat. 10 a.m.-5 p.m. and Sunday noon-4 p.m. (by appointment in October and for special tours). Admission is $1 for adults, 75 cents for senior citizens, and 50 cents for children.

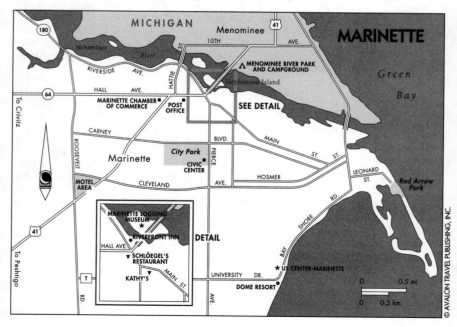

One of the paper industry's giants is in Marinette. **Scott Worldwide,** tel. (715) 735-7510, ext. 2207, 3120 Riverside Ave., offers tours of its mammoth operation June through Labor Day *by appointment* Mon.-Friday. They're free, but some rules hold: no kids under 12, no open-toed footwear, and no cameras.

The area rivers—the Peshtigo and the Menominee—both make for good rafting with some adequate whitewater. Contact the local tourist office or the County Parks Office, tel. (715) 732-7530, for maps and information. Red Arrow Park and Seagull Bar are unspoiled public beach areas not far from town. Seagull Bar is a narrow spit jutting into Green Bay where you're guaranteed tourist-free sunning. To get there, follow Leonard Street east from Ogden Street.

Accommodations

US 41 (Marinette Avenue) on the south side entering town offers the most accommodations. At 1301 Marinette Ave., the **Chalet Motel,** tel. (715) 735-6687, (800) 272-9928 for reservations, charges $30 s, $44 d (good winter rates) and includes free movies.

Right in the heart of downtown, left off US 41 onto Riverside Ave. along the Menominee River, the **Best Western-Riverfront Inn,** 1821 Riverside Ave., tel. (715) 732-0111, offers rooms from $75 s or d, more for an actual river view.

Riverside Avenue is also the site of the attractive **Lauterman Guest House Inn,** 1975 Riverside Ave., tel. (715) 732-7800, with seven exquisite rooms with private baths as well as two whirlpools. Rates are $70 d.

At 751 University Avenue, the **Dome Resort Hotel,** tel. (715) 735-0533, offers quite a bit for $45 s, $50 d, including an indoor pool and miniature golf.

In town, Marinette operates a campground at the **Marinette City Park,** east a few blocks off US 41 along Carney Ave., tel. (715) 732-0558. Sites cost $8 and include showers. Marinette County also runs campgrounds, many near Crivitz, west of Marinette, and some excellent ones near the waterfalls. Contact the County Outdoor Recreation Office, tel. (715) 732-7530, for information.

Food

Marinette is close to yooper country—a yooper would be a resident of Michigan's Upper Peninsula—so pasties, a regional specialty, are pervasive. (Your best bet, though, is to cross into Menominee to sample them.) Across from City Hall is exactly what you'd expect to find in a renovated historic red-brick district—**Kathy's On The Square Bakery and Coffee Shop,** in Dunbar Square. It's got fresh baked goods and good coffee. Hours are daily 7 a.m.-5 p.m. except Saturday 7 a.m.-3 p.m. (closed the first Monday of the month). From $3.

The cheapest eats in town might be at the **Old-Style Deli Counter,** on US 41 (Hall Ave.) after it bears left near the river. Those who crave greasy-spoon eats should head for the **Mickey-Lu Bar-B-Q,** 1710 Marinette Ave., tel. (715) 735-7721, which has been dishing out charbroiled sandwiches for five decades and mixes the best malts. From $2.

Similarly priced but a definite step in another direction, **Memories Restaurant,** 1378 Main St., tel. (715) 735-3348, is a '50s-style diner with a from-scratch menu, including good homemade bread and pie. It opens at 6 a.m. (7 a.m. on Sunday).

Near the US 41 juncture with the river, **Schlöegel's Restaurant,** 1828 Hall Ave., tel. (715) 735-5084, offers lots of good homemade food, especially the New England clam chowder and Swedish fare. From $3. The **Rail House Brewery,** 2029 Old Peshtigo Rd., tel. (715) 732-4646, has a wide variety of continental cuisine along with its own beers. From $5.

Marinette's finest restaurant is **The Flying Dutchman,** 751 University Ave., tel. (715) 732-3930, with a supper-club menu of seafood, chicken, pasta, and, of course, steaks. The bay view is quite nice. From $5.

Services and Information

The **Marinette Chamber of Commerce and Visitor Center,** tel. (715) 735-6681 or (800) 236-6681, www.mari.net/marinette, is at 601 Marinette Ave. in a bright little house open 10 a.m.-5 p.m.

Transportation

There is no more Greyhound service to Marinette; the White Pine service from Green Bay to Calumet, Michigan, stops at the Peshtigo pharmacy, six miles south.

There is no air service in Marinette, but Menominee does serve as a United Express Airlink, with two weekday flights (coming and going) to Chicago and Milwaukee, and three weekday flights to Lansing, Michigan, out of the Twin County Airport, 2801 N 22nd St., tel. (906) 863-1210.

MARINETTE COUNTY

The county seat is most often a base for exploring what people really come for—the waterfalls and other natural areas in the rest of this gargantuan county. One of the largest in the state, it's ensconced between the ribbony Menominee River/Michigan border to the east and the north-to-south demarcation of the Nicolet National Forest.

US 141, running north out of Green Bay to Iron Mountain, Michigan, is the main thoroughfare through the county, but even that has a way-off-the-beaten-path feel to it; nothing approximates a large town along any of the byways. It's a great place to leaf through the priceless county-road Wisconsin Atlas and Gazetteer and nose out all the waterfalls and whitewater photo ops. Besides the hydrophilic recreation, there are some blue-ribbon muskie and fly-fishing waters and the highest concentration of trout streams in the state.

Peshtigo River: Parkway Road

Dropping in latitude faster than any river in the state and featuring one of the longest stretches of active whitewater in the Midwest, the winding Peshtigo River begins in the north-central portion of Wisconsin near Crandon, bisects the Nicolet National Forest, and really gathers steam as it crosses into Marinette County. The river links small communities (and outstanding natural areas) along the way to Crivitz and Peshtigo—the largest towns in the county besides Marinette—before emptying into Green Bay. Best of all, Wisconsin Public Service owns much of the flowage area and keeps it wild, so shoreline visual clutter is kept to a minimum. Four hydroelectric dams, built partially to regulate the water levels in the area, are available for tours and don't detract much from the visual superlatives. To be frank, this stretch isn't much for whitewater aside from the county parks. Unless you're going to experience the river from a raft, the Peshtigo is more accommodating to the fisher along this route. South of Goodman and McClintock Parks, few auto stop-offs offer views of rapids or anything very ambitious—unless you like dams, that is.

Most everything is accessible via officially designated RR 32. Its 26.5 miles start at Good-

PESHTIGO RIVER AND PARKWAY ROAD

man Park Road in the north, thence to Parkway Road, and end at CR W in the south. Three good county parks are passed, along with the Peshtigo and Thunder Rivers and lots of established forest land. The only downside is the egregious plastering of signs along the route.

Note: Marinette County parks charge $1 for a day-pass; these can be used at all parks during a 24-hour period. Camping is additional.

The northwestern section of the county, approximately 20 miles northwest of Crivitz, combines stands of forest, acre after acre of whitewater, and flowages chock-full of fish. Beginning near the Athelstane County Forest Area, the whitewater starts at **Taylor Rapids.** There's camping available here at **Goodman Park** (featuring Strong Falls) as well as farther downstream at **McClintock Falls Park.** Both county parks offer sites for $6. Goodman Park tends to close in spring due to runoff, but the rapids are worth the effort. McClintock Park is actually separated by a couple of miles from the small campground (in a hollow off the road; good waterside sites are somewhat close together and have vault toilets) and feels the most primitive of all the county parks. The river is cut into two, then three ribbony channels around little islets on which stand cairn-like fireplaces, grill rings, and even stone and log shelters. The falls here aren't legendary but they're decent, and you'll often find few folks here.

The river then passes through Wilson Rapids and the river-runner's big-gulp, Roaring Rapids (you won't see it from your car on Parkway Road), before reaching the apex, Caldron Falls and 1,200 acres of flowage deemed Class-A1 muskie fishing. A few state records have been plucked from the area in past years.

After passing **Old Veteran's Lake Campground** (little seclusion and a river view for $6), you'll come to **Twin Bridge County Park.** This is the best spot besides the High Falls Dam to check out the 1,750 acres of blue-ribbon fishing in the High Falls Flowage. The campground has three rings of sites ($6)—avoid those closest to the river and picnic area; head instead for the secluded overlook area. The High Falls area is particularly popular for tourists because of the preponderance of downscale resorts in the area, and the rocky islands and channel formations in the flowage. (Anglers also pull out lunker walleyes with astonishing regularity.)

You'll see more intimidating cascades at Veteran's Falls in **Veteran's Memorial Park,** off Parkway Road along the Thunder River. Steep steps lead to a bridge above the rapids (a good photo opportunity), or clamber down slippery rocks to the lower level. The river's roaring section closes out at Johnson Falls and Sandstone Flowage, a wilderness-quality fly-fishing-only stretch along Medicine Brook.

River Running: The Peshtigo is obviously popular with kayakers, canoers, and rafters, and there are plenty of camping and fishing opportunities. Mapping out the details of the trip is beyond the scope of this book, so in addition to the usual caveat of "know what you're doing before you do it," contact the proper authorities before setting out. The **Marinette County Outdoor Recreation Office,** P.O. Box 320, Marinette, WI 54143, tel. (715) 732-7530, will likely refer you to private area operations. **Kosir's Rapid Rafts,** HCR, Box 172A, Athelstane, WI 54104, tel. (715) 757-3431, and **Thornton's Raft Co.,** HCR 1, Box 216A Parkway Rd., Athelstane, WI 54104, tel. (715) 757-3311, are campgrounds-cum-resorts offering cottages and bars and restaurants, swimming beaches, and the like. Kosir's operates mid-May through September with four trips Saturday and three the rest of the week; prices are $18 per person, $15 on weekdays. They will also take you down the Menominee. Thornton's two-a-day trips mid-May through September increase to three a day during the summer; the cost is $18, and you can get your trip videotaped. (Thornton's is unmistakable for the funky rattletrap gray-and-red schoolbuses running rafters to and fro.) Both operations also offer spring trips for $30.

One hands-on way to get into the water is through the **American Outdoor Learning Center,** P.O. Box 133, Athelstane, 54104, tel. (715) 757-3811, an outdoors-skills organization heavy on whitewater rafting and canoeing, but also into other disciplines as well.

Other Practicalities

The area between Caldron Falls Reservoir and High Falls Flowage will likely have more tourists, as the rock formations and islands along the riverway make popular photo stops. **Eagle Resort,** tel (715) 757-3331 or (920) 437-0831; **Peshtigo River Resort,** tel. (715) 757-3741;

Pine Acres Resort, tel. (715) 757-3894; Popp's Resort, tel. (715) 757-3511 or (715) 757-349; and about a million others are found here also. Most offer boat rentals or fishing, and some rather good deals can be found; Popp's has two-person cottages for $43. Small resorts, restaurants, bait shops, etc., are found all over this area, the only place where the visual litter of touristdom unfortunately takes over. The entertainment runs the gamut from basic country-music-and-fish-fry to world-famous hog wrestling at the Caldron Falls Bar.

Crivitz

It's hard to believe tiny Crivitz (just over 1,000 residents) is the hub of the county. It's the center for supplies and communications in the area, and most resorts use the town as a base. In addition to the usual collections pertaining to early area history, the Crivitz Museum, tel. (715) 854-3278, open May-Oct. Wed.-Sat. noon-4 p.m., features some unique exhibits on the early days of the area's resort industry. On South Avenue off US 141, look for the weathered old buildings standing together, perhaps precariously, a few blocks after the turnoff.

Besides the Peshtigo River resorts and camping areas, Crivitz is the main town for big Lake Noquebay to the east. There's plenty of good fishing, and east of the lake you'll find a state wildlife area and a stretch of county forest. There are also plenty of resorts in the lake area.

If resorts aren't your style, west of town five miles along CR W you'll find the Schaffer Park Motel, tel. (715) 854-2186, in a good location right on the Peshtigo River. Rooms start at $42 (two- or three-night minimum on weekends in summer), and riverside campsites are also offered. The supper club here is also highly touted.

The Peshtigo River Campground, one and a half miles south on US 141, tel. (715) 854-2986, has separate tent sites for $15 and up. Open seasonally. West of Crivitz, take CR X to Boat Landing #3 Rd., take that south to Archer Rd.; there, the High Falls Family Campground, tel. (715) 757-3399, has tent sites for $11-14.

For information on the Peshtigo River area, your best bet is to contact the Crivitz Recreation Association, N9661 Parkway Road, Crivitz, WI, 54114, tel. (715) 757-3651, or (715) 757-3253, for a 24-hour recorded message.

Wausaukee

The nearest community to Newton Lake and Little Newton Lake, Wausaukee has limited tourist offerings. McNeely's Old Store, 723 Main St., tel. (715) 856-5831, right along US 141, predates the roaring '20s. This old-time drugstore still has the old tin roof and original fixtures, along with general-store wares and wizened locals offering tourist information. It closes up tight come winter.

Paesano's Resort, tel. (715) 757-2122, is right on the lake and offers cottages from $45 d up to $315 a week for a six-person cabin. Open year-round. In town, the charming Hotel Wausaukee, 502 Main St., tel. (715) 856-5316, is a century-plus-old clapboard hotel turned into a B&B-style inn, with a lumber industry museum and gallery inside. Rollo's, tel. (715) 856-5966, is an always-packed carnivore's delight; ribs, and lots of them, are the specialty. The Wausaukee Bowl serves up a perch and walleye fish fry.

East of town on the Menominee River, Bear Point Motel and Yacht Club, tel. (715) 856-5092, is notable mainly because it's the "hook-and-line" sturgeon fishing center of Wisconsin. Rooms go from $25 to $40. Tinier yet, little Athelstane, a westward jaunt off US 141 on CR C, has Wolf Rock Resort and Campground, tel. (715) 757-3561, cheap at $5 per site, and also offering cabins.

Pembine/Amberg

North out of Wausaukee are Amberg and Pembine. Amberg's got what many people consider to be the best of the waterfalls in Marinette County. Dave's Falls, south of town on CR V, was named after a 19th-century lumberman who lost his life clearing a logjam in the river.

The Amberg Museum, on CR V, tel. (715) 759-5484, is a better-than-average small-town historical society museum, displaying lumber industry and settler artifacts, along with the town's granite quarrying story, an old fire truck (my favorite), and zillions of excellent photos. It's open Memorial Day through Labor Day Sat.-Sun. and holidays 10 a.m.-2 p.m. and is free.

If camping in the area isn't for you, head to Iron Mountain. But if Pembine's it, the Grand Motel, at the junction of US 8 and US 141, tel. (715) 324-5417, has rooms $28-42. The town's cafe closed up shop, so you're relegated to a local tavern's half-pound burgers or a very nice family restaurant on the north edge of town, offering great daily specials (look for the campground next to it).

Other County Waterfalls

Right in Amberg itself, **Dave's Falls County Park** has a short but steep hoof down to the rapids. According to lore, the falls claimed the life of a lumberman who ventured too far out trying to unsnag a logjam a century ago. Camping isn't permitted here, but just northwest of town on Town Corner Lake (and in the Town Corner Lake Wildlife Area), the **Tranquil Vista Campground,** tel. (715) 324-6430, has tent sites from $6 and hiking trails. This beautiful park offers rock formations adorning the banks and a whole series of rapids, and a few winding trails with enough views to occupy the better part of a couple of hours.

Midway between Amberg and Pembine on US 141 is most folks' favorite area for waterfalls. **Twelve Foot Falls,** tel. (715) 732-7530, offers campsites for $6; banner trout fishing on the Pike River, and access to other great cascades; Eighteen Foot Falls is about a mile away. The problem is, you're going to get lost trying to find them all—Bull Falls, Eight Foot Falls, Horseshoe Falls (great, but really tricky to find), and 12- and 18-Foot Falls. Most—but not all—are reasonably well marked, but only if you approach in one direction. But what the heck, that's what exploring is all about. For a surefire way to get to 12- and 18-Foot Falls, just head to Lily Lake Road off of US 8 and follow the signs down the gravel, dirt, and occasionally paved road.

A personal favorite, Long Slide Falls, is along a leisurely drive northeast out of Pembine on Morgan Park Road. A quarter-mile from the pulloff area, the Pembonwon River is channeled over a 50-foot drop, and the water's great in summer. You can climb down right atop the main roaring channel—magnificent. Smalley Falls is just upstream, but many of the trails are as yet unmarked. A few miles east you'll find **Morgan Park,** tel. (715) 732-7530, a county park with campsites for $8. (If you're coming from Pembine, ignore the larger green highway signs directing you east off the road; continue until you see a tough-to-spot green and white road sign that says "Morgan Park Road"—this leads first to the falls, then to the park.)

The best, or at least most isolated, rapids aren't even in Wisconsin—at least the access road isn't. Journey up the remaining leg of US 141 and just before you reach Niagara, veer onto US 8 and cross into Michigan. Just south of Norway, Michigan, Piers Gorge offers a secluded, fantastic hike alongside the Menominee river, especially early in the morning.

Marinette County Bicycling

Marinette County puts out an excellent, detailed (text and map) brochure on bike routes throughout the county. Routes range from 20 to 50 miles, and if you don't mind a few miles of gravel here and there, you can cool off in all those waterfalls (that's not an official recommendation, mind you). Routes include the very popular **Menominee River Century Loop**—one of the better ones in the Midwest, a 25- to 70-mile route—and the secluded **Pembine/Amberg Loop.** Luckily, most routes traverse only a few miles of stressed-out max-traffic roads. For more information, contact **Marinette County Tourism,** UW Extension-BK, P.O. Box 320, Marinette, WI 54143, tel. (800) 236-6681.

NICOLET NATIONAL FOREST AND VICINITY

The eastern swath of Wisconsin's modestly epic national forest, Nicolet—named for the first intrepid European to arrive in Green Bay in 1634—may appear slightly smaller in size than the western Chequamegon, but is by no means a lesser forest. All things considered, it's very nearly the state's perfect approximation of the "great north woods experience." North to south, the forest abuts the Upper Peninsula of Michigan and stretches south as far as the northwestern tier of Oconto County—some 666,000 acres in all, with 1,300 miles of fishable stream and over 1,200 lakes, many grade A1 for lunkers. These verdant expanses were set aside by the federal government as early as 1933 and the inception of early New Deal works, and just in the nick of time. The Nicolet today encompasses three primitive wilderness areas (some 35,000 acres) holding stands of majestic trees—some just a scant few—that somehow managed to escape logging a century ago; trees 200 to 400 years old are found in the forest.

No exact figures are available, but a personal observation is that the Nicolet National Forest is less cluttered than the Chequamegon. Often the backroads sectors of the forest are absolutely vacant and even on weekends, precious few folks are around. Hike into one of the admirable wilderness areas and you're guaranteed seclusion.

Francophiles and smarty-pants tourists will do the correct local "Nick-oh-LAY" take on the name, as it was affixed after the French explorer. Don't be surprised, though, to hear "Nickle-ETT" from more than a few—mostly puzzled visitors, but I swear I've heard a couple of locals utter it at gas stations.

Cradle of Rivers
The Nicolet has rightfully been given the moniker "Cradle of Rivers," acting as the headwaters (or at least major conduit) for several of the state's renowned wilder rivers, including the Pine, Popple, Pike, Wolf, Wisconsin, and Peshtigo. The more sedate Brule is a canoeist's dream. This forest gave rise to the Wisconsin Wild River System.

Recreation
Over 800 miles of trails wind through the 666,000 acres on 32 trails of varying length. Only one, Lakewood's Maranatha Ski and Horse Trail, is for *neither* hikers nor mountain bikers. Designed predominantly for hikers in the summer and skiers in the winter, more and more miles are being converted for mountain bikes (and there are miles of logging skid roads, old railroad grades, and abandoned truck trails to explore on your own, though no maps have been made showing all of them. No fees are assessed, and access is not restricted as long as you're on national forest lands). Snowshoeing isn't unheard of alongside the trails. Though beyond the scope of this book, the forest does maintain over 500 miles of signed and groomed snowmobile trails, as well as additional hundreds of miles of unplowed off-road terrain. The best thing to do is contact local chambers of commerce, who can put you in touch with area snowmobile aficionados. (Or contact the **Paul Bunyan Rider Snowmobile Club** in Lakewood, 715-276-7539; this number also doles out info on snow conditions on the trails.)

Fishing? With the headwaters of the Wolf River, and the Wisconsin, the lazy Brule, fishy Popple and Oconto, and wild Peshtigo Rivers running through it, Nicolet is an angler's paradise. Everywhere you pull off within the forest's confines you'll find boat landings. Some lakes are non-motorized use only; be certain you know what the restrictions are.

These same rivers also have given rise to an increased interest in canoeing the Cradle of Rivers. Most parts of the Pine and Brule Rivers are good for beginners, as well as part of the Peshtigo segment. More advanced paddlers usually head for the Wisconsin, Deerskin, Popple, Oconto, and Wolf Rivers. The Wolf is nationally recognized for its aggressive fast waters (and thus is better suited for rafts). The closest rentals are in Eagle River at **Hawk's Nest Eagle River Canoe Outfitters,** 6141 WI 70 West, Eagle River, WI 54521, tel. (715) 479-7944 or (800) 688-7471, which also has over-

ICE AGE TRAIL

Serpentining and switchbacking for more than 1,000 miles across the state, north to south to north again, then a sharp bend west, Wisconsin's epic Ice Age National Scenic Trail is a 1,200-mile course skirting morainic topography left behind by the state's four glacial epochs. It's also an ongoing project, started at the grassroots level in the late 1950s and today still being pieced together inch by inch by volunteers. When county chapters have finally cobbled together enough municipal, county, and state forest land with donated private land for right-of-way, Potawatomi State Park in Door County will be linked with Interstate State Park between Minnesota and Wisconsin on the St. Croix National Scenic Riverway via one continuous footpath.

A Geological Primer

Glaciation affected all of the Upper Midwest and Northern Plains, but nowhere is it more exposed than in Wisconsin. Southwestern Wisconsin's Driftless Area is also the only purely unglaciated region on the planet surrounded by glacial till. For two million years, global climatic patterns have shifted wildly between deep-freeze and moderation. Within the periods of plunging temperature, four primary glacial advances penetrated Wisconsin. The ultimate period, the Wisconsin, began 25,000 years ago and crawled across the two-thirds of the state northwest to southeast before pulling back. The glacier's advance wasn't stopped but was redirected a bit by the existent uplands of the state; six lobes were channeled. One, the Green Bay Lobe, with little to impede it, penetrated as far south as Janesville in southeastern Wisconsin. And as they advanced and retreated, the lobes carved, scoured, dug, dropped, filled in, and, in short, cooked up the state's modern topography.

The Ice Age Scientific Reserve

Technically, the trail is but a segment of the Ice Age National Scientific Reserve, established by congressional fiat in 1971 after decades of wrangling by ardent trekker and forward-thinking ecologist Ray Zillmer of Milwaukee. Zillmer's brainchild didn't receive full national park status as he'd hoped, but he did get something truly unique in the national park system—this reserve of nine units statewide, linked by eons of geology. When the reserve was dedicated in 1971, Congress left the trail to be developed locally, which it has been since 1975.

The reserve's nine units are scattered along the advance of the glacial periods and highlight their most salient residuals. Numerous other state and county parks, equally impressive geologically, fill in the gaps, creating a concatenate showcase of geology. Kames, eskers, drumlins, moraines, kettles, and all the glacial effects are highlighted in the units on the east side of the state. From Devil's Lake west, the absolute magnificence of bluffs, dells, and

(continued on next page)

ICE AGE TRAIL

(continued)

gorges carved by meltwaters of the glaciers becomes apparent.

The Trail

At the time of writing, 650 miles of Ice Age National Scenic trails had been established and maintained either by the National Park Service or by county chapters or state parks. The longest established stretches come in the Chequamegon and Nicolet National Forests, along the Sugar River Trail in southwest Wisconsin, through the Kettle Moraine State Forest, and along the Ahnapee State Trail in the Door Peninsula. Certain counties and localities—near Rib Lake, for example—have magnificent stretches. Hiking the whole thing is possible and has been done about a half-dozen times, though it takes about three months and oodles of patience attempting to circumvent cityscapes where particular segments have not yet been opened.

Camping is currently a problem along the route if you're outside an established park or forest. Some managing authorities permit it without hesitation; other places you'll find no spots for too many miles. Do not trespass to camp, or attempts to finish the trail will suffer as private landowners balk at helping inconsiderate trekkers.

Information

Unfortunately, it's difficult to gather information on any of the dozens of trail segments. Writing the National Park Service or the Wisconsin DNR will get you a basic map and that's it. County and local municipal information, or advice on whom to contact at the moment, is available through the nonprofit Ice Age Park and Trail Foundation, which accepts donations of money, land, and time for the trail; contact the organization at 207 E. Buffalo St., suite 515, Milwaukee, WI 53202.

night trips into the Rainbow Flowage and on the Wisconsin River.

Camping

Twenty-two campgrounds are established within the national forest, most in the northern half, fewer in the south around Lakewood. A handful of primitive hike-in sites are found in the wilder regions of the Blackjack Springs and Headwaters Wilderness areas in the Eagle River District and in the Whisker Lake Wilderness in the Florence District. Less ambitious "walk-in" sites are also found at Fanny Lake in the Lakewood District and Perch and Lauterman Lakes in the Florence District. These offer roads ending one-quarter to one-half mile away, and all equipment must be carried in. Best of all, these wilderness and walk-in sites are free, though no water is available. Donations to the walk-in and wilderness sites are optional but a good idea, invaluable for perpetuating these opportunities for others.

Reservations are available at some sites at Franklin Lake campground in the Florence/Eagle River District and Boulder Lake (small and large groups) in the Lakewood District. Depending on the amenities provided in each campground, rates range $8-12. Reservations can be made at

tel. (877) 444-6777 or www.reserveusa.com a minimum of five days prior to arrival and a maximum of 240 days in advance. The fee is $9 in addition to the site fee.

Technically, camping is allowed on any square foot of national land as long as it is federal land and as long as you're 150 feet from water. No fees or registration are required, but common sense and zero-impact camping rules must prevail. Over 250 primitive "dispersed" sites are available if you're leery of crashing through the underbrush and camping with the Sasquatches in the dense forest; contact the appropriate ranger stations for specifics.

Fees

In addition to campsite fees, a $3 parking fee is necessary for boat landings, beaches, trailheads, and some remote campsites.

Information

The Nicolet National Forest is parceled into three districts (the addresses and phone number are listed below, in the individual sections covering each district): Lakewood, Laona, and Florence/Eagle River. Figuring out which area you may be interested in and *then* contacting the nearest ranger station may be worth your while, as the central HQ is somewhat limited in its information distribution. The forest headquarters is located at 68 S. Stevens St., Rhinelander, WI 54501, tel. (715) 362-1300 or TDD (715) 362-1383.

Three-dollar USGS topo maps for all quadrangles of the Nicolet National Forest are available from the main headquarters. The office also has a simpler map designed more for recreational use, also three dollars.

LAKEWOOD DISTRICT

Mountain

A gas station for every member of the community, that's what Mountain feels like. In addition to a garage for the County Highway Department and quite a few boarded-up buildings, Mountain is a good stocking-up spot (at the catch-all general store). Cozy is the **WinterGreen B&B,** 16330 Thelen Rd., tel. (715) 276-6885. Four large rooms, each with private bath and sitting area, are avail-

Mountain fire lookout tower

able in a modern-rustic home set amongst trees. Rates run $65-90. Another B&B option, **Ärhus** (that'd be Danish), 15434 Maiden Lake Rd., tel. (715) 276-6713, also known as the Big House, was built during Prohibition as a hunting lodge. Five rooms share two baths; rates from $65.

Lakewood

Lakewood is but a few souls larger than Mountain but is considered the heart of this district, perhaps because within a short radius of Lakewood are over 60 prime fishing lakes. The only highlight besides the auto tour is a restored 1881 logging camp at McCauslin Brook Golf Club. Apparently, the camp is one of the oldest of its kind in the U.S., though I suspect one in Minnesota may be older. Another unknown sight, the **Woodland Trail Winery,** at Big Hill Road and WI 32, tel. (715) 276-3668, makes wine out of Wisconsin-grown fruit, including some interesting whites. Free tours and samples are available; open daily 9 a.m.-6 p.m.

There are not many places to stay, and five miles east of town along CR F is **Waubee Lodge Resort-Motel, Supper Club and Cocktail Bar,** tel. (715) 276-6091 or (800) 4-WAUBEE, a much better choice than anything in Lakewood. Offering plenty of family-style cottages and, this being northern Wisconsin, even mobile homes. The supper club is particularly popular. Lodging rates run $40-85, with multi-day minimums in summer. A mile south of Lakewood a good supper club, **Maiden Lake Supper Club,** tel. (715) 276-6479, offers a rustic bar next to a fireplace and serves excellent walleye and Angus steaks nightly from 5 p.m.

For information on Lakewood, contact the Chamber of Commerce, 1559 Maiden Lake Rd., tel. (715) 276-6500.

Recreation

Eight trails are scattered throughout the southernmost of Nicolet's districts. A few hardly qualify as hiking experiences. The one-and-a-quarter-mile **Quartz Hill Trail,** south of Carter via WI 32, takes hikers along both sides of the highway up somewhat steep McCaslin Mountain. The trail passes a marker describing the quartz-quarrying operations of early Ojibwa and, on the opposite side, one of the few remaining fire-spotting towers left in the forest. An even shorter hike is the one-mile (or less) **Chute Pond,** south of Mountain on WI 32 for three and a half miles, then west onto Parkway Drive. The short, steep climb rises to a splendid overview offering good views of the surrounding countryside. Boulder Lake Campground also has a flat two-miler, alternating trail and bog boardwalk.

The primary trailhead of **Lakewood Cross-Country Ski Trail** is at McCaslin Brook Country Club, east of Lakewood via CR F. Covering rolling hills for the most part, some areas are for the hardcore. For the Thoreau in all of us, the wondrous **Jones Spring Area,** is a hands-off, motors-off, wild area accessed most easily from CR T, west of Lakewood, to Fanny Lake. These 2,000 primitive acres feature three lakes, overlooks, an Adirondack shelter, pack-in hiking campsites, and wood duck boxes. The wildlife is truly puzzled by the sight of hikers. The **Nicolet Nordic Ski Trail** (actually five loops) is accessed west of Mountain via CR W to McComb Lake Road. Eleven miles of mostly easy terrain make up the trails. **Popple Ridge,** with a trailhead off WI 64 east of Langlade, has 15 miles of old truck trails often used by snowmobiles in winter and hikers in summer. If nothing else, hike the abandoned railroad grade of the Chicago-Northwestern Railroad, 22 miles across the forest.

Of the hiking and skiing trails above, Lakewood and Nicolet Nordic allow mountain bikes. The Boulder Lake Campground Trail does, too, though at two miles it's hard to break a sweat.

Skiers only are allowed on the **Maranatha Ski Trail,** north of Langlade via WI 55, then right two miles down Sawyer Lake Road, featuring four miles of trails for all levels of experience. One section of the trail even crosses Rose Lake, and you had better check the ice before venturing across.

The Wolf River technically does not flow through the Nicolet, but skirts the far southwest boundary. Part of the National Wild and Scenic River System, the river really hasn't gathered kinetic energy in these parts but is still better suited in many places for rafts. Thus, it is a good idea to contact a local raft operator for details. It starts as a minor stream 20 or more miles from the Michigan border on its 200-mile tumble to Lake Winnebago. After joining with another river (around Lily), the Wolf is suddenly transformed into a 150-foot-wide leviathan. A 400-foot drop

over 30 miles doesn't sound like much, until you see it. (For more detail, see the "Shawano" and "Menominee Indian Reservation" sections in the "East Central Waters" chapter.)

Canoeists should be prepared for fairly tame waters until Lily, when things change rapidly. Do not canoe beyond Markton and into the Menominee Indian Reservation without checking local regulations first.

The Oconto River flows through the area, but extended trips should really be tackled only by advanced canoers. The stretch south of Mountain and above Chute Pond alone has 15 rated rapids. Small sections are OK for rafting, canoeing, or tubing, but check with the ranger station for specifics. During low water periods, recommended areas are from CR F downstream to Tar Dam Road and from Chute Pond to Suring. The ranger station has excellent maps and detailed information for each segment of the Wolf and Oconto Rivers. Avail yourself of this information; as the rangers point out, "Many a canoe has been totaled on these stretches."

Almost every lake within the forest confines has an access point, even if it is privately owned. **Archibald Lake,** the largest at 448 acres, features a few islands in the middle. **Fanny Lake** is motor-free, making it popular with canoers. **Sawyer Lake** and **Jessie Lake** are joined by a tranquil channel. **Boulder** and **Maiden** Lakes are smashingly clear all the way to the bottom.

Lakewood Auto Tour

Seventeen highlighted natural and historical points dot these 65 miles in and around Lakewood, Townsend, and Mountain. (Factoring in getting lost, it's a conservative 80 miles, which can be done in one shot, but trying to do it all at once can be hot, dusty, and even a bit tedious.) The local chamber of commerce has detailed maps of the tour, and you'll need one, as driving directions alone would require an entire chapter. It is, happily, well marked by the powers that be, so risk of getting lost has been cut down substantially.

The tour begins at the Lakewood Ranger Station south of Lakewood and proceeds to the north edge of town to Archibald Lake Road. There are signs to the **Cathedral of Pines,** an impressive name for an uninspiring stand of pines—uninspiring on the surface, that is. These trees represent some of the oldest standing wood in the Nicolet, if not Wisconsin, trees left standing from the last century and early part of the 20th century. Even more appealing, around 100 nesting pairs of Great Blue Herons predominate the local region, a rookery.

The **Jones Spring Impoundment** is a rather dull name for an excellent site—a large earthen dam blocking off a creek to form an impoundment and wildlife haven area. Sitting quietly, you might spy wood ducks taking advantage of one of the many wood duck boxes scattered throughout the area.

Right off WI 64, the Natural Red Pines at stop #7 are a stand of impressive, rich red sentinels, interesting as descendants of the seed stock of the forest trees from pre-European days. Most red pines in other places are transplanted.

My personal favorite is stop #9, the **Mountain Fire Lookout.** Go into Mountain on WI 32, left onto CR W, then another immediate left onto Old 32 to the tower. A handful of miles later, actually in the town of Riverview, you'll come to the access road. Along with Carter's, this is what remains of the network of 20 fire-spotting towers throughout the region, built in the 1930s by the Works Progress Administration. For a time, some towers were used as relay stations for the sheriff's department, but eventually all save this one and Carter's were dismantled. The total height of the tower plus elevation is 880 feet—and what a climb it is, eye-popping and creaky in a strong wind—none too comforting.

The **Waupee Flowage,** stop #11, is off CR W and Grindle Lake Road, then down a short trail. It's serene and isolated—you'll likely be alone here—and there are painters' aesthetics and a tranquil platform designed to expedite the nesting of osprey (also drawing bald eagles) and a solitary campsite.

To reach my next personal favorite from Waupee Flowage, head back to CR W, then left on La Fave Road. Turn left onto Holts Ranch Road (the maps say right) to stop #14—the **Logging Camp.** These eerie stone ruins of a late-19th-century logging camp are now choked with weeds and brambles. The camp is in the middle of nowhere and makes a great walk in the late afternoon sun; bring your camera. The white pines across the road were untouched in the last century; as the maps say, "try envisioning an entire state full of them."

After crossing the steel-framed girder bridge spanning the Oconto River, you reach a prime jumping-off spot for hiking the Lakewood Trails, just east of Lakewood.

Camping
Boulder Lake, via CR WW off WI 55 or CR T, is the Nicolet's largest and most popular campground. Its 89 sites are large and, for the most part, secluded. Spread underneath towering thin trees, there are some excellent lakeside sites—24 are reservable. The 362-acre lake has plentiful walleye, northern pike, and bass, and there is a hiking trail through the area.

Boot Lake is approximately half the size and also has nice lakeside sites, though it's not as private as it could be. To get there, take CR T out of Townsend and follow the signs. A hiking trail leads across the highway to **Fanny Lake,** the only developed campground within the Jones Spring Natural Area. The free sites are walk-in only, with no water, and registration is necessary at the Lakewood Ranger Station. The Jones Spring Area is 2,000 acres of semi-wild land. For tranquility, the nonmotorized area is tough to beat.

The most primitive campground, **Bagley Rapids,** south of Mountain along WI 32, has 30 sites and not much else. It's primitive, but great for rafting and canoeing as it's on the Oconto River. All Lakewood campgrounds provide pit toilets only.

Information
The **Lakewood Ranger Station,** tel. (715) 276-6333 or TDD (715) 276-3909, is located on the south edge of Lakewood at 15805 WI 32. Open 7 a.m.-4 p.m. in high season, lesser hours other times.

LAONA DISTRICT

Laona
One rather mundane story explicating this town's name has it that was the name of the daughter of a local businessman (sigh). Unassuming Laona is the first community greeting visitors to the Nicolet via US 8 from the east. The number-one highlight in town is the **Lumberjack Special** at the **Camp Five Museum Complex.** Getting to the museum necessitates clambering aboard a

railway buff's dream—the wheezy old Vulcan 2-6-2 steamer. The center houses a 1900s general store, a main exhibit center full of rail memorabilia, a nature center, a blacksmith's shop, a surrey forest tour operation, and a farm corral (hands-on for the children). Visitors can even buzz through rice banks and a natural bird refuge on the Rat River via pontoon boats. Four departures Monday through Saturday (10:30 a.m.-2 p.m.) mid-June through the last Saturday of August. Museum and train cost $14 adults, $9 ages 13-17, less for younger children. For information, call (715) 674-3414 summer, (715) 845-5544 winter.

Equally impressive, if not a bit somber, the once-majestic **MacArthur Pine** is a 420-year-old white pine that narrowly sidestepped the buzzsaws but has started to show the ineluctable ravages of time. Once much taller (the tallest of its kind in the world at over 165 feet), it's been trimmed down to around 100 feet (losing a few feet every year) by lightning, though it still boasts a 17-foot circumference and some 7,500 board feet of lumber. Located west of Newald off Forest Road (FR) 2167, the drive covers a rutted gravel road—not particularly fun if it's been raining.

The cheapest accommodations in town are the $10 beds at the AYH **Laona Hostel,** right along US 8, tel. (715) 674-2615, with beds for 12 in two dorm rooms. Private rooms are available. Office hours are 8-10 a.m. and 6-11 p.m. Also available are boat rentals, a kitchen, linen rental, and canoe and ski rentals. Reservations are a good idea; no credit cards accepted.

Recreation

One-half mile south of Laona on WI 32, a Civilian Conservation Corps (CCC) trail passes through what's called the Old School Forest. Other minor trails include the **Dendro-Eco Trail,** less than a mile along the Peshtigo River (the trailhead is north three miles via US 8, then east four miles on FR 2131); the **Halley Creek Bird Trail,** off CR H east of Laona via FR 2136, is a one-miler traversing four distinct habitats; the **Knowles Creek Interpretive Trail** is less than a mile along a 200-acre wetlands impoundment. There's a viewing platform and numerous nest boxes and dead trees for cavity-nesting birds; to get there, go east from Wabeno via CR C, and follow the signs.

Popular and easily accessible, the **Laura Lake Trail** is adjacent to the campground of the same name, north and east of Laona 14 miles on US 8, then five miles north on FR 2163. It's just over two miles, but worth it, passing through spinneys of hardwood and hemlock. The **Michigan Rapids Trail** is a pretty hike along the Peshtigo River, bypassing Armstrong Creek. To get to the trail, head north out of Laona via US 8 to FR 2131, then right a half mile on FR 2134.

The only trail in this district for skiers and bikers in addition to hikers is the **Ed's Lake National Recreation Trail,** a six-miler following old railroad grades. One loop features an Adirondack shelter. To get there, follow CR W between Crandon and Wabeno—you can't miss the sign.

One section on the Peshtigo River is prime for beginners: two miles northwest of Cavour you can put in at Big Joe Campground (off WI 139); exit downstream at the Cavour CCC bridge, a trip of some seven and a half miles, and just after the bridge there's a nature trail and primitive campsite. The rest of the river can be challenging and even downright dangerous. Check with the ranger station for water conditions and quality tips.

Camping

The largest and most popular of the district's five campgrounds, **Laura Lake,** is a secluded group of 41 sites nestled between two lakes. There is a two-mile trail encircling one lake, and electric motors only are allowed on the lakes, so peace is somewhat ensured.

In the northwest section of the district, along WI 32 near Hiles, tiny **Pine Lake** has 12 sites along the shore of one of the forest's largest lakes. A sandy beach, great fishing, and low numbers of people make it worth checking out, especially during the week.

Southwest of Wabeno, along WI 52, isolated **Ada Lake** is a peaceful campground of 20 sites, and the trout are plentiful. **Bear Lake,** with its 27 sites, is good for trout fishing on the Rat and Peshtigo Rivers and offers good walk-in sites and great views. The final campground, **Richardson Lake,** four miles west of Wabeno via WI 52, is your standard-issue National Forest Campground. The campgrounds in the Laona district run $8-12.

Information

The **Laona Ranger Station** is along WI 8, tel. (715) 674-4481, Route 1, Box 11B, Laona, WI 54541.

FLORENCE/EAGLE RIVER DISTRICT

Phelps

About the only community of any size in the Eagle River District is **Phelps,** offering, in this author's humble opinion, the best community lakeview in the forest. The town also has perhaps the most quintessentially Wisconsin motel, the **Lakeview,** tel. (715) 545-2101, with 12 clean, understated rooms complete with creaking fans, refrigerators (it is designed for anglers, after all), and a decorating sense straight out of the '50s. Plus, the house mutt, Peabrain, is a treasure. Rooms run $26-45. There's also a dive shop located in Phelps, where the highway bends.

Whatever you do, don't miss the **Lac Vieux Desert,** north on CR E. Muskie anglers go berserk in these waters, haunted by the most ferocious of lunkers. This is also the headwaters of the Wisconsin River.

Florence and Spread Eagle

Spread Eagle sits at the tip of one of the most diverse ecosystems in the state—one of the few remaining plains areas. There is also a small chain of nine lakes, reportedly frequented by Al Capone and other nefarious underworld figures during Prohibition. On US 2/141, actually closer to Florence, you'll find **The Chuck Wagon,** tel. (715) 696-6220, a rustic log structure once part of the northland's tourist camp network and now a rustic tavern and eatery, open daily for lunch and dinner. Florence, the underpopulated county's seat, has a worthy B&B that seems to have been renovated right out of an old motel building, as well as one of the smallest, oldest, and not-to-be-messed-with county jails in Wisconsin—a scant 24 by 30 feet—built like a tomb in 1889 and now on the National Register of Historic Places. Self-guided tours of the jail and the stately courthouse are available. Keyes Peak Ski Hill is

west of town, and there's a superlative view of the area from a pulloff along the way. The ski hill, tel. (715) 528-3207 or (715) 528-3228, has four runs; the longest is 1,750 feet and drops 250 feet. One rope tow and one chairlift carry skiers up the mountain. Rentals, instruction, and cross-country skiing are other options. Open Friday noon-9 p.m. and weekends 10 a.m.-9 p.m.

Scenic Drive

Officially designated Wisconsin Rustic Road #34 departs Alvin and traverses portions of Lakeview Drive, Carey Dam Road, and Fishel Road. There's nothing breathtaking along the nearly nine-mile route, but it's secluded and a nice northern forest experience on the whole. The road is unpaved and narrow as hell, so take it easy—especially when the trees seriously crowd the road and vision is obstructed.

Recreation: Florence Area

Besides the Eagle River district, the Florence district offers the most recreational opportunities, including trails and isolated backwoods logging roads, and a personal favorite for canoeing—the Brule River, which also forms the northern border of the **Whisker Lake Wilderness,** the district's mammoth spread of almost primeval wilderness. Access is easiest west of Florence approximately 11 miles; head north off WI 70 on FR 2150 to the entrance station. The tract covers some 7,500 acres, and there is a stand of virgin pine and hardwood. Whisker Lake is the area for dispersed camping.

The district's highlight, the grand **Lauterman National Recreational Trail,** offers nine total miles for hikers, bikers, and skiers, connecting Lauterman Lake with the Chipmunk Rapids and Pine River Campgrounds, and also with Perch Lake in the north. You'll find generally moderate to hilly terrain in substantially dense forests along these trails. There are three loops, with one "bunny" trail. Lauterman Lake has five walk-in campsites available (free), and an Adirondack shelter is also along the trail near the lake.

Very much a personal favorite, the **Perch Lake Trail,** is just over a mile from the quiet Whisker Lake Wilderness. For total seclusion, the five primitive campsites here can't be beat.

The aptly named **Ridge Trail,** accessed west of Florence 16 miles via WI 70, then left and one mile down FR 2450, winds along an aspen ridge and the Pine River. **Assessor's Trail** plunges deep into hemlock stands so thick you'll feel the light fading.

Not to be confused with the Bois Brule River in far northwestern Wisconsin is the sedate, comfy Brule River. Doubling as the Wisconsin/Michigan border, the river runs through splendid wilderness areas and offers killer trout fishing. Tons of access points exist at both Nicolet Forest Service sites and county parks along its banks. The Brule is decidedly lazy for most of its length and has the most dependable water levels of any in the forest. Popular put-in sites are found at Brule Lake, northwest of Nelma or along CR A, the latter passing the Brule River Campground (another put-in spot). Take-out is usually at a park near WI 139 and Forest Road 2150, in the vicinity of the Whisker Lake Wilderness Area. The only touchy point on the river runs below the Brule River Dam, technically out of national forest confines, where the Michigamee and Brule Rivers join to form the Menominee. You most definitely do not want to take a canoe through here.

The Pine and Popple Rivers run through the district, and sections of both are part of Wisconsin's own Wild River System. They also traverse what might be the state's most primitive wilderness. Water levels are generally best from late April to early June. For beginners on the Pine, the short spell around the Chipmunk Rapids Campground, accessed off WI 70 via Forest Road 2156, is a good bet; Section Two of the Pine River has some Class IV-V mandatory take-outs, so don't screw around on this river. The Popple River is even more widely diverse in skill level required, so check day-to-day conditions with the ranger station. If you can swing some sightseeing in addition to the frenetic rapids, the residuals of old logging dams are found en route. *Neither river should be explored without first checking specifics.*

Recreation: Eagle River Area

Two good wilderness areas are found in the district for those seeking solitude. Seven miles northeast of Eagle River is the 5,800-acre **Blackjack Springs Wilderness Area.** Highlights include four large clear springs forming the headwaters of Blackjack Creek, along with a lake and assorted streams, some of which produce lunker trout.

The wonderful 20,000-acre **Headwaters Wilderness,** 16 miles southeast of Eagle River (producing the wild Pine River), holds some of the largest and oldest trees in the national forest and Wisconsin. (One stand is accessed via the Shelp Lake Trail. See "Scott Lake Trail," below.) The area is characterized by muskegs and bogs alternating with forested swamps and a few dense uplands.

The most popular trails are undoubtedly those of the **Anvil Lake National Recreation Trail,** 12 excellent miles of CCC trails for hikers, skiers, and mountain bikers. Pay attention to the skill levels required—the Devil's Run is aptly named. Dramatic plunges and tons of rutted tree roots will dismount you or snag your ski tip. An easy trail to the east connects with a moderate loop around Upper Nine-Mile Lake; a log shelter with a fireplace stands at the junction. Traditional-style skiing and ski skating are allowed. There is excellent wildlife viewing in the area—watch for the woodland warbler. To get to the Anvil system, simply head east out of Eagle River via WI 70 nine miles to the primary trailhead; or, backtrack less than a mile to FR 2178 (Military Rd.) and head south less than a mile along the top segment of the officially established forest natural history auto tour.

The Anvil trail system connects with the **Nicolet North Trail System,** 15 miles of trails also for bikers, skiers, and hikers. There are fewer steep hills here. This system in turn connects to the **Hidden Lakes Trail,** 13 miles for hikers only. The actual trailhead for Hidden Lakes is midway on the Franklin Nature Trail (departing from the Franklin Lakes campground), passing Butternut Lake and Luna-White Deer Campground as well as pinprick lakes and mighty hemlock stands. You can camp at several established sites, or rough it at any of the tiny lakes. Hardcore hikers can forge on all the way to the Anvil Trail, or return to the Franklin Lake boat ramp. The North Branch of the Pine River must be forded, as there is no bridge; expect six to eight inches most of the year.

Tiny Phelps has a short but secluded one-mile trail for traditional skiing and hiking—take CR E north one-half mile to Sugar Maple Road, then right for another half mile. The **Franklin Nature Trail** is only one mile long, but impressive—some of the hardwood and hemlock spinneys are over 400 years old. Plank walks across a bog and some above-average lake views are pluses. Take WI 70 east of Eagle River for eight miles to FR 2178 (Military Road); turn right and follow the signs to the campground. The **Sam Campbell Memorial Trail** (interpretive) is named for a local naturalist and writer who used nearby Vanishing Lake for inspiration and contemplation; go east from Three Lakes via WI 32 to Military Road, then left four and a half miles to FR 2207, then north to the trailhead. The quarter-mile traipse through the aftermath of the 1986 1,200-acre charring of the Spring Lake area makes an eerie walk. Off FR 2178 north of WI 32, look for signs to the trailhead. A favorite of mine is the half-mile **Scott Lake Trail,** winding through 300-year-old stands of white pine, then via a short trail to Shelp Lake and outstanding bog environments. You'll be alone except perhaps for an ornithologist or two. Head east of Three Lakes via WI 32 and south five miles to Scott Lake Road, then left for four miles. Finally, if you're interested, you can witness how the USFS manages timber resources on the **Argonne Experimental Forest Trail,** a so-called living laboratory of less than a mile with over a dozen markers explaining (or justifying) in some detail how the forest is used. The road is east of Three Lakes via WI 32.

Campers at Spectacle or Kentuck Lakes (see below) also have a two-plus miler winding along the old Thunder Lake Railroad grade, once a primary conduit for shipping logs to the local sawmills.

The Eagle River District's Auto Tour is precisely 15 miles longer than the Lakewood tour, but the sights are basically the same—a mélange of natural history, topographical sights, and the historical museum in Three Lakes. It also essentially covers every trail and natural area mentioned in this text. Pick up a brochure for the whole tour from the Eagle River Ranger Station. For those without much time, just take a spin through the forest nine miles east of Eagle River off WI 70 via the old **Military Road,** FR 2178, and **Butternut Lake Road,** a nice forest-

in-a-nutshell trip through splendid scenery. Old Military Road, once called the Lake Superior Trail, is the modern result of a trail that's been in use for millennia—first by the nomadic early Native American tribes, then by explorers, trappers, and miners, and, finally, of course, by the U.S. military.

Most of the Pine River is tranquil from the put-in site along Pine River Road, but there are some notable rapids after WI 55, and a few portages are mandatory (bypassing Class IV-V lovelies) later in the trip in the Florence District, so be forewarned. The Eagle River District section offers a few looks at the remnants of old sawmills on the banks.

Camping: Florence Area

A personal favorite in the district is the carry-in **Brule River** campground, right on the Wisconsin-Michigan border north of Alvin via WI 55. Set in a lovely red pine and balsam grove are 12 sites ($8) that don't get used much. Also isolated but heavily used, **Stevens Lake** is 16 miles southwest of Iron River, with only six sites.

Contiguous **Chipmunk Rapids Campground** ($8) and **Lost Lake Campground** ($8), off WI 70 via Forest Road 2450, are 18 miles southwest of Florence. Chipmunk offers six sites adjacent to the Lauterman National Recreation Trail and offers its own artesian drinking well at a carry-in site along the Pine River. A one-mile trail (and road) connects Lost Lake, bustling with 27 sites, short walking trails, and an interpretive trail through a 150-year-old stand of hemlock and pine. No motors allowed, so it is quiet.

Morgan Lake ($8) is 11 miles southeast of Long Lake via FR 2161, with 18 campsites and electric motors only allowed on the lake. There is a small beach here, and the district's only reservable site—for groups.

Florence has two free campgrounds designated as walk-in only. It's a short walk—the road extends within a half-mile of the five sites. **Perch Lake,** one of the most popular and secluded campgrounds, is located a quarter-mile from the Whisker Lake Wilderness, which is rich in bass and bluegill, and you'll also hear loons. **Lauterman Lake** is somewhat better known. As part of the Lauterman National Recreational Trail, it's also more popular. The lake is full of northern pike, bass, and perch.

Camping: Eagle River Area

Anvil Lake is the most accessible of the district's nine campgrounds, nine miles east of Eagle River right atop WI 70, with just 18 mediocre sites. One positive is access less than a mile away to the grand Anvil Lake trail systems and the scenic drive accessed across the road.

The largest campground is **Franklin Lake,** along the Heritage Drive Scenic Byway (Forest Road 2181), with 77 sites, a beach, a lake trail, interpretive center, nature programs, and trailhead for a Nature Lakes Trail. Historic log and stone structures dot the campground, and the whole area is on the National Register of Historic Places. The lake is a mammoth one at 880 acres. Trails also connect this to Anvil Lake Campground and to the nearby **Luna-White Deer Lake Campground,** 36 sites sandwiched between the lakes. No motors are allowed on these lakes, so these are quiet sites.

The largest lake in the Nicolet, Lac Vieux Desert's 2,853 acres were fished by the Ojibwa before Europeans found these headwaters of the Wisconsin River. Also one of the most popular campgrounds, you'll see lots of rustic resorts dotting the shoreline. This is one of my favorite areas for exploring and photos—the opportunities are endless. The muskie fishing is great here, too.

Sister campgrounds **Spectacle Lake** and **Kentuck Lake** are 16 miles northeast of Eagle River via WI 70. Spectacle is a family favorite for its 500-foot beach, and Kentuck is known for its fishing—walleye, muskie, and bass.

Another favorite, **Laurel Lake,** offers 12 campsites and access to the massive Three Lakes-Eagle River chain of lakes. Two minuses—there is no beach here, and motorboats are allowed.

The primitive **Windsor Dam** campsites are intended primarily for anglers and hunters. Semi carry-in, the eight sites are secluded along the North Branch of the Pine River.

Information

The **Florence Ranger Station** is at WI 70 and US 2, Florence, WI 54121, tel. (715) 528-4464 or TDD (715) 528-5298. The Florence County Parks Department is also located here, with an interpretive center for visitors.

The **Eagle River Ranger Station,** tel. (715) 479-2827 or TDD (715) 479-1308, is on the north end of town along Wall St. (Box 1809), Eagle River, WI 54521.

VICINITY OF NICOLET NATIONAL FOREST

Antigo

Twenty miles west of the lower reaches of the forest, little Antigo marks your entry into ginseng country near Marathon County. It's worth a side trip for any angler, checking out **Sheldon's Inc. Mepps Fishing Lures.** (Any fisher worth his weight knows who they are.) Tours of the fishing lure plant are offered year-round, and anglers spend most of the time ogling the lunkers on display. Free tours are offered in winter weekdays at 10 a.m. and 2 p.m.; May-Dec. tours run weekdays three times 9-11 a.m. and 1:30 and 2:30 p.m.

Antigo also features the free **Langlade County Historical Museum,** on 6th Ave., open May-Aug. Tuesday, Thursday, and Sunday in the afternoons. At 7th and Superior Streets (look for the library) stands the **F.A. Deleglise Cabin,** an 1878 log structure where the town's founder lived.

Mole Lake Indian Reservation

The Sokaogon (Mole Lake) Band of Lake Superior Chippewa occupies the smallest reservation in Wisconsin—3,000 acres west of the national forest. Known informally as the "Lost Tribe" for its lengthy peregrination before arriving here and battling the Sioux for control of the area (and because the 1854 federal treaty signed was lost in a shipwreck on Lake Superior). The name "Sokaogon" means "Post in the Lake" and refers to the appearance of a petrified tree in the midst of a nearby lake, perhaps auguring the end of the band's wandering.

A ferocious battle with the Sioux in 1806—over 500 died—produced a significant home for the Sokaogon. The land here is the most abundant in *manomin* (wild rice) in Wisconsin. The beds around the village of Mole Lake are among the last remaining ancient stands of wild rice.

THE LAKES DISTRICT: NORTHEAST

From Tomahawk in the south, draw a line northwest to Hurley. Make another line from Tomahawk northeast to the far northwestern corner of the Nicolet National Forest at Land O' Lakes. The area outlined subsumes the Northern Highland American Legion State Forest and is one of Wisconsin's two northern "lakes districts," essentially one spread of water, with seemingly a lake for every resident (many lakes remain unnamed). In terms of lakes per square mile, the region is surpassed only by areas in northern Canada and Finnish Lappland. In the three major counties in the district (Iron, Vilas, and Oneida), lakes or wetlands make up almost *40%* of the surface area. Considering that these primeval pools of glacial hydrology are ensconced almost wholly within state and county forest land, the area is a perfectly realized great north woods escape.

TOMAHAWK

Somnolent Tomahawk lies 20 miles southwest of Rhinelander on the mighty Wisconsin River and is a cheery, engaging place if not aesthetically captivating. Set a few miles west of US 51, it's predominantly flat and lacks trees. But beyond the surface appearance, Tomahawk is a modest resort town in its own right, nestled near the confluence of four northern rivers and not far from an array of fish-heavy lakes.

Named for an oddly configured nearby lake, Tomahawk's lumber industry at one time rivaled any town to the north. From humble beginnings—one structure did duty as a saloon, eatery, and whatever else was needed—the city exploded with the arrival in 1886 of the railroad. The bust came as quickly as the boom, and the population left to follow the receding timberline.

The **Tomahawk Chamber of Commerce** is on 4th, tel. (715) 453-5334 or (800) 569-2160. Open weekdays 9 a.m.-5 p.m., Saturday till 1 p.m.

Sights
Adjacent to the chamber office, a small **historical center** displays a collection of homesteading and lumber artifacts and structures. Open daily during summer 10 a.m.-4 p.m. Free.

Regularly scheduled nature seminars, outdoors workshops, and scientific courses are given at **Treehaven**, tel. (715) 453-4106, a natural resources education and conference center on 1,500 acres. Sporadic naturalist-guided hikes, family nature courses, and even concerts are ongoing. Call to see what's cooking while you're around.

If you're here in fall, check out the local Harley-Davidson plant's sponsored Colorama tours—and there's also the excellent Yesteryear ethnic festival.

The best side road in the region is wondrously scenic WI 107, hugging the Wisconsin River south to Merrill—a great stretch of eye candy.

There's an inordinate number of okay golf courses and the free **water ski show** in Tomahawk, the Kwahamot—Tomahawk reversed—is held Tuesday, Thursday, and Saturday evenings Memorial Day-Labor Day at the Bus. 51 Bridge.

Tomahawk is also the endpoint of the seven-mile multipurpose **Hiawatha Trail.** Leading to Lake Nokomis, the trail departs a park on the west side of town off Somo Avenue.

Side Trip
Southeast of Rhinelander some 20 miles are tiny Pelican Lake and Jennings. The latter features what some consider to be the most authentic example of late-19th-century settler architecture, the 1899 **Mecikalski Stovewood Building.** Also called "cord wood" or "stack wall," the style of architecture refers to the short end-cut logs which are "stacked" and bonded with mortar or clay, generally a foot or more thick. Cord wood construction was economical and practical, not necessitating entire log lengths. The practice is decidedly American, and 19th-century Wisconsin was prime country for it; over 60 structures were built using this method, though this is the best example and the only commercial building known to be constructed in this style. After years of neglect, the Kohler Co. kicked in funds for restoration, and the building is now listed on the National Register of Historic Places. Tours are given summers Thurs.-Sat. 10 a.m.-3 p.m. and Sunday 1-4 p.m.

Accommodations

You'll find exceedingly attractive lodgings in Tomahawk—better on average than many better-known resort towns. On Bus. 51 N. is the pinnacle of Tomahawk lodgings, **The Bridge Inn,** tel. (715) 453-5323. The rooms have real wood paneling, a balcony, and all overlook the Wisconsin River (you can see the water-ski shows). The inn also features a popular restaurant. Rooms start at around $40.

There are also plenty of resorts on any of the lakes nearby, some 45 within easy distance. Rates run $360-1,000 per week for a two-person cabin, and most resorts in these parts accept single-night stays. One longstanding resort, **Lakewood,** tel. (715) 453-3750, on Lake Nokomis, has the lion's share of resort activity. Featuring modern two- to four-bedroom cottages for two to 10 people, the resort offers good spring and fall rates.

Food

For breakfast, try the classic **La Nou's Old Town Pub and Eatery,** 204 W. Wisconsin, in an early-century pharmacy gussied up just a touch. The menu is basic—casseroles, for goodness' sake—but just sitting in all that oak is restful enough. Open for breakfast and lunch weekdays from 5:30 a.m., weekends from 6:30 a.m. From $4.

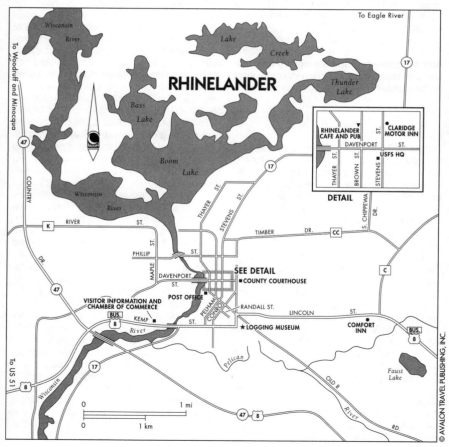

© AVALON TRAVEL PUBLISHING, INC.

Recently face-lifted, **The New Bootleggers,** along Bus. 51 N. at CR L, tel. (715) 453-7971, serves a full menu from 5 p.m. daily except Monday, Sundays from 4 p.m. The dining room is right on Lake Nokomis, and plenty of snowmobiles pull right up at the door. Live entertainment is provided Friday and Saturday. From $4.

Hearty family fare is served at the **Primetime Family Restaurant,** on Bus. 51 north of town, daily from 6:30 a.m. Baked ham, mashed potatoes, meatloaf, Scandinavian-style Swiss steak, and, believe it or not, a hot dish of the day—this is the Midwest, after all—are menu staples. This place is so popular, local radio stations broadcast the menu. From $3.

RHINELANDER

Another northern Wisconsin logging and lumber boomtown, Rhinelander is also a gateway of sorts—to water (the confluence of the Wisconsin and Pelican Rivers in town and all those lakes to the north) and to forests (the Northern Highlands American Legion State Forest to the northwest, the Nicolet National Forest to the northeast). The town is a kind of microcosm of the lakes region as a whole—some 230 lakes lie within a 10-mile radius of downtown.

The Sioux used the sandy promontory at the rivers' confluence for a seasonal base, and later, in 1870, a young explorer spied the same spot and envisioned sawmills atop the tame rapids.

With an injection of cash from a somewhat skeptical family, young Alexander Brown found himself the owner of what was originally called Pelican Rapids. A bit of expedient gladhanding (naming the town for a railroad magnate) paid off. The railroad laid its lines right through town, cementing Rhinelander's future.

One sawmill each year was the town's average, and the local waterways were soon choked with northern timber. Rhinelander later diversified into papermaking, making use of what the mills discarded, and it's still a primary industry in town.

Sights

Downtown, a block off Bus. 8, the **Rhinelander Logging Museum,** tel. (715) 369-5004, is actually two museums in one. Fitting for the theme of the museum are the logging equipment and photos, all exhibited in an old logging camp dining hall. Other buildings on the grounds include an old schoolhouse and the old Rhinelander depot, with lifelike period dummies and a new HO-scale model railroad downstairs. Across the grounds, the **Civilian Conservation Corps Museum** features photos and memorabilia on the history of the CCC. Strewn about the grounds you'll find an assortment of logging flotsam: a 40-ton narrow-gauge railroad, one of six used in the area; one of the last wood-sheath designed cabooses, built in 1913; an adze-hewn dugout canoe; road icers (used to make ruts easier for sleds to transverse); a rutter (for making the ruts for the icers to, well, ice); and a bateau, a long boat used on

Railroads were integral to Rhinelander's early economy.

log drives, usually housing the cook. The museum is free and open Memorial Day-Labor Day daily 10 a.m.-5 p.m.

Consolidated Papers, Inc. offers a 17-mile industrial forest (not an oxymoron!) tour 10 miles east of Rhinelander. The front end is the company's pine seeding greenhouse on US 8, near Monico. From there, tours lead through the 95,000 acres of company forest, with explication of modern industrial forestry throughout. The forest is open to public recreation, including cross-country skiing in winter on old logging trails and some groomed trails. Brochures are available at the chamber of commerce. Open to the public May through mid-September.

The easiest freebies are the **Hodag Water-Ski Shows,** Sundays and Thursdays at 7:30 p.m. mid-June through mid-August, at Hodag Park on Boom Lake, and the **Oneida County Courthouse** downtown (by day, scope out the murals of homesteading life; by night, the Tiffany glass on the dome radiates an amber light).

Accommodations

The ever-busy **Claridge Motor Inn,** 70 N. Stevens, tel. (715) 362-7100 or (800) 528-1234, is a low-slung Best Western with a popular restaurant. Rates start at $55 s, $65 d.

Probably the most efficient resort operation around, **Holiday Acres,** four miles east along US 8 (then follow the signs), tel. (715) 369-1500 or (800) 261-1500, is a high-gear family resort well known among generations of north woods vacationers. The more than 1,000 acres feature a motor lodge, spiffy cottages (many with fireplaces), and the Three Coins, a dining room among the most popular in the north. The resort's recreational list boggles the mind—three tennis courts, you-name-it water sports, indoor pool, nature and jogging trails, and access to 1,000 miles of snowmobile trails. There's even an up-and-coming Rhinelander mountain-bike race held here. Rates start at $85 per day, $345 per week.

Another good family resort that won't dent the pocketbook, **Kruse's Pinewood Lodge,** 4129 Lake Thompson Rd., tel. (715) 369-5585 or (800) PINEWOOD, is run by a family in the Rhinelander resort business since the 19th century. Lodge rooms ($325 d per week) and cabins are available. Cabins for two to eight are available, and $900 to house for eight for a week isn't bad.

A high number of return visitors stay at **Feases' Shady Rest Lodge,** off US 8 east of town on Shady Rest Rd., tel. (715) 282-5231 or (800) 477-3229. Very modernized contemporary cottages, along with luxurious suites and spacious lodge rooms—all right atop the lake—are available. Rates start at $75 per day, $345 per week.

Food

Not a cafe and more than a pub, the landmark of landmarks in the northland, **Rhinelander Cafe and Pub,** 30 N. Brown St., tel. (715) 362-2918, has been in business since 1911 and today is the must-see dining experience in the region. The huge, hall-style dining room is buttressed by the original diner counter. It's dark as can be, but try to scope out the varied accoutrements on the wall, nautical memorabilia, muskie photos, and newspaper reviews of the place. The extensive menu runs the range of simple sandwich baskets to diverse daily concoctions—chicken Oscar, for example. Prime rib, steaks, and duck are still the specialties. SRO is the norm. Open daily, 7 a.m.-10:30 p.m. From $5.

You'll find nice atmosphere along with steaks, seafood, chicken, and chops—and a nice pasta primavera—at the **Al Gen Supper Club,** a half-mile east of Sunrise Plaza, off Bus. 8 on the east side of town, at 3428 Faust Lake Rd., tel. (715) 362-2230. From $6.

Earning a mention for backwoods ambience and a nightly entertainment schedule, **Holiday Acres-Three Coins Dining Room,** is four miles east on US 8 (then follow signs), tel. (715) 369-1500. The generations-old dining room specializes in seafood and offers a wide range of music, from jazz to standard oldies. Open daily 5:30-10:30 p.m., lesser hours in winter. From $8.

Entertainment and Events

Mid-July features Rhinelander's version of a music blowout—the three day **Hodag Country Festival** (or Hodag Days), drawing many national country acts. In late September or early October, **Oktoberfest** arrives, bringing all the beer and polkas you'd expect.

Recreation

The **Camp 10 Ski Area,** tel. (715) 362-6754, is seven miles south of town. Two T-bars service a vertical drop of just over 250 feet and a short

HODAG

It certainly can't rival the mythic proportions of Yeti of the Himalayas, or even big-toed Sasquatch in the Pacific Northwest, yet Rhinelander's own crafty backwoods prehistoric relic, the Hodag, has been legendary in its own right. Some have regarded it as akin to the jackalope—that hybrid of horned and long-eared fauna populating tourist towns everywhere west of the Mississippi, though, oddly enough, spotted only by the grizzled denizens of local shot-and-a-beer joints. Others swear to their graves that something monstrous, something mysterious, populates the great north woods around Rhinelander.

It all started in 1896, when local pioneer (or opportunist) Gene Shepard showed up in town with a photograph of what he claimed was a ferocious beast that had sprung at him in the forest. It's got it all: seven feet long, with a leathery body, seemingly half reptilian and half leonine, with tusks like sharpened walrus tusks, razor-sharp claws, a coniform row down the back worthy of a Triceratops, and horns large enough for a Brahma bull.

The news hit the town like a wildfire. Rumors spread—supposedly the beast had been caught licking up the last offal of a white bulldog, its favorite meal. Before panic could subside, Shepard and a crew of hearty lumberjacks formed a posse and hit the woods to try and capture it, which they supposedly did, with chloroform and a long pike, after trapping it in a cave. Shepard threw it in a pit behind his house, and no one seemed to notice that nobody but he could look at it. When the jig was about to be up, Shepard claimed the Hodag escaped. All the local pets were scooped up and locked in attics before Shepard finally, somewhat reluctantly, admitted the hoax. He had constructed the beast of animal parts, steel, and ox hides.

It never quite left the psyche of the local community, however. The symbol of Rhinelander today, the Hodag, is everywhere. Hodag is the high school nickname and mascot. Parks and businesses are named after it. Check out the history and the hoax at Rhinelander's Logging Museum, or another replica at the local chamber of commerce. The coolest souvenir in the northlands is a Hodag sweatshirt.

Whatever one's take on the paleolithic varmint, it may soon be official, in a manner of speaking. In 1994, the Wisconsin Legislature introduced a bill that would make it the "official mythical beast" of Wisconsin; it was kicked around but never became law.

BRIAN BARDWELL

run, about a third of a mile. Open Dec.-March. Rentals and instruction are available.

Services and Information

The **Rhinelander Chamber of Commerce,** tel. (715) 362-7464 or (800) 236-4386, www.ci.rhinelander.wi.us, is at Sutliff Ave off US 8 West, a handful of blocks from the central area.

Transportation

Rhinelander is served by **Greyhound,** with a stop at the Downtown Motel, 15 E. Anderson St., tel. (715) 362-2737.

The **Rhinelander/Oneida County Airport,** tel. (715) 365-3416, is served by **Northwest Airlink,** tel. (800) 225-2525; **United Express,** tel. (800) 241-6522; and **Skyway Airlines** (only in summer), tel. (800) 452-2022. All the major car rental agencies operate out of the airport.

EAGLE RIVER

Some would say Eagle River isn't properly within the lakes district—the Nicolet National Forest even named one of its districts for the town, after all. They cavil, I say. If you look at a map, Eagle River splits the two regions apart, so it could go either way. However, it is closer to the Northern Highland American Legion State Forest (and is surrounded by lakes).

Eagle River was apparently named in the 1850s by a pair of itinerant trappers camped along the river who marveled at the number of eagle pairs along the river. Eagle River grew up as a lumber town, but before it waned it got the drop on all the rest of northern Wisconsin in reshaping itself into tourist destination number

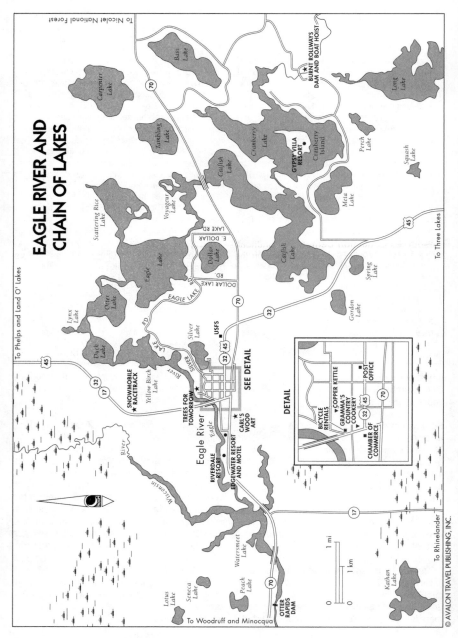

EAGLE RIVER AND CHAIN OF LAKES

To Nicolet National Forest

To Phelps and Land O' Lakes

To Three Lakes

To Rhinelander

To Woodruff and Minocqua

Bass Lake

Long Lake

BURNT ROLLWAYS DAM AND BOAT HOIST

Carpenter Lake

Tombling Lake

Cranberry Lake

Cranberry Island

GYPSY VILLA RESORT

Perch Lake

Squash Lake

Scattering Rice Lake

Catfish Lake

Voyageur Lake

Meta Lake

LAKE RD.

E. DOLLAR

DOLLAR LAKE RD.

Dollar Lake

Catfish Lake

Eagle Lake

EAGLE LAKE RD.

Spring Lake

Gordon Lake

Lynx Lake

Otter Lake

Duck Lake

Yellow Birch Lake

SILVER LAKE RD.

Silver Lake

USFS

SNOWMOBILE RACETRACK

TREES FOR TOMORROW

SEE DETAIL

Eagle River

Eagle River

CARL'S WOOD ART

RIVERDALE RESORT

EDGEWATER RESORT AND MOTEL

Wisconsin River

River

Watersmeet Lake

Lotus Lake

Seneca Lake

Peach Lake

OTTER RAPIDS DAM

Kathan Lake

DETAIL

BICYCLE RENTALS

COPPER KETTLE

GRAMMA'S COUNTRY COOKERY

CHAMBER OF COMMERCE

POST OFFICE

1 mi

1 km

© AVALON TRAVEL PUBLISHING, INC.

one, establishing winter recreation areas years before surrounding communities.

Its tourism development was perhaps a foregone conclusion, given that it lies along a chain of 28 lakes following the Eagle River—considered the longest such interlinked chain of freshwater lakes in the world. Because precious few portages exist after linking up with the Wisconsin River, you could paddle all the way to the Big Easy.

But it is winter that really sets Eagle River apart from the rest of the dime-a-dozen summer retreat towns—in particular, snowmobiling. The community's absolutely frenetic international snowmobile races in January are perfectly quintessential for the north woods.

Sights

Much of the town's focus is on active rather than passive pursuits, but the **Trees for Tomorrow Resources Education Center,** 611 Sheridan St., tel. (715) 479-6456, is worthwhile. On the south bank of the Eagle River, this WPA-funded facility dates from the '30s. A self-guided nature trail snakes through a demonstration forest, and there are some impressive outdoor skills or natural sciences seminars and other hands-on programs (for a fee). Guided tours happen Tuesdays and Thursdays in summer. Open year-round 8 a.m.-5 p.m. Free. The Eagle River Historical Museum is also on the grounds.

The Northwoods Children's Museum, 346 West Division St., tel. (715) 479-4623, has lots of hands-on activities for kids, great news for frazzled parents. You can even harvest cranberries from a bog. Hours are Mon.-Sat. 10 a.m.-5 p.m.

Don't miss **Carl's Wood Art Museum,** tel. (715) 479-1883, two blocks west of McDonald's. If not for the seeming thousands of hand-hewn (actually, chainsaw-hewn) burls, then go for the enigmatic Carl himself. Mr. Schels, an immigrant from Bavaria (in 1920), slowly migrated to the north woods and the life of a trapper, logger, sawmill operator, and, somehow, wood folk artist. The grounds are guarded by a nearly three-*ton* grizzly bear and a twenty-five-foot wooden chain, each link some 30 pounds. The rest form a bizarre mélange of fauna and miscellaneous objects and structures. The place is strangely appealing. Open Memorial Day weekend through second weekend in October Mon.-Sat. 9 a.m.-5 p.m., Sunday 10 a.m.-4 p.m.

Don't leave Eagle River without checking out Carl's Wood Art Museum.

In Three Lakes, south of town, **Three Lakes Winery,** tel. (715) 546-3080, is located in an old railroad depot at 6971 Gogebic Street. Tours and tastings are free, and there are some fantastic local cranberry wines (and they should be—this region produces more of the tart berries than anyplace else). Self-guided tours are available in late summer and early fall. Open daily 9 a.m.-5 p.m., lesser hours for tours.

Chain of Lakes: Lots of resorts line the hundreds of miles of shoreline on the chain's 28 lakes. An interesting self-guided water tour is a boathouse tour; the local chamber of commerce has a detailed brochure of all these historic structures. If you're not setting up house in one of the cottages or resorts, head for the **Burnt Rollways Reservoir,** made up of 20 of the lakes and maintained by the Wisconsin Valley Improvement Company. At over 7,626 acres, with 106 miles of shoreline, it's one of the region's most popular boating and fishing areas. These lakes are in turn linked to the Eagle chain of eight lakes by way of the historic Burnt Rollways boat hoist—dating from 1911—at a damsite between Long Lake and Cranberry Lake. (By the way, the name Burnt Rollways comes from the revenge exacted on a work boss who couldn't pay some loggers; they torched his logs stacked on the rollway.) There is a small fee for passage, and rest rooms are available at the hoist itself. Open from Memorial Day weekend to September. For information, contact the company at (715) 848-2976.

The next point of interest along the chain is another dam—the **Otter Rapids Dam and Hydroelectric Power Plant,** a turn-of-the-century power plant still cranking out electricity. This is the beginning of the long series of dams and assorted river blocks on the Wisconsin River, which have given it the nickname "Hardest-Working River in the Country." Self-guided tours are available; call for verification, tel. (715) 536-7289.

Recreation
Recreation on water is the focus in these parts, and the list generally begins with fishing. Anywhere along the massive Eagle Chain or Burnt Rollways Reservoir, muskie, walleye, and bass predominate. The Eagle River information center acts as a clearinghouse for information regarding local guides. Your best bet is to contact the **Eagle River Area Guides** association, tel. (715) 479-8804, with a membership of 25, for a listing of all current guides.

If you're heading out on your own, boat rentals are available from **Heckel's,** 555 W. Division St., tel. (715) 479-4471 or (800) HECKELS, or on Lynx Lake at **Uttech's Holiday Harbor Marina,** tel. (715) 479-7788. Generally, $25 can secure a 14-foot aluminum fishing boat and motor for one day. For tackle, you can't do much better than **Chain O'Lakes Mobil,** 1970 US 45 N., tel. (715) 479-4688; open 365 days per year at 6 a.m., it's got the area's largest selection.

Pick up a copy of *Fishing Hot Spots,* tel. (715) 479-5568, a series of angling guides mapping out every lake in Wisconsin. The series is produced out of this area and is available throughout the region at sporting goods stores or bookshops.

Three Lakes maintains a five-km ski trail, starting at the town high school. One half of the trail is novice-friendly, and the rest is a tad more difficult; it's groomed for both diagonal and skating styles.

The best skiing is found at the **Nordmarka** ski trails, operated at the Eagle River Golf Course on McKinley Boulevard. The Nordic trails are for all levels, no charge. A sister operation offers the excellent **Razorback Ridge** trails (12 miles), a short drive west of Sayner along CR N (try McKays Corner Store for parking). You'll find eight loops here, from two to seven miles. These double as mountain bike trails. Bike rentals are available at **Chain of Lakes Cyclery,** 107 Rail-

road St., tel. (715) 479-3920. You can get a mountain bike for $12 per day.

The courthouse in Eagle River also has Vilas County Forestry Department maps of county ski trails if they're not available at the information center.

You'll find rentals, sales, and instruction, as well as trails, at the **Eagle River Nordic Ski Center,** east of Eagle River off WI 70 East on Crossover Road.

If you're not up for paddling the 28 lakes yourself, a few operations lead easy trips down the Wisconsin River. For the extremely inexperienced, **Hawk's nest,** tel. (715) 479-7944, offers tranquil runs down the Wisconsin, of two winding but tame segments between Rummels Road and River Road along US 45. Also operating leisurely trips but really set up for guided, fully outfitted backcountry tours, **Rohr's Wilderness Tours,** tel. (715) 547-3639, is headquartered in Conover. It'll go pretty much anywhere in northeastern Wisconsin or the Upper Peninsula and also operates whitewater instruction courses. Rohr's also has a rustic campground on site.

It is beyond the scope of this book to detail the massive networks of snowmobile trails to the east and west (and through) Eagle River. One point to mention: lots of local groups offer tours, including **Decker Sno-Venture Tours,** tel. (715) 479-2764, rated number one almost annually by *Snowgoer* magazine, beating out weighty competitors such as Yellowstone Tour and Travel and Togwotee's Sno World. It covers Eagle River, Wisconsin, the Great Lakes, the Midwest, the U.S., and the world.

Accommodations
Resorts predominate to the extent that the local chamber of commerce has dispensed with any text in its visitors booklet, and simply lists page after page after page of glossy resort photo ads. In town there are a few basic motels, some right on the Eagle River, many with boat docks. The cheapest you'll find is likely the **Riverdale Resort,** tel. (715) 479-4373 or (800) 530-0019, with outhouse-size cabins and rooms starting under $30. The rooms, a few with kitchenettes, are clean and comfortable (and large), so don't go by outward appearances.

Many of the motels and (what claim to be) resorts right downtown are genuinely nice, including

Edgewater Inn, 5054 US 70 West, tel. (715) 479-4011, with charming rustic rooms and cottages overlooking the water that include continental breakfast. Rates run $40 s, $45 d year-round.

Also west along WI 70, the condo-style **Eagle River Inn,** tel. (715) 479-2000, has basic rooms, suites, condos, and some kitchenette units available. Full recreation amenities—indoor pool, sauna, hot tub, racquetball court, and boat docking are provided, as well as heated kennels for pets. The restaurant features reputable German food. Rates start at $90, $150 for suites.

Kudos to the **Gypsy Villa Resort,** tel. (715) 479-8644 or (800) 232-9714, which merits special mention for its attention to families—a top cottage resort. Fourteen very secluded villas stretch throughout isolated Cranberry Island; all have a few hundred feet of their own water frontage, including a private beach. A centrally located rec and exercise room, plenty of outdoor activities, and a new tennis court are available. Many of the villas also come with their own pontoon boat and electric motor. One- to four-bedroom villas run $345-1,800 per week and sleep two to six persons.

Also well regarded, **Chanticleer Inn and Resort,** 1458 Dollar Lake Rd., tel. (715) 479-4486, offers some motel rooms, 10 or so cottages, and 20 townhouses. Right on the chain of lakes, it offers tennis courts, an adjacent golf course, sand beaches, and plenty of rentals. The dining room is exceedingly popular. Rates run from $80 s or d in the motel, and weekly rates are available.

A mile from Eagle River on Yellow Birch Lake, the **Cranberry Inn Resort,** tel. (715) 479-2215, offers cabins and B&B lodgings. A special draw is the Finnish-style sauna, built of local wood and stone and complete with showers, kitchen, library, and deck (it's also open to the public for a fee). The resort sits on a one-time homesteading tract, with the coach house and barn renovated into simple accommodations. B&B rates run $88 per night, two-night minimum. A long-weekend cabin special runs four days and three nights for $165, and a fisher special for three days and two nights runs $400. Group sauna events and daily, weekly, or even monthly rates are also available.

You'd swear that **Fernwood and Wildwood** cabins, 16 miles northwest of Eagle River on Upper Buckatabon Lake, tel. (715) 479-5712, date from the 19th century. Nope, they're new but brilliantly put together with knotty logs, true antiques, and narrow spiral stairs to cramped but cozy lofts. Upper and Lower Buckatabon Lakes are in the *Fishing Hot Spots* series for muskie. Canoes are provided for exploring the lagoon and lakes, and the cabins share a sandy beach. Three bedrooms and a loft in each, with two bathrooms and more; it costs $900 per week for up to six persons, significantly less in low seasons.

Food

The cuisine isn't legendary, but it is better than you'd expect. Exceedingly diminutive **Fay's Dinky Diner,** across from the information depot at 121 Railroad St., is a favorite. That's not an unfair pejorative, since the diner—all four stools and three booths of it—is one of the most cramped you'll ever experience. You could pretty much reach over and crack your own eggs from the stools, and you will likely be enlisted to pour java. A tad more spacious with equally downhome fare, **Gramma's Country Cookery,** 107 Railroad St., serves famous chicken dumpling soup and great daily specials and now has an all-you-can-eat fish fry Wednesday and Friday for under six bucks. Both from $2.

The **Copper Kettle,** 207 E. Wall St., tel. (715) 479-4049, is one of the more famous eateries in Eagle River and serves standard family-style food along with some oddball variations, including the "Braunwich"—braunschweiger, hard-boiled-egg, tomato, and bacon. It also boasts that it is the "Pancake Hall of Fame" to prodigious cake eaters. The menu is as thick as a brick. Serving daily 6 a.m.-9 p.m. From $3.

Families are the focus at the Pine-Aire Resort and Campground's **Logging Camp Kitchen and Still,** 4443 Chain O' Lakes Road, tel. (715) 479-9208. Copious breakfasts, lunches, and dinners are served piping hot in an 1890s logging camp atmosphere. Beyond that the place gets pretty busy—ventriloquists, folksy folk singers, dances, beach parties, fishing workshops, sporadic kids-only events, and various other distractions are the rule while you chow down. From $7.

If you're paying attention, you cannot miss **Alexander's Pizza,** on Railroad St., tel. (715) 479-7363, and its ad barrage. You've gotta respect any pizza joint that uses University of Wisconsin business school surveys in its ads. Plenty of healthful toppings cover these wood-fired pizzas. Alexander's also offers sandwiches, pool tables, and a game room. The pizza at the **Colonial House,** 125 Railroad St., tel. (715) 479-9424, gives it a run for its money, and truth be told, the classic old-time ice cream parlor look gives it a leg up in atmosphere. Homemade soups and pies, and lately full dinners, are on the menu. The ice cream here will clog the arteries. From $4 at both.

You'll find more pan-style pizza and a bit more Italian food at the **Pasta Cottage,** 1265 Catfish Lake Rd., off WI 70 East, tel. (715) 479-2388, serving homemade ravioli that's worth the sled trip (Trail #10 if you're interested). Open from 4 p.m., closed Tuesdays. From $5.

Captain Nemo's, 3310 WI 70 East, tel. (715) 479-2250, is housed in a structure long known by locals as a supper club. Eight enormous aquariums contain muskie, walleye, northern pike, panfish, and bass. Charbroiled steaks and trout (tank to table) are the mainstays and the chef's specialty is Cajun. Open daily except Monday from 5 p.m. From $6.

Folks rave about the dining room/supper club of **The Chanticleer Inn,** 1458 Dollar Lake Rd., tel. (715) 479-4486. The casually elegant atmosphere is nice, and you can't beat the waterside view. Myriad preparations begin with chicken, and the stuffed cheese ravioli, grilled swordfish, and veal marsala are noteworthy. From $6. The **White Spruce Inn,** along US 45 North, tel. (715) 479-9090, is billed as the birthplace of the first European child in Eagle River. If that isn't enough, it was later made the first schoolhouse in town. The inn is known today for hardwood-smoked ribs and steaks, and Monday features an all-you-can-eat shrimp boil. From $6.

Entertainment and Events

Don't plan on finding any thumping discos anywhere close. You'll find a live DJ Friday and Saturday nights at **Reflections** nightclub, 2230 US 45, tel. (715) 479-8711, and one or two dumb "exotic dance" clubs that are bad beyond words.

Every January throngs of aficionados of Wisconsin's de facto pastime—snowmobiling—descend on Eagle River for a weekend of cacophonic, boisterous revelry, an Indy 500 of supercharged sleds. The **World Championship Snowmobile Derby.** Held at the "Best Little Racetrack in the World" and originally designed to bring in more winter tourists—it had a ready-made half-mile oval track—the derby grew to epic proportions when sponsors like Valvoline noticed the deep devotion to the activity and started injecting money into the deal. Fast forward three decades and you've got the most important snowmobile championship race in the world—almost 400 racers in 20 classes compete for nearly $90,000 in prize money. Getting a pitside seat is truly a dramatic experience—the ice kicked up by the 400-pound missiles stings your face—and words fail the shaking ground, smoke, and steam from the sleds. The operation is getting so big that luxury-box suites now line the press box.

Thursday night qualifier races are generally free and recent night racing has become a smash hit with the crowds. Otherwise, time trials are held on Thursday, followed up by two days of elimination heats and another crowd favorite, the Can Am Challenge, pitting six Canadian drivers against six American foes. For the loudest din and fastest machines, don't miss the Formula III title races.

Attendees have other choices besides the races themselves. The weekend sees dozens of manufacturers, tour operators, and sponsors bringing in state-of-the-art equipment for demonstrations and some hands-on opportunities. Clubs operate tours into the nearby forests, and you might get lucky and hook up with one of the racers. The loudest cheers erupt when a member of the Green Bay Packers shows up. For information on the event, contact the derby office at P.O. Box 1447, Eagle River, WI 54521, tel. (715) 479-4424. Figure $40 for a three-day pass, with daily passes also available.

A follow-up event in Eagle River is March's **24 Hours of Eagle River,** a Le Mans-esque endurance test along the half-mile oval on 440 cc stock sleds for $50,000 in purse money. Hardcore race fans up for the duration can get free shuttles to and from an area casino every two hours. A summertime version, known as the "hauling grass" (also a verb) race, takes place in August.

Eagle River's other big snow-season draw, the **Klondike Days** festival, is generally held at the end of February. Everyone comes to see the World Championship Oval Sled Dog Sprints—billed as "the fastest sled dog racing in the world"—on the same track as those monster machines of the previous month. This is not some tongue-in-cheek laugh-fest; four-, six- and ten-dog teams compete over two days in three classes for $20,000 in purse money—no small potatoes. Other features include demonstrations and competitions in old logging-era skills, chain saw "cut-offs" to a rendezvous, and a log pull (draft horse teams of 3,300 pounds and up). There is also a living history museum and Native American cultural demonstrations are also held, especially traditional dancing and storytelling.

Anglers own the summer, and their own crown jewel is August's **National Championship Muskie Open,** and a serious deal it is. Hundreds of anglers populate the local lakes and riverways for this catch-and-release competition.

Services and Information
The original railway depot in downtown Eagle River has been renovated and turned into the chamber of commerce's **information center,** 116 S. Railroad St., tel. (715) 479-8575 or (800) 359-6315, www.eagleriver.org. The office maintains a **24-hour events hotline** at (715) 479-5001. For 24-hour snow conditions, call (715) 479-5185.

Transportation
There is no Greyhound service to Eagle River. The closest you can get is Rhinelander, some 23 miles south. The airport offers **Trans North Aviation,** tel. (715) 479-6777, with regularly scheduled flights to and from Chicago's Palwaukee Airport from both Eagle River and Minocqua/ Woodruff during the summer, daily Thurs.-Fri. and Sun.-Mon. for $260 roundtrip.

NORTHERN HIGHLAND AMERICAN LEGION STATE FOREST

Most of the lakes region is subsumed by this largest of Wisconsin's state forests—220,000 acres. Its proximity to the frenetic tourist towns of Minocqua and Woodruff undoubtedly make the forest the state's most frequented, with an estimated 1.5 million visitors per annum. Initial machinations for setting aside land to protect the streamflow at the headwaters of the Flambeau, Wisconsin, and Manitowish Rivers began

just after World War I and final establishment came in 1925. Today, anglers rival pleasure boaters and canoeists for the 54,000 acres of surface water on 930 lakes and 250 miles of rivers and streams.

This is muskie country. Other anglers may claim to be looking for other lunkers, but everybody knows that most are secretly lobbing and reeling hoping for that Moby Muskie trophy. The region is at friendly war with the Hayward area for bragging rights.

Camping
There are almost 1,000 sites at 18 campgrounds in the forest, so unless you show up unannounced over Memorial Day or the Fourth of July (and maybe even late July), you'll probably find someplace to throw your tent. Five wilderness camp areas are available, and, unlike most places, they can be reserved. The most impressive feature of this state forest is the network of primitive wilderness canoe campsites—100 in all.

Trout Lake is the largest lake in the forest and has two developed campgrounds; needless to say, they're popular—the one farther north is much better. The sparsely wooded campsites are a downer, though the lake is nice and does offer a great hiking trail. **Clear Lake,** an apt name, is just east of Minocqua and may be the most popular, with tons and tons of pleasurecrafters. A good thought is to stake out a highnumbered campsite—the higher the number, the more secluded. Also, winter camping is permitted at Clear Lake. **Indian Mounds** is atop Tomahawk Lake, definitely one of the Minocqua Chain's most popular lakes, evidenced by large numbers of boaters. But, the sites are large and secluded and a couple are walk-in only. A personal favorite is **Cunard Lake** in the west-central forest. The 36 sites are isolated, and there is good canoeing between Cunard Lake and Sweeney Lake via a creek. **Firefly Lake** is quiet—no motors allowed—but way too popular at peak periods.

A nightly fee is charged, usually $8-12. Contact the Woodruff Area HQ, below. Reservations are accepted at Crystal Lake, Big Muskellenge Lake, and Clear Lake and Firefly family campgrounds.

Unlike canoe campsites, the 13 primitive wilderness sites can be reserved (for dates less than two weeks in length, Memorial Day through Labor

Day). **Allequash Lake** (four sites), between Minocqua and Boulder Junction east of CR M, is an hourglass shaped lake, one bay allowing electric motors only, so go for site #1. Undeveloped **Day Lake** (two sites) is south of North Creek Road between CR M and H and permits electric motors only. **Nebish Lake** (two sites) is three miles east of CR M on Nebish Road. This is an experimental research lake, so anglers must register before and after landing their boats. The most popular, **Clear Lake** (four sites), four miles east of Minocqua off CR J and not to be con-

fused with the other family campground, is often full, and offers hand-pumped water. Go for site #1, as it's most isolated from the others. In off-season times, campers cannot reserve sites and must self-register; for the Clear Lake sites, you must self-register at the Clear Lake Campground off Woodruff Road. For other campgrounds, register at the North Trout Lake Campground on CR M.

Recreation

The connected lakes and the streams and rivers within the forest's confines are a canoeist's

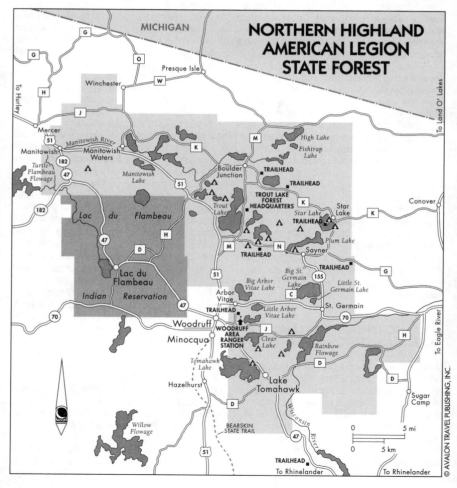

NORTHERN HIGHLAND AMERICAN LEGION STATE FOREST

© AVALON TRAVEL PUBLISHING, INC.

dream. There are three separate lake chains in the forest, and the Eagle River chain of 28 lakes to the east is believed to be the longest in the world. Nineteen wilderness lakes in the Vilas and Oneida County sections of the forest are absolutely free of visual shoreline pollution and have no road access (85 percent of the region is government owned); a good example is Salsich Lake near Star Lake. An additional 40 lakes are development-free but have some road access; the most popular is probably Allequash.

Over 100 free canoe-in wilderness campsites are found within the forest. No reservations are accepted, so canoe in and see what you can find. The trip is not challenging, just endless.

The most popular canoe trip in the forest is doubtlessly on the **Manitowish River,** spanning 44 miles from High Lake, northeast of Boulder Junction, all the way to the Turtle-Flambeau Flowage through extras like wild rice beds. Three maintained portages (the longest is 1,700 feet) are the toughest part of the languid, wide river. Put-in is at the High Lake boat landing on the south side of Highway B, and the trip is usually divided into four segments: High Lake to Fishtrap Dam; to CR K; to US 51; then to Murray's Landing. The HQ can help you plan alternate canoe routes; there are certainly enough options. The easiest would be to put in at WI 182 on the Bear River and exit at Murray's Landing, three hours of the easiest canoeing you'll ever do.

Not to be confused with the wilderness sites mentioned under "Camping," above, the Northern Highland American Legion State Forest (NHALSF) allows dispersed camping along the Lumberjack Trail or along any of the labyrinthine network of snowmobile trails. A permit (free) must be obtained at either ranger station prior to setting out; in the summer, contact stations are at Crystal Lake and Clear Lake. Camping is permitted anywhere, but you must be 50 feet from the trail and 200 feet from any water source. Use your head, of course, and leave no trace that you were there.

The key to the forest is the 18-mile **Bearskin State Trail** for hikers/bikers, linking Minocqua and Harshaw in Oneida County via an old railroad grade. The trail crosses Bearskin Creek nine times and has more lake frontage than you'll likely see anywhere else. Access points are at Lakewood Road, Church Road, Blue Lake Road, and the easiest, off US 51 in Minocqua, behind

the post office. At the far end in Oneida County, parking is available at CR K, six miles north of Heafford Junction. You'll need a pass if you're biking, $3 daily.

Nine primary hiking/skiing trails wend their way through the forest, ranging in length from two miles (the appropriately named **Schlecht**—that's "bad" in German—a bruising trail, with steep inclines) to 13 miles on the **Lumberjack Trail,** a wilderness track through the oldest timber in the forest as well as some recently logged areas. The Lumberjack also links to the **Escanaba,** a 12-mile trail past five lakes offering excellent scenery and some challenging grades. A shelter with fire ring is also found en route. The best trail for the beginning skier (and the only one allowing skating), the **McNaughton Trail,** is a scenic charmer 13 miles south of Woodruff on WI 47 then west on Kildare Road; this trail can take you all the way to Rhinelander. Scenic hardwood surrounds Shannon Lake on the **Shannon Lake Trail,** three miles north of St. Germain on WI 155 to Lost Lake Drive S., then north to Found Lake Road, then a couple of miles more to the trailhead. Many say their favorite is **Statehouse Lake,** a couple of miles of excellent riverside views along a section of the Manitowish River, then delving into the forest. To get there, head two miles west of Manitowish Waters on US 51, then east on Old 51 for a mile.

Note: The Vilas County Forestry Department also maintains an amazing number of hiking/skiing trails, a couple overlapping the state forest's. The county Advertising and Publicity Department, tel. (715) 479-3649, has photocopies outlining the 18 trails it maintains. Trails vary in length from a mile and a half to over 13 miles.

Four cross-country/hiking trails do triple duty as off-road cycling options within the forest— **McNaughton, Madeline Lake, Lumberjack,** and **Shannon Lake,** all described above. The four trails total 33 miles, 51 if you include the Bearskin State Trail out of Minocqua.

But these are only the established trails. Myriad logging trails wind throughout the forest, and these are definitely on-limits for bikers. The only taboo routes are nature trails. An estimated total of 800 miles of off-road trails exist.

Information

The most visited ranger station in the forest is the **Woodruff Area HQ,** at 8770 CR J, Woodruff, WI, 54568, tel. (715) 356-5211. But the main HQ is actually the **Trout Lake** office northeast of Woodruff off US 51 and CR M; the telephone number there is (715) 385-2727. Hours are Mon.-Fri. 7:45 a.m.-4:30 p.m. Before contacting any office, it might be worth your while to pinpoint exactly where in the forest you're interested in going. One of the district offices may have the maps or logistical information you're looking for and may thus save you time and travail.

Mercer

One of the most photographed sights in the state, **Claire de Loon,** is a gigantic loon guarding the roadway outside Mercer's tourist information cabin. They're loon-happy around these parts, or maybe just friendly, because they're sure chatty and solicitous at the welcome center, tel. (715) 476-2389, open daily 10 a.m.-4 p.m. in summer. The tiny cabin offers visitor information and posts vacancies in the area. **The Great Northern,** tel. (715) 476-2440, is a spiffy place and bills itself as "the motel that's also a wildlife gallery"—that's right, the Great Room displays a whole horde of dead fauna from around the globe, including a walrus.

Mercer also provides entry into the amazing Turtle-Flambeau Flowage, out of town via CR FF. Oodles of lodges and cabins are found en route to Butternut.

Manitowish and Manitowish Waters

These sister communities lie a handful of miles apart via US 51 at the far northwestern corner of the State Forest and were named in a linguistically bastardized way for *manitous,* the spirits that populate the region according to the Ojibwa. Set on a minor chain of 14 lakes and assorted wetlands, the communities are tourism centers in summer, and the other economic base is cranberries. The cranberry marshes near Alder and Little Trout Lakes outside of town are the highest-producing bogs in the nation; tours are available July-Oct. on Friday mornings, call (715) 543-8488 for information.

The **Manitowish River Trail** is a 20-mile novice-level canoe trip from the US 51 bridge in Manitowish Waters into

the wild Turtle-Flambeau Flowage. Rustic campsites (no water) are found on the way, and the Iron County chambers of commerce have good maps and instructions available.

But people really know little Manitowish Waters as the hideout of John Dillinger, another mobster who hid out in the north woods during Prohibition. **Little Bohemia Lodge** is where Dillinger, Babyface Nelson, and two others blazed their way out of an FBI raid in 1934, killing two mobsters, an FBI agent, and a local constable, and catching national attention. Bullet holes and assorted gangster detritus are still visible, and the lodge is still in operation—"The Hideout" is now a two-bedroom cabin on Little Star Lake—and has a restaurant serving dinner April-Jan., plus lunch during the summer. From $11. (Incidentally, Dillinger wasn't the inspiration for.30/.30 Road in town—it was the northland's obsession with hunting.)

For other practicalities, the **Pine Baron** restaurant serves beef Wellington, venison, pheasant, buffalo, as well as pasta and Philly cheesesteak sandwiches. It's also the only place around for decent espresso and cappuccino. The saloon/motel **Pea Patch Inn,** has the best sense of humor around (billed as the "best motel and saloon by a dam site"; Saturdays are Peanut Days, so throw the shells on the floor). Both offer menu items from $4. For legendary portions, the great **Swanberg's Bavarian Inn,** tel. (715) 543-2122, has been around since the '40s and offers outstanding German cuisine (lunch and dinner) in a laid-back atmosphere. From $4.

For something besides Midwestern, check out the wondrous **Blue Bayou Inn,** tel. (715) 543-2537, right on Lake Manitowish at the US 51 Spider Lake Bridge. The inn serves Creole and Cajun to die for in a cozy, romantic restaurant. From $14.

Rates in Manitowish are similar to the rest of the lakes region; some are seasonal, usually April to mid-October, and some stay open for snowmobile season. Rates vary from $300 per week for a clean, spartan housekeeping cabin to $900 for a spacious, luxurious multi-person unit. An excellent lodging option with an equally fabulous dining room, **Voss' Birchwood Lodge,** south on US 51, tel. (715) 543-8441, has been in the same family since around the turn of the century. The stately, rustic main lodge has a large, warm fireplace and there are also large guest cottages. Rates go from $75 daily if you can get it to $600 and up for weekly cottages. One of the newer lodges in Manitowish Waters, the **Aberdeen,** along Twin Pines Rd., tel. (715) 543-8700, sits on 100 acres along the chain of lakes. On Manitowish Lake you'll also find the modestly upscale **Fox Point,** tel. (715) 543-2075 or (800) 644-3699, with a motel, suites, and cabins from $60 to $115 per night for rooms right on the lake. The cabins have fireplaces, and there's a poolside cocktail lounge. On Wild Rice Lake—the only lodge on the lake—longstanding **Copp's Cabins,** tel. (715) 385-2373, has offered a cottage and cabins since World War II. Clean and not too modern, the place is cheery enough to have evening campfires. Rates run $550-800 per week.

Also south of town, off Powell Road, the **Powell Marsh Goose Refuge** contains native grains and grasses luring one of the only groups of sharp-tailed grouse in northern Wisconsin.

The **Manitowish Waters Chamber of Commerce,** tel. (715) 543-8488, is on US 51 North, in the community center on Airport Road. Open high-season weekdays 10 a.m.-3:30 p.m., Saturdays 10 a.m.-2 p.m., lesser hours off-season.

Presque Isle

Northeast of Manitowish Waters and technically outside the state forest, Presque Isle was dubbed "Almost an Island" by French Explorers. The maze-like streams and lake chains gave the land a resemblance to an island within a flowage. It calls itself Wisconsin's "Last Wilderness," which is true enough, considering the prime location between the 200,000 acre Northern Highlands American Legion State Forest and Michigan's massive Ottawa National Forest.

The village today is sleepy enough but does get its share of the summer tourist trade. The behemoth sawmills have long since departed, and the state has put their old grounds to use as the world's largest **walleye hatchery,** producing millions of walleye for transplanting to area lakes. The walleye is the number-one game fish in the

state. The requisite museum—the **Presque Isle Heritage Museum,** tel. (715) 686-2910, is on Main Street, with a general assortment of historical wares. Open Memorial Day through September daily 10 a.m.-2 p.m. Free.

Beacon Point Resort, on Presque Isle Lake, tel. (715) 686-2233, offers six units, including a private home, and a large beach. Rates run $600-800 per week. At a stunning location on the lake—an isolated promontory with over 4,000 feet of shoreline—the **Bay View Lodge,** tel. (715) 686-2448, offers year-round one-, two-, and three-bedroom cottages. On the cheaper end, the **Ox-Bow Lodge,** tel. (715) 686-2212 or (800) 476-1541, is a seasonal operation with enough options for a daily rate of $55 and up or weekly rentals from $260. Similarly, the family-oriented **Lynx Lake Lodge,** tel. (715) 686-2249 or (800) 882-LYNX, has weekly rentals from around $480 for a two-bedroom cottage and plenty of boats, canoes, etc. Some late spring and fall multi-day packages are available. The dining room at the Lynx has a seafood smorgasbord on Friday, and the Sunday brunch smorgasbord will fill you up.

Also a lodge but more famous for its copious German food and heaps of *gemütlichkeit,* the **Carlin Club Lodge,** tel. (715) 686-2255 or (800) 562-5900, is a year-round motel/lodge and a boisterous dining room with seriously good food. Polka bands swing into action, and if you're around in early August, stop by for the rollicking "Oktoberfest in August" blowout, featuring a huge beer tent, polka music, and tons of bratwurst. From $5.

The **Presque Isle Chamber of Commerce,** tel. (715) 686-2910, is right along Main Street and open weekdays except Thursday 10 a.m.-3 p.m.

Boulder Junction

One word: muskie. That's pretty much the obsession around Boulder Junction, locked in mortal, if benign, competition with Hayward, on the other side of Northern Wisconsin. The town touts itself as the "Muskie Capital of the World," as does its rival, and with nearly 200 lakes surrounding the town, you'll get the chance to meet your Pleistocene match somewhere.

Boulder Junction is hardly a bopping town, but once you've spun around these parts a bit, you'll understand why it is the de facto heart and soul of the northern part of the great north woods—suddenly you're in a bigger-than-it-seems zone of chi-chi coffee shops, boutiques, cafes, and even—gasp—a bookstore. And yet it's as northwoods as it gets. This refreshing atmosphere of northwoods personality with muskie madness impelled *Sports Afield* to dub Boulder Junction one of "America's Greatest Outdoor Sports Towns." It is a great place to come in out of the wilderness for an afternoon and recharge with something less gruff than silty cowboy coffee.

Muskie fishing is a big deal. Any lodge or cabin operation worth its salt has fishing equipment and a boat for guests, 90% of whom want to fish. Guide services for just about anything—snowmobile and canoe trips besides fishing—can be arranged through the local chamber of commerce. Like with lodging, checking out a number of guides thoroughly is worth the time.

Boulder Junction, in an admirable display of civic ambition, maintains its own **Boulder Area Trail System** for mountain bikes and hikers. The initial trail opened in late 1994, and more are being created all the time. The trails start right at the visitor center. (The paved Trout Lake bike trail also starts here, so be sure which one you're on.) One leg of the B.A.T.S. trail veers north, but it doesn't matter, since both legs eventually join up anyway. Mileage markers are posted every quarter-mile, and maps are available at the information cabin. Near Boulder Junction is the largest wilderness area donated to the Nature Conservancy in the U.S.—2,189 acres with 15 wild lakes. It's the **Catherine Wolter Wilderness Area,** open to low-impact recreation.

Wherever you stay is definitely going to provide canoes, Alumacraft, bass boats, or even pontoon boats. But should you just want a half-day rental as you whiz on through, **McCormack's Cisco Chain Marina,** northeast of town along CR B, tel. (715) 547-3761, rents pontoon boats, fishing boats, canoes, and motors, and offers full- and half-day rentals.

Right in town, both the **Northern Highland Motor Lodge,** tel. (715) 385-2150, and the **Boulder Junction Motor Lodge,** tel. (715) 385-2825, have rooms from $55. The former has an indoor pool and whirlpool, the latter rooms with hot tubs and a fireplace in the lobby; for an extra $10, you'll get a "deer-viewing" room in the back.

However, nobody comes to the north woods to stay in a motel (not unless they're fleeing a freezing-cold weekend in a campground, that is, and splurging on hot water and cable TV). Twenty or so lakes dot the countryside around Boulder Junction, and dozens of lodges run the gamut from dirt-cheap mom-and-pop operations to cushier condo-esque digs. Rustic and charming, the five cabins at the **Whispering Pines Resort,** tel. (715) 385-2425, are sans frills. Four basic cabins each sleep four and run $420 per week ($71 per day), and the newer cottage has two bedrooms and a loft with a fireplace for $600 per week.

One place that does allow single-night stays is the **Evergreen Lodge,** tel. (715) 385-2132, on Little Crooked Lake. Very cozy and modern housekeeping cabins are available, sleeping up to four people for $410-1,040 per week. They offer some meal plans.

White Birch Village, tel. (715) 385-2182, offers 10 clean, modest homes with decks, and some with fireplaces. The lowest you'll pay for a double is around $580 per week in prime season, $790 for four people.

Trout Lake is for serious anglers and **Skaley's North,** tel. (715) 385-2480, does right by fishers. Five cabins, all holding four to six persons, start at $540 per week. The lake is almost wholly owned by the government, so shoreline clutter is kept to a minimum.

These are but a few. Contact the Boulder Junction visitor center, tel. (715) 385-2400, to get a complete listing, and do your homework. Often people will find a perfectly suitable place, hit it off with the owners, and wind up returning annually for the rest of their lives.

The most ambitious and creative food in the entire state forest—if not all of Northern Wisconsin—is found right downtown in Boulder Junction at the **Guide's Inn,** at the corner of CR M and Center St., tel. (715) 385-2233. The owner and chef, a fellow of the American Culinary Federation, creates outstanding continental cuisine, as well as inventive dishes based on traditional northwoods fare—a Black Forest schnitzel, for example, as well as a variety of seafood and pasta. Even the ice cream is made on-site. Open daily for dinner, and it's worth it to stand in line for this food. From $9.

It's hard to compete with that, but downtown Boulder Junction offers a whole range of other places to eat, from the simple to the eclectic. All of the offerings will fill you up for around five bucks. For early morning bites, the place to go is **The Granary,** tel. (715) 385-2035, a newer log place with prodigious breakfasts along with burgers and sandwiches for lunch. Open at 5:30 a.m. Ditto for **The Outdoorsman,** tel. (715) 385-2826, a breakfast-lunch joint open at 7 a.m. in an older log cabin with a fieldstone fireplace. At Main and CR K, the **Ruffed Grouse** prepares three full squares a day, with decent pizza to boot. Open 6:30 a.m. to 9 p.m. daily.

For a worthy Friday fish fry in a true Wisconsin atmosphere, **Pope's Gresham Lodge,** tel. (715) 385-2742, sits on Lower Gresham Lake.

In the locally popular is-it-a-tavern-or-a-restaurant category, the best-known is probably the **Boulder Beer Bar and Restaurant,** tel. (715) 385-2749, serving homemade pizza, pasta, chili and, according to a well-informed source, the Northland's best potato wedge fries. The homey restaurant (with a fireplace) has a contiguous bar serving over 450 brands of beer. From $4.

You can't miss the **information center,** right on CR M, tel. (715) 385-2400, www.boulder-jct.org, in a renovated log cabin. Besides lots of information, the center's got a cozy living room atmosphere, so pull up a chair and peruse the brochures. Open 9 a.m.-5 p.m. weekdays, 10 a.m.-4 p.m. weekends, Sundays until 3.

St. Germain

Due east of Woodruff and Minocqua is St. Germain—originally St. Germaine, apparently after a French soldier in the late 1600s who married an Ojibwa woman and settled with the tribe. The "e" was inexplicably dropped later, and now lives *in perpetua* only as the name of the Indian chief statue at the information center. The proximity of the three towns makes things a tad more congested than, say, the Presque Isle area, but certainly still tranquil. St. Germain recently got the new **Snowmobile Racing Hall of Fame,** tel. (715) 479-5466, formerly in Eagle River. The cool memorabilia includes old sleds, uniforms, and even a roster of 31 inductees (thus far). You can also watch action-packed videos of famous races, focusing logically on the granddaddy race over in Eagle River in January. Naturally, you can sled right to the entrance in winter. Open 9 a.m.-5 p.m. year-round. Free. In early 2000

ground was broken on a new huge complex two miles to the west. It will feature "Sled World," a sort of Hard Rock Cafe for sled-heads.

As for accommodations, contact the chamber of commerce at (800) 727-7203 for a guide to all of the options. Ten lakes surround the community, the biggies being Big and Little St. Germain Lakes. You'll find cabins advertised from $50 per night, though many places only rent by the week in summer. Unless specified otherwise, all lodgings listed here are open year-round.

Right on WI 70, the **Hearthside Inn,** tel. (715) 479-2500, offers rooms from $48 (casually posh and worth the dough). The best of all is probably the luxurious **Whitetail Inn and Lodge,** tel. (800) 236-0460, at the junction of CR C and WI 70 West. The lodge has cozy modern rooms and a host of amenities including exercise room, laundry room, pool, and one of the better restaurants in the region. Doubles run $95 a night, $600 a week, and up; some Luxury Deluxe Suites can handle four and run $195 a night, $1,150 a week.

A sketch of what's available on Big and Little St. Germain Lakes includes the recently renovated **Black Bear Lodge,** tel. (800) LODGE-40, in business since the turn of the 20th century. Ten units including the main lodge start at $550 a week in summer, with daily rates in winter. Excellent cabins for the money and one of the best beaches in the area are found at **Esch's Serenity Bay,** tel. (715) 479-8866, with four-person units from $950 a week as the baseline rate. Two places heavy into family rentals include **Stiemke's Resort,** tel. (715) 479-4946, with three- to five-bedroom units from $600; and the **Idle Hours Resort,** tel. (715) 542-3765 or (800) 221-7699, which even puts out its own 20-page "newsletter"—you'll find just about every lodging option imaginable here, starting with a one-bedroom unit from $590 per week.

Besides the dining room at the Whitetail Lodge, you'll find the usual assortment of supper clubs in and around St. Germain. **Eliason's "Some Place Else,"** at the junction of WI 70/155, tel. (715) 542-3779, has a good dinner menu that isn't all that expensive and some live entertainment Fridays and Saturdays, including Betty Jean on the Hammond organ. Around since the Roaring '20s, the **Clear View Supper Club,** on Big St. Germain Lake, tel. (715) 542-

3474, is a casual place with a carnivorous menu, specializing in ribs and steaks. Both from $6.

The **St. Germain chamber of commerce,** at WI 70 East and WI 155, tel. (715) 542-3423 or (800) 727-7203, is open Mon.-Sat. 10 a.m.-4 p.m., Sunday 10 a.m.-1 p.m.

Sayner

Sayner is a must-see if for no other reason than the **Vilas County Historical Museum,** WI 155, tel. (715) 542-3388, and the exhibit on the pride and joy of the area, local eccentric-made-good Carl Eliason, the inventor of the snowmobile back in 1924 (see special topic). Otherwise, you'll find the usual slew of logging detritus, an interesting doll collection, an odd display of outboard motors, some decent wildlife exhibits (except the bear traps), and a fascinating look at the area's fishing guide history. Well worth a peek if you're in the area. Open 10 a.m.-4 p.m. daily, Memorial Day through the town's Colorama weekend in autumn. The museum is free, but donations are appreciated.

One lodge people mention breathlessly, **Froelich's Sayner Lodge,** tel. (715) 542-3261 or (800) 553-9695, is on Plum Lake. The resort has been offering vacationers a place to crash since the 1890s, and the Froelich family has operated the lodge since the 1950s. Rates start at $65. Open late May-October 1.

You'll find the oddest dining experience around at **Weber's Wildlife Game Farm,** tel. (715) 542-3781, a favorite pit stop of local snowmobilers. Down a burger or pizza and watch the wildlife show. Weber's is a weird amalgam of taxidermy display and private zoo. The farm is a mile south of Sayner along WI 155 at CR C.

The **Sayner Chamber of Commerce,** 203 Main St., tel. (715) 686-2910, also functions as Star Lake's chamber. Open 10 a.m.-3 p.m., closed Monday.

Star Lake

Check out the **Star Lake Forestry Plantation,** on the remains of an old lumber camp on the lake. The plantation, begun in 1913, was the first attempt at silviculture in northern Wisconsin, a phenomenally successful venture, considering the forest is still around. Also in the area also you'll find the **Star Lake-Plum Lake Hemlock Natural Area,** one of the state forest's 14 state

natural and scientific areas—this one 550 acres of middle- to late-middle-aged growth forest.

A lodge of some repute in Wisconsin, **Hintz's North Star Lodge,** on CR K, tel. (715) 542-3600 or (800) 788-5215, was once a grand old logging hotel, catering later to the Chicago railroads. The lodge offers 15 housekeeping units and two new lake homes, both with whirlpools. The lodge, however, is most popular for its cuisine—a homey eatery since before the turn of the century. Try creative Midwestern cooking, including the best pot roast around and, of course, worthy walleye. Rates start at $95 d, with multi-night minimums.

The **Whippoorwill Inn,** 7919 CR K on the lake, tel. (715) 542-3333, is a lavishly appointed B&B, with five rooms in an almost 10,000-square-foot log dwelling. No creature comfort is left undone, and exquisite food is served. Rates start at $95.

For hardcore north woods Wisconsin lodging—where they advertise spartan cabins as "well and sturdily built" and "4-*men* cabins"—try the **Silver Muskie Resort,** tel. (715) 542-3420. The name lets you in on its usual repeat customers—anglers and hunters. This place is dirt cheap for the location at $325 per week for a one-bedroom cabin, all the way to $510 for a three-bedroom.

Lake Tomahawk

There's not much to mention in this tiny town other than the **Shamrock Bar,** which houses what is supposedly the world's longest muskie; if that doesn't wow you, it's also got karaoke. Lake Tomahawk also hosts a semi-legendary duck race and maintains a tiny museum—the **Northland Historical Society Museum** is open Friday and Saturday 2-5 p.m. in summer, with exhibits on local history. North of town via WI 47 to the state forest campground you'll find the **Lake Tomahawk Mounds,** four earthen mounds dating from A.D. 1000. **Lake Tomahawk Canoe Headquarters,** on WI 47, tel. (715) 277-2405, offers 17-mile canoe trips down the Wisconsin River for $30.

The **Lake Tomahawk Chamber of Commerce,** tel. (715) 277-2602, is on Bradley St., next to the True Value. Open Monday, Wednesday, and Thursday 9 a.m.-5 p.m., Friday and Saturday 9 a.m.-8 p.m., and Sunday until 6 p.m.

SNOWMOBILE CENTRAL

Wisconsinites had been toying with varieties of homemade "snow machines" for some time before something inspired Carl Eliason to strap a small gas-powered boat engine onto a toboggan, pound on some turnable skis, and let himself loose across the ice near Sayner, Wisconsin, in 1924. Voila!—the first modern snowmobile, which he patented in 1927. Things haven't been quite the same around these parts since. Wisconsin has one of the most active populations of snowmobilers of any state. Over 25,000 miles of well-tracked trails are maintained by dozens and dozens of snow clubs throughout the north. And these are just maintained trails; Wisconsin Trail #15 bisects the state southeast to northwest—a seeming million frozen miles aboard a sled. *Snowgoer* magazine readers consistently rate northeast Wisconsin tops in the country.

How serious is snowmobiling in these parts? Don't be surprised to see a line of the buzzing machines scraping to a halt next to you in the Citgo station, filling up for the next several miles. Restaurants, pubs, and assorted businesses even post advertisements along snowmobile trails. Across northern Wisconsin, any lodging worth anything either caters to snowmobilers exclusively—with rentals, linked trails on-site or nearby, guided tours—or at least offers special snowmobile rates. And snowmobile clubs are everywhere, grooming and tracking the lengths of the trails.

But snowmobile aficionados, like motorcycle purists before them, have battled some serious image problems. Many people regard them as single-browed Cro-Magnons out to despoil the bucolic landscape. 'Bilers of the true kind cringe at the antics of the few yahoos, the ones fueled as much on Leinenkugel's lager as they are by the feeling of frigid air cutting through the mask. The snowmobile clubs of Wisconsin are on the whole a respectable, devoted bunch who do as much charity work as they do trail maintenance. However, in a time-honored tradition, making "pit stops" generally translates as bar-hopping. And there are many morons zipping home after the bars close or after a festival aboard a 400-pound missile. Some 30 snowmobilers die every year on the trails and lakes. The good news is that the number decreases almost annually.

If you're really down with the sledding culture, head for St.Germain, home to the **Snowmobile Racing Hall of Fame.** At the time of writing, a massive new complex—replete with *Planet Hollywood*-type theme restaurant—was being built.

snowmobile capital of the world

Land O' Lakes

Although Land O' Lakes is technically outside the auspices of the Northern Highland American Legion State Forest and is indeed far closer to the Nicolet National Forest, the town is pulled spiritually toward the state forest by the chains of lakes to the south and west of it, linking it with its lake brethren inside the forest proper.

Aptly named Land O' Lakes couldn't be in a more prime location—a quarter-mile or so from the buzzing highway. To the east is Lac Vieux Desert, the headwaters of the Wisconsin River and its toiling route southward. To the west (actually, in full circumference) are an almost incalcuable number of those famous little pools of water lined with resorts and summer cottages, including the 17-lake, 150-mile-long Cisco Chain, the second-longest chain of lakes in Wisconsin (and a historic route of natives and early explorers). Water is the inescapable ethos underpinning this district; west of Land O' Lakes along CR B is the true continental divide and separation point for watersheds flowing to the Mississippi, Lake Superior, and Lake Michigan. A marker near Devils Lake shows the precise spot.

Land O' Lakes is the only town in the region and therefore has a large number of stocking-up grocery stores, taverns, restaurants, and other assorted trappings of a tourist area. No trouble finding a lake to canoe or fish, or finding a trail to snowmobile—115 km of well-marked local trails link up with the 600 miles in Vilas County as a whole (Lake Superior-affected meteorological caprice dumps 200 inches of snow in the area).

Crossing over into Michigan off CR B via CR Z, Hwy 535 leads you into the **Sylvania Wilderness Area**, an established recreation area some 21,000 acres large, dotted with almost 40 lakes. Camping is available. A visitor center is located in Watersmeet. While in Watersmeet you could check out the puzzling **mystery lights** that have been intermittently observed over the past dozen years. Go north on US 45 out of Watersmeet to Paulding, then west on Robbins Pond Road. Park anywhere and head for a hill. The freaky lights appear to wasp up and out of the woods, where they hang for up to 15 minutes; some say they resemble a star but are very amber-colored.

Rohr's Tours operates a guided wilderness tour service. Tours last from a few hours to a few days. It's mainly canoeing via the Lac Vieux Desert, but there are also outings to lakes and rivers throughout northern Wisconsin and the Upper Peninsula. Rohr's also leads hiking and backcountry ski tours. The service maintains its own primitive campground and offers complete outfitting and paddling instruction courses. For more information, contact: R.W.T., 5230 Razorback Road, Conover, WI 54519, tel. (715) 547-3639.

Top notch Land O' Lakes lodging is in the historic **Gateway Lodge**, at the junction of US 45 and CR B, tel. (715) 547-3321 or (800) 848-8058, a two-story landmark built way back when and reaching a zenith in the 1930s and 1940s, when Hollywood bigshots used to stay. It's real-deal rustic but you don't have to worry about mice chewing holes in your bags. The cozy lobby is dominated by an enormous stone fireplace, and it's gotten around to getting an indoor pool, hot tub, and redwood sauna. A nine-hole golf course is across the way, and one of the largest trap and sporting clay ranges in the Midwest is here. An excellent restaurant is also on-site. You may get to see the resort accordionist, who's been playing here for over 50 years. Weekday studio rates can dip as low as $50, $10 more for a suite. Weekly rates from $370.

The **Sunrise Lodge**, 5894 West Shore Dr., off CR E., tel. (715) 547-3684 or (800) 221-9689, on the west shore of Lac Vieux Desert, has a fresh-scrubbed woodsy feeling in its 20 one- to seven-bedroom units, including four executive homes. Plenty of home-cooked food is offered in the dining room and bakery. Recreation abounds, with its own exercise and nature trails in addition to the 4,600-acre lake. Rates from $65 s or $85 d on a European Plan, with some good weekly rates.

On Mamie Lake in the Cisco Chain is **Bent's Camp Resort**, tel. (715) 547-3487, equally famous for its lodge pub and its sandwiches and fish fries. The resort has nine one- to three-bedroom log dwellings; one lodge room is available year-round. There's also a bait and tackle shop. Full, full service, like traditional resorts.

A summer stop-off for four decades is the soft-serve joint **Dari-Maid**, right downtown. The soft-serve is now 96% fat-free—some things do change. Otherwise, good burgers, standard fries, and the like. From a buck.

Supper clubs dot the area, and you'll be hard-pressed to have a better time than at the always boisterous **Bear Trap Inn,** tel. (715) 547-3422, a couple miles west on CR B. It's one of the oldest eateries in Land O' Lakes, so you'll still hear expressions like "wet your whistle" while waiting at the bar for a table. When you do sit down, go for the grilled scallops. Lively big band music completes the effect. Open Tues.-Sat. The poorly spelled **Tia Juana Supper Club,** US 45 and CR E, tel. (715) 547-3900, has been serving very little Mexican food since 1929. Specialties include ribs, lamb chops, and pan-fried walleye. Open daily at 5 p.m. Both from $5.

Enjoy the best Bloody Marys for miles at the **Black Oak Inn,** 5407 CR B, tel. (715) 547-3705, which also has a popular Friday fish fry, along with burgers and sandwiches. From $5. Speaking of imbibing, for a true-blue north woods experience, head along the South Shore Road of Lac Vieux Desert, out of Phelps, to the **Hillside Resort.** It's about as woodsy as it gets.

The local **chamber of commerce** maintains a tiny information booth at the junction of CR B and US 45. Open seasonally. Call (800) 236-3432 or (715) 547-3432 for more information.

MINOCQUA/WOODRUFF

Location, location, location. That pretty much sums up these contiguous communities set amidst the lushness of state and county forest greenery. Some 3,200 lakes are essentially the heart, soul, and nerve center of this district, though Eagle River may dispute this. Only some 4,500 souls occupy the twin burgs (Minocqua dominates—heck, it even seems cosmopolitan compared to Woodruff), but they're drowned annually by a sea of southlanders come summer, with minor relief after Labor Day prior to the first snows and the ineluctable advance of the buzzing hordes of snowmobilers. (Just check out the gas stations—they're everpresent, and every one of them is the size of a Wal-Mart superstore.) The town of Arbor Vitae—literally, "tree of life," named for the plethora of white cedar all around used by French explorers to ward off scurvy—is also considered part of the two.

It is a conduit to the north woods for many travelers, so expect a lot of minivans and kids.

Though you might anticipate a foot-first leap into price-gouging or choking, polluted gridlock, that's not at all the case. The two towns are pros at channeling the swells of mad traffic and equally mad travelers remarkably efficiently. It's low-stress for such a popular place.

History

Like any northern town of yesteryear, Minocqua got its start in the logging heyday as a not-uncommon Sawdust City full of timbercutters and sawmill workers. Dammed waterways didn't suffice, so a railroad race was on, won eventually by the Chicago, Milwaukee, St. Paul and Pacific Railroad Company, which laid the final tie in 1887. Seemingly before the final spike was struck, the opportunists and job seekers appeared. Minocqua was established first, spreading eventually into the odd-shaped peninsula jutting into the Minocqua Lake—one reason it's dubbed "The Island City." It wasn't quite a risque conglomeration of speakeasies, saloons, and poker game shootouts, but there was enough fast money to make things interesting. A year later, the squatters and workers in rough camps to the north of Minocqua were thrown out by the solicitors for the Milwaukee, Lake Shore, and Western Railway Company, which set about platting little Woodruff. Sister cities were born.

Almost serendipitous was the "discovery" of the towns as summer getaways. The railroads were soon hauling tourists as the boarding-house operators swiftly changed signs from seeking sawmill workers to attracting tourists. In fact, the trains chugging out of Chicago became known as the "Fisherman's Special" and "Northwoods Hiawatha."

Since those heady early days, it's been tourism all the way for the two towns. And with the paradisiacal location, a bust cycle is hard to imagine. With 95% of Woodruff area and 80% of Arbor Vitae in local, state, or federal lands, and thus off-limits to development, it's hard to go wrong if you love the outdoors.

Sights

In Woodruff, the **Dr. Kate Museum,** 923 2nd Ave., tel. (715) 356-5562, doubtlessly gets a lot of attention now, thanks to the success of the television show *Dr. Quinn, Medicine Woman.* Kate Pelham Newcomb, the "Angel on Snow-

MINOCQUA, WOODRUFF, AND ARBOR VITAE

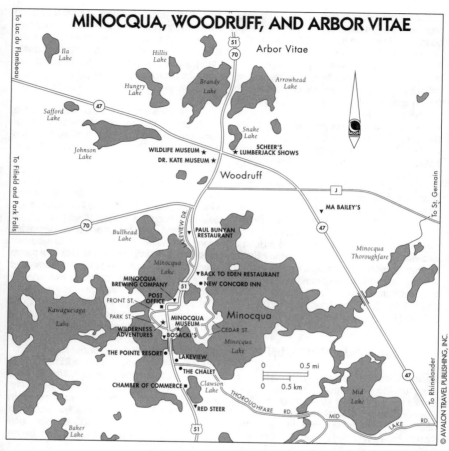

shoes," was a hardy country doctor tending to isolated trappers and settlers in the area early in the 20th century. She became a household name when she tirelessly attempted to gain support for a simple rustic hospital in Woodruff. Schoolchildren throughout the township and beyond initiated what became known as the "Million Penny Campaign." Television picked up the story and the world was galvanized. Woodruff got its hospital—over $20 million was raised. The museum also features exhibits on railroads, timber, farming, and some good stuff on tourism, as well as excellent displays on women in World War II and the 1950s. It's open late May through

Labor Day, weekdays 11 a.m.-4 p.m., sporadic hours otherwise. The somewhat less impressive **Minocqua Museum,** along Chicago Ave., tel. (715) 356-7666, is also called the Bolger Memorial Building. The exhibits change annually and are always fascinating glimpses into the Island City's recent past. Open summers Tues.-Fri. 10 a.m.-4 p.m. Both museums are free.

Family vacationers go nuts for **Scheer's Lumberjack Shows,** tel. (715) 356-4050, right off the main drag in Woodruff. World champion lumberjacks run through the tricks of the trade in a rollicking show. A personal fave is speed climbing; other skills are logrolling, cross-cut sawing, canoe jousting, axe throwing, chopping, and running the boom. Yanko the camp cook does his spiel of gabbing and singing. Kids' Day is Wednesday, with prizes galore. Lots of music on Thursday. The grandstand is covered, so it's on rain or shine. Showtimes are Tues.-Thurs. and Saturday at 7:30 p.m., with matinees at 2 p.m. (except Saturday), early June-late August. Admission is $7.

Children especially like **Jim Peck's Wildwood Wildlife Park,** two miles west via WI 70, tel. (715) 356-5588, a cross between a petting zoo and educational center. More than 110 species of fauna, most tamed, are dispersed over the spacious grounds. Boat rides, nature hikes, and educational programs are regularly scheduled. Open mid-May through mid-October daily 9 a.m.-5:30 p.m. Admission is $7 adults, $5 children.

Others prefer to witness wildlife rehabilitation and wilderness return facilitation at the **Northwoods Wildlife Center,** 8683 Blumstein Rd. and WI 70 West, tel. (715) 356-7400, designed as equal parts hospital and education/research center. During summer, the center is open for tours Mon.-Sat. 10 a.m.-4 p.m. Or, check out one of the planet's largest and most high-tech cool-water fish hatcheries, the **Woodruff State Fish Hatchery,** southeast of Woodruff via WI 47 and CR J, tel. (715) 358-9215. Established around the turn of the century, the hatchery goes at a rate of almost 50,000 per year. King muskie holds court here—it ought to—this hatchery developed methods to "farm" these fish. Walleye and northern pike are also raised. Guided tours are given weekdays at 11 a.m., including aquarium rooms and a trophy room. Open Memorial Day through Labor Day. Free.

A whole slew of family amusement centers, replete with cacophonic go-carts or interminable holes of mini-golf and indigestible hot dog stand-style food are available through the area. None is particularly memorable. The most comprehensive is probably **Circle M Corral,** a few miles west via WI 70, tel. (715) 356-4441. Prices for individual attractions vary; none of it is cheap. Open at 10 a.m. daily in summer.

Both the Rainbow and Willow Reservoirs offer thousands of acres of true wilderness areas, which are dwindling in the state. Between them there's 10,000 primeval water acres and 150 miles of unadulterated shoreline. Canoeing couldn't be better for wildlife watching. **Rainbow Flowage** has an almost unheard-of concentration of eagles and osprey, with 16 pairs of osprey alone. **Willow Flowage** has 10 pairs of osprey and an almost equal number of eagles; it also has the county's only waterfall—Cedar Falls, on the Tomahawk River. To get there, take Cedar Falls Road out of Hazelhurst. You may even see the odd wolf pack. In 1998 the state of Wisconsin plunked down nearly $10 million to buy the Willow Flowage to retain its wilderness status.

Scenic Drives

West of Minocqua along WI 70 brings you to Mercer Lake Road, one endpoint for another grand Rustic Road, this one accessing the Bearskin State Trail. It loops for almost 10 miles along innumerable lakes and hardwood spinneys before crossing the remains of the old railroad tracks that carried in the early throngs of tourists. Mercer Lake Road eventually links up with Blue Lake Road (head east) and crosses the Tomahawk River; in the middle is an optional length of Sutton Road, which leads back to WI 70. Along this section look for the remains of early-century cabins built by homesteaders.

Hazelhurst

Ten miles south of Minocqua are a handful of attractions in Hazelhurst. Top draw is perhaps the *Wilderness Queen,* a luxury cabin cruiser plying the 7,000 acres of the **Willow Reservoir,** an eerily quiet region within 100,000 acres of forest; as mentioned above, the state of Wisconsin recently purchased the lot of it, and nature lovers all over the state rejoiced. The Willow is a great place to ogle osprey, an oft-seen bird species in these parts, and has a sizable number of eagles as well. The *Wilderness Queen* has myriad tours (basic tour is $9.50 adults, $6.50 children) including lunch, brunch, and dinner tours; there's also a dessert cruise and the usual moonlight tour. Fall color tours are particularly worth it. Entertainment may include banjo music or singalongs.

The **Warbonnet Zoo,** along US 51, tel. (715) 356-5093, has pens of various species of deer (black and Sika deer) as well as African transplants like eland, niligia, and auodads, not to mention the more mundane macaws, wolves, and tigers in between. Also offered are go-carts, pony rides, mini-golf, and a cafe. Open May-Sept. daily 9 a.m.-8 p.m. Admission is $5 adults, $4 ages 15 and under. **Journey into the Wild Museum,** also on US 51, tel. (715) 356-4496, displays all these creatures once they're dead. Some 1,100 preserved animals in various poses. Open May-Oct., varying hours. Admission is $5.50, $4 students.

Accommodations

An almost mind-boggling array of lodging options exists in the Minocqua-Woodruff-Arbor Vitae region. At last count, there were over 32 lakes within the parameters of Minocqua, so you get the idea of how many subsequent accommodations are out there.

There is no consolidated number to call for placement. You can show up unannounced and the chamber of commerce will do its best to place you, but the area does fill up, despite the thousands of bed spaces. Winter and summer are the worst; you'll most likely find something in fall and spring. You'll find weekly rentals for $325 and weekly rentals for $2,200. And everything in between. Plan ahead. Contact the chamber for a complete listing and start making calls. It pays off to spend your money in a place whose owner you truly like; many a lifelong friend has been made this way. The list below is in no way comprehensive.

Minocqua, Arbor Vitae, and Woodruff have around a dozen basic motels, including the best bet for budget travelers, the **Chalet Motel,** tel. (715) 356-3003, just north of the visitor information center. Clean, quiet and cheap, around $35 or less all year.

Also good right between Woodruff and Minocqua is the **New Concord Inn,** tel. (715) 356-1800 or (800) 356-8888, on Lake Minocqua. Rooms run from $59. Meticulously clean rooms overlooking Lake Minocqua are at the **Aqua Aire Motel,** tel. (715) 356-3433, with rates from $45 s or 60 d.

Best of all within the Minocqua city limits is **The Pointe Resort Hotel and Conference Center,** tel. (715) 356-4431, a first-class condo resort on a minor hillock overlooking Minocqua Lake Bay, with a view of the island. Spacious studio and one- or two-bedroom condo suites are excellently appointed. All have private lakeside balconies or patios. A full list of recreational extras is also available. Rates from $99 in high season. Along similar lines is the more venerable **Beacons,** 8250 Northern Rd., tel. (715) 356-5515, with its landmark boathouse on Minocqua Lake. Around in some fashion since the early 1900s, today it's a lakeside condo resort with one- to two-bedroom units available. Nightly rates start at $110, weekly rates from $575.

One resort that accepts daily stays is **Island Cove Resort,** 8616 Lakeview Dr., tel. (715) 356-5026, with some motel type rooms from $50 along with lakeside units. Some of the units on the lake have fireplace suites. Worthwhile sunset views. Weekly rates start at around $420.

Private homes and cottages are generally a guaranteed way to get that solitude you've been pining for, since you're the only guest. The chamber of commerce in Minocqua also has lists of these. Some include **Northern Memories,** on Ike Walton Lake, tel. (414) 251-1753, a secluded log home with a sandy beach; **Spielhaus,** on Mercer Lake, tel. (708) 253-2253, a spacious private home with a deck; and **Davis' Cedarhaus,** tel. (715) 342-9798, a cedar chalet on Squirrel Lake that can sleep up to ten.

Whitehaven, 1077 CR F, tel. (715) 356-9097, is a 1920s mansion originally constructed for a Chicago industrialist who summered in the area. It features mission-styled arch windows, a capacious great room with a cathedral ceiling and stone fireplace, and a deck overlooking the lake. Four rooms are available for guests, with rates from $70. **Tamarack,** 7950 Bo-di-Lac Dr., tel. (715) 356-7124, is a huge home made of 150-year-old hand-hewn logs; there's a fireplace and grand deck overlooking Squirrel Lake. It's $100 for a room here.

Food

The institution of institutions in Wisconsin's far north has got to be **Bosacki's,** north end of the US 51 bridge in Minocqua, tel. (715) 356-5292, a rambunctious place absolutely overflowing with tourists come summer, and only slightly less full of grizzled snowmobilers in winter. Opened in an 1896 building in 1917, the fourth generation of the Bosacki family is now running the place. How amazingly popular is the place? When a boat fire and subsequent explosion ravaged the original building, petitions circulated—

classic Minocqua eats

all the way to Russia and Israel—for the family to rebuild; almost 15,000 people signed. Today Bosacki's has a tackle-and-bait, marina, and water-ski operation right on the premises, along with a guide service; it's advertised as accessible "by land, air, sea, or water." The food is exceedingly popular—standing room only for Friday fish fries (no reservations), so popular they're also served on Wednesday. If nothing else, just bend an elbow at the famed hand-carved 1903 Brunswick oak bar in back for homemade candies or dreamy hot fudge sundaes. From $4.

You'll probably hear the stories of **Ma Bailey's,** 8591 Woodruff Rd., tel. (715) 356-6133, a popular Woodruff supper club that was once, a long long time ago, a house of ill repute. No one's quite sure when Ma and her husband arrived-sometime in the 1920s- and started up a bordello. Facing jail time, Ma turned on the charm, convincing the magistrate that her poor health would make it too much of hardship to spend any time in the clink. And it worked—no stint in the hoosegow for Ma Bailey. Today, the restaurant's entrée names are embarrassingly tacky—Dolly's Delectable Duck, Boom-Boom's BBQ Ribs, the Happy Hooker special of the day. But the decor is lively, the place boisterous, and it's tough to beat for a fun night out. The owner might even tickle the ivories. Go east off of US 51 onto CR J to Woodruff Road. Open daily except Wednesday at 5 p.m.; closed Mon.-Wed. in winter. From $5.

Another venerable Minocqua supper club is the aptly named **The Red Steer.** An 18-oz.

porterhouse tops the list, along with a good tenderloin en brochette. Two blocks south of the US 51 bridge, tel. (715) 356-6332, it's open daily from 4:30 p.m. From $4.

Solem's Norwood Pines, two miles west along WI 70, tel. (715) 356-3666, is a supper club with the best piano bar singalongs of any joint in the area. Meals in summer are served on a screened deck over Patricia Lake. Open daily from 4:30 p.m., closed Monday in off-season. From $9.

Back to Eden, 8524 US 51 North in the Olde Minocqua Boardwalk, tel. (715) 356-1103, is an amazing anomaly—a vegetarian restaurant and natural foods store in the land of the corn-fed steer and deep-fried fish. Excellent soups, salads, sandwiches, and desserts—all cholesterol free. Extending that, there are also some vegan specialties and non-dairy soft serve. It's open for lunch and dinner daily except Saturday. Closed late October through May. From $4.

Another of the finest restaurants in the state is **Jacobi's** 9820 Cedar Falls Rd., a quarter-mile from downtown in Hazelhurst, tel. (715) 356-5591, right along the Bearskin State Trail. Located in a classic backwoods inn (upscale tavern, more like it), dating from the 1930s, the place has begun to garner gourmet nods from far, far away. The list of jaw-drop entrées is long—the house specialty is garlic-stuffed tenderloin, for example. For a splurge night, this place is it. Open daily for dinner in summer, closed Monday and Tuesday in winter. From $8.

LOONS

It is an incredible experience, the shrill call of a loon—part whistle, part warble, part music—dancing across the placid waters of a lake. Northern Wisconsin is one of the few remaining refuges of loons. These short-tailed, brilliant-black-headed, fish-eating, diving birds are threatened more and more each year, often by the very people who come to observe them. Shoreline development has caused the greatest crisis. Water and air pollution, along with toxins migrating through the food chain, even unknowing harassment by recreational lake users, have taken their toll.

The northeastern Wisconsin counties of Vilas and Oneida have close to 2,000 loons. The Turtle-Flambeau Flowage has the largest number of common loon nesting sites found anywhere. The common loon, found on Wisconsin waters, is one of the genus *Gavia—Gavia immer,* one of four species and the only one outside of northern Canada and Alaska. It is the head that is most striking—an obsidian green, with a narrow, pointed beak. The neck will be ringed in a thick band of white. The body is powerful and streamlined, usually black and white. Most are at least two feet tall and weigh around 10 pounds, with an angelic wingspan of about five feet.

With rigid bone structure and rear-located, powerful legs, loons can dive as deep as 200 feet for a full 10 minutes searching for fish, frogs, crayfish, insects, or other aquatic delicacies. When it wants air instead of water, it "sprints" across the water surface for almost a quarter-mile, gathering speed for flight. The only time a loon comes ashore is to nest; its oddly shaped body is decidedly not for land-lubbing, to the point that loons often have to remain half-in, half-out of the water, resting their chests on the shore. Ferociously territorial, only one nesting pair of loons will occupy a lake, except for unusually large lakes, which might have two. Loons migrate in winter, most going to the southern Atlantic coast.

Scientists have classified loon "speak" into four categories: wails, hoots, tremolos, and yodels. The former two are what you'll probably hear at your campsite. The wails and hoots both indicate either concern when separated from a mate or an expression of interest in something. The latter two are defensive cries.

Superb Sicilian-style food at **Mama's,** WI 70 West, tel. (715) 356-5070, doling out Italian food on Curtis Lake since the early 1950s. Try the pepper steak. There's also good pizza, and the Wednesday buffet is a treat for the wallet. Lunches are served on weekdays. From $4 at lunch, $8 at dinner.

Perhaps most legendary are the copious feeds at **Paul Bunyan's Cook Shanty,** on US 51 between Minocqua and Woodruff, tel. (715) 356-6270, the place with the gargantuan Paul and Babe the Blue Ox out front. It's also the quintessential north woods dining experience for a family. Lumberjack-style breakfasts, lunches, and dinners (until 9 p.m.) in old-style cook shack decor. New are the feed-your-face Friday fish fries. Open daily May-October.

Pub grub and brewery tours are dispensed at Minocqua's newest eatery, the **Minocqua Brewing Company,** US 51, tel. (715) 358-3040, which has lots of sandwiches and a few meat-based entrées. From $5.

Entertainment and Events

In downtown Minocqua, the **Landmark,** a funky old 1889 structure hosts live blues bands Monday, Friday, Saturday, and some Wednesdays. Thursday has comedy shows, and Tuesday is free pool and all-you-can-eat buffalo wings. Standard bar grub otherwise.

The **Northern Lights Playhouse,** tel. (715) 356-7173, performs Broadway musicals and some non-musicals June to October in Hazelhurst. Shows are daily, some with matinees; it's often matinees only in September. Every Wednesday and Saturday brings children's theater. Tickets are $14.25 adults, $12.80 for seniors and students, and $8 for children 12 and under.

Recreation

A true gem of Minocqua is the **Minocqua Winter Park and Nordic Center,** tel. (715) 356-3309, rated in the top 10 in the Midwest and offering 70 km of Piston Bully grooming with tracks for striding and skating, as well as three short loops for children. Thursday and Friday nights a mile-and-a-half loop is lighted. It also operates an open telemarking slope. The chalet has a modest cafe, day lodge, and full-service ski shop. It's located west of town six miles off WI 70 along Squirrel Lake Road. A daily pass for adults is $5 midweek, $6 weekend and holiday; a three-day pass is $15. Children 12-18 $3/4; children 6-11 $1/2. Full-day ski rentals are $10 for traditional skis, $17 for skating skis.

Bike supplies and rentals are available at a couple spots, including **B.J.'s Sportshop,** tel. (715) 356-3900, along US 51 North. A few operations conduct horseback riding, including **Circle M Corral,** tel. (715) 356-4008.

Guided **fishing** is a serious industry in Minocqua. In Vilas County alone, which encompasses much of the forest land and tons of the lakes, during one Muskie Marathon, anglers registered 1,672 muskies totaling 22,000 pounds. Many local pros stake their livelihoods on bringing up lunker muskies or walleye; some dabble in bass or northern pike as well. A good guide is an intensely personal, some say spiritual, thing. The local chamber of commerce maintains lists of guides, individual or operations. Getting to the know the guide a bit first can save a lot of grief and make a trip much more fun, even if you don't catch your trophy.

One well-regarded operation is that of the 10 or so serious pros at **Strictly Walleye/Muskie Headquarters,** 8600 US 51 North, tel. (715) 356-9229, so efficient they manage to put out a 16-page newsworthy paper. A couple world record holders are on staff, and all the guides have been on these lakes for decades.

Services and Information

The **Minocqua-Woodruff-Arbor Vitae Area Chamber of Commerce,** along US 51, tel. (800) HI-NORTH, www.minocqua.org, is not far from the Red Steer Supper Club. It's open weekdays 9 a.m.-5 p.m., Saturday 9 a.m.-3 p.m., and Sunday noon-4 p.m. and is definitely well stocked with information. If it's closed there's a small 24-hour computer kiosk outside to link up with local places to stay. These hours diminish somewhat in the off-season. If you're heading out into the wilderness, it's a good idea to pick up a **topographical map,** sold at a shop on the south side of US 51/70, across from the Holiday service station.

The Woodruff **post office** is on WI 47, right off US 51. The Minocqua post office is an immediate right turn after US 51 bends south to hit the main drag.

Transportation

Greyhound stops once daily in Minocqua at the Hardee's restaurant, junction of highways 51 and 70. Service is slim and getting slimmer. To Rhinelander the bus leaves at 8 a.m., takes 45 minutes and costs $9.

Trans North Aviation, tel. (715) 479-6777, operates out of both Eagle River and Minocqua/Woodruff. During summer, it offers one flight daily Thurs.-Fri. and Sun.-Mon. to Chicago's Palwaukee Airport; the fare is $260 roundtrip.

LAC DU FLAMBEAU INDIAN RESERVATION

Wisconsinites unfortunately got to know the Lac du Flambeau Reservation all too well in the late '80s during furious confrontations between Ojibwa spearfishers and local sportfishers. Edgy and tense in the beginning, while federal courts pondered old treaties, disputes over spearing rights versus nonnative rights reached a head with ugly episodes of violence at boat landings and scores of arrests.

Tensions have eased somewhat, though as recently as the winter of 1995 the Ojibwa alarmed northern residents again with their claims to take 100 percent of their limit of walleye, which the Wisconsin DNR said would effectively eliminate any sportfishing in the region other than catch-and-release. The Ojibwa in turn were angered by what they considered railroading by the state government, which demanded the Ojibwa drop the quota or the state would start meddling into gaming receipts. Though it never came to pass, it did shed light once again on things that seemingly never change.

The Sioux Indians originally controlled the current Ojibwa reservation. A strategic location at a midpoint between the Montreal River route from the Wisconsin River to Lake Superior as well as the Chippewa River to the Mississippi, it was finally wrested by the Ojibwa around 1650. Lac du Flambeau ("Lake of the Torches") is what the bewildered French first said when they saw the Ojibwa spearfishing in birchbark canoes in the inky black night, lit only by their torches. The largest Native American group never to be forcibly removed from their state territory, the Ojibwa reservation status was established in 1854 with the LaPointe treaty, signed on Madeline Island. It became a general case of federal mismanagement, as usual. The Depression-era WPA guide to Wisconsin took the government to task for conditions on the reservation:

In a report published in 1934 the Land Planning Committee . . . discusses this as an outstanding example of mismanagement of Indian affairs . . . for 25 years the reservation was held in trust by the Government, which permitted outsiders to log off the timber, thus depriving the Indian owners of the only valuable property they had. By 1914 lumbering ceased, and the Indians were left unemployed on denuded land. Eventually each Indian received a small tract, virtually worthless for farming, not large enough to be used for grazing or forestry.

Life on the reservation is better today, though certainly not perfect, judging from the events surrounding spearfishing sites. Ojibwa population today hovers around the 2,500 mark, with tribal enterprises including a well-respected traditional Ojibwa village, a cultural center and museum, pallet manufacturing, a mall, a fish hatchery, and a casino.

Sights
Waswagoning (Wa-SWAH-gah-ning) is a meticulous recreation of an Ojibwa village spread over 20 acres along Mov-

ing Cloud Lake. An amazing place, devoid of tackiness, its name means the same as the Francophone Lac du Flambeau. Various birchbark lodges dot the landscape, connected by trails, each lodge offering demonstrations on aspects of Ojibwa culture—winter maple camps, tanning, birchbark canoe building, wigwam making, specialty dances or weaving, among others. There's even a teaching lodge designed for instructional purposes; the directors even plan to delve into Ojibwa philosophies and the sacred side, including the sweat lodge. Still very new, the area is under constant growth. With the isolated trails and moving lake-edge scenery, the whole is quite effective. There is precious little like it for itinerant tourists. Tours are available 10 a.m.-4 p.m. daily, Memorial Day-Labor Day, with rates of $7 adults, $5 children and seniors 65 and over. To get there, go west on WI 47 to CR H, then a third of a mile. For information, call (715) 588-3560.

Not to be confused with this is the **Lac du Flambeau Chippewa Museum and Cultural Center,** tel. (715) 588-3333, just south of the Indian Bowl in downtown Lac du Flambeau. The history and culture of the Lac du Flambeau Band of Chippewa is detailed through the most comprehensive collection of Ojibwa artifacts anywhere, with most emphasis from the French fur trade days. Exhibits are sectioned into four seasons. A century-plus-old 24-foot dugout canoe is the favorite attraction, as are ceremonial drums and some clothing. A record sturgeon pulled from the Flambeau lakes is also on display. Tours are available daily and occasional workshops are conducted, with hands-on demonstrations. Open May 1-Oct. 31 Mon.-Sat. 10 a.m.-4 p.m., until 7 p.m. on powwow nights. Admission is $2 adults, $1 children 5 to 15.

Lac du Flambeau Reservation operates its own **fish hatchery,** along WI 47 to the north, tel. (715) 588-3303, raising millions of walleye, muskie, and trout. Scheduled tours are available May-Aug. on Wednesday 1-3:30 p.m. Trout fishing for a fee is available daily, with no license required.

Events
The Lac du Flambeau Indian Bowl hosts **pow-wows** mid-June-mid-Aug., Tuesday at 7 p.m.

Recreation
The Lac du Flambeau **marina** has access to the 10-lake chain Lac du Flambeau sits on. The Bear and Trout Rivers are good ways to explore most of the lakes, which are very canoe-friendly. The Lac du Flambeau chamber of commerce has a good map marking sites of historical in-terest along the routes, from the crucial water routes via the Bear River to sites of early trading posts, Indian camps from earliest settlement periods, battle sites, forts, Indian boarding schools, and the largest lumber yard in Wisconsin. You can also pass by Medicine Rock, on which Ojibwa made offerings; and the legendary "Crawling Rock," a series of rocks which were purportedly dropped as stepping stones by a warrior fleeing a charging bear; others say it's because one rock seems to move across the water.

TROUBLE IN PARADISE

It all began in the early 1970s, with the arrest of two members of the Lac du Flambeau Ojibwa Reservation who had crossed reservation borders to fish walleye. A class-action suit followed, and the debate set forth: What, if any, residual fishing rights do Wisconsin Native Americans possess in ceded territory? And who is to decide?

The case—and others following it—landed in federal courts, where it has been ever since, for over two decades now. (The court decisions actually cover a broad range of issues, including the sensitive Great Lakes commercial fisheries, but most people focus solely on the spearfishing issue.) The federal judge in the original case ruled against the Ojibwa, but that decision was overturned in 1983 in what became known as the Voigt decision. The Native Americans had the right, apparently, to exercise treaty rights granted in the 1830s and 1840s. The generally worded land-cession treaties formed the crux of the debate—one 1842 treaty states unequivocally that the Natives have rights to use off-reservation lands "until required to move by the President," which never happened.

Still, courts have tussled, lawyers have caviled, and since that 1983 decision, the Ojibwa have, come spring and fall, returned to the waters and, using traditional-style tridents, harvested walleye and a few muskies. In essence, the decision stated that Native Americans are entitled to first fishing and to a 100% take of off-reservation lakes, so long as the practice doesn't harm the resources.

During the first off-reservation season in 1985, 2,914 fish were taken; that figure rose steadily to an average high of 26,477 in 1988. Of those fish, 82% were males. The number of Native American participants rose from an original 194 to 426. The protests were on. The most famous group was Stop Treaty Abuse (STA), which garnered the most press coverage, good and bad. The basic arguments against Indian spearing are that it's unfair special privilege, the night-fishing disrupts the spawning of walleye (in fact, most lakes in the 1840s didn't even *have* walleye), and that if the Ojibwa take their limit, the result would be a zero limit on walleye for non-Indian anglers. (In the great north woods, that is tantamount to treason.)

Resort owners, anglers, and citizens, shellshocked by the very idea of all of it, didn't know what to do. Some contacted legislators, some organized committees, some went so far as to actually communicate with the Ojibwa, and still others squared off with the Indians at boat landings, where tension ran thick and more than a few incidents of violence ensued, spring after spring. Millions of dollars were spent in police overtime, and hundreds of arrests were made. At one point, the Wisconsin governor had to appear on television to beg the protestors to stay away from the landings.

Things calmed down until 1995, when the issue flared up again. First, the Menominee Nation in the southeast expressed a desire to reassert treaty rights over commercial fishing throughout a tremendously large expanse of northern Wisconsin, Michigan, and Lake Michigan. That winter, the Lac du Flambeau band of Ojibwa again considered a 100% take on off-reservation spearing. In 2000, federal courts blocked the tribes from their plans. Another din ensued, though this time a zero-limit for walleye was but a minor issue. Though the government denies it, the Ojibwa claim the state tried to railroad them into dropping their walleye limit by suggesting it would start looking closely at casino revenues if they didn't. Many believe opposition to Indian spearfishing presently has less to do with the walleye than it does resentment over the mere image of nouveau-riche Indians with loaded casino coffers.

The mesotrophic, spring-fed lakes of the Lac du Flambeau chain are also prime muskie waters—three world class records for line fishing have been recorded around here.

Lac du Flambeau

The town of Lac du Flambeau is virtually in the middle of the reservation, set amidst five lakes.

Approximately 30 lodging choices are spread throughout the 10 lakes in the vicinity of the reservation. The venerable **Dillman's Sand Lake Lodge,** tel. (715) 588-3143, is synonymous with North Woods Wisconsin. Currently the lodge offers B&B and regular lodge accommodations, in addition to comfortable rustic cabins perfect for families. And there's always something to do at Dillman's—the lodge often sponsors bike tours, and the Dillman's Creative Arts Foundation puts on a dinner theatre in conjunction with the University of Wisconsin-Stevens Point. And the amenities would take a page to list; over its 250 acres is everything one could want to do. There's also a sports program for children come summer. Rates run from $60 to $400.

Also in Lac du Flambeau is spiffy, luxurious **Fence Lake Lodge,** tel. (715) 588-3255, with one- to five-bedroom hilltop duplexes, vacation homes, and two popular, well-liked restaurants. Very modern rooms, nothing much rustic here. The place recently expanded greatly, so all you could imagine is now here. Rates start at $80 a day, $520 a week.

The **chamber of commerce,** tel. (715) 588-3346, is at Jeanne Murray's Country Casuals on Main Street. It's open 9 a.m.-5 p.m., Mon.-Sat. and noon-4 p.m. Sunday.

TURTLE-FLAMBEAU FLOWAGE

Bookending the western side of the Northern Highland American Legion State Forest is the "Crown Jewel of the North"—also called Wisconsin's version of the Boundary Waters Canoe Area of northern Minnesota. Of all Wisconsin's numerous flowages, reservoirs on major river chains, the Turtle-Flambeau is perhaps the wildest and most primitive, though a contrived version. The majority of its shoreline is in state hands and thus off-limits to development—in fact, many of the lakes in the flowage have only one (or no) resorts or cottages on them.

The area was originally dammed in 1926 by endless public and private endeavors to regulate water supply and secondarily supply power. With the Turtle backed up behind the "Hoover Dam of Iron County," the waterways of the Bear, Manitowish, Turtle and Flambeau Rivers became enmeshed. The resulting 20,000-plus acres, one of the larger bodies of water in the state, has never gotten the same attention as other regions of Wisconsin—thankfully so, say many. To keep it as close to wilderness as possible, in 1990 the state of Wisconsin bought the whole mess, lock, stock, and barrel. Nine lakes, numerous creeks, three rivers—backcountry lovers find it all orgasmic. Virtually all flora and fauna native to the state is here in spades, with the granddaddy sportfish, the lake sturgeon, also prowling the waters. The highest number in the state of nesting pairs of eagles, loons, and osprey are on the property.

The flowage is broached primarily via Mercer and Manitowish Waters on the north side, Springstead in the east, and Butternut/Park Falls on the west. The latter two towns are covered in the Northwest Wisconsin chapter.

Note: CR FF is a grand bicycle route stretching between Butternut and Mercer. Winding, rustic, and not too heavily laden with traffic, it's got some wearied sections of road, but overall isn't too bad.

Canoeing

The canoeing is superlative in the flowage—as close to alone as you could hope to be in many areas. The north fork of the Flambeau River is a 26-mile trip from the flowage to Park Falls; almost two dozen rapids are transgressed en route. Eight hours is average for this one. Rapids run Class I and Class II.

The **Bear River Trail** is a 25-mile trip, reasonable for novices, that leaves southwest of Lac du Flambeau on Flambeau Lake, with one easy rapid; eventually it joins up with the Manitowish River and lolls into the town of Manitowish.

The heart of the flowage is traversed by two popular trails: the **Manitowish Route** and the **Turtle River Route.** The former is 10 miles from Murray's Landing, west of Manitowish, to Turtle Dam on the east side of the flowage. It isn't difficult, per se, but water levels fluctuate and it's tough-going, orienting wise. A compass and the ability to read one are recommended. The Turtle River Route is from Lake of the Falls County Park at CR FF to Turtle Dam on the west side. This is an easy, one-day access.

Accommodations

Many simple North Woods-style cabins, lodges, and resorts line the southwestern section of the flowage, essentially trailing CR FF from Butternut to Mercer. The places are no frills, precisely the way it's supposed to be. Included within is the **Lake View Resort,** on Bastine Lake, tel. (715) 476-2506. The cabins here are modern and cozy with all possible amenities, along with a swimming beach. A lounge is on-site. Daily rates available, weekly rates from around $400. Right nearby are similar digs at **Idle Shores Resort,** tel. (715) 476-2504, with one- to three-bedroom cottages. This one is open May to October only.

Good is the year-round **Daly's Cedar Lodge,** also on Bastine Lake, tel. (715) 476-2511, with a rich lodge and rustic log cottages available. Light housekeeping and some meal plans are available.

For those who would rather rough it, over a dozen established campsites are found along the flowage, many on little islets dotting the reservoir—that's the best camping. The eastern bulbous portion of the Chequamegon National Forest is also right nearby. Contact any of the area's chambers of commerce for specifics on regulations and precise locations—some of the sites are not easy to find. Sites are first-come, first-served.

Information

Further details on the area can be gained from the **Turtle-Flambeau Flowage Club,** 6365 O'Meara Rd., Butternut, WI 54514, tel. (715) 476-2506.

THE IRON RANGE

Hurley and even smaller Montreal lie in the midst of the mighty Penokee Iron Range as well as the over-the-border Gogebic Iron Range, the last and most massive of the Upper Peninsula's three prodigious iron deposits, long since depleted. The range, to many Wisconsinites, has been unfairly relegated to backwater status—too many news reports in southern Wisconsin mentioned the population flight from Iron County in the bad old days of economic decline. And while it is true the county ranks pretty low in population and thus doesn't have the infrastructure taxes to pretty things up as the richer areas to the southeast do, Iron County has important history and even some outstanding topography. The Turtle-Flambeau Flowage is one of the most wilderness-like stretches of any northern river, and Iron County competes squarely with across-the-state rival Marinette County for numbers of cascades. Marinette may have more, but no falls beat Iron County's for sheer height and isolation.

The Flambeau Trail

Native Americans followed a route from Saxon Harbor northwest of Hurley, portaging canoes and beaver pelts between their villages and Northwest Fur Co. Trading Posts. The 90-mile trail from Madeline Island to Lac du Flambeau became the crucial Flambeau Trail, followed in due course by explorers, trappers, traders, and the U.S. military. The whole thing is mapped out now, passing Superior Falls at the first take-out point. **Little Finland,** one of the last and best bastions of hardy *Suomi* mining heritage in the Upper Midwest, houses the National Finnish-American Cultural Center—here check out the Finnish-style fish-tail construction of adhering beams, which once stood in Ashland's bay as an ore dock. Also, head five miles south of Hurley to the corner of Dupont and Rein Roads, where you'll see a huge stone barn designed by a Finnish stonemason. The trail later passes the **continental divide;** the northern waters above the divide were unnavigable, necessitating this 45-mile portage to southern-flowing streams. Finally, the trail reaches the Turtle-Flambeau Flowage area at the reconstructed **Mercer Depot**—now a historical society office—before heading into Manitowish and the trail's debouchment toward Lac du Flambeau.

HURLEY

Living museum Hurley, population 1,800, sure had some big britches in its headier early days. The little town—more or less a sister city to boomtown Ironwood, Michigan, across the border—arose a century ago on the iron riches taken from the subterranean veins of the mammoth Gogebic and Penokee Iron Ranges, the former accounting for almost 40% of the Upper Peninsula's economy at its zenith (some 350 mines tore through the subterranean stretches). White pine wealth followed later. "Lusty infants on a diet of lumber and iron ore," the old WPA guide noted.

What really set Hurley apart from other boomtowns was its unimaginable bacchanalia, for which it became legendary. At its sybaritic zenith, more than 75 saloons lined the aptly named Silver Street, wooing the 7,000-odd salty miners and loggers. The same WPA guide quotes the prevailing wisdom along the logger/miner transient railway: "The four toughest places in the world are Cumberland, Hayward, Hurley, and Hell, and Hurley is the toughest of 'em all." It is against a background of such legend that Wisconsin native and Pulitzer Prize-winner Edna Ferber set the harrowing, only slightly fictionalized account of the brutal Lottie Morgan murder, *Come and Get It,* in Hurley.

Things tamed somewhat with the waning fortunes of ore and receding lines of timber—not to mention Prohibition. Many saloons and dance halls boarded up tight. The rest, however, went backroom or simply hibernated while the mobsters used Hurley as a haven during Prohibition. When Prohibition was repealed, the town again saw a throwback to drinking and debauchery—even *more* drinking halls lined the raucous Silver Street.

Things have finally cooled off in tough-as-hell Hurley; in fact, you'd be hard-pressed to find anything rowdier along Silver Street than an occasional argument over a Packer game in a local tavern. To be sure, though, Silver Street hasn't lost all of what made it (in)famous. As recently as the late 1980s, the City Council was divided over how (or whether) to close down the more exotic clubs on the lower blocks of Silver Street. Otherwise, Hurley finds itself wrapped in lore and history—proudly so—with its grand old courthouse,

the warehouse of historical trappings, and as the nucleus of a winter recreation paradise.

Sights

The *grande dame* of Iron County is the somewhat wearied but eminently proud **Iron County Courthouse,** tel. (715) 561-2244, now doubling as the county's repository of historical artifacts. It is indeed a leviathan—a turreted and steepled structure full to overflowing with Iron County memorabilia throughout its multi-layered interiors. Built in 1893 for a princely $40,000 and sold later to the county, the courthouse stands gracefully behind the town atop a small rise. You could spend an entire afternoon poking around this place. A personal favorite is the mock-up of a Silver Street saloon on the top floor, using carved bars from one of those that made the town legendary. Or visit on a Saturday and you might see volunteers using original turn-of-the-century Scandinavian-style rag-rug weaving looms. Local craftsmen have also built replicas of model homesteads, schools, and a post office. Exhibits range from coins, lace, and old typewriters to the original courthouse clock, dating from 1893. The basement has a morgue—seriously—with a tin casket, cooling board, altar, and requisite old Bible. Open year-round Monday, Wednesday, Friday, and Saturday 10 a.m.-2 p.m. Free, but donations are requested.

A mile west of town is the art-deco **Cary Mine Building,** west on WI 77 to Ringle Dr., the epicenter of mining operations for 80 years.

Waterfalls

Iron County boasts over 50 waterfalls, from the wilderness-accessible to the roadside. It's the highest concentration in the Midwest. The highest are personal favorites **Potato River Falls** and the hard-to-find **Superior Falls,** both a respectable 90 feet. To reach the Potato River Falls, head west; south of US 2 in Gurney is a sign to Potato River Falls along a gravel road. Magnificent upper and lower falls don't see many folks, so the trails are great for exploring. There's also rustic camping. Continuing on down WI 169 will bring you to Wren Falls, with great trout fishing and more primitive camping, though a meager 15-foot drop for the falls. Superior Falls is west of Hurley 12 miles, then north on WI 122 for 4.2 miles. Cross the Michigan border, go half a mile, and turn left on a gravel road (it's easy to miss—keep your eyes peeled). There's a parking area and signs to the great, chuffing 90-foot cascade raining into Lake Superior.

The east branch of the Montreal River has **Peterson Falls** (35 feet) and **Spring Camp Falls** (20 feet). The west branch has **Kimball Park Falls,** with a series of riffles; 15-foot **Gile Falls** (check out the large waste rock tailing piles across the way); and **Rock Cut Falls.** The latter is generally regarded as tops in the county. To get to Rock Cut, go west on WI 77, then left on 9th Ave. to a stop sign. Turn left onto Division St. for a block. Go straight through the stop sign. CR D will curve, so veer off it straight onto an unnamed gravel road, and drive one more mile to a T-intersection. Go right onto a gravel road to the ATV trail. Park here and walk left on the trail to the ridge.

The Turtle River in the Mercer area also has three oft-visited falls, including the ever-popular **Lake of the Falls,** with rustic camping. The Upson area has two cascades, **Rouse Falls** and **Little Balsam Falls,** which are accessible only with some orienteering. Easier and equally lovely falls can be found along the Black River Parkway north of Ironwood and Bessemer, Michigan, north of Hurley in the Upper Peninsula.

The **Wisconsin Travel Center,** along US 51/2, offers detailed directions for each waterfall.

Accommodations

Hurley's got a few budget motels, but you'd do best to head east into Ironwood, MI, along US 2; there you'll find some good $35 rooms, and many of those motels have Finnish-style saunas. In Hurley near the Wisconsin Travel Center the **Holiday Inn,** 1000 US 51 N, tel. (715) 561-3030, has rooms from $50 s, $65 d. It features a pool, sauna, whirlpool, and restaurant.

You can even rent **The Granite House,** tel. (715) 561-2963, a turn-of-the-century, five-bedroom granite house, fully furnished.

For **camping,** the closest county park is Weber Lake, west of town on WI 77, right on CR E. Sites are $7. Another is at **Saxon Harbor,** at Lake Superior off US 2 onto WI 122. This is really for RVs, though. A private option is **Frontier Bar and Campgrounds,** tel. 715-893-2461, on US 2 W. at WI 169 junction.

Food

There's nothing of much culinary interest in Hurley. Downtown along Silver Street you'll find about a dozen assorted watering holes, restaurants, or combinations of both. **Cardo's Cafe** sure isn't much to look at inside but offers decent omelettes and good pasties. From $3. **Silver Dragon,** tel. (715) 561-9807, is the best Chinese eatery, with a good-sized menu of pan-Cathay entrées. From $5. Also along Silver Street, **Freddie's Old Time Saloon and Hall of Fame,** tel. (715) 561-5020, has great character—it's full of antiques and original fixtures—and a complete menu. Enjoy the only charbroiled steaks around, along with some decent steamed seafood and ribs, at **Branding Iron Supper Club,** tel. (715) 561-4562, open from 5 p.m. daily. From $4. Off Silver St., there's Italian and American fare at **Liberty Bell Chalet,** 109 5th Ave., tel. (715) 561-3753. From $4.

Entertainment and Events

Bars and taverns worth mentioning line the historic five blocks of the downtown Silver Street area.

The oldest marathon in the state and second-oldest in the Midwest (dating from 1969) is the **Paavo Nurmi Marathon,** named, appropriately, for a Finn—dubbed the "Flying Finn" for his numerous Olympic gold medals—and run in August. It's a good place to feast on pasties and *mojakaa,* a beef stew. Thanks to all the snow, Hurley holds its **Red Light Snowmobile Rally** earlier than most, in mid-December.

Recreation

This is Big Snow Country, so snowmobiling is king—bigger even than skiing. Over 350 miles of groomed trails are spread throughout the vicinity, and rentals are available in Hurley. The town even maintains a **24-hour recreation hotline** at (715) 561-FUNN for updates on snow conditions.

The **Whitecap Ski Area,** tel. (715) 561-2227, is in Montreal to the west. Thirty-three runs ribbon through a 400-foot vertical drop, with the longest some 5,000 feet. It's serviced by one quad, one triple, and four double chairlifts and a couple of tow ropes. Snowboarding is allowed. Open daily 9 a.m.-4 p.m. Lift tickets cost $30 adults, $25 ages 12 to 17 on weekends and holidays, about five bucks less during the week. Even larger operations are across the border in the Upper Peninsula.

Three cross-country trails are maintained in the vicinity totaling some 40 miles. Contact the Iron County Development Zone Council, tel. (715) 562-2922, for information. The trails are maintained by donations.

A magnificent trail network for bikers is the 300-mile **Pines and Mines Mountain Bike Trail System,** operated jointly by Michigan, Wisconsin, and the USFS and running through the carpets of forests in Iron County and the Upper Peninsula. Michigan has two good ones—the **Ehlco Tract Complex** and **Pomeroy/Henry Lake** set of gravel roads. Iron County has the third section, an amazing spider web of trails and road leading along old railroad grades, logging roads, and roadways, passing historical sites (in particular the Plummer mine headframe) and tons of forests, streams, and even waterfalls. Those in incredible shape could even make it all the way to Mercer, or west to Upson and beyond. Thirteen of the best waterfalls are accessible via this system. Most trails are suitable for beginners to intermediate bikers, but trail #6 (Montreal to Weber Lake)—a trail that really makes you want to take it—is excruciating, if not hellish, as is trail #13 (Hogs Back) from south of the Gile Flowage to Island Lake Road. For info or maps, contact the Hurley chamber of commerce, tel. (715) 561-4334, or the Pines and Mines Mountain Bike Trail System, P.O. Box 706, Ironwood, MI 49938.

Services and Information

The **Hurley Chamber of Commerce,** tel. (715) 561-4334, www.hurleywi.com, is at 316 Silver Street.

Pick up valuable information and get a bathroom stop at the fresh-looking **Wisconsin Travel Information Center,** tel. (715) 561-5310, along US 51 North. This center has the same information on Hurley as the chamber of commerce downtown and, inexplicably, some that the downtown office doesn't have. Staff can point out directions to nearby sights, too. On the grounds of the travel center is a minor museum relating the town's mining past—walk through a sundial explication of the local mines, check out some gargantuan mining drill remnants, or take a gander at the dozens of artifacts donated to the museum by area families. Open April through late May daily 8 a.m.-4 p.m.; through September Mon.-Sat. 8 a.m.-6 p.m. and Sunday until 4 p.m.; through October 30 daily 8 a.m.-4 p.m. (perhaps longer on Friday); thereafter, Tues.-Sat. 8 a.m.-4 p.m.

VICINITY OF HURLEY

Montreal

Along the way to Montreal, note exceedingly diminutive Pence, with over 20 log structures of all sorts visible from the road. This is one of the largest concentrations of such architecture in Wisconsin.

Once peopled by company miners living in squat white shotgun shacks, Montreal today is a living microcosm of the area's heritage. Long ago it was the site of the world's deepest iron ore mine, memorialized with a marker along WI 77. Once the only completely planned and platted company town in Wisconsin, the whole place is on the National Register of Historic Places. Mining is gone but not forgotten—it lives on in the only extant mining headframe west of town, the **Plummer Mine Headframe.** Eighty feet tall and imposing as ever, it's one of the truer pieces of history you'll see around. An interpretive park surrounds it.

Accommodations in Montreal are limited to **The Inn,** 104 Wisconsin Ave., tel. (715) 561-5180, a 1913 B&B built by the Montreal Mining Co. for workers. Plenty of family antiques and quilts adorn the interiors. Rates from $55.

NORTHWESTERN WISCONSIN

Enormous northwestern Wisconsin defies any attempts to capture it in thumbnail sketches. Within one grand region, the northwest offers everything that the rest of the state can boast—millions of acres of local, county, state, and federal forest verdance; superb littoral stretches of Lake Superior; a National Scenic Riverway buttressed in the south by the Great River Road; unrivaled wilderness flowages; the Duluth-Superior inland harbor; and one of the greatest concentrations of lakes in the world.

The northwestern reaches are also known as Indianhead Country, ostensibly because the northern stretch of the St. Croix River and the Bayfield Peninsula form a Native American chief gazing westward. That may be a bit of a stretch, but it does lend a touch of romanticism to the region.

EAU CLAIRE AND VICINITY

The city of "Clear Water" is the largest community in northern Wisconsin and lies at a strategic point in the Chippewa River Valley, at the confluence of the Chippewa and Eau Claire Rivers. Busy and pretty, it's bigger (56,000 and change) than anybody in the state realizes. With an eclectic economy and a University of Wisconsin satellite campus, the city's got a solid economic base bolstered by the city's gateway status.

History

The first timber opportunists likely came snooping as early as 1822, and one hardy family erected a rough cabin near the mouth of the Eau Claire River in 1832. The first mills went up in 1845, and immigrants poured in, eventually settling three separate villages. By the Civil War, over two dozen sawmills were shrieking all night long,

pushing three million board feet of logs through per hour at peak production. In total, Eau Claire would process 46 million board feet of lumber, which explains its nickname, "Sawdust City."

Eau Claire went through the usual lumber boomtown throes—a saloon for every five residents. Worse were the internecine timber squabbles and violent flare-ups the city fought with upstream rival Chippewa Falls over strategic and valuable water rights. Eau Claire's powers had the forethought to harness the local rapids for hydroelectric power, one reason it would eventually eclipse Chippewa Falls up the river when the timber vanished. Eau Claire also lay close enough to the south's agrarian industry to diversify into vegetable processing, an industry in which the city is considered a national leader.

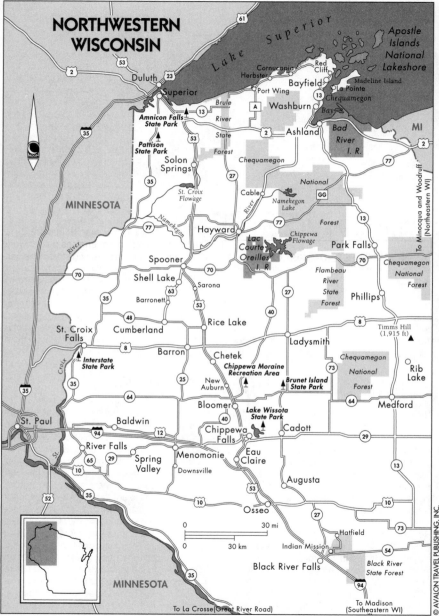

SIGHTS

Carson Park

The hub of Eau Claire's tourist attractions is Carson Park, a 134-acre peninsular playground jutting into Half Moon Lake west of downtown. The park road swoops up and along minor bluff lines and through some fairly impressive woodsy areas. The primary attraction is the **Chippewa Valley Museum**, tel. (715) 834-7871, with award-winning displays on the valley's Ojibwa culture as well as explication on the city's growth during European incursion. Of note are the 21-room dollhouse and an anachronistic ice cream parlor. Also on the grounds is the Anderson Log House, an 1850s two-story home designed in Swedish architectural style; and a one-room schoolhouse, the Sunnyview School, dating from 1882 and

also available for tours. Both are open May-Sept. (until October for the Anderson house) and come with admission to the museum. The museum is open Tues.-Sun. 1-5 p.m., daily 10 a.m.-5 p.m. in summer; admission costs $3 adults, $1 children.

The **Paul Bunyan Logging Camp**, tel. (715) 835-6200, a replica of an 1890s camp, features an interpretive center with unusual and wonderful file footage of logging operations among its timber paraphernalia. The camp structures include a bunkhouse, dingle, filer's shop, cookhouse, barn, tons of heavy equipment, and, of course, the requisite Paul Bunyan and Babe the Blue Ox statue. The museum is open daily April through Labor Day 10 a.m.-4:30 p.m., the rest of the year Tues.-Fri. 1-4:30 p.m. and weekends 10 a.m.-4:30 p.m. Admission is $3 adults, $1.50 children.

The **Chippewa Valley Railroad** offers rides on a half-mile 16-gauge line through the park. The two coal-fired steam engines pull all-wood 1880s passenger coaches, two streamline passenger coaches, a gondola car, a caboose, and a couple of steel coaches. One of the best specimens of state rail history—the Soo Line 2719 steam locomotive—is displayed. Trips run Sunday noon-5 p.m. Memorial Day through Labor Day and cost $1 adults, 50 cents children 12 and under.

Carson Park is also the home of the **Eau Claire Cavaliers** baseball team. Long a bastion for the boys of summer, Eau Claire has fielded semi-pro teams since the early 1900s. Burleigh Grimes, a northwestern Wisconsin boy done good, pitched for the Eau Claire Bears and later in the pros before being enshrined in Cooperstown in 1964. The Cavaliers are a semi-pro team made up of local and regional players, some with minor-league experience. A statue of Hank Aaron now stands at the entrance to the stadium. Hammerin' Hank got his professional baseball start in Eau Claire in 1952 with the Eau Claire Bears. This team still exists and shares time in Carson Park, but this manifestation is composed mostly of former high school and American Legion players.

In addition to the trappings of touristdom, Carson Park is the city's primary recreational spot, with dozens of ballfields, stadiums, courts, and trails. The Birch Creek Picnic Area is especially nice.

NORTHWESTERN WISCONSIN HIGHLIGHTS

American Birkebeiner, Hayward/Cable
Amnicon Falls State Park, Superior
Apostle Islands National Lakeshore
Carson Park, Eau Claire
Chequamegon National Forest
Copper Falls State Park, Mellen
Dells Mill, Augusta
Flambeau River State Forest, Park Falls
Gandy Dancer Trail, St. Croix Falls
Jacob Leinenkugel Brewing Company,
Chippewa Falls
Lake Superior Big Top Chautauqua,
Bayfield
Madeline Island, Bayfield
National Freshwater Fishing Hall of Fame,
Hayward
Pattison Falls State Park, Superior
Sigurd Olson Environmental Institute,
Ashland
Soo Line Ore Dock, Ashland
SS *Meteor*, Superior
**St. Croix Falls/Namekagon National Scenic
Riverway**
The Hideout, Couderay
The Norske Nook, Osseo
Timm's Hill County Park
Wisconsin Concrete Park, Phillips

Historic Homes and Walking Tour

Eau Claire has entire blocks of extant historic structures and homes dating from lumber-baron days. Many remain despite the town's being partially burned out by the periodic conflagrations that plagued every "sawdust city" in northern Wisconsin. City fathers had had enough of it by the end of the Civil War and passed the first of many "fire-proof building" ordinances, which essentially preserved the city's structures for modernity.

At the corner of Lake and Farwell Streets is the linchpin of historic architectural displays, the **Schlegelmilch House,** tel. (715) 832-7028. The 1871 edifice is modest but obviously belonged to a well-to-do family; it was the first to be built out of stone. The public can only tour the house on group tours or special events.

University of Wisconsin-Eau Claire

The lovely UW-Eau Claire campus is south of the Chippewa River and downtown via State Street at 105 Garfield Ave., tel. (715) 836-2637. On campus, the **Newman Clark Bird Museum** is an odd, circular structure housing a respected ornithological collection of 530 species. A **planetarium** with a star show and regular lectures, and a nice **greenhouse** on the fifth floor of the Phillips Science Hall, featuring a tropical rainforest, a dry climate, and other botanical exhibits, can also be found here. The **Foster Art Gallery** has two major shows annually and permanent smaller exhibits.

All are free, though hours vary. An **arboretum** sprawls over 200 acres and has self-guided trails.

Side Trips

Lots of outstanding road trips exist in the Eau Claire area. The most promising is to Augusta, 20 or so miles to the southeast via US 12. Easily one of the most photographed gems along the route is the **Dells Mill,** three miles north off WI 27 on CR V, tel. (715) 286-2714. This eye-catching 1864 mill and museum, set along engaging Bridge Creek, is predominantly a museum, but some grinding is still done on site. The remarkable thing about the mill is that its five structures are constructed solely of hand-hewn timber joined only by wooden pegs. Inside you'll find over 3,000 feet of belting and 175 water-forced pulleys. The museum is open daily May-Oct. 10 a.m.-5 p.m. Admission is $7 adults, $3.50 students 6-18, and $1.50 children.

Augusta is in a region rich in Amish culture. **The Wood Shed,** 105 W. Lincoln St., tel. (715) 286-5404, has 10,000 square feet of folk art and Amish woodwork, quilting, wall hangings, baskets, rugs, dolls, and furniture. Open Mon.-Sat. 10 a.m.-5:30 p.m. The store arranges tours of the Amish countryside.

While in Augusta, head for **Chuck's Black Bear Supper Club,** north on WI 27, tel. (715) 286-2687. This excellent supper club, built in a log structure, oozes with regional character and offers all the usual culinary trappings of a Wisconsin supper club.

Cadott is approximately 15 miles east of Chippewa Falls on WI 29, at the junction with WI 27. You'll find a **veterans' tribute** featuring 43 flags, the first to honor Asian veterans of the Vietnam War. Another martial marker is along CR X in Cadott, this one honoring Lansing Wilcox, Wisconsin's last Civil War veteran. Four miles north from Cadott on WI 27, a trademark local sign informs you you're exactly halfway between the North Pole and the equator.

ACCOMMODATIONS

Clairemont Avenue

The **Eau Claire Motel,** tel. (715) 835-5148 or (800) 624-3763, 3120 E. Clairemont Ave., has a restaurant and continental breakfast and rates in the $30-35 range.

Closer to downtown at the western end of Clairemont Ave. is the **Ramada Conference Center,** 1202 W. Clairemont, tel. (715) 834-3181 or (800) 482-7829, with over 240 rooms, a full slate of amenities, and rates from $60.

After Clairemont bends to the north you'll find **Westgate Motel,** 1436 N. Clairemont Ave., tel. (715) 834-3580, offering low-budget rooms from $35 and up, with a free continental breakfast.

Downtown

Not too expensive and worth the money, the **Green Tree Inn Suites,** 516 Galloway St., tel. (715) 832-3411 or (800) 236-3411, is close to the downtown convention center and offers many two-room suites. From $40.

South

South Hastings Way has quite a few lodging choices. The cheapest is **Maple Manor Motel,** 2507 S. Hastings Way, tel. (715) 834-2618 or (800) 624-3763, with rooms from $35, some with kitchenettes. The rooms are oddly but appealingly detailed in Chippewa River Valley themes, and a made-to-order breakfast is included.

A very respectable operation is **Antlers,** 2245 S. Hastings Way, tel. (715) 834-5313 or (800) 423-4526, offering 33 rooms in a basic set-up. Rates start at $38 and include a continental breakfast.

Southwest

The cheapest rooms on Craig Road are at the **Exel Inn,** 2305 Craig Rd., tel. (715) 834-3193 or (800) 367-3935, offering some in-room whirlpools. Rates start at $38, including a free continental breakfast.

The **Comfort Inn,** 3117 Craig Rd., tel. (715) 833-9798 or (800) 221-2222, has an indoor pool, sauna, and rooms from $55 and up.

Bed and Breakfasts

Perched on a hillock with a commanding view of the Chippewa River Valley, **Fanny Hill,** 3919 Crescent Ave., tel. (715) 836-8184 or (800) 292-8026, rests amidst one of the largest flower gardens in the state (eight acres of Victorian gardens landscaped and adorned to match the season). The inn is a lovely, absolutely immense Victorian home. The 11 rooms are done in a variety of styles and start at $79. In addition, over 750,000 guests have come for the dining room and dinner theater combination.

Set along Otter Creek on 15 wooded acres, **The Atrium** is a half mile off of US 53 North on Prill Rd., tel. (715) 833-9045. Built around an atrium with 20-foot glass ceiling and featuring a fountain in the middle, the guest house interiors feature hand-stenciling and rustic antiques, including an antique pump organ in the parlor. Rooms start from $60.

Camping
East out of Altoona via CR Q, the **Beaver Creek Reserve** is actually an environmental education and outdoor recreation center on 360 acres. A nature center and observatory are also on the grounds. Contact the director's office, tel. (715) 877-2212, for camping availability. Two more campgrounds are found about a half hour east off US 12 and charge $12 for sites. You'd probably be better off just driving up through Chippewa Falls to Lake Wissota State Park for larger and better-maintained sites.

FOOD

Fanny Hill
Travel media and food scribes slobber and gush about the dining and drama combo at the Fanny Hill Inn. The dining is certainly worth the kudos. Seated in a tastefully decorated dining room offering superb views of the Chippewa Valley through floor-to-ceiling windows, diners get a true epicurean experience. In addition to the four-star international gourmet meal, a show—mysteries, comedies, and lots of musicals and music-based revues—is offered. Dinner and shows start at 6 p.m. Thurs.-Sat., 5 p.m. Sunday, and costs $20 for show only and up to $37 for dinner and show. Matinees are also held weekdays.

Family Restaurants
The best bet for road-weary families is the **Fireside**, 2831 Hendrickson Dr., tel. (715) 835-7397, open daily at 6 a.m. offering a budget-pleasing 32-item breakfast buffet on weekends 8-11:30 a.m. From $3.

So popular that it's now expanded throughout the valley, **Heckel's Big Steer Family Restaurant,** at 805 S. Hastings Way, tel. (715) 834-2076, and 1106 W. Clairemont Ave., tel. (715) 834-7101, has offered downhome cooking with enormous portions since 1961. The menu lists one page of breakfasts, one of sandwiches, and one of meat-and-potatoes dinners. From $3.

One place most folks don't know about is the **Red Brick Cafe,** 800 Wisconsin St., on the second floor of Building 2 in Banbury Industrial Mall. This is awesome Midwestern comfort food like pot roast, casseroles, and homemade soups. From $3.

Supper Clubs and American
Fischer's White House, 1920 S. Hastings Way, tel. (715) 832-9711, is a supper club specializing in aged steaks and pastas. The bread and popovers are baked on-site, and a variety of eclectic seafood specialties spice things up. Dinner served daily. **Wally's Chalet,** 1505 N. Clairemont Ave., tel. (715) 832-0880, is still in operation after five decades. Thursday and Saturday prime rib and a Friday fish fry are Wally's specialties; open daily for lunch and dinner. Both from $5.

You could almost call the fare at the great **Sweetwater's,** 1104 W. Clairemont Ave., tel. (715) 834-5777, eclectic American. It serves outstanding gourmet wood-fired pizzas, lots of pasta, and creative takes on the usuals, including prime rib. From $4.

Pub Grub
Camaraderie, 442 Water St., tel. (715) 834-5411, is a bar-cum-cafe chock-full of fading photographs and boasting an antique Wurlitzer. The interior decor and accoutrements consist in part of recycled wood from Eau Claire and northern Wisconsin buildings. The casual restaurant has a large menu of salads, a page of sandwiches, and steaks and seafood, but the house specialty is fried cheese curds. Open daily for lunch and dinner, with daily specials. From $4.

Cafe
Excellent is the **Acoustic Cafe,** 505 South Barstow St., tel. (715) 832-9090, with great sandwiches, pitas, and the best coffee in town. Plus it's got reliable live music. From $3.

Barbecue
On the "other" side of the park, **Mike's Smokehouse and Roadhouse BBQ,** 2235 N. Clairemont, tel. (715) 834-8153, has way above average barbecue, excellent side dishes, and a festive atmosphere. It's a great place. From $3.

Asian

Two blocks south of the Holiday Inn-Campus, the **Yenking,** 2930 Craig Rd., tel. (715) 835-3348, has Sichuan, Hunan, and Cantonese along with house-specialty Peking dishes. Yenking also offers a good lunch buffet; open daily for lunch and dinner. From $5.

You'll find teppan-yaki and good seafood at **Tokyo,** 2426 London Rd., tel. (715) 834-0313, as well as traditional dining. The only Japanese restaurant in town, Tokyo is closed Monday, but open for lunch and dinner the rest of the week. From $6.

ENTERTAINMENT

A vaudeville "palace" and movie house in the Roaring '20s, the **The State: Regional Arts Center,** 316 Eau Claire St., tel. (715) 832-2787, has undergone a thorough makeover into a regional professional cultural center. Now home to local theater guilds, a children's theater troupe, and a symphony, it also features national touring acts.

Eau Claire is not exactly a hotbed of nightlife. The most buzzing place downtown is **The Corner Stone,** 304 Eau Claire St., tel. (715) 838-9494, a bar with live music. The **Acoustic Cafe** (see "Food") has folkier music; nearby on South Barstow is **Houligan's,** another bar with live bands. **Colby's Grille,** in the Holiday Inn, features jazz on Tuesday. The **Cabin,** at the university, is the oldest coffeehouse in Wisconsin, with folk, blues, jazz, and occasional comedy. The **Artists Series** has a school-year schedule of music, theater, and dance. For university information, call the activities and programs office at (715) 836-4833. Fanny Hill's dinner theater (see under "Food," above) is another good entertainment option.

EVENTS

During the third weekend in January, the **Winterfest** celebration in Carson Park features snow carving, children's slides, sleigh rides, outdoor sports, and a hot-air balloon race.

The largest country hoedown in Wisconsin is **Country Jam USA** in Eau Claire, held the third week of July. The biggest names in country

music kick up their heels for four days and turn Eau Claire into something decidedly different from its usual self. At about the same time, nearby Cadott hosts a **Rock Fest,** with dozens of national or prominent acts on their "second wind." Another large country music festival is **Country Fest** in nearby Cadott.

RECREATION

Chippewa River Trail

This nearly three-mile-long multi-use path runs through Eau Claire's urban river corridor. The river trail in turn joins with the larger **Chippewa Valley Trail,** which eventually leads through prairie, mixed forest, and agrarian patchworks to Menomonie and the **Red Cedar State Trail.** The Eau Claire trailhead is north of the Eau Claire River, then north on Barstow Street. You can access the river trail at Carson Park (a spur trail) or at UWEC. No trail pass is needed in the city, but a $3 daily pass is needed on the state trails. Get your bike rental at **Riverside Bike and Skate,** 902 Menomonie St., tel. (715) 835-0088, open daily.

Canoeing

The Eau Claire and Chippewa Rivers do have some fairly good, placid stretches, devoid of buzzing powercraft. Half Moon Lake around Carson Park is a perfectly refreshing one-hour wisp of a ride. Another common trip runs from the Paper Mill Dam on the Chippewa to Hobbs Landing, taking you through downtown. **Riverside Bike and Skate,** 902 Menomonie St., tel. (715) 835-0088, is open daily and rents equipment for all your recreation needs. It also offers pedal and paddle shuttles and tours.

SERVICES AND INFORMATION

The **Chippewa Valley Visitor Center,** tel. (715) 834-2345 or (800) 344-3866, www.chippewavalley.com, is at 3625 Gateway Dr., just off US 53 south of town at Golf Road. The spacious and well-stocked center has loads of information and the cleanest restrooms for miles. Open 8 a.m.-5 p.m. weekdays and 10 a.m.-3 p.m. weekends, it's also got a 24-hour vestibule with a direct-dial courtesy phone to area lodgings.

The main post office, tel. (715) 830-5300 or (715) 830-5707, is downtown at 126 N. Barstow

Street. Hours are 8 a.m.-4:30 p.m. weekdays and 9 a.m.-1 p.m. Saturdays. The LE Phillips Memorial **Library,** tel. (715) 839-5005, is at 400 Eau Claire Street. **Sacred Heart Hospital** is at 900 W. Clairemont Ave., tel. (715) 839-4222.

GETTING THERE AND AWAY

By Bus
The **Greyhound** station, tel. (715) 832-9707, is at 101 N. Farwell St. and is open from 7:45 a.m.-7 p.m. daily.

By Air
The **Chippewa Valley Regional Airport,** 3800 Starr Ave., tel. (715) 839-4900, is north of town off US 53. **Northwest Airlink,** tel. (715) 835-6166, operates a shuttle to the Minneapolis-St. Paul airport six times daily.

Eau Claire Passenger Service, tel. (715) 835-0399, also operates ground transportation between Eau Claire's Holiday Inn and the Minneapolis-St. Paul airport. Ten trips leave daily between 5:30 a.m. and 8 p.m., and a one-way ticket costs $25.

GETTING AROUND

Eau Claire City Transit, tel. (715) 839-5111, operates a 14-line bus system traversing the city and going into Altoona. Buses run 6 a.m.-6 p.m. weekdays, from 8 a.m. on Saturdays. Fares are $1 adults, 50 cents seniors. Bus lines #2 and #7 get somewhat close to Carson Park, while the green line, #4, operates around the university.

Cabco, tel. (715) 832-1573, is a 24-hour taxi service serving Eau Claire.

CHIPPEWA FALLS

Eau Claire may be the city of clear water, but its chief competitor today is the "City of Pure Water," so called for the natural springs that still feed into the beer that made it famous—Leinenkugel's (known as "Leinie's" in virtually every tavern north of Illinois). Those same springs feed the Chippewa River, which floated millions of board feet of cord wood down the Chippewa to the sawdust city of Eau Claire in the

previous century. The water in Chippewa Falls is claimed as the "purest" in the U.S.—just ask the locals. A private laboratory in Minneapolis was called in to settle a friendly feud between Deming, New Mexico, and Chippewa Falls in 1969. The lab gave a nearly perfect quality rating to Chippewa Falls' water—and it's been boasting about it ever since. Cray Computer is a more recent addition to the local economy. Chippewa Falls has also been noted by preservationists as one of the country's best preserved; in part due to this *Time* magazine rated it one of the country's top 10 small towns. The National Trust for Historic Preservation has called it one of the U.S.'s top 10 "Distinctive Destinations," based on historic structures maintained.

Sights
Walk into any tavern in the northwoods of Wisconsin and the beer of choice is indisputably Leinie's. The **Jacob Leinenkugel Brewing Co.,** WI 124 North, tel. (715) 723-5557, has been using the crystal clear waters of Chippewa Falls to brew beer since 1867, when it first opened as the Spring Brewery. It went from one brand of beer (400 barrels) its first year to nine premium brands, today sold throughout the region. Half-hour tours are given Mon.-Sat. June-Aug. and weekdays Sept.-May. Hours vary, but generally the gift shop stays open summer Mon.-Sat. 9:30 a.m.-3 p.m. and Sunday 11:30 a.m.-3 p.m. and tours leave whenever there are enough people—on a tighter schedule if demand warrants. Reservations aren't necessary, but on weekends they're a good idea. The tour is free and takes in the whole brewing process. Yes, free samples are offered at the end.

checking the brew at Leinenkugel's Brewery

You can actually view the primevally pure gurgling springs at the **Chippewa Spring House,** 600 Park Ave., tel. (715) 723-0872, one of the oldest landmarks in the valley and the community's first structure, built in 1836. A glass dome caps the icy water as it rises to flow toward the river, and you can still espy century-old hand-carved graffiti on the walls. Across the street is the **Chippewa Water Co. bottling plant,** started by poet Ezra Pound's grandfather and still in operation after more than a century. Samples are available.

The lumberman's mansion **Cook-Rutledge Home,** 505 W. Grand Ave., is a two-story red brick edifice featuring gingerbread trim and a veranda with extending porte cochere. The interiors are done in golden oak and stained-glass windows imported from Europe. The walls are covered with Lincrusta, an embossed linoleum, hand-painted to look like cordovan leather. Tours, taking in four rooms total, are available Thurs.-Sun. June-Aug. at 2 and 3 p.m. Admission is $3 adults, $1 ages 17 and under.

Housed in an old Notre Dame convent, the **Area History Center,** 123 Allen St., tel. (715) 723-4399, is repository of rotating exhibits. Check out the adjacent Goldsmith Chapel, an attraction in itself with ornate woodwork and stained-glass windows. Chippewa Falls' modern history is partially chronicled at the **Chippewa Falls Museum of Industry and Technology,** 21 E. Grand Ave., tel. (715) 720-9206. People are fairly surprised how important Chippewa Falls has been to the computer revolution; Cray Computers, builder of the world's most powerful supercomputers, was founded in Chippewa Falls. Besides the fascinating Seymour Cray Supercomputer Collection, visitors get a look at the history of manufacturing and processing in the city since the 1840s. Open Thurs.-Sat. 1-5 p.m.; admission is $3, $1 children.

Lake Wissota State Park sits opposite Chippewa Falls on the 6,300-acre lake created by the 1916 damming of the Chippewa River. Hydrophiles generally monopolize the park, but there are 11 miles of pretty flat trails along the shore or into the mixed marsh and prairie environment. A nature trail features 35 educational stops. There's great camping near the shore, and the park is maintained for winter camping also. The **Old Abe Trail** starts from here and runs 20 miles to Brunet Island State Park in Cornell.

Irvine Park is a local oddity—300 acres with a most impressive zoo, filled with native U.S. and exotic species. Also on the grounds you'll find a museum, an old schoolhouse, a 1936 fire truck, and antique machinery of all sorts. At Christmas, over 50,000 lights and 100 displays turn it into an old-time Christmas Village. The community pool, featuring a 160-foot slide, sits adjacent. Between the pool and the park sits the only public rose gardens between Madison and the Twin Cities, with 500 rose bushes and 300 lilies. Camping is available.

Accommodations

An inexpensive choice is the motel/supper club **Edelweiss,** north two miles on WI 124, tel. (715) 723-7881, with rooms starting at $30. The best rooms and most varied amenities are found at the **AmericInn,** 11 W. South Ave., tel. (715) 723-5711 or (800) 634-3444, with good rooms and an indoor pool, hot tub, sauna, and jacuzzi. Rates start at $60 and include a continental breakfast. Also try the brand-new **Country Inn by Carlson,** 1021 Park Ave., tel. (715) 720-1414, featuring rooms from $65.

Irvine Park offers camping right in town. **Lake Wissota State Park** has some excellent secluded campsites. The nearest private campground is **O'Neil Creek,** north on WI 124, then east on CR B, tel. (715) 723-6581, a four-season campground that also has cabins and plenty of rentals. Rates start at around $11 for a primitive site.

Food

The family restaurant of choice is absolutely **Olson's Ice Cream Parlor and Deli,** 611 N. Bridge St., tel. (715) 723-4331, a landmark since 1944 for its "Homaid" ice cream. It's got a basic lunch list of deli soups, salads, and sandwiches. Ice cream aficionado magazines have rated this place in the top 10 in the U.S.; you can observe the ice cream-making process through large windows. From $2.

The **Fill Inn Station,** 104 W. Columbia St., tel. (715) 723-8282, is a supper club-cum-family restaurant-cum-bar of choice. The menu isn't strictly supper club fare—you can get pizza and sandwiches as well as steak and seafood. From $5.

Another steakhouse, this one done up like a chalet, **Edelweiss,** north two miles on WI 124, tel. (715) 723-7881, offers great upstairs dining and outstanding German food on Saturday nights. From $6. Candlelight dining and even cruise dinners ($75 per couple) are found at **High Shores Supper Club,** 17985 CR X, tel. (715) 723-9854. From $6.

For prime rib every night and a legendary (locally) deck dining room, try the Chinese-American **Water's Edge,** CR S, tel. (715) 723-0161. The Friday fish fry and broasted chicken buffet is a great deal. From $5.

Cultural Events
The **Heyde Center for the Arts,** 3 High St., tel. (715) 726-9000, is housed in the former high school. It has regular live theater, musical performances, art shows, poetry, dance, and more.

Events
Among the largest fairs in Wisconsin, the Chippewa County Fair is held the second week of July in Chippewa Falls. Late August sees the celebratory blowout **Pure Water Days.**

Services and Information
The **Chippewa Falls Chamber of Commerce,** 10 S. Bridge St., tel. (715) 723-0331, www.chippewachamber.org, is open until 5 p.m. weekdays.

The **post office** is at 315 N Bridge St., tel. (715) 723-2894. The public **library,** tel. (715) 723-1146, is at 105 W Central Street. **St. Joseph's Hospital,** tel. 715-726-3220, is at 2661 CR I.

OSSEO

Osseo draws scads of travelers from around the world to one tiny little diner, the world-renowned **Norske Nook,** on 7th St., tel. (715) 597-3069, which arguably bakes the world's best pies. Celebrated by roadfood gourmands and good enough to get the owner on the old NBC *Late Night With David Letterman* show, the place could not be more underwhelming when first you walk through the door, looking like nothing more than a classic diner. But the food is unreal. They've got the obligatory heart-stopping breakfasts and the requisite Midwestern hot beef sandwiches. Occasionally a dinner special might feature something Scandinavian like *lutefisk.* But the pies! The pies are really the thing-a whole page of them. The strawberry pies have up to five pounds of strawberries. The Nook is *the* stop between Eau Claire and the Mississippi.

Since you're already in Osseo, stop by the **Northland Fishing Museum,** 1012 Gunderson Rd., tel. (715) 597-2551, an awesome repository of classic and antique fishing equipment, featuring one of the most extensive fishing lure collections in the world. The collection has some of the rarest lures ever manufactured in the U.S., along with a kitschy and hip hodgepodge of exhibits on every conceivable aspect of freshwater fishing. You want a rusted Evinrude? You got it. Open daily 9 a.m.-5 p.m.; admission is free.

MENOMONIE

One of the ubiquitous oddly spelled Wisconsin towns, Menomonie (Muh-NAH-muh-nee) was still one more lumber town alongside a floating log highway. But this was not your ordinary lumber town, it was *the* lumber town, the site of the world's largest lumber corporation at the time.

After Europeans began pushing Natives out of the area in 1822, the first makeshift lumber mill went into temporary operation near the conjoinment of the Red Cedar River and Wilson Creek. Local Natives weren't exactly enamored of the idea of another sawmill town, but the mill kingpins rammed the treaty through the federal Indian agent's office. Within four decades, business machinations had created Knapp, Stout & Co. Processing over five million feet of lumber, with 1,200 employees on 115,000 acres of land, it was the bigshot for a spell. Menomonie weathered the unavoidable crash by diversifying, mostly into dairy. Today, the city of 13,500 is a pleasant college town with a UW satellite campus.

University of Wisconsin-Stout
Named for its progenitor, a fantastically wealthy lumber magnate—the perceptive James Stout, who foresaw incipient timber unemployment—UW-Stout was founded as a private institution, the Stout Manual Training School. It was the first in the country to offer a curriculum designed specifically for industrial arts. The education-minded Stout also radically revamped local schools, shifting their emphasis toward practical, vocational education. UW-Stout today has nationally ranked programs and departments in industrial and vocational sciences and home economics. It is perhaps best known for its excellent hotel/restaurant hospitality program. It's also

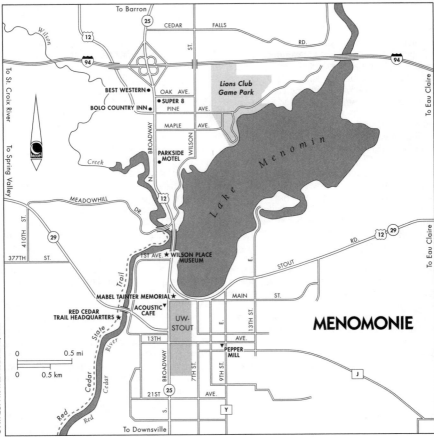

initiated the process to establish a Hmong Culture department. The Chippewa Valley has a large number of Laotian immigrants from the Vietnam era, and this program will be one-of-a-kind in the United States. It's also a pleasant little campus, full of thick-walled turn-of-the-century buildings.

Mabel Tainter Memorial
This enormous dark sandstone theater was deliberately contrived by its designer and builder in 1890 to do no less than "advance American architecture, society, education, and religion." It's a lofty, if not quixotic, memorial to the builder's daughter, a local aesthete, who died at 19. In Romanesque style, it smacks of a Thames-side

opera house—the interior is downright eye-popping. In relatively rare (for Wisconsin) Moorish style, the ornate auditorium has leaded glass; hand-stenciled coating on the walls, ceilings, and railings; carved woods from the area; brass fixtures; a wondrous Steere and Turner Tracker pipe organ; and very pricey old paintings. The building is open weekdays 8 a.m.-5 p.m., Saturday noon-5 p.m., and Sunday 1-5 p.m. Tours are offered daily at the top of every hour 1-4 p.m.; admission is $5 adults, $3 children.

Other Sights
The **Wilson Place Museum,** 101 Wilson Circle, tel. (715) 235-2283, is the sandstone home of

one of the founders of Menomonie, Capt. William Wilson. His descendants really did an overhaul around the turn of the century, adding a dozen fireplaces, a ballroom, and wraparound porches on each floor. Later descendants turned it into a quasi-Mediterranean villa. It's open spring and fall 1-5 p.m. on weekends. June-Sept., it's open 1-5 p.m. daily. Mid-November through the first week of January is the home's locally famous "Victorian Christmas," when it's open 1-8 p.m. Admission for guided tours is $5 adult, $2 children.

The newest attraction in Menomonie is the **Russell J. Rassbach Heritage Museum,** 820 Wakanda St., tel. (715) 232-8685. It's got a huge assortment of items pertaining to local history; highlights include a re-creation of a Victorian home, guns from a famed local bank robbery, mock-ups of original local cigar factories, a Civil War exhibit, a replica of the kitchen of the Caddie Woodlawn (see below) house, a 1931 four-door Nash sedan built in Kenosha, and displays on local Dunn County celebrities, in particular ex-major leaguer Andy Pafko. Hours are 10 a.m.-5 p.m. Memorial Day weekend-Labor Day, lesser hours thereafter. Admission is $4, $2 students and seniors, $1 children 6-12.

The local **Lions Club Park** keeps deer, elk, buffalo, pheasant, ducks, geese, and other native species, along with a short nature trail.

Scenic Drives
WI 25 to the south is a great little road trip, paralleling the Red Cedar River State Trail. Downsville, six miles south, offers the **Empire in Pine Museum,** WI 25, tel. (715) 644-8452. A huge, award-winning collection of lumbering artifacts and displays is housed on two floors. The holdings include an old blacksmith shop, muzzle-loading bunks, and a rare saw. A multimedia display portrays Knapp, Stout & Co.'s massive operations. The museum is open May-Oct., Tues.-Sat. noon-4 p.m. and Sunday 1-5 p.m. Admission is $2.

Eight miles south you'll find **Caddie Woodlawn Historic Park.** The character in the famed children's book, Caddie Woodlawn, was actually Caroline Augusta, who moved here with her family in 1857; her granddaughter, Carol Ryrie Brink, wrote the book. The family home, another old structure, and a log smokehouse now sit in this historic park.

West from Menomonie almost 20 miles, in Spring Valley, is a spelunker's delight—rare tri-leveled **Crystal Cave,** tel. (715) 778-4414. Thirty chambers of eerily chilly prehistoric silence are open for tours descending some 70 feet. Open weekends in April, then daily Memorial Day-Labor Day; admission is a stiff $8, $5 children 5-12.

Twenty-two miles west on I-94, then north a hop brings you to little **Baldwin.** The town's **Dutch windmill,** erected to memorialize the town's heritage, is worth the trip. An antique farm equipment museum can also be found in town.

Accommodations
The largest dose of chain motels comes at the junction of I-94 and WI 25, including the **Best Western Motor Lodge,** 1815 N. WI 12/25, tel. (715) 235-9651, with large rooms from around $50, an indoor pool, whirlpool, and restaurant.

The well-known **Bolo Country Inn,** 207 Pine Ave., tel. (715) 235-5596 or (800) 553-2656, not far away, offers 25 multifarious rooms ranging in size from a nook to capacious five-room suite. Each is cozy and tastefully decorated and receives a breakfast basket delivery each morning. The restaurant is one of the best in the valley. Rates from $60.

You'll find public camping at the U.S. Army Corps of Engineers' **Eau Galle Lake Recreation Area,** 18 miles west via WI 29, tel. (715) 778-5562. It's set on a 150-acre lake featuring a beach and surrounded by miles of trails.

Camping is also available at private local **Twin Springs Resort Campground,** north one mile on WI 25 then right on Cedar Falls Rd. 2.5 miles, tel. (715) 235-9321. This longstanding local campground offers tent and trailer sites starting at $13 for two persons ($10 solo); camping cabins are also available.

Food
Being a college—and thus bar—town, there is no shortage of bar and grills and downscale pub grub in town. There are also a large number of Chinese restaurants. **Log Jam,** 709 South Broadway St., tel. (715) 235-4792, is Menomonie's only brewpub, and it has lots of pizzas, sandwiches, a few Jamaican jerk choices, and some Southwestern items; there's also regular reggae music. From $4.

The family restaurant of choice seems to be the **Pepper Mill** at 1414 9th Street. Breakfasts, burgers, and salads are the norm here, not to mention enormous cinnamon and pecan rolls. Find family fare in a historic depot at the **Old Depot Cafe,** 2616 Hils Court, just north of Wal-Mart. Solid fare at good prices. From $4.

Eight miles west on US 12 is **The Knapp House,** tel. (715) 665-2261, with a popular Friday night buffet of chicken, seafood, and barbecued ribs; live entertainment is also provided. Saturday nights, as always, are prime rib nights. The specialty of the house is honey-glazed barbecued ribs. From $5. Also west of town, here along WI 29, is **Grazi's,** N5729 410th St., tel. (715) 232-8878, an excellent Italian eatery focusing on pastas, meat, fish, and even a few rewarding vegetarian options. The veal is recommended. Open for dinner Tues.-Saturday. From $8. One of the top 10 supper clubs in the state according to more than one foodie publication is the **Black Bear Cafe,** WI 27 North, tel. (715) 286-2687, south of town in Augusta. It's got a solid slate of ribs, steaks, seafood, chicken, and even a few Greek specialties. Open for dinner Tues.-Sat. and lunch and dinner Sunday. From $6.

The **Acoustic Cafe,** 102 West Main St., serves coffee and light fare and sporadically offers live music, as do other nearby bars. Also downtown is the **Blue Moon Cafe,** 815 Main St., where the organic vegetarian food is scrumptious. Both from $4.

The best meal to be found in Menomonie is at the **Bolo Inn,** an upscale supper club in a country inn on the north edge of town. Exquisite steaks are the rule here, along with the straight prime rib, chicken, and seafood necessities. Lunch entrées are actually quite a good bargain. Open daily for lunch and dinner. From $6.

Some have called **The Creamery,** tel. (715) 664-8354, in Downsville one of the top-shelf eateries in the state. The menu is "imaginative American" and varies season to season according to the vagaries of farmers' markets and the whims of the talented chefs. Entrées always feature lots of seafood, along with lamb, pork, veal, beef, and fowl. The structure itself was a genuine cooperative creamery, constructed in 1904. The restaurant is open for lunch and dinner Tues.-Sun., with a Sunday brunch, and there are also four lodging rooms. From $11.

Recreation

The **Red Cedar State Park Trail** departs the historic depot along the west edge of WI 29 in Menomonie and stretches nearly 15 miles south along the Red Cedar River to the **Dunville Wildlife Area.** The Menomonie depot dispenses $3 daily trail passes and offers local and trail information. A tiny interpretive center inside exhibits local flora, fauna, and railroad heritage. The trail spins through Menomonie's Riverside Park and the first of a dozen bridges before passing what's known as a "weeping" rock wall. Irvington, where legend tells of gold buried along the riverbank by fleeing French soldiers is next, followed by Downsville and an old cut-stone quarry. The route ends at the Dunnville Wildlife Area, accessed via CR Y, and features an old 860-foot-long railroad bridge along this final leg. You can also link up with the final southern segment with the Chippewa River Trail to Eau Claire. You can also canoe/kayak/tube the Red Cedar River from Menomonie. Rentals, trail passes, inner tubes, and even a bike museum are found at the **Red Cedar Outfitters,** tel. (715) 235-5431, at the Menomonie trailhead. Rates are, in general, $5 per hour to $13 per day for a bike, $25-32 per day for a canoe; the company has great "Surf and Turf" options where you canoe down the river and bike back. There's even a restaurant if you're hungry.

Hoffman Hills State Recreation Area lies east via I-94, then north on WI 40. Set on 700 acres, there are 10 miles of multi-use trails but no camping.

Services and Information

You'll find local tourism information at the **Menomonie Area Chamber of Commerce,** 700 Wolske Bay Rd., tel. (715) 235-9087 or (800) 283-1862. The best website is the one covering the whole valley (www.chippewavalley.net) but you can email the chamber directly: chamber@menomonie.com.

Transportation

Greyhound stops at Video Biz, 1302 N. Broadway, tel. (715) 235-5571. At least two buses per day head for Minneapolis ($19). Verify the bus stop location with the chamber of commerce, as things change a lot.

BLACK RIVER STATE FOREST AND ENVIRONS

The Black River Valley contained the most pine trees per settlement in the state when the first sawmill was opened in 1839. Before the last trees were clearcut, over 50 sawmills were whining away 24 hours a day. In total, lumber companies felled and processed 4.9 *billion* board feet of lumber here. Iron ore smelting has also been a local industrial linchpin since 1856; tons of taconite pellets are still mined in open pits.

The forest was once the prime hunting grounds for the Winnebago, whose hegemony once stretched west throughout the region. Forcibly relocated to northeastern Iowa and later a South Dakota reservation before making a long migration back to Wisconsin, they defied attempts to remove them again.

A rolling area of relatively low hills enhanced by a few castellated spikes of sandstone and limestone, the forest itself covers 66,000 acres and is in turn surrounded by 120,000 acres of county forest. The state forest is still prime hunting grounds, offering arguably the best white-tailed deer hunting in Wisconsin.

Green Gold

One Jackson County economic oddity—speaking on a national scale now—is sphagnum moss, commercially produced nowhere except this pocket of western Wisconsin. Rejuvenating itself rapidly in the boggy and marshy areas on the western fringe of the Sand Counties, it can hold 20 times its weight in water and keeps nursery plants and flowers alive during shipping and hydroponic gardening, not to mention being used for surgical dressings. Road-trip throughout Jackson and Monroe Counties (the Tomah area to the southeast is prime) and you're sure to see moss being pulled and baled. Harvest is non-stop labor from spring through the first freeze, and a few towns in the area have tours outlined.

Wazee Trail

The local chambers of commerce have detailed maps of the Wazee Trail, a 62-mile auto tour through the Black River region along historic Native American routes. A new wildlife area and trail center is being planned along the route at an old iron mine. **Dike 17** is a waterfowl haven on the route with an observation tower. Twelve miles of the trail are established as an official Wisconsin "Rustic Road." If you get lost, just look for white numbered signs shaped like pine trees.

The River

The Black River—named for the water's black hue, caused by a high iron content—cuts across Wisconsin's central plain and western upland regions. Unlike most waterways in the glacially carved northern reaches, the river cuts for the most part through a steep trench with relatively few marshy areas or lakes (though it is surrounded by those moss-rich swamps). From the Clark County line, where the forest begins, the river channel cuts through sandstone, revealing underlying granite along a 40-mile inlier.

Besides fishing for muskie, walleye, and smallmouth bass, most visitors come to the Black River to paddle; 75 river miles are canoeable in the immediate vicinity on two river forks and numerous tributaries. Trips are most common out of Hatfield. A trip all the way to the Mississippi River is possible, requiring about five very casual days.

Halls, Morrison, and Robinson Creeks and the East Fork of the Black River offer more challenging rapids. Above Lake Arbutus upstream to WI 95 is expert-rated during high water; when the water is low, there are far too many large rocks to make a descent.

The lower Black is exceedingly sedate, with a gentle bottom. The stretch south of Black River Falls to the Melrose Bridge offers lots of great fishing and a canoe campground island. One of the most popular stretches of water is the float upstream from Black River Falls between Hall's Creek and a dam, where you exit the water to your left. If you really want to go casual, tubers generally take two hours to leisurely float from Irving Landing to Lost Falls. Another popular day trip is the 24-mile drift from Lake Arbutus near Hatfield to Hoffman Wayside on WI 54—it takes an overnight stay, and camping is available on Hawk

Island (the only place besides sandbars). In high water, some rapids can be too much for neophytes. As always, get a complete water conditions update before you set out. Complete rentals and an outfitter operation can be found at **Riverview Inn, Supper Club and Outfitter,** tel. (608) 488-5191, in North Bend, with one- to three-day trips on the river, shuttle included. A one-day rental starts at $25; you can get a canoe/dinner for two special for $40. You can also get rentals at **Lost Falls,** N2974 Sunnyvale Rd., tel. (800) 329-3911; they start at $22.

Wazee Lake

East of Black River Falls a number of miles is primevally icy Wazee Lake, which is 350 feet deep with no outlets; it's also incredibly clear. Diving and snorkeling are popular. Get rentals at **Wazee Sports Center,** W10120 WI 54, tel. (800) 940-6042, a few miles away from the Wazee Lake Recreation Area. There's plenty of camping available here.

Other Recreation

The Black River State Forest has 35 miles of mountain-bike trails, with trailheads at Castle Mound and Pigeon Creek campgrounds, and at Smrekar and Wildcat cross-country ski trail parking lots. The cross-country ski trails—highly rated by ski bums, by the way—are five miles north of Millston. The Wildcat trail parking lot is four miles northeast on North Settlement Rd., and the Smrekar lot is four miles east on CR O. Twenty-four miles of ski trails loop through the forest; some are advanced-only, so know before you go. You can find an old cemetery just south of the junction of the Central and North Trails, as well as an old root cellar, and the East Trail passes the remnants of an old farmstead. The Central Trail features its own self-guided nature trail. *Trail passes are required;* they cost $3 per day.

The county is constantly establishing more trail routes along iron mine trails in county forest land. Hundreds of miles of state and county forest logging roads are open to bikes.

State Forest Camping and Backpacking

Three family campgrounds are located in the state forest. **Pigeon Creek,** in the southeastern sector of the forest, is two miles northeast of Millston on N. Settlement Road. This is the least impressive of the campgrounds. Slightly better maintained, more secluded sites are found at **Castle Mound,** one mile east of Black River Falls, and **East Fork,** two miles southeast of Hatfield along the river. Reservations are taken at Castle Mound. Park stickers ($4 resident) and camping fees ($7 residents, $9 nonresidents) are necessary. You'll also find canoe campsites south of Black River Falls. Failing these there are a dozen more private or public campgrounds scattered throughout Jackson County; Wazee Lake Recreation Area is closest to Black River Falls. The chamber of commerce has a great county map highlighting all of them.

Primitive backpacking is also available, and a permit is necessary. You can't camp anywhere you want, so get details from the forest HQ. Though the forest looks small and rather mundane as a "working forest" (meaning that it's managed for timber extraction), it is easy to get off-track here. Take a compass and know how to use it.

Information

The **Black River State Forest HQ,** tel. (715) 284-1400 or (715) 284-4103, is at the junction of WI 54 E and I-94. It's open weekdays 7:45 a.m.-4:30 p.m. The **Black River Falls Chamber of Commerce,** 336 N. Water St., tel. (800) 404-4008, www.blackrivercountry.com, also maintains some information. To get there, head north onto WI 27 off WI 54 a quarter mile.

Black River Falls

Black River Falls is your quintessential Our Town kind of community, set beside the river. There's the local history collection at the historical society, though you'll have to check with the chamber of commerce first, since it's not open often. The chamber can also point out a few area highlights like the scenic views from Bell Mound or the Native American petroglyphs at Gullickson's

Glen. The atavistic **Pioneer Brewing Co.,** (715) 284-7553, is at the intersection of East 4th and Pierce Streets. It, well, "pioneered" western Wisconsin's brewing industry when it opened in 1856. It lasted until Prohibition killed it off; it later was a turkey factory and landmine manufacturing plant during the Korean War. In 1996 it reopened as a brewery and today produces a lager and pale ale. Tours are available.

One future note: the area has been mulling over a proposed nine-story, beer stein-shaped convention center and community building, with a pub in the lid, of course. Nothing concrete yet, but rumors are delicious enough for roadside attraction aficionados.

West of town on WI 54 is the **Rustic Mill,** the local supper club of choice for prime rib—six nights a week—and the Friday fish fry. The place is full of exceedingly gregarious locals. Try the apple-cranberry pie. Closed Tuesday. From $6. **Pete's** is south on WI 27 and offers sandwiches and a Friday fish fry, along with weekend entertainment. From $4. **Molly's Grill** in downtown Black River Falls offers Chinese, Mexican, Cajun, and Italian, depending on the night, and even has Door County-style fish boils on Friday. Saturday night it's the usual slow-roasted prime rib. This is the huge-and-hearty breakfast spot of the town as well, serving food daily 6:30 a.m.-10 p.m. From $4. The local roadfood-quality cafe is the **Country Cafe** farther up Main, with straight low-budget cafe fare but also a few specialty concoctions, including a fabulous stew. From $3.

Hatfield

Sitting on popular Lake Arbutus, one of the few dam-formed lakes along the Black River, the town is the gateway to numerous resorts in the area (all of which help the town's population swell from 50 to nearly 5,000 in summer). Most resorts are on the southwest perimeter of the lake, along CR K and CR J, including the **Pine Haven Resort,** tel. (715) 333-5724. Also along the shore is the **Russell Park Campground,** a county park with over 175 campsites and a sandy beach. A state forest campground is on the lake's east side, as is another county campground.

Hatfield's genuine roadside attraction is the **Thunderbird Museum and Shops,** tel. (715) 333-5841, almost two dozen rooms covering every conceivable topic—geology, Native Americans, copies of historic documents, world collectibles, old country stores, a church, dolls, old phone switches, a depot, a hand-carved fireplace, and much, much more. More is better here—this is a pack rat's dream, with some splendid and unique history despite the clutter. Open Memorial Day-Labor Day daily 9 a.m.-5 p.m.; admission is charged.

In Hatfield, **The Palms Supper Club,** CR K, tel. (715) 333-5823, has been the local choice for dining since the '30s. It's also the most, er, distracting. Each dining room is absolutely chock-full of knickknacks and doodads.

Cataract

East of Cataract the **Little Falls Railroad and Doll Museum,** CR B to WI 11, has hundreds of dolls in rotating exhibits. The working train displays are cool, as are the thousands of old, old books and magazines. Some prefer the **Paul and Matilda Wegner Grotto** not far away from Cataract via WI 27 south, then west on WI 71. It's a garden of concrete sculpture decorated with thousands of glass shards in the usual grotto theme of religion and patriotism.

Indian Mission

The Ho Chunk Nation (Winnebago) has no reservation lands and now holds title to some 2,000 acres of land in the Jackson County area. Over Labor Day, Memorial Day, and Thanksgiving weekend, the nation holds **powwows** at Red Cloud Memorial Park. There is also a small cultural museum and, four miles east of Black River Falls on WI 54, a **casino.**

NORTHWESTERN LAKES

Erect a radar base in Eau Claire, where US 53 branches north from the interstate, and the sweep of the beam as it rotates clockwise between nine and noon reveals another massive concentration of primeval glacial pools. Second in density only to Wisconsin's other lake district, in the northeast, but second to none in sheer numbers, the area features arguably the state's best muskie fishing and the country's first established scenic riverways.

ST. CROIX
NATIONAL SCENIC RIVERWAY

The St. Croix National Scenic Riverway is one of a dozen so designated in the federal Wild and Scenic Riverway System. It was also the first, officially promulgated in 1968 by Congress, containing 252 miles of the Upper and Lower St. Croix Rivers and the entire Namekagon River. Though not technically a part of the system, the Brule River was and is a de facto link in the chain. With only a short portage between the Brule and St. Croix, this was the most crucial waterway between the Great Lakes and the Mississippi River. Though brown for most of its length in the south (tannic acid leaches into the water from decaying pine and tamarack nee-

dles), the riverway is one of the "healthiest" in the U.S. in terms of biology and bio-diversity.

The St. Croix is a schizophrenic river, split into regions at St. Croix Falls. The Upper St. Croix and Namekagon Rivers, though neither is technically classified as whitewater, are the more challenging and isolated for canoeists, drifting and paddling through an expansive river valley streaked with creeks and dotted with thousands of glacial lakes and tracts of second-growth forest. The Lower St. Croix, by the time it departs St. Croix Falls, has become an old man—somnolent and wide, full of sandbars and backwater sloughs and for the most part used by power boats.

Camping is free and allowed at innumerable primitive sites along the riverway, as well as a few state parks with established campgrounds. Camping is usually limited to one night at one site in most places; and there's a *maximum* total of 21 nights May 15-September 15. Water is sometimes problematic as not all campsites have it available. A filter is a good idea, and boil it for 30 minutes before drinking or cooking with it.

Upper St. Croix and Namekagon Rivers
The St. Croix River begins as a humble, ribbony creek flowing from Upper St. Croix Lake in a muskeg forest between Gordon and Solon

A tourist paddleboat plies the St. Croix River.

Springs. It navigates 102 miles on its course to Prescott, but after just 20 miles it links up with the Namekagon River, its main tributary. The Namekagon starts as a chilly trout stream at a dam northeast of Cable, within shouting distance of the Chequamegon National Forest. Wending through forested valleys in relatively primitive conditions, both have a few low and medium hazards, but even at spring runoff high-water periods, neither is classified as a white-water river. For pure backwoods isolation, the Namekagon can't be beat.

The Upper St. Croix is generally much shallower and narrower than the Namekagon. The only stretch guaranteed to allow canoes is the stretch below the CCC bridge. To get to Riverside and the Namekagon confluence is generally recommended as a two-day trip, best done in spring for high water. Novice canoeists might also have some trouble with rapids, which in spring can change from Class I to Class III. In all, there are dozens of rapids from the Gordon Dam to the CCC bridge. There are seven established access points along the river before it joins with the Namekagon; three are parks offering primitive **camping** (Louise Park and Schoen Park, 10 and 12 miles from Gordon Dam respectively, also have vehicle camping access). Near the St. Croix headwaters, a county park in Solon Springs offers an established campground ($8) on Lake St. Croix. The park also contains Solon Springs' claim to fame—the **Lucius Woods Performing Arts Center,** a rustic outdoor amphitheater featuring established musical acts on weekends; tickets are generally $6 and up. (This is also the summer home of the Duluth Symphony Orchestra.) For eats in Solon Springs, you can grill your own steaks at the **Village Pump,** or try **Prevosts,** once an old-time tavern, now a good cafe with homemade pasties. Out of town, **Smithy's Supper Club,** 10814 US 53, tel. (715) 378-2241, sits in a garden area with a gurgling brook.

The Namekagon changes from an icy, extremely isolated trout stream with a dense coniferous forest crowding its sandy banks, to a somewhat wider channel through marshes and swamps. The river contains one hairpin turn after another, and that's why canoeists love it so much—no boaters. Along the route are four dam-created flowages, and water levels are marked on bridges. When the water level falls below the .6 mark, canoeing will be tough. For water conditions, call (715) 635-8346.

Generally, paddlers take the river in three segments. From its source at the Namekagon Dam northeast of Cable, the 33-mile stretch to Hayward takes two days and is best done May-June; spring water runoffs can raise levels and change Class I rapids to Class II or even III. Mostly streamlike with a few rapids, the route also covers a few lakes. There are eight access points passed en route, with camping at three; the first two require a portage, the last is at Hayward Landing.

The second trip is between Hayward and Trego, the most developed 34 miles on the whole upper stretch. The route is mostly narrow, with consistent water and a good gradient. It has few rapids, but these can be tough for novices. You'll find **camping** at Earl Park and in Trego, where the town park has vehicle access to the river.

Trego, at the Great South Bend of the river, was once a ready-made campsite, used by the original Ojibwa inhabitants, followed up by *voyageurs* and fur traders. Johnathan Carver in 1767 and Henry Schoolcraft in 1831 also slept on sandbars here. Today, the town is the site of the **Namekagon Visitor Center,** tel. (715) 635-8346, north of town on US 63. It offers slide shows on the river and the old fur trade, along with logging exhibits; a couple of displays are hands-on. There are also plenty of maps and straight dope on the river from chatty hosts. The center's open Memorial Day-Labor Day, daily 8 a.m.-4:30 p.m. The town itself is essentially not much more than a few services and a huge number of **river outfitters,** which offer rentals and shuttles for a minimum of $17. These include **Namekagon Outfitters,** tel. (715) 635-2015 or (800) 547-9028.

Below Trego, a trip of 40 miles spins to Riverside. The most backwoodsy part of the entire system, it's thus the most popular weekend excursion. The narrow channel is flanked by steep sandy banks and trees and is made interesting by serpentine turns. Four **campsites** are passed along the way, the last in Riverside.

Confluence

Near Riverside, the two rivers join and form the Upper St. Croix National Scenic Riverway proper, a wider, more sedate, but no less scenic stretch leading to St. Croix Falls. The first trip is usually a two-day trip to Nelson Landing, bypassing Minnesota's St. Croix State Park along the way. Just south of Danbury, and stretching all the way past Grantsburg, you'll pass the long, sinuous **Governor Knowles State Forest,** with 33,000 acres of great canoeing and hiking (some 40 miles total on two 20-mile trails that trace the bluffline above the river), and some primitive but established campsites along the river. (Dispersed backpacking is allowed by permit.) Nine access points are scattered along the route and camping is found at a handful of places, mostly near Nelson's Landing; the camping at the mouth of the Yellow River is by fee. Just downriver from the confluence, Big Island has a riverine campground, though it may be off limits if the water level is too high. Danbury has **canoe rentals** at Yellow River Campground, tel. (715) 656-4402, among others. Gulden's offers two-hour trips from $15; a four-day rental costs $100, shuttle included.

Resorts surround the hundreds of Burnett County lakes. **Ike Walton Lodge,** tel. (715) 866-7101, east of WI 35 and Danbury, is perfectly representative—heavy on the fishing and snowmobiling. Cottages start at $40/250 daily/weekly; there is also an air-conditioned motel unit with an indoor pool and hot tub for the same rate. Some 10-person suites go for $100 a night.

East of Danbury and easily missed are the 11 separate communities spread through four counties and composing the **St. Croix Indian Reservation.** Often called the "Lost Tribe" due to its dispersion, another tribal community is across the St. Croix River in Minnesota, and the tribal headquarters is to the southeast, near the village of Hertel. Casinos in Turtle Lake and Danbury are tourist attractions, and an annual late-August **Wild Rice Powwow** is a popular draw. The whole region east of Danbury along WI 77 is dubbed the "Fishbowl" for its preponderance of glacial pools and the teeming panfish in them.

For a good side trip, head for **Crex Meadows Wildlife Area** east of the landing near Phantom Flowage along CR F. This 30,000-plus-acre spread features 250 species of birds, including nesting herons, sharp-tailed grouse, sandhill cranes, trumpeter swans, rare colonies of yellow-headed blackbirds, and a dozen species of duck. A pack of timber wolves have crossed into Wisconsin from Minnesota and reportedly taken hold in the area. The prairielands contain over 200 of the last vestiges of pure prairie plant in the state. There is an interpretive center on-site, with self-guided auto tours. Visitors can also canoe, and some limited camping is allowed Sept.-December. Crex Meadows is a thoroughly captivating place.

Between Nelson's Landing and WI 70 is some of the fastest water on the river; the rapids are generally Class I, though they, too, increase in difficulty during the spring thaw. You can definitely cover this stretch in a day. Campsites are found at four or five places en route, half in Minnesota, and there are also a half-dozen access points.

West of Grantsburg in Minnesota on MN 70 is another **information center,** open Memorial Day-Labor Day. Grantsburg itself is a pleasant one-horse town. The only tourist trap is the nearly eight-foot talking wooden statue of "Big Gust," the likeness of a local historical figure; check him out at the Village Hall. The village also hosts its summertime **Snowmobile Watercross** in July, when snowmobile pilots attempt to skim their machines across a downtown lake. There are plenty of classic little greasy spoons here.

Five miles east of Grantsburg in tiny Alpha is the **Burnett Dairy Cooperative.** A group of almost 300 local dairy farmers, it won a World Championship in 1988 for one of its 50 varieties of cheese. Twenty-one miles east and north near Webster you'll find **Forts Folle Avoine,** a historical park comprising mock-ups of the 1802 fur trading posts of XY Company and the Northwest Fur Company, along with a reconstructed Ojibwa village. Costumed docents banter in period lingo—right down to bad Cajun chatter. The museum and archaeological exhibits are impressive, and the best eats around are found here; the dining room serves up synchronous fare, from wild rice pancakes to "wilderness stew." The park is open Memorial Day-Labor Day, Wed.-Sun. 9 a.m.-5 p.m. Admission is $5, $3 for children ages 5-12.

From here, things get congested canoe-wise, but the scenery stays splendid. You'll wisp past sandy bluffs etched with goat prairie and multi-hued rocks. State parks, forests, and wildlife areas line the Wisconsin and Minnesota shores. **Fish Lake Wildlife Area** appears three miles south of Grantsburg; the 15,000-acre refuge covers eight flowages and one natural lake, all in a glacial lake basin, and offers walking and driving tours. The 40-mile trip to St. Croix Falls is slow and wide and can be done in either two or three days, depending on how leisurely you split things up. The final miles loll along the flowage created by the St. Croix Falls Dam. Ten campsites, most of them on the Minnesota side, are accessible along the route.

St. Croix Falls

Your arrival in St. Croix Falls, the largest community along the river, is marked by the **River Headquarters,** tel. (715) 483-3284, just off of WI 87 north of town. It's open daily May-Oct., Mon.-Fri. the rest of the year. In high season, the hours are 8:30 a.m.-5 p.m., until 6 p.m. Fri.-Sunday. Inside you'll find maps, exhibits, toilets, and plenty of information.

You've got a mile-long portage ahead of you (on the Minnesota side) around the NSP Dam if you plan to continue on the river.

The Polk County Information Center south of town on WI 35 is the terminus for the **Gandy Dancer Trail** (named for the "Gandy Dancers," or railroad workers who used Gandy tools), a multi-use trail atop an abandoned rail line. The trail stretches 98 miles to Superior, crossing over the St. Croix River and into Minnesota before cutting back into Wisconsin; one trail highlight is a 350-foot bridge crossing the river. The trail passes through nine cities and villages, and a trail pass is required—$3 a day or $10 a year.

Also along WI 35, one block north of the main entrance to the state park, **Quest Canoe Rental,** tel. (715) 483-1692, offers canoe shuttle trips in and around the state park and up or down the river. A daily rental starts at around $15, shuttle included.

In St. Croix Falls, the **Fawn Doe Rosa Park** contains a wildlife display featuring "Big Louie," a 1,200-pound Kodiak bear, and a hands-on menagerie. The park also has a picnic area, pony rides, a chuck-wagon drive-in, and tacky

the Devil's Chair

gifts. Open daily mid-May through mid-October. It's located two miles east on WI 8.

The best accommodations locally are at the **Dalles House,** a block south of the US 8 and WI 35 junction, tel. (715) 483-3106. Large, clean units and an indoor pool and sauna are available, with rates from $50. The restaurant is also popular. The St. Croix area is absolutely loaded with B&Bs; the Polk County Information Center has brochures. For food, the **Valley Family Restaurant** has all the pancakes you can stuff in for 99 cents and homemade soups and dinner specials. It's open daily for breakfast, lunch, and dinner. Four miles east on WI 8 is **Wayne's,** a 24-hour joint with decent food, including a Wednesday fish fry, its own smoked meats, and delectable homemade strawberry pie.

Interstate State Park

Interstate State Park is south of the "falls." (Before you ask, there are no falls, at least not since the construction of the dam.) Wisconsin's first state park, established in 1900, Interstate has perhaps the most magnificent examples of glacial topography outside of Devil's Lake or Door County. Glacial runoff was so ferocious that it sluiced superb river gorges right through the area's billion-year-old basaltic lava. The parks—one each in Minnesota and Wisconsin—were formed in part to prevent Minneapolis opportunists from exploiting the traprock in the gorge walls for roadbuilding. The gorges here in the mid 19th century held the world's largest logjam—150 million board feet, jammed together for three miles upriver, taking 200 men six weeks to disentangle.

The Dalles of St. Croix, a 200-foot gorge of basalt palisades below the falls, makes a resplendent backdrop for canoeists and also draws rock climbers on both sides of the channel. The **Potholes Trail** is a funky traipse along rounded chasms formed by glacial backwash. Along other trails, oddball hoodoo formations appear; the most photographed is probably **Old Man of the Dalles,** and you'll see why. (Three other formations are seen from the river south of here, including a 60-foot-high "Devil's Chair"; "The Cross," some 15 feet high; and "Angle Rock," at the sharp bend in the river.) A dozen trails snake for a total of eight miles through the 1,400-acre park. The final link in Wisconsin's **National Ice Age Scientific Reserve,** the park has an interpretive center with exhibits, films, displays, and even a mural or two. It's open year-round, Memorial Day weekend-Labor Day daily 8:30 a.m.-4:30 p.m. weekends, lesser times the rest of the year. The family campgrounds have great isolated camping and a nice sandy beach not far away. No organized tour boats leave from the Wisconsin side, but the Taylor Falls, Minnesota, docks have **tour boats** plying the waters in and around the rocky cliffs.

Lower St. Croix River

The Lower St. Croix wasn't added to the National Scenic Riverway until 1972. Beginning at the St. Croix Falls Dam, it runs 52 miles to Prescott, where it flows into the Mississippi River. This stretch is much wider, deeper (down to 100 feet), and slower than the upper section. It is navigable for canoes until the Apple River, after which pleasure crafters squeeze out other types of recreational vehicles—canoes are definitely unwelcome. On the way to the Apple River, there are no rapids, but plenty of back channels and sloughs. Water levels are always dependable in the main channel, not at all trustworthy in the backwater reaches. Though the channel is also clogged with powerboat pests, the whole stretch is wake-free, so at least you won't get swamped. Camping is available at two Minnesota sites (one a state park with fees) and at the Somerset Landing, near the mouth of the Apple River.

Osceola, five miles downstream from St. Croix Falls, was named for an Indian chief. The name was originally Leroy, and old Leroy wouldn't allow the change until he was paid two sheep. Downtown, a flight of wooden stairs climbs to **Cascade Falls,** or you can just wander through the charming town and stop for a look-see at the **Emily Olson House,** which doubles as the local historical society quarters. The **ArtBarn,** tel. (715) 294-ARTS, is a renovated barn housing galleries, a theater, workshops, and more. There's a statue of **Chief Osceola** and a large **state fish hatchery** also in town. The chugging steam engines of the **Osceola and St. Croix**

Railway, tel. (800) 643-7412, depart from the old depot just off WI 35 downtown. The old trains steam on 90-minute roundtrips to Marine-on-St.-Croix, Minnesota, at 11 a.m. and 2:30 p.m., and 45-minute tours to Dresser at 12:45 p.m. Fares are $6-12 depending on age. Tours are given Saturday, Sunday, and holidays May 27-Aug. 27 and Sept. 30-Oct. 29. A special July 4th train goes to Amery for fireworks, and fall color tours are offered throughout September on weekends. A mile north of town is a **campground** popular with road-tripping bicyclists.

Two miles below Osceola, a sharp left cut in the river marks the dividing line between the Sioux and Ojibwa nations under 1837 treaties. The river spins for 10 more miles, passing a Minnesota state park and great old Marine-on-St.-Croix, Minnesota, before the mouth of the Apple River appears. Canoeists should disembark here, or try going up the Apple River. Tons and tons of tubers will be winding their way downstream against you; so many people "tube the Apple" that *Life* magazine put the event in its pages in 1941, and the press has dutifully shown up ever after. You'll pass through the **St. Croix Islands Wildlife Refuge** before entering the Apple river, and if you can make it against the current, little **Somerset** waits upstream a handful of miles. There's not much in Somerset, historically known for its moonshine operations, but today the town has frog legs and pea soup; it's famed for both culinary delights. The former culinary concoction can be sampled at **River's Edge** in town, the latter at an annual town festival. Still farther east (no, you can't paddle there), **New Richmond** is home to the **New Richmond Heritage Center,** featuring an Italianate farmhouse and a smattering of 19th-century buildings; there are hiking trails on the grounds as well.

Beyond Stillwater, Minnesota, the river widens into what is known as **Lake St. Croix**—at times up to 7,400 feet across. The next Wisconsin community above Lilliputian size, **Hudson,** so called for the area's close resemblance to the Hudson River Valley of New York, started as a trading outpost and steamship supply point. This eye-catching river town (pop. 6,400), Wisconsin's fastest-growing municipality, has a relatively famous **octagon house,** 1004 Third St., dating from 1855. This erstwhile home of a local judge is done in period style, and a Victorian garden surrounds the outside and leads to the carriage house. Tours are offered May-Oct., Tues.-Sat. 11 a.m.-4 p.m., and Sunday 2-4:30 p.m.; admission is $3 adults, $1 teens, 50 cents children. The chamber of commerce offers free maps to other 19th-century structures in the downtown area. You'll also find the **Phipps Center for the Arts,** a well-regarded performing arts facility offering numerous cultural productions. Off Buckeye Street downtown is an outstanding cliffside park. To the east, **Willow River State Park,** 2,800 modest acres along the eponymous river, offers a few waterfalls. The area was once used as an entryway to burial grounds. Three dams form three separate flowages in the park. Fewer than 10 miles of trails—they're each under two miles—twist south of Little Falls Lake; the best is **Little Falls Trail.** A nature center doubles as a ski hut come winter, and this is one of the few parks with winter camping. Rates are $8 for the family campground, and a park sticker is required for vehicles.

Cozy B&Bs are found in every direction. The most apparent is huge **Phipps Inn,** 1005 Third St., tel. (715) 386-0800 or (888) 865-9388, not far from the octagon house. Built in 1884, this beacon-bright white, 1884 Italianate has more fireplaces than most B&Bs have rooms. Rates start at $119. The remaining half dozen places offer unmemorable accommodation, including the cheapest—**Royal Inn,** 1509 Coulee Rd. on the north side of I-94, tel. (715) 386-2366, offering bare-bones rooms for under $45. The **Comfort Inn,** 811 Dominion Dr., tel. (715) 386-6355, has solid rooms with rates from $55 and offers a pool and whirlpool.

For food, there's a fairly wide variety. **Dibbo's,** 517 Second St., has homemade daily specials and great pies. Warehouse-size dining rooms greet you at **Sunsets,** 500 1st St., tel. (715) 386-4001, with soups, salads, and sandwiches at lunch and steak and seafood come dinnertime. **Barker's** (no phone) is a spacious place in an old building with booths. It has lots of burgers and sandwiches, along with lots of beers. Sandwich specials are creative—like chicken with peanut-chipotle sauce. Barker's makes its own cheesecakes. No credit cards. **Mama Maria's,** tel. (715) 386-7949, is an Italian place with good food, like chicken in champagne sauce. Both are on the main drag (WI 35).

A **Wisconsin Information Center,** tel. (715) 386-2571, is located east of town on I-94; it's open May-Oct. Mon.-Sat. 8 a.m.-6 p.m. and Sunday until 4 p.m., Tues.-Sat. only thereafter. The **Hudson Chamber of Commerce,** tel. (715) 386-8411 or (800) 657-6775, www.pressenter.com/~hudsoncc/, is downtown at 502 Second Street.

River Falls

The St. Croix River doesn't run through or even near River Falls, but WI35 does, and you'll likely pass through if you're traveling the St. Croix Riverway or the Great River Road. Ten miles southeast of Hudson along WI 35, the town of 10,000-and-change got its start when the first settler, a Connecticut Yankee, wrote back to the East, "I think I have found the New England of the Northwest." That part is debatable, but the settlers came in droves, creating yet another sawmill town, with a few brick kilns and sauerkraut factories thrown in for good measure.

It's an attractive town, and the *other* river in these parts, the Kinnickinnic, parses it into equal segments. The Kinnickinnic River pathway passes historical sites and developments on its traipse through the town. The stone buildings—the bricks baked right here—have their original superficialities, down to glass transom windows. Along Main Street itself, **00 Lures,** 214 N. Main St., is a world-renowned fishing-lure maker. The **Falls Theater** at 105 South Main St. is the epitome of an anachronism. This old movie theater features first-run flicks for the princely sum of $2 adults, $1 children.

River Falls' largest draw today, though, is a state enemy—the Kansas City Chiefs hold summer **football training camp** at UW-River Falls late July through late-August. The Chiefs are part of the very popular "Cheese League," NFL teams that take advantage of the moderate climate and cheap rents at state schools to practice. If you're around in midsummer, the town is bedecked in Chiefs red. You can watch practices most days in the morning after 8:30 a.m. and again at 3 p.m. They're free.

The cheapest local lodging is found west along WI 29 (adjacent to campus) at **Motel River Falls,** tel. (715) 425-8181, with rates starting around $30. The **Knollwood House,** Knollwood Drive at N8257 950th St., tel. (715) 425-1040, is a B&B in an 1886 brick farmhouse. A radiant heat sauna, a pool, solarium, and golf green are nice extras. Rooms start at $95.

You'll find consistent Midwestern fare at the **Clifton Hollow Supper Club,** west of town on CR F, tel. (715) 425-7323, offering the Wisconsin cuisine triumvirate of a Friday fish fry, Saturday prime rib, and Sunday brunch. From $10.

The Main Street area has a few decent cafes and light meal places—**Mary's Cafe,** 206 N. Main, has four good burgers for $2.25! **Java Hut,** 417 S. Main St., has good food and coffee; it also presents eclectic music on a regular schedule. Vegetarians will love **Pearl's Kitchen,** located inside the Whole Earth Grocery; it's got great veggie soups, salads, and sandwiches, and most items are made from organic ingredients. From $4.

Unique is the **UW-River Falls Falcon Foods,** just off the Spruce St. entrance to campus, south of Kargest Gym. This student-operated dairy and meat facility has 65 flavors of wonderful Wisconsin ice cream, fresh cheese, and delicious smoked meats. It's great. From $3.

THROUGH THE FISHBOWL: US 53 TO SUPERIOR

Folks were mighty happy when the feds allowed speed limits to be jacked up to 65 mph on four-lane highways. Not that US 53 is at all unsightly for most of the drive, but most residents have driven it a million times. Along the route to Superior, US 53 bypasses little "node" communities, each on its own string of lakes dotted with rustic family and fishing resorts. Veer west off the highway and you'll pass through the "Fishbowl," an area with one of the highest concentrations of glacial lakes in Wisconsin, full to the brim with panfish. To the east of US 53, the state is covered with a carpet of state and federal verdance.

New Auburn

Nine miles east of New Auburn on CR M, the **Chippewa Moraine Unit** is one of the nine reserve chain links on the trans-state scientific reserve. Nearly six miles of nature trails wend through 4,000 acres; a blue heron rookery is visible on an easy one-hour hike. The rest of the trails present you with an obvious glacial topography, and a few glacial pools are canoeable. The **interpretive center** is wonderful, chock-full of hands-on stuff and exhibits, and the staff is wonderfully chatty. The building itself is perched on an ice-walled lake plain; it won a Governor's Award for design, and it's apparent why when you get there. The center is open daily 8 a.m.-4:30 p.m. if volunteers are available. From the deck, you can get a view of South Shattuck Lake, a kettle or ice-block lake. But be forewarned, the black flies reach biblical-plague proportions on the trails around the center.

To the east, the reserve is connected to **Brunet Island State Park** by a 20-mile segment of the Ice Age Trail;. There is no camping allowed along the trail yet, but give them time. Chippewa County holds 23 miles of the Ice Age Trail, most of it well marked. It's a great riverine thumb of a park, set between the confluence of two rivers, south of the Holcombe Flowage. You can knock off the trails without breaking much of a sweat. Chippewa County Forest lands line the area between the state park and the Ice Age Reserve Unit, offering dozens of miles of trails, most of which are unfortunately open to braying off-road vehicles. The canoeing's lazy and fine, and the campsites line a sinuous, marshy sand spit smack at the water's edge. (Sites #25-75 are the best.)

Chetek

Once a community with one of the country's largest lumber companies, Chetek is much more tranquil today. Dozens and dozens of local resorts line 128 miles of lake shoreline on a six-lake chain. There's little else unless you count the **Hydro Lites,** a local water-ski team, as an attraction, or the **ice races** across the lake, held every Sunday after the ice freezes. A hole-in-the-wall **historical museum,** found along Moore Street, is open summers Wednesday and Friday 1-5 p.m.

One of the most luxurious inns in Wisconsin is found in Chetek. **Canoe Bay,** 115 S 2nd St., tel. (715) 924-4594, is owned by Relais & Chateau, a chi-chi organization representing the grandest lodges in the world. The architecture of the cottages was inspired by—but not done by—Frank Lloyd Wright. The fixed-price menu is to die for in this area. Rates start at $250, but you're not paying for posh—you're paying for peace of mind, and you've got it here.

ROADKILL

Every year, the great debate: to kill or not to kill deer in the north woods. Long a cultural aspect of rural communities, if not a rite of passage, the practice has become the target of animal rights protestors, who argue that it is both cruel—for obvious reasons—and unnecessary, as the deer population is grossly exaggerated.

Yet driving south to north in Wisconsin, then back again, you can experience the insanely high numbers in herds (and carcasses roadside). In one traverse of the state you'll likely slam on the brakes at least once, trying to avoid thumping a deer. The modern rite of passage for "my first deer" no longer necessarily implies one downed with a weapon.

Deer Displacement
Northern Wisconsin has always had great hordes of deer in its epic tracts of forest. The most telling evidence of deer overpopulation comes from southern Wisconsin. A century ago, as the last of the forests were clearcut, the white-tailed deer in southern Wisconsin was hunted to near extinction. However, the fecund croplands and suburban gardens that replaced the meadows and forests have also lured huge numbers of deer back, to the point that some suburban areas ringed with rural lands have higher deer concentrations than public parklands. Some wildlife biologists now worry that the social carrying capacity of the land, or the number of deer that humans can tolerate, has been maxed out in the south, while in the sparsely populated north, the reverse is true—the biological carrying capacity is bulging at the seams. The primary cause is once again a lethal modern combination of an abundance of crops available for the deer to eat and refusal to allow hunting on private land, which results in no thinning of the herd. And it's not the same old divisions in this debate—some environmentalists are pro-deer hunting, as enormous deer populations destroy fragile and rare flora in winter feeding.

The Numbers
The Department of Natural Resources estimates the deer herd at anywhere between 1.5 and 1.9 million, or one for every four residents of the state. It was 1.8 million in 1999. Things were so bad in 1996 that the DNR instituted an unheard-of early-October gun season for does and fawns, designed to thin herds to manageable levels; this has continued annually, along with extending periods in November, all to no avail. Annually, over 20,000 car-deer crashes are reported; since these are only the investigated ones,

---

An **information booth,** tel. (800) 224-3835, sits at the entrance to town east of US 53.

Barron
Them ain't chickens you see, but tom turkeys. Seemingly millions of them are kept at the **Jerome Foods processing plant,** one of the largest on the planet. With 1,800 employees, it's one of the region's crucial economic linchpins. Not in Barron itself but west of Cameron along CR W is the **Pioneer Village Museum,** 1870 13 1/2 Ave., tel. (715) 458-2841, a jumble of nearly 30 historic county structures, with a depot, church, jail, school, homestead farm, and more. It's open Thurs.-Sun. 1-5 p.m. and costs $2 adults, $1 children.

Rice Lake
The largest community until you hit Superior, Rice Lake is named for the ancient beds of *manomin* that once lined the shores of the lake.

The **Bayfield Trail,** along Lakeshore Drive, is an old Indian pipestone and wild rice trade route; watch for a historical marker on the lakeshore. Also along Lakeshore Drive you'll find a burial mounds park with a dozen extant mounds—there were once almost 70.

The **Red Barn Theater,** two miles northeast on WI 48, tel. (715) 234-8897, is a popular local theatrical house with five shows running throughout the summer, from dramas to farces. Tickets cost $11. A gift shop-cum-wildlife museum, **Bear Paw Co.,** at the junction of US 53 and WI 48, tel. (715) 236-7300, features black bears poking at you from behind gift sweaters and mountain goats overlooking everything from high above.

The Red Cedar River, if gushing chamber of commerce boostings are to be believed, contains more fish than any similarly sized body of water in the state. They're at least half right—the bass fishing is blue-ribbon. Rice Lake is the ter-

you can probably safely double that number. In fact, in a handful of counties, car-deer crashes outnumber all other crashes combined. Things have gotten so bad that the state has had to contract private services to travel around tagging and bagging the carcasses. There ends up being so much more work than they thought, the private companies often lose lots of money but can't get out of their contracts with the state. Exact figures are impossible to calculate—insurance claims vary wildly—but a conservative estimate puts the damage total, including cars and agricultural losses, at around $100 million per year. Thankfully, less than two percent of car-deer crashes result in human injury or fatality. Still, in 1999 six people were killed and 841 were injured out of 47,555 people who were involved in deer-car crashes; these numbers were increasing by around five percent per annum.

Preventive Maintenance

Communities have tried everything: frightening deer away, fencing, relocation, and even organized hunts. The DNR and local groups have decided that relocation is far too expensive and offers no guarantees since stress can kill the deer in transit. Besides, suburban feeding has lured far more deer back.

If you're driving in Wisconsin, face the fact that at some point you're going to meet a deer on a highway. October and November are the worst months statistically, but May and June are pretty bad, too, as fawns are starting to get their legs and move around. You could see one anytime. April through August, crashes happen mostly after 8 p.m.; the rest of the year, they typically occur 5-7 p.m. Deer, like any wildlife, are most active around dawn and dusk, but they are active day and night. Most crashes occur on *dry* roads on mostly clear days. And the old adage about them freezing in the headlights is absolutely true; that's why "shining" deer—an illegal hunting practice—is so effective. The best thing you can do is pay close attention, don't speed, and keep an intelligent stopping distance between you and the next car. Use your peripheral vision and if you see one deer, expect more. If one appears, hit it—sadly, it's the safest thing to do for you and for all other traffic.

minus of one of Wisconsin's newest multi-use trails. The **Wild Rivers Trail** stretches 96 miles through three counties. North of Rice Lake on CR SS is the western endpoint of the **Tuscobia State Trail,** another rails-to-trails project. This one is the longest in Wisconsin, stretching 76 miles east from US 53 to Park Falls. Part of the route is an official Ice Age Trail Segment. Golfers might like the **Tagalong Golf Course and Resort,** tel. (715) 354-3458, modeled after St. Andrews Course in Scotland. The resort is nice, but it only accepts travelers on package plans in summer months.

There are half a dozen motels in town itself, half are chains. Of those that aren't, **Currier's Lakeview,** 2010 E. Sawyer St., tel. (715) 234-7474, warrants the most notice, a two-story complex with an ersatz A-frame at one end. Some of the myriad lodgings have extra rooms or kitchenettes. Boats and a dock are right out back on the lake. There's also a sauna and free conti-

nental breakfast. High-season rates are as low as $40 weekdays but jump much, much higher on Friday and Saturday.

Northeast of Rice Lake, the land is peppered with more lakes and flowages, all dotted with family resorts. One that stands out, **Stout's Lodge,** northeast via US 53 and CR V, tel. (715) 354-3646, sits on an island in Red Cedar Lake. Constructed laboriously by hand in 1900 out of logs and imported four-inch-thick floor planks and carved beams, the lodge was modeled after famous Adirondack resorts. Massive boathouses, servant and guest quarters, a pistol range, a bowling alley, and a central hall were constructed. It is 26 acres of prime seclusion—there's even a bird sanctuary with its own eagle nest. The resort's restaurant is highly regarded, offering the finest dining in the area using fresh local produce and game. This resort is so intriguing that guided tours including lunch are offered by reservation.

Try the newer branch of the famed **Norske Nook,** 2900 Pioneer Avenue. It remains to be seen if it can duplicate the culinary feats of its Osseo location. **Lehman's,** 2911 S. Main St., tel. (715) 234-2428, is the local supper club of choice, with good steaks since 1934. From $5. There are also free municipal band concerts Thursday nights downtown.

The Blue Hills

Blue Hills Country lies due east of Rice Lake and into Rusk County. These hills are far older than either the Rockies or the Appalachians and were at one time higher than the Rockies— at least until the glaciers lumbered in and shaved them down. The best place to see them is northwest of Weyerhauser, which will also lead you to the endpoint of the Blue Hills segment of the **Ice Age Trail.** Tracing the edge of the Chippewa Lobe, from the last glacial period, it's also part of the Tuscobia State Trail. Along the way, the oddball topography of felsenmeer (literally, "sea of rocks") can be seen, formed by excessive frost, which created hundred-foot, steep, rocky grades. There are 12 miles of trails in the Blue Hills, open for biking, hiking, and cross-country skiing. **Christie Mountain** is a downhill ski operation with a 350-foot vertical drop and 10 4,000-foot runs.

Cumberland

Cumberland is beautiful side trip west from Rice Lake via WI 48 if for no other reason than all the lakes in the area. That's not to mention the late August celebration of the underappreciated orange tuber at rollicking **Rutabaga Days.** The **Tower House** downtown is in an impressive historic structure offering Italian and American food, including a Sunday Italian smorgasbord and Saturday barbecue ribs. Open daily for three squares.

Spooner

With 350 lakes and the wild and woolly Namekagon River within shouting distance, Spooner is yet another gateway to family northwoods resorts. An attractive little town of just under 2,500, it's the kind of place where the shops are housed in those ersatz log structures—but on the whole done tastefully.

Since 1953, Spooner's annual zenith has come during the second week of July when it hosts the **Heart of the North Rodeo.** Wisconsin isn't exactly prime rodeo country, but this PRCA-sanctioned granddaddy is legitimate, drawing top professional rodeo champions. It is among the nation's top 100 rodeos and one of the oldest on the Mississippi. Some 3,000 contestants vie in men's and women's championship categories; the purse is $30,000. Performances generally start at 7:30 p.m. Friday and Saturday and 2 p.m. Sunday, and a parade is held on Saturday at 1:30 p.m. General admission is $11 adults, $5 ages 12 and under; a season pass is $22 adults, $12 ages 12 and under. For information, call (800) 367-3306.

A couple of alternative attractions exist during other times or for PETA members. Downtown Spooner's **Railroad Memories Museum,** tel. (715) 635-2752, is housed in an old Chicago & Northwestern depot, filled with the usual stuff, but seven rooms of it. The holdings include a model railroad display, a video room, photos, watches, uniforms, and four original cars. Open Memorial Day through Labor Day daily 10 a.m.-5 p.m. Admission is $3 adults, 50 cents children. The **state fish hatchery,** a half mile west of US 63 on US 70, is now among the world's largest freshwater rearing stations. It's got educational displays, exhibit ponds, and observation areas and is open for viewing any weekday. Tours are given weekdays at 10 a.m. and 2 p.m. mid-April through late September. Free.

Spooner is also on the 96-mile-long **Wild Rivers Trail,** which stretches through three northern counties on an old railroad bed.

Area resorts are too numerous to list with any degree of accuracy here. Contact the **information center,** tel. (715) 635-2168 or (800) 367-3306, along River Street in Spooner, for complete listings. Long Lake is one of the largest and most popular resorts in the area.

Side Trips

Nearby Shell Lake has the ho-hum **Washburn County Historical Museum** but also offers the very interesting **Museum of Woodcarving,** US 63 North, tel. (715) 468-7100. This is the largest collection of woodcarvings in the world, done by one person—a local teacher—over a span of 30 years; the masterpiece is the incredibly detailed *Last Supper,* which took four years to finish. Joseph Barta, the inspired artisan, also fancied himself something of a poet. This is the kitsch trip of the whole region. Open May through late October daily 9 a.m.-6 p.m. Admission is $4, $2 children under 13.

Cheery **Barronett,** farther south, has more than its share of galleries and antique stores. Genuinely eye-catching ornate and intricate carvings are found at **Carrousel Creations,** along US 63, tel. (715) 822-4189. This operation re-stores any antique wood but specializes in old carousel animals. Its custom home-interior and business-sign carving is well known.

Southeast of Spooner, near Sarona, via CR D and CR P is the **Hunt Hill Audubon Sanctuary,** tel. (715) 635-6543, a 400-acre environmental education center and retreat camp featuring nature trails and canoeable lakes. Nature programs and extended educational series are ongoing.

SUPERIOR

The tip-of-an-arrowhead where Wisconsin and Minnesota share Lake Superior comprises Wisconsin's blue-collar harbor town, Superior.

Poor Superior, the little sibling of the amiable Twin Ports, often gets a bad rap when compared with prim, postcard Duluth, etched into the rufescent palisades across the harbor. Superior, many jaded travelers sneer, proffers not much more than mile after mile of drab, eye-level aesthetics typical of an ore town—endless coal foothills, the forlorn natural graffiti of iron oxide, a clunky patchwork of rail lines, ore docks and cranes, and too much fencing. Worse, owing to its lower elevation, Superior seems to catch all of the climatic flotsam that slides off the bluffs and across the harbor. While the sun shines on the crown of Duluth, Superior sulks in a shroud of fog and a perceived shortage of trees.

That said, the phlegmatic port town is not at all distressed by apparent contrasts. It is unvanquishably proud of its position, along with Duluth, as one of the busiest deepwater harbors in the nation. Its also one of the farthest-inland and deepest freshwater ports worldwide and the largest harbor on the Great Lakes, shipping umpteen million tons of ore and grain annually.

Off the industrial straightaways, Superior reveals not only grand stretches of classic Lake Superior history but, real truth be told, tons of trees—it's got the largest municipal forest in the United States. And don't let the curmudgeons sully Superior's image—it was nice enough for President Calvin Coolidge to relocate the White House here in 1928.

History
The spits extending from Wisconsin and Minnesota form a natural breakwater, which pro-vided protection for French boats exploring the area. While traversing the length of the St. Louis River in 1662, Pierre Esprit Radisson camped at the site, and a decade later, the explorer who gave Superior's sister city its name—Daniel Greysolon, Sieur du Lhut—purportedly established a trading post here. The Sault Canal opened Lake Superior to oceangoing traffic and opportunistic investors, and Superior found itself settled for good in 1852. The isolated city grew in fits and starts, the population exploding with every rumored railroad advance. When the railroad finally arrived, in 1881, Superior was firmly established as a friendly rival to Minnesota's Duluth. Immigrants, mostly Finns and Poles, poured in to mine and work the docks as stevedores. Within a decade, shipping had increased by 4,000%.

To become the "Pittsburgh of the West," an old guidebook recalls, was Superior's ultimate goal, with hopes of steel mills raised adjacent to the railroad and docks. But Duluth's direct access to larger ore ranges to the west precluded U.S. Steel from opening shop here. Superior was content to become the region's major rail hub. Later, Superior's shipyards would develop the first "whaleback," a massive ore carrier.

SIGHTS

Barker's Island/SS *Meteor*
The ready-made starting point for most travelers is the narrow sandbar between Duluth's Park Point strand and the Wisconsin mainland. Most start from the Superior visitors bureau on US 53, connected to the island by a road and footpath. Good for a leg stretch, the few hundred

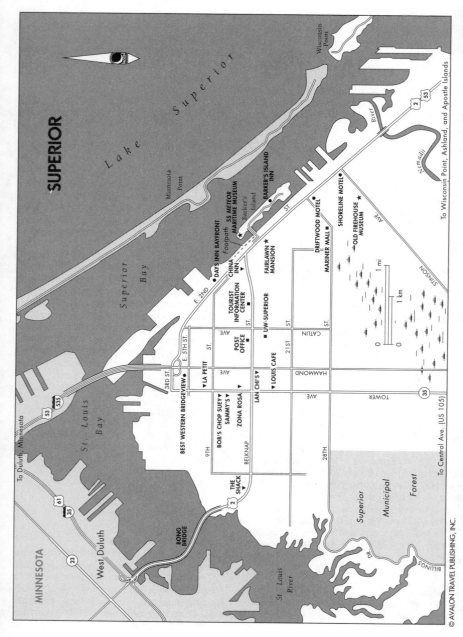

SUPERIOR

Lake Superior

Superior Bay

St. Louis Bay

MINNESOTA

West Duluth

To Duluth, Minnesota

Minnesota Point

Wisconsin Point

Barker's Island

Nemadji River

To Wisconsin Point, Ashland, and Apostle Islands

DAYS INN BAYFRONT

SS METEOR MARITIME MUSEUM

Footpath

CHINA INN

BARKER'S ISLAND INN

FAIRLAWN MANSION

TOURIST INFORMATION CENTER

DRIFTWOOD MOTEL

SHORELINE MOTEL

MARINER MALL

OLD FIREHOUSE MUSEUM

UW-SUPERIOR

POST OFFICE

BEST WESTERN BRIDGEVIEW

LA PETIT

LOUIS CAFE

LAN CHI'S

BOB'S CHOP SUEY

SAMMY'S

ZONA ROSA

THE SHACK

BONG BRIDGE

Superior Municipal Forest

St. Louis River

To Central Ave. (US 105)

E. 2ND ST.

E. 5TH ST.

3RD ST.

9TH

BELKNAP

HAMMOND

CATLIN

TOWER

28TH

21ST ST.

STINSON AVE.

BILLINGS DR.

© AVALON TRAVEL PUBLISHING, INC.

1 mi
1 km
0
0

yards trace Superior Bay, cross a bridge, and lead directly to a state-of-the-art **marina**. With over 400 slips, it's the largest marina on the Great Lakes and among the largest freshwater marinas in the world. **The Barker's Island Inn** is also on this edge of the island, along with scads of children's play areas, mini-golf, and assorted tourist-trap curios straight out of a carnival midway dotting the walkway. Free summertime **concerts** are held here June-Sept. some evenings. Barker's Island is also the point of departure for the **Vista Fleet,** tel. (218) 722-6218, a posh cabin cruiser line with three ships. Tours take in the Duluth Aerial Lift Bridge, the Duluth Ship Canal, Port Terminal dock, all of Barker's Island, the Blatnick Bridge, and the world's largest coal docks, then pass into the St. Louis River to watch taconite being loaded at the Mesabi Iron Ore docks. From Superior, two-hour cruises depart late May through mid-October. In high season, mid-June through early September, tours leave every two hours 10:30 a.m.-6:30 p.m. Rates for basic sightseeing cruises in all seasons are $9 adults, $4 children. Moonlight cruises (same prices), lunch cruises ($14/$6), and specialty dinner cruises ($25-35 adults, $11-16 kids) are also offered. Note that some tours depart from the D.E.C.C. dock in downtown Duluth across the harbor.

Moored permanently and gracefully on the west end of the island, its anchor rammed into the earth, is the crown jewel of the island. The **SS** *Meteor* **Maritime Museum,** tel. (715) 392-5742 or (800)

942-5313, is the only extant whaleback freighter on the Great Lakes of the type designed and built in Superior's early shipyards. Built and launched into the bay in 1896 by the American Steel and Barge Co., the ship is a direct descendant of the even more massive "lakers" that prowl the channels of the Twin Ports. Tours are the only way to see inside and are offered daily mid-May to late September, 10 a.m.-5 p.m., until 6 p.m. in July. Admission is $5 adults, $4 seniors, $3 children 6-12; a family rate of $15 is available.

Fairlawn Mansion

Directly opposite Barker's Island, between US 2 and 21st St., stands what is undoubtedly one of the most opulent mansions constructed during northwestern Wisconsin's heyday. Built in 1890, it was home to lumber and Vermilion Range iron ore magnate Martin Thayer Pattison, later Superior's second mayor. The 42-room mansion-cum-landmark, 906 E. 2nd St., tel. (715) 394-5712, with a distinctive steeple worthy of any basilica, serves as the historical museum of Douglas County. The ground floor is a meticulous reconstruction of the period's lavish detail, down to fine etching on glass and wood. The second floor is devoted to the ethnography of the region, dating back to the Ojibwa and Sioux. The top floor follows a century and a half of logging, sawmills, railways, shipping, and mining. The museum is open daily year-round 9 a.m.-5 p.m.; admission is $7 adults, $6 students and seniors, $5 children 6-12 and $20 family.

the leviathan
S.S. Meteor

Old Firehouse and Police Museum

Turreted and, appropriately, a brilliant fire-engine red, Superior's turn-of-the-century firehouse has been co-opted a bit by their municipal servant brethren, the police, and turned into the Old Firehouse and Police Museum, 23rd Ave. E. and 4th St., tel. (715) 392-2773. The museum houses a whole bunch of kid-friendly antique equipment including a 1906 pumper, some police vehicles, lots and lots and lots of guns, more guns, an old jail cell—did I mention guns?—photos, and a thorough collection of photographs. Open June-Aug. 10 a.m.-5 p.m.; admission charged.

The Dukes

The Twin Ports are chummy enough to co-support a pro baseball team—the Duluth-Superior Dukes, members of the Northern League. Unaffiliated with the major leagues and generally equated with the minor leagues' AA level, the Northern League gave Henry Aaron his start, in Eau Claire. The Twin Ports franchise has been called the "flagship franchise" of this league by its own commissioner due to its history and connection to its home community—even more than the St. Paul franchise. The Dukes play their games across the harbor in Duluth's Wade Field May-September. Contact the tourist center for a schedule and ticket information.

The Docks

The docks in Superior are among the busiest in the world, and the **Burlington Northern Taconite Ore Docks** are indeed the largest in the world. Not all are available for public viewing, but the Burlington docks have allowed observation. Inquire at the visitor center for access.

Wisconsin Point

Just east of Superior, off US 2 at Moccasin Mike Rd., a narrow sandbar breakwater acts as a protective lip to the large harbor. The formation is the largest semi-natural breakwater in the world and offers a wild, off-the-beaten path snoop into the great harbor. It's a quiet, isolated place with innumerable forks, pulloffs, dead ends, and where-the-hell-am-I turnoffs. The highlight of the excursion is the **Superior entry lighthouse.** No tours are available, but you can get fairly close.

Pattison State Park

It wouldn't be a trip to Superior without a side trip to this jewel of the state park system, featuring the graceful, thundering 165-foot Big Manitou Falls. It's the highest cascade in Wisconsin—one of the highest in the eastern U.S.—and the reason most people visit.

Archaeological evidence points to human habitation on this site as far back as nine millennia ago, 1,000 years after the retreat of the last glaciers. Copper from the half-billion-year-old Douglas Fault gave rise to the region's primary Paleo-Indian occupation. The Old Copper Culture groups populated the area as far back as 5000 B.C., scavenging the cupric bluffs in the park. Copper fever later brought European neophytes hoping to exploit veins, transforming the area into a warren of shafts, tunnels, and sluices. In the park today, the residual effects of mining can still be seen, including the triangular hole at the base of Big Manitou and a network of old trenches, pits, and foreboding shafts.

Bisecting the park, the Black River actually looks like dark beer, at times even refracting reddish hues due to oxides in the area's soil. Flowing 22 miles toward Lake Superior from Black Lake, along the Wisconsin-Minnesota border, it was dammed in the 1800s by lumbermen to avoid damaging logs by tumbling them over the great falls. In 1928, another dam was built, and the result is a 27-acre lake the color of stout with good swimming. Though it doesn't affect the lake, the DNR dumps lampricidic chemicals above Big Manitou Falls regularly to kill sea lampreys, which infest the tributaries of Lake Superior. The lamprey, one of the Great Lakes' most pernicious parasites, travels upriver to spawn and die, and the falls work well to mix the chemicals.

Ten miles of trails head in all directions, and the most popular is also the easiest. The **Big Falls Trail** leaves the parking area not far from a nature center that doubles as a park shelter. At half a mile, it's a minor traipse to get a good photo of the big beast of a waterfall. Trailing the west side of Interfalls Lake, formed by a CCC dam on the Black River, is **Little Falls Trail,** a longer trail at three miles roundtrip, but to decidedly smaller falls—some 30 feet. At the halfway point you can cross back to the other side and return via the short **Beaver Slide Nature Trail** or branch off and continue southward along an old **logging** camp trail, which loops around the Black River in the park's southern tier.

This southern region also has spur trails to the **backpack camping area,** offering three sites, which can be reserved, and primitive conditions. The family campground in the north end of the park has 60 sites—30 reservable—with showers in summer.

Of the 50-odd species of mammal in the park, the rare timber wolf and moose have been sighted—very rarely. Clever and diligent spotters should keep their eyes peeled—and keep their distance.

Amnicon Falls State Park

Twelve miles southeast along well-traveled US 2/53 is Amnicon Falls (also on the Tri-County Recreational Trail), another prime piece of geology created by the Douglas Fault. A half billion years ago, the fault cracked and settled, forming the channel of the weak-tea-colored Amnicon River. The Amnicon splits around an island and flows over three impressive falls, each nearly 30 feet high. More falls form during high water runoff, as the river drops precipitously on its course through the park—180 feet in just over one mile. The river's "root beer" color is caused by tannic acid leached from decaying vegetation in the nearby bogs and is a prime reason for the park's popularity with photographers come sunset. The watershed, including the park, contains the only native muskie population in northwestern Wisconsin, and the warm Amnicon itself is a primary spawning run (the name even means "place where fish spawn") for coho, chinook, rainbow trout, and with smelt from Lake Superior.

Leading to the island is the park's famed bowstring covered bridge (also called the Horton, after its designer) spanning 55 feet below Snake Pit Falls. A minor, sweatless loop trail begins here, and on the other side of the covered bridge another short trail descends to a picnic area. A **nature trail** leaves from the campground and heads toward a decaying sandstone quarry that dates from the late 1880s.

The family campground has 36 sites, most of them at least partially secluded and half of them reservable.

ACCOMMODATIONS

Under $50

Most lower-end lodging options are strung along US 2/53 east of town, including the **Shoreline Motel,** 2302 E 2nd St., tel. (715) 398-6688, which has rooms for around $36 s. If you follow US 2 as it becomes Belknap Street downtown you'll pass three or four more nondescript but perfectly adequate budget motels.

$50 to $100

A good choice on the west side, near the Bong Bridge and thus an easy skirt into Duluth, is the newer **Best Western Bay Walk Inn,** 1405 Susquehana, tel. (715) 392-7600. To get there, continue west of the US 2/Belknap St. bridge split-off. Modestly upscale rooms start at $60 during high season.

covered bridge,
Amnicon Falls
State Park

WISCONSIN'S WHITE WHALE

Every autumn, the well-nigh-impossible pursuit of the white whale of Wisconsin, the muskellunge (hereafter muskie) ineluctably turns the most rational of anglers into raving Ahabs or Don Quixotes. It's more than just a fish. It's an obsession, a mental or mythical construct that life can only rarely approximate. Why go to Baja to fight a sailfish when you can hook a muskie and be in for the ride of your life at a fraction of the price? Once hooked, these primeval behemoths can imitate the acrobatics of any marlin—or play smart and lie low on the bottom, sailor-knotting your test line into ribbons around your own prop. Averaging an hour or more to spot from the boat when hooked, the muskie is a formidable opponent for the average angler.

Boulder Junction and Hayward are locked in a friendly competition over bragging rights to the title of "Muskie Capital of the World." Wisconsin's Vilas County and its western lake groupings now make a fairly decent living leading frothing anglers out into prime muskie territory, where 50-inchers are sought

in maniacal fantasies. But they'll be hard-pressed to land one. It takes an average of 100 hours just to get a nibble, and the average required 10,000 casts is too much for all but the most obsessed. (Packer great Brett Favre purportedly hooked one on his second cast; it happened during the Packers' blessed 1996-97 Super Bowl season, so it makes sense.) Once hooked, a muskie can toy with you for up to 45 minutes, tugging at but never quite taking the bait; once it does, you'd better not have anywhere to go in the near future.

The Creature
The word "muskie," though the genus *Egsox masquinongy* faintly resembles the modern moniker, is still of doubtful etymology. The Ojibwa had a close cognate, which essentially translated as "ugly fish." Fossil evidence suggests that muskies migrated eons ago from oceans to inland seas. Three basic types of muskie exist: the aforementioned basic species, or Great Lakes muskie; an Eastern, or Ohio, version; and a loathed mutation of a muskie and the northern pike, the Tiger Muskie. A true muskie has dark vertical markings on a lighter background, but the only way to truly distinguish it from a northern pike is by its lack of scales on the lower gill cover. The muskie is torpedo-shaped

---

On Barker's Island, the **Inn and Conference Center,** tel. (715) 392-7152 or (800) 344-7515, offers 115 varied units with a splendid view of the bay and Park Point in Minnesota. The complex has a nice indoor pool, whirlpool, sauna, and game room, along with outdoor tennis courts. Rates start at $65, $140 for a suite.

The **Days Inn-Bayfront,** right near the fork in Highways 2 and 53, tel. (715) 392-4783, is a good bargain, with spacious, well-maintained rooms and a view. There's a pool, whirlpool, sauna, and restaurant. Rates start around $75 in summer, lots less in off seasons.

Houseboat
Out on Barker's Island, the **Gull Wing II,** tel. (715) 398-3986, has houseboat rentals, with daily or weekly rates.

Camping
The closest public camping is found at Amnicon Falls State Park, the next closest at Pattison

Falls State Park. Reserve sites at 888-WI-PARKS (www.wiparks.net); reservations cost $9.50. A private campground is located not far from Amnicon at the junction of US 2 and US 53. In a pinch, there's also **Manitou Valley Campground,** tel. (715) 399-8696, on WI 35 13 miles south of Superior.

FOOD

Coffee Shops
Get good java at **Le Petit,** 1220 Tower Ave., tel. (715) 392-5515, which also has a deli and sandwich menu. From $3.

Family Style
Ever popular, the **Town Crier,** 4927 E. Second St., tel. (715) 398-7521, features colonial/Yankee decor and atmosphere. Hearty, well-prepared specialty skillet meals—pork chops, chicken, ground beef, steak, or codfish—come sizzling

and absolutely rock solid, with pointed pelvic and pectoral fins set close together, giving it a streamlined speed unmatched in aquatic species. The mouth contains a jaw wrapped halfway around the head and the largest canine teeth of any freshwater fish. Those teeth can be used to attack mammals and birds as large as a muskrat; more than one puzzled fisher has pulled out a skeletal smaller fish chewed up by a muskie while on the line.

Muskie are born in multiples and grow fast—up to 30 inches and seven pounds in five years. The state record is a whopping 69-pounder taken in 1949 from a dammed section of the Chippewa River near Hayward; thus began the rivalry with the Boulder Junction area, which probably has more muskie in more of its lakes.

Prior to the advent of stocking by the DNR, begun back in 1899, the muskie was in gradual but constant decline. Muskies have overcome quite a few obstacles in the past half-century—not limited to extreme popularity among anglers, heavily sedimented lakes, and lakeshore overdevelopment. Catch-and-release imperatives have ameliorated things somewhat. Stocking has resulted in a plethora of muskie in certain waters, despite the insanely high cost of raising fingerling muskies. One-quarter of the current population has been raised through stocking, much of it in the headwater regions of the Chippewa, Flambeau, and Wisconsin Rivers. The DNR even stocks them in the central and southern waters of the state.

On the Water

Ask a dozen old-timers how to land a muskie and you'll get a dozen different answers. Patience is the most important trait an angler can bring to the encounter. Millions of years of predatory evolution have given the mighty muskie an important genetic advantage over most fishers. You might like to enlist the aid of a local guide.

The prime muskie season is May-Nov., and many swear October's the optimal time. Muskies are coolwater fish and thus do better on the fringes of early May and fall. The lure doesn't much matter—the bigger and juicier looking, the better—just keep it active. And get a heavy test line. Some old-timers still use "row-trolling." Motor trolling, thankfully, is illegal. The muskie can be found just about anywhere—drop-offs, weed beds, shallow bays—anywhere there's food.

And if you do land a legal muskie (32 inches), consider letting it go anyway. Only 10% of muskies reach that legal limit, and only a small percentage live 15 years. With proper photographic records, exact replicas can be built for show. And certainly don't eat the Big One—old-time muskies can be laced with PCBs.

onto the table with a medley of lightly sautéed veggies. Otherwise, a decent variety of rich, carnivorous entrées, a bit of seafood, a dozen sandwiches, and breakfast whenever it strikes your fancy. Open 6 a.m.-11 p.m., until midnight in summer. From $4.

Afterwards, it's not uncommon to see families head for **Bridgeman's Restaurant and Ice Cream Parlor,** tel. (715) 392-1372, in the Mariner Mall along 28th Street. The standard family menu offers good sandwiches. The in-store bakery and ice cream are well worth the trip. From $2.

Greek

Louis' Cafe, 1602 Tower Ave., tel. (715) 392-3058, bills itself as a Greek eatery and does have a slate of authentic Greek cuisine. But it's really a classic 24-hour diner (except Sunday, when it closes at 10 p.m.) with famous pancakes served all day. From $2.

Asian

Nearly a dozen Asian restaurants are found in Superior (pretty remarkable for a city of its size). **Lan Chi's,** 1320 Belknap St., tel. (715) 394-4496, offers mostly Vietnamese fare, heavily influenced by Chinese. Go for the *ga xao xa ot,* traditional chicken and lemongrass that's hot as the dickens, or the sweet and sour chicken meatballs, *ga xao chua ngot.* Lan Chi's is open from 11 a.m. daily, noon Sundays. From $5.

The most varied Cathay cuisine is found at **China Inn,** 15 Belknap St., tel. (715) 392-3434. They cover every regional style, including Hong Kong and Hunan, and the place is always full of locals. From $4.

Italian

Superior has three or four decent family-style Italian restaurants, none a *trattoria* or anything, but dependable nonetheless. **Sammy's Elbo Room,** 1309 Tower Ave., tel. (715) 392-3829, has been around awhile and offers homemade Italian entrées as good as anyone's. The lunch and dinner specials change often and are a good bargain. From $5.

Mexican
Not exactly south-of-the-border, but passable Mexican fare is found at **Zona Rosa,** 1410 Tower Ave., tel. (715) 392-4821. Some American dishes are also available. Open daily for lunch and dinner.

Barbecue
You'll find straight smokehouse classics alongside supper club fare at the very good **Shack,** 3301 Belknap St., tel. (715) 392-9836, with more solid seafood and steaks. Locally, this place owns bragging rights to barbecued ribs and Caesar salads. Thursday nights, the Shack cooks up a Scandinavian-style fish boil and has a popular Sunday brunch as well. Most consider this the finest place to eat in Superior; carnivores certainly think so. Open daily for lunch and dinner. From $6.

ENTERTAINMENT AND EVENTS

University of Wisconsin-Superior
The University of Wisconsin-Superior, between US 2 and 21st St., and accessed via Catlin St., has a **theater** performing three to five shows annually. The **music department** also has shows scheduled throughout the school year. On the third floor of the Holden Fine and Applied Arts Center you'll find the school **art gallery,** containing student, faculty, and guest works. For information, call (715) 394-8101.

Nightlife
Not much, despite a student population. The **Bayfront Blues Saloon,** 1807 N. 11th St., tel. (715) 392-6400, has all blues all the time and is so popular it is now the site of a huge blues festival in summer.

RECREATION

Charter Fishing
With the largest harbor in the world, you wouldn't expect anything less than a thriving business catching lake lunkers. Most guides depart Barker's Island for half- and full-day trips and return laden with walleye, lake trout, steelhead, German brown, and king and coho salmon. Many also offer guided river excursions for trout and salmon, particularly on the Brule River toward Ashland and the Root River. The St. Louis River estuary also boasts some of the best walleye takes in North America. For a lake outing, expect to pay $245 for a half-day, $350 for a full day with up to six in the boat.

Charter fishing is an intensely personal endeavor, so researching your operation beforehand is a must. For a good bet, contact the **Lake Superior Charter Captains Association** via the local information bureau, tel. (800) 942-5313.

Superior Municipal Forest
The largest municipal forest in the U.S. spreads across the western fringes of Superior. Easily accessed via Billings Dr., which parallels the St. Louis River, or Wyoming Ave. off 28th St., or even Tower Ave. heading south, the 4,500-acre spread includes 28 km of hiking and ski trails.

Tri-County Corridor
The corridor is a multi-use recreational trail paralleling US 2 east to Ashland. The best part of the trail is just east of Superior at Wisconsin Point. The trail is a major link to a handful of other trails in Douglas, Bayfield, and Ashland Counties. To get there, head out from the tourist information center on the Osaugie Trail where it crosses the Nemadji River, and continue past a great ore dock lookout before hooking up with the corridor.

SHOPPING

Berger Hardware
Old-as-the-hills Berger Hardware, along Tower Avenue in Superior's north end, is the place for the most ardent of pack rats. Stroll around the creaky aisles and scope out the scads of wares circa WW II, possibly earlier. No one's ever counted exactly how many, um, things are crammed in the store, but it's easily in the hundreds of thousands.

SERVICES AND INFORMATION

The **Superior and Douglas County Visitors Bureau**, tel. (715) 392-2773 or (800) 942-5313, www.visitsuperior.com or www.superiorwi.com, was relocating from Barker's Island to a spot along Belknap Street not far away and is exhaustively stocked with the local dope plus statewide information.

The central **post office**, tel. (715) 394-6643, is at 805 Belknap Street. The public **library** is at 1530 Tower Ave., tel (715) 394-5860. For a clinic, try **Mariner Medical Clinic,** 109 N. 28th St E, tel. (715) 395-3900.

TRANSPORTATION

The city is no longer served by **Greyhound;** you'll have to go to Duluth. This is odd since any buses coming from the south have to pass through Superior; alas, they don't stop so you'll have to disembark in Duluth's somewhat grimy west end, then catch a local bus back.

Superior is served by the **Duluth Transit Authority,** tel. (218) 722-7283. Bus lines 16 and 17 cross the bridges between the twin cities. Fares are $1 for adults.

The area is served by Badger Taxi, tel. (715) 394-5555.

THE LAKE SUPERIOR COAST

Wisconsin is capped in the far north by the serpentine Lake Superior coastline. There are those who say that the entire Wisconsin experience can be had in but two counties—albeit biggies—Bayfield and Ashland, whose perimeters enclose a national lakeshore (including an archipelago), two Indian reservations, arguably the best concentration of waterfalls in the state, and a chunk of the massive Chequamegon National Forest.

The Snow Belt

Lying on the wrong side of Lake Superior as far as weather is concerned, most of Bayfield County sits in the massive cleft of a promontory extending dangerously far, climatically speaking, into Lake Superior. The peninsula watches helplessly as Alberta Clippers race unimpeded across the Canadian Plains, swoop down the precipitous Minnesota escarpments along the north side of the lake, and drop about 120 inches of snow each year, if not more. Bayfield County has been known to get two feet in March, when the rest of the state—including parts just 30 miles inland—gets less than an inch. During the other minor seasons, a day of azure skies and high clouds can be followed by a shrouded, spitting gale racing out of nowhere.

Yet the big lake is also palliative to the climate. The layering effect around the oversized county moderates things enough to allow for a multi-hued patchwork of farm and fruit orchards in the bucolic agrarian stretches, with zillions of apple blossoms blazing come spring and fruit stands in every direction in summertime.

BAYFIELD

This gateway village is right out of a Currier & Ives print, the sandstone bluff offering a commanding view of the Apostle Islands. The town is gatekeeper to superlative Bayfield County, a mix of island-dotted seascapes, Great Lakes thunderheads, and pastoral dairyland, all populated by fishers and farmers, a host of new artisans, and a few tourist-minded businessfolk. It is quite likely the most aesthetically realized village in the state; the *Chicago Tribune* in 1997 dubbed it the "Best Little Town in the Midwest." Most of the hillside mansions, virtually all on the National Register of Historic Places, were built from the earthtone and pastel brownstone underlying the Apostle Islands archipelago, and every hairpin turn on WI 13 reveals a spectacular lake panorama.

Early Woodland and Ojibwa Indians had long occupied the outlying islands before French Jesuits erected and abandoned numerous "parishes" down the coast of Chequamegon Bay. Originally settled by Europeans in the 1850s, it was a muscles-and-sweat village of loggers, commercial fishing families, and dock workers; it was discovered soon enough by well-to-do merchant-shipping families who first arrived in the early 1890s seeking a climatically equable northern resort on the big lake.

Sights

The Apostle Islands obviously dominate the local scene. In addition, though, one major highlight is found at the "Carnegie Hall of Tent Shows." The **Lake Superior Big Top Chautauqua,** is equal parts vaudeville, minstrel and thespian troupe, and folkways preservation. It all takes place under Big Blue, a 60- by 150-foot tent presided over by the distinctive voice of chief ballyhooer Warren Nelson; well, actually, the original Big Blue burned in 2000 and the new one isn't exactly the same color as the original. A night's slate of entertainment might feature national folk, country, or bluegrass artists; guest lectures; and dramas recounting Chequamegon Bay history. Throughout the season, the performances are broadcast on Wisconsin Public Radio. Plenty of food and drink is available on-site. Performances are given daily at either 7:30 or 8:15 p.m. and cost $18 adults, $8 children 12 and under for reserved seats, $12 adults, $4 children for open seating; some big-name acts will command higher prices. Tickets are usually, but not always, available at the door; for ticket information, call (715) 373-5552 or (888) 244-8368. To get there, take WI 13 south to Ski Hill Rd., then follow the signs to the base of Mt. Ashwabay.

Downtown Bayfield's **Heritage Museum,** 100 Rittenhouse Ave., tel. (715) 779-3272, features temporary exhibits on local history. Much more apropos to the area is the **Bayfield Maritime Museum,** next to the Madeline Island Ferry Dock with displays on the ecosystem and species of Lake Superior, knot tying, Native American fishing, and local history. You can also ogle an original Chequamegon Bay tug and parts from other local boats. The museum quite literally opened the day we visited to update this book, so more will no doubt be on offer when you visit. It's scheduled to be open daily during the summer and perhaps lesser times in spring and fall.

The **Bayfield Winery,** CR J, tel. (715) 779-5404, is nearly three miles northwest of town. It produces traditional hard ciders, meads, and country wines from mostly locally grown fruits and honey; there's also a farm and 20 acres of wildflowers. Open daily 10 a.m.-5 p.m. May-Oct.

You'll find *lots* of boat ride options—sail or otherwise. Check "Apostle Islands National Lakeshore" later; you'll likely have even more options by the time you read this.

Accommodations

Bayfield doesn't come cheap following April. Expect to pay $60 or more if you just show up in town, and there are times when rooms might be hard to root out. A multi-night minimum stay is often necessary in peak periods, particularly on weekends. The chamber of commerce, at the corner of Manypenny Ave. and Broad St., can help phone around to see what's available.

The cheapest rooms you're going to find are south of town on WI 13. The **Seagull Bay Motel,** tel. (715) 779-5558, is a clean and comfy place with conscientious owners. Rates start out around $40, even in peak season, and top out at $65. Off-season rates are a steal. Some units have kitchenettes.

Directly across from the Madeline Island Ferry are the varied rooms and suites at the **Harbor's Edge Motel,** tel. (715) 779-3962, a historic harborfront clapboard building. Rooms run $55 and up.

Arguably the grandest view of the lakeshore is found south of town at the cozy country-style **Apostle View Inn,** tel. (715) 779-3385, with six units set far back from the road. This is a very well-maintained property with rates from $71.

Another comparative bargain, the accommodations at the **Winfield Inn,** tel. (715) 779-3252, run $61-82 for basic rooms; $90 and up for kitchenette units. Set on three acres just a few blocks north of town, the rooms are spread out through a couple of buildings. Rooms on the upper level and lakeside offer resplendent views, as does the outdoor sun deck. It was recently undergoing a renovation so should be even more appealing.

Across from the city dock you'll find what amounts to condo rentals at the **Bay Front Inn,** tel. (715) 779-3880, offering 10 units with private decks and a continental breakfast. Some rooms have jacuzzis. Rates run from $90.

Throw a rock in Bayfield and you'll hit an 1850s brownstone refurbished into a creature-comforts-outfitted B&B. The quintessential Bayfield experience is at the **Old Rittenhouse Inn,** Rittenhouse Ave. and Fourth St., tel. (715) 779-5111 or (888) 644-4667, an enormous old place with 20 meticulously restored rooms spread through three Victorians, all with working fireplaces. Rooms start at $99.

The mainland unit of the Apostle Islands National Lakeshore does *not* have campsites. Between Washburn and the Red Cliff Indian Reservation, however, you'll find a dozen campgrounds, many operated by local communities; a personal fave are the lakeside sites at Little Sand Bay, only $6 but tough to get in summer sometimes. Between Bayfield and the Little Sand Bay Visitor Center at Red Cliff is the **Red Cliff Marina and Campground,** with a spacious spread right on the water. A mile and a half south toward Bayfield is the **Dalrymple Campground,** Bayfield City Hall, tel. (715) 779-5712, offering 30 rustic sites ($10) overlooking the water. South of Bayfield, the **Apostle Island View Campground,** tel. (715) 779-5524, is well run and features a separate tent area. Rates start at $12. To get there, head south on WI 13 to CR J, then follow the signs.

Food

While in Bayfield, indulge in at least one of the area's two culinary trademarks—whitefish livers and fish boils. Eating whitefish livers started as a tradition a century ago when boats were landing millions of pounds of whitefish. A local restaurant, Greunke's, is credited with getting tourists in on the act sometime in the '60s. The livers are generally sautéed with onions and sometimes green peppers, though individual styles vary.

Quaint little eateries, espresso shops, and casually upscale cafes line every block of Bayfield, and you can even get a burger and a beer, too. A couple of java joints are in town, including **Morningstar,** across from the chamber of commerce. Open daily at 7:30 a.m. except Wednesday.

One of the longest-established places in town, the **Pier,** tel. (715) 779-3330, offers straight, well-prepared family fare. including soups, sandwiches, homemade baked goods, and ice cream for the little ones. Open at 6 a.m. daily. From $4.

The menu is trendy but the atmosphere amusing at laid-back **Maggie's,** 257 Manypenny Ave., tel. (715) 779-5641, offering creative sandwich and ethnic fare. An incalculable number of pink flamingos adorn the interior. Open 6 a.m.-11 p.m. in summer, shorter hours otherwise. From $4.

The landmark of sorts in Bayfield is funky old **Greunke's,** 17 Rittenhouse Ave., tel. (715) 779-5480. The place that purportedly started the whole whitefish liver thing is still the place in the village to sample it. The Civil War-era structure still has a sheen of originality to it—down to the heavy wooden doors and a century or more of detritus on the walls. The menu lists an excellent array of seafood and some steaks, or you can simply get a chicken breast sandwich. Greunke's is the place for the local fish boil, served Thurs.-Sun. in season, and is also the place for breakfast, as it's usually crammed with locals. From $5.

An enthralling epicurean experience, the six-course, all-night meals from the **Old Rittenhouse Inn** have been called the most memorable in the state. The fare spans the culinary spectrum but gives a hearty nod to creative Midwestern fare, made with as many area ingredients as possible. The remarkably ambitious menu changes constantly—for a splurge, this place is highly recommended. Open nightly May-Oct., weekends thereafter. Reservations are necessary. From $15.

Nightlife

Everybody's pretty much tuckered out from paddling come nightfall, so there's not a lot to do, but **Mama Get's,** 200 Rittenhouse Ave., has live music nightly.

Events

The Bayfield area, tourist haunt that it is, has ongoing events throughout the year. The coolest, personally speaking, is late February's **Apostle Islands Sled Dog Race.** The biggie is October's **Apple Fest,** a blowout feting apples, a fruit integral in all its forms to the local economy. Earlier, in September after Labor Day, a more subdued event—though it's getting fairly sizable now—showcases the area's lighthouses. A cool schooner race takes place in late September.

Recreation

Tours to the Apostle Islands are detailed under "Apostle Islands National Lakeshore," below. (The local Apostle Islands cruise concessionaire has a website: www.apostleisland.com.) Do-it-yourself boaters are in a prime spot—Bayfield is home to the country's largest fleet of bareboat charter operations; marinas are so packed that some have ridiculously long waiting lists for slips.

That leaves charter fishing as the most popular local pastime requiring any effort, and there is no shortage of local charters. Other options include biking up and around the coastal interior behind Bayfield. A magnificent day trip on a bike wanders the uplands overlooking the town—take Washington, Rittenhouse, or Manypenny Avenues. All of these roads afford grand views and, one way or the other, lead to the golf course and CR J. CR J, Betzhold Road to the north, and WI 13 take in many of Bayfield's orchards and 500-foot lake views and provide a cool breeze the whole way.

There are other established trails around Bayfield. The easiest is the gorgeous **Iron Bridge Trail,** winding up into the hills from the north end of Broad Street, offering a superlative view from a wooden bridge and landscaped terraces. The **Railroad Trail** begins at the corner of 3rd and Manypenny and traces the shoreline to Port Superior three miles south, with great mini-palisades and sandy nooks along the way. **Trek and Trail,** a local kayak and dog-sled tour operator, has bikes for rent.

If you don't want to exert yourself, **Apple Wagon Tours,** tel. (715) 779-3335, offers guided tours taking in all those fabulous orchards, yes, but also historic sites and scenic views. Rates and times vary but in summer are available daily.

South of Bayfield, **Mt. Ashwabay Ski Area,** tel. (715) 779-3227, is a downhill ski operation with 13 runs, some modestly expert. Even better, 40 km of cross-country ski trails are open. Rentals and instruction are available, and a 1,500-foot T-bar and four rope tows line the hills. Rates here are the cheapest in northern Wisconsin, around the $15 level, plus $10 for rentals. Open Wednesday and weekends, with evening hours Wednesday and Saturday.

You can go wreck-diving near the islands—there are 25 established hulls littering the lake bottom; several around Sand, Long, and Stockton Islands are popular. The *Coffinberry* is still visible on the surface and is a popular snorkeling destination. All divers must register with the NPS Headquarters. See "Apostle Islands National Lakeshore" for dive charters.

Services and Information

The **Bayfield Chamber of Commerce,** at the corner of Manypenny Avenue and Broad St., tel. (715) 779-3335 or (800) 447-4094, www.bayfield.org, has lengthy resource lists for accommodations and assorted tours. For information on the Apostle Islands, though, you need to head for the Apostle Islands Headquarters up the hill.

Transportation

The **BART** bus system, offering service from Red Cliff south to Ashland, has a terminal in Bayfield. The first bus arrives in Bayfield at 7:05 a.m., the last at 5:50 p.m., running a staggered schedule. From Ashland, the first bus northbound leaves the hospital at 7:55 a.m. Going from Ashland to Bayfield costs all of $2. The bus will stop anywhere along the route that doesn't create a safety hazard. For information, call (715) 682-9664.

ROAD-TRIP: WI 13 TO SUPERIOR

Here's where the windshield vistas become worthy of Ansel Adams—the modest Bayfield County mosaic of orchards, multi-hued patches of unidentified crop, enormous rolls of hay, dilapidated one-eyed shotgun shacks weathering by the side of the road, or even an abandoned Chevy truck rusting in the cattails. WI 13 eases out of Bayfield and whips along the coastline, coming out almost as far west as Superior—some 80 miles and totally worth the effort. These parts were settled predominantly by Finnish and other Scandinavian immigrants pushing west out of the Michigan's Upper Peninsula around the middle of the 19th century. They would eventually spread through the ore docks and shipyards of Superior and into the mines of the Mesabi and Vermilion Iron Ranges in Minnesota. A number of their homesteads can still be seen poking through the weeds along the route.

West of Red Cliff and the mainland unit of the Apostle Islands National Lakeshore, lots of tiny side roads poke their way north from WI 13, leading to assorted points and promontories. Some end at established picnic areas near beaches, others offer miles of gravel just to reach an overrated boat landing.

Red Cliff Indian Reservation

Less than 10,000 acres in size, the Red Cliff Reservation of the Lake Superior Chippewa hugs the shoreline starting three miles north of Bayfield and wraps around the point of the peninsula, a magical stretch of lakefront property. The reservation was established by the legendary Ojibwa Chief Buffalo, who stoically and respectfully resisted U.S. federal attempts to appropriate Ojibwa lands thought to contain a wealth of copper ore. At one point, this band of Ojibwa and the band at Bad River belonged to the La Pointe Band, which separated in the 1840s to the present locations. The **Buffalo Art Center** holds a collection of traditional and contemporary Ojibwa art and hosts cultural events throughout the year. The reservation has its **Isle Vista Casino,** tel. (715) 779-3712, as well as a **marina** and adjacent **campground** with resplendent views of Basswood and Madeline Islands. Another campground, farther from the madding crowds, at Point Detour, features a reconstructed Chippewa village. The reservation's **pow-wow** takes place over the Fourth of July weekend.

Cornucopia

The Depression-era WPA state guidebook described the "stiff gray fishing nets hang drying on big reels; weathered shacks crowd to the shore line with its old docks; thousands of gulls flash white against the sky." The northernmost community in Wisconsin, edging out Red Cliff by a scant few feet, Cornucopia features hands down the best sunsets on Lake Superior—this is the place in Wisconsin everyone thinks is his or her secret getaway. There is a **marina and public harbor,** as well as, oddly enough, a used book shop, along with a handful of gift shops. Cornucopia is also becoming something of an artists' colony. The best sight not relating to the lake is the onion dome of a Greek Orthodox church. In early August the community has a huge **fish fry.**

The **Village Inn,** tel. (715) 742-3941, is an unassuming little country inn and restaurant that may offer the most quintessential Lake Superior experience—fish boils and whitefish livers; also try the fish chowder. The cozy rooms start at $55, or around $300 per week, and lunch and dinner are served daily. **Swenson Cottages** are out of town at the Siskiwit River Falls (to get there, take CR C from the west). Finding them may require extra time and crossing private property, but stick to CR C as the bridge spans the river and you'll get there.

Fish Lipps has basic sustenance and arranges charters; it's a good spot to rub shoulders with locals.

Herbster

Unincorporated Herbster, situated at the mouth of the Cranberry River, features a small **recreation area** right on the lake, which leads to the **Beach Resort,** offering cabins and a minor motel. Exit Herbster via Bark Point Rd., which leads to a tall promontory overlooking Bark Bay and far into the lake. There is also gorgeous scenery to the west of town. In Herbster proper, the beachfront park offers outstanding **camping,** tel. (715) 774-3411, and a fishing dock and boat launch.

Port Wing

More cabins, camping, and boat moorings can be found at Port Wing to the west. This long established farming town was heavily settled by Finnish immigrants expanding westward from their original bases in Michigan. Other than that, the town boasts the state's first consolidated school district (a radical idea for 1903) and the first school bus, both of which—or at least decent mock-ups thereof—are displayed in a town park. Today, it offers mostly sportfishing charters, a couple of bars, and some stores and gas stations. West of Port Wing is another motel/campground/cafe, but even better, a marked detour leads to **Brule Point,** down a pocky gravel road scratched out of rough lakeside wetland. There are lots of pulloffs along the way, and a picnic area and great beach at the end. The place is isolated and usually less than populated, even in high summer season.

A few miles west of Port Wing, at the junction with Falls Road, the Iron River crosses WI13. A left turn on Falls Road leads to **Orienta Falls** of the Orienta Flowage.

Brule River State Forest

For no apparent reason, WI13 turns sharply to the south and trims the edge of this relatively unknown Wisconsin State Forest, punctuated by lowland spruce, paralleling the deep Brule River channel from its headwaters near the St. Croix Flowage into Lake Superior. The spring-fed river lies in an expansive bed of the huge flowage, which at one time drained enormous glacial Lake Duluth.

Historically the river was the most vital link in the chain of waterways between Lake Superior and the Lower Mississippi River, requiring only a short portage from the Brule to the St. Croix River. Daniel Greysolon, Sieur du Lhut made the river well known in his 1680 writings. Chief Buffalo (of the Red Cliff area) and a band of Ojibwa warriors crushed a much larger contingent of Sioux in 1842 near the town of Brule. In more recent history, the river has been more or less taken over by the U.S. presidency. Five U.S. presidents have fished its blue-ribbon trout waters. So enamored of the Brule was Calvin Coolidge that in 1928 he essentially relocated the already relocated White House to a nearby lodge. It's thus been dubbed the "River of Presidents." Donated by a lumber company a century ago and maintained for some logging, the often forgotten forest is ecologically sound enough to contain two protected State Natural Areas.

Today canoeists and trout aficionados make up the bulk of casual users. The area around the community of Brule and the lower riverway is much more placid, dropping three feet per mile through mostly evergreen and bog. After passing the Copper Range Campground and boat launch the river gets serious, dropping almost 20 feet per mile inside steep banks and incessant rapids (80 in all). The area betwixt US 2 and Stone's Bridge is the most popular, with proud stands of trees and lots of tranquility. Not surprisingly, this is where the presidents summered. Whatever you do, contact the ranger station in Brule, south of the US 2 and WI 27 junction, tel. (715) 372-4866, for maps and camping information. Outfitters near the town of Brule include **Brule Country Canoes and Kayaks,** tel. (715) 372-8588.

Hikers will find one super nature trail at the Bois Brule Campground, south of US 2, and extended snowmobile/ski trails to trek almost the entire length of the river; one 26-miler heads to St. Croix Lake. Old logging trails branch out in myriad patterns throughout Douglas County.

Campers have two fairly primitive campgrounds to choose from; one is south of US 2 not far from the ranger station and the other is four miles north of Brule via CR H. No reservations are accepted.

To Superior

There's nothing dramatic along the rest of the route until the road graces the banks of the Amnicon River. A couple of miles prior to the intersection with US 2, you'll find a pulloff offering a great view of a traditional **Finnish windmill.** Built in 1904 and used to grind wheat, it's not in operation but hasn't been allowed to decay.

WASHBURN

Washburn, poised between larger Ashland to the south, and mighty-mini Bayfield and the Apostles to the north, seems to get little respect from the tourism community. Consider that the town of Washburn isn't even in Washburn County. It's in Bayfield County—it's the county *seat*—though most visitors would never guess it. Nevertheless, the town is quite agreeable and pleasant, with a couple of surprisingly good restaurants and some picturesque shoreline. It's a good place to stay for budget-conscious travelers scared off by Bayfield's prices (and full rooms).

Sights

The best thing to do is walk along the town's **lakeshore parkway walking trail** stretching from Pump House Road in the northeast of town to Thompson's West End Park. Downtown, the **Washburn Historical Museum and Cultural Center** is an unmistakable soft brownstone that was once a bank. Various art exhibits, concerts, lectures, and more are offered there year-round. Open generally Memorial Day-Labor Day 10 a.m.-4 p.m. Free.

North of town along WI 13, the **Washburn Fish Hatchery,** tel. (715) 779-5430, offers ex-

Once a bank, this brownstone now houses the Washburn Historical Museum and Cultural Center.

BRIAN BARDWELL

hibits on Lake Superior fish species and stocking methods. Open daily April-December.

On Bayfield Street in the central part of town you'll find an odd biological specimen—the **Lombardy Poplar.** This state champion tree has defied odds by living—and growing—for 80 years, despite the fact that this species is generally short-lived. This one, an exotic European import, has hung on to produce a trunk 52 inches in diameter.

Accommodations
There are but a few motels in town. The cheapest, quite a decent deal, are the rooms at the **Redwood Motel and Chalets,** 26 W. WI 13, tel. (715) 373-5512. Basic rooms, some with kitchenettes, run $50 s or d in summer. East from WI 13 is the local **Super 8,** tel. (715) 373-5671, with basic rooms from $70 s or d in summer.

Two fine public campgrounds are right on the water in Washburn. **Memorial Campground** on the northeast side of town has 48 sites interspersed among huge pines and also, believe it or not, a lighted tennis court and cable TV hookups at each site. On the southwest side of town, **Thompson's West End** offers 45 sites, a boat launch, and artesian well. Neither community campground takes reservations; both are open mid-April through mid-October. Failing these, there are a couple of public campgrounds north and south of town from around $6. The USFS campgrounds are well marked but most don't know about the **Big Rock County Camp-** ground on the Sioux River; to get there go three miles northwest of town on CR C, then right on Big Rock Road.

Food
On its way to becoming something of a landmark on the road to the Apostles, the **It's A Small World Restaurant,** right on WI 13, tel. (715) 373-5177, offers a careful and wondrous blend of Midwestern and international foods. Different cultural cuisines are featured each week in a choice of two entrées—*coq au vin,* perhaps, or maybe beef tournedos, and the next week a *rouladen.* Otherwise, Small World prepares a unique hodgepodge of sandwich blue plate and a touch of vegetarian. Its claim to fame is the "Oddball Burger," so called not because of its ingredients—it's a doctored Swiss cheeseburger, essentially—but because of its creator, one Mr. Oddball who used to run the joint and was known for his billiards exploits. Open daily, it's definitely the roadfood stop of choice south of Bayfield. From $4.

You can get decent Mexican food at **Cantina del Norte** on the south side of town on WI 13. It's worth a trip if you're averse to deep-fried foods—everything here is baked. From $4.

Transportation
Washburn is served by the **Bay Area Rural Transit (BART)** buses that run between Ashland and Bayfield. The first southbound bus leaves at 7:25 a.m.; first bus northbound comes in at 8:25 a.m. To Ashland is $1.20; to Bayfield $1.

ASHLAND

The largest town in far northern Wisconsin, Ashland sits propitiously at the base of Chequamegon Bay. A permanent Lake Superior stop-off since 1854, the town became a transportation point for millions of tons of ore extracted from the Penokee-Gogebic Range of Hurley and Michigan's Upper Peninsula. Pierre Esprit Radisson and Medard Chouart entered Chequamegon Bay as far back as 1659, landing somewhere between Ashland and Washburn. Their crude lean-to shelters were replaced a handful of years later when French Father Claude Allouez built the first mission among the Ojibwa, abandoned in 1669.

The city quickly roared to a peak after 1854, when Asaph Whittlesey erected a rough cabin and started to establish a far-flung outpost. The city grew exponentially with its transportation capabilities—by the 1890s Ashland was shipping twice the tonnage of Milwaukee, Duluth, and Superior combined.

All that has changed, though the town's 9,000 hardy souls hang on to a varied industrial base and one of the bay's best recreational fishing locations. Touted as the "Garland City of the Inland Seas"—not an exaggeration but not exactly noticeable—it's a sedate town chock-full of old rail lines, stained wood docks, aging trestles, and a stretch of lakeshore that offers some superb vistas.

Sights and Recreation

The Olympus-sized **iron ore dock** juts 1,800 feet into Chequamegon Bay. Wisconsin's wonder of the world once stuck out half a mile. Forty feet above water, it's supported by 576,000 cubic pounds of stone and the equivalent of 45 miles of pine trees driven 16 to 22 feet into the floor of the bay. This marvel of 19th century engineering took nine years to construct, 1916-25. Then and now the largest of its kind in the world, Ashland once had five of them in town, each shipping a million or so tons annually. Those born and raised in the area tell stories of knuckleheads clambering all about it, even swimming its entire breadth underwater through the beams—illegal and questionable in its wisdom. Instead, it's loads of fun just wandering around the causeways behind the Hotel Chequamegon and near Ashland Marina, Kreher Park, Maslowski Beach Park, or down any side streets east of downtown. When rain clouds beckon and fog banks roll in, the massive dock looks positively threatening.

The spanking new, grand **Northern Great Lakes Visitor Center,** west of town at the junction of US 2 and WI 13, tel. (715) 685-2680, is an impressive piece of architecture and construction, a multi-leveled educational center focusing on the region's ecosystem and history. A multi-media introduction produced by Bayfield's Big Top Chautauqua chronicles the area's cultural history. Other exhibits examine the cultural history and environmental issues of the region known as the Great Lakes Pinery from Michigan's upper peninsula to Minnesota; they all put the lie to the derisive nickname once applied to the region: "The Godforsaken Waste." The top level provides a stunning view of the area. The center runs admirable educational programs, even exciting on-the-water paddle programs are common. Trails meander about outside. It's open daily June-Oct. 9 a.m.-6 p.m., until 5 p.m. rest of the year. Free.

Northland College is located along Ellis Avenue (WI 13) south of downtown, tel. (715) 682-1233. Despite the name, the college isn't the northernmost institute of higher learning in the state, but it is ensconced in the north woods, a primary inspiration for its eco-minded coursework. Locals refer to the school's students as tree huggers—a term of endearment. Case in point, the **Sigurd Olson Environmental Institute** is here, a think-tank and educational center for environmental studies, named in honor of the pioneering ecologist who was born and raised in the Ashland area. The institute offers displays about Olson and the school's pioneering environmental activism. Nature photography and woodcarvings get the most display space. Lovely Ashland brownstone is scattered across the campus in turn-of-the-century buildings. The institute is open weekdays 8 a.m.-4 p.m., perhaps odd hours when school is not in session. Note that a $12 million renovation was in the works to re-create the institute into the **Center for Science and Environment** by the time this book hits press.

The **Ashland Historical Museum,** in the columned, 23-room antebellum mansion at 522 Chapple Ave., is full of Ashland historical tidbits, period room mock-ups, photographs, maps, manuscripts, and a doll collection. Open Mon.-Fri. 10 a.m.-4:30 p.m., and Saturday until 2 p.m.

Along US 2 East in Ashland off Bay View Park is what's known locally as **Tern Island,** an island producing two-thirds of the common terns in the Lake Superior region. Jutting into the waters from the park is a reconstructed section of the Ashland Pier, one of the five ore docks built in the previous century. Ashland's **parks** are particularly appealing—a host of them spread along the lip of the lake. Most contain absolutely frigid-looking beaches and great picnicking. Maslowski Beach on the west side offers the best views, arguably the best sand stretches, and a bubbling artesian spring. West of town off Turner Road you'll find Prentice Park, connecting with Superior via the **Tri-County Recreation Trail,** a 60-mile biking/hiking/snowmobile trail that spins through Fish Creek Slough. There are more artesian wells here for the parched (if you're into artesian wells, the Ashland Water Utility oversees one of the largest in North America), and some decent camping. The park's wildlife includes a local rarity, mute swans, often with baby cygnets, and tame deer are kept penned in the park's confines. **Maslowski Beach** has a commemorative marker of the first cabin built in Wisconsin by Europeans, erected by Radisson and De Grossilliers in 1658.

Ashland and Iron Counties boast one of the highest concentrations of waterfalls in the state. Almost two dozen are within a quick drive of Ashland; Potato River Falls are especially worth seeing. Many of the waterfalls are covered under "Hurley," in the "Northeastern Wisconsin" chapter.

Accommodations

Find great rooms and decidedly different but tasteful decor at **Anderson's Chequamegon Motel,** west on US 2, tel. (715) 682-4658. Rates start at $39 in summer. Similar prices are offered at the very good **Crest Motel,** US 2 and Sanborn Ave., tel. (715) 682-6603. This motel has absolutely the best view of any until you get to Bayfield.

The best option in Ashland is unquestionably the **Hotel Chequamegon,** 101 US 2 W, tel. (715) 682-9095. It was rebuilt after a 1950s fire, and the attention to original detail is astonishing; you'd swear this eye-catching remake is the original. At one time, the Hotel Chequamegon was the most opulent along Lake Superior, if not the entire Northwest region. Sixty-five rooms of various incarnations—simple single to suite with jacuzzi, are all appointed in period detail and offer tons of character. There are also an indoor pool, whirlpool, sauna, exercise room, and two well-regarded dining rooms. Worth the splurge. Rates start at $85 s/d.

West of town off Turner Rd., **Prentice Park** has 10 tent campsites (a few sites for small campers). Fret not if the park is full, since you're centrally located for camping. To the south and southwest are northern tracts of the Chequamegon National Forest.

Food

Locals hang at the outstanding **Golden Glow Cafe,** 519 Main St. W, tel. (715) 682-2838, a block south of US 2. Doubling as an ice cream parlor, the joint genuinely has a cozy halcyon glow to it, and it's huge inside—a scuffed Formica counter stretches interminably past diners. The menu lists straight up egg-based breakfasts along with standard diner lunches and dinners. The cafe offers decent daily specials, homemade pies, and a popular Friday fish fry.

The meal of choice for many in the area is found at the restored 19th century **Depot,** 400 3rd Ave. W, tel. (715) 682-4200. Ornate glass and mirrors and rich original woods fill the interior, and a museum-quality collection of railroad artwork hangs on the walls. The menu is Midwestern eclectic—mostly carnivorous, exquisitely well-prepared dishes. The depot doesn't come cheap but it's worth it. From $10. The **Railyard Pub** is now on site as well, pumping out its own English-style ales and serving pub grub. Outside, the mammoth locomotive is the only 10-wheel drive ever made.

Not far away at 211 Chapple Ave. is the wondrous **Black Cat Coffee House,** which has gourmet coffee but warrants a visit for its excellent vegetarian cuisine, including creative pizzas. You can also get beer, and it has live music most weekends. From $3.

The **Molly Cooper** restaurant at the Chequamegon Hotel serves food all day, offering homemade soups—great chowder—salads, sandwiches, and entrées like bruschetta, eggplant, shrimp linguine, and an excellent baked whitefish. A separate dining room at the hotel serves dinners. From $5.

Services and Information

Ashland's visitors bureau—also known as the **Apostle Islands Country Visitors Bureau**—tel. (715) 682-2500 or (800) 284-9484, www.travelbayfieldcounty.com, is at 805 Lakeshore Drive.

Transportation

Ashland is the southern terminus for **Bay Area Rural Transit (BART),** tel. (715) 682-9664, which stretches north to Bayfield. Ashland's hospital serves as the terminal, and the first bus departs, heading north, at 8:05 a.m. No stops are scheduled downtown until around

2:30 p.m., but you can board downtown or anywhere else along the route as long as the driver doesn't have to make a dangerous stop. The fare to Bayfield is $2.

There is spotty **Greyhound** service but currently no local depot; call (800) 231-2222 for information.

BAD RIVER INDIAN RESERVATION

The Mauvaise ("bad") River was aptly named by the French, disgusted at its treacherous navigation. The treaty of 1854 relaxed the federal government's intractable stance on moving Native Americans west of the Mississippi—due in no small part to the Herculean efforts of the Ojibwa. The Loon Clan of Lake Superior Ojibwa were allowed to settle here, along they river which they renamed *Mushkeezeebi,* or Marsh River, along with a small contingent on Madeline Island. At 123,000 acres, the 1800 descendants of the clan live on the largest Indian reservation in Wisconsin. It stretches for 17 miles along Lake Superior and over 100 miles inland, including the superb Kakagon Sloughs, a 7,000-acre wetland of virginal wild rice beds, noted as a National Natural Landmark for its *manomin* (wild rice) and its waterfowl population. Some have called it "Wisconsin's Everglades," and it isn't much of a stretch. Bad River's wood products factory, run by the reservation, produces log home kits.

APOSTLE ISLANDS NATIONAL LAKESHORE

If the Bayfield peninsula in the north is Wisconsin's crown, then the jewels of that crown (a cliché, but befitting) are the nearly two dozen pastel-hued sandstone islands of one of the nation's few national lakeshores. This coastal treasure, misnamed by overzealous or perhaps innumerable French Jesuits, is to many the most precious region in Wisconsin. The inverse of the fierce nor'easters tearing across the lake, the periods when Lake Superior shows placidly equable spirits appear to deposit droplets of mercury atop the surface of a glistening mirror. The area is a magnificent Great Lakes hodgepodge of geology, climate, anthropology, history, and flora and fauna unrivaled anywhere on the inland seas.

Bayfield, the postcard-pleasant coastal village across the bay from Madeline Island is inextricably linked to the Apostles—it's the departure point of the ferry, so you can't get to the islands without visiting Bayfield. Plus, once you get there, you'll want to spend a couple of extra days, because Bayfield is so quaint.

NATURAL HISTORY

Geology
Superficially, the islands represent yet another example of glacial imperiousness—the flat-topped, waxy looking islands appear scraped into horizontal symmetry by ice floes. The islands do show a simple "veneer," as one geologist has noted, of glacial wash, yet the remainder of their composition, save for diminutive Long Island, is billion-plus-year-old pre-Cambrian bedrock of one of three types: salient Oriental sandstone; Devils Island sandstone; and Chequamegon sandstone. Glacial action was key in carving channels between the individual islands over separate encroachments, depositing silt and rocks on the lake bottom; any bluffs

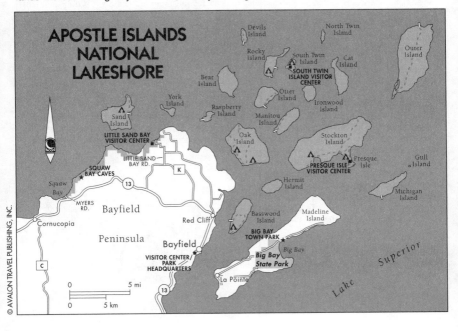

SMOKEY BEAR AND FRIENDS

Wisconsin's secondary mammal is the lumbering, doe-eyed *Ursus americanus,* the black bear. Should you venture to northern—and, given population numbers, even central—Wisconsin, chances are good you'll spot one; go to the Bayfield Peninsula or the Apostle Islands and camp and I can practically guarantee a sighting.

Now, is this a good thing, or a bad thing? Depends who you are, one supposes, but most important is probably what you're doing at the time.

Talking about black bears is a good news/bad news deal. No one's ever been killed by a black bear in Wisconsin, but attacks do happen. In 2000 a young boy was dragged into the woods while in his sleeping bag, even as his father frantically beat the bear with a fiery log; the boy required major reconstructive surgery, and the bear was euthanized. In 1999 a woman was killed in the Great Smoky Mountains, the 25th documented victim of a black bear since 1900 in North America.

At Least They're Not Grizzlies . . .

An adult black bear averages 50-74 inches in length and 250-350 pounds. Female bears are a bit less in length but half as heavy. But they can come close to grizzly-esque proportions: in 1963 a black bear weighing 700 pounds was killed in Wisconsin.

Stocky or bulky is often used to describe them; they usually sport Homer Simpson bellies of fat. Their legs are short and sturdy; they walk on the soles of their feet like humans. Many have tan patches across the nose; one-quarter of the state's bears have white chest markings. They're omnivores, which means they eat everything—flora and fauna. This explains why they're so fond of garbage dumps and camping coolers.

It's the claws, the jaws, and the speed that give hikers and campers pause. The non-retractable claws are perfectly adapted for foraging, digging, ripping, and, gulp, climbing. The jaws aren't as terrifying as those of a grizzly, but if a black bear bares teeth, you'll soil yourself. They can run 30 miles per hour, so don't even think of running.

Distribution

Traditionally Wisconsin's black bears have been found roughly north of a line from St. Croix Falls along the Mississippi east to Green Bay. Numbers have exploded from 5,000 to nearly 14,000, so they're migrating south again and have been seen in Adams County in south-central Wisconsin. Currently there is no hunting season on bears, but given the numbers, that could change.

Run Or Climb . . . Or Neither?

The old joke: the black bear will come up the tree after you, the grizzly bear will just knock it down. Seriously, knowing what to do and what *not* to do is paramount. Inquire about recent bear activity. Look for bear activity on the trail: scat, diggings, torn-up logs (they love mealy ants and worms), turned over logs. Carry a bandana, shirt, or hat to drop or distract the bear. Leave your backpack on for added protection. Also pray that you never come between a mama bear and her cubs.

Camp in open areas away from trails, thick brush, berry patches, or spawning streams. At the campsite, food is what can kill you. Store food and all odorous items by hanging at least 10 feet above the ground, four feet from the top and side supports, at least 100 yards from your tent. Strain all dishwater and store with garbage; dump water and store garbage 100 yards from your tent. Do not sleep in the same clothes you cooked in. Do not take anything odorous—like chocolate, toothpaste, etc.—into your tent, or don't be surprised if a bear sticks his head in and says, "Got any chocolate?"

If you meet a bear, *do not run; it may incite aggression.* Chances are a black bear will be more afraid of you than you are of it . Talk to the animal in a calm, low voice while slowly backing away. If it attacks, try to scare it away by shouting, making noise, or throwing small stones. Always fight back with a black bear.

PAUL B. JOHNSON/CALIFORNIA DEPARTMENT OF FISH AND GAME

on the mostly flat islands are moraines. As the last glacier retreated almost 10 millennia ago, all but one of the islands were covered by enormous lakes. These primeval lakes receded, and Lake Superior found its present form. Superficial wave and wind carving actions molded the islands into their present appearance.

Climate

The islands take the brunt of legendary Superior storms squarely on the chin. To this day, ships still drop their "hooks" in the leeward, rain shadow side of any of the islands to escape fierce nor'easters that might suddenly swell up. Thence, you can expect capricious weather patterns, and like the mainland, a hell of a lot of snow—around 120 inches average in these parts. The islands themselves, far enough off the mainland to lose much of its protective cover, can experience varying climatic patterns of their own. Island flora, for example, take an extra couple of weeks to bloom after mainland wildflowers have already blazed. But Gitchee Gumee (a Native American-derived name for Lake Superior) can also have a positive spin— those gale-producing waters ameliorate unpleasant heat. While the inland swatches of northern Wisconsin are roasting at 100 degrees Fahrenheit, campers on the islands will need a sweater come dusk. Hands down the best summertime sleeping climate for campers anywhere in Wisconsin is found in the Apostle Islands.

Average high temperatures in summer rarely top 80 degrees Fahrenheit, with nighttime lows in the 50s. Winter temperatures can plunge into the negative teens (and worse with wind chill), though the mean temperature is moderated somewhat by the lake. Spring and fall are the toughest seasons to peg. One day will offer halcyon warmth and azure skies, followed by a pelting slush the next day with winds in excess of 30 knots and six-foot swells on the lake.

Flora and Fauna

The islands support a remarkable ecological diversity, amazing considering how ravaged they were by humans for over a century. Some of the most pristine stands of old growth northern mesic and boreal forest and not a few threatened or endangered plant species thrive in the unique island microclimate. In all, 16 Wisconsin State Natural Areas, officially off-limits, are interspersed through the islands. They contain myriad northern forests, bogs, lake dunes, and lagoons.

Migratory birds have become a primary reason for many tourists to visit the islands. Over 100 species in all inhabit the islands. Gulls, mostly herring gulls, are absolutely everywhere; 98 percent of Wisconsin's herring gull and tern population resides on the Lake Superior coast in and around these islands. Great blue herons and two species of cormorants are protected in two areas, and bald eagle nests can be found in a couple of spots. Even pelicans have been introduced. Wolves were exterminated in the 1950s, but are making a comeback in the north, so who knows if they'll reappear here. Deer overran the islands to the extent that organized hunting charters were hired to thin the herds early in the century. They too were hunted far beyond their biological capacity to rebound but are managing a slow comeback. A delight on Stockton, Sand, and a few other islands are beaver colonies—a pertinent mammal, so crucial to the settlement and exploration of the region.

The most salient species on the island is the black bear, found on a handful of the islands, including Stockton, which has one of the highest concentrations in the United States. Most of the islands have abundant blueberries, so it isn't quite a surprise to find Smokey and pals swimming the straits in search of food.

HUMAN HISTORY

Paleo-Indians entered the region perhaps as soon as the glaciers left the horizon. The chain of islands has seen occupations—permanent or otherwise—of Huron, Sioux, Fox, and later Iroquois, all arriving to exploit the phenomenal wealths of game and fish. But, it was indisputably the Ojibwa, who once held sway from the eastern portion of Michigan's Upper Peninsula south to Milwaukee, whose hegemony mostly shaped the human history of the Apostles. Prior to the enraptured Jesuits christening the islets biblically, Ojibwa myths recounted the creation of the islands—a nature-creator hurled enormous sticks or stones (accounts vary) at a fleeing animal, splashing into the glacial lakes and creating the archipelago.

Black Robes and Beaver

As with the rest of New France, the wilds of what would become Wisconsin were only secondarily analyzed for commercial purposes—at least until the wealth of beaver became apparent (and Paris dandies made them the fashion rage). At this point, the race was on between the Quebec governor, who wanted to woo the Natives with iron goods, and the Black Robes, who wished to save those Natives from fire and brimstone.

Call it a draw in the long run, but the early sway fell to buck-toothed tree-cutters. The Apostles would eventually become the westernmost shipping point for beaver pelts along the fabled "Voyageur's Highway" along the northern Lake Superior coast. Another route crossed Lake Superior to the area west of Hurley, leading 4,000 miles to Montreal. The fur trade reached its zenith prior to the Revolutionary War and didn't ebb until the 1840s.

Fishing

The economic linchpin to Lake Superior's south shore was commercial fishing, which caught on quickly with the decline of the beaver industry, around 1830. Enormous stocks of whitefish and herring were netted, processed, and shipped from the islands; despite the dearth of overland transportation, the Apostles were a mainstay in the U.S. fishing industry. Semi-permanent fish camps dotted the islands, net sheds lined the shores, and it became such an industry that a thriving cooperage (barrel-making) industry also developed. An annual fishing season would net almost eight million pounds of fish. The last fishing camps withered away on the islands in the 1950s, when invasion of the Great Lakes by the parasitic sea lamprey choked off fish populations. On Wisconsin's Lake Michigan shore, fishing of a different sort—sportfishing—would replace commercial fishing and in some ways has become more large scale.

Quarries

Sandstone from the Apostles helped rebuild Chicago after the Great Fire. Buildings from the Milwaukee County Courthouse to entire city blocks in Chicago and other Midwestern cities owe their construction to the ruddy brownstone culled from quarries on a handful of the Apostle Islands. Following the Civil War and spanning some 30 years, the quarries were massive operations and fed the local economy until steel-girder construction obviated the need for stone. Hermit Island has the best residual quarry; a visit to the Apostle Island HQ in Bayfield offers an up-close peek at the lustrous stone, dubbed second-best in the U.S. by architectural and construction firms.

Shipping

Mention the Great Lakes, particularly Lake Superior, and associative synesthesia sets in: foghorns, hurricane force gales, flickering ship lights, and rocks littering shoals. The Apostle Islands have the highest concentration of lighthouses in the United States, due in large part to the necessities of fish delivery to eastern and southern population centers and the sociopathic nature of the lake. A lighthouse keeper in the Apostles once reported over 125 ships in deepwater lanes at the same time. The Apostles are still a vital link in the North American shipping chain.

Ships always had trouble with the shallow sandbars and tempestuous weather, running aground with alarming regularity. In part it was inevitable, as ships had to run close to shore for protection, and that's a dangerous proposition when sailing through two dozen blocks of stone. One gruesome tale involved a ship in a fierce storm washing ashore with the frozen corpses of sailors lashed to the masts, surviving the winds but not the hypothermia that followed. Twenty-five documented wrecks litter the lake bottom. The first lighthouse went up in 1857 on Michigan Island; by 1891 a half dozen lights had been constructed on the islands, which made them the primary shipping landmark across Lake Superior. Today, iron ore, wheat, and coal are the primary cargoes of the massive beasts prowling the shipping lanes. But they are far surpassed by more modest boating pursuits—pleasure yachters, whose numbers are so great that marinas in the Apostles have unheard of waiting lists for slips.

Logging

Seemingly incongruous but bitterly ironic is the fact that the Apostle Islands today have some of Wisconsin's most breathtaking old growth northern forest. And this despite the fact that most islands were depredated by the lumber saw by the 1930s during the dreadful timber epoch. To the timber industry in the 1880s, the Apostles seemed ready-made, as virgin tracts of red and white pine and hemlock, all floating soft woods, lay yards from a natural waterway; even in winter, logs could be stacked atop the ice and floated toward shore come spring. Eventually, the soft woods were eliminated and the sawyers set their sights on the hardwoods, which required transport. Only those particularly steep-sided islands—North Twin, for example—managed to bedevil the cutters. The era's mindset of "all for us," resulted in clearcutting so extensive that in 1930, when the National Park Service made research inquiries into National Park Status at Herbert Hoover's behest, the Superintendent derided those who had even made the request. So denuded were the islands (fires subsequent to clearcutting all but moonscaped most islands) that the National Park Service felt they were unrecoverable.

The logging heritage made a return in the mid-1990s, when an entrepreneur log salvager got permits to raise, one by one, the millions of red oak, maple, birch, hemlock, cherry, and elm logs that sank during transportation a century ago but haven't rotted on the lake bottom because of the cold and low oxygen levels. Up to 30,000 logs per year will be raised; once surfaced, old tie hack engravings and markings are still visible. These pristine logs are in high demand from woodworking and timber industries worldwide. Others are more apprehensive about once again taking advantage of a lost resource.

Tourism and National Lakeshore Status

Great Lakes mariners had always known about the salubrious environment of the Apostle archipelago, and many of the well-to-do shipping bigwigs became enamored of the place and began making pilgrimages here as early as the 1850s. (The first newspaper travelogues appeared at about the same time.) When the railroad arrived in Bayfield in the early 1880s, the town was soon earmarked for tourism. Major resorts went up, and attempts were made to raise hotels and resorts on Madeline and Sand Islands but eventually fell through.

As far back as 1891, Northwestern Wisconsin communities had been pushing for the establishment of the islands as a national park. Calvin Coolidge, who relocated the White House to Superior in the late 1920s, wholly supported the idea. The initiative was initially rejected because the NPS feared the islands would never heal sufficiently from logging exploitation. Nothing much came about until the 1960s, when U.S. senator and former Wisconsin governor Gaylord Nelson, the same man who would later help spearhead the National Ice Age Scenic Trail, brought John F. Kennedy to the Apostles to trumpet federal recognition—one of the earliest environmental speeches by a U.S. politician. Richard Nixon eventually signed the documents on September 26, 1970.

THE ISLANDS

There are 22 islands in the Apostle Islands chain. Twenty-one of them, along with a 12-mile chunk of shoreline, belong to the National Lakeshore. They range in size from three-acre Gull Island to 10,000-acre Stockton Island. Madeline Island is not included, as it's got year-round residents. Many of the islands have alternate local appellations, so take notes so you always know which island you're asking about.

All but two of the islands are open for some sort of exploration—those that aren't are off-limits as flora or fauna preserves. This still leaves a heap of land to cover. Some are primitive and wild, others are almost like a mini state park. Some are reached daily via Bayfield shuttles, while others are off the beaten track and require a kayak, private boat, or an expensive water taxi from Bayfield. Poking around the Apostles is the most fun some people ever have in Wisconsin.

Over 50 miles of hiking trails can be found on the islands, mostly on old overgrown logging roads. Looking at the map of an island, you're likely to presume that skirting the perimeter would be a great day hike. Don't bet on it. Not only are many shoreline areas off-limits to protect flora or fauna, many of the islands aren't as tame as they look. Many explorers and hikers have been dizzyingly lost in a gorge overnight. If you want to hack your own trail, obtain a USGS topo map, take a good compass, and be prepared to sleep at least one night with the bears.

Transportation to Stockton, Manitou, Oak, Raspberry, and Sand Islands, often tours or shuttles, is covered under "Transportation" in the "Practicalities" section, below.

Stockton Island

Stockton Island and its twin, Presque Isle, is the largest island in the National Lakeshore. Five millennia ago, Stockton Island and Presque Isle were separated by a channel. Over time, currents deposited silt and sand and a land-locking sandbar arose, and vegetation followed. At just over 10,000 acres it is easily the most developed and highly visited island; half of the camping in the archipelago is done here. Historically it has always drawn the largest crowds as well, beginning 3,000 years ago with Native Americans and ending with post-Civil War logging and fish camps and a sandstone quarry operation. For a spell, plans to establish ranches were also considered, giving an indication as to its size. Stockton Island features a beach, 15 miles of hiking, 20 campsites (primitive sites on the north side at an early 20th century logging camp), a ranger station, and one of the superlative sights in the chain—the **Stockton Island Tombolo State Natural Area.** ("Tombolo" is Italian for "mound" but really translates as "overgrown sandbar.") Today it's not only one of the most popular hiking trails but also leads to a **visitor center** (open late May-early Sept., daily 8 a.m.-4:30 p.m.) and a fascinating scientific area. As a protected area it provides refuge for two threatened sedge species and the English Sundew, all thriving in a diverse 680-acre ecosystem. The highest concentration of black bears in the U.S. is found on Stockton Island, numbering just under three dozen.

Oak Island

It's the tallest of the chain, with steep-sided 250-foot ravines etched across its surface, and a maximum elevation approaching 500 feet—so tall it protruded above the post-glacial lake that submerged the chain. Oak Island's 5,100 or so acres are the inverse of Stockton Island's development. Rustic and tough, this spunky island is the one crowd-haters should head for. There are only about 11 miles of trail, but they're steep, unforgiving, and great fun. Hikers have been lost for days at a time wandering the mini-gorges. The Apostles may look diminutive, but they've got adventure. *Note: not only is off-trail trekking possibly hazardous, but it may be illegal, as some areas are sporadically off-limits to protect nesting eagles.*

Historically of interest are the pirates that plagued the shoreline, hiding in Oak's rugged topography. Frustrated loggers later followed and established five separate lumber camps. (One guy took up residence on a sand spit for 25 years, becoming known affectionately as the "King of Oak Island.") Their artifacts still lie about the island. The cliffs are ringed by sandy spits and some superb beaches. Boaters have a dock, and campers will find superb sites—one at a sand spit a mile east of the dock, a couple to the west of the dock. There is another campsite on the north bay, and the northern perimeter offers a great vista. Black bears are ubiquitous so take care with food supplies. Oak Island is also the best place in Wisconsin for winter camping!

Raspberry Island

Small at only 296 acres, Raspberry is one of the most popular islands. Its 1860s **lighthouse** is the second-tallest in the region. The cliffs here include uncommon clay-lined sandstone and 275 acres of forest containing the Canada yew, less and less common as deer herds proliferate unchecked on the islands. A short trail leads from the dock to the lighthouse. Sand spit campsites are now closed due to the establishment of an 11-acre protected Sand Spit Natural Area. Campers must now stay at least 100 feet from shore. This is the one tour where the NPS really pulls out all the stops, down to the period-costume detail and an re-creation of the lighthouse keepers' gorgeous gardens. Docents lead tours on-site constantly late May-late September.

Sand Island

On the western fringe of the chain and fully out of any peninsular windbreak, Sand Island's ecosystem supports a thriving, oddball flora. It's also got a commanding stretch of sea caves on the east side. Sand Island, almost 3,000 acres, was the only island besides Madeline to support a village, this one a community of 100, mostly fishing families. It was big enough to have a post office. Sand Island was also home to a thriving resort, in operation from 1885 to 1910—the largest and most popular resort in the chain. Historically significant structures are still visible along the coast. Most visitors dock at East Bay and trudge 40 minutes along a suck-soil trail (when it rains), once an established Bayfield

County Road, past a rusted auto hull to an 1881 Norman Gothic brownstone **lighthouse.** Ninety acres of the island is a State Natural Area, predominantly northern wet mesic forest, which holds 250-year-old white pine spinneys. Two grassy camping sites are found near the east dock and two additional group camps are on the island. More black bears reside here, so campers should take care with the food.

Manitou Island

This 1,300-acre island is one of the flattest and least enthralling topographically. The island's fishing camp rivals the one on Little Sand Bay in its exhaustive renovation. A ranger resides on the island, leading hordes of friendly tourists on short tours. A short trail leads from the dock past archaeological excavation sites of Woodland Indians. Manitou is the only island accessed every day by some sort of tour or shuttle.

Basswood Island

Basswood Island was the granddaddy (from 1868) of this archipelago's brownstone quarries, shipped around the country for city halls and major construction projects; the underbrush hasn't even established a hold over the enormous slabs of stone. The nearly 2,000-acre island was also temporarily populated by homesteaders and fishers in semi-permanent camps up through the late 1930s. Campers will find four sites on the south end of the island (no water); two more are 200 hundred yards south of the dock and do have water, and there is a group site here also. Seven total miles of trails wend through the island. There is no shuttle service here, but it is just a stone's throw from Buffalo Bay at Red Cliff, so kayaking or boating are easy alternatives. Along the coast, you'll see hoodoo-like rock formations.

Devils Island

The northernmost island—and as far north as Wisconsin goes—takes it squarely on the chin from Gitchee Gumee come storm season. It's a crucial, and tricky, turning point on shipping lanes on the way to the Duluth-Superior harbors. The rough waters and mercilessly pounding waves are responsible for the prime draw of the island, the **Devils Island Cliffs State Natural Area**— five acres of exposed cliff, subterranean blowholes, and blufftop boreal forest. The underground

chasms underlining the island produce rhythmic booms and whumps that reportedly scared the bejesus out of early visitors; lighthouse keepers reported ferocious extravasations of foamy water during high wave storms. Endangered plants clinging to the cliffs include butterwort and hair-like sedge. An 1891 third-order fresnel lighthouse sits atop the cliffs and, at the right angle at sunset, a killer photo opportunity presents itself. With the exception of Raspberry Island, this may be folks' favorite lighthouse; there was a huge hullabaloo when the Coast Guard announced plans to dismantle it (it was restored instead). The rest of the island is preserved as part of the Apostle Islands Maritime Forest Natural Area, with old-growth boreal forest in stands across the extent of the island. A boat dock is found at the south end of the island and a one-mile trail leads to the lighthouse. Alternately, a rock "landing" is not far from the lighthouse, but landing is extremely tricky. There is only one campsite, and no well for water is provided. Tour boats ply the waters around Devils Island, but none have scheduled stops.

Outer Island

Outer Island is perhaps the one Apostle most littered with the detritus of human occupation, the result of decades of logging and fish camps. At 8,000 acres, it's the second-largest in the group. The south end of the island is the best place to hang out, with sand dunes and spits forming a lagoon nearly a mile long. The entire spit area is part of the protected 232-acre Apostle Islands Sandscape Natural Area, a bizarro mélange of coniferous forest, lagoon, pine barrens, and bogs, containing the rare dragon's mouth orchid; migrating birds also use the spit in spring and fall. Another 200-acre spread, of old growth northern mesic hemlock, may be the most extensive in the Great Lakes to survive logging and deer damage. Clay bluffs recede along the western coast. One solitary sand spit campsite is found on the southern edge of the forest; no water is provided, and it's a seven-mile hike. There are no scheduled shuttle stops here, but there is a dock adjacent to the lighthouse on the north side.

Rocky Island

Shuttles forsake tadpole-shaped Rocky Island, well named for the cliff-walled shoreline on the southern end. The 1,100-acre island has a dock on the eastern side, where the cliffs subside and the clay turns to sand. A smattering of extant structures from fish camps still lie in the weeds and along an established trail. Twenty acres of the island are protected as the Rocky Island Cuspate Unit Natural Area, juxtaposing beach dune and bog. Two campsites (no water) are strung along less than half a mile south of the dock and four more trail along the "tail" of the island north of the dock.

Rocky Island is a chip shot across the channel from South Twin Island, and the two are one of the most popular pairs of islands in the archipelago, despite the fact that South Twin already has a twin.

South Twin Island

In precise topographical contrast to Rocky Island, this sister-of-sorts sits across the narrow channel. The least rocky island in the chain, it's mostly flat and sandy—and diminutive, a mere 360 acres. Despite the lack of craggy belvederes or yawning sea caves, enough folks still visit to warrant a visitors center next to the dock on the west side, though "visitors center" may be overstating it somewhat. Five campsites line the shores around the spits near the dock. No shuttles dock here.

Hermit Island

Hermit Island, if for no other reason than its name, is a perennial favorite of visitors plying the waters on boat cruises. Named for a cooper who arrived from the upper peninsula of Michigan, Wilson (just Wilson) had been jilted severely there, and many took that to be the source of a certain pernicious misanthropic nature. During his spell of solitude, only one man, an Indian from Red Cliff, was allowed to visit him. All others were driven off by gunfire, including tax collectors, who had come nosing around after apocryphal-or-not stories surfaced that "Wilson" had squirreled away a fortune on the island. Upon his death the island was swarmed with bootyhunters who dug it up en masse, but to no avail. Later, a brownstone quarry was established, and a few gargantuan blocks of stone lie tumbled about on shore. On the southern side on calmer days the old ribs from a loading pier can be seen in the shallow brownish water. There is no es-

tablished shuttle itinerary, and there is no dock here, but camping is possible.

The Untouchables

Eagle Island is an off-limits protected Critical Species Natural Area, with large numbers of sensitive nesting herring gull and double breasted cormorant colonies. Gull Island's three acres is also part of this unit, and a 500-foot buffer zone is strictly enforced for boaters May 15-Sept. 1 during prime nesting season. Warmly rufescent **North Twin,** an almost perfect example of northern boreal biome (inhospitable to logging and thus untouched), is also hands-off.

There are additional established Scientific Areas on many of the islands that are also off-limits, so don't go tramping off the path without first checking with a contact station.

Remaining Islands

The largest remaining island, **Michigan Island,** at almost 1,600 acres has a mile or so of trails and a lighthouse to snoop around, along with one sand spit campsite (no water) on a small lagoon. Relatively undisturbed, this island is good for those with a Robinson Crusoe bent hoping to camp on an isolated sand spit and hack through unmarked trails.

Ironwood Island really did once have Ironwood, but once the local timber industry got going, it didn't last long. A few decaying structures lie about the island. One very primitive campsite sits on a sand spit to the south, or you can follow a few old trails, which are not maintained but still passable.

Otter Island is also fairly substantial at 659 acres and contains historically significant Native American encampments, along with the usual logging and fishing camps. There's now a dock and camping on the southeast corner.

Cat Island used to house a modest hotel and resort, along with a quarry. There's nothing much now except for a few beaches in the south, some roads, and more weatherbeaten old dwellings. The dispersed camping here is quite good.

Sometimes one island, sometimes two over time—water levels fluctuate—**York Island** is essentially a long, narrow spit popular with kayakers. You'll find more dispersed camping here.

Bear Island is geologically noteworthy as the second-tallest island in the chain behind Oak

Island. Now 250 feet above water, its steep, lovely cliffs form coves and descend to rocky shores. Over 400 acres of the island are protected old and recovering northern mesic and wet-mesic forest—part of the Bear Island Hemlocks and Perched Bog Unit. You'll find more dispersed camping here.

An island, yes, but **Long Island** smacks more of a breakwater or displaced sand spit poking out of the water, precluding entrance to Chequamegon Bay south of Madeline Island. A breeding ground for endangered piping glover, it isn't technically possible to visit. You can skirt the perimeter to view a couple of lighthouses, keeping the buffer zone in mind.

MAINLAND UNIT

Little Sand Bay is the beginning of the federally protected shoreline on the other side of the peninsula, 13 miles northwest of Bayfield and directly across from Sand Island. To get there, take WI 13 to CR K, then Little Sand Bay Road. Here you'll find yet another National Park Service **visitor center,** open Memorial Day-Labor Day and the last three weeks of September, 9 a.m.-5 p.m. Featuring a dock and scattered displays on fishing, shipping, and tourism, the center particularly rehashes the story of the *Sevona,* a 3,100-ton steamer that was slammed to a watery grave in 1905 in the channel separating the shore from Sand Island. Up-to-date weather and channel information is available at the center also. Adjacent to the visitor center is the restored **Hokenson Brothers Fishery,** at the base of the oddly configured dock. Named for the three brothers who operated the commercial fishery in the '30s and '40s, the park service restored every inch of the buildings into a living museum of sorts—taking in the whole of the process, including the nets, the fishing tug *Twilite,* and the processing area. The old boat sits on the beach, and assorted buildings contain relics and interpretive displays: a herring shed, a carpenter's shop, blacksmith forge, a net twine shed, and an ice house. Free 45-minute ranger-led tours depart regularly. A community **campground** here is cheap and has good views, though you're pretty close to neighbors.

A ribbony strand of beach runs along the coastline, offering nifty views of Sand Island.

Squaw Bay

No established trails lead along the 13-mile coastline surrounding Squaw Bay, northeast of Cornucopia; get there by driving along WI 13 and cutting down one of a few roads that dead-end at or behind the waterline—none are developed. The best way to see the two-mile-long spread of absolutely wild sea caves and natural arch-shaped hoodoos in the sandstone is from a kayak, paddling right into the yawning chasms. Easily one of the most photographed sights in the peninsula, the caves soar to heights of 65 feet in some sections. See "Transportation" under "Practicalities," below for tours.

PRACTICALITIES

Camping

Seventeen of the archipelago's islands are accessible for campers. All are primitive sites, and some islands have dispersed camping. Stockton Island now has one handicapped accessible site.

All campers must register at the Apostle Islands HQ, at the corner of 4th and Washington Streets high above the harbor in the Bayfield County Courthouse (June-Sept. register also at the Little Sand Bay Visitor Center). Permits cost $15 and can be used for up to 14 consecutive nights of camping for one to seven people and can be obtained up to one month in advance. All groups of seven or more must register as a group, and facilities for groups are only found on Stockton, Sand, Oak, and Basswood Islands. The fee system allows for reservations: call (715) 779-3397, ext. 6.

Most beaches, unless stated otherwise, are off limits. All camping must be 100 feet from any water or road or trail. No dispersed camping within view of any building or within one-quarter mile of any designated campsites. In short, if you wonder about it, you probably can't. Always ask first.

Garbage and fires are also big problems. Be prepared to go sans flames and pack out your garbage. Water is available at some, but not all, campsites.

The mainland unit of the Apostle Islands Lakeshore does not have an established campground, which always seems to puzzle travelers. Just southeast of the visitors center in Russell,

LYME DISEASE

Since the first diagnosed case of this bacterial plague was isolated in Lyme, Connecticut, in 1975, it has spread across the U.S. and is now found on the Pacific coast; it is the fastest growing insect-borne infectious disease in the country, despite the fact that Lyme Disease cases are decreasing in the rest of the country. In Wisconsin, however, almost 3,000 cases of Lyme Disease have been diagnosed; annually the state sees 500 cases. But these are only the reported cases; many more go unreported and untreated.

The cause of Lyme Disease is *Borrelia burgdorferi,* carried and transmitted to humans via the *Ixodes dammini,* or deer tick. The deer tick is *not* the only tick (or, some think, insect) to carry the bacterium, but in Wisconsin it is the primary carrier. Distinguishing the maddeningly small deer tick from the more ubiquitous dog tick is easy. The deer tick is exceedingly small—the head and body, two to four mm, are only slightly larger than a sesame seed—and reddish brown and black. Dog ticks are twice the size and brown, usually with white markings on the back. Deer ticks are concentrated most heavily in the northwestern quadrant of Wisconsin but have been reported as far south as the counties bordering Illinois and Iowa and as far east as the Wolf River watershed.

Prevention

Lyme disease is as preventable as malaria, if you use common sense. Deer ticks are active year-round, so you've always got to be aware. Deer ticks cannot fly or jump. They cling to vegetation and attach themselves to objects pushing through. Always wear light-colored clothing, long sleeves, and long pants, and tuck the cuffs into your boots. A hat is always a good idea. Walk in the center of trails and avoid branches and grasses whenever possible. Check yourself and others *thoroughly,* paying particular attention to the hair. Children are always candidates for tick attachment. Check everybody every 24 hours, even if you haven't been in the deep woods. Studies have indicated that the deer tick must be attached to your skin for 24-72 hours before the bacterium is spread. Pet owners beware: domestic animals can develop Lyme disease, and this is not limited to hunting dogs, so check them as well.

People swear by insect repellents using DEET. But remember that DEET's cocktail of toxicology has caused death in children, and unsubstantiated reports have shown that high concentrations of it for long exposures can do very bad things to your nervous system. If you use DEET, buy it in concentrations of no higher than 20% for kids, 30% for adults. So-called "natural" repellents aren't very effective for ticks, black flies, or mosquitoes.

In 1998 SmithKline Beecham announced it had developed LYMErix, a Lyme-disease vaccine. The FDA's governing panel grudgingly okayed it, despite having serious reservations due to a lack of testing. The efficacy rate still only tops out at 79% after three expensive doses, and claims of the vaccine actually causing degenerative arthritis have surfaced. In short: it's probably better to skip the vaccine and use preventive measures.

Diagnosis and Treatment

Paramount: Do not panic every time you pull a tick out. The chances are good it's a dog tick, and even if it is a deer tick, it doesn't automatically guarantee Lyme disease. The best way to remove it if you do find one is to grasp it with tweezers as close to the skin as possible and tug it out gently. (Do not jerk or twist, because the head will come off and cause infection. Also, avoid the old method of using a match to "burn" them out; all this does is crisp it and leave the head in.) Disinfect the area thoroughly. You may want to save the tick's body in a plastic bag with a cotton ball soaked in alcohol. Wash your hands after removing the tick.

The disease generally progresses through three stages, which vary depending on how soon the disease is diagnosed and treated. The first stage is apparent when the characteristic red rash erythema chronicum migrans (ECM) appears, usually 3-32 days after the transmission. This is usually a red circular rash not necessarily around the infection site. Other signs are any combination of headache, chills, nausea, fever, aching joints, or fatigue, all of which may disappear and recur without regularity. Diagnosed within stage one, the disease is highly treatable with antibiotics.

If it progresses to stage two, weeks to months after exposure, complications with the heart and nervous system are manifest, including but not limited to heart block, meningitis, facial paralysis, encephalitis, and excruciating joint, tendon, or muscle pain. The most salient symptom in stage three is chronic arthritis, usually appearing a month to several years after initial transmission. Treatment in both stages is far more difficult than stage one and requires repeated treatments.

you'll find a community park with campsites. Another mile east of that there is a campground on the Red Cliff Indian Reservation, and just north of Bayfield is a private campground. There are 10 others on the peninsula.

Services and Information
The **Apostle Islands National Lakeshore Headquarters,** tel. (715) 779-3397, at the corner of 4th and Washington Streets, is high above the harbor in the huge and funky Bayfield County Courthouse. There are plenty of exhibits, displays, videos, and more. A very good gift shop sells books and related memorabilia on the islands. The center is open late April-late May daily 8 a.m.-4:30 p.m.; late May-early Sept. 8 a.m.-6 p.m.; early Sept.-late Oct. 8 a.m.-5 p.m.; the rest of the year Mon.-Fri. 8 a.m.-4:30 p.m.

Transportation
There are three main ways to the Apostle Islands. The most common, do-it-yourself options are discussed below. Shuttle tours and a water taxi are the other viable options. None are exactly cheap.

Most hikers and campers hop aboard the **Inner Island Shuttle** of Apostle Islands Cruise Service, tel. (715) 779-3925, www.apostleisland.com. This shuttle departs mid-June-early Sept. at 10:30 a.m. and 2 p.m. from downtown Bayfield with stops at Sand, Raspberry and Oak Islands. There are lighthouses to be toured along this route. It costs $24 adult, $13 children.

Many islands do have ranger-led tours, great relic fishing camps, logging detritus, hiking, or camping, but no public transport. Only about a third of the islands are covered by any commercial transportation; some are off-limits. The only option besides paddling or sailing yourself is to beg a prohibitively expensive charter from any local charter operator. A sample of fares, roundtrip to islands (based on one to six passengers, generally): Basswood (the cheapest), $60; Devils, $200; Outer, $300. Don't show up alone and hope to get to a fringe island with a pack anytime quickly.

Tours and Do-It-Yourself Transportation
The most common way to get around the islands is to do it yourself, whether via a sailboat or a sea kayak. Kayak and equipment rental is available in Bayfield at **Trek and Trail,** tel. (800) 354-8735, two blocks south of the dock for the Madeline Island Ferry. A four-hour basic kayak rental runs $25 single or $48 double, up to a three-day rental for $90 s or $175 d. All the equipment you need is available here too. It also provides shuttles up the coast for $15-25 and rents mountain bikes. Trek and Trail, a highly efficient operation, also rents cabins ($65-85) and leads very popular tours to the islands, including an introductory kayaking course ($30), a full-day Basswood Island paddle ($80), and multi-day island-hopping ($199-439), and its most popular course, an all-day sea caving trip for $79, departing daily at 9 a.m. No experience is required, but reservations most definitely are. Reservations are also necessary come winter for the thrilling **dog-sled tours** over the pack ice; two- and three-day trips are offered ($300/390) along with a day-trip combining dogsledding with an Ojibwa cultural experience. Other kayak rental operations are in Bayfield, including the Apostle Islands Cruise Service.

Two kayak launch points are located within the national lakeshore's mainland unit. Meyers Beach is a popular spot; the town of Russell maintains a kayak launch adjacent to its boat ramp at Little Sand Bay ($1), but you can launch free at Little Sand Bay along the beach to the west of the main NPS dock. You could even paddle the entire **Lake Superior Water Trail,** which stretches 91 miles along the coast between Port Wing and Ashland; this is part of an ambitious 3,000-mile-long trail taking in three U.S. states, Ontario, and many sovereign tribes. The Wisconsin section is a *tough* paddle, so make sure you're up to it.

Rent sailboats and find instruction—you'll be seaworthy in three days of lessons—from **Superior Charters, Inc.,** tel. (715) 779-5124 or (800) 772-5124, with over 50 boats in the marina, from 27 to 45 feet. **Sailboats Inc.,** tel. (800) 826-7010, also has sailing certification courses. Generally you can get certified in three days for around $800.

Apostle Islands Cruise Service, tel. (715) 779-3925, www.apostleisland.com, also offers the following tours from Bayfield. The **Stockton/Manitou Island Cruise** leaves late June-early September for those two islands at 1:30 p.m. daily, costing $23 adults, $12 children. For those not interested in hopping off, the aforementioned cruises will take you all over. But the main trip for sightseers, the **Grand Tour,** leaves Bayfield at 10 a.m. daily and spins around 20 of the islands. You'll see every sight possible without actually getting off the boat. The cost is worth it at $24 adults, $13 children. During peak season, there is occasionally a sunset cruise from Bayfield Tuesday and Thursday at 5:45 p.m. This heads to the Squaw Bay caves, then past Sand and Eagle Islands. A **Lighthouse/Squaw Bay** tour departs Wednesday and Friday at 5:45 p.m. and costs $24 adults, $13 children. The A.I. Cruise Service has special weekend **lighthouse tours** as well. Perhaps the favorite tour are the sailings aboard classic schooners, especially the 54-foot **Zeeto,** a three-masted 1870s Chappelle. Tours depart hourly 9 a.m.-6 p.m. late May-late Sept.; they cost $44.

Also departing Bayfield's city dock every day in summer at 9:30 a.m. and 1:30 p.m. are **sailboat rides** aboard a 1969 Morgan, the *Catchun-Sun,* tel. (715) 779-3111. There's a two-person minimum and tickets are $40 per person for a three-and-a-half-hour cruise. They also do overnights and charters. Five dollars more for the same time and same departures aboard the yachts of the *AniMashi,* tel. (888) 272-4548.

Shipwreck Tours: Twenty-two wrecks lie in the shallow waters in and around the Apostles. No real dive tours are organized in the archipelago, but **Roberta's,** tel. (715) 779-5744, has scuba diving charters. Divers must register with the park's headquarters; the HQ has materials for divers.

Warnings: Open canoes are not permitted on Lake Superior, and you'd be nuts to think you could use one. Even kayakers had better know what they're doing before they venture out. When Lake Superior looks placid, it still can hold lots of dangerous surprises—lake levels do change with barometric pressure and wind direction. In combination, a wind-set (caused by winds pushing water to one side of the lake) and extremely low pressure area will create a "saiche," a three- or four-foot drop in water level, followed by a sudden back-flow. Rare, but it could be a killer. Storms are severe and can crop up suddenly. Most occur in November, when the water is still warm and mixes with arctic air, but they can occur at any time.

MADELINE ISLAND

Settled around 1490 by Ojibwa coming from the Gulf of the St. Lawrence who eventually made the island their permanent tribal home and center of their creation-based religion, Madeline Island became the most crucial island link in the French network of commerce and transportation between the hinterlands of New France and Quebec. Later garrison commanders from 1693 set up deeper trading forays along the Mississippi Valley via the St. Croix River to the south. The post would ship such a wealth of beaver pelts that the market in Paris dipped. The British later overran the area and established their own forts.

The treacherously multisyllabic *Moningwu-nakauning,* or "Home of the Golden Shafted Woodpecker," was later refitted with the current Anglo-friendly name. After the arrival of the Protestant missionaries in 1830, a trader under the British married the daughter of a local chieftain and the church christened her Madeleine. The first tourists came aboard steamers in 1894, and within five years the first enclave of summer homes had been established.

A permanent population on Madeline Island precluded its inclusion into the National Lakeshore. Year-round numbers hover around 180, but it can swell fifteen-fold in summer, when residents—mostly well-to-do from the Twin Cities—flock to their seasonal homes. Though it is one of the fastest-growing tourist destinations in northwestern Wisconsin, don't go expecting Cape Cod or the Maine coastline. Disembarking the ferry, the "town" appears as but a minor strip of humble structures. Tooling around the island in a car takes a half hour tops, and nowhere will you find a concentration of buildings. That said, it's a perfectly realized "island getaway"—15 minutes from the mainland but thoroughly rustic and with a great state park to boot.

La Pointe

La Pointe is not much more than an assemblage of minor whitewashed structures housing basic restaurants, a museum, taverns, accommodations, and the few island services. A pair of long-term Twin Cities summerites established the island's **Historical Museum** in 1969, straight ahead and to the left off the ferry landing. The holdings are heavy on Ojibwa culture, missionaries, and the French fur trade—including real "black robes" worn by Jesuits—and John Jacob Astor's accounting papers. There's also a host of fishing flotsam. The musical, introductory slide show is always fun. Open Memorial Day-early Oct. 10 a.m.-4 p.m.; July-Aug., 9 a.m.-7 p.m.; admission is $5.50 adults, $2.75 children 12 and under.

Not far away is the **Lake View Schoolhouse,** a 19th century one-room schoolhouse restored and appointed with period furnishings by the historical society. Open June-Fall; admission is free.

Big Bay State Park
Two millennia ago, the land this park occupies was a shallow bay. Eons of lake action deposited sand, forming a barrier beach and then another and sealing off what is now Big Bay Lagoon, another of the archipelago's remarkable ecosystems. A half-mile or so boardwalk **nature trail** skirts the lagoon through a mishmash of bog and forest. The lagoon itself is languid and perfect for canoes. On the opposite side of the lagoon, the Ridge Trail leads to an indoor group camp through mostly coniferous forest. The best trail is the **Bay View Trail,** which traces the eastern promontory of the park, bypassing spectacular wave-hewn sandstone formations, sea caves, and plenty of crashing Lake Superior waves. The picnic area at the apex, where the trail hooks up with the **Point Trail,** might be the most popular in Wisconsin. The beach is the most popular point in the park, a mile and a half of isolation.

Camping is grand in the park; most sites are isolated from each other and if not, are secluded by dense spinneys. In all, 55 sites are available in the park. Some sites are pack-in, though I'd hesitate to call them backpacking. The Madeline Island Ferry dock posts site availability notices—get there way early July-early September. Reservations are available.

Other Sights
Heading east out of town along the main road, turn north on Old Fort Road to Madeline Island's **Indian Burial Ground,** returning to its natural state. Farther east, **Memorial Park** features a warming pond and is the burial place of O-Shaka, son of legendary Chief Buffalo, who preserved Native rights to lands on Lake Superior

and Madeline Island in 1854 treaties with the Federal government. Interred in the cemetery are many of the original 20,000 Ojibwa who populated the island when the French arrived. Michel Cadotte himself, the son of a local trader and the man who married Madeleine, is also buried here. Some of the graves date back three centuries—there should be no need to mention walking softly and acting dignified.

Accommodations
The most basic lodging is the clean and well-kept **Madeline Island Motel,** tel. (715) 747-3000, directly opposite the ferry landing, with rates from $60 s or $66 d in summer season, mid-June-mid-September.

A half block closer to the dock on the opposite side of the road is the **Island Inn,** tel. (715) 747-2000, with five relatively spacious rooms with refrigerators from $89 s or d. One building of the inn dates from the 1870s.

Without question the most hedonistic luxury accommodations are found at **The Inn on Madeline Island,** tel. (715) 747-6315 or (800) 822-6315, four blocks from the ferry. The inn is actually an island-wide assemblage of lakefront properties of all sorts, cabins in the woods, cottages overlooking the golf course, and some apartments and condos downtown. The inn also offers Har-Tru clay tennis courts for guests. Rates start at $75 per night for the most basic studio, rising to $1,500 per week for a huge lakefront private home. A mind-boggling array of choices are offered; get a brochure beforehand. Some excellent package deals are available, and off-season rates make it a bargain.

Besides Big Bay State Park, the island has **Big Bay Town Park,** seven miles out of La Pointe and north of the state park. Formed around another overgrown lagoon, the swampy confines of the park feature a wooden bridge and a long strand of beach. Canoeing and fishing are popular here, and there are some 40 campsites available, none reservable. Rates are $10 per site. Look for the sign at the ferry dock giving up-to-the-hour availability of campsites at Big Bay State Park and the municipal campground.

Food
Overlooking the Madeline Island Golf Course and the MI Yacht Club is a state culinary trea-

sure, **The Clubhouse,** tel. (715) 747-2612. The distinctive polygonal structure ought to augur what's really coming, a wondrous melange of Midwest and French haute cuisine. The menu jumps about with pleasant regularity: mixed north woods and cherried greens, grilled asparagus, smoked duck gorgonzola, trout, venison, and duck are just a few examples of the cuisine you're likely to experience—every possible ingredient comes from Wisconsin. *Wine Spectator* has given kudos to the establishment's wine list. Serving dinner weekends May, June, and October, Wed.-Sun. July-Aug., and Thurs.-Sun. in September. From $10.

Much more down to earth is the **Island Cafe,** tel. (715) 747-6555. With a screened-in porch, it's a great Sunday champagne brunch spot. Otherwise, it serves basic fare for breakfast, lunch, and dinner. The cafe also serves some vegetarian (even vegan) dishes—cinnamon-apple hummus, veggie burrito, etc.—and is a coffee shop of sorts. Open at 8:30 a.m. From $5.

Somewhere between supper club and casually upscale, **The Pub,** tel. (715) 747-6315, is the restaurant at the Inn of Madeline Island. It specializes in fish and lighter entrées for lunch. Serving breakfast, lunch, and dinner. It was undergoing extensive additions, so other options may exist by the time you read this. From $4.

Pizza, subs, and espresso somehow go together at **Grampa Tony's,** another seasonal establishment. The food here is no frills but solid. From $4.

Recreation

Mopeds and mountain bikes are the most popular way to take in the island. To the right of the ferry landing in the large blue building, **Moped Dave's Motion To Go,** tel. (715) 747-6585, rents mountain bikes for $6 an hour or $24 a day, mopeds for $12 hour; it also offers air tours.

In Big Bay Town Park, north of the state park, **Bog Lake Outfitters,** tel. (715) 747-2685, rents canoes, rowboats, paddleboats, and cabins. Paddling the lagoon is a popular pastime on the island. Rates are $8 hour, $25 half-day, $35 full-day, or $100 for a full week. Cabins start at $75 per day.

The Robert Trent Jones-designed course of the **Madeline Island Golf Course,** tel. (715) 747-212, is a 6,069-yard, par-71 gem, known for lake vistas and double greens; reservations are a good idea.

As part of the island yacht club, the **Apostle Island Yacht Charter Association,** tel. (715) 747-2983 or (800) 821-3480, has captained charters or bareboating on sailboats 27 feet and longer. The **Blue Waters Sailing School,** tel. (612) 559-5649, offers lessons and charters. The **Mainsheet Charter,** tel. (715) 747-212, has a 35-foot sloop for chartered four-hour sails around Basswood Island and back; myriad cruises are offered.

Services and Information

The **Madeline Island Chamber of Commerce,** tel. (715) 747-2801 or (888) 475-3386, www.madelineisland.com, only operates in season, Memorial Day-Labor Day, and doesn't carry a whole lot of information in any event. The ferry dock kiosk in Bayfield has all the brochures and straight dope you'll need.

Getting There

Late January usually until sometime in April, WI 13 becomes the state's only "ice highway"—a real, established state road plowed and maintained across the ice. During the holidays, Christmas trees mark the borders. At the book-end seasons when ice is forming or breaking up and thus too tender for cars, flat-bottomed air boats whiz across the short straits, and what an amazing ride that is.

The **Madeline Island Ferry,** tel. (715) 747-2051, departs from Bayfield beginning from first ice break-up; the trip takes 20 minutes. Through mid-April, there are eight departures daily 7:30

Madeline Island ferry

a.m.-5:30 p.m.; through mid-May, nine departures, plus three trips 8:30-11 p.m. Friday nights (daily after May 5); mid-May-late June, 19 departures 7:30 a.m.-11 p.m., plus an 11 p.m. and midnight Friday night departure; through September a 6:30 a.m. trip weekdays, otherwise 7:30-9:30 a.m. hourly, every half hour 9:30 a.m.-6 p.m., and hourly through 11 p.m., also Friday and Saturday midnight and 1 a.m. trips. Rates are $8.50 auto, $7.50 trailer, $10 pickup camper and RV, bicycles $1.75, motorcycles $5.25; passengers are extra—$3.75 ages 12 and over, $2 6-11, five years and under free. No reservations are accepted except for large groups or special vehicles.

Getting Around
Once on Madeline Island, the **Madeline Island Bus Tour,** operated by the ferry line, departs a half block to the right of the ferry dock. Tours take in the whole island and include some hiking. They're offered mid-June-mid-Aug. at 10:30 a.m. and 3:30 p.m. Rates are $8.50 adults over 12, $4 6-11, under five free.

CHEQUAMEGON NATIONAL FOREST

First the name. That's Shuh-WAH-muh-gun. It used to be *shee-KWAM-uh-gun,* and, for tourists, any approximation is okay. The name—Ojibwa for "land of shallow waters"—appears often across the northern tier of the state. A staggered series of four rough parallelograms stretching from the Bayfield Peninsula south 120 miles, the Chequamegon is Wisconsin's—and one of the Midwest's—largest national forest at just under 850,000 acres, larger than Rhode Island. It forms the eastern edge of the northwest region's vast lake-dotted expanses and is itself surrounded by county and state forest lands—essentially the entire northern "cap" of Wisconsin.

Natural History
The physical geography of the forest stretches along one-third of Wisconsin's north-south latitude and contains a diversity inherent to such a large area. The geology of the central patches includes some of the oldest formations in the United States, forming an 80-mile ridgeline—the Great Divide, which continues into Michigan—that separates basins draining north and south. The range, at one time higher than the Alps, held one of the U.S.'s greatest concentrations of iron ore. (Subterranean chasms still hold what is believed to be the planet's most comprehensive reserves of untouched taconite ore—3.7 billion tons) The ridges were formed billions of years ago by successive folding and faulting, pushing the volcanic material to the surface. Atop the black shell lies the residue of millions of years of marine sediment.

Unfortunately, 150 years of rapacious forest practices has, by most biologists' standards, affected the ecodiversity of the forest. Vast tracts of mixed forest have been replaced by fast-growing trees like aspen, and cutover land is left open for bird hunting. Somehow, there are still stands of old growth trees—some over 200 years old—in the forest.

Flora and Fauna
Two hundred twenty-nine species of bird inhabit the national forest as planted breeders, migrants, or permanent residents; you'll incessantly hear the forest called the "Ruffed Grouse/Muskellenge/etc. Capital of the World." Hundreds of mammal species also live within the forest's confines, including raccoons, squirrels, chipmunks, white-tailed deer, foxes, fisher and martins, and the odd beaver. The black bear population, particularly around Glidden, is the highest in the state. Two recent species reentries are worth noting. In 1995, the DNR released the first elk the Chequamegon has seen in a long time. The hope is that the elk population will become permanently established in the forest. So far, so good; numbers have increased quickly. The rare timber wolf does exist within portions of the park (and numbers are increasing quickly); consider yourself blessed if you spot one. Even once-doomed species like martens and fisher are rebounding.

The Chequamegon Forest has established five prime wildlife viewing areas: **Chequamegon Waters Flowage, Popple Creek and Wilson Flowage, Day Lake, Lynch Creek,** and **Moquah Pine Barrens.** All of these wildlife refuge areas

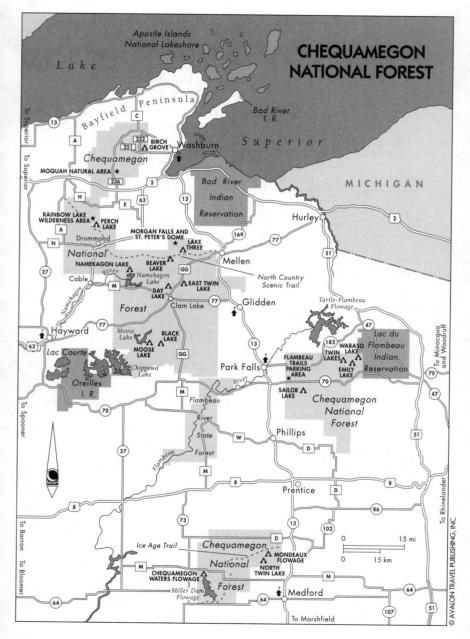

CHEQUAMEGON NATIONAL FOREST

Apostle Islands
National Lakeshore

Lake

Bad River
I. R.

Bayfield Peninsula

Superior

MICHIGAN

To Superior

13

A

252 BIRCH
GROVE

251

Washburn

Chequamegon

C

MOQUAH NATURAL AREA ★

236

2

Bad River
Indian
Reservation

Hurley

2

To Superior

H

E

63

13

77

51

RAINBOW LAKE
WILDERNESS AREA ★

PERCH
LAKE

169

A

N

Drummond

MORGAN FALLS AND
ST. PETER'S DOME

LAKE
THREE

27

National

NAMEKAGON LAKE

BEAVER
LAKE

Mellen

North Country
Scenic Trail

Namekagon
Lake

GG

River

Cable

M

DAY
LAKE

EAST TWIN
LAKE

Turtle-Flambeau
Flowage

To Minocqua and Woodruff

Forest

Namekagon

Clam Lake

77

Glidden

13

Hayward

77

Moose
Lake

BLACK
LAKE

GG

47

63

MOOSE
LAKE

Chippewa
Lake

182 WABASO
LAKE

TWIN
LAKES

Lac du
Flambeau
Indian
Reservation

Lac Courte

Oreilles
I. R.

Park Falls

FLAMBEAU
TRAILS
PARKING
AREA

EMILY
LAKE

70

70

River

70

47

M

SAILOR
LAKE

Chequamegon
National
Forest

27

Flambeau

River

State

W

Phillips

D

51

To Spooner

Forest

M

8

Prentice

D

8

To Barron

MOON

8

73

86

To Rhinelander

To Bloomer

Ice Age Trail

Chequamegon

D

102

0   15 mi

0   15 km

National

MONDEAUX
FLOWAGE

M

CHEQUAMEGON
WATERS FLOWAGE

Forest

NORTH
TWIN LAKE

M

Miller Dam
Flowage

64

64

Medford

107

51

To Marshfield

© AVALON TRAVEL PUBLISHING, INC.

have interpretive wayside exhibits; auto tour brochures describing the most commonly seen fauna can be obtained from ranger stations.

Human History

Ancient powwow sites or burial grounds sit adjacent to abandoned European homesteads decaying in the weeds, while gracefully rusting logging machinery lies nearby.

Archaeological evidence dates human occupation of the northern swath of the forest, near Chequamegon Bay, back as far as 1.000 B.C.— the early Woodland period Indians. Various Woodland tribes shared the mammoth spread until the 1490 arrival of the Ojibwa, whose hegemony extended over the forest—though there was sporadic competition with the Sioux—until the arrival of the Europeans. A strategic Indian trail stretched south from Chequamegon Bay to the Chippewa River headwaters. Jesuits and French *voyageurs* first penetrated the wilderness south of Chequamegon Bay in the 1650s; Radisson and De Grossilliers established the first aboriginal contact in 1659 near Hayward, just west of the forest.

The seemingly triple-thick forest canopy brought Wisconsin's largest share of timber opportunists, with full-scale logging beginning in the 1820s, upwards of 100 million board feet of lumber per year by the 1880s. Dams, reservoirs, mills, CCC camps—all still stand. The Chequamegon National Forest took shape in the 1930s, following repeated friendly invasions by the Civilian Conservation Corps and Works Project Administration, which established camp after camp for assorted trailbusters. National Forest status was started in part for recovery and protection from the ravages of timber exploitation.

RECREATION

Note that the national forest has a $3 daily fee for *some* places (beaches, boat launches, etc.) inside the forest, but not all. Basically, if you can park there, you need to pay the fee. Camping does not cost an extra $3.

Trails

The forest boasts two National Scenic Hiking Trails: the North Country and the Ice Age. Other trails total over 200 miles, all doubling as cross-country ski trails in winter; 50 miles of that total is tracked weekly.

The Chequamegon is a point of pilgrimage for mountain bikers. Most flock to the Cable and Hayward areas for the magnificent, 200-mile **Cable Area Mountain Bike Association** (CAMBA) trail system, most of which are not in the forest proper. Over 100 miles of trail "clusters" are currently maintained inside the forest, and there are hundreds of miles of service roads and logging roads that I've never been kicked off of. Trail clusters include a mix of single and double tracks and average 15-30 miles per cluster.

Five hundred miles of ATV and snowmobile trail are also within the forest.

Hydrophilia

The forest has 800-plus lakes, 411 larger than 10 acres, some of them unnamed. Lakes under 10 acres all go without names because there are so damn many. Officially, there are 632 miles of navigable river and stream inside the forest, including the best options—the Flambeau, Chippewa, and Namekagon Rivers. The latter is a federally recognized National Wild and Scenic River with Class Two and Three rapids. The former two offer similar challenging stretches of whitewater and are being considered for National Scenic Riverway status for their splendid wildlife habitats.

The Chippewa River is most popular along its East Fork but can become too shallow after June. The Namekagon begins at a dam northeast of Cable and spends very little time in the forest itself; it's covered in more detail under "Northwestern Lakes."

The South Fork of the Flambeau River begins at Round Lake, spanning the Park Falls district east to west before leaving the forest and bending southwest toward the Flambeau River State Forest and its confluence with the North Fork. The South Fork is famed for its diversity—equal parts sluggish and white-knuckle; in the lower stretches you definitely need to be prepared. You can paddle the entire Chequamegon section in a couple of leisurely days. The first dozen miles, to Cedar Rapids, is particularly popular. The second stretch out of the forest is perhaps the most diverse stretch, though it has some challenging sections before finishing in Fifield.

Fishing: With all those rivers, streams, and lakes, it's no wonder that landing a lunker is the number-one recreational activity in these parts. It's beyond the scope—or ability—of this book to suss out the whys and wherefores of fishing in the forest. According to statistics, the Clam Lake area offers the forest's highest concentration of lakes, containing the most consistent fish populations.

Scenic Drive

WI 77 spans the 29 miles between Glidden, on the eastern fringe of the park, to Lost Lake, in the western tier. Recognized federally as the Great Divide Scenic Byway, its stretches reveal systematic reforestation and an engaging mixture of natural history and immigrant settlement. Along the corridor, the highway crosses the Great Divide, creating drainage basins to the north and south. Stop in Clam Lake for a great **woodcarvers museum.**

ACCOMMODATIONS

Resorts

About a zillion resorts line the shores of Chequamegon lakes. You'll find the usual gamut, from 1920s era musty mom-and-pop operations to slick resorts. Thankfully, not many of those treacly Vail-style condo operations have infiltrated the forest yet. All resorts are outlined below in their respective districts.

Camping

The forest's five districts support 27 campgrounds of varying size—three to 94 sites—and seclusion; all but two are on lakes, and those two are on fishing rivers. Rates range $8-14 at all campgrounds, and reservations can be made at some campgrounds by calling (877) 444-6777 or on the Internet at www.reserveusa.com. You can reserve family sites up to 240 days in advance. Outside of Memorial Day, the Fourth of July, and Labor Day weekends, you're likely to find something open, somewhere in the forest, and even during those times sites are sometimes available. For the most part campgrounds require driving a few miles on gravel road, though all can handle trailer traffic.

Backcountry camping is free and permitted anywhere within the forest, as long as the site is at least 50 feet from any trail or water source. Also, 14 percent of the lands within the forest boundaries are privately owned, so make certain you are on public land before pitching a tent. Camping at any one spot is permitted for a maximum of 21 days. Note that campgrounds are maintained May 1 through mid-October, but you have every right to camp there at other times. You'll have to park your vehicle by the gate and lug your stuff in; you'll also have to provide your own water.

A caveat—carry a topo map and a compass. This isn't the Sierra Nevada, but you'd be surprised how fast you can get lost in the forest. "Without a trace" is emphasized here.

SERVICES AND INFORMATION

The **Chequamegon Forest Supervisor** office is at 1170 4th Ave. S., Park Falls, WI 54552, tel. (715) 762-2461. This office has basic information and maps. Contacting individual district ranger stations is a better way to get information on the specifics.

The Forest Supervisor's office has three basic maps available for purchase. The most basic is the 3/8 inch-per-mile visitor map ($3), which displays every recreational site in the forest and all lakes and streams, but should obviously not be construed as a map for wilderness travel. More detail is available on 1/2-inch-per-mile sheets ($3) used for administration in the forest, but no recreation sites or explicative detail is contained on them. Fifty-three gridded USGS topo maps ($3 each) are also available; the supervisor's office can send you a copy of the grid for ordering specific-area maps. For roughing it, these topo maps are indispensable.

PARK FALLS DISTRICT

The Park Falls District of the National Forest is the easternmost swath in Wisconsin, gracing the western edge of the Lac du Flambeau Indian Reservation and just a few miles to the east of the town of Park Falls. To the south is the Flambeau River State Forest.

Sights

The **Round Lake Logging Dam** was built in the 1880s on the South Fork of the Flambeau River to facilitate floating logs downstream. Long in disrepair after the last log sluiced through in 1909, it was "adopted" by local groups in the early 1990s and is still undergoing a careful facelift.

At the Smith Rapids Campground, the **Smith Rapids Covered Bridge** is somewhat of a tourist attraction in itself—the only covered bridge built in the state in a century. It's a Town Lattice Truss bridge with a modern twist—its use of glue-laminated lumber, allowing continuous chords on the top and bottom of the trusses.

The Park Falls District has four established wildlife viewing habitats: **Squaw Creek Waterfowl Area** and **Wilson** and **Popple Creek Flowages,** all accessible east of Fifield and south on FR 136; **Mackinnsy Slough Waterfowl Area** is east of Fifield on WI 70 to FR 144 north. All features tons of waterfowl and fur bearers, including large numbers of Great Blue Herons, American Bitterns, Belted Kingfishers, common loons, buffleheads, tundra swans, osprey, and eagles. At Popple Creek nests one of the only colonies of yellow-headed blackbirds in northern Wisconsin.

Recreation

The **Flambeau Trail System** offers more than 60 miles of trails for mountain bikes, horses, and ATVs. Smith Rapids bridge is found along one route, as well as ridgeline rides, a couple of impoundment flowages, and even an old log-driving dam. You can access the trail at Sailor Lake Campground, Round Lake, along Blockhouse Lake, or along WI 182 east of Park Falls. The Round Lake area is a non-motorized area and crosses footbridges and the old logging dam. Primitive campsites are found along the lake.

Five miles east of Fifield via WI 70 are the **Wintergreen** ski and hiking trails. Twelve miles east of Park Falls on WI 182 are seven miles of the **Newman Springs** ski, hiking, and mountain biking trails.

Camping

Sailor Lake is the largest and also the closest campground to Park Falls—east of Fifield seven miles on WI 70, then south of FR 139. You'll find shaded campsites here and a spur to a multi-use trail, usually with many ATVs. Farther east on WI 70 and then north on FR 148 is **Smith Rapids.** This campground is good for canoeists, as it's on the South Fork of the Flambeau River. Still farther east on WI 70, and then north on FR 144 and FR 142 are **Twin Lakes,** offering 17 sites (two fully accessible) on a 20-acre lake featuring good fishing and a tiny sandy strand of beach, and the decent **Emily Lake** campground to the east. Still farther east is the primitive, isolated **Wabasso Lake,** this one so secluded that the USFS is considering reinstating it as a walk-in-only campground.

BETWEEN THE DISTRICTS: PRICE COUNTY

Park Falls

Park Falls is the largest community on the fringes of the national forest, channeling loads of tourists through year-round. The town caters to shotgun-toting sportsmen looking for the *Bonasa umbellus* (Ruffed Grouse), as the USFS maintains over 5,000 acres of habitat near Park Falls. A gateway community, Park Falls is not only the headquarters of the Chequamegon, but also of the wild Turtle-Flambeau Flowage.

Four miles south in Fifield is the **Price County Historical Museum,** tel. (715) 762-4571, featuring historical flotsam housed in a Victorian Town Hall. Open June-Labor Day, Friday and Sunday 1-5 p.m.; admission is free.

Park Falls has **camping** at Hines Memorial Park downtown, situated right on the Flambeau River. Five motels are found in Park Falls; rates can dip below $20 in the off-season at some places. Simple, well-kept rooms are found at the **Mason Motel,** 798 WI 13, tel. (715) 762-3780, with rooms from around $30, also with an attached cafe and bar. The best place in town is likely the **Northway Motor Lodge,** south of town on WI 13, tel. (715) 762-2406 or (800) 844-7144, offering huge rooms, a sauna, hot tub, spa, and a free continental breakfast. Rates start at around $45.

Family Inn Supper Club, along N. 4th St., has a popular Sunday brunch. Four miles south of town is **Hick's Landing,** N12888 Hicks Rd. in Fifield, tel. (715) 762-5008, overlooking the national forest Sailor Creek Flowage. Serving classic Wisconsin rustic supper club fare since the early 1950s, the Landing's got killer steaks and lobster—it's one of the few places that still has traditional relish trays before the meal. From $6. Hick's Landing serves dinner daily except Monday. Northeast of Park Falls in Butternut is a good coffee shop and the largest Porterhouse steaks you'll ever see at the **Butternut Resort.**

Lots and lots of local resorts offer canoe shuttling and rentals, and a few rent mountain bikes. The **Tuscobia State Trail** runs along an abandoned railroad grade for 76 miles to Rice Lake. Linked with the Flambeau River Forest trails, its western end also comprises a segment of the Ice Age National Scenic Trail.

For information on the Park Falls Area, especially resorts on the lake chains, contact the **Park Falls Chamber of Commerce,** 400 S. Fourth Ave., Park Falls, WI 54552, tel. (715) 762-2703 or (800) 762-2709.

Phillips

Phillips' main claim to Badger fame is its utter destruction in an 1894 conflagration. Fires from three directions engulfed the town of 2,500, killing 13. It is also home to the fabled **Wisconsin Concrete Park.** Local logger, jack-of-all-trades, and folk artist-gone-overboard Fred Smith began in his old age to assemble images wrought from wire, concrete, glass, mirrors, shells, beer bottles, and assorted other stuff. Painstakingly creating humanoid and animal forms, he had singlehandedly created the world's largest collection—200 cowpokes, bulls, bears, farmers, beer wagons, and more—of concrete art by the time he died in 1976. The park is sort of an atheist's retreat from all those fervid stone religious grottoes spread across the Midwest. After Smith's death, decay and storm damage set in before the Kohler Foundation, the Wisconsin Arts Board, and the National Endowment for the Arts stepped in and began restoration. It's an eerie, personal place.

Phillips also annually fetes its ethnicity with a Czech festival in late June. An A-frame **information center** is open seasonally.

Phillips is also a town of cafes, with one nearly every 50 feet. The **Phillips Cafe** and **Barbara's Crystal Cafe** are within shouting distance of each other, and both offer standard Americana roadfood. The menu at the Phillips is a bit more adventurous, with a few alternatives for non-carnivores; it also has a Friday fish fry until 9 p.m. But the Crystal gets the local nod for breakfast, opening first, at 4:30 a.m.

Bloom's Tavern, 396 S. Avon Ave., definitely warrants a visit. This classic Wisconsin tavern dates from 1892 and is thus Wisconsin's oldest; it's also Leinenkugel Beer's oldest customer. However, its modern history has been more interesting. It's currently owned by Elvis Presley (seriously), who garnered international media attention in 1999 when he began somewhat quixotic political campaigns.

Flambeau River State Forest

This managed, multi-use 87,000-acre forest dates to a 1930 state attempt to preserve dwindling northern forests. Riparian stretches are the key to the forest—50 miles along the North and South Forks of the Flambeau River. Canoeing is the primary activity besides fishing, and the South Fork has some of the most perfect whitewater in Wisconsin. The timber's not bad either—one stretch along CR M is the largest virgin white pine stand in the state.

The North Fork's upper section is generally the tamest stretch of the river, parts of the southern section can be killer. The North Fork begins in the Turtle-Flambeau Flowage area (see the Northeastern Wisconsin chapter for details), and the channel itself and its banks northeast of Park Falls are technically part of the state forest. Marked river access for canoes is found along WI 70, six miles east of Loretta and Draper, 12 miles east of Winter, and 15 miles west of Phillips.

From CR F to the northeast, the river flows 13 miles to Park Falls. Along the way you'll see **Bear Skull Rock** with a cedar growing out of it, planted there by an explorer who purportedly witnessed an Ojibwa wrestle a bear at the spot. There are lots of rapids, but none are especially hazardous. After a portage around the Park Falls dam, the following dozen miles into the forest's main area offer no real dangers but great fishing. After WI 70, the wilderness area begins near Nine Mile Creek and continues to Babb's Island—an especially picturesque section. The current increases after Oxbo but there are no dangerous rapids. CR W appears eventually and it's a good spot to take out, since the State Forest HQ is found here.

Below Babb's Island it's prudent to stop in and get details about what lies ahead, as the more type-T rapids are soon to come.

The South Fork of the Flambeau River begins at Round Lake, spanning the Park Falls district east to west before leaving the forest and bending southwest toward the Flambeau River State Forest and its confluence with the North Fork. The South Fork is famed for its diversity—equal parts sluggish and hair-raising. In the lower stretches you definitely need to be prepared.

A half dozen larger lakes in the forest—a couple are designated wilderness lakes—are muskie rich. Besides fishing, a park highlight is **Big White Pine,** over 130 feet tall and 300 years old, off CR M.

Family camping is found at Connors Lake and Lake of Pines, both off of CR W. A dozen or so primitive canoe campsites (free) are also spread along both forks of the river, and backpackers can pick up a free dispersed camping permit. Eight or nine resorts and lodges are found along the riverway. The **Oxbo Resort,** tel. (715) 762-4786, offers cabins and a whole slew of canoe and bike rentals, along with a shuttle service. Most other resorts also have outfitting services.

Two primary trails wend through the forest. The **Oxbo** begins east of Oxbo on WI 70 and is 13 km long. Larger **Flambeau Hills** trail is nearby and stretches for 21 km. Trails also connect with country trails and the Tuscobia State Trail.

The forest **headquarters** is at the CR W crossing of the Flambeau River.

Timm's Hill

For most of its early statehood, Wisconsin's highest spot was believed to be Rib Mountain, near Wausau. Eventually, someone got around to the nitty gritty surveying work and discovered that Timm's Hill, 25 miles south of Phillips, was actually higher. Along WI 13 and WI 86, then down lovely rustic CR RR and surrounded by a county park, the hill sports a 45-foot observation tower and, after the wobbly climb, about the only truly vertiginous heights in the state. Just under 2,000 feet above sea level, the platform at the top at times holds enough day-trippers to warrant a numbering system. Hiking and ski trails wend around the base of the hill. Lining the access road to the park are a number of modest inns

and spartan cabins in quite picturesque locations, but camping is not allowed.

Rib Lake

Due south of Timm's Hill is a smattering of lakes, the nucleus of which is Rib Lake and the eponymous village. A very northern European busy-as-a-beaver place, the Rib Lake Area has a host of great lakes, resorts, and trails, including a maintained segment of the Ice Age Trail.

In the village itself you'll find a **campground** at Lakeview Park.

North of Rib Lake, between WI 102 and CR D, is Wisconsin's first established **Rustic Road.** This gravel ribbon stretches five miles past a handful of lakes (and one beach), resorts, and a scenic overlook.

The community-maintained **Jaycee Trail** is a system of interconnected hiking and ski trails to the north and east. The Jaycee links up with one of the better stretches of the **Ice Age National Scenic Trail.** Along the IAT to the west, you'll pass glacial eskers, a county forest (with a homesteader's cabin), and the **Deutsches Wiedervereinigkeits Brucke** (German Reunification Bridge), built by IAT volunteers to commemorate the German Volksmarch tradition, which reportedly inspired the Ice Age Trail movement. Two glacially formed "mountains" are strewn with glacial boulders (erratics) and offer nice views from the top. If you're up for it, a hike to the western end of Rib Lake's IAT segment brings you to a Great Blue Heron rookery. Beyond there lies East Lake, a glacial pothole lake almost totally undeveloped and open for wilderness camping.

East on the Ice Age Trail you'll find parking to access the local trails, for north-south watershed line markers, a trailside shelter, an enormous erratic boulder some 20 feet across, and a marker pointing out an old logging "sleigh road" linked to the IAT. The Jaycee Trail branches here, continuing with the IAT, but if you stay on the Jaycee you'll pass an almost perfectly preserved logging camp, including a well, bunkhouse, cook shanty, and root cellar. The trail along here is an old "tote road," a supply route between logging villages. Eventually, the Jaycee Trail links back up with the IAT, passing scores of logging camps, bridges, farmsteads, gravel pits, and tanning bark camps. The

IAT/Jaycee then connects with the Timm's Hill National Trail leading directly to Timm's Hill.

Ladysmith

Though Ladysmith is well west of any of the national forest along US 8, it does sit along the banks of the Flambeau River. Environmentalists abhor the area because of the **Ladysmith Mine,** the state's last—and largest—copper mine. The mine has begun scaling back production, and by the time this book is published, the company says the mine will be returned to its natural, pre-settlement state. During its production life, almost two million tons of ore were extracted. Otherwise of interest, county heritage is on display at the **Historical Society** at the Rusk County Fairgrounds, open weekends 12:30-4:30 p.m.

MEDFORD DISTRICT

Sights

The Medford District is in the far southern area of the national forest, separated from the rest of the forest by the Flambeau River State Forest and an entire county. The chief draws for most travelers are the Ice Age National Scenic Trail and the **Mondeaux Flowage and Recreation Area.** The local concessionaire building is an original structure built by the CCC during the 1930s and inside are a few exhibits detailing the Corps' work with the WPA during the Great Depression. When the 400-acre flowage was cleared and flooded by a coffer dam 1936-38, the CCC built up numerous camphouses, beaches, and playgrounds. The area has been called one of the most perfect examples of New Deal works in the Midwest.

Recreation

Mondeaux Flowage and the recreation area constitute one of the Chequamegon's most popular attractions. The concessionaire building above rents small boats for row-fishing; four campgrounds and three boat landings line the northern half of the flowage. The **Ice Age Trail** from the east loops north around the flowage before heading west, totaling some 40 miles through the district. The easiest access is at the Mondeaux Flowage and Picnic Point and Spearhead Point

campgrounds. Primitive campsites are scattered along the route (no running water), and remember that you can camp anywhere you like as long as it's 50 feet off the trail and 200 feet from water. Numerous trailheads are scattered along the trail. East of Mondeaux Flowage, there is a parking area at the junction of Forest Roads 101 and 563. Other parking is found to the west: on CR E, north of FR 102; west of there along FR 102, which also accesses the Birch Lake trail and leads to a seven-mile **interpretive loop** with a primitive campsite; along FR 108, which accesses the same loop trail; and the popular **Jerry Lake** parking area, along FR 571, north of CR M.

Another impoundment—over 2,700 acres along the Yellow River—is known for wildlife habitat in the Beaver and Bear Creek Waterfowl Management Areas. Of the waterfowl, tundra swans, sandhill cranes, and double-crested cormorants make up the most interesting snag dwellers. This place is also quite popular for with canoeists. One thing to note: a motorized trail accesses the flowage from the east, so don't be surprised to hear braying ATVs off in the distance. It's something to consider.

North of WI 64 four miles along FR 119 is the **Perkinstown Winter Sports Area,** a tubing hill (small fee) and 12 miles of cross-country skiing. The area also features a chalet serving food. Open weekends 11 a.m.-4 p.m. The **Sitzmark Ski Trail,** as the primary trail is known, stretches all the way to the Chequamegon Waters Flowage.

The Jump River is one of the forest's primary canoeing rivers. While not a section amateurs want to challenge, the Big Falls are worth a stop. Just north of the district boundary along CR N, south of Kennan, **Big Falls County Park** is one of the prettier stretches of river in this district.

Out of the town of Medford and running 25 or so miles to the north is the **Pine Line,** a wilderness trail off-limits to ATVs. Aptly named, there are epic stretches of dark green conifer as far as the eye can see. Access points are also found along the way in Ogema and Prentice.

Camping

Medford District campgrounds are quite munificent—there's free firewood at most in the district, and all but Kathryn Lake are reservable. The only warm showers in the Chequamegon National Forest are found at the **Chippewa Camp-**

WHOSE FOREST IS IT, ANYWAY?

The Chequamegon National Forest is an expansive spread of very young verdance, still incompletely recovered from clearcutting practices first begun in the 1820s. And as the forest matures, the age-old battle of who controls the forest and for what purpose is being fought stridently here. The combatants are the usual players: sportsmen, environmentalists, federal land managers, and loggers.

The forest and its myriad uses come under the auspices of the USFS. Environmentalists bemoan the Forest Service's Ecosystem Management practice of replacing original woods with faster-growing stands of evergreen (easier to recover from logging) and its catering solely to hunting and timber interests at the expense of the forest's dwindling diversity. Environmentalists say that the USFS casually throws around "old growth" as if Wisconsin were the Amazon basin; those same environmentalists also point out the very apparent systematic reforestation of the Chequamegon. The USFS shoots back that not only do bylaws of national forests insist the forest be maintained for multi-use purposes, but that the economy of northern Wisconsin demands it. Lost in the bureaucratic shuffle, as always, are the fauna.

In 1990, the Sierra Club and a consortium of University of Wisconsin researchers filed a lawsuit against the USFS, charging that it violated federal laws mandating the preservation of biodiversity. A federal judge ruled against the plaintiffs, stating that the actions by forest managers were neither "arbitrary nor capricious." Environmentalists deplored the decision and pointed out that while the USFS may not intentionally degrade the environment, by trying to be all things to all people with its management practices, the forest suffers.

The battle is far from over. Forward-looking wildlife biologists and forest management experts have called for radical experimentation in the Chequamegon. This would entail establishing enormous tracts of hands-off wilderness, to be left untouched except by casual recreationalists and Mother Nature. This, supporters say, would enable the ecosystem to rebuild a semblance of old growth, which has been lost, and allow the reintroduction of vanished species such as the moose.

Environmentalists were pleasantly surprised when the Clinton Administration in 2000 imposed a freeze on road building in 33 million acres of federal forests; this temporary hands-off rule was to give the USFS time to develop a final proposal on the remaining 160 million acres of federal—and thus public—land so that damaging and unnecessary roads wouldn't be built. This wouldn't affect Wisconsin's federal forest land, because no roads were planned during the trial period. Furthermore, a Chequamegon-Nicolet National Forest spokesperson said only 312 miles of roads had been built 1986-1996, but the forest had reclaimed nearly 600 miles in the same time. Thus the state's federal lands were already becoming more "wild." (Environmentalists don't buy the statement at face value, of course.)

---

ground, on the Chequamegon Waters Flowage in the southwestern part of the district. Ninety sites sit along the 2,714-acre flowage; many of these, including four sites for disabled campers, can be reserved. There are also a couple of swimming beaches and access to a motorized trail. To get there, follow CR M to the west side of the district, then south on FR 1417.

East of this campground on CR M, the campground at 60-acre **Kathryn Lake** is perfectly adequate.

The remaining four campgrounds are packed close together in the northeastern section, along the Mondeaux Flowage, roughly between CR D and CR E. They are all fine, but quite popular is **Picnic Point Campground,** on FR 106 off FR 1563. Its three small sites are right on the Ice Age National Scenic Trail. Most popular perhaps in all of the national forest are the campsites at **Spearhead Point** a couple of miles north on FR 106. Also accessing the Ice Age Trail, its 27 sites are on prime flowage access, and three are available for reservation by disabled visitors. **Eastwood Campground** is on the flowage shoreline accessed via FR 104. The 22 sites here are relatively well shaded, and access for the Ice Age Trail is just up the road.

Services and Information
The **Medford Ranger District Office,** tel. (715) 748-4875, is at 850 N 8th St., WI 13, Medford, WI 54451.

Medford

Medford is one endpoint (the terminus is along Allman Street) to the 26-mile-long **Pine Line Recreation Trail;** the other is in Prentice. The northern tier of the trail runs through the terminal moraine of the last glacial period, through hardwood forests, cedar swamps, and rich bog land. There's a **tourist information office** at the corners of WI 13 and WI 64.

GLIDDEN (GREAT DIVIDE) DISTRICT

Sights and Recreation

The **Penokee Overlook,** four miles west of Mellen along CR GG, is an easy stroll up a few stairs for a top-notch view of billion-year-old hummocks. Speculators began trickling into the region—technically part of the Penokee-Gogebic Iron Range—in the 1880s to sniff about for profit possibilities. Within two decades, tons of raw iron were being mined per year. Before the bottom fell out in 1912 and things finally closed up tight in the Great Depression, 300 million tons of ore were shipped from the Wisconsin-Michigan range. You can also access the **Penokee Trail System** near the overlook.

Close by you'll find **St. Peter's Dome** and **Morgan Falls.** Standing 1,710 feet above sea level, the "dome" is the aptly named second-highest point in the state. On a clear day, three states are visible from the crown. It's a rocky two-mile hike with lots of unsure footing. Morgan Falls drop a frothy but tame 80 feet over onyx-colored granite. A trailhead leaves the parking area, then forks in opposite directions to the falls and the dome. A number of stream crossings are necessary to get to St. Peter's Dome, so be forewarned, but the walk to the falls is none too challenging. To get there, take FR 199, via CR C out of Mellen.

Most popular with families, the **Day Lake Recreation Area** is now a 640-acre lake but once was marshland along the Chippewa River. A campground, picnic area, and short **nature trail** are found here. To visit, head west of Glidden along WI 77 to CR M toward Cable.

West of Mellen along CR GG, then north quite a way on FR 187 is the **Veikko** trailhead, a three-and-a-half-mile intermediate trail with a couple of good views of Morgan Creek as it twists toward Morgan Falls. South of Clam Lake a mile or so via CR GG is the trailhead for the **West Torch River,** with 12 miles of trails.

Southwest of Mellen via CR GG is a lovely backwoods drive. It wisps along the Penokee Range past oodles of wildlife, including a chance to see Wisconsin's only **elk herd.**

Camping

The largest campground in the Glidden District is **Day Lake,** a mile north of Clam Lake on CR GG. This campground has a boat launch on a 600-acre muskie-laden lake; you can land a trophy from the pier. There are also reservable sites accessible to disabled campers. Nearby off CR GG then onto FR 190 is **East Twin,** much less frequented but with more good fishing. East of Clam Lake on CR M, then south on FR 166 and east on FR 164 you'll find **Stockfarm Bridge,** with seven very secluded sites in a copse of red pine. This is a pack-out campground used mostly by canoers, as it lies right along the Chippewa River. All but the latter have reservable sites.

The remainder of the campgrounds in the district are west of Mellen via FR 187 and 198. The most popular is **Lake Three,** with its eight campsites in a hardwood setting. Most come because the campground is on the North Country National Scenic Trail; there's also the nice view of the lake, and the Penokee Overlook isn't far away. The North Country Trail is also connected to the **Beaver Lake** campground, on FR 198. The fishing here includes channel catfish.

Services and Information

Information on the Glidden District is available from the **Glidden District Ranger Station,** P.O. Box 126, Glidden, WI 54527, tel. (715) 264-2511.

HAYWARD (GREAT DIVIDE) DISTRICT

Sights

One of the forest's established wildlife viewing areas is the **Lynch Creek Habitat,** west of Clam Lake via WI 77, then north on FR 203. Four species of nesting duck, mallards, Great Blue herons, beaver, otter, fox, raccoons, deer, and even coyote are primarily spotted. Two accessible trails wind through red pine to viewing platforms.

Recreation

Of the national forest's over 550 documented historic sites, the Hayward District has by far the most at 100. Many of the best preserved are the skeletal remnants of Swedish farmsteads now aging in the weeds in the depths of the forest. The highlight of the Hayward District, the **North Country Scenic Trail** (NCST), passes quite a few of them, mostly in the Marengo River Valley. The NCST is the forest's twin crown jewel to the Ice Age Trail. Entering the forest a couple of miles west of Mellen, it stretches for 60 miles through the forest and exits five miles southwest of Iron River. Like the IAT, it is a work in progress, and a dandy one at that. When completed, it will be the longest unbroken walking path in the U.S. at 3,200 miles, stretching from Crown Point, New York, to Lake Sakakawea, North Dakota, where it will link with the Lewis and Clark, then Pacific Crest Trails. The Chequamegon National Forest walking trail, in fact, inspired the whole trail and lent its name. This route undoubtedly includes the most varied topography and scenery the national forest has to offer: the billion-year-old Penokee Range; two dozen named lakes, streams, and rivers, and dozens more unnamed; and not one but two huge wilderness areas. The **Porcupine Wilderness** is 4,450 acres of rolling uplands, wetland, and swamp, and is totally motor-free. Six lakes larger than five acres and lots of ponds are also found within. Porcupine Lake covers 75 acres and, along with the tributaries, is full of trout. Four established campgrounds are found along the trail, along with one primitive site on Tower Lake. Adirondack shelters can be used just west of Mellen near the Penokee Mt. Ski Trails. Contact the district office for map specifics and trailhead parking. It is generally well marked.

Around **Black Lake** and leading from the campground, an interpretive trail details the lake's pine and hemlock "Eras," starting around 1880 and lasting until the Great Depression.

The **Rock Lake Trail Cluster** is a system of six interconnecting loops for hikers, skiers, and mountain bikers. The trails, ranging in length from 1.2 to 10 miles, cater to all skill levels. This is one of the most well-regarded networks in the forest. To get there, head eight miles east of Cable along CR M to the parking lot.

Camping

The Hayward District has what may be the most primitive camping experience in the park. **Black Lake,** 26 miles east of Hayward to the junction of CR B, CR W, and Fishtrap Rd., then north on Fishtrap Rd. to FR 173. This rustic campground has 25 sites plus three very primitive pack-in sites. Fourteen sites are reservable, and there is an interpretive trail in circumference of the lake.

Not far from Black Lake, **Moose Lake** is accessed via FR 174 and FR 1634 off WI 77 east of Hayward. Seven of the 15 sites here are reservable, and the fishing is not bad.

Seventeen miles east of Cable on CR M, then north on CR D, and west on FR 209 is **Namekagon,** offering 33 campsites and full of RVs. Accessed easily from here are biking trails and the North Country Scenic Trail. Sites here are also reservable.

Services and Information

The **Hayward District Ranger Station,** tel. (715) 634-4821, is north off of US 63 (well-marked), Route 10, Box 508, Hayward, WI 54843.

WASHBURN DISTRICT

Sights

The stands of Norway and red pine in this district of the forest were among the purest and densest ever found (and exploited) during the last century. The **Drummond Rust-Owen Mill Reservoir** is the last residual of a sawmill dating from 1883. Built from fieldstone and displaying a unique conical silo, it was used to power the mills in Drummond—one of the largest 50-odd lumber towns that sprouted in northern Wisconsin. The reservoir saved the little town from fire on two occasions. Though the roof has fallen and weeds are encroaching, the walls for the most part are structurally sound. It's just west of town adjacent to FR 223, north of US 63.

Recreation

The enormous 6,600-acre **Rainbow Lake Wilderness Area** lies southwest of Delta along FR 228. Off-limits to motorized anything, it's prime backwoods land for hikers and canoers. The North Country Trail cuts through for six miles; Tower Lake, one of the forest's most isolated, is linked to the trail by an access route. Reynard and Wishbone Lakes are good for canoers and birders and are also linked to the North Country Trail by a spur. The best access to the wilderness is via the Perch Lake Campground.

The **Valkyrie** multi-use trail, is accessed west of Washburn off CR C. It has four interconnecting loops ranging from 2.6 to 4.6 miles for hikers, skiers, and mountain bikers. One of the most respected trail systems in the forest, it departs near the Mt. Valhalla Winter Sports Area (an old ski jump hill), which has a chalet. Loops twist in every conceivable direction from here.

The **Drummond Trail,** also multi-use, is east of Drummond along FR 213, or accessed from the south at the Lake Owen Picnic shelter. Over 15 miles of trails make up this network. The North Country Scenic Trail intersects a Chequamegon Area Mountain Bike trail network northwest of town; the trailhead is at Drummond Town Park on Lake Drummond.

Camping

The closest campground to Washburn and definitely the most popular in the district is **Birch Grove,** 12 miles west of Washburn via Wannebo Rd. and FR 252 and 435 (well-marked). There are some decently secluded sites here on a long lake, and, man, are loons loud around

here. The Valhalla Trail is accessible from here for hikers and mountain biking—it starts from Mt. Valhalla, which has snowmobiling, cross-country skiing, ATV trails, hiking, biking, and horseback riding.

East of Iron River along US 2 to FR 234 is **Wanoka Lake,** popular with bikers traveling the Tri-County Corridor stretching from Ashland to Superior. The lake is rife with trout.

Two campgrounds in the district accept reservations. Six miles north of Drummond on FR 35 is the **Perch Lake** campground, on a 75-acre bass lake. This one is crowded as it's close to the North Country trail (though not *on* it) and the Rainbow Lake Wilderness, not to mention trout fishing in the White River. The **Two Lakes** campground is five miles southeast of Drummond and among the largest campgrounds in the Chequamegon with 90 sites. Always popular, this one is smack between two lakes, with an interpretive trail and seven walk-in primitive sites. The North Country Trail is nearby, and Porcupine Lake Wilderness Area is easily accessible from here.

Services and Information

The **Washburn District Ranger Station,** tel. (715) 373-2667, is right along WI 13 near the historical center in the old brownstone in town, P.O. Box 578, Washburn, WI 54891.

HAYWARD-CABLE

Bookended by US 53 to the west and the national forest to the east, the Hayward-Cable stretch of US 63 and its environs is probably the most visited area in the northwestern lakes region. Seventeen miles may lie between them, but they're in the same breath locally. Surrounded by county and federal forest, and bisected by the Namekagon (the north fork of the St. Croix National Scenic Riverway), the area's got lakes and chains of lakes in every direction, and a decided recreational bent.

HISTORY

Archaeological evidence shows human occupation on present day Lac Courte Oreilles Indian Reservation dating to 5000 B.C. The Namekagon River was a strategic Ojibwa transportation route when French (and later British) trappers hiked or paddled in to barter fur and iron. Henry Schoolcraft spent a good deal of time in the area in an 1831 journey down the Brule-St. Croix Riverway to the Mississippi.

Hayward at one time was a planetary timber big shot, its boom status starting in 1880 when a lumberman—named Hayward—set up the first of many lumber mills. (Cable, an afterthought as a community today, actually arose first, as a railroad center and headquarters.) Hayward's ribaldry and raucousness when timber laborers came roaring into town to spend their pay was unrivaled by any mining or lumber boomtown anywhere (and fully detailed by national media). Timber still plays a role in the local economy, but the area has fully embraced tourism. The first resort went up on Spider Lake in 1885, and the area's never been the same. The little—population still under 2,000—town swells with tourists in both summer and winter. Even the governor maintains a "Northern Office" in Hayward.

Sneeze and you'll miss Cable—nothing more than a snack bar and service center, a lonely cafe, a few B&Bs on the main drag, and a couple of other businesses and resorts not far off the highway.

SIGHTS

Shameless kitsch or north woods work of art? Judge for yourself the 143.5-foot-tall muskie and other assorted behemoths in the fiberglass menagerie outside the **National Freshwater Fishing Hall of Fame,** just off WI 27 onto CR B, tel. (715) 634-4440, in Hayward. Kids will make a beeline to climb the planet's only four-and-a-half-story climbable muskie—you can snap a photo of the kids in the "jaws." The muskie's innards are also a museum. The real museum is serious business, a four-building repository of freshwater fishing history and records. Holdings include an eye-catching historical collection of 5,000 lures, hundreds of antique rods and reels, an equal number of outboard motors, depth finders, bilge pumps (some from naval vessels), and 400 mounted fish, including a world record. A newer addition is the "bobbing boat," a 10-foot sleigh-like boat with a handle for ice-pushing and oars for rowing. Twin theaters feature videos detailing the fishing industry, and researchers can utilize the library. Open daily mid-April through November 1, 10 a.m.-5 p.m. Admission is $4.50, $3 kids 10-17, $2 children under 10.

A mile south of Hayward on CR B at the Lumberjack Village Pancake House, **Scheer's Lumberjack Shows,** tel. (715) 634-5010, go down mid-June through late August, Monday, Wednesday, and Friday at 7:30 p.m., with Tuesday and Thurs.-Sat. matinees. Speed climbing, team sawing, axe throwing, and canoe jousting are contrived solely for familial delight; past features have pitted teams from other countries against the U.S.A.'s finest. Admission is $7, less for seniors, $5 for children under 12. Arrive early and get a camphouse lumberjack meal of barbecue, home-smoked meats, and German apple pancakes; including dinner the cost is $9 adults, $4 children under 12.

Scheer's shows are held in the "Bowl," an 1890s holding area for logs being floated south to mills. Now it's the site of the Scheer's and even a logrolling school—that's how big timber still is around here. Across the street and detailing that history is the **Sawyer County Historical Museum,** tel. (715) 634-8053, with quite a lot of regional exhibits inside. Admission is $1 adults, 50 cents children.

Another logging camp bunkhouse-style smorgasbord is piled onto the tables at **Historyland Cook Shanty,** a mile east on CR B, tel. (715) 634-2579, with roast beef of all types and good potato pancakes. Straight-up prices are $9 adults, $8 seniors, $6 and under for kids. Surrounding the restaurant is a free **logging camp and museum** with timber industry memorabilia strewn about the grounds, including rusting equipment pulled from local forests. Open daily May through mid-September, 8 a.m.-8 p.m.

A mile and a half south of town on US 63, the **Wisconsin Tree Nursery** covers 132 acres with self-guided trails. Open May-Sept. Mon.-Fri. 8 a.m.-4 p.m.

South on WI 27 is the family-specialty **Wilderness Walk,** tel. (715) 634-2893, a 35-acre wildlife menagerie and petting zoo, with walking trails and some local art exhibits. The wildlife pens include a new mountain lion exhibit. It also has an Old West Town. Admission is $5.50, $4 kids under 12.

Cable has the **Natural History Museum,** a couple of blocks east of US 63, with mostly wildlife exhibits and some summer lectures. Of special interest is a permanent exhibit on the Eastern timber wolf. Open June-Sept. Tues.-Sat. 10 a.m.-4 p.m. and Sunday 10 a.m.-2 p.m.

Vicinity of Hayward

It's ostensibly a supper club (with decent food at that), but most come to **The Hideout,** 17 miles southeast of Hayward via CR B, CR NN, and CR CC, tel. (715) 945-2746, to see the lair of "Scarface" Al Capone. The northern lakes of Wisconsin were rife with Windy City wiseguys in the '20s and '30s, and this is likely the best extant example of their sanctuaries. Situated within 400 acres of pines on a hill overlooking an icy unnamed lake, the fieldstone buildings and their interiors were incredible works of art, considering the isolation. The main lodge features a hand-hewn, 100-ton stone fireplace. A wooden spiral staircase was crafted in Chicago and transported here. The dining room and bar were built in what was likely the most ornate garage ever constructed in the lakes region of the state. Also still intact are the machine-gun turret manned by thug bodyguards, a bunkhouse, and an eerie "jail." There's even a doghouse built for Capone's German shepherds. Tours are given daily noon-7 p.m. June-Sept., Fri.-Sun. in May (fall and spring hours vary); admission is $7.50 adults, $3.50 children 6-11. The dining room serves steaks, chicken, chops, worthy Italian food, and a decent fish

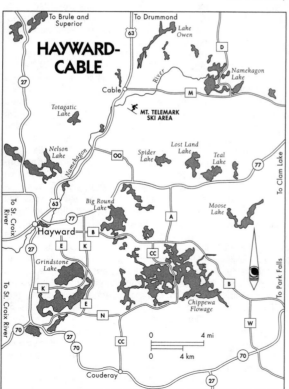

the biggest muskie of 'em all, Hayward

fry. The flapper memorabilia and decor here are pervasive.

Chippewa Queen Tours, tel. (715) 462-3874, offers two-hour narrated tours of the Chippewa Flowage. Tours operate out of Treeland Resorts and leave Monday, Wednesday, and Friday at 11 a.m. in summer; after Labor Day through the first weekend in October there is also a 2 p.m. Saturday tour; a 2 p.m. Sunday tour is offered Memorial Day through the first weekend of October. Dinner tours in summer leave at 5 p.m. Wednesday and Saturday. Fares are $9 adults, $6 children. See "Recreation" for more information on the flowage.

ACCOMMODATIONS

This author stopped counting after reaching 150 resorts and motels in the area. The Hayward-Cable region is considered also to include the villages and towns of Clam Lake, Drummond, Grand View, the Namekagon River, and the Chippewa Flowage area, itself the size of a city-state. Every conceivable type of lodging is available in the area—youth hostel, private and public campgrounds, dispersed and canoe campsites, fleabag motels, posh suites, historic B&Bs, and classic north woods "resorts." One thing the area noticeably lacks is a preponderance of those ersatz condo ghettoes sprouting up to make the local area look like a silly copy of Vail.

If you show up unannounced during summer, you'll likely nail down some accommodation, but you may not be able to be picky. If you're going to be around for the festivals, especially the Birkebeiner ski race, plan way ahead. And note that most, but by no means all, lodging options remain open year-round.

Hotels and Motels
Probably the cheapest all year is on the west side of US 63—the **Aspen Inn,** tel. (715) 634-4884, offering rooms for around $30 in the off-season if you're lucky. A smashingly good little place is the **Edelweiss,** also south on WI 27, tel. (715) 634-4679. There are only a few rooms, but they're extremely well kept and somewhat private. Rates hover around $40 s and $50 d all year.

The **Northern Pines International Inn,** tel. (715) 634-4959, is not far from the Edelweiss, and couple of the rooms have kitchens; there are also an indoor pool and sauna. Rates are $55 s or d.

Most comprehensive is **Country Inn and Suites by Carlson,** just south on WI 27, tel. (715) 634-4100, with large rooms and a ton of amenities. Rates are $68 and up s or d. The restaurant here is very good.

Resorts
Resorts in the Hayward-Cable area run the range of dusty old cottages that look as if they were built in the '30s by the CCC to sybaritic digs that look suspiciously like modified condos. The cheapest you'll find is around $260 per week for the bare-bones mom-and-pop outfits, but there is no upper level in this stratosphere. Pay around $400 per week for a one- or two-bedroom cabin and you're pretty much guaranteed solid lodging. Surprisingly, many places around these parts do not have a high-season ban on one-night rentals, though on weekends that may change suddenly, depending on demand.

The Chippewa Flowage southeast of Hayward has the most lodging options in the area, simply because it's so damn big. Organized and with-it, **Treeland Resorts,** tel. (715) 462-3874, date from 1928 and today offer the most luxurious digs around. A couple dozen posh cedar-lined vacation homes and newer motel suites make up the lodging options. The restaurant is well regarded, and the lodge operates wilderness lake tours through the flowage. Weekly rates start at $590.

Dun Rovin Lodge, tel. (715) 462-3834, is the showiest place on the Chippewa Flowage and has rates starting at around $440 per week. There's a taxidermy display, including the flowage's world record 70-pound muskie, and the flowage's aquatic life is displayed in 6,000-gallon tanks. Around 20 remodeled cabins are available, and there is a restaurant. Treeland and Dun Rovin both offer motel units as well. Figure on rooms starting around $40 and heading up to $75.

The Chippewa and Big and Little Moose Rivers flow in and out of Moose Lake in the Chequamegon National Forest, a perennial area favorite. **Virgin Timber Resort,** tel. (715) 462-3269, has eight one- to four-bedroom, one- or two-story cabins, all with fireplaces. Rates are $390-740 weekly for two to eight people.

A well-run resort operation also in the Chequamegon National Forest is **Lost Land Lake Lodge,** tel. (715) 462-3218, offering one- to three-bedroom well-kept cabins on spacious, isolated grounds. The restaurant here is quite good also. Rates are $515 and up for weekly rentals. In the same conglomeration of lakes you'll find the excellent **Ross' Teal Lake Lodge,** tel. (715) 462-3631, an old-style lodge from the mid-1920s that started as little more than a fishing camp. (The family's been in the business so long they once housed Abe Lincoln.) Two dozen one- to four-bedroom cottages are available, all with a cool screened porch. The restaurant is a fine option for local dining. Weekly rates are available; daily rates fluctuate between $120 and $160 in summer and fall.

An excellent lodge in the Cable area, the **Lakewoods Resort,** east of Cable on CR M, tel. (715) 794-2561 or (800) 255-5937, is plunked between the Rock Lake Primitive Area and Lake Namekagon in the Chequamegon National Forest. The condos and plush lake homes here won't bust the bank. An 18-hole golf course, indoor and outdoor pools, tennis courts, a sand beach, and an excellent restaurant make the rates ($70 and way up) more than decent.

Also on Lake Namekagon, the Bavarian **Garnisch Lodge,** tel. (715) 794-2204 or (800) 794-2204, is a whitewashed main lodge trimmed in brown and offset by two housekeeping homes—one in rustic Swiss style, the other with a castle facade. The lodge rooms have private baths and huge stone fireplaces, while the two homes offer two or five bedrooms, all in distinctive styles. Rates start at $80 in the lodge, $260-600 for the homes for two nights.

Historic Inns

The **Lumberman's Mansion,** 4th St. and Kansas Ave., tel. (715) 634-3012, was well known before it was even finished. A regional newspaper back in 1887 said this: "When completed, it will be the finest house in town and one of the best on the line." It underwent a careful renovation in 1989 when new owners planned to convert it into an inn; restorers consulted with local historical troves and even interviewed local old timers to ascertain exact specifications and the materials used in the original construction. The owners use all Wisconsin furnishings. Rates are a reasonable $75-90.

East of Cable in the Chequamegon National Forest, the **Spider Lake Lodge,** tel. (715) 462-3793 or (800) 653-9472, is a rustic 1923 lodge hand-hewn from forest logs dragged in on horse sleighs. You can still see the axe marks between the logs. A massive fieldstone fireplace sits in the center of the lodge's main room. Rooms run $75-90.

Camping

The Hayward vicinity offers 17 private campgrounds alone; factor in the half dozen communities of the Cable area, and there are easily 30 resorts or camping-only operations where you can pitch a tent. **Lake Chippewa Campground,** 13 miles east on CR B, then five miles south on CC, tel. (715) 462-3672, is perfectly representative of the area's camping-only options—secluded sites with the usual sandy beach, recreation activities, and boat rentals, with sites costing $14-23. But why on earth would you want to stay there?

You've got over a million square acres of county, state, and federal forest around you.

Hostels

Chez Perry, two miles east of Cable on CR M, tel. (715) 798-3367, is a member of the American Youth Hostels. The facility has 52 beds and stays open all year. Rates are $13 for AYH members.

FOOD

Quick Bites and Greasy Spoons

The only worthy greasy spoon in town is the **Moose Cafe,** 100 Dakota Ave., tel. (715) 634-8449, with the requisite faded newsprint in the counter and jokesters sipping coffee. The cafe serves straight-up cafe food with great homemade daily specials. Open daily 5 a.m.-9 p.m. Next door in the **Moccasin Bar** check out a world-record muskie display, a five-foot, 67-pounder; all the beers on tap are made in Wisky, too.

Resorts

Some resort dining rooms could be mistaken for standard family fare eateries, a couple bend toward Teutonic fare, a couple offer "lumberjack"-style dining, and there is of course the classic Wisconsin supper club, a few in business since way back when and still allowing resort guests to pour their own brandy Manhattans on the honor system.

You'll find old-fashioned Wisconsin north woods hospitality at **Ross' Teal Lake Lodge,** tel. (715) 462-3631, along with exquisite prime rib and fresh fish. The Angus steaks are worth noting at **Treeland,** tel. (715) 462-3874, and its Chippewa Flowage dinner cruises can't be beat. Treeland's restaurant deserves note if only for its nightly 30-plus item salad and fruit bar. It's also got an ice cream parlor. **Lost Land Lake Lodge,** tel. (715) 462-3218, also has garnered some attention for its supper club fare, especially the fish fry. The house specialty of roast honey duck is worth the trip, as is the wild rice soup.

Technically not in a resort, the **Flat Creek Eatery** at the Country Inn and Suites by Carlson, tel (715) 634-4100, is likely Hayward's finest food choice—an eye-poppingly creative variety of eclectic food, inspired in part by a visiting chef

program. The house chef also coordinates a national wild game cooking competition at the eatery, held in late April with over 120 national chefs entering the preliminary round. From $5.

Supper Clubs

The **Fireside**—locals may still refer to "Tony's Fireside" in honor of the longtime owner who died in 1994—has been serving the locals in some incarnation since the Depression. The Fireside still has its rustic feel, serving the usual supper club steaks, chops, and chicken. There are also a few creative additions including some Norwegian and vegetarian entr'es. Eight miles south on WI 27, then east on CR K, tel. (715) 634-2710. Open daily for dinner. From $6.

A large array of steaks—including a whopping 22-ounce Porterhouse—are found at **Club 77,** tel. (715) 462-3712, seven miles east on WI 77. Walleye, salmon, and assorted other seafood are also well prepared, as are the great house specialties—roast duck and steak Diane. From $6.

Since 1934, folks have streamed to **Turk's Inn,** a couple of miles north on US 63, tel. (715) 634-2597, for the hand-cut and aged steaks. Turk's also makes good shish-kebob and cheese *burek.* Open daily for dinner. From $7.

At 212 Main St., **Karibalis,** tel. (715) 634-2462, (or "Karb's") is something between a family restaurant and a supper club. Three meals a day and summertime Sunday brunch are offered. Open 8 a.m.-10 p.m. From $6.

German

The **Maximilian Inn,** tel. (715) 865-2080, serves Teutonic fare as well as a variety of continental cuisine, south on WI 27. From $6.

ENTERTAINMENT AND EVENTS

Entertainment

Hayward isn't the hedonistic, piano-pounding saloon town it once was, but there are always a couple of joints around that have sporadic live music in summer. **Uncle Al's** downtown features live entertainment on weekends, and **Cruzin'** on the east end of US 63 has '50s music.

Everybody hits the **Moccasin Bar** at the corner of WI 27 and US 63 to see the world-record muskie. You can also head out CR B to a **wildlife**

THE BIRKIE

In the depths of winter in 1973, 53 local ski aficionados headed northeast out of Hayward and skied their tails off 52 km to the Telemark Resort in Cable. They were attempting, for whatever reason, to re-create the famous Norwegian **Birkebeiner** race, an annual celebration of the desperation skiing of a duo of Norwegian militiamen trying to save the life of the country's infant king. The 53 didn't know what they were starting.

Within two decades the Birkie, as it's affectionately known, has become the Super Bowl, if you will, of Nordic skiing. Annually in late February, around 7,500 skiers (a children's race gets 1,700 entries) from around the world—especially Norway—turn up in the small communities of Hayward and Cable. The DYNO American Birkebeiner—its official name—is now the largest and most prestigious ski event in North America. They do it for the spirit of the thing. They sure don't do it for the dough—a relatively paltry $7,500 for the winner, but still an improvement, since no money at all was offered until 1996. What was originally a one-day cavort in the snow has turned into a three-day blowout, featuring the main Birkie, a 25-km *kortelopet*, or half-race, and a delightful children's race, the Barnebirkie. Events kick off with a 10-km torch-lit race Thursday evening, following the afternoon sprint races down Hayward's Main Street. Snowshoe races are part of the fun on Friday. A personal fave is the huge spaghetti feed on Friday night at the Telemark Lodge.

museum and bar, which has purportedly the world's most exhaustive muskie collection. Admission to the museum is $3 adults, $2 children.

Events

It's not as prestigious as Eagle River's snowmobile blowout, but Hayward's **Winterfest** does have world championship snowmobiling, with drag races and speed races.

Hayward also bills itself as a rival for Boulder Junction's claim of "Muskie Capital of the World." (A world record was caught here, which facilitates bragging rights.) The muskie is celebrated the third week of June in the **Muskie Festival,** featuring lumberjack competitions, live music, street dances, a powwow, and, of course, fishing competitions. The largest parade in northern Wisconsin also files through Hayward's downtown.

The third weekend of July Hayward hosts the **Lumberjack World Championships;** no joke, the competition is televised on ESPN. The pro competition features chopping, sawing, tree-climbing, and the perennial crowd pleaser, log rolling—all great fun. Early morning events include displays, demonstrations, chainsaw carving, and some hands-on chopping booths.

Northeast of Cable is little Grand View, which hosts early August's **Firehouse Fifty,** the oldest and largest on-road bike race and tour in the Midwest. Spectators will find unbeatable scenery along the forest roads.

The largest off-road bike race in the U.S. goes down near the Telemark Lodge the second weekend after Labor Day, the **Chequamegon Fat Tire Festival.** Umpteen thousand riders will gear up, ride, and party hard for this one, a 40-miler through the forest. Non-participants can take organized trail rides through the system on the Friday before the event.

RECREATION

CAMBA Trails

Hands down the most comprehensive trail system for off-road bike riders in the Midwest is the **CAMBA** (Cable Area Mountain Bike Association) trails. Over 200 total miles utilize old logging roads, ice-sled byways, and whatever ridgelines the glaciers left behind (and add to that about a lifetime's worth of forest roads not technically part of the system). The system is organized into six separate clusters, each with single and double track and totaling 25-40 miles. Trail conditions are varied—carpets of leaves, boggy and sandy muck, rutted dirt, and the occasional frightening python-sized tree root hidden beneath topcover. Two clusters—**Namekagon** and **Drummond**—are actually within the Chequamegon National Forest. The Namekagon trails might be the most popular, with both the easiest and most difficult trails in the forest (Patsy Lake and Rock Lake, respectively), as well as accessing the semi-primitive Rock Lake Area and the remoter regions of the forest. The Drummond trails have the easiest area riding and pass even more lakes. The most challenging rides come along the **Esker Trail** in the Cable cluster or the **fire tower trail** in the Seeley cluster, which also has grand Namekagon River Valley views and traces the Birkie ski course through a cranberry bog. The longest cluster, the **Delta,** has some killer trails and arguably the best views—along the White River Valley—also accessing the North Country National Scenic Trail. The **Cable Cluster** traces the course of the Fat Tire racecourse and the Birkie course. Dozens of operations in the area have biking supplies and rentals. **New Moon,** tel. (715) 634-8685 or (715) 798-3811, has operations at both ends of the Birkie Ski Trail—one along US 63 N in Hayward, the other in Cable out of the Telemark Lodge. Detailed trail map sets are available for $5 from local merchants, or via the CAMBA direct, P.O. Box 141, Cable, WI 54821, tel. (715) 798-3833 or (800) 533-7454; CAMBA can also provide information on the huge Fat Tire Festival and occasional off-road races.

Chippewa Flowage

Abutting the Chequamegon National Forest and the Lac Courte Oreilles Indian Reservation is Wisconsin's third-largest lake (and largest wilderness lake), the 15,300-acre Chippewa Flowage (lovingly, the "Big Chip"). Not as wild as the Turtle-Flambeau Flowage, it nonetheless is a grand piece of property, jointly managed by the state DNR, the USFS, and the Lac Courte Oreilles Anishnabe Nation. This labyrinthine waterway is surrounded by 233 miles of variegated, heavily wooded shoreline, an endless array of points, bays, stagnums, sloughs, and seemingly hundreds of isolated islands. Primitive camping is permitted on the islands, but the 18 sites are first-come, first-served. There is no dispersed camping, but you will find a couple of private operations on the shoreline. Nearly every species of bird and mammal indigenous to northern Wisconsin is found within the acreage. The flowage is also a nationally known muskie lake and no slouch for walleye. The world-record muskie was caught right here in 1957.

Canoeing

The 98-mile-long Namekagon River is the northern tributary of the federally established St. Croix National Scenic Riverway System, and it flows smack through the Hayward-Cable area, its headwaters at the Namekagon Lake dam northeast of Cable. The river is no white-knuckler, though some high-water periods create medium to high hazards. For the most part, it's an exaggerated trout stream running a wide river valley and dammed into four flowages. River trips are generally classified into three segments: the dam to Hayward (33 miles); Hayward to Trego (35 miles); and Trego to Riverside (40 miles). This last section is basically development free.

Visitors centers in Hayward and Cable have detailed maps and camping information. Rentals in Cable are available at **Big Brook Bait,** tel. (715) 798-3310; in Hayward at the local **KOA Campground,** tel. (715) 634-2331, or **New Moon Bike Shop,** tel. (715) 634-8685. The USFS ranger office in Hayward has maps, though the real information center for the river is west, in Trego, tel. (715) 635-8346. The headquarters, in St. Croix Falls, can be reached at tel. (715) 483-3284.

Fishing

To cover all the area's fishing options would be a book in itself. Consider interviewing for a guide through the **Guide Service, Inc.,** tel. (715) 462-3055.

Downhill Skiing

Telemark Resort, east of Cable on CR M, tel. (715) 798-3811 or (800) 472-3001, has a downhill ski area with 10 runs—two beginner, five intermediate, and three advanced—and equipment rentals ($16). The hills are serviced by five ropes, chair lifts, and T-bars. Lift tickets are $26.

SERVICES AND INFORMATION

The **Hayward Visitors Information Center,** a block north of the US 63/WI 27 junction, tel. (715) 634-8662 or (800) 72HAYWARD, www.haywardlakes.com, is open weekdays 9 a.m.-5 p.m. and scattered weekend hours.

TRANSPORTATION

Denizens of the Mini-Apple can get to Hayward, but no one else can, as there's no longer any inter-city bus service. **Northern Wisconsin Travel,** tel. (715) 634-5307, operates bus shuttles to and from Minneapolis' airport serving Spooner, Rice Lake, Cumberland, Turtle Lake, Amery, and New Richmond en route. Buses leave Hayward at 7 a.m. Tuesday, Thursday, and Saturday at 7 a.m. A one-way ticket to Minneapolis is $39, less 10 percent for seniors.

Once in Hayward, **Cindy's Taxi,** tel. (715) 634-2989 or 1-492-0020 (cell phone), drives local or long-distance trips at a flat rate of $1 per mile, $3 minimum.

LAC COURTE OREILLES INDIAN RESERVATION

Southeast of Hayward and sandwiched between two lakes and the Chippewa Flowage, the Lac Courte Oreilles ("Lake of the Short Ears") Indian Reservation is a 31,000-acre federal trust reservation, home to the Lac Courte Oreilles Band of Lake Superior Chippewa, who arrived at these lakes sometime in the mid-18th century. But the area's human occupation dates back much farther—more than 7,000 years. Copper arrowheads have been unearthed on an isthmus between two local lakes. The North West Fur Trading Company established a trading post on a nearby lake in 1800, creating a European and native presence before the treaties with the federal government were finally signed in 1825, 1837, and 1842, which permanently placed the band here. With a tribal membership of 5,000, the population on the reservation itself is around 3,000. You'll find the usual casino, but the reservation's location adjacent to the Chequamegon National Forest, the expan-

sive Chippewa Flowage, and within the hundreds of lakes and lake chains also give it a strategic importance for outdoors lovers. The reservation's radio station, WOJB (FM 89), is about the only thing worth listening to in the region.

Sights and Activities
The tribe holds an annual **Honor the Earth Traditional Powwow** the third week of July; other powwows are scheduled for Veterans Day and Thanksgiving.

North of the powwow grounds along Trepania Rd./Indian Route 17 is the **Ojibwa Cultural Village.** A series of wigwams sit in a forested setting, and visitors are guided through a group of educational displays on Ojibwa heritage, from wild-rice fanning to blanket weaving. Some of the activities are hands-on, and visitors can also sample traditional foods.

During summers at the Appa-Lolly Ranch and Riding Stables you'll find the weekly **Summer Days Powwows,** held Wednesdays at 6:30 p.m. early June through mid-August, featuring drum and Ojibwa dance troupes and the main attraction—Ojibwa riders and horses in full dress. Admission is $6 adults, $3 children 5 and over. The ranch also offers overnight camping trips, three-hour ride programs, picnic lunch rides, and more. For information, call (715) 634-5059 or (800) 9-PONY-UP.

Also on the reservation, along CR E, the **St. Francis Solanus Indian Mission** is a site dating from the mid-19th century. The buildings include a rectory, a convent, and school. Inside you'll find assorted Native American artifacts. Open daily.

SOUTHWESTERN WISCONSIN

Ten thousand years ago—as the icy bulldozers of the ultimate glacial epoch gouged their way across the hemisphere—for whatever reason, two adjacent thrusting lobes were rerouted by the declensions of natural valleys (and immovable quartzite). The forks twisted around the natural borders of southwestern Wisconsin but never encroached on the interior—as had none of the previous mantles of glaciers. The inspiring result is Wisconsin's Driftless Area, encompassing nearly one-quarter of the state's geography—four times the square mileage of Connecticut—and the world's only pocket of land completely surrounded by glacial drift.

The Western Uplands physiogeographic re-gion nicely encompasses this entire Driftless Area. Early geologists to the state remarked on the region's similarities to the Cumberland plateau in the Appalachians. An oddball topo-graphical hodgepodge, the swooping "coulees" in the upper quarter are the uplands' most salient feature, marked by ambitious valleys so impos-ing and eye-catching that early Wisconsinites could find no English-language equivalent. In the north, northern and southern biotic regions in-termingle. Farms predominate today where mines once took ore. The rolling, variegated ter-rain, splattered with red barns and roads slowed by chugging tractors, is likely the most quintes-sentially rural in America's Dairyland.

ALONG THE WISCONSIN RIVER

THE LOWER WISCONSIN STATE RIVERWAY

In 1989, the Wisconsin Legislature gave final approval—after seven hard-fought years—to a proposal by environmentalists, the DNR, a few politicos, and local residents officially establish-ing the 92.5-mile Lower Wisconsin State River-way. From Sauk Prairie, in south-central Wis-consin just north of Madison, to its confluence with the Mississippi River, it's definitely an "Old Man River," shuffling instead of rushing, lolling in-stead of cascading. It's also the longest re-maining undammed stretch of river in Wisconsin.

A grand achievement of common sense and civic middle-ground cooperation, these 92 miles couldn't have been better chosen. Precious little development has occurred along the shorelines here already, and the establishment of the river-

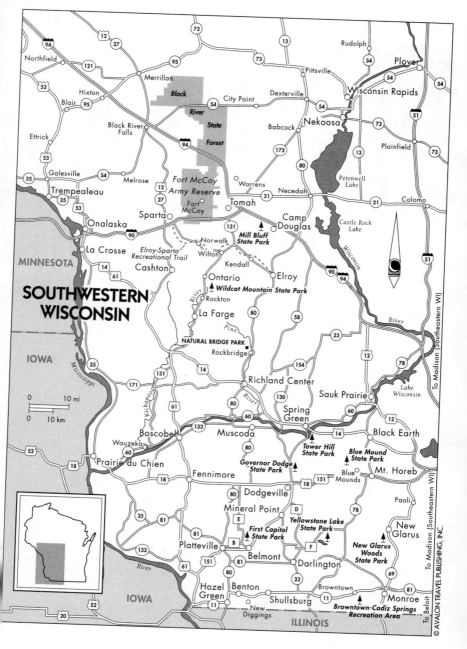

SOUTHWESTERN WISCONSIN

MINNESOTA

IOWA

IOWA

ILLINOIS

SOUTHWESTERN WISCONSIN HIGHLIGHTS

Badger Mine, Shullsburg
Cheese Days, Monroe
Elroy Sparta Recreational Trail
House on the Rock, Spring Green
Kickapoo River Watershed, Ontario
Lower Wisconsin State Riverway, Sauk City
Mustard Museum, Mount Horeb
Taliesin, Spring Green
The Mining Museum, Platteville
Wildcat Mountain State Park

way guards its pristine beauty. Ultimately the state hopes to own up to 80,000 acres of riverfront property; half that is now under state control.

The riverway subsumes nineteen official Natural Areas as diverse as Bakken's Pond near Spring Green, to the haunting battlefield park of the Battle of Wisconsin Heights. It has been called one of the most amazing conglomerations of natural history, ecology, state and Native American history, recreation, flora and fauna, and topography in the Midwest. All told, 40,000 acres are included. Shoreline incursion is barred, keeping the bluffs and greenery intact, and any off-bank timber extraction has to first pass muster with a tough advisory-board review. About 350 species of flora and fauna are found inside the riverways parameters. Sixty or more threatened or endangered species reside within its boundaries, as do 35 flora species specific to the unglaciated Driftless Area.

The riverway is also very much a work in progress. Development of new campgrounds, rustic or otherwise, will be taking place, as will a scattering of new boat landings. Most are to be concentrated on the Sauk City-Spring Green upper third, and gradually less as the river rolls southwest toward Wyalusing State Park. The stretch south and west of Boscobel is earmarked for primitive status.

Highlights

Four miles south of Sauk City is the ever-inspiring **Ferry Bluff,** just off WI 60. From the bluff, the Baraboo Range is visible to the east, as is Blue Mound to the south. Many disembark in Spring Green for an extended stay. Near the Lone Rock Boat landing is a protruding cliff called **Devil's Elbow** for its hazardous navigation and numerous wrecks. The **Avoca Prairie,** seven miles west of the WI 133 Lone Rock bridge, is almost 1,000 acres of wet-mezic prairie, the largest tallgrass-prairie remnant east of the Mississippi River. (Turn north off WI 133 onto Hay Lane Rd., past Marsh Creek to the parking area; be very aware of wet conditions or you will get stuck.) You'll pass two of the last extant hand-operated draw-span bridges built by the railroads prior to reaching Bear Creek. After passing Richland City, **Bogus Bluff** comes into view, rich with apocryphal tales of subterranean riches, as well as splendid views. **Muscoda** is the only town of any size before Boscobel, and to the west is the **Blue River Sand Barrens,** a genuine desert— cacti, snakes, and a species of lizard all live here. (On the other side of the river, along WI 60, you can hop into legendary **Eagle Cave** for a small fee; look for Eagle Cave Road.)

Canoeing

Spring Green marks the southern end of the most populated segment of the 92-mile riverway; Sauk Prairie, 25 miles away, is the northern terminus. Two-thirds of the river's users are active between these points.

The whole of the thing can be canoed, as there is nary a dam, cascade, rapids, or portage; this is the longest unimpeded stretch of river in the Midwest. Currents range from five mph on the upper reaches to an absolutely slothful one to two mph near Muscoda. Spring Green to Boscobel is active enough, but beyond Boscobel you'll be alone. Many Spring Green area travelers pitch a tent at Tower Hill State Park, then access the river via the park's creek. Other popular access points include Peck's Landing, beneath the WI 23 bridge; and the Lone Rock Landing, just east of the WI 130 bridge.

Canoe operations offering trips on the Wisconsin are listed below under "Sauk Prairie."

Swimming

No matter what you see the locals doing, respect this river. There are monthly drownings in the summer because someone was messing around and got careless. The sandbars make for enticing swimming targets or beach-the-canoe-and frolic spots, but the current is misleadingly slow. At three to five mph it doesn't seem like much, but the layered currents can drag you under. Worse, river fluctuations create deep sinkholes, which can neither be seen nor predicted by observing the current—step in one and say bye-bye. Swim only at established beaches or at least wear a flotation device. If you have to bop off a sandbar, always wade upstream, and be certain that everyone is aware that the killer side of a sandbar is downstream. If you are sucked in, do not try to return to where you entered and do not treat it like a rip tide and cut at a 90-degree angle. Go with the flow and angle toward the closest shore.

Fishing

Gamefish are present in the Wisconsin River's main channel, but panfish predominate on poles and are especially pervasive in the sloughs and bayous off the river channel. Gamefish include channel and flathead catfish, sauger, bass, pike, and the everpresent walleye. Check locally for regulations and take limits. For serious anglers, it might be worth a 17-mile drive east along US 14 to Black Earth Creek, one of the top 100 trout streams in the country, with more than 1,500 brownies per mile.

Camping

Free dispersed camping is allowed on all state-owned lands, whether inner-stream islands or banks. Trouble is, it isn't always easy to know what land is in state hands—*check locally before setting camp.* In certain areas, only sandbars are not privately owned, and thus, those are what you've got. They're grand, Huck Finnish ways to experience the river, but then again, this is a river and water levels fluctuate sand bars disappear, so keep aware. *No glass containers whatsoever are allowed.*

Information

The Wisconsin Department of Natural Resources produces outstanding publications on the riverway, including maps heavy with background reading. It can be found at Tower Hill State Park, DNR offices along the route, or various shops or chambers of commerce. The latter offices have enough accompanying local maps and brochures to cobble together a nice booklet for your trip. Otherwise, contact the Wisconsin DNR ahead of time, Box 7921, Madison, WI 53707, tel. (608) 266-2181.

SAUK PRAIRIE

Sauk Prairie is actually two tiny communities—Sauk City and Prairie du Sac—at the southern endpoint of the Lake Wisconsin Region. Both take their toponymical inspiration from the Sauk tribe, and both cropped up about the same time. In the 1840s, Upper and Lower Sauk were founded by Hungarian immigrant and dandy Agoston Haraszthy, before he lit out for California to become the "Father of the California Wine Industry." Sauk City managed to one-up Prairie du Sac by incorporating first, making it Wisconsin's oldest incorporated village. (It also gained famed throughout Europe as one of the country's last bastions of Freethinkers.)

The cities were inspiration for native son August Derleth, the verbose wordsmith who championed the common Wisconsinite (his "Sac Prairie" stories were obviously modeled on the area). The two towns are also known for eagle watching. The ice-free and calm, free-flowing waters of the lower Wisconsin River (courtesy of power plants and dams) and notched sandstone bluffs for roosts have given rise to a phoenix-like reappearance of endangered bald eagles. Of the state's nearly 600 nesting pairs of eagles, up to 10% are concentrated in the Sauk Prairie stretch of river.

Sights and Recreation

View the **eagles** in January at several sites: next to the Firehouse Restaurant (viewing scopes offered) in Praire du Sac, which has an information kiosk; Veterans Park, which has in-car-only viewing; a mile north of Prairie du Sac then onto Dam Road to the hydroelectric plant; and if you're feeling ambitious, head out CR PF, where you might get a gander at eagles feeding on farmland flotsam.

Among the most popular wineries in Wisconsin, **Wollersheim Winery,** WI 188, tel. (608) 643-6515, is also one of the oldest. Ensconced in a lovely valley along the Wisconsin River (great vistas, and lots of chances to see eagles),

Wollersheim has been producing wines since before the Civil War and now accounts for over half of the wine produced in Wisconsin. The antebellum buildings, limestone aging caverns, and vineyards are an official National Historic Site. Popular and fun volunteer grape harvesting and stomping weekends are held in autumn. The winery is open year-round 10 a.m.-5 p.m., with tours offered mid-May-October daily, hourly 10:15 a.m.-4:15 p.m., lesser hours off season. Tours cost $2.50 for adults 12 and over, free for children accompanied by an adult.

Northwest of Sauk Prairie approximately 10 miles is a day-use and seasonal state park focused on the only natural bridge in Wisconsin, **Natural Bridge State Park.** Crags and battlement outcroppings such as this are found throughout the state's Driftless Area. Generally sandstone, or sandstone and limestone, on a first glance they might remind you of the rises and spires of the American Southwest. This wind-eroded hole in a sandstone promontory measures 25 by 35 feet and is one of the oldest sandstone natural features on the planet. Stratigraphic dating has also revealed Paleo-Indian encampments as far back as 12,000 years—among the oldest sites in the Upper Midwest. A couple of trails wind through the park's 60 acres and a natural area within. By the way, north of the park you'll find **Orchard Drive** (and parts of Schara and Ruff Roads), one of Wisconsin's official Rustic Roads. This six-miler serpentines through grand glacial topography and plenty of wildflowers. This is as off-the-beaten path as it gets.

The most humbling site in central Wisconsin is the **Black Hawk Unit** of the Lower Wisconsin State Riverway, one of 26 units between the Prairie du Sac dam and the Mississippi River. The unit is of archaeological note for the rare linear-type effigy mounds from the Late Woodland Period (between 600 and 1300 A.D.), found only in the quad states region including southwestern Wisconsin. Arrayed to align with the sun at summer solstice, they are primarily in the form of birds and mammals, and a few are reptiles. Unfortunately, that splendid and cryptic history is overshadowed by the massacre that occurred along the park's northern perimeter—the **Battle of Wisconsin Heights**—between Fox-Sauk warriors and a militia that had pursued them across the state. The park has over 15 miles of eerily quiet trails, leading from the archaeology of the effigy mounds to the site of the battle and even past late 19th-century log buildings put up when the land was part of a working farm and recreational resort. To get there, take US 12 south to CR Y and west to WI 78, then go south a mile to the parking area.

Sauk Prairie is a good spot to indulge in a favorite pastime on the lower Wisconsin—canoeing. Next to the Spring Green area, this might be the most popular segment of the river. The float from around WI 60 and back to town is easiest; otherwise, you could theoretically go all the way to Spring Green. If you do, primitive camping is allowed on sandbars and is without question the most enthralling way to experience the river. Figure $30 for a canoe rental and shuttle service on a leisurely, two-and-a-half-hour trip; a four-night trip all the way to the Mississippi can go as high as $150. Both **Brice's Blackhawk River Runs,** tel. (608) 643-6724, and **Sauk Prairie Canoe Rental,** tel. (608) 643-6589, offer rentals and trips.

Sauk Prairie is also the proud parent of the annual **Wisconsin State Cow Chip Throw,** held Labor Day weekend. At the **Riverview Ballroom,** built in 1942 and overlooking the Wisconsin River, you can dance to country music Friday nights on the largest dance floor in southern Wisconsin.

Accommodations

You can find low rates and superior quality rooms at the **Skyview Inn,** junction of US 12 and CR PF, tel. (608) 643-4344 or (800) 525-8875. It offers a spacious, grassy setting and one suite with a jacuzzi. Rates start at $40 in summer, dipping to $30 off-season.

Newer, the **Cedarberry Inn,** 855 US 12, tel. (608) 643-6625 or (800) 342-6625, offers clean and comfortable rooms and a few very nice suites. The inn also has an indoor pool, sauna, and workout room. Rates from $55 s or $65 d.

Food

Leystra's Swistyle Venture Restaurant, 200 Phillips Blvd., Sauk City, tel. (608) 643-2004, serves basic cafe fare in a century-plus-old wagon-and-blacksmith shop turned dairy turned diner. It's popular locally for its ice cream menu and "cheese chalet" of regional cheese offerings.

Otherwise, you'll get hearty Midwestern breakfasts, lunches, and dinners. From $4.

Inarguably the best eagle-watching is right inside **The Firehouse,** 540 Water St., Prairie du Sac, tel. (608) 643-2484, with a resplendent view of the Wisconsin River. The food is a touch above basic supper club fare, especially the excellent steak Diane. CJ's also offers some ambitious stir-frys, duck, a local-favorite wiener-schnitzel, and even "Milwaukee-style" potato pancakes. CJ's is closed Monday; dinner otherwise, and Sunday brunch. From $4.

Another fantastic steak option—with an excellent 20-ounce Porterhouse—**Green Acres,** WI 78 and US 12, tel. (608) 643-2305, is a supper club with a sense of humor (hence the name). Steaks to kill for, but the stuffed trout is to die for. From $6.

The dense German food at the **Dorf Haus** includes real-deal Teutonic specialties—wiener schnitzel a la Holstein (topped with an egg), cured-Bavarian-style pork shank, sauerbraten, and even *leberkaese* (pork and beef loaf)—this is likely one of the few spots in the state you'll see it. Special Bavarian smorgasbords are offered the first Monday of every month year-round and the first and third Mondays in summer. Along CR Y in diminutive Roxbury, tel. (608) 643-3980. From $8.

Between Prairie du Sac and Merrimac along WI 78 and overlooking Lake Wisconsin, **The Oaks,** tel. (608) 643-6723, is another superlative restaurant. It offers very impressive continental fare and adventurous regional game dishes— lapin *Chasseur* (that's rabbit to you and me) and broiled venison roast in a vinaigrette sauce, as well as a host of pastas and locally favored ribs, broasted chicken, and veal liver. The house specialty, blackened prime rib, is outstanding. Open summers for lunch Tues.-Sat., dinner daily, lesser unspecific hours off-season. There's also a grand Sunday brunch and an all-day fish fry come Friday. From $8.

SPRING GREEN

Tracing the final relaxing course of the Wisconsin River westward, the first community, little Spring Green, isn't even right on the river, though most presume it is. From a satellite view, Spring Green is nestled and locked into the crook on the north side of a river bight, surrounded by the lushest green imaginable.

It's close enough for rivertown status, however, and that prime, luck-of-the-draw geographical plunk-down on the edge of the Wyoming Valley has given Spring Green the edge on any tourist town around. Famed Wisconsin curmudgeon Frank Lloyd Wright found the area's beauty to fit his architectural visions so well he founded a groundbreaking design school here and lived here for five decades.

Spring Green began as a squat grouping of simple log cabins that served as a shipping point for hogs and cattle. Over the decades, however, the town of Spring Green has become a serious tourist town—full of crafts and antique shops, art galleries, upscale eateries, and even a renowned outdoor theater group, the American Players Theater. Combined with that are a host of river rats paddling through the tame lower segment of the Wisconsin River and a lot of Wright devotees trooping around to view The Master's works. Yet there's still a large sense of pastoral simplicity. Farmers still roll tractors down the roads and through town. Indeed, the town has been way ahead of the pack on balancing development with preservation; expansion of village roadwork to handle the traffic clogging WI 23 and US 14 coincided with equal-sized projects to build ponds, wetlands, and a wildlife area on the south side, a green tension line of sorts. In fact, hot commodity Spring Green didn't get a stoplight along busy US 14 until 1995. (It was first mentioned in 1948.)

Sights

Throw a dart blindfolded in the Spring Green area and it'll hit the word Wright. In 1911, three miles south of Spring Green's village center in the Jones Valley, Frank Lloyd Wright began work on **Taliesin** (Welsh for "Shining Brow") on the homestead of his Welsh ancestors. He had already made quite a name and reputation for himself in Wisconsin and in architectural circles, both good and bad. An unabashed, monumental egoist, Wright in his lifetime had a profound artistic and architectural influence upon the Badger State. He also enraged proper society with his audacity and uncanny ability to *épater les bourgeois,* that is, to stroke his own famed who-gives-a-damn-

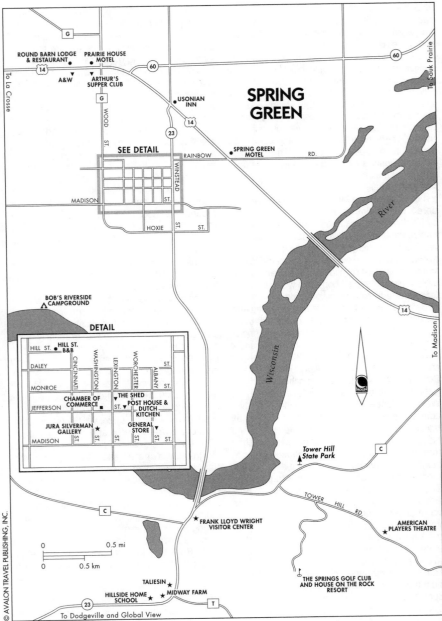

SPRING GREEN

To La Crosse

ROUND BARN LODGE & RESTAURANT
PRAIRIE HOUSE MOTEL
A&W
ARTHUR'S SUPPER CLUB
USONIAN INN
SPRING GREEN MOTEL
SEE DETAIL

WOOD ST.
RAINBOW
WINSTEAD ST.
MADISON
HOXIE ST. ST.

To Sauk Prairie

River
Wisconsin

BOB'S RIVERSIDE CAMPGROUND

DETAIL

HILL ST.
HILL ST. B&B
DALEY
CINCINNATI
WASHINGTON
LEXINGTON
WORCHESTER
ALBANY ST.
MONROE
CHAMBER OF COMMERCE
THE SHED
POST HOUSE & DUTCH KITCHEN
JEFFERSON
JURA SILVERMAN GALLERY
GENERAL STORE
MADISON

To Madison

Tower Hill State Park

FRANK LLOYD WRIGHT VISITOR CENTER

TOWER HILL RD.

AMERICAN PLAYERS THEATRE

0   0.5 mi
0   0.5 km

TALIESIN
HILLSIDE HOME SCHOOL
MIDWAY FARM

THE SPRINGS GOLF CLUB AND HOUSE ON THE ROCK RESORT

To Dodgeville and Global View

© AVALON TRAVEL PUBLISHING, INC.

what-they-think predilections. When he wasn't dashing off preternaturally radical designs, he was alternately a deadbeat dad, a browbeater, and—one dare say—a megalomaniac. And one who cut a figure with his everpresent cape and porkpie hat. As he said, "I had to choose between hypocritical humility and hated arrogance."

Wright stressed the "organic" in everything, and his devotion to the natural world predated environmental consciousness by generations (though the Japanese had it figured out millennia before Wright visited Tokyo and apparently had an epiphany). "Space is a breath of art," he once wrote. Taliesin is a perfect example—gradually pulling itself along the crown of a hill, not dominating the peak.

For whatever understated beauty he engendered, he remains an enigmatic figure, loathed by his detractors. His adoring minions will never forgive the state of Wisconsin for not giving him his due during his stormy life. His most famous exchange occurred over a client phoning Wright to inform him that rainwater was dripping on his table in his new Wright home. To which the master purportedly replied, "Move your table."

Before Wright left the state for the Southwest, Taliesin was established as the preeminent architectural design school. Today thousands of acolytes (not really an exaggeration) study under the Taliesin Fellowship. The 600-acre grounds consist of his residence, Taliesin; Hillside Home School, a boardinghouse for a school run by an aunt; a home built for his sister (Yan-Y-Deri, Welsh for "under the oaks"); a windmill (his first commissioned project); and Midway Farm, all built between 1902 and 1930 while Wright and his associates operated his studio and workshop from the main building. Locally quarried sandstone is the predominant rock, and everywhere, those unmistakable Frank Lloyd Wright roofs. The visitor center, heretofore the planet's only Frank Lloyd Wright-designed restaurant, was constructed out of a popular Spring Green diner from the '40s, using steel trusses scavenged from the WW II-era aircraft carrier USS Ranger. A small and wonderfully eclectic cafe still operates at one end, serving breakfast and somewhat light lunches (a best bet for creative food that won't bust the bank). The visitor center also offers a splendid, stadium-size view out across the river. The visitor center, more like a gift shop, is open daily May-Oct. 8:30 a.m.-5:30 p.m., weekends only 10 a.m.-4 p.m. in April and Nov.-December.

The grounds are accessible daily 8:30 a.m.-4 p.m. May-Oct. and weekends 10:30 a.m.-1:30 p.m. in April and November. Myriad tours are available, including a popular two-mile sweatless stroll throughout the estate. You'll view the lovely aesthetics of the Wright-landscaped countryside but no interiors. It costs $15 (more on weekends), $5 12 and under, with tours departing daily beginning May 1, 10:45 a.m. and 1:45 p.m. Tours of the Hillside Studio and Theater cost $10 ($5 kids) and depart daily May-Oct. 10 a.m.-4 p.m. Two other tours require reservations. The two-hour House Tour departs daily May-Oct. at 9:30 a.m. and 1:30 p.m.; it costs $40 on weekends. The biggie is the Estate Tour, a four-hour sweaty traipse around the entire grounds; refreshments are served. These depart Tuesday, Thursday, and Sunday May-Oct. at 8:30 a.m. and cost $60. Other tour options appear during peak periods.

When you tire of Frank Lloyd Wright, consider the local traditional-minded **American Players Theatre** nearby. Since 1980 and its first performance of A Midsummer Night's Dream, APT has created a cult following of sorts for its broad palette of offerings, and for its accessible direction. Carved into a hillside with gracefully aging seats, it is really the only way to experience something akin to the carnage in Henry V—a steamy August evening with nighthawks swooping and actors literally crashing through the underbrush. It's still casual classics—blue jeans and shorts are de rigueur for a goodly portion of every crowd—but no longer will the hasty patchwork of the side stage be apparent. The theater offers up first-rate catered dinners pre-show, picnic grounds, a shelter, and a concession stand. Performances rotate Tues.-Sun., with matinees Saturday. The season runs mid-June to early October. Tickets range from $22 to $35. For schedules and tickets, call the box office, tel. (608) 588-2361. Located three miles south of Spring Green, adjacent to the golf course.

In the mid 1800s, what is today **Tower Hill State Park** was the site of a major lead-shot-production operation. The major supplier to U.S. forces prior to the Civil War would have hit the big time as cannonballs started to fly across the Mason-Dixon line, but it went belly up in competition with farther-flung and cheaper facilities, all made possible by the railroad. The old shot tower and smelter have been refurbished, and it's a cool (literally and figuratively) traipse down into the cooling tank, where the lead pellets fell 180 feet to the bottom, rounding and cooling as they went. A narrow gouge cut into the bluff accesses the chamber. Camping is prime—only 15 wooded sites, first come, first served. Get one of the two that overlook Mill Creek, which runs into the Wisconsin River—great for canoes. To get there, head south out of Spring Green for two miles, then turn east (left) onto CR C.

House on the Rock

Wisconsin's very own House on the Rock absolutely defies lexical trickery in nailing it down. Novella-length magazine articles have gushed about the, well, left-handed grandeur and spectacle of its true-blue Americana, anything-can-happen overkill. The greatest of all these had to be *National Lampoon's* write-up in the early 1990s, when one of its columnists happened upon the joint whilst en route to an otherwise mundane Windy City wedding. A near-religious epiphany ensued over this Shangri-La—contrived solely to club tourists over the head aesthetically. This is the grandest shakedown of them all in Dairyland, mere miles from the amok-dom of the Wisconsin Dells. Best of all, it all goes down less than 10 miles from that enclave to natural architecture—that altar to an ego, that House that Wright Built—Taliesin, in Spring Green.

Come to Wisconsin and you absolutely cannot miss this eighth dimension tourist trap's ad barrage—Wisconsin's version of a two-drink minimum. Way back in the 1940s, otherwise-sane

the House
on the Rock

Alex Jordan literally stumbled over a 60-foot candle-like outcropping in the Wyoming Valley. Intending to construct a weekend retreat and artists' haven, Jordan somehow or other wrestled the original structure into completion atop the chimney. Bit by bit, this architectural gem began to transmogrify into what it is today—the original house atop the rock, plus several other mind-blowing rooms and add-ons, all stuffed with the detritus that Jordan accumulated over a lifetime, much of it museum-worthy in quality or scope.

The catalogue: Mill House, Streets of Yesterday, Heritage of the Sea, Pizza Atrium, Transportation Building, Music of Yesterday, World's Largest Carousel (20,000 lights and 275 handcrafted wooden animals, not one of which is a horse), Organ Room (three of the world's greatest right here), Doll Houses, Circus Room, Weapons Exhibit, Oriental Collection, Armor Collection, Crown Jewel Collection, Doll Carousels, and Village Periods. The best? Try the loopy Infinity Room, a glassed-in room that spikes out 218 feet over the valley floor. The newest attraction is the Transportation Room, offering a complete gander at the House in all its glory. And how about the holiday season's 6,000 Santas? But a list doesn't do it justice—it isn't just a selection of junk; it's a wild, shotgun-spattered Attic of the Damned. Is it art? Is it a giant Rorschach test of the mental wilds of an inspired eccentric? Well, equal parts all, perhaps, but an indescribable feeling of visionary honesty pervades the place—never a feeling that it's all a sham or simple stupid overindulgence. The method to the madness is there.

Many visitors overlook what a remarkable artistic and design achievement it was for Jordan to create the grounds and structures. Jordan never failed to think of how the visitor would see it all, from the 30-mile-panorama observation decks to the floral displays. The House on the Rock truly befuddles most who experience it. Those devoted to tackiness have found their Mecca; and best of all, even jaded tourist hacks have to shake their heads and grin.

You can experience all of this March 15 through the last weekend in October. High season hours are 9 a.m.-dusk June-Sept., last tickets sold at 5:30 p.m., lesser hours for the rest of season. Also, special holiday season tours are offered mid-November through early-January, 10 a.m.-4 p.m. Admission is a stiff $19.50 adults, $11.50 ages 7 to 12, $5.50 ages 3 to 6. Holiday tours start at $10. Located south of Spring Green along WI 23, tel. (608) 935-3639.

Accommodations

The local lodging listings consist of more B&Bs than motels and hotels, so don't bet on finding too much budget lodging in Spring Green, at least not between Memorial Day and Labor Day. The closest you'll come is the very good **Usonian Inn**, at the junction of US 14 and WI 23, tel. (608) 588-2323, with rooms from around $40 if you're lucky.

The landmark of sorts in town proper is the **Round Barn Lodge**, along US 14, tel. (608) 588-2568, advertised really as more than it is—a motor lodge with decent rooms and some one- and two-bedroom units. Though the salient rondure came from a Frank Lloyd Wright associate, it doesn't always translate to the rooms. The erstwhile dairy barn is now a popular restaurant. Amenities include two pools, whirlpool, saunas, and a rec room. Rates from $75 s or d.

Perhaps more appealing for Wright aficionados is the **Spring Valley Inn**, at the junction of US 14 and CR C, tel. (608) 588-7828, designed by Taliesin Associates, Wright's design center. With its steeple-like upthrust, you can't miss it, and its location right at the entrance to the valley is secluded but still prime. Large rooms, with an indoor pool, whirlpool, sauna, rec room, and 28 km of groomed cross-country ski trails for guests. The restaurant features Italian cuisine along with local microbrews, alfresco by a huge stone fireplace. An information center for the valley is within, as is a gift shop heavy on Wisconsin provisions. Rates from $85 s or d.

Not designed by Wright, but again by an "associate," you'll find fine lodgings indeed at the **Prairie House Motel**, US 14, tel. (608) 588-2088 or (800) 588-2088. A countryside setting, comfortable rooms, a cozy atrium with a gently sloping wood-wainscoted ceiling, a whirlpool, sauna, and exercise room are all offered. Basic rates of $60 s or d.

The coziest resort around is indisputably **The Springs Golf Club and House on the Rock Resort,** 400 Springs Dr., tel. (608) 588-7000 or (800) 822-7774, an all-suite luxury spread with a 27-hole Robert Trent Jones, Jr., championship course out your window. A decided bent for the recreation-minded pervades—hiking to mountain biking to tennis as well as the duffer's dream course. Rates from $165 s or d.

In the heart of Spring Green is the **Hill St. B&B,** 353 Hill St., tel. (608) 588-7751, a Queen Anne from 1904 with ornate handcrafted woodwork. Seven bedrooms are in this large complex, five with private bathrooms. Rates from $70.

You'll find an artistic air at the log cabin **Silver Star**, 3852 Limmex Hill Rd., tel. (608) 935-7297, displaying professional regional photographers' works within its chic cafe/coffeehouse and in all the rooms—minor museums of historical photographic figures. My personal favorite is the FSA Suite, dedicated to the Farm Security Administration photographers. It's all spread out over 300 acres of farmland; sticklers for tradition are happy to find a cozy main room with large fieldstone fireplace. Rooms run $95-135.

For the best **camping** head to Tower Hill State Park, south out of Spring Green two miles, then east (left) onto CR C. If it's full, head southwest to Governor Dodge State Park, or north 10 miles past Plain along WI 23, then take CR N and CR G to Sauk County's White Mound Park. For tenters in Spring Green is **Bob's Riverside Camp,** S13220 Shifflet Rd., tel. (608) 588-2826, offering canoe rentals.

Food

You'll discover an intriguing assortment of classic roadfood—quality eats, typical Midwest supper clubs and wannabe chi-chi restaurants in Spring Green. For a real "I went there" type meal, check out the basic cafe in the **Frank Lloyd Wright Visitors Center Riverview Terrace.** The place originally was an old diner, and Wright redesigned it to be a restaurant. Light foods only—ranging from delectable breakfast (French toast to bread pudding) to variegated salad styles to quiche and stuffed Wisconsin trout for lunch. Serving from 9 a.m.-5 p.m. daily. Fantastic vista of the river. From $4.

The local **A&W,** corner of WI 60 and US 14, has throwback window bellhop service along with a playground. From $2. Find basic grub at **The Shed,** 123 N. Lexington St., west of WI 23, offering sandwiches and a few dinner entrées—some vegetarian—ranging from chicken to rack of ribs and lasagna, as well as some vague Mexican dishes and pizza. From $4. But if you want some cafe advice, head east 11 or so miles along US 14 to Black Earth and the not-to-be-missed **Lunch Bucket Cafe,** the only game in town and a classic breakfast and lunch small-town diner.

A natural foods cafe and grocery, the **General Store** serves up light lunch specials (Monday, Wednesday, and Friday) and copious weekend breakfasts. Also a good place to score that espresso drink. Along Albany, one half block south of Jefferson. From $4.

Originally constructed in 1914 as a dairy barn, the distinctive circular construction of the **Round Barn,** along US 14, tel. (608) 588-2568, is an orientation device as well as a culinary institution in Spring Green. Over 200 round barns existed at one time in Wisconsin, now sadly dwindling in number. Built to save on expensive construction materials and to redirect strong winds; they also, the rumor goes, prevent the devil from finding a corner to hide in. The environs are certainly topnotch—the upsweep of the barn roof and its original rafters are still visible through a window that was originally a hay chute. Hearty Midwestern fare is served three times a day (vegetarians are not left out). A menu staple is the Round Barn Casserole, ham and chicken in a cheddar cheese sauce, slathered onto fresh broccoli and toast points and served with cranberry sauce. From $6.

Post House and Dutch Kitchen Restaurant, 127 E. Jefferson St., downtown, is another venerated tradition in Spring Green. Dating from 1857, it's the oldest continuously operating restaurant in the state. Fowl or fish, pork or prime rib, and anything in between can be found on the menu. The picturesque outdoor garden and cocktail area were designed by a Wright contemporary. Open daily, except Monday Nov.-March. From $5.

Events
The last full weekend of June, Spring Green hosts the **Spring Green Arts and Crafts Fair,** with 250 Midwest artisans and craftspersons setting up temporary booths throughout the village.

Shopping
In a city creaking with artisans and galleries, the Wisconsin artists showcase at the **Jura Silverman Gallery,** 143 S. Washington St., tel. (608) 588-7049, has managed to make quite a name for itself. Art furniture, slumped glass, handmade-paper art, photography, prints, paintings, watercolors, hand-bound books, carving, jewelry, and a whole lot more by Wisconsin artists, showcased in a 1900 cheese warehouse. Open Wed.-Sun. 10 a.m.- 5:30 p.m.

Definitely not from cheesehead artists, but from the other side of the planet, the wares at the world crafts dealer, **Global View,** tel. (608) 583-5311, off of CR C along Clyde Road in a reconverted barn, are not your usual import-export, they-don't-know-any-better, Asian "crafts." Global View maintains a reference library and location photographs of the source of each item, if not of the artists themselves, and tours to meet the artists are also organized here.

The whole of the Wisconsin River Valley can be thought of as one big farmer's market. Summertime vegetable stands crop up every half mile or so, or turn up in autumn for pumpkins as big as a kid.

Services and Information
Contact the **Spring Green Chamber of Commerce,** P.O. Box 3, Spring Green, WI 53588, tel. (608) 588-2042 or (800) 588-2042. Also check its website at www.springgreen.com.

WEST TO THE MISSISSIPPI

Muscoda
The story goes that the Fox and Sauk who lived in encampments on this site lent the descriptive moniker *mash-ko-deng,* or "meadow of prairie" to their home. Over time this transmuted into the present "Muscoda." Perhaps a more logical source is Henry Wadsworth Longfellow's "Hiawatha", which includes the line, "Muscoday, the meadow." Longfellow at least got the pronunciation to fit the spelling; most massacre it into "Mus-KOH-duh." It's "MUS-cuh-day." Whatever the linguistic gymnastics, its early buildings, dating from the 1830s, can be seen closer to the river, built before the town relocated.

Sleepy little Muscoda gets its kicks as the "Morel Mushroom Capital of the World." The tasty mushroom, tough to find but worth the woods-scouring, is feted annually with a festival in May. You might also stop by relic-quality **Tanner Drug Store** along N. Wisconsin Ave., a working drug store with original oak and pine counters and some antiques. Right on the river at **Victoria Park** outside of town sits the Muscoda Prairie, a lovingly restored stretch of prairie along the Lower Wisconsin State Riverway; all the work was done by volunteers and it's great! A **campground** is here.

An optional jaunt between Muscoda and Boscobel is to cross the river to WI 60. Six miles west at Eagle Cave Road is the state's largest onyx cave, **Eagle Cave,** discovered in the 1840s by a puzzled bear hunter who couldn't figure out where his quarry had gotten to. There's also a good **campground** here.

Boscobel

Back on the south side of the river, charming little Boscobel's location was pegged as *bosquet belle,* or "beautiful woods"—by Marquette and Joliet, who passed through in 1673. It's legendary for turkey hunting and canoeing but another claim to perpetuity is the Christian Commercial Travelers Association. That'd be the Gideons to you and me, founded in downtown's stone Hotel Boscobel in 1899. The story goes that two devout Christian salesmen were forced to double up in the hotel, in famous Room 19, and got to discussing how tough it was to be a God-fearing traveling man, especially in hellhole rivertowns, and hatched the idea of an interdenominational fraternity for travelers. Hoteliers and innkeepers, only too happy to encourage more saintly pursuits, cooperated. By 1914, almost a quarter-million Bibles had been placed from sea to shining sea. The old stone hotel still stands today. Purchased in the early '90s and de-mothballed, it currently is a restaurant whose menu features ethnic varieties. From $5.

Various other structures are under restorative saws and blades, including the **Antique Mall,** housed in an old creamery; and the railroad depot across the street, which is also a mini-museum and the offices of the chamber of commerce. (If you want tourist information, the chamber of commerce has some, but head for Dick's Supermarket—look for signs off WI 133—which has the same brochures available for much longer hours.) An old **Grand Army of the Republic** building—the only surviving Wisconsin GAR building—on Mary Street houses a Civil War museum, open by appointment. The "Old Rock Schoolhouse," also in Boscobel, 207 Buchanan St., is a renovated Romanesque Revival limestone structure.

A number of decent places to sleep can be found in Boscobel, including **Hubl's Motel,** along WI 60, tel. (608) 375-4277, with a decent location right on the river, important as this is prime canoeing country. Some rooms with kitchenettes, boat rentals, and rates from $30.

In one of the oldest buildings in town, the aptly named **Unique Cafe,** 1100 Wisconsin Ave., tel. (608) 375-4465, features killer pies, from-scratch cafe food, and an amazing assortment of "memorabilia" gathered by the proprietor. It's a genuinely interesting place to sit and eat and look around. It also has a decent Sunday brunch. From $2.

Fennimore, 10 miles south of Boscobel, was once a major player in the lead trade. People generally stop by to see the **Fennimore Doll Museum.** The displays of tractors, trucks, cars and more from various museums is ever-increasing. The museum, 1140 Lincoln Ave., tel. (608) 822-4100, is open daily Memorial Day through December, 10 a.m.-4 p.m. Admission is $3, $1 under 18.

Visit too the up-and-coming **Fennimore Railroad Museum,** 610 Lincoln Ave., tel. (608) 822-6319, down the street. Smaller steam engines ride on a 15-inch track, and children can ride. The claim to fame here is the "Dinky" narrow gauge trains that once crisscrossed the area. The "Dinky" is significant as one of the most extensive operations in the state—16 total miles throughout the Green River Valley, and famed for its horseshoe curve, necessitated by the grade of the valley. It also operated far longer than most narrow gauge railroads—finally shut down for good in 1926. Open Memorial Day-Labor Day, 10 a.m.-4 p.m., admission by donation.

The Silent Woman, 1096 Lincoln Ave., tel. (608) 822-3782, if not the best supper club in the southwest, then it's close, with a superlative atmosphere. The capacious courtyard is indoors but you'd swear it wasn't, with a pumped-in stream running through it. Real plants and greenery line the banks. Steaks, a host of seafood, chicken, and a veal entrée are offered. Ten cozy guest rooms run $52 for a basic room, $82 for a semi-suite, and $132 for a two-room suite. Open for breakfast, lunch, and dinner Tues.-Sat., Sunday for brunch 10 a.m.-2 p.m., Monday for dinner only.

Wauzeka

Backtrack through Boscobel and cross the river, then head west along WI 60 toward the Mississippi. At the midpoint is flyspeck Wauzeka, site of the **Kickapoo Indian Caverns** tourist trap. Geologically significant for their size—larger than better-known caverns throughout southwestern Wisconsin—and historically significant for sheltering the eponymous Indian tribe, the onyx caverns weren't discovered until the 19th century and weren't really explored (other than by curious local kids, no doubt) until much later. The present-day cavern tour offers cool, dinosaur-esque pools and a crystalline-faced wall which would look quite stunning if it weren't for the gaudy lighting scheme ("Do you see a hamburger in that?" "No."). But the musty gift shop, cloying shtick, and not-their-fault over-worked guides can be a bit of a downer. At W200 Rhein Hollow Rd., tel. (608) 875-7723 (follow the signs, which you cannot miss). Open for tours mid-May-Labor Day, 9 a.m.-5 p.m., admission charged.

From Wauzeka, it's only about 10 miles west to Prairie du Chien and the Mississippi River. Prairie du Chien is covered in the "Great River Road" chapter.

THE OLD MILITARY ROAD

Essentially a cobbling together with logs of ancient Indian trails south of the Wisconsin River, the historic Old Military Road, the first overland link east to west in the state, constructed in 1835-36 by soldier labor, used to stretch as far as Prairie du Chien. Today, you're as likely to see recreational bicyclists along the route as you are cud-chewing bovines, as the Verona-Dodgeville Military Ridge State Trail covers the distance on an abandoned railroad bed.

MOUNT HOREB

The "Trollway," as the main drag in predominantly Norwegian Mt. Horeb is known, is reminiscent of a northern European mountain village. Predating statehood, Norwegian and Swiss (and a few Irish) farmers staked out the rolling ridges and valleys around these parts, and the town grew to be the largest community in the

area. The surrounding countryside, not to mention the main drag, shows a thoroughly northern European brick-and-frame architecture and not a few log structures and octagonal barns. It's also a node on the Military Ridge State Trail, and the ride from town to Blue Mound State Park is an enjoyable couple of hours.

Attractions

Mount Horeb may be a quaint conglomeration of Pippi Longstocking-esque architecture and summertime festivals, but it's also fast becoming known as the place where "mustard happens." At the not-nearly-famous-enough **Mt. Horeb Mustard Museum,** 109 E. Trollway, tel. (608) 437-3986, you're greeted at the door by cheery, delightfully irreverent hosts, their lapels exclaiming, "Just let us know if you need any condiment therapy." And all this because of one of those accursed, classic Boston Red Sox September Swoons—Bill Buckner's infamous boot of that

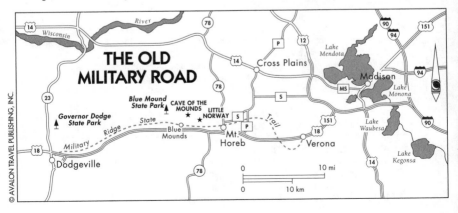

troll on the Trollway, Mount Horeb

World Series Game 6 groundball, snatching defeat from the jaws of victory for the hapless Bosox. Barry Levenson, a lawyer prior to that moment, became an apostate to the game. In a scene from a twisted *Field of Dreams,* Barry wandered into a late-night grocery store where the mustard jars were heard to say, "If you collect us, they will come." So he decamped to a small town in southwestern Wisconsin and opened this eccentric museum featuring the underappreciated spice. What better place to open a mustard museum than a state where bratwurst is king? All kidding aside, this is a serious place, with over 2,000 mustards on display. It's also the world's largest mustard retailer—400 to purchase and one hundred to sample. Ladysmith, WI's, own Royal Bohemian Triple Extra Hot Horseradish Mustard is the hottest. The museum has even sponsored National Mustard Day, heretofore known as August 5. One of the most enjoyable stops in southwestern Wisconsin, the Mustard Museum is a must-see. Always free, and open 10 a.m.-5 p.m. every day all year.

The **Mt. Horeb Area Historical Museum,** at the corner of Main and 2nd, tel. (608) 437-3645, is housed in the old municipal building. This 1918 home features a dozen rooms that regularly change themes. Open Fri.-Sun. 12:30-5 p.m. Memorial Day through Labor Day.

North and west of town along CR JG is **Tyrol Basin,** 3487 Bohn Rd., tel. (608) 437-4135, a

ski/snowboard area with 12 slopes, a maximum run of half a mile, a tame 300-foot vertical drop, rentals, instruction, snowmaking, and a tow rope and two triple chairlifts. It offers free beginner lessons and there's a halfpipe for gonzos. Open Dec.-March weekdays 10 a.m.-10 p.m., weekends from 9 a.m.

Mount Horeb hosts the **Wisconsin Old Time Scandinavian Fiddle Fest** at Tyrol Basin every July. Speaking of Scandinavians, there are more Scandinavian gift huts than trolls in this town. The largest is **Open House Imports,** 308 E. Main St., with an absolutely mind-boggling array of Scandinavian gifts including crystal, porcelains, gnomes, Bastad clogs, and Sølje jewelry.

Accommodations

The **Karakahl Inn,** 1405 US 18/151, tel. (608) 437-5545 is not your average Best Western. The buildings, constructed in the mid-1960s, were designed as a retreat for patients of famed chiropractor Clarence Gonstead. Shaped like a fierce Viking ship, it supposedly follows the dictums of Frank Lloyd Wright. Scandinavian fare is served in the restaurant, and the room decor is thoroughly modern. The inn offers an indoor pool and sauna. Rates from $59 s, $69 d.

Food

Folks in these parts really line up at **Schubert's,** tel. (608) 437-3393, across from the museum to mustard. Thick, chunky wood booths, original tin ceilings, and an old soda fountain make up the interior. Standard farm-country cafe breakfasts, lunches, and dinners are offered. Extra entrées feature Norwegian meatballs, roast pork, Swiss steak, corned beef and cabbage, catfish, ribs and kraut, and the occasional beef stew. Schubert's also has *limpa,* a Swedish rye bread, for which it is justifiably famous. There's a fish fry every Wednesday and Friday from 11 a.m. This is probably the most authentic small-town coffee-klatch eatery along Old Military Road. From $3.

Housed in an old cheese factory just across from the parking lot of the Military Ridge State Trail, the **Mount Horeb Pub and Brewery,** tel. (608) 437-4200, has a casual menu of good sandwiches and carnivore-based fare in a very pleasant atmosphere—especially when you've just ridden 25 miles on a bike! Open daily for lunch and dinner. From $4.

North out of Mount Horeb 10 miles along CR S and CR P is little Cross Plains, on US 14, and one of the state's great roadhouses—**Pott's Inn,** tel. (608) 798-1626. The bar offers basic food but is best known for a consistent array of live music in every genre imaginable. Regular Dixieland every other Sunday.

About the same distance to the southwest via US 18/151 and WI 78 in don't-blink-or-you'll-miss-it Daleyville is **Moen Creek Homestead,** CR JG, tel. (608) 437-4141. The Homestead features creative Midwestern cuisine—buffalo is not uncommon, and organic vegetables are grown on the grounds.

BLUE MOUNDS AREA

Three short miles west of Mount Horeb, the town, centered between three highlights on the Old Military Road, began as a tiny mining encampment. After an ungodly amount of lead was extracted from its ground, Blue Mounds became the site of a strategic U.S. Army fort, built to protect settlers.

Nissedahle

Transliterated, roughly, as "Valley of the Elves" (actually Nissedal, but better known as "Little Norway") and tucked into the rain shadow edge of big Blue Mound next to a bubbly spring, this outdoor living museum features over a dozen log buildings from a Norwegian homestead. The log cabin features a real sod roof, and the spring house, built atop the spring and acting as a refrigerator of sorts, displays a gorgeous triumvirate of cupolas. The massive Norway Building, a replica of a 12th-century Norway *stavkirke,* or stave church, replete with Cathay-esque steeples and dragon heads, relocated to Wisconsin from the World's Columbian Exposition of 1893. Antiques abound throughout the grounds, including the original manuscript of an Edvard Grieg musical composition dating from 1873, not to mention hand-carved skis, and intricate rosemaling. The interiors of the buildings house what is arguably the most exhaustive display of Norwegian-American culture in the United States. The site is open daily 9 a.m.-7 p.m. July-Aug.; 9 a.m.-5 p.m. in May-June and Sept. 1-late October. Tours depart regularly with costumed docents. Admission is $8, $7 seniors, $3 children 12 and under.

Blue Mound State Park

In the annals of his exploratory journeys down the lower Wisconsin River in 1776, Jonathan Carver detailed extensively the "mountains" due south of the river. This most salient upthrust of the surrounding hills can appear quite steely blue. The highest point in southern Wisconsin at 1,719 feet above sea level, Blue Mound doesn't exactly spur migratory peregrinations, but it does have a commanding view of some lush countryside. (And it's rumored to hold Native treasure.)

Note the singular Blue Mound park and the plural Blue Mounds town; no historical mistake, there are in fact two mounds—the shorter eastern twin is now Brigham County Park in Dane County. It too offers superlative ganders across the valleys, along with camping. Both are multi-layered candy drops of geology, capped by Niagara dolomite limestone.

Blue Mound had always been a landmark for Native Americans traversing the hills on their way to the northwest side of Madison's Lake Mendota (they were enamored of its vistas long before Carver—the Winnebago called it "High Place with Beautiful View"). The U.S. military appropriated the footpath for a section of the military road to Fort Winnebago in Portage, and after outliving its military purpose, the diminutive community of Pokerville sprouted up and built a half-oval racetrack (!) around the crown—today it's the road through the picnic area.

One of the extras at this park is a real swimming pool. For the more ambitious, a number of trails wind throughout the area. One short trail links the park to the Military Ridge State Trail, or you can hike east along the ridge to the short Walnut Hollow Trail, or the two-mile Pleasure Valley Trail—short but with a few challenging sections. Mountain bikers are allowed on the ridge trail, Walnut Hollow Trail, and Pleasant Valley Trail, which heads north to the John Minix Trail for a total of just over four miles. At the time of writing the park was building a trail specifically for mountain bikers.

The state park is of particular interest today as it's the only park in close proximity to the Military Ridge State Trail with camping—78 sites are available, more than half by reservation. Sites are $10, plus a daily entrance sticker.

Cave of the Mounds

Like the Blue Mound of Blue Mound State Park, Cave of the Mounds, tel. (608) 437-3038, is freakish, yet another residual of the eons-old cementation process. Acidic groundwater, ebbing through subterranean fissures, cleaned out soluble limestone but couldn't penetrate the thicker layers. Over time, a natural cave formed (another cave, Lost River Cave, exists near Blue Mound State Park).

The cave is an oddity in other ways as well. Though the area above the subterranean caverns was settled, mined, plowed, and grazed starting as far back as 1828 (making the homestead the oldest in the county), these caves weren't discovered until 1939 (blastings for a quarry created an entrance). It took until the 1980s for geologists to explore enough for the U.S. Department of the Interior to declare it a National Natural Landmark. It's better known as the "jewel box" of large caverns, neither as large nor as famous as others, but, as the Chicago Academy of Sciences called it, "the significant cave of the upper Midwest."

The tours feature the usual low stoops on cement walkways, the flashlight-in-the-face style lectures, zillions of stalactites and stalagmites, primeval pools, and the inevitable kaleidoscopic lighting techniques. The constant 50° is a wonderful heat-beater in summer. The farm grounds up top, with a few assorted gardens, now make for great walking and picnicking.

An annual event is the performance of the *Song of Norway,* a romantic musical tracing the life of Norwegian composer Edvard Grieg, performed on an outdoor stage.

The caverns are open for tours, at 15 minute intervals mid-March through mid-November, daily 9 a.m.-7 p.m. summers, until 5 p.m. the rest of the year. It's open weekends only in winter. Admission is $10 adults, $5 children 12 and under. The tour includes a slide presentation before setting out. It's located three miles west of Mount Horeb—you can't miss the signs.

DODGEVILLE

The name "Dodge" is big in these parts—all thanks to one man, Henry Dodge, second in omnipresence perhaps only to James Doty, the eventual judge and politico who wangled for Madison to become the state capital. A miner, Dodge became a leading figure in the Black Hawk War, which thrust him into regional prominence. Capitalizing on his fame, he was elected Wisconsin's first Territorial Governor. Dodgeville today is a small town of just under 4,000 people at a primary highway intersection, the crook of Highways 18 and 151. It's a bit somnolent but not forlorn—the downtown district has been touted for its careful balance of historic preservation. Dodgeville is one of the two largest communities, along with Platteville, between Madison and the Mississippi.

Sights

The second-largest state park in Wisconsin and definitely worth any recreation buff's time, massive 5,000-acre **Governor Dodge State Park,** lies north just a bit out of town via WI 23. Built around a homesteader's 160 acres and later, two man-made lakes, the park has just about everything a visitor could want, including some noticeable examples of Driftless Area terrain, particularly the bluff rises visible from throughout the trail system. Naturalist-led hikes are scheduled during summers, and this is also a favorite park for horse lovers—they've got 22 miles all to themselves. Otherwise, 35 miles of multipurpose trails wind throughout the woodlands, open meadows, and around the two lakes.

The easiest trail is the two-mile **White Pine Nature Trail,** beginning and ending at the Enee Point picnic area, with only a couple of steep scree-laden areas. The longest is the **Lost Canyon Trail,** an eight-miler starting at Cox Hollow beach and winding through woods and down into Lost Canyon, past waterfalls, and on to Twin Valley Lake. Two trails, totaling 10 miles, are also open to mountain biking. The longer is the seven-mile **Meadow Valley,** appropriately named for the terrain, with precious few wooded ridges. The shorter, three-mile **Mill Creek Trail** is more popular, mostly owing to the fact that it hooks up with the popular **Military Ridge State Trail.** Thirty-nine miles total from Dodgeville east to Verona, the trail passes through Barneveld, Blue Mound State Park, Blue Mounds, and Mt. Horeb, trailing the old Military Road. Between Dodgeville and Mt. Horeb, the trail skirts the top of Military Ridge, the watershed between the Wisconsin

River to the north and the Pecatonica and Rock Rivers to the south. The trail is wide and easy, with a two to five percent grade, and passes primarily through bucolic moo-cow ranges. But there're plenty of woods, prairies, wetlands, and the Sugar River Valley—and almost 50 bridges. One problem: no camping anywhere along the trail, but about halfway a short trail does lead to camping at Blue Mound State Park. Trail passes are required—$3 per day, or $10 per season, and are available anywhere along the trail.

Governor Dodge State Park has about a million campsites, many of them in quite impressive secluded sites. Six backpack sites are also available. Campsites are $10, plus a daily admission sticker.

Dodgeville is nationally known for one thing— **Land's End**, Land's End Lane, off King Street, north of US 18, tel. (608) 935-9053, one of the most popular mail-order outfits in the country. Tours departing the visitor's center are available Mon.-Fri. 8 a.m.- 5 p.m., Saturday 9 a.m.-2 p.m.; take in a video and a short tour of the facility.

The Museum of Minerals and Crystals, north on WI 23, tel. (608) 935-5205, also known as the Nature's Miracle Museum, has some 3,500 striking geologic specimens, including Smithsonian-quality fluorites, Mexican geodes, and calcite from the legendary Sweetwater Mine in Missouri. A popular sideshow is the black-light room—a peek at lots of bizarre geology under a fluorescent light; or, perhaps you'd enjoy the planet's only collection of faceted lead crystals, canary-yellow man-made lead alloy used for nuclear reactor windows. A look at the lovely mosaic of 1,000 stone pieces forming an image of legendary racehorse Man O' War is worth the price of admission. Open April 1-Nov. 15, daily 9 a.m.-5 p.m. Admission $4, $3.50 seniors, $3 ages 6 to 18. Horse rides are available at a stable also on site—guided one- and two-hour rides through Governor Dodge State Park depart hourly April 1-Nov. 15.

A free gander at the residual of Dodgeville's lead-mining days, the **first slag furnace**, sits along East Spring Street, next to the lumber yard. Extra lead was extracted from molten waste rock, and according to period reports the glow could be seen for miles.

The Greek Revival limestone courthouse, the oldest in the state, is open to self-guided walking tours during business hours.

Outside of Dodgeville west on US 18, then north on WI 80 to Highland brings you to the **Spurgeon Vineyards and Winery,** 16008 Pine Tree Rd., tel. (608) 929-7692, where sixteen acres of vines are turned into award-winning reds and whites. Winery tours and free tastings are available. Open April-Oct. 10 a.m.-5 p.m. daily; rest of year on weekends only.

Accommodations

It would be nearly impossible to miss the regionally famous **Don Q Inn,** WI 23 N, tel. (608) 935-2321 or (800) 666-7848, one of Wisconsin's most "distinctive" lodging options. You can't miss the landmark C-97 Boeing Stratocruiser parked out front. How about the trademarked "FantaSuites": Caesar's Court, Tranquility Base moon landing, and a hot-air balloon gondola are the wilder ones. Some rooms are the real thing— the original, the Steeple, is an 1872 church steeple; the erstwhile Dodgeville Station of the Chicago and Northwestern Railway now also houses several rooms. The pool is half indoor, half outdoor and truly one of a kind. The restaurant is built into an old local barn crammed full of relics from the past century. The stained glass, originally pulled from Deusenberg cars, is the work of a local artisan, and the tables were handmade by local craftsmen. All this can be yours for the kitsch-worthy price of $55 per night and up.

For **camping,** head immediately to Governor Dodge State Park, and if it's full (unlikely, unless it's a holiday weekend), drive north to Spring Green and Tower Hill. Still nothing? One private campground, **Hide-A-Way Acres,** tel. (608) 935-5019, is adjacent to Governor Dodge. There is also **Tom's Campground,** 2751 CR BB, tel. (608) 935-5446, with a separate tenting area and a rustic stone cottage available for rental.

In the opposite direction, west along US 18 for 10 miles and then north for seven more along WI 80 and CR BH you'll find **Blackhawk Lake Recreation Area,** 2025 CR BH, tel. (608) 623-2707, a large campground of open and wooded sites on a 600-acre lake. Fishing is prime here, though a 300-foot beach also makes swimming popular. Occasional naturalist films, talks, and hikes departing the small nature center are offered. Of the 123 sites, 67 are reservable.

The **Folklore Village Farm Hostel,** 3210 CR BB, six miles east of downtown Dodgeville off US

18/151, tel. (608) 924-4000, is a farmland experience of fiddle, accordion, and the rural life. Almost 100 acres, the farm features a huge activities center (it's the best wedding site in southwestern Wisconsin), an 1893 school, a one-room church, old Danish and Swedish bunkhouses, and a farmhouse. Myriad workshops or events in dance, music, material arts, and foods are offered—including a great weekly community potluck dinner. As part of the farm, American Youth Hostels offers accommodations. Bunkhouse beds costs $10, and linen rentals are available. Reservations are essential.

Food

For a supper club, it's **Thym's,** north a mile on WI 23, tel. (608) 935-3344, offering kitchen-cut steaks and the usual assortment of other meats and seafood—try the hickory-smoked pork chops—plus some pastas. Open for lunch and dinner weekdays, dinner only Saturday, and brunch and dinner on Sunday. From $6.

The dining room of the **Don Q Inn** is also popular, serving entrées such as seafood Alfredo, rack of ribs, roast duck, or even Chateaubriand. From $6.

Directly across from the Iowa County Courthouse is the **Courthouse Inn,** tel. (608) 935-3663, with one of the largest menus in town for lunch and dinner. There's a whole page devoted to sandwiches—hot beef, turkey club, or hot meatloaf—and a handful of dinner platters, including liver and onions. Breakfast is served all day. From $5.

For dessert, try the only old-fashioned **soda fountain** in the county, at the Corner Drug Store. Up the street, the **Quality Bakery** has Cornish pasties and saffron buns. From $3 for both.

Shopping

Of all the antique shops in the region, **Carousel Collectibles and Antiques,** 121 N. Iowa St., tel. (608) 935-5196, may be the farthest gone into its own world. The specialty of the house is carousel art, from antique carousel woods to new, five-foot-high carousel horses, and tons of carousel gift items. Proprietors also do carousel restoration.

Information

Located along WI 23, north of US 18/151 a bit, you'll find the **visitor center** side-by-side with the Iowa County Historical Society Museum, both open seasonally, daily May 1-Oct. 31.

The **Dodgeville Chamber of Commerce,** 178 N. Iowa St., tel. (608) 935-5993 or (877) 863-6343, www.dodgeville.com, is open approximately the same times.

THE LEAD ZONE

And there's gold in them thar hills. Well, not precisely "Au", but wealth of a sort. The hills around these parts were the first reason—the *real* reason—any white interloper who wasn't seasonal or a soldier stayed for long. Natives had been scavenging lead deposits in the area—so rife that lead littered the topsoil. The earliest European to cash in on the ready-made ore, Nicholas Perrot, started bartering with the Natives around 1690. A century later perceptive homesteaders quickly turned mining-opportunists and wound up as the first "Badgers." Mines were hewn into the sides of hills every which way one looked. Accidentally forming the first cohesive region in the state, these early pioneers solidified an economy of sorts and in many respects got the state on its feet.

The results were staggering—the War of 1812 had precluded any large-scale operations, but the region still poured forth a half million pounds of lead prior to U.S. appropriation of the Northwest Territory following the war. Only 200 intrepid miners populated the region when the federal government began to stick it to the Fox, Sauk, and Miami Indians. By 1830 that number had grown to almost 10,000. Some 350 mining permits were granted annually, and 52 smelters were in operation—and this predated any treaties with the Fox or Sauk. It's no surprise, then, that these once fierce protectors of the French lead mines suddenly felt they had been cheated and no longer agreed to cooperate. The resulting Black Hawk Wars flared on and off until the U.S. Army slaughtered Black Hawk's band at the Battle of Bad Axe near Prairie du Chien.

Settlers then began to pour in. The population of the lead region jumped to over 15,000 by 1833. By the 1840s, the area was the U.S.'s leading lead producer. All from what was by then known as the Upper Mississippi Valley Lead-Zinc District. By the mid-1840s railroads had stretched far enough to transport cheaper lead from other areas, and the mining petered out. An atavistic boom in zinc would recharge some mining but, by that point, agriculture—fueled by an influx of Swiss and German settlers in the mid-1800s—supplanted ore extraction as the primary industry. The territory became a leading wheat producer until an epidemic of cinch bug closed out the crop. The Swiss and Germans, along with Irish and Yankee settlers, helped the area bounce back with the dairy industry.

MINERAL POINT

Only 2,400 friendly souls, yet what a huge place Mineral Point really is, in many ways the heart and soul of the state's heritage. The name was no fluke—ore fever coursed through the region when a prospector discovered huge deposits under Mineral Point Hill. Hordes of Cornish immigrants took right to the hills. Tirelessly scratching into the hillsides, they even scraped gouges into the bluffsides where they could rest and escape the elements. Many thus believe Mineral Point to be the origin of the nickname "badger," as these ubiquitous holes and the miners in them were dubbed.

Soon the heart of the region, it was in Mineral Point that the Territory of Wisconsin was established on July 4, 1836. Elected governor Henry Dodge maintained the political and economic spheres of the territory from temporary offices while Madison was being built. A second mining boom hit in the 1870s, when "dry-bone," or zinc carbonate, once tossed aside by lead miners, was found to be metal-rich. The railroads rolled through, and Mineral Point soon had the largest zinc operation in the U.S.; it persisted (more or less) through 1979, when the last mine closed down after 150 years.

Over 500 structures in this small town still stand on 1837 plattings. Most buildings contain locally quarried limestone and feature Cornish designs, and all date from the century after 1830. The main drag, High Street, is undergoing an extensive and careful facelift. The town's gemlike status has impelled a renaissance of sorts, with benign hordes of artisans relocating to Mineral Point and setting up studios, shops, and galleries. ("Art" or "gallery" or "antiques" is affixed to absolutely everything; don't be surprised to see "bar-antiques.")

The pervasiveness of "shake rag" this and "shake rag" that stems from a Cornish tradition. At noontime, wives summoned their husbands home from the mines by waving dishcloths. The name stuck.

Sights

Pendarvis and the Merry Christmas Mine, 114 Shake Rag St., tel. (608) 987-2122, is judged by many as the most thorough and best preserved view of the region's mining heritage. While the rest of this historic district was being demolished in the 1930s for scavenged building blocks, a foresighted local purchased some of the rundown Cornish cottages and set to renovating. Pendarvis operated for decades as a reputable Cornish eatery before being donated to the State Historical Society in 1970. Quite small actually, the complex has a long three-unit rowhouse, the oft-photographed Polperro House, and stone-and-

log cottages (six structures in all), linked together by narrow stone paths through gardens.

Even better might be the stroll up, over, and through Mineral Point Hill and the Merry Christmas Mine on a set of trails snaking up from the back of the parking lot. Miners took 80 years to get around to this side of the hill, firing up the lanterns about 1906 and mining for seven years in the largest zinc operation in the area. Assorted hulks of rusting equipment and over 100 abandoned crevice shafts dot the 43 acres. Native prairie restoration is ongoing, and big bluestem is already blooming again.

The complex is open May-November. Guided tours led by garbed docents depart regularly (schedule varies) daily 9 a.m.-5 p.m., last tickets sales at 4 p.m. Admission is $7.50 adults, $3.50 children 3-12, and $6.75 seniors.

Up Shake Rag Street from Pendarvis is another group of stone and stone-and-log dwellings

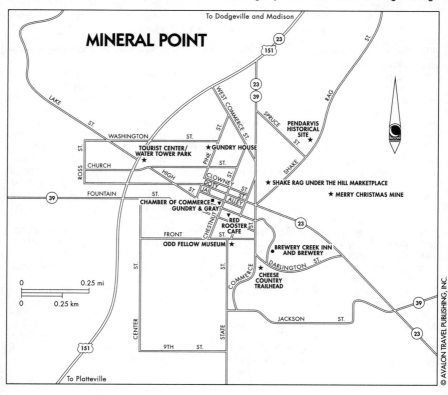

originally put up by Cornish immigrants in the 1830s—**Shake Rag Under the Hill Marketplace,** tel. (608) 987-3499, self-titled as "a traditional marketplace" and organized atop a site settled by Cornish potters, weavers, and other artisans 150 years ago (even Wisconsin's first pottery). Seven historic structures, including one of the oldest log cabins in the state, are surrounded by tailored gardens. Inside, artisans and crafters display and sell their wares—linens, pottery, jewelry, and more. You can even stay the night on the three acres on one of three B&B rooms and a cottage. Open daily May-Oct., weekends through December.

Two blocks east of the tourist information center is the **Gundry House,** 234 Madison St., tel. (608) 987-3670, a cut sandstone and limestone Victorian built in 1867 by prominent local merchant, Joseph Gundry, notable because his business featured the local-legend "Pointer Dog" statue. Otherwise, it's an impressive home with period furnishings, offering tours Thurs.-Sun. 1-5 p.m. May-Nov. for an admission fee.

Not many get around to the 1838 **Wisconsin Odd Fellow Museum,** Front and State Streets, tel. (608) 987-3093, the first Odd Fellow Hall west of the Allegheny Mountains. Built and dedicated by Thomas Wildey, founder of the Order, it's the only hall dedicated by him and still standing. The large building includes quite a bit of furniture extracted from other lodges, including the Noble Grands Chair from an Iowa Lodge. Open June-Labor Day, 9 a.m.-5 p.m. by appointment. Free.

If you're up for a road-trip, 13 miles east of town is Hollandale, a mile west of which along WI 39 is **Grandview,** the erstwhile home of folk artist Nick Engelbert. Engelbert, an immigrant dairy farmer turned self-taught artist, in the 1930s began to transform his artistic visions into concrete, glass, and stone and scattered them throughout the gardens around his farm. It's a great mini-trip and a splendid look at rural folk art.

Tours
View the anachronisms of Mineral Point via horse-drawn buggy from **Byrne Livery,** tel. (608) 987-2692. The main, narrated trip takes in Shake Rag Street, with a stop at Shake Rag under the Hill, Pendarvis, Walker Hotel, and the downtown district. Tours are generally offered in summer 10

a.m.-4 p.m. or by appointment. The short tour is generally $7, a longer option around $11, half price for children under 10.

Accommodations
There's just one non-B&B or historic inn accommodation in town. The **Redwood Motel,** US 151 North, tel. (608) 987-2317 or (800) 321-1958, has distinctive exteriors (that look more Swiss than anything), along with tastefully done rooms from around $35 s, $45 d, and also a restaurant.

The town's newest lodging is the **Brewery Creek Inn,** tel. (608) 987-3298, built in a 145-year-old stone warehouse. Some rooms have whirlpools and/or fireplaces. Rates from $95. The complex also has a brewpub and popular restaurant. Speaking of brewing, the **House of the Braumeister,** tel. (608) 987-2913, once housed the chief brewmaster of a local brewery. The 1900 Queen Anne has golden oak woodwork and lovely beveled leaded glass windows. Rates from $65.

Right into the cliffsides surrounding town and hewn from limestone blocks, the **Walker House,** No. 1 Water St., tel. (608) 987-3794, has original fixtures in the Cornish Miner's Pub—oak beams and stone caves. Surviving since 1836, it's the oldest operating hotel and restaurant in Wisconsin, today offering a *prix fixe* six-course dinner Thurs.-Sat. nights. Reservations are required. Beware: rumors persist that the spirit of a convicted murderer haunts the premises.

The closest public **campground** is found at Governor Dodge State Park in Dodgeville. East and south of Mineral Point along CR S and CR D you'll find **Shady Acres,** tel. (608) 776-2565. Ten minutes past that along CR D and CR F is **Yellowstone Lake State Park,** a modest state park with 128 campsites, showers, a good fishing lake, and eight miles of hiking trails. A wildlife reserve is also part of this 2600-acre park. Sites cost $8, plus a daily park sticker.

Food
Better get used to hearing *figgyhobbin* (alternately *figgihobbin*), because you'll see the word incessantly. Yes, it is of course a Cornish dish, and no, it isn't the roast beast the name connotes. It's actually a pastry of raisins and walnuts, and it's quite rich. Other Cornish food

might include saffron cakes, Mawgan meatballs, and pasty.

See above for the popular brewpub and restaurant at the **Brewery Creek B&B.** Once a county bank, the **Red Rooster Cafe,** 158 High St., tel. (608) 987-9936, is a one-of-a-kind roadfood-quality eatery where diners sit at a horseshoe-shaped counter on old red vinyl and chrome swivel chairs underneath a coffered ceiling. The menu features pasties, and a whole lot of standard cafe fare, but enough non-standard items to make it worth your while. Open daily from 5 a.m., weekends from 7 a.m., until 5 p.m. From $3. Slightly more modern and a bit more gourmet on the sandwich side—also with great coffee—is **Gundry and Gray,** 215 High St.; open daily 10 a.m.-7 p.m., it's got great comfy chairs and a pleasant atmosphere—great for relaxing after strolling through all those antique shops. From $3.

And that's it. Mineral Point in previous years had two excellent gourmet restaurants, but at research time, both had closed. (One was being renovated into another B&B and, possibly, restaurant.) A pub and steakhouse was scheduled to open after this book was published.

Entertainment

The **Mineral Point Opera House,** 139 High St., tel. (608) 987-2642, features a slate of live performances, mostly folk, during its May-Oct. season. The **Mineral Point Theatre,** once a major stop on the Midwest theater tour, now shows movies on weekends, as well as occasional theatrical presentations by the local Shake Rag Players and some traveling shows. Renovations are planned and more live events are proposed for the future.

Shopping

Get ready to unshackle the calfhide. Ever since some pioneering artisans discovered the tasteful architecture and low-key small-town tranquility in the '40s, Mineral Point has been a hotbed for Wisconsin artisans. Over 40 galleries and studios populate the town, and more seem to spring open annually. One weekend each October southern Wisconsin artisans open their studio doors for back-room views of the artistic process; Spring Green and Baraboo participate, but Mineral Point is the place to start any tour. The three-day festival is a great combination of art and halcyon autumn.

The most prominent group, the **Jail Alley Shops,** is a row of 1840s structures constructed mostly by municipal employees. There is no jail, at least not any more; the courthouse and subsumed jail sat where the Mineral Point Civic Center and Theatre now stand.

Johnston Gallery, 245 High St., tel. (608) 987-3787, showcases the works of over 120 artists. Open daily 10 a.m.-5 p.m. all year.

For antiques, try **Livery Antiques,** 303 Commerce St., tel. (608) 987-3833, a group mall with 15 dealers represented. You can find tramp art to quilts to toys and more. You want it, they'll find it.

Services and Information

The **Mineral Point Chamber of Commerce** maintains a little cabin/cottage in Water Tower Park, right along US 151, open 9 a.m. to 5 p.m. during summer. Alternately, stop by the office itself right at 237 High St., tel. (608) 987-3201, where the eternally solicitous staff will chat you up and give you the lowdown.

PLATTEVILLE

The name doesn't exactly flow like honey, does it? Ask a Wisconsinite and Platteville won't make the short list of charming cities. Which isn't to demean the underrated town—it is as pleasant as any hilly, agrarian town you'll find. But it is overlooked by most, except those historically bent travelers who know it for what it is.

It began as Platte River Diggings. The earliest Caucasian to show interest in the lead was Emmanuel Metcalf, a trapper who found a store of lead in an animal den. The progenitor proper of the town, Major John Rountree, arrived and purchased the load in 1827 and had the hilly patterns of the new town configured after Yorkshire, where the planner was from. The christening name—Platteville—was inspired by the long, gray, end-result "bowls" of the lead smelting process practiced by the Native Americans. While the lead lasted it turned Platteville into "the present metropolis of the lead industry," as the old guidebooks referred to it. As the nucleus for the tri-state mining industry, it became home to the country's first mining college—immortalized by the world's largest "M" east of town atop Platteville Mound. At 214 by 241 feet, the letter dominates the slope and is illuminated twice annually by UW-Platteville students.

Attractions

The most exhaustive examination of the lead and zinc industry in the region is found at the **Bevans Lead and Mining Museum,** 385 E. Main St., tel. (608) 348-3301. Dating from 1845, the Bevans mine was the regional golden goose, as it were, pushing out two million pounds per year. Guided tours include a walk 50 feet into the clammy mine, then into the shafts for simulations of the mining process. A return to the top includes nifty displays, dioramas, and artifacts, not excluding the Native Americans' contributions to the industry. Top it all off with a hop aboard a genuine 1931 mine locomotive for a chug around the grounds, perhaps to the contiguous **Rollo Jamison Museum,** best described

as a world-class junk collection with a keen eye on history. Jamison was a lifelong pack rat who amassed some 20,000 various pre-1900 items, all centered on the idea of practical application in people's lives. Keep in mind that the detailed exhibits of carriages and tools, and the general store, kitchen, and parlor mock-ups are the work of a single man. The top floor of the Jamison Museum features the Rountree Gallery, displaying the work of area artists. These museums are open May-Oct. daily 9 a.m.-5 p.m., weekdays 9 a.m.-4 p.m. the rest of the year. Admission is $4 adults, $3.50 seniors, $2 children and includes entrance to both museums. The changing exhibit galleries are open at no cost Nov.-April.

Mitchell-Rountree Stone Cottage, at the corner of Lancaster and Ann Streets, is the oldest surviving homestead in Platteville, and one of the oldest in the state. Built in 1837 by Rev. Sam

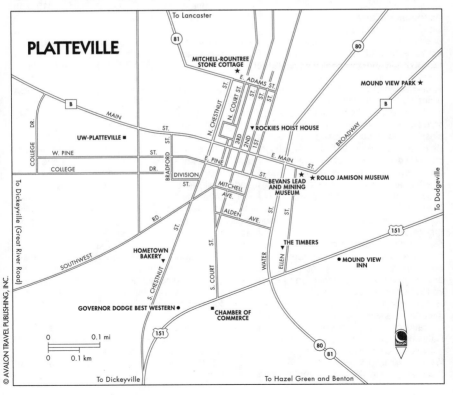

Mitchell, a local veteran of the Revolutionary War, and distinctively constructed after the Tidewater Virginia style, replete with dormer windows, it is made of two-foot-thick locally quarried dolomite Galena limestone. Free guided tours are given daily Memorial Day-Labor Day.

The University of Wisconsin-Platteville, the first normal school in Wisconsin, and its Center for the Arts hold theatrical performances. The theater, an exact duplicate of London's Cottlesloe Theatre in the National, adds atmosphere. Call the center, tel. (608) 342-1298, for details.

The town goes absolutely bonkers come mid-summer when the behemoth Chicago Bears, hated enemies of the beloved Pack, show up in July or August for the summertime Cheese League **training camp** at UW-Platteville. Call the chamber of commerce for exact dates and times.

Accommodations

Coming from Madison along US 151, the most practical lodging option is also the most economical—**Mound View Inn,** right along US 151, tel. (608) 348-9518, with rates from $40 s or $50 d. The inn offers very spacious, well-kept, and attractive rooms for the money; some hot tub and whirlpool suites are available.

The most logical option for anyone spending time on the UW-Platteville campus would be the close-by **Governor Dodge Best Western,** tel. (608) 348-2301 or (800) 528-1234, a huge complex with decent rooms at $55 s, $72 d. It also offers a heated indoor pool, whirlpool and sauna.

A true and significant slice of history is found at Platteville's **Walnut Ridge,** 2238 CR A, tel. (608) 348-9359. These three meticulously restored buildings date from the very beginnings of the lead era, including an 1839 miners' bunkhouse relocated from British Hollow, now a bungalow; and an immigrant family's house-barn for a kitchen. Not the usual motley arrangement of mismatched antiques—here you'll sleep in real, believe it or not, rope beds, and bathe in tin bathtubs. A country-style shop on the premises sells country antiques, dried flowers, and other rustic influences for the home. Rates here run $130.

Platteville allows camping downtown—more or less—at **Mound View Park,** at the corner of Madison St. and CR B. Contact the police department, tel. (608) 348-2313, to verify this before staking out. Electricity and showers are available, and a pool is nearby. The park may or may not allow tent campers. Otherwise, the closest public campground is the **Grant River Recreation Area** (see "Potosi," in the "Great River Road" chapter).

Food

Get a quick bite at the bakery-cum-cafe **Hometown Bakery,** featuring a small dining area for deli salads, fresh sandwiches, tons of Shullsburg, WI cheese, and homemade soup in bread bowls. At 615 Chestnut St. on top of the hill behind McDonald's. Open from 5 a.m. Mon.-Sat., 7 a.m. Sunday. Drive-through is also available. From $3.

Try the "Wun-Doe-Burger," and other assorted pub grub at the lunch joint **Rockies Hoist House,** 90 N. 2nd St., tel. (608) 348-7819, with live entertainment weekly. From $4.

Travel around southwestern Wisconsin and you'll notice there's no German food. The notable exception is **Arthur Haus,** nine miles north of Platteville at 9315 WI 80, tel. (608) 348-7899, featuring a copious spread of German essentials. Open Wed.-Sat. 5-10 p.m., Sunday brunch and dinner. From $8.

Hands down the best restaurant in Platteville, and some say the region, **The Timbers,** 670 Ellen St., tel. (608) 348-2406, is a redwood-and-stone structure ensconced in a grove overlooking a small dale. Cuisine-wise, it has one of the most extensive menus in the state—over 100 well-prepared entrées covering a broad spectrum of tastes, including vegetarian. Even greater attention is paid to the centerpiece theater pipe organ, a truly grandiose opulent thing, supposedly the largest ever built—come in Saturday night for a performance. The club's noteworthy chef garnered acclaim, taking home the culinary equivalent of the Vince Lombardi Trophy—his Cornish pasty was judged the best in Wisconsin. Open daily for lunch and dinner, and Sunday for brunch. From $4 lunch, $10 dinner.

Services and Information

The **Platteville Chamber of Commerce,** tel. (608) 348-8888, www.platteville.com, is at 275 US 151 N. and maintains a visitors information center, open weekdays 9 a.m.-5 p.m.

PLATTEVILLE VICINITY

Belmont

Don't blink or you'll whiz right past what is likely Wisconsin's smallest state park—**First Capitol Historic Park,** located seven miles east of Platteville along County Roads B and G. The glad-handing politics of pork were alive and well in Wisconsin long before it was even a state. The powers that be finagled microscopic Belmont into accepting territorial-capital status, even though it appears that most of the early leaders had no intention of keeping it here. The status lasted one short 45-day session in 1836, but they managed to push through 42 bills. Folks in 19th-century Wisconsin often kept animals inside for warmth, and the government here was no exception. The hogs, chickens, and cows that stunk up the overhead gallery in the original building are long gone now (legislators would stir up the piggies below with long poles when things weren't going their way), as is the edifice. Two buildings do remain and are now restored and feature small exhibits on early 19th-century Wisconsin and a diorama of the first Capitol. Free, it's open summers daily 10 a.m.- 4 p.m., tel. (608) 987-2122.

Up the road a half mile is the **Belmont Mound State Park,** a day-use park with some trails leading to the mound itself. The mound was used by the first legislators as a landmark while traversing the prairies to find Belmont, no doubt wondering the entire way what in the hell they were doing there in the first place.

Shullsburg

This Tinytown with the inspirational street names of Charity, Friendship, Justice, Mercy, Hope, and Judgment (and the inexplicable Cyclops), Shullsburg was founded by a trader and platted by a priest. The city still has a 19th-century feel, with four dozen or so museum piece—mostly Vernacular—buildings along its Water Street Commercial Historic District, built mostly between 1840 and the turn of the 20th century. Hopefully, tactless gentrification and clapboard fakeries won't run amok to despoil this town's tourism potential.

Back in the 1820s, a group of brothers established the Badger Lot Diggings, hand-dug and worked by Cornish miners for 30 years before petering out. It has since been converted into a walk-through museum of mining life known as the **Badger Mine.** Tours descend the same 51 steps the miners took into the ore shafts, extending some quarter-mile into the hillsides—you're left on your own if you wish, unheard of in these litigious times. Other lead mines exist and are open to the public, but none this extensive. The museum features replicas of the mining camp, and the odd Civil War-era piano lies about; keep an eye open for Jefferson Davis' John Hancock on the old Brewster Hotel register book. Open Memorial Day-Labor Day, daily 10 a.m.-4 p.m., admission is $4 adults, $2.50 children above 6. Outside of town to the south is Gravity Hill, a supernaturally charged hill where cars drift backwards up a hill, or so it appears. Ask for directions in town.

The best grub in town is found at **The Brewster Cafe,** 208 W. Water St., just off WI 11, tel. (608) 965-4485. Renovations to the 1880s creamery have been finished and the gem of a cafe also has a sister-operation cheese store. Pasties supplement the cafe fare. It's open Sun.-Thurs. 8 a.m.-10 p.m., Friday and Saturday until 11 p.m. From $3. The Badger Mine has its old sign, bullet-riddled in a holdup gone shoot-em-up. The food is well prepared and the atmosphere is the real thing. And an old-fashioned **soda fountain** is at the local drug store.

Benton

In this former mining hub once named Cottonwood Hill, all that's left are the tailing piles. Benton is the final resting spot of Friar Samuel Mazzuchelli, the intrepid priest and architectural maven who designed two dozen of the regional buildings and communities (and gave Shullsburg its sweet street names), buried in St. Patrick Church cemetery. The church itself was the first stone structure in the area, and Mazzuchelli's restored home is on the church grounds; ask at the new rectory for tour details. Mazzuchelli's 1844 masterpiece, the church of St. Augustine, is in New Diggings, about five miles southeast, the priest's last still-intact wood structure. The weathered wood of the church gives it an almost ethereal quality. Only one mass a year is held here on the last Sunday of September at 2:30 p.m. Otherwise, it's open Sundays 1-4 p.m. late May-late September. If religious peregrination doesn't compel you, the New Diggings Inn

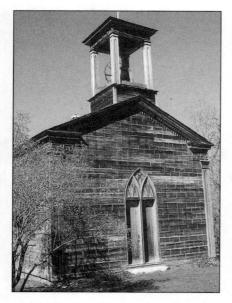

the 19th-century church of Father Samuel Mazzuchelli

has occasional weekend hootenannies.

Travelers in Benton might be more interested in the ugly shenanigans that went along with the mining; learn about them at the truthfully named **Swindler's Ridge Museum,** named after a nearby bluff notorious for thievery. The complex features three museums in the original mining complex; two mines are now restored as working models of sorts. An 1851 schoolhouse full of Civil War-era stuff is also on the site, as is Father Mazzuchelli's original rectory. Open Memorial Day-Labor Day, Fri.-Mon. 10 a.m.-4 p.m., admission by donation.

Hazel Green

They should have called this place "Point of Beginning," since that's exactly what it was. In 1831, a U.S. land commissioner sank a post and constructed a mound around its intersection with the 4th Meridian. Every single piece of surveyed land in the state of Wisconsin is referenced from this point. It's marked along WI 80, south of town. (Actually, it's more of a sweaty, half-hour trudge to find the damn thing.) Wisconsin's only disputed non-natural border (Wisconsin has

three short, arbitrary border segments—one with each neighboring state) was the segment near Hazel Green separating Illinois from what was then Michigan Territory.

More colorful is the story of the naming of the town. An 1820s feud between two rival miners prompted its first name, "Hardy's Scrape," which didn't seem to please the denizens of the town too much—they changed it to "Hard Scrabble." Still no go, so in 1838 with official incorporation, a more mellifluous name was chosen, and there went all the fun.

About the only thing to do in Hazel Green is head down to the **Opera House and Old Town Hall,** 2130 N. Main St., on the National Register of Historic Places and featuring an ice cream and antique shop. Stroll through the auditorium, which was the original stage and has a new hand-painted curtain. Open daily 1-9 p.m.

Equally historic are two cozy B&Bs—the wonderfully original 1846 **Wisconsin House Stage Coach Inn,** 2105 Main St., tel. (608) 854-2233, a multi-level abode framed in native oak with clapboard siding and six over six windows, and **DeWinters of Hazel Green,** 22nd at Main St., tel. (608) 854-2768. Both have rates starting around $55. The Wisconsin House Inn, lore has it, was the only thing left standing after an 1876 tornado leveled everything else in the village; it's also a fine fixed-price-menu eatery for dinners on Saturday.

Darlington

Approximately 16 miles southeast of Platteville, this impeccably preserved anachronism along the Pecatonica River features wide streets and a host of extant preserved architecture. The **Lafayette County Courthouse,** 627 Washington St., is the only courthouse in the U.S. built using the funds of a solitary individual. And, foot for foot, there is arguably more mural space in this courthouse than any other in the state. A few blocks away is the **Lafayette County Historical Museum,** with model trains, railroad history, and some interesting pearling displays. Open Memorial Day-Labor Day.

Nine miles north of Darlington is the **Prairie Springs Hotel,** one of the earliest buildings in the region. It's one of the most unusual, well built in the southern vernacular style by an early miner turned soldier and local leader. It's currently being restored.

SWISS VALLEY

South of Madison through Verona along WI 69 you'll find Green County, which might as well be called "Little Switzerland" for its preponderance of Swiss heritage. The Swiss culture shows itself most prominently in New Glarus, an amazing alpine village seemingly forgotten by time. In Monroe, farther south, world-famous Swiss cheese is created thanks to a sub-strata of limestone-soil laying under the local landscape, allowing a certain digestive process by which cows produce creamy gold, the necessary first ingredient for Swiss cheese.

In the '30s, Monroe cheesemaking had grown so prodigious that a postmaster in Iowa grew weary of the waftings of ripe Monroe Limburger passing through his tiny post office. The Depression-era WPA guide captured the moment:

[C]heese was stoutly defended when Monroe's postmaster engaged in a sniffing duel with a postmaster in Iowa to determine whether or not the odor of Limburger in transit was a fragrance or a stench. Well publicized by the press of the Nation, the duel ended when a decision was reached which held that Limburger merely exercised its constitutional right to hold its own against all comers.

Paoli

Before reaching Green County, you pass through some ready-made Sunday drive country and charming towns, including the quaintest of them all, Paoli. Known mostly for its somnolent waterside small-town appeal, and now, due to its renovated, grand 1864 Paoli Mill, full of shops. Next door is an outstanding gallery of 125 Midwest artisans working in virtually every medium. Even if artistry isn't your thing, the assortment's insight into regional arts and crafts is worth a look. At 6858 Paoli Rd., tel. (608) 845-6600.

NEW GLARUS

In 1845, a group of 190 Swiss left the Canton of Glarus during an economically devastating period. Scouts dispatched earlier had quite literally stumbled into southwestern Wisconsin and marveled at its similarities to Switzerland—nestled in the crook of a short but steep valley, with a natural rise in the center. The settlers suffered the usual travails of any group pushing out across a country with horses and wagons, beginning with the disappearance of the two guides who were to lead them to the site. Disheartened after waiting some time, some members of the group returned to Switzerland. Others simply mixed into the toiling immigrant labor forces of the East Coast. By the time the guides reappeared, the number of Swiss settlers had dropped to almost 100. Arriving just before fall, the group lived together in a rough shelter until temporary lodgings could be hacked from the wilds. The Swiss farmers attempted to follow the instructions of other Wisconsin farmers and grow wheat, but were unaccustomed to growing the grain and, returning to dairy, they soon began to pique interest in the east for their trademark cheeses.

New Glarus today is a cute, Swiss-looking town carved into a small rise off the main highway. Its living anachronism status—full of white-and-brown architecture, umlauts and scrolled Swiss-German sayings, gift shops every 10 feet, a Swiss festival what seems like biweekly, and Swiss music piped throughout the village—sounds dangerously close to tacky tourist trap. Fear not—it's done with class.

Attractions

One word can fully encapsulate this town. Festivals. Celebratory shindigs feting the Swiss heritage are held continually. The big draw is the **Wilhelm Tell Pageant,** held on Labor Day since 1938. Virtually the whole town puts on the *lederhosen*—half of the town in the grandiloquent play of Swiss independence that nobody in the other half can understand but enjoys nonetheless. It's quite something to see hundreds of New Glarus residents in costume running through the woods and across the fields. (English versions are also performed.) The real Independence Day, or *Volksfest,* is celebrated with another festival, this one on the first Sunday in August. Swiss consular officials and other dignitaries often make happy appearances. The best act was the young children's yodeling choir; this is a long-lost art recently brought back by local schools. June features a first-week **Polkafest**, a real hoot; and another popular drama during the **Heidi Festival**, on the last full weekend of the month. Winter's most popular event is the **Winter Festival**, and, of course, an obligatory **Oktoberfest** goes down in early October. Most of the festivals feature arts and crafts fairs, street dances, polkafests, Swiss flag throwing (don't ask), yodeling (of course), *thalerschwingen* (let the locals tell you),

or any combination of the above. Figure $5-8 for tickets to most events.

Up the hillsides you'll find 13 buildings comprising the **Swiss Village Museum**, 612 7th Ave., tel. (608) 527-2317, centered around flower gardens and an educational exhibit detailing the Swiss immigrant movement to New Glarus. Buildings include a one-room log cabin, a *Käserei* (cheesemaker), *Schmiede* (blacksmith shop), *Wehr Haus* (fire house), *Krämerei* (general store), and a *Druckerei* (print shop). One of the newest outbuildings is a Swiss-style bee

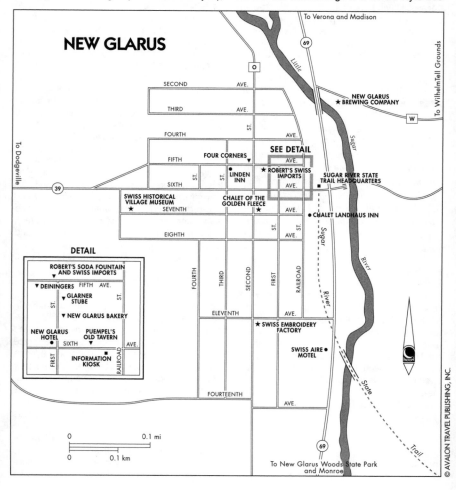

house, and sausage and smokehouse. Period demonstrations from cheesemaking to quilting are offered, and local schoolchildren sometimes attend class in the old schoolhouse. A display on the Glarner industries of Sap Sago cheese, slate, and fabrics was donated from Glarus, Switzerland. Tours are guided by local residents and given daily May 1-Oct. 31, 9 a.m.-4:30 p.m. Admission is $6, $2 ages 12 and under.

The **Chalet of the Golden Fleece,** 618 2nd St., tel. (608) 527-2614, is a Bernese Mountain-style chalet built in 1938 by Edwin Barlow, the founder of the village's *Wilhelm Tell* tradition. Within the three creakingly full floors are a huge assortment of European and immigrant everything-but-the-kitchen-sink, featuring noteworthy artifacts like Gregorian chants written on parchment from the 15th century, Etruscan earrings, and a watch that once adorned the wrist of King Louis XVI. If for no other reason, the museum is worth the insight into Swiss architecture and folk art. Open daily May 1-Oct. 31, 10 a.m.-4:30 p.m. Admission is $3 adults, $1 children 17 and under and students.

Like the rest of the nation, Wisconsin has gotten caught up in the micro- or home-brew trend. New Glarus has, in this, my humble opinion, the best of the new small-town breweries, the eponymous **New Glarus Brewing Co.,** turning out the appealing Edel Pils—the "People's Beer"—year-round, along with four seasonal beers. You can't get by without at least one Uff Da Bock, in season. The *braumeister,* trained in Europe, reaps accolades and ribbons at every World Beer Championship; sample his work at local taverns as far away as Madison. Do stop by the brewery for its tasting room and views of the brewery process. Along CR W at WI 69, tel. (608) 527-5850.

The Swiss penchant for fabric no doubt led to the development of the town's oldest business, the **Upright Swiss Embroidery Factory,** 1100 Second St., tel. (608) 527-2515, turning out embroidered fabric on two gigantic 22-ton looms imported from Switzerland. Get a free gander at the thousands of "cooperating" needles weekdays 8 a.m.-4 p.m.

Three miles or so northwest via CR O is the massive **Swiss Valley Orchard,** tel. (608) 527-5355, a spread of over 2,000 dwarf apple trees and the best apple pastries you'll find. The operation also features hayrides and a brat house,

grilling bratwurst. Open weekends only late June through late August 11 a.m.-6 p.m., then daily through the first week of November.

Once a dense wood impeding travel to and from Milwaukee, and arguably the best state park campsites in this part of Wisconsin, are found at **New Glarus Woods State Park,** tel. (608) 527-2335. The smallest state park for the time being, the Woods offers but 32 rustic campsites—some bike-in only—with no showers or electricity. The 11 hiking miles are excellent, through dense woods or deep valleys. The state is toying with the idea of expanding the park, inevitable since New Glarus is the western endpoint of the **Sugar River State Trail,** a 23-mile path from New Glarus to Brodhead along the Sugar River ravine. A leisurely, one-percent grade groomed trail, the whole shooting match is part of the Ice Age National Scenic Trail. In Brodhead, lots of secondary trails branch off, including one to the popular "Half-Way Tree"—a spot used as a landmark by the Winnebago, who knew this point was equidistant between the Mississippi River and Lake Michigan. Bicycles are available for rent at the refurbished New Glarus depot, the trail headquarters. Assorted private campgrounds are located along the route. The fee is $3 daily, $10 annually for the trail.

In the vicinity of the park off CR H on the way to Blanchardville is a gorgeous official state Rustic Road; great for a Saturday drive.

Accommodations

The cheapest lodging in New Glarus is the **Swiss-Aire Motel,** WI 69 south of town, tel. (608) 527-2138 or (800) 798-4391, a basic but very good motel with a heated pool, continental breakfast, and located right on the Sugar River Trail. Rates from $61, but these drop precipitously Nov.-April.

Right in the heart of the village is the **New Glarus Hotel,** 100 6th Ave., tel. (608) 527-5244, with room rates from $45. But there's also the legendary Swiss cuisine (from a Swiss chef) and boisterous polka dancing, as well as the more subdued Ticino Pizzeria.

The most distinctive inn is the **Chalet Landhaus,** 801 WI 69, tel. (608) 527-5234 or (800) 944-1716, built in rustic, traditional Swiss style. The main room features a bent staircase, Swiss detailing, and a fireplace. Rooms have balconies strewn with geraniums, and there are a few suites available with whirlpools. Rates from $50 s or $60 d.

The **Country House Inn,** 180 WI 69, tel. (608) 527-5399, is three miles north of town on 50 acres of wooded meadow. Tons of antiques adorn this 1892 farmhouse, which offers breakfast at a harvest table under candlelit chandeliers. Rates from $75.

Food
The eateries listed below offer any number of Swiss cuisine items. One unique drink is *rivela,* a malted, milky, alcohol-free, sweet sports drink of sorts popular in Switzerland.

Ruef's Meathouse offers real-deal Swiss. Ruef's smokes its own meats and makes *kalberwurst* and *landjaegers.* You can also get your hands on real Swiss cheese in many other places. The best for variety might be **Prima Käse,** W6117 CR C, Monticello, tel. (608) 938-4227, a cheesemaker just 10 minutes away in Monticello and the U.S.'s only maker of wheel and Sweet Swiss cheese.

For delectable Swiss-style baked goods, the **New Glarus Bakery,** 534 First St., tel. (608) 527-2916, is the only stop necessary. The Swiss-trained bakers turn out the house specialty, "Alpenbread," but you might also find *stollen,* a dense, *two-pound* bread concoction of raisins, spices, marzipan, and almonds, often served at the end of meals or as the centerpiece at brunches.

The **Four Corners,** 200 5th Ave., tel. (608) 527-2244, has been on the scene since 1880, with house specialties of *kalberwurst,* veal sausage simmered in beer with a light gravy; *schublig,* a Swiss sausage simmered in beer; *sauerbraten,* marinated beef roast in red cabbage and sauerkraut; and even a corned beef dinner. Open daily with a full breakfast, lunch, and dinner menu. There's an outdoor steak fry Wednesdays in summer. From $4.

Along the main drag, you'll find **Glarner Stube,** 518 1st St., tel. (608) 527-2216, a restaurant site dating from 1901, specializing in fondue (cheese cooked in wine), *Schublig, Kalberwurst,* and *Genschnitzelettes* (tender veal sautéed in white wine sauce). Open for lunch and dinner Tues.-Thurs. until 8 p.m., until 9 p.m. Fri.-Sat., and until 8 p.m. Sunday. Closed Monday. From $13 for dinner. A few blocks up the road is **Flan-**

nery's, a supper club heavy on the American, with live music most weekends. From $5.

Very new to the New Glarus scene, **Deininger's,** 119 Fifth Ave., tel. (608) 527-2012, was opened by Chicagoans who wanted that great culinary opportunity in the countryside. An outstanding restaurant with continental-Swiss-German heavy-fare, it's already standing room only on weekends, and worth it to splurge. Open for lunch and dinner Monday and Thurs.-Sat., lunch only Tuesday. Open for brunch on Sundays. Closed Wednesday. From $10.

For a cool-off after the Sugar River Trail, stop by the **soda fountain** at Roberts Swiss Imports, which also has some soups and homemade cookies.

The requisite watering hole in New Glarus is the classic 1893 tavern, **Puempel's Old Tavern.** This is the real thing, with the original back bar, dark woods, high ceilings, and the real draw—patriotic folk-art murals painted in 1913 by Andrea Hofer.

Services and Information
The exceedingly tiny New Glarus **information kiosk,** right at the entrance to town off WI 69, is open seasonally during regular business hours. For more information, contact New Glarus Tourist Information, tel. (608) 527-2095 or (800) 527-6838, www.swisstown.com.

MONROE

Monroe's first cabin went up in 1835, and the town initially became a polarized village, one end called Monroe, the other New Mexico. Geographical prudence won out and Monroe was rechristened in 1839. Swiss settlers first concentrated on wheat and left the cheesemaking to home industry, but shrewd outsiders let the county in on the little gold mine they were sitting on just prior to the crack in the state's wheat industry. Interest in the East grew fast, very fast; by the 1880s, some 75 area cheese factories were producing Swiss, Limburger, Gruyere, and other of the more odoriferous varieties of cheese.

How serious is cheese in Monroe? Besides seeing "Swiss Cheese Capital of America" everywhere, the biannual Cheese Days draws in over 100,000 people for equal parts revelry, ed-

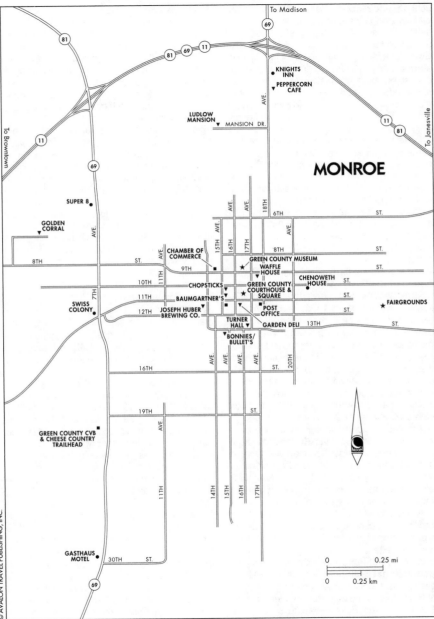

MONROE

To Madison

To Brownton

To Jonesville

KNIGHTS INN
PEPPERCORN CAFE

LUDLOW MANSION
MANSION DR.

SUPER 8

GOLDEN CORRAL

CHAMBER OF COMMERCE

GREEN COUNTY MUSEUM
WAFFLE HOUSE

CHOPSTICKS

CHENOWETH HOUSE

GREEN COUNTY COURTHOUSE & SQUARE

BAUMGARTNER'S

SWISS COLONY

POST OFFICE

FAIRGROUNDS

JOSEPH HUBER BREWING CO.

TURNER HALL

GARDEN DELI

BONNIES/BULLET'S

GREEN COUNTY CVB & CHEESE COUNTRY TRAILHEAD

GASTHAUS MOTEL

0   0.25 mi
0   0.25 km

ucation, and respect. Monroe has one of the country's only Limburger cheese factories, and the only Swiss and Gruyere cheese factory still using traditional copper vats is in Monroe. The Swiss Colony, Inc., the largest local employer, started back in 1926 as the first mail-order cheese business and is now one of the largest nationwide. Appropriately, the local high school nickname is the "Cheesemakers"—how's a Monroe Cheesemakers sweatshirt for an ineffably kitschy souvenir?

Beyond the cheese, Monroe has long been regarded—along with New Glarus—as top-shelf picturesque in Wisconsin. An official from the National Trust for Historic Preservations once said it best, "If you put up a fence around Monroe, you could charge admission to get in."

Note: Listen to the Swiss Program, still heard on local radio station WEKZ 1260 AM, around 1 p.m. Mon.-Sat.

Sights
Monroe is perfect for walking around. The nucleus is the stately, almost baroque **Green County Courthouse** with a quad-faced clock—freshly buffed for the city's 1995 sesquicentennial celebrations—on the Yankee-style square. The courthouse is now over the century mark and the people of Monroe are as proud of that structure as anything else. The architecture of Monroe displays an intriguing blend of subtle Swiss, common worker bungalow, and gingerbread Victorian, plus the odd octagon house or two. Free walking-tour brochures are available from the Monroe Chamber of Commerce.

The countryside no longer reeks of cheese, and there are far fewer than 200 factories churning out wheels of Swiss. None receives more attention than **Alp & Dell**, 657 2nd St., north of WI 69 bypass, tel. (608) 328-3355 or (800) ALP-DELL. Carpeted walkways with large viewing windows overlook the famed copper vats, this being the only remaining cheese factory still using traditional copper. Open daily, Mon.-Sat. 8 a.m.-5 p.m., Sunday 10 a.m.-5 p.m., summer hours generally extended.

Starting in Monroe, the **Cheese Country Recreational Trail** rides 47 miles of railroad bed abandoned in 1985 after hauling thousands of tons of lead and zinc from the lead region. The multipurpose trail—sad to say, lots of

ATVs—parallels the Pecatonica River and touches the edge of Cadiz Springs State Park and its two lakes. A historic 440-foot skeletal bridge is just west of Browntown; the remainder of the trail, passing through Browntown, South Wayne, Gratiot, Darlington, Calamine, and finishing in Mineral Point, has an additional 55 or so overpasses. Darlington has refurbished its depot into a historic museum. Gorgeous sections of this trail pass through native grass prairie and magnificent stands of oak. Bikers should be cautioned that sandy spots plague the trail. In Calamine, the trail links up with the **Pecatonica River State Trail,** which itself runs across the Bonner Branch Valley fork of the Pecatonica and leads to an additional 200 miles of trails. A hefty $6 trail fee is assessed for any wheeled vehicle or horse, with stickers available at most gas stations near the trail. Bike rentals are available at the Gasthaus Motel. Monroe is planning a parking lot in town and/or a branch of the trail right downtown and headquartered in the old Monroe Depot.

Monroe's simple but engaging **Green County Historical Museum,** 1617 9th St., tel. (608) 325-2609, has the usual displays of local memorabilia, with special exhibits on cheese factories past and present, and an anachronistic red schoolhouse. Open Memorial Day-Labor Day, weekends 2-5 p.m., admission $1 adults, 50 cents children.

See rare (today) Old World alpine Swiss cabinetry and folk painting from Gottlieg Brändli and Janeen Joy, 508 17th Ave., tel. (608) 325-6681. Gottlieg, a former *Bauernmalerei,* or Swiss-German folk artist immigrant, has lectured on the stylistics of Alpine design at the Smithsonian. Their custom design work can be viewed at the shop, or drive up to New Glarus to see more of it. The studio is open 8 a.m.-6 p.m. weekdays, Saturday by appointment.

Accommodations
The cheapest digs are found at the **Knights Inn,** 250 N. 18th Ave., tel. (608) 325-4138, which has a basic motel section and another wing with slightly larger rooms. Whatever you get, it's a deal at around $30 s or $59.

Similarly priced is the **Gasthaus Motel,** 685 WI 69 South, tel. (608) 328-8395, a well-spruced little place with the usual extras like free coffee, free local calls, and a bonus of bike rentals.

The best lodging in town is found at the **AmericInn**, 424 WI 69 North, tel. (608) 328-3444, with attractive rooms in a large complex, featuring a heated indoor pool, whirlpool, and game room. Rates from $60 s or d.

A spectacular—and huge—B&B is **Chenoweth House**, 2004 10th St., tel. (608) 325-5064, an 1887 beaut with four rooms and rates from $85. The **Ludlow Mansion B&B**, 1421 Mansion Dr., tel. (608) 325-1219, has luxurious suites and a plus of a recognized dining room. Its rates are from $90.

The **Browntown-Cadiz Springs Recreation Area** is seven miles west of Monroe via WI 11 but has no camping facilities. The **Green County Fairgrounds**, along 25th Ave. between 9th and 13th Streets, has 100 sites (and showers)—not the best, but it's only $7. The nearest last-chance public campground would be New Glarus Woods State Park back up in New Glarus, or Yellowstone Lake to the northwest.

For a private campground, the very small **Cadiz Hills**, west on WI 11, tel. (608) 966-3310, has 25 sites and a small separate tenting area. Rates run $10-12, and there's also a small petting zoo and some nature trails.

Food

A prerequisite while in Monroe is the local delicacy, the Swiss cheese sandwich, at **Baumgartner's**, tel. 325-6157, a Wisconsin institution since 1931, directly across from the courthouse. It's a cheese store (a mammoth "We Ship Anywhere" operation) and locally favorite tavern, though which came first is anybody's guess. Walk in and peruse the cheese or buy some outstandingly anachronistic post cards of local cheese factories. Through the swinging saloon doors you'll enter a six-decade-old Shangri La of small town life—a long polished bar, wooden-flat ceiling, horn racks, and mural-maps of Wisconsin. Be daring and go native—try limburger and braunschweiger, just like the locals. From just over a buck. Food is served daily 'til 9 p.m. For just a shot-and-a-beer, head for the friendly **Ludlow's Tavern** on the west side, with the best jukebox in Monroe.

More local flavor at the wonderful **Turner Hall**, 1217 17th Ave., tel. (608) 325-3461, which serves lunch from noon daily and offers a Friday night fish fry. Great basic Midwestern fare along with some creative Swiss-style food. There's even a great Swiss *Rathskeller* and bowling alley. Show up for polka dances Sunday. From $3.

For great Chinese—Hunan, Sichuan, a small amount of Cantonese, and great Shanghai—next door to Baumgartner's is **Chopsticks**, 1021 16th Ave., tel. (608) 329-7900, offering a lengthy list of interesting entrées, decently prepared. Open for lunch Tues.-Sun., dinner only Fri.-Sat. Closed Mondays. From $5.

Bonnie's, 1301 15th Ave., tel. (608) 325-1331, atop what was the town's first hotel, sits on an enclosed balcony. It offers basic sandwiches, soups, and salads, but it's a killer place to have lunch. A tad more upscale, **Bullet's**, on the main floor, specializes in pizza along with family-style food. Both from $5.

On the outskirts of town near the junction of Highways 11/81 and 69 stands the **Peppercorn Cafe**, tel. (608) 329-2233. An understated supper club, with sandwiches for lunch and for dinner, fajitas, pizza, pastas, Angus steaks, and prime rib, along with creative chef specials. The custard bread pudding here brings people from other states. Open Mon.-Sat. for lunch and dinner. Closed Sunday. From $5.

Cozy and comfy meals in a mansion are found at the **Ludlow Mansion**, 1421 Mansion Dr., tel. (608) 325-1219, with several dining rooms and a split-level cocktail lounge.

The cheapest grub you'll find is at the **Waffle House**, 1014 17th Ave., with cheap 7-11 a.m. breakfast specials, including oatmeal. Beyond that, it offers a basic cafe menu, with a popular fish fry. Open daily 7 a.m.-5 p.m. Mon.-Thurs. and Saturday, until 7 p.m. on Friday, and until 3 p.m. Sunday. From $3.

A tad more ambitious, the **Garden Deli**, 1713 11th St., offers a basic menu mostly of healthful sandwiches and from-scratch soups and salads.

Entertainment and Events

Cheese Days, held the third weekend of September *of even numbered years,* has feted "Cheese Country" since 1914 with celebratory fairs, Swiss musicians, fun runs, a street dance, a carnival, exhibitions, an absolutely enormous cheese-flavored parade, and tons and tons of Swiss and limburger (including a 200-pound wheel produced on the square over the weekend). In the off-years the town has launched a new **blues festival.** Another huge event is late June's **balloon rally.**

The **Monroe Arts Center,** 1315 11th St., tel. (608) 325-5700, has a full schedule of music, storytelling, theater, and more throughout the year.

Shopping

Well, tours would be more appropriate, and they are available, but factory outlet pricing is available at **Swiss Colony,** 1112 7th Ave., tel. (608) 328-8400, a good place to pick up cheese, sausage, pastries, and assorted specialty food gifts.

Services and Information

The **Monroe Depot,** 2108 7th Ave, tel. (888) 222-9111, www.greencounty.org, is a county tourist information center, as well as the trail headquarters of the Cheese Country Recreational Trail and a museum and heritage center to cheesemaking.

The **Chamber of Commerce** is just west of the Green County Museum and is open weekdays 8 a.m.-4 p.m.

CRANBERRY COUNTY

The word "cranberry" in southwestern Wisconsin essentially means Monroe County and its primary community, Tomah; it lies south of Minneapolis and east from La Crosse. The county is one of the top producers of cranberries in the nation—28.5 million pounds annually. An enormous military installation, legendary bike trails, and even an occasional Amish settlement also crop up.

TOMAH

Sights

The cranberry heritage is best viewed 12 or so miles to the north (along CR E) in Warrens at the **Warrens Expo,** tel. (608) 378-4878—you can't miss the signs. A hands-on museum devoted to the cranberry is a fun place with a businesslike approach to a vital, local industry. The museum has locally designed and built cranberry plucking and processing apparatuses, from hand rakes to horse clogs and water wheels. Cranberry ice cream can be sampled in the gift shop. Open April-Oct., daily 10 a.m.-4 p.m. Admission is $5 adults, $3 children.

Warrens' annual **Cranberry Festival** is one of the most popular in the state. A red explosion with cranberry products as far as the eye can see, it's a good time to take a bog tour. Organized tours on bike are offered over Memorial Day. Twenty- to 30-mile tours roll through cranberry marshes, sphagnum moss drying beds, Great Blue Heron nesting sites, and old European (and one Mormon) homesteading enclaves. Sag wagons are provided. The Expo has excellent fold-out maps and brochures to it on your own.

Back in Tomah proper, head to Milwaukee

Street and Superior Avenue—better known as "Gasoline Alley", after local boy-done-good Frank King's comic strip, which used Superior Avenue as its inspiration. At the far end of Superior Avenue is Gillett Park, which houses the **Little Red Schoolhouse,** a Civil War-era one-room schoolhouse of which locals are particularly proud. At 306 Arthur St. stands the **Harris G. Allen Telecommunication Museum,** tel. (608) 374-5000, a collection of exhibits, including about a jillion antique, international, or bizarre phones and classic switchboards tracing the telephone industry. Open April-Oct., Tues.-Sat. 9 a.m.-4 p.m. Admission is free, tours are $2.

Practicalities

Tomah offers basic lodging, and a whole slew of it, given the city's strategic highway location. Most are located off the interstates on Highways 16, 12, or 21. The cheapest is likely the **Park Motel,** on US 12 north of I-90, tel. (608) 372-4655. A locally owned and meticulously attended place, it'll have rooms for around $45 in high season, much less off-season.

One rather unique option is the **Lark Inn,** 229 N. Superior Ave., tel. (608) 372-5981 or (800) 447-LARK, with a wide range of options from basic housekeeping units and comfy suites to a grouping of log cabins. All offer microwaves and refrigerators and are tastefully adorned with country quilts and antiques. A deli on-site features 24-hour room service. Rooms run from $49 s, $55 d.

You'll find camping in the Black River State Forest's two campgrounds, or, along the way to the state forest, **McMullen County Park,** along CR O, with a 600-acre spread with hiking trails.

Enjoy European cuisine buffet-style at **Burnstad's European Village and Cafe,** Highways 12 and 16 E, tel. (608) 372-3277, in a comfy, low-key environment, with homemade soups and breads. There's also a gourmet gift shop with Wisconsin and Amish goods. It's set in a "village" with cobblestone walkways, an ersatz German *Bahnof* and village with a whole bunch of shops specifically dedicated to relieving you of your dollars.

Services and Information

The well-stocked **Tomah Chamber of Commerce,** 306 Arthur St., tel. (608) 372-2166 or (800) 948-6624, www.tomahwisconsin.com, has lots of information and brochures. It has particularly good auto/bike tour maps.

SPARTA

Sights

Bike trail capital—it's on the La Crosse River and Elroy-Sparta State Trails—Sparta is great for a cyclist's trail-end cooldown. Canoeing is also good along the La Crosse River all the way to the Mississippi; Perch Lake and east are class A trout waters. Sparta has an only-weird-if-you-think-about-it Siamese museum and the **Deke Slayton Memorial Space and Bike Museum,** 208 Main St., tel. (608) 269-0033, devoted to the local boy turned NASA astronaut . . . and bicycling, since it is one hub of Wisconsin biking. More eye-catching is amazing **F.A.S.T Corp.,** northeast of Sparta in Angelo, along WI 21—that's "Fiberglass, Animals, Shapes, and Trademarks" to you and me. Chances are you've spotted one of the 20-foot fiberglass sculptures of animals, logos, etc. at a business somewhere. The grounds are often liberally strewn with the product, which is why locals refer to it as the "Sparta Zoo."

Even farther north along WI 27/71 is another roadside-kitsch attraction—the **Paul and Matilda Wegner Grotto,** two miles south of Cataract, a half-mile west of the 71/27 split, another in southwestern Wisconsin's lengthy list of folk-art mini-masterpieces. These concrete sculptures with broken glass and crockery facades are, like the Dickeyville grotto, imbued with equal parts patriotism and religious fervor. On-site now are an American flag, a chunky-looking birdhouse, and a 12-foot concrete replica of a '30s-era Bremen ocean liner, along with more quotidian religious icons. The Prayer Garden, Glass Church, and Peace Monument defy description. The philanthropic Kohler Foundation rehabilitated the site and donated it to the county. The grotto, tel. (608) 269-8680, is open during daylight hours and is free.

Even the town library is worth a look, built to resemble a Roman temple with an open palladian portico and short Ionic support columns. The red sandstone **Monroe County Courthouse,** also in Sparta, shows Romanesque Revival inspiration and features a lovely tower with open oriel windows and three gabled pavilions. (The local chamber of commerce has walking tour brochures.)

North of town is the **Monroe County Local History Room,** on CR B, a museum and library detailing the county's history. Open weekday business hours.

If you're looking for bike rentals or shuttles, **Out Spokin' Adventures,** tel. (800) 4WEBIKE, has everything you'll need; it also offers tours.

Practicalities

Sparta has plenty of motels, most along W. Wisconsin St., including the **Spartan,** 1900 W. Wisconsin St., tel. (608) 269-2770, with basic rooms from $30. A unique B&B is **Justin Trails,** 7452 Kathryn Ave., tel. (608) 269-4522, a combination country B&B, Nordic ski area, and even pro disc golf course; it's been noted by oodles of national media. Rates from $80. For a more unusual B&B, St. Mary's, south via WI 27 and CR X, has the century-old St. Mary's church. Sitting atop a commanding ridge, the Convent House has been turned into a B&B, and the preserved architecture of the church is lovely.

FORT McCOY

The only U.S. Army installation in Wisconsin sits around the community of Fort McCoy, almost the geometric center of the county. Totaling some 60,000 acres, the fort is a primary Army Reserve mobilization and training center for 120,000 active and reserve military members; it was well known to Wisconsinites as a Cuban Resettlement Center in 1980. While this isn't particularly impressive to many travelers, the two recreation areas with-

AMISH COUNTRYSIDE

Beginning in the mid-1960s, "pioneer" Amish began setting up homesteads in southwestern Wisconsin. Coming from Amish enclaves across the nation—particularly Pennsylvania, Ohio, and Indiana—they were primarily fleeing stratospheric land prices, urban encroachment on their pastoral way of life, and, some cynics add, droves of camera-toting tourists, too many of whom had seen the movie *Witness*.

With a verdant landscape resembling the eastern Appalachians, southwestern Wisconsin was a logical settling site. Pockets of Amish farms were soon established mostly in Vernon, Trempealeau, and Taylor Counties, along with some in Monroe County. Puzzled dairyland farmers didn't know what to make of it all. The Amish were welcomed at first—the region was in an economic depression, and the injection of hard work and cash was much appreciated. But welcome soon turned to uneasiness when the Amish started to "pester" (as locals said) folks incessantly for rides or to use the phone, and when it was discovered that these ardent home-schoolers might be costing the townships state educational aid.

Amish and Mennonites

There are approximately 100,000 Amish spread across North America today, and many more Mennonites, who are often mistaken for Amish. Both groups trace their existence to the 1600s and a sub-split from the Swiss Anabaptists in a dispute over baptism. At the time, authorities started executing them for heresy. They escaped into neighboring countries, where they were also persecuted, and another split took place in a group that fled to the Alsace region of modern France. There, in 1693, a more hard-line, conservative faction of the original Swiss group broke off, eager to pursue its own excommunication and social shunning practices. That group took the name Amish after Alsatian leader Jacob Ammann and also adopted his severe, distinctive clothing and facial hair codes. Mennonites are thus a distant relation.

Life and Ethic

The crux of Amish life is a strong community, based on two central tenets: separation and obedience. Separation (from the outer community) is necessary as the "outside" is inherently distracting; people on the outside aren't evil, just pawns in modernity's

dehumanizing processes. Obedience is an even stronger aspect of Amish life. The Amish live by an ethereal concept called *gelassenheit*, very roughly translated as "yielding" or "submission to an authority." This is part of the *Ordnung* ("Order"), the unwritten collection of social mores to which each member must subscribe. This closed society is far more enigmatic than anyone could have guessed.

There are many kinds of Amish. Old Order Amish are more conservative, but bit by bit more progressive communities are taking hold. For example, some will ride in automobiles, although they still won't drive them; some will use electricity, if it isn't theirs; some own property, etc. All Amish still cultivate the ethic of hard work, thrift, and community support.

Though most people recognize the Amish by their black horse-drawn carriages, more widely discussed are the dictums regarding electricity. Most, but not all, electricity is banned in Wisconsin Amish communities. Electricity plays a significant role in Wisconsin Amish history for one big reason: milk. America's Dairyland understandably has rather stringent rules pertaining to milk storage and transport. The Amish, if they wanted to conduct commercial operations, had to be up to code, impossible without electricity. After years of negotiations, agreements involving diesel engines and other alternate methods were reached.

Persecuted for religious practices in previous centuries, the Amish are now facing criticism from the U.S. government for their educational practices. High school education is prohibited by strict Amish sects; in the 1950s, Amish fathers were imprisoned for refusing to send their children to the ninth grade. Other families were prosecuted for illegal home schooling. Eventually, the Amish sought to establish their own schools, and many did, though they failed to comply with state regulations in many instances. In 1972 the Supreme Court ruled against the Amish schools, but by then there was no turning back. When the Wisconsin government attempted to abolish them, public furor forced them to back off. The issue still hasn't been settled to the contentment of all parties.

Wisconsin Amish Today

Amish settlements can be found across the entire western and central portions of Wisconsin—as far east as the Wolf River, as far north as northwestern Wisconsin's Lakes District, and almost to the Illinois border. Population estimates are tough to fix precisely, but it's close to 8,000 statewide, plus another 1,500 or so close-Christian-cousin Mennonites. Most are still concentrated in Vernon County—La Farge and Ontario are the largest centers for Amish agriculture in the state.

The Amish are particularly well known for their Old World craftsmanship. Bent-hickory furniture is a staple of regional shops, as are the meticulously handcrafted quilts. Home-based bakeries and other cottage industries are found along every country road. And though most of the time there's relative harmony, cultural flare-ups do occur.

In several incidents in the mid-1990s, Amish families suffered attacks. There are obvious cultural differences with the potential to cause conflict. In the worst, a woman was sexually assaulted and a horse was killed in a drive-by shooting. Unwilling to draw attention by reporting such crimes, the Amish nonetheless couldn't contain

all of the information. It became apparent that these were far from isolated incidents. Harassment by locals was not uncommon. For the above crimes, a young ignorant local was prosecuted and convicted, but it failed to comfort the Amish.

On the other hand, there are those times when the small communities rally around the Amish. After a century of state-level opposition to home schooling in every state, the Amish once again faced bureaucratic nightmares in Wisconsin when they tried to build their own school. Public support exerted such force that the state government was more or less obliged to grant special exemptions to the group. More recently, in a move that no doubt smoothed some of the cultural impasses, the Amish were instrumental in defeating plans for an Air National Guard low-level training zone through the valleys across southwestern Wisconsin.

AFZR-XO-PA, Fort McCoy, WI 54656, tel. (608) 388-2407.

in the confines are. Whitetail Ridge Recreation Area has a small downhill/ cross-country ski hill with a tubing slope, snowmobile trails, and a chalet. Pine View Recreation Area has a beach, boat rentals, mini-golf, and a large campground. A rather comprehensive **historical center** is also located on the base. The historical center is open Monday, Wednesday, and Friday 11 a.m.-1 p.m. and is free.

For more military history, head east along I-90/94, to Camp Douglas and the **Volk Field Air National Guard Training Site Museum,** an 1890s-era log cabin housing a full history of the National Guard, from the Civil War to the present. Open Wed.-Sun., it's free. The library onsite is particularly well regarded for its research archives. The camp also offers tours of the facilities—you can even watch bombing runs. The Hardwood Air-to-Ground bombing range is open Tuesday 12:30-8:30 p.m. and Wed.-Sat. 7:30 a.m.-4 p.m. For more information, call the museum, tel. (608) 427-1280 or (608) 565-2884 for a recording; the bombing range's number is (608) 427-1271.

For information on the recreation areas or a multi-page brochure on a driving tour of the facility, contact the Fort McCoy Public Affairs Office,

Mill Bluff State Park

Along US 12/WI 16 near Camp Douglas and Volk Field is the underappreciated Mill Bluff State Park. A geologist's palette, Mill Bluff is one of the region's only true mesas; most others are a hodgepodge of smaller outcroppings more appropriately called buttes, or the rarer pinnacle (such as Mill Bluff's Devil's Needle). The park is dominated by the nucleus, inspiring Mill Bluff, so high that when glacial Lake Wisconsin covered all of the central portion of the state, this mesa and the assorted buttes around it were rocky islands. The top is reached via stone steps etched into the side by the CCC in the '30s. The bizarre conglomeration is the residual geology of the Dresback Group, upper Cambrian-era formations of more impenetrable sandstone, resulting in rocks that tend to weather vertically. The geology is so diverse in this park that it was chosen as one of the nine units of the Ice Age National Scenic Trail. The prehistory is as crucial as the rocks—petroglyphs have been found on bluff faces. A hiking trail snakes along the top of the bluff, and a small pond offers a beach. The campground ($8 sites, plus daily sticker) has two dozen sites, none reservable.

ELROY-SPARTA RECREATIONAL TRAIL

In a state that popularized the "rails-to-trails" system, the big daddy, the one that pioneered them all, is the nationally known Elroy-Sparta Recreational Trail. Thirty-two plus miles between sleepy Elroy and Sparta were converted from the 1870s railroad bed of the Chicago Northwestern Railroad. The project was completed in 1967, and the trail is oh-so-easy limestone screenings and a wide, wide trail; plank-covered and rail-guarded bridges; and no tough grades at all (three percent throughout). The trail, virtually surrounded by wildlife refuge lands, roughly parallels WI 71 and dances with the headwaters of the Kickapoo River, along with the Baraboo River and numerous trout-laden creeks.

Yet what really draws over 70,000 riders to the trail annually are the three otherworldly railroad tunnels, hand-carved out into massive limestone rises for the railroad. Two tunnels are a mere quarter-mile, but the other—the terrifying Norwalk Tunnel—is a full three-quarters of a mile of drippy, spelunkers'-delight darkness. There are no lights so bring a flashlight—and a jacket, it's 50-some degrees in there. All bikes must be walked. It's an ineffable experience—the light at the ends of the tunnel disappears and all you can hear in Tunnel #3 are the overhead natural springs cascading through the faults worn in the cement over the passage of time. The tunnels took two to three laborious years each to bore out in the 19th century, and at present it can feel like it takes that long to get through. Tunnel #3 still has the old "keeper's shack" in which a solitary— I daresay lonely—watchman kept vigil on the thunderous doors, clapped shut between trains during winter to protect the tunnels from heaving and cracking due to winter cold.

Particulars

The trail is open for riders (and hikers, technically) May 1-Oct. 31. Trail passes are required for all riders 18 and over; hiking is and always will be free. Daily passes cost $3 or $8 annually. Rentals and repairs are available at all communities along the route. Of note is Kendall, offering an electric vehicle for people with disabilities, and a drop-service for a nominal fee.

One-Horse Towns

Kendall's historic railroad depot is now the headquarters for the state trail (with an electric cart allowing visitors with disabilities to use the trail); it serves as a repository for trail information, as well as being a small museum. Camping at the village park is available, and Kendall, the most "cosmopolitan" along the route, also has a B&B, a motel, a restaurant (the Midway Supper Club), not to mention one of the best Polkafests in Wisconsin (October).

Wilton serves up a copious, farmhand-sized pancake breakfast every Sunday morning Memorial Day-Labor Day; the village park also offers a public campground. (Another campground is directly on the trail—the Tunnel Campground, where sites cost $15.) Wilton offers bike rentals and has, a mile south, a habitat for rare wood turtles.

In addition to the epic tunnel, **Norwalk** also offers easy access to Tunnel #2 (that is to say, for lazy bones just looking for photos). North of town, a flood control dam has created an additional recreation area. Right on the trail you'll find the Norwalk Cheese Factory, open Mon.-Sat. 7 a.m.-4 p.m.

Elroy

Elroy is the hub of two additional trails—the **400 State Trail** (not 400 miles) stretching to Reedsburg, and the **Omaha Trail**, a 12.5-mile sealcoated trail to Camp Douglas. The 400 has public camping in the largest village along its length, Wonewoc, also offering five restaurants. The coolest accommodations along the trail are the domed units at Union Center's **Garden City Motel**, tel. (608) 462-8253. Wonewoc also has an interpretive nature trail as well as a camp hall of the Modern Woodmen of America at CR EE and CR G, tel. (608) 983-2352. The century-old landscape murals covering the entire interior were restored by the Kohler Foundation. *Quite* a trip, visually. Open June-Aug. Saturday 1-3:30 p.m. or by appointment. La Valle's Hemlock Park, west of town, has great sandstone bluffs for hiking, as well as lakes on either side. The Omaha Trail features another monster tunnel, some 875 creepy feet long. Both trails require use fees of $3 per day, $8 per season.

The lovely common area of central Elroy links all three trails and features an old depot chock-full of rentals and information for bikers, along with public restrooms. Rentals cost $4 per hour, with a maximum of $12 for a 24-hour period. Call (608) 462-BIKE for information. Saturday nights during summer, the live entertainment is a real hoot.

Off your bike, the almost-microscopic **Elroy Museum,** in an old Masonic temple, is open May-Sept. weekends 1-4 p.m. Replicas of the famed Deusenberg 11 automobile are made at **Deusenberg Motors,** 1006 Academy St., tel. (608) 462-8100. Tours are available by appointment. The Deusenberg plant is the smallest auto manufacturing plant in the U.S., pushing out precious few of the $150,000 cars.

For practicalities, the **Elroy City Park,** on WI 80/82 on the edge of town, offers a swimming pool and is a good place for a shower. Camping is $6. **Thompson Park,** a mile north on WI 71, has primitive camping; access is by foot or bike only through a high culvert under WI 71. **Waarvik's Century Farm,** N4621 CR H, tel. (608) 462-8595, is a fourth-generation family B&B with a separate house and a log cabin, offering a bike shuttle service and rates of $45-125. A nearby motel is the **Valley Inn Motel,** along WI 80 S., tel. (608) 462-8251, with rooms from $30.

COULEE RANGE

Best representing what southwestern Wisconsin is all about is likely north of the Wisconsin River and east of La Crosse—part of Monroe and all of Vernon and Richland Counties. Well within the topography of the challenging coulee country, the area also features excellent state parks, interesting architecture, glimpses of Amish life, and even classic pastoral grazing land.

Scenic Drives
Pick any country road and it will roll, dip, turn back on itself, then seemingly forget itself in gravel and dissipate into something else—but always run along (or over) a creek or past a dilapidated homesteader's cabin, a rusted wreck, an Amish home-bakery, bent-stick furniture maker, or black horse buggy, and through fields of trillium.

The Ontario-La Farge stretches (north of Richland Center), around Wildcat Mountain State Park, are a perfect encapsulation of everything the region offers. Two state-designated Rustic Roads also run within these parameters. The shorter **Tunnelville Road** begins along WI 131 south of La Farge and twists for almost three miles to CR SS. Spectacular countryside wildflowers (including beds of trillium) line Tunnelville, and there are few people. More popular is the nine-mile trail including Lower Ridge, Sand Hill, and Dutch Hollow Roads, all off WI 131. Dutch Hollow Road is right at the southern tip of Ontario-Amish country. Fantastic old-style architecture can be seen all along this road, as well as some contour farming. CR

D, east of Cashton, has the **Wisconsin Hill and Valley Cheese Factory,** an Amish-owned cheese factory and outlet center. Open Mon.-Sat. 9 a.m.-4 p.m., with cheesemaking tours in the early afternoons.

KICKAPOO RIVER WATERSHED

WI 131 runs the course of the Kickapoo River watershed south from Tomah through Wilton (also grazing the Elroy-Sparta Recreational Trail), past the rivers headwaters north of Ontario and Wildcat Mountain State Park, and into undiscovered federal "wild" lands before hitting its southern half around Soldiers Grove, a total of 65 miles. The Kickapoo River, which doesn't even stretch as far north as Tomah when you total the serpentine bights and watery switchbacks, tops out at 120 miles. Thus it has become known as the crookedest river in the nation, as one soon discovers when canoeing.

The original inhabitants of most stretches were the Algonquian Kikapu. The word *Ki-Ka-Pu* translates roughly as "one who travels there, then here", describing quite well both the rolling river as well as the peripatetic Native American tribe (which wound up in the Texas-Mexico region).

The southern villages are covered in other sections—Soldiers Grove, Gays Mills, Viroqua, and Westby in the "Great River Road" section, and Wauzeka in "Along the Wisconsin River." All of these areas offer canoeing on their respective stretches.

Canoeing

Of all the canoeable waterways in the state, many hydrophiles would finger the Kickapoo as numero uno. The water is always low, challenging canoeists only during springtime meltoffs or summer deluges (at which time it can exceed the banks and become unruly), and the scenery is superb—craggy, striated bluffs with pockets of goat prairie, oak savanna, and pine. The Ocooch Mountains along the West Fork are legendary.

Escape the madding crowd and head for the depths of the Kickapoo River Impoundment area at Rockton. Or head south to La Farge, and beyond to almost 9,000 acres under the auspices of the federal government and hands off to development. Until July 1995, that is. The federal government reached an agreement with the Wisconsin Legislature to hand over 8,500 acres to the state. For two decades, the feds had hemmed and hawed and vacillated over whether to dam the Kickapoo near La Farge, hoping to put a damper on spring floods and create a lake and recreation area. Opposed by some environmentalists, the project never got far off the ground, and as this book goes to press the land is in the hands of the state. Currently there are no plans for the land beyond returning some 1,100 acres to the Ho Chunk Nation. Also, there have been no reports of anybody being tossed off this land in limbo, though prudence dictates checking first if you're hoping to leave the river.

The West Fork draws lots of serious anglers, and the main fork is almost perfect for lolling rolls. If you do want to start in Ontario (easiest for novices, as the outfitters are all right there), figure 12 hours (more if you like to take your time) to get to La Farge; most operations take you halfway, to Rockton.

La Farge is small, but the countryside, the largest Amish farming area in the state, does have the wonderful **Trillium** B&B, E10596 Salem Ridge Rd., tel. (608) 625-4492, a private cottage with nook-sized rooms and zillions of cushiony pillows. A huge porch sits in front, and the cottage also has a stone fireplace. Appropriately named as well, the farm sits on 85 acres of trillium-strewn meadow, forest, and an organic garden. Rates from $55.

Most campers go to Wildcat Mountain State Park. A single primitive site is located just north of bridge 5 (but you cannot get there via motor vehi-

cle). Another federally run primitive campground is on CR P, adjacent to bridge 10. A third is approximately one and a half hours of canoeing below bridge 13. All are free. La Farge's Village Park has primitive sites and does charge a few bucks.

WILDCAT MOUNTAIN STATE PARK

This is the best secret state park in Wisconsin. It ain't for nothing that the Wisconsin Department of Natural Resources has called this little park one of its "undiscovered gems." Nobody knows about it, but it's always full of people—go figure.

The topography is splendid. Canoe the languid Kickapoo a stone's throw from Amish enclaves and some of the southern state's most unique ecosystems. This is even the only state park that caters to equestrians.

Much of the park's interior is established as a wildlife refuge, and due to the topography, other areas remain untouched, alive with native flora and fauna. Along the line of demarcation separating biotic zones, the natural areas include plant and tree life from northern and southern Wisconsin, some of them rare stands.

Canoeing

The Kickapoo grazes the far northwestern perimeter of the state park, then bends away and doubles back into the park's interior. The canoe landing is south through the park on WI 33, next to a shelter.

Trails

The shortest of three exceedingly short hikes is the **Ice Cave Trail,** located south off WI 33 onto CR F. You could broad-jump to the end of this trail, featuring a natural rock depression into a sandstone bluff (resembling a cave). A spring coursing across the top freezes like an enormous icicle in winter, periodically remaining icebound until June. Just over a mile in length, the **Hemlock Nature Trail** leaves from the picnic area and canoe landing south off WI 33. It leads into the Mt. Pisgah Hemlock Hardwoods Natural Landmark Area and ascends the mini-mighty mountain to the modest pinnacle at 1,220 feet, offering the best views in the park. The trail is marked with almost 30 signs pointing out the natural valley oddities the trail cuts through—

almost primeval flora dots the trailsides—look for wild ginseng and trillium, as well as shaggy mane and puffball fungi (not found in too many other places). The longest trail, **Old Settler's,** begins at the northern end of the upper picnic area on Wildcat Mountain. The trail incorporates pathways foot-hewn by homesteaders heading for nearby farmlands and offers above-average scenery and somewhat sweaty terrain. Twelve miles of trails are set aside for horses.

Camping
The main campground offers 30 sites, but it isn't much to ballyhoo. Though it's atop the crown of the mound and a few spots have grand views, the sites for the most part aren't all that wooded. Half are reservable. Not far beyond the park's canoe landing, and east of WI 131, is a primitive campsite. One of the only horse campgrounds in a state park is located in the northern sector.

RICHLAND CENTER

Suffrage and Frank Lloyd Wright are the focal points of Richland Center's heritage, underpinned by the surrounding dairy operations, for

---

SUFFRAGETTE CITY

You know you're in southwestern Wisconsin when you see the words "Wright" and "Frank Lloyd Wright" every which way you turn. But in his birthplace, Richland Center, many citizens would much rather discuss the city's other claim to fame—its heritage as the hotbed of radicalism in the late 19th century and arguably the birthplace of women's suffrage. Almost immediately upon being founded, Richland Center became a major site of the suffrage movement.

This was due to the many women recently successful in the Temperance movement, who turned their sights onto an equally egregious American predisposition. No doubt feeling influenced by the many suffrage clubs in the town, Richland Center gradually took what would be quite shocking moves in contemporary terms. The town was one of the few to allow women to work in the newsrooms of the local papers. Richland Center fiercely debated the inclusion of a suffrage clause in its charter when the city finally incorporated in 1887; it didn't pass, but that galvanized the movement even more.

Ada James

Ada James
Ada James, a pioneer in U.S. women's suffrage, was born in Richland Center, the daughter of a founding member of one of the original Women's Clubs in the state ("women's club" being code for nascent feminism). Abetted by her mother and other "radical" women, James was a political progressive from the start, destined by a familial predilection for activism. In 1910, she founded the Political Equality Club and instituted an unheard-of notion for the time—grassroots campaigning. At the time, suffrage was decidedly a pastime for the wealthy.

James' uncle was the first politician in Wisconsin to submit a suffrage referendum. It failed. Her father, David James, submitted a bill for suffrage when he was sent to the state senate in 1910. He narrowly missed. Having failed in securing that watershed accomplishment at the state level, Ada was ultimately successful in dispatching her father to Washington to present Wisconsin's 19th Amendment ratification papers, giving women the right to vote. This shocked the powers that be in the nation's capital. Most assumed Wyoming would be the first state to force the issue. It was widely believed Wisconsin's progressives talked the talk but rarely walked the walk regarding real change for women.

As a direct result, some four decades later Dena Smith was elected state treasurer in 1960, the first woman elected to a statewide office in Wisconsin. James herself never held elected office but for a short time was involved with the state Republican Party. She held a lifelong affiliation with the League of Women Voters.

which the town is the commercial center. The area was first settled by Yankees and settlers from the British Isles in the two years following statehood; dairy was almost immediately the number one industry. Frank Lloyd Wright was born here in 1869, and several of the community's buildings were designed by the famed architect. Ada James, a pioneer in U.S. women's suffrage, was also born in Richland Center; she led a second wave of women's rights campaigners to its ultimate fruition with the passage of the 19th Amendment.

Sights

Designer Frank Lloyd Wright dubbed it his "Mayan House," and the red-brick **A.D. German Warehouse,** with its flat roof and cement frieze, does show some temple overtones. Designed and built in 1915, during what many experts have called the zenith of his artistry, it is one of few surviving structures of this period. Wright forsook all interior walls and a cooling system, both radical for the time. Today the warehouse has a gift shop, tourist information center, a small theater on the ground floor, and a Frank Lloyd

Wright museum and gallery on the second. Guided tours by appointment only, call (608) 647-2808 for information.

At the end of W. 2nd St., take a stroll across the Pine River via a pedestrian footbridge. It seems you're right atop the water and makes for a great picture. Also get a gander at the whole town from **Miner Park** on a bluff overlooking the town.

Rockbridge is a well-named spot five miles north of town. Right off WI 80 is legendary **Natural Bridge Park,** right in the Pine River Valley. Eons of erosion subtly hewed a chasm, then a tunnel, out of the rock. The site is of historic significance, as it was one of the shelters for Blackhawk and his band in their doomed flight from the U.S. Army in 1832. Camping is allowed, but only with pre-registration (register at the Natural Bridge Store, tel. (608) 647-4673).

In addition to the famed natural bridge, along CR SR you'll find another oddity, **Steamboat Rock,** as they say around here, "drydocked above the Pine River." A final rock whittled into the regional menagerie is **Elephant Rock,** viewed along WI 58—ask for directions at the local tourist office.

the A.D. German Warehouse

GREAT RIVER ROAD

This famed road stretches from the source of the Mississippi River in Lake Itasca, Minnesota, and parallels the Ol' Miss all the way to New Orleans. The 85 miles of the Great River Road north from La Crosse are unquestionably the best-known stretch of the road, but the roadway that broaches Wisconsin, Illinois, and Iowa near Dubuque (not even a town shows up on the Wisconsin side), and follows a patchwork of state and county roads north to La Crosse is serious road-tripper mileage in itself. Along the way it bypasses wacky religious grottos, anachronistic Big River ferries, more than one historically and archaeologically significant settlement, and, halfway to La Crosse at Prairie du Chien, the conjoinment of the Wisconsin and Mississippi Rivers. An alphabet-soup jumble of roads is involved in the southern stretch, so if you think

you're lost (you likely won't be), just look for the green and white wheelhouse signs, which mark the way in the southern stretches (no longer apparent in the northern half).

The towns along the River Road are tidy, north-to-south platted hamlets with the river as Main Street, some but certainly not all prettied up for river road traffic. There is little auto traffic along the whole route, but no matter where you are along the road, freight trains roar by with alarming regularity (and speed), the sound clashing with the barges chugging along the river.

TO THE WISCONSIN RIVER

From Dubuque—that's East Dubuque, in Illinois—the road spins out of sight of the river for the first handful of miles, and there's really not much to see until you get to Dickeyville. Just across the border into Wisconsin, you'll pass a Wisconsin Travel Information Center. Stop in mid-May through August daily 8 a.m.-6 p.m., the rest of the year 'til 4 p.m.

Potosi
Highway 61 departs Dickeyville, passes through Tennyson—which you won't much notice—then heads to WI 133 and on the way to Potosi, the state's self-proclaimed "Catfish Capital." The town proudly boasts the longest main street in the

---

GREAT RIVER ROAD HIGHLIGHTS

Dickeyville Grotto, Dickeyville
Eagle-watching, Cassville
Granddad's Bluff, La Crosse
Stonefield, Cassville
Villa Louis, Prairie du Chien
Wyalusing State Park, Wyalusing

world without an intersection—that's three miles without a stop, or even a glance sideways at a cross street. Potosi was the earliest in the state to open a mine, and the last to close one; a nearby mine shut operations in 1960. The town name even means "mineral wealth." "Badger huts," the hastily constructed sleeping and breaktime quarters that lead miners burrowed into hillsides and inspired the state's nickname, can still be seen in the bluffs above the town. The largest port on the upper Mississippi (predating statehood) and the lead mines supplying Union forces (and, some say, the Confederates) solidified the local economy to the extent that Potosi real estate was the most valuable in the state by 1850. The **Dutch Hollow Rock House,** built in 1847, is the Wis-

DICKEYVILLE GROTTO

The over-the-top marriage of jingoism and religious reverence, the Dickeyville Grotto is one of innumerable Midwest grottoes constructed around the turn of the century, when a papal blessing allowed many religiosos to go off the deep end and build what became serious tourist attractions. Constructed around an Italian-carved statue of the Virgin Mary cradling Jesus, the Dickeyville Grotto was the 10-year devotional labor of Reverend Father Mathias Wernerus. Like other grottoes, it is an odd—some say distasteful, others say divine—aesthetically challenging assemblage of broken glass, tile, stone, gravel, petrified wood, shells, and even gems, affixed to virtually every nook and cranny of the place. Linings are even done in onyx.

The disquieting part for some is the patriotic wall displaying Abe Lincoln and George Washington next to Christopher Columbus, not to mention the Stars and Stripes joined with the Vatican's standard. The rear is buttressed by a wall of saints. Flower beds explode in color come spring. And this just begins to describe the visual business.

Some view religious grottoes as an embarrassment to the devout, others will road-trip through two states to pick up a tacky souvenir, and still other find them truly inspirational. Whatever the case, this is the souvenir spot of the Great River Road. The grounds at the grotto, 305 W. Main St., are open all the time. Free tours are available daily June-Aug. 9 a.m.-5 p.m., and weekends May, September, and October the same hours.

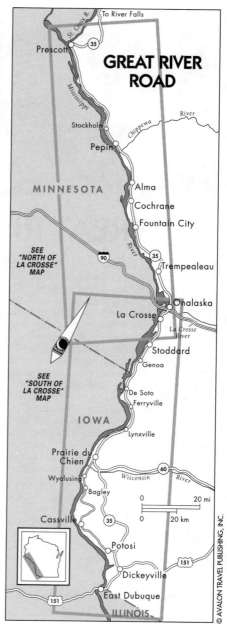

© AVALON TRAVEL PUBLISHING, INC.

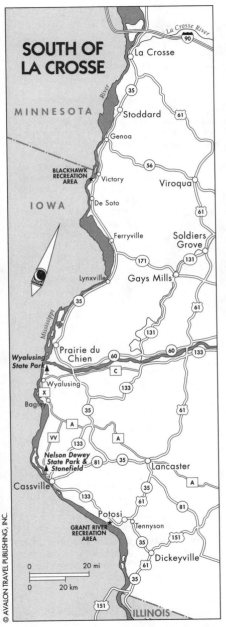

SOUTH OF LA CROSSE

La Crosse River

La Crosse

MINNESOTA

Stoddard

Genoa

BLACKHAWK RECREATION AREA

Victory

Viroqua

IOWA

De Soto

Ferryville

Soldiers Grove

Lynxville

Gays Mills

Prairie du Chien

Wyalusing State Park

Wyalusing

Bagley

Nelson Dewey State Park & Stonefield

Lancaster

Cassville

Potosi

Tennyson

GRANT RIVER RECREATION AREA

Dickeyville

0   20 mi
0   20 km

ILLINOIS

consin turn on the George Washington-slept-here approach—only here it was John Wilkes Booth.

Real grimy history can be found at the **St. John Lead Mine,** along WI 133 on Main St., tel. (608) 763-2121, purportedly the oldest lead mine—and thus permanent commercial enterprise—in the state. Hand-dug into what the Native Americans termed "Snake Cave", the site was visited by Nicholas Perrot prior to the turn of the 18th century. Tours take in the entire mine and offices (get a gander at the shingles). A fee is charged, and take a jacket—it can get chilly in there.

Also at the mine you'll find a canoe rental operation, with drop-and-paddle unguided trips on the Grant and Big Platte Rivers. Rentals are for a full day regardless of your itinerary and cost $11-16 per canoe per day, life preservers extra. The trip on the Grant is the long one at 37 total miles (18 hours), on the Big Platte it's shorter (16 miles) and has slow water the whole way. Primitive camping is available along the entire stretch, but get advice from the canoe rental operators as to where it's best to pitch a tent.

South of Potosi along WI 133 is the **Grant River Recreation Area,** tel. (608) 763-2140, a U.S. Army Corps of Engineers-maintained riverside campground ($10) open early April-late October.

North of Potosi a mile, then east on Hippy Hollow Road brings you to the **British Hollow Smelter,** the last of its kind in this region. With a 200-foot underground chimney thrust deep into the hillside, the smelter was once one of the largest around.

Restaurants abound in the Potosi area, but wherever you eat, sample the Mississippi catfish (as if they'd let you avoid it). The main street features a bunch of supper clubs, and you'll find more places to eat in Tennyson.

Triangular brown and yellow signs, marking an **auto tour** that takes in all regional points of historical significance, line the roads around Potosi and Tennyson.

Lancaster

You may as well take a side trip on your way to Cassville, since you won't see the river anyway. Lancaster, known as the "City of the Dome", is an 11-mile jump up the road. Once you espy the glass-and-copper topped dome of the courthouse, modeled after St. Peter's Basilica, you'll know why. Check out the murals of regional history inside the courthouse (done by Franz Rohrback,

EAGLE-WATCHING

The bald eagle, on the federal government's endangered species list since 1972, is making a dramatic reappearance in many places. One of the primary eagle habitats is the Lower Wisconsin State Riverway, starting in Sauk City in south-central Wisconsin and stretching to the confluence of the Mississippi River. South of here to the state line, the Upper Mississippi Wildlife Refuge is another, and the Cassville area is one of the best areas to view eagles within that region. Having rebounded from perilously low levels, Wisconsin now has almost 600 eagle nesting sites, a sevenfold increase in a quarter-century. Though eagles are still getting pushed out by development, poached by knuckleheads, electrocuted by power lines, and poisoned by toxic fish, the future isn't quite so grim.

Bald eagles really aren't bald; that falsecognate word came from the Middle English ball(e)d—"white spot." The much more impressive scientific name, Haliaetus leucocephalus, roughly translates as "white-headed sea bird." The average mature bald eagle has a wingspan of six to eight feet and weighs up to 15 pounds. Females on average are noticeably larger. Adults have the snow-white head and tail, a brown body, and yellow bill, feet, and eyes. Younger birds have more white mixed in with the brown coat—the younger, the whiter. The white head doesn't fully appear until the bird is four or five years old. Eagles travel 30-40 mph in flight but in dives can eclipse 100 mph. Their vision is six times more acute than a human's.

Eagles generally live 30-50 years, though in the wild that number has slowly dropped. Generally, nesting pairs mate for life; females lay one to three eggs in March, and both birds incubate the eggs. One nest weighed in at two tons.

Habitat and Viewing

The primary reason for Cassville's preponderance of bald eagles is its location. Situated near lock and dam #10 along the Mississippi River, and with two riverside power plants, the town has open water year-round, necessary for attracting eagles. Furthermore, the craggy variations in southwestern Wisconsin's topography allow for maximum isolation in eagle nesting sites. Finally, fish are attracted to the warm waters of the power plant discharge, so food is readily available.

In the winter, Cassville can have as many as 200 eagles in one location; as many as 10 will stay in the region for the summer, with the rest moving back north to northern Wisconsin or the Upper Peninsula of Michigan. They do not migrate per se; they simply move south in winter for food and stop when they find it. Best sites around town to view the eagles are the Wisconsin Power and Light Co. generating station along CR VV northwest of Cassville (look for the road marked "Boat Landing") and the bluffs of Nelson Dewey State Park, also accessed from CR VV. Back in town, simply follow the road closest to the river and you'll spot dozens of them. The other power plant is on the south side of town, via WI 133.

One obscure spot is six miles north of Nelson Dewey State Park along CR VV, then west on Duncan Road. The **Eagle Valley Nature Habitat-Glen Haven** is a grouping point for up to 1,000 birds in winter. Don't expect a sparkling visitor's center; it's nothing but tranquil Mississippi River banks and lots of eagles on 1,500 acres.

who also did huge murals in the State Capitol rotunda). Or get a gander at the Civil War Monument and G.A.R. display on the grounds, the first such memorial in the United States. Public areas have innumerable historical monuments, including not one but two of the state's first governor, Nelson Dewey, who's buried in a nearby cemetery. A block east of the courthouse is the **Cunningham Museum,** the local take on a historical society museum, loaded with martial history and an interesting exhibit on the state's earliest African-American settlement.

Cassville

With a solitary general store after its founding in 1831, Cassville, 16 miles west of Potosi along

WI 133, played second fiddle to the larger lead-mining boomtown. But locals championed the village for capital status anyway. The California gold rush eventually helped end the mining riches of Potosi; worse, the Grant River had silted so badly that it was essentially unnavigable. Cassville took over the crucial river traffic control and soon eclipsed its neighbor.

River transportation began with a ferry as far back as 1836, and today the **Cassville Car Ferry** still plows across the Mississippi into Iowa. This is one of the few remaining river ferries in the U.S. (another is in Merrimac, Wisconsin); the paddle-wheel and horse-and-treadmill versions have finally been retired, but it's still a tri-states area tradition during the May-Oct. season. This one decidedly ain't free—$10 per car, $5 motorcycle, $2 bicycle, $1 walk-on. Prior to Memorial Day, the ferry makes trips Sat.-Sun., then daily until Labor Day when it reverts to the weekend schedule. Hours are 9 a.m.-9 p.m. The departure point in Cassville is Riverside Park (featuring an effigy mound in the shape of an eagle); the last ferry returns from Millville, Iowa, at 8:40 p.m.

The big draws for Cassville are the **Stonefield** agricultural heritage and village life museum, and across the road Nelson Dewey State Park, both a mile north of town. Through a gate a guide leads tours of a contiguous 1900 farmstead and the "innovations" (antique equipment and designs) of the time. Farther along across Dewey Creek (through a covered bridge) are the 30 reconstructed buildings done up as an explicatory showcase of turn-of-the-century Midwest village life: broom factory, meat market, cheese factory, barbershop, creamery, and more. The highlight of the whole shebang is the home site of Wisconsin's first governor, Nelson Dewey, next to the state park entrance. The original building was mostly lost in an 1873 fire, but enough millwork and detail work was saved to reconstruct it following his death. It's a particularly rare architectural specimen—southern plantation amidst pastoral dairyland, fitting the mold of rural gothic, a leading design of the time, though not in Wisconsin. Dewey meticulously planned his rustic vision of a gentleman's retreat down to the stone fences snaking through the fields, also done to give local masons jobs. Stonefield also holds disparate events ranging from parlor and lawn games, scavenger hunts and storytelling days for kids, and great dairy

heritage or threshing festivals. Open daily late May-early October. May-June and Sept.-Oct. it's open 10 a.m.- 4 p.m., until 5 p.m. rest of season. Tours are given hourly. Admission is $7.50 for adults, $3.50 for children 5-12.

Nelson Dewey State Park is a 750-acre plot hewn from the original 2,000 acres of the Dewey family spread along Dewey Creek, one of the only large plantations in the Upper Midwest. The nucleus of the park is the restored homestead, but most visitors head up to the majestic belvedere bluffs for miles-long vistas of the Mississippi River valley. Along the bluffs you'll see groupings of prehistoric **Indian mounds,** the two most prominent at the cliff top (no effigy mounds, such as those found up the road in Wyalusing State Park). Mostly conical in shape, these rare constructions are puzzling for their chain-like arrangement. A seven-acre bluff facing southwest above the river encompasses the Dewey Heights Prairie; a dry, limy prairie set aside by the state as a scientific reserve in 1952. There is a short trail through the prairie, a 40-site (two walk-in) campground ($10 resident plus $5 daily sticker fee) in a walnut grove along the creek, and three brief miles of trails along the bluffs.

The always-helpful chamber of commerce has brochures for a **historical walking tour** of Cassville, taking in historic structures. Most are currently in use for purposes other than their original designs, including the Denniston Building, once a proud and opulent hotel built by Nelson Dewey and eventually turned into apartments.

Events: One of the largest assemblages of bald eagles along this stretch of the Mississippi River (one link in a massive national wildlife refuge) is on display in January during **Bald Eagle Days.** The late January weekend features lectures, public viewings, live bird displays (including horned and screech owls, red-tail hawks, kestrels, and peregrine falcons in addition to eagle varieties), hayrides, guided bus trips (for a fee), and slide shows.

In July, national attention focuses on Cassville's **Twin-O-Rama,** feting multiple births from across the country since 1929. It's a photo-op from heaven for three days—a town populated wholly by twins and triplets.

Practicalities: On the south side of town, off on Jack Oak Rd., is **Eagle's Roost Landing,** tel. (608) 725-5553, a motel with the bonus of riverside cabins. Rooms start at $45 for a double in the motel, $65 for a cabin big enough for four people. A marina out back has a slip that can handle just about any normally sized boat and offers boat and motor rentals (from $10 per day). The Eagle's Roost also has houseboats for rent, one 45-footer and a 50-footer with most everything you need included in the price: $925 for a four-day rental or weekend, $1,500 weekly. The 1855 **Geiger House,** 401 Denniston St., tel. (608) 725-5419, was built on land belonging to then-Governor Nelson Dewey. Three rooms with two shared baths are $70 s or d. Originally raised as a riverboat boardinghouse, the **River View B&B,** 117 W. Front St., tel. (608) 725-5895, has an outdoor hot tub and four rooms with two shared baths. Rates run $60.

None too many cafes in this town. In fact, there's only the classic cafe **Robbin's Nest,** 115 E. Amelia St., once the town bank, with a standard cafe menu to go with the robin's-egg-blue dining room. Cozy and quiet. Open 6 a.m.-2 p.m. weekdays, 7 a.m.-2 p.m. weekends.

Bagley

County Roads VV and then A lead out of Cassville through deep, winding valleys—a pretty drive to Bagley and Wyalusing. The former features some of the best river-views along the route, the latter offering a sandy swimming beach; neither is very large. Wyalusing, once a rousing 600 people, now counts a dozen permanent residents. In comparison Bagley looks absolutely worldly, and in fact there is a bar in Bagley that has a large world map full of pushpins left by international visitors. Bagley also has two large **campgrounds**—your best bet for a place to pitch a tent if Wyalusing State Park up the road is full.

Wyalusing State Park

Judged by many travelers to be the most scenic of Wisconsin's state parks, the site was ready-made for park status high above the confluence of the Wisconsin and Mississippi Rivers. Perhaps the most historically significant park in the region, it was here where Father Jacques Marquette and Louis Joliet discovered the upper Mississippi in 1673. It's also the western terminus of the 92-mile lower Wisconsin State Riverway, the undammed and wild lowest portion of the river, now protected from development. The most popular spot in the park is Point Lookout, 300 feet above the rich blue waters of the two rivers. Sixteen impeccable miles of trails branch and twist through variegated topography. **Sentinel Ridge Trail** passes effigy mounds from three distinct native settlement periods—not to mention the heavy population of wild turkeys. (The mound groupings within the park are architecturally significant because of their thorough preservation.) Along the Wisconsin River is a trail following segments of a real-life immigrant path; another wagon trail loops back to the main trails and goes past a settler's semi-permanent "pit stop" point. Canoeists have marked routes totaling 20 miles along the backwater sloughs of the Mississippi; fishing is excellent, especially for walleye. Winter camping is permitted, and a trail is open for cross-country skiing.

This is superlative hiking but none too special camping. Two huge campgrounds offer some 130 sites and community showers; group camps feature indoor dorms. Campsites are in the open and closely grouped—no rustic solitude. Campsites cost $10; a park sticker is an additional $5 per day.

PRAIRIE DU CHIEN

After the strategic viability of the Fox and Wisconsin River corridors were called into question following the establishment of Fort Howard in Green Bay, it was just a matter of time before the military started hacking a road and stringing forts through the wilderness to put a damper on the pesky Indians—and the British and French interlopers. Prairie du Chien, chronologically the second-oldest settlement after Green Bay, would become the westernmost point of that chain of forts, one of four built on the site.

Native Americans originally inhabited the islands in the Mississippi River channels. Nicholas Perrot showed up not long after Marquette and Joliet and may or may not have erected a fort on one of the islands, by now a main node on the fur-trade network and populated by bartering Native Americans and itinerant French. Several thousand Indians may have been living in the area by the time the first Europeans showed up, around the start of the American Revolution. The name comes not from a ubiquity of prairie rodents, but from a respected Indian chief, honored by French settlers. It was at one time a major "clamming" center—clams were all the rage as buttons, and the oysters could command thousands in eastern markets.

Prairie du Chien today could visually define what a Mississippi River town is all about, equal parts somnolent village and proud, historical tourist stop. The backdrop of high, craggy bluffs is set off nicely by meticulously landscaped street corners—flowers bloom at every one of them. Rows of willow trees frame an appealing diversity in home architecture.

Villa Louis
One of the state's most respected historical sites, under the auspices of the State Historical Society of Wisconsin, is Villa Louis, in its time likely the most ostentatious and opulent home in all the Upper Midwest. The extended plot of land on St. Feriole Island was originally the site of Fort Shelby, constructed immediately after the War of 1812 to protect the river channels and lucrative trade routes from the British. (Native Americans had used the island for numerous burial mounds, and the structures were built right atop some of them.) In 1840, Hercules Dousman, a phenomenally wealthy (he's known as Wisconsin's first millionaire) fur trader with the American Fur Co., originally built a simple home—the House on the Mound, in a nice slap to the face of Native Americans in the area—on the original Fort Crawford site. His son, H. Louis Dousman, for whatever impels otherwise rational folks to do such things, decided to raise the most palatial estate of them all. Like all great acts of such caliber, this one went belly up. Dousman died soon after the house's completion, and his wife and family couldn't keep up the payments. Following World War I, it started on a merry-go-round of different uses, including a boarding school, before finally being turned over to the city in the 1930s for a museum. In 1995 the estate became an even more marvelous glimpse at the region's past, when extensive (and expensive at $2 million) restoration work was begun in an attempt to correct earlier historical renovations; the friendly invasion force even used the original designs and

Villa Louis

implements, some in vaults in London. Even better, curators have managed to relocate original art work or furniture scattered all over the world and have descendants will it back to the estate. The complex includes the old carriage house and historical artwork detailing local history. There is also a fur trade museum and assorted other original buildings. The museum is open May-Oct. daily 9 a.m.-5 p.m., with tours conducted at regular hours through 4 p.m. Admission is $7.75 adults, $7 seniors, and $3.50 children 5-12. The grounds are always open, and nearby on the same island is a Victorian historical education walk.

Other Sights
Somewhat lesser known is the **Prairie du Chien Museum at Fort Crawford**, tel. (608) 326-6960, the remainder of the fort where Black Hawk surrendered, closing the final battle of the Indian wars east of the Mississippi. On the site of the second Fort Crawford, both Zachary Taylor and Jefferson Davis spent military service time. The more intriguing segment of the museum, "Medical Progress," features Dr. William Beaumont's experiments on the human digestive system (on an Acadian fur trader with an untreatable belly wound) in the 1830s. Establishing not a few modern physiological practices in the process, Beaumont tied bits of food to surgical string to time the digestive process of the willing patient—200 times. Among the results: the first recorded temperature of the human stomach. Other exhibits trace Wisconsin medical history as well as display antique medical instruments or practices. Of great interest are the exhibits on Native American herbalist practices. Other buildings focus on regional history, particularly the Blackhawk War; fascinating is the look at Mississippi clamming, an erstwhile local industry. The three-building complex at 717 S. Beaumont Rd. is open May-Oct. Wed.-Sun 10 a.m.-5 p.m. Admission is $3 adults, $2.50 children 12 and under.

The **Old Rock School**, on the edge of downtown, is considered the oldest surviving school structure in Wisconsin. A military memorial was put up on the grounds in the 1990s.

Accommodations

Most of Prairie du Chien's accommodations are strung along WI 60 to the east, or north and south along the Great River Road (Marquette Road).

South Marquette Road has the lion's share of places to stay, most of them chains. Extremely nice—award-winning, in fact—is the **Bridgeport Inn,** tel. (608) 326-6082 or (800) 234-6082, with an indoor pool, spa, whirlpool suites, and a continental breakfast included. Rooms are $70 and up. Of the three other extremely cheap but exceptional locally owned motels to the south, try the spotlessly clean and charming **Holiday Motel,** 1010 S. Marquette Rd., tel. (608) 326-2448, with rooms starting at $36; many are decorated in historical themes.

For RVs, **Frenchman's Landing Campground,** tel. (608) 874-4563, seven miles north on WI 35, is the only campground in the area with sites on the river. Tent dwellers' best bet besides Wyalusing State Park is **La Riviere Park,** on Vineyard Coulee Rd. off WI 18 on the south end of town, offering primitive camping and nature trails through some native prairie swaths where you might spot a rare poppy wallow flower, once thought wiped out by agriculture.

Food

You'll note the amazing number of places dishing up or selling the local specialty—Mississippi catfish, smoked or fresh—or even the odd purveyor of turtle meat.

A Sunday institution of sorts in the tri-states area is a leisurely drive to Prairie du Chien to sample the slider-burgers at **Pete's,** a dainty burger-only joint built out of a caboose right downtown, serving Fri.-Sun. A couple of bucks will fill you up. Another with a lock on the local eaters-out is the **Hungry House,** at the junction of Highways 27 and 35. It has outstanding homemade pies and soups; the fresh catfish fries are equally renowned. From $3.

The venerable **Kaber's,** at the corner of Blackhawk and Main Streets, tel. (608) 326-6216, has been around since the '30s and still serves up standard supper club fare. Open at 4 p.m. daily. From $6. **Jeffers Black Angus,** tel. (608) 626-2222, a slightly more elegant supper club, is a couple of miles south, across from the airport. From $8. Likely the best view from any supper club is at **The Barn,** featuring a woodsy dining room decor, a cocktail lounge, a Sunday brunch,

and bluff vistas. Three miles north along Main St., tel. (608) 326-4941, it serves brunch only on Sunday, but check with them, this may expand.

The oddest bar around is the **St. Feriole Railroad** along Water St., a tavern built right into an old railroad car.

Events

Prairie du Chien, over Father's Day, hosts one of the Midwest's largest **Rendezvous,** when buckskin-clad and beaver hat-adorned trapper, trader, and soldier wannabes congregate for a long weekend of food and festivities. The similar **Civil War Encampment** takes place in late July and the biggest of them all, the **Villa Louis Carriage Classic,** comes up in September.

Services and Information

At the bridge along WI 18 is another **Wisconsin Travel Information Center,** open summers Mon.-Sat. 8 a.m.-6 p.m. and Sunday 9 a.m.-5 p.m. otherwise April-Oct. daily 9 a.m.-5 p.m.

WISCONSIN RIVER TO LA CROSSE

The 60-odd miles separating Prairie du Chien's Villa Louis and La Crosse are the most underrepresented mileage on the Great River Road. Which isn't to say the Tinytowns don't warrant mention, they're simply the ones that lie the lowest or spruce themselves up the least for tourist traffic. Also on the positive side: the road itself winds through some of the most appealing, challenging terrain on the route, flanked by vaulting bluffs and right-atop-the-railway river views.

Lynxville

The highway changes out of Prairie du Chien, to WI 35—and only WI 35 goes all the way to La Crosse. Fifteen scenic but otherwise uneventful miles later is Lynxville, described by an old tour guide as "another faded village on a river bluff." Soporific today, the shells of old standing structures used to serve a regional purpose. In the 19th century as Prairie du Chien, and Cassville to the south, developed into primary river ports, Lynxville's railroad dominated, at one time the railroad hub south of La Crosse. The largest log raft ever on the Mississippi River was put together and floated from the quay here in 1896, a monstrous beast at 250 feet wide, 1,550 feet long, and comprised of 2.3 million board feet (rivaling the barges of today). All in all, the town back then was probably eight times as large as it is today, with many residents living on then-extant islets dotting the river before locks and dams flooded them out. The village today sits at the southern cusp of the lake created by engineers a generation ago, a river lake stretching 17 miles north to De Soto. Lynxville offers a dearth of practicalities—a tavern, gas station, an antiques shop, and very basic sustenance dining, and some decent river scenery along **Lock and Dam #9.** Most unique is **Hubbard's Fishing Float and Diner.** When you arrive at Gordon's Bay boat landing, just raise the flag and the float boat will come down on the hour to get you.

Leaving Lynxville, a choice—north along WI 35 through a historical recreation area and more old river towns, or east to loop through rolling hills for some S-curve road routes to classic southwestern Wisconsin river villages. This is the area to pull out the county road maps and snoop around atop the blufflines; lots of grand river vistas are apparent north of Lynxville.

Side Trip

North of Lynxville, head east 13 miles miles along WI 171 through Mt. Sterling into the topography of green gumdrops that the region is known for. Mount Sterling has little other than a cheese factory specializing in award-winning goat cheese. Another unknown Wisconsin writer—Ben Logan—grew up in the surrounding coulees and wrote a touching memoir, *The Land Remembers.* Eventually, you'll come to **Gays Mills,** legendary for its apple orchards. Just after the turn of the 20th century the state of Wisconsin scoured the southern tier of the state for promising orchards in which to plant experimental apple trees. The coulee valleys between the Wisconsin and Mississippi Rivers turned out to be perfect for the hardy fruit. Come spring and fall, photo road-trippers flock to the blossoms or the harvesting. Along WI 131 (which you'll need for the next stop) is **Log Cabin Village,** tel. (608) 735-4341, a grouping of original structures from the region. Open May-Oct. 8 a.m.-10 p.m.; tours are available by appointment.

North from Gays Mills along WI 131 takes you directly to the cutting edge community of **Soldier's Grove,** notable as the only solar-powered community you'll probably ever see. Lying in a dangerous flood plain in a cleft along the Kickapoo River, Soldier's Grove was incessantly lapped at by floodwaters before a new dike was built in the '60s. Naturally, not too long after that, in 1978, the town was devastated by a flood. Picking up the pieces and moving to higher ground, the town had the commendable foresight to plan its current eco-friendliness—all of the buildings of **Solar Town Center** are heated at least 50% by the sun. The martial moniker inspired the park south of town, designed as a war memorial to local and regional veterans. For practicalities, there is the **Old Oak Inn,** along WI 131 S, tel. (608) 624-5217, offering a heated pool and good rooms from $40 and up. It also serves outstanding meals; open daily except Tuesday.

Out of town along WI 61, the highway leads to **Viroqua,** one of the prettiest towns in southwestern Wisconsin; its Main Street has undergone a careful restoration. Along Main Street, the **Sherry-Butt House,** run by the county historical society, was constructed southern-style in 1870 and has been occupied by only two families since. Open Sunday 1-5 p.m. Tours are also available for an old country church and one-room school along Broadway. Call (608) 637-7396 for information. Otherwise, there's not a damn thing to do in Viroqua other than wander around, go to the last county fair of the season in the state (September), or watch an occasional yet outstanding demolition derby.

Out of Viroqua, WI 56 cuts back to the Great River Road, or you can head up to Westby, another of the "New Norways" in southwestern Wisconsin, for a stop at the indescribably wonderful **Borgen's Norwegian Cafe and Bakery,** or the luxurious **Westby House,** 200 W. State St., tel. (608) 634-4112, an antiques-laden B&B that has a dining room open for lunch and dinner.

Ferryville

Back on the River Road, Ferryville can't rival downriver Potosi for the longest main street without an intersection, but it's got a fairly long main street itself—it is in point of fact recognized as the longest in any town or village with only one street. (Apocryphal or not, the more colorful stories tell it that local laws allowed for the dispensation of liquor only every mile; saloonkeepers dutifully measured exactly one mile between each.) They should have kept the original name—Humble Bush—because that's sure what it is today. Instead, economic pragmatists had their way when the riverboats began crossing between here and

Iowa. Ferryville's big claim to fame is cheese, dispensing cheese in myriad outlets, including the huge **Ferryville Cheese Retail Outlet,** with over 100 varieties to pick from. It's also a good spot to pick up Amish or country-style quilts, and stop by the Swing Inn to get a peek at the four-foot-plus rattlesnake skin, taken from surrounding hills, which are rumored to be rife with rattlers. The village allows free camping in the park at the south end of the village; otherwise, the **Grandview,** tel. (608) 734-3235, has the best rooms, from $38. Or, the **Mississippi Humble Bush B&B,** tel. (608) 734-3022, has four rooms and a large loft for dorm-style group lodging. Rooms from $65.

De Soto

Nine more miles of railroad accompaniment brings the road to De Soto, named for you-know-who, the European commonly held as the first to espy the Mississippi River (and who eventually wound up in its watery clutches—his soldiers depositing his body there to protect it from the "desecration of savages") back in 1541.

The martial devotion of the local cafe befits De Soto, which, along with Victory four miles up the road, served as the western endpoints to one of the state's least proud moments, the pursuit of Chief Black Sparrow Hawk (immortalized erroneously as Blackhawk) and his Sauk and Fox Indians across the state, culminating in the Battle of Bad Axe at the mouth of the river of the same name, two miles north. The battle had two effects: it ended serious Indian resistance, and, when Blackhawk became a nationally prominent figure, a flood of settlers poured into the state. Today, the U.S. Army Corps of Engineers has established a somewhat somber **park** at the battle site with riverfront camping (sites are $8 and reservable; call 877-444-6777), a sandy beach, and a slew of historical sites. Various educational and campfire programs are ongoing throughout the summer. Ironically, two miles to the north, Victory was named in honor of Black Hawk's defeat.

Genoa

Three miles north of Victory opens the mouth of the Bad Axe River proper, near Genoa, an untouched classic river town. Trading outposts were raised in the 1840s, and the town grew with a decided Italian flavor as many early settlers were Italian fishermen who started out as lead miners in Galena, IL, before migrating here for the fishing. The Bad Axe River allowed the Dairyland Power Cooperative to begin the first rural electric (here, hydroelectric) project in western Wisconsin. The state's first nuclear power plant was also located here, built in 1967 and taken off line in 1987. Fishing is key here, with one of the upper Mississippi's best walleye runs; there's even a barge anchored below the lock for fishing—**Clement's Fishing Barge,** tel. (608) 689-2382. Barges, found along many of the locks, are a great way to actually get on the river to fish, and they can be downright cheap, under $10 as a rule. Much of the fish is stocked by the **Genoa Fish Hatchery,** actually located closer to Victory. Another of the "largest anywhere" variety of fish hatcheries the state seems to specialize in, this one is the most diverse, raising cold- and warm-water fish. Open Mon.-Fri. 7 a.m.-3:30 p.m. Otherwise, Genoa's **Lock and Dam #8** is one of the river's best for viewing "lock throughs" as the ships pass.

Accommodations and catfish-cheek dinners are found at **Big River Inn,** tel. (608) 689-2652, with rooms from $32. Five-buck (or less) emergency camping is available at Engh's Fish Market, offering showers and electricity for RVs only. Tenters should head to Stoddard.

Stoddard

North of Genoa, the river views turn downright splendid, and pulloffs are pocked into the roadside. Midway between Genoa and Stoddard is an outstanding drive, off the road to the east, to an abandoned quarry, now the Old Settlers Overlook, some 500 feet above the river. Before the construction of Genoa's lock and dam, Stoddard wasn't even close to the Mississippi, but upon completion of the dam almost 20,000 acres of bottomland was covered, and suddenly Stoddard could call itself a riverboat town, along with a super view of the town park across one of the river's widest stretches. There's great ornithology along the Coon Creek bottoms; the area is protected federal refuge land.

Stoddard has one of the best county parks in the state-**Goose Island,** with over a thousand acres, six miles of trails, and more than enough camping. Also find campsites at **Stoddard Park.**

LA CROSSE

It would be nearly impossible to go away from a trip to La Crosse without some sort of regard for the landscape. The folks are friendly, too, but man, that topography just sort of grips you. The castellated and craggy circumference of one of Wisconsin's prettiest cities, spread along the Mississippi River, is often voted number one by Midwestern travel mavens as far as aesthetics goes, not to mention the views those heights proffer. Even Mark Twain, after a visit, referred to it as "a choice town." Buffalo Bill Cody found the town so much to his liking that he brought his Wild West Show back again and again, and he eventually purchased part of Barrons Island.

Situated where the mini-mighty La Crosse and Black Rivers flow into the Mississippi, La Crosse is situated below one of the Mississippi's major bights, allowing heavy commercial traffic. Here, the prairie, and thus all paths on it, literally march to the river's edge. (And Native American legend holds that it is an area of "No Wind"—and the locals will inform you that no tornadoes have ever occurred at the confluence.) The initial name—"prairie la crosse"—affixed in the early 1680s, stuck a century later when equally puzzled French trappers saw the Winnebago playing the fast-paced game of lattice-head sticks, permanently infusing the original name with cruciform symbolism. The equally apropos nickname "Gateway City" is a more mundane take on what the city became known for.

One of the wide channels islands impelled bigbritches, 18-year-old New York dreamer Nathan Myrick to alight from a federal keelboat in 1841 and erect a rough-hewn cabin on what today is Pettibone Park and begin commerce with the Winnebago. Despite the prime location, permanent settlement was a hard sell and in 1848 still only a hardy two dozen people were permanently ensconced on the hard-working shoreline.

Following statehood, the village suddenly became a town with a huge influx of German and Scandinavian immigrants, many lured by the Rhine-like aesthetics. During the Civil War and despite a regional depression, La Crosse found its position solidified by the natural waterways. Traffic was impeded along the Mississippi, and

the government needed routes via La Crosse. This situation would continue through World War I and convince the U.S. government to reinvest in Mississippi-channel transportation following that. Eventually, La Crosse became the major link in the Mississippi network between St. Paul and Iowa. With the river traffic came the railroads, and everyone knows what that can do to a simple town's desire for permanence. Breweries arose to reinvigorate the community—chiefly four large-scale breweries, making the city for a long time one of the state's brewing cornerstones.

SIGHTS

Granddad's Bluff

This famed rock upthrust, towering (for Wisconsin, anyway) over 550 feet above the back haunches of La Crosse is without question the number one scenic spot in western Wisconsin. Overlooking three states (Wisconsin, Minnesota, and even Iowa—a viewing radius of some 40 miles) and the Mississippi Valley, the bluff is a perfect representation of the 15-million-year-old geology of the Mississippi Valley. Don't go expecting Rocky Mountain panoramas, but on a clear day, when the muggy August weather doesn't vaporize the whole thing into a translucent haze, the view can be superlative. To get there, follow Main Street east until it becomes Bliss Road.

Museums and Historic Structures

A stroll through La Crosse offers an eyeful of superb structural facades in every direction, and plenty of museums. Chief among these is the **Hixon House,** 429 N. 7th St., tel. (608) 782-1980, an opulent Italianate mansion originally built for Gideon Hixon, yet another timber magnate. With nary a reproduction within, the place is beloved by Victorian buffs. Woodworkers will appreciate the variegated native Wisconsin woods used for the interiors. The flaxen-colored home stands amid brilliant gardens and adjacent to a meticulously preserved wash house. What everyone actually remembers is the intriguing "Turkish Nook"—inspired by a late 1890s

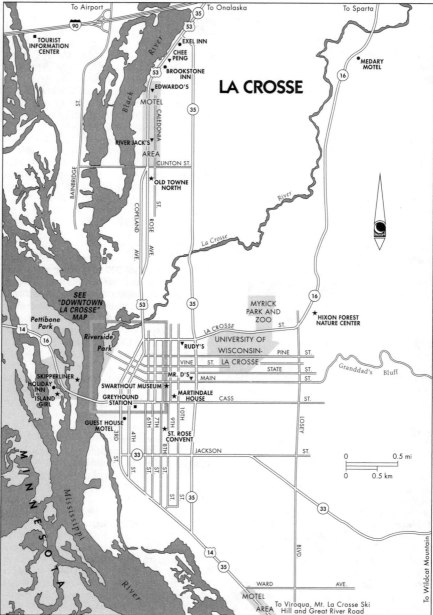

LA CROSSE

To Airport
To Onalaska
To Sparta

TOURIST
INFORMATION
CENTER

MEDARY
MOTEL

EXEL INN
CHEE
PENG
BROOKSTONE
INN
EDWARDO'S
MOTEL

RIVER JACK'S

OLD TOWNE
NORTH

CLINTON ST.

CALEDONIA
AREA

COPELAND AVE.
ROSE AVE.

BAINBRIDGE

Black River

La Crosse River

SEE
"DOWNTOWN
LA CROSSE"
MAP

Pettibone
Park

Riverside
Park

MYRICK
PARK AND
ZOO

HIXON FOREST
NATURE CENTER

RUDY'S

UNIVERSITY OF
WISCONSIN-
LA CROSSE

PINE ST.
VINE ST.
STATE ST.
MAIN ST.
CASS ST.

Granddad's Bluff

SKIPPERLINER
HOLIDAY
INN
ISLAND
GIRL

SWARTHOUT MUSEUM
GREYHOUND
STATION

MR. D'S

MARTINDALE
HOUSE

GUEST HOUSE
MOTEL

ST. ROSE
CONVENT

JACKSON ST.

3RD ST.
4TH ST.
6TH ST.
7TH ST.
8TH ST.
9TH ST.
10TH ST.

LOSEY

0   0.5 mi
0   0.5 km

MINNESOTA

Mississippi River

BLVD.

WARD AVE.

MOTEL
AREA

To Viroqua, Mt. La Crosse Ski
Hill and Great River Road

To Wildcat Mountain

© AVALON TRAVEL PUBLISHING, INC.

predilection for everything Oriental—a room worthy of a sultan. The house is open Memorial Day-Labor Day daily 1-5 p.m., with admission of $4 adults, $3 seniors, $2 children.

New to La Crosse is the **Children's Museum of La Crosse,** 207 5th Ave., tel. (608) 784-2652, a three-floor blowout of hands-on fun for kids; parents might like some of the multimedia stuff, too. Open Tues.-Sat. 10 a.m.-5 p.m., Sunday noon-5 p.m.; admission is $3.50.

Brand new is the **Museum of Modern Technology,** 149 Sixth St. South, tel. (608) 785-2340, dedicated to preserving the history of science since the Middle Ages. It's appropriated a lot of astronaut Deke Slayton memorabilia from nearby Sparta (he was raised in Sparta), along with lots of U.S. bicycling history stuff (hard to figure the technology connection there). You'll find lots of traveling Smithsonian exhibits too. Hours are Tues.-Sat. 10 a.m.-5 p.m., Sunday 1-5 p.m.; admission is $3, $2 children.

The University of Wisconsin-La Crosse has an **archaeological museum and lab,** near 17th and State Streets. You can watch scientists at work processing artifacts from the region. Open weekdays 9 a.m.-4:30 p.m.; free.

At 9th and Main Streets in the library, the **Swarthout Museum,** tel. (608) 782-1980, is a more comprehensive museum look at local and regional history, traced all the way back to prehistoric times, also featuring more river life. One area lets kids try on period clothing. Open Tues.-Fri. 10 a.m.-5 p.m., weekends 1-5 p.m.; closed Sundays June-August. Free.

Not a museum really but an art gallery centered around the work of a prominent local artist, the **Sampson Gallery,** 600 N. 3rd St., features local, regional, and international artists. A heritage center here focuses on Wisconsin heritage, quite an interesting visual display of the state.

The **La Crosse Doll Museum,** 1213 Caledonia St., tel. (608) 785-0020, is in the heart of Old Towne North and contains nearly 7,000 dolls dating all the way back to Pre-Columbian periods. Its Norman Rockwell display is one-of-a-kind. Open Mon.-Sat. 10 a.m.-5 p.m., Sunday 11 a.m.-4:30 p.m. Admission is $3.50, $1 12 and under, $8 family.

On the grounds at Riverside Park is the **RiverUSA Museum,** tel. (608) 782-1980, a local historical repository for La Crosse and Mississippi River history. The museum has a bent for riverboats, including a somber exhibit on the *War Eagle.* The ship caught fire and sank in the Black River in 1870 and pretty much completes the city's riverboat history. Open daily 10 a.m.-5 p.m.

Scenic Drives

There are a few good drives in the area starting with the **Mindoro Cut.** The southern terminus is northeast of La Crosse in West Salem, then stretches up to Mindoro. A massive project when undertaken around

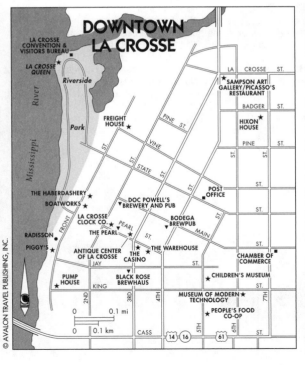

the turn of the century, the road was literally shorn into a ridge between the La Crosse and Black River valleys. The Cut was considered one of the most ambitious hand-carved roads in the U.S. when it was finished in 1906. Even with modern, leviathan earth-movers and assorted belching technology, it's a marvel.

Three other routes, established as state "Rustic Roads"—and three outstanding ones at that—are definitely among the best in the state. CR MM begins at the junction of US 14 and US 61 east of La Crosse, and stretches along Morman Coulee Creek Valley. The trip features eye-catching vistas of the Mississippi Valley and passes the wildlife refuge at Goose Island and the first area mill site, dating from 1854. The state brochure also touts the local temperature inversions, which can produce dense fogs and an opaque sort of atmosphere.

Rustic Road #31 starts in West Salem at the exit off I-90 running through city streets and outskirt roads and passing the Hamlin Garland Homestead, a few parks, and the local octagon house. While in West Salem, check out the Neshonoc Dam, Mill, and Powerhouse, all examples of 19th-century residual architecture.

My favorite starts northwest of Holmen on Amsterdam Prairie Road and Old 93, adjacent to the Van Loon Wildlife Area, which sits between the east and west channels of the Black River. The trip features plenty of charming river-valley views but also actually allows for a short walk—along McGilvray Road, also known as "Seven Bridges Road." The bowstring arch construction of the bridges has placed it on the National Register of Historic Places.

Riverside and Other Parks

La Crosse seems to have a park for every resident of the city, including funky river island parks. Chief among them is Riverside Park, and guess where it's located. Home to the La Crosse Convention and Visitors Bureau office, it's also got a 25-foot, 25-ton sculpture, *Hiawatha,* towering over the confluence of the Black, La Crosse, and Mississippi Rivers. Updated local takes on the legend say that the statue acts as a talisman against natural calamity. Not to be outdone is the *La Crosse Eagle,* an even taller sculpture overlooking the river. The park is also a departure point for *La Crosse Queen* Riverboat cruises and is equally good for just sitting and scoping out the riverway. On the grounds too you'll find the **Riverside Museum,** tel. (608) 782-1980 (see "Museums and Historic Structures," above).

Myrick Park, along La Crosse St. (WI 16) in the northern section of town, is famous for its zoo. Tiny, the zoo holds fewer than 20 species, mostly North American, with an odd monkey or two for good measure, and a petting zoo on-site. Newer and quite amazing is the "Kid's Coulee"—a multi-tiered child-designed playground absolutely full of bizarre contraptions and physically challenging get-ups. The zoo is open May-Oct. daily 9 a.m.-6 p.m. (the park itself

steamy summer view of the La Crosse River valley from Granddad's Bluff

is open 8 a.m.-8 p.m. daily) and is free. A nice trail system runs side-by-side with the park.

Riverboat Tours

Two replicas call the dock at Riverside Park home. The *La Crosse Queen* is, engineering-wise, true to the past. Its propulsion is generated wholly from its split stern-wheeled design. (Most contemporary takes on the old ships have "free" paddlewheels, which look nice, but the ship has modern screws underneath for real power.) The *Queen* meanders ever so surely up the main channel of the Mississippi into Minnesota Territory on the way to Dresbach, Minnesota, and Lock No. 7—a one-and-a-half-hour tour. Three-hour jaunts for the real river rat stretch along a segment of Ol' Miss that features an anachronistic swing bridge, a wildlife refuge, and some outstanding bluff areas; a buffet is served on this cruise. Weekend dinner cruises and Sunday brunch tours are also available. The *Queen* runs June-late Oct., generally at 11 a.m. and 1:30 p.m., with an additional tour at 3:30 p.m. starting in June. In high season the three-hour tour also starts at 9 a.m. on Wednesdays. Tickets are $10 adults (12 and over) for a short sightseeing trip, $5 children; $30 adults for the four-hour trip. For information, call (608) 784-2893.

Docked in proximity is the other well-known paddlewheeler redux, the *Julia Belle Swain,* this one driven by a pair of reciprocating steam engines pulled from another paddlewheeler. This boat is for serious river-lovers, specializing in two-day excursions complete with continental breakfast, lunches, dinner, and accommodations and tours on the long trip downriver to Prairie du Chien and back. The shortest excursion is a wonderful fall-color tour. Rates are $44 adults, $21 children, including lunch; basic sightseeing cruises are $12 adults, $8 children. The two-day jaunt costs $229 adults, $99 children, based on double occupancy. Call (608) 784-4882 or (800) 815-1005 for information.

Most modern of all is the *Island Girl,* a sleek cabin cruiser with some of the most popular—and award-winning—dinner cruises in the area. It operates out of the Bikini Yacht Club along Park Plaza Drive (across the Cass St. Bridge, behind the Holiday Inn). The lengthy list of tours includes breakfasts, dinners, moonlight cruises, sightseeing, and even sporadic "murder mystery" or themed nighttime jaunts. The food is superb on the dinner cruises—a different entrée nightly, Italian to chicken Oscar to Chateaubriand. Trips are offered May-Oct., most (sightseeing, dinner, and moonlight) running Wed.-Sat., fewer trips Sun.-Tues., though a brunch trip is available on Sunday. Basic sightseeing trips of two hours cost $11, or dinner cruises are $27. A host of others stand somewhere between. Sightseeing cruises generally run at 12:30 p.m. and/or 3 p.m. daily.

City Tours

Downtown La Crosse comprises one of the largest historic districts in the state of Wisconsin. Well-done walking-tour maps of the historically and architecturally significant downtown sites in La Crosse are available through the La Crosse Historical Society, tel. (608) 782-1980. Those less invigorated can pick up **auto tour** tapes at the Convention and Visitors Bureau in Riverside Park.

Or, just hop aboard the local **trolleys,** which run every 15 minutes through the downtown area, the riverfront, and occasionally north to Old Towne North and UW-La Crosse, passing nearly every major sight. It's a great and cheap tour. The loop runs all summer (May 30-Sept. 2) 11:30 a.m.-1:30 p.m. Tues.-Fri, with extended times Thursday evenings and Saturdays. Fares are all of 25 cents.

Mary of the Angels
Chapel at St. Rose Convent

Since August 1, 1878, two or more Franciscan sisters from this convent have kept a continuous prayer vigil, dedicated to the community and the world. Known as the "Perpetual Adoration", the vigil has been well documented in international media. The Mother-House itself is quite impressive—a grand mash of Corinthian and Romanesque styles. Intricate southern German stained glass and Italian marble line the interiors, with intricate bronze pieces and mosaics handmade by international artists. Guided tours ($1) are available. The convent is located at 715 S. 9th Street.

The St. Rose Grotto and its Virgin Mary have fallen on hard times, but a better one is the **Grotto of the Holy Family,** 10 miles east on WI 33 in St. Joseph, at the Franciscan Sisters of St. Joseph's Ridge (believe me, you can't miss the kitschy beckoning). Saints and Mary, Mary and the saints; wearied and either tacky or reverent. Still, it's one of the largest in western Wisconsin. The grounds are open for viewing Mon.-Sat. 9-11 a.m. and 1-3 p.m., on Sunday afternoon.

ACCOMMODATIONS

Downtown
Most inexpensive downtown and definitely one of the most precious motels anywhere in the state is the **Guest House Motel,** 810 S. 4th St., tel. (608) 784-8840 or (800) 2RHOUSE. As they say, a touch of Britain in La Crosse—owned by an English couple, the Guest House is trim and meticulously cared for. A coffee shop is on the premises. Outdoor heated pool. Rates from $38.

Also downtown, this one on the city side of the Cass St. Bridge, is the excellent **Radisson,** 200 Harborview Plaza, tel. (608) 784-6680 or (800) 333-3333, with superb river views, a pool, sauna, exercise room, and well-known dining rooms. Rates from $99.

Across the bridge is the **Holiday Inn,** 529 Park Plaza Dr., tel. (608) 784-4444, even closer to the river. Two pools, a sauna, exercise room, boat dock, domed recreation area, and more are offered here. This is also the departure point for the *Island Girl* cabin cruiser. Rates from $92 s or d.

Outskirts
Most hotels and motels are grouped on the north side of town along Rose Street (WI 53) and along the south side along Morman Coulee Rd. (WI 14/35/61). A good chain is **Exel Inn,** 2150 Rose St., tel. (608) 781-0400, with rates from $39. The best of all hotels might be the **Brookstone Inn,** 1830 Rose St., tel. (608) 781-1400, a modern inn with a small heated indoor pool and some exercise equipment. Rates from $57.

On the south side, eight basic accommodations are strung along Morman Coulee Rd. (WI 35), between the 3300 and 5200 blocks, with nary a chain operation among them. At the northern end is the **Welch Motel,** 3643 Morman Coulee Rd., tel. (608) 788-1300, where you get cable TV in your room. Starting from $35.

One good motel stands on the east side—the **Medary Motel,** 2344 WI 16, tel. (608) 781-7381, offering impeccably clean, basic but large rooms. Rates from $38. Alternately, at N3080 WI 16, the **Nuttleman Motor Lodge,** tel. (608) 782-0297, has 15 units with decent views of the bluffs; separate cabins are also available.

B&Bs
The **Martindale House,** 237 S. 10th St., tel. (608) 782-4224, is an 1850 Italianate mansion that looks like an architectural version of a Russian Nesting Doll set. Four rooms are appointed in individual styles: French, English, Martindale, and Scandinavian. A carriage house suite comes with a hot tub. Rates run $89-155.

Houseboats
A unique local vacation is to rent a houseboat and take to the waters of any of the triumvirate of rivers. Boats vary from 43 to 53 feet long and feature a wide variety of amenities; some are absolutely posh. You can't beat plowing the waters of the Mississippi in your own hotel room. Fuel, water, fishing supplies, refrigerators, ranges, cooking utensils, showers, carpeting, heaters, decks, Weber grills, and more are standard for all boats. Operations offering houseboats include **Fun 'N the Sun,** 1312 Herman Court, Onalaska, tel. (608) 783-7326, which has immaculate boats starting at $1,150 for a three-day, $1,270 four-day, or $1,895 for a seven-day rental during high season, considerably less in the off season.

Camping
You're in good hands—La Crosse takes its camping so seriously that the department overseeing the county parks actually advertises. Better than 90 percent of state campgrounds, the huge **Goose Island Campground,** tel. (608) 788-7018, is three miles south along WI 35. Over 400 sites—rustic to drive-through—are available here ($13), with a new cedar-log store, a nice sandy beach, and the cleanest bathrooms you will likely ever see. Its location can't be beat—on the backwaters of the Mississippi River bordering a wildlife refuge full of egrets and eagles.

A bit smaller but equally well taken care of by the county is **Veteran's Memorial Park,** off WI 16 between La Crosse and West Salem, right atop the La Crosse River, tel. (608) 786-4011. Rates are also $10.

Closest to town is the private **Pettibone Park Resort,** three miles west just over the Cass St.

Bridge, tel. (800) 738-8426. The campground is smack dab next to the Holiday Inn—rates are $18.

Neshonoc Lakeside Campground, tel. (608) 786-1792, offers two hundred sites located on a picturesque lake. About two miles east of West Salem on WI 16, the campground offers watercraft rentals, a pool, showers, and lots of extras. Rates from $17.

FOOD

Mr. D's

Mr. D's, West and State Streets, is a non-standard family cafe, the quintessential breath of fresh air. Start with 30 omelette combinations, and you're free to construct your own. More than 100 sandwiches are available, all on fresh-baked breads. A gazillion soups range from beer-cheese to Crab Chowder and a must-be-seen-to-be-believed loaf-a-soup. Best of all, it's done with a thoroughly unpretentious air—a most informal place. Oh yeah, the donuts are killer, with an all-night carryout window dishing 'em out starting at 9 p.m. Absolutely recommended. Open Mon.-Sat. 4:30 a.m.-4 p.m., Sunday 5 a.m.-1 p.m. From $4.

Institutions

Renowned eatery **The Freight House,** 107 Vine St., tel. (608) 784-6211, is a 120-year-old edifice with the original old swooping beams that line the high walls, now set off by lovely blonde wainscoting. This erstwhile brick storage structure for the Chicago, Milwaukee and St. Paul Railroad is on the National Register of Historic Places; it was redesigned into an upscale restaurant in the 1970s. Famed for its naturally aged and hand-cut steaks, it also offers a tremendous selection of seafood entrées (it brags of its Alaskan King Crab); and a respectable wine list is available. All this amidst a slew of railroad mementos including an antique railroad car parked in front in which Buffalo Bill Cody once rode. If nothing else, perch at the bar and watch the barkeeps climb the ladder up the immense back wall. Open nightly for dinner. From $9.

Not quite historic but indisputably legendary is La Crosse's other claim to fame as far as national press goes—the ineffable **Piggy's On Front,** 328 Front St., tel. (608) 784-4877, specifically contrived for the engorgement of the car-

nivore. In possession of a gaggle of awards from media, professional culinary associations, and regional "best of" surveys, the restaurant does up hickory-smoked barbecue ribs as well as anybody. Achingly good pork cuts and steaks are also par for the course here, and it's one of the only places to get smoked prime rib. The decor is first rate—dark woods, antiques, stained glass, chandeliers, and dining rooms right atop the Mississippi River. Piggy's even has a century-old tiger skin back bar—a subdued kind of festive boisterousness prevails. A piano bar is now on the premises. Open for lunch (from $4) and dinner (from $9) daily, with a Sunday brunch.

Fine Dining

The Radisson Hotel's **Boatworks,** 200 Harborview Plaza, tel. (608) 784-6680, is among the finer restaurants in La Crosse. Appetizers like mushrooms Lorenzo bode well for exquisitely prepared entrées like duck and shrimp sauté or lobster. A mesquite-seared yellowfin tuna with tequila-peppercorn sauce is equally memorable. From $7. The hotel's **Haberdashery** is a pub with upscale pub grub.

Asian

Chee Peng, a newer arrival, is the only Asian alternative to Chinese—this one Chinese-Thai. At 2240 Rose, along US 53 North, next to Shopko. Open daily for lunch and dinner. From $4.

Brewpubs

La Crosse has three good ones right downtown. At 3rd and Jay Streets the **Black Rose Brewhaus,** tel. (608) 796-2337, has its own specialty beers along with German cuisine alongside traditional pub grub; there's also a Friday night fish fry and Sunday morning Bavarian brunch. The other two are **Bodega Brew Pub,** 122 S. 4th St., tel. (608) 782-0677, and **Doc Powell's Brewery and Pub,** 200 Main St., tel. (608) 785-7026. The Bodega's bar is particularly nice, right aside the brass kettles, with a nice vintage bottle collection. Doc Powell's Brewery makes its own breads and has a lunch and dinner menu. From $4.

Italian

Adjacent to the local Sampson Art Gallery, the wannabe hip **Picasso's,** 600 N. 3rd St., tel. (608)

784-4485, is heavy on Nouveau American cuisine, with a special bent for Italian. Pastas, creative sandwiches, and full dinner entrées—chicken Tetrazzini to curried lobster—as well as deli meats, cheeses, and salads are offered. Lots of froufrou coffee, too. Service has been spotty, and despite the tasteful decor, the layout still seems like it was once a Denny's. Nonetheless, it's a creatively offbeat meal for the money. Breakfast, lunch, and dinner daily. From $5.

Not Italian per se, but **Edwardo's** offers some decent pasta entrées along with legendary wood-fired pizzas. At 1930 Rose St., tel. (608) 783-7711. From $5.

Vegetarian and Natural Foods
The **People's Food Co-op,** on 5th Ave., has a deli with some quick vegetarian options, along with natural foods and a bakery. From $3.

Something Else
Along WI 33 west of town is the **Ridge View Inn,** tel. (608) 788-6431, a restaurant next to a working dairy farm. The copious farmhand meals are worth note, but of highest repute are both the splendid view across the La Crosse River Valley (one can see all the way to the Mindoro Gap ridge) as well as the on-site Bahr-Jungen Farm Museum, one of western Wisconsin's largest conglomerations of antique farm equipment, from tractors to milking equipment. Open daily except Monday for dinner, and Sunday for lunch. From $6.

Desserts and Car Hops
A treat for anyone is **The Pearl,** a 1930s-style soda fountain and confectionery along Pearl Street downtown. Besides homemade ice cream in the shakes, malts, and phosphates, there's a respectable selection of candies.

Updating that by about two decades is **Rudy's,** 10th and La Crosse Streets, tel. (608) 782-2200, a '50s-era drive-in with Super Burgers, assorted chicken sandwiches, hot dogs, and the requisite roller-skating car hops. Best of all—root beer brewed daily. The Rudy family has been in the drive-in industry for over six decades, so you can pretty much trust them. Open March-Oct., daily 10 a.m.-10 p.m. Both from $3.

ENTERTAINMENT

Pump House
The local clearinghouse **Pump House Regional Center for the Arts** is a stately 19th-century Romanesque Revival structure, La Crosse's first water pumping station. Art galleries within feature revolving multimedia exhibits and live music throughout the year—folk, mostly. The center also features lots of lectures, and plays by the local troupe Pegasus Players, tel. (608) 784-7342. At 119 King St., open Tues.-Sat. 9 a.m.-5 p.m.

The Pump House also has an updated list of arts events via the telephone—(608)784-ARTS, or check out *Steppin' Out,* an up-to-the-month brochure of cultural events, available at the Convention and Visitors Bureau in Riverside Park and at a number of other venues.

Other Cultural Events
Norskedalen Nature and Heritage Center has a full slate of live performances and lectures. The two colleges—UW-La Crosse, tel. (608) 785-8900, and Viterbo College, tel. (608) 791-0491—also have regularly scheduled theatrical and musical performances.

The **La Crosse Symphony** season usually spans five events, Nov.-May. in the Viterbo College Fine Arts Building.

Enjoy freebie concerts from the La Crosse Concert Band on Sundays, summers in Riverside Park, or at the summertime Sunset Jazz Series.

Live Entertainment
A number of pubs downtown offer live music on a changing schedule, including jazz, mostly at **Bodega Brew Pub,** 122 S. 4th St., tel. (608) 782-0677, and **Doc Powell's Brewery and Pub,** 200 Main St., tel. (608) 785-7026. **River Jack's,** 1835 Rose St., tel. (608) 781-7070, a restaurant and bar, has assorted live acts.

Techno, industrial, ska, punk, and DJs are all found at the **Warehouse,** 328 Pearl St., tel. (608) 784-1422, all ages. The coolly named "Vatican PX" shop on-site sells indie record-label stuff and leatherwear.

Bars

La Crosse for a time had somewhat of a reputation for carousing—in fact, the downtown 3rd Street district was once a statistic right out of the Guinness Book—most bars per capita. Later on, a debauched annual festival turned violent and was canceled. The demise of this festival, an enforced drinking age, and general student ennui have curtailed most of the rowdiness, but with a UW school here, you're never far from a watering hole or an entertaining bar-time parade of inebriated students.

Pearl Street and environs generally offers something, whether a pub or a nightclub. Highly recommended by those who know is the jazz aficionado's dream joint, **The Casino,** with a great long bar and good jazz collection, and it's easily spotted by the sign "Good Drinks, Bad Service" out front.

EVENTS

Granddad's Bluff

In addition to the two listed below, La Crosse celebrates its heritage with Riverfest, a July gathering mostly of music performances.

Oktoberfest

It's not surprising to discover that the largest German-heritage festival in the Midwest is held in Wisconsin. La Crosse's legendary blowout, held the last week in September and first week in October, features a 7:30 a.m.-midnight slate of beer, polka, beer, varied music, beer, and a host of family events—sports to carnivals to parades. Almost half a million people attend this one, including a number of German musical acts. Some events require tickets, others are free.

Jazz Festival

This up-and-coming, decade-plus-old jazz festival, with almost a dozen bands on a handful of stages, is held at the Oktoberfest grounds, Freight House Restaurant, and Radisson Hotel. Tickets are generally $13 at the gate, less with advanced purchase; $60 gets you into everything.

SPORTS AND RECREATION

Trails

The city of La Crosse has a notable network of trails stretching from the Mississippi River all the way to the bluffs guarding the town, following the La Crosse River through marsh and bottomland. Canoe trails also snake through these sloughs down toward Ol' Miss. Departing Riverside Park, the main trail swoops up through the northern part of town, crosses WI 35, and then branches—either north to Red Cloud Park, or south in innumerable directions. Most keep on the main trail to Myrick Park and the UW-La Crosse vicinity. From there, it's just a hop over to the **Hixon Forest Nature Center** and its trails. The Hixon Center acts as the nucleus of an intricate network of hiking and cross-country ski trails throughout the city. The nature center itself, at 2702 Quarry Road, off WI 16, has two short nature loops, and is open weekdays 11 a.m.-4 p.m. and weekends 1-4 p.m. Most go for the webwork of varied Hixon Forest Trails, snaking in every conceivable direction through the 630 acres of prairie and bluff.

It sounds like quite a feat, but walking the entire River-Bluff Trail takes only two to three hours. From there, however, it can take a week to explore all of the other possibilities. Sumac Trail is the main artery into the forest and other trails. From there, it's possible to get to **Lookout Point** and, after hooking up with Bicentennial Link, **Birch Point.** Both offer superlative gazes across "goat" prairie—that is, sad residuals of once-proud oak savannas, left only because they were too steep for agricultural plows. The best trail is the Log (or Oak) Trail, which hooks up to Granddad's Bluff Park, with the most commanding view of all. Of historic note is the junction of Gully and Cellar Trails—a man-made cave was found by archaeologists when the trail network was being developed, and the best guess is that the site was a large brick kiln in the 19th century.

MISSISSIPPI BARGES

In the logging heydays, gargantuan log rafts were lashed together and floated downriver to markets. The largest ever built on the Mississippi was an amazing one built near Lynxville, Wisconsin, in 1896—it measured 260 feet wide and 1,550 feet long. (That's over 2.5 *million* board feet of lumber.) Monstrous river barges, though no longer made of logs, still prowl the waters, running grain, coal, chemicals, oil, and cement all the way to the Big Easy. A quarter-mile-long towboat, which actually pushes the barges, can generate 6,250 horsepower and move 22,500 tons, or 990 semi trucks, in one load. Wisconsin moves two million tons of cargo in and out of the state each year. With a typical stopping distance of over a mile, commercial barges obviously have right of way in the channels.

These leviathans are also somewhat controversial. A vital element in the transportation of domestic goods, they have a serious impact on the waterways. Dredging has to be done to guarantee the depth of the channel, and shipping companies have quite a bit of sway in the operation of locks and dams, trying to cut the time required to pass through the lock systems. Critics say the barges abrade the shoreline not only with their own wakes, but also by pushing other crafts closer to shore. Currently the Corps of Engineers has a plan to redo the locks to allow even larger barges to pass through; this, not surprisingly, has met with environmental furor.

La Crosse River Trail: The Mississippi River region has an absolute plethora of state multipurpose trails, many of the rail-to-trail variety. The **La Crosse River State Trail** is a 22-miler on the packed limestone screenings spanning the abandoned grade of the Chicago and Northwestern Railroad. The western trailhead isn't in La Crosse technically, but in Medary, northeast of La Crosse along WI 16. The eastern terminus is the Bicycle Capital of the U.S., Sparta. Two public and one private campground are found along the route. The topography varies from prairie remnant to agricultural expanse to trout streams and wetlands; keep your eyes peeled for osprey nests or Neshonoc geese. Hardcore cyclists can hook up with both the Elroy-Sparta and Great River Trails,

totaling some 75 miles of linked trail in all. Trail passes ($3 daily, $10 annually) are required for any rider 16 and older.

Boat Rentals
SkipperLiner of the Bikini Yacht Club, 621 Park Plaza Dr. (behind the Holiday Inn), tel. (608) 784-0556, is a full-service marina, restaurant, bar, showroom (with live entertainment), and convenience store. Rentals include bass and pontoon boats, waverunners, canoes, and even bicycles. Four-hour rates and daily rates are available. A four-hour waverunner rental runs $80; a canoe $25; a bicycle is $15 for a day.

Mt. La Crosse
Ski bums have this mini mountain, with a 516-foot vertical drop, 17 trails, a mile-long run, three chair lifts, snowmaking, and ski lessons. The ultimate trail is called Damnation!—but I don't know that I'd flee in terror. The Swiss chalet features the "St. Bernard Room" full of items highlighting the largest of man's best friends. The hill is open November-mid-March, tel. (608) 788-0044 or (800) 426-3665.

SHOPPING

There's a huge conglomeration of chi-chi antiques and crafts shops in Old Towne North along Caledonia Street; also, the **Antique Center of La Crosse,** 110 S 3rd St., tel. (608) 782-6533, has three floors and some 75 boutiques of anachronisms—the largest collection in western Wisconsin. Even the building is an antique, a century-old Queen Anne structure.

The **La Crosse Clock Co.,** 125 S. 2nd St., tel. (608) 782-8200, is about the most interesting local operation, one of the largest collections of clocks in the Midwest. The shop also features German cabinetry. The prices are quite low here.

The local **farmers' market** takes place in summer from 6 a.m. on Saturday in the downtown square off State Street.

SERVICES AND INFORMATION

The **La Crosse Convention and Visitors Bureau,** tel. (800) 658-9424 or (608) 782-2366, www.explorelacrosse.com, is in Riverside Park, not far from the large eagle statue and adjacent to the paddlewheel docks. Lots of good information here. The RiverUSA museum is in the same complex. Hours are for the museum part are Memorial Day-Labor Day, 10 a.m.-5 p.m. daily, though some offices are open at 8 a.m.

Additionally, the state of Wisconsin maintains a **Wisconsin Travel Information Center** a mile east of the Minnesota border on I-90, open regular business hours with the usual clean restrooms and pamphlet-filled interiors.

The **post office** is at 425 State St., tel. (608) 782-6034. The **library**, tel. (608) 789-7100, is at 800 Main Street. WLSU (88.9 FM) is the station for public radio.

TRANSPORTATION

Bus

The local bus station, tel. (608) 784-5510, is at the corner of 4th and Cameron Streets. An example of a fare: to Minneapolis ($36) one bus a day leaves at 2:25 p.m.

Train

The **Amtrak** depot, tel. (608) 782-6462, is at 601 Andrew Street. The Empire Builder Chicago-Seattle line makes stops twice daily, departing westward at 7:11 p.m., eastward at 10:45 a.m., though you should double-check. To Milwaukee costs $54.

Air

The **La Crosse Municipal Airport,** tel. (608) 789-7464, is at 2850 Airport Dr. (northwest out of town near Onalaska) and is served by **Northwest Airlink,** tel. (800) 872-7245; **American Eagle,** tel. (608) 781-7570; and **Skyway,** tel. (608) 781-4775.

Local Transport

The local public **bus service** (MTU), tel. (608) 789-7350, operates routes from 5 a.m.-10:40 p.m. weekdays, until 7:40 p.m. on Saturdays, and until 6:40 p.m. on Sundays. Rates are 75 cents for adults, 60 cents for children. The terminus for all lines is the corner of 5th and State Streets downtown. UW-Lacrosse is served by Route 1.

VICINITY OF LA CROSSE

M&M Ranch

The largest menagerie of live exotic animals in the Midwest is found at this spread off I-90 in Rockland, WI. Over 700 llamas, miniature donkeys and horses, a macaw, Highland cattle, Angora goats, potbellied pigs, pygmy hedgehogs, and a resident and popular camel named Erkel live and graze on the ranch. Tours are available by appointment and cost $5, $2 for children. Contact the La Crosse Convention and Visitors Bureau.

Norskedalen

The 400-acre "Norwegian Valley", under the auspices of the UW-La Crosse Foundation, is a hodgepodge nature and heritage center in Coon Valley, approximately 16 miles southwest of La Crosse. Beginning in the late 1970s as an outdoor laboratory in an arboretum, it grew to include many surrounding Norwegian and Bohemian homesteader lands. Guided tours are offered May-Oct. Mon.-Sat. 9 a.m.-4 p.m., from 10 a.m. Saturday, and Sunday noon-4 p.m.; the

rest of the year it's open lesser hours. A visitors center is open year-round Mon.-Sat. 9 a.m.-4:30 p.m. and Sunday noon-4:30 p.m., with cultural exhibits and displays. Also on-site you'll find a pioneer homestead with tours available May-October. Plenty of ongoing events take place throughout the year, including Sunday lecture forums, movies, and storytelling; threshing bees; *Sankt Hans Dag,* an ancient Scandinavian summer solstice festival; old-time music jamborees; and classes in ecology and Norwegian language. Most popular are the nature trails snaking throughout the arboretum, open for hiking, snowshoeing, and skiing. Daily admission is $4 adults, $2 children 17 and under, $10 family. For information, call (608) 452-3424.

Hamlin Garland Homestead

Six miles west of La Crosse is the small town of West Salem, known for no other reason than as the boyhood home of Wisconsin native and Pulitzer Prize-winner Hamlin Garland. Born in

1860, Garland was among the first—if not the first—writers to use Midwest farm life as a central focal point, in particular creating strong female characters. Writing mostly as a social realist, he later turned to a style that pulled no punches in its grim land—and human—scapes of the Midwest; he undoubtedly had a profound effect on August Derleth. Virtually unread in his lifetime until being awarded the Pulitzer Prize in 1922, he is now remembered mostly for *A Son of the Middle Border*, a bittersweet fictionalization of growing up on a coulee country farm. Published in 1917, it was reissued in 1995 by Penguin Books as a Penguin Classic. His homestead is at 357 Garland St. and is listed as a National Historic Landmark. Tours are offered Memorial Day-Labor Day, 10 a.m.-5 p.m., and cost $1.

West Salem also has the **Palmer-Gullickson Octagon House,** 358 N. Leonard St., impressive enough as octagon houses always are. This one was once the sumptuous home of Dr. Mary Lottridge, purportedly the second woman to finish medical school in the United States. Open summers 10 a.m.-5 p.m.

ONALASKA

Onalaska lies north of La Crosse at the hook in the Mississippi that forms the eponymous Onalaska Lake and Spillway—much enamored by anglers, who take a huge number of sunfish from the waters. The oddball name, inspired by a late 18th-century poem (spelled "Oonalaska" in that usage), is one of three in the United States. The other two are in Texas and Washington, but Wisconsin's "Oonalaska" was the first.

Sights

Onalaska is technically the southern terminus of the **Great River State Trail,** a 24-mile, multi-purpose, crushed limestone rail-to-trail paralleling the Mississippi River on an easy three percent grade. Along the way, the trail passes through bottomlands, modest swamps (white oak trees native), and prairies, then travels atop majestic bluffs in Perrot State Park, a magnificent side trip off the trail. The northern terminus is the 6,000-acre Trempealeau Wildlife Refuge. Dozens of great partially forged iron bridges (under careful restoration by the DNR and private contractors) are scattered along the route, and the trail also passes through lovely Trempealeau. One frightening highlight is the still-active Burlington Northern railroad line directly next to the trail. Another highlight is the Midway Prairie, a small swath of extant virgin prairie north of the trail, now maintained by the U.S. Fish and Wildlife Service. (It's north of the CR Z crossing and is marked.)The trailhead is at Hilltopper and Oak Forest Drive, exit 35N off I-90. Trail passes are required for bikers—$3 per day, $10 per season—and are available in town.

Practicalities

The local **Lumber Baron Inn,** 421 2nd Ave. N., tel. (608) 781-8938, is a mammoth 1888 B&B dream home replete with carriage house. Rooms start at $70.

There are excellent restaurants in Onalaska. **Seven Bridges Restaurant** along WI 35, tel. (608) 783-6101, is a thoroughly Midwestern supper club wrought from stone and offering a commanding view of Lake Onalaska. Straight supper club fare—steaks and seafood, with some chicken and pork. From $6. Intriguing too is **Marge's Lakeview,** N5135 WI 35, tel. (608) 781-0150, a family-style eatery offering three squares a day of chicken and dumplings, fish, shrimp, and chicken, and the specialty of the house—buffalo. Some Wisconsin-oriented dishes are occasionally prepared as well. Open from 5:30 a.m.-2 p.m., daily, 5-9 p.m. also Tues.-Fri. From $5.

Some have called **Traditions,** 201 Main St., tel. (608) 783-0200, one of the best restaurants in the state. Housed in an old bank building, it offers consistently excellent creative cuisine; there's a good wine list as well. The menu changes weekly so you'll find something good whenever you show up. Open for dinner Tues.-Saturday. From $15.

BACK ON THE RIVER ROAD

Getting from La Crosse and Onalaska back onto the Great River Road can be a bit messy, at least for those who cringe at the thought of four-lane anything. Eventually, however, after a few exits and left turns, you'll be skirting the river's edge under the curl of the bluffline. Follow WI 35 around the edge of Lake Onalaska, an enormous pool formed above Lock and Dam No. 7. Acre for acre the lake is one of the most active fishing spots on the Mississippi River. A loop onto the alphabet-jumble of county roads to the west, most of which begin with or include a "Z," can get you to Trempealeau, about 15 miles north of Onalaska (likely via CR XX through New Amsterdam). Whatever route you choose, you'll whip through the town of Midway first.

Once just another railway node, the town is noteworthy today for the Sand Lake Bison company, one of the most comprehensive operations in the U.S. to raise pure-bred American Bison. West of town along CR Z you'll find a public campground. Heading out of Midway on the "Z" highways again, you can explore along the southern tier of marshy Black and Mississippi River bottomland in the Van Loon Wildlife Area, a hot spot of canoeing, fishing, and primitive camping. Whichever highway you choose, you'll travel through a salient "terrace" on the way to Trempealeau. The Mississippi River bottomland on either side of road is part of the protected Brice and Amsterdam Prairies, and CR Z actually dead-ends at the Trempealeau Wildlife Refuge, so you'll have to backtrack to CR XX to return to the Great River Road.

For a short side trip, take WI 53/35 out of Midway to Old 93 Road, which leads to Amsterdam Prairie Road. The ride twists through gorgeous homestead farmland, a few stands of trees, and along blufflines before reaching McGilvray Road, at this point just a foot path. Also known as Seven Bridges Road, the official state "Rustic Road" features historic bowstring arch-truss bridges.

TREMPEALEAU

From a distance, it's impossible to miss the imposing bluffs along the Mississippi floodplain above tiny Trempealeau. So eye-catching were they that both the Winnebago and French referred to the "bump" at the northern end of the bluffline—now, of course, Trempealeau Mountain—either as "Soak Mountain" or "Mountain in the Water."

The town was founded by a combination of American Fur Company operatives from Prairie du Chien, displaced Acadians, and the odd Kentuckian. Even William Cullen Bryant was an early admirer of the local landscape. Early settlers were no less enamored; a local minister spent feverish years honestly trying to prove that Trempealeau was the site of the Garden of Eden.

Trempealeau never amounted to much in the world of river transportation. Even with the arrival of the railroad, it was more low-key backwater than bustling cargo center. Still, the town had a busy, attractive Main Street, which, save for six buildings, was completely razed by an 1881 conflagration. Those half dozen buildings were relocated, spruced up, and now form the lovely backbone of the village of Trempealeau, officially recognized by the National Register of Historic Places.

Lock and Dam #6 in Trempealeau is one of the best sites to get an operations level gander at a dam. From the tower right over the water, you could damn near hop aboard a passing boat. The lock and dam, including an earth dam extending all the way to the Minnesota shore, completed in 1936, cost an astonishing $5 million. A public fishing barge is moored below the dam.

South of Trempealeau you'll find a chain of seven spring-fed lakes, two in yet another fish and wildlife refuge. This is the area for canoeing, and assorted private cabins on stilts over the marshy waters are available; most are decidedly low-key.

To get on the water, the village has a public marina (no rentals); the Trempealeau Hotel has canoes and bicycles for rent. If you need to rent a boat, contact *Larry's Landing*, tel. (608) 534-7771. Canoeists can have a field day on Mississippi backwater trails networking in all directions. The best is the Long Lake Trail, a two-hour jaunt through the swampy sloughs of the national wildlife refuge. For those intimidated by sandbar swimming (it can be dangerous), the community offers an Olympic-sized swimming pool.

Practicalities

The reason everyone should take a spin to Trempealeau is the flaxen-yellow **Trempealeau Hotel**, 150 Main St., tel. (608) 534-6898, one of Wisconsin's most endearing anachronisms and the *grande dame* of this stretch of the river road. There's a wonderful lack of "renovated" feel to the place—it's still got too much charm. The owners have thankfully resisted the generally addictive impulse to transmogrify a cool old haunt into a syrupy B&B with prices hiked way up. The eight, tight upstairs rooms share a bath, not unlike a European-style hotel, and get this, they run only $30. A quaint one-bedroom cottage with private sun deck is available riverside for around $100; newer luxury suites have jacuzzis, fireplaces, and great views for $120 weekends.

Wall to wall with locals and itinerant tourists, the hotel's equally famed restaurant offers traditional soups, salads, steaks, sandwiches—try the Walnut Burger; plus odds and ends like fajitas, burritos, a large assortment of vegetarian-friendly entrées, and fish boils in the summer. A regular schedule of live entertainment, including a reggae festival and Memorial Day blues bash, is offered in the outside beer garden. The hotel rents bikes and canoes and can help arrange local river and refuge tours.

Perrot State Park

Over the winter of 1685-86, fur trader Nicholas Perrot wintered at the confluence of the Trempealeau and Mississippi Rivers. Archaic Indian encampments and Hopewell burial mounds have been excavated here and dated to 5000 B.C., though many were damaged by settlers and their plows. Known as the Trempealeau Bluffs, the crown of the ridge swells up to 500 feet above the bottomland of the Mississippi River, which once arched to the *east* of the bluffs before glacial silt deposits channeled the river into creek beds and redirected it onto its present course. Three miles of plain now separate the cliff line from the Wisconsin uplands to the east.

Brady's Bluff is the crown jewel of the four primary bluffs, a towering 520-foot terrace rising steeply above the flood plain, accessed between the east and north entrances. Climbing up

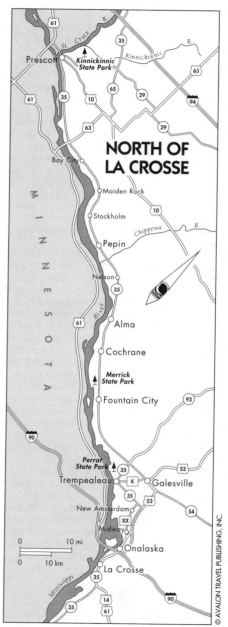

NORTH OF LA CROSSE

© AVALON TRAVEL PUBLISHING, INC.

Brady's Bluff is essentially a sweaty Geology 101; you'll pass 600 million years of geological stratification. Two trails, to the north or south, lead up the hill, and magnificent vistas are found at the top. Trempealeau Mountain though, that landmark beckoning to Native and settler alike, is even more intriguing. A fragmented part of the bluffline, it is now an island sitting in the Trempealeau River bay off the Mississippi River, albeit a rock island some 384 feet high. There are no established trails on the rock. Of the remaining bluffs, only Perrot Ridge, 507 feet high, is reached by a trail (but not to the summit). The mile-and-a-half route starts at the east park entrance and skirts the concavity of the ridgeline. An east-branching trail then traipses past Eagle, Chicken Breast, and Heald's Bluffs before looping back past pimple-sized (in comparison) Bald Knob.

The Great River State Trail, a multi-use, screened gravel trail, tangentially scrapes the northern park boundary; a linking trail leads from the park's campground. This 24-mile trail is detailed above under "Onalaska," in the "Vicinity of La Crosse" section.

Besides hiking trails, the park has nearly 10 miles of cross-country ski trails, some groomed and tracked. Canoeists can even launch from the campground and follow an established canoe trail through Trempealeau Bay. Whatever you do, do not leave the bay and head out into the river, unless you've got superhuman strength.

To the north along West Prairie Road (which leads back to WI 35/54) is the 5,600-acre **Trempealeau National Wildlife Refuge,** a major link in the Mississippi River migratory flyway. Predominantly marshy wetland in the backwater sloughs of the Mississippi, the preserve also has site-specific tracts of sand prairie and bottomland hardwood forest. Herons, bald eagles, and egrets are commonly spotted within the refuge. A five-mile auto tour accesses two shorter nature trails open to hikers. Get off the beaten path by hiking along the spider web of old dikes and service roads dating from the 1930s. Be careful though, lots of the heath now shrouds old ditches, and man-trap-sized holes have snared more than a few. Bikers are not allowed off-road within the refuge. The refuge is open seven days a week during daylight hours; the park HQ, tel. (608) 539-2311, is open Mon.-Fri. 7:30 a.m.-4 p.m.

Perrot State Park offers 97 campsites, 37 of which are reservable. Most are decently isolated in hardwood nooks, and a few lucky campers get riverside sites (#44-60). Standard rates ($8) apply for camping, plus an admission sticker ($5).

Side Trip

Take CR K northeast out of Trempealeau to trim and busy **Galesville**, parked in a crook of bluffs overlooking Lake Marinuka, a town that gets a side-trip nod for one of the best little cafes in western Wisconsin. **Backyard Patio Cafe** is housed in a deliciously historic old pottery shed on Mill Road along Beaver Creek. Veg-head sandwiches and numerous entrées, all with vague international hints, are on the menu here along with lots of creative but casual fare. Live music is regularly offered on Fridays and Saturdays—heavy on folk and bluegrass. It was only open weekends on last visit.

Not far from the cafe is lovely **High Cliff Park** and an anachronistic wobbly footbridge and path along a bluff, leading to a spring.

Otherwise, Galesville is chockablock with gingerbread Victorian and Queen Anne mansions; the Town Square and assorted streets are on the National Register of Historic Places. The **AA Arnold Farm,** on the north side of town, is a magnificent Italianate edifice dominating the surrounding farmland. An even more impressive architectural wonder is the farm's indoor silo.

To get back on the river road (WI 35), take WI 93/54 west out of Galesville.

FOUNTAIN CITY AND NORTH TO ALMA

There's not much to see between the fringes of the Trempealeau Wildlife Refuge and Fountain City, just 15 miles of tedious, mostly off-the-river roadway. But Fountain City's **Eagle Bluff,** the highest point on the Upper Mississippi River at 550 feet, and one of many imposing sandstone rises in the vicinity, commands the same attention as Trempealeau's bluffs. Another bluff in the area is claimed by locals to resemble an Indian chief's head. And the city (nay, village) seems carved right out of the steep-walled cliffs, descending down into the postcard-quality town. The squat bungalows and their lawns, the tiniest pea patch-

THE MIGHTY MISSISSIPPI

Factoring in length, surface area drained, discharge, and minutiae elements, the Mississippi River takes the bronze medal worldwide in river status. It's generally listed as the third-longest river in the world at 2,350 miles, though some say the Missouri River headwaters would jack that number up to 3,890 miles. More impressive, its wildly tornadic-shaped drainage basin spreads across 30 U.S. states and creeps into two Canadian provinces, draining 41% of the U.S.'s water.

The Wisconsin-Minnesota Mississippi trench runs for more than 200 miles from Prescott, Wisconsin, to East Dubuque, Iowa, with average widths ranging from one to six miles and blufflines rising to nearly 600 feet above the floodplain. The Upper Mississippi's bluffs are the most salient features and distinguish the Mississippi from other major rivers with their lack of a vertiginous backdrop. Instead, a series of craggy "terraces" is punctured occasionally by breaks. Henry Schoolcraft's 1821 exploratory journals go on at length about the "giddy heights" and "beautiful lands." Unlike the forested swaths on the Minnesota side, the Wisconsin bluffs, facing west and thus drier, are grassier and rockier, and the surrounding prairie can resemble regions of the West.

European Discovery

The Ojibwa called it *Messippi*—appropriately, "Big River." Lookout Point in Wyalusing State Park overlooking the confluence of the Wisconsin and Mississippi Rivers was purportedly the first vantage point over the Ol' Miss for Father Marquette and Louis Joliet, who wrote on July 17, 1673, of their "joy that cannot be expressed" at finally espying the rumored Great River. After exploring as far south as Arkansas, the pair realized they had found the link-up with the Gulf of Mexico and thus proved a waterway existed between Acadia and the Gulf. Explorers such as Pierre Radisson and Daniel Greysolon du Lhut quickly followed up and mapped the northernmost reaches of the Mississippi and St. Croix Rivers, still searching for the fabled Northwest Passage. Nicholas Perrot laid claim to all lands drained by the Mississippi for France in 1686 with the establishment of a fur trade outpost/fort near Pepin.

Fur traders and trappers were the first to make use of Wisconsin's riverside. The first permanent settlement came near Prairie du Chien and gradually inched northward. Larger boats displaced Native canoes for transporting beaver and iron goods. Wisconsin's epic northern tracts of timber and their exploitation coincided roughly with the explosion of lead mining in the southwest. The Chippewa, Buffalo, St. Croix, and tributaries drain most of northern Wisconsin via the Mississippi and, for a time, Wisconsin sawmills and log transportation villages controlled the vast industry. By statehood, over 30 sawmills were buzzing logs on these three river systems. Between 1837 and 1901, over 40 million board feet had been floated down the Mississippi from Wisconsin.

Modern Mississippi

Mark Twain would hardly recognize the river of his mind's eye, barefooted boys mucking about in mudflats. During the Civil War, the river and in particular La Crosse, Wisconsin, was invaluable to Union transportation networks. At one point, over 1,000 steamships plied the waters of the Mississippi between Wisconsin and points south. Following the Civil War, river traffic for commercial purposes soared, and with that came the need for the government to manipulate the riverway to allow for expanded traffic as the nation sprawled westward. Low water in dry season obstructed traffic, as did snags, rocks, and logs.

The primary change in the river's natural history came in 1930, with the first locks and dams built by U.S. Army Corps of Engineers. Ten locks and dams form the western boundary of Wisconsin between Prescott and Dubuque, Iowa. These diggings and dammings changed the ecology of the river; instead of a free-flowing body of water with a mind of its own, an ersatz mocha-colored chain of lakes, each 15 to 30 miles long, was formed above dam lines, with sloughs and tidepools below. The sludgy backwater regions are amazing, swamp-like groupings of lake and pond, up to 200 in a given 20-square-mile area.

Environmental Issues

Those early machinations had malignant ramifications. As the waters were corralled, and ebbed into sluggish lakes and pools, sediment dropped and gradually squeezed out the riparian aquatic life. To make matters worse, expansion precluded river protection, so factories discharged effluents directly into the water, sewer lines ran right into tributaries, and agricultural pesticides and fertilizer seeped in, forming a lethal cocktail.

Now, biologists fret that the five-decades-old "lakes" are gradually exhausting their livability and becoming inhospitable to aquatic life. Sedimentation—mostly due to agricultural runoff—remains a vexing part of the problem. More worrisome is flooding. The dams may ensure commercial traffic year-round, but that's only for the dry season. They do nothing to control flooding, and as the massive Midwestern floods of the mid-1990s proved, dikes and levees have severe limitations. The Army Corps of Engineers is currently embroiling itself in more controversy. In 1993 the Corps spent $50 million to explore expanding the locks so barges could fit through in one piece.

They ultimately decided it was acceptable; then federal whistleblower suits were filed alleging improprieties and general data fudging. This fiasco caused American Rivers to put the Mississippi on its "endangered rivers" list. Environmentalists have heard it before; the Corps of Engineers is one of the densest layers of bureaucracy and is often criticized. River lovers say the Wisconsin stretch of the Mississippi, already the most dammed section of the whole river, should be allowed to return to its pre-settlement natural state by just ripping the locks out and shipping by rail (which would be cheaper by most estimates). Some backwater areas would be allowed to dry out, preserving the ecosystem for following floods.

Recreation

Today, most of Wisconsin's segment of the Mississippi is protected as part of the Upper Mississippi National Wildlife Refuge. The refuge, stretching 261 miles south of the mouth of Wisconsin's Chippewa River, is the longest refuge in the U.S.; it was established by congressional fiat in 1924. Some say this happened just in time, as Wisconsin had lost 32% of its wetlands by then. This refuge is a crucial link in a migratory flyway including points south to the Gulf of Mexico or the Atlantic seaboard.

And while recreation brings in over $1 billion a year to regional coffers and has become the essential lifeblood to this portion of the river in many ways, some claim the darting jet-skis and wake-inducing pleasure craft are abrading the shoreline and causing untold damage to the aquatic ecosystem.

For anglers, catfish are the prized possession, but walleye and sauger are what you'll probably catch. Still, the waters are rife with catfish, and a catfish fish fry is a Great River Road classic. The area of Genoa has one of the best walleye runs on the Mississippi. Oddball creatures include the paddlefish and the infrequent snapping turtle.

es of verdance imaginable, back into the windward side of the big bluff as it curves along the river. Smacking a bit of the European feel of New Glarus or Mount Horeb in southwestern Wisconsin, Fountain City has more of a Mediterranean island fishing village atmosphere, though there are more than a few pockets of Berne-style Swiss architecture. Founded by a wintering river trader in 1839 with an eye for aesthetics, the town was named for rivulets of spring water cascading out of the "hard heads," or sandstone bluffs. The waters at one time ran off the bluffs and through the streets—no longer, however, as the springs were capped and turned into fountains. The scenery turns downright thrilling around Fountain City all the way to Prescott.

Merrick State Park

North of Fountain City, the Mississippi River widens to almost two miles due to damming. Right along the **Whitman Dam State Wildlife Area** is one of the smaller—320 acres—state parks in the northwestern part of the state. Merrick nonetheless has prime waterfront property, and blue herons frolic on the marshy backwater islands. There is only one short (1.4-mile) hiking trail; boating is king, with boat moorings right at the campsites.

You'll find perfect water's edge campsites here, separated into north and south campgrounds; the southern side's campsites are much better. Half of the campsites are available for reservation.

Other Sights

Most just go onto **Lock and Dam 5A,** which forms another pool north of town. A viewing platform available to the public has the honor of being the only **floating bar** on the Mississippi, the Dam Saloon, which also has fishing for $6.

Handfuls of crafts, antiques, and "used" detritus can be found in Fountain City. Of particular note is the shop of **Leo Smith,** a folk art woodcarver of national repute. At 121 S. Main St., tel. (608) 687-6698, the shop is open daily by chance, late morning to whenever.

The most unusual tourist attraction in Fountain City, the **house with a rock in it,** is north along WI 35. In 1995, a 50-ton boulder fell off the majestic bluffline and smashed into a house at the base. The owners decided to turn it into a bizarre tourist attraction. Open March-Nov. 10 a.m.-6 p.m., admission charged.

River City Kayaks, tel. (608) 687-8158, is right downtown and has kayak rentals.

Practicalities

The tiny **Fountain Motel,** tel. (608) 687-3111, has perhaps the best location of any motel on the road. Set back from traffic at the base of the bluff, the hotel offers clean rooms from $38.

Mississippi River channel catfish is the meal of choice in town, served at all the local eateries. **Lettner's,** at the corner of Main and Liberty, is a combination old-fashioned ice cream parlor, laundromat, and antiques and junk (or "junque") store.

Enjoy rubbing elbows with the locals at bars? You can't go wrong in Fountain City. The **Monarch** tavern downtown is a classic Wisconsin tavern with original dark wood interiors and, seemingly, the original bottles that went with it; it's also got the most popular lunch-dinner restaurant in these parts. From $4.

Cochrane

North of town seven miles along WI 35, then onto Prairie Moon Rd., is another folk-art oddity. The **Prairie Moon Museum and Sculpture Garden,** a hodgepodge of human (or animal) concrete figurines and a kind of folk-art stone wall, were all created by a local artist. Cochrane itself (pop. 475) breezes by, offering not much else to corral your attention than the local **high school,** tel. (608) 687-4391, which offers a taxidermy display of local fauna, including eagles and a rare albino deer rumored to have lived in the surrounding hills for years until it was eventually hit by a car. Call for viewing times.

The only game in town for lodging, and a good place to eat (and dance) is the **Cochrane Inn,** tel. (608) 248-2999, downtown, with live entertainment at times.

Buffalo City

Immediately north of Cochrane and just off the road, Buffalo City was for a long time the smallest incorporated city in the U.S. (now pop. 915). There's not much to do other than spend time in a host of **city parks,** one of which contains the original 1861 jail. Riverside nature trails are in the works for a new 10-acre wooded park.

The restaurant of choice is the **Mississippian,** 8th and WI 35, tel. (608) 248-2464, an 1891 saloon and dance hall converted into a fish house and restaurant in the '30s. It's straight supper club cuisine, steaks to seafood. Open year-round Monday and Wed.-Fri for lunch and dinner, Sat.-Sun. for breakfast, lunch, and dinner. Closed Tuesday. From $4.

ALMA

Most diminutive Mississippi River towns are essentially long stringy main drags across the tracks from the big river, offering perhaps a few modest bungalows backed up to or even hewn into the bluffs. Alma forms so gradually that it's really tough to gauge exactly where the city starts. Tough, that is, until you get a gander at weathered Twelve Mile Bluff standing guard. Mississippi river pilots at one time used the bluff as a landmark and navigational aid. Founded in the 1850s by Swiss immigrants who set up a supply depot for riverboats, and later the site of an enormous sawmill, this tranquil little town of understated houses and worn but proud main street structures makes for a good midpoint siesta or overnight between La Crosse and Prescott. Ever so long, it's a prime strolling town, and aerobically inclined wanderers have a ready-made workout, huffing up the steps etched into the bluffs. And for scenic drives, the "dugways," what locals call roads that wind through the bluff country backing east off the river, can't be beat.

Sights

Lock and Dam 4 sits across the street from the busiest part of the "center" of town. It's got the requisite observation platform and the largest fishing float on the river; it costs $9 per day, shore-to-float launch included, and night fishing is available too. Most anglers pull in northern pike, walleye, bass, and the ubiquitous catfish. A small eatery serves up breakfasts and quick orders. Right above the town off of CR E is likely the best public park along the road—**Buena Vista Park,** perched 500 feet above the water.

This is also the vantage point to see thousands of migrating **tundra swans,** which pass through during spring and fall and lay up in the sloughs north of town. Alternately, Rieck's Lake Park north of town has a wildlife observation deck atop the water.

Accommodations

North of town a mile is a cheap motel; a few miles north of that are the motel units and cabins at **Reidt's,** tel. (608) 685-4843, with some kitchenettes and rates from $38.

People come to stay in Alma's funky historical hotels and B&Bs. The steal of the whole trip are the $25-and-up rooms at the Italianate **Laue House,** tel. (608) 685-4923, on the south edge of town. Originally built by Fred Laue, a German immigrant whose sawmill essentially gave life to the city, it has been updated but definitely not over-renovated—no frills, but it's engaging. A variety of rooms, from a tiny one-person alcove to a huge room for four overlooking the river, are available with rates of $16-35. Laue House also rents canoes.

Historic lodging is also found at the **Burlington Hotel,** tel. (608) 685-3636, on the north side of the village; and at the **Sherman House,** tel. (608) 685-4929, a great old farmers' hotel with modest units (some with kitchens) and a coffee shop. Both offer rates starting at $25 or so—you read that right. In the very center of it all is a gift shop/gallery/B&B, the **Gallery House,** tel. (608) 685-4975, which hosts lots of special weekends—Murder Mystery, Anniversary, and the like. If you still can't make up your mind, the innkeeper of the **Tritsch House B&B,** 601 South 2nd St., tel. (608) 685-4090, completed Le Cordon Bleu basic cuisine training, so you know the full breakfast will be grand. From $65.

Three miles south of the town center is a **campground,** tel. (608) 248-2454. It's better suited for RVs; tent campers would be happier in Merrick or Perrot State Parks, though some of the tent sites are rustic, as they say. Rieck's Lake Park north of town has a couple dozen sites.

The Alma Marina, tel. (608) 685-3333, also has **houseboats** for rent and, because of Alma's central location, there are no locking delays for almost 45 miles. Three- to seven-day rentals are offered, and with a group it can work out to no more than $20 per person, per day.

Food and Drink

Pier 4 Cafe, tel. (608) 685-4923, features a screened-in porch, river-lock views, and lumbering freight trains whizzing by just a few feet away. It's a personal favorite spot for unique atmosphere in the state. Straight cafe fare with a decent variety sets itself apart from greasy egg monotony; it also offers lunches and a fish fry on Friday. From a couple of bucks.

Folks rave about the food at the simple-looking **Alma Hotel Restaurant and Bar,** 201 Main, tel. (608) 685-3380, usually mentioning the great pies or carnivorous daily specials—meat with "hot" in the title being a Midwestern staple. Open daily 6 a.m.-8 p.m. From $4.

Another classic hotel with a supper club-style dining room, the **Burlington Hotel,** 809 N. Main St., tel. (608) 685-3636, is a good bet for steaks, chicken, and seafood. From $6 at dinner.

TO PEPIN

Skirting the wetlands doused by seepage from Buffalo Slough, on which Rieck's Lake Park sits, the roadway is hacked out of a bluff face or supported by concrete pylons atop mucky soil where "burrow pits" were dug out of the land, the deposits creating an adjacent higher roadbed.

At the mouth of the Buffalo River is what's known as **Buffalo Slough;** the site is historically the most significant from lumber's heyday. A staggering amount of timber was floated down the Chippewa, St. Croix, and Eau Claire Rivers and was collected and stored in enclosed ponds here. For a spell, the powers that be in the "Buffalo" virtually controlled the northern timber industry, inciting Wisconsin's version of a range war between the mills of the upper Chippewa River and the Buffalo Slough mills. Even after a grudging agreement was reached, heading off full-scale violence, the ponds at the slough still had a firm grip over the industry. One river, the Chippewa, drained one third of northern Wisconsin and led directly to Buffalo Slough.

An additional few miles up the road is **Nelson,** crowded along a bluffline so high that hang gliding and soaring above town is becoming something of a draw. About the only other draw is the family-owned **Nelson Cheese Factory,** south of town on WI 35, tel. (715) 673-4725, dispensing cheddar, Colby, Monterey Jack, and squeaky cheese curds since the 1850s. It's open daily 9 a.m.-7 p.m. and offers tours. South of town you'll find excellent cabins at **Cedar Ridge Resort,** tel. (608) 685-4998, which sleep up to six and are fully furnished; rates are $365/65 weekly/daily and include a boat rental. One enormous "loft" building is gorgeous and sleeps 11; the $700 weekly price tag isn't too bad, then. The property consists of almost four acres and 300 feet of shoreline.

Tiffany Bottoms Wildlife Area

This area is known for the confluence of the Chippewa and Mississippi Rivers, a magnificent marsh-island dotted wetland, north of town a few miles and spreading over 12,500 acres from Mississippi and up the Chippewa River valley. WI 25 branches north from WI 35 and hugs the perimeter, passing two noticeable coulees. Neither paved road penetrated these capacious tracts of water-pocked bottomlands until WPA and CCC projects in the '30s. There are a dozen or more boat landings along both highways, and an undeveloped network of "trails"—mostly those old logging roads—branches all over the place (outstanding for berry picking and inward contemplation). Amateur shutterbugs should have a field day with the ambient sunset beams playing havoc on the oddball topography's colors. Primitive camping is allowed with a permit; contact the DNR office in Alma, tel. (608) 685-6222, in the county courthouse.

PEPIN

Back on the roadway, it's little wonder some have dubbed the stretch in and around Nelson and Pepin the most perfectly realized stretch of the Great River Road, visually speaking. When the U.S. government made the heavy decision to dam the Mississippi and transform it from a free-flowing river ecosystem into a sluggish series of lakes, it had already been second-guessed by geology. Glacial retreat and their "wash" had deposited silt at the mouth of the Chippewa River, eventually backing up enough water to form a 22-mile-long by 2.5-mile-wide winding gem of a lake, **Lake Pepin.** William Cullen Bryant wrote that Lake Pepin "ought to be visited in the summer by every poet and painter in the land." Father Hennepin later dubbed it, somewhat cryptically, the "Lake of Tears." Lake Pepin is so unique geologically that for years in the early 20th century Wisconsin and Minnesota authorities quibbled as to where, exactly, the river channel—and thus the state boundary—lay.

Wide—by Great River Road standards—Pepin is in something of a prime location, ensconced within virginal heaths, while a stone and wood gate stands to welcome visitors, giving you an idea of the personality of the place.

Pepin is also lousy with "Little House" affixations. Laura Ingalls Wilder, the author of the "Little House" books, was born on a homestead

Laura Ingalls Wilder park

nearby in 1867, and the villagers are not about to let you forget it.

Sights

Seven miles northwest of town via CR CC (or Sand Ridge or Short Cut Roads, both of which join the county road) is the **Laura Ingalls Wilder Little House,** a cabin and wayside picnic grounds spread out over a handful of acres. Nothing much to see here but the shell of a building, a couple of rooms, and some memorabilia on the walls. Back in town there is a **Pepin Historical Museum,** better known as the **Laura Ingalls Wilder** museum, along WI 35. Open daily May-Oct. 10 a.m.-5 p.m., it's full of displays and memorabilia pertaining to the woman in the famed line of books. Also on WI 35, in the village center park, is the 1886 **Pepin Depot Museum,** chockablock with railroad memorabilia, a gift shop, and a ticket office that has been completely redone. Open April 1-Oct. 31 daily 9 a.m.-5 p.m.

The year 1995 saw the inaugural season of professional theater along the Great River Road. The **Lake Pepin Players,** tel. (715) 442-3109 or (800) 823-3577, perform out of a theater on Second Street, occasionally featuring nationally known faces in some plays. Performances are held June-mid-Oct., Thurs.-Sun., with matinees on Thursdays and Sundays. Ticket prices generally run $14 adults, less for students, seniors and children.

Pepin has one of the most substantial **marinas** along the northern segment of the Great River Road.

Practicalities

Pepin's got a romantic feel to it, and three historic B&Bs are found here, including the **Summer Place,** 106 Main St., tel. (715) 442-2132, with a great arbor deck overlooking Lake Pepin and rates from $115.

Across the street from the Bumble Bee Motel and Campground is a true indicator that you're in a Mississippi river town—the **Park View Cafe** not only serves up roadfood quality hash, but also dispenses live bait.

Near the marina is one of the county's best-known eateries, the **Harbor View Cafe,** tel. (715) 442-3893. Somewhat upscale continental and creative international cuisine is the ticket here, and this is definitely the place to go for something

other than eggs or a hot beef special. The menu changes daily. You'll have an hour wait ahead of you, but trust me, it's worth it. Closed April and late Nov.-early March, otherwise open for lunch and dinner; open for breakfast on Sunday March-late November. From $9.

STOCKHOLM

The name of this place belies its actual size, in the top five for dearth of population in Wisconsin. But what an unbelievable amount of stuff this town of less than 100 people has to offer—artists and galleries (even Mississippi pearls, extinct since dredging reduced the numbers in the 1930s appear in shops), upscale eateries, not to mention an espresso shop. It's definitely worth a stop, even just to marvel at the extant architecture.

The name was no accident. Scandinavian settler Eric Peterson showed up in 1851 and stuck around; others from his hometown of Kalskoga arrived soon after, making it one of the oldest Swedish settlements in the state. The toponymy is a loopy mishmash of river jargon and "-son" appellations.

Sights

Well, there's nothing to do here really, other than to snoop around the tomes of history and a few Swedish artifacts at the **Swedish Institute** under the old Post Office; there is the obligatory **historical museum,** open Sunday 1-5 p.m. Shopping is the real lifeblood of the town. A collection of artisans and galleries line the few streets. Amish quilts and furniture are but two highlights. An annual art fair, organized back in the '70s by artisans attracted to the gorgeous river scenery, has become a huge event.

A mile south of town is a **historic overlook** at the site of a 1686 fort built by Nicholas Perrot. From here the French laid claim to all of the Mississippi's drainage—"no matter how remote"—for King Louis XIV.

Practicalities

The **Stockholm Village Park** has a boat ramp, swimming area, and **camping** for $9. You have to register at a couple of the cafes nearby; if you don't, they'll charge you an extra $5 in the park.

The **Merchant's Hotel,** tel. (715) 442-2113,

dates from 1867 and seemingly not much has changed about the place. Swedish heritage but with a '40s ambience—the four rooms (two with a river view) have shared bath, porch, and full kitchen. Rooms are $50, open April-November. For rooms inquire at Stockholm Antiques. An additional B&B, the four-square home **Hyggelig Hus,** tel. (715) 442-2086, offers, as you might guess from the name, a Scandinavian experience including copious Swedish breakfasts. Rates from $85.

For food, the **Bogus Creek Cafe** has soups, salads, fresh specialty bread sandwiches, and great garden seating. From $4.

TO PRESCOTT

Out of Stockholm, the remaining 30 or so miles to Prescott whip through a handful of unassuming towns, many of which aren't at all apparent. As Lake Pepin bends northwest at the base of an enormous bluff, the appellation of the next village, Maiden Rock, gets a visual aid. A Native American "maiden" preferred a plunge off the crown of the hill to an arranged marriage. Today, it's a typically sleepy little village with a riverside campground, a couple of nondescript eateries, and a couple of B&Bs, including the classic **Harrisburg Inn,** tel. (715) 448-4500. "A view with a room," they say, quite correctly, all for $88. Maiden Rock is also another artistic enclave on Lake Pepin. North of town is a wayside with unsurpassed lake vistas and the Rush River, an excellent trout stream.

The next tinytown, Bay City, is often overlooked entirely. Sitting at the head of Lake Pepin, it was a key transit point for shipping fish to Chicago. Later, it had a dubious honor as the location of the county's first murder. About all it's got going for it now is an operating mine chugging away, a few assorted businesses, and a clean campground.

West of Bay City in the main channel of the Mississippi River lies Trenton Island, regularly swallowed by Mississippi River mud floods. Still, none of the 100 residents will leave—a cogent reminder of the river's irresistible nature and the unvanquishable attitude of residents descended from pioneers hardy enough to hack a home out of a wilderness. In the early 1990s, state and county officials began—imperiously, say locals—to "prod" the residents into relocation and government buyouts. Underestimating the obdurate pride of the islanders, the federal government claims that unless Pierce County removes the people—and counties with similar flood-prone stretches downstream do the same—none will be eligible for disaster-relief money. The island has a number of businesses—a campground with a horrible view, and a tavern/bait shop/burger joint with a deck.

PRESCOTT

The road gets serious after Bay City and is a downright roller coaster past Diamond Bluff. Up and up and up, then a stomach-churning descent with spectacular scenery the whole way. You'll eventually come to the sentinel town of Prescott, the westernmost community in the state and the point at which the disparately colored Mississippi and St. Croix Rivers merge into one mighty waterway. The city is one of the original communities on the western edge of Wisconsin planned by a freelance Indian agent named Philander Prescott, acting as point man for controlling interests back east as well as profit-seeking soldiers at Fort Snelling near present-day St. Paul. Prescott was soon dwarfed by St. Paul to the west, but its strategic location ensured permanence nonetheless.

Prescott is where the Ol' Miss begins its run along the Wisconsin border but, heading north, the river roads roll on—this time tracing the St. Croix National Scenic Riverway, the top half of Wisconsin's "West Coast."

Sights

The best point to view the confluence is **Mercord Park,** high above the town. The steely blue hues of the St. Croix, seen in the right light, seem impossibly different from the silty Mississippi; on joining, the Miss's waters dominate. In the park you'll find a restored 1923 bridge **gearhouse,** the first control unit of the bridge spanning the Wisconsin-Minnesota border. The original reduction gears and electric motor have also been refurbished, and period photos now line the interior. The house is open and staffed May-Oct. on Fri.-Sun. afternoons.

North of town via CR F is the superb 1,150 delta acres of the St. Croix and Kinnickinnic River confluence at **Kinnickinnic State Park.** Likely the most unique camping option in the area is found here—all sites are designed along sandy spits and are only accessible via the water. There is little or no development in the wooded areas of the park, which makes it quite an attraction; real development for the park is ongoing, so roads and trails are going up incessantly. The chilly waters of the Kinnickinnic favor trout fishing. Canoeing should be limited to the Kinnickinnic as well; leviathan barges give narrow berth to tiny craft in their way.

Accommodations

Prescott offers precious few accommodations. The **River Heights Motel**, 1020 US 10, tel. (715) 262-3266, has 23 rooms overlooking the St. Croix River. Otherwise, there's the **Arbor Inn**, 434 N. Court St., tel. (715) 262-4522, a B&B with rates from $125.

    Kinnickinnic State Park has boat-in campsites.

Food

Centrally located and with a killer view, the **Steamboat Inn,** tel. (715) 262-5858, is at the US 10 bridge crossing into Minnesota. The fare is solid, with chicken, steaks, and seafood. Stairs lead past an alfresco deck to the banks of the St. Croix and the restaurant's "riverboat," which offers lunch or dinner cruises. Open for staggered seasonal hours, with lunch and dinner weekdays April-Oct., year-round dinners and Sunday brunch. From $5.

    In the 200 block of Broad St. North, on the boardwalk downtown, are a couple of simpler options. **Papa Tronnio's** has pizza from scratch is the specialty. In the same block you'll find the **Courtyard.** This cozy, garden dining room doesn't forget it's in the Midwest—there's a "casserole of the day." Lunches served Tues.-Sun., dinners Thurs.-Sat. Both from $4.

    East of town in the undulating coulees midway between Prescott and Ellsworth on US 10 is **The Virginian,** tel. (715) 425-5600, going on 40 years as a supper club heavy on steaks seared right before your eyes. Mixing the best Manhattans for miles, the club also has displays of antique clocks and ceramic liquor decanters. From $8.

Services and Information

The **Welcome and Heritage Center,** 233 Broad St. N, at the corner of Highways 10 and 35, tel. (715) 262-3284 or (800) 4-PIERCE, has travel information as well as displays of local history. It's open weekdays 10 a.m.-3 p.m.

BOOKLIST

If you're in Madison and are serious about reading Wisconsin-oriented books, eschew bookstores and head directly to the State Historical Society Museum, across from the State Capitol. The gift shop is even better in scope than the library.

REQUIRED READING

Leopold, Aldo. *A Sand County Almanac*. New York: Oxford University Press, 1949. An absolute must-read for anyone who considers himself or herself to be at all attuned to the land. Also an education for those superficial enough to think central Wisconsin is a vast nothingland.

Ostergren, Robert C. and Vale, Thomas R., ed. *Wisconsin Land and Life*. Madison: University of Wisconsin Press, 1997. This amazing book came out in 1997 and was instantly regarded as the most perfect synthesis of natural history and cultural geography that has ever examined the Badger state. Written by two prominent UW-Madison geography professors. This heavy but eminently readable book covers climate, geology, climate, flora and fauna, settlement patterns and cultural geography, regional economies, and changing landscapes, both cultural and ecological.

DESCRIPTION AND TRAVEL

Lyons, John J., ed. *Wisconsin. A Guide to the Badger State*. American Guide Series, Works Projects Administration, 1941. From the mother of all guidebook series, the Wisconsin edition, nearly six decades old, is still the standard for anyone interested in the history, natural history, and culture of the state. Check the library or used bookstores.

Middleton, Pat. *Discover! America's Great River Road*. Stoddard, WI: Heritage Press, 1989. It also includes three other states, but it's Wisconsin-heavy and of note for its sidebars about local history and inclusion of personal narrative.

OUTDOORS & ENVIRONMENT

Benyus, Janine M. *Northwoods Wildlife: A Watcher's Guide to Habitats*. Minocqua, WI: NorthWord Press, 1989. A detailed, clearly written, down-to-earth book using wildlife habitats as a starting point for exploring the Upper Midwest. Ecology for idiots, this is a wonderful, informative handbook to carry along.

Olson, Sigurd. *Collected Works of Sigurd Olson*. Stillwater, MN: 1990. Wisconsin's seminal ecologist besides Aldo Leopold, Olson had as much influence as his more famous contemporary. This is an excellent overview of his life's work, writings that show an incredible depth of ecological awareness but are very approachable for a layperson.

Rulseh, T., ed. *Harvest Moon, A Wisconsin Outdoor Anthology*. Stoddard, WI: Lost River Press, 1993. Some of Wisconsin's finest outdoor writers are featured in an anthology that's dense but surprisingly accessible. The Wisconsin ethos—we are connected to nature—is strong in this book.

Umhoefer, Jim. *Guide to Wisconsin Outdoors*. Minocqua, WI: NorthWord Press, 1990. A complete—and very heavy—listing of all the state and federal lands in Wisconsin, park by park and forest by forest. Updated regularly enough to be worth your while if you're going to spend much time in the woods.

HISTORY

The History of Wisconsin. Madison: State Historical Society of Wisconsin, 1973-1988. A massive, multi-volume, encyclopedic examination of the state's history.

Nesbit, Robert. *Wisconsin: A History*. Madison: University of Wisconsin Press, 1989. For those with too little time, money, or inclination for the state historical society's version, this is standard reading.

McAnn, D. *The Wisconsin Story: 150 Years, 150 Stories*. Milwaukee: Milwaukee Journal Sentinel, 1998. In contrast to the previous two scholarly, somewhat dry reads is this great book, excellent because most articles are about historical minutiae most folks have never heard about but are fascinating highlights to the general history books. Well-written and engaging, it's probably your best bet for an easy vacation read.

FOLKLORE

Leary, J. *Wisconsin Folklore*. Madison: University of Wisconsin Press, 1998. This wonderful book runs the gamut of Wisconsin culture: Linguistics, storytelling, music, song, dance, folk crafts, and material traditions. The chapter on Milwaukee-isms is worth the price of the book. The Smithsonian has even recognized the uniqueness of the book.

NATURAL HISTORY

Finley, Robert W. *Geography of Wisconsin: A Content Outline*. Madison: College Printing and Press, 1965. Written by a University of Wisconsin geography professor, this softbound text, found only in libraries, is the best resource for non-scientists. Full of clear maps, it also includes data on climate, agriculture, and topography.

Green, William, et al., eds. "Introduction To Wisconsin Archaeology." *The Wisconsin Archaeologist* (Sept.-Dec. 1986, Vol. 67, no. 3-4). Clearly written.

Martin, Lawrence. *The Physical Geography of Wisconsin*. Madison: University of Wisconsin Press, 1965. This is the granddaddy of all Wisconsin geography books, first published in 1916 and updated in subsequent editions.

Paull, R. and R. *Wisconsin and Upper Michigan Geology*. Dubuque, IA: Kendall/Hunt Publishing Co., 1980. One in a highly popular series of road guides to geology. These guides have less jargon than a textbook but still adequately cover the complexities of the topic.

Reuss, Henry S. *On The Trail of the Ice Age*. Sheboygan, WI: Ice Age Park and Trail Foundation, 1990. A good compendium of the oddball geology of the state and the effort to establish the Ice Age National Scenic Trail. Plus, buying it supports a good cause.

Schultz, Gwen. *Wisconsin's Foundations*. Dubuque, IA: Kendall/Hunt Publishing Co., 1986. An excellent primer on the geology of Wisconsin and, more important, its effects on Wisconsin's geography and geocultural history.

PEOPLE

The State Historical Society has produced brief booklets profiling every immigrant group in Wisconsin. They're available from the State Historical Society Museum in Madison for $2-3 each.

Bieder, Robert E. *Native American Communities in Wisconsin, 1600-1960*. Madison: University of Wisconsin Press, 1995. The first and, really, only comprehensive, in-depth look at Native Americans in the state.

Freeman, L. *Belle: the Biography of Belle Case La Follette*. Beaufort, SC: Beaufort Books, 1986. An excellent compendium of information on Belle La Follette, women's suffragist and wife and trusted legal advisor to Progressive Governor Robert La Follette.

Maxwell, R.S. *La Follette and the Rise of the Progressives in Wisconsin*. Madison: State Historical Society, 1956. A fine account of Robert La Follette, the much-beloved Progressive Party politician of the late 1800s and early 1900s.

McBride, G. *On Wisconsin Women*. Madison: University of Wisconsin Press, 1993. An excellent newer book, this is one of few sources of information about many of the important women in the state's history.

Meine, C. *Aldo Leopold: His Life and Work.* Madison: University of Wisconsin Press, 1988. The best book on ecologist Aldo Leopold—see special topic "Sand County Sage" for more on Leopold.

O'Brien, M. *McCarthy and McCarthyism in Wisconsin.* Columbia, MO: University of Missouri Press, 1980. The best book that focuses on Senator Joe McCarthy and his effects on the state, rather than the national ramifications of his actions.

Ritzenthaler, Robert E. *Prehistoric Indians of Wisconsin.* Milwaukee Public Museum Popular Science Handbook Series no. 4, 1979. This nifty little booklet, written in layperson's prose, is a condensed introduction to the earliest of Wisconsin's natives.

Rovere, R.H. *Senator Joe McCarthy.* New York: Harper & Row, 1959. This book is as good as any covering his biographical information, but it has the interesting quality of having been written soon after McCarthy's actions, so it's not filtered through late 20th century historical and social concepts.

Tanner, T., ed. *Aldo Leopold: The Man and His Legacy* Ames, IA: Iowa State University Press, 1988. Another good choice, containing multidisciplinary examinations of his life, studies, and effects.

Weisberge, B.A. *The La Folletes of Wisconsin.* Madison: University of Wisconsin Press, 1994. A good resource.

Zaniewski, R. *Atlas of Ethnic Diversity in Wisconsin.* University of Wisconsin Press. 1998. This outstanding (and huge) tome is the best ever produced covering the peoples of Wisconsin. It's coffee-table-sized, it's got excellent color graphics, and it's terribly expensive. Check the library.

LITERATURE

Boudreau, Richard, ed. *The Literary Heritage of Wisconsin: An Anthology of Wisconsin Literature from Beginnings to 1925.* La Crosse, WI: Juniper Press, 1986. A condensed version of the state's literary canon.

Stephens, Jim, ed. *The Journey Home: The Literature of Wisconsin through Four Centuries.* Madison: North Country Press, 1989. A remarkable multi-volume set of Wisconsin literature, tracing back as far as the trickster cycles of Native Americans. Rich with obscure minutiae, this tome is not readily obtainable for those of modest means but is of paramount importance to anyone hoping to get a complete overview of Wisconsin letters, history, and culture.

Taylor, Bruce. "Wisconsin Poetry." *Transactions.* (vol. 2, special edition). Madison: Wisconsin Academy of Sciences, 1991. An anthology of recent Wisconsin poets.

Vukelich, George. *North Country Notebook.* Madison: North Country Press, 1987. This is a collection of conversations, serialized in newspapers, among a hodgepodge of know-it-alls ("Steady Eddy" and others) sitting around up in the north woods yakking about the world. In 1995, Vukelich, Wisconsin's own, passed away.

Wilder, Laura Ingalls. *Little House in the Big Woods.* New York: Harper Collins Children's Books, 1953. While no one would think it, the series was actually inspired by Wisconsin; Laura Ingalls Wilder was born in a small cabin near the Mississippi River town of Pepin, the source material for many of the books' events.

Xan, Erna Oleson. *Wisconsin, My Home.* Madison: University of Wisconsin Press, 1975. Details of an immigrant settler's life in the Fox River Valley.

CUISINE

More and more cookbooks detail Midwestern cuisine. Any bookstore worth its salt will have great selections on regional cooking.

Allen, T. *Wisconsin Food Fests*. Amherst, WI: Amherst Press. 1995. Terese Allen is one of Wisconsin's most noted food writers, so look for her name in bookstores. This book is best for travelers; you can always find a fest somewhere close to you—a good way to sample a sesquicentennial of ethnic cooking.

Apps, Jerry. *Breweries of Wisconsin*. Madison: University of Wisconsin Press, 1992. This amazing book came out and surprised everyone—a thorough examination of the culture of beer in Wisconsin as had never been done before. Part history of beer, part cultural synopsis, with detailed examinations of major Wisconsin brewers past and present.

Boyer, D. *Great Wisconsin Taverns*. Black Earth, WI: Trails Book Guides, 1999. The name pretty much says it all. It sounds hokey, but the author, a professional folklorist and storyteller, made his peregrinations around the state—not to mention a predilection for imbibing—into a wonderful, offbeat guidebook.

Hachten, Harva. *The Flavor of Wisconsin*. Madison: State Historical Society of Wisconsin, 1981. A dense volume cataloging all—and this means all—the ethnic groups of the state and their contributions to the cuisine.

Raetz Stuttgen, Joanne. *Cafe Wisconsin*. Minocqua, WI: NorthWord Press, 1993. The author is a folklore expert who, while in graduate studies at Indiana University, managed to take two years off to write a highly readable and enjoyable analysis of every good greasy spoon and cafe in the state. The last chapter is a well-written sociological examination of the cultural and social milieu of the *kaffeeklatsch* and the greasy spoon.

GREEN BAY PACKERS

Sadly, I've never found a good one. Oh, the facts are there in all the books, but most read dry as toast or are just poorly written. There's never been a book that's managed to capture the absolute fervor of the Packers and their fans and combine it with rich historical detail.

INDEX

BREWERIES

EVENTS

LIGHTHOUSES

M

ODDLY UNIQUE

THEATER ARTS

ZOOS

ABOUT THE AUTHOR

A NATIVE CHEESEHEAD, Thomas Huhti has spent most of his life in Wisconsin, save for a year in Duluth, Minnesota. During that exile he studied and played a lot of hockey, then returned to finish a degree in Linguistics, English, and (almost) Chinese at the University of Wisconsin.

It was during college that he first wound up in East Asia, where he discovered a latent preference for movement and developed a serious case of anywhere-but-here. He went back for a two-year stint in Taiwan, Hong Kong, and the PRC on a language and research fellowship. He eventually made a solo tour circumnavigating the globe, fleeing graduate school and jumpstarting a nascent writing career.

He has contributed research, gruntwork, or writing to both new books and updates of books on China, Thailand, Burma, the Philippines, French Polynesia, Canada, and the United States. Prior to writing *Moon Handbooks: Wisconsin,* he completed roadwork for *Moon Handbooks: Northern Mexico* and *Baja* and was a contributing writer to Avalon Travel Publishing's *Road Trip: USA.*

A self-confirmed "white punk on sports," he would always rather be playing ice hockey. But shagging fly balls, snaring smashmouth grounders, or catching passes are fine, too, whenever he's not barreling around the world with a backpack. He balances everything with epic bouts of loafing, movies, and reading. He is a dog person.

FOR TRAVELERS WITH SPECIAL INTERESTS

GUIDES

The 100 Best Small Art Towns in America • Asia in New York City
The Big Book of Adventure Travel • Cities to Go
Cross-Country Ski Vacations • Gene Kilgore's Ranch Vacations
Great American Motorcycle Tours • Healing Centers and Retreats
Indian America • Into the Heart of Jerusalem
The People's Guide to Mexico • The Practical Nomad
Saddle Up! • Staying Healthy in Asia, Africa, and Latin America
Steppin' Out • Travel Unlimited • Understanding Europeans
Watch It Made in the U.S.A. • The Way of the Traveler
Work Worldwide • The World Awaits
The Top Retirement Havens • Yoga Vacations

SERIES

Adventures in Nature
The Dog Lover's Companion
Kidding Around
Live Well

Rick Steves shows you where to travel

and how to travel—all while getting the most value for your dollar. His Back Door travel philosophy is about making friends, having fun, and avoiding tourist rip-offs.

Rick's been traveling to Europe for more than 25 years and is the author of 20 guidebooks, which have sold more than a million copies. He also hosts the award-winning public television series *Travels in Europe with Rick Steves*.

RICK STEVES' COUNTRY & CITY GUIDES

Best of Europe
France, Belgium & the Netherlands
Germany, Austria & Switzerland
Great Britain & Ireland
Italy • London • Paris • Rome • Scandinavia • Spain & Portugal

RICK STEVES' PHRASE BOOKS

French • German • Italian • French, Italian & German
Spanish & Portuguese

MORE EUROPE FROM RICK STEVES

Europe 101
Europe Through the Back Door
Mona Winks
Postcards from Europe

WWW.RICKSTEVES.COM

ROAD TRIP USA

Getting there is half the fun, and Road Trip USA guides are your ticket to driving adventure. Taking you off the interstates and onto less-traveled, two-lane highways, each guide is filled with fascinating trivia, historical information, photographs, facts about regional writers, and details on where to sleep and eat— all contributing to your exploration of the American road.

"Books so full of the pleasures of the American road, you can smell the upholstery."
~ BBC radio

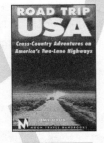

THE ORIGINAL CLASSIC GUIDE
Road Trip USA

ROAD TRIP USA REGIONAL GUIDE
Road Trip USA: California and the Southwest

ROAD TRIP USA GETAWAYS
Road Trip USA Getaways: Chicago
Road Trip USA Getaways: New Orleans
Road Trip USA Getaways: San Francisco
Road Trip USA Getaways: Seattle

www.roadtripusa.com

MOON HANDBOOKS

provide comprehensive coverage of a region's arts, history, land, people, and social issues in addition to detailed practical listings for accommodations, food, outdoor recreation, and entertainment. Moon Handbooks allow complete immersion in a region's culture—ideal for travelers who want to combine sightseeing with insight for an extraordinary travel experience.

USA

Alaska-Yukon • Arizona • Big Island of Hawaii • Boston
Coastal California • Colorado • Connecticut • Georgia
Grand Canyon • Hawaii • Honolulu-Waikiki • Idaho • Kauai
Los Angeles • Maine • Massachusetts • Maui • Michigan
Montana • Nevada • New Hampshire • New Mexico
New York City • New York State • North Carolina
Northern California • Ohio • Oregon • Pennsylvania
San Francisco • Santa Fe-Taos • Silicon Valley
South Carolina • Southern California • Tahoe • Tennessee
Texas • Utah • Virginia • Washington • Wisconsin
Wyoming • Yellowstone-Grand Teton

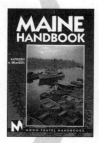

INTERNATIONAL

Alberta and the Northwest Territories • Archaeological Mexico
Atlantic Canada • Australia • Baja • Bangkok • Bali • Belize
British Columbia • Cabo • Canadian Rockies • Cancún
Caribbean Vacations • Colonial Mexico • Costa Rica • Cuba
Dominican Republic • Ecuador • Fiji • Havana • Honduras
Hong Kong • Indonesia • Jamaica • Mexico City • Mexico
Micronesia • The Moon • Nepal • New Zealand • Northern Mexico
Oaxaca • Pacific Mexico • Pakistan • Philippines • Puerto Vallarta
Singapore • South Korea • South Pacific • Southeast Asia • Tahiti
Thailand • Tonga-Samoa • Vancouver • Vietnam, Cambodia and Laos
Virgin Islands • Yucatán Peninsula

www.moon.com

U.S.~METRIC CONVERSION

1 inch	= 2.54 centimeters (cm)
1 foot	= .3048 meters (m)
1 yard	= 0.914 meters
1 mile	= 1.6093 kilometers (km)
1 km	= .6214 miles
1 fathom	= 1.8288 m
1 chain	= 20.1168 m
1 furlong	= 201.168 m
1 acre	= .4047 hectares
1 sq km	= 100 hectares
1 sq mile	= 2.59 square km
1 ounce	= 28.35 grams
1 pound	= .4536 kilograms
1 short ton	= .90718 metric ton
1 short ton	= 2000 pounds
1 long ton	= 1.016 metric tons
1 long ton	= 2240 pounds
1 metric ton	= 1000 kilograms
1 quart	= .94635 liters
1 US gallon	= 3.7854 liters
1 Imperial gallon	= 4.5459 liters
1 nautical mile	= 1.852 km

To compute celsius temperatures, subtract 32 from Fahrenheit and divide by 1.8. To go the other way, multiply celsius by 1.8 and add 32.

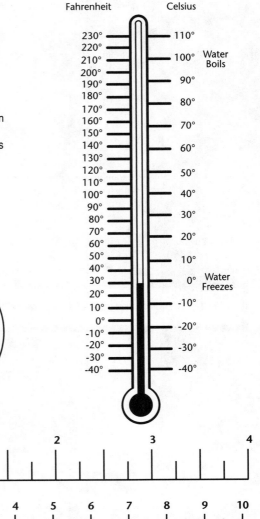

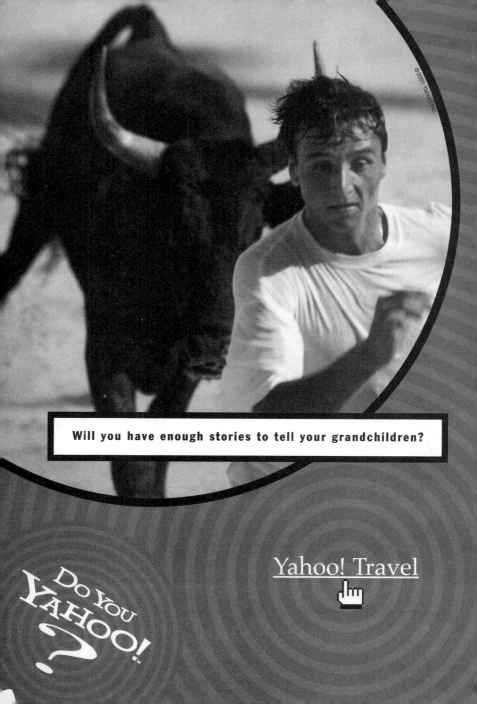

Will you have enough stories to tell your grandchildren?